7 Steps To Getting A Job With The Fede

1 Identifying the Job Titles
That Are Right for You

2 Finding the Right
Hiring Pathways

3 Collecting Vacancy
or Test Information

4 Familiarizing Yourself
with Vacancy Information

5 Completing Your Examination
(Application or Test)

6 Preparing for Your Interview

7 Considering an Offer

WORKING
FOR
YOUR UNCLE
The Complete Guide to Finding a Job with the Federal Government

by the Editors of the
FEDERAL JOBS DIGEST

Breakthrough
Publications, Inc.

For information address:

Breakthrough Publications
310 N. Highland Avenue
Ossining, New York 10562

Manufactured in the United States of America

Library of Congress Catalog Card Number: 93-070670

ISBN: 914-327-72-0

ACKNOWLEDGMENT
The editors wish to acknowledge with gratitude the United States Office of
Personnel Management, Washington, D.C., for its help in compiling the information supplied in this book.

Contents

Introduction

FEDERAL EMPLOYMENT

So you want to work for the Federal government! More than 3 million people just like you have found Federal service an arena full of challenge, diversity, and advancement opportunity unparalleled in the private sector. Those 3 million employees make the Federal government bigger than the top six or seven private-sector employers combined!

Nearly every private-sector occupation has its counterpart in the Federal government. There are lawyers, laborers, doctors, dentists, electricians, engineers, police, painters, scientists, secretaries, computer operators, clerks, editors, and accountants—to name fewer than 1% of the jobs. In addition, the Federal government employs people in many unique occupations, such as Federal law enforcement, justice, defense, and diplomacy. All told, there are over 2,000 different Federal occupations, with about 70% of the work force white collar and 30% blue collar.

The Federal government hires at all levels of experience and salary. At one end of the hiring spectrum, there are entry-level jobs requiring little or no experience, some of which bring in annual salaries of over $20,000. At the other end of the spectrum, there are senior-level executive positions requiring a high degree of experience and education; these command top salaries of $115,700. Of course, all levels between those two extremes—both white- and blue-collar positions that demand specialized administrative, professional, or technical skills—are hired as well.

While earning salaries comparable to those of their nongovernment counterparts, Federal workers enjoy benefits that far outweigh many private-sector companies. Liberal vacation and sick leave, the chance to choose from many excellent health insurance plans, and a generous retirement plan help make Federal employment particularly attractive. Adding to the rich rewards of Federal service is the opportunity to apply your special skills, day in and day out, to serving the needs of your country.

With such a large and varied work force, the government is constantly seeking new employees. New employees fill about 550,000 vacancies a year due to retirements alone. They move into jobs left by workers promoted to higher-level positions or who leave Federal service altogether. It's easy to see why the government must pursue recruitment activity unparalleled by any other employer in the United States.

Like any other job market, the openings in the Federal service come and go. You have to stay on top of the market and apply for positions that come in your field as they occur. Federal employment opportunities are usually not listed in the classified section of the newspaper or handled by private personnel agencies. You must track them down yourself. Your persistence is likely to pay off in a rewarding government job, complete with job security and promising promotion potential.

This book is designed to explain how you can go about landing your first government job—or, if you are already an employee of the Federal government, how to seek promotion. It explains how the government goes about hiring people and shows you how to make sure your Federal job application gets the notice it deserves.

Now, a word of encouragement. The Federal hiring process is probably unlike any you've ever seen. Sometimes it may seem much slower or more complicated than those used by organizations in the private sector. It's an immense undertaking that seeks out many different kinds of applicants for hundreds—even thousands—of jobs in many different Federal departments, agencies, bureaus, and organizations.

As you begin reading this book, try not to get overwhelmed by the application process. Be prepared to proceed through this complicated and sometimes confusing process. You may become frustrated at times, but you will, in all likelihood, be rewarded in the end by making a successful application. The effort required is not small, but the reward is worth it.

Note: Because the agency is the most common government administrative office, this book, to avoid confusion and needless repetition, will use the term **"agency"** when referring to any administrative office within the government, whether it officially be called a department, bureau, organization, or agency.

MERIT PRINCIPLES AND THE HIRING PROCESS

Now we must add another factor that differentiates the Federal government from other employers. The government follows a set of legally prescribed personnel rules and regulations, one of the most important of which is law 5 U.S. C. 2301, requiring that:

Recruitment, selection and advancement should be from qualified individuals from all segments of society and should be determined solely on the basis of relative ability, knowledge, and skills, after fair and open competition which assures that all receive equal opportunity. All applicants and employees should receive fair and equitable treatment without regard to political affiliation, race, color, religion, national origin, sex, marital status, or handicapped condition, and with proper regard to their privacy and constitutional rights.

In order to ensure that these so-called *merit principles* are applied consistently and completely over the Federal work force, a complex and elaborate hiring system has been devised by the Federal government. Called the *merit system*, it is the centerpiece of all Federal employment procedures.

The emphasis on the merit system results in a very important distinction between the Federal hiring process and that of the private sector. It is important to understand this distinction in order to make an effective Federal job application. Private-sector employers are able to use subjective, *qualitative* factors as their main and often only selection criteria—to hire someone simply because they "feel good about that person," because "he has the background we're looking for," or because "she really made a good impression." There is nothing wrong with this process: Private-sector employers are within their rights to hire anyone they please so long as their hiring policies are not discriminatory. However, this puts a lot of emphasis on the job interview, turning personal salesmanship, appearance, presentation, and style into major factors in the hiring process.

This is not the case in the Federal hiring process. Federal employers must justify their hiring decisions largely on *objective* criteria. They must hire not on the basis of a person's presentation or salesmanship, but "solely on the basis of relative ability, knowledge, and skill." To this end, Federal employers do not hire candidates for positions in the regular civil service without first assigning them a numerical score, or *rating*. Assigning these scores and ranking their recipients are the basis for much of the Federal hiring system. Only those applicants with sufficiently high numerical scores are offered jobs, with preference going to those scoring highest.

Ratings are based on how well candidates either perform on a written test or present their qualifications on a standard application form. Great personal appearance, stylish manner, or good conversation mean comparatively little in the Federal hiring formula; a high rating means a great deal more. Federal job seekers should bear this in mind and treat any tests or application forms they encounter as worthy of serious attention.

HOW TO USE THIS BOOK

It is very difficult to explain how to obtain a Federal job in a way that will always be relevant for everyone. The Federal government hires people in so many different fields and at so many different career levels that information important to one group is useless to another. Our objective in this book, then, has been to include all the information necessary to help everyone, but to organize it in such a way that any particular reader does not have to wade through irrelevant material. General information thus appears in the main text; more specific information—including pay schedules, job descriptions, statistics, and contact information—is presented in the extensive appendixes. Thus the main text explains what *everyone* should do whereas the appendixes help you determine specifically what *you* should do.

In organizing the information in this book, we have broken the application process into seven steps, which are outlined in the Overview. All Federal job seekers need to follow these seven steps, although the manner in which each will follow them may differ considerably. Each step is presented in its own chapter, and each of these chapters refers the reader to one or more of the appendixes. In addition, there is a Glossary that defines many words or expressions used in the Federal hiring process.

A major purpose of this book is to help you attain the most positive evaluation possible from your prospective Federal employer, whether based on a written test or an application form. Such an evaluation will not only help you land the Federal job you want, but will also determine the salary you receive: *Generally, the more positive your evaluation, the higher your salary.* That is why this book goes into such great detail in helping you prepare your Federal application and comply with application procedure.

It would be perfectly natural for you to react to much of the material in this book with impatience. "Why do I need to bother with this or that detail?" you might ask. The answer is that it might add an additional point to your rating, and that one point can make the difference in whether or not you are selected for a job. Our advice to you is this: Be patient and detailed oriented; it will pay off.

Overview: Seven Steps to Federal Employment

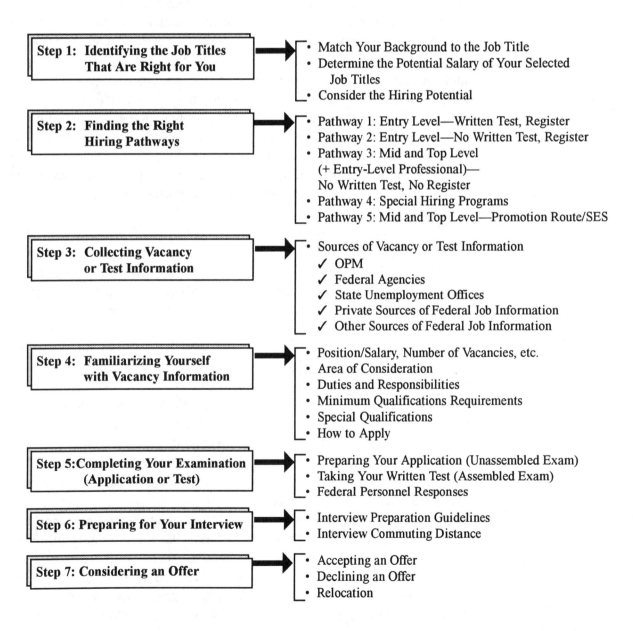

Step 1: **Identifying the Job Titles That Are Right for You**
- Match Your Background to the Job Title
- Determine the Potential Salary of Your Selected Job Titles
- Consider the Hiring Potential

Step 2: **Finding the Right Hiring Pathways**
- Pathway 1: Entry Level—Written Test, Register
- Pathway 2: Entry Level—No Written Test, Register
- Pathway 3: Mid and Top Level (+ Entry-Level Professional)— No Written Test, No Register
- Pathway 4: Special Hiring Programs
- Pathway 5: Mid and Top Level—Promotion Route/SES

Step 3: **Collecting Vacancy or Test Information**
- Sources of Vacancy or Test Information
  - ✓ OPM
  - ✓ Federal Agencies
  - ✓ State Unemployment Offices
  - ✓ Private Sources of Federal Job Information
  - ✓ Other Sources of Federal Job Information

Step 4: **Familiarizing Yourself with Vacancy Information**
- Position/Salary, Number of Vacancies, etc.
- Area of Consideration
- Duties and Responsibilities
- Minimum Qualifications Requirements
- Special Qualifications
- How to Apply

Step 5: **Completing Your Examination (Application or Test)**
- Preparing Your Application (Unassembled Exam)
- Taking Your Written Test (Assembled Exam)
- Federal Personnel Responses

Step 6: **Preparing for Your Interview**
- Interview Preparation Guidelines
- Interview Commuting Distance

Step 7: **Considering an Offer**
- Accepting an Offer
- Declining an Offer
- Relocation

There are seven steps that you must take in order to secure a Federal job. This chapter discusses each of these steps in brief, giving you an overview of the entire process. How you are best to accomplish each of these steps is explored in detail in subsequent chapters. For now, just take some time to become acquainted with the types of activity involved in successfully pursuing Federal employment.

STEP 1: IDENTIFYING THE JOB TITLES THAT ARE RIGHT FOR YOU

Step 1 on the road to your Federal job is to identify the Federal job titles in which you have an interest and for which you are qualified. You may wonder why this step is even necessary. After all, many job seekers who have worked in the private sector throughout their careers have come to expect the prospective employer to match them to a job title, and many companies will do this. In fact, there is a type of resume, perfectly acceptable to the private sector, that begins not with a job title but merely with a statement of objective; the company then routinely matches the applicant to its available positions. It is of the utmost importance to recognize that this process does not take place in the Federal government. If you do not specifically identify the job title for which you are applying, your application will be returned without consideration.

Having realized that it is you who must identify the appropriate and desirable job title, you may believe that the choice is obvious. "I am an accountant," you might say; "I am a carpenter," or "I am a clerk." You can be sure that just about every job title that exists in the private sector also occurs in the Federal government—most likely, including your present one. However, you may also be qualified for many more job titles than the one with which you most readily identify. For example, someone with a background in accountancy might qualify for such job titles as Auditor, Financial Institution Examiner, or Tax Technician in addition to Accountant. Likewise, a carpenter should consider not only Carpenter but also, say, Wood Working Machine Operator, and a clerk should explore such job titles as Mail and File Clerk, Clerk-Typist, and Data Transcriber. Not to know all the job titles for which you are qualified is to miss a lot of opportunities.

In choosing which Federal job titles to pursue, it is important to be clear what each one actually entails. A job title in Federal service can have a very different meaning from the same job title in the private sector, and some can be downright confusing. Consider, for instance, the word "secretary." In the private sector, a secretary is usually one who assists one or more executives. Although there certainly are such secretaries in the Federal government, there are also "secretaries" who direct offices, organizations, or even entire governmental departments—for example, the Secretary of Defense. A job seeker who knows the precise wording of the appropriate Federal job title would be able to apply for the specific kind of secretarial job he or she has in mind.

Another important part of selecting a job title is determining the prospects for a successful application-that is, how likely you are to get the job. Many job titles see little hiring activity simply because the government employs few people in that occupation. Sometimes openings in a given occupation are filled through a special hiring program, with those jobs being reserved for, say, veterans or Native Americans (that is, American Indians). Consequently, you should find not just one but all the job titles that are appropriate for you. There is no limit to the number of job titles for which you may apply, and the more you pursue, the better your chances of obtaining a Federal position. The chapter on Step 1 goes into detail to help you identify which job titles are right for you with regard to your qualifications, your interests, and your chances of being hired. It also describes the pay schedules that determine what salary may be expected for various positions.

Early in this chapter, you will be introduced to four "exemplary candidates"—a secretary, a recent college graduate, a graduate student in business, and a technical blue-collar worker. Their progress in obtaining jobs in the Federal government will be followed throughout each of the remaining steps.

STEP 2: FINDING THE RIGHT HIRING PATHWAY

The next step on the road to finding a Federal job is to discover the hiring pathway you will need to travel to your goal. A pathway (our term, not the government's) is the set of procedures an applicant must follow to be considered for a position. The Federal job applicant's life would be simple if there were only one standard way to apply for a Federal job. In the private sector the application procedure is fairly routine: The candidate either makes a phone call or mails a letter and resume to set up an interview; during the interview, the candidate presents his or her credentials; and the company responds with a decision by letter or phone call. The procedure is usually the same for all applicants to a given company, and is quite similar from one company to another. This is not the case in the Federal government.

There are several reasons for the diversity of application procedures in the Federal government: the enormity of the enterprise, the legal requirements with which it must comply, and the many different labor market conditions encountered by Federal employers. The chapter on Step 2 presents an overview of the Federal employment system, outlines the types of civil service, describes the components of its hiring procedures—ratings, registers, applications, tests, and so on. It then explains which pathways cover what kinds of job titles, whether white collar, blue collar, or those in the high-level Senior Executive Service. Once you have a good understanding of the material covered by this chapter, the challenging complexities of the Federal job application process may no longer seem quite so formidable.

STEP 3: COLLECTING VACANCY OR TEST INFORMATION

A Federal job opening is called a vacancy. By law, every opening in Federal service must be announced so that interested candidates can come forward for consideration, and anyone who does so and is qualified will be considered fairly. However, no job seeker will be considered for a Federal job unless he or she is responding to a specific government announcement and following its application instructions. You cannot simply send in an application assuming that there is a corresponding position open, or that you will be kept on a waiting list, or *register*, until one becomes available. You must instead obtain a copy of the announcement for the position in which you are interested—or at least know what it says—and follow the instructions regarding how and when to apply.

There are several kinds of job-related announcements and publications, and more than one may be vital to your job search. The chapter on Step 3 outlines the types of information they cover—including what qualifications are required for a position—and discusses how to go about getting hold of them.

STEP 4: FAMILIARIZING YOURSELF WITH VACANCY INFORMATION

Having obtained announcements regarding current openings in the Federal civil service, it is important to ensure you understand the information they present. What kind of salary is being offered? How long do you have before your application is due? What forms do you have to send in? Who will be considered for the job, and what qualifications must they have?

The chapter on Step 4 takes you through the various parts of a common type of announcement—the Vacancy Announcement—and shows how to determine the answers to these questions and others. It then introduces you to a number of forms often encountered in the Federal hiring process.

STEP 5: COMPLETING YOUR EXAMINATION (APPLICATION OR TEST)

At this point most job seekers will either have to take a written test or send in a detailed, standard application form called the *SF-171*. Some may end up doing both, since those who do sufficiently well on a test to merit further consideration will probably be asked to fill out this application. A well written application or high test score goes a long way to ensuring Federal employment.

The chapter on Step 5 opens with a detailed discussion of how best to complete the SF-171. (Worksheets provided in an appendix help you match your work experience to the qualifications of the job for which you are applying.) Also explored are cover letters and Federal *performance appraisals* (and acceptable nongovernmental alternatives). The process of preparing for and taking a written test is then outlined, as is the application process for the Senior Executive Service.

After successful completion of the written test or application form, the candidate may be called for an interview—the next step in the employment process.

STEP 6: PREPARING FOR YOUR INTERVIEW

In the private sector the interview is conducted early in the hiring process; in the Federal civil service, the interview is only conducted toward the end of that process. A candidate who is being interviewed for a Federal position can assume that he or she is under careful consideration and has a very good chance to be appointed.

Interviews cover a wide range of topics and have different purposes depending on the occupation in question. In some cases, they are merely to ensure that you understand what a job entails, allow you to see the agency's facilities, and clear up any loose ends, including questions about the likelihood of your promotion. In other cases, the interview is very much a part of the screening process and is used to evaluate the candidate's probable performance on the job.

STEP 7: CONSIDERING AN OFFER

A candidate who receives an offer of employment is usually given a deadline for responding, and should specifically accept or decline the offer by that time; thereafter, the position will be offered to another candidate. Although turning down an offer will generally not prevent a candidate from being considered for another position, it is wise to give a sound reason for declining.

A good way to choose among multiple offers is by considering their relative promotion potential. Often, an agency will outline a promotion path in order to make the job more attractive to a desirable candidate. It is also important to understand the ramifications of the various types of appointment that may be offered, which are reviewed in this chapter.

Step 1: Identifying the Job Titles That Are Right for You

Purpose: To help you identify the Federal job titles appropriate for you and for which you will apply. Even if your job title choices seem obvious, we recommend that you read this chapter and do the exercises: You are likely to find (as do most people) that you are qualified for more job titles than you thought. Having additional job titles for which to apply will often improve your chances of obtaining a Federal position quickly.

Associated appendixes:
A   Job Title Matching Guide
C   Selected Occupations and Their Hiring Pathway Factors
J   Geographic Location of Federal Employment
K   White-Collar Occupations in Federal Service
L   White-Collar Occupations in Federal Service by Selected Agency
M   White-Collar Occupations in Federal Service by Grade
N   Wage Grade Occupations in Federal Service
O   Wage Grade Occupations in Federal Service by Selected Agency

THE IMPORTANCE OF DETERMINING THE JOBS FOR WHICH YOU QUALIFY

The first question you must address to begin finding a Federal job is this: For which job titles do you want to apply? Selecting the specific job titles in which you are interested is a very important step in the Federal employment process. This is not the case in the private sector, where most job seekers need only pick an industry or an occupation, paying little attention to the actual title of the job for which they apply.

For example, Joe decides that he wants to work in the newspaper industry and that he would like a job in the editorial department. So he sends a résumé and a cover letter to the editor of his town newspaper, *The Small-*

Town News, expressing his desire to work for that newspaper and stating his willingness to do anything that the editor sees fit. The editor, Mr. Jones, likes Joe's letter and résumé and calls him in for an interview. The editor is impressed with Joe's sincere interest in the newspaper business and decides to hire him. Mr. Jones figures that his associate editors can use some help in editing, the copy chief deserves some assistance with trafficking galleys, and that the reporters need someone to answer their phones while they're out getting stories. Mr. Jones gives these duties to Joe and calls him an Editorial Assistant. Joe has his job in the newspaper business and *The Small-Town News* has a new staff member.

The Federal government does not generally accept applications from interested job seekers, or *candidates,* and match them to the jobs that best suit them; instead, candidates apply for specific job titles in the Federal government. This means that before you apply you must know which job title or titles are appropriate for you.

Virtually every job that exists in the private sector, from Custodian to Nuclear Engineer, exists in the government as well. This is why finding the Federal job titles for which you qualify can be a truly daunting task. If you are not careful, your best Federal job opportunities may be hidden from you; as a result, you may apply for the wrong job title. Recall also that, as was mentioned in the Overview, a job title in Federal service can have a very different meaning from the same job title in the private sector. Moreover, some job titles may seem vague and others misleading. You must therefore be certain you understand what a given job title entails. For example, a Document Analyst may sound like someone who extracts and evaluates information in reports and other documents—perhaps new laws or even job applications; instead, what a Document Analyst actually does is determine document authenticity and source, detect signs of tampering, and restore unreadable text. This requires detailed knowledge of handwriting analysis, typewriters, printing processes, inks, and papers—hardly the job one might have first suspected from its title. Similarly, a Preservation Packager, who might sound like someone involved in packaging foods to prevent spoilage, actually deals in applying coatings and other materials to machine parts and tools.

Although you may qualify for as many as 25 or more Federal job titles, you must apply for each job title individually. Say you apply for a job as a Secretary, but your work experience also qualifies you to be a Clerk-Typist; even though there may be openings for Clerk-Typists, you will not be considered for a Clerk-Typist position until you actually apply for one. As was noted earlier, the government will not match you to a job; it will only consider you for a job for which you apply.

The best way to give yourself an edge in securing a Federal job is first to determine for which job titles you qualify, and then to ascertain which of these offers you the greatest chance of getting hired. The following section is designed to help you successfully match your specific background to the Federal job titles for which you are best qualified.

MATCH YOUR BACKGROUND
TO THE JOB TITLE

The number and types of job titles for which you qualify will depend on your previous experience and/or educational background. It is therefore helpful at this point to construct a personal biography containing pertinent information about your education and any work or volunteer experience.

Let's first take a look at the examples below—biographical sketches of four individuals with various levels of education and work experience. Each of these people qualifies for a number of different Federal job titles, some of which may be obvious, others somewhat surprising. On the other hand, they may not qualify for some job titles that you *might* have expected. Let's introduce you to them now.

EXAMPLES

Janet is a secretary with a high-school diploma. She has been at her present job for six years and earns $26,500. In addition to her regular secretarial duties, which include word processing, data entry, and steno dictation, Janet also writes her own correspondence and helps plan, manage, and schedule her employer's business meetings, conferences, and travel reservations. Janet types 60 words per minute and takes dictation at 80 words per minute. At her previous jobs she worked as a receptionist, payroll clerk, clerk-typist, order processor, and file clerk. Janet hopes that with all of her office management experience she might qualify for an administrative office position.

Michael is a recent college graduate with a liberal arts degree. He maintained a grade-point average (GPA) of 3.0 while he majored in history and minored in criminal psychology. He is not sure if he wants to pursue a career in office management or in something more dramatic, like law enforcement. He types well and is a good organizer.

Helen has a B.S. in Business Administration with a minor in Accounting. She also speaks fluent French, which she learned as an exchange student in college. Presently, she is nearing completion of her work toward a master's degree in Financial Management and is a part-time bookkeeper for a mortgage company in New York City. Helen plans to build a career in finance, preferably on the West Coast. She is interested in a job with some travel potential, which the Federal government, with offices across the country and around the world, might well be able to offer.

Jeff, a Vietnam veteran who served as a radar technician in the Army, has worked as an electrician for the past eight years; his most recent annual earnings were $27,300. He has a high-school diploma plus a certification as an air conditioning repair technician. Before becoming an electrician, Jeff had a series of different jobs including building superintendent, construction worker, building framer, and carpenter. He enjoys working with his hands, but blue-collar jobs in the private sector are often seasonal, with poor benefits and retirement packages. Jeff, 47 years old and with a couple of school-age children, is looking to the government for more security and regular paychecks.

Now try to draw up a personal biography of your own, summarizing your life experience as well as your career goals. Start with your job experience, paid or volunteer, listing your most recent job first. Then add your educational credits, which include any certificates, advanced degrees, foreign languages, and so on. Perhaps you are a veteran, or disabled, or a student, senior citizen, retired person, someone just reentering the job market for the first time in ten years, or a noncitizen. Write down whatever information could be pertinent: It may be important to your job search and may even indicate special programs for which you are eligible.

Now let us look at Appendix A (Job Title Matching Guide, p. 125). This appendix provides sample personal biographies, including work experience and educational background, and matches them to current Federal job titles. The first column gives the Applicant Category (that is, describes a type of candidate: "Recent College Graduate, Accounting," "Ex-Housewife," and so on). Column 2 contains the Applicant Description, one or more brief bios that help define the Applicant Category of column 1 (such as, "John is a skilled and experienced journeyman carpenter"). The Job Title/Occupation Recommendation is given in column 3. Let us see how the four job seekers of our earlier examples match up to column 1, Applicant Category.

> Column 4 of **Appendix A** refers to relevant occupational groups described in Appendix B and will be helpful in Step 2; but it is not needed for Step 1, which we are now considering.

EXAMPLES

Janet readily finds a match for her background in the "Clerical, Skilled" category (p. 134).

Michael will find a close match with "Recent College Graduate, Liberal Arts" (p. 127).

Helen's matching biography is "Recent College Graduate, Accounting" (p. 130).

Jeff's background compares well with "Blue Collar, Experienced Trade, Journeyman" (p. 135).

Note that these may not be the *only* categories that fit our examples. Jeff would also match (though not as closely) with "Armed Services, Enlisted Vietnam Era or Later"; and Helen, who speaks fluent French and wants to travel, might also look under "Recent College Graduate, Overseas Interest." This multiplicity of category is not unusual. Job seekers who have many years of work experience or otherwise complex backgrounds may find that they can fit into three or four categories, whereas those who are entering the job market for the first time will probably find that fewer categories fit their backgrounds.

With your own personal biography in hand, you should now carefully review the different categories and descriptions in columns 1 and 2 to see how many may apply to you. It is important to be both creative and accurate

Occupational codes refer to the General Schedule (GS) and Wage Grade (WG) Schedule, job-classification and pay systems that cover most Federal jobs. See "Determining the Potential Salary . . . ," p. 16.

when doing this: Consider all realistic possibilities, but do not pretend to yourself that you belong in a category if you really do not.

Having chosen the appropriate Applicant Category(ies), move on to the third column, Job Title/Occupation Recommendation, which lists several suggested Federal job titles and their *occupational codes*.

The categories in Appendix A are intentionally broad in order to represent as many different backgrounds as possible. Just because your background fits a particular category does not mean that you will qualify for, or be interested in, all the job titles listed therein: They are simply recommendations, intended only to give you an idea of the kinds of job title that are appropriate for you, as a starting point for your own further analysis.

Until a few years ago, persons applying for administrative jobs took a written test and were placed on a register which covered many jobs in many agencies. Now, those jobs are filled in a similar manner to higher-grade positions. That is, they are filled under case examining procedures, usually one job at a time.

Let's look more closely at each of our four examples and see how they approach the challenge of job title selection:

EXAMPLES

Janet finds (in Appendix A, p. 134) that her extensive office experience qualifies her for many different job titles. Secretary, Management Assistant, Administrative Officer, Support Services Specialist, and Miscellaneous Administration are the suggestions that interest her.

Michael finds that even with his very general education he is eligible to apply for many administrative jobs at the entry (trainee) level: Air Traffic Controller, Foreign Service Officer, and various Law Enforcement occupations. Michael remembers reading that because of new initiatives, the Immigration and Naturalization Service will be hiring several thousand border patrol agents during the next several years, so he keeps that occupation in mind.

Helen, with her business and accounting background, should investigate a range of occupations in banking and finance, including Accountant, Auditor, Financial Analyst, Financial Research Assistant, Budget Analyst, and Financial Institution Examiner.

Jeff's broad work experience may qualify him for a number of job titles: Electrician, Carpenter, Maintenance Mechanic, and so on.

Appendixes K and N list **General Schedule and Wage Grade Schedule jobs**, respectively. Jobs in the **U.S. Postal Service** (and some others) are outside both of these systems, but are discussed in Appendix B.

The job titles suggested in Appendix A are by no means the only ones for which you, or our sample applicants, may qualify. To broaden the list of Federal jobs that are appropriate based on your present work experience—or to find out more about a recommended job title—refer to Appendix K (White-Collar Occupations in Federal Service) and/or Appendix N (Wage Grade Occupations in Federal Service), which list and briefly describe most types of jobs in Federal service. By reviewing the outlines in either appendix, you can identify more fully the specific occupations that match your qualifications.

Let's see how our four exemplary job seekers would go about this. Each of our white-collar job seekers—Janet, Michael, and Helen—should look through Appendix K carefully. Jeff, a blue-collar worker, should get started in Appendix N.

EXAMPLES

Let's begin with Janet. On page 608 of Appendix K, Janet finds a list of all white-collar jobs organized into what the government calls *occupational groups,* each of which covers a number of *job series.* Janet can see that the General Administrative, Clerical, and Office Services Group contains many job title series that might be of interest to her. To determine if her office management experience qualifies her for jobs in a specific series— for instance, the Management Clerical and Assistance Series (GS-344)— she can look up the general series description on page 624. Janet finds that her experience planning, managing, and scheduling her employer's daily routine indeed sounds quite similar to the duties described for this series. Encouraged, Janet continues to peruse the lists (and the index) to find as many applicable job title series as possible. She notes, however, that the description of Administrative Officer (GS-341)—one of the job titles recommended by Appendix A—indicates that previous government experience is probably a requirement. Her chances of getting this particular job, she realizes, are therefore slim.

Michael looks for additional job series of interest in the Business and Industry Group and, since he minored in criminal psychology, in the Investigation Group as well.

Helen looks not only in the Accounting and Budget Group, but also in the General Administrative, Clerical, and Office Group. In addition, because of her foreign language background, she checks the Information and Arts Group, where she is intrigued by the job title Language Specialist.

In Appendix N, Jeff finds an index of Wage Grade (blue-collar) occupations, with their occupational codes, starting on page 722. Immediately, he sees the job title Air Conditioning Equipment Mechanic, 5306. In addition, he thinks his military experience as a radar technician might qualify him for a job in the Electronic Equipment Installation and Maintenance Family, 2600. A quick check of the general description on page 725 confirms his feelings. Jeff should continue to look through the entire list to make sure that he checks out each family in which he might locate additional job titles.

> A job series (or *series of classes*) comprises those job titles related closely enough to be designated by the same number in the Federal job classification system. Job series and job title are often correlated simply: For example, in the Physics Series the job title is Physicist. But there are so many employees in the General Administrative, Clerical, and Office Services Group that its series names do not reflect all its job titles: A job vacancy might therefore be listed simply as "clerical, relying on an **occupational code** for clarification.

> Note that **Wage Grade positions** are listed in *job families* instead of *occupational groups.*

Although your own personal educational background and job experience may vary considerably from those of our examples, the steps you take in determining the job titles for which you qualify will basically be the same. Take your time. Review all the occupational groups (or job families) listed: There may be jobs of which you are not aware that match your background quite closely.

If you are interested in a career change at this time, you might want to determine which other occupational groups might interest you. It is important to remember, however, that the government seeks to match closely work experience and job title. Thus, having the experience to be at the mid- or upper-administrative level in one occupational group does not necessarily qualify you to be an administrator in a different one: You might instead have to start in an entry-level, trainee position to gain the necessary basic qualifications in a new field.

It is important to note that Appendixes A, K, and N can only indicate whether you *generally* qualify for a certain job title or series; they cannot guarantee that you *specifically* qualify for a given vacancy or even a given agency. Work-experience requirements, especially for mid- and upper-level positions, may be quite precise and stated in a vacancy announcement or other informational document.

> **Vacancy announcements** and other sources of qualifications information are described in Step 3.

You should now have found a number of job titles for which you think you may qualify. It is also important to consider where you are likely to fit into the government's hierarchy for those job titles, in terms of position and salary. In Federal service, salary—a major concern to most job seekers—is linked directly to grade level.

DETERMINING THE POTENTIAL SALARY OF YOUR SELECTED JOB TITLES

Grade levels are established by agencies based on the duties and responsibilities of the positions being filled. Your experience and training will determine the level(s) for which you qualify. Some positions may be filled at a single grade, and others may be filled at several grades when the agency is willing to consider applicants with different levels of experience. Sometimes, agencies establish career ladders. Career ladders consist of a full performance level or journeyman level and one or more lower graded positions. An applicant hired at a level below the full performance level can be promoted to higher levels provided he or she progresses satisfactorily and meets the agency's requirements for promotion.

Government tables showing salaries for each grade level are called *pay schedules*. Each pay schedule has its own set of grade levels; that is, level 5 on one schedule does not correspond to level 5 on another. However, two different jobs at level 5 *on the same schedule* are seen as equivalent in terms of occupational development and job responsibility, and thus entail the same salary.

> Your grade level will determine the salary you are paid. See Appendix F for sample pay schedules; local variations (see text) can be obtained from OPM service centers and personnel offices at Federal agencies.

In most pay schedules, grade levels are further divided into salary *steps*. As a rule, an employee's salary starts at step 1 (the lowest) and is raised to the next step in that grade level periodically. These "within grade increases" occur more frequently for the lower steps (every 52 weeks for the three lowest steps of General Schedule grades) and less frequently for the higher steps (156 weeks for the top three steps of General Schedule grades). For wage grade positions, the increase from step 1 to 2 occurs after only 26 weeks. In

some cases if the Government determines that an applicant has superior qualifications and requires a higher salary to match current income or a job offer
from the private sector, the salary may be set at a step above the first step.

The pay schedule covering most white-collar positions is the *General
Schedule (GS)*. This has 15 grade levels, divided into three main career levels: *Entry level* comprises the first seven grade levels (GS-1-7), *mid level* the
next five (GS-8-12), and *top level* the highest three (GS-13-15). The vast
majority of new hires each year occur at entry level. An employee in a nonprofessional position (such as a clerk) is said to reach *full performance level*
upon acquiring the full range of skills for his or her job title; this may be at a
grade as low as GS-4 or as high as GS-7, depending on the job.

Generally grades GS-1, 4, 6, 8, and 10 are reserved for clerical and tech-
nician-type positions and GS-5, 7, 9, 11, and 12 for administrative and professional positions. Applicants for administrative positions can qualify either
on the basis of a college degree or experience. Professional positions usually
have a positive education requirement meaning that applicants may not substitute experience for specific education requirements such as a degree or
prescribed course work in a particular subject area. Strict rules govern the
relation of duties and responsibilities to salary and grade level.

> **Educational qualifications**
> for General Schedule grade
> levels are outlined in
> Appendix M.

Above the General Schedule is the *Senior Level Pay Schedule (SLPS)*.
This schedule has a minimum salary (120% of GS-15, step 1) and a maximum
salary (equivalent to level IV of the Executive Pay Schedule, discussed below) but no grade levels: An individual's pay may fall anywhere within the
prescribed range. The SLPS includes two parallel subscales: SL (for managers and administrators) and ST (for scientific, medical, legal, and other technical professionals). Sample job titles are Senior Advisor to Commissioner,
Special Assistant to Commissioner (SL); and Soil Scientist, Senior Electronic
Engineer (ST).

Also above the General Schedule is the *Senior Executive Service (SES)*,
which comprises most of the top supervisory and managerial jobs in the Executive branch of the government (aside from presidential appointees). There
are some 8,600 SES positions, with such titles as Branch Director, Associate
General Counsel, Assistant Commissioner, Chief Financial Officer, Assistant
Legal Advisor, and Deputy Inspector General. These require a high degree of
expertise, usually in more than one discipline, and often entail multiple advanced degrees and supervisory experience. The SES has six grade levels,
but these are essentially unlinked to duties and responsibilities (unlike those
in the General Schedule); instead, one's grade is determined by whatever
factors the hiring agency deems important personal work experience, private-sector pay for a similar position, agency size, difficulty in filling the position, and so on. The system is designed to encourage and reward professional excellence in those who set policy and administer programs at the
highest levels of government. Those who perform successfully may receive
special annual bonuses; those found unsatisfactory will be removed. In 1997,
SES pay rates ranged from $97,000 for level 1 to $115,700 for levels 5 and 6.
Note, levels 5 and 6 are the same because no SES pay level may exceed Level

Locality pay is the percentage by which General Schedule salaries are increased depending on where the position is located. The country is divided into 30 locality areas, and each has a different percentage.

For more on "**plums**," see *The Plum Book,* available from the Superintendent of Documents at the Government Printing Office. ISBN 0-16-0537-32-0.

IV of the Executive pay schedule. SES pay rates are augmented by the same *locality pay* percentages as the General Schedule.

The *Executive Schedule* has five levels, numbered EX-I–V, with the *lowest* number reflecting the *highest* salary. There are fewer than 1,000 employees in this schedule. Level I of the schedule includes such positions as heads of cabinet agencies. In 1997 the pay rate for Level I was $148,400.00, and the pay rate for Level V was $108,200.00. Unlike the SES and the General Schedule, Executive pay rates are not augmented by locality pay. As can be seen from Appendix F (Federal Salary Rates), there is some overlap in salaries between the Executive Schedule and the SES pay system. Almost all positions at the Executive Schedule are presidential appointments requiring Senate confirmation. Such political appointments (informally called *"plums"*) may also occur in the SLPS or SES, and tend to change with each new Administration, if not each presidential term.

Blue-collar fields in Federal service are referred to as Wage Grade occupations and are covered under the *Wage Grade (WG) Schedule.* There are five standard career levels (A–E). The first two career levels are *developmental*; that is, the employee is still learning the skills necessary for the job. At the lowest level (A), called *helper* (corresponding to grade levels WG-1–5), the employee receives on-the-job training. The next career level (B) is called *apprentice*, entails both on-the-job training and classroom instruction, and corresponds to WG-6–8. Once past apprenticeship, the employee becomes a *journeyman* (C) and is considered to have all the appropriate skills (that is, to be at *full performance level*, WG-9–11). The next two career levels have their own subscales in the Wage Grade system: Wage Leader and Wage Supervisor. Leader (D) is similar to the title of foreman in the private sector and corresponds to WL-1–15. *Supervisor* (E), the highest Wage Grade career level, is for those who hire, promote, and fire Wage Grade workers. This represents WS-1–19. (These Wage Grade career levels are sometimes abbreviated H, A, J, L, and S.) Salaries in all Wage Grade categories are adjusted to local private-sector hourly rates for comparable job titles, and thus vary from region to region.

Since grade levels usually represent a *range* of salaries (as shown by the sample pay schedules of Appendix F), it is possible to get a pay increase without being promoted (that is, by moving to a higher pay step, not a higher grade); this is called a *within-grade increase.* As explained above, it may even be possible, under certain circumstances, to negotiate a higher within-grade starting salary. Also, although most Federal salaries are strictly determined by grade level, extreme shortages of qualified applicants can affect the pay schedule in a given area. Higher pay (via *special salary rates*) may apply to specific job titles for which the demand is high. In these situations, the first step of the grade will be equal to a higher step of the normal pay scale. Some occupations such as medical officers have special pay scales which are applicable worldwide not just in a particular location.

Although the General Schedule is a national pay scale, it is augmented by *locality pay.* The country is divided into 30 locality pay areas, and the General Schedule rates are increased by a specific percentage. These percentages are reviewed each year. In 1997 the increases over the basic General Schedule ranged from 4.81% to 11.52%.

When applying for a Federal job, you *must* stipulate not only the precise job title for which you are applying but also the minimum grade level you will accept. At this point, therefore, you should begin to consider which grade level might be most appropriate for each of the job titles in which you have shown an interest.

EXAMPLES

Janet, with six years of secretarial experience, could certainly get a job at entry level GS-5, but that would probably mean a significant cut in salary for her: On the basic General Schedule, in 1997, GS-5 starts at $19,520.00. Even in Houston which has a locality pay augmentation of 11.52%, the highest in the country, her salary would only be $21,768.00. The top of GS-5 on the basic General Schedule in 1997 is $25,379.00. Therefore, with locality pay augmentations, her salary would be above $26,500.00. Thus, if an agency determined that Janet had superior qualifications, it could offer her a salary at the top step of GS-5 to match her current salary. However, this does not often happen for secretarial positions, and Janet should not plan on it. In 1997, GS-7 begins at $24,178.00, so for some localities Janet's salary would be at or above $26,500.00. However, Janet feels that her experience might land her a position at GS-8, whose starting salary is the clearly preferable $26,777.00 plus locality pay augmentation. GS-9 with a starting salary of $29,577.00 plus locality pay augmentation would even be better for Janet.

Michael understands that, with a bachelor's degree but no job experience, he should stick to GS-5 or GS-7, both of which are entry level. (As it happens, all but a very few entry-level positions for Air Traffic Controller are at GS-7.)

Helen, having some work experience and well on her way to a master's degree, considers herself at just about mid-career level. She suspects, therefore, that GS-7 or even (with her degree) GS-9 are appropriate for her. In addition, by contacting OPM or Federal agencies directly, Helen learns that a nationwide shortage of Accountants has led to their having special salary rates in some locations. (Step 3 contains more information on how to obtain job information.) In a location where a special rate is applicable, she would receive either the special rate or the basic General Schedule salary plus the locality pay augmentation which ever is greater. On the other hand, she finds there would be no such special rates for a Financial Analyst, another job title she is considering. Therefore, for this job, she would receive the basic General Schedule rate plus the applicable locality pay augmentation.

Jeff, with experience in several blue-collar jobs and expertise relevant to two job titles (Electrician and Air Conditioning Equipment Mechanic) is clearly at least a journeyman (WG-9–11); however, to obtain the salary he needs, he should try to qualify as a leader. This he can do by applying at WL-12, the low end of the leader scale, for a position as Electrician.

Note that you may have nothing to lose by applying for jobs you feel are equal to or somewhat below your present level: They can serve as stepping-stones to higher-level positions. Federal employers, like many in the private sector, generally prefer promoting a current employee to hiring someone new.

Of course, if you are qualified for one of those top Federal jobs with annual salaries of $90,000+ a year, by all means apply; but to apply for jobs for which you are not qualified, or to request a salary far more than is appropriate based on your experience and training, is to waste your time and ultimately to discourage yourself.

> **Promotion potential** and other factors that may refine **grade level choice** are discussed in greater detail in the upcoming section "Grade Level: External Hiring vs. Internal Promotion (p. 21).

CONSIDER THE HIRING POTENTIAL

While you may be qualified for 20 or more different Federal job titles, not all will offer equal hiring prospects. This section is designed to help you narrow your choices to those job titles that will offer you the best chances of becoming a Federal employee. Factors that affect the hiring potential of a job title include these six:

1. the occupational group (or job family) in which the job title appears;
2. the grade level (which affects both the number of positions available and whether they are likely to be filled by new hires or promotions);
3. the universality of the job title (how many agencies have such positions);
4. the geographic location(s) in which you are willing to work;
5. your citizenship; and
6. whether you are a veteran of the U.S. armed forces.

OCCUPATIONAL GROUP/JOB FAMILY

> The relative sizes of **occupational groups/job families** are shown in Appendixes L and O.

The Federal government hires workers in just about every conceivable occupation and at every level of experience. Some occupational groups, however, contain more employees than others: The General Administrative, Clerical, and Office Services Group is the largest, comprising roughly 700,000 employees; the Film Processing Family is one of the smallest, with only 100 employees. Clearly, the larger the group, the more vacancies and the greater opportunity to be hired.

There are also more opportunities in fields where positions are difficult to fill. These include the professional occupations (such as engineering, accounting, and computer science), skilled blue collar (journeyman), and health care.

GRADE LEVEL: EXTERNAL HIRING VERSUS
INTERNAL PROMOTION

When an agency announces a job vacancy it also designates who is eligible for consideration for that position. Sometimes an agency will limit the pool of applicants for a job title to current employees, to former employees who are eligible to be reinstated, or only to employees of that particular agency. The agency is indicating that it would prefer to promote someone from within the government rather than seek someone from the outside. This is especially true for positions in the mid- and upper-grade levels, where a particular position requires knowledge that can only be obtained through previous government employment. For instance, Air Traffic Controllers at the Federal Aviation Administration are rarely hired at the GS-9 level from outside the agency; they must have on-the-job experience at the GS-5/7 levels in order to qualify for the next promotional step.

> **Promotion** is also discussed in Step 2; see the section "Status versus Nonstatus Candidates (p. 33).

Generally speaking, the higher the grade level, the lower the likelihood of external hiring. Like most organizations, the Federal government tends to hire at entry level and promote from within for upper-level jobs. The extent to which new hires are concentrated at the lower grades varies considerably from one occupational group to another. In clerical and administrative fields, prior experience in government is often considered a prerequisite to an upper-level position, as it is for most supervisor-level blue-collar positions. Upper-grade-level external hiring is much more prevalent for specialists with counterparts in the private sector; that is, those in professional and technical fields such as engineering, math and science, computer science, law, accounting, health care, and skilled blue-collar work (for leader-level positions).

Appendix C (Selected Occupations and Their Hiring Pathway Factors) provides an employment overview of many popular Federal job titles (listed alphabetically in the first column, "Occupational Series # / GS Level"). The last two columns show whether the primary hiring focus is external (via new hires) or internal (via promotion) at various grade levels. The "Hiring Volume columns indicate how many people are hired at those grade levels.

EXAMPLE

Janet, you'll recall, would much rather be hired at the GS-9 level than at GS-7. One of the job titles she is considering is Management Assistant, GS-344, which was recommended in Appendix A. However, checking this job title in Appendix C (p. 211), she finds that at GS-9 the hiring volume is low and the primary hiring focus internal; thus she would probably have to apply at GS-7—where the hiring focus is external, though the hiring volume is still low—and, if hired, await a promotion to GS-9. This is not the case for the job title Secretary (p. 214), which she is also considering: The hiring focus for Secretaries is either external or mixed, and the hiring volume medium to high, at all grade levels shown.

In the same way, compare the job titles for which you feel qualified with the hiring volume indicated in Appendix C. Note, however, that this appendix contains only a representative sample of the Federal, white-collar job titles for which readers may qualify: A more complete listing, offering a detailed breakdown by grade level of people employed in various job titles (that is, *incumbents*, not merely new hires), is found in Appendix M (White-Collar Occupations in Federal Service by Grade). Some job titles, such as Management Clerical and Assistance (GS-344), have large concentrations of employees in one or two entry-level grades but dramatically fewer employees (if any) as grade level increases. This indicates that most new hires are at the lower grades, with higher grades reached by promotion. On the other hand, a smoother distribution of employees among grade levels, as for Computer Specialist (GS-334), indicates that external hiring occurs at both lower and upper grades.

Also given in Appendix M are the median and average grade levels for each job title. The *average (mean) grade* is determined much as you would figure out the average value of the coins in your pocket. The *median grade,* however, divides all people with the same job title into two roughly equal groups; thus, a median of 11 for Archeologists (GS-193) means that there are as many of them in grades 1-10 as in grades 12-15. The median grade is considered to be the more accurate indicator of *promotion potential,* the likelihood of eventual promotion into an upper-level job. Clearly, the higher the median, the greater the promotion potential. Thus, if your eventual goal is an upper-level job, you should not expect to get there in a job title that has a low journeyman grade. This does not mean, however, that *starting* in such a job title would prevent you from reaching an upper-level job: Switching from one job title to another within a given occupational group (or job family) is routine in Federal employment.

EXAMPLE

Janet, through her perusal of Appendix K, has already identified which job titles in the General Administrative, Clerical, and Office Services Group (GS-300) might be most appropriate for her. She now looks up those job titles in Appendix M to see which have considerable enough numbers of employees to give her at least a fair chance of being hired. She notes that in Federal service there are about 100,000 Secretaries, 4,000 Support Services employees, and some 8,000 both in Management Assistant and in Administrative Officer positions. She concludes that all of these job titles offer at least some opportunity for new hires. However, their promotion potential varies considerably: Secretary has the least potential, with a median grade of 5; Administrative Officer has the most, with a median of 11.

Comparing several job title possibilities in Appendix M, Helen notes that both Accountant (GS-510) and Auditor (GS-511) have median grades of 12, whereas that of Financial Institution Examiner (GS-570) is 11 and that of Financial Analyst (GS-1160) is 13. Clearly, Financial Analyst has the greatest promotion potential.

UNIVERSALITY OF THE JOB TITLE

An agency's job types and hiring volume depend on its size and its particular mission. Some job titles, such as Financial Institution Examiner, occur almost exclusively at one or two agencies; others, such as Accountant and Secretary, are hired by virtually every Federal agency. The more agencies in which a job title occurs, the better your chances of finding an opening.

Appendixes L (White-Collar Occupations in Federal Service by Selected Agency) and O (Wage Grade Occupations in Federal Service by Selected Agency) can help indicate how widely a job title is distributed among agencies, and which agencies offer you the best job opportunities. Listing hundreds of job titles apiece (in occupational-code sequence), these appendixes show the number of people employed in each job title nationwide, and how many of those are employed at each of the 25 largest Federal agencies.

> **Appendixes L and O,** though the most recent agency breakdowns of this kind available, show data from late 1994.

EXAMPLES

Looking up the job title Accountant by its occupational code (GS-510), Helen learns from Appendix L that there are over 11,000 Accountants currently employed throughout the Federal government (see p. 678). In addition, she can determine exactly how many Accountants are employed at the 25 major Federal agencies nationwide. When she compares the statistics for Financial Institution Examiner (GS-570), Helen sees that there are only a little over 4,000 in the entire government, and only the Federal Deposit Insurance Corporation hires that job title in quantity. But though Accountant clearly offers more opportunities in the long term, 4,000 is still a substantial number, so even though FDIC is undergoing downsizing, Helen decides to add Financial Institution Examiner to her job title list. After all, the FDIC might be hiring now, and she wants to explore all avenues.

Similarly, Michael can compare Computer Specialist (GS-334; p. 675), with 44,000 presently employed throughout the government, and Education and Training (GS-1701; p. 689), with around 9,000 Federal employees. Michael should compare all the job titles he has picked to determine where his best opportunities exist.

Jeff, our blue-collar worker, finds (in Appendix O) that although many agencies need a few Wage Grade workers, the majority of blue-collar job titles in the Federal service are at Department of Defense (DOD) bases across the country. The other major hirers are the Department of Veterans Affairs (VA), the Tennessee Valley Authority (TVA), the General Services Administration (GSA), and the Department of the Interior. For example, checking Electronics Mechanic (WG-2604), Jeff finds that there are over 16,000 employed by the government, the majority of the positions being with either the Army, Navy, or Air Force. Likewise, there are over 5,000 Carpenters (WG-4607) employed by Uncle Sam, almost all of whom are civilians with the military organizations. However, Maintenance Mechanics (WG-4749) number over 11,000 and can be found in large numbers at other agencies besides the DOD, including the Department of the Interior, the GSA, and the Department of Transportation. Therefore, Jeff may have more initial success entering the Federal job system as a Maintenance Mechanic than as a Carpenter. However, if Jeff *lives near* a Department of Defense base, he should probably try to get a job there as an Electronics Mechanic.

Jeff's situation highlights the next important factor in considering hiring prospects: geographical location.

GEOGRAPHIC LOCATION

A major factor in determining the speed and success with which you secure a Federal job is where you are willing to work. The larger the area, the more opportunities are likely to await you. Clearly, the more Federal workers in an area, the more jobs and the better your chances of getting employment become. Most Federal jobs are in major metropolitan areas, with 11% of them in Washington, DC. But Federal jobs are spread across the country, even in some of the more remote areas, as well as overseas. Your Federal job application will include a question asking where you want to work; the less restrictive your choices, the better your chances of being hired quickly.

Data in **Appendix J** are for Standard Metropolitan Statistical Areas (SMSAs), which can comprise one or more cities.

Appendix J (Geographic Location of Federal Employment) provides an alphabetical listing of all the U.S. geographic areas that have Federal offices and gives the number of people presently employed by the Federal government in these areas. It will help you determine whether your locality offers sufficient opportunities for Federal employment.

EXAMPLES

Let's assume that Michael is interested in a job as an Air Traffic Controller, but lives in the relatively small town of Anderson, SC (p. 591), with a Federal work force of only 114. Needless to say, he must be willing to relocate to a larger metropolitan area with an airport, such as Atlanta, GA, or Washington, DC, if he ever hopes to land a job as a Federal Air Traffic Controller. In addition, job titles such as Air Traffic Controller, although found in virtually every state in the country, may only be needed in certain states at any given time.

If Michael decides to pursue a career as a border patrol agent, those positions are located primarily in the border states. Applicants such as Janet (clerical) and Helen (finance), whose job titles are in greater demand nationwide, are likely to determine that geography plays a less important role in their job search.

Geography is more important for Wage Grade job seekers like Jeff, who lives in Nebraska. He can see that his best opportunities are to be found in cities with DOD bases, such as Jacksonville, FL, Norfolk, VA, and Sacramento, CA. Moreover, if Jeff won't live near the coast, he is unlikely to get a job with the Navy.

CITIZENSHIP

As a very general rule, most Federal government jobs are restricted to U.S. citizens; however, there are several important exceptions. An agency may consider non-U.S. citizen applicants for *Competitive Service* positions only if it can demonstrate that after exhaustive recruiting efforts, it cannot locate qualified citizen applicants. If a noncitizen is placed in one of these positions, the position is taken out of the competitive service and placed in the excepted service. The noncitizen would not be able to move to other positions. Not open to noncitizens, however, are positions in law enforcement and those requiring security clearance. Many clerical or lower-level blue-collar jobs overseas are also open to noncitizens (see Appendix P).

> **Competitive Service** is defined in Step 2 (p. 34).

Agencies may also use *Excepted Service* jobs for the following noncitizens:

1. those owing permanent allegiance to the United States (such as residents of American Samoa);
2. aliens from Cuba, Poland, South Vietnam, countries of the former Soviet Union, or the Baltic countries lawfully admitted for permanent residence;

> **Excepted Service** is defined in Step 2 (pp. 34-5).

3. South Vietnamese, Cambodian, or Laotian refugees paroled in the United States after January 1, 1975;
4. Philippine, Israeli, and Irish citizens;
5. citizens of countries "allied with the United States in the current defense effort;
6. noncitizens who are translators (under temporary, 60-day appointments);
7. noncitizens who have applied for overseas Department of Defense jobs that do not require security clearance;
8. appointments in the field service not to exceed 60 days to meet emergencies; or
9. nationals of the People's Republic of China who qualify for adjustment of status pursuant to the Chinese Student Protection Act of 1992. A few agencies have special legislation which permits them to hire noncitizens even if they do not fall under one of the exceptions described above. For example, the Public Health Service can hire some scientists without regard to these restrictions. Such exceptions are extremely rare.

Non-Appropriated Fund (NAF) positions, jobs paid for by money other than that appropriated by Congress, are also open to noncitizens. They include jobs in military officer and enlisted clubs, which are funded by their patrons.

> **NAF** positions are discussed in Step 2 (p. 36).

Under most of these exceptions, noncitizens will be considered for employment under the same procedures as other applicants. However, agencies are permitted to establish policies which give priority to citizens ahead of noncitizens.

VETERANS

Veterans who meet certain standards receive many advantages in the Federal hiring process. One is that certain jobs are available *only* to qualified veterans (as long as enough of them are willing and able). These jobs are of two types: unskilled jobs for which almost anyone would qualify (such as Custodian, Messenger, and Elevator Operator) and job titles for which military service is a decided advantage (such as Military Pay Clerk, Electronics Mechanic, and Aircraft Mechanic). There are also programs that make other jobs available to veterans on a noncompetitive basis while providing vocational or scholastic education.

EXAMPLE

Jeff, having served on active duty in Vietnam, qualifies for a Veterans Readjustment Appointment (VRA). This may well give him an edge in getting that job as an Electronics Mechanic, since the Department of Defense has a particular interest in the VRA program. Also, having received a Purple Heart for being wounded in action, Jeff is entitled to preferential hiring treatment for positions in the regular civil service.

Special veterans hiring programs, including **VRA**, are discussed in Appendix Q.

Now that you have identified which job titles are appropriate for you, and which of those are more likely to land you a job, you are ready for Step 2 in your Federal job search.

HOW THE EXEMPLARY CANDIDATES APPLY STEP 1

The chart on the following page summarizes what each of the four exemplary candidates—Janet, Michael, Helen, and Jeff—accomplished by implementing Step 1.

Note, at one time the reference to administrative groups was very important. Each group covered different jobs, and applicants had to take separate tests for each group. Then a separate register was established for each group. Now that administrative jobs are filled by case examining (one position at a time), the groups are much less important. However, if the agency decides to use the administrative written test as part of the rating process, the test will still be different for each group.

Summary Table: The Exemplary Candidates at the End of Step 1

Exemplary Candidate Biography	Applicant Category (App. A)	Job Title & Series (Apps. A & K)	Grade (Apps. C &M)	Hiring Prospects (App. M)
Janet, secretary with high-school diploma; at present job for 6 years; earns $26,500; duties include word processing, data entry, & steno dictation; writes own correspondence; helps plan, manage, & schedule business meetings, conferences, & travel reservations; types 60 wpm; takes dictation at 80 wpm; previously worked as receptionist, payroll clerk, clerk-typist, order processor, & file clerk; hopes to qualify for an administrative office position.	Clerical/ Skilled	Secretary GS-318	5	Excellent
			7	Good
			9	Fair
		Support Services Spec. GS-342	7/9	Poor
		Management Asst. GS-344	7	Fair
			9	Poor
		Admin. Officer GS-341	7/9	Poor
		Misc. Admin. GS-301	7/9	Good
		Admin. Occupations	5/7	Fair
Michael, recent college graduate with liberal arts degree; maintained GPA of 3.0; majored in history, minored in criminal psychology; not sure if wants career in office management or in something more dramatic, like law enforcement; types well; is good organizer.	Recent College Grad.	Admin. Occup. Groups 2,3,4,6,7	5/7	Fair-Good
		Air Traffic Controller GS-2152	7	Fair
		Foreign Service Officer GS-130	7	Poor
		Intelligence Officer GS-132	5/7	Poor
		Personnel Asst. GS-203	5	Good
		Law Enforcement (Various)	5/7	Good
		Education (Various, GS-1700)	5/7	Fair
Helen, B.S. in Business Administration, minor in Accounting; speaks fluent French; nearing completion of master's degree in Financial Management; is part-time bookkeeper for mortgage company in New York City; plans to build career in finance, preferably on West Coast; interested in job with travel potential.	Recent College Grad. (Accounting, Liberal Arts, Overseas)	Accountant GS-510	5/7	Good
		Auditor GS-511	5/7	Good
		Financial Instit. Examiner GS-570	5/7	Fair
		Financial Analyst GS-1160	5/7	Poor
		Language Specialist GS-1040	5/7	Fair
		Foreign Service Officer	FP-7*	Poor
		Foreign Service Secretary	FP-9*	Good
Jeff, Vietnam vet, radar technician in army; electrician for past 8 years; most recent annual earnings $27,300; high-school diploma, certification as air conditioning repair technician was building superintendent, construction worker, building framer, & carpenter; enjoys working with his hands; 47 years old with school-age kids; wants security, regular pay.	Blue Collar/ Experienced Trade/ Journeyman	Electrician WG-2805	J/L	Good
		Carpenter WG-4607	J	Good
		A/C Equip. Mechanic WG-5306	J	Good
		A/C Equip. Operator WG-5415	J	Poor
		Electronics Mechanic WG-2614	J	Good
		Maintenance Mechanic WG-4749	J	Good

*Foreign Service positions have their own pay schedule and are not in the General Schedule; see Appendix F.

Step 2: Finding the Right Hiring Pathway

Purpose: To help you follow the proper sets of procedures—what we call *hiring pathways*—in applying for the job titles of interest to you. The first main section describes how the Federal employment system is set up and what factors affect the job market; the second introduces and explains the various components of Federal hiring procedures. These introductory sections, useful background for all readers, are especially important for those interested in pursuing a number of different job titles. The hiring pathways themselves are covered in a third section, designed to help you identify which sets of procedures are appropriate for you.

Associated appendixes:
  B   Selected Fields and Their Hiring Pathways
  C   Selected Occupations and Their Hiring Pathway Factors
  D   Federal Personnel Offices
  F   Federal Salary Rates
  P   Job Opportunities Overseas
  Q   Special Recruitment and Hiring Programs

In this step you determine what application procedures you will need to follow in making your application. This includes what application forms to file, where and when to file them, whether you will need to take a test, whether you are likely to be considered immediately or go on a waiting list, and many other pertinent questions. Life would be so easy for the Federal job seeker if only one application route were pertinent to all positions; but it is just not so simple.

To help you determine what application procedures apply to you, we have grouped them into five sets, which we call *hiring pathways* (or just *pathways*). These are described in the second half of this chapter. You will need to determine which of these pathways is appropriate for each position in which you are interested. To do this, it is important first to understand the structure of the Federal employment system and the various components of its hiring procedures.

THE FEDERAL EMPLOYMENT SYSTEM

FEDERAL AGENCIES AND OPM

The United States government is divided into three branches: the legislative, which enacts Federal laws; the judicial, which applies and interprets those laws; and the executive, which carries out (executes) those laws. In addition to the president and White House staff, the executive branch comprises many individual administrative offices, or *agencies*. Their official names may not include the word "agency"—some are called departments, bureaus, commissions, or boards—but all are considered agencies for the purposes of this book. Departments (such as the Department of State and Department of Defense) have cabinet status; that is, their chief officials—somewhat confusingly called *secretaries*—comprise the cabinet, which advises the president. All other agencies are considered to operate independently within the executive branch.

> With few exceptions, the job titles for which you will be applying with the help of this book are for positions in **executive branch** agencies. See Appendix D for a list of these agencies.

One independent Federal agency important to the Federal recruitment process, and to which we shall refer throughout this book, is the *Office of Personnel Management (OPM)*. OPM is the agency charged by law with the responsibility of overseeing all Federal personnel practices, including recruitment, to determine their compliance with statutes. Thus, other agencies must answer to OPM for their recruitment policies and practices. In addition to its oversight responsibilities, OPM performs many personnel functions, including recruitment for some of the other agencies.

THE FEDERAL JOB MARKET

Because the Federal employment system operates on such a tremendous scale—involving thousands of facilities nationwide and overseas and comprising hundreds of different organizations—it must advertise openings and recruit and hire people in ways markedly different from those of the private sector. It must also be able to adapt its recruitment methods and promotion policies to many different job market conditions. These conditions, like those of any market, are determined by the interaction of supply and demand. In some cases the supply of candidates exceeds the demand (*oversupply*); for others the demand exceeds the supply (*undersupply*). Cases in which the supply matches the demand are said to be in *equilibrium*.

Where an undersupply of candidates prevails, Federal employers try to attract candidates by making the application process as smooth as possible; after all, if applying for jobs is too difficult or inconvenient, job seekers can find other employers who will make life easier for them. However, where a candidate oversupply prevails, Federal employers are inclined to use application procedures that are efficient and cost effective, even though some candidates find these procedures difficult and inconvenient.

Although the Federal government is a very desirable employer, it must compete for employees with private-sector companies, big and small, and with state and local governments in the public sector. Throughout our discussion of application procedures, we shall refer frequently to the Federal government's need to compete for candidates.

Job markets may vary from job to job and place to place, and even for the same job title at different career levels. In addition, the many current Federal employees who also compete for government positions that become open, form an internal job market. Because Federal employers recruit candidates with different job titles, in different geographic locations, at different career levels, and from within their own ranks as well as outside of them, hiring procedures must be responsive to each of these factors. A new factor relates to downsizing which some Federal agencies have undergone. As the result of a presidential directive, agencies are required to give priority to surplus and displaced employees who apply for positions and are determined to be well qualified.

Job Titles and the Job Market

All Federal job titles can be divided into three categories that we shall call multiple-use, predominant-use, and unique-use occupations. A *multiple-use* occupation is one used by more than one agency. Examples are Secretaries, Computer Specialists, and Accountants. A *predominant-use* occupation is one used largely by a single agency. The Department of Agriculture, for example, is the predominant user of Soil Conservationists: Only a comparative handful are employed by the Army, Navy, and the Departments of Interior and Energy. Similarly, the Department of Veterans Affairs (VA) is the predominant user of health care professionals, even though there are thousands in the armed forces, the Department of Health and Human Services, and elsewhere. A *unique-use* occupation is found in one agency only. For instance, only the Treasury Department uses Bond Sales Promoters; and only the Department of Energy uses Nuclear Material Couriers.

Candidates for multiple-use occupations tend to be in the shortest supply because many agencies have to compete for candidates. Unique-use occupations, obviously, involve the least competition within the public sector. For most jobs, of course, the Federal government also has to compete with the private sector, which has its own demand for health care professionals, scientists, clerical workers, and so on. However, for some positions the Federal government has no competition; we shall call these *monopolized occupations.* Postal workers, Intelligence Agents, and Foreign Service Officers, to name a few, have no where to work but the government. Consequently, the supply of candidates for these positions greatly exceeds the demand. For example, sometimes hundreds of candidates compete for every single postal job opening. Likewise, some 20,000 candidates for Foreign Service positions vie for the 250 or so jobs that become available each year. The CIA probably holds the record: It is said to screen thousands of applicants for every Intelligence Agent position that opens. No doubt it is difficult for the CIA, with its national security focus, to have to screen so many candidates carefully; but for other Federal employers, monopolized positions can make recruitment easier, as the oversupply is very much in the government's favor.

Two examples illustrate how supply and demand can affect application procedures:

Because the supply of candidates for postal work greatly exceeds the demand, candidates are required to take a difficult written test, which is given only once every year or two in most places. They usually have only a few days to apply; if they miss the opportunity, they have to wait for the next exam. Even applying on time doesn't guarantee a chance to take the test: Instead, in many metropolitan areas, this is determined by lottery. Candidates who do get to take the test must generally score above 90 (if not above 95) to have much chance of an interview—for which they must wait, sometimes for over a year, to be called. Finally, after a successful interview, the candidates may be appointed postal workers. In such a candidate oversupply, the application process need hardly be easy or convenient for the job seeker.

A very different application process awaits candidates in occupations for which there is an undersupply. For example, because secretaries are in wide demand in both the private and public sectors, they are not required to take a written test, are hired on the basis of an application form, and often are put to work within days of applying. After all, even the Federal government must observe the laws of supply and demand.

Geographic Location and the Job Market

Although many Americans are willing to relocate to find a better job, most still prefer to remain near their homes. This is why the employment market is not so much a national market as a local one. Thus, for many job titles, job market conditions vary from one locality to another. Clerical workers are a case in point:

In some major metropolitan areas, clerical workers are in short supply; as a result, their application procedures are as easy and convenient as Federal employers can make them. The clerical written test is administered in many locations and as often as once a week. Because there are few candidates, agencies can often make employment offers within days after applicants obtain their test results. Even though applicants may have to take a written clerical test, they usually do not have to take a typing or stenography test. Agencies will usually accept self-certification although they have the option of requiring applicants to demonstrate their skills.

Candidates who make false claims on their applications will be discharged. In many suburban and rural areas, on the other hand, clerical workers are in oversupply. The application procedures are neither so easy nor so convenient. Written tests may be given only monthly, often at some distance from the candidate's home. Upon successful completion of the test, candidates are placed on a waiting list. Usually only the highest-scoring candidates are offered jobs, and even then they must often wait months for an offer.

Since local job market conditions can vary greatly from one area to another, it is generally impossible to describe Federal hiring procedures that are valid nationwide. This is especially true for multiple-use occupations, which are likely to occur in the private sector as well and thus lead to candidate undersupply.

When it has a monopoly on an occupation, however, the Federal government can enforce uniform application procedures. Hence the procedures for Air Traffic Controller, Border Patrol Agent, and Intelligence Agent are the same across the country. Even postal work, which is very localized—every city has its post office—uses basically the same application procedures nationwide.

Career Levels and the Job Market

Grade and **career levels** are described in Step 1; **salary rates** appear in Appendix F.

Generally, the higher the career level in Federal service, the more the market tends to place the Federal government at a disadvantage and favor the employee. This is because the pay differential between Federal and private-sector employment tends to increase (with the private sector paying more) as the career level rises.

Standards of Federal pay for entry-level General Schedule jobs are generally close to those in the private sector. However, there are important differences:

Positions that require little or no prior experience or education tend to pay higher in Federal service than in the private sector. For example, one need not have relevant education or work experience (though some *general* experience is required) to qualify as an Air Traffic Controller, Postal Worker, Correctional Officer, or other Law Enforcement Officer; yet starting salaries in these job titles are good compared to similar work in the private sector.

Many entry-level jobs that do require prior relevant education or experience, however, tend to pay somewhat less in Federal service than in the private sector. This is true of most entry-level jobs in the professions, sciences, other technical fields, and health care; but even in these fields the pay differential at the lower grades is not as great as at the upper levels.

As explained in step 1, there is the basic General Schedule, but the salaries are augmented by locality pay. For hard to fill positions, there are *special rates,* and as explained in Step 1, salaries are set either at the General Schedule rate as augmented by locality pay or the special rate whichever is higher. Wage Grade rates vary from one geographic area to another, depending on the wage prevailing locally in the private sector. Wage Grade candidates must therefore ask prospective employers what the hourly wage is to be for a position at a given grade level.

Special salary rates were mentioned in Step 1 (p. 16).

At entry level, Federal work may pay more than the private sector: The average annual salary of all Federal workers in all grades is some $31,000, whereas for private-sector workers it is only $28,000. At the mid- and upper-levels, however, Federal pay is often below that of the private sector. This puts the Federal government at a disadvantage to the private sector in recruitment. For example, the highest salary in the Federal civil service at this writing is $115,700 per year plus locality pay. (This is at level 6 of the Senior Executive Service, for jobs requiring neither presidential appointment nor Congressional confirmation; jobs that do carry such requirements are covered by the Executive Pay Scale, whose highest salary [at EX-1] is $148,400.) Top-level executives in the private sector make much more in many fields. Thus although there are many compensatory benefits in Federal employment—including superior job security, excellent retirement benefits, longer vacations, and more holidays—the supply of mid- and top-level candidates for many Federal positions is still lower than the demand.

See Appendix R regarding Federal **employment benefits.**

Status versus Nonstatus Candidates: The Internal Job Market

The condition of the internal Federal job market—that involving candidates who are already part of the Federal employment system—can best be characterized as one of equilibrium between supply and demand. Until a few years ago, there was a tilt toward the demand side. However, recently the government has undergone significant downsizing, so there is now a tilt toward the supply side. Between 1993 and 1997, the overall government work force was reduced by approximately 250,000. However, even with the downsizing, there is still a need for the government to fill many jobs each year. The Excepted Service is described later in this chapter; see "Types of Federal Civil Service."

Agencies may opt to fill many mid- and top-level positions *only* by promotion of current Federal employees. This is particularly true for mid- and top-level jobs in administrative and executive fields: Federal employers believe, as do employers in many industries, that only those employees with experience in the organization are qualified for these positions. Current Federal employees with potential for such promotion are said to have civil service *career (or competitive) status* and are called *status candidates.* Nonemployees or Federal employees hired under special programs that do not convey status (that is, the Excepted Service) are called *nonstatus candidates.* All in all, a great deal of promotion activity takes place within the Federal work force, and most Federal employers regularly need status candi-

Promotion is also discussed in Step 1 under "Grade Level: External Hiring vs. Internal Promotion (p. 21).

dates to fill mid- and top-level positions. The internal job market, then, can fairly be characterized as one of equilibrium between supply and demand. Application procedures for promotion are therefore reasonably convenient.

As mentioned in Step 1, because the Federal government is huge, it has more advancement opportunities than most private-sector employers; hence promotion is usually more rapid in Federal service than in the private sector. Generally, there are minimum time-in-grade restrictions that apply before promotion can be obtained; these vary by job title, but can be as little as a year. It should be emphasized, however, that all promotions are based on job performance, not on time-in-grade.

Like managers of any organization, Federal employers would like to promote from within when possible. Thus, opening a mid- or top-level position to both status and nonstatus candidates is an indication that the position is hard to fill internally; in other words, that there is an insufficient supply of mid- and top-level status candidates. Hiring procedures for such positions tend to be made as easy and convenient as the system will allow, with status candidates having the inside track.

TYPES OF FEDERAL CIVIL SERVICE

Almost all Federal civil service positions are classified as either Competitive Service or Excepted Service, depending on whether they are subject to or excepted from specific regulations and procedures established and administered by OPM. This classification (Competitive vs. Excepted) is important in that it partly determines the hiring method to be used to fill a job.

Competitive Service

> The competitive aspects of Competitive Service are explained below ("Components of Federal Hiring Procedures, p. 36). The various pay schedules are described in Step 1 (p. 16).

The vast majority of government civilian jobs are in the *Competitive Service*, under which fair and open competition among applicants is used to ensure equal employment opportunity. This means job applicants must compete with others seeking the same job under regulations and procedures established by OPM. Competitive Service positions are found throughout the two major pay schedules (General Schedule and Wage Grade) as well as in the higher Senior Level Pay Schedule. The Senior Executive Service is not officially part of the Competitive Service, but career SES positions are filled under competitive procedures that must conform to merit principles. About 10% of SES employees are political appointees, and they are not appointed under competitive procedures. (Note: Veteran Preference about which you will read more later does not apply to the Senior Executive Service.)

Excepted Service

> In **Appendix C**, the first two columns (Hiring System) show whether a listed job title is in the **Competitive** or **Excepted Service.**

Most civil service jobs that are not in the Competitive Service are in the *Excepted Service*. This comprises civilian positions in the executive branch of the Federal government that are specifically excepted from the Competitive Service—whether by statute, by the president, or by OPM—and are thus outside OPM's competitive hiring process. Student work-study positions are a good example. In addition, certain positions are *always* in the Excepted Service; these fall into three groups, called Schedules A, B, and C:

A. Positions (a) for which it is not practical to recruit through the regular competitive system, (b) that are not confidential or policy determining in nature, and (c) for which civil service examinations are not available or appropriate. *Examples*: Attorneys, Chaplains, Foreign Language Specialists, summer jobs for students, and positions held by noncitizens because there are no competitive service applicants as explained in step 1.

B. Positions (a) for which it is not practical to recruit through the regular competitive system, (b) that are not confidential or policy determining in nature, and (c) for which candidates must pass a *noncompetitive* examination. *Example*: employees in the College Students Cooperative Education Program (student trainees).

C. Key positions at the GS-15 level or below that (a) do not require an examination but (b) *are* policy determining or (c) involve a close personal relationship with the head of, or key officials of, an agency. Persons may be appointed by the head of the agency. Any position may be included in this schedule. *Examples*: Confidential Secretary, Special Assistant.

> You can find out from an agency whether a job for which you intend to apply is in the **Excepted Service**.

It is important to realize that Excepted Service positions can occur in agencies predominantly staffed by Competitive Service employees. The biggest advantage to these jobs is that they are generally easier to apply for and fill than those in the Competitive Service. You need not have competitive status. Excepted agencies may use streamlined rating procedures or may not even rate applicants at all.

The main drawback to the Excepted Service is that employees are not awarded all of the traditional rights, benefits, and protections commonly associated with competitive civil service employment. Among those missing is the opportunity to earn *career status,* which greatly increases the employee's ability to obtain a different or higher-level Federal job. Generally, those who wish to transfer to the Competitive Service must apply for a Competitive Service position as though they were total outsiders (but at least armed with some government experience); upon obtaining such a position, the employee then leaves the Excepted Service and is a new Competitive Service employee. However, Excepted Service employees under Schedules A and B may, in *some* cases, qualify for the Competitive Service automatically. This so-called *conversion* is available to Drug Enforcement Agents (after a year in the Excepted Service) and to those eligible for certain special hiring programs (such as student trainees, the handicapped, returning Peace Corps workers, and VRA appointees).

Step 7 explains special provisions which permit employees in some excepted agencies to transfer to the Competitive Service. This ability to transfer is based on statutory provisions or agreements between the agency and OPM.

> **Excepted agencies** are explained in the next subsection; **Competitive examining procedures** are covered below (p.40). The **SF-171** form is discussed in detail in Step 5 and shown in Appendix H.

> **Career status** is introduced above ("Status versus Nonstatus Candidates, p. 33). Advantages and drawbacks of the **Excepted Service** are further explored in Step 7.

> These and other special **hiring programs** are described in Appendix Q.

Keep in mind that the Excepted Service hiring process does have *some* merit system features; for instance, agencies are prohibited from showing favoritism or from discriminating against applicants. In fact, each excepted agency must establish written rules for Excepted Service hiring and apply those rules uniformly. If you request to see a copy of the agency's rules, it must show them to you.

Independent Employment Systems (Excepted Agencies)

A full list of **excepted agencies** appears in Appendix D.

Some job titles may be excepted from OPM regulations only in certain agencies. This is because several entire agencies—and therefore *all* job titles at these agencies—are excepted from the Competitive Service by law. These *independent employment systems*, or *excepted agencies*, include (but are not limited to) the U.S. Postal Service, the Foreign Service (under the State Department), the Federal Reserve System, the Tennessee Valley Authority (TVA), the FBI, the CIA, and the General Accounting Office (GAO). Candidates who want *any* position in an excepted agency—even a Data Transcriber, Motor Vehicle Operator, or other job title found also in nonexcepted agencies—must still apply to the agency itself.

Non-Appropriated Fund (NAF) Positions

A small group of Federal jobs (about 10,000 positions) is paid for by money not appropriated by Congress but earned by certain commercial services provided at military bases and other Federal work sites. These *Non-Appropriated Fund (NAF) positions* are therefore not part of the Federal civil service proper. Most are associated with the commercial services themselves, including military base post exchanges (PXs), commissaries, and officer and enlisted clubs. Such positions are particularly attractive to those just entering the Federal workplace because hirings tend to favor those new to the system; they are also open to noncitizens. Many of the positions within these activities involve the trade, craft, and labor jobs in the Federal Wage System, but some jobs in the General Schedule may be included as well. Although NAF positions may be advertised by Federal agencies in the same manner as regular civil service jobs, employees are not part of the Federal civil service and are not subject to the same requirements, benefits, or obligations.

COMPONENTS OF FEDERAL HIRING PROCEDURES

As we have said before, there is no single—let alone simple—way to apply for all Federal positions. However, although the procedures are many, the underlying objectives are closely interrelated. In this section you will come to understand several important aspects of Federal application procedures, including ratings, examinations, Examining Authority, eligibility, the Rule-of-Three, and registers.

RATINGS

The Federal government, you'll recall, is legally bound to observe a strict *merit system* of employment. This system requires that every applicant for a competitive Federal position be considered objectively. To provide an objective basis for the comparison of candidates for a specific position, each may be given a numerical score, or *rating*. The highest rating obtainable for most applicants is 100; but because certain veterans are awarded an additional 5 or 10 points under a special hiring program called *veterans' preference*, their highest possible rating is 110. The lowest score actually given is 70: Applicants who fall below this cutoff score are considered not qualified for the position being filled. Candidates are advised of their eligibility, and in some cases told their actual score, in a *Notice of Results*.

To appreciate the rating process fully, you must understand that for each position, there is a position description that describes the duties, responsibilities, and requirements for the position. Based on the duties, responsibilities, and requirements, the position is placed into a job series and given a job title and grade. OPM publishes qualifications standards for the various job series and grades. Applicants are evaluated against these standards to determine whether they meet minimum qualifications. In addition to the minimum standards published by OPM, agencies develop additional rating criteria which are intended to determine those applicants who will be best qualified for the position. The rating given a candidate is intended to reflect how well his or her education and/or prior experience meet the qualifications described for the given position *at a given grade level*. Thus by applying at a grade level truly justified by your education and work experience you should receive a solid rating; but your rating would drop were you to apply for the same job title at a higher grade.

Although it is impossible for us to reprint here the exact standard for every job title at every applicable grade level (they occupy several volumes in themselves), we have reproduced brief descriptions of all General Schedule and Wage Grade job titles in Appendixes K and N, respectively. These descriptions will give you some idea of the qualifications for job titles that interest you. OPM has made their standards more general recently, so there is more emphasis placed on the individual rating criteria developed by agencies for positions. For most General Schedule positions, you will meet the minimum OPM standard if you have at least 52 weeks of directly related experience which is equivalent to the next lower grade level. This does not mean that the experience has to be in the Federal government. Agencies will evaluate the experience you describe in your application and determine whether it is related to the position being filled and the level it is equivalent to. Particularly at the entry and mid-level grades, education may be substituted for experience. For Wage Grade positions, your experience will be evaluated to determine whether you have specific skills required for the position. Unlike the General Schedule, you do not have to have a specific amount of experience as long as your background demonstrates that you have the required

> The **merit system** is outlined in the Introduction. **Veterans' preference** is described in Appendix Q. The **Notice of Results** is explained in Step 5 (p. 101).

skills. Your goal, when you actually apply for a Federal job, is to show that you meet the standard and the criteria developed for the particular position.

EXAMINATIONS

As was mentioned in the Introduction, the Federal government employs more than three million people in over 2,000 different occupations. It hires 20,000 to 30,000 people each month, with more than 85,000 people applying for those jobs. At last count (which was several years ago), over one million applications for Federal employment had been received over the course of a year.

Given the scope of their operations, Federal employers have striven to make the process of evaluating and rating candidates—called *examination*— as quick and cost-effective as possible. Beginning several years ago, agencies were permitted to accept résumés instead of standard government applications (SF-171). Usually announcements will indicate the criteria that the agency is using to evaluate applicants. It is important that your résumé or application be tailored to address the criteria described in the announcement. For some jobs, you may be required to take a written test or complete a supplemental application form designed for the position being filled.

Assembled versus Unassembled Exams

One method of examining candidates is to give a written test; this, in fact, was once the only method used to examine candidates for Federal service. It is still the principle method used in many city and state governments, but it is now used only for a small percentage of Federal positions. The test for clerical positions is one of the few written tests still used by the Federal government. Until several years ago, recent college graduates applying for entry-level administrative positions had to take a written test, (the ACWA exam), but testing is now only used in the rating process at the option of the hiring agency. OPM reports that few if any agencies avail themselves of that option. A written test is called an *assembled exam* because candidates assemble in a room to take it.

Written tests have important advantages for Federal employers. When properly designed they are fair to all candidates. Also, they are relatively inexpensive to score, and can generally be scored quickly by computer. However, written tests also present a serious problem for Federal employers: They are very unpopular with candidates. If there is a competition from the private sector for these candidates, some may decide against seeking Federal employment rather than be bothered with taking a test.

The other type of examination is called an *unassembled exam* because candidates need not assemble in order to take it. This method is based on an application form that the candidate completes at home and submits by the filing deadline, or *closing date,* along with any supporting materials required (for instance, a college transcript or proof of professional license). An unassembled exam is scored just as rigorously as an assembled exam and should be thought of as a take-home test. There are two types of unassembled exams: closed-end and open-end.

Closed-end forms allow only answers of the multiple-choice variety. This has mostly fill-in-the-circles type answers that can be scored (rated) quickly and inexpensively by computer. Multiple-choice questions relate to facts about the candidate's education and prior job experience; there is little chance to enhance one's background as might be done with a résumé. Agencies can use computerized forms to examine for any position. Much of the examining which OPM does for agencies uses this method. The Administrative exam now uses this approach for each position an agency is filling. As noted above, in addition to this, agencies have the option of using a written test for Administrative positions but rarely do.

Open-end forms, on the other hand, allow unlimited commentary. The most common example of this type used to be the Standard Form (SF-)171: Application for Federal Employment. Federal agencies are no longer permitted to require that you complete this application. However, since many agencies are still very familiar with it and since it provides a structured approach for you to describe your background, it still is very helpful for you to be familiar with it. Since the SF-171 is no longer published, you may not be able to obtain an actual copy of it. However, the information contained in step 5 will enable you to develop an application which contains all the pertinent information you need to apply for a position. You must be sure, however, to review vacancy announcements carefully to ensure that you address any requirements that may be applicable to the job for which you are applying. If you feel more comfortable with actually using a published form, OPM does have an optional application form for Federal Employment (OF 612). This form requests much of the information which the SF-171 asks for, but it is not quite as detailed. Most of the chapter on Step 5 is dedicated to filling it out, and work sheets are provided in Appendix I. The most important parts of the SF-171 relate to prior job experience, descriptions that should be concise, but can be as long as the candidate desires. This provides ample opportunity to relate any information that may improve the candidate's rating. Open-end forms have a serious drawback for Federal employers: They are expensive and time consuming to score, especially on a large scale, as each must be evaluated individually by a trained examiner. However, they do enable candidates to relate their specific education and work experience to the positions for which they are applying.

Group versus Case Examining: Managing Applicant Supply

Depending upon the number of vacancies that occur (or are expected to occur) for a given job title and grade level over a relatively short time, Federal employers will take one of two approaches: group or case examining. This decision may determine what type of examination you will be asked to take (assembled or unassembled, closed- or open-end); however, it will not affect the way in which your examination is rated.

Group examining is for positions that come open regularly (are "active") and whose qualification standards are not so specialized as to be extremely restrictive—many entry-level positions, for example. The likely recurrence of openings means that some form of inventory of candidates, such as a *register* (see p. 40), may be kept. Group examining may involve assembled and/or unassembled exams.

Agencies and OPM are now doing much more case examining than ever before, and it can be used for many types and levels of positions. Virtually all case examining is done by unassembled exam using the SF-171, résumés, the OPM Optional Application Form for Federal Employment, or any other application form applicants choose to submit (and related supporting forms submitted by the candidate). This gives the applicant ample opportunity to present information about prior experience, which is the main qualification for most nonentry-level positions. It is important to reiterate that whatever form your application takes, you must be sure to provide the information required in the vacancy announcement. Generally agencies are not permitted to require a particular form or format, but in some cases, agencies may have approval to use specific forms which can be entered into an automated system. In those cases, you must use only that form.

The period between a position's opening and closing dates—the *filing period* or *application window*—is chosen to elicit a sufficient, yet manageable, number of applications. For instance, if too much interest is anticipated in a position, the filing period is kept short and given a definite closing date, to limit the number of forms received by the deadline; but if an applicant undersupply is expected, the filing period will be less restrictive (with a closing date of either "continuous" or "open until filled"). Managing applicant supply is particularly important when using résumés or other narrative application formats, since rating this open-end examination is expensive and time consuming, and government policy is to give every candidate examined at least a preliminary evaluation.

> Types of **closing dates** are described in Step 4 (p. 79).

EXAMINING AUTHORITY: TO WHOM DOES THE CANDIDATE APPLY?

The legal authority to develop examinations, whether tests or application forms, and to evaluate and rate candidates who take them is called *Examining Authority.* This authority originates in the Office of Personnel Management (OPM). Until 1996, OPM did much of the examining itself, so most applicants applied directly to it even though the positions were in other agencies. In 1996, Congress mandated that OPM must delegate most examining authority to agencies, so most applicants will now apply directly to the agencies which are filling the positions. OPM can still do some examining for agencies if those agencies reimburse OPM for the cost, so in some situations you may still have to apply to OPM. Agencies may enter into agreements with agencies other than OPM to do examining for them, so it is possible that you will apply to one agency for a position in another agency. Agencies may enter into such agreements to gain greater efficiency. For example, if one agency has many positions and another has only a few, it may be more efficient for the agency with a few positions to reimburse the other agency for examining services rather than to provide those services itself. OPM still must do all the examining for administrative law judge positions. These are high-level positions involved in the adjudication of various matters such as disability claims with the Social Security Administration. There are between 1,000 and 2,000 of these positions in the Federal government. Anyone interested in such a position would have to apply directly to OPM. The concept of Examining Authority pertains only to the Competitive Service (including the SES); it is not relevant to Excepted Service, excepted agency, or Non-Appropriated Fund positions.

Delegated Examining Authority

When examining authority is delegated to agencies, OPM does not give up its oversight responsibility, but periodically audits the operation of agency examining units.

Direct Hire Authority

You may occasionally hear the term *direct hire authority.* When OPM had most of the examining authority, this was an important authority. Where there was a shortage of applicants, OPM would give agencies direct hire authority, so they could recruit and hire applicants without going to OPM. Since agencies now already have delegated examining authority, it is no longer necessary for OPM to give them direct hire authority. In other words, agencies already have all the authority they need to recruit and hire applicants.

| **Agency addresses** are listed in Appendix D. |

ELIGIBILITY AND THE RULE-OF-THREE

A candidate who passes a Federal examination, whether assembled or unassembled, is called an *eligible*, as he or she is eligible to receive an offer of employment, or *appointment*, for the job title and grade level covered by the exam. When the number of eligibles is about the same as or less than the number of openings for that job title and grade level, all eligibles can be offered employment.

However, when there are more than three eligibles for any opening, the three most highly rated must be considered first. This is called the *Rule-of-Three.* Under this rule, the agency can then appoint any of the three eligibles regardless of their relative ratings; however, it cannot (without documented justification) appoint a nonveteran if a veteran is among them and is the higher rated. Except for scientific and professional positions at GS-9 and above, veterans with compensable disabilities of 10% or more are placed ahead of all other candidates as long as they meet minimum qualifications. For example, a

Who has **Examining Authority** for a position in which you are interested? See Appendix C and/or write your local Federal Job Information Center. (**OPM Service Centers** are discussed in Step 3 and listed in Appendix D.)

10% compensably disabled veteran with a score of 80 would still be placed ahead of other candidates with scores of 95 and 100. For scientific and professional positions at GS-9 and above, 10% compensably disabled veterans are placed according to their scores and do not float to the top. Should the agency find all three wanting in some respect, it can (with documented justification) ask to consider the next three most highly rated eligibles.

REGISTERS

When Registers Are Used

When there are more eligibles than openings, a question arises: Should the names of those not needed now be saved for future use? In practice, the answer is that the names of eligibles will not be saved if no substantial future demand for those eligibles is anticipated—that is, if the job title for which those eligibles have been rated is not an active one. In the case of inactive job titles, Federal employers prefer to recruit from scratch next time rather than try to maintain a list. Lists are perishable: Eligibles find other employment, relocate, or simply lose interest. However, if substantial near-term demand for eligibles is indeed anticipated, such a list—called a *Register of Eligibles* (or just *register*)—or a competitor inventory will be kept. Registers are generally maintained for a given position, that is, for a single job title and grade level. OPM is phasing out the use of registers, and there is much more case examining than ever before.

Because registers save recruiting time, Federal employers would like to have them for every position that regularly comes open. However, in many fields not enough candidates can be found to maintain a register. So, in practice, Federal employers can maintain registers only for job titles and grade levels for which an applicant oversupply condition prevails. For reasons explained above, these are mostly at entry level and, to a much lesser degree, at mid level.

Applicant oversupply conditions are discussed in the section on "The Federal Job Market."

Another reason that registers are only infrequently maintained at mid level and never at top level is these positions are much less active than those at entry level. Candidates for mid- and top-level positions would have to wait so long for selection that the register would become old and of little value. Thus registers are impractical for most of these positions, and candidates are *case examined* instead. However, after filling a case-examined position, OPM or the hiring agency may decide to maintain an *applicant supply file* at the local level. This is a list of candidates who are *likely to qualify* (based on a preliminary evaluation of their examinations) but have *not yet been rated*: Actual rating is deferred until there is a new opening, since each position in a given job title at GS-9 and above is somewhat distinct, and candidates must be rated with regard to its *special qualifications*.

Case examining is introduced earlier in this chapter (p. 39)

Step 4 (p. 83) explains **special qualifications**.

How Registers Are Used

Registers used to be very common when OPM did most of the examining, but now they are relatively uncommon. When OPM or an agency does establish a register, it will work as described below. Eligibles are assigned a place on the register (that is, *ranked*) according to their ratings. The top-ranked candidate is the one with the highest rating; the lowest-ranked candidates have ratings of 70. (The one exception is for veterans with 10% compensable disabilities who float to the top as explained above.) Eligibles remain on the register until being referred to a Federal employer for an interview. This referral process is called *selection*. An eligible on a register is available for selection if he or she is still interested in the position in question and has not accepted other employment. However, an eligible cannot be referred off a register to be interviewed by more than one agency at a time.

Since the *Rule-of-Three* requires that three candidates be considered at a time, an agency requesting eligibles off a register receives a list of the three highest-ranked candidates willing to work in that agency's geographic area. Each of these candidates is, for the time being, referred to that one agency only. The agency must either appoint one of the three or have a good reason for declining them all, including hard evidence relating to the candidates' inability to perform the job. As in case examining, the agency can then appoint any of the three candidates regardless of their relative ratings, but cannot appoint a nonveteran (without documented justification) if a higher-rated veteran is among them. The two candidates who are not appointed are returned to the register and again ranked according to rating; they will be referred to the next requesting agency without prejudice.

Candidates who are offered an appointment but decline the offer are also returned to the register; but they too must have good reasons for declining. Such reasons might relate to serious commuting problems, a specific work schedule, or the duties entailed at a particular facility. However, reasons for declining related to job title or salary that would apply to *all* positions for which the register is maintained may result in an eligible's removal from it. Note that *failure to respond* to a job offer will also lead to a candidate's removal from a register. Removal from a register in no way restricts an applicant from applying in response to another open vacancy announcement even at the same agency.

How high one's rank must be in order to be referred off a register quickly—or for that matter, to be selected at all—varies greatly from register to register. In particular, it depends on the relationship between the supply of eligibles on the register and the demand for them. In high-demand, low-population registers (for example, those for health care professionals), even eligibles with ratings as low as 70 may be called quickly. On the other hand, in low-demand, high-population registers—postal registers being the best example—eligibles will not be selected without ratings in the high 90s.

> Recall that **ratings** below 70 are not given; instead, applicants are notified that they did not pass the examination and told when they may retake it.

> The **Rule-of-Three** is introduced above (p. 41).

> Special hiring programs for **veterans** are explained in the section on Pathway 4 below and in Appendix Q.

Name Requests Off a Register

One way to improve your chances of working for the agency you want in an occupation for which registers are maintained by OPM is to get the agency itself to want you: That way, once you are rated and listed on an OPM register, the agency can request you by name. Such a *name request* will ensure that you are referred directly to that agency as soon as your name comes "within reach"—that is, when you are among the three top-rated candidates on the register (in accordance with the Rule-of-Three).

After phoning the agency to ascertain precisely whom you should contact, *write* that individual of your desire to work there. In general, agencies prefer candidates that express interest in them, and they will be responsive to your inquiries if they anticipate a need for the job title(s) in which you are interested.

If the agency is genuinely interested in you and would be willing to make a name request on your behalf, you will want to ensure that your name comes to the top of the register as soon as possible. One way to do this is to indicate a *narrow* geographic preference when you apply for your rating. Name requests once were a common procedure when there were many OPM registers. Since there are very few registers now and most examining is done through individual vacancy announcements, the name request procedure will not help in most cases. Usually, you will have to apply in response to a specific announcement, but if there is a register, the use of a name request may improve your chances for being hired.

Opening and Closing of Registers

Registers are periodically opened or closed to new candidates. A register opens when vacancies exist and the old register is worn out—that is, when either all the eligibles have been referred off it or those still listed have lost interest or cannot be contacted. Generally, registers are considered worn out after one to three years.

A common misconception about Federal recruitment is that candidates can come forward to be examined at any time for any job title. If candidates are not needed at the time, this thinking goes, they will be assigned to waiting lists (that is, a register). This is not so. One reason, noted above, is that registers are not maintained for every position. Another is that, even when a register is maintained, candidates can come forward only when that register opens. If a register is closed, then (excepting certain veterans) no candidates for that position and grade level will be examined. Application forms (SF-171s) submitted when the register is closed will be returned unevaluated with a note that says, "No openings exist at present for the job title in question."

When Federal employers decide to open a register, they announce examinations for the job title and grade level covered by it. Many candidates confuse an announcement to be examined for a register with an announcement to be considered for immediate appointment. The best way to determine if the application you are filing is for immediate appointment or for a register is to

> Veterans with 10-point disability **veterans' preference** (see Appendix Q) are examined even after a register is closed.

ask the Examining Authority. When enough eligibles have been assigned to the register to provide for one- to three-years' anticipated demand, the register is again closed: No further examinations are given and no additional eligibles are added to the register (excepting certain veterans, as noted earlier) until the next time that the register is opened.

> **Examining Authority** is explained earlier in the chapter.

Though some registers open as infrequently as every three years, once a year is probably about average for most. However, there are registers that are always open. Again, it is the relationship between the supply of candidates and the demand for them that determines the frequency with which the register opens, how fast candidates move off the register and, as we have seen, whether a register is kept at all. Occasionally, a register will stay closed for many years because the agency is able to locate enough candidates from other sources. In 1997 the Air Traffic Controller register had been closed since 1992, and FAA did not anticipate opening it. If the supply of applicants is in equilibrium with the demand for them, the register will be open continuously or frequently, candidates will move off it quickly, and possibly even low ratings will result in selection. If, on the other hand, an oversupply of candidates prevails, the register will open infrequently, candidates will be referred off it slowly, and only those with the highest ratings will be selected.

Having now investigated the structure of the Federal employment system and the various components of its hiring procedures, we can enumerate the five hiring pathways promised at the opening of this chapter.

THE FIVE PATHWAYS INTO FEDERAL SERVICE

To simplify matters, we have grouped all hiring procedures into five typical sets of procedures, which we call *hiring pathways*. The first three apply to first-time Federal employees; the fourth applies to both first-time and current Federal employees; and the fifth applies to current Federal employees specifically. Your comprehension of this discussion will be enhanced by referring to the table on p. 46 entitled "Pathways into Federal Service."

> Note that **hiring pathway** is not an official Federal term; it is used here to represent a procedural road to an appointment.

Let's describe each pathway so that you will be able to determine which is (or are) most appropriate for you.

PATHWAY 1: ENTRY-LEVEL WRITTEN TEST, REGISTER

This first pathway into Federal service is intended for entry-level, nonstatus candidates interested in occupations for which there is an oversupply of applicants. It is characterized by two procedures: Candidates may be required first to take a written test (assembled examination); then, if they pass, they are assigned to a register. Most of the tests for these job titles are conducted by the agencies with the openings.

> **Status vs. nonstatus** is discussed on p. 33.

PATHWAYS INTO FEDERAL SERVICE

PATHWAY	CANDIDATES	JOB TITLES	EXAMINING AUTHORITY		EXAMINATION METHOD		REGISTER			APPLICANT SUPPLY	
			OPM	AGENCY	ASSEMBLED WRITTEN	UNASSEMBLED NONWRITTEN	NAT'L	LOCAL	NONE	OVER	EQUILIBRIUM
#1 WRITTEN TEST REGISTER	ENTRY LEVEL NON-STATUS	Postal	X	X	X			X		X	
		Clerical/Secretarial	X	X	X	X		X			X
		ACWA* (60 Titles)	X		X		X			X	
		Treasury Enforcement	X	X	X		X			X	
		Foreign Service		X	X		X			X	
		Border Patrol	X		X		X			X	
		Air Traffic Controller	X		X		X			X	
		Federal Apprentice Exam									
#2 NO WRITTEN TEST REGISTER	ENTRY LEVEL NON-STATUS	Accountant	X	X		X	X		X		X
		Engineer	X	X		X	X		X		X
		Mathematician	X	X		X	X		X		X
		Physical Scientist	X	X		X	X		X		X
		Life Scientist	X	X		X	X		X		X
		FBI, CIA, DEA, DIA	X	X		X	X			X	
		Technical/Trade	X	X		X		X		X	
		Correctional Officer		X	X	X		X			X
#3 NO WRITTEN TEST NO REGISTER	MID, TOP LEVEL NON-STATUS	Secretarial/Clerical	X	X		X			X		X
		White Collar/Professional	X	X		X			X		X
		Computer Science	X	X		X			X		X
		Technical	X	X		X			X		X
		Health Care Professional	X	X		X			X		X
#4 SPECIAL HIRING PROGRAMS	ENTRY, MID, TOP STATUS/ NON-STATUS VETERANS (ALL); ENTRY, NON-STATUS, VETERANS (VIET), DISABLED, NATIVE AMERICANS, STUDENTS	All / Can Apply for all some especially reserved	X (All Agencies Participate in programs)	X	X (Add 5, 10 points)	X (No Exam)	X	X	X (Cannot be passed over without justification)		X
#5 PROMOTION ROUTE	MID, TOP LEVEL STATUS	All		X		X			X		X

Federal employers can require a written test for these job titles at entry level and be certain that there will be enough applicants. In fact, the onerous nature of the written test serves to screen out some candidates, thus reducing the number who need to be examined and ensuring that only the more motivated will apply. The oversupply of applicants also results in the use of a register, as more than enough candidates to fill existing openings pass the test and become eligibles.

Pathway 1 applies only to a relatively small number of job titles—those covered by the Postal Service, entry-level clerical and secretarial, and the Foreign Service Officer and Air Traffic Controller. Occasionally an agency will develop a written test for some of its positions, but this is rare because gaining approval for a new written test is difficult. The Immigration and Naturalization Service has developed a test for many of its positions such as border patrol agents.

Postal Service

The pay differential between Federal service and similar work in the private sector favors the employee; that is, salaries in the Postal Service are much higher than they are for related private-sector positions. Also, entry-level postal positions have neither specific education nor prior experience requirements. For these reasons, an enormous oversupply of applicants exists for jobs in the Postal Service.

> See Appendix B, p. 194, for more on the **Postal Service.**

To deal with this huge oversupply, the Postal Service attempts to screen out as many applicants as it can through administrative procedures. There is a different test for each main entry-level job title, and an exam is scheduled only when more employees are actually needed in that job title in the given location—every nine months to three years in most areas. In many cases the examination announcement provides an *application window* (time between opening and closing dates) of only a few days: Candidates who do not file applications within that brief time frame are out of luck until the next announcement.

Postal tests are conducted and registers maintained by the Postal Service on a local basis: Usually, the area covered is a county. Although the test is difficult, many candidates pass, and sufficient numbers do extremely well. Having passed the test, candidates usually remain on the register for months (but sometimes even longer). Only the highest-ranking applicants are selected, with ratings often no lower than 95; some preparation for the test is therefore recommended. Many candidates take a prep course, which can be quite expensive; others use a prep book (study guide) that contains sample tests. A good prep book is probably as effective as a course and is considerably less costly.

> A **sample postal exam** appears in Appendix E.

As was mentioned earlier (in "Job Titles and the Job Market"), the application for the exam in metropolitan areas is treated as a lottery ticket: Only those who win the lottery are awarded a seat for the test. In less populated areas, where there are fewer candidates, a lottery is usually not conducted:

> **Study guides** are discussed in Step 5 (p. 99).

All applicants are allowed to take the test. There are also fewer candidates in areas where private-sector salaries are high, as there is less of a pay differential between the Postal Service and similar work in the private sector. This means that registers are less populated, ratings necessary for selection are lower, and time on the register is reduced. One strategy for obtaining an appointment to the Postal Service, therefore, is to apply for the test in an area that is less populated or of higher private-sector income than where you would actually prefer to work. Once you receive an appointment and are a Postal Service employee, the potential for transferring to your preferred work area is good. A postmaster would prefer a job be filled by an experienced employee than by a trainee.

Clerical and Secretarial

See Appendix B, p. 159, for more on **Clerical and Secretarial.**

There are sixty or so different job titles grouped under the General Administrative, Clerical, and Office Services Group (for clerical and secretarial), including some computer-oriented positions (such as Computer Operator and Computer Aide and Technician). They are the one exception to the general Pathway 1 rule of applicant oversupply: In actuality, clerical and secretarial candidates are in oversupply in some geographic areas (small cities and suburban and rural areas) and in undersupply in others (large metropolitan areas). Applicants for lower-level clerical positions will have to take a written test. OPM or in some cases individual agencies administer the test. After you take the test, you will receive a notice of results with your score. OPM does not maintain registers of clerical applicants, but depending on the supply of applicants, individual agencies may maintain their own registers. You can be placed on an agency's register by applying directly to that agency. Your placement on the register will be based on your score on the test. Agencies must honor that score even if you took the test at another agency. Agencies which do not maintain registers will announce individual positions. You must apply for these specific positions. Your rating will be based on your score on the written test. Because there are many types of clerical positions with specific requirements, you must meet the specific requirements of the position being filled in addition to passing the written test. In rare situations, agencies may receive special authority to fill clerical positions without using the written test. In these situations, the agency will develop rating criteria based on the experience and education of applicants. At the time of the writing of this book, OPM was very reluctant to permit agencies to use alternative procedures to the written test.

Candidates with a bachelor's degree can bypass the written test if they apply for clerical positions GS-5 via Pathway 3.

Foreign Service

See Appendix B, p. 168, for more on the **Foreign Service.**

Although employees at U.S. embassies abroad include personnel with secretarial, medical, or communications skills, they are not, strictly speaking, members of the Foreign Service. The Foreign Service Exam is therefore intended only for candidates who wish to be Foreign Service Officers. Such officers with the State Department engage in international diplomacy (the so-called Diplomatic Corps); those with the Department of Commerce are involved in economic aspects of overseas trade; and those with the U.S. Information Agency (USIA) disseminate information regarding U.S. society and culture. The chance of gaining such an appointment can be described as a shot in the dark at best: Over 20,000 applicants take the test each year, but only about 250 are appointed. Clearly, if you are interested in a Federal job, Foreign Service Officer should not be the only job title you pursue.

Air Traffic Control

Although FAA uses a register for Air Traffic controller positions, as noted above, that register has been closed since 1992, and as of 1997, FAA did not anticipate opening it.

Law Enforcement

Although there is an applicant oversupply for job titles in these areas, the supply of candidates is not overwhelmingly large compared to the demand, which is strong and steady: Many entry-level law enforcement employees are hired each year. Note that entry-level law enforcement positions with *excepted agencies* (FBI, CIA, etc.) are pursued via Pathway 2 (see p. 50); however, those at other agencies are covered under Administrative careers, and hence by Pathway 3.

See Appendix B for more on **Law Enforcement** (p. 175)

Positions such as border patrol agents in the Immigration and Naturalization Service are covered by a written test and fall under Pathway 1. The recruitment processes for law enforcement positions are complex. Candidates must first take the unassembled administrative exam, and they usually *also* must complete some applications forms. Thereafter, they may be selected for an interview, which is much more important for these job titles than for most other Federal positions, as the panel tends to have a clear conception of the kinds of people who are likely to be successful on the job. Candidates who pass the interview stage are given extensive background checks, some of which may take as long as six months. Those with backgrounds deemed acceptable are sent to training school, and only upon successful completion of training are they given permanent appointments. For every fifty applicants, one is finally appointed to a position.

Technical and Trade

Every technical or trade occupation, from Electronic Technician to Welder, occurs in Federal service. "Technician" job titles are in the General Schedule; trade job titles are Wage Grade. The Federal government employs substantial numbers of people as technicians or trade workers—roughly 30% of the Federal work force is Wage Grade—though positions are often concentrated in a few agencies. Hence there is generally a predominant Wage Grade employer in a given geographic area—usually a Department of Defense (DOD) agency, although the Department of Veterans Affairs (VA) and the General Service Administration (GSA) may also have many trade workers in an area.

Like most other jobs, these jobs are filled by agencies using case examining. If one employer is predominant in an area, other agencies in that area may but are not required to have the predominant agency do examining on a reimbursable basis.

Candidates may have to wait many months to be selected for apprentice programs. Those who are eventually hired become Wage Grade apprentices, receiving on-the-job training and classroom instruction.

PATHWAY 2: ENTRY LEVEL—NO WRITTEN TEST, REGISTER

This pathway is intended for entry-level, nonstatus candidates interested in occupations for which the supply of candidates is larger than *or* in equilibrium with the demand. For most of these positions, the private sector tends to pay more than the Federal government, so the supply of candidates relative to the demand is much smaller than for Pathway 1. Job titles covered by this pathway use an unassembled exam (application form) instead of a written test, and maintain a register.

Let's consider the various categories of job titles covered under this pathway.

Law Enforcement and Intelligence at Excepted Agencies

Several law enforcement job titles are in excepted agencies—the FBI, CIA, and National Security Agency (NSA), for example. These agencies are not under OPM jurisdiction and operate independently.

Since many people find positions at these agencies attractive, there is an oversupply of candidates. The application procedures for law enforcement positions at excepted agencies are not easy and usually involve many steps. Generally, they include an unassembled exam that measures candidates against stringent standards. Successful candidates are then usually assigned to a register, which can be slow moving. A very demanding interview follows for those who are referred off the register. These law enforcement positions require a thorough background check, which can take six months or longer. Candidates who make it that far receive tentative appointments and attend a special agency-operated training school; permanent appointment coincides with graduation. The number of candidates who begin the application process is very large compared to the number who receive permanent appointments. The CIA probably has the record: Many thousands begin the process for every one who becomes a CIA Agent.

Technical and Trade

Technician is a term used in General Schedule job titles to denote a worker in a professional field who is at a level somewhat below that of a full professional. For example, an Engineering Technician is someone who works in the engineering field without being a fully qualified, professional Engineer. Other common job titles of this type include Forestry Technician, Soil Conservation Technician, Medical Technician, Surveying Technician, Electronic Technician, Photographic Technician, and Psychology Technician. There are no written tests or national registers for these job titles; they are filled by case examining.

Delegated Examining Authority is discussed on p. 41.

Professionals (Excluding Health Care and Attorneys)

Federal employers require substantial numbers of professionals in the following fields: accountancy and auditing, engineering, mathematics (and related fields, such as statistics and operations research), and the physical and life sciences. However, as there is also much steady demand for such professionals in the private sector, the Federal government often faces a shortage of candidates for its openings in these fields. Consequently, Federal employers try to make the application process as easy and convenient as possible for these candidates at entry level by forgoing a written exam and allowing hiring via Pathways 2 and/or 3.

Pathway 2 would be used at the option of an individual agency if it chose to establish its own register for any of these positions. The agency would have the option of requiring applicants to submit narrative applications and assign the ratings on the basis of the information contained in the applications or alternatively develop a computerized form (closed-end unassembled exam) which could be more quickly scored. Most positions are filled under Pathway 3.

Note: For these job titles, see also Pathway 3.

PATHWAY 3: MID- AND TOP-LEVEL (+ ENTRY-LEVEL PROFESSIONAL)—NO WRITTEN TEST, NO REGISTER

This pathway is characterized by use of an unassembled exam (application form) instead of a written test and by the absence of registers. It now applies to most first-time Federal employees. As explained previously, agencies now do most of their own examining. Most of this examining is on a case-by-case basis. Among others, it applies to first-time Federal employees at mid- and top-career levels and to entry-level professionals for which a master's or doctoral degree or a license is required.

Because the pay differential between Federal service and the private sector is quite substantial for many of the job titles covered by this pathway—especially in top-level, white-collar positions—candidates are in short supply. You might want to approach the local agency office first, to see whether they are presently hiring; but note that the national headquarters may have jurisdiction with regard to higher-grade positions.

Mid- and Top-Level Clerical and Secretarial

Experienced Secretaries and Clerical candidates with advanced skills (such as word processing and steno) are in demand in most geographic areas. To apply for any of these job titles at mid- or top-level, approach any agency of interest and inquire about openings. If there are any, you will be examined by the agency using your résumé or other narrative application form. If you cannot find an agency with an opening, contact one of the job information sources described in step 3.

A bachelor's degree entitles you to apply at GS-5 via this pathway.

Business and Industry White Collar

White-collar candidates with mid- and top-level skills (GS-9–15) in business and industry are in regular demand. Job titles include both general business occupations (such as Purchasing and Quality Assurance) and occupations within industries of interest to the Federal government (such as Transportation Industry Analyst). However, many in these general administrative and executive positions are first hired at entry level and promoted to mid and top levels from within; few are hired into other fields (such as clerical) at entry level and promoted into administrative or executive job titles.

Technical and Trade

The demand by Federal employers for experienced white-collar candidates in technical fields such as electronics and telecommunications is strong and steady; so is the demand for experienced blue-collar candidates in the building, repair, and maintenance trades. However, there is little demand in many of the hundreds of other Wage Grade fields.

Trade job titles are concentrated in fewer agencies than most other occupations in Federal service. Demand for these job titles is geographically sensitive: Although there may be no openings in many regions, in others, jobs may be plentiful. Candidates should find out from one of the sources discussed in step 3 what agencies hire in their job title. At worst, candidates willing to relocate should be able to find employment.

Professionals (Excluding Health Care and Attorneys)

As you'll recall, entry-level candidates in these fields (accountancy, biology, engineering, etc.) can apply using Pathway 2 and/or Pathway 3 (and we recommend using *both*). Under Pathway 3—which is also appropriate for these professionals at mid- and top-levels—candidates usually complete an open-end, unassembled exam (a résumé or other narrative application) and apply directly to any agency with an opening. The agency rates the candidates and selects those it wishes to interview. Note: at the option of the agency, it may use a computerized as opposed to a narrative application form. This option requires more candidate effort than Pathway 2, since not every agency contacted will have an opening; however, it can result in faster appointment, and enables candidates to choose the agencies with which they wish to interview.

Licensed Health Care Professionals are in great demand in Federal service. Agencies that have these professionals include the Department of Veterans Affairs, the Department of Defense, the Department of Health and Human Services (including its Indian Health Service), and the Bureau of Prisons. Because competition from the private sector for health care professionals is keen, candidates can approach any facility or headquarters personnel office of any of the above agencies for employment information. Some central agency personnel offices will pass on a candidate's name to facilities in his or her geographic area. In many cases, only a résumé need be submitted. Rapid consideration is assured in almost all occupations. Demand is highest for Medical Officers, Nurses, Physical Therapists, Pharmacists, and Physician's Assistants. (Note that Physician's Assistants must be willing to work in prison environments.)

Computer Science

Mid- and top-level Computer Specialists and Computer Scientists, including programmers, analysts, and designers, are in great demand by many Federal agencies. Although all agencies employ people in this field, not every facility will offer this kind of employment. Prospects for quick processing of the candidate's application are good.

PATHWAY 4: SPECIAL HIRING PROGRAMS

The American people, acting through Congress, have decided that selected groups of citizens deserve preferential treatment in Federal recruitment, retention, and promotion. The largest of these groups comprises veterans of military service; others include students, the severely disabled, returning Peace Corps and VISTA volunteers, and Native Americans. This pathway applies to those designated to receive such preferential treatment.

Special hiring programs developed for these groups include both status and nonstatus candidates. There are two program types: ratings enhancement and noncompetitive.

Rating Enhancement

Rating enhancement programs are all veteran-oriented and operate within the Competitive Service by (actually or effectively) adding points to applicants' ratings. Veterans follow Pathways (1, 2, and 3) in the same way as other candidates, applying for whatever job titles are of interest to them, but are treated differently in two important respects:

1. Either 5 or 10 points are added to whatever rating the candidate would have received otherwise, in accordance with the veterans' preference rules. (This is the rating enhancement per se.)

> **Veterans' preference** is covered in Appendix Q.

2. The Rule-of-Three is also changed such that the Federal employer cannot offer the appointment to a nonveteran if a veteran is among the three and has a higher ranking.

These preferences for veterans apply to appointments made through examinations both assembled and unassembled. They do not apply to promotions and other internal actions. Agencies filling excepted service positions from outside the agency must also give preference to veterans. Very large numbers of veterans gain Federal appointment this way.

Noncompetitive

> Specific **noncompetitive programs** are discussed in Appendix Q.

In some instances, some or all of the application procedures we have discussed may be suspended and appointments made noncompetitively. Such appointments are thus in the Excepted Service rather than the Competitive Service. Several programs apply to specific groups, including Vietnam-era veterans, students, disabled individuals, and Native Americans. What these programs have in common is that they suspend the competitive examination process: Candidates are neither examined, rated, nor assigned to registers. If a position is open, they can receive appointment solely by qualifying for inclusion in the program. (If no position is open, candidates will not be appointed even if they do qualify for the program.)

Agencies that have a particular interest in a given program will regularly reserve positions for them. For example, DOD has a particular interest in the Veterans Readjustment Appointment (VRA) program. The Bureau of Indian Affairs and the Indian Health Service must give absolute preference to Native Americans. This means that they must hire a qualified Native American ahead of any other applicant. Many agencies are interested in student programs, and often convert students to career status upon graduation.

Positions filled through noncompetitive programs are almost always at entry level. In most cases, individuals in the program are not eligible for promotion beyond GS-9; they can, however, apply for appointment to positions above GS-9 under the same application procedures as other candidates—that is, by leaving the program (and hence the Excepted Service) and taking their chances on competitive appointment.

Candidates who think they might qualify for one of these special hiring programs can get general information about them from the information sources described in step 3. Agencies have coordinators for these programs (usually at their Washington, DC headquarters) whose job includes helping candidates apply for them. Names of these coordinators can be obtained by contacting the personnel office of the agency.

The supply of candidates who wish to be included in these programs varies considerably. Some programs—those for Native Americans, for example—are under utilized for some occupations and in some locations. On the other hand, there is an oversupply of candidates for the student programs. In the case of a candidate oversupply, those who qualify compete *among themselves* for the positions. Early application is an important element of success, and candidates are advised to stay in close touch with agencies and program coordinators to learn when openings occur.

Outstanding Scholar

The Outstanding Scholar Program applies to entry level administrative positions at grades 5 and 7. If an applicant has a grade point average of 3.5 or better or finished in the top 10% of his or her class, he or she can be appointed to one of these positions without any further competition. The appointment would be in the Competitive Service. (Because grade point averages are rounded off to the first decimal place, an individual with a GPA of 3.45 actually qualifies under this program.) This program does not apply to any other positions.

PATHWAY 5: MID- AND TOP-LEVEL— PROMOTION ROUTE/SES

This pathway, like Pathway 3, is characterized by use of the unassembled exam and by the absence of registers. However, it applies only to current employees, not to those seeking their first job in Federal service (with the one exception of the Senior Executive Service). This is why we have called it the "promotion route." It covers all job titles at the mid- and top-level grades.

Promotional Strategies

Unlike their private-sector counterparts, Federal managers cannot promote employees entirely at their own discretion. The principles of the merit system apply to candidates for promotion just as they apply to candidates for first-time appointment. Each application for a promotional position must be examined objectively and compared to those of other candidates. Whoever gets the appointment must be one of the best qualified candidates. In practice there is often no competition for the promotional position because it is not widely advertised. The announcement of the opening may be as discreet as a notice on a bulletin board. Often no candidate comes forward except the one for whom management intends the promotion. Another device for maximizing the chances of management's candidate is to write the job qualifications in such a way that the most qualified person turns out to be the person for whom the position is intended. (These are called "wired jobs.") In these ways Federal managers are able to secure promotion for the people they feel deserve it.

It should be noted, however, that many positions regularly come open for which the manager's have no candidates in mind. In these cases, the selection process is similar to that of Pathway 3 in that applicants are rated for individual positions based on their experience and education. However, in the internal promotion process, the rating process also includes the applicants' performance appraisals and awards which they have received. Finally, the internal promotion process does not use the Rule of Three and veterans preference. The best qualified candidates are referred to a selecting official who can select any of them. A best-qualified list may have 10 or more candidates. As we explained earlier, at one time there was a greater demand for applicants for mid- and top-level positions than the supply. However, because of Government downsizing and the effort to eliminate managerial layers, this is no longer the case. There are still many opportunities for promotion, but often there are many applicants for each vacancy. In addition, agencies must give priority to their surplus employees who are facing separation because of downsizing. If one of these employees applies for a position and is determined to be well qualified, he or she must be given priority. (See "Status versus Nonstatus Candidates.") Only candidates with previous experience in the Federal government, or in some cases, in the specific department or agency, will be considered for many of these positions, especially those in the executive and administrative fields.

Application procedures for internal promotion are usually made as easy and convenient as possible. For most positions the application procedures require only an unassembled exam and no register, almost invariably a résumé or other narrative application form. Some agencies are experimenting with skills banks by which employees do not have to apply for positions. They are rated and ranked for promotion on the basis of the information which the agency already has on file. If your agency uses such an approach, you must ensure that your file is kept current by adding information on any new experience and training you have obtained. Frequently the filing period is open-ended (open until filled).

Bypass Strategies

In some cases, the procedural problems presented in our discussion of Pathways 1 and 2 can be circumvented by using Pathway 5 to obtain the same job titles. This may be possible for the administrative job titles covered under Pathway 3, and for the entry-level technical and trade job titles covered under Pathways 2 and 3. Of course, you cannot be hired *directly* into those job titles as a first-time Federal employee without using those procedures; however, by selecting an *alternative* occupation temporarily—one that has an easier pathway—you may be able to become a Federal employee quickly and seek *promotion* into the job title originally sought. For example, for white-collar work, the easiest entry-level job in which to gain appointment is a clerical position; from there the candidate may be able to gain promotion into one of the administrative job titles without having to complete an exam. Likewise, a candidate interested in a hard to crack, Wage Grade occupation may be able to obtain appointment more quickly in a related technical or trade field as a *helper* (apprentice) at the blue-collar entry level—and then seek promotion into the occupation originally sought. Just which Wage Grade and technical occupations are harder or easier to enter varies from one geographic area to another: Candidates should explore conditions locally by contacting potential employers.

Naturally, such a strategy should not be left to chance: Promotions of this kind are at the discretion of management. Consequently, candidates should determine in advance if promotion from clerical to an administrative title, or from helper in one field to journeyman in another, is possible or likely in the agency of interest.

Contacting potential employers is discussed in Step 3.

SES Recruitment

One important exception to the policy of promotion from within for administrative and executive positions is the Senior Executive Service. Its policy is to recruit a minimum of 10% of its members from the private sector, so as to bring fresh ideas and new talent to government. The pathway into the SES is similar to the pathway a top executive would take in a private-sector job. Dealings are direct with the hiring agency, whose executive office candidates are asked to phone for details regarding the position being offered. The recruitment process generally involves résumés, employment narratives (sometimes standardized in application format), and interviews. Overseas Federal positions are generally pursued via Pathway 5 since almost all such positions are filled by those previously employed by the U.S. government. Because Federal employers abroad are responsible for transporting new employees and their household goods to their locations and the cost of which is substantial—they want to be sure that those employees will perform satisfactorily. Successful prior Federal service would seem to be their best assurance of this. Consequently, candidates for positions overseas should first obtain a position with a Federal employer in the United States using Pathway 1, 2, or 3.

Note that most transfers or new hires sent to locations abroad are professionals. Clerical staff, maintenance, and other blue-collar service people are generally recruited from among local nationals.

For more on **Federal jobs overseas,** see Appendix P.

HOW THE EXEMPLARY CANDIDATES APPLY STEP 2

Let's turn to the four exemplary candidates we met in Step 1 of the Federal Job Search process—Janet, Michael, Helen, and Jeff—to see how they use the information we have just presented.

EXAMPLE: JANET

Janet, you'll recall, has a secretarial background. If you will refer to the chart on page 27, you will see that in Step 1 Janet had identified six job titles as appropriate for her at various grade levels, and had determined the hiring prospects for each. She now looks at her selection again, this time from the perspective of the pathways she will need to take to apply for these positions.

Since Janet is currently working, she does not want to take a cut in pay; she would, however, be willing to work for the Federal government at her current salary, because she believes that its benefits package is generally superior to the benefits available to her in the private sector. Hence the lowest grade level Janet will accept is GS-7, though she would certainly prefer 8 GS-8 or 9. She realizes that she could probably obtain an appointment very quickly in almost any of the job titles she had identified if she would accept a GS-5. However, since she already has a job, the speed with which she could obtain an appointment is not critical to her. Consequently, rather than apply at the entry level for any of the titles she has selected (Pathway 1), Janet decides to apply at the mid-level via Pathway 3. This also means she will not be pursuing Administrative occupations.

Janet realizes that Pathway 3 is comparatively easy and convenient for the candidate. After reading this chapter, she believes that the agencies in her area (Denver, CO) are likely to do their own examining for the job titles in which she is interested.

EXAMPLE: MICHAEL

Our next exemplary candidate is Michael. If you refer again to the chart (p. 27), you will see that Michael has identified seven job titles and grade levels that he feels are appropriate for him. He has also determined the hiring prospects for each of these titles. Michael is very attracted to Federal careers that he considers glamorous. He would very much like to be a diplomat in an exotic country, a border patrol agent, or an agent for the CIA, FBI, or DEA. Work as an Air Traffic Controller also seems exciting and interesting. However, having considered the information in this chapter, he has decided to approach the prospects of these glamorous careers realistically. He understands that to apply for many of the job titles in which he is interested he is required to take a written test. Since he is located in a semirural section of South Carolina, he would have to travel to the nearest large city in his state to take any of these tests; this would require a whole day of his time.

He is also considering a career in the private sector and must devote energy to that job search as well. Michael decides that taking the Foreign Service exam isn't worth his time: 250 hires out of 20,000 candidates seems a bit too much of a long shot for him. He also decides that the prospects of becoming a CIA agent are too remote. Likewise, he decides to forget about being an FBI or DEA agent, since he sees from the writeup in Appendix B that he does not really have the background they require. Since the Air Traffic Controller register is closed, he gives up on that possibility. He decides that he will take the written test for border patrol agent.

Michael decides to pursue one other idea. He noted in reading about Pathway 5 that status candidates can be promoted into administrative job titles without taking an exam. He thinks he should explore the possibility of being hired by some agency in a clerical job title: Perhaps he can persuade the prospective manager of his department into agreeing to promote him into an administrative title after a few months. He believes he could qualify easily for a clerical position, since he is a good typist and is well organized. Pathway 3 is applicable here: Since Michael has a bachelor's degree, he will not need to take the clerical exam.

Each position Michael will pursue, then, is covered either by Pathway 1 or 3. Satisfied that his thinking is sound, he is ready to go on to Step 3.

EXAMPLE: HELEN

As shown in the chart on page 27, Helen has identified seven job titles she feels are interesting and for which she believes she could qualify. She is now ready to apply what she learned from this chapter.

Helen has always wanted to travel to interesting places. She learned French because she is interested in French culture and because she realized that French is spoken in many countries throughout the world. One of her career plans is to use her proficient French and business education to secure a business- or commerce-oriented position with the U.S. government abroad. Helen is very proud to be an American and would consider being a diplomat for her country a great honor; therefore she decides to take the Foreign Service Exam even though she knows that scoring well enough for selection is a long shot.

She also sees in Appendix B that being a Secretary in the Foreign Service might be an interesting alternative to Foreign Service Officer. Foreign Service Secretaries are in demand, and she could use that position as a springboard to one in trade-oriented foreign affairs. Her skills would surely qualify her, and the chances of her being sent to a French-speaking country are good (though she understands that the State Department will not guarantee a particular duty station).

Of course, with her educational background and work experience, Helen feels she has a better chance at any of the occupations in Appendix B's Accounting and Budget Group. Among these she gives particular consideration to Financial Institution Examiner, a job title that involves a lot of travel, which appeals to Helen. However, she notices that Financial Institution Examiner is listed in Appendix B as an administrative job title: To be hired at entry level (GS-5/7), she might need to go through an examining process if a job is announced. She is concerned about getting a job fairly quickly. She will be receiving her master's degree in a few months and wants to have a job lined up well before she graduates. Consequently, she decides not to pin her hopes on finding an administrative job, but she will keep her eyes open for announcements. However, the education qualifications tabulated in Appendix M (p. 695) indicates that she would qualify at GS-9 once she has her master's in Finance. She will keep her eyes open for announcements of GS-9 positions.

Helen also decides to give up on Language Specialist and Financial Analyst as job titles because she feels (based on Appendix M) that the hiring prospects are just not good enough.

The Accountant and Auditor job titles look like they could lead to quick appointment, and she can apply at GS-7 or even GS-9, since her master's degree is pending. She sees that for professional job titles such as these she can use either Pathway 2 or 3, each of which has its advantages. It will depend on whether any agencies set up their own registers. If none does, she will have to use Pathway 3 and apply for individual announcements. Pathway 2 would be easier: She would need only to apply for an agency's register and be considered for all jobs in that agency. The jobs in which she is most interested are: Foreign Service Officer, Foreign Service Secretary, Accountant, and Auditor.

EXAMPLE: JEFF

Unlike the other candidates we have been following, Jeff is not pursuing work in the private sector. Jeff is now 47 and has been working in the private sector all his adult life. At one time he hoped that he would make a lot of money there, but that has not happened. Now his goals have shifted. Although still concerned with making a good salary, he is primarily concerned with excellent job security, a sound retirement plan, and good health benefits. He believes that a job with the Federal government is the answer.

Jeff feels relocating is not a good option for him. His children are in school and his family is involved in the local area. Unfortunately, he lives a considerable distance from a major city, and is not sure how much Federal activity takes place in his area. He does know, however, that there is an Air Force base about 40 miles away.

You will note from the chart on page 27 that Jeff found six job titles for himself based on his work in Step 1. Appendix O (Wage Grade . . . by Selected Agency) gives the following numbers of positions in the Air Force (upon which Jeff will probably have to rely for a job, given his location): Electronics Mechanic, 5,511; Electrician, 1,197; Air Conditioning Equipment Mechanic, 1,077; Carpenter, 1,055; Maintenance Mechanic, 957; and A/C Equipment Operator, 71. These numbers indicate Electronics Mechanic as Jeff's best bet, although Electrician (for which he can apply at leader level) and several other job titles might also work out, depending on the state of the job market in his area.

Reviewing what he learned about Pathways 1–3 in this chapter, Jeff feels that he is in good shape. He probably fits into Pathway 3 because he has advanced skills in several trades that are in demand. However, Jeff had discovered in Step 1 (from reading Appendix Q) that he qualifies under the Veterans Readjustment Act, which might also present an opportunity for him. In the first place, since the Department of Defense has a particular interest in the VRA program, it might give him an extra advantage in pursuing Electronics Mechanic or Electrician positions. Moreover, although he has always worked with his hands and enjoyed his jobs, under VRA he could be trained in another field—perhaps a white-collar occupation—that would not be as hard on him physically as are his Wage Grade occupations.

Since Jeff is not dividing his job search effort between the private and public sectors, he decides that he can afford to make the effort to pursue all the Federal job titles for which he qualifies. He plans to use Pathway 3 for the skilled trade and technical job titles, and to look into the VRA program, as covered under Pathway 4.

All four exemplary candidates are now ready for Step 3—obtaining job vacancy information about the job titles they have selected.

Summary Table: The Exemplary Candidates at the End of Step 2

Step 1					Step 2		
Exemplary Candidate	Applicant Category (App. A)	Job Title & Series (Apps. A & K)	Grade (Apps. C & M)	Hiring Prospects (App. M)	Pursue?	Grade Pathway	
Janet	Clerical/ Skilled	Secretary GS-318	5	Excellent	✓	GS-7/9	3
			7	Good			
			9	Fair			
		Support Services Specialist GS-342	7/9	Poor	✓	GS-7/9	3
		Management Asst. GS-344	7	Fair	✓	GS-7/9	3
			9	Poor			
		Admin. Officer GS-341	7/9	Poor			
		Misc. Admin. GS-301	7/9	Good	✓	GS-7/9	3
		Administrative Occupations	5/7	Fair			
Michael	Recent College Grad.	Admin. Occup. Groups 2,3,4,6,7	5/7	Fair-Good	✓(Grp. 3)	GS-5	1
		Air Traffic Controller GS-2152	7	Fair	✓	GS-7	1
		Foreign Service Officer GS-130	7	Poor			
		Intelligence Officer GS-132	5/7	Poor			
		Personnel Asst. GS-203	5	Good			
		Law Enforcement (Various)	5/7	Good	✓(Cler.)†	GS-5/7	3
		Education (Various, GS-1700)	5/7	Fair			
Helen	Recent College Grad. (Accounting, Liberal Arts, Overseas)	Accountant GS-510	5/7	Good	✓	GS-7/9	2
		Auditor GS-511	5/7	Good	✓	GS-7/9	2
		Financial Instit. Examiner GS-570	5/7	Fair	✓	GS-9	3
		Language Specialist GS-1040	5/7	Fair			
		Financial Analyst GS-1160	5/7	Poor			
		Foreign Service Officer	FP-7*	Poor	✓	FP-7*	3
		Foreign Service Secretary	FP-9*	Good	✓	FP-9*	3
Jeff	Blue Collar/ Experienced Trade/ Journeyman	Electrician WG-2805	J/L	Good	✓	WG-J/L	3
		Carpenter WG-4607	J	Good	✓	WG-J	3
		A/C Equip. Mechanic WG-5306	J	Good	✓	WG-J	3
		A/C Equip. Operator WG-5415	J	Poor	✓	WG-J	3
		Electronics Mechanic WG-2614	J	Good	✓	WG-J	3
		Maintenance Mechanic WG-4749	J	Good	✓	WG-J	3
					✓(VRA appt.)		4

*Foreign Service positions have their own pay schedule and are not in the General Schedule; see Appendix F.
†Michael is hoping for a clerical position from which to pursue administrative job titles.

Step 3: Collecting Vacancy or Test Information

Purpose: To help you collect information regarding the job titles and pathways that are appropriate for you, including listings of current openings.

Associated appendixes:
- D   Federal Personnel Offices
- G   Sample Vacancy Information
- H   Application Forms
- P   Job Opportunities Overseas
- Q   Special Recruitment and Hiring Programs

Collecting vacancy information is a vital and necessary step in the application process. Although you now know which pathway(s) to take, you still need timely information explaining how to follow a pathway to the specific job title(s) in which you are interested: what openings there are, where and when to apply, what application form to use, and the duties and qualifications of the job title(s). There are several major sources for this information, and various means of conveying it. Let us begin with the sources.

SOURCES OF VACANCY OR TEST INFORMATION

Federal employers hire several hundred thousand people every year, including temporary and part-time employees. Available jobs are announced by more than 1,500 personnel offices. Given the job(s) in which you are interested, and therefore the pathway(s) you will pursue, you may find it useful to draw on more than one of the following informational sources. When doing so, it is important to be aware of their advantages and limitations: No single source of Federal job information is all inclusive.

FEDERAL JOBS ON-LINE

The editors of the *Federal Jobs Digest* newspaper and this book, *Working for Your Uncle,* have an internet site for job information which can be accessed by typing **http://www.jobsfed.com.** It contains information on employment procedures and vacancy announcements from Federal agencies. Federal agencies which are recruiting for competitive service positions from outside the agency or for SES positions provide electronic versions of their vacancy announcements. The *Federal Jobs Digest* then puts the announcements on its internet site. In theory, you can find out every competitive service vacancy for which agencies are recruiting externally. Agencies are not required to provide information on vacancies for which recruitment is limited to the agency. In addition, they are not required to provide information on excepted service vacancies although some of them do as a way of reaching the largest possible audience.

You will be able to download some vacancy announcements from the internet, and for some positions, you will be able to actually file an on-line application. The site also contains information on special employment programs such as programs for veterans.

The site has some text-only components which are accessible to visually impaired persons who are using speech programs with their computers. The internet site also has links to other sites throughout the Federal Government.

AUTOMATED OPM

For those applicants who have a computer and a modem but no internet access, OPM maintains computer bulletin boards. The jobs bulletin board in Macon, Georgia has job listings from throughout the country. To access this bulletin board, dial 912-757-3100 and follow the prompts to register.

OPM's Main Street Bulletin Board in Washington, D.C., 202-606-4800 provides a gateway to the Macon Jobs bulletin Board. It also contains a lot of information concerning employment regulations etc. However, most of the information is designed for personnel specialists, and applicants may find it too technical. Unless you are in Washington, D.C., and want to save the long distance charges associated with calling Macon, you should go directly to the Macon Bulletin Board instead of going through Main Street. This is because using Main Street as a gateway to Macon is a slower process than going to Macon directly.

OPM has set up touch screen information sites in its service centers and other offices. In addition, many Federal agencies also have these touch screens. You will be able to obtain vacancy information and information on employment procedures from these screens. However, as noted above, you will not be able to receive employment counseling from a live person. You should check in your local phone book to see if your city has an OPM office. If it does, you should call to determine whether the office has a touch screen facility. You can also check with Federal personnel offices in your area to see if any of them have the OPM touch screens.

OPM's Career America Connection allows you to obtain vacancy information and information on employment procedures using an automated telephone response system. The Career America Connections are maintained by local OPM offices and generally only have information on vacancies in a particular region as opposed to nationwide. To find the phone number for the Career America Connection in your area, you should look in the white pages of your phone book under Career America Connection, Office of Personnel Management Jobs, or Federal Job Information. Appendix D contains a list of the OPM service centers with their Career America Connections. Not all areas will have a Career America Connection. In Washington, D.C., the Career America Connection number is 202-606-2700.

OPM's Macon, Georgia Service Center has a Career America Connection which has nationwide vacancy information. It is the only one of the Career America Connections with nationwide information. In addition, this number provides limited capability to speak with a job information counselor. The phone number for the Macon Career America Connection is 912-757-3000.

You probably have noticed that there are no 800 phone numbers. Because of funding reductions, OPM no longer has 800 numbers for job information.

FEDERAL AGENCIES

The second major source of Federal job information is the Federal agencies themselves. Every agency (department, bureau, and so on) within the Federal government has its own personnel office that publicizes job information. (Of course, OPM itself is a Federal agency; however, here we refer to all agencies except OPM.) Information provided by agency personnel offices can also be evaluated with regard to our five hiring pathways:

Pathway 1 (entry level—written test, register): As previously explained, the use of government-wide registers is decreasing. Even for entry-level positions, most agencies now do case examining and have information only on the positions for which they are recruiting. If one or more agencies has combined resources to fill vacancies or paid OPM to maintain registers for them, the agencies would have information on these registers. The Postal Service which maintains its own registers will have information on its jobs, and FAA will have information on Air Traffic Controller positions for which it maintains its own register. Note, as explained in step 2, as of the writing of this book, FAA's register was closed, and the agency did not anticipate opening it. Note, neither the Postal Service nor the FAA are in the competitive service. FAA used to be, but in 1996 Congress authorized it to establish its own personnel service. Therefore, even though we are mentioning them in this hiring pathway, they are like other excepted agencies that maintain their own employment registers.

Pathway 2 (entry-level—no written test, register): For some unique- or predominant-use job titles, agencies are the best sources of job information. Examples of unique-use employers on a national level are the intelligence and law enforcement agencies. If you are interested in being an agent for the FBI, CIA, the Drug Enforcement Agency (DEA), or U.S. Customs, contact the agencies in question. When a particular employer is a predominant user of a position, you should start with that employer. It is possible that other agencies may be obtaining their examining services from that employer for a fee. If this is the case, the predominant employer could give you information on jobs which other agencies have. However, lower-use agencies are not required to obtain the service from the predominant user, so you may end up having to contact each user for information. For example, a predominant local employer, such as a defense base, might be the best source of information about openings for some positions in a particular geographic area.

Pathway 3 (mid- and top-level [+ entry-level professional]—no written test, no register): Job titles are well covered. As was mentioned in the previous section, some of these jobs are hard to fill because candidates are in short supply; agencies (and, in some case, OPM Service Centers) are busy recruiting. These positions will usually be filled by case examining, making the agency the primary source of information.

Pathway 4 (special hiring programs): Some agencies are closely connected with certain programs, such as the Department of Defense (DOD), which does a great deal of hiring under veterans programs, including VRA. In fact, some openings with DOD are especially identified as suitable for VRA candidates, and candidates would do well to contact the VRA Program Coordinator at any large Federal facility in their area (whether or not it is in the DOD). Agencies have coordinators to assist individuals with disabilities. These coordinators can help disabled applicants locate the best opportunities, and they can explain some special appointing authorities which may be helpful to some individuals. At the Indian Health Service of the Department of Health and Human Services and the Bureau of Indian Affairs of the Department of the Interior, Native Americans receive preference in hiring. If a Native American is qualified for a position, he or she must be selected ahead of persons who are not Native Americans. These two agencies can provide additional information on how this preference works and the requirements which must be met to claim it.

Program Coordinators are usually located at larger Federal facilities.

Pathway 5 (mid- and top-level—promotion route/SES): Job information is readily available. A given agency is certainly well able to provide candidates who already work for it with information about promotions. However, many Federal employees routinely transfer from one agency to another. In these cases, employees find job information more difficult to obtain. Those seeking *merit promotion*—that is, promotion within the Competitive Service based on qualifying past experience—would do well to identify agencies for which they would like to work and stay in touch with them to learn about upcoming job announcements. Of course, given that there are hundreds of agencies and thousands of facilities, this can be a very difficult task. Candidates can narrow the field significantly by learning which agencies and facilities employ the job titles and grade levels of interest to them.

Many agencies have automated telephone systems which provide job information. You should be able to learn about which agencies have such systems by contacting local personnel offices. In addition, most agencies are establishing internet sites which include job information. Experienced internet users will probably have no problem locating this information by searching on such words as jobs or Federal employment information. For most agencies you can get to the main internet site by using the initials of the agency followed by dot gov. Most sites begin with http://www. followed by the initials.gov. For example, http://wwwdhhs.gov for the Department of Health and Human Services, nasa.gov for the National Aeronautics and Space Administration, doe.gov for the Department of Energy, dot.gov for the Department of Transportation and dod.gov for the Department of Defense, etc.

Note that information about job vacancies at any *excepted agency* should *always* be obtained by contacting its personnel office directly. An agency should also be contacted directly regarding job opportunities overseas (see Appendix P).

STATE EMPLOYMENT OFFICES

The third source of Federal job information is state employment offices (job service offices, or state employment service offices as they are called in many states).

OPM furnishes these offices the information that it receives from agencies concerning competitive service vacancies. Since the information is usually provided electronically, it is fairly up to date. Agencies with excepted service positions are not required to provide vacancy information to OPM or to state employment offices. They will do so only when they feel that these sources would be helpful in the recruitment process. Employment offices will not have information on vacancies which agencies are filling internally, and they probably do not have much information on special Federal hiring programs. Some, however, may be able to assist the applicants to access OPM's bulletin boards or internet site.

> **Excepted agencies** are discussed in Step 2 (p. 35) and listed in Appendix D.

PRIVATE SOURCES OF FEDERAL JOB INFORMATION

You, the reader, have probably realized by now that obtaining Federal job information can be a time-consuming and often frustrating business. You will not be surprised to learn that private companies have come into being to make the Federal job hunting effort easier. The publisher of this book is also the leading publisher of Federal job information through its *Federal Jobs Digest (FJD)*, available at newsstands and many libraries or by subscription.

This newspaper publishes the Federal Job Opportunities Listing from OPM plus information obtained directly from Federal agencies regarding additional jobs not listed with OPM. *FJD*'s direct contact with agencies also provides information on job titles the agencies intend to fill by promoting current Federal employees. It is thereby able to provide fairly comprehensive information on job openings covered by all five hiring pathways. Each listing includes agency name, job title, grade level, filing date, application address, phone number, and name of contact.

Federal Jobs Digest is published fortnightly (though only once in December) and has a special section announcing postal exams, another on the Senior Executive Service, yet another for VA jobs, and one for jobs with the Federal government overseas. Openings geared to special hiring programs are highlighted in occasional articles.

Another private source of Federal job information is the newsletter *Federal Career Opportunities*, which can be found in some libraries.

OTHER SOURCES OF FEDERAL JOB INFORMATION

Student recruitment programs are discussed in Appendix Q. Students may learn about special college recruitment programs through their school's job placement office. High school and college students who want summer jobs may get information from their guidance counselors (as well as from an OPM Service Center or Career America Connection).

Finally, even with all the other outlets at its disposal, the Federal government additionally advertises some positions in newspapers and magazines and on radio and television. Clearly, a position must be quite hard to fill before ads are placed in the media (as they often are for health care professionals).

SUMMARY

Vacancy and test information sources are summarized in the table entitled "Finding the Right Vacancy Information. Because no one source of Federal job information is all inclusive, the serious Federal job candidate would do well to use more than one. A relatively comprehensive source such as OPM's bulletin board, internet site, or its telephone Career America Connection and a private source such as the *Federal Jobs Digest* should be consulted. In addition, candidates should be in direct contact with the personnel offices of Federal agencies that offer them the best opportunities. As for special hiring programs, their objectives and compliance procedures are so diverse that there can be no single approach to finding pertinent job information. Candidates interested in these programs should study them (starting with Appendix Q) and use whatever informational source seems most appropriate for the program for which the candidate qualifies.

Summary Table: Finding the Right Vacancy and Test Information

Pathway			Vacancy/Test Information	
No.	Type	Position Type	Source	Type
1	Written test, register	Entry level	OPM Service Center Agency State unemployment office *Federal Jobs Digest*	Application package (test card enclosed) Job vacancy listing
2	No written test, register	Entry level	OPM Service Center Agency State unemployment office *Federal Jobs Digest*	Application package (Form B and/or SF-171 enclosed) Job vacancy listing
3	No written test, no register	Mid/top level [+ entry-level professional]	OPM Service Center Agency *Federal Jobs Digest*	Vacancy Announcement (with SF-171) Job vacancy listing
4	Special hiring programs	Various	OPM Service Center Agency	Applicable forms Applicable forms
5	Promotion route/SES	Mid/top level	Agency *Federal Jobs Digest*	Vacancy Announcement Job vacancy listing

TYPES OF VACANCY OR TEST INFORMATION

The Federal government has a variety of test, job vacancy, and job description information that it provides to prospective employees. Such information comes in many shapes and sizes, from a one-page application with an attached test card to a twenty-page color brochure. This section discusses the four most common forms: test scheduling cards, Competition Notices, Vacancy Announcements, and career brochures. It also briefly describes OPM's *Qualifications Standards Operating Manual* and *X-118C,* definitive governmental tomes that may be cited in other informational documents. Let's take a look at each to see what they are, how they may be obtained, and how they relate to each pathway.

TEST SCHEDULING CARDS

A test scheduling card may be issued to anyone who indicates a desire to apply for a position requiring an assembled examination (written test) as per Pathway 1. It can be obtained either from OPM or from an agency that has a job vacancy covered by the test. For example, the test scheduling card for the

Test Scheduling Cards
are further discussed in
Step 4; samples are shown
in Appendix H.

border patrol agent test can be obtained by writing to the Immigration and Naturalization Service. However, as OPM reduces its job information capability and agencies like FAA do more of their own examining, you would be better off to write directly to the agency.

COMPETITION NOTICE

A Competition Notice is to announce actual or anticipated job vacancies within broad occupational groups. Whether called an Examination Announcement, Civil Service Announcement, or just plain Announcement, the Competition Notice may be issued by OPM and often used to compile a Register of Eligibles from which agencies will request referrals. A Competition Notice also lists required forms, provides a filing address, and designates the *application window* (opening and closing dates) during which applications will be accepted for any one of the thousands of Federal job vacancies each year.

Some application windows are very short (one or two weeks); others are indefinite (until further notice). As a general rule, the length of the application window is determined by the number of vacancies and the difficulty with which they are filled. For example, a Competition Notice for Carpenter at WG-11—a job with relatively few vacancies in relation to the number of people who apply—may have an application window of two weeks or less. On the other hand, one for Chemical Engineer at GS-5/7—a job title with many vacancies difficult to fill and very specific educational requirements may be listed as open until further notice.

Sample **Competition
Notices** are located in
Appendix G.

Generally, Competition Notices apply to professional or technical occupations at entry level. As more examining authority has been delegated to agencies, there are fewer Competition Notices. The more common vehicle is a Vacancy Announcement either for a specific vacancy or for a group of vacancies. Thus, the line between Competition Notices and vacancy announcements has become blurred. You just need to read the document carefully to determine what it is and what the requirements are.

VACANCY ANNOUNCEMENT

Unlike a Competition Notice issued by OPM for broad occupational groups, a Vacancy Announcement is issued by an individual agency and usually covers one job title only (but not necessarily only one position). A Vacancy Announcement may be generated by agency headquarters to fill vacancies in that job title all across the country, or by a regional agency office only for vacancies in a particular region or even a single facility. It is almost always associated with case examining rather than use of a register.

Sample **Vacancy
Announcements** are
located in Appendix G.

Vacancy Announcements usually go into greater detail concerning job location, promotion potential, duties and responsibilities, minimum qualifications, ranking factors, and application procedures than do Competition Notices. For the more basic qualifications of specific white- or blue-collar job titles, Vacancy Announcements often refer applicants to *OPM's Qualifications Standards Operating Manual* or *Handbook X118-C*, respectively.

CAREER BROCHURE

If you are unable to find any current vacancy information for the job title(s) in which you are interested, it may be simply because no positions in that occupation are presently open. However, do not be discouraged: Use this time to do some advance research of the duties and qualifications agencies require for the job title(s) for which you want to apply. Then, when vacancies do occur, you will be more knowledgeable about the types of individuals agencies seek to attract.

Career brochures, published by the agencies themselves, are a valuable source of such information. They must be requested directly, and in writing, from the agencies that generally hire in your field, that are usually more than happy to mail them to you. Whether comprising four black-and-white pages or twenty in color, career brochures provide a general overview of an agency's mission, its major career paths, and the minimum qualifications for those paths. They also mention a headquarters personnel office to contact and, if the agency is quite large, may list the addresses of regional personnel offices as well.

OPM'S *QUALIFICATIONS STANDARDS OPERATING MANUAL* AND *HANDBOOK X118-C*

Remember, general descriptions of white- and blue-collar occupations appear in Appendixes K and N, respectively. Agency addresses are listed in Appendix D. Some Vacancy Announcements avoid detailed explanations of minimum job requirements by citing one of two large and comprehensive Federal publications: OPM's *Qualifications Standards Operating Manual* which covers white-collar occupations or *Handbook X-118C (Blue-Collar Occupations in Federal Service)*. (Note: as explained in step 2, the standards for white-collar positions are more general than they used to be, so it is more likely that for these positions, the vacancy announcement will have detailed information on the requirements of the position and not simply refer you to OPM's Operating Manual.) These are in loose-leaf format, as they must be updated periodically. Although neither book contains government secrets, it may require some research on your part to locate copies. A good place to check is the agency personnel office where you wish to apply. In addition, the reference section of a public library or nearby college or university library might well have copies. Wherever you find them, expect to use them on the premises, as they generally cannot be checked out. In addition, you may find a manual entitled *Position Classification Standards*, which contains detailed information on duties responsibilities, qualifications requirements and grade level criteria for Federal occupations. You can purchase a CD Rom which contains qualification and classification standards by contacting the Government Printing Office.

Ranking factors are described in Step 4 (p. 83). **OPM's Qualifications Standards Operating Manual and Handbook X118-C** are discussed below.

HOW THE EXEMPLARY CANDIDATES
APPLY STEP 3

Let's pick up the four exemplary candidates where we left them at the end of Step 2 (see "Summary Table: The Exemplary Candidates at the End of Step 2, p. 62) to see how they use the information provided in this chapter.

EXAMPLE: JANET

By the end of Step 2 Janet had reduced her Federal job search to four job titles. Her objective in Step 3 is to collect the job information that applies to each of these. Janet had noted that the job titles and grade levels she selected are covered by Pathway 3. From the present chapter (including the chart "Finding the Right Vacancy and Test Information on p. 69), Janet learned that information for such job titles is available from three sources:

1. OPM;
2. the agencies that hire employees in the job titles in question; and
3. the *Federal Jobs Digest (FJD)*.

Janet believes that the jobs in which she is interested might be filled by case examining. Janet calls OPM's Career America Connection in her area, and learns that several agencies have vacancies as well as an ongoing need for some of the positions in which she is interested. She also learns that OPM is doing recruitment and examining for several of the agencies. She leaves a message on the Career America Connection telephone line and requests application materials and vacancy announcements. In addition, she accesses OPM's internet site and downloads several vacancy announcements. She writes letters to several agencies which seem to have an ongoing need to fill positions in which she is interested. These are addressed "Attn: Personnel Department, Secretarial and ask whether there are openings in any of her four possible job titles. She receives *application packages* from four of them. Perusing the latest issue of *FJD*, which Janet found at her local library, she sees an opening for a Secretary at an agency about a 35-minute commute from her house. She phones the Personnel Specialist named in the listing. The specialist thanks Janet for her call and sends her an application package.

> An **application package** (or qualifications information package) tells you the qualifications required for a given job title and provides your application form(s).

EXAMPLE: MICHAEL

By the end of Step 2, Michael was left with three options to pursue (see table on p. 62). Air Traffic Controller is covered by Pathway 1. Because FAA is now an excepted agency, Michael contacts that agency directly to learn about air traffic controller positions. Michael will have to contact individual agencies or use one of OPM's information sources to determine whether any agencies are recruiting for any administrative positions. During the past several years, only a small number of administrative positions have been filled. Michael also writes to the Immigration and Naturalization Service to obtain information on the test for border patrol positions.

Next, even though he prefers an administrative position, Michael wants to pursue his idea of applying directly to an agency (via Pathway 3) for a job in a clerical field, from which he could later *transfer* to an administrative title (probably Contract Specialist, GS-1102). His reasoning is that because few administrative positions are filled, his opportunities will be limited. In addition, when agencies do fill administrative-type positions, they prefer to use the outstanding scholar provisions which permit direct hiring of applicants without any sort of examining process. Because Michael did not have a 3.5 grade point average and did not finish in the top 10% of his class, he would not qualify for the outstanding scholar program. If an agency were to fill an administrative position without using the outstanding scholar program, it would issue an announcement. Michael and other applicants would provide information on their backgrounds in a prescribed format, and OPM would score this information using an administrative rating scale. Michael would not necessarily have to take a written test unless the agency asked that it be administered as an additional rating factor. The agency would have to pay OPM for all the services related to rating and ranking Michael and other applicants. This is another reason why agencies don't like to fill administrative positions unless they can use the outstanding scholar provisions. This alternative approach, even though it seems the long way around, may actually result more quickly in an administrative job. Using the phone book that covers both his own county and three others around him, Michael locates six local Federal agency offices. Two of these are offices of the Department of Agriculture and do not seem large enough to have any administrative job titles. Michael calls all four remaining agencies and asks to speak with the Personnel Specialist who handles white-collar professional positions. Although one of the specialists is abrupt, cutting short the conversation even before Michael can present his idea, the other three do listen. Two of these reject his idea, saying they have no openings at present and do not anticipate any in the near future: There is a job freeze at their facilities. However, the Personnel Specialist at the local Department of Energy office is interested in Michael's qualifications and suggests that he take the clerical test given twice a month by OPM in the county seat. It is a walk-in exam: No reservation is needed. Michael decides to give it a try.

EXAMPLE: HELEN

Helen decided in Step 2 to pursue four job titles. Foreign Service Officer is covered by Pathway 1; Accountant and Auditor are covered by Pathway 3; and Foreign Service Secretary which she is pursuing at GS-9, is covered by Pathway 3.

To obtain information on the Foreign Service Officer position and exam, Helen writes to the Department of State in Washington, DC (as instructed on p. 165 of Appendix B) and requests an application package.

Helen realizes that as explained in step 2, OPM no longer maintains national registers for accountant and auditor positions as they once did. This makes her job search effort much more difficult particularly because she wants to relocate. She calls OPM's Career America Connection in Macon, Georgia which has vacancy information from throughout the country. She also writes to agencies' headquarters in Washington, D.C. to get the addresses of personnel offices in the areas where she would like to move, and she also asks for any information the headquarters offices have concerning vacancies in those areas. Helen also contacts a local state employment office and learns that she can visit that office and obtain information on vacancies throughout the country which OPM has provided electronically. If Helen has internet access, she will be able to obtain vacancy information from the comfort of her home. Helen realizes that consulting the *Federal Jobs Digest* which she finds in her college placement office is another way to locate openings in other areas of the country. Seeing many openings listed for Accountants and Auditors at GS-7 and GS-9, to augment her job search she phones four agencies in places where she feels she would like to live. All four send her application packages.

To pursue her interest in a Foreign Service Secretary position, she also writes to the State Department (a different office than that handling the Foreign Service Exam; see Appendix D, p. 224). The State Department responds with an application package within three weeks.

EXAMPLE: JEFF

As of the end of Step 2, Jeff was considering six job titles, all of which were covered by Pathway 3; in addition, he had decided to look into the VRA program (Pathway 4). Since his job search is very important to him, Jeff decides to use all available sources for Pathway 3 job title information: OPM's job information sources, the agencies, and *Federal Jobs Digest* (as per the chart on page 69). He calls the Career America Connection phone number in his area to determine whether there are vacancies for jobs in which he is interested. He learns that there are vacancies for air conditioning equipment mechanic, and he leaves a recorded message requesting an application package which is sent to him. He also learns that the Air Force base 40 miles from where he lives has continuing announcements for positions in which he is interested although it may not necessarily have specific vacancies at this time. He calls the base and asks to speak to the Civilian Personnel Office; once connected, he asks to speak with the Personnel Specialist in charge of Wage Grade positions. This specialist confirms the openings for Air Conditioning Equipment Mechanics and identifies current openings in two other job titles of interest to Jeff, Electrician and Electronics Mechanic. He also confirms that the base has Delegated Examining Authority for these job titles and so does not use OPM to recruit for them. Jeff asks the specialist to send him information and an application package for all three job titles; it arrives in the mail a few days later.

To explore his possibilities under the VRA program, Jeff again calls the Career America Connection in his area, and he hears a recorded message which confirms the information about the program contained in Appendix Q. Jeff realizes that VRA appointments are arranged by individual agencies, many of which are in the Department of Defense; he must contact VRA coordinators at these agencies to determine if any openings exist for which he might qualify. Phoning the Air Force Base with which he had already spoken, Jeff asks to speak with the VRA coordinator. He finds that the base does not have one, but that such a service is provided by another Personnel Specialist who is on vacation. It takes Jeff some time to reach him, only to find out that no openings presently exist in the VRA program at the base. Conversion, introduced in Step 2 (p. 35), does apply to VRA positions.

Jeff, having subscribed to *FJD*, finds in its listings an opening that was earmarked for the VRA program at a DOD agency in a large city in his state some 70 miles from his home. The phone number is given in the listing. Jeff reaches the agency's VRA coordinator and is told that he would be considered for this Excepted Service position. The job title is Quality Assurance Specialist, GS-1910 (a white-collar job); the field specialty is electrical equipment. The position would start somewhere in the range GS-5 9 and have potential for promotion to higher grade levels; at GS-9, according to the VRA coordinator, his position could even be *converted* to the Competitive Service. Jeff feels he has a good chance to get this job. He asks the VRA coordinator to send him the application package; it arrives a few days later.

All four candidates are now ready for the next step in the application process: analyzing the job information they obtain.

Step 4: Familiarizing Yourself with Vacancy Information

Purpose: To help you analyze the application packages—that is, the Federal employment information and application forms—you collected in Step 3. A sample Vacancy Announcement is analyzed in detail, and the application forms you are most likely to fill out are introduced and explained.

Associated appendixes:
- F   Federal Salary Rates
- G   Sample Vacancy Information
- H   Application Forms

So far we have discussed the importance of finding the right job titles, determining the hiring pathways for those jobs, and how to obtain Federal job vacancy information.

ANALYZING VACANCY ANNOUNCEMENTS

As discussed in the chapter on Step 3, Vacancy Announcements are issued by individual agencies and usually cover one job title only. Although the style of Vacancy Announcements may vary from agency to agency, all contain several distinct components, and many include vast amounts of Federal jargon. This section takes you through a sample Vacancy Announcement virtually line by line to show you exactly how to interpret it. By the end, you should be comfortable with any Vacancy Announcement you encounter during your quest for a Federal job. Although some of the information presented is already familiar from previous chapters, a little repetition at this point might be helpful: Consider this a brief review of much of what we have covered—a chance to put it all together in your mind.

The actual Vacancy Announcement we are going to use as our example is the one on page 461 for Wildlife Biologist, which is relatively complete. The rest of the sample Vacancy Announcements in Appendix G contain similar information, though there are variations in the way it is presented.

POSITION/SALARY

Each position on a Vacancy Announcement is delineated by its job title, occupational code, and grade level(s). The *job title* is the formal name of a position as determined by official classification standards (in this case, Wildlife Biologist). The *occupational code* is a code assigned to a Federal *job series,* each series comprising one or more job titles. The code includes an abbreviation indicating which Federal *pay schedule* is applicable to the job: GS for General Schedule (white collar), WG for Wage Grade (blue collar), and so on. The occupational code for Wildlife Biologist is GS-486, the job series being Wildlife Biology. (Recall from Step 1 that the wording of job title and job series may not always match up this precisely: For example, job title Support Services Specialist is in the Office Services Management and Supervision Series, as indicated by its occupational code, GS-342.)

The *grade level* indicates the applicable salary range within the indicated pay schedule, and represents the level of training and/or work experience required for the position. A job may be advertised at a specific level, such as GS-7, or on a flexible scale depending on the qualifications of the applicant. For example, a grade range of GS-7/9/11 means that the job can be filled by a qualified applicant at grade level GS-7, GS-9, or GS-11. Such flexibility may be an indication that more than one position is to be filled (see "Number of Vacancies," below). Alternatively, it may mean that a position offers good chances of promotion to the highest-level grade advertised (see "Promotion Potential," below).

To see what salary you would receive if hired at any given grade level, refer to the current pay schedules in Appendix F. (Because salary levels for Wage Grade positions are area-specific—based by OPM on private-sector wage rates prevailing locally for similar jobs—Appendix F can provide only a sample Wage Grade schedule.) Note that grade level salaries are subdivided to delineate *within-grade (step) increases* for satisfactory performance: For example, a job at step 1 of GS-5 in Washington D.C. indicates an annual salary of $20,908 (the basic General Schedule Salary of $19,520 plus the 7.11% locality pay augmentation whereas the annual salary at step 7 would be $25,092 (the basic General Schedule rate of $23,426 plus the 7.11% locality pay augmentation. Keep in mind that as explained in step 1, these salaries will vary by location. For example, in New York City, those salaries would be $21,306 and $25,569 respectively. New employees are generally hired at step 1 of a grade level (though higher starting steps may occasionally be negotiated); increases are awarded at specific time intervals (52 weeks for each of steps 1–3, 104 weeks for steps 4–6, and 156 weeks for steps 7–9), and thus reflect length of service.

Note also that higher-level Wage Grade positions (leader and supervisor) are designated WL and WS.

Appendix F also shows the pay schedule for jobs in the Senior Executive Service (SES), as well as that for the Postal Service. In addition, pay schedules are presented for fields with *special (advanced) salary rates,* including Foreign Service Officers, other Foreign Service employees, and various health care professionals. Special salary rates are authorized from time to time when there are too few qualified applicants to fill the jobs advertised. There are also special salary rates for some other occupations, for example, clerical workers in major metropolitan areas, where the cost of living is high. Your local OPM office or agency personnel office can tell you which job titles, if any, currently have special salary rates in your area.

According to the General Schedule provided on p. 284, the annual salary for the exemplary Wildlife Biologist position at the GS-15 level would be $70,894 plus the locality pay augmentation for the area in which it is located.

NUMBER OF VACANCIES

A Vacancy Announcement may be used to seek applicants for one or more positions. A multiple Vacancy Announcement may mean either that the agency has an immediate need for a number of qualified candidates or that a future need is anticipated. Thus you may be applying either to fill an actual, specific vacancy or simply to be evaluated and placed in an applicant supply file for that job title.

The broad range of grade levels in the sample Vacancy Announcement for Architect, GS-808-7/9/11–13, strongly suggests that more than one position is at stake. However, since the number of vacancies is not mentioned on the announcement for Wildlife Biologist, and there is only one location indicated, we can pretty much assume that this announcement is for one job vacancy only.

PROMOTION POTENTIAL

Many Vacancy Announcements indicate the promotion potential of the position for which applicants are being recruited: For the Wildlife Biologist example, it is GS-15. This means that once in the job you may be promoted (in increments) up to that grade after a specified length of time (often as little as one year) at each previous grade without having to compete with others for the position. Even though promotions are not automatic or an entitlement, it is a tremendous advantage to be able to be promoted without competition.

However, in contrast to promotions, you are entitled to within-grade increases if your performance is satisfactory, and they are automatic for employees with satisfactory performance ratings. Even if an announcement includes no explicit statement regarding promotion potential, you should by no means dismiss the idea of promotion. Once you have received enough professional training and/or experience at your current classification level—certain *time-in-grade restrictions* are intended to prevent excessively rapid promotions—you may be either moved to the next step in your current position (the within-grade increase discussed above under "Position/Salary") or promoted to the next higher grade. As was mentioned earlier, when a Vacancy Announcement lists several grade levels, the position is likely to offer good chances of promotion to the highest-level grade advertised. In addition, once eligible for promotion, you can apply for a new position that has been announced at a higher grade.

ANNOUNCEMENT NUMBER

Most Vacancy Announcements are identified by a number. This number is important for two reasons:

1. You must write it on your application so the personnel official can accurately identify the opening for which you are applying.
2. If you need to contact a personnel office for more information, or request a copy of the announcement or any required supplemental forms, you can refer to this number to avoid confusion or misunderstanding.

The announcement number for the sample Vacancy Announcement for Wildlife Biologist is 92-042.

OPENING DATE

This is the date on which a hiring agency begins accepting applications for the job. The opening date for the Wildlife Biologist vacancy is April 6, 1992. If the words "Opening Date" do not actually appear on a particular Vacancy Announcement, it is safe to assume that applications have been accepted since the "Issue Date" (or simply "Date"): Only very rarely does a position open some time after an announcement is issued; for obvious reasons, it cannot open beforehand.

CLOSING DATE

Closing dates are very important: If your application does not arrive in time, it will simply not be considered. Closing dates are expressed in one of several ways:

1. by the last date on which the application will be accepted by the personnel office;
2. by the last date the application can be postmarked;
3. as "open until filled," usually meaning "open until a suitable candidate is found," which might occur within a few days (but sometimes meaning that the issuing agency anticipates periodic vacancies for this type of position and will continue to accept applications until they are no longer necessary); or
4. as "continuous," usually meaning that the position will be kept open for an extended period (often a year or longer) because multiple candidates are needed but relatively few are expected to apply.

In our sample Vacancy Announcement, the closing date is April 27. Its importance is emphasized at the bottom of the announcement, under "How to Apply": Agency personnel officials have underlined that the "application must reach the issuing office by the closing date." This means that it must be *in their hands,* not merely postmarked, by April 27.

If there is little time before the closing date of a job that interests you, contact the personnel office to which you will send your application to see whether there is any flexibility in the deadline: Closing dates for hard-to-fill jobs are often extended.

LOCATION/ORGANIZATION

Each announcement states the geographic location of the position as well as the division or office within the agency in which the position exists. In cases of multiple vacancies, the locations of positions may vary: An agency may be seeking candidates for similar jobs in San Francisco, Atlanta, Philadelphia, New York, Denver, and Washington, DC. It is therefore important to indicate on your application the location(s) of the positions in which you are interested.

The only location mentioned for the Wildlife Biologist position is in Jamestown, ND; that, therefore, was the only location where the agency had a vacancy for that job title when it issued the Vacancy Announcement.

NATURE OF APPOINTMENT

Several kinds of appointment are available in the Competitive Service, and these are specified on a Vacancy Announcement. Two types of shorter-term appointments are the following:

For more on **types of appointments,** see Step 7 (p. 120).

temporary limited (or simply *temporary*) *appointments,* which usually last one year or less and involve no promotion or transfer rights; and
term appointments, which may last between one and four years and have limited promotion privileges within the agency. Persons given term appointments may be promoted to other term positions, but they may not be promoted to permanent positions.

In Appendix G, the Vacancy Announcements for Equal Employment Manager, GS-260-13, and Laborer Leader, WG-03502-3, both specify temporary appointments.

The vast majority of new full- and part-time government employment comprises *career-conditional appointments.* Employees must demonstrate satisfactory work performance for three years, the first of which is probationary, before being granted *career appointments.* Employees with career appointments enjoy the full range of rights and privileges associated with Federal employment. Upon leaving the system, they may retain competitive status forever; whereas career-conditional employees who leave the government retain competitive status for three years only (unless they are veterans in which case they would also retain competitive status for ever). This retention of competitive status, or *reinstatement eligibility (RE)*, allows a return to Federal employment without a repetition of the competitive examining process.

AREA OF CONSIDERATION

Each announcement also indicates who is eligible to be considered for the job vacancy, which is determined by the recruiting agency. Some vacancies are restricted to certain types of applicants, including the following:

agency affiliated—applicants currently or formerly employed by a specified agency, generally the agency issuing the Vacancy Announcement (though former volunteer work with an agency such as the Peace Corps may also be relevant);

career status—current Federal employees who have worked a predetermined amount of time (usually three years) in a given job title;

career-conditional—current Federal employees who have not yet worked long enough at their present jobs for full career status;

competitive status—Federal employees currently in either career or career-conditional positions (or former Federal employees with reinstatement eligibility);

department only—applicants affiliated with a particular department of the executive branch (almost always the department to which the agency issuing the announcement belongs);

handicapped (often noting level of severity);

Indian preference—Native Americans;

nonstatus—nonemployees (first-time hires) or Federal employees hired under special programs that do not convey status (that is, the Excepted Service);

Notice of Rating/Results—applicants already rated or otherwise found eligible for the particular job title;

reinstatement eligible—former employees who retain their competitive status

transfer eligible—current Federal employees who have worked a predetermined amount of time (usually one year) in a given job title and are eligible for promotion transfer; and

veterans (possibly citing specific hiring programs, such as VRA).

> See the earlier section "Nature of Appointment" regarding **reinstatement eligibility** (p. 80).

> Such **notices** are described in Step 5 (p. 101).

In addition, an agency may specify a *geographic* area of consideration, usually meaning that applications will be accepted only from applicants within a certain commuting distance or region near the job location. This is done when the agency believes it will not have to go far to find a suitable candidate and wishes to restrict the number of applications it has to process. Registers are described in Step 2 (p. 42).

In our example of Wildlife Biologist, the area of consideration is (Federal) government-wide and includes career-status (and, according to the "General Information," career-conditional) Federal employees. The "General Information" section encourages applications from the handicapped, certain veterans, and others to whom special hiring programs apply.

Sometimes a Vacancy Announcement will include the notation, "An OPM register may also be used. What this means is that qualified applicants— including first-time hires—will be sought from a register if none is found inside either the hiring agency or another government agency. Such cases demonstrate the importance of being rated and placed on a register if one is maintained for the position in which you are interested: You never know when an agency might need someone with your particular expertise, and you could be selected for consideration even without having ever seen a particular Vacancy Announcement. Also, once you have your Notice of Rating in hand, name requests are discussed in Step 2 (p. 44). You can apply directly to an agency and (at the agency's discretion) be *name requested* off the register. Because the use of OPM registers is decreasing, this avenue will be less available than in the past. However, an agency may maintain its own register or an applicant supply file, and if a vacancy announcement indicates that it does, you should submit your application for consideration for future vacancies.

DUTIES AND RESPONSIBILITIES

A brief overview of the general duties and responsibilities of the position is almost always stated on the Vacancy Announcement. This important information can help you determine if the job really interests you. If it does, the duties and responsibilities statement will help you tailor your application so as to reflect your ability to perform these duties.

The rundown on duties and responsibilities for the sample Wildlife Biologist position is quite extensive, giving any applicant a very good idea of just what the job entails. Note, however, that not all Vacancy Announcements are quite as informative as this one.

MINIMUM QUALIFICATIONS REQUIREMENTS

Federal Vacancy Announcements often itemize, in detail, the *minimum* or *basic qualifications* for the job title at entry level. In other cases, they outline these qualifications briefly and refer to the full description found in either OPM's *Qualifications Standards Operating Manual* which contains minimum qualification requirements for General Schedule positions or *Handbook X-118C* which contains minimum qualifications standards for blue collar (wage grade) positions. This information is very important: If your qualifications do not meet the minimum qualifications officially established for the job, your application will not be considered further. As explained in step 2, OPM has revised its qualification standards for General Schedule positions to make them very general. Therefore, agencies must flesh them out on their announcements. The agency will usually describe requirements which amplify or add to the minimum requirements contained in OPM's standards. You must meet these additional requirements.

The Wildlife Biologist announcement lists detailed minimum qualifications, gives acceptable alternatives, and even explains what is meant by "professional experience." However, it also mentions that Federal personnel offices have copies of OPM's *Qualifications Standards Operating Manual* should you wish to research the qualifications further.

SPECIAL QUALIFICATIONS

Special qualifications, which may be listed in the Vacancy Announcement under such headings as "Knowledge, Skills, and Abilities" (KSAs), "Ranking Factors," "Evaluation Factors," or "Selective Placement Factors," refer to qualifications for a job title beyond the minimum or basic ones. These are usually used for positions at the mid- and upper-administrative levels (GS-9 and above) to attract candidates whose qualifications best match those required for a particular position. They may also be used to differentiate positions with the same job title but different areas of specialization (say, a Computer Specialist with expertise in aerospace programming versus one with an extensive background in data base applications). A good rating for a mid- or upper-level position depends on your ability to demonstrate that you satisfy the special qualifications outlined on the Vacancy Announcement. Your application package will receive closer consideration if you highlight these special qualifications either on your application or on any separate forms that the agency may require.

The announcement for Wildlife Biologist lists these qualifications under "Quality Ranking Factors," and explains that the KSAs by which you will be ranked are on the supervisory appraisal form on the reverse of the announcement (not reprinted in the appendix).

HOW TO APPLY

The announcement will always tell you what forms to submit as part of your application. This application material frequently consists of a Standard Form-171, a résumé, or narrative application and a performance appraisal (both of which are explained in the section on forms below). The announcement will also state the address to which the completed forms should be sent. Copy this address carefully: The Federal government is a large and complex organization, and the omission of one letter or number in a mailing address may mean your application is never received by the correct office.

The Wildlife Biologist announcement indicates that a resume or other narrative application, performance appraisal, and other materials are required, and provides the correct address in Washington, DC to which they should be sent.

> Federal employees must not send applications in franked (prepaid, government) envelopes. Such use of government mail is improper, and the applications will not be considered. Some agencies will accept applications by fax or electronic mail. If the announcement does not specify that these are acceptable, you should check with the personnel office before using one of these methods.

APPLICATION FORMS YOU MAY ENCOUNTER

By now it should be clear that there is no one way to do anything in the Federal employment system; so it should come as no surprise that, depending on the job title(s) for which you apply, there are various forms that you may have to fill out. Some individuals may find that only one form is necessary, whereas others may have to fill out quite a few. Generally, the higher the grade and the more complex the job, the more supplementary forms you will be required to complete. The forms most commonly encountered are discussed in the following subsections; samples (blanks) are provided in Appendix H. Note that *some* of the forms shown in Appendix H may be photocopied and used; the exceptions are fill-in-the-circles computer forms (or "bubble sheets"), for which an original must always be submitted.

An agency may require an applicant to fill out a special application form or forms in addition to, or in lieu of, those forms outlined below; if so, the agency will so inform you when you apply.

TEST SCHEDULING CARD (OPM FORM 5000 A/B)

The test scheduling card is basically a registration form for any written test you may be required to take, and can be obtained either from an OPM office or from an agency that has a job vacancy covered by the test. OPM or agencies may use other registration forms. For entry-level job seekers with little or no applicable experience (like our exemplary candidate Michael), this will probably be the first Federal form that must be completed; fortunately, it is also the simplest. Space is provided for your name, address, date of birth, social security number, veteran's status, and citizenship. The form lists test locations and which job titles are covered by the exam. In addition, it may provide pertinent information concerning any minimum qualifications or additional application procedures. The government will return your completed test scheduling card to you with the date, time, and place where you are to take the written test for which you have applied. OPM and agencies are phasing out the use of the form and substituting other methods of registration such as by phone.

APPLICATION FOR FEDERAL EMPLOYMENT, STANDARD FORM (SF-)171

Filling out the **SF-171** is discussed in depth in Step 5. **Worksheets** to help you organize your previous work experience and present it effectively on the SF-171 are provided in Appendix I.

The SF-171 (see p. 488) used to be the application form required for most Federal jobs. It is a standard form (unassembled exam), used instead of a résumé, on which you must detail your education, work experience, volunteer work, any special honors or recognition you have received, foreign language skills, professional certifications, and other information. In the past all of our exemplary candidates would have been likely to fill out the SF-171 at some point during the application process. As explained in step 2, agencies no longer may require the SF-171. Applicants may still use it or OPM's Optional Application form (OF612). Applicants may also use resumes, but if you use a resume, you must be sure to include all the information required by the announcement. You must be sure to address the qualifications requirements described on the announcement. You may wish to attach separate sheets to your resume that highlight each qualification factor described on the announcement. Some agencies may have obtained special approval to require a specific application form. If they require a specific form, this will be stated on the vacancy announcement. Note, however, that you usually do not need to submit a Standard Form, résumé, or application to OPM or an agency just because a test scheduling card is returned to you; once you have taken the test and been rated, however, an agency may well require a resume or application when it considers you for employment. Sooner or later, virtually every candidate fills out a resume or narrative application: How you complete this unassembled exam is extremely important and, in large measure, determines your chances of getting a Federal job.

EMPLOYMENT AVAILABILITY STATEMENT, FORM A

Candidates for a position may find other employment, relocate, or simply lose interest in the job: Therefore, when an agency or OPM wishes to confirm that they are still available for and interested in a given position, it mails them Form A. This appears in two formats: "key entry," the older, more commonly used version, on which the information requested must be written in or typed; and the newer, scannable version shown on page 494.

OCCUPATIONAL SUPPLEMENT, FORM B
(OPM FORM 1203)

A Form B is a standardized, fill-in-the-circles computer form that OPM and some agencies are using instead of narrative applications for some entry-level (GS-5/7), white-collar job titles in Federal service. Some agencies and OPM are using similar forms for higher-grade positions too. It is designed so that an applicant's job experience, education, and geographic preference for a job title or occupational group can be computer scanned rather than reviewed by OPM or agency officials. This allows the automatic and more efficient processing of thousands of applications received by the government each year for entry-level positions that utilize registers but no written test. It also can be used for other positions, when agencies have many vacancies and receive many applications. The Form B is also known as OPM Form 1203, in which case an alphabetical code is added to indicate the job titles specified (1203-J for Accountant and Auditor, for example; see samples on p. 517).

> Because it is to be computer scanned, any **Form B** you submit must be an original, not a photocopy.

EXAMPLE

Helen may use a Form B or similar form if the agencies to which she is applying are using automated procedures to fill their entry-level accountant positions. If some agencies are buying their examining service from OPM, OPM would probably use the form.

PERFORMANCE APPRAISAL FORM (PA)

For more on **performance appraisals,** see Step 5 (p. 97).

This type of form is used for all permanent positions government-wide in an annual, ongoing review of a Federal employee's work; it may also be requested as part of the hiring process. If you are a current Federal employee and seeking either a promotion (even if noncompetitive) or a different job title within the government, your performance appraisal should be filled out by your present supervisor. For new hires, a letter of reference from a current or former employer (or a peer in your field) is often requested in lieu of a performance appraisal. An agency may have its own version of this form.

SUPPLEMENTAL QUALIFICATIONS STATEMENT, FORM 1170

Special qualifications are explained on p. 83.

Supplemental qualifications statements can be used in addition to the SF-171 if you need additional space to document your educational background or other qualifications. Three examples of these forms are shown in Appendix H: One is Form 1170/17, List of College Courses and Certificate of Scholastic Achievement, which recent college graduates might need to use; the others are Supplemental Qualifications Forms for Secretary and Nursing positions. Such forms would be used to outline an applicant's special qualifications (such as experience in using word-processing software or caring for the elderly). Even if the announcement does not request these specific forms, you must read it carefully to determine whether the information is still required. For example, the agency may want information concerning your college courses even though it is not asking for the form mentioned above.

HOW THE EXEMPLARY CANDIDATES
APPLY STEP 4

Let's rejoin the four exemplary candidates where we left them at the end of Step 3 and follow them along as they apply the information they learned in this step.

EXAMPLE: JANET

Janet has written to six agencies within commuting distance and asked them for any information on openings in the four job titles of interest to her. Four of these agencies sent application packages. In addition, Janet found another vacancy listing in the *Federal Jobs Digest,* and the agency with that vacancy also sent her an application package. Note, because agencies usually cannot require specific application forms, many will no longer send out a specific application package. They may just send you the Vacancy Announcement.

Janet reviews the five similar application packages she has received from the agencies. All contained one or more Vacancy Announcements. The Department of Health and Human Services (HHS) sent her announcements for all four of her chosen job titles: Secretary, GS-318-7/9; Misc. Administration, GS-301-7; Support Services Administration (or Specialist; the title may vary), GS-342-9; and Management Assistant, GS-344-9. An FBI office and a USDA Forest Service office each sent her Vacancy Announcements for the first two of these job titles. The remaining two agencies—a Naval Training Center and an office of the Department of Housing and Urban Development (HUD)—sent her announcements for only the first job title. The HHS and FBI sent a performance appraisal. In addition, the FBI and the Forest Service sent her colorful career brochures about their agencies, and the FBI package included a personalized letter soliciting her application.

Janet decides this all looks promising. She notices that two of the Secretary Vacancy Announcements have closing dates of "Continuous," and that all but one of the others list closing dates of "Open Until Filled." (The exception—the Forest Service announcement for Misc. Administration— gives a closing date 11 days away.) Because most of the announced jobs say "Open Until Filled" or "Continuous," Janet reasons correctly that these agencies might be having trouble filling the jobs currently open. On the basis of this evaluation of the situation, she decides to apply for only three or four of the positions and then wait to see what happens: Perhaps she will find a job right for her from among those few. She selects the two agencies that had sent her career brochures—the FBI and the Forest Service—because she feels this gesture (plus the personalized FBI letter) shows a bit more enthusiasm for her application.

Janet then further analyzes the total of four Vacancy Announcements she had received from these two agencies, comparing the important information they contain (see table, "Janet's Vacancy Announcement Comparison," p. 88). The most noticeable difference is that the Misc. Administration positions both start at higher salaries and have greater promotion potential than do the Secretary positions. At the same time, however, the area of consideration for both of the former are restricted to current employees of the respective agencies. Perhaps, Janet muses, these Misc. Administration announcements had been sent her by error; or perhaps these positions had been open for a while and, since suitable candidates had not yet been found, the agencies had decided to lift the restrictions and consider all candidates. She phones the receptionist in the personnel offices of both agencies to ask whether the areas of consideration had been changed. The receptionist at the Forest Service responds that the job, listed as "Open Until Filled," had since been filled via promotion of an agency employee. The FBI receptionist says that the Personnel Specialist in charge of the position is at a conference and will not be back for several days; Janet should apply anyway and see what happens.

Janet is disappointed that the promotion potential indicated on the Vacancy

Table: Janet's Vacancy Announcement Comparison

Job Title	GS Series	Agency	Starting Grade	Promotion Potential	Area of Consideration	Closing Date	Ranking Factors
Secretary	318	FBI	GS-5/7	GS-8	All sources	Continuous	none
Secretary	318	Forest Svc.	GS-5/7	GS-8	All sources	Continuous	none
Misc. Admin.	342	FBI	GS-9	GS-13	Current agency employees	11 days	N/A
Misc. Admin.	342	Forest Svc.	GS-9	GS-13	Current agency employees	Open until filled	N/A
(added upon further consideration)							
Mgmt. Asst.	344	HHS	GS-9	GS-9	All sources	Open until filled	N/A

*Janet realizes on reading the Vacancy Announcement that the ranking factors apply only to those with previous Federal experience, which she does not have.

Announcements for the two secretarial jobs is no higher than GS-8. What is worse, she would have to accept a position at GS-7 to start and wait for promotion to GS-8. However, in reading over the career brochures and other material the agencies sent, Janet finds some encouraging information. Reading between the lines, she gathers that she *might* even be able to negotiate a beginning salary above the usual General Schedule starting level (step 1) for first-time Federal employees. This is because she has excellent qualifications which are probably superior to most of the other applicants. If the agency agrees, it can set a salary at a higher step in order to match her existing income. This makes the salary situation possibly more enticing. Janet also learns from reading the application packages that Secretaries can take advantage of the many training courses offered without charge to Federal employees. By taking these courses she could qualify for a more advanced position in Federal service.

Based on her analysis of the application material she had received, Janet decides to apply for both positions open at the FBI and the one still open at the Forest Service. In addition, to increase her chances of an administrative job at GS-9, she decides also to apply to Health and Human Services (HHS) for their Management Assistant position (GS-344-9).

EXAMPLE: MICHAEL

At the end of Step 3, Michael had decided to take the border patrol agent exam. He has since received a registration form from the Immigration and Naturalization Service and a test schedule. He notes that the test will be given the following month in a city about two hours away from his home. He sees no problem in filling out the registration form, as the information it calls for is quite straightforward.

Meanwhile, in case he has no success in locating an administrative position and does not pass the test to gain quick appointment as a border patrol agent, Michael has taken the clerical exam given by OPM on a walk-in basis in a YMCA about an hour from his home in a nearby county seat. Michael also knows that even if he does well on the border patrol exam, the required interview and background investigation would probably take a while. A few days later, Michael receives a Notice of Results declaring that he has passed. He mails a photocopy of this to an agency with whom he had spoken about obtaining an administrative position through transfer, and includes a cover letter expressing his interest in working there. The agency, an office of the Department of Energy, sends him an SF-171, a Form 1170/17, and a Vacancy Announcement for a GS-303 Misc. Clerk and Assistant position. The Vacancy Announcement is quite general: The closing date is "Continuous, the grade level GS-4, no promotion potential is given, and the area of consideration is "All Sources in Commuting Area; the duties description is also quite general, and no special qualifications or ranking factors are included. Michael concludes from reading the Vacancy Announcement that the position is a kind of catchall office assistant job; but he decides to complete the SF-171 and Form 1170/17 and await the response.

EXAMPLE: HELEN

At the end of Step 3, Helen had received application packages from four agencies around the country for Accountants or Auditors. She had also written to the State Department regarding both Foreign Service Officer (and its exam) and Foreign Service Secretary.

Of the four agencies who sent her application packages, two included a career brochure and a Vacancy Announcement—one for Auditor and one for Accountant. From the remaining two agencies she received one Vacancy Announcement apiece for Accountant positions. All four application packages included SF-171s. Seeing the response of these agencies, Helen surmises that there is no shortage of jobs for Accountants or Auditors. Hence, she now decides she can afford the luxury of choosing where in the country she would like to work, which is in the Los Angeles area. (Ideally, of course, she would prefer to work overseas, which is why she is also pursuing Foreign Office positions; but she also had always wanted to live in Southern California.)

Of the four agencies that responded to her calls, one is a Naval Weapons Support Center near Los Angeles. Helen decides that this is the only one of the four to which she will respond. It had sent her a Vacancy Announcement for an Auditor GS-511-5/7/9 with an "Open" closing date, area of consideration noted as "All Sources," and various qualifications and ranking factors.

She receives from the State Department a 5000 A/B test scheduling card with which to apply for the Foreign Service Exam. This is self-explanatory, and she completes and returns it.

The application package she receives from the State Department regarding Foreign Service Secretary includes a career brochure for the Foreign Service, for the Foreign Service Secretary position, and an SF-171. On perusing the information, Helen sees that this type of information differs in an important aspect from that in the Accountant Vacancy Announcements she had read. The Vacancy Announcements had each described one position and was specific about the duties and qualifications of that job. This information instead described a class of positions. Although the jobs of Foreign Service Secretaries posted around the world were sure to differ from one another, the State Department was not recruiting one position at a time (which is why a Vacancy Announcement had not been used): They were recruiting candidates who could fill any one of these positions. The information also points out that candidates for this job title must be available to work wherever required by the State Department, and so are not allowed to express any geographic preference.

EXAMPLE: JEFF

At the end of Step 3, Jeff had received an application package (which included general information and Vacancy Announcements for an air conditioning equipment mechanic, an electrician, and an electronics mechanic from the Air Force Base he had phoned. He had also made contact with a VRA coordinator at a DOD agency in a city some 70 miles from his home, who sent him an application package for quality assurance specialist, a white-collar job.

The vacancy announcements from the Air Force base say precisely what qualifications each job required at different career levels. Jeff sees that he qualifies at the level of leader for Electrician, equivalent to the foreman level at which he is currently working. Although he would probably qualify as a journeyman for Air Conditioning Equipment Mechanic or Electronic Mechanic, Jeff realizes (after checking the Wage Grade pay schedule also provided by the Air Force base) that he would have to take a considerable cut in pay at these levels. Consequently, Jeff decides to apply only for the position of Electrician.

From his VRA contact at the DOD's Defense Logistics Agency office 70 miles away, Jeff receives not only a Vacancy Announcement for Quality Assurance Specialist GS-1900-5/7/9, but also a VRA brochure, and an agency brochure. Jeff realizes that under the noncompetitive VRA program he would be examined with regard only to his qualifications for the program, not for the position. However, he decides that any background he could show to support his qualifications for the job title might help his chances at getting the VRA appointment; after all, more than one veteran might be trying for the job. Jeff studies the Vacancy Announcement and confirms (via "Area of Consideration") that it is open to VRA appointment. Under "Duties," Jeff sees that the position concerns inspection of electrical equipment—equipment with which he had worked for years.

Jeff decides to complete two SF-171s: one for the Electrician job and one for the VRA position. He is ready to start the next step in the Federal employment process.

Step 5: Completing Your Examination (Application or Test)

Purpose: To help you with the Federal examination—whether an application form or a written test required for the position(s) in which you are interested. For many Federal positions competition is keen; even a slightly higher score on your test, or a subtle improvement to your application, can make the difference in obtaining an appointment or in qualifying at a desired grade level.

Associated appendixes:
E Selected Federal Tests
G Sample Vacancy Information
H Application Forms
I SF-171 Experience Block Worksheets
J Geographic Location of Federal Employment

PREPARING YOUR APPLICATION (UNASSEMBLED EXAM)

As previously explained, the most common application form used to be the SF-171. Agencies can no longer require this form. They must accept résumés or other narrative application forms. Only where agencies have special approval or where an automated system is being used can agencies require a specific application. However, the principles which applied to proper completion of the SF-171 will still help you to prepare a strong application. In whatever form, your application will probably be the first paperwork seen by your prospective Federal employers. For most job titles, it is the primary document upon which one's rating will be based.

FILLING OUT THE SF-171

This section, in conjunction with Appendix I (SF-171 Experience Block

Worksheets) will walk you through the process of filling out an SF-171. Do not rush this crucial step in the application process: It is best to read through the entire section and do the worksheets in Appendix I before actually trying to fill out the form. A thorough understanding of the process can save you time and increase your chances of receiving a higher rating. It may then be wise to fill out a practice copy of the form, using pencil or pen. We highly recommend, however, that the *final* version of your SF-171 be either type-written or produced via personal computer (PC). Good computer software is now available for this purpose, and some Personnel Specialists report being impressed by computer-generated, laser-printed applications.

If you are applying for more than one register or job title, you will have to submit a separate SF-171 for each one; however, because much of the information you provide will be the same on each application, you can type it once onto a "master SF-171, to be photocopied and completed for each specific job title. Using photocopies of a master SF-171 in this way is completely acceptable, provided they are clear and legible and that each one you submit has an original signature. The creation of master and subsidiary SF-171's is facilitated, of course, by the use of PC software. Bear in mind that complet-ing and submitting an SF-171 is rarely a one-shot deal. More often, it is an ongoing process in which you apply for every appropriate job title or vacancy you find desirable until you finally receive an acceptable job offer.

A copy of an actual SF-171 is provided in Appendix H (p. 488) and may be photocopied and filled out, whether for practice or actual submission. The form is divided into a series of numbered items, or blocks, to which the com-mentary below is keyed. (Block 24 is additionally discussed in detail in Ap-pendix I.) Be sure *also* to read the instructions provided with the form by the government.

Block 1: When you complete your master copy of the SF-171, leave this blank: You will need to insert different job titles and announcement num-bers for each register or vacancy for which you are applying.

Blocks 2–9: Make sure to keep your master copy of the SF-171 up to date regarding any changes in address or phone number. Should your address or telephone number change *after* you submit an SF-171, notify the orga-nization to which you sent the application as soon as possible. You can do this by submitting a letter stating the changes which have been made.

Block 10: This area is for current or former Federal employees so that the personnel office can decide whether you qualify as a status applicant. If you served as a volunteer in the Peace Corps, VISTA, or ACTION, be sure to indicate that here.

Blocks 11–16: In general, to enhance your job opportunities, demonstrate as much flexibility as possible in response to these questions. You can *maxi-mize* your job opportunities by indicating: that you are available for tem-porary appointments of any duration; that you will accept a job anywhere; that you are available for unlimited travel; and that you are available for any part-time position.

In **block 11,** former Peace Corps, VISTA, or ACTION volunteers should note: "Eligible for noncompetitive appointment as Peace Corps/ VISTA/ACTION volunteer."

In **block 12,** enter the lowest *grade* you will accept rather than the lowest *pay*, since pay rates within each grade change from year to year, and your application may be under active consideration during such a change.

Listing the lowest grade level for which you qualify will not keep you from being considered for higher-grade-level jobs for which you may also qualify. For example, if you qualify at GS-9 but indicate the lowest grade you will consider as GS-7, you can be considered for job vacancies at both the GS-7 and GS-9 levels. However, if you list the highest grade at which you qualify as the only grade you will accept, you will not be considered for any lower-grade positions. Thus if the lowest grade you will accept is GS-9, you will not be considered or rated for any vacancies at the GS-7 level.

Blocks 17–22: These are mainly to determine whether you are eligible for veterans preference, discussed briefly in Step 2 (under "Pathway 4") and in detail in Appendix Q. (Conditions for qualifying are also listed in the instructions that accompany the SF-171.) The term *compensably disabled* means that an individual receives a Federal pension in compensation for a disability incurred during military service (whether or not in combat). The *Purple Heart* is awarded to all armed forces members wounded or killed in action; their wounds need not have been permanently disabling. If you are either compensably disabled or a Purple Heart recipient, you should not only indicate this in block 22, but must also file a Form SF-15 (Application for 10-Point Veterans' Preference) in order to receive full credit for your military experience. Note that even if you do not claim veteran's preference you must still complete **block 22** (mark "no preference")—even if you never served in the U.S. military (**block 17**)!

Block 23: Obviously, if you are currently employed and do not want your employer to know that you are job hunting, answer "No" here.

Block 24: This work experience block is generally the most important part of the SF-171, comprising the primary information OPM or the hiring agency will review to determine your qualifications for employment. Although the instructions given in this section suffice for most entry-level applicants, we *strongly suggest* that you also use the worksheets in Appendix I if you have not done so already. These worksheets specifically address how to match your work experience to the government's *job qualifications* and thereby maximize your rating potential.

> **Job qualification** info sources are covered in Step 3 (under "Types of Vacancy or Test Information").

List your *current or most recent* job or volunteer experience first (block 24A), followed by your next most recent job, and so on. You must also account for any periods of unemployment.

If you held *more than one job* at the same time, list first the one that ended most recently. If you currently hold more than one job, list first the job you consider most important or career enhancing.

List *volunteer activities* in the same chronological order as jobs. Volunteer work often demonstrates skills that supplement those appearing in the description of your jobs. Experience gained doing volunteer work is credited in the same manner as experience gained from employment.

If you need more experience blocks to document your past employment, use the SF-171-A Continuation Sheet included with the SF-171 (on the back of the instructions). If you need more room to describe your job, you may continue the description on white, 8½" × 11" sheets of paper. These should be inserted by cutting open the SF-171 where indicated (at the top of its third page) and attaching the additions with strips of transparent adhesive tape. Supplemental sheets should reference the experience block on the SF-171 to which they relate, and each sheet should include your full name, Social Security number, and the announcement number or job title. In addition, if the Vacancy Announcement lists specific knowledges, skills, abilities, or other criteria which will be used to evaluate candidates, you should include separate sheets which address each of these.

When describing your work experience, use *active verbs*—words like "organize," "maintain," "retrieve," "propose," and "implement." These convey an active, aggressive approach to your job and create a strong impression of your responsibilities and accomplishments.

List the *current telephone number,* if known, of your immediate supervisor in each job that you describe, even if that person has left the organization since supervising you.

The key "description of work" sections ask you to describe the duties, responsibilities, and accomplishments you had in each job. You will enhance your chances of being hired if you include evidence that you have expanded your capabilities and assumed greater responsibilities or more demanding duties within each job, as well as from one job to the next. What projects did you follow through to completion? By what percentage did you increase office productivity? Include everything you can to improve your rating.

Blocks 25–30: For some candidates—for example, recent college grads with a degree in engineering or accounting but little work experience these education blocks can be just as important as **block 24.** If you have the specific degree and/or number of credits in a particular concentration required by the job(s) for which you are applying, make sure you include that information here. If you are substituting work experience for education, specify what experience you are substituting for what educational requirement.

Block 31: Any additional noncollegiate training relevant to the job(s) for which you are applying should be listed here—for example, a course in word processing you took at a business school or in an adult education class. Be sure to include any military schools you attended and explain, in civilian terms, what skills you gained. Training received during actual military service, such as in radio and other communication, may also be useful and should be described here.

Block 32: Try to put *something* in this block. It is one of the few places on the SF-171 where the government gives you the chance to distinguish yourself from other applicants. If you have published an article, received a patent for an invention, or joined a scientific or professional organization, be sure to mention it. Awards may include those from businesses ("Salesperson of the Month"), unions, or other organizations (social, religious, or fraternal). Scholastic awards, such as honors or fellowships, are also noteworthy, as are any related to special skills, such as foreign language proficiency, writing, music, and so on.

Block 33: This is important if you are applying for a job with a minimum typing speed requirement. Note that candidates hired but found to have made any false claims on their applications will be discharged.

Block 34: For some jobs (health care professional, engineer, accountant, pilot, air conditioning repair technician, etc.) special certificates will be a qualifying factor and an integral part of your rating. In other instances, they may interest a personnel official and show that you have many skills and talents in addition to those that qualify you for the job. Be sure to include your driver's license for any job title that entails driving (Messenger, Construction Controller, Motor Vehicle Operator, etc.).

Block 35: The ability to read and/or write in more than one language can be a valuable asset when working for the government. Bilingual proficiency may be required for some job titles, including Translator (the most obvious), Border Patrol Officer, Customs Enforcement Officer, Foreign Service Officer, and a few in the Education series.

Block 36: Make sure the addresses and telephone numbers you give for your references are current. Select individuals who know you well and will give you good recommendations. It is advisable to ask their permission before including them as references.

Block 37: In most cases you must be a U.S. citizen to be hired. Important exceptions are discussed in Step 1 (p. 25).

Blocks 38-45: Answering "Yes" to any of these questions does not mean you are ineligible for a Federal job; however, it does mean that you must provide details in **block 45.** You may also wish to explain the circumstances of your "Yes" answer in a *cover letter* you submit with your SF-171. Because the JF-171 is no longer used, you may not be required to answer all these questions when you submit your application. The Vacancy Announcement will indicate which if any of these questions must be answered with your application materials. Even though you may not be required to answer these questions at the time of your application, you may be required to answer them or similar questions prior to your selection being made final, so you should be prepared to deal with the issues covered by these questions.

> **Cover letters** are discussed in a separate section (p. 97).

Block 46: If you are receiving a Federal civilian or military pension, you are still eligible to apply for Federal employment, but accepting Federal employment may affect your pension. In most cases, while you are working for the Federal government, your salary would be reduced by the amount of your Federal pension. If you are receiving retired military pay, that pay would be reduced while your are working. For extremely hard to fill positions, an agency may be able to obtain special approval from OPM for you to receive both your full Federal salary and your full pension. If this is important to you, you should not begin working until such approval is obtained, and you have seen written confirmation from OPM to the agency.

Block 47: Here you are asked about Federally employed family members so that the examiner can determine compliance of your candidacy with nepotism laws. Questions will be raised if either the Personnel Specialist or your prospective supervisor is related to you.

Blocks 48–9: Leave these blocks (Signature and Date) blank on your master SF-171: Although the application you submit may be a photocopy, your signature (and therefore the date) must be an original.

PERFORMANCE APPRAISALS

In addition to the SF-171, almost all agencies require applicants to provide some kind of job evaluation from a current or former supervisor, or someone else familiar with the employee's performance in Federal parlance, a *performance appraisal (PA)*. Occasionally, an agency may ask for a PA on its own special form; if so, this will be sent to you with the Vacancy Announcement.

About once a year, each current government employee receives such an official evaluation of his or her ability to meet job requirements. If you are already a Federal employee, the agency to whom you are applying often will require a copy of your most recent PA, which usually must be dated within the past year. If you are not a Federal employee, you probably have no such appraisal to submit; however, you can submit a document that serves the same purpose, such as:

1. an *evaluation from your current employer,* including the length of time that you have worked for the company, the title of your most recent job, the basic duties and responsibilities of the position, and how well you have succeeded in carrying them out;

2. a *letter of recommendation* from someone—such as a teacher, professor, former employer, or respected industry peer—who knows you well enough to comment on your employment qualifications.

Clearly, if you do not want your current employer to know of your job search, you should consider the second alternative. In either case, the requirement that the document be dated within the past year is somewhat relaxed.

If a PA is required and yours is unfavorable, consider attaching a note explaining the circumstances leading to the unfavorable evaluation. Remember to be tactful: Attacking your supervisor may jeopardize your chances of employment. Sometimes, it is possible to withhold an unfavorable PA until you are called for an interview. If an agency permits you to delay presenting the PA until that time, you can explain the reasons for the unfavorable report in person.

Even if a job announcement does not request a PA, you may want to consider submitting a favorable one (or a substitute document) anyway, as it will help distinguish you from other job applicants. PAs are especially important at the lower-grade levels, particularly if they relate directly to the job(s) for which you are applying. They may be less significant at higher levels, where education and experience receive at least as much weight in the rating process.

WHEN AND HOW TO WRITE A COVER LETTER

Cover letters are generally unwelcome at Federal personnel offices, especially regarding entry-level positions, because they slow down the evaluation process; they are more useful (and sometimes specifically requested) for upper-level positions, including those in the SES. A cover letter should not be submitted with a Form B (Occupational Supplement), since it is your rating, not your writing, that matters when applying for inclusion on a register. Nor is a cover letter usually advisable for an SF-171: Your form should be sufficiently clear and compelling to distinguish you as one of the top candidates for the job without further explanation or elaboration. However, a cover letter containing additional, *pertinent* information—addressed either to Personnel Specialist/(job title) or the specific individual noted on the job announcement—may be appropriate in certain instances when submitting an SF-171:

If, because of an imminent application deadline, you are unable to tailor your SF-171 to include any special or additional qualifications required for a position, you may wish to prepare a cover letter explaining briefly the extent to which you are in fact able to meet those particular qualifications.

Likewise, if there is something in your application that might raise questions in the mind of a personnel official—if you have not been employed for a considerable length of time, are entering the job market for the first time later in life, or are trying to change occupations or revert to an occupational field in which you had worked previously—a cover letter may be useful in explaining these special circumstances. (An unfavorable performance appraisal or a "Yes" answer in any of blocks 38 45 on your SF-171 may also merit a cover letter.)

If you are applying directly to an agency with which you have made substantial previous contact, you may wish to address a cover letter directly to the officials to whom you have spoken, recalling the nature of your discussions.

A cover letter is also a good idea if you are interested in working in a particular agency or at a specific regional office but do not know whether any Vacancy Announcements have been issued under which you might be considered. The letter—addressed to the Director of Personnel, in this instance—should explain your interests and ask about the prospects for such employment in the near future. In this way, the agency will learn of your availability and your qualifications, and should let you know if any specific job opportunities currently exist or are anticipated.

Some application instructions, particularly for administrative positions at the GS-12 level and above, specifically request a cover letter in which you are expected to highlight certain professional and managerial qualifications that illustrate your ability to handle the responsibilities of the job.

If you do decide to include a cover letter, use it to create a positive first impression with the personnel officials who will review your application. Bear these points in mind:

1. Keep it *short*, no longer than two single-spaced typewritten pages. The government values clear and concise writing.
2. Do *not* turn the cover letter into a sample of your professional (say, legal or administrative) writing: The job announcement will specifically request a writing sample if one is required.
3. Do *not* use the cover letter to prove you meet the general job qualifications: This should be done on the SF-171 and specified forms or attachments.
4. If you highlight your ability to meet the job's *special* requirements, evaluation factors, and ranking factors, do so in the order in which they appear in the announcement. Each statement should be a separate paragraph. Do *not* simply repeat, word-for-word, information you already included on your SF-171; instead, relate your background and abilities directly to the specific factors being addressed.
5. *Type* or *word-process* the cover letter neatly onto standard 8½" × 11" bond (not erasable or onion-skin) paper, or standard-sized personalized stationery, on one side of the paper only. Proofread it carefully and correct any errors, preferably by retyping (rather than using correction fluid).
6. Date and sign the letter. Be sure to include a full return address, so that Federal correspondence can reach you promptly, and a daytime telephone number where you can be contacted.
6. Do not attach the letter to your application; simply fold the two together and mail in a standard (no. 10) business envelope, keeping a copy for your files.

TAKING YOUR WRITTEN TEST (ASSEMBLED EXAM)

As was discussed in Step 2 (Pathway 1), entry-level, nonstatus candidates interested in occupations for which there is a considerable oversupply of applicants will have to take a written test, usually (but not always) conducted by OPM, before being placed on a register. Such entry-level job titles, which comprise a great many new hires into Federal service annually, include those in the administrative field or Federal Apprenticeship programs, the Postal Service, and law enforcement, and clerical and secretarial positions (except where in undersupply; see p. 31), as well as Air Traffic Controller and Foreign Service Officer.

In order to take an exam, you will almost always have to make a reservation in advance. This is done by getting a test scheduling card (OPM Form 5000 A/B) or comparable form (OPM and some agencies are starting to use procedures by which you can register electronically or by phone) from either OPM or an agency with a vacancy covered by the test. Fill out this simple form and mail it in before the closing date. It will be processed and returned to you with the date, time, and place where you are to take the written test for which you have applied. In *some* areas—and then only *some* of the time—the clerical exams may be given regularly enough to be taken on a walk-in basis (that is, without a reservation); if you intend to take one of these tests, call the local Career America Connection number if there is one for your area or contact a Federal personnel office in the area to see how they are handled in your area. One other aberration you should bear in mind: In metropolitan areas, an application for a postal exam is treated as a lottery ticket, with only those who win the lottery getting to take the test.

Specific tests are discussed at length in Step 2 (pp. 45-50); see Appendix E for **sample exams**.

Along with your test schedule information you may be sent a brochure that describes testing procedures and provides sample test questions (see Appendix E). You will be strongly advised to arrive early (which is good advice), and told to bring a No. 2 pencil but *nothing else:* no calculators, scrap paper, study guides, or other aids. Your pencil should be wooden (not mechanical), sharpened, and have a working eraser—in case you need to change any of your responses on the computer-scannable answer form. Do not bring food—no test runs longer than four hours, and no provision is made for a meal period.

The **test scheduling card** is discussed in Step 4 (p. 84).

OPM guidelines provide for special testing for disabled applicants, using such aids as readers for the blind and interpreters for the deaf. The tests themselves may be modified tests if necessary, and extra time allotted to complete them (including an optional meal break). If you are a disabled individual and will need special accommodation, you should contact OPM or the agency administering the test well ahead of time.

Postal exam details are covered in Step 2 (p. 47).

Some exams are relatively difficult, as shown by the samples provided in Appendix E. To maximize your rating, and therefore your chances of being promptly referred off the register, it might be worthwhile to prepare for the examination by obtaining a *study guide* (prep book). Such guides are available from various publishers (Breakthrough Publications, Simon & Schuster, and others) for many Federal exams and allow you to practice on additional sample tests. Check the reference section of a well-stocked bookstore or ask your local librarian. *Preparatory courses* are also available for some exams, such as those for the Postal Service; these can be quite expensive and are not necessarily more effective than a good prep book.

APPLYING FOR THE SENIOR
EXECUTIVE SERVICE

As mentioned in Step 2 (p. 57), applying for a position in the Senior Executive Service is like applying for a job as a top executive in the private sector; you deal directly with the hiring agency, and you may phone them for details, and initially submit a résumé with a cover letter. If you are responding to a specific Vacancy Announcement, the announcement will describe the specific competencies that you need to address. If the agency is interested, you may be asked to fill out additional application material. An SES application requires you to relate your background and abilities to both the special technical qualifications demanded by the specific position and to six managerial qualifications, or Executive Competency Review Factors. This is done in an employment narrative, a six-question supplemental statement (also known as a KSA, for knowledge, skill, and ability), for which the agency may have special forms. Your technical qualifications are reviewed by the agency; your managerial qualifications, however, must be approved by an OPM qualifications review board. These managerial qualifications are as follows:

1. *integration of internal and external program policy issues*—seeing that key national and organization-wide goals, priorities, and other issues are taken into account in carrying out the responsibilities of the immediate work unit.
2. *organizational representation and liaison*—establishing and maintaining relationships with key individuals and groups outside the immediate work unit and serving as spokesperson for one's unit and organization.
3. *direction and guidance of programs, projects, or policy development*—establishing goals and the structure and processes necessary to carry them out.
4. *resource acquisition and administration*—obtaining and allocating the resources necessary to support program or policy implementation.
5. *utilization of human resources*—seeing that people are appropriately employed and treated fairly and equitably.
6. *review of implementation and results*—seeing that plans are implemented or adjusted as necessary and that the appropriate results are being achieved. Although the exact wording of these supplemental six questions may vary with the particular SES vacancy, the basic approach to drafting your response is the same: Analyze each question, determine its intent, and develop a focused and concise answer. A less formal, more personal response is appropriate in this context, and the use of first-person pronouns is recommended ("As CEO, I . . . "). Answers should provide specific examples, but should not exceed a page apiece. Be sure to read the Vacancy Announcement carefully, as it may require a specific format. A sample SES employment narrative is reproduced on p. 102, along with some useful explanatory comments.

FEDERAL PERSONNEL RESPONSES

Once you submit your application or take your written test, either OPM or the Federal agency will usually respond by sending you some sort of notice. These may be either preprinted forms or correspondence on agency letterhead. There are four basic types of Federal personnel response at this stage:

1. If you have applied to a *national* register, whether by written test (Air Traffic Controller, postal worker, etc.) or by Form B a *Notice of Results–Rating* is sent to indicate that you have been assigned to such a register, and advise you of your rating and the grade level at which you have qualified. It does not, however, indicate your *ranking*—that is, how high or low on that register your name appears (not even in terms of percentile). As was explained in Step 2, ratings below 70 are not given; instead, applicants are notified that they did not pass the examination and told when they may retake it.

2. *A Notice of Results–Eligibility* is sent to say you have been found eligible for the job title for which you have applied and have been assigned to either a local register or an *applicant supply file*. Rating is postponed until an actual position becomes available, since your score may vary depending on the special qualifications of that position.

3. If you are being *referred off* an OPM register, you will be sent an *Employment Availability Statement* (or *Form A*). This will tell you which agency is considering hiring you for what position, and ask that you respond if you are still available for the job.

4. *The Acknowledgment of Application Receipt* states that your application has been received; it says nothing about whether it has been rated or even considered, and therefore provides no clue as to your eligibility. It does, however, advise you if there is a problem with your application, such as a missed deadline, incorrect addressee, or incomplete or illegible form. If your application is fine, you may later be notified to report for a written test, or told to call for an interview, or sent an Employment Availability Statement, or advised that the job has been filled. Alternatively, you might receive no further correspondence in which case you should assume either that the job has been filled or that the opening was canceled. Cancellations occur when current agency employees assume the duties of the vacant position or, for example, new budget restrictions make it impossible for the agency to fill the job, obviating the need to hire someone new.

> **Applicant supply files** are described in Step 2 (p. 42).

HOW THE EXEMPLARY CANDIDATES
APPLY STEP 5

EXAMPLE: JANET
When we left Janet at the end of Step 4, she had analyzed all the Vacancy Announcements she had received as a result of contacting local agency

SES Questions and Sample Answers

1. Integration of internal and external program/policy issues.

This question asks for experience which demonstrates an ability to take diverse factors, both within the organization and its various components, and within the industry and the environment. This might include economic and regulatory issues effecting operation.

"As CEO of General Widgets, I chaired senior staff meetings directing the development of manufacturing and marketing strategies for all makes and models. This required the consideration of such issues as fluctuating costs of raw materials, labor rates and attitudes, the quality and cost of competition, changing import and export regulations, and environmental and safety regulations governing the industry.

"I was responsible for final determinations regarding the allocation funds, capital investments, model initiation and discontinuation, and plant expansion and closing. These determinations were based upon the analysis of such factors as raw data from each individual cost center, the results of market analysis for diverse regions, the results of safety or emissions testing for specific products, among other indications of profitability."

2. Organizational representation and liaison.

This is used to determine an ability to speak for your activity. This ability requires a highly developed skill in written and oral communication; an in-depth understanding of your organization's goals, priorities, capabilities, and limitations; as well as an advanced degree of decision-making authority. This could be illustrated as follows:

"With GW, I held ultimate responsibility for all public affairs operations. Additionally, I represented the corporation in high profile media events, stock holders meetings, and Congressional hearings on industry concerns. I directed labor negotiations in complex or potentially volatile situations, and represented the corporation at industry conferences and trade negotiations worldwide.

"I coordinated teams in contract negotiations with Japanese auto manufacturers to facilitate the development of foreign-built models. I directed liaison efforts between U.S. designers and Japanese manufacturing engineers to insure productive and effective communications. This involved development of highly proficient translation facilities to enable efficient exchange of technical information."

3. Direction & guidance of programs, projects, or policy development.

The answer to this question indicates your ability to shape the direction of your organization.

"As CEO of a multi-million dollar widget manufacturing and distribution corporation, I was ultimately responsible for the development and implementation of all programs, projects and policy. I reviewed proposals and accompanying technical and financial documentation, made determinations regarding all corporate activities.

"I conceived of the foreign-built models program to increase sales, and have spearheaded operations to bring Japanese manufacturing techniques and technology to U.S. plants. I reviewed proposed projects such as plant construction, marketing incentives, and financing packages; and made final determinations regarding modification, authorization, or rejection.

"I developed corporate policies in response to a changing regulatory, economic, technological, and competitive environment. I initiated policy development activities, reviewed proposals, and authorized final policy implementation."

4. Acquisition and administration of financial and material resources.

This question will be used to evaluate your ability to provide your organization with all its operating requirements within a large bureaucratic environment. This includes such duties as financial projections, budgetary requests and justification, as well as procurement through standard and innovative channels.

"As Manager of the New Model Design Facility, I was responsible for the development of overall facility budgetary requests based upon comprehensive line-item budgets at the project level. I directed the development of financial and accompanying documentation to justify all requests. I then presented and defended these requests before the Board of Directors. The competition for funding was often fierce and required a highly developed ability to speak persuasively.

"As CEO of GW, I was responsible for final determinations regarding allocation of funds, capital investments, and manufacturing plant expansion and closing. My activities in this arena determined funds availability for a variety of programs and projects, and my decisions could make the difference between profitability and failure of entire product lines.

"In my position as CEO, I directed the development of procurement policies and procedures to ensure the integrity of all acquisition activities. This included channels for procurement and location of emergency supplies, equipment, and materials. Source selection standards and procedures were delineated, and competitive bid procedures defined. I directed procurement negotiations for high dollar value items and material, and ensured acquisition at the most cost effective rate possible."

5. Utilization of human resources.

This is an open-ended question which can deal with most any aspect of personnel management and supervision. It is particularly vital to convey an ability to use available personnel to their fullest potential. This could be illustrated by employee development programs, affirmative action programs, and Equal Employment Opportunity programs. It would also include activities which reduced turn-over or increased morale. Additionally, the Federal personnel system is based upon performance standards; if you have any experience in the development of the standards, it should be mentioned here. The following is an abbreviated example. This question could typically take an entire page.

"As CEO, I was ultimately responsible for all human resource management activities. I directed the development of policies and programs including innovative employee development programs to increase the representation of minorities and women in senior management positions. This was done by intensified recruiting at the entry level at minority universities, and subsequent training programs to facilitate promotion.

"I directed all union negotiations and labor actions. A great deal of diplomacy was required to ensure maximum utilization of resources under the restrictions of union contract terms. I personally negotiated plant closings and other unpopular, high profile actions, ensuring the cooperation of the union at other facilities.

"Directed human resource managers in the development of performance standards for occupational fields. HR policy included individual performance standards and production quotas; I reviewed proposed policy and authorized all modifications."

6. Review of implementation results.

This asks for a demonstrated ability to monitor and evaluate your organization's operations. It could be illustrated by examples of organizational/management analysis projects involving surveys, studies, or audits. Quality assurance systems would be another example of this activity.

"I have throughout my career recognized the importance of systems and procedures to facilitate quality control, product integrity, and program-auditing functions. As CEO, I have administrated a Quality Assurance System with a budget in excess of $500 million. This is a far reaching program which monitors the quality of our various products from raw material and parts through depreciation and aging in use. I have been personally involved in the making process for this program, determining appropriate evaluative exercises and opportunities.

It is GW policy that all programs and projects include evaluative systems and procedures at all stages from conception to close-out. This ranges from market surveys and feasibility studies to audits in progress and upon conclusion. Reporting standards are an integral part of all activities, and I utilize these reports to identify areas requiring additional review."

offices. She had decided to respond regarding four positions: Secretary (GS-318-5/7) and Misc. Administration (GS-342-9) at the FBI, Secretary (GS-318-5/7) at the Forest Service, and Management Assistant (GS-344-9) at the Department of Health and Human Services (HHS). From her analysis she had suspected that she had little chance of getting the Misc. Administration position, which seemed to have been designed for a current agency employee. However, she felt there was nothing to lose by applying: This job was more desirable than the Secretary positions because it had much higher promotion potential. Janet hopes to show on her application that she is indeed capable of performing such a job satisfactorily.

Janet uses a word-processing program on her personal computer to prepare her application material, which she then carefully types onto her "master SF-171." She finds that her answers are the same for all four applications except for job title (block 1) and those questions that related to her previous experience (block 24); these two blocks, then, are the ones she leaves blank on her master application, filling them in only on the copies she will actually submit.

In block 12, which asks, "What is the lowest pay you will accept?" She replies GS-7 *in all cases:* This gives her the option of being interviewed at GS-7, but does not preclude her from being considered at GS-9 if she is found qualified. In block 13 she lists the city in which she lives (Denver, CO) as her geographic preference. Although not fond of travel, she decides to check the box that indicated she would accept unlimited travel (block 16, line c), thinking this answer might enhance her odds of getting to the interview stage—at which point she could discuss the travel issue, if there was one. For block 32 (special skills, awards) she describes her computer-related abilities, including familiarity with the DOS operating system, Windows 95, several word-processing programs, and two data base programs. As for awards, Janet searches her memory and comes up with two: a Secretary of the Month Award from one of her earlier jobs, and an Achievement Certificate after taking a week-long course on how to operate various data base programs.

In block 24 she tailors her responses to each of the four different jobs. Using Worksheet 1 in Appendix I, Janet analyzes the duties and responsibilities of the jobs she has held and notes her accomplishments in each of them. On Worksheet 2 she analyzes the skills required for each of the four jobs for which she is applying, including both the basic skills and the ranking factors or special qualifications. She then matches her previous experience as closely as possible to the requirements of the job (Worksheet 3). For each of the Secretary positions she is able to cite previous duties, responsibilities, and accomplishments that match all of the qualifications sought, whether basic or special. However, for the Misc. Administration and Management Assistant jobs, she is able to match her previous experience only to the basic skills sought: The ranking factors for both of these jobs are beyond her experience, and clearly apply to people who have already held similar positions with the agencies offering them. Janet is somewhat discouraged by this realization, and feels she will have little chance of being appointed to either administrative job at GS-9; but since she has come this far, she decides to go ahead and submit all four applications.

When filling in block 24 for her two Secretary applications, Janet finds there is not enough room on the SF-171 for all of her answers. Therefore, she cuts the SF-171 open with a pair of scissors, inserts extra paper to lengthen the room allotted to block 24, and tapes the form back together. In addition she writes a short cover letter to the FBI explaining that she is submitting two different applications. Because she does not want the examiners to think that she hadn't understood the restrictions of the area of consideration for the administrative positions—that the jobs were intended for current employees—she explained that she was enclosing her applications on the possibility that no status candidate would be found.

The Forest Service had also sent Janet two other forms: a Form 1170/17 (List of College Courses and Certificate of Scholastic Achievement) and a performance appraisal form. On the first, she fills in the titles and grades of several courses she had taken at a local community college. She cannot complete the Federal PA form because she has never held a Federal job; instead, Janet sends along a letter of recommendation she had received from a former employer.

For the Management Assistant job, Janet briefly describes on her SF-171 all the management-related experiences, courses, and training sessions she can recall ever having. She even throws in a public speaking course she once took at the YWCA.

Having now completed her application packages and cover letters, Janet lets them sit on her desk at home for two days, in case any further ideas occur to her; none do, so she mails them all and waits to see what happens.

Some three weeks later she receives letters from both the FBI and the Forest Service asking her to call for an appointment to be interviewed for the secretarial positions. No mention of the Misc. Administration position is made by the FBI; however, the HHS does send an Acknowledgment of Application Receipt regarding the Management Assistant spot.

EXAMPLE: MICHAEL

The Immigration and Naturalization Service to which Michael sent his test registration card for the border patrol agent test returns the card in about two weeks. It shows that he is scheduled to take the border patrol agent exam in the first week of the following month. The INS also sends a descriptive package for the test, including sample questions. After looking over these samples, Michael decides the exam is difficult and will require some study. At his local bookstore he buys a study guide for the border patrol agent test. He studies the border patrol agent test guide.

When he takes the border patrol agent test several weeks later, Michael finds that the guide has been helpful, if only in preparing him for the nature of the test and the types of questions. He thinks he does well on the exam, and indicates on it that he would work anywhere in the United States, believing (correctly) that this will enhance his chances of appointment.

Some five weeks after taking the exam, Michael receives a Notice of Results–Rating: He has passed the air traffic controller test, scoring 91. He is pleased with this result. A couple of weeks later, the Immigration and Naturalization Service sends him a career brochure on the boarder patrol agent position along with additional application materials. The materials look like they will take hours to complete. He has meanwhile received an offer from one of the private-sector companies by whom he had been interviewed, and is beginning to think that the Federal application process is more trouble than it is worth. Giving some additional thought to his career plans, however, Michael realizes that the private-sector position he has been offered is not very stimulating: It is as a Securities Representative and entails a lot of time cold-calling potential securities customers. Being a border patrol agent seems a lot more exciting and a lot more important, so he decides to complete the application materials after all.

The duties and qualifications of the border patrol agent, described in the career brochure he was sent, seem to emphasize the abilities to make decisions and handle stress. In using the Appendix I worksheets to complete block 24 of his SF-171 or provide the equivalent information in a different form, Michael decides to emphasize aspects of his experience— such as his year as a Boy Scout leader that demonstrate he is capable of handling responsibility and stress.

Two weeks after sending off his completed forms, Michael receives a notice to call for an interview regarding a border patrol agent position.

A second aspect of Michael's Federal job search was his effort to bypass the cumbersome procedures for administrative jobs. To this end he had been speaking to a Power Administration Office of the Department of Energy about a clerical position from which he might transfer to an administrative-type position. By the end of Step 4, Michael had already passed the clerical test suggested by the agency and received a Vacancy Announcement for Miscellaneous Clerk and Assistant, GS-303, which cited only the most basic clerical skills.

Michael decides that, with some minor modifications to block 24 (and, of course, a change of job title in block 1), (or equivalent modifications to other application materials if he did not use the SF-171), he can submit the SF-171 or other application materials he has just completed for the boarder patrol agent job. In block 24 he includes more description regarding the part-time jobs he has held, and his accomplishments in these positions, to show his qualifications for an clerical position. Two weeks after he sends off this SF-171, he receives a notice to call the DOE for an interview appointment.

After a couple of phone calls, Michael has two interviews set up with the Federal government: one for a clerical job with the Department of Energy, and another a few days later for border patrol agent.

EXAMPLE: HELEN

By the end of Step 4, Helen had returned a 5000 A/B card for the Foreign Service Exam. This has resulted in a seat to take the Foreign Service Exam, which is given once a year, usually in December. Upon reviewing the sample questions that came with the package, Helen realizes that she might not have a very good chance of scoring well on the test: It seems to favor candidates with backgrounds in liberal arts subjects, and has many questions related to history, political science, and law. Although Helen had studied business law in conjunction with her accounting courses, she had taken only survey courses in the other subjects. Nevertheless, she decides to take the test. For several weeks before her exam, she works with the sample questions in a study guide she has found in the library. On the day of the test, she travels to Albany, the capital city of her state, and takes the exam in a large armory with hundreds of other candidates. When her Notice of Results-Rating arrives about five weeks later, she is pleased to see that she has done well with an 89; however, there is no indication of what percentile this score represents.

Also in Step 4, Helen received a Form B or equivalent type form from the Department of the Interior for Accounting/Auditor positions. Helen learns that the agency will be filling these positions throughout the country and that OPM will be doing the examining for the agency. She is also advised that the Naval Weapons Support Center has accounting positions but that it will be doing its own examining. She is told that for this agency she needs to submit a narrative application describing her education and experience. She is also advised that she must submit a narrative application for the Foreign Service Secretary position. She now sets out to complete these forms.

The Form B seems pretty straightforward, and is in fill-in-the-circles format to facilitate computer analysis. According to Appendix B, her chances of finding an Accountant or Auditor job in almost any area of the country are good. She considers the possibility of getting a Federal job in New Orleans, which has a large French-speaking population; but Appendix J (Geographic Location of Federal Employment) shows many more Federal employees, and hence job opportunities, in and around Los Angeles. Given her desire to relocate to the West Coast, Helen declares under geographic preference that she would only be interested in the L.A. area. The rest of the form deals with her educational background. She is pleased she had taken so many classes and done well in them, and is sure she will qualify as a GS-9. Five weeks after submitting her Form B, she receives a Notice of Results-Rating showing that she had indeed qualified at that grade level. Several weeks later she receives an Inquiry of Availability (Form A) from the Los Angeles office of the National Park Service, an agency in the Department of the Interior, regarding her availability for a position as Accountant. She calls the Personnel Clerk whose name appears on the inquiry, and is told that a phone interview can probably be arranged with the Personnel Specialist who is handling the position; in the meantime, she should complete an SF-171 or other narrative application and send it to the agency. Helen gives the Personnel Clerk the fax number for her college placement office; the next day Helen gets a faxed Vacancy Announcement. That same day she also learns that the Defense Contract Audit Agency in San Diego is recruiting for an auditor position. (DCAA). She phones them, and they send her a Vacancy Announcement for an Auditor position with an "open" closing date.

Helen now has to complete SF-171s, résumés or other narrative applications for four different positions: Auditor at the Defense Contract Audit Agency, Accountant at the Park Service, Auditor at the Naval Weapons Support Center, and Foreign Service Secretary. Helen sees that the Vacancy Announcements for the first three positions are very similar, with "Open" closing dates and areas of consideration listed as "All Sources." Promotion potential, however, is much higher for the Navy job: GS-15 versus GS-13 for the DCAA job and GS-12 for the Park Service. Also, although the basic duties are the same for all three jobs, the special qualifications differ somewhat, as the actual responsibilities of an Auditor vary from those of an Accountant. Judging from the Vacancy Announcements, each Auditor position seems to be one of many through which the Navy and Defense Contract Audit Agency supervise their contracts with suppliers. The Park Service position, on the other hand, seems to be one of only a few general Accountants with broader responsibilities who supervise all of the financial activities of the Park Service in California.

Since she has never held a professional, full-time accounting position and is still in school, Helen believes she might be most likely to obtain either position on the basis of her forthcoming master's degree, not her previous job experience. Nevertheless, based on her new understanding of the two jobs, Helen does somewhat tailor her block 24 answers to correspond to their qualifications. Even though she is not required to complete a SF-71, she decides to follow that form because it will provide structure for her application. (after using the Appendix I worksheets). In the SF-171s for the Navy and Defense Auditor positions, she emphasizes her summer job auditing at a large CPA firm. In the one for the Accountant position at the Park Service, she highlights her present part-time bookkeeping for a mortgage company, as well as her several years of part-time (volunteer) bookkeeping for her church.

Helen decides to complete her Foreign Service Secretary SF-171 differently than those she was filling out for Accountant and Auditor positions: Each job title requires its own approach. For Foreign Service Secretary, Helen emphasizes some part-time work she had done of a clerical and secretarial nature at the university bursar's office, but still mentions her auditing and accountancy experience. In block 32 (awards/special skills) she stresses her fluency in French and her word processing ability. Helen says in block 16 that she is available to work anywhere required by the State

Department.

Some two weeks after mailing her completed SF-171s, Helen hears from three of the agencies. From the Foreign Service she receives a Form A (Employment Availability Statement) asking whether she is still interested in the position of Secretary. She phones the personnel office and is told (by one of the secretarial staff) that an interviewer who is touring the country will be in her state the following month. An interview is arranged. Helen also sets up phone interviews with the Park Service and the Naval Weapons Support Center, each of which has sent similar inquiries.

Having heard nothing from the Defense Contract Audit Agency even after an additional two weeks of waiting, Helen sends them a written inquiry as to the status of her application. The DCAA responds with a form saying they have no current openings for Auditor in that office. This she interprets correctly to mean that the job for which she applied has been filled.

Helen realizes she has yet to be offered an interview for a position as Foreign Service Officer. She supposes her rating of 89, as good as it was, must not have been high enough to do the trick in this very competitive field. Still, she has managed to set up three other interviews, and now plans to prepare for them.

EXAMPLE: JEFF

As of the end of Step 4, Jeff had two SF-171s to complete: one for the Electrician job at an Air Force base about 40 miles away, and another for the VRA position of Quality Assurance Specialist at the Defense Logistics Agency in a large city about 70 miles away. Like Helen, Jeff decides to use the SF-171 because it will help him to structure his application in an orderly manner. In addition, a personnel specialist advises him off the record that because most personnel specialists and supervisors are familiar with the SF-171, they find it easier to work with than a résumé. Because he does not type, Jeff makes four photocopies of a blank SF-171, intending to fill out two of them by hand (one for each of the two agencies) and have a friend type each onto the remaining two blank copies.

Reading the SF-171 instructions, Jeff discovers that 10 veterans preference points will be added to any rating he gets because of his Purple Heart. Jeff will indicate his veterans preference in block 22. The instructions on the SF-171 say that an additional form—an SF-15 (Application for 10-Point Veterans Preference)—must be filed in order for Jeff actually to claim credit for those points. He phones the Air Force base to obtain this form, and makes a copy; this way, he can submit one with each SF-171.

Jeff, like our other exemplary candidates, makes good use of the worksheets of Appendix I. For instance, referring to the information he received regarding the Electrician job, which states clearly the qualifications at each career and grade level, he finds (on Worksheet 3) that the qualifications at leader level seem to match the job he now has with a local electrical contractor. He thus tries to emphasize this in block 24 of his Electrician SF-171. In block 32 (awards/special skills), Jeff emphasizes his abilities with all kinds of power tools, even mentioning that has a shop in his basement where he does wood and metal work. (He also mentions his Purple Heart in this block, along with several other military citations and awards he had received.)

The Vacancy Announcement for Quality Assurance Specialist lists a number of basic and special qualifications in the area of purchasing, inspection, and grading of electrical equipment. On his SF-171 for this position, Jeff tries to show that he has solid experience as a buyer of electrical equipment. He reasons that, even though he has VRA eligibility, he may still have to compete with other eligible Vietnam veterans.

Jeff mails his two SF-171s and, within three weeks, receives letters of response inviting him to interviews for both positions. He is now ready for Step 6 in the employment process.

Step 6: Preparing for Your Interview

Purpose: To help you prepare for the interview that results either when your application has been favorably received or your name has been referred off a register.

Associated appendixes:

D   Federal Personnel Offices
K   White-Collar Occupations in Federal Service
N   Wage Grade Occupations in Federal Service

HOW IMPORTANT IS THE INTERVIEW?

Even though candidates for Federal service are interviewed only if they have already been found largely qualified for a position, interviews are still critical to the Federal hiring process. As in the private sector, the interviewer explains the type of work required by the job and attempts to discern an applicant's motivation, basic intelligence, work habits, common sense, and other attributes and abilities germane to successful performance.

> See the section on **law enforcement interviews** below.

It is important to note that referral off a register does not automatically lead to an interview. An agency may decline to interview or appoint any of the three candidates referred to it for consideration (but must have a good reason for rejecting them all).

When the government has large numbers of positions to fill—say, for Clerk-Typist or Data Transcriber—the interview and the candidate's rating on the written test are given about equal weight in the hiring process. This means that even the most highly rated candidate may not win an appointment if he or she does poorly at the interview. On the other hand, if an agency's need for employees is such that it cannot afford to reject any qualified referred candidate, it may decide to hire one even without an interview. In these cases—which are quite rare—either the position is routine (such as clerical) or the candidate's credentials are well established (such as a certified CPA, practicing lawyer, or graduate engineer).

When there is no test involved, or when there are few jobs to be filled, the interview can take on broader meaning and consequences. Under these circumstances, an agency requests to interview when you are one of the top two or three candidates actively being considered for the job. The final outcome—who gets the job—may rest on how well your interview goes. The applicant who makes the best personal impression, or shows the most interest in the position or enthusiasm for the agency, might well be chosen over others with equally impressive resumes or higher ratings (although a nonveteran cannot be appointed over a higher-rated veteran without justification). The higher the grade level of the job, and thus the more skill required, the more important the interview may be.

INTERVIEW PREPARATION GUIDELINES

As in the private sector, first impressions are very important. The following are *essentials* for a good interview:

proper attire (jacket and tie for men, skirt and blouse or suit with skirt for
    women, and no sneakers for either);
a clean, well-groomed appearance; and
punctuality (arriving ten minutes early).

In addition, agency personnel officials prefer applicants who show an interest in, and knowledge of, their agency. A little research into an agency's background can help convey that you are interested in working there, and your enthusiasm may prove contagious. This can be especially helpful if you are competing with many other candidates. The other applicants may have no particular interest in the given agency, and their comparative indifference may become apparent in their interviews.

In order to show yourself to your best advantage, also be prepared to:

further clarify, in detail, your current and previous work experience and/or
    education;
explain any weaknesses or gaps in your job history;
outline personal or career goals in the framework of the job for which you are
    being considered; and
discuss how you can positively impact the agency's work environment.

Remember, this interview may be your only opportunity to impress agency officials with your own unique personality. Make the most of it!

INTERVIEW COMMUTING DISTANCE

If you are a very highly qualified candidate for a hard-to-fill job title but do not live within commuting distance of the personnel office, agency officials may decide to interview you over the phone. If so, prepare just as carefully as you would for meeting face to face: A phone interview can lead directly to your being hired.

Sometimes an agency prefers to interview in person even though extensive travel time is involved. If your interview with a government agency requires travel outside your normal commuting area, be sure to inquire whether your pre-employment expenses will be reimbursed. Such reimbursement is subject to the discretion of the hiring agency, but is usually made based on the lack of availability of likely candidates nearby. Thus, if you have been chosen for an interview even though you live far away, you are a candidate for reimbursement.

Because they may not have a large enough pool of qualified candidates locally, some agencies (usually located in Washington, DC) dispatch traveling interviewers to meet with eligibles nationwide. In such cases a candidate may have to wait several months for an appointment, but the interview is likely to be conducted in Federal facilities near his or her home.

Many agencies send out college recruitment teams to interview interested students on campus, especially as part of designated Career Day programs. An increasingly popular Federal recruitment vehicle is the *job fair,* usually featuring positions for which agencies are experiencing candidate shortages. Held in large cities and announced in the media, job fairs allow applications to be filed and interviews held on the spot.

LAW ENFORCEMENT INTERVIEWS

In law enforcement, an area with rapid turnover and a high rate of burnout (in both the public and private sectors), it is important to weed out individuals who show clear signs of not being able to handle the stress of dealing with possible life-and-death situations on a daily basis. The so-called *structured interview* associated with positions related to law enforcement (Correctional Officer, Deputy U.S. Marshal, FBI Agent, etc.) is considered a fair and proven method. Only a few are chosen from the many candidates who apply.

A structured interview can be quite extensive and demanding. Often the applicant is interviewed by a team of staff members that might include a prospective supervisor, a psychologist, and a personnel official. The applicant is engaged in conversation to ascertain his or her attitudes about various circumstances that might arise in the course of duty, and is asked what he or she might do in a particular situation. For example, a potential Deputy U.S. Marshal might be asked what he would do if a dangerous prisoner he is escorting out of the state suddenly escapes during a transfer to another plane at a crowded airport. The would-be Correctional Officer might be asked how he would deal with a racial flare-up that occurs when the inmates are not in their cells but in the prison gymnasium. Likewise, an applicant for DEA Agent might be asked to delineate what situations seem dangerous enough to merit the use of firearms even when innocent bystanders may be injured.

Remember, these are only examples: The actual questions and scenarios are changed regularly so that no candidate can achieve an unfair advantage by knowing someone who had been interviewed earlier. Also, there are no "correct" answers established for these questions and situations; rather, the interviewers observe your reactions to being put on the spot. Are you alert and thoughtful? Do you answer perhaps too quickly? Do you seem trigger-happy, always ready to use force? Are you not forceful enough? Do you consider the safety of others? Do you show racial bias? Do your answers suggest possible criminal tendencies of your own? Even body language can be important; for instance, hand-wringing, nervous tremors, or sweating may suggest an insufficient ability to cope with stress.

HOW THE EXEMPLARY CANDIDATES APPLY STEP 6

EXAMPLE: JANET

At the end of Step 5, Janet had set up interviews at local offices of the FBI and the Forest Service. Before going to these interviews, she studies the career material that both agencies had sent her. She also seeks additional, noncareer-oriented information at her public library. There she is referred to a book called the *Federal Directory,* which lists the headquarters of each agency. Writing to their respective public affairs offices, Janet identifies herself simply as an interested citizen and asks to be sent information about each agency's current mission and concerns. From this new material she learns a good deal: For example, one of the issues the FBI is currently facing is how to handle increasing workload with a minimum increase in costs. The Forest Service, she discovers, also faces cost issues and is involved in a controversy on the proper use of public land.

Janet's interviews are both relatively informal and receptive in tone. Each Personnel Specialist offers her the position of Secretary at GS-7 at the outset of the interview, including the 8% locality augmentation in her city. (Both offers are subsequently confirmed by official letter.) Note, at times, the supervisor of the position being filled may offer you the position. In most agencies, even though the supervisor makes the selection, only an authorized member of the personnel office is permitted to make a formal employment offer. Therefore, you should always check with the personnel office if an offer comes from another source. Janet tells each that she is enthusiastic about the agency and its work. She then spends a couple of minutes demonstrating her knowledge of each agency's mission and the issues it faces, discussing these with the interviewer, who seems pleased. At the FBI interview she mentions that her father and

> **Agency headquarters** are also listed in Appendix D.

uncle had both been police officers.

Janet lets each agency know that she is also considering an offer from the other. She says her decision will be strongly influenced by her starting salary and promotion potential, and asks each interviewer whether she will be able to start at higher than step 1 of level GS-7; both reserve comment until they refer with a supervisor. She says she realizes from the Vacancy Announcements that the promotion potential of the positions they are offering is GS-8; however, she explains, this is not satisfactory, as she is already earning a salary comparable to that level. Both interviewers react sympathetically to her stated goal of promotion into an administrative or management position, and explain in detail the many opportunities for free training in specialized fields available to secretaries in their agency through OPM. Both also say they will consult with their supervisors about the possibility of her being promoted to a Management Assistant (GS-344-9), Misc. Administration (GS-342-9), or even Administrative Officer (GS-341-9) position.

When Janet phones these two Personnel Specialists after a few days to discuss this possibility again, their responses arc pretty similar: Their supervisors have agreed to start her at GS-7 step 2, $24,984 plus the locality pay augmentation for her city, but cannot guarantee that she would be promoted to an administrative or management position; however, they feel that the chances of her being so promoted within about a year are pretty good. The Forest Service interviewer agrees to start Janet in an agency department where she could learn the Management Assistant's job. The other interviewer points out that the FBI is much bigger than the Forest Service, and that she would have as good a chance for promotion with the FBI as anywhere. Janet thanks them for their efforts and promises to give them an answer within two days. In the next day's mail, she receives a written offer from each agency confirming the content of their phone discussions.

EXAMPLE: MICHAEL

While waiting for his interviews with the INS for the border patrol agent position and with the Department of Energy (DOE) for the clerical position, Michael does some homework. He reviews information that he has obtained on border patrol positions and is reminded that the interview may be rigorous. He feels well prepared.

To ready himself for the DOE interview, Michael makes a special trip to the agency, wearing a suit and tie. He tells the lobby guard that his business in the building is to pursue employment, and goes to the public affairs office. He tells the receptionist that he is a job candidate who wants to familiarize himself with the agency's mission, and spends an hour or so reading the material on display in the reception area.

When he returns on the day of his interview, everything seems to go well. Michael demonstrates his knowledge of the agency and its current objectives. He meets the Personnel Specialist with whom he had previously spoken about the possibility of transferring into an administrative job title once he had gained status as a clerical employee. The interviewer explains that the agency cannot guarantee such a promotion, but would be willing to start Michael in an important clerical position at GS-5 from which he could learn the job of a Budget Analyst. With just one year's work experience on top of his B.S. degree, Michael would qualify for this position at level GS-7—and have a good shot at an appointment, since openings occur regularly. The interviewer tells Michael to respond within two weeks. His interview with the INS is only a few days away.

Despite warnings, Michael is quite surprised by his interview with the INS for border patrol agent positions. His DOE interview had been rather informal, but at the INS he faces not an individual but a panel of interviewers, each of whom seems to have a specific role. The moderator explains at the outset that one of the purposes of the interview is to determine how well applicants handle stress. Questions are put to him in rapid-fire sequence, and at times Michael feels as if he is under investigation. What has he done to deserve this, he wonders? He isn't being paid to be here! Later, Michael hopes his annoyance and frustration during the interview had not shown.

EXAMPLE: HELEN

At the end of the last step in the employment process, Helen had set up interviews with three agencies of interest to her. Two of these—those for the Naval Weapons Center in Los Angeles and the National Park Service's L.A. office—were to be conducted by phone. The third, for the position of Foreign Service Secretary, was to be with the agency's traveling interviewer. Helen prepares for these interviews by studying the career material that all three had sent her; this, she finds, explains each agency's mission quite well. Moreover, the Vacancy Announcements they had supplied clearly explained the duties of the positions.

A Personnel Specialist from each of the first two agencies telephones at the time appointed, and these specialists turn the interview over to the supervisors of the positions being filled. Helen discusses the jobs at length with each interviewer and feels that she is demonstrating her ability to perform the auditing or accounting work involved. She asks each about promotion potential: What time in grade is required before promotion is possible? What historically was the promotion record for agency employees in the position in question?

The Navy interviewer reads her an impressive statistic called the promotion rate, which gives the percentage of employees in the Auditor position for which she is applying who had been promoted in the previous year. At his agency the promotion rate is 34%—much higher than the average of 23% for Auditors in Federal service. Navy Auditors do very well, he says, and particularly so in his agency. Assuming she does her job well, Helen should expect regular promotion and increased responsibility.

The Park Service interviewer also professes good promotion potential at that agency. He points out that the Park Service is nowhere near as big an agency as the Navy, and so one cannot fairly compare promotion rates. However, he says, the Park Service is an agency very well liked by its employees: Helen would have very high job satisfaction.

The traveling Foreign Service interviewer tells Helen about the exciting and satisfying career available to a Foreign Service Secretary, and says Helen is a very good candidate: Her educational level is higher than most, and her French is certainly an asset. The interviewer regrets that the agency could not guarantee that Helen would be sent to a French-speaking country; but Helen, she says, is sure to find the environment stimulating wherever she is sent. When asked about Helen's chances of being appointed as an Foreign Service Officer, the interviewer says that her office has no control over that register: Helen just has to wait and see whether she is called. A referral off that register could take many months, she says.

Within three weeks Helen receives written offers of appointment from all three agencies, giving her five days to respond.

EXAMPLE: JEFF

At the Air Force base to which he has applied as an Electrician, Jeff meets the Personnel Specialist with whom he had first spoken. She describes the salary, benefits, work schedule, and other particulars of the job, and answers Jeff's questions relating to seniority considerations and how the pension system works. In particular, Jeff wants assurance that the work is steady and year-round. She responds that there have been no layoffs for several years, nor any discussion of closing the base. Jeff also meets the job supervisor with whom he would be working if hired. He shows Jeff around one of the buildings and explains the kind of work they do. Jeff shows that he understands the work and will have no problems acting as foreman of a crew.

Within a week, Jeff is offered (first by phone, then by mail) an appointment for the position of Electrician WG-2805. His title would be Leader at grade level WL-12, paying about $2 an hour less than he now makes; on the other hand, it is steady year-round work, could lead to promotion, and offers better benefits than he presently has.

Jeff's meeting with the VRA interviewer at the Defense Logistics Agency also goes well. The interviewer too had served in Vietnam, and he and Jeff had had similar experiences. Jeff tells the interviewer about the wound he had received and about the resulting Purple Heart. The interviewer, who had seen this award noted on Jeff's SF-171, had verified it in his military records.

About a month after his interview, Jeff receives notice that he has been accepted into the VRA program and will be trained for the position of Quality Assurance Specialist (GS-1910). He would be paid at the GS-7 level and be eligible for promotion to GS-9 in one year.

Jeff sits down to decide which job to take.

Step 7: Considering an Offer

Purpose: To help you consider any Federal job offer you may receive, compare it to any others you may have received, and decide whether or not to accept it.

Associated appendixes:
F   Federal Salary Rates
M   White-Collar Occupations in Federal Service by Grade
R   Federal Benefits and Work Conditions

CONSIDERING AN INDIVIDUAL OFFER

If you have followed the procedures laid down in this book, sooner or later you will probably be offered a Federal job (sooner in the case of an applicant undersupply, later in an oversupply). Your application may be rated promptly and lead to an interview at which you are made an offer—a matter of weeks. Even in a shortage situation, however, do not assume that no job offer is forthcoming until three or four months have elapsed. If the candidate supply is roughly the same as the demand (equilibrium), you may want to allow for a longer wait—at worst, up to a year. If you have applied or tested for a position for which applicants are in oversupply, do not give up hope of an offer until at least six months have passed: Offers have been known to come through up to two years after the initial examination!

Once an offer has been made, you will have to decide whether to accept the position, to decline and wait until another offer is made, or to pursue additional avenues of Federal employment. Most likely, you will be given a deadline for responding. If you have not specifically accepted or declined the offer by that time, the agency may well offer the position to another candidate.

ACCEPTING AN OFFER

Should you decide to accept an offer of Federal employment, first phone your personnel contact at the agency to let them know. This gives you an opportunity to confirm the terms of your appointment, including the starting date. After phoning in your acceptance, be sure to confirm it in writing immediately, citing all the specifics of the offer. It is a good idea also to attach to your acceptance letter a copy of the government's written offer.

DECLINING AN OFFER

If you are offered a job without having been referred off a register—that is, if you had submitted an application and were *case examined*—you will be simply asked to explain your reasons, which may be based on whatever criteria you choose. Of course, rejecting an offer might create some prejudice against you regarding other appointments at the same agency—especially if the same Personnel Specialist is handling them. You will not even be kept in the agency's applicant supply file. However, turning down an appointment at one agency will not prevent you from pursuing another position—even a similar one—at another agency.

If, on the other hand, you are offered a job after having been referred to the agency off an OPM register of eligibles, declining the appointment can have more serious repercussions. As was mentioned in Step 2 (p. 42), your name can be removed from a register, and thus excluded from further referrals to other agencies, if you are unwilling to accept a reasonable offer of employment. Remember, registers are maintained by job title and grade level: If your reasons for declining apply just as well to the other positions on the register, further offers may not be forthcoming.

RELOCATION

Should you be offered a job that requires relocation, ask about the reimbursement of relocation costs. If you are not a current Federal employee, relocation reimbursement can cover the travel and transportation expenses for you and your family. If your are a current Federal employee or a former Federal employee being reemployed within one year of being separated by reduction in force, reimbursement for relocation can cover more items such as real estate expenses and temporary quarters. The agency will determine whether to pay relocation expenses on the basis of its recruitment difficulties. These determinations are generally discretionary with an agency. If an agency pays your relocation expenses, you will have to sign an agreement to remain in Federal service for a year. If you leave before that year, you will have to repay the expenses reimbursed by the Government unless your departure is beyond your control such as because of serious illness. The agreement to remain in Federal service does not require you to stay with the agency that reimbursed your expenses. You can move to another Federal agency, and you would not be required to repay anything to the agency which originally hired you. If costs exceed reimbursement, there are also tax deductions that Federal employees can claim for moving expenses due to employment-prompted relocation. Relocation costs and tax deductions are governed and regularly updated in the Federal Travel Regulations.

CONSIDERING MULTIPLE OFFERS

If you have done a particularly good job of preparing your applications and being interviewed, you may receive several offers of Federal employment. Job title, salary, and geographic location are perhaps the most obvious factors to consider when comparing offers; another is promotion potential. Appendix M (White-Collar Occupations in Federal Service by Grade) is one means of weighing the likelihood of promotion, and how far up the ladder one may eventually go, for two or more different job titles. Another is to compare the responses of your interviewers to questions regarding promotion. Personnel Specialists examine promotion trends at their agencies and may be able to relate some useful and encouraging statistics—for instance, the *promotion rate,* which gives the percentage of employees in a given position who were promoted during the previous year. The higher a promotion rate, the more likely your chance of moving up on the career ladder. Agencies often offer recruitment bonuses for hard to fill positions. You may be able to negotiate a recruitment bonus. Agencies may pay a bonus up to 25% of the salary of the position. This is a one-time payment. Bonuses can be given to individuals with excellent qualifications for hard to fill positions. If you receive a bonus, you will have to sign an agreement to remain in Federal service for a specified time, often 1 year.

Another important aspect to consider is whether a given position is in the Competitive or Excepted Service. In the Competitive Service, advancement to career status (generally within three years) provides you with seniority and job tenure throughout the Federal civil service system. As a status employee you can apply for promotion into any competitive position throughout the system. In addition, if your agency experiences cutbacks—known officially as *reductions in force,* or RIFs—you may secure appointment at another agency. Excepted Service employees have no such transfer rights, and must respond to RIFS by seeking alternative appointments starting from scratch.

Some Excepted Service employees receive certain benefits to the same extent as those in the Competitive Service: They are eligible for leave, injury compensation, retirement, unemployment compensation, and life and health insurance, just as any other Federal worker. (Benefits in the Excepted Service vary from agency to agency; ask for an explanation of benefits before accepting an appointment.) They also receive performance ratings and may qualify for training or incentive awards. When a job title is in the Excepted Service (or an entire agency is excepted), special pay rates may apply; some of these are shown in Appendix F. However, many excepted positions are in the General Schedule or wage grade pay systems, and employees in those

See Step 2 regarding the **Excepted Service** (p. 34) and **excepted agencies** (p. 35-6; also see list in Appendix D).

positions are paid like their counterparts in competitive service positions.

The biggest disadvantage of the Excepted Service is that you cannot acquire competitive status while in it. Acquiring such status would first require your reclassification into the Competitive Service. Unless yours is a position that allows for *conversion,* this process is by no means automatic: You must apply for a Competitive Service position in the usual way, be awarded an appointment, and leave the Excepted Service. Being in the Excepted Service thus may limit your ability to advance your Federal career—unless you hold a job title that is *always* excepted (such as Attorney).

The *types* of appointments offered may also have a bearing on your promotion potential. In the Competitive Service, *temporary appointments* involve no promotion or transfer rights, and term appointments provide promotion privileges only to other term positions within the agency; both of these also entail limited benefits. It is the more usual *career-conditional appointments* that lead to *career appointments,* and thus the full range of rights and privileges associated with Federal employment, including *reinstatement eligibility*—the ability to be reappointed without reexamination. Nonveterans with career-conditional appointments are reinstatement eligible for three years; career-conditional veterans and career-status employees have lifetime reinstatement eligibility.

In the Excepted Service, an appointment may be without time limitation, *temporary* (1 year or less), or *time limited* of more than 1 year. Unlike term appointments in the Competitive Service, this latter type of appointment can be for any length of time not just a maximum of 4 years. Employees on appointments without time limitation or appointments of more than 1 year earn comparable benefits to employees in the Competitive Service related to retirement, and health and life insurance. As previously explained, however, even employees on appointments without time limitation do not acquire any type of status. Therefore, they cannot transfer to Competitive Service positions without competing as if they were applying for a Federal position for the first time.

In the case of a reduction in force, Excepted Service employees compete for retention only with other excepted employees, so their retention possibilities are often less than for employees in the Competitive Service. In addition, because they don't have competitive status, their opportunities for placement with other agencies are less than for employees in the Competitive Service. There are some agencies such as the Postal Service, the Tennessee Valley Authority, the General Accounting Office and segments of the Department of Veterans Affairs, which are excepted from the Competitive Service but have special agreements with OPM or special statutory authority which permit their employees to transfer to the Competitive Service without competing. You should inquire of your agency whether it has such an agreement. Each agreement is different, so you should obtain the specific provisions of your agency's agreement. For example, some agreements permit movement if there is no break in service which would not help employees separated by reduction in force while other agreements permit movement for up to 1 year fol-

Conversion to the Competitive Service is described in Step 2 (p. 35).

These **appointment types** are introduced in Step 4 (p. 80). **Benefits** are discussed in some detail in Appendix R.

Step 2 describes **Excepted Service Schedules A-C** (p. 34) and **independent employment systems** (p. 36).

lowing separation. You should try to obtain a copy of the agreement or applicable law to show to any Competitive Service agency to which you apply because some agencies in the Competitive Service aren't even aware of these agreements.

One other factor that differentiates various types of appointments in the Federal civil service is the issue of *appeal rights:* the rights of an employee to appeal to the Merit Systems Protection Board regarding an imposed disciplinary action, such as a reduction in grade (demotion), temporary suspension, or dismissal. These rights apply to career and career-conditional appointments in the Competitive Service after employees complete a 1 year probationary period. They also apply to veterans in some Excepted Service positions who have completed 1 year of service, and they apply to nonveterans who have completed 2 years of current continuous service in some excepted positions. For example they apply to Schedule A and B positions, but they do not apply to Schedule C positions. They apply to some but not all positions in the Postal Service. Many excepted agencies such as the Central Intelligence Agency have special statutory authority which exempts all their employees from being able to appeal to the Merit Systems Protection Board.

The various types of appointments and their tenure, reinstatement eligibility, appeal rights, and benefits are summarized in the table "Appointments in the Competitive and Excepted Services" (p. 122).

Once you have decided which position to accept and advised the agency of your decision, be sure to notify the other agencies as well: The fact that you have taken a Federal appointment elsewhere is quite an acceptable reason for having to decline their offers.

HOW THE EXEMPLARY CANDIDATES APPLY STEP 7

EXAMPLE: JANET

Janet considers the offers she has received from the FBI and the Forest Service. Both involve the same salary, the same promotion potential (GS-8), and more or less the same promises with regard to promotion to an administrative or management position. The major difference is that the FBI is an independent employment system, so its employees are ineligible for career status; the position at the Forest Service, however, is a career-conditional appointment in the Competitive Service, and thus offers better job security. Also, once employed by the Forest Service, Janet could pursue promotion through that agency or any other in the Competitive Service; at the FBI, opportunities for advancement would pretty much have to come from within that excepted agency itself, and her tenure would apply to that agency only. Still, Janet thinks the FBI is sufficiently large to have plenty of advancement potential, and she feels strongly about its mission: Law enforcement has been a tradition in her family.

Table: Appointments in the Competitive and Excepted Services

Service	Type of Appointment	Tenure (RIF Protection)	Reinstatement Eligibility	Appeal Rights	Benefits
Competitive	Career	Group 1 (max. protection)	Lifetime	All	All
	Career-conditional	Group 2 (veterans given pref.)	Nonveterans–3 years Veterans–lifetime		
	Term	Group 3	None	All	All if appt. for 2-4 years None if appt. for <1 year
	Temporary	None	None	None	All after 1 year None before 1 year
Excepted	Schedule A	Laid off first if position also found	None	Veterans after 1 year, limited	All
	Schedule B	in the Competitive Service	None	appeal rights Others, none	All
	Schedule C	None	None	None	All
	Time-limited	None	None	None	Same as for Comp. Svc.
	Temporary	None	None	None	Same as for Comp. Svc.
Indep. Employ. System	Permanent	Within agcy.	Within agcy.	Within agcy.*	All
	Temporary	None	None	None	Same as for Comp. Svc.

*Cannot appeal to Merit Systems Protection Board but can appeal to the agency's own review board.

Janet decides to accept the FBI position. She phones the Personnel Specialist who had conducted her interview to inform him of her decision and confirm the terms of her appointment—job title, salary, and appointment type—as they were stated in her appointment letter: Secretary GS-318-7, step 2, career conditional. She also double-checks her starting date. These details confirmed, she then notifies the FBI in writing of her acceptance of the position, reiterating for the record the terms of her appointment and starting date, and attaching a copy of the FBI's written job offer. Janet then phones (and later writes) the Forest Service to thank them for their offer, which she declines. Finally, several days later, she receives an official letter confirming her FBI appointment.

EXAMPLE: MICHAEL

Michael receives a letter from the INS thanking him for the time he devoted to pursuing a career with the agency, but stating that it cannot offer him a border patrol agent position at the present time (without spelling out the reasons). Michael is disappointed: He had already been imagining himself on the job, helping to make the borders safe. He believes he would have done the job well, and his parents and friends would certainly have been impressed. However, after awhile, Michael begins to reconsider his rejection by the INS. Perhaps they knew what they were doing; perhaps he would not have made a good border patrol agent. The consequences of being a bad border patrol agent were not pleasant to contemplate.

Michael has been checking various sources for administrative vacancies. He found a contract specialist, but when he called the agency, they advised him that they had hired an applicant eligible for the outstanding scholar program.

Meanwhile, he receives a letter from the Department of Energy offering him the clerical position he had discussed. However, his disappointment with the INS and the administrative positions process have put a damper on his enthusiasm for Federal employment, and he phones the Department of Energy to decline their offer.

A few weeks later, Michael accepts a job with an office supply company in his area, becoming manager of its order processing department.

EXAMPLE: HELEN

Helen thinks long and hard about the three offers she has received from Federal agencies. The Navy Auditor job seems to offer the best promotion potential, the Park Service Accountant position the most satisfaction, and the Foreign Service Secretary position the greatest potential for excitement. Meanwhile, having waited about four months with no word of a Foreign Service Officer position, Helen concludes that her chances of being offered a job in the diplomatic corps are remote.

For most of the five days she has been given to choose among her offers, Helen thinks she is going to accept the Foreign Service Secretary position; however, she finally realizes that the Foreign Service is an independent employment system and that her chances for promotion are not great. Rereading the material she had received with her application package, she concludes that almost all the top Foreign Service positions go to Foreign Service Officers, and she would probably remain a Secretary, or at most a mid-level Administrator, throughout her career with the agency. This is not what she had earned a master's degree to achieve. She therefore decides to give up on the idea of a glamorous Foreign Service career: She will accept one of the other two positions and travel abroad during her three weeks of Federal vacation time. In fact, now that she thinks about it, she might well transfer to a position with the Federal government overseas. The Foreign Service wasn't the only Federal presence abroad: The Navy has offices all over the world.

At the last minute, the Navy offers Helen a recruitment bonus equal to 20% of the salary for her position. The Park Service Personnel Officer, when asked, says his agency just cannot afford to match this offer, but would try to make her relocation as easy as possible any other way they could.

Helen decides to accept the Navy position because it seems to offer the best career track. Not only is it bigger than the Park Service, with more offices and more top-level positions, but with offices abroad it provides more direct access to employment overseas. To pursue a position in a foreign country while employed at the Park Service would necessitate transfer to another agency (once she has competitive status). To obtain such a position from the Navy, on the other hand, would simply entail a transfer within the *same* agency.

Helen writes the Navy accepting the Auditor position and confirming the terms of the offer (with a copy of their offer attached). Two weeks after receiving her master's degree, she bids farewell to New York and heads for Los Angeles and the start of a career in Federal service.

EXAMPLE: JEFF

Jeff compares his two job offers. He notes that the Electrician position is in the Competitive Service, whereas the VRA position at the Defense Logistics Agency is in the Excepted Service. However, studying the material he has received about the VRA program, he sees that it provides for conversion to a position in the Competitive Service after two years on the job (at the agency's discretion). So, in this case, accepting employment in the Excepted Service would not leave him at a disadvantage.

The VRA job represents a great opportunity to become a white-collar professional. If he does manage to be appointed to the Competitive Service as a Quality Assurance Inspector—a position for which the VRA program will train him—Jeff's ultimate promotion potential under VRA is GS-12. This represents a lot more money than he would be able to earn even if promoted to the supervisory level as an Electrician.

However, if he accepts the Electrician position he will immediately be classified as career-conditional in the Competitive Service which, being a veteran, entitles him to lifetime reinstatement rights, should he be laid off; and in three years he will have tenure. Under VRA, however, he will have to wait two years to convert to the Competitive Service. The security he is seeking seems closer at hand with the Electrician position.

In the final analysis, Jeff accepts the Electrician position for personal reasons. Those 70 miles to the Defense Logistics Agency just seem too long a commute, and his family is still too young to be relocated—Lorrie, his high-school-age daughter, had become frantic at the mere suggestion. Jeff writes to his contact at the Defense Logistics Agency declining the VRA appointment. In his explanation he states how much he appreciates the opportunity that the VRA program had offered: It made him feel much better about his having served in Vietnam.

Appendix A: Job Title Matching Guide

This appendix will be useful in matching your qualifications to appropriate Federal job titles. To use it, place yourself in one or more of the applicant categories found in the first column. (Column 2, "Applicant Description," can help you categorize yourself.) Then read the recommendations in column 3 to determine the job titles, occupations, and programs for which you might be eligible. These recommendations are intended only as a starting point for your own analysis. Not all of them may be equally applicable to your situation; nor are they by any means the only job titles for which you may be qualified.

The fourth column refers you to one or more of the in-depth occupational studies presented in Appendix B.

> The importance of knowing the **job titles** for which you qualify is covered in Step 1 (p. 10). Appendixes K and N provide **brief descriptions** of job titles in Federal service.

CONTENTS

Applicant Category	Applicant Description	Job Title/Occupation Recommendation	See in Appendix B
Recent College Graduate, Liberal Arts	*George graduated from State University this past May with a Liberal Arts degree. His GPA is 3.5.* *Eleanor received her Master's degree this past January in Liberal Arts.* Note: *Under the Outstanding Scholar Program (see Appendix Q), George can apply to agencies directly. His educational experience qualifies him at the GS-5 or 7 level, depending on the job qualifications.* *Eleanor will have to apply to individual agencies for which she wants to receive a rating. Agencies determine the need of testing on an individual basis. Her Master's degree would qualify her at the GS-7 level.*	GS- (various) Administrative occupations GS-2152 Air Traffic Controller GS-130 Foreign Service Officer GS- (various) Law Enforcement occupations	Administrative Air Traffic Control Foreign Service Law Enforcement
Recent College Graduate, Overseas Interest	*Derek graduated from an Ivy League school with a degree in political science and would like to work for the State Department or Information agencies.* *Margaret has a degree in Russian and would like some overseas work as well. She also types 40 wpm.*	GS-130 Foreign Service Officer GS-1040 Language Specialist GS-132 Intelligence Operations Specialist (Overseas) GS-950 Paralegal Specialist GS-1035 Public Affairs Specialist GS-1001 International Radio Broadcaster GS-1045 Translator	Foreign Service Public Information Intelligence Administrative, Legal Administrative Public Information Intelligence

Applicant Category	Applicant Description	Job Title/Occupation Recommendation	See in Appendix B
Recent College Graduate, Health Care	*Maria recently graduated from a local college with a nursing degree.*	GS-610 Nurse (all fields)	Health Care
		GS-602 Medical Officer (all fields)	Health Care, Research and Administrative
	Lisa is a Medical Doctor (or Dentist, Pharmacist).	GS-680 Dental Officer	
		GS-660 Pharmacist	
	Virginia has a two-year associate degree in Health Care.	GS-621 Nurse Aid/Assistant Operating Room Nurse Assistant Licensed Practical Nurse	
Recent College Graduate, Health Technology	*Tom recently graduated from college with a specialized degree in in a technical health field.*	GS-661 Pharmacy Technician	Health Care
		GS-631 Occupational Therapy Technician	
	Note: *There are more tham 6,000 openings every year in the health technology field in the Federal sector. Job opportunities exist in every state.*	GS-681 Dental Assistant	
		GS-699 Health Aid & Technician	
		GS-603 Physician's Assistant	
		GS-682 Dental Hygienist	

Applicant Category	Applicant Description	Job Title/Occupation Recommendation	See in Appendix B
Recent College Graduate, Engineering	*Lorraine is a recent college grad with a bachelor's degree in Engineering.*	GS-800 Engineer All disciplines including: Aerospace, GS-861 Agricultural, GS-890 Architect, GS-808 Biomedical, GS-858 Chemical, GS-893 Civil, GS-810 Electrical, GS-850 Environmental, GS-819 Industrial, GS-896 Mechanical, GS-830 Mining, GS-880 Naval Architect, GS-871 Nuclear, GS-840 Petroleum, GS-881 Safety, GS-803	Engineers Public Information (VOA) Foreign Service Law Enforcement (FBI)
Recent College Graduate, Sciences	*Joseph has just graduated with a bachelor's degree in Science.*	GS-401 Biological Sciences GS-028 Environmental Protection Specialist GS-1310 Physical Sciences GS-1320 Chemistry GS-408 Ecologist	Science, Food Inspection Science Administration
Recent College Graduate, Computer Science	*Jonathan has recently graduated from college with a bachelor's degree in Computer Science.*	GS 334 Computer Specialist GS-1550 Computer Scientist GS-332 Computer Operator	Computer-Related Fields

Applicant Category	Applicant Description	Job Title/Occupation Recommendation	See in Appendix B
Recent College Graduate, Mathematics	*Ruth has just graduated from college with a bachelor's degree in Mathematics.*	GS-1520 Mathematician GS-1530 Statistician	Mathematics and Statistics
		GS-334 Computer Specialist	Computer-Related Fields
		GS-570 Financial Institution Examiner	Business and Finance
		GS-(various) Law Enforcement	Law Enforcement
		Program Analyst	
Recent College Graduate, Accounting	*Martin has just graduated from college with a degree in Accounting.*	GS-510 Accountant GS-511 Auditor GS-570 Financial Institution Examiner GS-1160 Financial Analyst GS-504 Financial Research Assistant GS-560 Budget Analyst	Business and Finance

Applicant Category	Applicant Description	Job Title/Occupation Recommendation	See in Appendix B
College Student– Part-Time Cooperative Intern	*Lindsay is a sophomore at New Dominion University. She is looking to work part-time in a cooperative or intern program with an agency in Denver.* Note: *Lindsay is in luck. Most agencies try to recruit their cooperative students in their sophomore year. After that, the opportunities tend to dwindle.*	Any cooperative or intern jobs offered through the College Placement program at school.	Contact the College Placement Officer and apply for a cooperative or intern job with a local Federal agency *no later than* sophomore year.

Applicant Category	Applicant Description	Job Title/Occupation Recommendation	See in Appendix B
Career Entry Office, Soft Skills	*Melissa has a high school diploma. She worked in an office as an assistant to a photographer. She has no specialized skills and is looking for her first job with advancement potential. She would like to learn a technical skill.* Note: *The soundest advice for Melissa would be to go back to school to learn that technical skill. If that is not feasible, her chances might be better if she took a clerical job in an agency, excelled in her work, and got selected for a promotional development program.*	GS-322 Clerk-Typist GS-318 Secretary (Typing/Steno) GS-356 Data Transcriber Postal worker Administrative occupations	Clerical Postal Service Administrative (except group 7)
Career Entry, Nonoffice, Unskilled	*Frank is 18, grew up in an urban environment, and has a high school diploma. His only work experience is in fast-food restaurants. He does not want to work in an office.* Note: *Agencies within the Department of Defense have excellent apprenticeship programs. The Navy, with its shipyard maintenance setup, would be a good place to start. The training program is highly selective, but excellent.*	GS-085 Guard GS-083 Police Officer WG-3502 Laborer WG-6907 Warehouse Worker WG-7408 Food Service Worker WG-5703 Motor Vehicle Operator Postal worker	Law Enforcement Wage Grade Postal Service

Applicant Category	Applicant Description	Job Title/Occupation Recommendation	See in Appendix B
Career Re-Entry	*Jayne has spent 14 years raising her two children, who are now old enough to fend for themselves while she reenters the work force. She hasn't worked in an office for 18 years and has no current word-processing or steno. She can type 40 wpm.*	GS-322 Clerk-Typist GS-318 Secretary (Type/Steno) GS-356 Data Transcriber Postal worker	Clerical Postal Service
	Note: *Women in this position could qualify for a Clerk-Typist job at the GS-2/3 level or as a Secretary, GS-3. Higher starting salaries are possible for those who worked before raising their children.*		

Applicant Category	Applicant Description	Job Title/Occupation Recommendation	See in Appendix B
Clerical, Skilled	*Dorothy has been working in an office for the past fifteen years. She has a high school diploma and recently completed a two-year associate degree in Office Management and Computers. She can type 60 wpm and take dictation and shorthand.* *She has worked her way up to Administrative Assistant, but her company is moving out of the state and she doesn't want to relocate.*	GS-301 Misc. Administration GS-318 Secretary GS-344 Management Assistant GS-341 Administrative Officer GS-342 Support Services Specialist Postal worker Administrative occupations (except Group 7)	Clerical Postal Service Administrative
Clerical, Unskilled	*Gloria lives in a large city and has a high school diploma. Her only work experience was a position at a supermarket. She would like secretarial or clerical work.* Note: *Gloria must be able to type at least 40 wpm to qualify for any clerical job. She can be eligible for secretari-al work if she has at least six months of experience. Any knowl-edge of shorthand would enhance her chances of being hired without previous work experience.*	GS-305 Mail and Clerk GS-322 Clerk-Typist Postal worker	Clerical Postal Service

Applicant Category	Applicant Description	Job Title/Occupation Recommendation	See in Appendix B
Blue Collar, Experienced Trades Worker (Journeyman)	*John is a skilled and experienced journeyman in carpentry [also applicable to any skilled trade] and wishes to work in that field for the Federal govern- ment. He seeks steady work.* *Note:* *A more complete listing of such jobs is provided in Appendix N.*	WG-2805 Electrician WG-4607 Carpenter WG-3603 Mason WG-2614 Electrical Equipment Repair	Wage Grade
Blue Collar, Inexperienced Trades Worker	*Tony has a high school diploma with a specialty in technical skills (e.g., auto, electronics, welding). He would like to become a journeyman in a skilled trade. However, local private-sector companies are not accepting new employees currently, and he wants to gain experi- ence in his occupation right away.*	WG-4749 Maintenance Worker WG-4742 Utility Systems Repairer WG-4206 Plumber WG-4102 Painter WG-4204 Pipefitter	Wage Grade, Military Base Occupations Wage Grade

Applicant Category	Applicant Description	Job Title/Occupation Recommendation	See in Appendix B
Midlife Career Changer, College Degree, Business Experience	*Chris is 43, has a college degree, and is unsatisfied with his career in manufacturing management. He is looking for a totally different field, but can't afford to start at entry level.* **Note:** *Chris should take some encouragement from the knowledge that the government tries to match its salaries with the private sector. His experience qualifies him for a mid-level salary in Administrative and Management jobs and Program Analyst positions with a variety of agencies.*	GS-301 Misc. Administration and Programs GS-345 Program Analyst GS-1152 Production Control Specialist GS-1910 Quality Assurance Specialist GS-1640 Facility Manager	Administrative, Clerical, Military Base Occupations Administrative Business and Finance Administrative
Midlife Career Changer, College Degree, Ex-Business Owner	*Marcus, after owning his own paper products business, has sold out at 57. He is financially independent and seeks an interesting and challenging Federal job to occupy his time. He doesn't mind starting in an entry level position.* Note: *Marcus would qualify for many grades, ranging from GS-7 to some SES (Senior Executive Service) positions depending on his qualifications and for what jobs he applies.* 　　*Since Marcus is financially independent, he might want to consider applying for a job with the Peace Corps.*	*In addition to* the jobs titles above, Marcus is qualified for the following: GS-1140 Trade Specialist GS-1160 Financial Analyst GS-1910 Quality Assurance Specialist Peace Corps (unpaid) Administrative occupations	 Administrative Business and Finance, Administrative Peace Corps Administrative

Applicant Category	Applicant Description	Job Title/Occupation Recommendation	See in Appendix B
Midlife Career Changer, Nonoffice Work, Unskilled Blue Collar	*Hank is 31 and has worked in a variety of jobs such as truck driving, car repair, and construction. He has no specialized skills and is looking to do something other than clerical work.*	WG-5703 Motor Vehicle Operator	Wage-Grade, Military Base Occupations
		WG-3566 Custodian	Wage Grade
		WG-7408 Food Service Worker	
		WG-3502 Laborer	
		WG-3809 Mobile Equipment Metal Mechanic	
		Postal worker	Postal Service

Applicant Category	Applicant Description	Job Title/Occupation Recommendation	See in Appendix B
Midlife Career Changer, Ex-Salesperson/Marketing	*Matthew was just laid off after 12 years with the advertising agency Layne, Webster, and Ritter. He is 38 years old. He wants out of sales and marketing, and into some Federal job at anything other than entry level.*	GS-301 Misc. Administration and Programs	Administrative, Clerical, Military Base Occupations
		GS-343 Management Analysis Officer	Administrative
		GS-345 Program Analyst	Administrative
	Note: *This situation tends to be a problem since people like Matthew usually make high salaries but have little experience that the government can use. Depending on his managerial experience, he may qualify for a number of positions at mid-level (GS-9/11) salaries; however, competition from those already in the government can be quite stiff.*	GS-1140 Trade Specialist	Business and Finance, Administrative
		GS-1035 Public Information Specialist	Writing and Public Information
		GS-1082 Writer-Editor	
		Postal Worker	Postal Service
	In this situation, Matthew may have to consider accepting a job at a lower GS level and take advantage of on-the-job training as a path toward advancment in the Federal government.		

Applicant Category	Applicant Description	Job Title/Occupation Recommendation	See in Appendix B
Midlife Career Changer, Ex-Teacher	*Peter taught science for 14 years at a local high school and is now looking for white collar work, not teaching.*	Administrative occupations	Administrative
		GS-1520 Mathematician	Mathematics and Statistics
	Note:	GS-1550 Computer Scientist	Computer-Related Fields, Mathematics & Statistics, Military Base Occupations
	A good place for an ex-teacher to start would be entry level positions at the GS-5/7 level.		
		GS-401 Biological Scientist	Science
	Potential government occupation is dependent upon background. Those who taught Math or Science, for instance, could be hired at the GS-9 level. Those who were in Administration, might be able to find administrative jobs at the GS-11 level.	GS-1301 Physical Scientist	Science
		GS-301 Misc. Administration and Programs	Administrative, Clerical, Military Base Occupations
		GS-334 Computer Specialist (depending on experience)	Computer-Related Fields, Administrative

Applicant Category	Applicant Description	Job Title/Occupation Recommendation	See in Appendix B

Educator	*Phylicia has a Ph.D. in Early Childhood Education and a Masters in Public Education Systems.*
	
	Note:
	Phylicia's Ph.D. would qualify her for most GS-11 positions.
	    Teaching tops out at the GS-11 level. Depending upon her experience, she could go higher in other educational areas. The educational research field, for example, has positions up to GS-15.
		GS-1710
		Educational and Vocational Training
		
		GS-1724
		Elementary Teaching
		
		GS-1720
		Education Program Specialist
		
		GS-1730
		Education Research Analyst
		
		GS-639
		Educational Therapist
		    Academic
		    Commercial
		    Science
		    Fine Arts
		    General
			Education/Training

Applicant Category	Applicant Description	Job Title/Occupation Recommendation	See in Appendix B
Real Estate Practitioner	*Fran has worked for the past 10 years in real estate. She would like Federal employment that takes into consideration her real estate professional certification.* Note: *Any experience in appraising and/or assessment would increase her hiring qualifications.*	GS-1176 Building Management GS-1173 Housing Management GS-1102 Contract Specialist GS-1170 Real Estate Specialist GS-1171 Appraiser	Business and Finance, Administrative

Applicant Category	Applicant Description	Job Title/Occupation Recommendation	See in Appendix B
Noncitizen, Professional	*Muhammad is an Engineer (or Scientist, Mathematician, or health care professional). He has a work visa, but no citizenship and none in sight. He wants to work for the Federal government.* Note: *In order to be employed by the Federal government in the Competitive Service, one must be a U.S. citizen. A noncitizen can be hired into the Excepted Service, if there are no U.S. citizens qualified and available to do the work.* *Mohammed has a good chance because his specialty is in demand. If hired, he would receive an excepted Schedule A appointment to work. He still would not be eligible for the Competitive Service, however, unless he were to become a citizen.*	GS-800 Engineer GS-1520 Mathematician GS-1530 Statistician GS-602 Medical Officer GS-1302 Physical Scientist GS-028 Environmental Protection Specialist GS-401 Biologist GS-334 Computer Specialist	Engineers Mathematics and Statistics Health Care Science Administrative Science, Food Inspection Computer-Related Fields
Noncitizen, Nonprofessional	*Sergei is a noncitizen, whose occupation is a laborer. He wants to work for the Federal government.* Note: *Because he is a noncitizen his chances of being hired by the Federal government are practically nil, especially in his occupation.*	None	None

Applicant Category	Applicant Description	Job Title/Occupation Recommendation	See in Appendix B
Pre-Retiree (late fifties), Office Professional	*Anthony is 59 and is looking for work for the next 6 years. He was a consultant (or Fortune 500 middle management, or banking/finance, or self-employed businessmen, etc.) He will consider anything, provided he doesn't have to relocate.* Note: *The Federal government does not discriminate because of age.* *Applicants will be considered regardless of age even if over 65. However, Anthony should be very careful not to tell any prospective employer that he plans on working only for six years. That might hurt his chances of finding a job.*	GS-301 Misc. Administration and Programs GS-345 Program Analyst GS-1160 Financial Analyst GS-1150 Industrial Specialist GS-570 Financial Institution Examiner	Administrative, Clerical, Military Base Occupations Administrative Business and Finance, Administrative
Pre-Retiree (late fifties), nonoffice/Blue Collar	*Hector worked in his own gasoline station and mechanic department for 30 years. He needs a salary until his social security kicks in.* Note: *Since he owned his own business, Hector might qualify for work as an Equipment Specialist or in General Facilities Management-type jobs in addition to any automotive related jobs.* *The Federal government does not discriminate because of age.*	WG-5823 Auto Mechanic WG-5703 Motor Vehicle Operator WG-5803 Heavy Mobile Equipment Mechanic WG-4749 Maintenance Mechanic	Wage Grade Wage Grade, Military Reserve Technician Occupations Wage Grade, Military Base Occupations, Military Reserve Technician Occupations Wage Grade, Military Base Occupations

Applicant Category	Applicant Description	Job Title/Occupation Recommendation	See in Appendix B
Retiree, White Collar	*Arthur worked for 45 years for 1st National Bank, first as a Teller, then Loan Officer, then Manager. He is retired and looking for any job to occupy his time. Even an entry-level job would be acceptable.* Note: *The Federal government does not discriminate because of age. Even applicants over 65 will be considered.*	GS-300 Clerical (various) GS-1165 Loan Specialist GS-570 Financial Institution Examiner Accountant Budget Analyst	Clerical Business and Finance, Administrative
Retiree, Blue Collar	*Thomas is 66 and is now searching for any kind of work full- or part-time, permanent or temporary, that is nonoffice. He worked for 32 years in an auto plant.* Note: *The fact that Thomas is over 62 raises some question. Is he eligible for Social Security? If he is, this could affect the number of hours that he may work. Also, is he collecting a pension from a previous job? That too may affect his working status.* *He might have better opportunities if he only seeks part-time or temporary work. This would relieve the government of paying full benefits and probably increase his chances of landing a job.* *The Federal government does not discriminate because of age.*	WG-5823 Automotive Mechanic WG-3566 Custodial Worker WG-7408 Food Service Worker WG-5703 Motor Vehicle Operator Postal worker	Wage Grade Wage Grade, Military Base Occupations Wage Grade Wage Grade, Military Reserve Technician Occupations Postal Service

Applicant Category	Applicant Description	Job Title/Occupation Recommendation	See in Appendix B
Armed Services, Enlisted, Vietnam Era or Later	*Greg has spent the past 17 years working in gas stations. He is a veteran of the Vietnam War.* Note: *Greg is entitled to Veterans' Preference points due to his military background. In addition, because he saw action in Vietnam, he also qualifies for benefits under the Veterans Readjustment Act. This means that, for jobs for which he qualifies, Greg can be appointed by a Federal agency without taking a competitive exam.*	WG-5823 Auto Mechanic WG-5803 Heavy Mobile Equipment Mechanic WG-5703 Motor Vehicle Operator WG-3502 Laborer Positions in the Army Reserve Technicians Program	Wage Grade Wage Grade, Military Base Occupations, Military Reserve Technician Occupations Warge Grade, Military Reserve Technician Occupations Wage Grade Military Reserve Technician Occupations
Armed Services, Enlisted, Recently Discharged	*Phil has just received his honorable discharge from the Navy. He is 22 and has some technical-radar experience.* Note: *Phil might consider an apprenticeship program with the Department of Defense. Phil should also look into a position with the DOD that directly relates to the job(s) which he did while in the Navy.*	GS-856 Electronic Technician GS-390 Communications Relay Operator GS-394 Communications Clerk (inc. Radio Broadcast Technician) Postal worker Various Army/Air Force Reserve Technician positions Administrative occupations	Engineering Public Information Postal Service Military Reserve Technician Occupations Administrative

Applicant Category	Applicant Description	Job Title/Occupation Recommendation	See in Appendix B
Armed Services, Officer, Recently Discharged	*Roland has left the Army with the rank of Major at age 38. As a Captain he was a front-line infantry officer and wonders if the Federal government could use his skills as a manager, leader and motivator.*	GS-301 Misc. Administration and Programs	Administrative, Clerical Military Base Occupations
		GS-235 Employee Development and Training	Administrative
		GS-342 Support Services Specialist/ Supervisor	
	Note: *Roland would probably qualify for Administration/ Management positions from GS-7 up to GS-13. The lower he is willing to start, the more openings would exist. The variety of occupations for which he could qualify depends on his experience in the Infantry. If he has worked on the development of Training Programs, he might be able to find a job involving employee development or training. Likewise, any experience in personnel may keep Roland involved with the military as a Military Personnel Management Specialist, for example.*	GS-201 Personnel Management Specialist	
		Various positions within the Army Reserve Technicians Program	Military Reserve Technician Occupations

Appendix B: Selected Fields and Their Hiring Pathways

Step 2 discussed the five hiring pathways used by the Federal government:
1. written test, register (entry level)
2. no written test, register (entry level)
3. no written test, no register (mid/top level + entry-level professional)
4. special hiring programs
5. promotion route/SES (mid/top level).

This appendix provides specific examples of how these hiring pathways are used for some of the major job titles and occupational groups in the Federal government today. For each occupational group, it covers how many people are currently employed, which job titles are most in demand, and which pathways are most often used for recruitment.* (To determine which agencies do the most hiring, consult Appendix L, Federal Occupations by Selected Agency.) It can either be used in conjunction with Appendix A, where specific pathway recommendations are paired with specific job titles, or stand on its own as a source of important occupational information.

Not every job title or occupation is covered in this appendix. If the job title for which you want to apply is not discussed, you should nevertheless investigate the hiring prospects and pathways through other channels (see Step 3) before applying for a vacancy. Remember, the more you know and understand the job prospects, the more you will able to make intelligent, well-informed choices about which Federal jobs you should pursue.

One note about the statistics presented in this appendix: The low and high grades for various job titles have been selected to show the range of grade levels for 98% of those employed in a given occupation. By disregarding the anomalous 2% of Federal employees at grades very much out of the mainstream—whether abnormally high or low—we hope to present a clearer picture of what grade expectations are reasonable.

> *Note:* **Addresses** for all **agencies** mentioned in this appendix, as well as for **OPM Service Centers**, are listed in Appendix D.

> * *Source:* OPM's Office of Workforce Statistics, <u>Central Personnel Data File Report for Fiscal Year 1996</u>.

CONTENTS

ADMINISTRATIVE

GROUP AND SERIES

Each listing shows GS series, job title, and number of employees. Job titles with the highest demand are shown in capital letters.

Group 1: Health, Safety, and Environmental

0018	Safety and Occupational Health Management	4,175	0673	Hospital Housekeeping Management	288
0023	Outdoor Recreation Planning	656	0685	Public Health Program Specialist	1,511
0028	Environmental Protection Specialist	5,254			

Group 2: Writing and Public Information

1001	General Arts and Information	2,863	1147	Agricultural Market Reporting	157
1035	Public Affairs	3,928	1412	Technical Information Services	1,080
1082	Writing and Editing	1,482	1421	Archives Specialist	850
1083	Technical Writing and Editing	1,279			

Group 3: Business, Finance, and Management

0011	Bond Sales Promotion	99
0106	Unemployment Insurance	N/A
0120	Food Assistance Program Specialist	N/A
0346	LOGISTICS MANAGEMENT	10,933
0393	Communications Specialist	N/A
0501	FINANCIAL ADMINISTRATION AND PROGRAMS	8,207
0560	BUDGET ANALYSIS	12,778
0570	Financial Institution Examining	2,391
1101	GENERAL BUSINESS AND INDUSTRY	18,903
1102	CONTRACT AND PROCUREMENT SPECIALIST	28,564
1103	Industrial Property Management	757
1104	Property Disposal	1,008
1130	Public Utilities Specialist	599
1140	Trade Specialist	641
1145	Agricultural Program Specialist	505
1146	Agricultural Marketing	529
1149	Wage and Hour Law Administration	50
1150	Industrial Specialist	1,957
1160	Financial Analysis	1,110
1163	Insurance Examining	63
1165	Loan Specialist	3,618
1170	Realty	3,304
1171	Appraising and Assessing	914
1173	Housing Management	2,387
1176	Building Management	1,122
1910	QUALITY ASSURANCE SPECIALIST	10,040
2001	GENERAL SUPPLY	3,806
2003	SUPPLY PROGRAM MANAGEMENT	4,977
2010	INVENTORY MANAGEMENT	6,175
2030	Distribution Facilities and Store Management	781
2032	Packaging	327
2050	Supply Cataloguing	476
2101	Transportation Specialist	7,314
2110	Transportation Industry Analysis	126
2125	Highway Safety Management	278
2130	Traffic Management	1,775
2150	Transportation Operations	963

Group 4: Personnel, Administration, and Computer Occupations

0142	Manpower Development	461
0201	PERSONNEL MANAGEMENT	10,717
0205	Military Personnel Management	1,675
0212	Personnel Staffing	2,273
0222	Occupational Analysis	40
0223	Salary and Wage Administration	147
0230	Employee Relations	1,786
0233	Labor Relations	1,098
0235	Employee Development	2,241
0244	Labor Management Relations Examining	394
0246	Contractor Industrial Relations	103
0301	MISCELLANEOUS ADMINISTRATION AND PROGRAMS	39,606
0334	COMPUTER SPECIALIST (TRAINEE)	53,480
0341	ADMINISTRATIVE OFFICER	7,703
0343	MANAGEMENT ANALYSIS	38,215
0345	PROGRAM ANALYSIS	313
1715	Vocational Rehabilitation	646

Group 5: Benefits Review, Tax, and Legal

0105	SOCIAL INSURANCE ADMINISTRATION	24,742
0187	Social Services	534
0526	Tax Technician	4,235
0950	Paralegal Specialist	4,469
0962	CONTACT REPRESENTATIVE	15,025
0965	Land Law Examining	284
0967	Passport and Visa Examining	1,009
0987	Tax Law Specialist	373
0990	General Claims Examining	2,835
0991	Worker's Compensation Claims Examining	787
0993	SOCIAL INSURANCE CLAIMS EXAMINING	1,897
0994	Unemployment Compensation Claims Examining	69
0996	Veterans Claims Examining	3,292
0997	Civil Service Retirement Claims Examining	N/A

Group 6: Law Enforcement and Investigation

0025	PARK RANGER	4,740
0080	SECURITY ADMINISTRATION	5,947
0132	Intelligence	3,760
0249	Wage and Hour Compliance	987
1169	INTERNAL REVENUE OFFICER	7,934
1801	General Inspection, Investigation and Compliance	6,901
1811	CRIMINAL INVESTIGATOR	22,184
1812	Game Law Enforcement	387
1816	Immigration Inspection	3,895
1831	Securities Compliance Examining	200
1854	Alcohol, Tobacco, and Firearms Inspection	751
1864	Public Health Quarantine Inspection	32
1889	Import Specialist	1,283
1890	Customs Inspector	6,698

Group 7: Positions with Positive Education Requirements

0020	Community Planning	518	0184	Sociology	48
0101	Social Science	5,430	0190	General Anthropology	65
0110	ECONOMIST	4,753	0193	Archeology	791
0130	Foreign Affairs	2,249	1015	Museum Curator	356
0131	International Relations	74	1420	Archivist	465
0140	Manpower Research and Analysis	25	1701	GENERAL EDUCATION	
0150	Geography	296		AND TRAINING	2,663
0170	History	615	1720	Educational Research & Program	394
0180	Psychology	3,568			

GRADE LEVELS: GS-5–7

QUALIFICATIONS

Any interested citizen is qualified to take one or more Administrative tests. Generally, they are taken by recent college graduates and those about to graduate with bachelor's degrees. A degree is *required* only for job titles in Administrative Group 7.

HIRING PATHWAYS: 3, 4, 5

A method for Groups 1–6 (Pathway 4 Special Hiring Programs), which is popular with Agencies is the *Outstanding Scholar Program (OSP)*. Applicants with an overall academic grade-point average (GPA) of 3.5 or better may submit an SF-171 and Form 1170/17 (List of College Courses) as part of an application package. Those who wish to apply under OSP can approach any agency of interest to them and inquire about Administrative openings. Outstanding scholars can be hired directly by the agency at GS-5/7 level.

A third method (Pathway 5) is *transferral* into an Administrative career position from another Federal job. Current Federal employees need not take an Administrative exam, but can apply directly to the agency with the opening, outlining their qualifications on their SF-171s; as always, experience is a substitute for education as a means of qualifying for a position. Given this option, a longer-term strategy for obtaining an Administrative appointment is first to obtain a Federal position in a non-Administrative job title (say, Clerical), fulfill the minimum time in grade (usually about a year), and then apply for transfer into an Administrative position.

Job titles in Group 7 are in low demand and infrequently open. Interested candidates should approach agencies directly (Pathway 3) in hope of finding a vacancy. They can then apply using an SF-171 or a Federal Resume. To see which agencies hire for a given Group 7 job title, check Appendix L (White-Collar Occupations by Selected Agency) or write your local OPM Service Center.

AIR TRAFFIC CONTROL (ATC)

There are currently 23,910 Federal Air Traffic Controllers, all hired exclusively by the Federal Aviation Administration (FAA). Their specific duties depend on whether they work at an en route center, flight service center, or airport control tower:

At *en route centers,* Air Traffic Controllers give aircraft instructions, air traffic clearance, and advice regarding flight conditions. Controllers use radar to track all flights within the center's assigned air-space, typically 100,000 square miles. The staff at an en route center can range from 300 to 700, with 8,000 working in such centers nationwide.

At *flight service centers,* controllers provide assistance to pilots on terrain, weather peculiarities, preflight and inflight weather information, indications of turbulence and icing, and other other information important to flight safety. Altogether, approximately 4,000 Air Traffic Controllers work in service centers, which usually employ 10–70 apiece.

At *airport control towers,* specialists direct air traffic around airports in the air and on the ground, handling a 3–30-mile range. Controllers give pilots taxiing and takeoff instructions, provide air traffic clearances, and ensure separation between landing and departing aircraft. The number of controllers at each tower facility ranges from 10 to 150, with 9,000 working in towers at virtually every airport nationwide.

SERIES, GRADE LEVELS, AND PROMOTION POTENTIAL

GS Series	Job Title	Positions/ People Employed	Grade Level			Promotion Rate (%)
			Low	High	Average	
2152	Air Traffic Controller	23,910	GS-7	GS-15	GS-12.1	14

> Additional **transportation** job titles are listed in Appendix K under GS-2100, Transportation Group.

QUALIFICATIONS

To qualify applicants must be under 30 years of age and meet one of the following criteria:

1. Pass the written test with a rating of 75.1 or above and have either (a) three years of general experience, (b) four years of college, or (c) any combination of college and experience totaling three years.

2. Pass the written test with a rating of 70 or above and have a bachelor's degree plus either (a) one year of graduate work or (b) superior academic achievement (GPA of 3.0 or better overall, or of 3.5 or better in one's major).

3. Pass the written test with a rating of 70 or above and have either (a) civilian or military facility rating in ATC involving the active control of aircraft, (b) past or present air carrier dispatcher certificate, (c) past or present instrument flight rating, (d) past or present FAA certificate as a navigator/bombadier, (e) past or present pilot rating with 350 hours of flight time, (f) past or present rating as an Aerospace Defense Command Intercept Director, or (g) specialized experience in military or civilian ATC work.

PATHWAY: 1

All applicants are required to take the Air Traffic Controller written aptitude test administered by OPM for the Federal Aviation Administration. Interested applicants can obtain an application for the exam from the nearest OPM Service Center (see list in Appendix D) or by writing directly to the FAA:

FAA Aeronautical Center
P.O. Box 24082
ATT: AAC-80
Oklahoma City, OK 73125.

Air Traffic Controller positions have been open frequently during the past several years because the FAA is increasing the size of its Air Traffic System. When open, a request for an application will be fulfilled with a test scheduling card (5000 A/B); when not open, no tests will be scheduled. Exams are generally given at least every three months at some 50 test centers around the country. Candidates who score above 90 generally have a good chance to be selected to receive a request for an SF-171.

Applicants with satisfactory SF-171 ratings are required to report to a nearby air traffic facility for an interview. This is to ascertain that the applicants possess the personal characteristics required of an Air Traffic Controller, such as motivation, practical intelligence, and the ability to speak distinctly and concisely.

Candidates who pass the interview undergo medical examination. Under requirements established by OPM, incidence of any of the following is disqualifying:

1. pychosis or neurosis;
2. substance dependence, whether to alcohol, narcotics, or nonnarcotic drugs;
3. any mental or personality disorder determined to constitute a hazard to flight safety according to a Federal Air Surgeon;
4. diabetes mellitus;
5. any organic, functional, or structural disease, defect, or limitation determined by a Federal Air Surgeon to constitute a hazard to air safety.

There are also strict vision standards: Optical requirements for applicants who plan to work at airport control towers or en route centers include (corrected) vision of 20/20 or better in each eye separately; if glasses or contact lenses are required, refractive error in each eye must not exceed ±5.50 diopters of spherical equivalent or 3.00 diopters of cylinder. The optical requirements for positions at flight service centers are not quite as rigorous: Applicants must demonstrate distant and near vision of 20/20 in at least one eye; if glasses or contact lenses are required, a refractive error exceeding ±8.00 diopters necessitates ophthalmological consultation.

All applicants who pass the medical examination must then undergo a security background investigation, which delves into matters of questionable conduct, reliability, character, trustworthiness, and loyalty to the United States government.

Candidates who get this far are sent to the FAA Academy in Oklahoma City to enter a 16-week training and screening program designed both to train candidates to perform the work and to weed out inappropriate persons. During their training, candidates are paid at the GS-7 level. About 54% of those attending the school make it through. Upon graduation candidates are promoted and report to their first duty station at the GS-9 level.

BUSINESS AND FINANCE

This category covers two white-collar occupational groups: the Accounting and Budget Group and the Business and Industry Group. The Federal government employs more than 122,935 people in the former and over 92,809 in the latter.

SERIES

Note that some series listed in Appendix K have, over the years, been absorbed into other job titles; a more up-to-date listing of job titles is that given in Appendix M. Job titles with the highest demand are capitalized.

Accounting and Budget   122,935

0501 Financial Administration and Programming (*or* General Accounting Clerical and Administration)	0540 Voucher Examiner
	0541 Fiscal Auditing (GAO)
	0544 Payroll
0503 Financial Clerical and Assistant	0545 Military Pay
0504 Budget and Accounting	0547 Benefit-Payment Roll
0505 Financial Manager	0560 Budget Analyst
0510 ACCOUNTING	0570 Financial Institution Examiner
0511 AUDITING	0590 Time and Leave
0512 INTERNAL REVENUE AGENT	0592 Tax Examiner
0525 ACCOUNTING TECHNICIAN	0593 Insurance Accounts
0526 Tax Technician	0599 Financial Management Student Trainee
0530 Cash Processor	

Business and Industry   92,809

1101 General Business and Industry	1146 Agricultural Marketing
1102 CONTRACTING AND PROCUREMENT	1147 Agricultural Market Reporter
1103 Industrial Property Manager	1149 Wage & Hour Law Administrator
1104 Property Disposal	1150 Industrial Specialist
1105 PURCHASING	1152 Production Control
1106 PROCUREMENT CLERICAL AND ASSISTANT	1160 Financial Analysis
	1161 Crop Insurance Adminstrator
1107 Property Disposal Clerical and Technician	1162 Crop Insurance Underwriting
	1163 Insurance Examiner
1130 Property Utilities Specialist	1165 Loan Specialist
1135 Transportation Industry Analyst	1169 Internal Revenue Officer
1140 Trade Specialist	1170 Realty
1144 Commissary Store Manager	1171 Appraising and Assessing
1145 Agricultural Program Specialist	1173 Housing Manager
	1176 Building Manager

1199 Business & Industry Student Trainee

GROUPS, GRADE LEVELS, AND ~~PROMOTION POTENTIAL~~

GS Series	Job Title	Positions/ People Employed	Grade Level Low	High	Average	Promotion Rate (%)
Accounting and Budget		122,935	GS-4	GS-15	GS-8.5	18–25
Business and Industry		92,809	GS-4	GS-13	GS-9.5	20–25

QUALIFICATIONS

GS-5: bachelor's degree in appropriate field
GS-7: master's degree and/or one year of related work experience
GS-9–15: advanced degrees and/or additional work experience (vary)

PATHWAYS: 1, 2, 3

Candidates with the minimum qualifying degree can often be hired directly (Pathway 3). Those who lack that degree must apply to take the Administrative Group 3 test (Business, Finance, and Management Group), receive a rating, and be listed on a register (Pathway 1). They can then wait to be referred from the register and/or apply directly to agencies (the name request route; see Administrative, p. 43).

Sometimes, if a large number of vacancies is anticipated, a register without test is assembled (Pathway 2). In such instances, a rating is required before an applicant can be seriously considered for a position.

Although a number of job titles in these groups have come under Direct Hire Authority at one time or another, the actual job titles and agencies that are currently participating is subject to change due to fluctuations in supply and demand. Interested applicants should contact their local OPM Service Center or agency personnel offices to ascertain which pathways are currently being used for which positions.

Because these occupational groups are so diverse, it is too difficult to describe fully all the available pathways and how each agency recruits its employees. However, to give some an idea of how agencies hire in the areas of business and finance, several occupations in the Accounting and Budget Group are highlighted below.

According to the latest available statistics (FY1997), agencies employing the largest number individuals in the 500 series are in the Departments of Treasury (25,000+), Defense (Army [14,000+], Navy [10,000+], Air Force [6,000+]), and Veterans Affairs (3,000+); for further information, see Appendix L.

ACCOUNTING AND AUDITING

Accountants and Auditors design accounting systems and procedures, evaluate financial performance, and assist in program management and control. Many Accountant or Auditor positions in Federal government require a great deal of travel.

Special salary rates, higher than those of the standard General Schedule, apply in many major metropolitan areas. Opportunities are excellent, and most qualified candidates receive offers.

Series, Grade Levels, and Promotion Potential

GS Series	Job Title	Positions/ People Employed	Grade Level			Promotion Rate (%)
			Low	High	Average	
0510	Accountant	12,524	GS-5	GS-15	GS-11.3	18
0511	Auditor	12,786	GS-5	GS-15	GS-11.3	9
0525	Accounting Technician	17,932	GS-4	GS-9	GS-5.9	16

Qualifications

Accountant or Auditor

GS-5: at least a bachelor's degree, including (or plus) 24 credits in Accounting; or four years equivalent experience in the Accounting field

GS-7: additional year of professional or graduate experience; or a bachelor's degree with a GPA of 3.5 or above

GS-9: additional two years of professional or graduate experience (relative to GS-5)

GS-11+: additional three years professional or graduate experience (relative to GS-5)

Accounting Technician

GS-4: two years of general office experience

GS-5: additional one year of specialized work-related experience

GS-7: three years of additional specialized experience (relative to GS-4)

GS-8+: four years of specialized work experience (relative to GS-4)

Pathways: 2, 3

Accountant or Auditor

OPM has given Direct Hire Authority to all agencies for Accountants and Auditors. Applicants may approach any agency to inquire about vacancies, and apply directly by using the SF-171 and the Form 1170/17. Trainee positions are not filled via any special hiring programs. Agencies hiring the most Accountants and Auditors include those in the Departments of Treasury, Defense, Agriculture, and Health and Human Services.

Those who wish broad geographic coverage for their applications at the GS-5–9 levels can be placed on a centralized (OPM) national register. Applications in this case are made with the Form B for Accountants, which can be obtained from any OPM Service Center or by writing to:

The **Form B** in Appendix H (p. 517) is a sample only; you must submit an original of this or any computer-scanned forms.

OPM Staffing Services Center
Examining Office
P.O. Box 9800
Macon, GA 31298

Applicants then send their completed Form Bs to the same Macon address in order to be rated and be placed on a register.

Accounting Technician

Accounting Technicians may be hired either directly by agencies or through OPM. They are most frequently hired for the Departments of Treasury, Defense, Agriculture, and Health and Human Services. Registers of qualified candidates are compiled when there is an applicant oversupply. Contact your local OPM Service Center for information on hiring in your area.

FINANCIAL INSTITUTION EXAMINER

The government employs over 4,000 Financial Institution Examiners, all but a few of whom are with either the Federal Deposit Insurance Corporation (FDIC) or the Treasury's Office of the Controller of the Currency (OCC). Their job is to review the safety and soundness of a financial institution, such as a bank, savings and loan, or credit union. (The stock market is also examined, via the Security and Exchange Commission.) Very heavy travel is required: Examiners frequently spend three or four nights a week away from home. Because turnover in this field is rapid, promotion potential is good.

Series and Grade Levels

GS Series	Job Title	Positions/ People Employed	Grade Level		
			Low	High	Average
0570	Financial Institution Examiner	2,389	GS-5	GS-15	GS-10.3

Qualifications

Candidates must have a bachelor's degree with at least 24 credits in business courses, six of which must be in Accounting. Three or more years of nonclerical bank experience also qualify.

Pathways: 1, 2

Some Financial Institution Examiner positions are filled by applying directly to the agency. In this case, candidates are not required to take a test; instead they apply to the FDIC or OCC using an SF-171 and, upon achieving a rating of 70 or above, are placed on registers maintained *independently* by the two agencies. Candidates who apply via the Outstanding Scholar Program (see Appendix Q) go to the head of these registers.

CLERICAL

This is the largest job category in Federal government, with over 450,000 employees. Every Federal facility employs people in clerical occupations. New employees can start with no experience at GS-1, or with up to three years of experience at GS-5. Advancement potential is high, as rapid turn-over presents many opportunities. Free training courses are offered to clerical and secretarial employees in many fields to improve their skills and increase their chances for promotion. Specific job descriptions are given in Appendix K.

MAJOR SERIES, GRADE LEVELS, AND PROMOTION POTENTIAL

GS Series	Job Title	Positions/ People Employed	Grade Level			Promotion Rate (%)
			Low	High	Average	
0301	Misc. Admin. & Programs	39,632	GS-4	GS-15	GS-11.5	19
0303	Misc. Clerk & Assistant	52,641	GS-1	GS-14	GS-5	20
0305	Mail and File Clerk	11,442	GS-1	GS-13	GS-4	14
0312	Clerk-Steno. & Reporter	177	GS-3	GS-13	GS-4.5	3
0322	Clerk-Typist	2,372	GS-1	GS-11	GS-3.5	2
0335	Computer Clerk & Asst.	6,926	GS-1	GS-13	GS-6	18
0356	Data Transcriber	3,135	GS-1	GS-10	GS-4	57

QUALIFICATIONS

Clerical candidates are hired at any level in the range GS-1–7; qualifications for each level are listed below:

GS-1: no experience
GS-2: three months of office experience | written
GS-3: six months of office experience | test
GS-4: one year of office experience | required
GS-5: three years of relevant work experience or bachelor's degree
GS-6: four years of office experience or bachelor's degree
GS-7: five year of office experience or bachelor's degree plus one year of office experience

PATHWAY: 1

Candidates at GS-1 are qualified without experience and do not have to take a written test; application can be made directly to agencies with openings. Most clerical new hires are at GS-2–4, for which candidates are required to take a written test. The exam is given frequently in metropolitan areas both by the OPM and by agencies, often administered on a walk-in basis at prescribed hours. The test is less available in suburban and rural areas and in smaller cities and towns. Contact your local OPM Service Center to obtain a test schedule and location. In certain instances, the examining authority (OPM or the hiring agency) may require clerical applicants to file a Form B for testing purposes.

Clerk-Typists, Clerk-Stenographers, Data Transcribers, and other clerical candidates are in high demand in most metropolitan areas, and hiring prospects are good. Interested applicants should contact either their local OPM Service Center or any agency in their area. In undersupply conditions, the examination is often waived and a personal statement obtained from the applicant that he or she has the qualifications sought, including typing speed. If the claims made on the statement are proved to be false, however, the candidate may be discharged.

SECRETARY

The duties of a Federal secretary include typing, taking dictation, filing, correspondence, work flow management, and so on.

Series, Grade Levels, and Promotion Potential

| GS Series | Job Title | Positions/ People Employed | Grade Level | | | Promotion Rate (%) |
			Low	High	Average	
0318	Secretary	69,184	GS-4	GS-9	GS-5.6	15

Qualifications

Applicants must have a certified typing proficiency of at least 40 wpm, plus work experience as outlined above

Pathways: 1, 2, 3

All agencies hire many secretaries, and such hiring is done at the local level: There are no national registers for Secretaries or other clerical support personnel. As with all other clerical positions, hiring pathways differ depending on local job-market conditions. A written test of basic English comprehension and math is prescribed for candidates at the GS-2–4 levels; but, as for other clerical positions, this test may be waived. Most agencies in major metropolitan areas have Direct Hire Authority for Secretaries because the demand is so high. Where there is a surplus of applicants, a local Register of Eligibles is compiled, and qualified applicants are called for interviews as the need arises. Contact your local OPM Service Center or Federal agencies directly to ascertain the paths currently being used in your area.

COMPUTER-RELATED FIELDS

There are three distinct, computer-related career areas in Federal service, each with its own qualifications and hiring pathways:

1. clerical (GS-1–5), with employees largely performing data-entry functions and operations (Data Transcriber, Computer Clerk, Computer Operator, and Assistant);
2. entry-level professionals (GS-7+) in programming, analysis, and design (Computer Specialist, Computer Operator, and Computer Scientist); and
3. mid- and top-level professionals in programming, analysis, and design (Computer Specialist, Computer Engineer, Computer Scientist).

Job descriptions are provided in Appendix K.

SERIES, GRADE LEVELS, AND PROMOTION POTENTIAL

GS Series	Job Title	Positions/ People Employed	Grade Level			Promotion Rate (%)
			Low	High	Average	
0332	Computer Operator	4,908	GS-4	GS-11	GS-7	15
0334	Computer Specialist	53,475	GS-5	GS-15	GS-11.4	14
0335	Computer Clerk & Asst.	6,926	GS-3	GS-11	GS-6	18
0356	Data Transcriber	3,135	GS-3	GS-5	GS-3.8	57
1550	Computer Scientist	3,094	GS-9	GS-14	GS-11.6	11

QUALIFICATIONS

Data Transcriber/Computer Operator/Computer Clerk: see "Clerical."

Computer Specialist

GS-5: bachelor's degree in any field
GS-7: one full year of graduate study in any field and/or one year of related work experience
GS-9+: advanced degrees and additional work experience, which varies widely depending on job title and agency-specific duties

Computer Scientist

GS-5: bachelor's degree including at least 30 credits in a combination of mathematics, statistics, and computer science
GS-7: one full year of graduate study in addition to a bachelor's degree and one

year of related professional work experience

GS-9: graduate degree or equivalent academic courses plus two years of related professional work experience

GS-11: Ph.D. or equivalent academic courses and three years of related work experience

GS-12+: various additional requirements depending on agency-specific duties

PATHWAYS: 1, 2, 3

Pathway 1 is used for candidates in computer-related fields at the clerical level (Computer Clerk, Data Transcriber, Computer Operator; see "Clerical" section).

Pathway 2 is often used for entry-level professional positions in the computer field and for Computer Operator (at GS-7 and above), as the job market for these positions is generally characterized by applicant oversupply in most areas. There is no written test, but candidates may be rated (via Form B) and placed on a register. Applicants should contact their local OPM Service Center to determine the current state of the job market.

For mid- and top-level computer professionals in Federal service, pathway 3 applies. Higher-echelon computer programmers, analysts, and designers are generally in short supply, so the job market is in these candidates' favor. They can make direct contact with agencies and apply using the SF-171. The nearest OPM Service Center will supply a list of local agencies that hire such computer professionals.

EDUCATION/TRAINING

Over 30,000 people are currently employed in education and training occupations in the Federal government. Many such positions involve program research and development (R&D) and implementation for schools at the elementary, secondary, and college level. Educators are also hired for vocational training (for example, military training instructors), as well as for actual hands-on classroom teaching (at DOD Dependent Schools overseas and the Bureau of Indian Affairs' schools in the United States).

SERIES, GRADE LEVELS, AND PROMOTION POTENTIAL

GS Series	Job Title	Positions/ People Employed	Grade Level			Promotion Rate (%)
			Low	High	Average	
1700	Education	18,092	GS-4	GS-14	GS-9.4	10–24

QUALIFICATIONS

GS-5–7: bachelor's degree and one year of teaching experience or a minor in education

GS-8–11: master's degree or related work experience

GS-12+: Ph.D. and/or additional related work experience

PATHWAY: 3

All educators are hired directly by agencies with job openings. Educators with extensive experience in project development and implementation may be hired by the Department of Education. The DOD hires many primary and secondary school teachers to teach the children of military personnel who have been stationed overseas (Dependent Schools). The Bureau of Prisons also hires many teachers, particularly those with experience in adult education, English as a Second Language (ESL), and vocational training. The Bureau of Indian Affairs directly hires teachers for its schools on reservations, which are mostly in the Southwest and Northeast (qualified Native American candidates receive preference). Application packages can be obtained by writing to these agencies.

Recent college grads interested in educational research and program analysis may apply to the Department of Education regarding its Career Intern Program (see Appendix Q).

ENGINEERS

Currently there are over 160,000 engineers employed by the Federal government nationwide. The demand for engineers is so great that some agencies offer one-year paid sabbaticals for further education in one's field of expertise or for broadening one's knowledge in other engineering fields. Special salary rates have also been instituted to compete more aggresively with the private sector.

Engineering specialties in short supply include Civil, Environmental, Mechanical, Electronics, Nuclear, Aerospace, Chemical, Industrial, Construction, and Architecture.

SERIES, GRADE LEVELS, AND PROMOTION POTENTIAL

GS Series	Job Title	Positions/ People Employed	Grade Level			Promotion Rate (%)
			Low	High	Average	
0802	Engineering Technician	18,593	GS-3	GS-13	GS-9.5	13
0803	Safety Engineer	527	GS-5	GS-15	GS-12.1	9
0804	Fire Prevention Engineer	157	GS-7	GS-14	GS-12.2	13
0806	Materials Engineer	1,143	GS-7	GS-15	GS-12.2	13
0807	Landscape Architect	663	GS-5	GS-15	GS-11.3	9
0808	Architect	1,877	GS-7	GS-15	GS-11.9	9
0809	Construction Controller	2,383	GS-4	GS-13	GS-9	11
0810	Civil Engineer	12,756	GS-7	GS-15	GS-12	13
0817	Surveying Technician	608	GS-3	GS-18	GS-5.4	17
0818	Engineering Drafter	399	GS-3	GS-9	GS-6	7
0819	Environmental Engineer	5,328	GS-5	GS-15	GS-11.8	14

0828	Construction Analyst	316	GS-7	GS-13	GS-11.2	17
0830	Mechanical Engineer	10,641	GS-5	GS-15	GS-11.6	10
0840	Nuclear Engineer	2,360	GS-5	GS-15	GS-12	8
0850	Electrical Engineer	4,194	GS-5	GS-15	GS-11.7	13
0854	Computer Engineer	2,458	GS-7	GS-15	GS-12.3	15
0855	Electronics Engineer	25,456	GS-5	GS-15	GS-11.9	15
0856	Electronics Technician	11,345	GS-5	GS-14	GS-10.8	10
0858	Biomedical Engineer	289	GS-5	GS-15	GS-11.3	12
0861	Aerospace Engineer	8,228	GS-7	GS-15	GS-12.5	17
0871	Naval Architect	852	GS-7	GS-15	GS-12.4	11
0873	Ship Surveyor	147	GS-9	GS-14	GS-12.2	8
0880	Mining Engineer	299	GS-9	GS-15	GS-12.2	3
0881	Petroleum Engineer	345	GS-7	GS-15	GS-12.4	8
0890	Agricultural Engineer	357	GS-7	GS-15	GS-11.3	9
0892	Ceramic Engineer	46	GS-9	GS-15	GS-12.9	12
0893	Chemical Engineer	1,155	GS-7	GS-15	GS-12	8
0894	Welding Engineer	52	GS-7	GS-15	GS-11.8	11
0895	Industrial Engineering Techn.	1,525	GS-5	GS-13	GS-9.8	7
0896	Industrial Engineer	1,833	GS-5	GS-15	GS-11.4	11
0899	Engrg. & Arch. Student Trainee	544	GS-2	GS-12	GS-4.2	76

QUALIFICATIONS

GS-5: bachelor's degree
GS-7: bachelor's degree and one year of experience or work on a master's degree
GS-9+: vary widely depending on the position

PATHWAYS: 2, 3

> The **Form B** in Appendix H (p. 501) is a sample only; you must submit an original of this or any computer-scanned forms.

OPM has granted Direct Hire Authority to all agencies for qualified candidates. In addition, there is a national register, or *Automated Applicant Referral Service (AARS),* available for those who wish broad geographic consideration. To be listed on the AARS list, candidates must fill out a Form B, which is available from the nearest OPM Service Center. Mail the completed form to:

OPM Staffing Services Center
Examining Office
P.O. Box 9105
Macon, GA 31297-5099

FIRE PROTECTION AND PREVENTION

Most of the 10,000 Firefighters, Fire Communications Operators, Fire Protection Inspectors, and Fire Protection Specialists employed full-time by the Federal government are in the Department of Defense, although there are also some in the Department of Veterans Affairs (VA) and the Forest Service.

The Forest Service also hires approximately 5,000 *seasonal* Firefighters, mainly at GS-3–5, to work during the months of May through September.

Many of these are college students, some of whom upon graduation go on to permanent positions as Firefighters with the Forest Service.

Firefighters at the DOD combat fires involving structures, including ships and industrial plants, and those resulting from aircraft crashes and other operational accidents; they also rescue crew and/or passengers from crashed or burning aircraft and drive motorized equipment. Forest Service Firefighters, not surprisingly, combat forest fires.

Fire Communications Operators operate telegraph, telephone, and radio equipment to receive and transmit alarms and messages in text or code. They must be knowledgeable not only in communications operations but also in firefighting techniques, to facilitate the dispatching of firefighting personnel and apparatus.

Fire Protection Inspectors investigate, detect, and initiate action to eliminate fire hazards. They also review construction projects for adherence to fire codes, and give lectures and conduct training classes in fire prevention.

Fire Protection Specialists (often called Fire Marshals) develop plans and standards for firefighting and fire prevention programs, and perform technical and Administrative functions related to the organization, training, and maintenance of firefighting units at the headquarters levels.

Fire Chiefs are responsible for the management of a program of fire prevention and protection. They lead and direct firefighters in the suppression of fires and saving of lives and property, and are responsible for the overall supervision and management of a fire department.

SERIES AND GRADE LEVELS

Because agency statistics are compiled for OPM on a series-number basis, no breakdown of positions/people employed, average grade level, or promotion rate is available for the various job titles that comprise GS-0081.

GS Series	Job Title	Grade Level	
		Low	High
0081	Firefighter	GS-3	GS-5
0081	Supervisory Firefighter	GS-6	GS-10
0081	Fire Communications Operator	GS-4	GS-7
0081	Fire Protection Inspector	GS-5	GS-9
0081	Fire Protection Specialist	GS-5	GS-13
0081	Fire Chief	GS-6	GS-12

QUALIFICATIONS

GS-3: one year of general work experience

GS-5: at least two years of firefighting experience plus one year of general work experience

GS-7+: qualifications vary greatly depending on job title and agency specifics.

PATHWAYS: 2, 3

The overwhelming majority of Firefighter positions are with the DOD at Army, Navy, and Air Force bases. Both the DOD and VA have Direct Hire Authority for all job titles at their facilities, so applicants are not required to take a written test. Sometimes, if a large number of positions are going to be filled, a Register of Eligibles is assembled based on SF-171 ratings; applicants are then called for interviews in rank order as vacancies arise (Pathway 2). When there are few vacancies, registers are not used; applications are rated and qualified applicants are interviewed immediately (Pathway 3).

The Forest Service and the Park Service both hire Firefighters on a seasonal basis, in addition to a few on a full-time, permanent basis. Both agencies have Direct Hire Authority for all firefighting positions, maintaining their own registers and conducting their own recruitment (usually during January–March, as for their other summer positions).

FOOD INSPECTION

The USDA's Food Safety and Inspection Service (FSIS), with a staff of nearly 10,000, is one of the largest public health agencies in the world. Its job is to ensure that the meat and poultry we eat is safe. Consequently, the FSIS employs Food Inspectors, Food Technologists, Veterinarians, Microbiologists, and Chemists, as well as Clerical/Administrative support staff.

The largest group comprises the more than 6,000 Food Inspectors at over 50 locations throughout the country. They protect against the distribution of substandard meat and poultry by inspecting animals at commercial slaughterhouses before and after slaughter. Other Food Inspectors work at processing plants, overseeing operations to ensure that canned and packaged products are properly processed and accurately labeled.

Food Inspectors often work in highly mechanized plants and may have to perform their duties near moving machinery, on slippery floors, and in extreme conditions (temperature, noise, odor). To ensure that applicants can withstand the rigors of the job, all candidates are required to undergo an extensive medical exam. Positions are most frequently filled in New York, Massachusetts, North Carolina, California, Nebraska, and Kansas.

SERIES, GRADE LEVELS, AND PROMOTION POTENTIAL

GS Series	Job Title	Positions/ People Employed	Grade Level			Promotion Rate (%)
			Low	High	Average	
1863	Food Inspector	6,582	GS-5	GS-12	GS-7.9	6

QUALIFICATIONS

To qualify for a Food Inspector position, applicants must first pass the FSIS exam (score at least 70 points). In addition, a candidate must have:

GS-5: a college degree in a relevant field such as zoology, biology, chemistry, veterinary medicine, food technology, or appropriate agricultural subjects, *or* three years of related work experience (say, as a veterinary assistant; in field disease control; at a public stockyard, ranch, farm, or hatchery; or in livestock or poultry slaughtering and/or processing).

GS-7: an additional year of experience that demonstrates knowledge of Federal regulations governing the food industry, or additional education at the rate of one year for nine months of the required additional experience.

PATHWAY: 1

All applicants must take the FSIS exam, receive a rating, and then be placed on a Register of Eligibles from which the names of candidates are selected in rank order. To obtain an application package and test scheduling card, write:

U.S. Department of Agriculture
Food Safety and Inspection Service
P.O.B., Examining Unit (P)
Butler Square West, 4th Floor
100 N. Sixth Street
Minneapolis, MN 55403

FOREIGN SERVICE AND ASSOCIATED

Strictly speaking, the term "Foreign Service" only applies to Foreign Service Officers (the "Diplomatic Corps"), who work for the Department of State, the U.S. Information Agency (USIA), or the Department of Commerce. Those in the State Department deal with diplomatic relationships between governments; USIA Officers are involved with the dissemination of information about our country through the foreign news media; and those in Commerce act as liaisons between local businesses and American companies, encouraging trade and business between the United States and the host country. In a looser sense, however, the Foreign Service is often taken to include the various support personnel required to run such enterprises, such as those with secretarial, medical, or communications skills, for a total of 8,780 employees (3,758 of whom are support personnel).

The **Foreign Service** is also covered in Step 2 (p. 48).

When considering a Foreign Service career, bear in mind that the average Foreign Service employee spends 25 years with the department and 60% of that time abroad. All candidates for the Foreign Service—whether Foreign Service Officer, Nurse, Communications Electronics Officer, or Secretary—must be willing to accept assignments at any of over 240 U.S. embassies and consulates overseas or in Washington, DC. Over the course of a career, assignments might include countries with politically unstable environments, harsh climates, or health or security hazards.

Only after a first tour of duty may one bid for specific available posts.

All job titles in the Foreign Service are on a pay schedule separate from the rest of the government (and hence have no GS series/grades). Current pay rates for Foreign Service Officers are shown in Appendix F; pay rates for other positions vary greatly according to job title, responsibilities, and the candidate's education and previous work experience. In addition, higher salaries apply in designated hardship posts. The government pays travel expenses to and from the locations overseas and, in most cases, covers housing, medical, and educational expenses.

Below is a list of the job titles most common in the Foreign Service. In-depth coverage of Foreign Service Officer follows, as do descriptions of the opportunities for Foreign Service Secretary and Communications Electronics Officer. All inquiries regarding Foreign Service Officer (and its exam) should be addressed to the State Department; application packages for all job titles listed can be obtained by contacting one or more of these agencies:

Department of State	Department of Commerce	U.S. Information Agency
Recruitment Div. FSBE	Room 3226	Special Recruitment Div.
P.O. Box 12226	14th & Constitution Avenue	301 4th Street, NW
Arlington, VA 22219	Washington, DC 20230	Washington, DC 20547

MAJOR JOB TITLES

Foreign Service Officer	Engineering Officer	Communication Electronics
Foreign Service Secretary	Communications Officer	Officer
Diplomatic Courier	Support Communications	Medical Officer
Diplomatic Security Officer	Officer	Nurse Practitioner

FOREIGN SERVICE OFFICER

Foreign Service Officers work in political, economic, counseling, and Administrative fields in Washington, DC, and U.S. embassies and consulates abroad. Because of the rapidly evolving nature of foreign affairs, Foreign Service Officers are needed with expertise not only in the traditional areas of diplomacy, but also in a variety of new areas—ocean fishing disputes, toxic waste dumping, earth sciences, terrorism, and international narcotics trafficking, to name a few. Although roughly 250 officers are commissioned each year, some 20,000 candidates take the test; clearly, only those with the most outstanding scores are selected off the register. There are currently 5,022 Foreign Service Officers.

Qualifications

All candidates for the position of Foreign Service Officer must pass the Foreign Service Exam, be a U.S. citizen of at least 20 years of age at the time of application, and successfully pass security and medical checks before assignment.

Pathway: 1

All candidates for Foreign Service Officer must first contact the State Department (at the address given above) to obtain application packages and test scheduling cards for the Foreign Service Exam. When applying to take the exam, applicants must indicate for which of the three agencies they are interested in working. (The USIA and Department of Commerce do hire Foreign Service Officers, but the majority of such positions are with the State Department.) Those who successfully complete the stringent application process will then be placed on the Foreign Service Officer register for the agency or agencies chosen, and contacted when there is a vacancy.

The Foreign Service Exam is given every year; the most recent one was given in November 1992 and required half a day (about four hours) to complete. Part I tests the applicant's basic knowledge of crucial domestic and foreign institutions and concepts; some of the fields covered are history, economics, geography, business and finance, political science, current events, international relations, general management, and comparative cultures. Parts II and III test an applicant's writing ability and verbal/numerical reasoning competency. The final section, a biographical questionnaire, measures an individual's experience, skills, and achievements. Though a bachelor's degree is not a requirement for taking the exam, candidates who score highly usually do have degrees and a broad knowledge of U.S. and world history, foreign policy, international economics, and foreign cultures.

Based on the exam results, the Foreign Service annually invites some 3,000 candidates to be interviewed at a regional assessment center (Boston, Chicago, Atlanta, Dallas, Los Angeles, or Washington, DC). The interview process usually lasts a full day, and candidates must cover their own expenses. Included are two written exercises and an oral exam; in addition, candidates must participate in a group effort with five other applicants to demonstrate their presentation, negotiation, and consensus-building skills. Factors used in grading candidates include their judgment, analytical ability, political and cultural sensitivity, and self-confidence. Approximately 20% of those invited to the assessment center will be chosen for a Register of Eligibles. Most people who actually land positions as Foreign Service Officers have been through the assessment process two or three times.

FOREIGN SERVICE SECRETARY

Foreign Service Secretaries perform duties beyond those normally associated with the secretarial profession. Assignments may include handling official telegraphic messages and diplomatic pouches. At a post of any size, a Secretary may be requested to work with high-level delegations, perhaps related to visits by the President, Secretary of State, or other dignitaries. Experienced secretaries can reportedly receive starting salaries as high as $24,772. Candidates can advance to the next pay level in one year, and can earn extra pay by passing qualifying tests in a foreign language during the first 30 days of training.

Qualifications

Candidates must be U.S. citizens and at least 21 years old at the time of appointment. In addition, they must have a high school diploma, two years of secretarial experience (or a combination of further education and work experience), the ability to type 60 wpm, experience with word processors and/or computers, and a general knowledge of world events. Although candidates do not have to undergo security checks, they must have a complete medical checkup.

Pathway: 2

The **special address** for Foreign Service Secretary applications to the **Department of State** is given in Appendix D (p. 227).

No exam is required. Candidates apply directly via the SF-171 to any or all of the three hiring agencies previously mentioned. Qualified applicants are placed on a register and contacted as the need arises; at that point, they must interview with the Foreign Service Board of Examiners (as must all candidates for all Foreign Service positions).

COMMUNICATIONS ELECTRONICS OFFICER

Communications Electronics Officers are responsible for the installation, maintenance, and repair of telecommunications equipment, ranging from telephones to sophisticated computer networks. Salaries start at approximately $28,050 and go as high as $37,467.

Qualifications

Candidates must be U.S. citizens and at least 21 years old at the time of appointment. They must also be able to type 40 wpm (there is *no* waiver for this typing requirement), and pass medical and security checks before assignment. A minimum of two years of specialized experience and an associate degree in applied science from an accredited college or university is required; however, successful completion of additional technical training or college courses in related fields may substitute for specialized experience on the basis of one year of full-time education for six months of experience.

Pathway: 2

No exam is required. Candidates apply directly via the SF-171 to any or all of the three hiring agencies previously mentioned. Qualified applicants are placed on a register and contacted as the need arises; at that point, they must interview with the Foreign Service Board of Examiners.

FORESTRY

Several different opportunities exist for individuals who wish to do work associated with the natural environment for the Federal government. The USDA's Forest

Service and Soil Conservation Service, the Department of Interior's National Park Service, and the Department of the Army all have positions that involve working on national lands and waterways. (The Army Corps of Engineers is responsible for over eight million acres of parks in the South and Southwest.) Both professional and technical positions are continuously being filled, and both full-time and seasonal work is available at many locations.

SERIES, NUMBER EMPLOYED, AND PROMOTION POTENTIAL

GS Series	Job Title	Positions/ People Employed	Grade Level			Promotion Rate (%)
			Low	High	Average	
0025	Park Ranger	4,740	GS-3	GS-14	GS-7.1	18
0457	Soil Conservationist	4,314	GS-5	GS-14	GS-10.3	9
0458	Soil Conservation Tech.	1,452	GS-3	GS-8	GS-6	12
0460	Forester	4,422	GS-5	GS-15	GS-10.9	7
0462	Forestry Technician	7,309	GS-2	GS-11	GS-5.4	14

PATHWAY: 2

Park Rangers, Soil Conservationists, and Foresters are hired by the Forest Service, Army, Soil Conservation Service, and National Park Service. Soil Conservation Technicians and Forest Technicians are hired by the Soil Conservation Service and Forest Service, respectively. All of these agencies have Direct Hire Authority for these positions; however, because so many applications are received, each agency usually assembles registers of qualified applicants to be contacted when vacancies arise. Applicants should contact the hiring agencies directly for application forms.

> **Park Ranger** is profiled under "Law Enforcement."

FORESTER

Foresters, hired exclusively by the National Forest Service, are responsible for managing the nearly 200 million acres of the National Forest System, where work sites can vary from glaciers to rainforests. Foresters, of whom there are presently 5,393, play an important role in organizing and handling such resources as water, soil, air, range, fish, wildlife, timber, wilderness, and minerals. Key duties include valuing and purchasing land, preparing and reviewing plans for special studies, and inspection of recreational and mineral projects.

Qualifications

Most Foresters are hired by the Forest Service at the trainee level, usually GS-5 or 7, directly out of college. Graduates must have a degree in forestry or a related field. Course history must include study of the management of renewable resources, forest biology, and forest resource measurements and inventory. Applicants who do not have a college degree may substitute related environmental work experience for education to qualify.

FORESTRY TECHNICIAN

Forestry Technicians assist Foresters by providing information on public lands for visitors, maintaining campground areas, handling vegetation, and assisting with forest fires.

Qualifications

Technicians enter the Forest Service anywhere from GS-2 up to GS-5, depending on a combination of related work experience and education.

SOIL CONSERVATION TECHNICIAN

Soil Conservation Technicians assist Soil Conservationists by helping to install equipment needed to follow through on the latter's recommendations. Typical tasks might include the design and implementation of land-saving practices such as waterways, terraces, and contour strip-cropping.

Qualifications

Candidates should have a knowledge of farm or ranch operations. Any additional related work or educational experience makes an applicant more attractive to the hiring agency.

HEALTH CARE

Over 140,000 health service practitioners are employed in Federal service. Of these some 51,000 are Nurses, 30,000 are Nursing or Dental Assistants, 10,000 are Medical Officers, 8,000 are Dental Officers, 6,000 are Medical Technicians, 3,000 are Pharmacists, and 2,000 are Physical Therapists.

Health care professionals work in Department of Defense hospitals and medical facilities, VA hospitals, Indian Health Service hospitals and clinics, at National Institutes of Health (NIH) facilities, and for the Federal Bureau of Prisons.

MAJOR SERIES, GRADE LEVELS, AND PROMOTION POTENTIAL

GS Series	Job Title	Positions/ People Employed	Grade Level			Promotion Rate (%)
			Low	High	Average	
0602	Medical Officer	8,804	GS-12	GS-15	GS-14.7	2
0610	Nurse (all types)	6,978	GS-6	GS-13	GS-10.4	8
0621	Nursing Assistant	12,660	GS-3	GS-7	GS-4.4	4
0633	Physical Therapist	587	GS-7	GS-12	GS-9.5	13
0645	Medical Technician (all types)	1,871	GS-3	GS-9	GS-5.7	8
0660	Pharmacist	4,230	GS-9	GS-14	GS-11.2	4
0680	Dental Officer	794	GS-12	GS-15	GS-14.6	3
0681	Dental Assistant	2,421	GS-3	GS-6	GS-4.6	7

> For additional health care **job titles** and their descriptions, see Appendix K.

QUALIFICATIONS

Medical Officer/Dental Officer

GS-11: Candidates require an M.D., D.M.D., or D.D.S. degree from an accredited medical school. For positions involving patient care responsibility, candidates must have a permanent, current, full, and unrestricted license to practice medicine in a U.S. state or territory, the District of Columbia, or the Commonwealth of Puerto Rico.

GS-12+: Additional experience is needed, appropriate to the position being filled.

> More on **qualifications** for health care positions is given under "Nursing" and "Medical Technician and Related" (p. 175).

Physical Therapist

GS-5: Candidates must have successfully completed an accredited curriculum in physical therapy and have a clinical affiliation.

Higher grade levels additionally require:

GS-7: one more full academic year of graduate education

GS-9: master's degree or equivalent

GS-11: Ph.D. or equivalent

GS-12: varies depending on agency

Pharmacist

GS-7: Candidates must have a bachelor's degree from an approved pharmacy school, have completed one year of internship, and be licensed to practice pharmacy in a U.S. state or territory, the District of Columbia, or the Commonwealth of Puerto Rico. Higher grade levels additionally require:

GS-9: one more year of postlicensure professional pharmacy experience or equivalent educational experience

GS-11: two more years of graduate work or equivalent

GS-12+: varying degrees of supervisory experience

Dental Assistant

GS-2: high school diploma

GS-3: one year of dental assistance/hygiene program or equivalent

GS-4: two years of dental program or equivalent

GS-5–6: courses in dental assistance/hygiene directly related to intraoral procedures.

PATHWAY: 3

Health care professionals are in great demand by the Federal government. In particular, Medical Officers, Nurses, Pharmacists, and Physical Therapists are in a position to walk into virtually any facility and be hired on the spot. Those who wish to avail themselves of a central register can apply directly to the Department of Veterans Affairs or through OPM using a Form B. Geographic area of preference can be indicated on the form; interested Federal employers will contact the applicant.

All agencies have Direct Hire Authority for these positions. Applicants may directly contact any hiring agency or DOD branch to inquire about medical vacancies and facilities. A list of DOD bases is provided in Appendix D.

NURSING

Nursing is one of the highest-demand occupations nationwide, and the Fed-eral government is no exception. There are currently more than 200,000 vacancies today, and this number is expected to reach 600,000 by the mid to late 1990s. A nurse can literally walk into a Federal agency, be interviewed, and get hired on the spot. Most hiring occurs at the GS-9/11/12 levels. All agencies that employ nurses offer special salary rates, which vary regionally and according to nursing speciality. It is not uncommon for nurses in large metropolitan areas to earn $30,000–40,000 a year at entry level. Benefits for nurses (and some others) include flexible hours and advanced training and/or graduate school paid for by the agency. Marketable job titles include the following:

Clinical Nurse	Psychiatric Nurse	Research Nurse
Commodity Health Nurse	Nurse Anesthetist	Nurse Consultant
Occupational Health Nurse	Nurse Educator	Nurse Midwife
Operating Room Nurse	Nurse Practitioner	Nurse Specialist

Qualifications

Candidates require a bachelor's degree in science (B.S.), plus

GS-5: six months of professional experience or one year of graduate-level education

GS-9: one year of experience or a master's degree

GS-11: two years of experience or three full years of graduate education

Pathway: 3

All agencies have been granted Direct Hire Authority for Nurses. Agencies hiring the most nurses include the Department of Veterans Affairs, Indian Health Service, National Institutes of Health, Bureau of Prisons, and the Department of Defense. Interested applicants are urged to contact the personnel office of the agency for which they would like to work, and/or to contact their local OPM for a Competition Notice for nurses and a list of agencies hiring in their area.

MEDICAL TECHNICIAN AND RELATED

There are more than 6,000 openings for Medical Technicians and other nondegree health care workers in the Federal sector every year. Job opportunities exist in every state. The most common job titles include the following:

0603	Physician's Assistant	0661	Pharmacy Technician
0621	Nursing Assistant	0682	Dental Assistant
0631	Occupational Therapy Technician	0699	Health Aid Technician
0645	Medical Technician		

Qualifications

GS-1: no specialized experience

GS-2: one-half year of general laboratory (or applicable medical) experience or a high school diploma

GS-3: one year of study that includes at least six credits in chemistry, biology, or other job-specific subjects

Pathways: 2, 3

Depending on geographic market conditions and the particular speciality, agencies may either have Direct Hire Authority for such positions (Pathway 3) or use a register without test assembled by a local OPM (Pathway 2). Agencies that hire the most health technicians include the VA, Indian Health Service, NIH, Bureau of Prisons, and the Department of Defense. Contact your local OPM Service Center and/or the agencies directly to find out which pathways are being used in your area.

INTELLIGENCE

Excepted agency positions are discussed in Step 7 (p. 120).

Most Federal employees in the intelligence field work in the following excepted agencies:

Central Intelligence Agency (CIA)
National Security Agency (NSA)
Federal Bureau of Investigation (FBI)

The remainder are hired through the Administrative program to work in these Competitive Service agencies:

See the "**ACWA**" section in this Appendix.

Defense Intelligence Agency
Departments of the Army/Navy/Air Force
Bureau of Intelligence and Research (Department of State)
Department of Energy
Department of Treasury

SERIES, GRADE LEVELS, AND PROMOTION POTENTIAL

The number of people in each job title is classified: Employee counts and grade-level averages are available only for each series as a whole. Promotion rates are unavailable.

GS Series	Job Title	Positions/ People Employed	Grade Level		
			Low	High	Average
Competitive Service					
0132	Intelligence Operation Specialist	N/A	GS-5	GS-15	GS-11
0132	Intelligence Research Specialist	N/A	GS-5	GS-15	GS-11
0134	Intelligence Aid and Clerk	N/A	GS-3	GS-10	GS-6.7
Excepted Service					
0132	Intelligence Operations Officer	N/A	GS-5	GS-15	GS-11
0132	Intelligence Research Officer	N/A	GS-5	GS-15	GS-11
Total (Competitive and Excepted)					
0132	(all relevant titles)	3,760			GS-11.7
0134	(all relevant titles)	288			GS-6.7

QUALIFICATIONS

Applicants for Intelligence Officer/Researcher/Specialist must must not have reached their 35th birthday at the time of assignment, and have at least a bachelor's degree with high academic performance. Work experience or graduate-level education enhance one's application. Applicants undergo a rigorous battery of intelligence, psychological, and medical tests, as well as a detailed investigation into past activities. Applicants for Intelligence Aid and Clerk should see the "Clerical" section in this Appendix.

PATHWAYS: 1, 3

For Competitive Service positions applicants would be well advised to use the Outstanding Scholar Program (OSP) or "name request" method, as competition for these positions is keen.

> **OSP** is discussed in Appendix Q; **name requests** are explained in Step 2 (p. 43).

Those interested in applying to excepted agencies should contact them directly. The screening process for intelligence jobs in these agencies is extremely elaborate and may require months to complete. Very few applicants are selected: Some observers report that thousands are considered for every one who eventually becomes an Intelligence Officer.

> A list of **Excepted Service** agencies appears in Appendix D.

LAW ENFORCEMENT

Law enforcement is one of the largest career fields in Federal service, with over 74,000 employees. Many positions in this field occur in the regular Competitive Service; many others are in specialized law enforcement agencies. Most professional law enforcement positions in the Competitive Service—that is, those that require a college degree or its equivalent—are in Administrative program Group 6, Law Enforcement and Investigation. Various other Competitive Service positions in law enforcement are recruited either through the OPM via Pathway 2 or by agencies directly via Pathway 3. Below is a general review of the most common job titles in the law enforcement field in Federal service. Individual descriptions for most of these job titles can be found in Appendix K. All but one (FBI Agent) are in the Competitive Service.

SERIES AND PATHWAYS

GS Series	Job Title	Pathway	Section(s) Where Discussed
0007	Correctional Officer	3	Corrections
0025	Park Ranger	1	Park Service/Administrative
0080	Security Administration	1	Administrative
0082	Deputy U.S. Marshal	3	Deputy U.S. Marshal
0083	Police	2	Police and Guard
0085	Guard	2	Police and Guard
1169	Internal Revenue Officer	1	Internal Revenue Service/Administrative
1810	General Investigator	1	Administrative
1811	DEA Agent	3	Drug Enforcement Agent
1811	FBI Agent	3	Federal Bureau of Investigation
1811	Internal Revenue Agent	3	IRS Agent
1811	Secret Service Agent	3	Secret Service
1811	Treasury Enforcement Agent	1	Treasury Enforcement Agent
1816	Immigration Inspection	1	Immigration & Naturalization/Administrative
1854	Alcohol, Tobacco, & Firearms Insp.	1	Alcohol, Tobacco, & Firearms Insp.
1890	Customs Inspector	1	Administrative
1896	Border Patrol Agent	1	Immigration & Naturalization/Administrative

ALCOHOL, TOBACCO, AND FIREARMS INSPECTORS

Inspectors at the Bureau of Alcohol, Tobacco, and Firearms enforce firearms laws and examine the production, use, and distribution of alcohol and tobacco. They break up interstate arson schemes, suppress illicit distilled-spirit trafficking, and combat the interstate trafficking of contraband tobacco and explosives. A full-field background investigation, drug tests, and medical exam are conducted before qualified applicants are appointed.

CORRECTIONS

Correctional Officers supervise, guide, and ensure the custody of criminal offenders in Federal prisons. They are hired by the Federal Bureau of Prisons (BOP), and the need for them is constant. Because their work is so demanding, Correctional Officers have a career ladder enabling them to reach GS-13 faster than other Federal employees. The position of Correctional Officer starts at GS-6, but after six months of satisfactory service a Correctional Officer can qualify for an "advanced promotion" to GS-7. Although Correctional Officers do not usually carry firearms while on the job, *all* Federal Corrections personnel, including Accountants and Food Service Workers, are required to take a three-week training session at the Federal Staff Training Center in Glynco, GA.

The Bureau of Prisons, the fastest growing Federal agency today, offers many unique and challenging job opportunities. Although most new hires are Correctional Officers, there is a need for those with expertise in over fifty different occupational groups, including health care, social work, accounting, marketing, sanitation, food service, personnel, administration, education, and recreation. Many Correctional Officers go on to other areas within the BOP, the most notable being Case Treatment Specialist (Case Manager) at the prison sites. In addition, many Correctional Officers become Shop Foremen and Supervisors for BOP's Prison Industries Division (trade name UNICOR), which runs inmate work programs in over 70 shops nationwide. These shops manufacture a diverse line of products—furniture, mattresses, textiles, electronic cable assemblies, and so on—that can only be sold to government agencies. The Department of Defense is a major contractor for UNICOR products.

Series, Grade Levels, and Promotion Potential

GS Series	Job Title	Positions/ People Employed	Grade Level			Promotion Rate (%)
			Low	High	Average	
0007	Correctional Officer	11,935	GS-6	GS-11	GS-7.6	32

Qualifications

Note: Applicants not already in Federal law enforcement must not have reached their 35th birthday at the time of appointment.

GS-6: bachelor's degree and one year of graduate education related to law enforcement or a combination of education and work experience, such as counseling in welfare or social services (such as employment for three and a half years in rehabilitation, corrections, or a related field)

Pathway: 3

All applications, including those initially sent to a local prison facility (except for Clerical positions, which are hired by local prisons), are sent to BOP headquarters in Washington, DC. Once rated, candidates are referred in rank order to prisons with job vacancies. Applicants can receive the current list of BOP job vacancies nationwide and an application package either by contacting a local prison facility or by writing to:

Bureau of Prisons
Special Examining Unit, Room 400
320 First St., NW
Washington, DC 20534

DEPUTY U.S. MARSHAL

Deputy U.S. Marshals perform a wide range of law enforcement duties, including serving warrants, tracing and arresting persons wanted under court warrants, seizing and disposing of property under court orders, and providing for the physical security of jurors and key government witnesses and their families. Deputy Marshals are required to carry firearms and be proficient in their use, operate motor vehicles, and work irregular hours as necessary. Performance of these duties may involve personal risk, considerable travel, and arduous physical exertion.

Series, Grade Levels, and Promotion Potential

Deputy U.S. Marshals are hired at GS-5/7 and promoted up to GS-11; at that point they can compete for higher-level jobs as Criminal Investigators (GS-1811); they seldom become U.S. Marshals, since those positions are appointed directly by the president. There are currently 2,315 full-time Deputy U.S. Marshals.

GS Series	Job Title	Positions/ People Employed	Grade Level			Promotion Rate (%)
			Low	High	Average	
0082	Deputy U.S. Marshal	2,315	GS-5	GS-11	GS-9.2	65

Qualifications

Candidates must pass the Deputy U.S. Marshal's Exam plus have either a bachelor's degree or a combination of education and work experience totaling at least three years.

Pathway: 1

Applicants should contact their local OPM and ask to fill out a 5000 A/B, the exam request form. The test is given in an area when a sufficient number of individuals have signed up to take it.

DRUG ENFORCEMENT AGENT

The Drug Enforcement Agency (DEA) investigates and prosecutes those who take part in the promotion, distribution, and sale of illegal drugs. DEA Agents are Criminal Investigators (GS-1811) who specialize in drug-related criminal activity.

Series, Grade Levels, and Promotion Potential

GS Series	Job Title	Positions/ People Employed	Grade Level			Promotion Rate (%)
			Low	High	Average	
1811	DEA Agent	N/A	GS-7	GS-15	GS-12.1	30

Qualifications

Note: All first-time applicants for Federal law enforcement positions must be no more than 35 years of age at the time of appointment.

GS-5: bachelor's degree with a minimum GPA of 2.95 or three years of general work experience, or a combination of education and work experience of at least three years

GS-7: one year of graduate level study or of specialized work experience (such as investigative experience as a member of a military intelligence or criminal investigation, or the preparation of comprehensive documented reports and responsibility for testifying in court)

GS-9: two years of graduate study in a field related to law enforcement or of specialized work experience in law enforcement, so as to yield a total of five years education and/or work experience

GS-11+: combined education and related work experience totaling at least six years

Pathway: 3

Applicants should write directly to the DEA, which has Direct Hire Authority for DEA Agents:

Drug Enforcement Administration
Special Agent Recruiting Unit
1405 I Street, NW
Washington, DC 20537

FEDERAL BUREAU OF INVESTIGATION

FBI Special Agents conduct surveillance, investigate suspects and witnesses, and apprehend fugitives and criminals. They are paid at the GS-10 level upon admittance for training at the FBI Academy in Quantico, VA, and can advance to GS-13 through field assignment work. Depending upon assignment, Special Agents can make up to $66,522 in metropolitan areas in as few as three years. Promotions are available into supervisory, executive, and management positions. The FBI, an excepted agency, also has a constant need for clerical and technical support staff.

> **Excepted agency positions** are discussed in Step 7 (p. 120).

Series, Grade Levels, and Promotion Potential

GS Series	Job Title	Positions/ People Employed	Grade Level			Promotion Rate (%)
			Low	High	Average	
0318	Secretary	1,218	GS-4	GS-9	GS-5.6	22
0322	Clerk/Typist	789	GS-2	GS-6	GS-3.6	15
0334	Computer Specialist	413	GS-5	GS-15	GS-11.4	23
0800	Engineer (various specialties)	510	GS-4	GS-15	GS-11.3	12–32
1040	Language Specialist	322	GS-7	GS-15	GS-10.4	22
1811	Special Agent	10,400	GS-7	GS-15	GS-12.1	30

Qualifications

Requirements for applicants to obtain a spot on the FBI Special Agent register are quite rigorous. All candidates must be U.S. citizens between the ages of 23 and 35, have a bachelor's degree, and qualify for one of these five entry-level programs:

> **FBI positions** other than Special Agent are covered in applicable sections throughout this appendix.

law: a J.D. (Jurist Doctorate) degree from an accredited law school
accounting: B.S. degree with a major in accounting and eligibility to take the CPA exam
engineering/science: B.S. in engineering, computer science, or physical science
language: proficiency in one of the languages needed by the FBI, which currently include various Asian languages (including several Chinese dialects), Russian, Spanish, and Arabic
diversified: bachelor's degree in any discipline plus three years of full-time work experience, or a master's degree with two years of full-time work experience

Pathway: 3

Because it is an excepted agency, the FBI conducts all its own hiring for all positions. In recent years it has decentralized its hiring, so individuals can now apply directly to any of its 56 field offices nationwide. An FBI phone number appears in every phone book in the country; alternatively, you may write to the FBI headquarters address given in Appendix D.

IMMIGRATION AND NATURALIZATION

The two major law enforcement occupations at the Immigration and Naturalization Service (INS) are Border Patrol Agent and Immigration Inspector.

Border Patrol Agents detect and apprehend aliens who have entered the country illegally, as well as persons who smuggle such aliens in. Enforcement duties are carried out by patrol and surveillance, primarily along international boundaries and coastal areas.

Immigration Inspectors interview persons who seek to enter, reside in, or pass through the United States, and inspect records of their citizenship staus to determine whether they are legally eligible to enter. A key responsibility of Immigration Inspectors is to prevent the entry of those who are legally ineligible. Work is primarily at ports of entry, whether by land, sea, or air.

Series, Grade Levels, and Promotion Potential

GS Series	Job Title	Positions/ People Employed	Grade Level			Promotion Rate (%)
			Low	High	Average	
1816	Immigration Inspector	3,894	GS-5	GS-14	GS-8.6	25
1896	Border Patrol Agent	5,368	GS-5	GS-14	GS-9.6	42

Qualifications

Border Patrol Agent

GS-5: a minimum of one year of experience that demonstrates the ability to take charge, maintain composure, and make sound decisions in stress situations (such as work as a claims adjuster, building guard, or customer relations)

GS-7+: responsible law enforcement or other experience and/or education and training that conferred the ability to make arrests, use sound judgment in the use of firearms, analyze information rapidly, and so on (such as correctional or rehabiliation work involving criminal offenders)

Immigration Inspector

GS-5: three years of general experience that confers the ability to deal with others face to face, learn and interpret facts, and seek cooperation in following procedures and regulations (such as clerical or technical work that involved screening of records, applications, or tax returns, or the clerical aspects of credit or security investigations)

GS-7+: specialized experience that required knowledge and application of laws, regulations, and instructions pertaining to admitting or excluding persons seeking to enter the U.S. (such as law enforcement or welfare work that included dealing with questions of citizenship or alien status)

INTERNAL REVENUE SERVICE

The Internal Revenue Service employs over 120,000 people nationwide and maintains seven regional offices and 63 field offices. Its major law enforcement job title is Special Agent (Criminal Investigations). These agents are Accountants who specialize in criminal investigation. They are involved in cases where "true criminal intent" is already suspected, such as money laundering schemes; conduct investigations of alleged criminal violations of Federal tax laws, particularly those relating to income and wagering or gaming devices; make recommendations with respect to criminal prosecution; prepare comprehensive technical reports, including accounting analyses and summaries; and assist the U.S. Attorney's office in the preparation of cases prior to and during trial. Special Agents are authorized to carry firearms and must be in top physical condition. They are often recruited from the ranks of other government law enforcement agencies, such as the FBI, Secret Service, or Customs Service.

Series, Grade Levels, and Promotion Potential

GS Series	Job Title	Positions/ People Employed	Grade Level			Promotion Rate (%)
			Low	High	Average	
1811	IRS Special Agent	10,000	GS-7	GS-15	GS-12.1	30

Qualifications

GS-5: three years of accounting and business-related experience, with study successfully completed in a college or university substituted at the rate of one year of academic education for nine months of general experience (provided study included courses in accounting and related business or law subjects totaling at least 24 credits, with at least 15 credits in accounting)

GS-7: additional one year of specialized experience (such as criminal investigative or comparable experience) that required the collection, assembly, and development of factual evidence and other pertinent data using investigative techniques; the making of oral and written reports; and the analysis and evaluation of evidence to arrive at sound conclusions

GS-9+: additional qualifications depending on the specific job

Pathway: 3

Special Agents are hired directly by the IRS office that has the vacancy. Job opportunities will differ depending on office location. Interested applicants should contact a local IRS office (listed in the local telephone book), or write to the IRS headquarters in Washington, DC (see Appendix D), for a list of IRS offices nationwide.

PARK SERVICE

The National Park Service maintains, protects, and oversees operations at all national parks. There are currently over 4,000 full-time Park Rangers working in such parks. In an average year the Park Service also hires roughly 4,000 seasonal Rangers, most of whom help the permanent Rangers at popular vacation spots. Rangers' duties cover four general areas:

1. *visitors services,* such as protecting all visitors, helping with information, and handling guided tours;
2. *enforcement of park regulations,* especially those regarding campsites and fires;
3. *search and rescue* of individuals who get lost or trapped in some remote location; and
4. *emergency medical care* in response to the many accidents that can happen in the wilderness.

Series, Grade Levels, and Promotion Potential

GS Series	Job Title	Positions/ People Employed	Grade Level			Promotion Rate (%)
			Low	High	Average	
0025	Park Ranger	4,740	GS-3	GS-14	GS-7.1	18

Qualifications

GS-3: one year of general experience or one year of college with six credits in related subjects (such as those listed below)

GS-4: one year of specialized experience or two years of college-level study related to such subjects as natural science, natural resource management, earth science, archeology, or recreation management, or a combination of education and experience

GS-5: two years of specialized experience or a bachelor's degree in a related field, or a combination of both education and work experience

GS-7: three years of related work experience or an additional year of college study at the graduate level, or a combination of both

GS-9: four years of related work experience or a master's degree in a related field, or a combination of both

GS-11+: five years of specialized experience or a combination of work and education

POLICE AND GUARD

Almost every Federal facility employs some of the more than 15,000 uniformed Police and Guards in the government.

Series, Grade Levels, and Promotion Potential

GS Series	Job Title	Positions/ People Employed	Grade Level			Promotion Rate (%)
			Low	High	Average	
0083	Police	5,932	GS-3	GS-11	GS-5.7	20
0085	Guard	3,613	GS-2	GS-11	GS-5	9

Qualifications

Police

GS-3: one year of postsecondary education (that is, above high school), with at least six credits of study pertinent to law enforcement or half a year of general work experience

GS-4: two years of postsecondary study,with at least 12 credits in subjects related to law enforcement or one-half year of specialized law enforcement experience

(*Note:* Specialized experience, at this or any grade for which it may be required, includes work as an active member of a Federal, state, municipal, or local police force, or comparable experience [say, as a military police officer] that involved responsibility for maintaining order and protecting life and property and has provided knowledge of law enforcement methods.)

GS-5+: a B.S. degree in Police Science or one year of equivalent work experience at the next lowest grade

Guard

Note: Competition for Guard positions is restricted by law to persons entitled to Veterans Preference *as long as* such applicants are available for appointment. Moreover, a candidate must have:

> **Veterans Preference** is described in Appendix Q.

GS-3: one year of postsecondary education (that is, above high school), with at least six credits of study pertinent to guard work or one-half year of general work experience.

GS-4: two years of postsecondary education or one-half year of specialized work experience such as work with a Federal, state, municipal, local, or private protective organization that involved the protection of property against hazards such as fire, theft, damage, accident, or trespass or maintaining order and protecting life—including service in the military or Coast Guard or, for hospital security guards, experience as a psychiatric nursing assistant—or one and a half years of general work experience

GS-5+: at least one year of equivalent work experience at the next lowest grade

Pathways: 2, 3

Job market conditions for these job titles vary considerably. In some areas state and municipal salaries are considerably higher than Federal salaries and candidates are in short supply; in others, however, candidates are in oversupply. Candidates should check with their local OPM Service Center to determine the situation in their areas. The Veterans Administration is a major employer of Police and Guards, and candidates can directly contact a local VA hospital or medical center regarding these positions.

SECRET SERVICE

The two law enforcement positions for which the Secret Service recruits are Special Agent and Uniformed Officer.

Special Agents' primary responsibility is the protection of the President and Vice President and their immediate families. They also enforce laws relating to the counterfeiting of money and other government documents, and investigate reports of credit or computer fraud as well as forged checks and bonds. Special Agents are rotated among these various investigative and protective missions during the course of their careers. Successful candidates begin training at the Federal Law Enforcement Training Center in Glynco, GA, at the GS5/7 level. Agents can be promoted up to GS-12 in as little as three years. Opportunities above GS-12 are based on merit.

Uniformed Officers, most of whom are assigned to Washington, DC, are responsible for policing the White House complex, Main Treasury Building, and other presidential offices. Their starting salary is approximately $29,000. Until 1970 Uniformed Officers were actually part of the District of Columbia's Police Department assigned to Federal buildings; although now Federal employees, they are still paid out of funds (designated by Congress) from that department, and thus have the unique job series designation LE (Law Enforcement).

The Secret Service, like other law enforcement agencies, also hires per-sonnel in many support fields, such as Computer Programmers, Engineers, Accountants, and Clerical (see the list in the FBI profile in this appendix).

Series, Grade Levels, and Promotion Potential

Series	Job Title	Positions/ People Employed	Grade Level			Promotion Rate (%)
			Low	High	Average	
GS-1811	Special Agent	2,000	GS-7	GS-15	GS-12.1	30
LE-0083	Uniformed Officer	1,100	GS-3	GS-13	GS-6	28

Qualifications

All Secret Service Special Agents must be under the age of 37 to apply, have a bachelor's degree or three years of related work experience, and pass the Treasury Enforcement Exam.

All applicants for Uniformed Officer positions must be under 37, have a high school diploma, and pass the Civil Service Exam administered exclusively by the Secret Service.

Pathways: 1, 3

The Secret Service has Delegated Examining Authority for both Special Agents and Uniformed Officers, and so can administer the tests and maintain the registers for both occupations. However, sometimes the OPM tests, rates, and registers applicants for Special Agent. Therefore, applicants must either contact a local Secret Service field office or write to Secret Service headquarters (address in Appendix D) to ascertain which method is being used locally .

The Secret Service uses standard civil service hiring pathways for all office support job titles for which it hired.

TREASURY ENFORCEMENT AGENT

Treasury Enforcement Agents are employed by the Internal Revenue Service, U.S. Customs Service, and the Bureau of Alcohol, Tobacco, and Firearms. The majority work with the IRS as Special Agents.

For the most part, Treasury Enforcement Agents perform the same duties as Criminal Investigators, looking into alleged criminal violations of Federal tax laws. Most investigations involve laws pertaining to income, wagering, and gaming devices. Agents also make recommendations to aid in the prosecution of alleged violators assist U.S. Attorneys in the preparation of cases and during trials, and prepare comprehensive reports, such as accounting analyses and summaries.

Series, Grade Levels, and Promotion Potential

GS Series	Job Title	Positions/ People Employed	Grade Level			Promotion Rate (%)
			Low	High	Average	
1811	Treasury Enforcement Agent	15,000	GS-7	GS-15	GS-12.1	30

Qualifications

Applicants must have accounting and business-related experience, such as knowledge of commercial auditing principles and the demonstrated ability to analyze accounting and bookkeeping records. Other areas considered by Federal employers include knowledge of capital markets and structure, management of both short- and long-term financial accounts, and business law. Specialized experience in the criminal investigative field should include the documented ability to exercise inititative and resourcefulness in the gathering of key evidence for legal proceedings. Applicants should be experienced in a variety of investigative techniques, and have no physical ailments that may inhibit the performance of duties.

Pathway: 1

All candidates must take the OPM Treasury Enforcement Agent Exam. This is offered quite infrequently, as there are thousands of eligible applicants currently on OPM registers. Interested individuals can ask their area OPM Service Center when the exam will be offered.

LEGAL

Most legal careers in Federal service are highly specialized, involving such functions as Social Security Administration, Claims Examining, Contract Admininstration, or Worker's Compensation Claims Examining. However, others are more generalized, including General Attorney, Paralegal Specialist, and Legal Clerk and Technician. These and other legal job titles are described in Appendix K.

There are over 81,000 people employed in legal careers in Federal service. Agencies that hire the most legal personnel are in the Departments of State, Defense (Army, Navy), Justice, Interior, Health and Human Services, Veterans Affairs, and Labor.

MAJOR SERIES, GRADE LEVELS, AND PROMOTION POTENTIAL

GS Series	Job Title	Positions/ People Employed	Grade Level			Promotion Rate (%)
			Low	High	Average	
0105	Social Insurance Admin.	24,740	GS-7	GS-14	GS-10.5	9
0526	Tax Technician	4,234	GS-7	GS-11	GS-8.9	25
0904	Law Clerk	15	GS-9	GS-12	GS-10.8	6
0905	General Attorney	18,068	GS-11	GS-15	GS-13.5	14
0950	Paralegal Specialist	4,467	GS-5	GS-14	GS-10	23
0962	Contact Representative	15,022	GS-4	GS-13	GS-6.8	22
0963	Legal Instruments Examiner	2,122	GS-3	GS-13	GS-6.3	24
0986	Legal Clerk and Technician	9,067	GS-4	GS-11	GS-6.3	22
0987	Tax Law Specialist	371	GS-9	GS-13	GS-12.9	5
0990	General Claims Representative	2,821	GS-4	GS-13	GS-7.9	21
0991	Worker's Comp. Examiner	785	GS-7	GS-14	GS-11	17
0993	Social Insur. Claims Exam.	1,896	GS-5	GS-13	GS-9.4	4
0996	Veterans Claims Examiner	3,290	GS-5	GS-14	GS-10.3	27

QUALIFICATIONS

General Attorney

GS-9: law degree from an accredited college or university, member of the
bar
GS-11: additional one year of professional legal experience
GS-12+: additional qualifications varying with specific agency duties

Law Clerk

GS-9+: same as for General Attorney, except not required to be a member of the
bar; however, a nonmember who receives appointment must be admitted to
the bar within 14 months to retain his or her position

PATHWAYS: 1, 3

Direct Hire Authority is in effect governmentwide for all General Attorney and Law
Clerk positions. These are Excepted Service positions at all agencies, and special
salary rates apply. All other positions use Pathway 1, via either the Administrative
program or the Clerical exam, as outlined below.

Pathway 1	Job Title
Administrative	Social Insurance Administration, Tax Technician, Paralegal Specialist, Contact Representative, Tax Law Specialist, General Claims Representative, Worker's Compensation Examiner, Social Insurance Claims Examiner, Veterans Claims Examiner
via Clerical	Legal Instruments Examiner, Legal Clerk and Technician

LIBRARIANS

The Federal government employs over 3,000 Librarians nationwide, in every major department and agency. There are positions at all grade levels for librarians who specialize in a particular subject matter or area of expertise. Some of the more common specializations include:

Biological Sciences	Engineering	Education
Physical Sciences	Business and Industry	Fine Arts
Medical Sciences	Law	Music
Social Sciences	Humanities	

The agencies that hire the most Librarians are the Departments of Veterans Affairs, Defense, Agriculture, Commerce, Health and Human Services, Justice, and Interior.

SERIES, GRADE LEVELS, AND PROMOTION POTENTIAL

Additional job titles in GS-1400, **Library and Archive Group,** are listed in Appendix K.

| GS Series | Job Title | Positions/ People Employed | Grade Level | | | Promotion Rate (%) |
			Low	High	Average	
1410	Librarian	1,751	GS-7	GS-15	GS-11.3	12

QUALIFICATIONS

GS-7: bachelor's degree with 24 semester hours in library science plus one year of professional experience

GS-9: master's degree plus one year of supervisory or Administrative experience

GS-11: in addition to the above, a doctoral degree or three years of graduate education in library science

GS-12+: additional Administrative or managerial experience related to area of expertise and various other agency-specific requirements

PATHWAYS: 1, 2, 3

All of the agencies listed have some Direct Hire Authority for Librarians. Interested candidates should contact these agencies directly or check with their local OPM Service Center to find which agencies in their area hire Librarians and what hiring pathways have been authorized. Applicants for all grades who qualify on the basis of experience are required to pass a subject-matter test in library science; however, no test is required of those who have a master's degree.

MATHEMATICS AND STATISTICS

There are over 15,000 people currently employed throughout the Federal government in mathematics- and statistics-related occupations. Since qualified applicants are scarce, OPM has given Direct Hire Authority to most agencies for positions in these fields.

According to OPM, Mathematicians are those who "plan, direct, conduct or assist in the performance of scientific, analytical or developmental work or basic or applied research in the mathematics field." By comparison, statisticians do "professional work or provide professional consultation requiring the application of statistical theory and technique in the collection and compilation analysis and interpretation of quantitative information in such areas as the biological, social and physical sciences, engineering, agriculture, and administration." The exact nature of the job depends largely on the agency for which one is working.

Mathematical Technicians and Statistical Assistants perform basic computational operations in a support capacity.

The agencies that hire the most in these occupations are the DOD (Army, Navy, Air Force), Defense Intelligence Agency, Census Bureau, Environmental Protection Agency, Department of Interior, Department of Transportation, Internal Revenue Service, and Social Security Administration.

SERIES, GRADE LEVELS, AND PROMOTION POTENTIAL

GS Series	Job Title	Positions/ People Employed	Grade Level			Promotion Rate (%)
			Low	High	Average	
1510	Actuary	175	GS-7	GS-15	GS-12.6	18
1515	Operations Research Analyst	3,476	GS-7	GS-15	GS-12.8	11
1520	Mathematician	1,688	GS-7	GS-15	GS-12.3	6
1521	Mathematics Technician	23	GS-3	GS-11	GS-6.5	8
1529	Mathematical Statistician	1,057	GS-5	GS-15	GS-12	10
1530	Statistician	2,466	GS-7	GS-15	GS-12	9
1531	Statistical Assistant	1,126	GS-3	GS-11	GS-5.9	18
1550	Computer Scientist	3,094	GS-7	GS-15	GS-11.6	11

QUALIFICATIONS

Professional Positions

GS-5: bachelor's degree in related field

GS-7: master's degree and/or one year of related work experience

GS-9+: advanced degrees and additional work experience, varying widely depending upon the position and/or agency

Technician or Assistant

GS-3: written test is required (see "Clerical" section) plus one year general work experience

GS-4: two years total work experience, six months specialized experience
GS-5: three years total work experience, one year specialized
GS-6: four years total work experience, two years specialized
GS-7: five years total work experience, three years specialized
GS-8+: six years total work experience, four years specialized

PATHWAYS: 1, 3

As mentioned earlier, there is Direct Hire Authority in most areas and at most agencies for Mathematicians and Statisticians. Therefore, those with qualifying degrees should contact the personnel offices of the agencies mentioned to explore hiring possibilities. In addition, computerized regional registers (via Form B) offer broader geographic consideration to Mathematicians at the GS-5/7 levels. To apply for register consideration, write:

> OPM Staffing Services Center
> P.O. Box 9105
> Macon, GA 31297

For Technician and Assistant positions it is best to contact a local OPM Service Center to ascertain which agencies are hiring in your area and what pathways are currently being used. Generally it is a combination of Direct Hire Authority (Pathway 3) and register with test (Pathway 1), depending on the need for qualified personnel and the level of the for which application is being made.

MILITARY BASE OCCUPATIONS

In addition to the uniformed military forces staffing the hundreds of military bases operated by the Departments of the Army, Navy, Air Force, and the Coast Guard, many civilian workers are employed. Most of these civilian positions are in the Competitive Serice and are filled through normal civil service processes.

Military bases employ both white- and blue-collar workers. In fact, most blue-collar positions that occur in the Federal government are located on military installations. The white-collar positions are those normally associated with office operation. Some commonly occurring DOD white- and blue-collar occupations are listed below:

SERIES AND JOB TITLES

More **job titles** appear under "Military Reserve Technician Occupations."

WG (Blue Collar)

2810	Electrical Worker (High Voltage)	4749	Maintenance Mechanic
3314	Instrument Maker	5803	Heavy Mobile Equipment Mechanic
3566	Custodial Worker	6907	Warehouse Worker
4742	Utility Systems Repairer	8852	Aircraft Mechanic

GS (White Collar)

0085	Security Guard	0525	Accounting Technician
0086	Security Clerical & Assistant	0602	Medical Officer
0120	Food Assistance Program Specialist	0620	Licensed Practical Nurse
0204	Military Personnel Clerk & Techn.	0800	Engineer (all disciplines)
0318	Secretary	1340	Meteorologist
0322	Clerk/Typist	1550	Computer Scientist
0510	Accountant	1701	General Education and Training

QUALIFICATIONS

Qualifications for these white- and blue-collar positions at military bases are the same as if they were at nonmilitary Federal facilities.

PATHWAYS: 1, 2, 4

For many positions on military bases and other installations, the base may be the unique or predominant employer in the area; hence most of these positions are covered by Direct Hire or Delegated Examining Authority. Often the local OPM Service Center's involvement in the military base recruitment process may be limited to helping with shortage category occupations. Most military facilities maintain an on-base Civilian Personnel Office (CPO) whose function is to recruit and examine candidates for white- and blue-collar positions. Interested candidates should contact these offices directly. A list of military bases is provided as part of Appendix D.

MILITARY RESERVE TECHNICIAN OCCUPATIONS

The Army and Air Force operate extensive reserve programs, staffed by both uniformed military forces and civilian workers (8,000 in the Army's program, 9,700 in the Air Force's). Many of the civilian employees double as military reserve forces; that is, although their main occupations are their civilian positions, they are also members of the Army or Air Force Reserve. As civilian workers they pursue their white- or blue-collar occupations—almost always located on military bases—in the same manner as other civil service employees. As members of the Air Force or Army Reserve, they are required to participate in reserve operations, which include one weekend of duty per month and two weeks of duty each year (usually in the summer). Reserve Technicians are paid both for their civil service job and additionally for their reserve work.

The Army Reserve Technician Program (ARTP) recruits year round, hiring more than 1,000 individuals annually. It operates under a mandate to have all budgeted positions filled by the end of every fiscal year.

Most ARTP vacancies are for *Unit Administrators,* GS-5/7. Duties include payroll managing, supply requisition, facility administration, and any Administrative duties that the Unit Commander feels is necessary for the successful operation of the unit.

SERIES AND JOB TITLES

Some commonly occurring Reserve Technician occupations are listed below. They are not to be confused with other civil service positions on military bases, discussed in the preceding section on "Military Base Occupations," that are not included in the Reserve Technician program.

WG (Blue Collar)

2604	Electronics Mechanic	5716	Heavy Mobile Equipment Operator
2650	Electronic Integrated Systems Mechanic	5801	Heavy Equipment Mover
		5803	Heavy Mobile Equipment Mechanic
4848	Mechanical Parts Repairer	6641	Ordnance Equipment Mechanic
5378	Powered Support Systems Mechanic	8602	Aircraft Engine/Propeller Mechanic
5703	Motor Vehicle Operator	8852	Aircraft Mechanic

GS (White Collar)

0080	Security Specialist	0301	Staff Administrative Assistant
0132	Intelligence Operations Specialist	0303	Unit Administrator
0205	Military Personnel Officer	0801	General Engineer
0301	Disaster Preparedness Technician	1035	Public Affairs Specialist
0301	Executive Officer	1702	Training Technician

GRADE LEVELS: GS-5–15, WG-2–15

PATHWAY: 3

Candidates should directly contact one of the Air Force or Army Reserve Civilian Personnel Offices (CPOs) listed below for application forms and information regarding procedures required.

Army Reserve Technician Program (ARTP) Recruitment Offices

Following is a listing of the addresses and phone numbers of the ten mainland ARTP recruitment regions. The standard abbreviations preceding each address designate the state or other geographical area covered by a given office. Some regions overlap.

DC, DE, MA, MD, NJ, NY, PA, VA, WV
  CPO
  ATTN: AFKA-ZI-CP
  Ft. Meade, MD 20755-5035

AR, IL, KS, LA, MO, NE, NM, OK, TX
  CPO
  ATTN: Military Technician Examiner
  Ft. Sam Houston, TX 78234-5000

NY (northwest)
  CPO
  ATTN: AFZS-CP
  10th Mountain Div. and Ft. Drum, NY
  13602-5000

AZ, CA (south), NV
  CPO
  ATTN: AFZW-GC-CP
  7th Infantry Div. and Ft. Ord, CA
  93941-5700

AL, FL, GA, KY, MS, NC, PR, SC, TN
  Recruitment and Placement Division
  Reserve Examining Branch
  Ft. McPherson, GA 30330-5000

CO, IA, MT, ND, SD, UT, WY
  CPO
  ATTN: AFCZ-CP-R
  4th Infantry Div. and Ft. Carson, CO 80913-5000

IA, IL, IN, OH, MI, MN, MO, WI
  CPO
  ATTN: AFZR-CP
  Ft. McCoy, WI 54656-5000

CT, MA, ME, NH, RI, VT
  CPO
  ATTN: AFZD-CP-PSD5
  Ft. Devens, MA 01433-5240

CA, NV, OR, WA
CPO
ATTN: AFZM-CP
Presidio of San Francisco, CA 94129-5000

OR, WA
CPO
ATTN: AFZH-CP
I Corps and Ft. Lewis, WA 98433-0128

Air Force Reserve Technician Program Recruitment Office

U.S. Air Force Reserve
Special Examining Unit
451 College Street
P.O. Box 9060
Macon, GA 31213

PEACE CORPS

VOLUNTEER POSITIONS

Each year the U.S. Peace Corps accepts applications to fill over 800 volunteer positions worldwide. Most are for two-year educational projects in one of more than 50 countries in Africa, Asia, and Eastern Europe.

QUALIFICATIONS

To teach math or science: a B.A./B.S. in Education and/or Math or Science
To be a teacher-trainer: an M.A.T.
To teach university English: an M.A./M.A.T. in English, TEFL, or Linguistics
To teach the blind or learning disabled: a B.A./B.S. in Special Education

RECRUITER (PAYING JOB)

On the paying side, the Peace Corps always has a need for Recruiters to recruit volunteers for the Peace Corps.

GRADE LEVELS

The Peace Corps is an excepted agency and therefore does not follow the General Schedule pay scale. Recruiters are normally hired at the FP-7 level, with a starting salary of roughly $21,900. Experienced applicants may start at approximately $26,600.

QUALIFICATIONS

Applicants should have three years of experience that provide a basic understanding of the principles of organization, management, and administration.

PATHWAY (ALL JOBS): 3

The Peace Corps has Direct Hire Authority for both its volunteer and paying jobs. Persons interested in either a volunteer or paid position with the Peace Corps should write:

> U.S. Peace Corps
> Office of Personnel
> Esplanade Mall
> 1990 K Street, NW
> Washington, DC 20526

POSTAL SERVICE

Post Offices are grouped into *Postal Section Centers,* headed by an **MSC.**

The U.S. Postal Service is the largest independent employment system (excepted agency), employing over 80,000 in professional positions and 710,000 in the nonprofessional positions generally referred to as *postal workers.* Professional jobs, which include those in computer-related, engineering, accounting, and some other fields, are generally concentrated in the Postal Headquarters in Washington, DC, as well as in *Management Sectional Centers (MSC).* The great majority of postal hiring is for nonprofessional positions.

JOB TITLES (POSTAL WORKERS)

Letter Carrier   Distribution/Machine Clerk
Postal Clerk   Rural Carrier
Mail Handler

JOB CATEGORIES

The Postal Service uses PS, not GS or WG, to designated its pay schedule (shown in Appendix F). Its employees are divided into three categories: Career Bargaining, Career Nonbargaining, and Casual.

Career Bargaining jobs include the most populated occupations, such as Clerk, Mail Handler, and Letter Carrier. Candidates must take the postal exam in order to be considered. Several of the occupations in this category have their own union to represent them in dealings with Postal Service management. Most employees in these positions are paid at the PS-5 level. These jobs start at about $25,828 and can go as high as $35,880 annually.

Career Nonbargaining positions include all management and Administrative positions, such as Postmasters and Supervisors and fall into this category. Many employees in these positions have been promoted from Career Bargaining jobs.

Casual jobs involve much the same work as Career Bargaining positions but are always part-time and last a maximum of 90 days. Individuals can be hired for two 90-day periods and one 20-day period over the course of a year. Salaries are paid on an hourly basis, with the rate being determined by location and demand (anywhere from $4.25 to $8.00 per hour). No exam is required.

QUALIFICATIONS

Any U.S. citizen is eligible to take the postal exam or work at a Casual postal job. There are no overall qualifications for those applying for a Career Nonbargaining position: Any standards to be met by those seeking such a professional (management/Administrative) job are established by the MSC or specific post office with the vacancy, and applicants should ensure they have the education and/or experience specified. Although many of these positions are filled via promotion from the Career Bargaining ranks, outside applicants are not required to take the postal exam.

PATHWAYS: 1, 2

Casual workers can simply apply at the local post office where they wish to work. They are usually in demand during heavy mail seasons, especially Christmas, and more frequently needed in large metropolitan areas.

The Postal Service recruits all new Career Bargaining and Career Nonbargaining employees through a selection process that includes a written exam. Applicants must be U.S. citizens at least 18 years of age and literate in English. The postal exam tests applicants' number-sequencing ability, reasoning powers, and English-language competence. Even applicants who have served as a Casual postal worker must take this exam in order to gain a permanent part- or full-time position.

> **Postal exams** are also discussed in Step 2 (pp. 47–8). A **sample** is shown in Appendix E.

Tests are not given on a regular basis; rather, each Postal Section Center (representing the first three digits of the ZIP code) schedules an exam only when it actually needs to hire more employees in a given job title for that region—every nine months to three years in most areas. Candidates must get a 5000 A/B card from a post office in the area covered by the exam, and submit it to the Postal Section Center conducting the test. Due to the large number of applicants, there is little advance notice given—usually only three to seven days. Candidates who do not file quickly will end up waiting for the next exam to be announced. In some large metropolitan areas the Postal Service announces not an exam but a lottery: The names of those who filed a 5000 A/B card are selected at random to determine who is to take the test.

Candidates interested in a job with the Postal Service must keep in close contact with the specific post office or Postal Section Center in which they are interested. Phone or visit every few weeks to determine when the next exam is scheduled. It is a good idea also to identify your local Management Sectional Center and request information about when tests will be scheduled in its Postal Section Centers. Generally, a Postal Section Center gives an exam every three years for each job title: Letter Carrier, Postal Clerk, Mail Handler, and Distribution/Machine Clerk. The entire hiring process is conducted exclusively by the Postal Service.

PUBLIC INFORMATION (WRITTEN/VISUAL/SPOKEN)

Two categories of public information occupations occur in Federal service: those requiring a skill that is generally acquired (such as writing), and those requiring a skill that is more specialized (such as illustration or photography). In either case the numbers of employees are small compared to other fields—about 22,000 all told—so employment opportunities are relatively few. All agencies use at least some personnel in these fields, with qualifications varying widely with regard to job title, agency, and grade level. The Voice of America (VoA, profiled below) hires those who specialize in the broadcast arts and sciences.

SERIES, GRADE LEVELS, AND PATHWAYS

| Series | Job Title | Positions/ People Employed | Grade Level | | | Pathway |
			Low	High	Average	
GS (White Collar)						
1001	General Arts & Information (*or* Int'l Radio Broadcaster)	2,861	GS-5	GS-14	GS-10.0	1 (Admin.) 3 (see VoA)
1020	Illustrator	671	GS-5	GS-12	GS-8.7	3
1035	Public Affairs	3,925	GS-5	GS-15	GS-11.2	1 (Admin.)
1060	Photographer	1,160	GS-4	GS-12	GS-8.4	3
1071	Audio-Visual Production	1,148	GS-5	GS-15	GS-11.1	3
1082	Writing & Editing	1,477	GS-5	GS-15	GS-10.3	1 (Admin.)
1083	Technical Writing & Editing	1,277	GS-5	GS-14	GS-10.7	1 (Admin.)
1087	Editorial Assistant	942	GS-4	GS-8	GS-5.6	3
WB (Blue Collar)						
0394	Radio Broadcast Technician	170	WB-2	WB-2	WB-2	3 (see VoA)

Candidates for such white-collar job titles under Pathway 3 should check Appendix L to ascertain which agencies hire for these positions on a national basis; a list of hiring agencies in their area can be obtained from their local OPM Service Center. Most positions in Illustration and Photography are with the Air Force, Army, and Navy, the Smithsonian Institution, and the Department of Interior's Forest Service. Candidates would do well to contact hiring agencies with regard to being "name requested" off the Administrative register.

> **Name requests** are explained in Step 2 (p. 43).

VOICE OF AMERICA

The Voice of America (VoA), the international broadcast arm of the U.S. Information Agency (USIA), accepts applications for Foreign Language Broadcasters as well as a number of technical support positions. The VoA is one of the largest broadcasting systems in the world, employing 2,500 people (1,784 in this country and 693 abroad) and reaching over 130 million listeners in 43 languages. It is supported by a worldwide network of news bureaus, correspondents, and relay stations.

Foreign Language Broadcasters serve as reporters, translators, editors, producers, and announcers. They research and write original material, as well as edit and provide reportorial coverage of news events in the broadcast language.

Broadcast Technician is a Wage Grade position and is therefore paid on an hourly basis.

Series and Grade Levels

Breakdowns for these job titles at the VoA alone are not available; data shown here are for the Federal civil service as a whole.

Series	Job Title	Positions/ People Employed	Grade Level		
			Low	High	Average
GS (White Collar)					
0334	Computer Programmer/Analyst	47,214	GS-3	GS-14	GS-11.4
0391	Communications Manager	2,625	GS-5	GS-14	GS-12.2
0801	General Engineer	19,624	GS-5	GS-14	GS-13
0850	Supervisor/Electrical Engineer	4,862	GS-5	GS-14	GS-11.7
0855	Electronics Engineer	27,475	GS-5	GS-14	GS-11.9
1048	Foreign Language Broadcaster	N/A	GS-5	GS-14	GS-10.1
WB (Blue Collar)					
0394	Radio Broadcast Technician	170	WB-2	WB-2	WB-2

Qualifications

Foreign Language Broadcasters: native fluency in the language in which they broadcast and proficient in written and spoken English, as demonstrated by successful performance on both a written exam and a voice audition

Engineers (various): bachelor's degree in Engineering plus a broad knowledge of broadcasting and related equipment

Broadcast Technician: technical experience that clearly demonstrates an understanding of radio broadcasting

Pathways: 2, 3

The VoA has Direct Hire Authority for all its positions. A register is used when it receives more applications than it has vacancies; qualified candidates are then contacted as positions open up. An application package, including forms and in-depth qualifications information, can be obtained by contacting the agency:

Voice of America/Office of Personnel
Delegated Competitive Examining Unit
Room 1543, 330 Independence Ave., SW
Washington, DC 20547
202-619-3117

SCIENCE

In addition to the over 140,000 people employed in various science-related job titles in health care professions (see "Health Care" profile), the Federal government also employs over 61,000 in the biological sciences, 43,000 in the physical sciences, and over 56,000 in the social sciences. These represent virtually every aspect of their respective fields, and include professional, technical, and Administrative positions.

In general, the more specialized the position and the higher the academic degree required to qualify, the more the position is in demand and the more likely there is to be Direct Hire Authority and special salary rates.

MAJOR SERIES, GRADE LEVELS, AND PROMOTION POTENTIAL

Although professional, technical, and Administrative scientific positions exist at virtually every agency, some specialize or use more of one type of scientist than another. The following is a breakdown of the major Federal science categories and the agencies that employ the largest numbers; additional job titles are listed in Appendix K.

GS Series	Group or Job Title	Positions/ People Employed	Average Grade	Promo. Rate (%)	Major Agencies
					USDA, Interior, HHS (Indian
0401	Biologist	7,701	GS-11.7	14	Health Serv.), Ctrs. for
0408	Ecologist	702	GS-11.8	17	Disease Control,
0430	Botanist	281	GS-11	18	Commerce, NIH, EPA, Nat'l
0440	Geneticist	258	GS-12.7	12	Sci. Foundation (NSF)

(Cont.)

(Cont.)

GS Series	Group or Job Title	Positions/ People Employed	Promo. Average Grade	Rate (%)	Major Agencies
0457	Soil Conservationist	4,314	GS-10.3	9	
0458	Soil Conservation Techn.	1,452	GS-6	12	
1310	Physicist	2,942	GS-13.1	5	Defense, USDA, Commerce,
1320	Chemist	5,937	GS-12	10	EPA, HHS, NSF, NASA,
1340	Meteorologist	2,998	GS-12	28	Tennessee Valley
1341	Meteorological Techn.	1,168	GS-9.7	14	Authority (TVA)
1360	Oceanographer	655	GS-12.5	10	
1370	Cartographer	4,097	GS-10.9	17	
1371	Cartographic Techn.	1,111	GS-7.5	12	
1386	Photographic Technol.	22	GS-12.1	4	
0101	Social Scientist	5,427	GS-11.5	14	Defense, Labor, Interior
0110	Economist	4,752	GS-12.5	13	(Bureau of Indian Affairs),
0180	Psychologist	3,565	GS-12.6	6	USDA, HHS, Justice, VA,
0181	Psychology Technician	699	GS-7	10	Ctrs. for Disease Control,
0185	Social Worker	4,985	GS-11.2	6	NSF
0189	Recreation Aid	1,241	GS-4	7	

QUALIFICATIONS

Professional

GS-5: bachelor's degree in appropriate field

GS-7: one year of graduate study or related work experience

GS-9: master's degree or two years of related work experience

GS-11+: additional advanced degrees and/or related work experience depending on with the responsibilities of the position

Technicians

GS-4: one and a half years of general work experience plus six months of related work experience

GS-5: two years of general plus one year of related work experience

GS-7: two years of general plus three years of related work experience

(One year of college-level course work is equivalent to nine months of work experience.)

Assistant or Aid

GS-1: no previous experience

GS-2: six months of general experience

GS-3: one year of general work experience

PATHWAYS: 2, 3

As with most positions that require either associate, bachelor's, or advanced degrees, there tend to be applicant shortages at one time or another at most agencies. Therefore, Direct Hire Authority is often used to facilitate recruitment. When there is an applicant oversupply, registers are assembled and qualified applicants contacted as vacancies arise. Interested applicants can apply directly to the agencies for which they wish to work and/or request information from local OPM Service Centers on which agencies are hiring and what pathways are being used.

SOCIAL SECURITY ADMINISTRATION

The Social Security Administration (SSA) distributes more than $40 billion in benefits to 200 million people across the United States. Most of these benefits are payable upon retirement, disability, or death of a spouse. The SSA's 1,300 offices nationwide also make Medicare payments. The agency currently has 65,000 employees and plans to stay at its current hiring average of slightly more than 5,000 new employees each fiscal year. The major job titles at the SSA are Contact Representative (Claims Representative, 14,000 at present) and Social Insurance Administrator (nearly 20,000 employed).

Social Insurance Administrators are primarily concerned with administering, planning, managing, and conducting the Federal Social Security insurance programs. SSA Administrators are responsible for deciding who is eligible for Social Security benefits and how much monthly benefits will be. They certify these payments to the Treasury Department, which then allocates the necessary funds.

Contact Representatives provide information and assistance to people with benefits-related problems, such as lost or late checks, incorrect payments, eligibility information, lost benefits cards, and so on. This job title is divided into two sub-groups: *Service Reps,* who deal with people face to face at SSA offices, and *Teleservice Reps,* who answer questions over the phone.

Since these positions are extremely agency-specific, few jobs in the private sector convey work experience that is related closely enough to qualify applicants for higher-level appointment. Therefore, most hiring occurs at the GS-5/7 levels in both occupations, and promotion is obtained from within.

SERIES, GRADE LEVELS, AND PROMOTION POTENTIAL

GS Series	Job Title	Positions/ People Employed	Grade Level			Promotion Rate (%)
			Low	High	Average	
0105	Social Insurance Admin.	24,740	GS-7	GS-14	GS-10.5	9
0962	Contact Representative	15,022	GS-4	GS-12	GS-6.8	22

PATHWAYS: 1, 3, 4

Those who qualify under OSP (Pathway 4) can apply directly to any local SSA office. Addresses can be found in local telephone directories or by writing to the SSA headquarters address listed in Appendix D.

SUPPLY AND INVENTORY

Currently there are over 24,000 Supply Clerks, Technicians, and Specialists in Federal service, the majority employed by the Department of Defense at military bases nationwide. However, every agency employs some people in this field to purchase, store, inventory, and dispose of supplies, from paper clips to office furniture, enabling the agency to function on a day-to-day basis. In addition to everday office equipment, DOD supply personnel process anything from hospital supplies to batteries, fuses, cables, and parts for military machinery, food for commissaries, and books and training manuals.

Supply Clerks are basically the same as any other Federal Clerk (see "Clerical") except that they must learn supply terminology in order to carry out their jobs.

Supply Technicians are assistants to Supply Specialists and must have a working knowledge of the concepts of supply procedures and practices. They implement the Supply Specialist's recommendations.

Supply Specialists are supervisors who coordinate supply networks and develop and recommend appropriate procedures for them.

SERIES, GRADE LEVELS, AND PROMOTION POTENTIAL

Because this particular series is divided into three categories, providing ac-curate grade-level averages and promotion rates for each is extremely problematic.

GS Series	Job Title	Positions/ People Employed	Grade Level			Promotion Rate (%)
			Low	High	Average	
2005	Supply Clerk		GS-4	GS-6		
2005	Supply Technician		GS-6	GS-8		
2005	Supply Specialist		GS-9	GS-13		
Series Overall		17,931			GS-6	12

QUALIFICATIONS

GS-4, Supply Clerk: see "Clerical" profile in this appendix

GS-6, Supply Technician: one year of general experience and three years of specialized, supply-related work experience

GS-9, Supply Specialist: five years of specialized, supply-related work experience that confers the ability to handle supervisory work duties

PATHWAYS: 2, 3

Most hires are by agencies in the Department of Defense (Army, Navy, Air Force, Defense Logistics Agency) and via Delegated Hiring Authority, although OPM also maintains registers for these positions. Candidates may apply to an OPM OPM Service Center or to the Civilian Personnel Office of a nearby DOD base or installation.

WAGE GRADE

The Federal government employs nearly 400,000 full-time Wage Grade (blue-collar) workers throughout the country. The Wage Grade classification means that employees in these job titles are paid an hourly wage, based on the hourly rate paid *locally* in the private sector for comparable job titles; thus the pay scale varies considerably depending on the location of the job. Wages are generally higher in metropolitan areas and lower in suburban and rural areas nationwide. There are over 400 Federal blue-collar job titles, generally divided into two classes: those that lead to journeyman career status (Electrician, Plumber, Painter, etc.) and those that do not (Motor Vehicle Operator, Gardener, Warehouse Worker, etc.).

> A sample **Wage Grade Schedule** is provided in Appendix F.

To reach the *journeyman* level, which is the equivalent of eligibility for state licensing in that particular trade, one must be apprenticed to a journeyman-level employee and receive a prescribed course of on-the-job training. This is important when considering a blue-collar career in Federal service because a WG-9 employee who has achieved journeyman status in his or her trade earns more than a WG-9 employee in a trade that does not progress to journeyman level. Thus a WG-9 Warehouse Worker earns less than a WG-9 Carpenter, since the carpentry job requires more specialized skills than does the warehouse job.

WAGE GRADE CAREER LEVELS

WG career levels are introduced in Step 1 (p. 17).

WG-1–5, *helper* (or *trainee*): receives on-the-job training

WG-6–8, *apprentice* (where applicable): receives on-the-job and classroom training leading from developmental to full-performance (journeyman) level

(In a nonjourneyman position, employees can progress to WG-6–8 through promotion.)

WG-9–11, *journeyman:* full performance, needs little or no supervision, equivalent to state licensure

WL-1–15, *leader:* foreman of a crew

WS-1–19, *supervisor:* able to promote, hire, fire, and evaluate workers

MAJOR WAGE GRADE (WG) SERIES

Each listing shows GS series, job title, and number of employees.

2604	ELECTRONICS MECHANIC	8,153	4701	Maintenance Operator	4,703
2610	Electronic Integrated Systems Mechanic	4,156	4749	MAINTENANCE MECHANIC	10,073
			5210	Rigger	3,286
2805	ELECTRICIAN	5,842	5306	Air Conditioning Equipment Mechanic	2,991
3414	MACHINIST	4,219			
3502	LABORER	10,721	5334	Marine Machinery Mechanic	5,453
3566	CUSTODIAN	10,783	5402	Boiler Plant Operator	3,503
3703	Welder	2,928	5703	MOTOR VEHICLE OPERATOR	6,527
3806	SHEET METAL MECHANIC	7,047	5716	Engineering Equipment Operator	2,638
3809	Mobile Equipment Metal Mechanic	839	5803	HEAVY MOBILE EQUIPMENT MECHANIC	9,766
3820	Shipfitter	3,228			
4102	PAINTER	3,718	5823	Automotive Mechanic	5,568
4204	PIPEFITTING	4,134	6907	MATERIAL HANDLER	15,584
4206	Plumber	1,925	7408	FOOD SERVICE WORKER	6,826
4607	Carpenter	4,727	8852	AIRCRAFT MECHANIC	11,368

Note: The job title Custodian is reserved for veterans as long as there are qualified veterans to fill the positions.

QUALIFICATIONS

Skilled Trades

These vary widely depending on the job title and grade level. For example, a Maintenance Mechanic at WG-7 would need a good working knowledge of at least two skills (carpentry, plumbing, painting, etc); at WS-11 supervisory experience would also be required.

Unskilled Trades

At entry-level (WG-2–4) no previous experience is necessary. A Motor Vehicle Operator must, of course, have a driver's license. A Warehouse Worker needs a strong constitution and the ability to follow verbal commands.

HIRING AGENCIES

Agency	WG Hires (% of Total)	Agency	WG Hires (% of Total)
Department of Defense (DOD)	76.6	Dept. of Veterans Affairs (VA)	8.6
Army	22.9	Tennessee Valley Authority (TVA)	3.0
Navy	29.4	Interior	2.9
Air Force	21.8	General Services Admin. (GSA)	1.4
Other Defense	2.5	Other	7.5

PATHWAYS: 2, 3

The Departments of Defense and Veterans Affairs do the majority of their own hiring. The TVA is an excepted agency and therefore conducts all of its own recruitment. The GSA and Interior generally list openings with the OPM and also hire directly for some occupations. Contact your local OPM Service Center, DOD bases, VA hospitals, and TVA, Interior, or GSA personnel offices to find out who presently has hiring authority for your job title. In addition, you may contact the headquarters offices listed in Appendix D.

Appendix C: Selected Occupations and Their Hiring Pathway Factors

The following chart, an employment overview of many popular Federal job titles, has six main column headings: Hiring System, Register Location, Test Requirements, Examining Authority, Hiring Volume, and Job Market.

Hiring System indicates whether a job is generally in the Competitive Service or the Excepted Service. The chart shows where the majority of the jobs are located, although many job titles do occur in both.

Register Location indicates whether lists of eligibles are kept primarily at local FJICs, at a centralized OPM location (a regional or national center), or not at all, which indicates that the decision is made case by case. Some job titles use both local registers and case examining, depending on the agency and position.

Test Requirements refer only to traditional, paper-and-pencil tests, not "examinations" in the larger Federal sense. The chart indicates whether the position entails an ACWA test, some other test, or does not generally require a written test.

Examination Authority indicates whether the occupation is generally recruited by OPM or more often involves Delegated Examining or Direct Hire Authority. When the categories are roughly even, the chart shows X's in both columns.

Hiring Volume is designated as "Many," "Some," or "Few," based on the number of people in each occupation. Those comprising 3,500 people or more are designated as having "Many" new hires; those with a total employee count of 2,500-3,499 receive a "Some" rating; occupations with less than 2,500 Federal employees are marked as "Few."

Job Market shows whether the bulk of the recruiting is "External," that is, due to the hiring of people from outside the Federal government (new hires); or "Internal," that is, due to hiring from among the ranks of current and former Federal employees.

> Appendixes L and O show **number of employees** in a given job title by agency.

This chart is an overview of selected occupations, meant only as to give you an idea of the many kind of information you need in order to make an informed decision about the job titles you decide to pursue, and to gauge the relative ease or difficulty with which you might land a Federal job. Note that some of this information is

OCCUPATION GRADE LEVEL	SERIES#	HIRING SYSTEM Competitive	HIRING SYSTEM Excepted	TEST REQUIREMENTS Other	TEST REQUIREMENTS No Test	HIRING VOLUME Many	HIRING VOLUME Some	HIRING VOLUME Few	RECRUITMENT FOCUS External New Hires	RECRUITMENT FOCUS Internal Promotion
Accountant	0510									
GS-5/7		X			X	X			X	
GS-9		X			X		X		X	X
GS-11+		X			X			X		X
Agriculture Commodity Grader	1980									
GS-5/7		X			X	X			X	
GS-9		X		X			X		X	
GS-11+		X			X			X		X
Agriculture Manager	0475									
GS-5/7		X			X	X			X	
GS-9		X			X	X			X	X
GS-11+		X			X		X		X	X
Air Traffic Controller	2152									
GS-5/7		X		X		X			X	
GS-9		X			X		X			X
GS-11+		X			X					X
Alcohol/Tobacco/Firearms Insp.	1854									
GS-5/7		X			X	X			X	
GS-9		X			X		X		X	
GS-11+		X						X		X
Animal Health Technician	0704									
GS-5/7		X			X	X			X	
GS-9		X			X		X		X	
GS-11+		X			X			X		X
Architect	0808									
GS-5/7		X			X		X		X	
GS-9		X			X		X		X	
GS-11+		X			X			X	X	
Archivist	1420									
GS-5/7		X			X	X			X	
GS-9		X			X		X			X
GS-11+		X			X			X		X
Art Specialist	1056									
GS-5/7		X			X		X		X	
GS-9		X			X			X		X
GS-11+		X						X		X
Astronomer/Space Scientist	1330									
GS-5/7		X			X		X		X	
GS-9		X			X		X		X	X
GS-11+		X			X			X	X	X
Attorney	0905									
GS-5/7			X		X	X	X		X	
GS-9			X		X	X	X		X	
GS-11+						X			X	X

OCCUPATION GRADE LEVEL	SERIES#	HIRING SYSTEM		TEST REQUIREMENTS		HIRING VOLUME			RECRUITMENT FOCUS	
		Competitive	Excepted	Other	No Test	Many	Some	Few	External New Hires	Internal Promotion
Audio-Visual Production	1071									
GS-5/7		X			X		X		X	
GS-9		X			X		X		X	
GS-11+		X			X			X		X
Biologist	0401									
GS-5/7					X		X		X	
GS-9		X			X		X		X	
GS-11+		X			X			X	X	
Border Patrol Agent	1896									
GS-5/7		X		X		X			X	
GS-9		X			X		X			X
GS-11+		X			X		X			X
Building Manager	1176									
GS-5/7		X			X	X			X	
GS-9		X			X		X		X	
GS-11+		X						X	X	
Business & Industry	1101									
GS-5/7		X			X	X			X	
GS-9		X			X		X		X	
GS-11+		X					X		X	
Clerk/Typist	0322									
GS-5/7		X		X		X			X	
GS-9		X			X	X			X	
GS-11+					X			X		X
Communications (General)	0392									
GS-5/7		X			X	X			X	
GS-9		X			X		X			X
GS-11+		X			X		X			X
Construction Control	0809									
GS-5/7		X			X	X			X	
GS-9		X			X		X		X	
GS-11+		X			X			X		X
Contract Specialist	1102									
GS-5/7		X			X	X			X	
GS-9		X			X		X		X	
GS-11+		X						X		X
Correctional Officer	0007									
GS-5/7		X			X	X			X	
GS-9		X			X		X			X
GS-11+		X			X			X		X
Criminal Investigator	1811									
GS-5/7		X			X	X			X	
GS-9		X			X		X		X	
GS-11+		X					X			X

OCCUPATION GRADE LEVEL	SERIES#	HIRING SYSTEM		TEST REQUIREMENTS		HIRING VOLUME			RECRUITMENT FOCUS	
		Competitive	Excepted	Other	No Test	Many	Some	Few	External New Hires	Internal Promotion
Customs Inspector	1890									
GS-5/7		X				X			X	
GS-9		X			X		X		X	
GS-11+		X			X		X			X
Data Transcriber	0356									
GS-5/7		X		X			X		X	
GS-9		X			X		X		X	X
GS-11+		X			X		X		X	X
Dental Assistant	0881									
GS-5/7		X			X	X			X	
GS-9		X			X		X		X	X
GS-11+		X			X		X		X	X
Deputy U.S. Marshal	0082									
GS-5/7		X		X		X			X	
GS-9		X			X	X				X
GS-11+		X			X		X			X
Ecologist	0408									
GS-5/7		X			X		X		X	
GS-9		X			X		X			X
GS-11+		X			X			X		X
Economist	0110									
GS-5/7		X			X			X	X	
GS-9		X			X			X		X
GS-11+		X			X			X		X
Educational Program Specialist	1720									
GS-5/7		X			X	X			X	
GS-9		X			X	X			X	X
GS-11+		X			X	X			X	X
Engineer (General)	0801									
GS-5/7		X			X	X			X	
GS-9		X			X	X			X	
GS-11+		X			X			X	X	X
Environmental Protection Spec.	0028									
GS-5/7		X			X			X	X	
GS-9		X			X		X		X	
GS-11+		X			X			X		X
Facility Manager	1640									
GS-5/7		X			X	X			X	
GS-9		X			X		X			
GS-11+		X			X			X		X
FBI Special Agent	1811									
GS-5/7			X		X			X	X	
GS-9			X		X		X		X	X
GS-11+			X		X					X

OCCUPATION / GRADE LEVEL	SERIES#	HIRING SYSTEM		TEST REQUIREMENTS		HIRING VOLUME			RECRUITMENT FOCUS	
		Competitive	Excepted	Other	No Test	Many	Some	Few	External New Hires	Internal Promotion
Financial Administrator	0601									
GS-5/7		X				X			X	
GS-9		X			X		X			X
GS-11+		X			X			X		X
Financial Institution Examiner	0570									
GS-5/7		X			X	X			X	
GS-9		X			X		X			X
GS-11+		X			X			X		X
Financial Manager	0505									
GS-5/7		X			X		X		X	
GS-9		X			X		X		X	X
GS-11+		X			X			X		X
Firefighter	0081									
GS-5/7		X			X	X			X	
GS-9		X			X		X		X	X
GS-11+		X			X			X		X
Food Inspector	1863									
GS-5/7		X			X	X			X	
GS-9		X			X		X		X	
GS-11+		X			X			X		X
Foreign Affairs Analyst	0130									
GS-5/7		X			X	X			X	
GS-9		X			X		X			X
GS-11+		X			X			X		X
Foreign Language Broadcaster	1048									
GS-5/7		X			X		X		X	
GS-9		X			X		X		X	X
GS-11+		X			X			X		X
Foreign Service Officer	(none)									
GS-5/7			X	X			X		X	
GS-9			X		X			X		X
GS-11+			X		X			X		X
Forestry Technician	0482									
GS-5/7		X			X	X			X	
GS-9		X			X		X		X	
GS-11+		X			X			X		X
Geographer	0150									
GS-5/7		X			X		X		X	
GS-9		X			X			X	X	
GS-11+		X						X		X
Geologist	1350									
GS-5/7		X			X	X			X	
GS-9		X			X		X		X	
GS-11+		X			X		X			X

OCCUPATION / GRADE LEVEL	SERIES#	HIRING SYSTEM Competitive	Excepted	Other	TEST REQUIREMENTS No Test	HIRING VOLUME Many	Some	Few	RECRUITMENT FOCUS External New Hires	Internal Promotion
Guard	0085									
GS-5/7		X			X	X			X	
GS-9		X			X		X		X	X
GS-11+		X			X				X	
Highway Safety Manager	2125									
GS-5/7		X			X	X			X	
GS-9		X			X		X		X	
GS-11+		X						X		X
Historian	0170									
GS-5/7		X	X		X		X		X	
GS-9		X	X		X		X			
GS-11+		X	X		X			X		X
Housing Manager	1173									
GS-5/7		X			X	X			X	
GS-9		X			X		X		X	X
GS-11+		X						X		X
Hydrologist	1315									
GS-5/7		X			X	X			X	
GS-9		X			X	X			X	
GS-11+		X			X		X			X
Illustrator	1020									
GS-5/7		X			X			X	X	
GS-9		X			X			X	X	X
GS-11+		X			X			X	X	
Immigration Inspector	1816									
GS-5/7		X			X	X			X	
GS-9		X			X		X		X	X
GS-11+		X					X			
Import Specialist	1889									
GS-5/7		X			X	X			X	
GS-9		X			X		X		X	X
GS-11+		X					X			
Industrial Hygienist	0690									
GS-5/7		X			X		X		X	
GS-9		X			X		X		X	X
GS-11+		X			X		X		X	
Industrial Property Manager	1103									
GS-5/7		X			X	X			X	
GS-9		X			X		X		X	X
GS-11+		X						X	X	
Insurance Examiner	1163									
GS-5/7		X			X	X			X	
GS-9		X			X			X	X	X
GS-11+		X						X		

OCCUPATION	GRADE LEVEL	SERIES#	HIRING SYSTEM		TEST REQUIREMENTS		HIRING VOLUME			RECRUITMENT FOCUS	
			Competitive	Excepted	Other	No Test	Many	Some	Few	External New Hires	Internal Promotion
Intelligence Aid/Clerk	GS-5/7	0134	X		X		X			X	
	GS-9		X		X			X		X	
	GS-11+		X			X			X		X
Internal Revenue Agent	GS-5/7	0512	X		X		X			X	
	GS-9		X			X	X				X
	GS-11+		X			X		X			X
Internal Revenue Officer	GS-5/7	1169	X				X			X	
	GS-9		X			X	X				X
	GS-11+		X			X		X			X
Interpreter	GS-5/7	1040				X			X	X	
	GS-9			X		X			X	X	
	GS-11+			X		X			X	X	
Investigator	GS-5/7	1801	X				X			X	
	GS-9		X			X		X		X	X
	GS-11+		X			X			X		X
Labor Relations Specialist	GS-5/7	0233	X				X			X	
	GS-9		X			X			X		X
	GS-11+		X			X			X		X
Landscape Architect	GS-5/7	0807	X			X		X		X	
	GS-9		X			X		X			X
	GS-11+		X			X			X		X
Land Surveyor	GS-5/7	1373	X			X		X		X	
	GS-9		X			X		X		X	
	GS-11+		X			X			X	X	
Laundry Plant Manager	GS-5/7	1658	X			X		X		X	
	GS-9		X			X		X			X
	GS-11+		X			X		X			X
Legal Clerk/Technician	GS-5/7	0988	X			X		X		X	
	GS-9		X			X		X			X
	GS-11+		X			X			X		X
Librarian	GS-5/7	1410	X			X		X		X	
	GS-9		X			X		X		X	
	GS-11+		X			X		X			X

OCCUPATION	SERIES#	GRADE LEVEL	HIRING SYSTEM Competitive	HIRING SYSTEM Excepted	TEST REQUIREMENTS Other	TEST REQUIREMENTS No Test	HIRING VOLUME Many	HIRING VOLUME Some	HIRING VOLUME Few	RECRUITMENT FOCUS External New Hires	RECRUITMENT FOCUS Internal Promotion
Loan Specialist	1165	GS-5/7	X			X	X			X	
		GS-9	X			X		X		X	
		GS-11+	X						X		X
Logistics Manager	0346	GS-5/7	X			X	X			X	
		GS-9	X			X		X			X
		GS-11+	X						X		X
Management/Program Analyst	0343	GS-5/7	X			X	X			X	
		GS-9	X			X			X	X	
		GS-11+	X						X		X
Manpower Development	0142	GS-5/7	X			X	X			X	
		GS-9	X			X		X		X	
		GS-11+	X						X		X
Mathematician	1520	GS-5/7	X			X	X			X	
		GS-9	X			X		X		X	
		GS-11+	X			X			X		X
Medical/Health Trainee	0699	GS-5/7	X			X	X			X	
		GS-9	X			X		X		X	
		GS-11+	X			X			X		X
Medical Illustrator	1020	GS-5/7	X			X		X		X	
		GS-9	X			X		X		X	
		GS-11+	X			X		X		X	X
Medical Records Librarian	0689	GS-5/7	X			X	X			X	
		GS-9	X			X	X			X	
		GS-11+	X			X	X			X	X
Medical Technician	0845	GS-5/7	X			X		X		X	
		GS-9	X			X		X		X	
		GS-11+	X			X		X		X	X
Messenger	0302	GS-5/7	X			X			X	X	
		GS-9	X			X			X	X	
		GS-11+	X			X			X	X	X
Metallurgist	1321	GS-5/7	X			X	X			X	
		GS-9	X			X	X			X	
		GS-11+	X				X				X

OCCUPATION / GRADE LEVEL	SERIES#	HIRING SYSTEM		TEST REQUIREMENTS		HIRING VOLUME			RECRUITMENT FOCUS	
		Competitive	Excepted	Other	No Test	Many	Some	Few	External New Hires	Internal Promotion
Meteorologist	1340									
GS-5/7		X			X	X			X	
GS-9		X			X		X		X	
GS-11+		X			X		X			X
Microbiologist	0403									
GS-5/7		X			X	X			X	
GS-9		X			X	X			X	
GS-11+		X			X		X		X	X
Misc. Administration/Program	0301									
GS-5/7		X			X	X			X	
GS-9		X			X		X		X	
GS-11+		X								X
Museum Specialist/Technician	1016									
GS-5/7		X			X				X	
GS-9		X			X				X	
GS-11+		X						X		X
Navigator	2181									
GS-5/7		X			X			X	X	
GS-9		X			X			X	X	
GS-11+		X			X			X	X	X
Nurse (All Specialties)	0610									
GS-5/7		X			X	X			X	
GS-9		X			X	X			X	
GS-11+		X				X			X	X
Nursing Assistant	0621									
GS-5/7		X			X	X			X	
GS-9		X			X		X		X	X
GS-11+		X			X			X		X
Nutritionist/Dietician	0630									
GS-5/7		X			X	X			X	
GS-9		X			X		X		X	
GS-11+		X			X			X	X	X
Oceanographer	1360									
GS-5/7		X			X	X			X	
GS-9		X			X	X			X	
GS-11+		X			X	X			X	X
Optometrist	0662									
GS-5/7		X			X		X		X	
GS-9		X			X		X		X	
GS-11+		X			X			X	X	X
Outdoor Recreation Planner	0023									
GS-5/7		X			X				X	
GS-9		X			X			X		X
GS-11+		X						X		X

OCCUPATION / GRADE LEVEL	SERIES#	HIRING SYSTEM		TEST REQUIREMENTS		HIRING VOLUME			RECRUITMENT FOCUS	
		Competitive	Excepted	Other	No Test	Many	Some	Few	External New Hires	Internal Promotion
Park Ranger	0025									
GS-5/7		X					X		X	
GS-9		X			X			X		X
GS-11+		X			X			X		X
Personnel Management Spec.	0201									
GS-5/7		X			X	X			X	
GS-9		X			X		X		X	
GS-11+		X						X		X
Pharmacist	0660									
GS-5/7		X			X	X			X	
GS-9		X			X	X			X	
GS-11+		X			X	X		X	X	X
Photographer	1060									
GS-5/7		X							X	
GS-9		X			X			X		X
GS-11+		X			X			X		X
Physical Scientist	1301									
GS-5/7		X			X		X		X	
GS-9		X			X		X		X	
GS-11+		X			X			X	X	X
Physicist	1310									
GS-5/7		X			X		X		X	
GS-9		X			X		X		X	
GS-11+		X			X			X	X	X
Police Officer	0083									
GS-5/7		X			X	X			X	
GS-9		X			X		X		X	X
GS-11+		X			X			X		X
Postal Worker	(None)									
PS-4/5			X	X		X			X	
PS-6			X	X			X			X
PS-7+			X	X				X		X
Printing Manager	1654									
GS-5/7		X			X	X		X	X	
GS-9		X			X		X	X	X	X
GS-11+		X			X			X		X
Procurement Analyst	1106									
GS-5/7		X			X	X			X	
GS-9		X			X		X		X	
GS-11+		X			X			X		X
Production Controller	1152									
GS-5/7		X			X		X		X	
GS-9		X			X		X			X
GS-11+		X			X			X		X

OCCUPATION / GRADE LEVEL	SERIES#	HIRING SYSTEM		TEST REQUIREMENTS		HIRING VOLUME			RECRUITMENT FOCUS	
		Competitive	Excepted	Other	No Test	Many	Some	Few	External New Hires	Internal Promotion
Program Analyst	0343									
GS-5/7		X				X			X	
GS-9		X			X		X			X
GS-11+		X			X		X			X
Psychologist	0180									
GS-5/7			X		X	X			X	
GS-9			X		X	X			X	
GS-11+			X		X	X			X	X
Public Affairs Specialist	1035									
GS-5/7		X			X	X			X	
GS-9		X			X		X			X
GS-11+		X						X		X
Purchasing Agent	1105									
GS-5/7		X			X		X		X	
GS-9		X			X		X		X	
GS-11+		X			X			X		X
Quality Assurance Inspector	1910									
GS-5/7		X			X	X			X	
GS-9		X			X		X		X	
GS-11+		X						X		X
Radio Operator	0389									
GS-5/7		X			X			X	X	
GS-9		X			X			X		X
GS-11+		X			X			X		X
Railroad Safety Inspector	2121									
GS-5/7		X			X		X		X	
GS-9		X			X		X		X	
GS-11+		X			X		X		X	X
Realty Specialist	1170									
GS-5/7		X			X	X			X	
GS-9		X			X		X		X	
GS-11+		X						X		X
Recreation Aid	0189									
GS-5/7		X			X		X		X	
GS-9		X			X		X		X	X
GS-11+		X			X		X			X
Sales Store Clerical	2091									
GS-5/7		X			X	X			X	
GS-9		X		X		X			X	
GS-11+		X			X			X	X	X
Secretary	0318									
GS-5/7		X		X	X				X	
GS-9		X			X		X		X	X
GS-11+		X							X	X

OCCUPATION / GRADE LEVEL	SERIES#	HIRING SYSTEM		TEST REQUIREMENTS		HIRING VOLUME			RECRUITMENT FOCUS	
		Competitive	Excepted	Other	No Test	Many	Some	Few	External New Hires	Internal Promotion
Security Administrator	0080									
GS-5/7		X				X			X	
GS-9		X			X		X		X	
GS-11+		X			X			X		X
Social Worker	0185									
GS-5/7		X			X	X			X	
GS-9		X			X		X		X	
GS-11+		X			X			X		X
Soil Conservationist	0457									
GS-5/7		X			X		X		X	
GS-9		X			X		X		X	
GS-11+		X								X
Speech Pathologist	0665									
GS-5/7		X			X	X			X	
GS-9		X			X	X			X	
GS-11+		X				X			X	X
Sports Specialist	0030									
GS-5/7		X			X			X	X	
GS-9		X			X			X		X
GS-11+		X			X			X		X
Statistician	1530									
GS-5/7		X			X	X			X	
GS-9		X			X	X			X	
GS-11+		X				X			X	X
Supply Clerical/Technician	2005									
GS-5/7		X			X		X		X	
GS-9		X			X			X		X
GS-11+		X			X			X		X
Teacher/Trainer	1710									
GS-5/7		X			X		X		X	
GS-9		X			X		X		X	
GS-11+		X						X	X	
Technical Writer/Editor	1083									
GS-5/7		X			X		X		X	
GS-9		X			X		X		X	
GS-11+		X					X			X
Telephone Operator	0382									
GS-5/7		X		X			X		X	
GS-9		X			X			X	X	
GS-11+		X			X			X	X	
Theatre Specialist	1054									
GS-5/7		X			X		X		X	
GS-9		X			X			X		X
GS-11+		X						X		X

OCCUPATION GRADE LEVEL	SERIES#	HIRING SYSTEM		TEST REQUIREMENTS		HIRING VOLUME			RECRUITMENT FOCUS	
		Competitive	Excepted	Other	No Test	Many	Some	Few	External New Hires	Internal Promotion
Trade Specialist	1140									
GS-5/7		X			X	X			X	
GS-9		X			X		X		X	
GS-11+		X						X		X
Traffic Manager	2130									
GS-5/7		X			X	X			X	
GS-9		X			X		X		X	
GS-11+		X						X		X
Veterinarian	0701									
GS-5/7		X			X		X		X	
GS-9		X			X			X	X	
GS-11+		X			X			X	X	X
Work Unit Supervisor	0313									
GS-5/7		X			X	X			X	
GS-9		X			X		X			X
GS-11+		X			X			X		X
Zoologist	0410									
GS-5/7		X			X			X	X	
GS-9		X			X			X	X	
GS-11+		X			X			X	X	

Appendix D: Federal Personnel Offices

The following is a list of addresses for all the major departments and agencies within the Federal government. Many have been granted Direct Hire Authority for certain positions, and therefore can be contacted directly by applicants seeking employment information. Phone numbers have not been supplied since they tend to change rather frequently.

Addresses are also supplied for military bases (important in the search for Wage Grade positions) and for OPM Service Centers throughout the United States and its territories. OPM Service Centers publish local listings of vacancies and registers, provide SF-171's and any additional application forms, and administer written tests. Many are only open certain hours of the day and on certain days of the week, so you may have to call more than once to get the information you are seeking.

Delegated Hiring Authority is described in Step 2 (p. 41).

OPM Service Centers are described in Step 3 (p. 64).

CONTENTS

CABINET AGENCIES

Department of Agriculture (USDA)
Administration Building
Personnel Operations Division, Rm. 31W
14th & Independence Avenue, SW
Washington, DC 20250

USDA Food Safety and Inspection Service (FSIS)
Personnel Division, Rm. 3133
14th St. and Independence Ave., S.W.
Washington, D.C. 20250

Meat and Poultry Regional Inspection Offices

Northeast	*Southeast*	*North Central*
7th Fl.	Room 299 South	11338 Aurora Ave.
1421 Cherry St.	1718 Peachtree St., NW	Des Moines, IA 50322
Philadelphia, PA 19102	Atlanta, GA 30309	

Southwest	*Western*
Room 5F41	Building 2C
1100 Commerce St.	620 Central Ave.
Dallas, TX 75242	Alameda, CA 94501

USDA Forest Service
Personnel Office
Rosslyn Plaza, Bldg. E
1621 N. Kent St.
Arlington, VA 22209

Forest Service Regional Offices

Eastern	*Rocky Mountain*	*Pacific Southwest*	*Southwestern*
Room 500	11177 West 8th Ave.	630 Sansome St.	Federal Building
Henry S. Reuss Federal Plz.	P.O. Box 25127	San Francisco, CA 94111	517 Gold Ave., SW
310 W. Wisconsin Ave.	Lakewood, CO 80225		Albuquerque, NM 87102
Milwaukee, WI 53203		*Southern*	
		1720 Peachtree St., NE	*Alaska Area*
Northern	*Intermountain*	Atlanta, GA 30367	Federal Office Building
Federal Building	Federal Building		Box 21628
P.O. Box 7669	324 25th St.	*Pacific Northwest*	Juneau, AK 99802-1628
Missoula, MT 59807	Ogden, UT 84401	333 SW First Ave.	
		P.O. Box 3623	
		Portland, OR 97208	

Farmers Home Administration
501 School St., SW
3rd Floor
Washington, DC 20024

USDA Soil Conservation Service
Attn: SEU
P.O. Box 37636
Washington, DC 20013

Department of Commerce
Office of Personnel, Rm. 5001
Herbert C. Hoover Building
14th Street & Constitution Ave., NW
Washington, DC 20230

Bureau of Census

Personnel Office, Rm. 3260
Federal Office Building No. 3
Suitland and Silver Hill Roads
Suitland, MD 20233

Bureau of Census Regional Offices

Atlanta
Suite 3200
101 Marietta St., NW
Atlanta, GA 30303-2700

Boston
Suite 301
2 Copley Place
P.O. Box 9108
Boston, MA 02117-9108

Charlotte
Suite 106
901 Center Park Dr.
Charlotte, NC 28217-2935

Chicago
Room 557
175 W. Jackson Blvd.
Chicago, IL 60604-2689

Dallas
Suite 210
6303 Harry Hines Blvd.
Dallas, TX 75235-5269

Denver
6900 W. Jefferson Ave.
P.O. Box 272020
Denver, CO 80227-9020

Detroit
1395 Brewery Park Blvd.
Detroit, MI 48232-5405

Kansas City
Suite 600
Gateway Tower II
400 State Ave.
Kansas City, KS 66101-2410

Los Angeles
Suite 300
15350 Sherman Way
Van Nuys, CA 91406-4224

New York
Room 37-130
Jacob J. Javits Federal Bldg.
26 Federal Plaza
New York, NY 10278-0044

Philadelphia
First Floor
105 S. 7th Street
Philadelphia, PA 19106-3395

Seattle
Suite 500
101 Stewart Street
Seattle, WA 98101-1098

National Institute of Standards and Technology (NIST)
Office of Personnel
Administration Building, Rm. A133
Gaithersburg, MD 20899-0001

National Oceanic and Atmospheric Administration (NOAA)
Human Resource Management Office
Silver Spring Metro Center 3
1315 East-West Highway
Room 13535
Silver Springs, MD 20910

Patent and Trademark Office
Crystal Park Bldg. 1, Room 700
2011 Crystal Drive
Arlington, VA 22202

Department of Defense (DOD)

The Pentagon, Rm. 32269
Office of Civilian Personnel
Washington, DC 20301

Office of Inspector General
Personnel and Security Div.
Operations Branch
400 Army Navy Drive
Arlington, VA 22202

Defense Contract Audit Agency
Office of Human Resources
Building 4, Room 4A415
Cameron Station
5010 Duke Street
Alexandria, VA 22304

Defense Intelligence Agency
Human Resources
3100 Clarendon Boulevard
Arlington, VA 22201-5300

Defense Mapping Agency
Personnel Office
8613 Lee Highway
Fairfax, VA 22031-2137

Department of the Army
Army Staff Civilian Personnel Office
Room 2E591, The Pentagon
Washington, DC 20310-6800

Department of the Navy
Human Resources Office - W
Washington Navy Yard
901 M St. SE, Bldg. 200
Washington, DC 20374-5050

Marine Corps Combat Development Command
Attn: Civilian Personnel Branch
H&S Battalion (Manpower)
Quantico, VA 22134-5001

Department of the Air Force
HQ USAF Civilian Personnel Office
AFDW/DPCS, Room 5E977, Pentagon
Washington, DC 20330-6420

Department of Education
Office of Personnel
Federal Office Building 6, Rm 1156
400 Maryland Ave., SW
Washington, DC 20202

Department of Education Regional Offices

Atlanta 101 Marietta Towers Atlanta, GA 30323	*Dallas* 1200 Main Tower Bldg. Dallas, TX 75202-4309	*New York* 26 Federal Plaza New York, NY 10278-0195
Boston J. W. McCormack P.O. and Courthouse Boston, MA 02109-4557	*Denver* 1244 Speer Blvd. Denver, CO 80204-3582	*Philadelphia* 3535 Market Street Philadelphia, PA 19104-3398
Chicago 401 S. State Street Chicago, IL 60605-1225	*Kansas City* 10220 N. Executive Hills Blvd. Kansas City, MO 64153-1367	*San Francisco* 50 UN Plaza San Francisco, CA 94102-4987 *Seattle* 915 Second Ave. Seattle, WA 98174-1099

Department of Energy
Office of Personnel
Forrestal Building
1000 Independence Ave., SW
Washington, DC 20585

Department of Health and Human Services (HHS)
Office of Personnel
Hubert H. Humphrey Building
200 Independence Ave., SW
Washington, DC 20201

HHS Regional Offices

Region I JFK Federal Bldg. Government Center Boston, MA 02203	*Region II* Jacob J. Javits Federal Bldg. 26 Federal Plaza New York, NY 10278	*Region III* Gateway Bldg. 3535 Market St, Phildelphia, PA 19104	*Region IV* 101 Marietta Tower Atlanta, GA 30323

Region V
105 West Adams St.
Chicago, IL 60603

Region VI
Cabell Federal Bldg.
1100 Commerce St.
Dallas, TX 75242

Region VII
601 East 12th Street
Kansas City, MO 64106

Region VIII
1961 Stout Street
Denver, CO 80294-3538

Region IX
50 United Nations Plaza
San Francisco, CA 94102

Region X
2201 Sixth Avenue
Seattle, WA 98121

Health Care Financing Administration
Office of Personnel and Recruitment
Central Building
7500 Security Boulevard
Baltimore, MD 21244-1850

Indian Health Service Regional Offices

South Dakota
Federal Building., Room 309
115 4th Avenue SE
Aberdeen, SD 57401

Maryland
Parklawn Building
5600 Fishers Lane
Rockville, MD 20857

Maryland
Twinbrook Parkway
12720 Twinbrook Parkway
Rockville, MD 20857

National Institutes of Health
Employment Office
Building 1, Room 1C27
9000 Rockville Pike
Bethesda, MD 20892

Social Security Administration
Office of Personnel
West High-Rise Building
6401 Security Boulevard
Baltimore, MD 21235

Department of Housing and Urban Development (HUD)

Office of Personnel
HUD Building, Rm. 2272
451 7th Street, SW
Washington, DC 20410

HUD Regional Offices

Atlanta
R. Russell Federal Bldg.
75 Spring St., SW
Atlanta, GA 30303

New England/Mass.
Thomas P. ONeill, Jr.
    Federal Bldg.
Room 375
10 Causeway St.
Boston, MA 02222-1092

Chicago
300 S. Wacker Drive
Chicago, IL 60606

Connecticut
330 Main St.
Hartford, CT 06106-1860

Denver
Executive Tower Bldg.
1405 Curtis St.
Denver, CO 80202

Fort Worth
1600 Throckmorton
Fort Worth, TX 76102

Kansas City
1103 Grand Ave.
Kansas City, MO 64106

New York
26 Federal Plaza
New York, NY 10278

Philadelphia
105 South 7th St.
Liberty Square Bldg.
Philadelphia, PA 19106

San Francisco
450 Golden Gate Ave.
San Francisco, CA 94102

Department of the Interior

Office of Personnel
Interior Building
849 C Street, NW
Washington, DC 20240

Bureau of Indian Affairs
Personnel Services Branch
Interior South Building
1951 Constitution Ave., NW
Washington, DC 20245

National Park Service
Personnel Division
Interior Building
1849 C St.
Washington, DC 20240

U.S. Fish and Wildlife Service
Office of Human Resources
Webb Building
4040 N. Fairfax Dr.
Arlington, VA 22203

Department of Justice
Personnel Office
Main Justice Building
10th Street and Constitution Avenue, N.W.
Washington, DC 20530

Bureau of Prisons Locations

Mid-Atlantic Region:
Alderson, WV
Ashland, KY
Beckly, WV
Butner, NC
Cumberland, MD
Lexington, KY
Manchester, KY
Memphis, TN
Milan, MI
Millington, TN
Morgantown, WV
Petersburg, VA
Seymour Jounson AFB, NC
Terre Haute, IN

Western Region:
Boron, CA
Dublin, CA
Eloy, AZ
Lompoc, CA
Los Angeles, CA
Nellis AFB, NV
Phoenix, AZ
Safford, AZ
San Diego, CA
Sheridan, OR
Terminal Island, CA
Tucson, AZ

Northeast Region:
Allenwood, PA
Bradford, PA
Brooklyn, NY
Danbury, CT
Fairton, NJ
Ft. Devins, MA
Ft. Dix, NJ
Lewisburg, PA
Loretto, PA
Minersville, PA
New York, NY
Otisville, NY
Ray Brook, NY

North Central Region:
Chicago, IL
Duluth, MN
Englewood, CO
Florence, CO
Greenville, IL
Leavenworth, KS
Marion, IL
Oxford, WI
Pekin, IL
Rochester, MN
Sandstone, MN
Springfield, MO
Waseca, MN
Yankton, SD

South Central Region:
Anthony, NM-TX
Bastrop, TX
Big Springs, TX
Bryan, TX
El Paso, TX
El Reno, OK
Ft. Worth, TX
Oakdale, LA
Oklahoma City, OK
Seagoville, TX
Texarkana, TX
Three Rivers, TX

Southeast Region:
Atlanta, GA
Eglin AFB, FL
Estill, SC
Guaynabo, PR
Jesup, GA
Marianna, FL
Maxwell AFB, AL
Miami, FL
Pensacola, FL
Talladega, FL
Tallahassee, FL

Bureau of Prisons
HOLC Building
Central Office/Personnel
320 First Street, NW
Washington, DC 20534

Prison Industries (UNICOR)
Human Resources Division
320 First Street, NW
Washington, DC 20534

Bureau of Prisons Regional Offices

South Central
4211 Cedar Springs Rd
Suite 300
Dallas, TX 75219

Southeast
523 McDonough Blvd., SE
Atlanta, GA 30315

Western
3rd Floor, 7950 Dublin Blvd.
Dublin, CA 94568

North Central
8th Floor
Gateway Complex Tower II
4th and State Ave.
Kansas City, KS 66101-2492

Northeast
U.S. Customs House
7th Floor
2nd and Chestnut Sts.
Philadelphia, PA 19106

Mid-Atlantic
Suite 100N
Junction Business Park
10010 Junction Dr.
Annapolis, MD 20701

Drug Enforcement Administration (DEA)
Office of Personnel
700 Army-Navy Drive
Washington, DC 20537

DEA Division Offices

Atlanta
75 Spring St., SW
Room 740
Atlanta, GA 30303

Boston
50 Stantiford St., Suite 200
Boston, MA 02114

Chicago
Suite 1200
John C. Kluczynski Fed. Bldg.
230 S. Dearborn St.
Chicago, IL 60604

Dallas
1880 Regal Row
Dallas, TX 75235

Denver
115 Inverness Dr. East
Englewood, CO 80112

Detroit
431 Howard St.
Detroit, MI 48226

Houston
333 W. Loop North
Suite 300
Houston, TX 77024-7794

Los Angeles
255 E. Temple St., 20th Floor
Los Angeles, CA 90012

Miami
8400 NW 53rd St.
Miami, FL 33166

New Orleans
Suite 1800, 3 Lakeway Center
3838 Causeway Blvd.
Metairie, LA 70002

New York
99 Tenth Ave.
New York, NY 10011

Philadelphia
Federal Bldg.
600 Arch St., Rm. 10224
Philadelphia, PA 19106

Newark
Federal Office Bldg.
970 Broad St., Room 806
Newark, NJ 07102

Phoenix
301 Westmount Place
3010 N. 2nd Ave.
Phoenix, AZ 85012

St. Louis
7911 Forsythe Blvd.
Suite 500
United Bank Bldg.
St. Louis, MO 63105

San Diego
402 W. 35th St.
National City, CA 91950

San Francisco
450 Golden Gate Ave.
P.O. Box 36035
San Francisco, CA 94102

Seattle
220 West Mercer St.
Suite 104
Seattle, WA 98119

Washington, DC
Room 2558
400 6th St. SW
Washington, DC 20024

Federal Bureau of Investigation (FBI)
Office of Personnel
J. Edgar Hoover FBI Building
9th Street & Pennsylvania Ave., NW
Washington, DC 20535

FBI Field Offices

Birmingham, AL	(205) 252-7705	St. Louis, MO	(314) 241-5357
Mobile, AL	(205) 438-3674	Las Vegas, NV	(702) 385-1281
Anchorage, AK	(907) 276-4441	Omaha, NE	(402) 493-8688
Phoenix, AZ	(602) 279-5511	Newark, NJ	(201) 622-5613
Little Rock, AR	(501) 221-9100	Albuquerque, NM	(505) 247-1555
Los Angeles, CA	(310) 477-6565	Albany, NY	(518) 465-7551
Sacramento, CA	(916) 481-9110	Buffalo, NY	(716) 856-7800
San Diego, CA	(619) 231-1122	New York, NY	(212) 335-2700
San Francisco, CA	(415) 553-7400	Charlotte, NC	(704) 529-1030
Denver, CO	(303) 629-7171	Cincinnati, OH	(513) 421-4310
New Haven, CT	(203) 777-6311	Cleveland, OH	(216) 522-1400
Washington, DC	(202) 324-6230	Oklahoma City, OK	(405) 842-7471
Jacksonville, FL	(904) 721-1211	Portland, OR	(503) 224-4181
Miami, FL	(305) 944-9101	Philadelphia, PA	(215) 629-0800
Tampa, FL	(813) 228-7661	Pittsburgh, PA	(412) 471-2000
Atlanta, GA	(404) 679-9000	Columbia, SC	(803) 254-3011
Honolulu, HI	(808) 521-1411	Knoxville, TN	(615) 544-0751
Chicago, IL	(312) 431-1333	Memphis, TN	(901) 525-7373
Springfield, IL	(217) 522-9675	Dallas, TX	(214) 720-2200
Indianapolis, IN	(317) 639-3301	El Paso, TX	(915) 533-7451
Louisville, KY	(502) 583-3941	Houston, TX	(713) 224-1511
New Orleans, LA	(504) 522-4671	San Antonio, TX	(512) 225-6741
Boston, MA	(617) 742-5533	Salt Lake City, UT	(801) 579-1400
Baltimore, MD	(401) 265-8080	Norfolk, VA	(804) 623-3111
Detroit, MI	(313) 965-2323	Richmond, VA	(804) 644-2631
Minneapolis, MN	(612) 376-3200	Seattle, WA	(206) 622-0460
Jackson, MS	(601) 948-5000	Milwaukee, WI	(414) 276-4684
Kansas City, MO	(816) 221-6100		

Immigration and Naturalization Service (INS)
Personnel Division
Chester A. Arthur Building, Rm 6023
425 I Street, NW
Washington, DC 20536

INS Regional Offices

Western	*Eastern*	*Central*
24000 Avila Rd.	70 Kimball Ave.	Room 2300
P.O. Box 30080	South Burlington, VT 05401	7701 N. Stemmons Freeway
Laguna Niguel, CA 92677-8080		Dallas, TX 75247

U.S. Marshals Service
Personnel Management Division
Lincoln Place 1
600 Army Navy Drive
Arlington, VA 22202

Department of Labor

Office of Personnel and Human Resources
Frances Perkins Building
200 Constitution Ave., NW
Washington, DC 20210

Department of State

Office of Personnel
Main State Department Building
2201 C Street, NW
Washington, DC 20520-2810

Trade and Development Program   *U.S. Mission to the United Nations*
Room 309, SA-16   799 United Nations Plaza
State Department   New York, NY 10017-3505
Washington, DC 20523-1602

Department of Transportation

Office of Personnel, Nassif Building
400 7th Street, SW
Washington, DC 20590

Federal Aviation Administration (FAA)
Personnel Offices
800 Independence Ave., SW
Washington, DC 20591

FAA Personnel Services Div.
Office of Aviation Careers   Mike Monroney Aeronautical Center
P.O. Box 26650, AMV-200   P.O. Box 25082
Oklahoma City, OK 73126   Oklahoma City, OK 73125

FAA Technical Center
Technical Building
Atlantic City, NJ 08405

FAA Field Installations

Alaskan
Box 14
Anchorage, AK 99513

Central
Federal Bldg.
601 East 12th St.
Kansas City, MO 64106

Eastern
Federal Bldg.
JFK International Airport
Jamaica, NY 11430

Great Lakes
2300 E. Devon Ave.
Des Plaines, IL 60018

New England
12 New England Exec. Park
Burlington, MA 01803

Northwest Mountain
1601 Lind Ave., SW
Renton, WA 98055

Southern
P.O. Box 20636
Atlanta, GA 30320

Southwest
P.O. Box 1689
Fort Worth, TX 76101

Western–Pacific
P.O. Box 92007
Worldway Postal Center
Los Angeles, CA 90009

Federal Highway Administration
Office of Personnel, Nassif Bldg.
400 7th St., SW
Washington, DC 20590

Federal Railroad Administration
Office of Personnel
Nassif Bldg.
400 7th St. SW
Washington, DC 20590

Federal Transit Administration
Office of Personnel
Nassif Building
400 7th St. SW
Washington, DC 20590

Maritime Administration
Office of Personnel
Nassif Bldg.
400 7th St. SW
Washington, DC 20590

National Highway Traffic Safety Administration
Office of Personnel
Nassif Bldg.
400 7th St. SW
Washington, DC 20590

Regional Offices

Region I
Transportation System Center
Kendall Square Code 903
Cambridge, MA 02142

Region II
222 Mamaroneck Av., Suite 204
White Plains, NY 10605

Region III
BWI Commerce Park, Suite L
7526 Connelly Drive
Hanover, MD 21076-1699

Region IV
1720 Peachtree Road, Suite 1048
Atlanta, GA 30309

Region V
18209 Dixie Highway
Homewood, IL 60430

Region VI
819 Taylor Street
Room 8A38
Fort Worth, TX 76102

Region VII
P.O. Box 412515
Kansas City, MO 64141

Region VIII
555 Lake Street, 4th Floor
Lakewood, CO 80228

Region IX
211 Main Street, Suite 1000
San Francisco, CA 94105

Region X
3140 Jackson Federal Bldg.
915 Second Avenue
Seattle, WA 98174

U.S. Coast Guard
Coast Guard Headquarters, Attn Personnel Office
2100 2nd Street, SW
Washington, DC 20593-0001

Department of the Treasury

Office of Personnel
Main Treasury
1500 Pennsylvania Ave., NW
Washington, DC 20220

Bureau of Alcohol, Tobacco, and Firearms
Personnel Division
650 Massachusetts Avenue, NW
Room 4170
Washington, DC 20226

Internal Revenue Service (IRS)
Human Resources Division
1111 Constitution Ave., NW
Washington, DC 20224

IRS Service Centers

Fresno, CA
5045 East Futler Avenue
Fresno, CA 93880
(209) 456-5454

Ogden UT
P.O. Box 9941, Mail Stop 1513
Ogden, UT 84409
(801) 620-6300

Cincinnati, OH/Covington, KY
P.O. Box 287, Stop 612
Covington, KY 41019
(513) 357-5559

Austin, TX
P.O. Box 934
Stop 1541, AUSC
Austin, TX 78767
(512) 477-5627

Andover, MA
P.O. Box 311
Andover, MA 01810
(508) 474-9675

Brookhaven, NY
P.O. Box 400
Holtsville, NY 11742
(516) 654-6055

Kansas City, MO
P.O. Box 24551
Kansas City, MO 64106
(816) 926-5558

Memphis, TN
3131 Democrat Road
Memphis, TN 37501
(901) 546-2130

Philadelphia, PA
P.O. Box 245
Bensalem, PA 19020
(215) 516-JOBS

Atlanta, GA
4800 Buford Highway,
Stop 79-A
Chamblee, GA 30341

Office of Comptroller of the Currency (OCC)
National Recruitment Coordinator
Human Resources Division
250 E Street, SW
Washington, DC 20219

U.S. Customs Service
Personnel Office
Gelman Building
2120 L Street, NW
Washington, DC 20037

U.S. Customs Regional Offices

Northeast
Room 801
10 Causeway St.
Boston, MA 02222-1056

Southeast
909 SE First Avenue
Miami, FL 33131-2595

New York
Suite 716
6 World Trade Center
New York, NY 10048-0945

North Central
9th Floor, 610 S. Canal Street
Chicago, IL 60607

Pacific
Room 705
1 World Trade Ctr.
Long Beach, CA 90831-0700

South Central
Room 337, 423 Canal St.
New Orleans, LA 70130-2341

Southwest
Room 1200
2323 S. Shepherd
Houston, TX 77019

Bureau of Engraving and Printing
Engraving and Printing Annex
14th and C Streets, SW
Washington, DC 20228

Federal Law Enforcement Training Center
Federal Law Enforcement Training Center
Glynco, GA 31524

Financial Management Service
Prince Georges Center II
3700 East-West Highway
Hyattsville, MD 20781

United States Mint
Judiciary Square Building
633 Third Street, NW
Washington, DC 20220

Bureau of the Public Debt
Hintgen Building
200 Third Street
Parkersburg, WV 26106-1328

U.S. Secret Service
Personnel Division, Rm 912
1800 G Street, NW
Washington, DC 20023

Department of Veterans Affairs
Office of Personnel and Labor Relations
VA Building, Room 055B
810 Vermont Ave., NW
Washington, DC 20420

INDEPENDENT AGENCIES

*Administrative Conference of the
    United States*
Gelman Bldg.
2120 L Street, NW
Washington, DC 20037

*Advisory Commission on
    Intergovernmental Relations*
Tech World Bldg.
800 K Street
Washington, DC 20575

African Development Foundation
1400 I Street, NW
Washington, DC 20005

*Agency for International
    Development (USAID)*
State Department Building
2201 C St., NW
Washington, DC 20523

Central Intelligence Agency (CIA)
Office of Personnel
725 17th St., NW
Washington, DC 20503

Commission on Civil Rights
624 Ninth St., NW
Washington, DC 20425

Commission of Fine Arts
441 F Street, NW
Washington, DC 20001

Commodity Futures Trading Commission
2033 K St., NW
Washington, DC 20581

Consumer Product Safety Commission
East West Towers
4330 East West Highway
Bethesda, MD 20814

Delaware River Basin Commission
25 State Police Drive
P.O. Box 7360
West Trenton, NJ 08628

Environmental Protection Agency
Office of Personnel
Waterside Mall Building
401 M Street, SW
Washington, DC 20460

EPA Regional Offices

Region I
Room 2203
JFK Federal Bldg.
One Congress St.
Boston, MA 02203

Region II
290 Broadway
New York, NY 10007-1866

Region III
841 Chestnut Street
Philadelphia, PA 19107

Region IV
345 Courtland St., NE
Atlanta, GA 30365

Region V
77 West Jackson St.
Chicago, IL 60604-3507

Region VI
Suite 1200
1445 Ross Avenue
Dallas, TX 75270-2733

Region VII
726 Minnesota Ave.
Kansas City, KS 66101

Region VIII
Suite 500, 999 18th St.
Denver, CO 80202-1603

Region IX
75 Hawthorne St.
San Francisco, CA 94105

Region X
1200 6th Ave.
Seattle, WA 98101

Equal Employment Opportunity Commission
1801 L Street, NW
Washington, DC 20507

Export–Import Bank of the United States
Lafayette Bldg.
811 Vermont Ave., NW
Washington, DC 20571

Farm Credit Administration
Farm Credit Bldg.
1501 Farm Credit Drive
McLean, VA 22102-5090

Federal Communications Commission
FCC Bldg.
1919 M Street, NW
Washington, DC 20554

Federal Deposit Insurance Corporation (FDIC)
Office of Personnel Management
550 17th Street, NW
Washington, DC 20429

FDIC Regional Offices

Atlanta
Suite 1200, Marquis One Bldg.
245 Peachtree Ave., NE
Atlanta, GA 30309-3415

Boston
Westwood Exec. Center
200 Lowder Brook Drive
Westwood, MA 02090

Chicago
Suite 3600
500 W. Monroe St.
Chicago, IL 60661

Dallas
Suite 1900, 1910 Pacific Ave.
Dallas, TX 75201

Kansas City
Suite 1500, 2345 Grand Ave.
Kansas City, MO 64108

Memphis
Suite 1900, Clark Tower
5100 Poplar Ave.
Memphis, TN 38137

New York
19th Fl., 452 Fifth Ave.
New York, NY 10018

San Francisco
Suite 2300, 25 Ecker St.
San Francisco, CA 94105

Resolution Trust Corporation
Office of Personnel
1777 F Street, NW
Washington, DC 20429

RTC Field Offices

Atlanta
South Tower
225 Peachtree St., NE
Atlanta, GA 30303

California
4000 MacArthur Boulevard
Newport Beach, CA 92660-2516

Dallas
3500 Maple Avenue
Dallas, TX 75219

Denver
Suite 800
Tower 3
1515 Arapahoe Street
Denver, CO 80202

Kansas City
4900 Main Street
Kansas City, MO 64112

Valley Forge
1000 Adams Avenue
Norristown, PA 19403-2402

Federal Election Commission
PEPCO Bldg.
999 E St., NW
Washington, DC 20463

Federal Emergency Management Agency
Federal Center Plaza
500 C St., SW
Washington, DC 20472

Federal Housing Finance Board
1777 F Street, NW
Washington, DC 20006

Federal Labor Relations Authority
607 14th Street
Washington, DC 20424-0001

Federal Maritime Commission
800 North Capitol St., NW
Washington, DC 20573

Federal Mediation and Conciliation Service
FMCS Bldg.
2100 K Street, NW
Washington, DC 20427

Federal Mine Safety and Health Review Commission
Riddell Building
1730 K Street, NW
Washington, DC 20006

Federal Reserve System
Bd. of Governors, Div. Human Resources
20th Street & C Streets, NW
Washington, DC 20551

Federal Retirement Thrift Investment Board
1250 H St., NW
Washington, DC 20005

Federal Trade Commission
FTC Bldg.
6th St. & Pennsylvania Ave., NW
Washington, DC 20580

General Accounting Office
Office of Human Resources
GAO Bldg.
441 G Street, NW
Washington, DC 20548

General Services Administration (GSA)
National Capital Region
18th & F Streets, NW
Washington, DC 20405

GSA Regional Offices

New England
Room 1075
Boston Federal Building
10 Causeway St.
Boston, MA 02222

Northeast and Caribbean
26 Federal Plaza
New York, NY 10278

Mid Atlantic
9th & Market Sts.
Philadelphia, PA 19107

Southeast
75 Spring St., SW
Atlanta, GA 30303

Great Lakes
230 S. Dearborn St.
Chicago, IL 60604

Heartland
1500 East Bannister Rd.
Kansas City, MO 64131

Greater SW
819 Taylor St.
Fort Worth, TX 76102

Rocky Mountain
Bldg. 41, Room 200
Denver Federal Center

P.O. Box 25006
Denver, CO 80225

Pacific Rim
525 Market St.
San Francisco, CA 94105

Northwest
GSA Center
Auburn, WA 98002

National Capital
7th & D Streets, SW
Washington, DC 20407

Government Printing Office
GPO Bldg. 3
North Capitol Street, NW
Washington, DC 20401

Inter-American Foundation
901 N. Stuart St.
Arlington, VA 22203

Interstate Commerce Commission
12th St. & Constitution Ave., NW
Washington, DC 20423

Library of Congress
James Madison Bldg.
101 Independence Ave., SE
Washington, DC 20540

Marine Mammal Commission
1825 Connecticut Ave., NW
Washington, DC 20009

U.S. Merit Systems Protection Board
Vermont Building
1120 Vermont Ave., NW
Washington, DC 20419

National Aeronautics and Space Administration
Office of Personnel and Human Resources
NASA Headquarters Building
Two Independence Square
300 E Street, SW
Washington, DC 20546-0001

NASA Research Centers

Ames Research Center
Moffett Field, CA 94035-1000
Dryden Flight Research Center
P.O. Box 273
Edwards, CA 93523-0273

Goddard Space Flight Center
Greenbelt Road
Greenbelt, MD 20771-0001

Goddard Institute for Space Studies
2880 Broadway
New York, NY 10025

Jet Propulsion Laboratory (JPL)
4800 Oak Grove Drive
Pasadena, CA 91109-8099

Lyndon B. Johnson Space Center
Houston, TX 77058-3696

John F. Kennedy Space Center
FL 32899-0001

KSV VLS Resident Office
Vandenberg AFB
P.O. Box 425
Lompoc, CA 93438

Langley Research Center
Hampton, VA 23681-0001

Langley Research Center Commercial Technology Office
Hampton, VA 23665-5225

Lewis Research Center
21000 Brookpark Road
Cleveland, OH 44135-3191

George C. Marshall Space Flight Center
AL 35812-0001

Michoud Assembly Facility
P.O. Box 29300
New Orleans, LA 70189

NASA Management Office
Jet Propulsion Laboratory
4800 Oak Grove Drive
Pasadena, CA 91109

Slidell Computer Complex
1010 Gause Boulevard
Slidell, LA 70458

John C. Stennis Space Center
MS 39529-6000

Wallops Flight Facility
Goddard Space Flight Center
Wallops Island, VA 23337-5099

JSC White Sands Test Facility
Johnson Space Center
P.O. Drawer MM
Las Cruces, NM 88004-0020

National Archives and Records Administration
8601 Adelphi Rd.
College Park, MD 20740-6001

National Credit Union Administration
1775 Duke St.
Alexandria, VA 22314-3428

National Foundation on the Arts and the Humanities
Old Post Office Bldg.
1100 Pennsylvania Ave., NW
Washington, DC 20506

National Labor Relations Board
Franklin Court Building
1099 14th St., NW
Washington, DC 20570-0001

National Mediation Board
1301 K Street, NW
Washington, DC 20572-0002

National Science Foundation
4201 Wilson Blvd.
Arlington, VA 22230

National Transportation Safety Board
490 L'Enfant Plaza East, SW
Washington, DC 20594

Nuclear Regulatory Commission
Office of Personnel Management
Two White Flint North Bldg.
11545 Rockville Pike
Rockville, MD 20555

Occupational Safety and Health Review Commission
One Lafayette Centre
1120 20th St., NW
Washington, DC 20036-3419

Office of Personnel Management
1900 E Street, NW
Washington, DC 20415

OPM Service Centers

Atlanta
Richard B. Russell Federal
Building
75 Spring Street SW, Suite 940
Atlanta, GA 30303

Chicago
John C. Kluczynski Federal
Building
DPN 30-3
230 South Dearborn Street
Chicago, IL 60604

Dayton
U.S. Courthourse & Federal
Building
200 West 2nd Street, Rm. 507
Dayton, OH 45402

Denver
12345 West Alameda Parkway
P.O. Box 25167
Denver, CO 80225

Detroit
477 Michigan Avenue, Rm. 565
Detroit, MI 48226

Honolulu
300 Ala Moana Blvd., Box
50028
Honolulu, HI 96850

Huntsville
520 Wynn Drive, NW
Huntsville, AL 35816-3426

Kansas City
601 East 12th St., Room 131
Kansas City, MO 64106

Norfolk
Federal Building
200 Granby Street, Room 500
Norfolk, VA 23510-1886

Philadelphia
William J. Green, Jr., Federal
Building
600 Arch Street, Room 3256
Philadelphia, PA 19106

Raleigh
4407 Bland Road, Suite 200
Raleigh, NC 27609-6296

San Antonio
8610 Broadway, Room 305
San Antonio, TX 78217

San Francisco
120 Howard Street, Rm. 735
San Francisco, CA 94105

San Juan
Federico Degatau Federal
Building
Carolos E. Chardon Street
Hato Rey, PR 00918

Seattle
700 5th Avenue, Suite 5950
Seattle, WA 98104-5012

Twin Cities
Federal Building, Room 503
One Federal Drive
Ft. Snelling, MN 55111-
4007

Washington, DC
1900 E Street, NW
Room 2458
Washington, DC 20415

Office of the Special Counsel
1730 M St., NW
Washington, DC 20036-4505

Overseas Private Investment Corporation
Office of Personnel
1100 New York Ave.
Washington, DC 20527

Panama Canal Commission
1825 I Street
Washington, DC 20006

Peace Corps
1990 K Street, NW
Washington, DC 20526

*Pennsylvania Avenue Development
Corporation*
1331 Pennsylvania Ave., NW
Washington, DC 20004-1703

Pension Benefit Guaranty Corp.
1200 K Street, NW
Washington, DC 20005-4026

Postal Rate Commission
1333 H Street, NW
Washington, DC 20268-0001

Railroad Retirement Board
844 N. Rush Street
Chicago, IL 60611-2092

Resolution Trust Company
801 17th St., NW
Washington DC, 20434-0001

Securities and Exchange Commission
450 5th Street, NW
Washington, DC 20549

Selective Service System
1515 Wilson Blvd.
Arlington, VA 22209-2425

Small Business Administration
Office of Personnel
409 3rd Street, SW
Washington, DC 20416

Social Security Administration
Office of Personnel
West High-Rise Building
6401 Security Boulevard
Baltimore, MD 21235

Smithsonian Institution
1000 Jefferson Drive, SW
Washington, DC 20560

Tennessee Valley Authority
Office of Human Resources
400 West Summit Hill Drive
Knoxville, TN 37902

Trade and Development Agency
1621 North Kent Street
Arlington, VA

*United States Arms Control and
Disarmament Agency*
320 21st Street, NW
Washington, DC 20451

United States Information Agency
301 4th Street, SW
Washington, DC 20547

*United States International
Development Cooperation Agency*
320 21st St., NW
Washington, DC 20523

*United States International Trade
Commission*
500 E Street, SW
Washington, DC 20436

United States Postal Service
475 L'Enfant Plaza, SW
Washington, DC 20260-0001

United States Soldiers' and Airmen's Home
3700 N. Capitol Street, NW
Washington, DC 20317

*United States Merit System Protection
Board*
1120 Vermont Ave., NW
Washington DC 20419

United States Sentencing Commission
One Columbus Circle NE
Washington DC 20002-8002

INDEPENDENT EMPLOYMENT SYSTEMS
(EXCEPTED AGENCIES)

The **Excepted Service** and **excepted agencies** are described in Step 2 (p. 34).

The following organizations—which also are listed above as either Cabinet or independent agencies—are *independent employment systems* (also called *excepted agencies*). *All* job titles at these agencies are excepted from the Competitive Service by law (that is, are in the Excepted Service).

Central Intelligence Agency (CIA)
Office of Personnel
725 17th St., NW
Washington, DC 20503

Defense Intelligence Agency
Human Resources
3100 Clarendon Boulevard
Arlington, VA 22201-5300

Federal Bureau of Investigation (FBI)
Office of Personnel
J. Edgar Hoover FBI Building
9th Street & Penn Ave., NW
Washington, DC 20535

Federal Reserve System
Personnel Division
20th Street & C Streets, NW
Washington, DC 20551

Foreign Service
14th St. & Constitution Ave., NW
Washington, DC 20230

General Accounting Office
Office of Human Resources
GAO Bldg.
441 G Street, NW
Washington, DC 20548

Library of Congress
James Madison Bldg.
101 Independence Ave., SE
Washington, DC 20540

National Security Agency
Fort George G. Meade, MD 20755-6000

Nuclear Regulatory Commission
Office of Personnel Management
Two White Flint North Building
11545 Rockville Pike
Rockville, MD 20555

Postal Rate Commission
1333 H Street, NW
Washington, DC 20268-0001

Tennessee Valley Authority
Office of Human Resources
400 West Summit Hill Drive
Knoxville, TN 37902

*U.S. International Development
    Cooperation Agency*
Main State Dept. Building
320 21st St., NW
Washington, DC 20523

U.S. Postal Service
475 L'Enfant Plaza, SW
Washington, DC 20260-0001
(or contact your local Postmaster)

*Veterans Administration Department of
    Medicine and Surgery*
VA Building
810 Vermont Ave., NW
Washington, DC 20420
(part of Dept. of Veterans Affairs; or
    contact VA hospitals nationwide)

Appendix E: Selected Federal Tests

Written tests are discussed in Step 2 (p. 38) and Step 5 (p.98)

Some 180 entry-level job titles, representing a great many new hires into Federal service annually, require a written test as part of the application process. Written tests enable the government to assess candidates' skills and aptitudes relevant to particular job titles, such as Air Traffic Controller, Foreign Service Officer, and clerical/secretarial positions, the Postal Service, and law enforcement. The exams presented in this appendix are only samples; those you may have to take may differ. Because such tests are unpopular with applicants, they are used only when there is an oversupply of candidates.

CONTENTS

Editor's Note: The selected Federal tests reproduced in this appendix are all currently in use. The dates on the first page of each exam are the dates noting when the test was originally published. For example, the Air Traffic Controller Exam dated August 1981 is still in use as of the date of publication of this second edition of Working for Your Uncle.

United States
Office of
Personnel
Management

AN 3675
August 1981

UNITED STATES OF AMERICA

OFFICE OF PERSONNEL MANAGEMENT

SAMPLE QUESTIONS FOR AIR TRAFFIC CONTROLLER EXAMINATION

The Air Traffic Controller Examination consists of three separate subtests. The first test is intended to assess Air Traffic Controller aptitudes. The second test is intended to assess the ability to perceive spatial relationships. The third test is intended to assess knowledges related to Air Traffic Control work. (These knowledges are not required to take the examination nor to be selected into an Air Traffic Controller position.)

The tests are scored by machine and therefore you will receive a separate answer sheet (i.e., separate from the test booklet which contains the questions). On this answer sheet you should carefully mark your answers by darkening the oval which represents the correct alternative to each question. A sample answer sheet is shown on page 3 in the section which deals specifically with the second test.

Test I

This test consists of drawings which simulate a radar scope depicting characteristic patterns of air traffic. Each problem contains a drawing of particular flight paths and aircraft flying on those routes. A table containing information about the altitude, speed, and route of each aircraft accompanies each drawing. Your task will be to answer questions which make use of this flight information. The questions ask for identification of potential mid-air collisions, differences in the routes of aircraft, distances between aircraft, compass headings of different aircraft, and changes in routes. Some preliminary instructions necessary to read correctly the information provided in the problems will be given to you at the test site before you actually start taking the test.

An example of the simulated radar scope and the table of flight information is given on the next page.

EXAMPLE

Flight Information			
Aircraft	Altitude	Speed	Route
10	5000	300	AHC
20	5500	300	EIHB
30	5000	450	DIJF
40	6000	450	BHJF
50	6000	300	GJHB

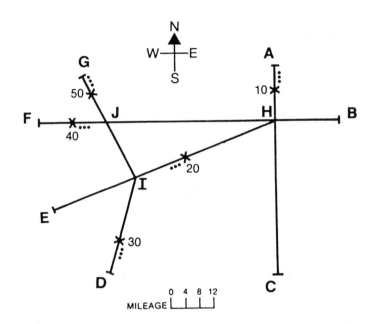

A typical example of the kind of information provided in the test problems is given above. The drawing shows the particular flight paths that aircraft must follow. Changes in routes can occur only at the intersection between two routes. Each x depicted on the routes represents an aircraft traveling in a particular direction indicated by the trailing dots.

To the side, a table containing critical flight information about each aircraft is provided. The number next to each x on the drawing allows the matching of the flight information to the correct aircraft. The flight information lists the altitude, speed in miles per hour, and route that each aircraft is flying.

Test II

In this test the questions deal with relationships among sets of figures and with relationships among sets of letters.

The sample questions on the next page illustrate the types of relationship which you will be asked to discover. A Sample Answer Sheet is provided to the right of the sample questions. You should mark your answers to the sample questions on this Sample Answer Sheet by darkening the oval corresponding to the letter of your answer for each question. The correct answers are given at the bottom of page 3.

SAMPLE QUESTIONS

Each of the first four questions has two boxes at the left. The symbols in the second box are different from the symbols in the first box. There is a relationship among the symbols within the first box and a relationship among the symbols within the second box. The relationship in the second box is similar but not identical to the relationship in the first box. Using these similarities and differences choose from the five lettered alternatives (A, B, C, D, E) the symbol that can best be substituted for the question mark in the second box. The correct answer is never based upon the series or progression of the symbols.

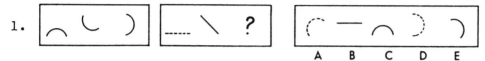

In question 1 all the symbols in the first box are curved while the symbols in the second box are straight. Of the lettered symbols in the third box, only B is straight, so B has been marked on the Sample Answer Sheet. (Note that although one symbol in the second box is made of dashes, the other is not, and so a dashed type of line is not the difference between the two boxes.) Now do questions 2 through 4.

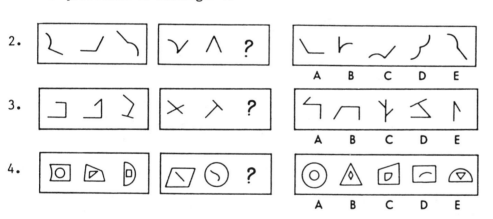

In each of the next five questions there are at the left a series of seven capital letters which follow some definite order and at the right five sets of two capital letters each. Look at the letters in the series and determine what the order is; then from the suggested answers at the right, select the set that gives the next two letters in the series. Next to the question number on the Sample Answer Sheet darken the oval that has the same letter as the set you have chosen.

5. X C X D X E X .... A) F X   B) F G   C) X F   D) E F   E) X G

The A space has been darkened for question 5 because the series consists of X's alternating with letters in alphabetical order. Now do sample questions 6 through 9.

6. A V A W A X A .... A) Z A   B) Y Z   C) Y A   D) A Z   E) A Y
7. A T T B S S C .... A) R R   B) R D   C) C R   D) D D   E) C C
8. A B D E G H J .... A) K L   B) L N   C) J M   D) L M   E) K M
9. A R C S E T G .... A) H I   B) H U   C) U J   D) U I   E) I V

Correct Answers to Sample Questions: 1-B, 2-B, 3-E, 4-D, 5-A, 6-C, 7-A, 8-E, 9-D.

<u>Test III</u>

In this test you will be asked to answer questions which entail knowledges which are related to Air Traffic Control work. The test is intended to serve as an indicator of the possession of these knowledges. However, possessing these knowledges is not required to take the Air Traffic Controller Examination, nor is it required to be selected for training into an Air Traffic Controller position.

The questions in this test deal with Air Traffic Rules, Air Traffic Procedures, Inflight Traffic Control Procedures, Communications Operating Procedures, Flight Assistance Service Procedures, Air Navigation and Aids to Navigation, and Aviation Weather.

☆U.S.G.P.O. —1981-720-067/6639

AN 3670
September 1976

SAMPLE QUESTIONS

The following sample questions show the types of questions that will be used in the written test. They show also how the questions in the test are to be answered. Read the directions carefully, then answer the questions, recording your answers on the Sample Answer Sheet on page 4. Then compare your answers with the Correct Answers to Sample Questions.

Each question has five suggested answers lettered A, B, C, D, and E. Decide which one is the best answer to the question. Then darken completely the space corresponding to the letter that is the same as the letter of your answer. Keep your mark within the space. If you have to erase a mark, be sure to erase it completely. Mark only one answer for each question.

Sample Questions I through III. In each of the sample questions below, select the one of the five suggested answers that is closest in meaning to the word in *italics*. Then darken the proper space on the Sample Answer Sheet.

I. The new training program is much better than any of the *previous* ones. *Previous* means most nearly

    A) abandoned   B) former   C) unused   D) recent   E) ineffective

Previous means coming or occurring before something else. Therefore, the correct answer is B.

II. The officer made several phone calls in an attempt to *verify* the report. To *verify* means most nearly to

    A) examine   B) explain   C) confirm   D) believe   E) improve

To *verify* means to prove or determine the truth or correctness of something. Therefore, the correct answer is C.

III. The driver's only *option* was to turn right at the intersection. *Option* means most nearly

    A) use   B) direction   C) hope   D) choice   E) opportunity

Option means something that may be or is chosen. Therefore, the correct answer is D.

Sample Questions IV through VI. In each of the next three sample questions, select the one of the five suggested answers that is best supported by the paragraph. Then darken the proper space on the Sample Answer Sheet.

IV. Just as the procedure of a collection department must be clear cut and definite, the steps being taken with the sureness of a skilled chess player, so the various paragraphs of a collection letter must show clear organization, giving evidence of a mind that, from the beginning, has had a specific end in view.

The paragraph best supports the statement that a collection letter should always
A) show a spirit of sportsmanship
B) be divided into several paragraphs
C) be brief, but courteous
D) be carefully planned
E) be written by the head of the collection department

The correct answer, D, is supported by the paragraph's statement that a collection letter should show clear organization and be written with a specific end in view. There is nothing in the paragraph to support alternatives A or E. Although the paragraph does imply that collection letters may contain several paragraphs (alternative B), it does not state that they *should always* be so divided. Also, the paragraph says nothing about the length or tone of a collection letter (alternative C), but only refers to the letter's clarity of thought and organization.

V. To prevent industrial accidents it is not only necessary that safety devices be used to guard exposed machinery, but also that mechanics be instructed in safety rules which they must follow for their own protection, and that the lighting in the plant be adequate.

The paragraph best supports the statement that industrial accidents
A) may be due to ignorance
B) are always avoidable
C) usually result from unsafe machinery
D) cannot be entirely overcome
E) usually result from inadequate lighting

The correct answer, A, is supported by the paragraph's statement that instructing mechanics in safety rules can help prevent industrial accidents, which implies that in some cases accidents may be due to ignorance of these rules. The paragraph does not support the statements that, in actual practice, industrial accidents are either *always* avoidable (alternative B) or that they cannot be entirely overcome (alternative D); it merely states the requirements of successful accident prevention. Although the paragraph does imply that industrial accidents can be caused by unsafe machinery (alternative C) and inadequate lighting (alternative E), it does not support the statements that such accidents *usually* result from these causes.

VI. Through advertising, manufacturers exercise a high degree of control over consumers' desires. However, the manufacturer assumes enormous risks in attempting to predict what consumers will want and in producing goods in quantity and distributing them in advance of final selection by the consumers.

The paragraph best supports the statement that manufacturers
A) can eliminate the risk of overproduction by advertising
B) distribute goods directly to the consumers
C) must depend on the final consumers for the success of their undertakings
D) can predict with great accuracy the success of any product they put on the market
E) are more concerned with advertising than with the production of goods

The correct answer, C, is supported by the paragraph's statement that although advertising gives manufacturers considerable control over the consumers' demand for their products, there are still big risks involved in producing and distributing their goods in advance of the consumers' final selection, which implies that manufacturers' ultimate success depends on the consumers. The paragraph's statement that there are such risks, in spite of advertising, contradicts alternatives A and D; nor is there any support for the statements that manufacturers distribute goods *directly* to consumers (alternative B) or that they are *more* concerned with advertising than production (alternative E).

Sample Questions VII through IX. Each of the next three sample questions contains five sentences. Decide which one of the five sentences would be most suitable in a formal letter or report with respect to grammar and usage. Then darken the proper space on the Sample Answer Sheet.

VII. A) The officer should of answered courteously the questions asked by the callers.
B) The officer must answer courteously the questions of all them callers.
C) The officer must answer courteously the questions what are asked by the callers.
D) There would have been no trouble if the officer had have always answered courteously.
E) The officer should answer courteously the questions of all callers.

The correct answer is E. Alternative A is incorrect because the word *have* should have been used instead of the word *of*. Alternative B is incorrect because the word *those* should have been used instead of the word *them*. Alternative C is incorrect because the word *that* should have been used instead of the word *what*. Alternative D is incorrect because the phrase *had have* is incorrect grammar; only the word *had* should have been used.

VIII. A) There are less mistakes in his work since he took the training course.
B) The training course being completed, he makes very few mistakes in his work.
C) Since he has completed the training course, he has made few mistakes in his work.
D) After taking the training course, his work was found to contain hardly any mistakes.
E) After he completed the training course, he seldom ever made any mistakes in his work.

The correct answer is C. Alternative A is incorrect because the word *fewer* should have been used instead of the word *less*. Alternative B is incorrect because poor word usage makes it seem as if *he* refers to *the training course*. Alternative D is incorrect because the word *few* should have been used instead of the phrase *hardly any*. Alternative E is incorrect because it is poor usage for the word *ever* to follow the word *seldom*.

IX. A) If properly addressed, the letter will reach my supervisor and I.
   B) The letter had been addressed to myself and my supervisor.
   C) I believe the letter was addressed to either my supervisor or I.
   D) My supervisor's name, as well as mine, was on the letter.
   E) My supervisor and me will receive the letter if it is properly addressed.

The correct answer is D. The word *me* should have been used instead of the word *I* in alternatives A and C, and instead of the word *myself* in alternative B. Alternative E is incorrect because the word *I* should have been used instead of the word *me*.

Sample Question X through XII. In each of the sample questions below, use your judgment and general knowledge to select the *best* or *most important* answer from the five suggested answers. Then darken the proper space on the Sample Answer Sheet.

X. From the standpoint of the prisoners, the *chief* advantage to be derived from a properly administered parole system is the
   A) freedom from fear of being returned to prison
   B) opportunity to adjust themselves to release from imprisonment
   C) removal of the temptation to commit crime
   D) reduced cost of supervising prisoners
   E) opportunity to save whatever they are able to earn

The correct answer is B. The *chief* advantage of a properly administered parole system from the prisoners' standpoint is the opportunity it provides them for information and assistance concerning their reentry into society. A parole system cannot guarantee that released prisoners will never return to prison in the future (alternative A), that they will not be tempted to commit crime (alternative C), or that they will have the opportunity to save whatever they earn (alternative E), since these possibilities are largely in the hands of the prisoners themselves. While alternative D may be a result of the parole system, it is not the chief advantage from the standpoint of the prisoners.

XI. An officer of the law may arrest a person without a warrant upon reasonable suspicion that the person has committed a felony. The *chief* purpose of this rule is to
   A) prevent the person's escape while his or her guilt is being investigated
   B) prevent the person from committing more crimes immediately
   C) give the person a chance to confess
   D) permit observation of the person's behavior
   E) increased the rate of arrest in proportion to the number of crimes committed

The correct answer is A. The *chief* purpose of arresting a person suspected of committing a felony is to insure that the suspect does not escape while further investigation takes place. While there may be some truth in all of the other alternatives, none of them can be considered to be the primary reason for this rule.

XII. Acquaintance with all types of ammunition commonly in use is extremely valuable to the worker in crime detection *chiefly* because
   A) all criminals possess this knowledge
   B) a broad background is desirable for success in investigative work
   C) the worker's safety is thus insured in time of danger
   D) the worker can thus eventually become a specialist in this line
   E) such knowledge often simplifies the problem of investigation

The correct answer is E. The *chief* advantage of familiarity with all types of ammunition for the worker in crime detection lies in the fact that such knowledge can be a valuable aid in discovering and following up clues during the process of investigation. Alternatives A and C are untrue, and while alternatives B and D may be true in some cases, neither one is the most important reason why acquaintance with ammunication is valuable to the worker in crime detection.

Sample Questions XIII through XV. Each of the sample questions below consists of five related events followed by five suggested orders in which the events could have occurred. Each suggested order represents the sequence in which the five sentences should be read, i.e., 3-5-1-2-4 indicates that the third sentence should be read first, the fifth sentence second, the first sentence third, etc. Select the one of the five suggested orders, lettered A, B, C, D, and E, in which the events most probably happened. Then darken the proper space on the Sample Answer Sheet.

XIII. 1. The maid discovered the body and called the police.
2. The police found Mary at the home of her sister.
3. A man was shot while swimming in his private pool.
4. A gun was found in Mary's pocketbook and was identified as the murder weapon.
5. The police questioned the maid and discovered that the victim had had a heated argument with his wife, Mary, the night before.

    A) 1-3-5-4-2   D) 1-5-2-4-3
    B) 3-5-1-4-2   E) 3-1-2-4-5
    C) 3-1-5-2-4

The correct answer is C. The most logical order of the five events is that first, the man was shot (3); second, his body was discovered by the maid and the police were called (1); third, the police questioned the maid and learned of the couple's argument of the previous night (5); fourth, the police found Mary at her sister's home (2); and fifth, a gun was found in Mary's pocketbook and identified as the murder weapon (4). The answer is not A because the maid could not have discovered the body (1) before the man was shot (3). The answer is not B because the police could not have questioned the maid (5) before she called them (1). The answer is not D because the first four events could not have taken place before the man was shot (3). The answer is not E because the police could not have looked for Mary (2) before learning from the maid that she was the victim's wife (5).

XIV. 1. In addition to the paper, a printing press and a stack of freshly printed $10 bills were found in Mr. Hayes' basement.
2. A detective saw Mr. Hayes leave a printing shop with a large package.
3. Mr. Hayes was arrested for counterfeiting and taken to the station.
4. The owner of the shop said Mr. Hayes had bought very high quality paper.
5. Mr. Hayes was under surveillance as a suspect in a counterfeiting case.

    A) 2-4-1-5-3   D) 2-5-1-4-3
    B) 5-2-4-1-3   E) 5-2-3-4-1
    C) 3-2-4-1-5

The correct answer is B. The most logical order of the five events is that first, Mr. Hayes was under surveillance (5); second, a detective saw him leave a printing shop with a large package (2); third, the shop owner said he had bought high quality paper (4); fourth, a printing press and freshly printed bills were found in Mr. Hayes' basement along with the paper (1); and fifth, he was arrested for counterfeiting (3). The answer is not A or D because the detective would not have seen Mr. Hayes leave the printing shop (2) if he had not been under surveillance (5). The answer is not C or E because Mr. Hayes could not have been arrested for counterfeiting (3) before any evidence was discovered (1).

XV. 1. The inspector realized that Ms. Smith was wearing a wig and had her searched.
2. The inspector decided to search Ms. Smith's luggage.
3. Although the inspector could not place the face, he knew that Ms. Smith looked familiar.
4. Narcotics were found sewn to the crown of Ms. Smith's wig.
5. The inspector found nothing in Ms. Smith's luggage, but her passport photograph revealed her identity as a suspected smuggler.

    A) 2-5-3-1-4   D) 3-2-5-1-4
    B) 3-1-4-2-5   E) 2-1-3-5-4
    C) 1-4-2-5-3

The correct answer is D. The most logical order of the five events is that first, the inspector saw that Ms. Smith looked familiar (3); second, he decided to search her luggage (2); third, he found nothing in her luggage but identified her from her passport photograph as a suspected smuggler (5); fourth, he realized that she was wearing a wig and had her searched (1); and fifth, narcotics were found in her wig (4). The answer is not A because the inspector would not have decided to search Ms. Smith's luggage (2) unless his suspicions were aroused by the fact that she looked familiar (3). The answer is not B, C, or E because the inspector would not have realized Ms. Smith was wearing a wig (1) before seeing her passport photograph (5).

Sample Answer Sheet	Correct Answers to Sample Questions
I A B C D E	I A ● C D E
II A B C D E	II A B ● D E
III A B C D E	III A B C ● E
IV A B C D E	IV A B C D ●
V A B C D E	V ● B C D E
VI A B C D E	VI A B C D ●
VII A B C D E	VII A B C D ●
VIII A B C D E	VIII A B ● D E
IX A B C D E	IX A B C ● E
X A B C D E	X A ● C D E
XI A B C D E	XI A B C D ●
XII A B C D E	XII A B C D ●
XIII A B C D E	XIII A B ● D E
XIV A B C D E	XIV A ● C D E
XV A B C D E	XV A B C ● E

EXHIBIT No. 3: CLERICAL TASKS TEST

DIRECTIONS AND SAMPLE QUESTIONS

This test contains four kinds of questions. There are some of each kind of question on each page in the booklet. The time limit for the test will be announced by the examiner.

Study the sample questions carefully. Each question has five suggested answers. Decide which one is the best answer. Find the question number on the Sample Answer Sheet. Show your answer to the question by darkening completely the space that is lettered the same as the letter of your answer. Keep your mark within the space. If you have to erase a mark, be sure to erase it completely. Mark only one answer for each question.

SAMPLE QUESTIONS

In each line across the page there are three names or numbers that are very similar.   Compare the three names or numbers and decide which ones are exactly alike. On the Sample Answer Sheet at the right, mark the answer—

A if ALL THREE names or numbers are exactly ALIKE
B if only the FIRST and SECOND names or numbers are exactly ALIKE
C if only the FIRST and THIRD names or numbers are exactly ALIKE
D if only the SECOND and THIRD names or numbers are exactly ALIKE
E if ALL THREE names or numbers are DIFFERENT

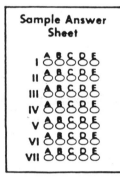

I. Davis Hazen	David Hozen	David Hazen
II. Lois Appel	Lois Appel	Lois Apfel
III. June Allan	Jane Allan	Jane Allan
IV. 10235	10235	10235
V. 32614	32164	32614

If you finish the sample questions before you are told to turn to the test, it will be to your advantage to study the code given above for A, B, C, D and E. This code is repeated on every page.

In the next group of sample questions, there is a name in a box at the left, and four other names in alphabetical order at the right. Find the correct location for the boxed name so that it will be in alphabetical order with the others, and mark the letter of that location as your answer.

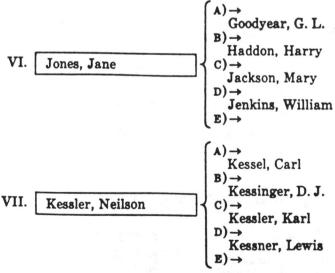

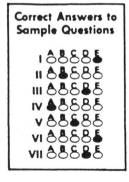

DO NOT OPEN THE TEST BOOKLET. TURN IT OVER WITHOUT WAITING FOR A SIGNAL, AND WORK THE SAMPLE QUESTIONS ON THE BACK PAGE.

In this booklet, the back page of the test is on page 28 (page 8 of Exhibit No. 3). Turn to page 28 and continue the sample questions. The test starts on page 22.

In questions 1 through 5, compare the three names or numbers, and mark the answer—
  A if ALL THREE names or numbers are exactly ALIKE
  B if only the FIRST and SECOND names or numbers are exactly ALIKE
  C if only the FIRST and THIRD names or numbers are exactly ALIKE
  D if only the SECOND and THIRD names or numbers are exactly ALIKE
  E if ALL THREE names or numbers are DIFFERENT

1. 5261383	5261383	5261338
2. 8125690	8126690	8125609
3. W. E. Johnston	W. E. Johnson	W. E. Johnson
4. Vergil L. Muller	Vergil L. Muller	Vergil L. Muller
5. Atherton R. Warde	Asheton R. Warde	Atherton P. Warde

In questions 6 through 10, find the correct place for the name in the box.

6. | Hackett, Gerald |
  A) →
      Habert, James
  B) →
      Hachett, J. J.
  C) →
      Hachetts, K. Larson
  D) →
      Hachettson, Leroy
  E) →

7. | Margenroth, Alvin |
  A) →
      Margeroth, Albert
  B) →
      Margestein, Dan
  C) →
      Margestein, David
  D) →
      Margue, Edgar
  E) →

8. | Bobbitt, Olivier E. |
  A) →
      Bobbitt, D. Olivier
  B) →
      Bobbitt, Olive B.
  C) →
      Bobbitt, Olivia H.
  D) →
      Bobbitt, R. Olivia
  E) →

9. | Mosely, Werner |
  A) →
      Mosely, Albert J.
  B) →
      Mosley, Alvin
  C) →
      Mosley, S. M.
  D) →
      Mozley, Vinson N.
  E) →

10. | Youmuns, Frank L. |
  A) →
      Youmons, Frank G.
  B) →
      Youmons, Frank H.
  C) →
      Youmons, Frank K.
  D) →
      Youmons, Frank M.
  E) →

GO ON TO THE NEXT COLUMN.

Answers

→ 11. Add: A) 55   B) 65
         4 3   C) 66   D) 75
       + 3 2   E) none of these
       ——

12. Subtract: A) 73   B) 79
         8 3   C) 80   D) 89
       −   4   E) none of these
       ——

13. Multiply: A) 281 B) 287
         4 1   C) 291 D) 297
       ×   7   E) none of these

14. Divide: A) 44   B) 51
                  C) 52   D) 60
       6 / 3 0 6 E) none of these

15. Add: A) 42   B) 52
         3 7   C) 53   D) 62
       + 1 5   E) none of these
       ——

For each question below, find which one of the suggested answers appears in that question.

16. 6 2 5 K 4 P T G

17. L 4 7 2 T 6 V K

18. 3 5 4 L 9 V T G

19. G 4 K 7 L 3 5 Z

20. 4 K 2 9 N 5 T G

Suggested Answers
  A = 4, 5, K, T
  B = 4, 7, G, K
  C = 2, 5, G, L
  D = 2, 7, L, T
  E = none of these

GO ON TO THE NEXT PAGE.

(Page 2 of Exhibit No. 3)

In questions 21 through 25, compare the three names or numbers, and mark the answer—
  A   if ALL THREE names or numbers are exactly ALIKE
  B   if only the FIRST and SECOND names or numbers are exactly ALIKE
  C   if only the FIRST and THIRD names or numbers are exactly ALIKE
  D   if only the SECOND and THIRD names or numbers are exactly ALIKE
  E   if ALL THREE names or numbers are DIFFERENT

21. 2395890	2395890	2395890
22. 1926341	1926347	1926314
23. E. Owens McVey	E. Owen McVey	E. Owen McVay
24. Emily Neal Rouse	Emily Neal Rowse	Emily Neal Rowse
25. H. Merritt Audubon	H. Merriott Audubon	H. Merritt Audubon

In questions 26 through 30, find the correct place for the name in the box.

26. Watters, N. O.
  A) →
    Waters, Charles L.
  B) →
    Waterson, Nina P.
  C) →
    Watson, Nora J.
  D) →
    Wattwood, Paul A.
  E) →

27. Johnston, Edward
  A) →
    Johnston, Edgar R.
  B) →
    Johnston, Edmond
  C) →
    Johnston, Edmund
  D) →
    Johnstone, Edmund A.
  E) →

28. Rensch, Adeline
  A) →
    Ramsay, Amos
  B) →
    Remschel, Augusta
  C) →
    Renshaw, Austin
  D) →
    Rentzel, Becky
  E) →

29. Schnyder, Maurice
  A) →
    Schneider, Martin
  B) →
    Schneider, Mertens
  C) →
    Schnyder, Newman
  D) →
    Schreibner, Norman
  E) →

30. Freedenburg, C. Erma
  A) →
    Freedenberg, Emerson
  B) →
    Freedenberg, Erma
  C) →
    Freedenberg, Erma E.
  D) →
    Freedinberg, Erma F.
  E) →

Answers

→ 31. Subtract:
      6 8
    − 4 7
    ——
    A) 10   B) 11
    C) 20   D) 22
    E) none of these

32. Multiply:
      5 0
    ×   8
    ——
    A) 400   B) 408
    C) 450   D) 458
    E) none of these

33. Divide:
    9 $\overline{)\,1\;8\;0}$
    A) 20   B) 29
    C) 30   D) 39
    E) none of these

34. Add:
      7 8
    + 6 3
    ——
    A) 131   B) 140
    C) 141   D) 151
    E) none of these

35. Subtract:
      8 9
    − 7 0
    ——
    A) 9   B) 18
    C) 19   D) 29
    E) none of these

For each question below, find which one of the suggested answers appears in that question.

36. 9 G Z 3 L 4 6 N

37. L 5 N K 4 3 9 V

38. 8 2 V P 9 L Z 5

39. V P 9 Z 5 L 8 7

40. 5 T 8 N 2 9 V L

Suggested Answers
  A = 4, 9, L, V
  B = 4, 5, N, Z
  C = 5, 8, L, Z
  D = 8, 9, N, V
  E = none of these

GO ON TO THE NEXT COLUMN.   **GO ON TO THE NEXT PAGE.**

In questions 41 through 45, compare the three names or numbers, and mark the answer—

A   if ALL THREE names or numbers are exactly ALIKE
B   if only the FIRST and SECOND names or numbers are exactly ALIKE
C   if only the FIRST and THIRD names or numbers are exactly ALIKE
D   if only the SECOND and THIRD names or numbers are exactly ALIKE
E   if ALL THREE names or numbers are DIFFERENT

41. 6219354	6219354	6219354
42. 2312793	2312793	2312793
43. 1065407	1065407	1065047
44. Francis Ransdell	Frances Ramsdell	Francis Ramsdell
45. Cornelius Detwiler	Cornelius Detwiler	Cornelius Detwiler

In questions 46 through 50, find the correct place for the name in the box.

46. **DeMattia, Jessica**

A) →
   DeLong, Jesse
B) →
   DeMatteo, Jessie
C) →
   Derby, Jessie S.
D) →
   DeShazo, L. M.
E) →

47. **Theriault, Louis**

A) →
   Therien, Annette
B) →
   Therien, Elaine
C) →
   Thibeault, Gerald
D) →
   Thiebeault, Pierre
E) →

48. **Gaston, M. Hubert**

A) →
   Gaston, Dorothy M.
B) →
   Gaston, Henry N.
C) →
   Gaston, Isabel
D) →
   Gaston, M. Melvin
E) →

49. **SanMiguel, Carlos**

A) →
   SanLuis, Juana
B) →
   Santilli, Laura
C) →
   Stinnett, Nellie
D) →
   Stoddard, Victor
E) →

50. **DeLaTour, Hall F.**

A) →
   Delargy, Harold
B) →
   DeLathouder, Hilda
C) →
   Lathrop, Hillary
D) →
   LaTour, Hulbert E.
E) →

GO ON TO THE NEXT COLUMN.

Answers

51. Multiply:
    6 2
×   5
—
A) 300 B) 310
C) 315 D) 360
E) none of these

52. Divide:

3 / 1 5 3

A) 41 B) 43
C) 51 D) 53
E) none of these

53. Add:
    4 7
+ 2 1
—
A) 58 B) 59
C) 67 D) 68
E) none of these

54. Subtract:
    8 7
− 4 2
—
A) 34 B) 35
C) 44 D) 45
E) none of these

55. Multiply:
    3 7
×   3
—
A) 91 B) 101
C) 104 D) 114
E) none of these

For each question below, find which one of the suggested answers appears in that question.

56. N 5 4 7 T K 3 Z

57. 8 5 3 V L 2 Z N

58. 7 2 5 N 9 K L V

59. 9 8 L 2 5 Z K V

60. Z 6 5 V 9 3 P N

Suggested Answers
A = 3, 8, K, N
B = 5, 8, N, V
C = 3, 9, V, Z
D = 5, 9, K, Z
E = none of these

GO ON TO THE NEXT PAGE.

In questions 61 through 65, compare the three names or numbers, and mark the answer—
  A if ALL THREE names or numbers are exactly ALIKE
  B if only the FIRST and SECOND names or numbers are exactly ALIKE
  C if only the FIRST and THIRD names or numbers are exactly ALIKE
  D if only the SECOND and THIRD names or numbers are exactly ALIKE
  E if ALL THREE names or numbers are DIFFERENT

61. 6452054	6452654	6452054
62. 8501268	8501268	8501286
63. Ella Burk Newham	Ella Burk Newnham	Elena Burk Newnham
64. Jno. K. Ravencroft	Jno. H. Ravencroft	Jno. H. Ravencoft
65. Martin Wills Pullen	Martin Wills Pulen	Martin Wills Pullen

In questions 66 through 70, find the correct place for the name in the box.

66. O'Bannon, M. J.
  A) →
  O'Beirne, B. B.
  B) →
  Oberlin, E. L.
  C) →
  Oberneir, L. P.
  D) →
  O'Brian, S. F.
  E) →

67. Entsminger, Jacob
  A) →
  Ensminger, J.
  B) →
  Entsminger, J. A.
  C) →
  Entsminger, Jack
  D) →
  Entsminger, James
  E) →

68. Iacone, Pete R.
  A) →
  Iacone, Pedro
  B) →
  Iacone, Pedro M.
  C) →
  Iacone, Peter F.
  D) →
  Iascone, Peter W.
  E) →

69. Sheppard, Gladys
  A) →
  Shepard, Dwight
  B) →
  Shepard, F. H.
  C) →
  Shephard, Louise
  D) →
  Shepperd, Stella
  E) →

70. Thackton, Melvin T.
  A) →
  Thackston, Milton G.
  B) →
  Thackston, Milton W.
  C) →
  Thackston, Theodore
  D) →
  Thackston, Thomas G.
  E) →

Answers

71. Divide:

    7 / 3 5 7

  A) 51   B) 52
  C) 53   D) 54
  E) none of these

72. Add:

      5 8
    + 2 7

  A) 75   B) 84
  C) 85   D) 95
  E) none of these

73. Subtract:

      8 6
    − 5 7

  A) 18   B) 29
  C) 38   D) 39
  E) none of these

74. Multiply:

      6 8
    ×   4

  A) 242   B) 264
  C) 272   D) 274
  E) none of these

75. Divide:

    9 / 6 3 9

  A) 71   B) 73
  C) 81   D) 83
  E) none of these

For each question below, find which one of the suggested answers appears in that question.

76. 6 Z T N 8 7 4 V

77. V 7 8 6 N 5 P L

78. N 7 P V 8 4 2 L

79. 7 8 G 4 3 V L T

80. 4 8 G 2 T N 6 L

Suggested Answers
  A = 2, 7, L, N
  B = 2, 8, T, V
  C = 6, 8, L, T
  D = 6, 7, N, V
  E = none of these

GO ON TO THE NEXT COLUMN.   **GO ON TO THE NEXT PAGE.**

In questions 81 through 85, compare the three names or numbers, and mark the answer—
   A   if ALL THREE names or numbers are exactly ALIKE
   B   if only the FIRST and SECOND names or numbers are exactly ALIKE
   C   if only the FIRST and THIRD names or numbers are exactly ALIKE
   D   if only the SECOND and THIRD names or numbers are exactly ALIKE
   E   if ALL THREE names or numbers are DIFFERENT

81. 3457988   3457986   3457986
82. 4695682   4695862   4695682
83. Stricklund Kanedy   Stricklund Kanedy   Stricklund Kanedy
84. Joy Harlor Witner   Joy Harloe Witner   Joy Harloe Witner
85. R. M. O. Uberroth   R. M. O. Uberroth   R. N. O. Uberroth

In questions 86 through 90, find the correct place for the name in the box.

86. | Dunlavey, M. Hilary |
   A) →
      Dunleavy, Hilary G.
   B) →
      Dunleavy, Hilary K.
   C) →
      Dunleavy, Hilary S.
   D) →
      Dunleavy, Hilery W.
   E) →

87. | Yarbrough, Maria |
   A) →
      Yabroudy, Margy
   B) →
      Yarboro, Marie
   C) →
      Yarborough, Marina
   D) →
      Yarborough, Mary
   E) →

88. | Prouty, Martha |
   A) →
      Proutey, Margaret
   B) →
      Proutey, Maude
   C) →
      Prouty, Myra
   D) →
      Prouty, Naomi
   E) →

89. | Pawlowicz, Ruth M. |
   A) →
      Pawalek, Edward
   B) →
      Pawelek, Flora G.
   C) →
      Pawlowski, Joan M.
   D) →
      Pawtowski, Wanda
   E) →

90. | Vanstory, George |
   A) →
      Vanover, Eva
   B) →
      VanSwinderen, Floyd
   C) →
      VanSyckle, Harry
   D) →
      Vanture, Laurence
   E) →

GO ON TO THE NEXT COLUMN.
(Page 6 of Exhibit No. 3)

Answers

91. Add: A) 53   B) 62
       2 8   C) 64   D) 73
     + 3 5   E) none of these
     —

92. Subtract: A) 7   B) 8
       7 8   C) 18   D) 19
     − 6 9   E) none of these
     —

93. Multiply: A) 492   B) 506
       8 6   C) 516   D) 526
     ×   6   E) none of these
     —

94. Divide: A) 71   B) 76
                  C) 81   D) 89
   8 / 6 4 8   E) none of these

95. Add: A) 131   B) 132
       9 7   C) 140   D) 141
     + 3 4   E) none of these
     —

For each question below, find which one of the suggested answers appears in that question.

96. V 5 7 Z N 9 4 T

97. 4 6 P T 2 N K 9

98. 6 4 N 2 P 8 Z K

99. 7 P 5 2 4 N K T

100. K T 8 5 4 N 2 P

Suggested Answers
   A = 2, 5, N, Z
   B = 4, 5, N, P
   C = 2, 9, P, T
   D = 4, 9, T, Z
   E = none of these

GO ON TO THE NEXT PAGE.

In questions 101 through 105, compare the three names or numbers, and mark the answer—

A if ALL THREE names or numbers are exactly ALIKE
B if only the FIRST and SECOND names or numbers are exactly ALIKE
C if only the FIRST and THIRD names or numbers are exactly ALIKE
D if only the SECOND and THIRD names or numbers are exactly ALIKE
E if ALL THREE names or numbers are DIFFERENT

101.	1592514	1592574	1592574
102.	2010202	2010202	2010220
108.	6177896	6177936	6177396
104.	Drusilla S. Ridgeley	Drusilla S. Ridgeley	Drusilla S. Ridgeley
105.	Andrei I. Toumantzev	Andrei I. Tourmantzev	Andrei I. Toumantzov

In questions 106 through 110, find the correct place for the name in the box.

106. Fitzsimmons, Hugh
- A) →
- Fitts, Harold
- B) →
- Fitzgerald, June
- C) →
- FitzGibbon, Junius
- D) →
- FitzSimons, Martin
- E) →

107. D'Amato, Vincent
- A) →
- Daly, Steven
- B) →
- D'Amboise, S. Vincent
- C) →
- Daniel, Vail
- D) →
- DeAlba, Valentina
- E) →

108. Schaeffer, Roger D.
- A) →
- Schaffert, Evelyn M.
- B) →
- Schaffner, Margaret M.
- C) →
- Schafhirt, Milton G.
- D) →
- Shafer, Richard E.
- E) →

109. White-Lewis, Cecil
- A) →
- Whitelaw, Cordelia
- B) →
- White-Leigh, Nancy
- C) →
- Whitely, Rodney
- D) →
- Whitlock, Warren
- E) →

110. VanDerHeggen, Don
- A) →
- VanDemark, Doris
- B) →
- Vandenberg, H. E.
- C) →
- VanDercook, Marie
- D) →
- vanderLinden, Robert
- E) →

GO ON TO THE NEXT COLUMN.

(Page 7 of Exhibit No. 3)

→ 111. Add:

$$7\ 5$$
$$+\ 4\ 9$$

Answers
A) 124 B) 125
C) 134 D) 225
E) none of these

112. Subtract:

$$6\ 9$$
$$-\ 4\ 5$$

A) 14 B) 23
C) 24 D) 26
E) none of these

113. Multiply:

$$3\ 6$$
$$\times\ 8$$

A) 246 B) 262
C) 288 D) 368
E) none of these

114. Divide:

$$8\ \overline{)\ 3\ 2\ 8}$$

A) 31 B) 41
C) 42 D) 48
E) none of these

115. Multiply:

$$5\ 8$$
$$\times\ 9$$

A) 472 B) 513
C) 521 D) 522
E) none of these

For each question below, find which one of the suggested answers appears in that question.

116. Z 3 N P G 5 4 2

117. 6 N 2 8 G 4 P T

118. 6 N 4 T V G 8 2

119. T 3 P 4 N 8 G 2

120. 6 7 K G N 2 L 5

Suggested Answers
- A = 2, 3, G, N
- B = 2, 6, N, T
- C = 3, 4, G, K
- D = 4, 6, K, T
- E = none of these

IF YOU FINISH BEFORE THE TIME IS UP, YOU MAY GO BACK AND CHECK YOUR ANSWERS.

In the following questions, solve each problem and find your answer among the list of suggested answers for that question. Mark the Sample Answer Sheet A, B, C, or D for the answer you obtained; or if your answer is not among these, mark E for that question.

VIII. Add:

$$\begin{array}{r} 2\ 2 \\ +\ 3\ 3 \\ \hline \end{array}$$

Answers
A) 44   B) 45
C) 54   D) 55
E) none of these

X. Multiply:

$$\begin{array}{r} 2\ 5 \\ \times\ \ \ 5 \\ \hline \end{array}$$

Answers
A) 100   B) 115
C) 125   D) 135
E) none of these

IX. Subtract:

$$\begin{array}{r} 2\ 4 \\ -\ \ 3 \\ \hline \end{array}$$

A) 20   B) 21
C) 27   D) 29
E) none of these

XI. Divide:

$$6\ \overline{)\ 1\ 2\ 6}$$

A) 20   B) 22
C) 24   D) 26
E) none of these

There is one set of suggested answers for the next group of sample questions. Do not try to memorize these answers, because there will be a different set on each page in the test.

To find the answer to a question, find which suggested answer contains numbers and letters all of which appear in the question. If no suggested answer fits, mark E for that question.

XII.   8 N K 9 G T 4 6

XIII.   T 9 7 Z 6 L 3 K

XIV.   Z 7 G K 3 9 8 N

XV.   3 K 9 4 6 G Z L

XVI.   Z N 7 3 8 K T 9

Suggested
Answers
$\begin{cases} A = 7,\ 9,\ G,\ K \\ B = 8,\ 9,\ T,\ Z \\ C = 6,\ 7,\ K,\ Z \\ D = 6,\ 8,\ G,\ T \\ E = \text{none of these} \end{cases}$

Sample Answer Sheet	Correct Answers to Sample Questions
VIII A B C D E	VIII A B C D E
IX A B C D E	IX A B C D E
X A B C D E	X A B C D E
XI A B C D E	XI A B C D E
XII A B C D E	XII A B C D E
XIII A B C D E	XIII A B C D E
XIV A B C D E	XIV A B C D E
XV A B C D E	XV A B C D E
XVI A B C D E	XVI A B C D E

After you have marked your answers to all the questions on the Sample Answer Sheets on this page and on the front page of the booklet, check them with the answers in the boxes marked Correct Answers to Sample Questions.

DO NOT OPEN THE TEST BOOKLET. YOU MAY STUDY THIS PAGE AND THE FRONT PAGE OF THE BOOKLET IF YOU FINISH THE SAMPLE QUESTIONS BEFORE THE TIME IS UP.

EXHIBIT No. 4:   HOW TO SCORE THE CLERICAL TASKS TEST

The correct answers to the questions on the sample Clerical Tasks Test are given below. On this test there is a penalty for wrong answers. The total score on the test is the number of right answers minus one-fourth of the number of wrong answers. (Fractions of one-half or less are dropped.) First count the number of correct answers you have made. Do not count as correct any questions with more than one answer marked. Then count the number of incorrect answers. Omits are not counted as wrong answers, but double responses do count as wrong. Multiply the total number of incorrect answers by one-fourth. Subtract this number from the total number correct to get the test total score. For example, if you were to answer 89 questions correctly and 10 questions incorrectly, and you omitted 21 questions, your total score would be 87. (89 minus one-fourth of 10 equals 87.)

Note to teachers: Exhibit No. 5 can be used for making a stencil to score this test by hand in the same manner as described for the Verbal Tasks Test. However, you must also count the incorrect responses. The number of wrong answers may be counted by marking with a colored pencil every unmarked opening that shows through the correct answer stencil when it is placed over the answer sheet. Then when the stencil is withdrawn the number of questions with wrong answers marked on the answer sheet can be counted. (Remember, if no alternative is marked, it is an omit. Omits are not counted as wrong answers. Double responses do count as wrong answers.) Another scoring method is to punch a "wrongs stencil" with holes for all alternatives except the correct answers. After using the correct answer stencil to count the right answers, use the wrongs stencil to count the number of incorrect answers.

SECTION 2

(Answer sheet with bubbled responses for questions 1–130, Test Series / Test Number grids, and the instruction: "Make no marks or entries in the columns to the right until you receive instructions from the administrator.")

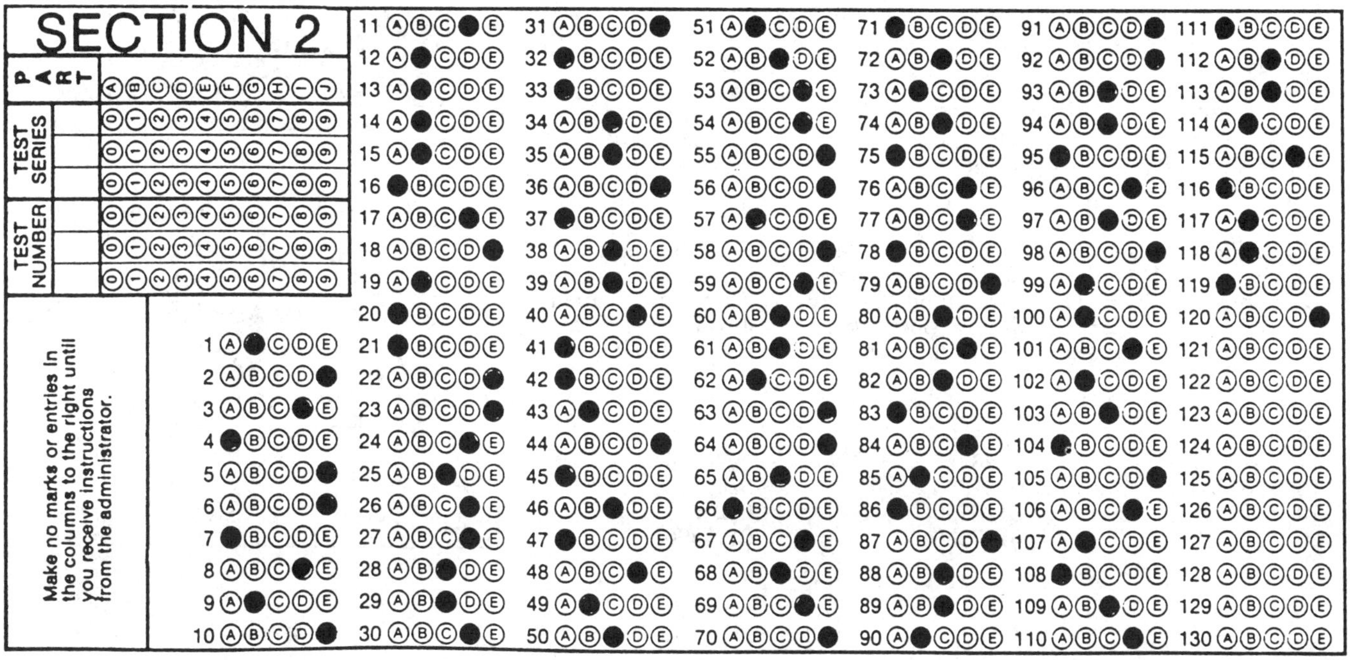

SAMPLE QUESTIONS

The following sample questions show types of questions found in the written test you will take. They also show how your answers to the questions are to be recorded on a separate answer sheet. The questions on the test may be harder or easier than those shown here, but a sample of each *kind* of question on the test is given.

Read these directions, then look at the sample questions and try to answer them. Each question has several suggested answers lettered A, B, C, etc. Decide which one is the best answer to the question. Then, in the Sample Answer Sheet box, find the answer space that is numbered the same as the number of the question, and darken completely the oval that is lettered the same as the letter of your answer. Then compare your answers with those given in the Correct Answers to Sample Questions box. For some questions an explanation of the correct answer is given immediately following the sample question.

Sample questions 1 through 20 require name and number comparisons. In each line across the page there are three names or numbers that are very similar. Compare the three names or numbers and decide which ones are exactly alike. On the Sample Answer Sheet at the right, mark the answer—

A if ALL THREE names or numbers are exactly ALIKE
B if only the FIRST and SECOND names or numbers are exactly ALIKE
C if only the FIRST and THIRD names or numbers are exactly ALIKE
D if only the SECOND and THIRD names or numbers are exactly ALIKE
E if ALL THREE names or numbers are DIFFERENT

1. Davis Hazen	David Hozen	David Hazen
2. Lois Appel	Lois Appel	Lois Apfel
3. June Allan	Jane Allan	Jane Allan
4. Emily Neal Rouse	Emily Neal Rowse	Emily Neal Rowse
5. H. Merritt Audubon	H. Merriott Audubon	H. Merritt Audubon

6. 6219354	6219354	6219354
7. 2312793	2312793	2312793
8. 1065407	1065407	1065047
9. 3457988	3457986	3457986
10. 4695682	4695862	4695682

11. Francis Ransdell	Frances Ramsdell	Francis Ramsdell
12. Cornelius Detwiler	Cornelius Detwiler	Cornelius Detwiler
13. Stricklund Kanedy	Stricklund Kanedy	Stricklund Kanedy
14. Joy Harlor Witner	Joy Harloe Witner	Joy Harloe Witner
15. R. M. O. Uberroth	R. M. O. Uberroth	R. N. O. Uberroth

16. 2395890	2395890	2395890
17. 1926341	1926347	1926314
18. 5261383	5261383	5261338
19. 8125690	8126690	8125609
20. 6177396	6177936	6177396

Sample Answer Sheet

```
   A B C D E          A B C D E
1  ○ ○ ○ ○ ○    11  ○ ○ ○ ○ ○
2  ○ ○ ○ ○ ○    12  ○ ○ ○ ○ ○
3  ○ ○ ○ ○ ○    13  ○ ○ ○ ○ ○
4  ○ ○ ○ ○ ○    14  ○ ○ ○ ○ ○
5  ○ ○ ○ ○ ○    15  ○ ○ ○ ○ ○
6  ○ ○ ○ ○ ○    16  ○ ○ ○ ○ ○
7  ○ ○ ○ ○ ○    17  ○ ○ ○ ○ ○
8  ○ ○ ○ ○ ○    18  ○ ○ ○ ○ ○
9  ○ ○ ○ ○ ○    19  ○ ○ ○ ○ ○
10 ○ ○ ○ ○ ○    20  ○ ○ ○ ○ ○
```

Correct Answers to Sample Questions

```
   A B C D E          A B C D E
1  ○ ○ ○ ○ ●    11  ○ ○ ○ ○ ●
2  ● ○ ○ ○ ○    12  ● ○ ○ ○ ○
3  ○ ○ ○ ● ○    13  ● ○ ○ ○ ○
4  ○ ○ ○ ● ○    14  ○ ○ ○ ● ○
5  ○ ○ ● ○ ○    15  ● ○ ○ ○ ○
6  ● ○ ○ ○ ○    16  ● ○ ○ ○ ○
7  ● ○ ○ ○ ○    17  ○ ○ ○ ○ ●
8  ● ○ ○ ○ ○    18  ● ○ ○ ○ ○
9  ○ ○ ○ ● ○    19  ○ ○ ○ ○ ●
10 ○ ○ ● ○ ○    20  ○ ○ ● ○ ○
```

Sample questions 21 through 30 require verbal skills.

Reading. In questions like 21 through 25, read the paragraph carefully and base your answer on the material given.

21. Probably few people realize, as they drive on a concrete road, that steel is used to keep the surface flat and even, in spite of the weight of buses and trucks. Steel bars, deeply embedded in the concrete, provide sinews to take the stresses so that they cannot crack the slab or make it wavy.

The paragraph best supports the statement that a concrete road
A) is expensive to build
B) usually cracks under heavy weights
C) is used exclusively for heavy traffic
D) is reinforced with other material

22. The likelihood of America's exhausting its natural resources seems to be growing less. All kinds of waste are being reworked and new uses are constantly being found for almost everything. We are getting more use out of our goods and are making many new byproducts out of what was formerly thrown away.

The paragraph best supports the statement that we seem to be in less danger of exhausting our resources because
A) economy is found to lie in the use of substitutes
B) more service is obtained from a given amount of material
C) we are allowing time for nature to restore them
D) supply and demand are better controlled

23. Through advertising, manufacturers exercise a high degree of control over consumers' desires. However, the manufacturer assumes enormous risks in attempting to predict what consumers will want and in producing goods in quantity and distributing them in advance of final selection by the consumers.

The paragraph best supports the statement that manufacturers
A) can eliminate the risk of overproduction by advertising
B) distribute goods directly to the consumers
C) must depend upon the final consumers for the success of their undertakings
D) can predict with great accuracy the success of any product they put on the market

24. What constitutes skill in any line of work is not always easy to determine; economy of time must be carefully distinguished from economy of energy, as the quickest method may require the greatest expenditure of muscular effort, and may not be essential or at all desirable.

The paragraph best supports the statement that
A) the most efficiently executed task is not always the one done in the shortest time
B) energy and time cannot both be conserved in performing a single task
C) a task is well done when it is performed in the shortest time
D) skill in performing a task should not be acquired at the expense of time

25. In the relations of people to nature, the procuring of food and shelter is fundamental. With the migration of people to various climates, ever new adjustments to the food supply and to the climate became necessary.

The paragraph best supports the statement that the means by which people supply their material needs are
A) accidental
B) varied
C) limited
D) inadequate

Vocabulary. For questions like 26 through 30, choose the one of the four suggested answers that means most nearly the same as the word in *italics.*

26. *Flexible* means most nearly
A) breakable   C) pliable
B) flammable   D) weak

27. *Option* means most nearly
A) use   C) value
B) choice   D) blame

28. To *verify* means most nearly to
A) examine   C) confirm
B) explain   D) guarantee

29. *Previous* means most nearly
A) abandoned   C) timely
B) former   D) younger

30. *Respiration* means most nearly
A) recovery   C) pulsation
B) breathing   D) sweating

Sample Answer Sheet	
21 A B C D E	26 A B C D E
22 A B C D E	27 A B C D E
23 A B C D E	28 A B C D E
24 A B C D E	29 A B C D E
25 A B C D E	30 A B C D E

Correct Answers to Sample Questions	
21 A B **C** D E	26 A B **C** D E
22 A **B** C D E	27 A **B** C D E
23 A B **C** D E	28 A B **C** D E
24 **A** B C D E	29 A **B** C D E
25 A **B** C D E	30 A **B** C D E

Sample questions 31 through 35 require reasoning skills. Each of these questions consists of two sets of symbols. Find the one rule that (a) explains the similarity of the symbols within each set, and (b) also explains the difference between the sets. Among the five suggested answers, find the symbol that can best be substituted for the question mark in the second set. In all these questions you will find details that have nothing to do with the principle of the question: to find the similarity between the symbols within a set and the difference between the sets.

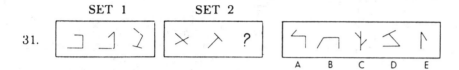

31.

The general rule for this question is that all the symbols are made up of lines that touch each other. The first set consists of symbols of three lines that touch. The second set consists of symbols of two lines that touch. Therefore E is the correct answer.

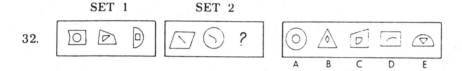

32.

The general rule for this question is that all the symbols are made up of two figures, one inside the other. The first set consists of figures each of which has a small closed figure inside. The second set consists of figures each of which has a line inside. Therefore D is the correct answer. The shape of the outer figure is a detail that has nothing to do with the problem.

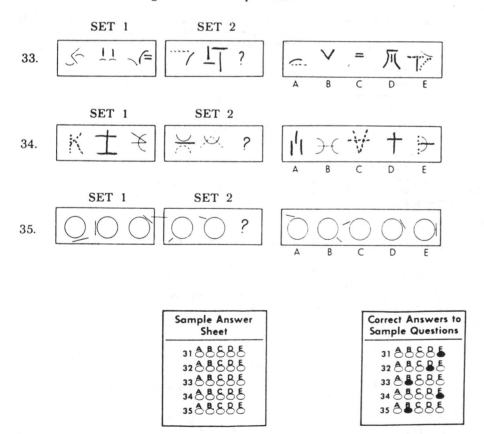

33.

34.

35.

Sample questions 36 through 48 also require reasoning skills. In each question there is at the left a series of numbers which follow some definite order, and at the right there are five sets of two numbers each. You are to look at the numbers in the series at the left and find out what order they follow. Then, from the suggested answers at the right, select the set that gives the next two numbers in the series.

Now do sample questions 36 through 48. Mark your answers on the Sample Answer Sheet.

36.   1 2 3 4 5 6 7.....................   A) 1 2   B) 5 6   C) 8 9   D) 4 5   E) 7 8

The numbers in this series are increasing by 1. If the series were continued for two more numbers, it would read 1 2 3 4 5 6 7 8 9. Therefore the correct answer is 8 and 9, and you should have darkened C on your answer sheet for question 36.

37.   15 14 13 12 11 10 9...............   A) 2 1   B) 17 16   C) 8 9   D) 8 7   E) 9 8

The numbers in this series are decreasing by 1. If the series were continued for two more numbers, it would read: 15 14 13 12 11 10 9 8 7. Therefore the correct answer is 8 and 7, and you should have darkened D for question 37.

38.   20 20 21 21 22 22 23.............   A) 23 23   B) 23 24   C) 19 19   D) 22 23   E) 21 22

Each number in this series is repeated and then increased by 1. If the series were continued for two more numbers, it would read: 20 20 21 21 22 22 23 23 24. Therefore the correct answer is 23 and 24, and you should have darkened B for question 38.

39.   17 3 17 4 17 5 17.................   A) 6 17   B) 6 7   C) 17 6   D) 5 6   E) 17 7

This series is the number 17 separated by numbers increasing by 1, beginning with the number 3. If the series were continued for two more numbers, it would read: 17 3 17 4 17 5 17 6 17. Therefore the correct answer is 6 and 17, and you should have darkened A for question 39.

40.   1 2 4 5 7 8 10....................   A) 11 12   B) 12 14   C) 10 13   D) 12 13   E) 11 13

The numbers in this series are increasing first by 1 then by 2. If the series were continued for two more numbers, it would read: 1 2 4 5 7 8 10 11 13. Therefore the correct answer is 11 and 13, and you should have darkened E on your answer sheet for question 40.

41.   21 21 20 20 19 19 18.............   A) 18 18   B) 18 17   C) 17 18   D) 17 17   E) 18 19

42.   1 20 3 19 5 18 7.................   A) 8 9   B) 8 17   C) 17 10   D) 17 9   E) 9 18

43.   30 2 28 4 26 6 24 ....   A) 23 9   B) 26 8   C) 8 9   D) 26 22   E) 8 22

44.   5 6 20 7 8 19 9..................   A) 10 18   B) 18 17   C) 10 17   D) 18 19   E) 10 11

45.   9 10 1 11 12 2 13 ....   A) 2 14   B) 3 14   C) 14 3   D) 14 15   E) 14 1

46.   4 6 9 11 14 16 19 ....   A) 21 24   B) 22 25   C) 20 22   D) 21 23   E) 22 24

47.   8 8 1 10 10 3 12 ....   A) 13 13   B) 12 5   C) 12 4   D) 13 5   E) 4 12

48.   20 21 23 24 27 28 32 33 38 39 ....   A) 45 46   B) 45 54   C) 44 45   D) 44 49   E) 40 46

Sample Answer Sheet	
36 A B C D E	43 A B C D E
37 A B C D E	44 A B C D E
38 A B C D E	45 A B C D E
39 A B C D E	46 A B C D E
40 A B C D E	47 A B C D E
41 A B C D E	48 A B C D E
42 A B C D E	

Correct Answers to Sample Questions	
36 A B ● D E	43 A B C D ●
37 A B C ● E	44 A B C D E
38 A ● C D E	45 A ● C D E
39 ● B C D E	46 A B C D E
40 A B C D ●	47 ● B C D E
41 A B C D E	48 ● B C D E
42 A B C ● E	

Sample Written Examination Questions

To familiarize you with representative types of questions used in the Foreign Service written examination, the following sample questions are provided. An answer key can be found on page 50.

KNOWLEDGE QUESTIONS
<u>Directions</u>: Each of the questions or incomplete statements below is followed by four suggested answers or completions. Select the one that is best in each case and then blacken the corresponding space on the answer sheet. Some sets of questions are presented with material such as reading passages, plans, graphs, tables, etc. Answers to such questions may require interpretation of the material and/or outside knowledge relevant to its content.

Knowledge Area: The historical antecedents of international affairs (e.g., Islam, colonialism, industrial revolution) to aid understanding of foreign governments and societies.

1. All of the following are necessary attributes of a nation-state EXCEPT

    (A) occupying a definite territory
    (B) having an organized government
    (C) using predominantly a single language
    (D) possessing internal and external sovereignty

2. Many of the developing nations that achieved independence after 1945 have become noted for their chronic instability. Which of the following factors generally contributes LEAST to this instability?

    (A) The rise of political factionalism
    (B) The large numbers of unassimilated ethnic and/or religious minorities
    (C) The artificiality of national boundaries drawn by former colonial rulers
    (D) The continued use of administrative systems inherited from colonial powers

Knowledge Area: World geography (e.g., location of countries, significant physical features, distribution of key natural resources, geography-based national rivalries and alliances) in order to understand the geographic context of foreign relations and U.S. foreign policy.

Questions 3 and 4 refer to the following map.

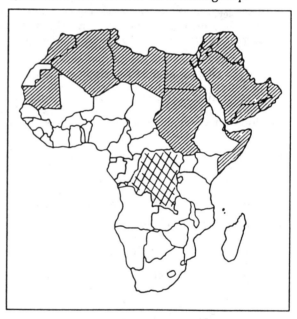

3. The cross-hatched country is a leading exporter of which of the following primary products:

    (A) Bauxite
    (B) Textile products
    (C) Copper
    (D) Diamonds

4. The shaded area on the map above identifies, as of the mid-1970's, members of which of the following?

   (A) The Organization of Petroleum Exporting Countries (OPEC)
   (B) The Arab League
   (C) The Central Treaty Organization (CENTO)
   (D) The Organization of African Unity (OAU)

Knowledge Area: Major events, institutions, and movements in the history of the United States (e.g., slavery, Constitutional Convention, Civil War, Great Depression, Civil Rights Movement) to facilitate understanding the U.S. system of government.

5. The Scopes trial of 1925 took on national significance because it

   (A) marked the first time that a U.S. court had ruled that the theory of evolution was correct
   (B) led to the first federal appropriation of aid for scientific research
   (C) symbolically pitted the new scientific outlook against the religious outlook of the Fundamentalists
   (D) was William Jennings Bryan's last major attempt to attract national attention in an attempt to capture the Democratic presidential nomination

6. The precipitous decline of the New World's indigenous population in the first century after its initial contact with Europeans was largely due to

   (A) disease
   (B) enslavement
   (C) warfare
   (D) famine

Knowledge Area: History of U.S. intellectual, artistic, and cultural life (e.g., literature, social philosophy, performing arts, sports, visual arts) in order to interpret U.S. cultural life for foreign nationals.

7. Who said, "In the future, everyone will be famous for at least 15 minutes?"

   (A) Mike Wallace
   (B) Andy Warhol
   (C) Barbara Walters
   (D) Marshall McLuhan

8. Milton Babbitt, John Harrison, Gunther Schuller, and John Cage are best known as

   (A) conductors of symphonic orchestras
   (B) ballet choreographers
   (C) playwrights
   (D) contemporary composers

Knowledge Area: Social, political, and economic trends in the United States (e.g., women and minority roles, demographic shifts, patterns of immigration, information age, biomedicine).

9. All of the following circumstances have contributed to the current emphasis on protecting the U.S. environment from toxic wastes EXCEPT:

   (A) Safe places to store toxic wastes in the United States have become scarce.
   (B) Research has increased knowledge of the toxicity of many widely used chemicals.
   (C) The amount of wastes of all kinds has grown.
   (D) Deregulation has made it easier for the public to purchase and use toxic substances.

10. In some areas of the United States, the presence of Southeast Asian refugees has produced considerable tension for which of the following reasons?

   I.   Fear of their impact on welfare rolls
   II.   Anti-Asian racism
   III. Resentment of their entrepreneurial competition
   IV.   Perceptions of them as clannish

   (A)   I only
   (B)   III only
   (C)   I and II only
   (D)   I, II, III, IV

Knowledge Area: Contemporary cultural trends in the United States (e.g., film, music, sports, magazines, newspapers, clothing and lifestyles).

11. Which of the following columnists is known for the conservative tone of his or her work?

   (A)   Russell Baker
   (B)   Carl Rowan
   (C)   Meg Greenfield
   (D   George Will

12. To the argument that television gives a truer account of what happens in a courtroom than does any other news medium, all of the following objections may reasonably be advanced EXCEPT:

   (A)   The television director, by choosing the image on which the camera focuses, engages in a process of selection just as a newspaper reporter or editor does.
   (B)   A pictorial medium has difficulty in dealing with abstract ideas, such as points of law, which are often the most important part of a court proceeding.
   (C)   Television inevitably becomes an "actor" in the courtroom proceedings and thereby changes the event as it records it.
   (D)   Television reporters, because they must concentrate on the technical and theatrical aspects of electronic journalism, have little time to master the complexities of a court case.

Knowledge Area: U.S. political process and its impact on policy (e.g., role of special interest groups, the media, political parties).

13. In the United States, campaigns for major public offices are increasingly being controlled by

   (A)   political action committees
   (B)   media consultants
   (C)   candidates' press agents
   (D)   local political party chairpersons

14. The major reason that it is easy to block a bill in Congress but difficult to enact one is which of the following?

   (A)   Well-organized opposing political parties in Congress
   (B)   The decentralized committee structure of Congress
   (C)   The influence of pork-barrel politics on congressional voting
   (D)   Institutional conflict between Congress and the President

Knowledge Area: U.S. Constitution and the structure of the U.S. Government (e.g., separation of powers, functions of cabinet departments, lawmaking, federalism, appropriation process).

15. Two key precepts of the Constitution that were not present in the Articles of Confederation were to

   (A)   buffer the government from the immediate impact of popular impulse and to extend the vote to all
   (B)   promote the power of individual states over that of the federal government and to keep the branches of the federal government separate but linked
   (C)   keep the President closely tied to the will of the majority and to promote the power of individual states over that of the federal government
   (D)   buffer the government from the immediate impact of popular impulse and to keep the branches of the federal government separate but linked

16. Which of the following statements is true about executive privilege?

    (A) It allows the President to withhold certain information from Congress and the courts.
    (B) It protects members of the executive branch from prosecution for any acts committed in the course of performing their jobs.
    (C) It is the concept that underlies the President's use of a pocket veto during a session of Congress.
    (D) It protects the members of the Cabinet when the President faces impeachment proceedings.

Knowledge Area: U.S. economic systems, its institutions and philosophical principles, to aid in interpreting U.S. policies and actions to foreign nationals.

17. If the Federal Reserve were to adopt an accommodative policy and then decrease the discount rate and buy government securities in the open market, it would most likely be responding to

    (A) rising interest rates by increasing the money supply
    (B) rising interest rates by decreasing the money supply
    (C) falling interest rates by increasing the money supply
    (D) falling interest rates by decreasing the money supply

18. In the United States, the last 25 years of the 19th century were characterized by several violent conflicts between capital and labor, which by 1900 resulted in

    (A) the use of federal court injunctions to jail strikers without a jury trial
    (B) the intensive participation of the American Federation of Labor (AFL) in politics
    (C) the unionization of the vast majority of factory workers
    (D) general acceptance of the closed shop by employers

Knowledge Area: U.S. educational system (e.g., public versus private institutions, scholarships).

19. All of the following were objectives of the common, or public school, movement of 1840-1860 EXCEPT:

    (A) primary school education for all white Americans regardless of sex
    (B) a professionally trained teaching force
    (C) establishment of a uniform national curriculum
    (D) introduction of a new pedagogy based on the idea that children were capable of infinite improvement

20. In the United States, at which of the following levels of education are there more privately than publicly controlled schools?

    I.   Elementary
    II.   Secondary
    III. Postsecondary

    (A) III only
    (B) I and II only
    (C) II and III only
    (D) I, II, and III

Knowledge Area: Foreign political systems (e.g., parliamentary, federal, dictatorship, one-party).

21. A major difference between U.S. political parties and political parties in European parliamentary systems is that

    (A) European parties are less ideologically rigid
    (B) U.S. parties have stronger local organizations
    (C) European parties exercise more discipline over their elected representatives in the legislature
    (D) U.S. parties better represent special interests

22. A distinguishing feature of the parliamentary form of government is that

    (A)   parliament is the sole repository of legitimacy and may not delegate governmental authority to regional or local units
    (B)   no final action may be taken on a bill until all members of parliament have had an opportunity to speak either for or against it
    (C)   members of the government are not allowed to take part in parliamentary debates that involve appropriations
    (D)   parliament has the power to require the prime minister to resign or call for an election

Knowledge Area: Basic principles of economics (e.g., supply and demand, money supply, international trade, comparative economic systems).

Question 23 refers to the following graph.

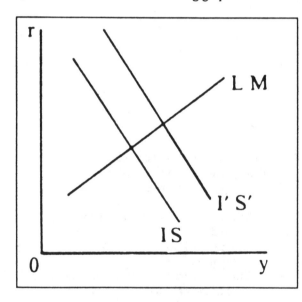

23. In the graph above, the shift of the IS curve to the new position, I'S', illustrates the Keynesian proposition that increases in both gross national product (GNP) and interest rates could result from increases in

    (A)   the money supply
    (B)   the demand for money
    (C)   government spending
    (D)   taxes

24. A "dirty float" system is one in which

    (A)   exchange rates are permitted to fluctuate freely
    (B)   governments act to influence the exchange value of their own currencies
    (C)   assets of foreign banks are undervalued
    (D)   exchange rates are determined by an automatic gold standard

Knowledge Area: Major contemporary international economic and commercial issues (e.g., unemployment, inflation, trade deficit, Third World debt) in order to understand the impact of economic conditions on a foreign country and on U.S. programs and policy interest.

25. To conform with the chronological sequence most commonly followed by U.S. manufacturers that are launching international operations, the activities below should be undertaken in which of the following sequences?

    I.   Establish a foreign sales branch.
    II   Initiate overseas assembly of parts manufactured in the United States.
    III.   Begin full-scale manufacturing overseas.
    IV.   Export U.S. goods through a foreign distributor.

    (A)   I, II, III, IV
    (B)   I, IV, III, II
    (C)   III, IV, II, I
    (D)   IV, I, II, III

26. All of the following statements concerning dumping in international trade are correct EXCEPT:

    (A)   It is defined as selling at less than fair value.
    (B)   It forms the basis for a claim in the World Court.
    (C)   It constitutes an unfair trade practice under GATT.
    (D)   It is subject to U.S. law.

ENGLISH EXPRESSION QUESTIONS

Directions: The following sentences contain problems in grammar, usage, diction (choice of words), and idiom.

> Some sentences are correct.
> No sentence contains more than one error.

You will find that the error, if there is one, is underlined and lettered. Assume that all other elements of the sentence are correct and cannot be changed. In choosing answers, follow the requirements of standard written English.

If there is an error, select the one underlined part that must be changed in order to make the sentence correct, and fill in the corresponding oval on the answer sheet.

If there is no error, mark answer space E.

EXAMPLES:

SAMPLE ANSWERS

I. He spoke bluntly and angrily to we
              A   B   C

    spectators.   No error
         D   E

I. Ⓐ Ⓑ ● Ⓓ Ⓔ

II. She works every day so that she would
         A   B   C

    become financially independent in her old
                D

    age.   No error
             E

II. ● Ⓑ Ⓒ Ⓓ Ⓔ

1. Paul Klee awaited many long years to receive the
              A   B

    recognition due him as a painter.   No error
                   C   D   E

2. Acting in skits or plays have frequently proved
                             A

    of great benefit to mentally ill patients,

    perhaps because such activity allows them to
        B   C

    act out their own inner conflicts.   No error
             D   E

3. According to the theory, some types of human
    A

    behavior once considered the result of great
             B

    psychological disturbance is in reality caused by
                              C

    a chemical imbalance within the body.   No error
                          D   E

4. The author's novels may seem somewhat old and
                          A   B

    musty, but their form survives in modern popular
              C   D

    novels.   No error
                E

5. No sooner had the Great Fire burned itself out
              A   B

    than plans were laid for the rebuilding of the city.
    C   D

    No error
    E

6. The candidate directed her appeal to the young
                          A

    once realizing that she could not win
         B   C

    without their votes.   No error
    D   E

7. Because of the increasing popularity of our
    A

    national parks, the park service must

    deal with the almost unsolvable problem of
                          B

    how you can let every visitor in and still keep
        C   D

    the wilderness intact.   No error
                               E

8. Herschel's catalogs of stars, first published in
                                  A

    the late eighteenth century, did much to progress
        B   C   D

    astronomy.   No error
                   E

Directions: In each of the following sentences, some part or all of the sentence is underlined. Below each sentence you will find five ways of phrasing the underlined part. Select the answer that produces the most effective sentence, one that is clear and exact without awkwardness or ambiguity, and fill in the corresponding oval on your answer sheet. In choosing answers, follow the requirements of standard written English. Choose the answer that best expresses the meaning of the original sentence.

Answer (A) is always the same as the underlined part. Choose answer (A) if you think the original sentence needs no revision.

EXAMPLE: SAMPLE ANSWERS

Laura Ingalls Wilder published her first book   Ⓐ ● Ⓒ Ⓓ Ⓔ
and she was sixty-five years old then.

(A) and she was sixty-five years old then
(B) when she was sixty-five years old
(C) at age sixty-five years old
(D) upon reaching sixty-five years
(E) at the time when she was sixty-five

---

9. Finally, public and legal pressures forced the auto manufacturers to abandon racing, and they would thus then develop more rapidly pollution controls and safety devices.

   (A) racing, and they would thus then develop more rapidly
   (B) racing and exchange it for more rapid development of
   (C) racing, and thus they would favor the more rapid development of
   (D) racing to be developing more rapidly
   (E) racing in favor of more rapid development of

10. Almost all folk singers have several ballads from the Child collection in their repertoires, whether they know it or not.

    (A) whether they know it or not
    (B) whether or not they know anything about it
    (C) whether knowing it or not
    (D) whether with their knowledge or without
    (E) whether knowingly or unknowingly

11. Because extremely low-frequency radio waves can penetrate deep water, much research has, as a result, been devoted to their potential use in underwater communications.

    (A) much research has, as a result, been devoted to their potential use in underwater communications
    (B) much research on their potential use in underwater communications has resulted
    (C) it has resulted in the devotion of much research to their potential use in underwater communications
    (D) devotion of much research to using them in underwater communications has taken place
    (E) much research has been devoted to their potential use in underwater communications

12. They have been sent to help people of developing countries, and much useful work has been done by members of the Peace Corps.

    (A) They have been sent to help people of developing countries, and much useful work has been done by members of the Peace Corps.
    (B) Members of the Peace Corps have been sent to help people of developing countries and much useful work has been done.
    (C) They have been sent to help people of developing countries, and members of the Peace Corps have done much useful work.
    (D) Sent to help people of developing countries, members of the Peace Corps have done much useful work.
    (E) Having been sent to help people of developing countries, much useful work has been done by members of the Peace Corps.

13. Horseshoe crabs are not crabs at all; its nearest living relative is the spider.

    (A) its nearest living relative is the spider
    (B) their nearest living relatives are the spiders
    (C) the nearest living relatives are the spider
    (D) their nearest living relative is spiders
    (E) its nearest living relatives are spiders

14. Drops of water acting like prisms refract sunlight, which process causes rainbows.

    (A) sunlight, which process causes
    (B) sunlight, and it causes
    (C) sunlight, which is the cause of
    (D) sunlight and thus cause
    (E) sunlight and this, therefore, causes

Directions: In each of the following questions you are given a complete sentence to be rephrased according to the directions that follow it. You should rephrase the sentence mentally to save time, although you may make notes in your test book if you wish.

Below each sentence and its directions are listed words or phrases that may occur in your revised sentence. When you have thought out a good sentence, look in the choices A through E for the word or entire phrase that is included in your revised sentence, and fill in the corresponding oval on the answer sheet. The word or phrase you choose should be the most accurate and most nearly complete of all the choices given, and should be part of a sentence that meets the requirements of standard written English.

Of course, a number of different sentences can be obtained if the sentence is revised according to the directions, and not all of these possibilities can be included in only five choices. If you should find that you have thought of a sentence that contains none of the words or phrases listed in the choices, you should attempt to rephrase the sentence again so that it includes a word or phrase that is listed.

Although the directions may at times require you to change the relationship between parts of the sentence or to make slight changes in meaning in other ways, <u>make only those changes that the directions require</u>; that is, keep the meaning the same, or as nearly the same as the directions permit. If you think that more than one good sentence can be made according to the directions, select the sentence that is most exact, effective, and natural in phrasing and construction.

EXAMPLE

I. <u>Sentence:</u>   Coming to the city as a young man, he found a job as a newspaper reporter.

Directions: Substitute <u>He came</u> for <u>Coming.</u>

   (A)   and so he found
   (B)   and found
   (C)   and there he found
   (D)   and then finding
   (E)   and had found

Your rephrased sentence will probably read: "He came to the city as a young man and found a job as a newspaper reporter." This sentence contains the correct answer: <u>(B) and found.</u> A sentence which used one of the alternate phrases would <u>change the meaning or intention</u> of the original sentence, would be a <u>poorly written sentence</u>, or would be <u>less effective</u> than another possible revision.

15. Root feeding is necessary for the survival of many old trees.

Begin with <u>Many old trees need.</u>

   (A)   for their surviving
   (B)   so they survive
   (C)   to survive
   (D)   in surviving
   (E)   as a survival measure

16. Only wealthy people can afford the luxury of hiring architects to design their homes.

Begin with <u>Hiring an architect.</u>

   (A)   and only
   (B)   therefore only
   (C)   luxury that only
   (D)   luxury; only
   (E)   something that only

17. In their book the term "institutionalized racism" was coined by Stokely Carmichael and Charles V. Hamilton in their book, *Black Power.*

Begin with <u>in their book.</u>

   (A)   has been coined
   (B)   they coined
   (C)   coined
   (D)   is coined
   (E)   was coined

18. The disturbance to the ecology of the area that the wastes from the new mill could create was mentioned in the article; however, greater emphasis was placed on the contributions that the mill could make to the economic development of the area.

Begin with <u>The article placed less.</u>

   (A)   rather than on the contributions
   (B)   than on the disturbance
   (C)   instead of the disturbance
   (D)   than on the contributions

19. The most extensive changes in the English language have come about through contact with different cultures, rather than through gradual changes in meaning.

Substitute <u>about, not through</u> for <u>about through</u>.

(A) but by contact
(B) but through contact
(C) rather by contact
(D) rather than by contact
(E) although through contact

20. Though, for the most part, German Shepards are intelligent and well-behaved, they often make difficult pets because of their tendency to recognize only one master

Begin with <u>The tendency</u>.

(A) it is often difficult for them
(B) for difficulty in their
(C) them often have difficulty with
(D) them difficult for
(E) them difficult

Directions: In each of the following questions you are given four sentences and a question that asks for the best sequence to make a clear, sensible paragraph. Choose the correct option that reflects the ordering of the sentences that represents the best order for a clear, sensible paragraph.

21. I.   Women are responsible for much of this wealth.
    II. Phyllis Wheatley, the poet, was one of the earliest to write of her life.
    III. Since the eighteenth century, Black women in America have been writing the stories of their lives.
    IV. Although most readers have heard of the lives of Booker T. Washington, Malcolm X, and Richard Wright, they are generally ignorant of the wealth of Black autobiography.

Which of the following presents the best sequence of the sentences above to make a clear, sensible paragraph?

(A) I, III, II, IV
(B) II, III, IV, I
(C) III, I, II, IV
(D) III, II, I, IV
(E) IV, I, III, II

22. I.   However, after Tito's death, the various, ethnic, linguistic, and religious groups in Yugoslavia began to assert their independence.
    II. Yugoslavia was formed as a federation of disparate states after the Second World War.
    III. The charismatic domination of Marshal Tito was the major force binding this federation.
    IV. In the last decade of the 20th century, the unity of Yugoslavia remains an open question.

Which of the following presents the best sequence of the sentences above to make a clear, sensible paragraph:

(A) I, IV, III, II
(B) II, I, III, IV
(C) II, III, I, IV
(D) IV, II, I, III
(E) IV, III, II, I

23. I.   No single group has been able to rest easy in its hegemony, however, because one or more of the other groups was always ready to dispute the first group's right to rule.
    II. The Middle East's relatively dense population, its scarcity of water and arable land, and its location in a crossroads between East and West, North and South, have all contributed to this conflict.
    III. Throughout recorded history, the Middle East has been an area of strife between peoples of different ethnic and religious backgrounds.
    IV. Persians, Kurds, Arabs, Jews, Turks, Christians, Shi'ite and Sunni Muslims, all have struggled to gain, hold, or regain power over the territory in the Middle East.

Which of the following presents the best sequence of the sentences above to make a clear, sensible paragraph?

(A) I, II, III, IV
(B) II, III, I, IV
(C) III, I, IV, II
(D) III, II, IV, I
(E) IV, II, III, I

SAMPLE TEST QUESTIONS ANSWER KEY

KNOWLEDGE TEST

1. C	11. D	21. C
2. D	12. D	22. D
3. C	13. B	23. C
4. B	14. B	24. B
5. C	15. D	25. D
6. A	16. A	26. B
7. B	17. A	
8. D	18. A	
9. D	19. C	
10. D	20. A	

ENGLISH EXPRESSION

1. A	11. E	21. E
2. A	12. D	22. C
3. C	13. B	23. D
4. E	14. D	
5. E	15. C	
6. B	16. C	
7. C	17. C	
8. D	18. D	
9. E	19. B	
10. A	20. E	

✤U.S. GOVERNMENT PRINTING OFFICE : 1991 292-913

MEMORIZING ADDRESSES

In this test you will be shown five (5) boxes numbered 1 to 5. Each box contains five addresses. Your objective is to remember where each address belongs. If you believe an address belongs in box 1, then darken in number (1) for that question on your sample answer page. If you believe an address belongs in box 2 then darken in number (2) for that question on your sample answer page and so on. Use the answer page found on page 000 to mark your answers for this first sample test on memorizing addresses. Use a pencil and mark only one answer per question.

1	2	3
3400 - 4300 Elm Powell 8100 - 8799 Castle Fletcher 6400 - 7299 Fern	7600 - 7999 Elm Marshall 2500 - 2999 Castle Lawrence 4200 - 5199 Fern	5500 - 6999 Elm Pleasant 1000 - 1999 Castle Kirk 7000 - 8999 Fern

4	5
1500 - 2299 Elm Chestnut 7500 - 7999 Castle Allendale 3000 - 3899 Fern	6000 - 6899 Elm Mystic 5000 - 5999 Castle Newport 2100 - 2999 Fern

TURN THE PAGE TO BEGIN THIS TEST.

DO NOT LOOK AT THIS PAGE ONCE THE TEST BEGINS.

SAMPLE TEST 1, SECTION (II) CLERK-CARRIER TEST
‒ ‒ ‒ ‒ ‒ ‒ ‒ ‒ ‒ ‒ ‒ ‒ ‒ ‒ ‒ ‒ ‒ ‒ ‒ ‒

MEMORIZING ADDRESSES
‒ ‒ ‒ ‒ ‒ ‒ ‒ ‒ ‒ ‒ ‒ ‒

1)	Kirk	41)	2100 - 2999 Fern
2)	4200 - 5199 Fern	42)	7500 - 7999 Castle
3)	7600 - 7999 Elm	43)	Powell
4)	Pleasant	44)	Newport
5)	Mystic	45)	5500 - 6999 Elm
6)	2100 - 2999 Fern	46)	Chestnut
7)	6400 - 7299 Fern	47)	1000 - 1999 Castle
8)	7500 - 7999 Castle	48)	3400 - 4300 Elm
9)	Fletcher	49)	Marshall
10)	Powell	50)	4200 - 5199 Fern
11)	5000 - 5999 Castle	51)	Mystic
12)	Marshall	52)	Kirk
13)	3000 - 3899 Fern	53)	Allendale
14)	6000 - 6899 Elm	54)	1500 - 2299 Elm
15)	3400 - 4300 Elm	55)	7000 - 8999 Fern
16)	1000 - 1999 Castle	56)	Marshall
17)	Lawrence	57)	6400 - 7299 Fern
18)	Chestnut	58)	Fletcher
19)	5500 - 6999 Elm	59)	Pleasant
20)	Newport	60)	7600 - 7999 Elm
21)	8100 - 8799 Castle	61)	Lawrence
22)	2500 - 2999 Castle	62)	3000 - 3899 Fern
23)	Allendale	63)	Powell
24)	1500 - 2299 Elm	64)	5500 - 6999 Elm
25)	7000 - 8999 Fern	65)	Chestnut
26)	Allendale	66)	2500 - 2999 Castle
27)	Newport	67)	4200 - 5199 Fern
28)	Kirk	68)	7500 - 7999 Castle
29)	7600 - 7999 Elm	69)	Marshall
30)	Pleasant	70)	Allendale
31)	3400 - 4300 Elm	71)	5000 - 5999 Castle
32)	1500 - 2299 Elm	72)	Lawrence
33)	6400 - 7299 Fern	73)	7000 - 8999 Fern
34)	Marshall	74)	3400 - 4300 Elm
35)	Powell	75)	Newport
36)	6000 - 6899 Elm	76)	Mystic
37)	8100 - 8799 Castle	77)	1000 - 1999 Castle
38)	Lawrence	78)	2100 - 2999 Fern
39)	4200 - 5199 Fern	79)	7600 - 7999 Elm
40)	1000 - 1999 Castle	80)	Kirk

END OF SAMPLE TEST 1
‒ ‒ ‒ ‒ ‒ ‒ ‒ ‒ ‒ ‒ ‒

MEMORIZING ADDRESSES
‒ ‒ ‒ ‒ ‒ ‒ ‒ ‒ ‒ ‒ ‒ ‒

SAMPLE ANSWER PAGE FOR SAMPLE TEST 1 SECTION (II) CLERK-CARRIER TEST

MEMORIZING ADDRESSES

1)	(1)	(2)	(3)	(4)	(5)	41)	(1)	(2)	(3)	(4)	(5)
2)	(1)	(2)	(3)	(4)	(5)	42)	(1)	(2)	(3)	(4)	(5)
3)	(1)	(2)	(3)	(4)	(5)	43)	(1)	(2)	(3)	(4)	(5)
4)	(1)	(2)	(3)	(4)	(5)	44)	(1)	(2)	(3)	(4)	(5)
5)	(1)	(2)	(3)	(4)	(5)	45)	(1)	(2)	(3)	(4)	(5)
6)	(1)	(2)	(3)	(4)	(5)	46)	(1)	(2)	(3)	(4)	(5)
7)	(1)	(2)	(3)	(4)	(5)	47)	(1)	(2)	(3)	(4)	(5)
8)	(1)	(2)	(3)	(4)	(5)	48)	(1)	(2)	(3)	(4)	(5)
9)	(1)	(2)	(3)	(4)	(5)	49)	(1)	(2)	(3)	(4)	(5)
10)	(1)	(2)	(3)	(4)	(5)	50)	(1)	(2)	(3)	(4)	(5)
11)	(1)	(2)	(3)	(4)	(5)	51)	(1)	(2)	(3)	(4)	(5)
12)	(1)	(2)	(3)	(4)	(5)	52)	(1)	(2)	(3)	(4)	(5)
13)	(1)	(2)	(3)	(4)	(5)	53)	(1)	(2)	(3)	(4)	(5)
14)	(1)	(2)	(3)	(4)	(5)	54)	(1)	(2)	(3)	(4)	(5)
15)	(1)	(2)	(3)	(4)	(5)	55)	(1)	(2)	(3)	(4)	(5)
16)	(1)	(2)	(3)	(4)	(5)	56)	(1)	(2)	(3)	(4)	(5)
17)	(1)	(2)	(3)	(4)	(5)	57)	(1)	(2)	(3)	(4)	(5)
18)	(1)	(2)	(3)	(4)	(5)	58)	(1)	(2)	(3)	(4)	(5)
19)	(1)	(2)	(3)	(4)	(5)	59)	(1)	(2)	(3)	(4)	(5)
20)	(1)	(2)	(3)	(4)	(5)	60)	(1)	(2)	(3)	(4)	(5)
21)	(1)	(2)	(3)	(4)	(5)	61)	(1)	(2)	(3)	(4)	(5)
22)	(1)	(2)	(3)	(4)	(5)	62)	(1)	(2)	(3)	(4)	(5)
23)	(1)	(2)	(3)	(4)	(5)	63)	(1)	(2)	(3)	(4)	(5)
24)	(1)	(2)	(3)	(4)	(5)	64)	(1)	(2)	(3)	(4)	(5)
25)	(1)	(2)	(3)	(4)	(5)	65)	(1)	(2)	(3)	(4)	(5)
26)	(1)	(2)	(3)	(4)	(5)	66)	(1)	(2)	(3)	(4)	(5)
27)	(1)	(2)	(3)	(4)	(5)	67)	(1)	(2)	(3)	(4)	(5)
28)	(1)	(2)	(3)	(4)	(5)	68)	(1)	(2)	(3)	(4)	(5)
29)	(1)	(2)	(3)	(4)	(5)	69)	(1)	(2)	(3)	(4)	(5)
30)	(1)	(2)	(3)	(4)	(5)	70)	(1)	(2)	(3)	(4)	(5)
31)	(1)	(2)	(3)	(4)	(5)	71)	(1)	(2)	(3)	(4)	(5)
32)	(1)	(2)	(3)	(4)	(5)	72)	(1)	(2)	(3)	(4)	(5)
33)	(1)	(2)	(3)	(4)	(5)	73)	(1)	(2)	(3)	(4)	(5)
34)	(1)	(2)	(3)	(4)	(5)	74)	(1)	(2)	(3)	(4)	(5)
35)	(1)	(2)	(3)	(4)	(5)	75)	(1)	(2)	(3)	(4)	(5)
36)	(1)	(2)	(3)	(4)	(5)	76)	(1)	(2)	(3)	(4)	(5)
37)	(1)	(2)	(3)	(4)	(5)	77)	(1)	(2)	(3)	(4)	(5)
38)	(1)	(2)	(3)	(4)	(5)	78)	(1)	(2)	(3)	(4)	(5)
39)	(1)	(2)	(3)	(4)	(5)	79)	(1)	(2)	(3)	(4)	(5)
40)	(1)	(2)	(3)	(4)	(5)	80)	(1)	(2)	(3)	(4)	(5)

ANSWERS TO SAMPLE TEST 1, SECTION (II) CLERK CARRIER TEST

MEMORIZING ADDRESSES

1)	3	41)	5
2)	2	42)	4
3)	2	43)	1
4)	3	44)	5
5)	5	45)	3
6)	5	46)	4
7)	1	47)	3
8)	4	48)	1
9)	1	49)	2
10)	1	50)	2
11)	5	51)	5
12)	2	52)	3
13)	4	53)	4
14)	5	54)	4
15)	1	55)	3
16)	3	56)	2
17)	2	57)	1
18)	4	58)	1
19)	3	59)	3
20)	5	60)	2
21)	1	61)	2
22)	2	62)	4
23)	4	63)	1
24)	4	64)	3
25)	3	65)	4
26)	4	66)	2
27)	5	67)	2
28)	3	68)	4
29)	2	69)	2
30)	3	70)	4
31)	1	71)	5
32)	4	72)	2
33)	1	73)	3
34)	2	74)	1
35)	1	75)	5
36)	5	76)	5
37)	1	77)	3
38)	2	78)	5
39)	2	79)	2
40)	3	80)	3

SAMPLE TEST 1, SECTION (II) DISTRIBUTION CLERK, MACHINE OPERATOR TEST

MATH PROGRESSIONS

In this test you will be given twenty-five (25) lines of numbers. The numbers on each line will be followed by a group of five (5) possible answers. You are to determine which answers best complete each line of numbers. Choose only one answer per question and mark that answer on the special answer page found on page 000. Use a pencil to record your answers. You have 20 minutes to complete this test.

1)	43	34	43	34	43	34	43	(a) 43 (b) 34 (c) 33 (d) 44 (e) 24

| 2) | 60 | 73 | 65 | 78 | 70 | 83 | 75 | (a) 75 (b) 78 (c) 88
(d) 87 (e) 67 |

| 3) | 16 | 27 | 37 | 48 | 58 | 69 | 79 | (a) 80 (b) 70 (c) 89
(d) 90 (e) 79 |

| 4) | 56 | 53 | 47 | 44 | 38 | 35 | 29 | (a) 23 (b) 24 (c) 25
(d) 26 (e) 27 |

| 5) | 29 | 49 | 69 | 39 | 9 | 29 | 49 | (a) 9 (b) 19 (c) 29
(d) 39 (e) 49 |

| 6) | 71 | 71 | 65 | 65 | 59 | 59 | 53 | (a) 59 53 (b) 53 47 (c) 53 53
(d) 47 53 (e) 47 41 |

| 7) | 35 | 36 | 37 | 25 | 26 | 27 | 15 | (a) 27 15 (b) 16 4 (c) 16 17
(d) 27 39 (e) 39 27 |

| 8) | 92 | 99 | 89 | 96 | 86 | 93 | 83 | (a) 90 80 (b) 83 80 (c) 83 83
(d) 80 83 (e) 80 80 |

| 9) | 84 | 77 | 79 | 72 | 74 | 67 | 69 | (a) 64 62 (b) 72 74 (c) 74 72
(d) 64 64 (e) 62 64 |

| 10) | 17 | 12 | 29 | 22 | 41 | 32 | 53 | (a) 40 65 (b) 44 65 (c) 65 44
(d) 43 65 (e) 42 65 |

| 11) | 22 | 22 | 16 | 22 | 22 | 16 | 22 | (a) 16 16 (b) 22 22 (c) 16 22
(d) 22 16 (e) 22 26 |

| 12) | 0 | 50 | 3 | 44 | 6 | 38 | 9 | (a) 23 21 (b) 32 12 (c) 12 33
(d) 12 15 (e) 32 26 |

13)	5	9	9	13	13	17	17	(a) 13 13	(b) 21 21	(c) 23 23
								(d) 21 17	(e) 17 21	
14)	48	61	44	65	40	69	36	(a) 40 73	(b) 43 73	(c) 73 32
								(d) 32 73	(e) 32 74	
15)	62	70	67	75	72	80	77	(a) 85 82	(b) 80 72	(c) 72 80
								(d) 82 85	(e) 85 90	
16)	53	0	58	0	63	0	68	(a) 73 78	(b) 73 9	(c) 0 78
								(d) 0 73	(e) 0 0	
17)	31	40	49	42	35	44	53	(a) 59 53	(b) 53 59	(c) 46 46
								(d) 46 44	(e) 46 39	
18)	77	57	75	59	73	61	71	(a) 63 69	(b) 69 63	(c) 69 65
								(d) 51 69	(e) 69 51	
19)	98	98	76	76	54	54	32	(a) 32 54	(b) 32 10	(c) 32 32
								(d) 10 32	(e) 54 32	
20)	1	16	31	23	38	53	45	(a) 60 52	(b) 52 60	(c) 37 52
								(d) 60 75	(e) 75 60	
21)	86	89	84	87	82	85	80	(a) 77 85	(b) 78 80	(c) 80 78
								(d) 83 78	(e) 83 75	
22)	25	50	75	25	50	75	25	(a) 25 50	(b) 75 25	(c) 50 75
								(d) 50 25	(e) 50 50	
23)	44	20	34	21	24	22	14	(a) 23 4	(b) 22 4	(c) 4 23
								(d) 13 12	(e) 23 24	
24)	63	56	49	42	35	28	21	(a) 15 8	(b) 14 8	(c) 15 7
								(d) 28 21	(e) 14 7	
25)	93	94	92	93	91	92	90	(a) 92 93	(b) 89 91	(c) 90 89
								(d) 91 90	(e) 91 89	

SAMPLE ANSWER PAGE FOR SAMPLE TEST 3, SECTION (I)

DISTRIBUTION CLERK, MACHINE OPERATOR TEST

MATH PROGRESSIONS

1 (a) (b) (c) (d) (e)   2 (a) (b) (c) (d) (e)   3 (a) (b) (c) (d) (e)   4 (a) (b) (c) (d) (e)   5 (a) (b) (c) (d) (e)

6 (a) (b) (c) (d) (e)   7 (a) (b) (c) (d) (e)   8 (a) (b) (c) (d) (e)   9 (a) (b) (c) (d) (e)   10 (a) (b) (c) (d) (e)

11 (a) (b) (c) (d) (e)   12 (a) (b) (c) (d) (e)   13 (a) (b) (c) (d) (e)   14 (a) (b) (c) (d) (e)   15 (a) (b) (c) (d) (e)

16 (a) (b) (c) (d) (e)   17 (a) (b) (c) (d) (e)   18 (a) (b) (c) (d) (e)   19 (a) (b) (c) (d) (e)   20 (a) (b) (c) (d) (e)

21 (a) (b) (c) (d) (e)   22 (a) (b) (c) (d) (e)   23 (a) (b) (c) (d) (e)   24 (a) (b) (c) (d) (e)   25 (a) (b) (c) (d) (e)

1 (a) (b) (c) (d) (e)   6 (a) (b) (c) (d) (e)   11 (a) (b) (c) (d) (e)   16 (a) (b) (c) (d) (e)   21 (a) (b) (c) (d) (e)

2 (a) (b) (c) (d) (e)   7 (a) (b) (c) (d) (e)   12 (a) (b) (c) (d) (e)   17 (a) (b) (c) (d) (e)   22 (a) (b) (c) (d) (e)

3 (a) (b) (c) (d) (e)   8 (a) (b) (c) (d) (e)   13 (a) (b) (c) (d) (e)   18 (a) (b) (c) (d) (e)   23 (a) (b) (c) (d) (e)

4 (a) (b) (c) (d) (e)   9 (a) (b) (c) (d) (e)   14 (a) (b) (c) (d) (e)   19 (a) (b) (c) (d) (e)   24 (a) (b) (c) (d) (e)

5 (a) (b) (c) (d) (e)   10 (a) (b) (c) (d) (e)   15 (a) (b) (c) (d) (e)   20 (a) (b) (c) (d) (e)   25 (a) (b) (c) (d) (e)

ANSWERS TO SAMPLE TEST 1

SECTION (I) DISTRIBUTION CLERK, MACHINE OPERATOR TEST

MATH PROGRESSIONS

1)	b	9)	e	17)	e
2)	c	10)	e	18)	a
3)	d	11)	d	19)	b
4)	d	12)	b	20)	d
5)	b	13)	b	21)	d
6)	b	14)	c	22)	c
7)	c	15)	a	23)	a
8)	a	16)	d	24)	e
				25)	e

ADDRESS CHECKING

In this test you are to determine if the two addresses are the same or different. If you believe the addresses are exactly the same, then darken in answer box (S) on your answer page. If you believe the addresses are different, then darken in answer box (D) on your answer page. Remember to use a pencil and mark only one answer per question. You have 5 minutes to complete this test.

1)	1039 Stratton Street	1039 Stratton Street
2)	23 Avenue L	14 Ave. L
3)	Livingston Road	Livingston Road
4)	54-87 Elm Drive	54-78 Elm Drive
5)	49587 Peters Lane	49857 Peters Lane
6)	70 West 14 Avenue	70 West 14 Avenue
7)	129 Oak Terrace	129 Oak Terrace
8)	Butte, Montana 59701	Butte, Montana 59701
9)	Avenue of the Americas	Avenue of the Americas
10)	2138 E. Clark Street	2138 East Clarke Street
11)	43 Reading Way	43 Reeding Way
12)	Route 25038	Route 25038
13)	144 South Dakota Street	144 South Dakota St.
14)	5 Newton Ln.	5 Newten Ln.
15)	26 N S E	26 N S E
16)	18 Maple View Drive	18 Maple View Drive
17)	60-55 Spruce Avenue	60-55 Sprace Avenue
18)	Ellison Dr. North	Ellison Dr. North
19)	82 4th Court	82 4th Court
20)	Ann Harbor, Michigan	Anne Harbor, Michigan
21)	Eastern Boulevard	Eastern Boulevard
22)	415 Sparrow Lane	514 Sparrow Lane
23)	22 Huntington Court	222 Huntington Court
24)	72-45 Irvington Street	72-45 Irvington Street
25)	945 Third Avenue	945 Third Avenue
26)	Stillwater, Oklahoma 74074	Stilwater, Oklahoma 74074
27)	36 Olmstead Road	36 Olmsteed Road
28)	R.F.D. 3280	R.F.D. 3280
29)	2118 Rochambeau Terrace	2118 Rochambeau Terr.
30)	South Clinton Apts.	South Clinton Apartments
31)	12 East 81 Street	12 East 18 Street
32)	Silver City, New Mexico	Silver City, New York
33)	Williamsburg, Virginia	Williamsburg, Virginia

34)	45803 Western Ct.	45830 Western Ct.
35)	8 Misty View Walk	8 Misty View Walk
36)	138 Jackson Street	138 Jacksen Street
37)	Becke Ave. West	Beck Ave. West
38)	2-13 Montgomery Avenue	2-12 Montgomery Avenue
39)	Blanchard Court	Blanchard Court
40)	48960 Cypruss Place	48960 Cypress Place
41)	Bar Harbour, Maine	Bar Harbor, Maine
42)	Twin Lakes North	Twin Lakes South
43)	562 Fleet Dr.	562 Fleet Dr.
44)	7477 Green Street	7477 Greene Street
45)	347-69 Cathy Lane	347-69 Cathy Lane
46)	696 Center Street	696 Centre Street
47)	27 Mockingbird Lane	27 Mockinbird Lane
48)	Jewel Road East	Jewel Road East
49)	55 President Ave.	55 President Ave.
50)	Baton Rouge, La. 70808	Baton Rogue, La. 78008
51)	83695 Brown Avenue	83695 Browne Avenue
52)	45618 Arlington Road	45618 Arlington Road
53)	3 West 23 Street	3 West 23 St.
54)	Whitman Square N. E.	Whitmann Square N. E.
55)	7 University Plaza	7 University Pl.
56)	Brooklyn, N.Y. 11208	Brooklyn, N.Y. 11208
57)	146 Potter Avenue	146 Porter Avenue
58)	2200 South Central Ln.	2200 So. Central Ln.
59)	19 Emerson Lakes	19 Emersen Lakes
60)	1552 Pennsylvannia Avenue	1525 Pennsylvania Ave.
61)	287 Elmira Loop	287 Elmira Loop
62)	790 McDonald Street	790 MacDonald Street
63)	Tyler, Texas 75702	Tyler, Tx. 75702
64)	Hollywood & Vine	Hollywood & Vyne
65)	4 Grace Alley	4 Grace Ally
66)	37 Hamilton Walk West	73 Hamilton Walk West
67)	Hardwick Manor East	Hardwick Manor East
68)	64306 Cranford Terrace	64036 Cranford Terrace
69)	Concord, Massachusetts	Concord, Massachusetts
70)	57 Maple Ave.	47 Maple Avenue
71)	823 Summit Place	832 Summit Place
72)	1234 DeKalbe Road	1234 DeKalb Road
73)	Piccadilly Square	Picadilly Square
74)	98345 Fennimore Street	98345 Fenimore Street
75)	Ocean Parkway	Ocean Parkway
76)	Lakeville, Conn. 06579	Lakeville, Conn. 06759
77)	2 Empire Blvd.	2 Empire Blvd.
78)	40 Rochester Drive	40 Rochester Drive
79)	1092 Saint Frances St.	1092 Saint Francis St.
80)	Boise, Idaho 83705	Biose, Idaho 83075

END OF SAMPLE TEST 1, SECTION (I) CLERK-CARRIER TEST

— —

ADDRESS CHECKING

— — — — — — — — —

34)	45803 Western Ct.	45830 Western Ct.
35)	8 Misty View Walk	8 Misty View Walk
36)	138 Jackson Street	138 Jacksen Street
37)	Becke Ave. West	Beck Ave. West
38)	2-13 Montgomery Avenue	2-12 Montgomery Avenue
39)	Blanchard Court	Blanchard Court
40)	48960 Cypruss Place	48960 Cypress Place
41)	Bar Harbour, Maine	Bar Harbor, Maine
42)	Twin Lakes North	Twin Lakes South
43)	562 Fleet Dr.	562 Fleet Dr.
44)	7477 Green Street	7477 Greene Street
45)	347-69 Cathy Lane	347-69 Cathy Lane
46)	696 Center Street	696 Centre Street
47)	27 Mockingbird Lane	27 Mockinbird Lane
48)	Jewel Road East	Jewel Road East
49)	55 President Ave.	55 President Ave.
50)	Baton Rouge, La. 70808	Baton Rogue, La. 78008
51)	83695 Brown Avenue	83695 Browne Avenue
52)	45618 Arlington Road	45618 Arlington Road
53)	3 West 23 Street	3 West 23 St.
54)	Whitman Square N. E.	Whitmann Square N. E.
55)	7 University Plaza	7 University Pl.
56)	Brooklyn, N.Y. 11208	Brooklyn, N.Y. 11208
57)	146 Potter Avenue	146 Porter Avenue
58)	2200 South Central Ln.	2200 So. Central Ln.
59)	19 Emerson Lakes	19 Emersen Lakes
60)	1552 Pennsylvannia Avenue	1525 Pennsylvania Ave.
61)	287 Elmira Loop	287 Elmira Loop
62)	790 McDonald Street	790 MacDonald Street
63)	Tyler, Texas 75702	Tyler, Tx. 75702
64)	Hollywood & Vine	Hollywood & Vyne
65)	4 Grace Alley	4 Grace Ally
66)	37 Hamilton Walk West	73 Hamilton Walk West
67)	Hardwick Manor East	Hardwick Manor East
68)	64306 Cranford Terrace	64036 Cranford Terrace
69)	Concord, Massachusetts	Concord, Massachusetts
70)	57 Maple Ave.	47 Maple Avenue
71)	823 Summit Place	832 Summit Place
72)	1234 DeKalbe Road	1234 DeKalb Road
73)	Piccadilly Square	Picadilly Square
74)	98345 Fennimore Street	98345 Fenimore Street
75)	Ocean Parkway	Ocean Parkway
76)	Lakeville, Conn. 06579	Lakeville, Conn. 06759
77)	2 Empire Blvd.	2 Empire Blvd.
78)	40 Rochester Drive	40 Rochester Drive
79)	1092 Saint Frances St.	1092 Saint Francis St.
80)	Boise, Idaho 83705	Biose, Idaho 83075

END OF SAMPLE TEST 1, SECTION (I) CLERK-CARRIER TEST

— —

ADDRESS CHECKING

— — — — — — — — — — — —

ANSWERS TO SAMPLE TEST 1, SECTION (I) CLERK-CARRIER TEST

ADDRESS CHECKING

1)	S		41)	D
2)	D		42)	D
3)	S		43)	S
4)	D		44)	D
5)	D		45)	S
6)	S		46)	D
7)	S		47)	D
8)	S		48)	S
9)	S		49)	S
10)	D		50)	D
11)	D		51)	D
12)	S		52)	S
13)	D		53)	D
14)	D		54)	D
15)	S		55)	D
16)	S		56)	S
17)	D		57)	D
18)	S		58)	D
19)	S		59)	D
20)	D		60)	D
21)	S		61)	S
22)	D		62)	D
23)	D		63)	D
24)	S		64)	D
25)	S		65)	D
26)	D		66)	D
27)	D		67)	S
28)	S		68)	D
29)	D		69)	S
30)	D		70)	D
31)	D		71)	D
32)	D		72)	D
33)	S		73)	D
34)	D		74)	D
35)	S		75)	S
36)	D		76)	D
37)	D		77)	S
38)	D		78)	S
39)	S		79)	D
40)	D		80)	D

SAMPLE QUESTIONS

The following sample questions show the types of questions found in the written test you will take. They show also how your answers to the questions are to be recorded. Read these directions carefully, then look at the sample questions and try to answer them.

Each question has several suggested answers lettered A, B, C, D and E. Decide which one is the best answer to the question. Then, in the Sample Answer Sheet box on each page, find the answer space that is numbered the same as the number of the question, and darken completely the oval that is lettered the same as the letter of your answer. When you are finished, compare your answers with the Correct Answers to Sample Questions.

Sample Questions 1 through 5—
Verbal Ability

Choose the one of the five suggested answers that means most nearly the same as the word in CAPITAL letters.

1. EMOLUMENT means most nearly
   A) benefit
   B) obligation
   C) option
   D) bribe
   E) memorial

2. SURVEILLANCE means most nearly
   A) confinement
   B) parole
   C) protection
   D) suspicion
   E) watch

3. SAPIENT means most nearly
   A) dependent
   B) flattering
   C) wise
   D) conceited
   E) interested

4. REMUNERATIVE means most nearly
   A) abusive
   B) mandatory
   C) adventitious
   D) profitable
   E) estimable

5. ACUMEN means most nearly
   A) experience
   B) confidence
   C) efficiency
   D) discernment
   E) toleration

Memory and Observation

Study carefully for about 5 minutes the photograph on page 6. After you have answered the next set of questions, you will be asked to recall what you saw in the photograph and answer some questions concerning it. While you are looking at the photograph, assume that you are in a position to see the scene just as it appears to you in the photograph.

Now answer Sample Questions 6 through 10.

Sample Questions 6 through 10—
Arithmetic Reasoning

Solve each problem and see which of the suggested answers A, B, C, or D is correct. If your answer does not exactly agree with any of the first four suggested answers, darken space E.

6. How much less is the postage on 1,000 circulars, weighing 2 ounces each, if mailed at the bulk rate of 19 cents a pound (with a minimum charge of 2¾ cents a piece) instead of the regular rate of 4 cents for each circular?
   A) $12.50   D) $22.00
   B) $15.00   E) none of these
   C) $17.00

Sample Answer Sheet

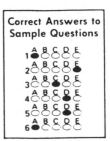

Correct Answers to Sample Questions

7. If X can check 80 records in 8 hours and Y can check 80 records in ¾ that time, how many hours will it take them working together to check the 80 records?
   A) 3½ hours
   B) 3³/₇ hours
   C) 4⁴/₇ hours
   D) 5 hours
   E) none of these

8. A clerk files papers at an average rate of 25 papers per minute. If an extra clerk, who can file at the same rate, is also assigned to the work, how many minutes will be required for the two clerks, working together, to file 5,400 papers?
   A) 80
   B) 108
   C) 216
   D) 434
   E) none of these

9. Mr. Wise, Mr. Vail, and Mr. Todd invested $7,000, $3,000, and $2,000 respectively in a partnership. If the annual profit of $6,000 is divided among them in proportion to their original investments, Mr. Wise will receive
   A) $ 500
   B) $2,000
   C) $2,500
   D) $3,500
   E) none of these

10. The safety rules of Factory X require that the operator of a certain machine take a rest period of 15 minutes after working 2 consecutive hours. If the workday consists of 3¾ hours in the morning, 30 minutes for lunch, and 4¼ hours in the afternoon, a job that requires 29 machine hours to complete will take the operator of this machine
   A) less than 3 days
   B) between 3 and 3½ days
   C) 3½ days
   D) between 3½ and 4 days
   E) none of these

Sample Questions 11 through 15—
Memory and Observation

Sample Questions 11 through 15 are based on the Sample Photograph that you have studied. Do not look at the photograph again.

11. Which one of the following appears in the Sample Photograph?
    A) an inkblotter
    B) a lamp
    C) a cup
    D) a telephone
    E) a typewriter

12. Which one of the following statements about the Sample Photograph is correct?
    A) There is a picture on the wall.
    B) There is a clock on the desk.
    C) Both men are writing.
    D) One man is writing.
    E) There is a pen stand on the desk.

13. The man with glasses appears to be
    A) reading a book
    B) talking on the phone
    C) reading a magazine
    D) writing a note
    E) reading a chart

14. What can be seen behind the woman and man on the left?
    A) a row of notebooks
    B) a telephone
    C) a chart
    D) a typewriter
    E) an adding machine

15. Which one of the following statements about the Sample Photograph is NOT true?
    A) There is a pencilholder on the table.
    B) The blinds are open.
    C) There is the number, 13, on a notebook.
    D) There is a metal incoming box.
    E) The cardboard box is in a box similar to the incoming box.

Sample Answer Sheet	Correct Answers to Sample Questions
7. A B C D E	7. A ● C D E
8. A B C D E	8. ● B C D E
9. A B C D E	9. A B C D ●
10. A B C D E	10. A B C ● E
11. A B C D E	11. A B ● D E
12. A B C D E	12. A B C D ●
13. A B C D E	13. A B C D ●
14. A B C D E	14. ● B C D E
15. A B C D E	15. A ● C D E

Sample Questions 16 through 20—Problems in Investigation

Sample Questions 16 through 20 are based on the following paragraph and statements. Read the paragraph and statements carefully and then answer Sample Questions 16 through 20.

On October 30, the Belton First National Bank discovered that the $3,000 it had received that morning from the Greenville First National Bank was in counterfeit 10-, 20-, and 50-dollar bills. The genuine $3,000 had been counted by Greenville First National Bank clerk, Iris Stewart, the preceding afternoon. They were packed in eight black leather satchels and stored in the bank vault overnight. Greenville First National clerk, Brian Caruthers, accompanied armor carriers James Clark and Howard O'Keefe to Belton in an armored truck. Belton First National clerk, Cynthia Randall, discovered the counterfeit bills when she examined the serial numbers of the bills.

During the course of the investigation, the following statements were made.

(1) Gerald Hathaway, clerk, of the Greenville bank told investigators that he had found the bank office open when he arrived to work on the morning of October 30. The only articles which appeared to be missing were eight black leather satchels of the type used to transport large sums of money.

(2) Jon Perkins, head teller, told investigators that he did not check the contents of the black leather satchels after locking them in the vault around 4:30 p.m., on October 29.

(3) Henry Green, janitor, said that he noticed Jon Perkins leaving the bank office around 5:30 p.m., one-half hour after the bank closed on October 29. He said that Perkins locked the door.

(4) A scrap of cloth, identical to the material of the armor carriers' uniforms, was found caught in the seal of one of the black leather satchels delivered to Belton.

(5) Brian Caruthers, clerk, said he saw James Clark and Howard O'Keefe talking in a secretive manner in the armored truck.

(6) Thomas Stillman, bank executive, identified the eight black leather satchels containing the counterfeit money which arrived at the Belton First National Bank, as the eight satchels which had disappeared from the bank office. He had noticed a slight difference in the linings of the satchels.

(7) Neil Nelson, bank accountant, noticed two 10-dollar bills with the same serial numbers as the lost bills in a bank deposit from Ferdinand's Restaurant of Greenville.

(8) Vincent Johnson, manager of Ferdinand's Restaurant, told police that Iris Stewart frequently dined there with her boyfriend.

16. Which one of the following statements best indicates that satchels containing the counterfeit bills were substituted for satchels containing genuine bills while they were being transported from Greenville to Belton?

    A) Statement (1)
    B) Statement (3)
    C) Statement (4)
    D) Statement (5)
    E) Statement (7)

17. Which one of the following statements best links the information given in statement (1) with the substitution of the counterfeit bills?

    A) Statement (2)
    B) Statement (3)
    C) Statement (4)
    D) Statement (5)
    E) Statement (6)

18. Which of the following statements along with statement (7) best indicates that the substitution of the counterfeit bills casts suspicion on at least one employee of the Greenville bank?

    A) Statement (1)
    B) Statement (2)
    C) Statement (3)
    D) Statement (5)
    E) Statement (8)

19. Which of the following statements would least likely be used in proving a case?

    A) Statement (1)
    B) Statement (3)
    C) Statement (4)
    D) Statement (5)
    E) Statement (7)

20. Which of the following statements best indicates that the substitution of the counterfeit bills could have taken place before the satchels left the Greenville bank?

    A) Statement (1)
    B) Statement (2)
    C) Statement (3)
    D) Statement (4)
    E) Statement (7)

Sample Answer Sheet	Correct Answers to Sample Questions
16 A B C D E	16 A B **C** D E
17 A B C D E	17 A B C D **E**
18 A B C D E	18 A B C D **E**
19 A B C D E	19 A B C **D** E
20 A B C D E	20 A **B** C D E

Sample Questions 21 through 25—
Spatial Perception

Sample Questions 21 through 25 are based on the four solid patterns below, lettered A, B, C, and D.

Each of the questions shows one of these four patterns cut into pieces. For each question, decide which one of the four patterns could be made by fitting all of the pieces together without having any edges overlap and without any spaces between pieces. Mark the letter of that pattern on the Sample Answer Sheet.

Some of the pieces may need to be *turned around* or *turned over* to make them fit.

A   B   C   D

21.

22.

23.

24.

25.

Sample Answer Sheet
21 A B C D E
22 A B C D E
23 A B C D E
24 A B C D E
25 A B C D E

Correct Answers to Sample Questions
21 A B C **D** E
22 A **B** C D E
23 A B **C** D E
24 **A** B C D E
25 A B **C** D E

Appendix F: Federal Salary Rates

For a discussion of these **pay schedules,** and of how **salary rates** are determined, see Step 1 (p. 16).

The following pay schedules show Federal salary rates for various types of positions. Salaries are constantly being upgraded. To obtain the latest, most accurate listings, contact your local OPM or VA office.

Beginning rates may vary according to job locations and candidate employment history. Some salaries are determined for the specific job at the time of hiring.

SELECTED FEDERAL WHITE COLLAR PAY SCHEDULE
GENERAL SCHEDULE BASE PAY
General Schedule salaries for those not covered by locaility pay. Effective for fiscal year 1998.

Step	1	2	3	4	5	6	7	8	9	10
GS-1	$12,960	$13,392	$13,823	$14,252	$14,685	$14,938	$15,362	$15,791	$15,809	$16,214
2	14,571	14,918	15,401	15,809	15,985	16,455	16,925	17,395	17,865	18,335
3	15,899	16,429	16,959	17,489	18,019	18,549	19,079	19,609	20,139	20,669
4	17,848	18,443	19,038	19,633	20,228	20,823	21,418	22,013	22,608	23,203
5	19,969	20,635	21,301	21,967	22,633	23,299	23,965	24,631	25,297	25,963
6	22,258	23,000	23,742	24,484	25,226	25,968	26,710	27,452	28,194	28,936
7	24,734	25,558	26,382	27,206	28,030	28,854	29,678	30,502	31,326	32,150
8	27,393	28,306	29,219	30,132	31,045	31,958	32,871	33,784	34,697	35,610
9	30,257	31,266	32,275	33,284	34,293	35,302	36,311	37,320	38,329	39,338
10	33,320	34,431	35,542	36,653	37,764	38,875	39,986	41,097	42,208	43,319
11	36,609	37,829	39,049	40,269	41,489	42,709	43,929	45,149	46,369	47,589
12	43,876	45,339	46,802	48,265	49,728	51,191	52,654	54,117	55,580	57,043
13	52,176	53,915	55,654	57,393	59,132	60,871	62,610	64,349	66,088	67,827
14	61,656	63,711	65,766	67,821	69,876	71,931	73,986	76,041	78,096	80,151
15	72,525	74,943	77,361	79,779	82,197	84,615	87,033	89,451	91,869	94,287

The bulk of Federal employees are paid as General Schedule (GS) employees. Upon appointment, the new federal employee is paid at Step 1 of the GS grade level at which he or she was hired: For example, an employee hired to fill a GS-5-level job would start with a salary of $18,340. After a specified waiting period, the employee is promoted to the next step within that grade, provided he or she has shown an acceptable level of confidence. The waiting period for promotion from each of the first three steps is 52 weeks; at the next three steps, it is 104 weeks; and at step 7 or higher 156 weeks.

SELECTED FEDERAL WHITE COLLAR PAY SCHEDULE
GENERAL SCHEDULE — WASHINGTON, DC. METRO AREA
Effective for fiscal year 1998.

Step	1	2	3	4	5	6	7	8	9	10
GS-1	$13,902	$14,366	$14,828	$15,288	$15,753	$16,024	$16,479	$16,939	$16,958	$17,393
2	15,630	16,003	16,521	16,958	17,147	17,651	18,155	18,660	19,164	19,668
3	17,055	17,623	18,192	18,760	19,329	19,898	20,466	21,035	21,603	22,172
4	19,146	19,784	20,422	21,060	21,699	22,337	22,975	23,613	24,252	24,890
5	21,421	22,135	22,850	23,564	24,278	24,993	25,707	26,422	27,136	27,851
6	23,876	24,672	25,468	26,264	27,060	27,856	28,652	29,448	30,244	31,040
7	26,532	27,416	28,300	29,184	30,068	30,952	31,836	32,719	33,603	34,487
8	29,384	30,364	31,343	32,323	33,302	34,281	35,261	36,240	37,219	38,199
9	32,457	33,539	34,621	35,704	36,786	37,868	38,951	40,033	41,116	42,198
10	35,742	36,934	38,26	39,318	40,509	41,701	42,893	44,085	45,277	46,468
11	39,270	40,579	41,888	43,197	44,505	45,814	47,123	48,431	49,740	51,049
12	47,066	48,635	50,205	51,774	53,343	54,913	56,482	58,051	59,621	61,190
13	55,969	57,835	59,700	61,565	63,431	65,296	67,162	69,027	70,893	72,758
14	66,138	68,343	70,547	72,752	74,956	77,160	79,365	81,569	83,774	85,978
15	77,798	80,391	82,985	85,579	88,173	90,767	93,360	95,954	98,548	101,142

SENIOR LEVEL (ST & SL)

Minimum $86,160
Maximum   115,700

The Senior Level is a sliding salary scale that replaces the old GS-16–18 levels which are now defunct. The two types of personnel covered are scientific and technical (ST) and managerial and advisory (SL). Agency heads determine salaries within the given minimum and maximum. As with the SES, there are no steps and the pay level is personal, not job-dependent. No more than one increase may be granted annually. Many employees who are paid at the Senior Level are special assistants and advisors to agency heads. In the case of scientific and technical employees whose skills are in high demand in the private sector, the ST scale is used to keep them working for the Federal government.

SENIOR EXECUTIVE SERVICE (SES)

ES-1	$101,667
ES-2	106,488
ES-3	111,310
ES-4	117,284
ES-5	121,267
ES-6	121,267

The Senior Executive Service is a gradeless system. Pay level is not job-dependent but set by the agency head based on an employee's experience and ability when the job offer is made—not unlike job offers in the private sector. No more than one increase a year may be granted. In addition to basic pay, Senior Executives also receive recruitment and relocation bonuses and retention allowances of up to 25% base pay if needed.

EXECUTIVE SCHEDULE

Level	Salary	Sample Job Title
EX-I	$148,400	Cabinet Secretary
EX-II	133,600	Department/agency head
EX-III	123,100	Chairman, Under Secretary (at indep. agencies, e.g., FTC, SEC, ICC)
EX-IV	115,700	Assistant Secretary of Department, Inspector General
EX-V	108,200	Top agency positions

The executive schedule pay system is for the top political appointee positions within the executive branch. Pay level is determined upon appointment. Appointments are made by the President and Congressional confirmation is required.

SALARY TABLE NO. 97-GS

1997 GENERAL SCHEDULE
INCORPORATING A 2.30% GENERAL INCREASE
Effective January 1997

ANNUAL Rates by Grade and Step

	1	2	3	4	5	6	7	8	9	10	Within-Grade Increase Amounts
GS-1	$12,669	$13,091	$13,512	$13,932	$14,355	$14,602	$15,017	$15,436	$15,454	$15,844	VARIES
2	14,243	14,583	15,055	15,454	15,628	16,088	16,548	17,008	17,468	17,928	VARIES
3	15,542	16,060	16,578	17,096	17,614	18,132	18,650	19,168	19,686	20,204	$518
4	17,447	18,029	18,611	19,193	19,775	20,357	20,939	21,521	22,103	22,685	$582
5	19,520	20,171	20,822	21,473	22,124	22,775	23,426	24,077	24,728	25,379	$651
6	21,758	22,483	23,208	23,933	24,658	25,383	26,108	26,833	27,558	28,283	$725
7	24,178	24,984	25,790	26,596	27,402	28,208	29,014	29,820	30,626	31,432	$806
8	26,777	27,670	28,563	29,456	30,349	31,242	32,135	33,028	33,921	34,814	$893
9	29,577	30,563	31,549	32,535	33,521	34,507	35,493	36,479	37,465	38,451	$986
10	32,571	33,657	34,743	35,829	36,915	38,001	39,087	40,173	41,259	42,345	$1,086
11	35,786	36,979	38,172	39,365	40,558	41,751	42,944	44,137	45,330	46,523	$1,193
12	42,890	44,320	45,750	47,180	48,610	50,040	51,470	52,900	54,330	55,760	$1,430
13	51,003	52,703	54,403	56,103	57,803	59,503	61,203	62,903	64,603	66,303	$1,700
14	60,270	62,279	64,288	66,297	68,306	70,315	72,324	74,333	76,342	78,351	$2,009
15	70,894	73,257	75,620	77,983	80,346	82,709	85,072	87,435	89,798	92,161	$2,363

SALARY TABLE NO. 97-ATL

INCORPORATING THE 2.30% GENERAL SCHEDULE INCREASE AND A LOCALITY PAYMENT OF 5.65% FOR THE LOCALITY PAY AREA OF ATLANTA, GA
(Net Increase: 2.80%)

Effective January 1997

	1	2	3	4	5	6	7	8	9	10
GS-1	$13,385	$13,831	$14,275	$14,719	$15,166	$15,427	$15,865	$16,308	$16,327	$16,739
2	15,048	15,407	15,906	16,327	16,511	16,997	17,483	17,969	18,455	18,941
3	16,420	16,967	17,515	18,062	18,609	19,156	19,704	20,251	20,798	21,346
4	18,433	19,048	19,663	20,277	20,892	21,507	22,122	22,737	23,352	23,967
5	20,623	21,311	21,998	22,686	23,374	24,062	24,750	25,437	26,125	26,813
6	22,987	23,753	24,519	25,285	26,051	26,817	27,583	28,349	29,115	29,881
7	25,544	26,396	27,247	28,099	28,950	29,802	30,653	31,505	32,356	33,208
8	28,290	29,233	30,177	31,120	32,064	33,007	33,951	34,894	35,838	36,781
9	31,248	32,290	33,332	34,373	35,415	36,457	37,498	38,540	39,582	40,623
10	34,411	35,559	36,706	37,853	39,001	40,148	41,295	42,443	43,590	44,737
11	37,808	39,068	40,329	41,589	42,850	44,110	45,370	46,631	47,891	49,152
12	45,313	46,824	48,335	49,846	51,356	52,867	54,378	55,889	57,400	58,910
13	53,885	55,681	57,477	59,273	61,069	62,865	64,661	66,457	68,253	70,049
14	63,675	65,798	67,920	70,043	72,165	74,288	76,410	78,533	80,655	82,778
15	74,900	77,396	79,893	82,389	84,886	87,382	89,879	92,375	94,872	97,368

NOTE: Locality rates of pay are considered basic pay only for certain purposes--see "1997 Salary Tables" cover sheet.

SALARY TABLE NO. 97-BOS

INCORPORATING THE 2.30% GENERAL SCHEDULE INCREASE AND A LOCALITY PAYMENT OF 7.97% FOR THE LOCALITY PAY AREA OF BOSTON-WORCESTER-LAWRENCE, MA-NH-ME-CT
(Net Increase: 2.58%)

Effective January 1997

ANNUAL Rates by Grade and Step

	1	2	3	4	5	6	7	8	9	10
GS-1	$13,679	$14,134	$14,589	$15,042	$15,499	$15,766	$16,214	$16,666	$16,686	$17,107
2	15,378	15,745	16,255	16,686	16,874	17,370	17,867	18,364	18,860	19,357
3	16,781	17,340	17,899	18,459	19,018	19,577	20,136	20,696	21,255	21,814
4	18,838	19,466	20,094	20,723	21,351	21,979	22,608	23,236	23,865	24,493
5	21,076	21,779	22,482	23,184	23,887	24,590	25,293	25,996	26,699	27,402
6	23,492	24,275	25,058	25,840	26,623	27,406	28,189	28,972	29,754	30,537
7	26,105	26,975	27,845	28,716	29,586	30,456	31,326	32,197	33,067	33,937
8	28,911	29,875	30,839	31,804	32,768	33,732	34,696	35,660	36,625	37,589
9	31,934	32,999	34,063	35,128	36,193	37,257	38,322	39,386	40,451	41,516
10	35,167	36,339	37,512	38,685	39,857	41,030	42,202	43,375	44,547	45,720
11	38,638	39,926	41,214	42,502	43,790	45,079	46,367	47,655	48,943	50,231
12	46,308	47,852	49,396	50,940	52,484	54,028	55,572	57,116	58,660	60,204
13	55,068	56,903	58,739	60,574	62,410	64,245	66,081	67,916	69,752	71,587
14	65,074	67,243	69,412	71,581	73,750	75,919	78,088	80,257	82,426	84,596
15	76,544	79,096	81,647	84,198	86,750	89,301	91,852	94,404	96,955	99,506

NOTE: Locality rates of pay are considered basic pay only for certain purposes-see "1997 Salary Tables" cover sheet.

SALARY TABLE NO. 97-CHI

INCORPORATING THE 2.30% GENERAL SCHEDULE INCREASE AND A LOCALITY PAYMENT OF 8.13% FOR THE LOCALITY PAY AREA OF CHICAGO-GARY-KENOSHA, IL-IN-WI
(NET INCREASE: 2.78%)

Effective January 1997

ANNUAL Rates by Grade and Step

	1	2	3	4	5	6	7	8	9	10
GS-1	$13,699	$14,155	$14,611	$15,065	$15,522	$15,789	$16,238	$16,691	$16,710	$17,132
2	15,401	15,769	16,279	16,710	16,899	17,396	17,893	18,391	18,888	19,386
3	16,806	17,366	17,926	18,486	19,046	19,606	20,166	20,726	21,286	21,847
4	18,865	19,495	20,124	20,753	21,383	22,012	22,641	23,271	23,900	24,529
5	21,107	21,811	22,515	23,219	23,923	24,627	25,331	26,034	26,738	27,442
6	23,527	24,311	25,095	25,879	26,663	27,447	28,231	29,015	29,798	30,582
7	26,144	27,015	27,887	28,758	29,630	30,501	31,373	32,244	33,116	33,987
8	28,954	29,920	30,885	31,851	32,816	33,782	34,748	35,713	36,679	37,644
9	31,982	33,048	34,114	35,180	36,246	37,312	38,379	39,445	40,511	41,577
10	35,219	36,393	37,568	38,742	39,916	41,090	42,265	43,439	44,613	45,788
11	38,695	39,985	41,275	42,565	43,855	45,145	46,435	47,725	49,015	50,305
12	46,377	47,923	49,469	51,016	52,562	54,108	55,655	57,201	58,747	60,293
13	55,150	56,988	58,826	60,664	62,502	64,341	66,179	68,017	69,855	71,693
14	65,170	67,342	69,515	71,687	73,859	76,032	78,204	80,376	82,549	84,721
15	76,658	79,213	81,768	84,323	86,878	89,433	91,988	94,543	97,099	99,654

NOTE: Locality rates of pay are considered basic pay only for certain purposes--see "1997 Salary Tables" cover sheet.

SALARY TABLE NO. 97-CIN

INCORPORATING THE 2.30% GENERAL SCHEDULE INCREASE AND A LOCALITY PAYMENT OF 6.75% FOR THE LOCALITY PAY AREA OF CINCINNATI-HAMILTON, OH-KY-IN
(Net Increase: 3.15%)

Effective January 1997

ANNUAL Rates by Grade and Step

	1	2	3	4	5	6	7	8	9	10
GS-1	$13,524	$13,975	$14,424	$14,872	$15,324	$15,588	$16,031	$16,478	$16,497	$16,913
2	15,204	15,567	16,071	16,497	16,683	17,174	17,665	18,156	18,647	19,138
3	16,591	17,144	17,697	18,250	18,803	19,356	19,909	20,462	21,015	21,568
4	18,625	19,246	19,867	20,489	21,110	21,731	22,352	22,974	23,595	24,216
5	20,838	21,533	22,227	22,922	23,617	24,312	25,007	25,702	26,397	27,092
6	23,227	24,001	24,775	25,548	26,322	27,096	27,870	28,644	29,418	30,192
7	25,810	26,670	27,531	28,391	29,252	30,112	30,972	31,833	32,693	33,554
8	28,584	29,538	30,491	31,444	32,398	33,351	34,304	35,257	36,211	37,164
9	31,573	32,626	33,679	34,731	35,784	36,836	37,889	38,941	39,994	41,046
10	34,770	35,929	37,088	38,247	39,407	40,566	41,725	42,885	44,044	45,203
11	38,202	39,475	40,749	42,022	43,296	44,569	45,843	47,116	48,390	49,663
12	45,785	47,312	48,838	50,365	51,891	53,418	54,944	56,471	57,997	59,524
13	54,446	56,260	58,075	59,890	61,705	63,519	65,334	67,149	68,964	70,778
14	64,338	66,483	68,627	70,772	72,917	75,061	77,206	79,350	81,495	83,640
15	75,679	78,202	80,724	83,247	85,769	88,292	90,814	93,337	95,859	98,382

NOTE: Locality rates of pay are considered basic pay only for certain purposes--see "1997 Salary Tables" cover sheet.

SALARY TABLE NOS. 97-CLE

INCORPORATING THE 2.30% GENERAL SCHEDULE INCREASE AND A LOCALITY PAYMENT OF 5.51% FOR THE LOCALITY PAY AREA OF CLEVELAND-AKRON, OH
(Net Increase: 3.12%)

Effective January 1997

ANNUAL Rates by Grade and Step

	1	2	3	4	5	6	7	8	9	10
GS-1	$13,367	$13,812	$14,257	$14,700	$15,146	$15,407	$15,844	$16,287	$16,306	$16,717
2	15,028	15,387	15,885	16,306	16,489	16,974	17,460	17,945	18,430	18,916
3	16,398	16,945	17,491	18,038	18,585	19,131	19,678	20,224	20,771	21,317
4	18,408	19,022	19,636	20,251	20,865	21,479	22,093	22,707	23,321	23,935
5	20,596	21,282	21,969	22,656	23,343	24,030	24,717	25,404	26,091	26,777
6	22,957	23,722	24,487	25,252	26,017	26,782	27,547	28,311	29,076	29,841
7	25,510	26,361	27,211	28,061	28,912	29,762	30,613	31,463	32,313	33,164
8	28,252	29,195	30,137	31,079	32,021	32,963	33,906	34,848	35,790	36,732
9	31,207	32,247	33,287	34,328	35,368	36,408	37,449	38,489	39,529	40,570
10	34,366	35,512	36,657	37,803	38,949	40,095	41,241	42,387	43,532	44,678
11	37,758	39,017	40,275	41,534	42,793	44,051	45,310	46,569	47,828	49,086
12	45,253	46,762	48,271	49,780	51,288	52,797	54,306	55,815	57,324	58,832
13	53,813	55,607	57,401	59,194	60,988	62,782	64,575	66,369	68,163	69,956
14	63,591	65,711	67,830	69,950	72,070	74,189	76,309	78,429	80,548	82,668
15	74,800	77,293	79,787	82,280	84,773	87,266	89,759	92,253	94,746	97,239

SALARY TABLE NO. 97-COL

INCORPORATING THE 2.30% GENERAL SCHEDULE INCREASE AND A LOCALITY PAYMENT OF 6.62% FOR THE LOCALITY PAY AREA OF COLUMBUS, OH
(Net Increase: 3.05%)

Effective January 1997

ANNUAL Rates by Grade and Step

	1	2	3	4	5	6	7	8	9	10
GS-1	$13,508	$13,958	$14,406	$14,854	$15,305	$15,569	$16,011	$16,458	$16,477	$16,893
2	15,186	15,548	16,052	16,477	16,663	17,153	17,643	18,134	18,624	19,115
3	16,571	17,123	17,675	18,228	18,780	19,332	19,885	20,437	20,989	21,542
4	18,602	19,223	19,843	20,464	21,084	21,705	22,325	22,946	23,566	24,187
5	20,812	21,506	22,200	22,895	23,589	24,283	24,977	25,671	26,365	27,059
6	23,198	23,971	24,744	25,517	26,290	27,063	27,836	28,609	29,382	30,155
7	25,779	26,638	27,497	28,357	29,216	30,075	30,935	31,794	32,653	33,513
8	28,550	29,502	30,454	31,406	32,358	33,310	34,262	35,214	36,167	37,119
9	31,535	32,586	33,638	34,689	35,740	36,791	37,843	38,894	39,945	40,996
10	34,727	35,885	37,043	38,201	39,359	40,517	41,675	42,832	43,990	45,148
11	38,155	39,427	40,699	41,971	43,243	44,515	45,787	47,059	48,331	49,603
12	45,729	47,254	48,779	50,303	51,828	53,353	54,877	56,402	57,927	59,451
13	54,379	56,192	58,004	59,817	61,630	63,442	65,255	67,067	68,880	70,692
14	64,260	66,402	68,544	70,686	72,828	74,970	77,112	79,254	81,396	83,538
15	75,587	78,107	80,626	83,145	85,665	88,184	90,704	93,223	95,743	98,262

NOTE: Locality rates of pay are considered basic pay only for certain purposes--see "1997 Salary Tables" cover sheet.

SALARY TABLE NO. 97-DFW

INCORPORATING THE 2.30% GENERAL SCHEDULE INCREASE AND A LOCALITY PAYMENT OF 6.40% FOR THE LOCALITY PAY AREA OF DALLAS-FORT WORTH, TX
(Net Increase: 2.46%)

Effective January 1997

ANNUAL Rates by Grade and Step

	1	2	3	4	5	6	7	8	9	10
GS-1	$13,480	$13,929	$14,377	$14,824	$15,274	$15,537	$15,978	$16,424	$16,443	$16,858
2	15,155	15,516	16,019	16,443	16,628	17,118	17,607	18,097	18,586	19,075
3	16,537	17,088	17,639	18,190	18,741	19,292	19,844	20,395	20,946	21,497
4	18,564	19,183	19,802	20,421	21,041	21,660	22,279	22,898	23,518	24,137
5	20,769	21,462	22,155	22,847	23,540	24,233	24,925	25,618	26,311	27,003
6	23,151	23,922	24,693	25,465	26,236	27,008	27,779	28,550	29,322	30,093
7	25,725	26,583	27,441	28,298	29,156	30,013	30,871	31,728	32,586	33,444
8	28,491	29,441	30,391	31,341	32,291	33,241	34,192	35,142	36,092	37,042
9	31,470	32,519	33,568	34,617	35,666	36,715	37,765	38,814	39,863	40,912
10	34,656	35,811	36,967	38,122	39,278	40,433	41,589	42,744	43,900	45,055
11	38,076	39,346	40,615	41,884	43,154	44,423	45,692	46,962	48,231	49,500
12	45,635	47,156	48,678	50,200	51,721	53,243	54,764	56,286	57,807	59,329
13	54,267	56,076	57,885	59,694	61,502	63,311	65,120	66,929	68,738	70,546
14	64,127	66,265	68,402	70,540	72,678	74,815	76,953	79,090	81,228	83,365
15	75,431	77,945	80,460	82,974	85,488	88,002	90,517	93,031	95,545	98,059

NOTE: Locality rates of pay are considered basic pay only for certain purposes--see "1997 Salary Tables" cover sheet.

SALARY TABLE NO. 97-DAY

INCORPORATING THE 2.30% GENERAL SCHEDULE INCREASE AND A LOCALITY PAYMENT OF 5.66% FOR THE LOCALITY PAY AREA OF DAYTON-SPRINGFIELD, OH
(NET INCREASE: 2.24%)

Effective January 1997

ANNUAL Rates by Grade and Step

	1	2	3	4	5	6	7	8	9	10
GS-1	$13,386	$13,832	$14,277	$14,721	$15,167	$15,428	$15,867	$16,310	$16,329	$16,741
2	15,049	15,408	15,907	16,329	16,513	16,999	17,485	17,971	18,457	18,943
3	16,422	16,969	17,516	18,064	18,611	19,158	19,706	20,253	20,800	21,348
4	18,435	19,049	19,664	20,279	20,894	21,509	22,124	22,739	23,354	23,969
5	20,625	21,313	22,001	22,688	23,376	24,064	24,752	25,440	26,128	26,815
6	22,990	23,756	24,522	25,288	26,054	26,820	27,586	28,352	29,118	29,884
7	25,546	26,398	27,250	28,101	28,953	29,805	30,656	31,508	32,359	33,211
8	28,293	29,236	30,180	31,123	32,067	33,010	33,954	34,897	35,841	36,784
9	31,251	32,293	33,335	34,376	35,418	36,460	37,502	38,544	39,586	40,627
10	34,415	35,562	36,709	37,857	39,004	40,152	41,299	42,447	43,594	44,742
11	37,811	39,072	40,333	41,593	42,854	44,114	45,375	46,635	47,896	49,156
12	45,318	46,829	48,339	49,850	51,361	52,872	54,383	55,894	57,405	58,916
13	53,890	55,686	57,482	59,278	61,075	62,871	64,667	66,463	68,260	70,056
14	63,681	65,804	67,927	70,049	72,172	74,295	76,418	78,540	80,663	82,786
15	74,907	77,403	79,900	82,397	84,894	87,390	89,887	92,384	94,881	97,377

NOTE: Locality rates of pay are considered basic pay only for certain purposes--see "1997 Salary Tables" cover sheet.

SALARY TABLE NO. 97-DEN

INCORPORATING THE 2.30% GENERAL SCHEDULE INCREASE AND A LOCALITY PAYMENT OF 7.06% FOR THE LOCALITY PAY AREA OF DENVER-BOULDER-GREELEY, CO
(NET INCREASE: 2.99%)

Effective January 1997

ANNUAL Rates by Grade and Step

	1	2	3	4	5	6	7	8	9	10
GS-1	$13,563	$14,015	$14,466	$14,916	$15,368	$15,633	$16,077	$16,526	$16,545	$16,963
2	15,249	15,613	16,118	16,545	16,731	17,224	17,716	18,209	18,701	19,194
3	16,639	17,194	17,748	18,303	18,858	19,412	19,967	20,521	21,076	21,630
4	18,679	19,302	19,925	20,548	21,171	21,794	22,417	23,040	23,663	24,287
5	20,898	21,595	22,292	22,989	23,686	24,383	25,080	25,777	26,474	27,171
6	23,294	24,070	24,846	25,623	26,399	27,175	27,951	28,727	29,504	30,280
7	25,885	26,748	27,611	28,474	29,337	30,199	31,062	31,925	32,788	33,651
8	28,667	29,624	30,580	31,536	32,492	33,448	34,404	35,360	36,316	37,272
9	31,665	32,721	33,776	34,832	35,888	36,943	37,999	39,054	40,110	41,166
10	34,871	36,033	37,196	38,359	39,521	40,684	41,847	43,009	44,172	45,335
11	38,312	39,590	40,867	42,144	43,421	44,699	45,976	47,253	48,530	49,808
12	45,918	47,449	48,980	50,511	52,042	53,573	55,104	56,635	58,166	59,697
13	54,604	56,424	58,244	60,064	61,884	63,704	65,524	67,344	69,164	70,984
14	64,525	66,676	68,827	70,978	73,128	75,279	77,430	79,581	81,732	83,883
15	75,899	78,429	80,959	83,489	86,018	88,548	91,078	93,608	96,138	98,668

SALARY TABLE NO. 97-DET

INCORPORATING THE 2.30% GENERAL SCHEDULE INCREASE AND A LOCALITY PAYMENT OF 8.14% FOR THE LOCALITY PAY AREA OF DETROIT-ANN ARBOR-FLINT, MI
(Net Increase: 3.14%)

Effective January 1997

ANNUAL Rates by Grade and Step

	1	2	3	4	5	6	7	8	9	10
GS-1	$13,700	$14,157	$14,612	$15,066	$15,523	$15,791	$16,239	$16,692	$16,712	$17,134
2	15,402	15,770	16,280	16,712	16,900	17,398	17,895	18,392	18,890	19,387
3	16,807	17,367	17,927	18,488	19,048	19,608	20,168	20,728	21,288	21,849
4	18,867	19,497	20,126	20,755	21,385	22,014	22,643	23,273	23,902	24,532
5	21,109	21,813	22,517	23,221	23,925	24,629	25,333	26,037	26,741	27,445
6	23,529	24,313	25,097	25,881	26,665	27,449	28,233	29,017	29,801	30,585
7	26,146	27,018	27,889	28,761	29,633	30,504	31,376	32,247	33,119	33,991
8	28,957	29,922	30,888	31,854	32,819	33,785	34,751	35,716	36,682	37,648
9	31,985	33,051	34,117	35,183	36,250	37,316	38,382	39,448	40,515	41,581
10	35,222	36,397	37,571	38,745	39,920	41,094	42,269	43,443	44,617	45,792
11	38,699	39,989	41,279	42,569	43,859	45,150	46,440	47,730	49,020	50,310
12	46,381	47,928	49,474	51,020	52,567	54,113	55,660	57,206	58,752	60,299
13	55,155	56,993	58,831	60,670	62,508	64,347	66,185	68,023	69,862	71,700
14	65,176	67,349	69,521	71,694	73,866	76,039	78,211	80,384	82,556	84,729
15	76,665	79,220	81,775	84,331	86,886	89,442	91,997	94,552	97,108	99,663

NOTE: Locality rates of pay are considered basic pay only for certain purposes--see "1997 Salary Tables" cover sheet.

SALARY TABLE NO. 97-HOU

INCORPORATING THE 2.30% GENERAL SCHEDULE INCREASE AND A LOCALITY PAYMENT OF 11.52% FOR THE LOCALITY PAY AREA OF HOUSTON-GALVESTON-BRAZORIA, TX
(Net Increase: 4.28%)

Effective January 1997

ANNUAL Rates by Grade and Step

	1	2	3	4	5	6	7	8	9	10
GS-1	$14,128	$14,599	$15,069	$15,537	$16,009	$16,284	$16,747	$17,214	$17,234	$17,669
2	15,884	16,263	16,789	17,234	17,428	17,941	18,454	18,967	19,480	19,993
3	17,332	17,910	18,488	19,065	19,643	20,221	20,798	21,376	21,954	22,532
4	19,457	20,106	20,755	21,404	22,053	22,702	23,351	24,000	24,649	25,298
5	21,769	22,495	23,221	23,947	24,673	25,399	26,125	26,851	27,577	28,303
6	24,265	25,073	25,882	26,690	27,499	28,307	29,116	29,924	30,733	31,541
7	26,963	27,862	28,761	29,660	30,559	31,458	32,356	33,255	34,154	35,053
8	29,862	30,858	31,853	32,849	33,845	34,841	35,837	36,833	37,829	38,825
9	32,984	34,084	35,183	36,283	37,383	38,482	39,582	40,681	41,781	42,881
10	36,323	37,534	38,745	39,957	41,168	42,379	43,590	44,801	46,012	47,223
11	39,909	41,239	42,569	43,900	45,230	46,561	47,891	49,222	50,552	51,882
12	47,831	49,426	51,020	52,615	54,210	55,805	57,399	58,994	60,589	62,184
13	56,879	58,774	60,670	62,566	64,462	66,358	68,254	70,149	72,045	73,941
14	67,213	69,454	71,694	73,934	76,175	78,415	80,656	82,896	85,137	87,377
15	79,061	81,696	84,331	86,967	89,602	92,237	94,872	97,508	100,143	102,778

NOTE: Locality rates of pay are considered basic pay only for certain purposes--see "1997 Salary Tables" cover sheet.

SALARY TABLE NO. 97-HOU

INCORPORATING THE 2.30% GENERAL SCHEDULE INCREASE AND A LOCALITY PAYMENT OF 11.52% FOR THE LOCALITY PAY AREA OF HOUSTON-GALVESTON-BRAZORIA, TX
(Net Increase: 4.28%)

Effective January 1997

ANNUAL Rates by Grade and Step

	1	2	3	4	5	6	7	8	9	10
GS-1	$14,128	$14,599	$15,069	$15,537	$16,009	$16,284	$16,747	$17,214	$17,234	$17,669
2	15,884	16,263	16,789	17,234	17,428	17,941	18,454	18,967	19,480	19,993
3	17,332	17,910	18,488	19,065	19,643	20,221	20,798	21,376	21,954	22,532
4	19,457	20,106	20,755	21,404	22,053	22,702	23,351	24,000	24,649	25,298
5	21,769	22,495	23,221	23,947	24,673	25,399	26,125	26,851	27,577	28,303
6	24,265	25,073	25,882	26,690	27,499	28,307	29,116	29,924	30,733	31,541
7	26,963	27,862	28,761	29,660	30,559	31,458	32,356	33,255	34,154	35,053
8	29,862	30,858	31,853	32,849	33,845	34,841	35,837	36,833	37,829	38,825
9	32,984	34,084	35,183	36,283	37,383	38,482	39,582	40,681	41,781	42,831
10	36,323	37,534	38,745	39,957	41,168	42,379	43,590	44,801	46,012	47,223
11	39,909	41,239	42,569	43,900	45,230	46,561	47,891	49,222	50,552	51,882
12	47,831	49,426	51,020	52,615	54,210	55,805	57,399	58,994	60,589	62,184
13	56,879	58,774	60,670	62,566	64,462	66,358	68,254	70,149	72,045	73,941
14	67,213	69,454	71,694	73,934	76,175	78,415	80,656	82,896	85,137	87,377
15	79,061	81,696	84,331	86,967	89,602	92,237	94,872	97,508	100,143	102,778

NOTE: Locality rates of pay are considered basic pay only for certain purposes--see "1997 Salary Tables" cover sheet.

SALARY TABLE NO. 97-HNT

INCORPORATING THE 2.30% GENERAL SCHEDULE INCREASE AND A LOCALITY PAYMENT OF 5.18% FOR THE LOCALITY PAY AREA OF HUNTSVILLE, AL

(Net Increase: 2.63%)

Effective January 1997

ANNUAL Rates by Grade and Step

	1	2	3	4	5	6	7	8	9	10
GS-1	$13,325	$13,769	$14,212	$14,654	$15,099	$15,358	$15,795	$16,236	$16,255	$16,665
2	14,981	15,338	15,835	16,255	16,438	16,921	17,405	17,889	18,373	18,857
3	16,347	16,892	17,437	17,982	18,526	19,071	19,616	20,161	20,706	21,251
4	18,351	18,963	19,575	20,187	20,799	21,411	22,024	22,636	23,248	23,860
5	20,531	21,216	21,901	22,585	23,270	23,955	24,639	25,324	26,009	26,694
6	22,885	23,648	24,410	25,173	25,935	26,698	27,460	28,223	28,986	29,748
7	25,430	26,278	27,126	27,974	28,821	29,669	30,517	31,365	32,212	33,060
8	28,164	29,103	30,043	30,982	31,921	32,860	33,800	34,739	35,678	36,617
9	31,109	32,146	33,183	34,220	35,257	36,294	37,332	38,369	39,406	40,443
10	34,258	35,400	36,543	37,685	38,827	39,969	41,112	42,254	43,396	44,538
11	37,640	38,895	40,149	41,404	42,659	43,914	45,168	46,423	47,678	48,933
12	45,112	46,616	48,120	49,624	51,128	52,632	54,136	55,640	57,144	58,648
13	53,645	55,433	57,221	59,009	60,797	62,585	64,373	66,161	67,949	69,737
14	63,392	65,505	67,618	69,731	71,844	73,957	76,070	78,183	80,297	82,410
15	74,566	77,052	79,537	82,023	84,508	86,993	89,479	91,964	94,450	96,935

NOTE: Locality rates of pay are considered basic pay only for certain purposes--see "1997 Salary Tables" cover sheet.

SALARY TABLE NO. 97-IND

INCORPORATING THE 2.30% GENERAL SCHEDULE INCREASE AND A LOCALITY PAYMENT OF 5.49% FOR THE LOCALITY PAY AREA OF INDIANAPOLIS, IN
(Net Increase: 2.74%)

Effective January 1997

ANNUAL Rates by Grade and Step

	1	2	3	4	5	6	7	8	9	10
GS-1	$13,365	$13,810	$14,254	$14,697	$15,143	$15,404	$15,841	$16,283	$16,302	$16,714
2	15,025	15,384	15,882	16,302	16,486	16,971	17,456	17,942	18,427	18,912
3	16,395	16,942	17,488	18,035	18,581	19,127	19,674	20,220	20,767	21,313
4	18,405	19,019	19,633	20,247	20,861	21,475	22,089	22,703	23,316	23,930
5	20,592	21,278	21,965	22,652	23,339	24,025	24,712	25,399	26,086	26,772
6	22,953	23,717	24,482	25,247	26,012	26,777	27,541	28,306	29,071	29,836
7	25,505	26,356	27,206	28,056	28,906	29,757	30,607	31,457	32,307	33,158
8	28,247	29,189	30,131	31,073	32,015	32,957	33,899	34,841	35,783	36,725
9	31,201	32,241	33,281	34,321	35,361	36,401	37,442	38,482	39,522	40,562
10	34,359	35,505	36,650	37,796	38,942	40,087	41,233	42,378	43,524	44,670
11	37,751	39,009	40,268	41,526	42,785	44,043	45,302	46,560	47,819	49,077
12	45,245	46,753	48,262	49,770	51,279	52,787	54,296	55,804	57,313	58,821
13	53,803	55,596	57,390	59,183	60,976	62,770	64,563	66,356	68,150	69,943
14	63,579	65,698	67,817	69,937	72,056	74,175	76,295	78,414	80,533	82,652
15	74,786	77,279	79,772	82,264	84,757	87,250	89,742	92,235	94,728	97,221

NOTE: Locality rates of pay are considered basic pay only for certain purposes--see "1997 Salary Tables" cover sheet.

SALARY TABLE NO. 97-KC

INCORPORATING THE 2.30% GENERAL SCHEDULE INCREASE AND A LOCALITY PAYMENT OF 5.10% FOR THE LOCALITY PAY AREA OF KANSAS CITY, MO-KS
(Net Increase: 3.01%)

Effective January 1997

ANNUAL Rates by Grade and Step

	1	2	3	4	5	6	7	8	9	10
GS-1	$13,315	$13,759	$14,201	$14,643	$15,087	$15,347	$15,783	$16,223	$16,242	$16,652
2	14,969	15,327	15,823	16,242	16,425	16,908	17,392	17,875	18,359	18,842
3	16,335	16,879	17,423	17,968	18,512	19,057	19,601	20,146	20,690	21,234
4	18,337	18,948	19,560	20,172	20,784	21,395	22,007	22,619	23,230	23,842
5	20,516	21,200	21,884	22,568	23,252	23,937	24,621	25,305	25,989	26,673
6	22,868	23,630	24,392	25,154	25,916	26,678	27,440	28,201	28,963	29,725
7	25,411	26,258	27,105	27,952	28,800	29,647	30,494	31,341	32,188	33,035
8	28,143	29,081	30,020	30,958	31,897	32,835	33,774	34,712	35,651	36,590
9	31,085	32,122	33,158	34,194	35,231	36,267	37,303	38,339	39,376	40,412
10	34,232	35,374	36,515	37,656	38,798	39,939	41,080	42,222	43,363	44,505
11	37,611	38,865	40,119	41,373	42,626	43,880	45,134	46,388	47,642	48,896
12	45,077	46,580	48,083	49,586	51,089	52,592	54,095	55,598	57,101	58,604
13	53,604	55,391	57,178	58,964	60,751	62,538	64,324	66,111	67,898	69,684
14	63,344	65,455	67,567	69,678	71,790	73,901	76,013	78,124	80,235	82,347
15	74,510	76,993	79,477	81,960	84,444	86,927	89,411	91,894	94,378	96,861

NOTE: Locality rates of pay are considered basic pay only for certain purposes--see "1997 Salary Tables" cover sheet.

SALARY TABLE NO. 97-LA

INCORPORATING THE 2.30% GENERAL SCHEDULE INCREASE AND A LOCALITY PAYMENT OF 9.46% FOR THE LOCALITY PAY AREA OF LOS ANGELES-RIVERSIDE-ORANGE COUNTY, CA, (INCLUDING SANTA BARBARA COUNTY AND ALL OF EDWARDS AIR FORCE BASE)
(Net Increase: 3.54%)

Effective January 1997

ANNUAL Rates by Grade and Step

	1	2	3	4	5	6	7	8	9	10
GS-1	$13,867	$14,329	$14,790	$15,250	$15,713	$15,983	$16,438	$16,896	$16,916	$17,343
2	15,590	15,963	16,479	16,916	17,106	17,610	18,113	18,617	19,120	19,624
3	17,012	17,579	18,146	18,713	19,280	19,847	20,414	20,981	21,548	22,115
4	19,097	19,735	20,372	21,009	21,646	22,283	22,920	23,557	24,194	24,831
5	21,367	22,079	22,792	23,504	24,217	24,930	25,642	26,355	27,067	27,780
6	23,816	24,610	25,403	26,197	26,991	27,784	28,578	29,371	30,165	30,959
7	26,465	27,347	28,230	29,112	29,994	30,876	31,759	32,641	33,523	34,405
8	29,310	30,288	31,265	32,243	33,220	34,197	35,175	36,152	37,130	38,107
9	32,375	33,454	34,534	35,613	36,692	37,771	38,851	39,930	41,009	42,088
10	35,652	36,841	38,030	39,218	40,407	41,596	42,785	43,973	45,162	46,351
11	39,171	40,477	41,783	43,089	44,395	45,701	47,007	48,312	49,618	50,924
12	46,947	48,513	50,078	51,643	53,209	54,774	56,339	57,904	59,470	61,035
13	55,828	57,689	59,550	61,410	63,271	65,132	66,993	68,854	70,714	72,575
14	65,972	68,171	70,370	72,569	74,768	76,967	79,166	81,365	83,564	85,763
15	77,601	80,187	82,774	85,360	87,947	90,533	93,120	95,706	98,293	100,879

NOTE: Locality rates of pay are considered basic pay only for certain purposes--see "1997 Salary Tables" cover sheet.

SALARY TABLE NO. 97-MFL

INCORPORATING THE 2.30% GENERAL SCHEDULE INCREASE AND A LOCALITY PAYMENT OF 6.74% FOR THE LOCALITY PAY AREA OF MIAMI-FORT LAUDERDALE, FL
(Net Increase: 3.07%)

Effective January 1997
ANNUAL Rates by Grade and Step

	1	2	3	4	5	6	7	8	9	10
GS-1	$13,523	$13,973	$14,423	$14,871	$15,323	$15,586	$16,029	$16,476	$16,496	$16,912
2	15,203	15,566	16,070	16,496	16,681	17,172	17,663	18,154	18,645	19,136
3	16,590	17,142	17,695	18,248	18,801	19,354	19,907	20,460	21,013	21,566
4	18,623	19,244	19,865	20,487	21,108	21,729	22,350	22,972	23,593	24,214
5	20,836	21,531	22,225	22,920	23,615	24,310	25,005	25,700	26,395	27,090
6	23,224	23,998	24,772	25,546	26,320	27,094	27,868	28,642	29,415	30,189
7	25,808	26,668	27,528	28,389	29,249	30,109	30,970	31,830	32,690	33,551
8	28,582	29,535	30,488	31,441	32,395	33,348	34,301	35,254	36,207	37,160
9	31,570	32,623	33,675	34,728	35,780	36,833	37,885	38,938	39,990	41,043
10	34,766	35,925	37,085	38,244	39,403	40,562	41,721	42,881	44,040	45,199
11	38,198	39,471	40,745	42,018	43,292	44,565	45,838	47,112	48,385	49,659
12	45,781	47,307	48,834	50,360	51,886	53,413	54,939	56,465	57,992	59,518
13	54,441	56,255	58,070	59,884	61,699	63,514	65,328	67,143	68,957	70,772
14	64,332	66,477	68,621	70,765	72,910	75,054	77,199	79,343	81,487	83,632
15	75,672	78,195	80,717	83,239	85,761	88,284	90,806	93,328	95,850	98,373

NOTE: Locality rates of pay are considered basic pay only for certain purposes--see "1997 Salary Tables" cover sheet.

SALARY TABLE 97-MIL

INCORPORATING THE 2.30% GENERAL SCHEDULE INCREASE AND A LOCALITY PAYMENT OF 5.58% FOR THE LOCALITY PAY AREA OF MILWAUKEE-RACINE, WI
(Net Increase: 3.72%)

Effective January 1997

ANNUAL Rates by Grade and Step

	1	2	3	4	5	6	7	8	9	10
GS-1	$13,376	$13,821	$14,266	$14,709	$15,156	$15,417	$15,855	$16,297	$16,316	$16,728
2	$15,038	$15,397	$15,895	$16,316	$16,500	$16,986	$17,471	$17,957	$18,443	$18,928
3	$16,409	$16,956	$17,503	$18,050	$18,597	$19,144	$19,691	$20,238	$20,784	$21,331
4	$18,421	$19,035	$19,649	$20,264	$20,878	$21,493	$22,107	$22,722	$23,336	$23,951
5	$20,609	$21,297	$21,984	$22,671	$23,359	$24,046	$24,733	$25,420	$26,108	$26,795
6	$22,972	$23,738	$24,503	$25,268	$26,034	$26,799	$27,565	$28,330	$29,096	$29,861
7	$25,527	$26,378	$27,229	$28,080	$28,931	$29,782	$30,633	$31,484	$32,335	$33,186
8	$28,271	$29,214	$30,157	$31,100	$32,042	$32,985	$33,928	$34,871	$35,814	$36,757
9	$31,227	$32,268	$33,309	$34,350	$35,391	$36,432	$37,474	$38,515	$39,556	$40,597
10	$34,388	$35,535	$36,682	$37,828	$38,975	$40,121	$41,268	$42,415	$43,561	$44,708
11	$37,783	$39,042	$40,302	$41,562	$42,821	$44,081	$45,340	$46,600	$47,859	$49,119
12	$45,283	$46,793	$48,303	$49,813	$51,322	$52,832	$54,342	$55,852	$57,362	$58,371
13	$53,849	$55,644	$57,439	$59,234	$61,028	$62,823	$64,618	$66,413	$68,208	$70,003
14	$63,633	$65,754	$67,875	$69,996	$72,117	$74,239	$76,360	$78,481	$80,602	$82,723
15	$74,850	$77,345	$79,840	$82,334	$84,829	$87,324	$89,819	$92,314	$94,809	$97,304

NOTE: Locality rates of pay are considered basic pay only for certain purposes--see "1997 Salary Tables" cover sheet.

SALARY TABLE 97-MSP

INCORPORATING THE 2.30% GENERAL SCHEDULE INCREASE AND A LOCALITY PAYMENT OF 6.53% FOR THE LOCALITY PAY AREA OF MINNEAPOLIS-ST. PAUL, MN-WI.

(Net Increase: 4.66%)

Effective January 1997

ANNUAL Rates by Grade and Step

	1	2	3	4	5	6	7	8	9	10
GS-1	$13,496	$13,946	$14,394	$14,842	$15,292	$15,556	$15,998	$16,444	$16,463	$16,879
2	15,173	15,535	16,038	16,463	16,649	17,139	17,629	18,119	18,609	19,099
3	16,557	17,109	17,661	18,212	18,764	19,316	19,868	20,420	20,971	21,523
4	18,586	19,206	19,826	20,446	21,066	21,686	22,306	22,926	23,546	24,166
5	20,795	21,488	22,182	22,875	23,569	24,262	24,956	25,649	26,343	27,036
6	23,179	23,951	24,723	25,496	26,268	27,041	27,813	28,585	29,358	30,130
7	25,757	26,615	27,474	28,333	29,191	30,050	30,909	31,767	32,626	33,485
8	28,526	29,477	30,428	31,379	32,331	33,282	34,233	35,185	36,136	37,087
9	31,508	32,559	33,609	34,660	35,710	36,760	37,811	38,861	39,911	40,962
10	34,698	35,855	37,012	38,169	39,326	40,482	41,639	42,796	43,953	45,110
11	38,123	39,394	40,665	41,936	43,206	44,477	45,748	47,019	48,290	49,561
12	45,691	47,214	48,737	50,261	51,784	53,308	54,831	56,354	57,878	59,401
13	54,333	56,145	57,956	59,767	61,578	63,389	65,200	67,011	68,822	70,633
14	64,206	66,346	68,486	70,626	72,766	74,907	77,047	79,187	81,327	83,467
15	75,523	78,041	80,558	83,075	85,593	88,110	90,627	93,145	95,662	98,179

NOTE: Locality rates of pay are considered basic pay only for certain purposes--see "1997 Salary Tables" cover sheet.

SALARY TABLE NO. 97-NY

INCORPORATING THE 2.30% GENERAL SCHEDULE INCREASE AND A LOCALITY PAYMENT OF 9.15% FOR THE LOCALITY PAY AREA OF NEW YORK-NORTHERN NEW JERSEY-LONG ISLAND, NY-NJ-CT-PA
(Net Increase: 3.34%)

Effective January 1997

ANNUAL Rates by Grade and Step

	1	2	3	4	5	6	7	8	9	10
GS-1	$13,828	$14,289	$14,748	$15,207	$15,668	$15,938	$16,391	$16,848	$16,868	$17,294
2	15,546	15,917	16,433	16,868	17,058	17,560	18,062	18,564	19,066	19,568
3	16,964	17,529	18,095	18,660	19,226	19,791	20,356	20,922	21,487	22,053
4	19,043	19,679	20,314	20,949	21,584	22,220	22,855	23,490	24,125	24,761
5	21,306	22,017	22,727	23,438	24,148	24,859	25,569	26,280	26,991	27,701
6	23,749	24,540	25,332	26,123	26,914	27,706	28,497	29,288	30,080	30,871
7	26,390	27,270	28,150	29,030	29,909	30,789	31,669	32,549	33,428	34,308
8	29,227	30,202	31,177	32,151	33,126	34,101	35,075	36,050	37,025	37,999
9	32,283	33,360	34,436	35,512	36,588	37,664	38,741	39,817	40,893	41,969
10	35,551	36,737	37,922	39,107	40,293	41,478	42,663	43,849	45,034	46,220
11	39,060	40,363	41,665	42,967	44,269	45,571	46,873	48,176	49,478	50,780
12	46,814	48,375	49,936	51,497	53,058	54,619	56,180	57,740	59,301	60,862
13	55,670	57,525	59,381	61,236	63,092	64,948	66,803	68,659	70,514	72,370
14	65,785	67,978	70,170	72,363	74,556	76,749	78,942	81,134	83,327	85,520
15	77,381	79,960	82,539	85,118	87,698	90,277	92,856	95,435	98,015	100,594

NOTE: Locality rates of pay are considered basic pay only for certain purposes--see "1997 Salary Tables" cover sheet.

SALARY TABLE NO. 97-PHL

INCORPORATING THE 2.30% GENERAL SCHEDULE INCREASE AND A LOCALITY PAYMENT OF 7.28% FOR THE LOCALITY PAY AREA OF PHILADELPHIA-WILMINGTON-ATLANTIC CITY, PA-NJ-DE-MD
(Net Increase: 2.66%)

Effective January 1997

ANNUAL Rates by Grade and Step

	1	2	3	4	5	6	7	8	9	10
GS-1	$13,591	$14,044	$14,496	$14,946	$15,400	$15,665	$16,110	$16,560	$16,579	$16,997
2	15,280	15,645	16,151	16,579	16,766	17,259	17,753	18,246	18,740	19,233
3	16,673	17,229	17,785	18,341	18,896	19,452	20,008	20,563	21,119	21,675
4	18,717	19,342	19,966	20,590	21,215	21,839	22,463	23,088	23,712	24,336
5	20,941	21,639	22,338	23,036	23,735	24,433	25,131	25,830	26,528	27,227
6	23,342	24,120	24,898	25,675	26,453	27,231	28,009	28,786	29,564	30,342
7	25,938	26,803	27,668	28,532	29,397	30,262	31,126	31,991	32,856	33,720
8	28,726	29,684	30,642	31,600	32,558	33,516	34,474	35,432	36,390	37,348
9	31,730	32,788	33,846	34,904	35,961	37,019	38,077	39,135	40,192	41,250
10	34,942	36,107	37,272	38,437	39,602	40,767	41,933	43,098	44,263	45,428
11	38,391	39,671	40,951	42,231	43,511	44,790	46,070	47,350	48,630	49,910
12	46,012	47,546	49,081	50,615	52,149	53,683	55,217	56,751	58,285	59,819
13	54,716	56,540	58,364	60,187	62,011	63,835	65,659	67,482	69,306	71,130
14	64,658	66,813	68,968	71,123	73,279	75,434	77,589	79,744	81,900	84,055
15	76,055	78,590	81,125	83,660	86,195	88,730	91,265	93,800	96,335	98,870

NOTE: Locality rates of pay are considered basic pay only for certain purposes--see "1997 Salary Tables" cover sheet.

SALARY TABLE NO. 97-PIT

INCORPORATING THE 2.30% GENERAL SCHEDULE INCREASE AND A LOCALITY PAYMENT OF 5.07% FOR THE LOCALITY PAY AREA OF PITTSBURGH, PA
(NET INCREASE: 3.22%)

Effective January 1997

ANNUAL Rates by Grade and Step

	1	2	3	4	5	6	7	8	9	10
GS-1	$13,311	$13,755	$14,197	$14,638	$15,083	$15,342	$15,778	$16,219	$16,238	$16,647
2	14,965	15,322	15,818	16,238	16,420	16,904	17,387	17,870	18,354	18,837
3	16,330	16,874	17,419	17,963	18,507	19,051	19,596	20,140	20,684	21,228
4	18,332	18,943	19,555	20,166	20,778	21,389	22,001	22,612	23,224	23,835
5	20,510	21,194	21,878	22,562	23,246	23,930	24,614	25,298	25,982	26,666
6	22,861	23,623	24,385	25,146	25,908	26,670	27,432	28,193	28,955	29,717
7	25,404	26,251	27,098	27,944	28,791	29,638	30,485	31,332	32,179	33,026
8	28,135	29,073	30,011	30,949	31,888	32,826	33,764	34,703	35,641	36,579
9	31,077	32,113	33,149	34,185	35,221	36,257	37,292	38,328	39,364	40,400
10	34,222	35,363	36,504	37,646	38,787	39,928	41,069	42,210	43,351	44,492
11	37,600	38,854	40,107	41,361	42,614	43,868	45,121	46,375	47,628	48,882
12	45,065	46,567	48,070	49,572	51,075	52,577	54,080	55,582	57,085	58,537
13	53,589	55,375	57,161	58,947	60,734	62,520	64,306	66,092	67,878	69,665
14	63,326	65,437	67,547	69,658	71,769	73,880	75,991	78,102	80,213	82,323
15	74,488	76,971	79,454	81,937	84,420	86,902	89,385	91,868	94,351	96,834

NOTE: Locality rates of pay are considered basic pay only for certain purposes--see "1997 Salary Tables" cover sheet.

SALARY TABLE NO. 97-POR

INCORPORATING THE 2.30% GENERAL SCHEDULE INCREASE AND A LOCALITY PAYMENT OF 6.13% FOR THE LOCALITY PAY AREA OF PORTLAND-SALEM, OR-WA
(Net Increase: 3.20%)

Effective January 1997

ANNUAL Rates by Grade and Step

	1	2	3	4	5	6	7	8	9	10
GS-1	$13,446	$13,893	$14,340	$14,786	$15,235	$15,497	$15,938	$16,382	$16,401	$16,815
2	15,116	15,477	15,978	16,401	16,586	17,074	17,562	18,051	18,539	19,027
3	16,495	17,044	17,594	18,144	18,694	19,243	19,793	20,343	20,893	21,443
4	18,517	19,134	19,752	20,370	20,987	21,605	22,223	22,840	23,458	24,076
5	20,717	21,407	22,098	22,789	23,480	24,171	24,862	25,553	26,244	26,935
6	23,092	23,861	24,631	25,400	26,170	26,939	27,708	28,478	29,247	30,017
7	25,660	26,516	27,371	28,226	29,082	29,937	30,793	31,648	32,503	33,359
8	28,418	29,366	30,314	31,262	32,209	33,157	34,105	35,053	36,000	36,948
9	31,390	32,437	33,483	34,529	35,576	36,622	37,669	38,715	39,762	40,808
10	34,568	35,720	36,873	38,025	39,178	40,330	41,483	42,636	43,788	44,941
11	37,980	39,246	40,512	41,778	43,044	44,310	45,576	46,843	48,109	49,375
12	45,519	47,037	48,554	50,072	51,590	53,107	54,625	56,143	57,660	59,178
13	54,129	55,934	57,738	59,542	61,346	63,151	64,955	66,759	68,563	70,367
14	63,965	66,097	68,229	70,361	72,493	74,625	76,757	78,890	81,022	83,154
15	75,240	77,748	80,256	82,763	85,271	87,779	90,287	92,795	95,303	97,810

NOTE: Locality rates of pay are considered basic pay only for certain purposes--see "1997 Salary Tables" cover sheet.

SALARY TABLE NO. 97-RCH

INCORPORATING THE 2.30% GENERAL SCHEDULE INCREASE AND A LOCALITY PAYMENT OF 5.27% FOR THE LOCALITY PAY AREA OF RICHMOND-PETERSBURG, VA
(Net Increase: 3.14%)

Effective January 1997

ANNUAL Rates by Grade and Step

	1	2	3	4	5	6	7	8	9	10
GS-1	$13,337	$13,781	$14,224	$14,666	$15,112	$15,372	$15,808	$16,249	$16,268	$16,679
2	14,994	15,352	15,848	16,268	16,452	16,936	17,420	17,904	18,389	18,873
3	16,361	16,906	17,452	17,997	18,542	19,088	19,633	20,178	20,723	21,269
4	18,366	18,979	19,592	20,204	20,817	21,430	22,042	22,655	23,268	23,880
5	20,549	21,234	21,919	22,605	23,290	23,975	24,661	25,346	26,031	26,716
6	22,905	23,668	24,431	25,194	25,957	26,721	27,484	28,247	29,010	29,774
7	25,452	26,301	27,149	27,998	28,846	29,695	30,543	31,392	32,240	33,088
8	28,188	29,128	30,068	31,008	31,948	32,888	33,829	34,769	35,709	36,649
9	31,136	32,174	33,212	34,250	35,288	36,326	37,363	38,401	39,439	40,477
10	34,287	35,431	36,574	37,717	38,860	40,004	41,147	42,290	43,433	44,577
11	37,672	38,928	40,184	41,440	42,695	43,951	45,207	46,463	47,719	48,975
12	45,150	46,656	48,161	49,666	51,172	52,677	54,182	55,688	57,193	58,699
13	53,691	55,480	57,270	59,060	60,849	62,639	64,428	66,218	68,008	69,797
14	63,446	65,561	67,676	69,791	71,906	74,021	76,135	78,250	80,365	82,480
15	74,630	77,118	79,605	82,093	84,580	87,068	89,555	92,043	94,530	97,018

NOTE: Locality rates of pay are considered basic pay only for certain purposes--see "1997 Salary Tables" cover sheet.

SALARY TABLE NO. 97-SAC

INCORPORATING THE 2.30% GENERAL SCHEDULE INCREASE AND A LOCALITY PAYMENT OF 6.56% FOR THE LOCALITY PAY AREA OF SACRAMENTO-YOLO, CA
(Net Increase: 3.03%)

Effective January 1997

ANNUAL Rates by Grade and Step

	1	2	3	4	5	6	7	8	9	10
GS-1	$13,500	$13,950	$14,398	$14,846	$15,297	$15,560	$16,002	$16,449	$16,468	$16,883
2	15,177	15,540	16,043	16,468	16,653	17,143	17,634	18,124	18,614	19,104
3	16,562	17,114	17,666	18,217	18,769	19,321	19,873	20,425	20,977	21,529
4	18,592	19,212	19,832	20,452	21,072	21,692	22,313	22,933	23,553	24,173
5	20,801	21,494	22,188	22,882	23,575	24,269	24,963	25,656	26,350	27,044
6	23,185	23,958	24,730	25,503	26,276	27,048	27,821	28,593	29,366	30,138
7	25,764	26,623	27,482	28,341	29,200	30,058	30,917	31,776	32,635	33,494
8	28,534	29,485	30,437	31,388	32,340	33,291	34,243	35,195	36,146	37,098
9	31,517	32,568	33,619	34,669	35,720	36,771	37,821	38,872	39,923	40,973
10	34,708	35,865	37,022	38,179	39,337	40,494	41,651	42,808	43,966	45,123
11	38,134	39,405	40,676	41,947	43,219	44,490	45,761	47,032	48,304	49,575
12	45,704	47,227	48,751	50,275	51,799	53,323	54,846	56,370	57,894	59,418
13	54,349	56,160	57,972	59,783	61,595	63,406	65,218	67,029	68,841	70,652
14	64,224	66,365	68,505	70,646	72,787	74,928	77,068	79,209	81,350	83,491
15	75,545	78,063	80,581	83,099	85,617	88,135	90,653	93,171	95,689	98,207

NOTE: Locality rates of pay are considered basic pay only for certain purposes--see "1997 Salary Tables" cover sheet.

SALARY TABLE NO. 97-STL

INCORPORATING THE 2.30% GENERAL SCHEDULE INCREASE AND A LOCALITY PAYMENT OF 5.18% FOR THE LOCALITY PAY AREA OF ST. LOUIS, MO-IL
(Net Increase: 2.75%)

Effective January 1997

ANNUAL Rates by Grade and Step

	1	2	3	4	5	6	7	8	9	10
GS-1	$13,325	$13,769	$14,212	$14,654	$15,099	$15,358	$15,795	$16,236	$16,255	$16,665
2	14,981	15,338	15,835	16,255	16,438	16,921	17,405	17,889	18,373	18,857
3	16,347	16,892	17,437	17,982	18,526	19,071	19,616	20,161	20,706	21,251
4	18,351	18,963	19,575	20,187	20,799	21,411	22,024	22,636	23,248	23,860
5	20,531	21,216	21,901	22,585	23,270	23,955	24,639	25,324	26,009	26,694
6	22,885	23,648	24,410	25,173	25,935	26,698	27,460	28,223	28,986	29,748
7	25,430	26,278	27,126	27,974	28,821	29,669	30,517	31,365	32,212	33,060
8	28,164	29,103	30,043	30,982	31,921	32,860	33,800	34,739	35,678	36,617
9	31,109	32,146	33,183	34,220	35,257	36,294	37,332	38,369	39,406	40,443
10	34,258	35,400	36,543	37,685	38,827	39,969	41,112	42,254	43,396	44,538
11	37,640	38,895	40,149	41,404	42,659	43,914	45,168	46,423	47,678	48,933
12	45,112	46,616	48,120	49,624	51,128	52,632	54,136	55,640	57,144	58,648
13	53,645	55,433	57,221	59,009	60,797	62,585	64,373	66,161	67,949	69,737
14	63,392	65,505	67,618	69,731	71,844	73,957	76,070	78,183	80,297	82,410
15	74,566	77,052	79,537	82,023	84,508	86,993	89,479	91,964	94,450	96,935

NOTE: Locality rates of pay are considered basic pay only for certain purposes--see "1997 Salary Tables" cover sheet.

SALARY TABLE NO. 97-SD

INCORPORATING THE 2.30% GENERAL SCHEDULE INCREASE AND A LOCALITY PAYMENT OF 7.07% FOR THE LOCALITY PAY AREA OF SAN DIEGO, CA
(Net Increase: 2.60%)

Effective January 1997

ANNUAL Rates by Grade and Step

	1	2	3	4	5	6	7	8	9	10
GS-1	$13,565	$14,017	$14,467	$14,917	$15,370	$15,634	$16,079	$16,527	$16,547	$16,964
2	15,250	15,614	16,119	16,547	16,733	17,225	17,718	18,210	18,703	19,196
3	16,641	17,195	17,750	18,305	18,859	19,414	19,969	20,523	21,078	21,632
4	18,681	19,304	19,927	20,550	21,173	21,796	22,419	23,043	23,666	24,289
5	20,900	21,597	22,294	22,991	23,688	24,385	25,082	25,779	26,476	27,173
6	23,296	24,073	24,849	25,625	26,401	27,178	27,954	28,730	29,506	30,283
7	25,887	26,750	27,613	28,476	29,339	30,202	31,065	31,928	32,791	33,654
8	28,670	29,626	30,582	31,539	32,495	33,451	34,407	35,363	36,319	37,275
9	31,668	32,724	33,780	34,835	35,891	36,947	38,002	39,058	40,114	41,169
10	34,874	36,037	37,199	38,362	39,525	40,688	41,850	43,013	44,176	45,339
11	38,316	39,593	40,871	42,148	43,425	44,703	45,980	47,257	48,535	49,812
12	45,922	47,453	48,985	50,516	52,047	53,578	55,109	56,640	58,171	59,702
13	54,609	56,429	58,249	60,069	61,890	63,710	65,530	67,350	69,170	70,991
14	64,531	66,682	68,833	70,984	73,135	75,286	77,437	79,588	81,739	83,890
15	75,906	78,436	80,966	83,496	86,026	88,557	91,087	93,617	96,147	98,677

NOTE: Locality rates of pay are considered basic pay only for certain purposes--see "1997 Salary Tables" cover sheet.

SALARY TABLE NO. 97-SF

INCORPORATING THE 2.30% GENERAL SCHEDULE INCREASE AND A LOCALITY PAYMENT OF 10.66% FOR THE LOCALITY PAY AREA OF SAN FRANCISCO-OAKLAND-SAN JOSE, CA
(Net Increase: 3.89%)

Effective January 1997

ANNUAL Rates by Grade and Step

	1	2	3	4	5	6	7	8	9	10
GS-1	$14,020	$14,487	$14,952	$15,417	$15,885	$16,159	$16,618	$17,081	$17,101	$17,533
2	15,761	16,138	16,660	17,101	17,294	17,803	18,312	18,821	19,330	19,839
3	17,199	17,772	18,345	18,918	19,492	20,065	20,638	21,211	21,785	22,358
4	19,307	19,951	20,595	21,239	21,883	22,527	23,171	23,815	24,459	25,103
5	21,601	22,321	23,042	23,762	24,482	25,203	25,923	26,644	27,364	28,084
6	24,077	24,880	25,682	26,484	27,287	28,089	28,891	29,693	30,496	31,298
7	26,755	27,647	28,539	29,431	30,323	31,215	32,107	32,999	33,891	34,783
8	29,631	30,620	31,608	32,596	33,584	34,572	35,561	36,549	37,537	38,525
9	32,730	33,821	34,912	36,003	37,094	38,185	39,277	40,368	41,459	42,550
10	36,043	37,245	38,447	39,648	40,850	42,052	43,254	44,455	45,657	46,859
11	39,601	40,921	42,241	43,561	44,881	46,202	47,522	48,842	50,162	51,482
12	47,462	49,045	50,627	52,209	53,792	55,374	56,957	58,539	60,122	61,704
13	56,440	58,321	60,202	62,084	63,965	65,846	67,727	69,608	71,490	73,371
14	66,695	68,918	71,141	73,364	75,587	77,811	80,034	82,257	84,480	86,703
15	78,451	81,066	83,681	86,296	88,911	91,526	94,141	96,756	99,370	101,985

NOTE: Locality rates of pay are considered basic pay only for certain purposes--see "1997 Salary Tables" cover sheet.

SALARY TABLE NO. 97-SEA

INCORPORATING THE 2.30% GENERAL SCHEDULE INCREASE AND A LOCALITY PAYMENT OF 6.62% FOR THE LOCALITY PAY AREA OF SEATTLE-TACOMA-BREMERTON, WA
(Net Increase: 2.47%)

Effective January 1997

ANNUAL Rates by Grade and Step

	1	2	3	4	5	6	7	8	9	10
GS-1	$13,508	$13,958	$14,406	$14,854	$15,305	$15,569	$16,011	$16,458	$16,477	$16,893
2	15,186	15,548	16,052	16,477	16,663	17,153	17,643	18,134	18,624	19,115
3	16,571	17,123	17,675	18,228	18,780	19,332	19,885	20,437	20,989	21,542
4	18,602	19,223	19,843	20,464	21,084	21,705	22,325	22,946	23,566	24,187
5	20,812	21,506	22,200	22,895	23,589	24,283	24,977	25,671	26,365	27,059
6	23,198	23,971	24,744	25,517	26,290	27,063	27,836	28,609	29,382	30,155
7	25,779	26,638	27,497	28,357	29,216	30,075	30,935	31,794	32,653	33,513
8	28,550	29,502	30,454	31,406	32,358	33,310	34,262	35,214	36,167	37,119
9	31,535	32,586	33,638	34,689	35,740	36,791	37,843	38,894	39,945	40,996
10	34,727	35,885	37,043	38,201	39,359	40,517	41,675	42,832	43,990	45,148
11	38,155	39,427	40,699	41,971	43,243	44,515	45,787	47,059	48,331	49,603
12	45,729	47,254	48,779	50,303	51,828	53,353	54,877	56,402	57,927	59,451
13	54,379	56,192	58,004	59,817	61,630	63,442	65,255	67,067	68,880	70,692
14	64,260	66,402	68,544	70,686	72,828	74,970	77,112	79,254	81,396	83,538
15	75,587	78,107	80,626	83,145	85,665	88,184	90,704	93,223	95,743	98,262

NOTE: Locality rates of pay are considered basic pay only for certain purposes--see "1997 Salary Tables" cover sheet.

SALARY TABLE NO. 97-DCB

INCORPORATING THE 2.30% GENERAL SCHEDULE INCREASE AND A LOCALITY PAYMENT OF 7.11% FOR THE LOCALITY PAY AREA OF WASHINGTON-BALTIMORE, DC-MD-VA-WV
(Net Increase: 3.33%)

Effective January 1997

ANNUAL Rates by Grade and Step

	1	2	3	4	5	6	7	8	9	10
GS-1	$13,570	$14,022	$14,473	$14,923	$15,376	$15,640	$16,085	$16,533	$16,553	$16,971
2	15,256	15,620	16,125	16,553	16,739	17,232	17,725	18,217	18,710	19,203
3	16,647	17,202	17,757	18,312	18,866	19,421	19,976	20,531	21,086	21,641
4	18,687	19,311	19,934	20,558	21,181	21,804	22,428	23,051	23,675	24,298
5	20,908	21,605	22,302	23,000	23,697	24,394	25,092	25,789	26,486	27,183
6	23,305	24,082	24,858	25,635	26,411	27,188	27,964	28,741	29,517	30,294
7	25,897	26,760	27,624	28,487	29,350	30,214	31,077	31,940	32,804	33,667
8	28,681	29,637	30,594	31,550	32,507	33,463	34,420	35,376	36,333	37,289
9	31,680	32,736	33,792	34,848	35,904	36,960	38,017	39,073	40,129	41,185
10	34,887	36,050	37,213	38,376	39,540	40,703	41,866	43,029	44,193	45,356
11	38,330	39,608	40,886	42,164	43,442	44,719	45,997	47,275	48,553	49,831
12	45,939	47,471	49,003	50,534	52,066	53,598	55,130	56,661	58,193	59,725
13	54,629	56,450	58,271	60,092	61,913	63,734	65,555	67,375	69,196	71,017
14	64,555	66,707	68,859	71,011	73,163	75,314	77,466	79,618	81,770	83,922
15	75,935	78,466	80,997	83,528	86,059	88,590	91,121	93,652	96,183	98,714

NOTE: Locality rates of pay are considered basic pay only for certain purposes--see "1997 Salary Tables" cover sheet.

SALARY TABLE NO. 97-RUS

INCORPORATING THE 2.30% GENERAL SCHEDULE INCREASE AND A LOCALITY PAYMENT OF 4.81% FOR THE LOCALITY PAY AREA OF REST OF U.S.

(Net Increase: 2.97%)

Effective January 1997

ANNUAL Rates by Grade and Step

	1	2	3	4	5	6	7	8	9	10
GS-1	$13,278	$13,721	$14,162	$14,602	$15,045	$15,304	$15,739	$16,178	$16,197	$16,606
2	14,928	15,284	15,779	16,197	16,380	16,862	17,344	17,826	18,308	18,790
3	16,290	16,832	17,375	17,918	18,461	19,004	19,547	20,090	20,633	21,176
4	18,286	18,896	19,506	20,116	20,726	21,336	21,946	22,556	23,166	23,776
5	20,459	21,141	21,824	22,506	23,188	23,870	24,553	25,235	25,917	26,600
6	22,805	23,564	24,324	25,084	25,844	26,604	27,364	28,124	28,884	29,643
7	25,341	26,186	27,030	27,875	28,720	29,565	30,410	31,254	32,099	32,944
8	28,065	29,001	29,937	30,873	31,809	32,745	33,681	34,617	35,553	36,489
9	31,000	32,033	33,067	34,100	35,133	36,167	37,200	38,234	39,267	40,300
10	34,138	35,276	36,414	37,552	38,691	39,829	40,967	42,105	43,244	44,382
11	37,507	38,758	40,008	41,258	42,509	43,759	45,010	46,260	47,510	48,761
12	44,953	46,452	47,951	49,449	50,948	52,447	53,946	55,444	56,943	58,442
13	53,456	55,238	57,020	58,802	60,583	62,365	64,147	65,929	67,710	69,492
14	63,169	65,275	67,380	69,486	71,592	73,697	75,803	77,908	80,014	82,120
15	74,304	76,781	79,257	81,734	84,211	86,687	89,164	91,641	94,117	96,594

NOTE: Locality rates of pay are considered basic pay only for certain purposes--see "1997 Salary Tables" cover sheet.

DEPARTMENT OF VETERANS AFFAIRS
HEALTH CARE PROFESSIONAL PAY SCALES

Health care professionals within the Department of Veterans Affairs are paid according to the rates below which differ by profession. Although most are paid at step 1 upon appointment, VA facilities have the authority to offer a higher starting step to applicants if necessary to secure their employment. This authority is granted by OPM according to geographic locale. As in the General Schedule, candidates apply to a specific grade when applying for a position. An applicant pursuing (for example) a Full Grade position will be paid at the starting salary of $40,298 if hired. Non-VA pay rates may vary; see, for example, the special salary rates on page 320.

Physicians

Grade	Minimum Salary for the Grade	Two-Year Periodic Step Increase Amount	Maximum Salary for the Grade
Chief	$79,894	$2,363	$101,161
Senior	69,270	2,009	87,351

Dentists

Grade	Minimum Salary for the Grade	Two-Year Periodic Step Increase Amount	Maximum Salary for the Grade
Chief	$74,394	$2,363	$95,661
Senior	63,770	2,009	81,851
Intermediate	54,503	1,700	69,803

Clinical Podiatrists & Optometrists

Grade	Step 1	2	3	4	5	6	7	8	9	10
Associate	$33,623	34,744	35,865	36,986	38,107	39,228	40,349	41,470	42,591	43,712
Full	40,298	41,641	42,984	44,327	45,670	47,013	48,356	49,699	51,042	52,385
Intermediate	47,920	49,517	51,114	52,711	54,308	55,905	57,502	59,099	60,696	62,293
Senior	56,627	58,515	60,403	62,291	64,179	66,067	67,955	69,843	71,731	73,619
Chief	66,609	68,829	71,049	73,269	75,489	77,709	79,929	82,149	84,369	86,589

Physician's Assistants & Dental Assistants

Grade	Step 1	2	3	4	5	6	7	8	9	10
Junior	$20,443	21,124	21,805	22,486	23,167	23,848	24,529	25,210	25,891	26,572
Associate	23,914	24,711	25,508	26,305	27,102	27,899	28,696	29,493	30,290	31,087
Full	27,789	28,715	29,641	30,567	31,493	32,419	33,345	34,271	35,197	36,123
Intermediate	33,623	34,744	35,865	36,986	38,107	39,228	40,349	41,470	42,591	43,712
Senior	40,298	41,641	42,984	44,327	45,670	47,013	48,356	49,699	51,042	52,385
Chief	47,920	49,517	51,114	52,711	54,308	55,905	57,502	59,099	60,696	62,293
Asst. Director	56,627	58,515	60,403	62,291	64,179	66,067	67,955	69,843	71,731	73,619
Director	66,609	68,829	71,049	73,269	75,489	77,709	79,929	82,149	84,369	86,589

SAMPLE VA NURSES LOCALITY PAY CHART

The Department of Veterans Affairs is currently having severe difficulties recruiting nurses. Consequently, VA nurses are paid on a geographically adjusted pay scale that authorizes different pay rates for each area of the country. Areas where recruiting is extremely difficult have relatively higher pay rates, which correspond closely to the area's top private rates. The following pay schedule illustrates rates in selected areas. A candidate, when hired, would be paid at step 1 of the grade at which he or she applied.

Grade	Step 1	2	3	4	5	6	7	8	9	10	11	12
Charleston, South Carolina												
1	$29,494	$30,378	$31,262	$32,146	$33,030	$33,914	$34,798	$35,682	$36,566	$37,450	$38,334	$39,218
2	37,336	38,456	39,576	40,696	41,816	42,936	44,056	45,176	46,296	47,416	48,536	49,656
3	43,465	44,768	46,071	47,374	48,677	49,980	51,283	52,586	53,889	55,192	46,495	57,796
4	51,376	52,917	54,458	55,999	57,540	59,081	60,622	62,163	63,704	65,245	66,786	68,327
5	74,346	76,576	78,806	81,036	83,266	85,496	87,726	89,956	92,186	94,416	96,646	98,876
Fayetteville, Arkansas												
1	$22,880	$23,566	$24,252	$24,938	$25,624	$26,310	$26,996	$27,682	$28,368	$29,054	$29,740	$30,426
2	35,310	36,369	37,428	38,487	39,546	40,605	41,664	42,723	43,782	44,841	45,900	46,959
3	46,749	48,151	49,553	50,955	52,357	53,759	55,161	56,563	57,965	59,367	60,769	62,171
4	58,312	60,061	61,810	63,559	65,308	67,057	68,806	70,555	72,304	74,053	75,802	77,551
5	67,057	69,068	71,079	73,090	75,101	77,112	79,123	81,134	83,145	85,156	87,167	89,178
Hampton, Virginia												
1	$27,776	$28,609	$29,442	$30,275	$31,108	$31,941	$32,774	$33,607	$34,440	$35,273	$36,106	$36,939
2	36,574	37,671	38,768	39,865	40,962	42,059	43,156	44,253	45,350	46,447	47,544	48,641
3	42,417	43,689	44,961	46,233	47,505	48,777	50,049	51,321	52,593	53,865	55,137	46,409
4	46,237	47,624	49,011	50,398	51,785	53,172	54,559	55,956	57,333	58,720	60,107	61,494
5	69,202	71,278	73,354	75,430	77,506	79,582	81,658	83,734	85,810	87,886	89,962	92,038
Louisville, Kentucky												
1	$28,810	$29,674	$30,538	$31,402	$32,268	$33,130	$33,994	$34,858	$35,722	$36,585	$37,450	$38,314
2	36,295	37,383	38,471	39,559	40,647	41,735	42,823	43,911	44,999	46,087	47,175	48,263
3	42,813	44,097	45,381	46,665	47,949	49,233	50,517	51,801	53,085	54,369	55,653	56,937
4	51,616	53,164	54,712	56,260	57,808	59,356	60,904	62,452	64,000	65,548	67,096	58,644
5	67,050	69,061	71,072	73,083	75,094	77,105	79,116	81,127	83,138	85,149	87,160	89,171
New York City, New York												
1	$40,227	$41,433	$42,639	$43,845	$45,051	$46,257	$47,463	$48,669	$49,875	$51,081	$52,287	$53,493
2	46,477	47,871	49,265	50,659	42,053	53,447	54,841	56,235	57,629	59,023	60,417	61,811
3	50,873	52,399	53,925	55,451	56,977	58,503	60,029	61,555	63,081	64,607	66,133	67,659
4	64,204	66,130	68,056	69,982	71,908	73,834	75,760	77,686	79,612	81,538	83,464	85,390
5	89,779	92,472	95,165	97,858	100,551	103,244	105,937	108,630	111,323	114,016	116,709	119,402
San Francisco, California												
1	$44,609	$45,947	$47,285	$48,623	$49,961	$51,299	$52,637	$53,975	$55,313	$56,651	$57,989	$59,327
2	52,480	54,054	55,628	57,202	58,776	60,350	61,924	63,498	56,072	66,646	68,220	69,794
3	57,203	58,919	60,635	62,351	64,067	65,783	67,499	69,215	70,931	72,647	74,363	76,079
4	62,351	64,221	66,091	67,961	69,831	71,701	73,571	75,441	77,311	79,181	81,051	82,921
4	81,081	83,513	85,945	88,377	90,809	93,241	95,673	98,105	100,537	102,969	105,401	107,833
Tampa, Florida												
1	$27,048	$27,859	$28,670	$29,481	$30,292	$31,103	$31,914	$32,725	$33,536	$34,347	$35,158	$35,969
2	34,387	35,418	36,449	37,480	38,511	39,542	40,573	41,604	42,635	43,666	44,697	45,728
3	43,395	44,696	45,997	47,298	48,599	49,900	51,201	52,502	53,803	55,104	56,405	57,706
4	53,426	55,028	56,630	58,232	59,834	61,436	63,038	64,640	66,242	67,844	69,446	71,048
5	71,057	73,188	75,319	77,450	79,581	81,712	83,843	85,974	88,105	90,236	92,367	94,498

FOREIGN SERVICE PAY CHART

DEPARTMENT OF STATE SALARY CHART EFFECTIVE JANUARY 1, 1996

The Foreign Service Pay Chart is used to determine the pay of Foreign Service personnel whether employed overseas by the Department of State or the Department of Commerce. (Effective the first day of the first applicable pay period beginning on or after January 1, 1996.)

	Class								
	1	2	3	4	5	6	7	8	9
Step 1	$69,300	$56,154	$45,502	$36,870	$29,876	$26,708	$23,876	$21,344	$19,081
Step 2	71,379	57,839	46,867	37,976	30,772	27,509	24,592	21,984	19,653
Step 3	73,520	59,574	48,273	39,115	31,695	28,335	25,330	22,644	20,243
Step 4	75,726	61,361	49,721	40,289	32,646	29,185	26,090	23,323	20,850
Step 5	77,998	63,202	51,213	41,498	33,626	30,060	26,873	24,023	21,476
Step 6	80,338	65,098	52,749	42,742	34,634	30,962	27,679	24,744	22,120
Step 7	82,748	67,051	54,332	44,025	35,674	31,891	28,509	25,486	22,784
Step 8	85,230	69,062	55,962	45,345	36,744	32,847	29,364	26,250	23,467
Step 9	87,787	71,134	57,641	46,706	37,846	33,833	30,245	27,038	24,171
Step 10	90,090	73,268	59,370	48,107	38,981	34,848	31,153	27,849	24,896
Step 11	90,090	75,466	61,151	49,550	40,151	35,893	32,087	28,685	25,643
Step 12	90,090	77,730	62,985	51,037	41,355	36,970	33,050	29,545	26,413
Step 13	90,090	80,062	64,875	52,568	42,596	38,079	34,041	30,431	27,205
Step 14	90,090	82,464	66,821	54,145	43,874	39,222	35,063	31,344	28,021

Foreign Service Officers assigned to domestic positions are entitled to locality-based comparability payments for their respective pay area. The locality pay percentages applied are the same as those applied to the General Schedule which are listed in the 1996 Locality Pay Areas With Respective Rates.

SENIOR FOREIGN SERVICE SCHEDULE

Pay for the Senior Foreign Service is establsihed by the President. The employees' basic pay may not exceed the pay for level IV of the Executive Schedule. In addition to the 1996 basic pay rates listed below, Senior Foreign Service employees are entitled to locality-based comparability payments for their respective pay area. The employees' locality rate of pay may not exceed the pay for level III of the Executive Schedule.

FE-1 .... $94,800
FE-2 99,300
FE-3 103,800
FE-4 109,400
FE-5 114,000
FE-6 115,700

POSTAL SERVICE PAY SCALES

POSTAL SERVICE (PS) SCHEDULE
Full Time Annual Basic Rates
Effective August 30, 1997

Much like the General Schedule, all Postal Service pay scales have grade levels (PS-1 – 10), each of which contains steps. PS steps run from AA to A to B to C to D and so on, up to the letter O. Therefore, an individual might say that he's paid at PS-4, Step J.

Full-time employees are paid by annual salary. The following shows four selected levels, from lowest to highest.

Grade	AA	A	B	C	D	E	F	G	H	I	J	K	L	M	N	O	Prev Step
1	22,090	24,389	28,451	28,515	31,585	31,796	32,007	32,217	32,426	32,637	32,847	33,058	33,269	33,476	33,688	33,898	211
2	22,401	24,737	26,851	28,960	32,093	32,321	32,548	32,775	33,005	33,231	33,459	33,688	33,914	34,144	34,371	34,597	227
3	22,731	25,110	27,277	29,443	32,643	32,888	33,137	33,379	33,627	33,870	34,119	34,363	34,609	34,854	35,100	35,344	249
4		25,077	27,742	29,969	33,240	33,505	33,772	34,038	34,301	34,567	34,833	35,100	35,307	35,632	35,897	36,161	267
5		26,541	29,391	31,679	33,886	34,171	34,458	34,742	35,029	35,314	35,600	35,887	36,171	36,459	36,743	37,029	287
6		28,097	31,141	32,321	34,582	34,893	35,204	35,512	35,824	36,134	36,442	36,754	37,065	37,375	37,688	37,998	311
7		28,680	31,805	33,019	35,337	35,671	36,004	36,339	36,676	37,007	37,343	37,675	38,009	38,345	38,678	39,011	333
8				33,603	36,145	36,508	35,870	37,232	37,597	37,958	38,323	38,683	39,047	39,409	39,770	40,135	365
9				34,420	37,027	37,421	37,812	38,205	38,594	38,985	39,376	39,770	40,160	40,555	40,948	41,338	391
10				35,280	37,958	38,381	38,802	39,226	39,650	40,071	40,494	40,918	41,339	41,763	42,186	42,608	424

Part-Time Regular Employees — Hourly Basic Rates

Grade	AA	A	B	C	D	E	F	G	H	I	J	K	L	M	N	O
1	10.62	11.73	12.72	13.71	15.19	15.29	15.39	15.49	15.59	15.69	15.79	15.89	15.99	16.09	16.20	16.30
2	10.77	11.89	12.91	13.92	15.43	15.54	15.65	15.76	15.87	15.98	16.09	16.20	16.30	16.42	16.52	16.63
3	10.93	12.07	13.11	14.16	15.69	15.81	15.93	16.05	16.17	16.28	16.40	16.52	16.64	16.76	16.88	16.99
4		12.06	13.34	14.41	15.98	16.11	16.24	16.36	16.49	16.62	16.75	16.88	17.00	17.13	17.26	17.39
5		12.76	14.13	15.23	16.29	16.43	16.57	16.70	16.84	16.98	17.12	17.25	17.39	17.53	17.66	17.80
6		13.51	14.97	15.54	16.63	16.78	16.93	17.07	17.22	17.37	17.52	17.67	17.82	17.97	18.12	18.27
7		13.79	15.29	15.87	16.99	17.15	17.31	17.47	17.63	17.79	17.95	18.11	18.27	18.44	18.80	18.76
8				16.16	17.38	17.55	17.73	17.90	18.08	18.25	18.42	18.60	18.77	18.95	19.12	19.30
9				16.55	17.80	17.89	18.18	18.37	18.55	18.74	18.93	19.12	19.31	19.50	19.69	19.87
10				16.96	18.25	18.45	18.65	18.86	19.06	19.26	19.47	19.67	19.87	20.08	20.28	20.48

PART-TIME FLEXIBLE EMPLOYEES — HOURLY BASIC RATES

Since most Postal Service employees start as flexible workers (16–32 hours a week, depending upon the workload of the particular post office where assigned), it is worthwhile to include here selected levels from the current pay schedule for flexibles. The grades and steps are the same as in the salaried schedule, but employees are paid on an hourly basis.

Grade	AA	A	B	C	D	E	F	G	H	I	J	K	L	M	N	O
1	1105	12.19	13.23	14.26	15.79	15.00	16.00	16.11	16.21	16.32	16.42	16.53	16.69	16.74	16.84	16.95
2	11.20	12.37	13.43	14.48	16.05	16.16	16.27	16.39	16.50	16.62	16.73	16.84	16.96	17.07	17.19	17.30
3	11.37	12.56	13.64	14.72	16.32	16.44	16.57	16.69	16.81	16.94	17.06	17.18	17.30	17.43	17.55	17.67
4		12.54	13.87	14.98	16.62	16.76	16.89	17.02	17.15	17.26	17.42	17.55	17.68	17.82	17.95	18.08
5		13.27	14.70	15.84	16.94	17.09	17.23	17.37	17.51	17.66	17.80	17.94	18.09	18.23	18.37	18.51
6		14.05	15.57	16.16	17.29	17.45	17.60	17.76	17.91	18.07	18.22	18.38	18.53	18.69	18.84	19.00
7		14.34	15.90	16.51	17.67	17.84	18.00	18.17	18.34	18.50	18.67	18.84	19.00	19.17	19.34	19.51
8				16.80	18.07	18.25	18.44	18.62	18.80	18.98	19.16	19.34	19.52	19.70	19.89	20.07
9				17.21	18.51	18.71	18.91	19.10	19.30	19.49	19.69	19.89	20.08	20.28	20.47	20.67

Step Income as Waiting Period

Steps (From-To)	AA-A	A-B	B-C	C-D	D-E	E-F	F-G	G-H	H-I	I-J	J-K	K-L	L-M	M-N	N-O	YRS.
Grades 1 - 3	96	96	88	88	44	44	44	44	44	44	34	34	26	26	24	14.9
Grades 4 - 7	90	90		44	44	44	44	44	44	44	34	34	26	26	24	12.4
Grades 8 - 10				52	44	44	44	44	44	44	34	34	26	26	24	8.8

The time between promotions is the same as described for salaried employees. Again the major raises occur at AA – D, with minimal advancements at D – O.

SPECIAL SALARY RATES
(EFFECTIVE JANUARY 1, 1996)
LAW ENFORCEMENT OFFICERS

As a result of the inherent danger of Federal law enforcement work, law enforcement officers are paid on a salary scale separate from and slightly higher than other Federal workers.

Law enforcement officers covered by this pay scale include FBI Agents, DEA Agents, Border Patrol Agents, INS Officers, and other officers discharged with upholding the law.

Grade	Step 1	2	3	4	5	6	7	8	9	10
GS-3	$18,229	$18.735	$19,241	$19,747	$20,253	$20,759	$21,265	$21,771	$22,277	$22,783
GS-4	20,469	21,038	21,607	22,176	22,745	23,314	23,883	24,452	25,021	25,590
GS-5	23,533	24,169	24,805	25,441	26,077	26,713	27,349	27,985	28,621	29,257
GS-6	24,814	25,523	26,232	26,941	27,650	28,359	29,068	29,777	30,486	31,195
GS-7	26,786	27,574	28,362	29,150	29,938	30,726	31,514	32,302	33,090	33,878
GS-8	27,921	28,794	29,667	30,540	31,413	32,286	33,159	34,032	34,905	35,778
GS-9	29,876	30,840	31,804	32,768	33,732	34,696	35,660	36,624	37,588	38,552
GS-10	32,900	33,961	35,022	36,083	37,144	38,205	39,266	40,327	41,388	42,449

MEDICAL OFFICER (NON-VA)

Medical officers who work not for the VA but for the Bureau of Prisons or the Department of Defense are paid according to the following schedule.*

Grade	Step 1	2	3	4	5	6	7	8	9	10
GS-11	$42,591	$43,712	$44,833	$45,954	$47,075	$48,196	$49,317	$50,438	$51,559	$52,680
GS-12	51,042	52,385	53,728	55,071	56,414	57,757	59,100	60,443	61,786	63,129
GS-13	60,696	62,293	63,890	65,487	67,084	68,681	70,278	71,875	73,472	75,069
GS-14	69,843	71,731	73,619	75,507	77,395	79,283	81,171	83,059	84,947	86,835
GS-15	75,489	77,709	79,929	82,149	84,369	86,589	88,809	91,029	93,249	95,469

*For Otisville, Pleasanton, Boron, Terminal Island, Los Angeles, Danbury, and New York City, the salary is increased an additional 8% for interim geographic adjustment.

PHYSICIAN'S ASSISTANT (NON-VA)

Federal physician's assistants working outside of the VA are paid according to the following schedule.*

Grade	Step 1	2	3	4	5	6	7	8	9	10
GS-7	$28,016	$28,773	$29,530	$30,287	$31,044	$31,801	$32,558	$33,315	$34,072	$34,829
GS-9	33,345	34,271	35,197	36,123	37,049	37,975	38,901	39,827	40,753	41,679
GS-11	40,349	41,470	42,591	43,712	44,833	45,954	47,075	48,196	49,317	50,438

*For Otisville, Pleasanton, Boron, Terminal Island, Los Angeles, Danbury, and New York City, the salary is increased an additional 8% for interim geographic adjustment.

WAGE GRADE PAY SYSTEM

The Federal Wage Grade pay system is used to compensate those Federal employees who perform what is traditionally considered "blue-collar" work. The Federal Prevailing Wage Rate Committee determines appropriate pay levels for the different regions of the country. Pay varies by region and is affected by prevailing rates paid in private industry.

The Wage Grade pay system comprises three schedules: Wage Grade, Wage Leader, and Wage Supervisor. The correct pay schedule for a worker is determined by whether he or she is a helper, apprentice, journeyman, leader, or supervisor. **Supervisors** direct all facets of an entire job from start to finish, while **leaders**—often called foremen in the private sector—direct a team of workers in a particular component of the job. **Journeymen** are full-performance workers who can perform their trade without supervision. **Apprentices** are those who are learning the trade. **Helpers** merely provide assistance to journeymen but are not learning the trade.

The Wage Grade schedule has eleven pay levels. The Wage Leader has fifteen pay levels. The Wage Supervisor schedule has nineteen pay levels. Pay level is determined by the job. For example, a Laundry Worker is classified at grade level 2, Laborer at level 3, and Electrician at level 15. A worker is therefore paid according to the appropriate pay level.

Each of these schedules has five steps, which represent time-in-grade pay increases given at fixed time intervals to employees who perform at a satisfactory level. Employees generally begin at step 1.

Each different occupation covered by the Wage Grade system has different levels of pay for helper, apprentice, and journeymen. Not all Wage Grade jobs have helpers or apprentices. For example, an electrician at the full-performance journeyman level is paid at Wage Grade level 11. An Electrician Helper receives compensation at Wage Grade level 1. A Laundry Worker has no helper or apprentice levels.

WASHINGTON, D.C.

Wage Grade	1	$7.58 to $8.58
	2	$8.64 to $10.08
	3	$9.49 to $11.10
	4	$10.39 to $12.12
	5	$11.26 to $13.16
	6	$12.14 to $14.19
	7	$13.01 to $16.16
	9	$14.64 to $17.11
	10	$15.45 to $18.06
	13	$17.89 to $20.87
	14	$20.58 to $24.03
	15	$21.49 to $25.07

WASHINGTON, D.C.

Wage Leader	1	$8.34 to $9.73
	2	$9.50 to $11.09
	3	$10.44 to $12.23
	4	$11.44 to $13.36
	5	$12.38 to $14.46
	6	$13.35 to $14.46
	7	$14.32 to $16.73
	8	$15.29 to $17.82
	9	$16.13 to $18.84
	10	$17.02 to $19.86
	11	$17.90 to $20.91
	12	$18.77 to $21.93
	13	$19.67 to $22.97
	14	$20.58 to $24.03
	15	$21.49 to $25.07

Appendix G: Sample Vacancy Information

This appendix presents samples of three kinds of vacancy-information documents: Qualifications Information Statements, Competition Notices, and Vacancy Announcements.

Qualifications Information Statements (QISs) provide detailed information about a specific occupation or job title, including its duties and responsibilities and the qualifications (both basic and special) sought in candidates. They are usually issued by OPM. To obtain copies of QISs not reproduced in this appendix, contact your local OPM Service Center or any agency that hires employees in those job titles.

Competition Notices are issued by OPM, either locally or nationwide, to indicate that it is accepting applications for a given job title via the procedures cited and during the prescribed period. Some give details about the job; others simply refer the candidate to a QIS. Competition Notices are often used to compile registers.

Vacancy Announcements are issued by individual agencies when they have either immediate or anticipated vacancies, and provide all the information a candidate needs in order to apply.

For more on **Competition Notices,** see Step 3 (p. 70).

Vacancy Announcements are introduced in Step 3 (p. 70) and discussed in detail in Step 4 (pp. 77-83).

The following announcements are representative of many different job titles from a wide range of agencies. Although the particular jobs in the Competition Notices and Vacancy Announcements will have been filled by the time this book goes to press, they are included here because they (1) present a variety of formats and terminology; (2) are indicative of the kinds of jobs that are frequently open; and (3) provide concrete examples of qualifications that are largely consistent over time and among agencies (especially for jobs below GS-9). A perusal of these documents may therefore help you find an appropriate job description and grade level.

Abbreviations: AD, salary is administratively determined, based on the difficulty and duties of the job; ES, Executive Service; GG, General Graded (special designation within FDIC, corresponds to GS); GM, managerial/supervisory position, paid on the GS scale; PG, pay system for jobs with the U.S. Government Printing Office; WL, Wage Leader; WS, Wage Supervisor.

CONTENTS

Accountant/Auditor Positions GS-5/7/9

Qualifications Information Statement
for Accountants, GS-510 and Auditors, GS-511

Each year the Federal Government hires about 1,300 accountants and auditors. About 80 percent are hired at trainee levels (30 percent at grade GS-5 and 50 percent at GS-7). The remaining 20 percent, who fill jobs requiring either experience or graduate education, are hired at grades GS-9, 11 or 12. This announcement explains what the qualification requirements are for jobs at grades GS-5/7/9 and describes how to apply for them.

Most accountants and auditors in the Federal Government do much the same work as those in large corporations in private industry. They design accounting systems and procedures, evaluate financial performance, and assist managers in program management and control.

The occupational specialties covered by this examination are Accountant, classified in the GS-510 series, and Auditor, classified in the GS-511 series. Although the two specialties involve different job duties, the qualification requirements are the same for both at the grade levels covered under this examination.

Some positions, especially those for auditors, require you to travel quite often.

Where the Jobs Are

There are approximately 22,000 accountants and auditors currently working in the Federal Government. Virtually every Federal agency employs at least one accountant or auditor. The agencies with the largest number of jobs are the Departments of the Army (3,000 jobs), Navy (1,500) and Air Force (1,500); various Department of Defense audit agencies (3,000); the Department of Health and Human Services (1,600); the Department of Energy (1,500); the Department of Agriculture (1,300); and the Department of Treasury (1,000). Special application procedures for some of these positions and for some other related positions are described at the end of this pamphlet.

Qualification Requirements

No written test is required. You will be rated on a scale of 70 to 100 based on the extent and quality of your experience and training. For positions in which you meet and deal with people, you may be required to show in an interview that you possess the personal qualities necessary for success in these positions.

Requirements by Grade Level
GS-5

Four full years of study in an accredited college or university which met all of that institution's requirements for a bachelor's or higher degree with a major in accounting

OR

Four full years of study in an accredited college or university which satisfied the requirements for a bachelor's degree and included or was supplemented by 24 semester hours in accounting or auditing subjects (up to 6 semester hours of the 24 may be in business law).

OR

At least 4 years of experience in accounting, which required the application of accounting theories, principles, and practices as evidenced, for example, by: the development or modification of systems, account classifications, or journals; designing financial reports; explaining the significance of financial data to operational concerns; or other work of a comparable nature. Such work must have been analytical or evaluative in nature and demonstrate the ability to apply the concepts, practices, and policies typically required in performing professional accounting work. College level education may be

substituted for experience. In crediting college level education toward the 4-year experience requirement, an academic year (30 semester hours or 45 quarter hours) is equivalent to 1 year of experience.

The background of candidates who qualify under this provision must also include one of the following:

1. Twenty-four semester hours in accounting or auditing courses (up to 6 semester hours may be in business law) of appropriate type and quality (NOTE: Resident or homestudy academic courses conducted by a Federal agency or a non-accredited institution that are determined to be fully equivalent to accounting and auditing courses in an accredited college may be accepted.); or,
2. Certification as a Certified Public Accountant obtained through written examination; or,
3. Recognized, well-established professional stature in a variety of highly responsible accounting functions in positions equivalent to GS-12 or higher, and (b) significant documented contributions to the accounting profession through publications, leadership in professional organizations development of new methods and techniques, or comparable achievements.

Applicants who qualify through a combination of college education and work experience and who meet the 24 semester-hour accounting coursework requirement, may use accounting technician work to meet the experience requirement. The accounting technician experience must include at least one year at the GS-5 or higher level and should indicate a potential for competent performance in a variety of types of professional accounting and auditing positions. Education must include at least 24 semester hours in accounting or auditing courses (up to 6 semester hours may be in business law) of appropriate type and quality.

GS-7

The same requirements for GS-5 PLUS at least 1 year of professional accounting or auditing experience; or 1 full academic year of graduate education in either accounting or auditing or related fields, such as business administration, finance, or controllership, or any equivalent combination of experience and graduate study. Generally, 24 semester hours, or 36 quarter hours, of graduate study is considered an academic year; however, if your school has a different standard, use it in reporting graduate study.

OR

Completion of all requirements for a bachelor's degree (including course requirements) as described for GS-5 and: qualification for Superior Academic Achievement as described below; or 12 months of student trainee experience in accounting or auditing in a work-study curriculum.

GS-9

The same requirements for GS-5 PLUS completion of a Master's Degree or 2 full academic years of graduate education in accounting or auditing or directly related fields, such as those listed under GS-7; or 2 years of additional professional accounting or auditing experience; or any time-equivalent combination of experience and graduate education. The experience must have included at least 1 year at a level of difficulty and responsibility comparable to the GS-7 level in the Federal service.

OR

A bachelor's degree which included or was supplemented by the required courses as described for GS-5, PLUS qualification for Superior Academic Achievement PLUS at least 1 year of subsequent professional accounting or auditing experience at a level comparable to GS-7 in the Federal Service.

Superior Academic Achievement Criteria

1. A "B" average (2.90 on a 4.0 scale—2.89 is not sufficient) for all courses completed at the time of application or for all courses completed during the last 2 years of the undergraduate curriculum; or
2. A "B+" average (3.5 on a 4.0 scale—3.49 is not sufficient) for all courses in accounting or auditing subjects completed at the time of application, or for all courses in accounting and auditing subjects completed during the last 2 years of the undergraduate curriculum; or
3. Standing in the upper third of your class based on completed work at the time of application.

United States
Office of
Personnel
Management

Salary

Federal salary rates are adjusted periodically. Current information regarding salaries may be obtained from Federal Job Information/Testing Centers.

Equal Employment Opportunity

All qualified applicants will receive consideration for appointment without regard to race, religion, color, national origin, sex, age, handicapping condition, political affiliation, or any other non-merit factor.

Where to Obtain Forms

All forms mentioned in this announcement are available from Federal Job Information/Testing Centers, which are located in many large cities across the country. They also have information on such subjects as kinds of appointments; veteran preference; and citizenship, age, and physical requirements. You can also obtain forms by writing the examining office at the address shown below under "Where to File."

How to Apply

There are two methods of applying for a job as an accountant or an auditor at GS-5 through GS-9. The first method is to file an application with the Office of Personnel Management (OPM) and establish eligibility on a list of qualified applicants. Federal agencies that do not keep their own lists of qualified applicants fill their job openings by asking OPM for the applications of the top-ranked candidates on OPM's list.

As only the highest ranking candidates are referred to the agency, it generally does little good to contact an agency until your application has been referred to it. Sometimes, however, there are shortages of candidates in some locales or agencies caused by jobs having special requirements that make them difficult to fill. Such special requirements could be willingness to travel extensively, or the ability to speak a foreign language (usually Spanish). If you meet these special requirements and want to work in a particular agency or installation, contacting that agency or installation's employment office might improve your chances of being offered a job. One of the ways to learn which, if any, agencies or locales have these hard-to-fill jobs is to inquire at a Federal Job Information/Testing Center. The second method of applying is to send your application directly to the agencies that keep their own lists of eligibles. Those agencies are listed at the end of this announcement, immediately preceding the geographic code list.

What to File

1. Standard Form SF-171, Application for Federal Employment. Provide information about professional memberships and offices held, honorary society memberships, or if you are a recent college graduate, about relevant extracurricular activities.
2. College Transcript or OPM Form 1170/17, List of College Courses. If you are sending a transcript of college courses, send it with your application. DO NOT have the school send the transcript directly to the examining office. Show all course titles, credit hours received, and the name of the school. If you are still a student, also include all courses you expect to complete (and the number of credits you expect to receive for them) within nine months of the date that you file your application.

If you are applying for GS-7 or -9 on the basis of superior academic achievement, you must complete part II of OPM Form 1170/17.
3. Occupational Supplement for Accountant/Auditor Positions, Form B (OPM Form 1203-J). Note the specific instructions under "How You Will Be Rated," above, and follow carefully the instructions on the form.
4. SF-15, Claim for 10-Point Veteran Preference. (If applicable)

Where To File

Send your application to:
The Office of Personnel Management
Staffing Service Center Examining Office
Box 9800
Macon, Georgia 31298-2699

This may be the upper third of your class in college or university or major subdivision (e.g., school of business administration); or
4. Election to membership in one of the national scholastic societies that meets the requirements of the Association of College Honor Societies other than freshman honor societies.

NOTE: Applications will be accepted from students who expect to complete, within 9 months, courses that would permit them to meet the requirements of this examination. As a senior student, you may be rated provisionally eligible under 1, or 2, above, if you had the required average in your junior year. You will have to submit evidence at the time of appointment that you maintained the required average in your senior year.

If 10% or more of your undergraduate coursework (credit hours) was graded on a pass/fail or similar basis, you may qualify for Superior Academic Achievement ONLY on the basis of membership in a national honorary scholastic society or class rank. If qualifying on the basis of class standing, you should obtain from an official of your school a letter that verifies your claimed class standing. The agency that hires you will require this letter at the time of appointment.

Foreign Education

Applicants who qualify on the basis of education in foreign colleges or universities are responsible for documenting that their education is equivalent to that provided by an accredited American college or university. The documentation may consist either of evidence that an accredited American college or university has accepted foreign coursework or degree(s) for advanced standing or a statement from a professional academic credential evaluation service or an accredited American college or university that it has evaluated the foreign education and found it to be acceptable.

How You Will Be Rated

Your basic eligibility and ratings for Accountant and Auditor positions at grades GS-5, -7 and -9 will be determined based on your experience, education and training as you describe them on the Occupational Supplement, Form B. Although the basic requirements for Accountants and Auditors are the same, you may receive different ratings for the two specialties if your background of education and experience is more closely related to one job than the other.

Your responses on the Occupational Supplement, Form B, an optical mark recognition form, are electronically scanned and fed into a computer which performs the calculations necessary to arrive at eligibility determinations and ratings for each of the two specialties and three grades you applied for. It is important that you complete the Form B carefully and accurately to assure that you receive proper credit for your education and experience and to avoid delays and lost opportunities for employment which will result if the data you enter on the form is inconsistent or is not clearly reflected in your narrative application forms—the SF-171 and your college transcript or course list.

Length of Eligibility

Once you are rated eligible and assigned ratings, you will be placed on the list of eligibles for one year. You may extend your eligibility by written request to the examining office between the 10th and 12th months of your eligibility. If you have acquired additional education or experience which would qualify you for a higher grade or earn you a higher rating, you may elect to submit a complete new application. Be certain to enter on the Form B both the information originally submitted and any new information.

Students

Applications will be accepted from currently enrolled students who expect to complete the qualifying coursework within nine months after filing their applications. While an agency may offer a job to a student on the basis of that application, the student may not begin work until all courses have been completed successfully.

Some Federal agencies conduct on-campus recruitment for accountants and auditors. For information about scheduled interviews with agency recruiters, students should contact their college's placement office. Many of these offices also have supplies of Federal employment application forms and related materials.

Other Opportunities For Employment in Accountant/Auditor Related Positions

Accountant/Auditor positions at grades GS-11 and above for most agencies are handled on a local basis by the Office of Personnel Management. Contact the Federal Job Information/Testing Center in the area in which you wish to work.

Geographic Code List

From the list below select up to 9 geographic locations where you are willing to accept employment. Indicate your choices by blackening the corresponding circles in the geographic availability item, page 3, item 15, or the Form B. Write "Macon" in the boxes provided for Examining Office.

Note that the State codes DO NOT cover locations within the state for which there are more specific city/county codes. Thus, if you wish to be considered for jobs anywhere in Alabama, select codes 01, 02 and 03. If you are available only for Montgomery, select only code 01. If you are available only for specific locations within the area covered by a code, enter that code and then write your specific geographic preferences in the availability block on page 1 of your SF-171 or in the continuation space on page 4. DO NOT WRITE ON THE FORM B.

Keep this list. You will need it to interpret the geographic codes which will appear on your notice of results to ensure that your choices were correctly entered in the computer.

Geographic Preference Codes for Accountant/Auditor Positions, GS-5/7/9

01	Alabama (all except)	33	Kansas	66	Ohio (all except)
02	Huntsville (Madison Co.)	34	Kentucky (all except)	67	Cleveland (Cuyahoga Co.)
03	Birmingham (Jefferson Co.)	35	Louisville (Jefferson Co.)	68	Dayton (Montgomery/Greene Co.)
04	Alaska	36	Louisiana (all except)	69	Oklahoma (all except)
05	Arizona (all except)	37	New Orleans (Orleans Co.)	70	Oklahoma City (Oklahoma Co.)
06	Phoenix (Maricopa Co.)	38	Maine	71	Oregon (all except)
07	Arkansas	39	Maryland (all except) (excludes D.C. suburbs)	72	Portland (Multnomah Co.)
08	California (all except)	40	Baltimore (Baltimore/Anne Arundel Co.)	73	Pennsylvania (all except)
09	Los Angeles (L.A./San Bernadino/Orange Co.)	41	Massachusetts (all except)	74	Philadelphia (Phila. Co.)
10	San Francisco Bay Area (Alameda/San Francisco Co.)	42	Boston (Suffolk/Middlesex Co.)	75	Chambersburg/Carlisle (Franklin/Cumberland Co.)
11	San Diego (San Diego Co.)	43	Michigan (all except)	76	Puerto Rico, U.S. Virgin Islands and Atlantic Overseas Locations
12	Sacramento (Sacramento Co.)	44	Detroit (Wayne/Macomb/Oakland Co.)	77	Rhode Island
13	Colorado (all except)	45	Minnesota	78	South Carolina (all except)
14	Denver Area (Denver/Boulder/Jefferson Co.)	46	Mississippi	79	Charleston (Charleston Co.)
15	Connecticut	47	Missouri (all except)	80	South Dakota
16	Delaware	48	Kansas City (Platte, Clay, Jackson Co.)	81	Tennessee (all except)
17	District of Columbia (Includes Charles, Montgomery and Prince George's Co. MD, also Arlington, Fairfax, Prince William, King George, Stafford and Loudoun Co. and Alexandria, Falls Church and Fairfax Cities, VA)	49	St. Louis (St. Louis Co.)	82	Memphis (Shelby Co.)
		50	Montana	83	Knoxville/Oak Ridge (Knox/Anderson/Roane Co.)
		51	Nebraska	84	Texas (all except)
		52	Nevada	85	Dallas/Ft. Worth (Dallas/Tarrant Co.)
		53	New Hampshire	86	Houston (Harris Co.)
18	Florida (all except)	54	New Jersey (all except)	87	San Antonio (Bexar Co.)
19	Jacksonville (Duval Co.)	55	Newark (Essex/Hudson Co.)	88	Utah (all except)
20	Miami (Dade Co.)	56	Ft Monmouth (Monmouth Co.)	89	Salt Lake City (Salt Lake/Davis Co.)
21	Pensacola (Escambia Co.)	57	New Mexico (all except)	90	Vermont
22	Georgia (all except)	58	Albuquerque (Bernalillo Co.)	91	Virginia (all except) (excludes D.C. suburbs)
23	Atlanta (Cobb/DeKalb/Fulton Co.)	59	New York (all except)	92	Norfolk/Portsmouth/Hampton/Newport News
24	Macon (Bibb/Houston Co.)	60	Manhattan (New York Co.)	93	Washington (all except)
25	Hawaii and Pacific Overseas	61	Other New York City (Bronx/Kings/Queens/Richmond Co.)	94	Seattle/Bremmerton/Tacoma (King/Kitsap/Pierce Co.)
26	Idaho	62	Long Island (Suffolk/Nassau Co.)	95	West Virginia
27	Illinois (all except)	63	North Carolina (all except)	96	Wisconsin
28	Chicago (Cook/Lake Co.)	64	Fayetteville/Jacksonville (Cumberland/Onslow Co.)	97	Wyoming
29	Rock Island (Rock Island Co.)	65	North Dakota		
30	Indiana (all except)				
31	Indianapolis (Marion Co.)				
32	Iowa				

Biological Sciences Positions, GS-5/7

Qualifications Information Statement

for
- General Biologists, GS-401
- Wildlife Biologists, GS-486
- Microbiologists, GS-403
- Fishery Biologists, GS-482

Qualification Requirements

No written test is required. You will be rated on a scale of 70 to 100 based on the extent and quality of your education and experience.

Requirements by Grade Level

GS-5 — Either A or B, below, satisfies the basic requirements, and is fully qualifying for the GS-5 grade level.

A. Successful completion of all requirements for a Bachelor's or higher degree from an accredited college or university with a major in the biological sciences or a related discipline such as oceanography or biochemistry. Except for the General Biologist option, there are specific coursework requirements for each option which are described in the next section. Degrees in other disciplines are qualifying if the specific coursework requirements are met.

B. A combination of college education and work experience which totalled 4 years and which provided a knowledge of the biological sciences equivalent to a Bachelor's degree in the field. This combination must have included or have been supplemented by the specific coursework required for each option. One academic year of college study (30 semester hours or 45 quarter hours) is equivalent to one calendar year of work experience for purposes of combining the two. The work experience may have been in any biological science discipline, but it must have been progressively responsible and include at least one year (if you need that much experience to qualify) equivalent to GS-4 level work in the Federal service.

GS-7 — One of the following is required in addition to the basic requirement:

A. One year of professional biologist experience. This experience must have been in or closely related to the discipline you are being rated for, and must have been equivalent to GS-5 level work in the Federal Service. Experience as a student-trainee may be used to meet this requirement, provided that it was in an appropriate biology discipline and was integrated with and complementary to your biology curriculum.

B. One academic year (24 semester hours or 36 quarter hours) of graduate study in a biological science discipline related to the specialty you are being rated for.

C. Any time-equivalent combination of A and B, e.g., 12 semester hours of graduate study and 6 months of experience.

D. If you qualify for GS-5 on the basis of a Bachelor's degree, you can qualify for GS-7 by meeting one or more of the following Superior Academic Achievement requirements:

1. A gradepoint average of "B" (2.90 or better on a 4.00 scale — 2.89 is not qualifying) for all courses completed at the time of application or for all courses in the last 2 years of the undergraduate curriculum

2. A gradepoint average of "B +" (3.50 or better on a 4.00 scale) for all courses in a qualifying biology major or for all such courses in the last two years of the undergraduate curriculum.

3. Standing in the upper third of the graduating class in your college or university or one of its major subdivisions, e.g., the School of Arts and Sciences.

4. Election to membership in one of the national scholastic societies which meets the requirements of the Association of College Honor Societies, other than freshman honor societies.

If 10 percent or more of your undergraduate courses were graded on a pass/fail or similar basis, you may not use gradepoint average to meet the Superior Academic Achievement requirements. You may qualify only on the basis of class standing or honor society membership. If you qualify on the basis of class standing, you should obtain an official notice from your school which verifies your class standing. An agency considering hiring you will require this proof at time of appointment.

Requirements by Specialty

General Biologist — There is no specific coursework requirement, but college study must have met the school's requirements for a major in biology or a related discipline, or have included or been supplemented by biology courses at an equivalent rate (6 semester hours per academic year, 24 semester hours for a full 4 year curriculum).

Microbiologist — study must have included at least 30 semester hours in biology, with at least 20 semester hours in microbiology, plus 20 semester hours in mathematics and the physical sciences which included at least one course each in mathematics and physics and one course in either organic chemistry or biochemistry.

Wildlife Biologist — biology courses must total at least 30 semester hours, which must include at least 21 semester hours in a combination of wildlife biology, zoology, genetics and ecology courses, with at least 9 of the 21 semester hours in wildlife biology; and at least 9 semester hours in botany courses.

Fishery Biologist — biology courses must total at least 30 semester hours, which must include at least 18 semester hours in any combination of fishery biology, zoology, and genetics courses with a minimum of 6 semester hours in fishery biology courses.

Applications from Students

Applications will be accepted from currently enrolled students who are within 9 months of completing educational requirements, and credit will be given for projected coursework and for Superior Academic Achievement; but you cannot begin work until you satisfy the hiring agency that you completed any claimed education, including all required courses, and maintained any claimed gradepoint average.

Foreign Education

Applicants who qualify on the basis of education in foreign colleges or universities are responsible for documenting that their education is equivalent to that provided by an accredited American college or university. The documentation may consist either of evidence that an accredited American college or university has accepted foreign coursework or degree for advanced standing or a statement from a professional academic credential evaluation service or an accredited American college that it has evaluated the foreign education and found it to be acceptable.

How You Will Be Rated

Your basic eligibility and numerical rating for the four Biological Science occupations at grades GS-5 and GS-7 will be determined based on your education and experience as you describe them on the Occupational Supplement, Form B. If you apply for more than one specialty, you will probably receive different ratings for each based on how closely related your background of education and experience is to each specialty. Numerical ratings will be the same for both grades in the same specialty.

Your responses on the Occupational Supplement, Form B, an optical mark recognition form, are electronically scanned and fed into a computer which performs the calculations necessary to arrive at eligibility determinations and ratings for each of the four specialties and two grades for which you apply. It is important that you complete the Form B accurately and carefully to assure that you receive proper credit for your education and experience and to avoid delays

United States
Office of
Personnel
Management

and lost opportunities for employment which will result if the data you enter on the form is inconsistent or is not clearly reflected in your narrative application forms — the SF-171 and your college transcript or course list.

Length of Eligibility

Once you are rated eligible and assigned ratings, you will be placed on the list of eligibles for one year from the date you indicate you are first available. You may extend your eligibility by written request to the examining office between the 10th and 12th month of your eligibility. If you have acquired additional education or experience which would qualify you for a higher grade or earn you a higher rating, you may elect to submit a complete new application. Be certain to enter on the Form B both the information originally submitted and any new information.

Salary

Federal salaries are adjusted periodically. Current information may be obtained from Federal Job Information Centers.

Equal Employment Opportunity

All qualified applicants will receive consideration for appointment without regard to race, religion, color, national origin, sex, age, handicapping condition, political affiliation or any other non-merit factor.

Where to Obtain Forms

All forms mentioned in this announcement are available from Federal Job Information Centers, which are located in many large cities across the country. They also have information on such subjects as kinds of appointments, veteran preference, and citizenship, age, and physical requirements. You can also obtain forms by writing the examining office at the address shown below under "Where to File."

How to Apply

Consult the Competition Notice (CN-0400) furnished with the application forms package to learn when applications will be accepted and if there are any restrictions on the specialties and locations for which you may apply. Then complete and submit the application forms following the instructions below. You will receive a Notice of Results, usually within three to four weeks.

Your name will be placed on the list of eligibles for biological sciences positions based on your numerical rating for the various specialties. As vacancies occur in Federal agencies, the highest standing eligibles available for the location and type of appointment will be referred for consideration. As only the highest ranking candidates are referred to the agency, it generally does little good to contact an agency until your application has been referred to it.

What to File

1. Standard Form 171, Application for Federal Employment (older editions are called Personal Qualifications Statement).

2. College transcript or OPM Form 1170/17, List of College Courses. If you elect to send a transcript, send it with your application; DO NOT have the school send the transcript to the examining office. If you fill out the course list, show course numbers and titles and credit hours received. If you attended more than one college, be sure it is clear where each course was taken. Note and follow the instructions on the Occupational Supplement, Form B. about cross-referencing coursework claimed on that form to your course list or transcript. If we cannot verify that you meet educational requirements, processing of your application may be delayed. If you are still in school, you may include courses you expect to complete in the next 9 months.

If you are applying for GS-7 based on Superior Academic Achievement, you must complete the Scholastic Achievement Section of OPM Form 1170/17.

3. Occupational Supplement for Biological Sciences Positions, Form B (OPM Form 1203-I). Read through the form before you start filling it out, and follow the instructions carefully. Be sure that entries on this form are consistent with information on other forms and that you cross-reference where requested to.

4. SF-15, Claim for 10-Point Veteran Preference (if applicable).

Where to File

Send your completed application to:

Office of Personnel Management
Staffing Service Center Examining Office
P. O. Box 9025
Macon, Georgia 31297-4599

Geographic Code List

From the list below select up to 9 geographic locations where you are willing to accept employment. Indicate your choices by blackening the corresponding circles in the geographic availability item, page 4, item 16, on the Form B., which will be sent to you when you are scheduled for the written test.

Note that the State codes DO NOT cover locations within the state for which there are more specific city/county codes. Thus, if you wish to be considered for jobs anywhere in Alabama, select codes 01, 02 and 03. If you are available only for Montgomery, select only code 01. If you are available only for specific locations within the area covered by a code, enter that code and then write your specific geographic preferences in the availability block on page 1 of your SF-171 or in the continuation space on page 4. DO NOT WRITE ON THE FORM B.

Keep this list. You will need it to interpret the geographic codes which will appear on your notice of results to assure that your choices were correctly entered in the computer.

Geographic Preference Codes Biological Sciences Positions, GS-5/7

01	Alabama (all except)
02	Huntsville (Madison Co.)
03	Birmingham (Jefferson Co.)
04	Alaska
05	Arizona (all except)
06	Phoenix (Maricopa Co.)
07	Arkansas
08	California (all except)
09	Los Angeles (LA) San Bernardino/Orange Co.)
10	San Francisco Bay Area (Alameda/San Francisco Co.)
11	San Diego (San Diego Co.)
12	Sacramento (Sacramento Co.)
13	Colorado (all except)
14	Denver Area (Denver/Boulder/Jefferson Co.)
15	Connecticut
16	Delaware
17	District of Columbia (Includes Charles, Montgomery and Prince George's Co. MD, and Arlington, Fairfax, Prince William, King George, Stafford and Loudoun Co. and Alexandria, Falls Church and Fairfax Cities, VA)
18	Florida (all except)
19	Jacksonville (Duval Co.)
20	Miami (Dade Co.)
21	Pensacola (Escambia Co.)
22	Georgia (all except)
23	Atlanta (Cobb/DeKalb/Fulton Co.)
24	Macon (Bibb/Houston Co.)
25	Hawaii and Pacific Overseas
26	Idaho
27	Illinois (all except)
28	Chicago (Cook/Lake Co.)
29	Rock Island (Rock Island Co.)
30	Indiana (all except)
31	Indianapolis (Marion Co.)
32	Iowa
33	Kansas
34	Kentucky (all except)
35	Louisville (Jefferson Co.)
36	Louisiana (all except)
37	New Orleans (Orleans Co.)
38	Maine
39	Maryland (all except) (excludes D.C. suburbs)
40	Baltimore (Baltimore/Anne Arundel Co.)
41	Massachusetts (all except)
42	Boston (Suffolk/Middlesex Co.)
43	Michigan (all except)
44	Detroit (Wayne/Macomb/Oakland Co.)
45	Minnesota
46	Mississippi
47	Missouri (all except)
48	Kansas City (Platte/Clay/Jackson Co.)
49	St. Louis (St. Louis Co.)
50	Montana
51	Nebraska
52	Nevada
53	New Hampshire
54	New Jersey (all except)
55	Newark (Essex/Hudson Co.)
56	Ft. Monmouth (Monmouth Co.)
57	New Mexico (all except)
58	Albuquerque (Bernalillo Co.)
59	New York (all except)
60	Manhattan (New York Co.) Other New York City
61	Bronx/Kings/Queens Richmond Co.)
62	Long Island (Suffolk/Nassau Co.)
63	North Carolina (all except)
64	Fayetteville/Jacksonville (Cumberland/Onslow Co.)
65	North Dakota
66	Ohio (all except)
67	Cleveland (Cuyahoga Co.)
68	Dayton (Montgomery/Greene Co.)
69	Oklahoma (all except)
70	Oklahoma City (Oklahoma Co.)
71	Oregon (all except)
72	Portland (Multnomah Co.)
73	Pennsylvania (all except)
74	Philadelphia (Phila. Co.)
75	Chambersburg/Carlisle (Franklin/Cumberland Co.)
76	Puerto Rico, U.S. Virgin Islands and Atlantic Overseas Locations
77	Rhode Island
78	South Carolina (all except)
79	Charleston (Charleston Co.)
80	South Dakota
81	Tennessee (all except)
82	Memphis (Shelby Co.)
83	Knoxville/Oak Ridge (Knox/Anderson/Roane Co.)
84	Texas (all except)
85	Dallas/Ft. Worth Dallas/Tarrant Co.)
86	Houston (Harris Co.)
87	San Antonio (Bexar Co.)
88	Utah (all except)
89	Salt Lake City (Salt Lake/Davis Co.)
90	Vermont
91	Virginia (all except) (excludes D.C. suburbs)
92	Norfolk/Portsmouth/Hampton/ Newport News
93	Washington (all except)
94	Seattle/Bremerton/Tacoma (King/Kitsap/Pierce Co.)
95	West Virginia
96	Wisconsin
97	Wyoming

BORDER PATROL AGENT
GS-5/7

QUALIFICATIONS INFORMATION STATEMENT

Duties

Border Patrol Agents are employed with the Immigration and Naturalization Service, Department of Justice, and are responsible for administering the immigration and nationality laws of the United States. Agents work to prevent smuggling and illegal entry of aliens into the country. Duties include patrolling areas to apprehend persons seen crossing the border; checking vehicles at check points; and inspecting and searching trains, buses, airplanes, ships, and terminals to determine citizenship and immigration status of passengers. Duties involve physical exertion under rigorous environmental conditions, and often require exposure to extreme weather conditions for extended periods of time.

Location of Positions

Initial duty locations are primarily along the United States - Mexico border in Arizona, California, New Mexico, and Texas. Assignment to a duty location is random. Requests for a preferred location may not be considered. In most instances, you will not be assigned to your hometown or within commuting distance of your hometown. Many posts are located in small, isolated communities.

Age

Public Law 100-238 established a maximum entry age of 37 for Border Patrol Agent positions. An age limitation in hiring established under Public Law 100-238 is regarded as an exception by law to the Age Discrimination in Employment Act.

You must not have passed your 37th birthday at the time you are hired. If you reach your 37th birthday without being hired, your name will be removed from the list of eligibles.

However, if you are over 37, or will shortly reach your 37th birthday, and have previously been employed in a Federal civilian law enforcement position covered under the special retirement provisions of Public Law 100-238, you are not subject to the age restriction. If you served in such a position, you should cite the reason for your exemption from the age restriction in an attachment to your application for the written test.

Qualification Requirements - Border Patrol Agent

Written Test

You must pass the Border Patrol Agent written test that measures your ability to learn and perform the duties of the position. In addition to the written test, there will be a written language test administered to assess individuals' ability to learn the Spanish language. This test is designed for those who have little or no proficiency in the Spanish language. Applicants who are fluent in the Spanish language will be given the choice to take the language test or a Spanish oral test at the time of the employment interview. You must pass either the language or Spanish oral test. You will not be permitted to take both.

General Experience Requirements (GS-5)

You must have had a minimum of one year of qualifying volunteer or paid experience, comparable in level of difficulty and responsibility to GS-4, which demonstrates your ability to perform as a Border Patrol Agent. Your experience, both volunteer and paid, must be clearly stated on the Application for Federal Employment, Standard Form 171, and must demonstrate that you possess the following qualities:

- Ability to take charge, maintain composure, and make sound decisions in stressful situations.

- Ability to learn law enforcement regulations, methods, and techniques through classroom training or on-the-job instruction.

- Ability to establish, maintain, and improve interpersonal relationships with a wide variety of people in all walks of life.

- Ability to gather factual information through questioning, observation, and examination of documents and records.

- Ability to learn to speak and read Spanish.

No additional experience is required for the GS-5 grade level.

Specialized Experience (GS-7 only)

One year of responsible law enforcement experience comparable in level of difficulty and responsibility to a GS-5, that required the exercise of tact, courtesy, and the ability to deal effectively with individuals or groups of persons; demonstrated ability as a competent law enforcement officer, including the ability to exercise sound judgement in the use of firearms; and, that conferred a knowledge of laws, regulations, precedent decisions, and instructions pertaining to law enforcement.

Quality of Experience

Your record of experience and training must show that you have the personal qualities and the abilities necessary for assignments appropriate to the duties and responsibilities of the position. Length of experience is of less importance than demonstrated success in positions of responsibility. Possession of the required length of experience will not by itself be accepted as meeting the experience and training requirements.

Spanish

The ability to read and speak Spanish at a level rated from good to excellent is required upon completion of the one-year probationary period.

Because all Border Patrol Agents must learn to speak and read Spanish, you must pass either the language test or the Spanish oral test. If you have a basic or no knowledge of Spanish, you may wish to take the language test. If you already read and speak Spanish, you may wish to take the oral test to demonstrate your proficiency in the language.

Substitution of Education For General Experience

One full academic year of college study leading to a bachelor's degree may be substituted for 3 months of general experience; 2 years for 6 months of experience; 3 years for 9 months of experience; and, 4 years for the entire year of general experience. Students who expect to complete their studies within nine months from the date of application, and who otherwise meet the requirements of the position, may be rated eligible and selected. However, they may not enter on duty until all educational requirements have been met.

Substitution of Education For Specialized Experience

Successful completion of graduate education in law or in a field related to law enforcement (e.g., police science) may be substituted for specialized experience at the rate of one full-time academic year of study, as defined by the educational institute, for one year of specialized experience.

Superior Academic Achievement

Applicants with a bachelor's degree may qualify for GS-7 if they meet one or more of the following criteria: (1) "B" average (3.00 or higher on a 4.0 scale) for all courses completed at the time of application or for all courses during the last 2 years of the undergraduate curriculum; (2) "B+" average (3.50 or higher on a 4.0 scale) for all courses in a related major field of study or all courses in a related major during the last 2 years of the undergraduate curriculum; (3) Rank in the upper third of the undergraduate class or major subdivision, e.g., School of Business Administration, School of Arts and Sciences; (4) Membership in a national honorary scholastic society (other than freshman society) which meets the requirements of the Association of College Honor Societies. If you qualify under this provision, complete Form OPM 1170/17, List of College Courses and Certificate of Scholastic Achievement. Grade-point averages should be rounded to one decimal place. For example, 2.95 should be rounded to 3.0 and 2.94 should be rounded to 2.9. Students who apply during their senior year may be rated provisionally eligible, but the agency will require proof of the final academic standing before appointment.

Physical Requirements

You must be physically able to perform all of the strenuous duties, under rigorous environmental conditions, involved in being a Border Patrol Agent. Duties require physical stamina in running long distances, climbing, jumping, etc., withstanding exposure to extreme weather conditions for extended periods; and standing/stooping for long periods of time. Irregular and protracted hours of work are required.

You will be required to pass a drug screening test.

Before entering on duty, you must undergo a thorough pre-employment medical examination and be found to be medically able to efficiently perform the duties of the position without hazard to yourself or others. The examination is given by a medical examiner and paid for by the U.S. Government.

A detailed list of the physical requirements may be obtained, if desired, from the Immigration and Naturalization Service, SEU, 425 I St., NW., Room 6023, Washington, D.C. 20536.

Special Requirements

The Border Patrol Agent position requires qualification in the use of firearms. You must demonstrate firearms proficiency for successful completion of training. Failure to do so will result in dismissal.

You must have a valid driver's license when you are hired. After you are hired, you must qualify to operate motor vehicles in accordance with applicable Government regulations.

Employment Interview

If you are selected as a candidate, you must demonstrate that you possess the abilities and characteristics important to Border Patrol Agent positions.

You will be given advance notice of the date and place of your interview and you must appear at your own expense. If, as a result of the interview, it is determined that you lack the qualities necessary for successful performance or you fail the Spanish oral test, you will be given an ineligible rating. (Refer to page 1, section on "Written Test" for additional information.)

Investigation of Suitability

All appointments are subject to a thorough investigation regarding qualifications, loyalty, honesty, integrity, and general characteristics. Evidence of habitual use of intoxicants to excess, disloyalty, moral turpitude, disrespect for law, failure to honor just financial obligations, unethical dealings or material misstatement of fact on the application for employment, and related documents will be considered sufficient reasons for rejection.

Training Progression

Soon after entering on duty, Border Patrol Agents are detailed to the Border Patrol Academy at the Federal Law Enforcement Training Center (FLETC) in Glynco, Georgia, for 18 weeks of intensive instruction in the history and responsibilities of the Service, immigration and nationality laws, Spanish, physical training, marksmanship, and other courses. Failure to successfully complete any part of the basic training program - including Spanish and physical training - will result in termination of employment. Each trainee must successfully complete a one-year probationary period. Post-Academy training will continue to prepare trainees for the probationary examinations, administered at 6-1/2 and 10 months after entry on duty.

Advancement

Initial appointments are at grades GS-5 and GS-7. Upon successful completion of the 6-1/2 month probationary examination, individuals hired at the GS-5 level are eligible for promotion to grade GS-7 and individuals hired at GS-7 are eligible for promotion to GS-9. Career progression to grade GS-9 generally follows after one year at the GS-7 level. Positions above this level are filled through Servicewide competition.

Basis of Rating

You will be rated on the basis of an evaluation of your experience, education and/or training; your written test score; and your success in passing the written language or Spanish oral test.

To receive an eligible rating, you must attain a rating of 70 or above on the written test, meet the experience and/or education requirements specified in this statement, and successfully complete either the written language test or Spanish oral test.

How and Where to Apply

You must obtain an OPM Form 5000-AB, Test Scheduling Card, from any Federal Job Information Center (FJIC) or by calling the College Hotline on 1-900-990-9200. (There is a $.40 a minute charge for the "Hotline" service.) FJIC's are located in principal cities across the country. They are listed under "U.S. Government" in metropolitan area telephone directories. If none is listed in your directory, you can call information for a large metropolitan area or you can contact your nearest State Job Service (or State Employment Security Office.) When completing the OPM Form 5000-AB, be sure to enter the city and state of the test location you prefer. If that location is not available, you will be scheduled at a nearby location. You must send the completed Form 5000-AB to the OPM Area Office servicing the test location which you have chosen. You will be sent other required application forms at the time you receive written notice of when and where to report for the written test.

Equal Employment Opportunity

All qualified applicants will receive consideration for employment without regard to race, color, religion, national origin, sex, or age, except as described above under "Age Restriction".

QUALIFICATIONS INFORMATION STATEMENT GS-300

FOR

CLERK

GS-5 and Above

DESCRIPTION OF DUTIES: The work of a Clerk essentially involves the orderly processing of the paper and performance of the routine work supporting the organization where employed. Among the basic duties performed by the Clerk are: (1) maintaining records; (2) receiving, screening, reviewing and verifying documents; (3) searching for and compiling information and data; (4) providing a central source of information on the activities of the organization orally and by correspondences; (5) preparing and/or verifying the validity of documents with which the organization is concerned.

EXPERIENCE AND EDUCATION REQUIREMENTS: The following table shows total amounts of experience required and allowable substitutions of education for that experience.

GRADE	SPECIALIZED EXPERIENCE	OR	EDUCATION
GS-5	1 year equivalent to GS-4	OR	4 years above high school
GS-6 and Above	1 year equivalent to next lower grade level	OR	Generally not applicable

Specialized experience is directly related to the position to be filled and has equipped the candidate with the particular knowledge, skills, and abilities to successfully perform the duties of that position. To be creditable, specialized experience must have been at least equivalent to the next lower grade level.

EDUCATION: Successfully completed education above the high school level in any field for which high school graduation on the equivalent is a prerequisite may be substituted for experience at grade GS-5. This education must have been obtained in an accredited business, secretarial, or technical school, junior college, college or university. One year of full time academic study is 30 semester hours, or the equivalent, of college or at least 20 hours of classroom instruction per week for approximately 36 weeks in a business, secretarial, or technical school.

Combining Education and Experience: Equivalent combinations of successfully completed education and qualifying experience may be used to meet total experience requirements at grade GS-5.

BASIS OF RATING: No written test is required. Applicants who meet the basic requirements will be rated based on an evaluation of their experience, education, and training as shown on their application forms.

EQUAL EMPLOYMENT OPPORTUNITY: All qualified applicants will receive consideration for employment without regard to race, religion, color, national origin, sex, political affiliation, age or other non-merit factor.

WHAT TO FILE: Application for Federal employment, SF-171; OPM Card Form 5001-BC; List of College Courses, OPM Form 1170/17; if appropriate; SF-15 with documentary proof required if you are claiming 10 point veteran preference (disability, widow, widower, spouse or parent); proof will be returned.

WHERE TO OBTAIN FORMS: You may obtain the required application forms from the U.S. Office of Personnel Management Area Offices at the addresses listed below:

James M. Hanley Federal Bldg.
100 South Clinton Street, Room 841
Syracuse, NY 13260

WHERE TO FILE:

U.S. OFFICE OF PERSONNEL MANAGEMENT
SYRACUSE AREA OFFICE
James M. Hanley Federal Building
100 South Clinton Street, Room 843
Syracuse, New York 13260

Computer Specialist Positions, GS-13, 14, and 15

Qualifications Information Statement

This pamphlet contains qualification requirements for Federal positions requiring computer skills at grades GS-13 through GS-15.

Specific, current information on how to apply, employment opportunities by occupation, geographic location and current salary levels is provided in recruitment information notices issued by U.S. Office of Personnel Management area offices.

You may obtain the application forms from any Federal Job Information/Testing Center (FJITC). These are listed in many cities under "U.S. Government" in the white pages of major metropolitan area telephone directories. You may also get the address of the nearest FJITC by contacting your local State Job Service (or State Employment Service) office.

Description of Work

The persons the Federal Government employs in the computer field advise on, supervise or perform work necessary to design and implement systems for solving problems or accomplishing work processes by the use of digital computers. These positions typically require knowledge of computer requirements and techniques.

There are six types of positions in the computer field in the Federal Government. Those types are described below.

Computer Systems Analysts are concerned with analysis of problems or processes and design of computerized systems for accomplishment of the work...Representative assignments include performance of feasibility studies for proposed computer applications in a subject matter area (e.g., payroll processing, control of incoming aircraft), development of an application's programming specifications, or analysis of existing applications systems to correct problems.

Computer Programmers are concerned with translating system designs into the plans of instructions and logic by which computers can produce the desired actions or products. Knowledge of a particular programming language (e.g., COBOL, FORTRAN) is an important consideration in recruitment for these positions.

Computer Programmer Analysts perform work which is a combination of Computer Systems Analyst and Computer Programmer duties.

Computer Systems Programmers are concerned with systems software. This typically involves maintenance and modification of assemblers, compilers, debugging routines, and similar internal computer programs necessary for the processing of other programs.

Computer Equipment Analysts are concerned with the selection or utilization of computer equipment. These positions do not involve design or repair of equipment. Concern is with the relative merits of equipment items (e.g., mainframe computers, disk memory devices, printers, terminals) and the arrangement of the items into equipment systems as appropriate to an organization's needs.

Computer Specialists perform work of a kind or combination of duties that does not fall under one of the above specializations but does have as the paramount requirement knowledge of computer requirements and techniques.

United States
Office of
Personnel
Management

Basic Qualification Requirements

- No written test is required for these positions.

- Have one year of experience which demonstrates accomplishment of computer project assignments that required a wide range of knowledges of computer requirements and techniques including knowledge of how the work is carried out in other organizations. For example, this level is shown by assignments where the person analyzed a number of alternative approaches in the process of advising management concerning aspects of ADP System design, such as what system configuration must be considered or what operating mode, system software, and/or equipment configuration is the most appropriate for a given project. In addition, the assignments will have involved performance of studies, such as feasibility studies, where alternatives were evaluated, reports prepared, and recommendations made. This one year of experience must have been comparable in difficulty and responsibility to the next lower grade in the Federal service.

General Information

Basis of Rating for Positions at GS-13, GS-14 and GS-15 Levels:

For grades GS-13 and above, applications will be reviewed as vacancies occur for which availability is indicated. You will be evaluated against the specific requirements of those positions and will then be ranked and referred for consideration if you are among the best qualified.

In the application forms, you are asked to indicate your grade level availability and specializations in which you have had substantial experience or education. You will be considered for the grades and occupational areas for which you indicate potential eligibility and availability.

Applicants who are graduates of foreign universities must show they have the required knowledges, skills, and abilities equivalent to that gained in accredited American colleges or universities by submitting one of the following:

1. Proof that the specific courses have been accepted for advanced credit in a subject area by an accredited U.S. college or university; or

2. Proof that a State university (U.S.A.) reports the institution as one whose transcripts are given full value, or full value in subject areas applicable to curricula at the State university; or

3. An evaluation of the coursework from an accredited American college or university or by an organization recognized as specializing in interpretation of foreign educational credentials; or

4. Evidence that clearly justifies a high evaluation of competence, such as a substantial record of experience, achievement, and publication in the appropriate field.

Length of Eligibility: Eligibility will be established for one year from the time you indicate you will be available for employment. Your eligibility will expire on the date shown on the front of your Notice of Results. To extend this period of eligibility, submit any new availability or qualification information during the last two months of your eligibility using the reverse side of your Notice of Results. If there are substantial changes in your qualifications, you should file a new application instead of extending your original eligibility.

Travel Costs: For some positions, the agency that hires you may pay your travel costs and the cost of transporting your household goods and personal belongings to your first post of duty. The agency will inform you whether this is the case.

Special Notice: The U.S. Office of Personnel Management furnishes information on Federal employment opportunities, qualification requirements, and application procedures without charge. Additional information about Federal employment, including Veteran Preference and other matters not included in this Statement, may be obtained from any Federal Job Information/Testing Center.

The U.S. Office of Personnel Management has no connection with any private employment agency or so-called "civil service" school. No "civil service" school or employment agency can guarantee that you will rank high enough on a list of eligible applicants to be offered a job with the Federal Government.

Equal Employment Opportunity: All qualified applicants will receive consideration for employment without regard to race, creed, color, religion, national origin, sex, or age.

United States
Department of
Agriculture

Food Safety
and Inspection
Service

Announcement No.
FSIS-1863-1

Food Inspector

Qualifications Information Statement

GS-1863-5 and 7

* Open Continuously

Description of Work

Food Inspectors in the Federal Government inspect the slaughter and processing of food animals in privately-owned meat or poultry slaughter and processing plants. They ensure that the product is fit for human consumption in compliance with Federal laws governing the wholesomeness and purity of meat and poultry products. This is accomplished through ante-mortem inspection involving a visual examination of the live animal or poultry prior to slaughter, and post-mortem inspection to determine that the product is not contaminated and that sanitation procedures are maintained.

Processing Food Inspectors inspect processed meat and poultry products, and all other ingredients contained in the final product. This includes frozen dinners, canned goods and cured and smoked products.

Federal Food Inspectors work in highly mechanized plant environments near operating machinery with moving parts; with poultry or livestock in confined areas; in extreme temperatures and on slippery floors. The duties often require working with sharp knives, hands in water, moderate lifting, and walking or standing for long periods.

As a Federal Food Inspector, you will be working in an ever-changing environment. Also, as a Federal official, you will be required to uphold the integrity of the regulatory process. You will acquire the skills necessary to balance the industry's desire for productivity against the public's right to protection against unsafe or inferior food products.

Location of Positions

The primary employer of Federal Inspectors is the U.S. Department of Agriculture's Food Safety and Inspection Service (FSIS), employing several hundred inspectors per year. Positions are located throughout the United States and Puerto Rico, at plants ranging from small facilities to large mechanized assembly line operations. Plants are located both in large metropolitan areas, as well as in rural locations, close to animal supply sources.

In addition, the Department of Commerce occasionally employs Food Inspectors at U.S. ports for fish inspection.

Training/Advancement

Most inspectors are trained in the slaughter inspection specialization, while the remainder specialize in processed products inspection. GS-5 level trainees perform the simpler inspection work and receive on-the-job training in the rules, regulations, techniques, and responsibilities of the position. Those assigned to slaughter inspection are trained to detect physical and behavioral abnormalities in live animals; and head, viscera and carcass irregularities that would make products unfit for human consumption. Those specializing in processed products are trained in food sanitation and processing operations, and the theories of public health sanitation applicable to food processing.

Food Inspector positions are filled at the GS-5 or GS-7 grade levels. If you are appointed at the GS-5 level, you will be eligible for promotion to GS-7 after one year of satisfactory performance. Opportunities above GS-7 are available through competitive promotion procedures.

* Certain locations and grades may close periodically. Amendments to this announcement will be available in Federal Job Centers, when locations or grades are closed.

Qualification Requirements

TO QUALIFY FOR THE JOB, YOU MUST PASS A WRITTEN TEST WITH A MINIMUM SCORE OF 70. Information on dates and locations of written tests is in the current amendment to this announcement, available at the address at the bottom of page 3, or at Office of Personnel Management Federal Job Information Centers.

GS-5

In addition to passing the written test, to qualify at GS-5 you must have three years of full-time experience as described below. This experience must have been obtained since your 16th birthday.

Acceptable Experience:

1. Experience with animals gained as a veterinary assistant or in field disease control.

2. Experience with livestock or poultry gained in a public stockyard; in manufacturing or preparing veterinary biological products; on a ranch, farm or hatchery; in poultry or livestock management; or other comparable activity.

3. Experience with livestock or poultry slaughtering/ processing; or in marketing or handling these products at sale points.

4. Experience in dairy, poultry, meat or other food processing settings where sanitation measures and quality controls are applied.

NOTE: Some jobs do not provide the type of experience that can be counted toward this requirement. Such jobs include laborer, guard, driver, or sales clerk positions in the activities described above. Only work directly involved with caring for animals or working with meat products will be credited.

GS-7

To qualify at the GS-7 level, applicants must meet the requirements described above, and must have had an additional year of experience which demonstrates the following knowledges and abilities:

1. Ability to carry out complete ante- and post-mortem inspections of meat animals and poultry; or ability to carry out complete inspections of meat, poultry, and fish processing; AND, regulations pertaining to meat, poultry, and fish processing; AND,

2. Knowledge of Federal laws and regulations pertaining to fitness of animals for human consumption; or, knowledge of Federal laws and

3. Knowledge of general sanitation practices, laws, and regulations governing the food industry; AND,

4. Ability to communicate effectively with supervisors and workers in the food industry.

Substitution of Education:

Satisfactory completion of a full 4-year course of high school study which included at least two 1-year courses in biology, general science, chemistry, appropriate agricultural subjects, or an equivalent combination of these, may be substituted for 1 year of the required experience. The application form (SF-171) must contain specific information about the courses, if they are substituted for experience.

Successfully completed study beyond high school may be substituted at the rate of one year for nine months of the required experience. This study must have included an average of six semester hours (or equivalent) per year in any combination of the following: zoology, biology, chemistry, veterinary medicine, food technology, or appropriate agricultural subjects.

Basis of Rating

Applicants who pass the written test and are eligible at the GS-5 level will be ranked according to their test scores. Applicants who are eligible at the GS-7 level, who pass the written test, will be rated based on an evaluation of experience and training, described in their application and Supplemental Qualifications Statement for Food Inspector.

Physical Requirements

Applicants must be physically and mentally able to efficiently perform the job functions, without hazard to themselves or others. These positions require good vision (including color), hearing, touch, and eye-hand coordination. If the use of a prosthesis or mechanical aid satisfactorily compensates for an impaired function, then applicants may not be automatically disqualified.

Some positions may require a valid state driver's license.

Conflict of Interest Policy

The Food Safety and Inspection Service prohibits the assignment of employees to any establishment where existing circumstances might prevent impartial performance of assigned duties. Such a situation is considered a conflict of interest. The following are specifically prohibited situations:

1. An appointment to perform official inspection or related duties at an establishment where you have been employed for more than 90 days during the past 3 years.

2. An appointment to perform these duties at an establishment, tenant, or subsidiary thereof, from which you receive an annuity or pension.

3. An appointment to any establishment which employs a member of your immediate family (i.e., parent, spouse, child, or sibling) or which employs other family members living in your household. These include immediate family in-laws, stepparents, stepchildren, grandparents and grandchildren.

4. An appointment to any establishment which employs your family member (above) in a supervisory, managerial, or policy making capacity, even if that person does not live in your household.

How to Apply

You will need to pass the written test only once, for both the GS-5 and GS-7 levels. To be scheduled for the test, complete the attached Test Scheduling Card, and submit to:

U.S. Department of Agriculture
Food Safety and Inspection Service
POB, Examining Unit
Butler Square West, 4th Floor
100 North Sixth Street
Minneapolis, MN 55403

FOOD INSPECTOR

1. NAME: (Last, First, MI)	2. DATE OF BIRTH (Month/Day/Year)

3. YOUR ADDRESS (Street and Number or R.D., City, State & ZIP Code)

4. TELEPHONE NO. (Including Area Code)

5. WHERE DO YOU WISH TO TAKE THE WRITTEN TEST?

DATE OF THIS APPLICATION (Month/Day/Year)

EXAM POINT

Form 10180 A

---

1. TITLE OF EXAMINATION	2. ANNOUNCEMENT NO.	3. YOUR TELEPHONE NO.
FOOD INSPECTOR		

4. Check here if you observe the Sabbath or religious holiday on a day other than Sunday (specify day) or have a disability that will require a special or individual testing arrangement. Specify the nature and degree of your disability and the special arrangement you will need. Attach another sheet if needed.

5. IN WHICH LOCATION DO YOU WISH TO TAKE THE TEST? *(City)* *(State)*

Your choice affects when you will be tested

·· SEE TEST CALENDAR.

6. ARE YOU A UNITED STATES CITIZEN?   ☐ YES   ☐ NO
NOTE: Only U.S. Citizens can be tested.

If you have performed active duty in the Armed Forces of the United States and were separated under honorable conditions, indicate periods of service.
From (Mo./Day/Yr.)   To (Mo./Day/Yr.)

Do you claim veteran preference? ☐ No ☐ Yes   If YES, based on:

☐ (1) Active duty in the Armed Forces of the U.S. during wartime or the period April 28, 1952 through July 1, 1955, (2) More than 180 consecutive days of active duty (other than for training) at least part of which must have been served after January 1, 1955 and before October 15, 1976, OR (3) Award of a campaign badge or service medal.

☐ Your Status as (1) A disabled veteran or a veteran who was awarded the Purple Heart for wounds or injuries received in action, (2) A veteran's widow who has not remarried, (3) The wife of an ex-serviceman who has a service-connected disability which disqualifies him for civil appointment, OR (4) The widowed, divorced, or separated mother of an ex-service son or daughter who died in action or who is totally and permanently disabled.

PRINT OR TYPE YOUR NAME AND ADDRESS

APPLICATION FOR WRITTEN TEST

FIRST, MIDDLE AND LAST NAME

NUMBER AND STREET, OR R.D. OR P.O. BOX NO.

CITY, STATE, AND ZIP CODE (required)

See Privacy Act Statement

Form 10180A

DO NOT WRITE IN THIS SPACE

When this card is returned to you, bring it with you when you report for the written test.

Cut along this line

Privacy Act Notice

This information is requested under the authority of sections 1302, 3301, and 3304 of Title 5 of the U.S. Code. These sections require the Office of Personnel Management to conduct examinations for competitive positions in the Federal Service. The information sought will be used to schedule you for a written examination, serve as an admission card to that exam, and to ascertain whether you may be affected by laws determining who may be tested or employed. Other possible uses of the data include disclosure to a source (e.g., former employer or a school) who is requested to furnish information about you that will assist in determining whether to hire you; to a Federal, state, or local agency for checking on law violations; or to the courts where the Government is a party to suits. Your social security number (SSN) is requested under authority of Executive Order 9397 which requires agencies to use the SSN as the means of identifying individuals in Government information systems. The furnishing of this information is voluntary.

How to Apply (continued)

Indicate only ONE test location in Block 5 of the application. Test Scheduling Cards must be postmarked no later than the first of the month preceding the month of the desired test. Applicants will be notified of the time and location approximately two weeks before the test is to be given. Application forms will be sent to you with the test confirmation. You must complete the forms and bring them with you to the test to be admitted. After the test, the results will be mailed to you. If you pass the test, and meet the experience and/or education requirements, your name will be placed on the List of Eligibles as discussed above. You will receive consideration for employment for a one year period, during which time the test may not be retaken.

General Information

Special Notice: The Office of Personnel Management has no connection with any private employment agency, so-called "civil service" school, or published study guide for Food Inspector. No "civil service" school, employment agency, or publication can guarantee that you will rank high enough on a list of eligible applicants to be offered a job with the Federal Government.

Equal Employment Opportunity: All qualified applicants will receive consideration for employment without regard to race, creed, color, religion, national origin, sex, age, or other nonmerit factors.

Mathematicians and Related Positions, GS-5/7

Qualifications Information Statement

This pamphlet contains the qualification requirements for Federal positions in mathematics and related fields at grades GS-5 and 7. The specific occupations are Actuary, Computer Scientist, Mathematician, Mathematical Statistician, Operations Research Analyst, and Statistician. Record your occupational specialty choices and qualification information on the Occupational Supplement for Mathematicians and Related Positions - 1500-X, Form B.

Current information on how to apply and salary levels is provided in the Competition Notice for Mathematicians and Related Positions (CN-1500). In some cases, positions in the occupations listed in this Statement may be filled by direct application to Federal agencies. Consult the Competition Notice or the Federal Job Information Center (FJIC) in the area where you wish to work to learn more about these opportunities.

You may obtain the Competition Notice and application forms from any FJIC. These are located in many cities across the country, and are listed under "U.S. Government" in the blue pages of major metropolitan area telephone directories. You may also get the address of the nearest FJIC by contacting your local State Job Service (or State Employment Security) Office.

Actuary (010)

Actuaries perform professional work in which they make use of mathematics and statistics, a knowledge of the economy, and sound financial and business methods. Their work relates statistical information on populations and their behavior to life, health, employment, and property risks and contingencies. From this information, insurance risks, premiums, and reserve funds for social insurance or annuity programs are developed. Actuaries also develop data to be used in projecting and planning the budget and operational needs of insurance programs.

Basic Qualifications Requirements for Actuary positions:

A. A Bachelor's or higher degree in an accredited college or university which includes course work in mathematics totaling at least 24 semester hours. The courses in mathematics must have included differential and integral calculus and, in addition, one or more courses in mathematics for which these courses are prerequisite, and 9 semester hours in statistics; or

B. Four years of progressive technical experience in actuarial support work or in mathematics, or an equivalent combination of education and experience. The experience or the combination of education and experience must include or been supplemented by either: (1) attainment of 60 credits for Society of Actuary (SOA) courses, or the successful completion of two actuarial examinations given by the Casualty Actuarial Society (CAS); or, (2) at least 24 semester hours in actuarial science, mathematics, and statistics as described above.

United States
Office of
Personnel
Management

Additional requirements: For grade GS-7 positions, to credit professional level experience, applicants must have a full 4-year course of study of the type described in paragraph A above.

Alternate requirements: For grade GS-7, a course of study as described in paragraph A and (1) attainment of 60 credits for SOA courses, or (2) successful completion of two of the CAS examinations.

Computer Scientist (020)

Computer Scientists perform primarily professional research or development work to evolve new concepts, methods, and techniques to store, manipulate, transform, and present information by means of digital computer systems. Such work embraces a wide range of activities that are either concerned with the development of new fields of computer science research or are responsive to problems arising from use of digital computers within the Federal service.

Basic Qualifications Requirements for Computer Scientist Positions:

* A Bachelor's or higher degree in an accredited college or university with a course of study that includes or was supplemented by 30 semester hours of course work in a combination of mathematics, statistics, and computer science that provided a thorough knowledge of the theoretical foundations and practical applications of computer science. At least 15 of the 30 semester hours must be in any combination of statistics and mathematics which included differential and integral calculus.

Mathematician (030)

Mathematicians plan, direct, conduct or assist in the performance of scientific, analytical or developmental work or basic or applied research in the field of mathematics.

Basic Qualification Requirements for Mathematician Positions:

* A Bachelor's or higher degree in an accredited college or university in mathematics or in a course of study that includes or was supplemented by 24 semester hours in mathematics; or

* A combination of education and experience which includes course work equivalent to a major in mathematics. The education and experience combined must total at least 4 years.

In either case, the coursework must have included differential and integral calculus and, in addition, four advanced mathematics courses which require calculus or equivalent mathematics courses as a prerequisite.

Mathematical Statistician (040)

Mathematical statisticians perform professional work involving the development and adaptation of mathematical statistical theory and methodology for a wide variety of statistical investigations. They investigate and evaluate the applicability, efficiency, and accuracy of the theory and methods used by subject-matter specialists or other statisticians in various statistical programs and studies. They usually have only incidental concern for the subject matter involved.

Basic Qualifications Requirements for Mathematical Statistician Positions:

* A Bachelor's or higher degree in an accredited college or university which includes 24 semester hours of course work in mathematics and statistics, of which at least 12 semester hours are in mathematics and 6 semester hours are in statistics; or

• A combination of education and experience which includes course work as described above. The education and experience combined must total at least 4 years.

Courses acceptable toward meeting the mathematics course requirement for qualifying under either provision must have included at least four of the following: Differential Calculus, Integral Calculus, Advanced Calculus, Theory of Equations, Vector Analysis, Advanced Algebra, Linear Algebra, Mathematical Logic, Differential Equations, or any other advanced course in mathematics for which one of these is a prerequisite. Courses in mathematical statistics or probability theory with a prerequisite of elementary calculus or more advanced courses will be accepted toward meeting the mathematics requirements, but the same course cannot be counted toward both the mathematics and the statistics requirement.

Any experience used in a combination with coursework to meet the above requirements should include evidence of professional statistical work (e.g., sampling; collecting, computing and analyzing statistical data; and, applying statistical techniques to data such as measurement of central tendency, dispersion, skewness, sampling error, simple and multiple correlation, analysis of variance and tests of significance). Work required in the processing of numerical or quantified information by other than statistical methods is not considered qualifying.

Operations Research Analyst (050)

Operations research analysts perform professional and scientific work requiring the design, development and adaptation of mathematical, statistical, and other scientific methods to analyze operational problems of decision-makers. Operations research analysts develop and conduct analytic studies to provide advice and evaluations of the probable effects of alternative solutions to these problems. The primary requirement of the work is competence in the rigorous methods of scientific inquiry and analysis rather than in the subject matter of the problem.

Basic Qualifications Requirements for Operations Research Analyst Positions:
• A Bachelor's or higher degree in an accredited college or university which includes 24 semester hours of course work in any combination of the following: operations research, mathematics, statistics, logic, and subject-matter courses which require substantial competence in mathematics or statistics.

Statistician (060)

Statisticians do professional work or provide professional consultation requiring the application of statistical theory and technique in the collection, compilation, analysis and interpretation of quantitative information in a variety of subject-matter fields including the biological, social, and physical sciences, engineering, agriculture, and administration.

Basic Qualifications Requirements for Statistician Positions:
• A Bachelor's or higher degree in an accredited college or university which includes 15 semester hours of course work in statistics (or in mathematics and statistics, provided 6 hours are in statistics), and 9 additional hours in one of the following: the physical or biological sciences, medicine, education or engineering; or in the social sciences including demography, history, economics, social welfare, geography, international relations, social or cultural anthropology, health sociology, political science, public administration, psychology, etc. Credit toward meeting statistical course requirements will be given for courses in which 50 percent of the course content appears to be statistical method, e.g., courses which include studies in research methods in psychology or economics such as tests and measurements or business cycles, or

courses in methods of processing mass statistical data such as tabulating methods or electronic data processing; or

• Coursework as described above, plus additional appropriate experience or education which, when combined with these courses, will total 4 years of education and experience.

The experience offered in combination with specified educational courses should include evidence of professional statistical work such as (1) sampling; (2) collecting, computing and analyzing statistical data; (3) applying known statistical techniques to data such as measurement of central tendency, dispersion, skewness, sampling error, simple and multiple correlation, analysis of variance and tests of significance.

Qualification Requirements for All Positions by Grade Level

GS-5 Positions:
• The basic requirements, as defined for each occupation, are fully qualifying at this level.
• Additionally, a graduate degree in the field (with or without an undergraduate degree that meets the basic requirements) is fully qualifying at this level.

GS-7 Positions: In addition to meeting the requirements for GS-5:
• One year of professional experience in an appropriate field comparable in difficulty and responsibility to GS-5 level work in the Federal service; or,
• One full academic year (as defined by the college or university) of graduate education in an appropriate field. (For Statistician positions only. When substituting graduate education for experience, the education must have included a course in statistical or related theory for which a knowledge of calculus is required.)
• Completion of all requirements for a Bachelor's Degree which meet one of the following Superior Academic Achievement standards:

1. A standing in the upper third of your college class or major subdivision (e.g., school of arts and sciences) at the time you apply;
2. A grade average of "B" (3.0 on a 4.0 scale) or its equivalent for all courses completed; (a) at the time of application; or (b) during the last 2 years of your undergraduate curriculum;
3. A "B+" (3.5 on a 4.0 scale) average or its equivalent for all courses completed in a qualifying major field of study, either: (a) at the time of application; or (b) during the last 2 years of your undergraduate curriculum; or
4. Election to membership in one of the national honorary societies (other than freshman societies) that meets the requirements of the Association of College Honor Societies.

If you apply based on Superior Academic Achievement, you must complete page 3, item 14, "Superior Academic Achievement," on the Occupational Supplement for Mathematicians and Related Positions - 1500X (Form B).

If more than 10 percent of your courses were taken on a pass/fail basis, your claim must be based on class standing or membership in an honorary society.

NOTE: Senior students, whose eligibility is based on all courses completed at the time of application (either 3.0 overall or 3.5 in the major field) are **not** required to submit evidence that they maintained the required average during their senior year. They may

Length of Eligibility: Eligibility will be established for 6 months from the time you are processed into the system. Your eligibility will expire on the date shown on the front of your Notice of Results (NOR). You may extend your period of eligibility if there are no changes in your qualifications by using the reverse side of your NOR and submitting it to the examining office identified on the NOR. If there are changes in your qualifications, you must file a new application.

Applications From Students: Application will be accepted from students who expect to complete any qualifying course work within the next 9 months. When filing the Form B, students should include course work they expect to complete within 9 months.

Travel Costs: For some positions, the agency that hires you may pay your travel costs and the cost of transporting your household goods and personal belongings to your first post of duty. The agency will inform you whether this is the case.

Special Notice: The Office of Personnel Management furnishes information on Federal employment opportunities, qualifications requirements, and application procedures without charge. Additional information about Federal employment, including Veteran Preference and other matters not included in this Statement, may be obtained from any Federal Job Information Center.

Civil Service Schools: The Office of Personnel Management has no connection with any private employment agency or so-called "civil service" school. No "civil service" school or employment agency can guarantee that you will rank high enough on a list of eligible applicants to be offered a job with the Federal Government.

Equal Employment Opportunity: All qualified applicants will receive consideration for employment without regard to race, creed, religion, national origin, sex, or age.

Geographic Availability: You will need the Geographic Code Listing, OPM Form 1205, to indicate your choices in item 4, "Geographic Availability", on the Form B. You may select one Zone and up to 9 geographic locations within the Zone where you wish employment consideration. If you wish to be considered for locations outside your selected zone, you must complete a separate Form B indicating the zone and the location(s).

For example, if you are interested in working in Alabama, which is in the Atlanta Zone, and Louisiana, which is in the Dallas Zone, you must complete a separate Form B for each zone. On the Atlanta application, if you are willing to work anywhere in Alabama, enter code 001; if you are interested in working only in northern Alabama, enter 002; or if you are available only in Birmingham, enter 004.

Note: If you have an overseas address and are unable to enter it as a deliverable address on page 2 of the Form B, enter instead an address in the United States where your mail can be sent.

---

be appointed on the basis of the average maintained during the first 3 years of college course work. On the other hand, senior students whose eligibility is based on courses completed during the final two years of the undergraduate curriculum (either 3.0 overall or 3.5 in the major field) may be rated provisionally eligible provided that they had the required average through their junior year. Evidence that the required average was maintained during the senior year will be required before an individual enters on duty.

General Provisions: The following provisions apply in crediting education or experience for any grade:

- For all grades, qualifying experience may be either paid or volunteer experience.

- Time spent in military service may be credited as an extension of experience gained immediately prior to entering the service or it may be credited on its own merits, whichever is more favorable.

- In order to qualify for most positions in research, development, evaluation or similar creative activities, completion of a full 4-year curriculum in an accredited college leading to a Bachelor's Degree in an appropriate field will normally be required.

General Information

Basis of Rating: No written test is required. If eligible, you will be assigned a numerical rating based on your qualifications (experience and education) as stated on the Form B. In the application forms you are asked to indicate your grade level availability and occupational specialties in which you believe you are qualified and wish to be considered. You will be considered by agencies for positions at the grade level(s) and occupational specialties selected. You should contact the OPM register holding office (or offices if you have eligibility with more than one office) if you decide that you are no longer available for a grade or discipline. *NOTE:* At the time of consideration for a position you will be asked to provide a copy of your SF 171, Application for Federal Employment, and OPM Form 1170/17, College Course List, or a resume that provides similar information to verify your claimed qualifications.

Foreign Education: Applicants who are graduates of foreign universities must show they have the required knowledges, skills, and abilities equivalent to that gained in accredited American colleges or universities by submitting one of the following:

1. Proof that the specific courses have been accepted for advanced credit in an appropriate subject area by an accredited U.S. college or university;

2. Proof that a State university in the U.S. reports the institution as one whose transcript is given full value or full value in subject areas applicable to curricula at the State university;

3. Proof the academic credit earned through a special credit program (e.g., College Level Examination Program) has been awarded by an accredited college, university, or institution;

4. Proof the courses have been evaluated and approved by a State department of education for a specific number of semester or quarter hours; or

5. Proof the course work was evaluated by an organization recognized for accreditation by the Council on Post secondary Accreditation as specializing in interpretation of foreign educational credentials.

For Grades GS-9 and Above: Contact the examining office having jurisdiction over the position for which you are applying.

Physical Sciences Positions, GS-5/7

Qualifications Information Statement

This pamphlet contains qualification requirements for Federal positions at grades GS-5 and GS-7 in the physical sciences. The *List of Disciplinary Fields and Occupational Specialties* on the last page of this pamphlet shows all of the disciplines and specialties covered, and may be used to record your academic major(s) and occupational choices on the application Form B.

Specific, current information on how to apply, employment opportunities by occupation and geographic location, and current salary levels is provided in the Competition Notice for Physical Sciences Positions (CN-1300). In some cases, positions in the occupations listed in this Statement may be filled by direct application to Federal agencies. Consult the Competition Notice or the Federal Job Information Center (FJIC) in the area where you wish to work to learn more about these opportunities.

You may obtain the Competition Notice and application forms from any FJIC. These are located in many cities across the country, and are listed under "U.S. Government" in the blue pages of major metropolitan area telephone directories. You may also get the address of the nearest FJIC by contacting your local State Job Service (or State Employment Security) Office.

Basic Qualification Requirements Applicable to All Positions and Grades

- Completion of a full 4-year or longer professional curriculum in an accredited college or university leading to a Bachelor's Degree with specific study in an appropriate field; or

- Completion of courses in an accredited college or university, consisting of lectures, recitations, and appropriate practical laboratory work in the specific field for which you are applying, plus appropriate practical experience or education which when combined with the coursework totals 4 years of education and experience. This combination must have provided technical and professional knowledge comparable to that acquired through successful completion of a 4-year college course. (For some positions, 4 years of appropriate experience, usually with proof of licensing, registration, or certification, is qualifying.)

Specific Coursework Requirements by Occupation

Astronomer and Space Scientist (010-018): a degree in one or any combination of astronomy, physics, mathematics, space science, or electronics which included courses in differential and integral calculus and 12 semester hours in astronomy and/or physics.

Cartographer (020-026): a degree in cartography or a major which includes or was supplemented by at least 30 semester hours in cartography and/or directly related sciences and related mathematics. Such course work includes, but is not limited to, astronomy, cartography, geodesy, photogrammetry, physical and geological oceanography, computer sciences, land surveying, geophysics, physical geography, and remote sensing. The 30 semester hours must include at least 6, but no more than 15 semester hours of college level, nonbusiness mathematics and statistics.

Chemist (030-052): a degree in a physical science, life science, or engineering which includes 30 semester hours in chemistry. The 30 semester hours must include 6 semester hours of physics and mathematics through differential and integral calculus.

General Physical Scientist (060-072): (These positions involve a combination of several physical science fields with no one predominant or a specialized field of physical science not identified with any other listed disciplines.) a degree in a physical science, engineering or mathematics that includes 24 semester hours in physical science and/or closely related engineering science such as mechanics, dynamics, properties of materials, or electronics.

Geodesist (080-083): a degree in geodesy or 30 semester hours in any combination of geodesy, mathematics, physics, astronomy, engineering science, surveying, geodetic surveying, photogrammetry, or geophysics. The coursework must have included differential and integral calculus.

Geologist (090-119): a degree in geology plus 20 additional semester hours in any combination of mathematics, physics, chemistry, biological science, structural, chemical, civil, mining or petroleum engineering, computer science, planetary geology, comparative planetology, geophysics, meteorology, hydrology, oceanography, physical geography, marine geology, and cartography.

Geophysicist (130-142): a degree which includes at least 30 semester hours in mathematics (including calculus), and the physical sciences (geophysics, physics, engineering, geology, astronomy, meteorology, electronics, etc.).

Health Physicist (150): a degree in a natural science or engineering which includes at least 30 semester hours in health physics, engineering, radiological science, chemistry, physics, biology, mathematics, and/or calculus. *Alternative to the above coursework:* Certification as a health physicist by the American Board of Health Physics plus appropriate experience and other education which provided an understanding of sciences applicable to health physics.

Hydrologist (160-170): a degree in a physical or natural science, or engineering, which includes at least 30 semester hours in any combination of courses in hydrology, the physical sciences, geophysics, chemistry, engineering science, soils, mathematics, aquatic biology, atmospheric science, meteorology, geology, oceanography, or the management or conservation of water resources. The coursework must include at least 6 semester hours in calculus (including both differential and integral calculus), and at least 6 semester hours in physics.

Land Surveyor (180): a degree in land surveying or civil engineering with a surveying option/emphasis. A civil engineering major must include at least 6 semester hours of surveying, 3 semester hours of land law, and 21 additional semester hours in any combination of the following: surveying, photogrammetry, geodetic surveying, geodesy, route surveying, remote sensing, cartography, survey astronomy, land information systems, computer aided mapping, aerial photo interpretation, and survey analysis and adjustments. *Alternative to the above coursework:* Current registration as a land

United States
Office of
Personnel
Management

surveyor in a State, Territory, or the District of Columbia, obtained through written examination, which meets the guidelines outlined in the National Council of Engineering Examiners (NCEE) Unified Model Law for Registration of Surveyors. Registrations granted prior to adoption of the Unified Law by the State, Territory, or the District of Columbia are not acceptable. To be considered equivalent to the NCEE Model law, registration laws must include the four options listed within the NCEE Unified Model Law in the section specifying "General Requirements for Registration" as a Professional Land Surveyor.

Metallurgist (190-192): a degree in metallurgy or metallurgical engineering which includes at least 20 semester hours in metallurgical subjects.

Oceanographer (200-209): a degree in oceanography or a major which includes 24 semester hours in oceanography or a related discipline such as physics, meteorology, geophysics, mathematics, chemistry, engineering, geology, or biology, plus 20 additional semester hours in any combination of oceanography, physics, geophysics, chemistry, mathematics, meteorology, computer science, and engineering sciences. Applicants who qualify on the basis of a major study in biology or geology must have at least 6 semester hours in the major directly concerned with marine science or 6 semester hours in oceanography; applicants who qualify on the basis of other physical science or engineering, must show differential and integral calculus and at least 6 semester hours in physics.

Physicist (220-243): a degree in physics or any degree with at least 24 semester hours in physics. The courses must include a fundamental course in general physics and, in addition, courses in any two of the following: electricity and magnetism, heat, light, mechanics, modern physics, and sound.

Qualification Requirements for All Positions by Grade Level

GS-5: The basic requirements are fully qualifying for GS-5 positions.

GS-7: The basic requirements for GS-5 plus one of the following:

- One year of professional experience in an appropriate field comparable in difficulty and responsibility to GS-5 level work in the Federal service; or

- One full academic year of graduate education in the appropriate field; or

- Completion of all requirements for a Bachelor's Degree which meets one of the following *Superior Academic Achievement* standards:

1. A standing in the upper third of your college class or major subdivision (e.g. school of arts and sciences) at the time you apply;

2. A grade average of 'B' (3.0 on a 4.0 scale) or its equivalent for all courses completed: (a) at the time of application; or (b) during the last 2 years of your undergraduate curriculum;

3. A 'B+' (3.5 on a 4.0 scale) average or its equivalent for all courses completed in a qualifying major field of study, either: (a) at the time of application; or (b) during the last 2 years of your undergraduate curriculum; or

4. Election to membership in one of the national honorary societies (other than freshman societies) that meets the requirements of the Association of College Honor Societies.

If you qualify on the basis of Superior Academic Achievement, you must complete page 3, item 14, "Superior Academic Achievement" on the Form B.

If more than 10 percent of your courses were taken on a pass/fail basis, your claim must be based on class standing or membership in an honorary society.

Note: Senior students, whose eligibility is based on all courses completed at the time of application (either 3.0 overall or 3.5 in the major field) are **not** required to submit evidence that they maintained the required average during their senior year. They may be appointed on the basis of the average maintained during the first 3 years of college course work. On the other hand, senior students whose eligibility is based on courses completed during the final two years of the undergraduate curriculum (either 3.0 overall or 3.5 in the major field) may be rated provisionally eligible provided that they had the required average through their junior year. Evidence that the required average was maintained during the senior year will be required before an individual enters on duty.

General Provisions: The provisions listed below apply in crediting education or experience for either grade:

- Qualifying experience may be either paid or volunteer experience.

- Time spent in military service may be credited as an extension of experience gained immediately prior to entering the service or it may be credited on its own merits, whichever is more favorable.

- In order to qualify for most positions in research, development, evaluation or similar creative activities, completion of a full 4-year curriculum in an accredited college leading to a Bachelor's Degree in an appropriate field will normally be required.

Patent Examiner/Advisor

In most cases, applicants qualify for patent examiner or patent advisor positions, if they meet the qualifications requirements for a physical sciences occupation. Professional experience in the examination or prosecution of patent application may be substituted for professional experience in physical sciences. In addition, to the basic requirements, the following substitutions of education or experience are allowed in qualifying for GS-7 only:

- One year of experience as a patent searcher for registered patent attorneys or agents;

- At least 6 full years of study leading to a J.D., LL.B. or higher degree from a recognized school of law; or

- Membership in the Bar of any State, Territory, or the District of Columbia.

To indicate availability for Patent Examiner or Advisor positions, mark the appropriate response in item 18, "Specialized Experience/Education," under Specialized Job Functions on the Form B. Patent Examiner/Advisor positions in engineering specializations are filled under the examining program for Professional Engineering positions.

General Information

Basis of Rating: No written test is required. If qualified for grades GS-5 or 7, you will be assigned a numerical rating and your name will be referred to hiring agencies in the order of your standing on a competitor inventory. Referrals to specific vacancies will be based on an evaluation of your experience, education, and training as shown on your Form B. NOTE: At the time of consideration for a position you will be asked to provide a copy of your SF 171, Application for Federal Employment, and OPM Form 1170/17, College Course List, or a resume that provides similar information to verify your claimed qualifications.

On the Form B, you are asked to indicate your grade level availability and occupational specialties in which you have had substantial experience or education. You will be

For example, if you are interested in working in Alabama which is in the Atlanta Zone and Louisiana which is in the Dallas Zone, you must complete a separate Form B for each zone. On the Atlanta application, if you were available anywhere in Alabama, you would enter code 001; if you were interested in working only in northern Alabama, you would enter code 002; or, if you were willing to work only in Birmingham, you would enter 004.

Note: If you have an overseas address and are unable to enter it as a deliverable address on page 2 of the Form B, enter instead an address in the United States where your mail can be sent.

List of Disciplinary Fields and Occupational Specialties

You may select any combination of 10 specialties and/or subspecialties from the list below. Indicate in item 16 on the Form B your choices of specialties for which you wish to be considered. Be sure to answer the seven questions for each specialty you have chosen.

Retain this list. You will need it to interpret your Notice of Results to ensure that the codes which have been entered in the computer file are the ones you selected and wish to be considered.

010 ASTRONOMY AND SPACE SCIENCE
011 Astrophysics
012 Celestial Mechanics
013 Photoelectric Photometry
014 Radioastronomy
015 Solar and Planetary Astronomy
016 Space Environment
017 Stellar Science
018 Stellar Studies

020 CARTOGRAPHY
021 Cartographic Programming
022 Image Processing
023 Photogrammetry
024 Photography
025 Photointerpretation
026 Remote Sensing

030 CHEMISTRY
031 Agricultural Chemistry
032 Analytical Chemistry
033 Biological Chemistry
034 Clinical Chemistry
035 Electron Microscopy
036 Enzymology
037 Forensic Chemistry
038 Genetics
039 General
040 Inorganic Chemistry
041 Immunology
042 Instrumentation
043 Metabolism
044 Neurological
045 Organic Chemistry
046 Physical Chemistry
047 Polymer Chemistry
048 Nuclear Chemistry
049 Radio Chemistry
050 Spectroscopy
052 Toxics

060 GENERAL PHYSICAL SCIENCE
061 Engineering Science
062 Environmental Science
063 Air Programs
064 Environmental Health
065 Geologic/Hydrologic
066 Environmental Impact - Water Quality
067 Environmental Pollution
   Monitoring/Regulatory Controls
068 Environmental Protection Technology
069 Hazardous Waste
070 Remote Sensing
071 Radiation (Radon)

072 Water Programs

080 GEODESY
081 Field Surveying
082 Physical Geodesy
083 Satellite Geodesy

090 GEOLOGY
091 Aerial Geology
092 Conservation Paleontology
093 Economic Geology
094 Engineering Geology
095 Environmental Geology
096 Geographic Information
   Computer Systems
097 Geomorphology
098 Geomorphology
100 Igneous Petrology
101 Marine Geology
102 Metamorphic Petrology
103 Mineralogy
104 Mineralogy and Crystallography
105 Mining
106 Neo-Tectonics
107 Organic Fuels
108 Paleontology
109 Petrology
110 Petrology
111 Planetary Geology
112 Quaternary Geology
113 Remote Sensing
114 Sedimentation
115 Sedimentary Petrology
116 Seismology
117 Structural Geology
118 Tectonic Geomorphology
119 Volcanology

130 GEOPHYSICS
131 Earthquake Seismology
132 Engineering Geophysics
133 Exploration Geophysics
134 Exploratory Seismology
135 Geophysical Instrumentation
136 Gravity
137 Magnetism
138 Satellites
139 Seismology
140 Solid-Earth Geophysics
141 Tectonic Physics

**150 HEALTH PHYSICS
(ALL SPECIALIZATIONS)**

160 HYDROLOGY
161 Aqueous Geochemistry
162 Erosion and Sedimentation
163 Evaporation and Transpiration
164 Flood Forecasting
165 Ground Water
166 Precipitation
167 Snow, Ice, and Permafrost
168 Surface Waters
169 Water Quality
170 Watershed Management

**180 LAND SURVEYING
(ALL SPECIALIZATIONS)**

190 METALLURGY
191 Extractive
192 Physical

200 OCEANOGRAPHY
201 Biological Oceanography
202 Geological Oceanography
203 Descriptive Oceanography
204 Ocean Bottom Processes
205 Physical Oceanography
206 Remote Sensing
207 Seabed
208 Surface and Near-Shore Process
209 Underwater Sound

220 PHYSICS
221 Acoustics
222 Atomic and Molecular Physics
223 Basic Properties of Materials
224 Chemical Physics
225 Chemical Physics
226 Electromagnetism
227 Electronic Components and Circuitry
228 Elementary Particles and Fields
229 Fluids and Gases
230 Heat
231 Instrumentation
232 Laser
233 Mathematical Physics
234 Mechanics
235 Microwave Physical Electronics
236 Nuclear Physics
237 Optical Physics
238 Plasma Physics
239 Quantum Physics
240 Radiology
241 Solar Physics
242 Solid State Physics
243 Thin-Film Circuitry

---

considered for the grades and occupational areas for which you indicate potential eligibility and availability.

Foreign Education: Applicants who are graduates of foreign universities must show the required knowledges, skills, and abilities equivalent to that gained in accredited American colleges or universities by submitting one of the following:

1. Proof that the specific courses have been accepted for advanced credit in an appropriate subject area by an accredited U.S. college or university;

2. Proof that a State university in the U.S. reports the institution as one whose transcript is given full value or full value in subject areas applicable to curricula at the State university;

3. Proof the academic credit earned through a special credit program (e.g., College Level Examination Program) has been awarded by an accredited college, university, or institution;

4. Proof the courses have been evaluated and approved by a State department of education for a specific number of semester or quarter hours; or

5. Proof the course work was evaluated by an organization recognized for accreditation by the Council on Post secondary Accreditation as specializing in interpretation of foreign educational credentials.

For Grades GS-9 and Above: Contact the examining office having jurisdiction over the position for which you are applying.

Length of Eligibility: Eligibility will be established for 6 months from the time you are processed into the system. Your eligibility will expire on the date shown on the front of your Notice of Results (NOR). You may extend your period of eligibility if there are no changes in your qualifications by using the reverse side of your NOR and submitting it to the examining office identified on the NOR. If there are changes in your qualifications, you must file a new application.

Applications from Students: Applications will be accepted from students who expect to complete courses that would permit them to meet the requirements for positions covered by this statement within the next 9 months. When filling out the Form B, students should include the courses they expect to complete within 9 months.

Travel Costs: For some positions, the agency that hires you may pay your travel costs and cost of transporting your household goods and personal belonging to your first post of duty. The agency will inform you whether this is the case.

Special Notice: The Office of Personnel Management furnishes information on Federal employment opportunities, qualifications requirements, and application procedures without charge. Additional information about Federal employment, including Veteran Preference and other matters not included in this statement, may be obtained from any Federal Job Information Center.

Civil Service Schools: The Office of Personnel Management has no connection with any private employment agency or so-called "civil service" school. No "civil service" school or employment agency can guarantee that you will rank high enough on a list of eligible applicants to be offered a job with the Federal Government.

Equal Employment Opportunity: All qualified applicants will receive consideration for employment without regard to race, creed, color, religion, national origin, sex, or age.

Geographic Availability: You will need the Geographic Code Listing, OPM Form 1205, to indicate your choices in item 4, "Geographic Availability," on the Form B. You may select one Zone and up to 9 geographic locations within the Zone where you wish employment consideration. If you wish to be considered for locations in other zones, you must complete a separate Form B indicating the zone and the location(s).

Professional Engineering Positions GS-5/7

Qualifications Information Statement

This pamphlet contains the qualification requirements for Federal positions at grades GS-5 and GS-7 requiring professional engineering skills. The *List of Disciplinary Fields and Occupational Specialties* at the end of this statement shows all of the disciplines and specialties covered, and is used to record your academic major(s) and occupational choices on the *Occupational Supplement for Professional Engineering Positions* - 0800-X, Form B.

Current information on how to apply and salary levels is provided in the *Competition Notice for Professional Engineering Positions* (CN-0800). In many cases, positions in the professional engineering occupations may be filled by direct application to Federal agencies. Consult the Competition Notice or the Federal Job Information Center (FJIC) in the area where you wish to work to learn more about these opportunities.

You may obtain the Competition Notice and application forms from any FJIC. These are located in many cities across the country, and are listed under "U.S. Government" in the blue pages of major metropolitan area telephone directories. You may also get the address of the nearest FJIC by contacting your local State Job Service (or State Employment Security) Office.

Basic Qualification Requirements

The primary method of qualifying for professional engineering positions is through successful completion of a full 4-year professional engineering curriculum (not engineering technology) leading to a bachelor's or higher degree in engineering in an accredited college or university. To be acceptable, the curriculum must:

- Be in a school of engineering with at least one curriculum accredited by the Accreditation Board for Engineering and Technology (ABET) as a professional engineering curriculum, or

- Include differential and integral calculus and courses (more advanced than first-year science or engineering) in five of the seven areas of engineering science or physics: (a) statics, dynamics; (b) strength of materials (stress-strain relationships); (c) fluid mechanics, hydraulics; (d) thermodynamics; (e) electrical fields and circuits; (f) nature and properties of materials (relating particle and aggregate structure to properties); (g) any other comparable area of fundamental engineering science or physics, such as optics, heat transfer, soil mechanics, or electronics.

Alternate Methods of Qualifying

If you do not meet the basic engineering requirements above, you may qualify for entry-level positions if you have four years of experience or an equivalent combination of education and experience that meets the requirements listed below.

Candidates may substitute for the basic requirement of at least 4 years of college-level education, training and/or technical experience that furnished (1) a thorough knowledge of the physical and mathematical sciences underlying professional engineering, and (2) a good understanding, both theoretical and practical, of the engineering sciences and techniques and their application to one of the branches of engineering. This knowledge and understanding must be equivalent to that provided by a full 4-year professional engineering curriculum with respect to (a) the knowledge, skills, and abilities required to perform professional engineering work in the specialty field of the position to be filled, and (b) the ability to develop and progress in a career as a professional engineer in the specialty field. The adequacy of such background must be demonstrated by one of the following:

- *Professional Registration:* Current registration as a professional engineer by any State, Guam, Puerto Rico or the District of Columbia. Absent other means of qualifying for engineering positions, those candidates who achieved such registration by means other than written test (for example, State grandfather or eminence provisions) are eligible only for positions that are within or closely related to the specialty field of their registration. For example, a candidate who attains registration through a State Board's eminence provision as a manufacturing engineer typically would be eligible only for manufacturing engineering positions.

- *Written Test:* Evidence of having successfully passed the Engineer-in-Training (EIT) examination or the written test required for professional registration, which is administered by the Boards of Engineering Examiners in the various States, District of Columbia, Puerto Rico and Guam.

Candidates who pass the EIT examination and complete all the requirements for a bachelor's degree in engineering technology (BET) that: a. included 60 semester hours of courses in the physical, mathematical and engineering sciences and in engineering as listed in the basic requirements; or, b. was in an accredited college or in a program accredited by the Accreditation Board for Engineering and Technology (ABET), may be eligible for certain engineering positions at GS-5. Eligibility is limited to positions that are within or closely related to the specialty field of the engineering technology program. Positions covered by the minimum educational requirement, which involve highly technical research, development, or similar functions requiring an advanced level of competence in basic science are excluded.

Because of the diversity in kind and quality of BET programs, graduates of other BET programs are required to complete at least one year of additional education or highly technical work experience of such nature as to provide reasonable assurance of the possession of the knowledge, skills, and abilities required for professional engineering competence. The adequacy of this background must be demonstrated by passing the EIT examination.

- *Specified Academic Courses:* Successful completion in an accredited college or university of at least 60 semester hours of courses acceptable for credit toward a B.S. in professional engineering, in the physical, mathematical and engineering sciences. These must have included the courses specified in the basic requirement above. The courses must also be fully acceptable toward meeting the requirements of a professional engineering curriculum as described in the basic requirements.

- *Related Curriculum:* Successful completion in an accredited college of a full 4-year or longer related curriculum leading to a bachelor's or higher degree in engineering technology or in an appropriate professional field, for example, physics, chemistry, architecture, computer science (not computer programming), mathematics, hydrology, or geology, may be accepted in lieu of a degree in engineering provided you have at least 1 year of professional engineering experience which was acquired under professional engineering supervision and guidance.

- *Completion of Advanced Engineering Degree:* Successful completion of an advanced degree in engineering which reflects the possession of the basic principals, concepts, and theories of professional engineering.

Qualification Requirements by Grade Level

GS-5: The basic requirements are fully qualifying for GS-5 positions.

GS-7: In addition to meeting the requirements for GS-5:

- One year of professional experience in an appropriate field comparable in difficulty and responsibility to GS-5 level work in the Federal service (if you have a professional engineering degree, up to 12 months of appropriate experience gained

United States
Office of
Personnel
Management

as a technician or technologist equivalent to the GS-5 level or higher, may be credited in qualifying for GS-7 engineer);

- One full academic year, or completion of the equivalent 30 semester hours, of graduate education in an appropriate field;

- Successful completion of a 5-year program of study (i.e., one designed to be completed in no less than 5 years) of at least 160 semester hours leading to a bachelor's degree in engineering in an accredited college or university;

- One year of appropriate student trainee experience or work experience in a cooperative work-study educational curriculum; or

- Completion of all requirements for a bachelor's degree that, by itself, is fully qualifying for the position (not a B.S. in engineering technology) which meets one of the following *Superior Academic Achievement* standards:

1. A standing in the upper third of your class or major subdivision (e.g., school of engineering) at the time you apply.

2. A grade average of "B" (3.0 of a possible 4.0) or its equivalent for all courses completed: (a) at the time of application; or (b) during the last 2 years of your undergraduate curriculum;

3. A "B+" (3.5 of a 4.0) average or its equivalent for all courses completed in a qualifying major field of study, either: (a) at the time of application; or (b) during the last 2 years of your undergraduate curriculum; or

4. Election to membership in one of the national honorary societies (other than freshman societies) that meet the requirements of the Association of College Honor Societies.

If you qualify on the basis of Superior Academic Achievement, you must complete page 3, item 14, "Superior Academic Achievement" on the Form B.

If more than 10 percent of your courses were taken on a pass/fail basis, your claim must be based on class standing or membership in an honorary society.

Note: Senior students, whose eligibility is based on all courses completed at the time of application (either 3.0 overall or 3.5 in the major field) are not required to submit evidence that they maintained the required average during their senior year. They may be appointed on the basis of the average maintained during the first 3 years of college course work.

On the other hand, senior students whose eligibility is based on courses completed during the final two years of the undergraduate curriculum (either 3.0 overall or 3.5 in the major field) may be rated provisionally eligible provided that they had the required average through their junior year. Evidence that the required average was maintained during the senior year will be required before an individual enters on duty.

General Provisions: The provisions listed below apply in crediting education or experience for either grade:

- For all grades, qualifying experience may be either paid or volunteer experience.

- Time spent in military service may be credited as an extension of experience gained immediately prior to entering the service or it may be credited on its own merits, whichever is more favorable.

- In order to qualify for most positions in research, development, evaluation or similar creative activities, completion of a full 4-year curriculum in an accredited college leading to a Bachelor's degree in an appropriate field will normally be required.

Patent Examiner/Advisor

In most cases, applicants qualify for patent examiner or patent advisor positions if they meet the qualification requirements for an engineering occupation. Professional experience in the examination or prosecution of patent applications may be substituted for engineering experience. In addition to the basic requirements, the following substitutions of education or experience are allowed in qualifying for GS-7 only:

- One year of experience as a patent searcher for registered patent attorneys or agents;

- At least 6 full years of study leading to a J.D., LL.B., or higher degree from a recognized school of law; or

- Membership in the Bar of any State, Territory, or the District of Columbia.

To indicate availability for Patent Examiner or Advisor positions, mark the appropriate response in item 18, "Specialized Experience/Education," under Specialized Job Functions on the Form B. Patent Examiner/Advisor positions in physical science specializations are filled under the examining program for Physical Science positions.

NOTE: Virtually all Patent Examiner/Advisor openings are in Washington, D.C. There are Patent Advisor positions in locations across the country, but there are very few vacancies.

General Information

Basis of Rating: No written test is required. If qualified for grades GS-5 or -7, you will be assigned numerical ratings and your name will be referred to hiring agencies in order of your standing on a competitor inventory. Referrals to specific vacancies will be based on or an evaluation of your experience, education, and training as shown on your Form B. NOTE: At the time of consideration for a position you will be asked to provide a copy of your SF 171, Application for Federal Employment, and OPM Form 1170/17, College Course List, or a resume that provides similar information to verify your claimed qualifications.

On the Form B, you are asked to indicate your grade level availability and occupational specialties in which you have had substantial experience or education. You will be considered for the grades and occupational areas for which you indicate potential eligibility and availability.

Foreign Education: Applicants who are graduates of foreign universities must show the required knowledges, skills, and abilities equivalent to that gained in accredited American colleges or universities by submitting one of the following:

1. Proof that the specific courses have been accepted for advanced credit in an appropriate subject area by an accredited U.S. college or university;

2. Proof that a State university in the U.S. reports the institution as one whose transcript is given full value or full value in subject areas applicable to curricula at the State university;

3. Proof that the academic credit earned through a special credit program (e.g., College Level Examination Program) has been awarded by an accredited college, university, or institution;

4. Proof the courses have been evaluated and approved by a State department of education for a specific number of semester or quarter hours; or

5. Proof the course work was evaluated by an organization recognized for accreditation by the Council on Post Secondary Accreditation as specializing in interpretation of foreign educational credentials.

For Grades GS-9 and Above: Contact the examining office having jurisdiction over the position for which you are applying.

Length of Eligibility: Eligibility will be established for 6 months from the time you are processed into the system. Your eligibility will expire on the date shown on the front of your Notice of Results (NOR). You may extend your period of eligibility if there are no changes in your qualifications by using the reverse side of your NOR and submitting it to the examining office identified on the NOR. If there are changes in your qualifications, you must file a new application.

Applications From Students: Applications will be accepted from students who expect to complete courses that would permit them to meet the requirements for positions covered by this statement within the next 9 months. When filling out the Form B, students should include the courses they expect to complete within 9 months.

Travel Costs: For some positions the agency that hires you **may** pay your travel costs and the cost of transporting your household goods and personal belongings to your first post of duty. The agency will inform you whether this is the case.

Special Notice: The Office of Personnel Management (OPM) furnishes information on Federal employment opportunities, qualifications requirements, and application procedures without charge. Additional information about Federal employment, including Veteran Preference and other matters not included in this Statement, may be obtained from any Federal Job Information Center.

Civil Service Schools: The Office of Personnel Management has no connection with any private employment agency or so-called "civil service" school. No "civil service" school or employment agency can guarantee that you will rank high enough on a list of eligible applicants to be offered a job with the Federal Government.

Equal Employment Opportunity: All qualified applicants will receive consideration for employment without regard to race, creed, color, religion, national origin, sex, or age.

Geographic Availability: You will need the Geographic Code Listing, OPM Form 1205, to indicate your choices in item 4, "Geographic Availability," on the Form B. You may select one Zone and up to 9 geographic locations within the Zone where you wish employment consideration. If you wish to be considered for locations outside your selected zone, you must complete a separate Form B indicating the zone and the location(s).

For example, if you are interested in working in Alabama, which is in the Atlanta Zone, and Louisiana, which is in the Dallas Zone, you must complete a separate Form B for each zone. On the Atlanta application, if you are willing to work anywhere in Alabama, enter code 001; if you will work only in northern Alabama, enter 002; or if you are willing to accept a job only in Birmingham, enter 004.

NOTE: If you have an overseas address and are unable to enter it as a deliverable address on page 2 of the Form B, enter instead an address in the United States where your mail can be sent.

List of Disciplinary Fields and Occupational Specialties

You may select any combination of 10 specialties and/or subspecialties from the list on page 6. Indicate in item 16 on the Form B your choices of specialties for which you wish to be considered. Be sure to answer the seven questions for each specialty you have chosen.

Retain this list. You will need it to interpret your Notice of Results to ensure that the codes which have been entered in the computer file are the ones you selected and wish to be considered.

LIST OF DISCIPLINARY FIELDS AND OCCUPATIONAL SPECIALTIES

010 AEROSPACE ENGINEERING
011 Aerodynamics
012 Aircraft/Airframe Systems/Structures
013 Aircraft Maintenance/Repair/Rework
014 Control and Guidance Systems
015 Flight Mechanics
016 Fluid Mechanics
017 Ground Support Equipment
018 Instrumentation (Aircraft)
019 Missile and Spacecraft Systems/Structures
020 Navigation and Guidance
021 Propulsion and Power
022 Stability, Control and Performance
023 Structural Dynamics/Aerodynamics
024 Theoretical Simulation Techniques

030 AGRICULTURAL ENGINEERING
(All Specializations)

040 BIOMEDICAL ENGINEERING
(All Specializations)

050 CERAMICS ENGINEERING
(All Specializations)

060 CHEMICAL ENGINEERING
061 Combustion
062 Electro-Chemistry
063 Heat and Fluid Flow
064 Instrumentation (Chemical Process)
065 Mass Transfer
066 Materials and Processing Engineering
067 Plant Design and Economics
068 Plastics, Polymers Coatings, Corrosion Control

070 CIVIL ENGINEERING
071 Structural Systems
072 City Planning
073 Hydraulic Structures
074 Plant and Facilities
075 Transportation Systems
076 Surveying and Mapping
077 Waterways, Harbors, Sea Platforms

080 COMPUTER ENGINEERING
081 Adaptive Software
082 Artificial Intelligence
083 Hardware
084 Information Structures
085 Systems Architecture/Design

090 ELECTRICAL ENGINEERING
091 Automatic Machinery
092 Instrumentation (Electrical Control)
093 Power Generation
094 Power Transmission/Distribution
095 Shipboard Electrical Systems
096 Solar Cells
097 Utilities/Facilities

100 ELECTRONIC ENGINEERING
101 Antennas and Propagation
102 Aerospace Test Equipment
103 Avionics
104 Circuit Theory
105 Command/Control Systems
106 Display Systems
107 Electro Acoustics
108 Electronic Device Circuitry
109 Electronic Instrumentation
110 Electro-Optics/Infrared
111 Fire Control Systems
112 Guidance Systems
113 Information Theory
114 IFF Systems
115 Integrated Circuits
116 Lasers
117 Logic Design/Circuitry
118 Medical Electronic Equipment
119 Microelectronics
120 Microwave
121 Navigation Systems
122 Pollution Monitoring Devices/Systems
123 Radar
124 Radio Communications
125 Semiconductor
126 Sensors/Transducers
127 Servomechanics
128 Shipboard Electronic Equipment
131 Simulated Training Devices
132 Solid State Devices
133 Sonar
134 Switching Systems
135 Tactical Data Systems
136 Telecommunications
137 Test Instrumentation
138 Transmitters/Receivers
141 Transmitter/Vacuum Tubes
142 Video Equipment
143 Wire Communications

150 ENVIRONMENTAL ENGINEERING
151 Air Pollution
152 Food Sanitation
153 Industrial Effluents
154 Noise Pollution
155 Solution Cost Monitoring
156 Sewage/Waste Disposal
157 Solid Waste Disposal
158 Water Pollution
159 Water Supply and Treatment

160 FIRE PREVENTION ENGINEERING
(All Specializations)

170 INDUSTRIAL ENGINEERING
171 Computer Assisted Design
172 Data Management System
173 Human Engineering/Ergonomics
174 Logistics
175 Materials Handling
176 Methods and Standards
177 Operations Analysis
178 Plant Layout
179 Production Planning
180 Quality Assurance/Control
181 Reliability
182 Safety Procedures
183 Test Range Operations
184 Time and Motion Study
185 Value Engineering
186 Work Simplification

190 MATERIALS ENGINEERING
191 Aerospace Metals
192 Aerospace Polymers
193 Ceramics
194 Construction Materials
195 Engineering Properties
196 Metals
197 Nonmetallic Inorganic
198 Nonmetallic Organic
199 Pavements
200 Petroleum
201 Physical Properties
202 Plastics
203 Refractory Compounds

210 MECHANICAL ENGINEERING
211 Air Conditioning
212 Actuation
213 Automotive Systems
214 Construction Equipment
215 Cranes and Hoists
216 Environmental Testing
217 Gas Turbines
218 Gear and Energy Resources
219 Heating and Ventilation
220 Heat Transfer
221 Hydraulic/Pneumatic Systems
222 Industrial Packaging/Preservation
223 Lubrication and Friction
224 Machinery and Machine Tools
225 Marine
226 Manufacturing
227 Ordnance/Weapon Systems
228 Power Plants
229 Pumps/Valves Theory
231 Shock/Vibration, Acoustics
232 Stress Analysis
233 Thermal Control
234 Tools and Gauges
235 Utility Systems/Facilities
236 Thermodynamics/Instrumentation

240 MINING ENGINEERING
241 Beneficiation
242 Coal
243 Health and Safety
244 Iron Ore
245 Non-Ferrous Metal Ores
247 Structures
248 Uranium and Radioactive Ores

250 NAVAL ARCHITECTURE
(All Specializations)

260 NUCLEAR ENGINEERING
261 Nuclear Production
262 Nuclear Explosive Effects
263 Nuclear Medicine
264 Nuclear Power Generation
265 Nuclear Power Supplies

270 OCEAN ENGINEERING
271 Deep Submergence Devices
272 Docks, Pontoons and Sea Platforms
273 Ocean Floor Studies
274 Ocean Wave Theory
275 Wave Wave Dynamics
276 Waterways and Harbors

280 PETROLEUM ENGINEERING
281 Asphalt Materials
282 Crude Petroleum
283 Liquefied Gas
284 Natural Gas
285 Refinery Products

290 SAFETY ENGINEERING
(All Specializations)

300 WELDING ENGINEERING
(All Specializations)

U.S. OFFICE OF PERSONNEL MANAGEMENT
NEW YORK CITY AREA OFFICE
Jacob K. Javits Federal Building
26 Federal Plaza
New York, New York 10278

QUALIFICATIONS INFORMATION SHEET
FOR
SECRETARY
GS-318

For current salary rates see the General Information Sheet for applicants.

Applications are being accepted only for the grade(s) and location(s) specified on the Federal Job Opportunities Listing.

DUTIES: Secretaries assist one or more persons by performing general office work auxiliary to the work of the organization. They serve as the principal office clerical or administrative support assistant in the office, operating independently of any other such position. The work requires knowledge of clerical and administrative procedures and requirements; various office skills, and the ability to apply such skills in a way that increases the effectiveness of others.

MINIMUM QUALIFICATION REQUIREMENTS: Applicants must have one year of specialized experience equivalent to the next lower grade in the Federal service which is in or directly related to the position to be filled and which has equipped the candidate with the particular knowledges, skills, and abilities to perform the duties of the position successfully. Positions at the lower grade levels consist primarily of clerical and procedural duties, while at the higher grades administrative support functions are more predominant.

NONQUALIFYING EXPERIENCE: Experience which has been limited to routine clerical work--such as referring telephone calls and visitors as a receptionist, timekeeping, simple filing and retrieving specifically requested data from files, typing--is not qualifying for Secretary positions at grade GS-5 and above.

SUBSTITUTION OF EDUCATION FOR EXPERIENCE: At the GS-5 level only, four years of successfully completed education above the high school level in any field may be substituted for the required specialized experience. The education must have been obtained in an accredited business, secretarial or technical school, junior college, college, or university. One full year of full-time academic study is 30 semester hours, 45 quarter hours, or the equivalent, of college, or at least 20 hours of classroom instruction per week for approximately 36 weeks in a business, secretarial, or technical school. Only education in excess of the first 60 semester hours (i.e., beyond the second year) is creditable toward meeting the specialized experience requirement; one full academic year of study (30 semester hours or the equivalent) beyond the second year is equivalent to six months of specialized experience. Education may not be substituted for the experience required at grades GS-6 and above.

PROFICIENCY REQUIREMENTS: For positions requiring TYPING (40 words per minute based on a five-minute sample with three or fewer errors) or STENOGRAPHY (40 words per minute typing speed AND 80 words per minute dictation speed), applicants must show possession of the required level of proficiency by (A) passing the appropriate performance test, (B) presenting a certificate of proficiency from a school or other organization authorized to issue such certificates, or (C) by self-certifying their proficiency. Federal agencies may verify proficiency skills of self-certified applicants by administering the appropriate performance test.

BASIS OF RATING: No written test is required. Applicants who meet the minimum qualifications will be rated on the degree to which they show possession of each of the following knowledges, skills, and abilities required by the position:

OPM-PHILADELPHIA REGION

1. Ability to Organize Effectively the Flow of Clerical Processes in an Office.
2. Ability to Design, Organize, and Use a Filing System.
3. Ability to Make Arrangements for Such Things as Travel, Conferences, and Meetings.
4. Ability to Locate and Assemble Information for Various Reports, Briefings, and Meetings.
5. Ability to Compose Non-Technical Correspondence.
6. Ability to Communicate Effectively Orally.

WHAT TO FILE: Applicants must submit: (1) a completed SF-171 (Application for Federal Employment), (2) Supplemental Qualifications Statement PYAO-573, (3) KEES Form A (OPM Form 1203-U), and if qualifying on the basis of education, (4) a completed OPM Form 1170/17 (List of College Courses) or transcript. If you are claiming 10-point veteran preference (disability, widow, spouse, etc.), SF-15 and documentary proof must also be submitted; original documents will be returned.

Failure to submit all of the required application forms may result in a lower rating than you deserve, a delay in rating, and lost job opportunities.

EQUAL EMPLOYMENT OPPORTUNITY: All applicants for Federal employment receive consideration without regard to race, religion, color, national origin, sex, political affiliation, age (with authorized exceptions), or any other nonmerit factor.

WHERE TO FILE: All necessary forms must be postmarked or received by the closing date shown on the Federal Job Opportunities Listing. Mail forms to:

U.S. Office of Personnel Management
New York City Area Office
Jacob K. Javits Federal Building
26 Federal Plaza
New York, New York 10278

GS-318

Form Approved
OMB. NO. 3206-0038

U.S. OFFICE OF PERSONNEL MANAGEMENT
NEW YORK CITY AREA OFFICE
Jacob K. Javits Federal Building
26 Federal Plaza
New York, New York 10278

SUPPLEMENTAL QUALIFICATIONS STATEMENT
FOR
SECRETARY
GS-318

COMPLETE AND RETURN THIS FORM WITH YOUR APPLICATION.

NAME _____
         (Last, First, Middle)

ADDRESS _____

CITY, STATE, ZIP _____

DATE OF BIRTH _____

SOCIAL SECURITY NUMBER _____
XXYYYXXXXXXXXXXXXXXXXXXXXXXXXXXXYYXXXXXXXYYXXXXXXYYXXXXXXXXXXXXX

GENERAL INFORMATION

This form should be completed if you are applying for Secretary, at grade GS-5 and above. In the spaces provided, answer all questions as completely as possible. A yes or no answer without the requested explanation may be disallowed. You must describe with specific examples the experience or education that supports a yes or no answer.

PLEASE TYPE OR PRINT YOUR RESPONSES LEGIBLY.

Your rating is based on information furnished in this Supplemental Qualifications Statement. There is no written test.

A false answer on this form may be grounds for not employing you or for dismissing you after you begin work.

ALL STATEMENTS ARE SUBJECT TO INVESTIGATION

XXYYYXXYXXXXXXXXXXXX.XXYXXXXXX.XXXXXXXXXXXXXXXXXXXXXXXXXXXXXXXXXX

OPM-PHILADELPHIA REGION
OPM FORM 1170

---

1. ORGANIZATIONAL SETTING

Check all blocks that describe an organizational setting where you have worked. Be sure to indicate the specific Experience block(s) on your SF-171 (Application for Federal Employment) where you gained this experience.

____ I worked for one person, who had no subordinate employees. SF-171 Block _____ .

____ I worked for one person, who has no subordinate employees but who was a member of a larger group (e.g., a partner in a law firm). SF-171, Block _____

____ I worked for several people, who had no subordinate employees but who were members of a larger group (e.g., several lawyers in a law firm). SF-171, Block _____

____ I worked for one person, who was the supervisor of a small organization of limited complexity. There were no subordinate supervisors. My boss directed the organization primarily through face-to-face meetings, and internal procedural and administrative controls were simple and informal. SF-171, Block _____

____ I worked for one person, who was the supervisor of a small organization of limited complexity. There were no subordinate supervisors, but the organization had extensive responsibility for the coordination of work outside of the immediate office (e.g., a Congressional liaison office, public affairs office, office of general counsel, personnel office, a scientific or research program office). As the secretary, I was responsible for establishing and maintaining numerous contacts outside of my immediate office for the purpose of coordinating substantive program work products, administrative details, and staff support responsibilities. SF-171, Block _____

____ The person I worked for was the Chief of an organization that was divided into subordinate units, each of which performed identical functions. SF-171, Block _____

____ The person I worked for was the Chief of an organization that was divided into subordinate units. Direction of the subordinate staff was exercised through intermediate supervisors, and the functions of the subordinate units differed from each other. There was a system of formal internal procedures and administrative controls, and a formal production or progress reporting system. As the secretary, I was required to establish and maintain frequent and substantive contacts outside of my immediate office, to coordinate numerous substantive administrative details in support of the organization's program, and to be conversant with not only the internal operations of my immediate office but also of its relationships and involvement with outside organizations. SF-171, Block _____

____ The person I worked for was the Chief of an organization that was divided into three or more subordinate levels including staff offices providing internal administrative support functions, such as personnel management, budget, procurement, management analysis, etc. My supervisor was responsible for decisions relating to the total management of my immediate office and its subordinate structure, including long-range planning, commitment of resources, program evaluation, relationships with other groups, etc. SF-171, Block _____

____ Other. SF-171, Block _____ . Please describe in detail.

II. ABILITY TO ORGANIZE EFFECTIVELY THE FLOW OF CLERICAL PROCESSES IN AN OFFICE.

Check all blocks that describe the work you have done. Be sure to indicate the specific Experience block(s) on your SF-171 (Application for Federal Employment) where you gained the experience.

A. Receptionist

___ I received telephone calls and visitors and referred them to the appropriate member of the staff to answer the question. SF-171, Block ___

___ I received telephone calls and visitors; personally answered questions regarding standard office procedures; referred other calls to staff members. SF-171, Block ___

___ I received telephone calls and visitors and screened them for my supervisor; personally took care of many matters and questions including answering substantive questions not requiring technical program knowledge; referred technical questions to appropriate staff office or employee according to the subject matter; referred only high-level or sensitive calls to my supervisor. SF-171, Block ___

B. Correspondence

___ I received and distributed incoming mail. SF-171, Block ___

___ I maintained control records on incoming correspondence and reports and notified staff members when due date was near. SF-171, Block ___

___ I typed correspondence and reports, proofreading my own work for errors in grammar, spelling, and punctuation. SF-171, Block ___

___ I performed typing, stenographic, and transcribing duties. SF-171, Block ___

___ I received and read incoming correspondence and reports, screened those items I could handle personally, and drafted replies to general inquiries and requests concerning procedural or administrative requirements of the office. SF-171, Block ___

___ I reviewed outgoing correspondence typed by others for procedural and grammatical accuracy. SF-171, Block ___

___ I reviewed outgoing correspondence prepared by members of the professional staff for procedural and grammatical accuracy, conformance with the general policy of the organization, factual correctness, and adequacy of treatment; advised the writer of any deviations or inadequacies. SF-171, Block ___

C. Office Management

___ I performed timekeeping duties and maintained leave records. SF-171, Block ___

___ I obtained the full range of office support services, such as mail, printing, maintenance, and supplies. SF-171, Block ___

___ I processed travel and expense vouchers. SF-171, Block ___

___ I requested various types of personnel training actions or services. SF-171, Block ___

___ I advised new clerical and professional employes regarding procedural and administrative matters. SF-171, Block ___

___ I advised clerks in subordinate offices of appropriate procedures. SF-171, Block ___

___ I shifted clerical work or clerical staff in subordinate offices to take care of fluctuating workloads. SF-171, Block ___

___ I advised secretaries in subordinate organizations concerning such matters as the information to be provided by the subordinate organizations for use in conferences or reports. SF-171, Block ___

___ I assisted my supervisor's professional subordinates in the procedural aspects of expediting the work of the office. SF-171, Block ___

___ I maintained information needed for budget purposes. SF-171, Block ___

___ I planned and arranged for the maintenance and preparation by others of information needed for budget purposes. SF-171, Block ___

___ I devised and installed new office procedures. SF-171, Block ___

___ I studied clerical activities in subordinate organizations and recommended to my supervisor specific restructuring of the way the activities were carried out. SF-171, Block ___

___ I studied and evaluated new office machines and recommended acceptance or rejection. SF-171, Block ___

D. Other. SF-171, Block ___
Please give specific examples of other experience or education that demonstrate your ability to organize effectively the flow of clerical processes in an office.

III. ABILITY TO DESIGN, ORGANIZE, AND USE A FILING SYSTEM.

Check all blocks that describe the work you have done. Be sure to indicate the specific Experience block(s) on your SF-171 (Application for Federal Employment) where you gained the experience.

___ I have worked with Subject files -- those in which materials are filed alphabetically by major division and specific subject heading. SF-171, Block ___

___ I have worked with Alphabetical files -- those in which materials are filed by key word in alphabetical order. SF-171, Block ___

___ I have worked with Decimal files -- those in which materials are assigned numbers in accordance with a prescribed classification system. The system provided for filing and retrieval according to major numerical families and subfamilies (e.g., 113.211 Energy, Petroleum, extraction techniques, etc.). SF-171, Block ___

___ I have worked with Alphanumerical files -- those in which materials are assigned letters and numbers (as in a Decimal system) but with more subdivisions. SF-171, Block ___

___ I have put materials in sequence order for filing, directly matched filing materials, and retrieved materials that have been specifically identified by someone else. SF-171, Block ___

___ I have performed filing tasks in subject or alphabetical files when this required knowledge of the units serviced and the subject matter being processed in order to distinguish materials which required different processing, to classify materials by subject matter, and to perform searches for materials that had been misfiled. SF-171, Block ___

___ I have classified and cross-referenced materials in decimal or alphanumeric systems that were extensively cross-referenced or when the subject matter of the materials was overlapping. SF-171, Block ___

___ I have monitored and purged files so that the orderly disposition of records as they become noncurrent could be accomplished. SF-171, Block ___

___ I have located and summarized information from files and documents when this required recognizing the relevancy of the information to the problem at hand. SF-171, Block ___

___ I have studied an existing file system and designed and established a new subject or alphabetical filing system. SF-171, Block ___

___ Based on deficiencies I have observed, I have designed and established a new decimal or alphanumeric filing system. SF-171, Block ___

___ Other. SF-171, Block ___
Give specific examples of your education or experience as a secretary that demonstrate your ability to design, organize, and use a filing system:

IV. ABILITY TO MAKE ARRANGEMENTS FOR SUCH THINGS AS TRAVEL, CONFERENCES, AND MEETINGS.

Check all blocks that describe the work you have done. Be sure to indicate the specific Experience block(s) on your SF-171 (Application for Federal Employment) where you gained this experience.

___ The travel arrangements I have made have been primarily domestic (within the United States). SF-171, Block ___

___ The travel arrangements I have made have been regularly both domestic and foreign. SF-171, Block ___

___ I primarily made travel arrangements through a travel agent. SF-171, Block ___

___ I prepared travel vouchers by estimating, computing, and verifying transportation, mileage, and subsistence costs. SF-171, Block ___

___ I made complete travel arrangements, including the planning of itineraries, selecting travel modes and carriers, routing to final destination, and purchasing tickets. SF-171, Block ___

___ I kept my supervisor's calendar, and scheduled appointments and conferences subject to my supervisor's approval. SF-171, Block ___

___ I kept my supervisor's calendar, scheduled appointments and conferences without prior approval, and saw that my supervisor was fully briefed on the matters to be discussed before the scheduled meeting. SF-171, Block ___

___ Based upon information provided by my supervisor concerning the purpose of the conference and people to attend, I made the necessary arrangements for conferences, including space, time, contacting people, and other matters; I assembled background material for my supervisor; I attended the meetings and reported on the proceedings. SF-171, Block ___

___ I noted the commitments made by my supervisor during conferences and meetings, informed the staff of those commitments, and arranged for the staff to implement them. SF-171, Block ___

___ I set up conferences requiring the planning and arranging of travel and hotel accomodations for conference participants based on a knowledge of the schedules and commitments of the participants. SF-171, Block ___

___ In addition to arranging conferences, I also arranged for a subordinate of my supervisor to represent the organization at a conference; these decisions were based on my knowledge of my supervisor's views. SF-171, Block ___

___ I assured that all of my supervisor's social obligations were met, arranged luncheons, issued invitations, insured proper seating arrangements, and insured that all details were covered (e.g., that guest speakers were invited sufficiently in advance, and that adequate provisions were made for protocol requirements) when necessary, I settled accounts with the restaurant, club, or caterer. SF-171, Block ___

___ Other. SF-171, Block ___
Give specific examples of your education or experience as a secretary that demonstrate your ability to make arrangements for such things as travel, conferences, and meetings:

V. ABILITY TO LOCATE AND ASSEMBLE INFORMATION FOR VARIOUS REPORTS, BRIEF-INGS, AND MEETINGS.

Check all blocks that describe the work you have done. Be sure to indicate the specific Experience block(s) on your SF-171 (Application for Federal Employment) where you gained the experience.

___ Upon request, I have retrieved specifically requested data from files. SF-171, Block ___

___ I have located and summarized information from files and documents when this required recognizing which information was or was not relevant to the problem at hand. SF-171, Block ___

___ I have arranged for the submission of information by other employees and assembled the material for my supervisor. SF-171, Block ___

___ I have developed material for my supervisor's use in public speaking engagements; after ascertaining the subject matter, I developed the background information and prepared an outline for the speech. SF-171, Block ___

___ Based on my knowledge of the organization and its history, I have handled sensitive assignments that involved gathering information from sources that were not initially known or was available in only one or a very few places. The subject matter was highly specialized and not a matter of widespread knowledge. Frequently the information was obtained orally from a variety of sources. I organized the material and drew my supervisor's attention to the most important parts. SF-171, Block ___

___ Other. SF-171, Block ___
Give specific examples of your education or experience as a secretary that demonstrate your ability to locate and assemble information for various reports, briefings, and conferences.

VI. ABILITY TO COMPOSE NON-TECHNICAL CORRESPONDENCE.

Check all blocks that describe the work you have done. Be sure to indicate the specific Experience block(s) on your SF-171 (Application for Federal Employment) where you gained this experience.

___ I have personally composed straightforward letters or memoranda that requested or provided factual information in proper English. SF-171, Block ___

___ I have personally composed letters to notify or to answer questions or complaints coming from members of the public regarding such matter as technical decisions, the status of one or more transactions, explanations of apparent delays, or information about a particular program. SF-171, Block ___

___ I have personally composed a wide variety of recurring internal reports and documents from information obtained from the staff, files, and other sources. SF-171, Block ___

___ I have signed out routine correspondence of a non-technical nature in my supervisor's name or in my own name as secretary to my supervisor. SF-171, Block ___

___ I have personally drafted letters of acknowledgment, commendation, notification, etc., when the need arose. SF-171, Block ___

___ On my own initiative I have observed the need for administrative or procedural notices or instructions to the staff, prepared the necessary issuances, and presented them to my supervisor for signature or signed them personally as the secretary. SF-171, Block ___

___ Other. SF-171, Block ___
Give specific examples of your education or experience as a secretary that demonstrate your ability to compose non-technical correspondence:

VII. ABILITY TO COMMUNICATE EFFECTIVELY ORALLY.

Check all boxes that describe the work you have done. Be sure to indicate the specific Experience block(s) on your SF-171 (Application for Federal Employment) where you gained the experience.

___ I have communicated orally with other people in order to exchange factual information. SF-171, Block ___

___ I have communicated orally with others in order to exchange substantive information regarding such matters as rules, procedures, regulations, programs, or benefits. SF-171, Block ___

___ I have made presentations at staff meetings. SF-171, Block ___

___ I have made presentations at large conferences. SF-171, Block ___

___ I have formally briefed the members of the staff or persons outside the organization on my supervisor's views on current issues facing the organization. SF-171, Block ___

___ Other. SF-171, Block ___
Give specific examples of your education or experience that demonstrate your ability to communicate effectively orally:

VII. SPECIALIZED SECRETARIAL EXPERIENCE

___ I have at least one year of experience as a Legal Secretary. SF-171, Block ___

Give specific examples of your experience that demonstrate your knowledge of legal terminology, legal forms, and legal processes and procedures.

___ I have at least one year of experience as a Medical Secretary. SF-171, Block ___

Give specific examples of your experience that demonstrate your knowledge of medical terminology and hospital or laboratory procedures.

___ I have at least one year of experience as a Technical Secretary. SF-171, Block ___

Give specific examples of your experience that demonstrate your knowledge of engineering or scientific terminology and research methods.

IX. EQUIPMENT AND PROFICIENCY.

___ I have used a manual typewriter. SF-171, Block ___

___ I have used an electric typewriter. SF-171, Block ___

___ I have used an electronic typewriter. SF-171, Block ___

___ I have used specialized wordprocessing equipment. SF-171, Block ___
    Specify types of equipment:

___ I have transcribed from a dictation machine. SF-171, Block ___

___ I have used a large mainframe computer. SF-171, Block ___
    Specify types of equipment:

___ I have used a personal computer(PC). SF-171, Block ___
    Specify types of equipment:

___ I have used PC software programs to do wordprocessing. SF-171, Block ___
    Specify programs used:

___ I have used PC software programs to do spreadsheets. SF-171, Block ___
    Specify programs used:

___ I have used PC software programs to do database management. SF-171, Block ___
    Specify programs used:

___ I have used PC software programs to do other functions. SF-171, Block ___
    Specify functions and programs:

___ I have used other specialized office equipment. SF-171, Block ___
    Specify equipment used:

My typing speed is ___ w.p.m.

My stenography speed is ___ w.p.m.

___ I have received the designation of Certified Professional Secretary (CPS) from the Institute for Certifying Secretaries of Professional Secretaries International. The date of my most recent certificate is ___.

X.   You may use this space to provide other examples of your education, training, and experience
     that demonstrate your ability to perform the work of a secretary:

After completing the application and this form, look them over carefully to make sure that you
have answered all items. Read the certification statement on this form and sign.

PRIVACY ACT INFORMATION

The Office of Personnel Management is authorized by section 1302 of Chapter 13 (Special Authority) and sections 3302 and 3304 of Chapter 33 (Examination, Certification, and Appointment) of Title 5 of the U.S. Code to collect the information on this form.

Executive Order 9397 (Numbering System for Federal Accounts Relating to Individual Persons) authorizes the collection of your Social Security Number (SSN). Your SSN is used to identify this form with your basic application. It may be used for the same purposes as stated on the application.

The information you provide will be used primarily to determine your qualifications for Federal employment. Other possible uses or disclosures of the information are:

1.   To make requests for information about you from any source (e.g., former employers or schools), that would assist an agency in determining whether to hire you;

2.   To refer your application to prospective Federal employers and, with your consent, to others (e.g., State and local governments) for possible employment;

3.   To a Federal, State, or local agency for checking on violations of law or other lawful purposes in connection with hiring or retaining you on the job, or issuing you a security clearance;

4.   To the courts when the Government is party to a suit; and

5.   When lawfully required by Congress, the Office of Management and Budget, or the General Services Administration.

Providing the information requested on this form, including your SSN, is voluntary. However, failure to do so may result in your not receiving an accurate rating, which may hinder your chances for obtaining Federal employment.

ATTENTION - THIS STATEMENT MUST BE SIGNED

Read the following paragraph carefully before signing this Statement

A false answer to any question in this Statement may be grounds for not employing you, or for dismissing you after you begin work, and may be punishable by fine or imprisonment (U.S. Code, Title 18, Sec. 1001). All statements are subject to investigation, including a check of your fingerprints, police records, and former employers. All the information you give will be considered in reviewing your Statement and is subject to investigation.

I certify that all of the statements made in this Statement are true, complete, and correct to the best of my knowledge and belief, and are made in good faith.

SIGNATURE(Sign in ink)   DATE SIGNED

OPM-PHILADELPHIA REGION

Technical Aids in Science and Engineering

Grades GS-2 and GS-3

Qualifications Information Statement

Description of Duties

Science and engineering aids work with professional and technical employees performing a wide range of nonprofessional support and technical assistance duties in research, development, testing, surveying, drafting, mapping, and many other activities in which the Federal government is engaged.

Qualifications Requirements

Except for the substitutions provided below, candidates must possess the following:

GS-2: Three months of appropriate experience
GS-3: Six months of appropriate experience

Appropriate experience is experience which provided a familiarity with the subject matter or processes of the position, and which demonstrates your ability to perform the duties of the position.

Substitutions of Education for Experience

If you are substituting post high school education for any part of the required experience, you must submit with your application a transcript or *List of College Courses* (OPM Form 1170/17) showing the courses completed, the length of each course, and the grade received.

One academic year of post high school education is equal to 30 semester hours, or 45 quarter hours, or 36 weeks in a technical or business school which included at least 20 hours of classroom instruction per week.

Construction Aid—GS-809

GS-2: High school graduation (or equivalent).
GS-3: Successful completion of one academic year of post-high school education which included at least 6 semester hours in courses such as drafting, surveying, mathematics, physical science, industrial technology, industrial arts, or pertinent technical courses such as electricity, material testing, or engineering mechanics.

Surveying Aid—GS-817

GS-2: High school graduation (or equivalent).
GS-3: Successful completion of one academic year of post-high school education which included a course in surveying, engineering, industrial technology, construction, physics, drafting, forestry, geography, navigation, cartography, physical science, or mathematics.

Engineering Drafting Aid—GS-818

GS-2: High school graduation (or equivalent).

Meteorological Aid—GS-1341

GS-2: High school graduation (or equivalent).
GS-3: Successful completion of one academic year of post-high school education which included at least one course in meteorology, mathematics, engineering, or physical science.

Engineering Aid—GS-802

GS-2: High school graduation (or equivalent).
GS-3: Successful completion of one academic year of post-high school education which included at least 6 semester hours in courses such as engineering, engineering or industrial technology, construction, physics, drafting, surveying, physical science, or mathematics.

Cartographic Aid—GS-1371

GS-2: High school graduation (or equivalent).
GS-3: Successful completion of one academic year of post-high school education which included at least 6 semester hours in courses such as astronomy, cartography, geodesy, geophysics, physical or geological oceanography, photogrammetry, computer science, land surveying, remote sensing, physical geography or mathematics (not more than 3 semester hours in math and statistics may be accepted).

Physical Science Aid—GS-1311

GS-2: High school graduation (or equivalent).
GS-3: Successful completion of one academic year of post-high school education which included at least 6 semester hours in courses such as physical science, engineering, or mathematics (except financial or commercial mathematics).

Hydrologic Aid—GS-1316

GS-2: High school graduation (or equivalent).
GS-3: Successful completion of one academic year of post-high school education which included a course in engineering, industrial technology, construction drafting, surveying, physical science, or mathematics.

Geodetic Aid—GS-1374

GS-2: High school graduation (or equivalent).
GS-3: Successful completion of one academic year of post-high school education which included at least 6 semester hours in courses such as geodesy, geography, cartography, physical science, engineering science, forest mensuration, surveying, or any branch of mathematics (except financial or commercial mathematics).

Basis of Rating

Your rating will be based on your written test results.

If you pass the written test, you will be issued a Notice of Results with numerical ratings of 70 to 100. The Notice of Results also will show the grades for which you are qualified and available, and the geographic areas for which you have indicated availability. With the Notice of Results, you will receive an explanation of the information contained on your Notice of Results. Please read that explanation carefully.

Students

If you intend to qualify on the basis of education and are still a student, but expect to meet the requirements for these positions within nine months, you may apply to take the written test. If you pass the test and meet all other requirements, you will be rated tentatively eligible for appointment. However, you may not begin working until you meet the education requirements.

Physical Requirements

For most positions, a physical impairment will not bar a person from employment, although it may be necessary to compensate for the condition by the use of adaptive devices. Some positions demand more strict physical requirements than others. For example:

- For Cartographic Aid positions involving the use of stereoscopic instruments, good vision in each eye, with or without glasses, and good depth perception are required.
- For Surveying Aid positions which require a high degree of mobility under difficult conditions, persons with an amputation of arm, hand, leg, or foot will not qualify. Also, vision in both eyes is required, as well as ability to distinguish basic colors.

Special Notice

The Office of Personnel Management furnishes information on Federal employment opportunities, qualification requirements, and application procedures without charge. Additional information about Federal employment, including Veteran Preference and other matters not included in this statement, may be obtained from any Federal Job Information Center. The Office of Personnel Management has no connection with any private employment agency or so-called "civil service" school. No "civil service" school or employment agency can guarantee that you will rank high enough on a list of eligible applicants to be offered a job with the Federal government.

Equal Employment Opportunity: All qualified applicants will receive consideration for employment without regard to race, creed, color, religion, national origin, sex, age, or any non-merit factors.

United States
Office of
Personnel
Management

QUALIFICATIONS   INFORMATION

SHEET

AIR CONDITIONING EQUIPMENT OPERATOR
WG-5415-9/10

DESCRIPTION OF DUTIES:

Air conditioning Equipment Operator positions involve the operation of air
conditioning systems for large buildings or complexes of buildings. Also
included are positions that involve the operation and regulation of cold
storage and specialized climate simulation facilities.

Jobs at the WG-9 level involve the operation of a centralized multiple zone air
conditioning plant that serves a building or complex of buildings. The air conditioning
plant consists of multiple chillers (compressors) or absorbers of large capacity
and performs various functions, such as heating, humidification, dehumidification,
filtration, ventilation, in addition to cooling. The operator can control the
separate zones from a master control panel or may perform the same functions from
local switches and gauges at the equipment site. Typical examples of equipment in
these systems include absorbers or centrifugal compressors, starters, circuit
breakers, condensers, evaporators, heat exchangers, chilled water and condensor
pumps, filters, fans, controls, motors, thermostats, humidifiers, cooling towers,
heating and cooling coils, recorders, and alarms. Typical measuring instruments
and testing equipment include flowmeters, recording meters, micrometers, psychro-
meters, velometers, and electronic leak detectors.

Jobs at the WG-10 level involve systems that are more complicated and difficult to
operate. Typical of this more complex level of work are plans that use high-
pressure steam-driven centrifugal compressors, or a combination of low pressure-
driven absorbers and high-pressure steam-driven compressors.

QUALIFICATIONS REQUIREMENTS:

No specific length of experience or training is required. Applicants must show,
however, that they have had training or experience of sufficient scope and quality
to provide them with the knowledges, skills, and abilities to operate two or more
utility systems.

BASIS OF RATING:

NO WRITTEN TEST IS REQUIRED. Applicants will be rated on the basis of an evaluation
of appropriate experience as described in their applications.

FORMS TO FILE:

Standard Form 171 (Personal Qualifications Statement), EWA-523 (Employment Availability
Statement), EWA-130 (Supplemental Qualifications Statement for Skilled Craftsman),
and EWA-130J (Attachment to Supplemental Qualifications Statement for Skilled
Craftsman) are required. If applications are currently being accepted, send completed
forms to Office of Personnel Management, Washington Area Office-SSX, P.O. Box 52,
Washington, D.C. 20044.

O C C U P A T I O N A L   D U T Y   S H E E T

CARPENTER WG-4607-7/9

DESCRIPTION OF DUTIES

Carpenters construct, alter, and repair buildings and structures, fittings, panels, partitions, and other wood or wood substitute articles.

Jobs at the WG-7 level require:

- The ability to measure and cut wood or wood substitute items in order to construct or repair products where appearance is not essential. Items constructed/repaired include scaffolds, staging parts, panels, bins, pallets, concrete forms, dry wall, sheathing, and roof decks.

- The ability to add, subtract, multiply, and divide, and work with simple fractions to plan and measure materials according to requirements and dimensions outlined in instructions.

- The ability to read, interpret, and apply simple blueprints and work sketches.

Jobs at the WG-9 level require:

- The ability to construct, alter, or repair items or structures where accuracy, spacing, and fit are essential, and structural soundness and appearance are important.

- The ability to construct items or structures where straight, angle, or curved cut must be exact, and assemble or installation are difficult.

- The ability to plan and complete projects from initial lay-out to final assembly.

- The ability to use more advanced shop mathematics to plan and compute more complex and exact projects with features such as arcs, tangents and circles.

- Tha ability to set-up, adjust and adapt hand and power tools to accomplish more difficult tasks such as laminating and bending; find-surfacing of materials; and cutting of bevels, rabbets, chamfers, dados, grooves and mitre joints.

- The ability to read, interpret, and apply complicated building plans specifications, blueprints, sketches, and building codes.

- The ability to determine the kind and type of materials and tools needed to complete a project.

QUALIFICATIONS REQUIREMENTS

No specific length of experience or training is required. Applicants must be able to show, however, that they have had training and experience of sufficient scope and quality to provide them with the knowledges, skills and abilities to perform the duties of the position.

BASIS OF RATING

NO WRITTEN TEST IS REQUIRED. Applicants will be rated on the basis of an evaluation of appropriate experience described in their application.

FORMS TO FILE

SF-171, Personal Qualifications Statement; EWA-130, Supplemental Qualifications Statement for Skilled Craftsmen; OPM Form 1203-U, Employment Availability Statement. If applications are currently being accepted, send completed forms to the U.S. Office of Personnel Management, Office of Washington Examining Services - WEC, P.O. Box 14179, Washington, D.C. 20044.

QUALIFICATION INFORMATION SHEET

COOK, WG-7404-5/8

DESCRIPTION OF DUTIES

Cook positions involve the cooking of regular or special diet foods and meals. This includes cooking meats, fowl, fish, and seafood; cooking frozen, canned, dried, or fresh vegetables; measuring and mixing ingredients for soups, stews, sauces, and special dishes; adding seasoning to food and regulating cooking temperatures.

Jobs at the WG-5 level involve a wide variety of simple cooking tasks without being told how to do the work, and without close review; in addition, some cooks at this level learn more difficult cooking under close supervision. Examples of cooking performed without detailed instructions are; assisting in grilling chops, steaks, poultry, and fish by watching while the items are cooking, turning as required, and removing when done; opening and heating canned vegetables or fruits; grilling pancakes, bacon and eggs to order; measuring weighing portions and ingredients as requied by recipe, formula, or diet; cooking cereal; beverages, toast, salads, gelatin, and sandwiches. Examples of cooking performed under close supervision are: adjusting recipes for the number of servings needed in quantity cooking; preparing convenience foods (instant mixes), prepackaged or canned foods when the recipe requires a few simple steps; cooking common or frequently used recipes for gravies, sauces, or soups; cooking fresh or frozen vegetables using techniques such as french frying, boiling, mashing, and whipping.

Jobs at the WG-8 level use a full range of quantity cooking procedures from the common or frequently used recipes to the new or complex recipes. Over a period of time, they prepare a full variety of meats, poultry, seafood, or both of the following; preparing a number of menu items for one meal when the work requires planning and coordinating a variety of steps to be sure that all items are ready for serving at the same time, or preparing menu items using special or difficult recipes involving many steps, ingredients or long preparation time.

QUALIFICATION REQUIREMENTS

No specific length of experience or training is required. Applicants must be able to show, however, that they have had training and experience of sufficient scope and quality to provide them with the skills, knowledges, and abilities to perform the duties of the position.

BASIS OF RATING

NO WRITTEN TEST IS REQUIRED. Applicants will be rated on the basis of an evaluation of appropriate experience as described in their application.

FORMS TO FILE

SF-171, Personal Qualifications Statement; SSW Form 13i-D, Supplemental Qualifications Statement for Cook; and EWA 523, Employment Availability Statement. If applications are currently being accepted, send completed forms to the U.S. Office of Personnel Management, Washington Area Office - SSX, P.O. Box 52, Washington, D.C. 20044.

QUALIFICATION INFORMATION

SHEET

Flatbed Cylinder Press Operator WG-4406-Ungraded

DESCRIPTION OF DUTIES

These positions involve the making ready and operation of a flatbed cylinder printing press to overprint the backs, faces, numbers, and seals on jobs as ordered, as well as the performance of other miscellaneous types of printing. Operators print from electrotype plates, Ludlow slugs, half-tones, numbering machines or other plates used on surface printing presses. Operators perform routine care, maintenance and adjustments for the press.

QUALIFICATION REQUIREMENTS

No specific length of experience or training is required. Applicants must be able to show, however, that they have had training and experience of sufficient scope and quality to provide them with the skills, knowledges, and abilities to perform the duties of the position. Required are the ability to operate a press equipped with numbering machines and skill in making adjustments necessary to ensure proper registration.

BASIS OF RATING

NO WRITTEN TEST IS REQUIRED. Applicants will be rated on the basis of an evaluation of appropriate experience as described in their application.

FORMS TO FILE

SF-171, Personal Qualifications Statement; EWA Form 130, Supplemental Qualifications Statement for Skilled Craftsman; EWA Form 130-P, Supplemental Qualifications Statement for Printing Occupations and EWA 523, Employment Availability Statement. If applications are currently being accepted, send completed forms to the U.S. Office of Personnel Management, Washington Area Office - SSX, P.O. Box 52, Washington, D.C. 20044.

Q U A L I F I C A T I O N   I N F O R M A T I O N
S H E E T

Heavy Mobile Equipment Mechanic, WG-5803-8/10

DESCRIPTION OF DUTIES:

Heavy Mobile Equipment Mechanics perform work involved in the repair and
modification of combustion-powered heavy duty vehicles and tractors. power
shovels, locomotives, combat tanks, cranes, large missle transporters, and
fire trucks. These vehicles have utility systems or special hydraulic, pneumatic, or mechanical systems, features, and controls which are designed for
construction, combat, earth moving, and ship loading, firefighting, and comparable
heavy duty industrial, or special applications.

Jobs at the WG-8 level require the adjustment, preventive maintence, repair,
replacement, and modification of engines, clutch assemblies, and braking systems.
The incumbent will assist higher grade mechanics in, but not limited to, the
follwing:

a. Preventive maintenance, major repair, replacement and modification of
    engines.
b. Rebuilding and/or replacement of clutch assemblies and braking systems.
c. Engine tuning, utilizing an analyzer.
d. Removal, rebuilding and/or replacement of transmissions, transfer cases,
    power take-offs, torque of converters and differential assemblies.

Workers at the WG-8 level perform without detailed instructions the less difficult
repair and maintenance tasks such as: cleaning carburetors; replacing points,
generators, starters, lights, batteries, spark plugs, tie rods, etc.; making
minor adjustments; repairing and maintenance of shop equipment.

Jobs at the WG-10 level require the repairing, overhauling, and rebuilding of
major assemblies, systems, and vehicles. The incumbent:

—   Traces and locates defects and causes of mechanical problems to determine
    type and extent of necessary repairs;
—— Selects and complies with appropriate repair specifications and
    procedures;
—   Fits and installs parts, such as pistons, valves bearings, gears, and
    cylinders, to appropriate tolerances; makes changes or modifications in
    accordance with specifications and guidelines; and
—— Connects, meshes, aligns, and adjusts items and systems to assure proper
    operation of the complete system or vehicle.

QUALIFICATION REQUIREMENTS:

No specific length of experience or training is required. Applicants must be able
to show, however, that they have had training and experience of sufficient scope
and quality to provide them with the skills, knowledges, and abilities to perform
the duties of the position.

BASIS OF RATING:

NO WRITTEN TEST IS REQUIRED. Applicants will be rated on the basis of an
evaluation of appropriate experience as described in their application.

FORMS TO FILE:

SF-171, Personal Qualifications Statement; and EWA Form 130, Supplemental Qualifications Statement for Skilled Craftsman; and EWA 523, Employment Availability
Statement. If applications are currently being accepted, send completed forms
to the U.S. Office of Personnel Management, Washington Area Office - SSX, P.O.
Box 52, Washington, DC 20044

QUALIFICATION INFORMATION

SHEET

LOCKSMITH WG-3817-9

DESCRIPTION OF DUTIES:

Locksmith positions involve the repair, overhaul modification, major reworking testing, and installation of a variety of locking devices typically found on doors, desks, compartments, mobile equipment, sages, vaults, and other secured locations. Also involved are the manufacture and duplication of keys, and the keying and combinating of locking mechanisms. Work requires a knowledge of the construction, operation, and functional characteristics of locking devices, and skill in manufacturing replacement parts, devising or changing combinations, establishing master keying systems, neutralizing lockouts, and a variety of installation and repair processes such as filing, drilling, and chiseling.

Jobs at the WG-9 level require skill in reworking, grinding, finishing substitute parts, and fabricating parts to close fits. WG-9 locksmiths improvise trade techniques to adapt locking mechanisms for uses to which they were not specifically designed or to hamper or prevent the use of standard neutralization techniques. Work often requires the development of drawings with sufficient detail to identify missing tolerances, dimensions, and critical parts. Locksmiths at this level are able to select appropriate materials considering such factors as needed strength and hardness, machining characteristics, and environmental factors. WG-9 locksmiths (work with a variety of equipment such as monitors, alarms, timing mechanisms and other items which make up a complete security or surveillance system.

QUALIFICATION REQUIREMENTS:

No specific length of experience or training is required. Applicants must be able to show, however, that they have had training and experience of sufficient scope and quality to provide them with the skills, knowledges, and abilities to perform the duties of the position.

BASIS OF RATING:

NO WRITTEN TEST IS REQUIRED. Applicants will be rated on the basis of an evaluation of appropriate experience as described in their applications.

FORMS TO FILE:

SF-171, Personal Qualifications Statement; EWA Form 130, Supplemental Qualifications Statement for Skilled Craftsman; and EWA 523, Employment Availability Statement. If applications are currently being accepted, send completed forms to the U.S. Office of Personnel Management, Washington Area Office - SSX, P. O. Box 52, Washington, D.C. 20415.

QUALIFICATION INFORMATION SHEET

RIGGER, WG-5210-8/10

DESCRIPTION OF DUTIES:

These positions involve nonsupervisory work involved in the selection, installation and use of cables, ropes, chains, and other weight handling gear to lift, move, and position heavy loads; and the assembly, repair, and installation of standing and running rigging used to support, secure, or operate equipment, machinery, and other items. This work requires a knowledge of rigging practices and weight handling techniques; the ability to plan and select the appropriate gear; and the skill to assemble, repair, and install rigging on a variety of objects.

Jobs at the GS-8 Level:

The WG-8 Rigging Worker selects and installs weight handling gear such as cables, ropes, slings, and chains used to lift, move, and position a variety of large and heavy equipment, machinery, and supply items. Objects to be moved are usually in open areas of shops, storage facilities, or loading docks, and are rigged for movement by crane or other mobile material handling equipment. The rigging worker cuts, splices, assembles, and repairs slings, nets, pendants, and other rigging gear used in day-to-day operations. He works under the supervision of a higher graded worker or a supervisor.

The GS-8 Rigger Worker uses a basic knowledge of established trade practices and techniques to select and install weight handling gear used in lifting, moving, and positioning a variety of large and heavy objects.

At this level the rigger must be skilled in using a variety of tools and equipment such as marlin spikes, fids, serving mallets, rigger's screw, and swaging machine to splice, form, and finish the rigging gear.

Jobs at the WG-10 Level:

The WG-10 Rigger plans, lays out, assembles, repairs, and installs complex weight handling gear and various standing and running rigging. In comparison with the WG-8 Rigging Worker who selects and installs weight handling gear for objects to be moved by crane or other mobile material handling equipment, the WG-10 Rigger uses equipment such as chainfalls, gin poles, tackle blocks, gallows frames, or combinations of these to rig and move objects through confined areas where cranes or other mobile material handling equipment cannot be used because of the object's size, shape, and location. In addition to the cutting, splicing, assembling, and repairing of standard weight handling gear done by the WG-8 Rigging Worker, the WG-10 Rigger makes and installs complex machinery, and other items having critical fit, tension, and operational requirements. He follows established rigging practices and procedures on his own and clears unusual problems with his supervisor.

QUALIFICATION REQUIREMENTS:

No specific length of experience or training is required. Applicants must show, however, that they have had training and experience of sufficient scope and quality to provide them with the knowledges, skills, and abilities to perform the duties of the position.

BASIS OF RATING:

NO WRITTEN TEST IS REQUIRED. Applicants will be rated on the basis of an evaluation of appropriate experience as described in their application.

FORMS TO FILE:

Standard Form 171 (Personnel Qualifications Statement), EWA-523 (Employment Availability), and EWA-130 (Supplemental Qualifications Statement for Skilled Craftsmen) are required. If applications are currently being accepted, send completed form to the Office of Personnel Management, Washington Area Office-SSX, Post Office Box 52, Washington, DC 20044.

QUALIFICATION INFORMATION

SHEET

SEWAGE DISPOSAL PLANT OPERATOR, WG-5408-7/8
SEWAGE DISPOSAL PLANT OPERATOR, WG-5408-9/10

DESCRIPTION OF DUTIES:

Sewage disposal plant operators maintain sewage disposal plants, pumping stations, substations and other equipment used in settling, disinfecting, and disposal of sewage and industrial wastes.

JOBS AT THE WG 7/8 LEVEL:

The duties of sewage disposal plant operators at this level include the implementation of written and oral instructions, following normal operating procedures; the reading of flow rates, elevations and totalizers; the performance of routine tests to determine type and strength of chemical reagents needed; the degree of acidity or akalinity of materials being processed; and the amount of solids to be removed; the operation of gates and valves controlling efflux and influx through knowledge of tank capacities; the performance of all operations involved in the primary treatment phase, including the operation of grit chambers, grease separators, imhoff tanks, pumps and valves; and adjustment and repair of equipment involved in the primary treatment such as grit chambers, bar racks, and imhoff tanks.

JOBS AT THE WG 9/10 LEVEL:

The duties of sewage disposal plant operators at this level include the implementation of normal operating procedures subject only to general supervision; the interpretation of charts, meters, and dials such as elevation and acid tank levels; the use of basic instruments, such as chlorimeters, hydrometers, and comparators; the separation of settleable matter from liquids; and the maintenance of oxidation levels.

EXPERIENCE REQUIREMENTS:

No specific length of experience is required. Applicants must show, however, that they have had training or experience of sufficient scope and quality to provide them with the knowledges, skills, and abilities to perform the duties of the position.

BASIS OF RATING:

NO WRITTEN TEST IS REQUIRED. Applicants will be rated on the basis of an evaluation of appropriate experience as described in their applications.

FORMS TO FILE:

Standard Form 171 (Personal Qualifications Statement), EWA-523 (Employment Availability Statement), EWA-130 (Supplemental Qualifications Statement for Skilled Craftsman), and EWA-130J (Attachment to Supplemental Qualifications Statement for Skilled Craftsman) are required. If applications are currently being accepted, send completed forms to Office of Personnel Management, Washington Area Office-SSX, PO Box 52, Washington, DC 20044.

BORDER PATROL AGENT
GS-5/7
(This is a Federal civilian law enforcement position.)

COMPETITION NOTICE:

The U.S. Office of Personnel Management will accept applications to take the written examination for GS-5/7 Border Patrol Agent positions in the Federal Government.

HOW TO APPLY

You must obtain an OPM Form 5000-AB, Test Scheduling Card, and a Qualifications Information Statement (QI-1896) from any Federal Job Information Center (FJIC) or by calling the College Hotline on 1-900-990-9200. (There is a $.40 a minute charge for the Hotline service.) FJIC's are located in principal cities across the country. They are listed under "U.S. Government" in metropolitan area telephone directories. If none is listed in your directory, you can call information for a large metropolitan area or you can contact your nearest State Job Service (or State Employment Security Office.) When completing the OPM Form 5000-AB, be sure to enter the city and state of the test location you prefer. If that location is not available, you will be scheduled at a nearby location. You must send the completed Form 5000-AB to the OPM Area Office servicing the test location which you have chosen. You will be sent other required application forms at the time you receive written notice of when and where to report for the written test.

ORAL INTERVIEW AND SPANISH LANGUAGE

An interview is required; and, you must know or learn Spanish as noted in the Qualifications Information Statement (QI-1896.)

MAXIMUM AGE LIMIT

Provisions of Public Law 100-238 allow the imposition of a maximum age for original entry into certain Federal law enforcement occupations. Border Patrol Agents are currently covered by such a restriction. The date preceding one's 37th birthday is the final date of entry as authorized by the Congress of the United States and as adopted by the U.S. Department of Justice.

If you are age 37 or older or will shortly reach your 37th birthday, but have previously served in a _Federal civilian_ law enforcement position which may exempt you from the original entry age restriction, please provide the following information: the name of the Federal agency where you worked; the title of your position; and the dates employed. Please attach this information to the completed Form 5000-AB.

WRITTEN TEST

You may take the Border Patrol Agent written test only once in a 6-month period. If you take it more often, only your first score will be counted. You can expect to receive a notice of rating within 6 to 8 weeks after your test date. Because of lead time requirements to schedule interviews and training, actual entry on duty is usually delayed for six to eight months after the notice of your score is received.

Along with the written test, there will be a written language test administered to assess individuals' ability to learn the Spanish language. This test is designed for those who have little or no proficiency in the Spanish language. Applicants who are fluent in the Spanish language will be given the choice to take the language test _or_ a Spanish oral test at the time of the employment interview. You must pass either the language or Spanish oral test. You will not be allowed to take both.

NOTE: Many candidates drop out of this program before entry on duty, and even before the interviews are scheduled. Stay interested and available.

JOB LOCATIONS: Most trainee Border Patrol Agent positions are located primarily along the United States-Mexico border in California, Arizona, New Mexico, and Texas. Many are in small, isolated communities.

How To Apply

Applicants are restricted to taking the test only once in a six month period. If the test is taken more than once in a six month period, only the first score will be recognized.

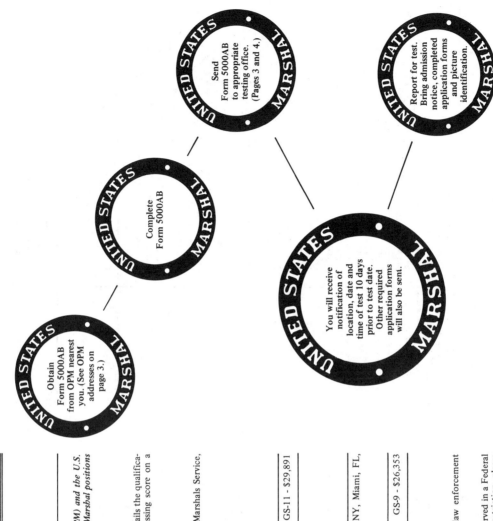

Obtain Form 5000AB from OPM nearest you. (See OPM addresses on page 3.)

Complete Form 5000AB

Send Form 5000AB to appropriate testing office. (Pages 3 and 4.)

You will receive notification of location, date and time of test 10 days prior to test date. Other required application forms will also be sent.

Report for test. Bring admission notice, completed application forms and picture identification.

Notice of Results

You may expect to receive notice of your test results approximately 10 weeks after your test date.

U.S. Department of Justice
United States Marshals Service

DEPUTY U.S. MARSHAL, GS-5/7
Announcement No. DUSM-01
Competition Notice

Effective   until further notice, the Office of Personnel Management (OPM) and the U.S. Marshals Service will accept applications to take the written examination for Deputy U.S. Marshal positions in the Federal government.

Qualification Requirements

The announcement accompanying this notice describes the duties of the position and details the qualifications required. In addition to meeting the qualifications, applicants must obtain a passing score on a written test.

Location of Positions

Deputy U.S. Marshal positions are located in the 94 U.S. Judicial Districts of the U.S. Marshals Service, which cover the 50 states, Puerto Rico, the Virgin Islands and Guam.

Salaries

REGULAR ANNUAL SALARIES FOR 1990

GS-5 - $16,305	GS-7 - $20,195	GS-9 - $24,705
		GS-11 - $29,891

SPECIAL ANNUAL SALARIES FOR 1990

Persons appointed to positions in Washington, D.C., Alexandria, VA, New York City, NY, Miami, FL, and Los Angeles, CA will receive the special salary rates below.

GS-5 - $19,025	GS-7 - $22,214	GS-9 - $26,353

Maximum Age Limit

Under Public Law 93-350, the maximum age for original entry into certain Federal law enforcement positions, including Deputy U.S. Marshal positions, is 34.

If you are age 35 or older or will shortly reach your 35th birthday, but have previously served in a Federal civilian law enforcement position which may exempt you from the original entry age restriction, please submit a copy of Standard Form 50 (Notification of Personnel Action) at the test site, indicating your employment in that position.

Form USM-12B

PRIOR EDITIONS ARE OBSOLETE AND NOT TO BE USED

OFFICE OF PERSONNEL MANAGEMENT
FEDERAL JOB INFORMATION/TESTING OFFICES

IF YOU WANT TO TEST IN	AND/OR YOU LIVE IN	SEND YOUR APPLICATION TO
— Los Angeles, CA	Los Angeles county	
— San Diego, CA	San Diego county	
— San Francisco, CA	Marin, San Francisco, San Mateo counties	
— Washington, D.C.	District of Columbia, Calvert, Charles, Frederick, Montgomery, Prince Georges, Arlington, Fairfax, Loudoun, Prince William, Stafford counties; Alexandria, Fairfax, Falls Church, Manassas and Manassas Park, VA	
— Miami, FL	Dade county	
— Chicago, IL	Cook, DuPage, McHenry counties	
— Boston, MA	Bristol, Essex, Middlesex, Norfolk, Plymouth, Suffolk, Worcester counties	
— Detroit, MI	Lapeer, Livingston, Macomb, Monroe, Oakland, St. Clair, Wayne counties	
— New York, NY	Bronx, Kings, New York, Putnam, Queens, Richmond, Rockland, Westchester counties	U.S. Marshals Service 600 Army Navy Drive Arlington, VA 22202-4210 Attn: Examining Unit. Suite 890
— Philadelphia, PA	Bucks, Chester, Delaware, Montgomery, Philadelphia counties; Burlington, Camden, Gloucester counties in New Jersey	
— Dallas, TX	Collin, Dallas, Denton, Ellis, Kaufman, Rockwall counties	
— San Antonio, TX	Bexar, Comal, Guadalupe counties	
— Houston, TX	Ft. Bend, Harris, Waller, Liberty, Montgomery counties	

ALABAMA
Huntsville:
Building 600, Suite 341
3322 Memorial Pkwy., South,
35801-5311
(205) 544-5802

ALASKA
Anchorage:
222 W. 7th Ave.
Box 22, 99513

ARIZONA
Phoenix:
U.S. Postal Service Building
Room 110
522 N. Central Ave., 85004
(602) 261-4736

ARKANSAS
(See Oklahoma listing)

CALIFORNIA
Los Angeles:
Linder Bldg., 3rd Floor
845 S. Figueroa, 90017
(213) 894-3360

Sacramento:
1029 J St., 2nd Floor, 95814
(916) 551-1464

San Diego:
Federal Bldg., Rm. 4-S-9
880 Front St., 92188
(619) 557-6165

San Francisco:
P.O. Box 7405, 94120
(located at 211 Main St.,
2nd Floor, Rm. 235)

COLORADO
Denver:
P.O. Box 25167, 80225
(303) 236-4162
(located at 12345 W. Alameda
Pkwy., Lakewood, CO)

For job information (24 hrs. a
day) in the following States,
dial:
MONTANA: (303) 236-4165
UTAH: (303) 236-4166
WYOMING: (303) 236-4166

For forms and local supplements
dial: (303) 236-4159

CONNECTICUT
Hartford:
Federal Bldg., Rm. 613
450 Main St., 06103
(203) 240-3263

DELAWARE
(See Philadelphia listing)

DISTRICT OF COLUMBIA
Metro Area:
1900 E St., N.W., Rm. 1416
Washington, DC 20415
(202) 653-8468

FLORIDA
Orlando:
Commodore Bldg., Suite 125
3444 McCrory Pl., 32803-3701
(407) 648-6148

GEORGIA
Atlanta:
Richard B. Russell Federal Bldg.
75 Spring St., S.W., 30303
(404) 331-4315

GUAM
Agana:
Pacific Daily News Bldg.,
Room 902, 96910
(671) 472-7451

HAWAII
Honolulu (and other Hawaiian
Islands and Overseas):
Federal Bldg., Rm. 5316
300 Ala Moana Blvd., 96850
(808) 541-2791
(808) 541-2784 - Overseas Jobs

IDAHO
(See Washington listing)

ILLINOIS
Chicago:
175 W. Jackson Blvd., Rm. 530
60604
(312) 353-6192

INDIANA
Indianapolis:
Minton-Capehart Federal Bldg.
575 N. Pennsylvania St., 46204
(317) 226-7161

IOWA
(See Missouri listing)
(816) 426-7757

KANSAS
Wichita:
One Twenty Bldg., Room 101
120 S. Market St., 67202
(316) 269-6794

In Johnson, Leavenworth, and
Wyandotte Counties, dial
(816) 426-5702

KENTUCKY
(See Ohio listing)

LOUISIANA
New Orleans:
1515 Poydras St., Suite 608
70112, (504) 589-2764

MAINE
(See New Hampshire listing)

MARYLAND
Baltimore:
Garmatz Federal Bldg.
101 W. Lombard St., 21201
(301) 962-3822

MASSACHUSETTS
Boston:
Thos. P. O'Neill Federal Bldg.
10 Causeway St., 02222-1031
(617) 565-5900

MICHIGAN
Detroit:
477 Michigan Ave., Rm. 565
48226, (313) 226-6950

MINNESOTA
Twin Cities:
Federal Building
Ft. Snelling, Twin Cities, 55111
(612) 725-3430

MISSISSIPPI
(See Huntsville, AL listing)

MISSOURI
Kansas City:
Federal Bldg., Rm. 134
601 E. 12th St., 64106
(816) 426-5702

St. Louis:
Old Post Office Bldg., Rm. 400
815 Olive St., 63101
(314) 539-2285

MONTANA
(See Colorado listing)

NEBRASKA
(See Kansas listing)

NEVADA
(See Sacramento listing)

NEW HAMPSHIRE
Portsmouth:
Thomas J. McIntyre Federal Bldg.,
Room 104
80 Daniel St., 03801-3879
(603) 431-7115

NEW JERSEY
Newark:
Peter W. Rodino Jr., Federal
Building
970 Broad St., 07102
(201) 645-3673
In Camden, dial (215) 597-7440

NEW MEXICO
Albuquerque:
Federal Building
421 Gold Ave., S.W., 87102
(505) 766-5583

In Dona Ana, Otero and El Paso
Counties, dial (505) 766-5583

NEW YORK
New York City:
Jacob K. Javits Federal Bldg.
26 Federal Plaza, 10278
(212) 264-0422

Syracuse:
James M. Hanley Federal Bldg.
100 S. Clinton St., 13260
(315) 423-5660

NORTH CAROLINA
Raleigh:
P.O. Box 25069
4505 Falls of the Neuse Rd.,
Suite 445, 27609
(919) 856-4361

NORTH DAKOTA
(See Minnesota listing)

OHIO
Dayton:
Federal Building, Rm. 506
200 W. 2nd St., 45402
(513) 225-2720

OKLAHOMA
Oklahoma City:
(Mail or phone only)
200 N.W. Fifth St., 2nd Floor
73102
(405) 231-4948

OREGON
Portland:
Federal Building, Rm. 376
1220 S.W. Third Ave., 97204
(503) 221-3141

PENNSYLVANIA
Harrisburg:
Federal Building, Rm. 168
P.O. Box 761, 17108
(717) 782-4494

Philadelphia:
Wm. J. Green Jr., Federal Bldg.
600 Arch St., Rm. 1416, 19106
(215) 597-7440

Pittsburgh:
Federal Building
1000 Liberty Ave., Rm. 119,
15222
(412) 644-2755

PUERTO RICO
San Juan:
Federico Degetau Federal Bldg.
Carlos E. Chardon St.
Hato Rey, P.R. 00918
(809) 766-5242

RHODE ISLAND
Providence:
John O. Pastore Federal Bldg.
Rm. 310, Kennedy Plaza, 02903
(401) 528-5251

SOUTH CAROLINA
(See Raleigh, NC listing)

SOUTH DAKOTA
(See Minnesota listing)

TENNESSEE
Memphis:
200 Jefferson Ave.
Suite 1312, 38103-2335
(901) 521-3956

TEXAS
Dallas:
(Mail or phone only)
Rm. 6B12, 1100 Commerce St.,
75242
(214) 767-8035

Houston:
(Phone-recording only)
(713) 226-2375

San Antonio:
(Mail or phone only)
6610 Broadway
Rm. 105, 78217
(512) 229-6611 or 6600

UTAH
(See Colorado listing)

VERMONT
(See New Hampshire listing)

VIRGINIA
Norfolk:
Federal Building, Rm. 220
Granby Mall, 23510-1886
(804) 441-3355

WASHINGTON
Seattle:
Federal Building
915 Second Ave., 98174
(206) 442-4365

WEST VIRGINIA
Phone only:
(513) 225-2866

WISCONSIN
Residents in Counties of Grant,
Iowa, Lafayette, Dane, Green,
Rock, Jefferson, Walworth,
Waukesha, Racine, Kenosha and
Milwaukee should dial (312)
353-6189 for job information.

All other Wisconsin residents
should apply to the Minnesota
listing or contact Federal Job information in their area.

WYOMING
(See Colorado listing)

COMPETITION NOTICE FOR MATHEMATICIANS AND RELATED POSITIONS, GS-5/7 with the United States Government

****
****

Positions Covered

This Competition Notice covers the following Mathematician and Related positions:

Actuary	Computer Scientist	Mathematician
Operations Research Analyst	Mathematical Statistician	Statistician

Best Opportunities: Employment opportunities vary by specialties and locations. However, the positions offering the best opportunities for employment are: Computer Scientist, Operations Research Analyst, and Mathematician.

Refer to the Qualifications Information Statement, QI-1500, for information concerning the required qualifications. This and other required forms are available from any Federal Job Information Center (FJIC). FJIC's are listed under "U.S. Government" in most metropolitan telephone directories. You may also call the College Hotline at 1-900-990-9200. (There will be a charge of 40 cents per minute for such calls.)

How to Apply

You will need the following materials to apply for the above mathematician and related positions:

- Occupational Supplement for Mathematicians and Related Positions - 1500X, Form B, OPM Form 1203-I,
- Qualification Information Statement for Mathematicians and Related Positions, QI-1500,

- Geographic Code Listing, OPM Form 1205,

Complete and submit a Form B for Mathematician positions, OPM Form 1203-I, to the **Office of Personnel Management, Staffing Service Center, Examining Office, P.O. Box 9105, Macon, GA, 31297-5099.** You may apply for consideration in more than one geographic zone, but you must submit an original Form B for each zone.

If you are claiming ten points veteran preference, you must complete and submit a Standard Form 15, Claim for 10-Point Veteran Preference, along with your Form B.

How Positions Are Filled

If you are eligible, your name will be placed on a competitor inventory and referred to agencies as vacancies occur. In addition, agencies are authorized to make immediate offers of employment to top ranking candidates. The rating needed to be hired directly will vary by location and specialty. If you are interested in working at a particular agency, you may want to contact the agency directly concerning employment prospects.

When you are contacted by a Federal agency for employment consideration, you will be asked to provide more detailed information about your background and qualifications. This normally will involve submitting a Standard Form 171, Application for Federal Employment, or a resume and OPM Form 1170/17, List of College Courses, or a transcript of college course work.

For positions at GS-9 and above, you must contact the OPM area office which covers the location where you want to be considered. Positions may be filled through OPM registers, through OPM issued recruiting bulletins, or through applying directly to an agency.

For GS-5 through GS-15 positions in Alaska and Hawaii (which includes the Pacific Overseas area), you need to contact the Anchorage Area Office and Honolulu Area Office respectively.

Entrance Salaries

GS-5	$16,305
GS-7	$20,195

Federal Agencies Maintaining Separate Competitor Inventories:

Positions with the National Aeronautics and Space Administration (NASA) GS-7/15 Aerospace Technologist positions with the NASA are recruited directly by each NASA installation. Contact the Personnel Office at the location where you wish to work. The addresses for the installations are:

Ames Research Center, Moffett Field, CA 94035
Dryden Flight Research Center, Edwards, CA 93523
George C. Marshall Space Flight Center, Huntsville, AL 35812
John F. Kennedy Space Center, KSC, FL 32899
Goddard Space Flight Center, Greenbelt, MD 20771
Langley Research Center, Hampton, VA 23665
Lewis Research Center, Cleveland, OH 44135
Johnson Space Center, Houston, TX 77058
National Space Technology Laboratories, NSTL. Station, MS 39529
Wallops Flight Facility, Wallops Island, VA 23337
Headquarters, NPH, Washington, D.C. 20546

The U.S. Government is an Equal Opportunity Employer

United States
Office of
Personnel
Management

COMPETITION NOTICE FOR PHYSICAL SCIENCE POSITIONS, GS-5/7 with the United States Government

****
****

Positions Covered

This Competition Notice covers the following Physical Science positions:

Astronomer   Geodesist   Land Surveyor
Cartographer   Geologist   Metallurgist
Chemist   Geophysicist   Oceanographer
General Physical Health Physicist Physicist
Scientist   Hydrologist

Best Opportunities: Employment opportunities vary by specialties and locations. However, the positions offering the best opportunities nationwide for employment are: Chemist and Physicist. Opportunities are good for Hydrologist in the Atlanta and Chicago Zones, and Cartographers and General Physical Scientists are in demand in the Washington, D.C. area.

Refer to the Qualifications Information Statement, QI-1300, for information concerning the required qualifications. This and other required forms are available from any Federal Job Information Center (FJIC). FJIC's are listed under "U.S. Government" in most metropolitan telephone directories. You may also call the College Hotline at 1-900-990-9200. (There will be a charge of 40 cents per minute for such calls.)

How to Apply

You will need the following materials to apply for the above physical science positions:

- Occupational Supplement for Physical Science Positions - 1300-X, Form B

- Qualifications Information Statement for Physical Science Positions,

- Geographic Code Listing,

Complete and submit a Form B for Physical Science, OPM Form 1203-K, to the **Office of Personnel Management, Staffing Service Center, Examining Office, P.O. Box 9105, Macon, GA, 31297-5099.** You may apply for consideration in more than one geographic zone, but you must submit an original Form B for each zone. (No photocopies of this form can be submitted).

If you are claiming ten points veteran preference, you must complete and submit a Standard Form 15, Claim for 10-Point Veteran Preference, along with your Form B.

How Positions Are Filled

If you are eligible, your name will be placed on a competitor inventory and referred to agencies as vacancies occur. In addition, agencies are authorized to make immediate offers of employment to top ranking candidates. The rating needed to be hired directly will vary by location and specialty. If you are interested in working at a particular agency, you may want to contact the agency directly concerning employment prospects.

When you are contacted by a Federal agency for employment consideration, you will be asked to provide more detailed information about your background and qualifications. This normally will involve submitting a Standard Form 171, Application for Federal Employment, or a resume and OPM Form 1170/17, List of College Courses, or a transcript of college course work.

For positions not covered by this competition notice and positions at GS-9 and above, you must contact the OPM area office which covers the location where you want to be considered. Positions may be filled through OPM registers, through OPM issued recruiting bulletins, or through applying directly to an agency. For GS-5 through GS-15 positions in Alaska and Hawaii (which includes the Pacific Overseas area), you need to contact the Anchorage Area Office and Honolulu Area Office respectively.

Entrance Salaries

* Special Salary Rates for Metallurgist Positions:		Entry Salary Rates for all other positions:	
GS-5	$19,805	GS-5	$16,305
GS-7	$24,532	GS-7	$20,195

*These rates apply only in the USA.

Federal Agencies Maintaining Separate Competitor Inventories:

Positions with the National Aeronautics and Space Administration (NASA) as GS-7/15 Aerospace Technologist positions are recruited directly by each NASA installation. Contact the Personnel Office at the location where you wish to work. The addresses for the installations are:

Ames Research Center, Moffett Field, CA 94035
Dryden Flight Research Center, Edwards, CA 93523
George C. Marshall Space Flight Center, Huntsville, AL 35812
John F. Kennedy Space Center, KSC, FL 32899
Goddard Space Flight Center, Greenbelt, MD 20771
Langley Research Center, Hampton, VA 23665
Lewis Research Center, Cleveland, OH 44135
Johnson Space Center, Houston, TX 77058
National Space Technology Laboratories, NSTL Station, MS 39529
Wallops Flight Facility, Wallops Island, VA 23337
Headquarters, NPH, Washington, D.C. 20546

Defense Mapping Agency (DMA) maintains a list of eligibles for Cartographer and Geodesist positions agency-wide at grades GS-5/15. Apply to DMA Aerospace Center, Staffing Division, Personnel Office, 2nd and Arsenal Streets, St. Louis Air Force Station, Missouri 63118. These jobs require a security clearance.

U.S. Department of Commerce's, National Oceanic and Atmospheric Administration (NOAA) maintain the list of eligibles for all Meteorologist positions government-wide at grade GS-5/15. Apply to the U.S. Department of Commerce, Eastern Administrative Support Center, NOAA, Special Examining Unit, 253 Monticello Ave., Norfolk, VA 23510.

U.S. Department of Agriculture (USDA) maintains the list of eligibles for Food Technologist positions government-wide at grades GS-5/12. Apply directly to the U.S.D.A. - F.S.I.S., P.O.B. - Examining Unit, Butler Square West, 4th Floor, 100 North Sixth St., Minneapolis, MN 55403. For GS-13/15 positions, contact your nearest FJIC.

The U.S. Government is an Equal Opportunity Employer

United States
Office of
Personnel
Management

COMPETITION NOTICE FOR PROFESSIONAL ENGINEERING POSITIONS, GS-5/7 with the United States Government

****

Positions Covered

This Competition Notice covers the following Professional Engineer positions:

Aerospace	Electronics	Naval Architecture
Biomedical	Environmental	Nuclear
Ceramic	Fire Prevention	Petroleum
Chemical	Industrial	Safety
Civil	Materials	Welding
Computer	Mechanical	
Electrical	Mining	

Best Opportunities: Employment opportunities vary by specialties and locations. However, the positions offering the best opportunities for employment nationwide are **Computer, Electrical, Electronics, and Mechanical** engineer. There are also good opportunities for Civil and Environmental Engineers in the Philadelphia and San Francisco Zones.

Refer to the **Qualifications Information Statement for Professional Engineering Positions (QI-0800, Rev. June 1989)** for information concerning the required qualifications. This and other required forms are available from any Federal Job Information Center (FJIC). These are listed under **"U.S. Government"** in most metropolitan telephone directories. You may also call the College Hotline at 1-900-990-9200. (There will be a charge of 40 cents per minute for such calls.)

How to Apply

You will need the following materials to apply for these positions:

- Occupational Supplement for Professional Engineering Positions - 0800X, Form B,

- Qualifications Information Statement for Professional Engineering Positions

  - Geographic Code Listing

Complete and submit a Form B for engineers, OPM Form 1203-C, to the **Office of Personnel Management, Staffing Service Center, Examining Office,** P.O. Box 9105, Macon, GA 31297-5099. You may apply for consideration in more than one geographic zone, but you must submit an original form for each zone. (No photocopies of this form can be substituted).

If you claim ten point veteran preference, you must include a completed Standard Form 15, Claim for 10-Point Veteran Preference, along with your Form B.

How Positions Are Filled

If you are eligible, your name will be placed on a competitor inventory and referred to agencies as vacancies occur. In addition, agencies are authorized to make immediate offers of employment to top ranking candidates. The rating needed to be hired directly will vary by location and specialty. If you are interested in working at a particular agency, you may want to contact the agency directly concerning employment prospects.

When you are contacted by a Federal agency for employment consideration, you will be asked to provide more detailed information about your background and qualifications. This normally will involve submitting a Standard Form 171, Application for Federal Employment, or a resume and OPM Form 1170/17, List of College Courses, or a transcript of college course work.

For positions at grade GS-9 and above, you must contact the FJIC which covers the location where you want to be considered. Positions are filled through OPM registers, through OPM issued recruiting bulletins, or through applying directly to an agency.

For GS-5 through GS-15 positions in Alaska and Hawaii (which includes the Pacific Overseas area), you need to contact the Anchorage Area Office and Honolulu Area Office respectively.

Special Entrance Salary Rates for Engineers

GRADE	Specialties		
	Mining	Petroleum	All Others
GS-5	$18,017	$20,780	$21,202
GS-7	$22,326	$25,739	$26,252

Federal Agencies Maintaining Separate Competitor Inventories

Positions with the **National Aeronautics and Space Administration (NASA)** as GS-7/15 Aerospace Technologist positions are recruited directly by each NASA installation. Contact the Personnel Office at the location where you wish to work. The addresses for the installations are:

Ames Research Center, Moffett Field, CA 94035
Dryden Flight Research Center, Edwards, CA 93523
George C. Marshall Space Flight Center, Huntsville, AL 35812
John F. Kennedy Space Center, KSC, FL 32899
Goddard Space Flight Center, Greenbelt, MD 20771
Langley Research Center, Hampton, VA 23665
Lewis Research Center, Cleveland, OH 44135
Johnson Space Center, Houston, TX 77058
National Space Technology Laboratories, NSTL Station, MS 39529
Wallops Flight Facility, Wallops Island, VA 23337
Headquarters, NPH, Washington, D.C. 20546

U.S. Department of Agriculture (USDA) maintains the list of eligibles for all Agricultural Engineering positions government-wide at grades GS-5/7. Apply to U.S. Department of Agriculture, Soil Conservation Service, P.O. Box 37636, Washington, D.C. 20013.

The U.S. Government is an Equal Opportunity Employer

United States
Office of
Personnel
Management

United States Office of Personnel Management

COMPETITION NOTICE

POSITION/SERIES/GRADE:	Secretary GS-0318-5/6/7/8 Number of Vacancies: Few	NOTICE NO. PM-9008
LOCATION: Eastern Massachusetts		OPENING DATE:
		CLOSING DATE:

DUTIES:

Secretaries in the Federal service assist one or more persons in an organization by performing general office work in an organization. Duties may include: providing telephone and receptionist services; maintaining attendance records; ordering office supplies, equipment repair, and printing services; reserving rooms for meetings; maintaining office filing systems, or designing and organizing filing systems; receiving and controlling incoming correspondence; reviewing out-going correspondence, reports, etc., for format, grammar, and punctuation, and removing typographical errors; composing non-technical correspondence; performing typing, stenographic, or transcribing duties; maintaining information needed for budget; making travel arrangements; arranging conferences; locating and assembling information for various reports, briefings, conferences, etc.; following up with staff members to insure that various commitments are met, etc.

QUALIFICATION REQUIREMENTS:

Applicants must have had one year of specialized experience directly related to the duties described above. The experience must have equipped candidates to successfully perform the duties of a Secretary and must demonstrate possession of the following knowledges, skills, and abilities essential to serve as a principal office assistant: (1) Ability to organize effectively the flow of clerical processes in an office, (2) Ability to organize and design a filing system, (3) Ability to make arrangements for such things as travel, conferences, and meetings, (4) Ability to locate things and assemble information for various reports, briefings, and conferences, (5) Ability to compose non-technical correspondence.

For each respective grade (GS-5/6/7/8) the required experience must have been equivalent to the next lower grade level in the Federal service.

Completion of four academic years of education in an accredited college or university may be substituted in full for grade 5 level positions. Education may not be substituted in full above grade 5.

For positions requiring typing, you must be able to type 40 words per minute. For most positions requiring stenography, you must be able to take dictation at 120 words per minute. In a few cases, only 80 words per minute is required.

A combination of education and experience may be used to meet the requirements at all grades.

For Secretary positions at the GS-2/3/4 levels, request a clerical package from the office mentioned below.

SUBMIT THESE FORMS:

o   SF-171, Application for Federal Employment;
o   SF-15, Application for 10-Point Veteran Preference (if applicable);
o   OPM Form 1203-AH;
o   PM0012, Supplemental Qualification Statement;
o   PM0012A, Geographic Code Listing.

MAIL COMPLETED FORMS TO:

Boston Area Office
U.S. Office of Personnel Management
Thomas P. O'Neill, Jr. Federal Building
10 Causeway Street
Boston, MA 02222-1031

ALL QUALIFIED APPLICANTS WILL RECEIVE CONSIDERATION FOR EMPLOYMENT WITHOUT REGARD TO RACE, CREED, COLOR, NATIONAL ORIGIN, OR ANY OTHER NON-MERIT FACTOR.

United States
Office of
Personnel
Management

Office of
Washington
Examining
Services

Washington,
D.C. 20415

Technicians in Engineering, Physical and Mathematical Sciences
Competition Notice:

All Grades and Options are Open

This list is used to fill technician positions at grades GS-4/12 in Washington, D.C., and Atlantic Overseas (opportunities are extremely poor for positions overseas). The jobs covered are:

Cartographic Technician
Construction Inspector
  Representative
Electronic Technician

Engineering Technician
Engineering Draftsman
Geodetic Technician
Hydrologic Technician

Industrial Engineering
  Technician
Mathematics Technician
Meteorological Technician

Office Draftsman
Physical Science Technician
Statistical Assistant
Surveying Technician

Refer to the Qualifications Information Statement for information about the qualifications required for each job.

Employment Opportunities

For each of the occupational specialties listed, the chart below shows what the past opportunities have been for being considered from this list. The chart uses the following codes to describe the general trends for hiring in the Washington, D.C., Metropolitan Area.

A. EXCELLENT—Most qualified applicants receive job offers.

B. GOOD—Most well-qualified applicants receive job offers.

C. FAIR—Some well-qualified applicants receive job offers.

D. POOR—Only a few of the best qualified applicants receive job offers.

E. ALMOST NONE—Opportunities are very limited.

Options	GS-4	GS-5/8	GS-9/12	Comments
Cartographic Technician	C	D	D	
Construction Inspector/Rep.	D	B	B	
Electronic Technician	C	B	B	
Engineering Draftsman	D	B	C	GS-4/9 only
Engineering Technician	C			
Aerospace		E	E	
Architecture		C	C	
Biomedical		D	D	
Chemical		E	E	
Civil		B	B	
Electrical		B	B	
Materials		C	C	
Mechanical		B	B	
Mining		E	E	
Naval Architecture		B	B	
Nuclear		E	E	
Petroleum		D	D	
Geodetic Technician	E	E	E	
Hydrologic Technician	D	E	E	
Industrial Engineer/Technician	D	D	D	
Mathematics Technician	E	E	E	
Meteorological Technician	D	C	D	
Office Draftsman	D	D		GS-4/7 only
Physical Science Technician	B			
Geology		C	E	
Geophysics		E	E	
Oceanography		E	E	
Chemistry/Biochemistry		B	D	
Health Physics		D	E	
Astronomy		E	E	
Pollution/Environment		D	E	
Physics		D	E	
Metallurgy		E	E	
Statistical Assistant		C	E	GS-5/12 only
Surveying Technician	E	E	E	

How to Apply: If you qualify for one or more of these positions, complete and submit the following forms:

Form B —Occupational Supplement for Engineering Technician (OPM Form 1203-Q)

Form A1—Applicant Data Sheet

SF-171 —Personal Qualifications Statement

OPM Form 1170/17—List of College Courses

These forms can be obtained from the Federal Job Information Testing Center in Washington, D.C.

Where to Apply: Completed forms should be sent to:

U.S. OFFICE OF PERSONNEL MANAGEMENT
OFFICE OF WASHINGTON EXAMINING SERVICES
P.O. BOX 14080
WASHINGTON, D.C. 20044

DEPARTMENT OF TRANSPORTATION

PROMOTIONAL AND CAREER OPPORTUNITIES

ANNOUNCEMENT NO: OST-92-026

ORGANIZATION OFFICE OF THE SECRETARY

POSITION Accountant, GS-510-11/12 or GM-510-13

OPENING DATE:

LOCATION O/Asst. Secretary for Administration, O/Financial Mgmt.

CLOSING DATE:

Working Capital Fund Div., Cost Analysis & Research Br.

AREA OF CONSIDERATION GOV'T-WIDE

CURRENT COMPETITIVE SERVICE STATUS EMPLOYEES OR THOSE WITH REINSTATEMENT ELIGIBILITY ONLY.

APPLICATIONS WILL BE ACCEPTED FROM HANDICAPPED APPLICANTS AND DISABLED VETERANS WHO ARE ELIGIBLE FOR EMPLOYMENT UNDER SPECIAL AUTHORITIES. PLEASE SPECIFY ELIGIBILITY FOR SUCH APPOINTMENT.

NOTE:

This position is covered under the Performance Management and Recognition System at the GM-13 level.

All applicants must meet the one year time-in-grade requirement.

If filled at the GS-11 or GS-12 level, this position has promotion potential to the GM-13 level.

DUTIES:

The incumbent serves under the Chief, Cost Analysis and Research, Working Capital Fund (WCF) and performs the following duties: (1) provides analyses of a wide variety of financial/accounting issues, systems, and operations including review of cost accounting and billing systems which may include revision of cost recovery methods, pricing formulas, and overhead allocations; (2) prepares financial statements; (3) evaluates programs and financial/ accounting operations and systems for effectiveness and efficiency; (4) provides consultation, advice, and technical support relative to the financial management and operation of the WCF; (5) develops and recommends financial, managerial, and process improvements to the operation of the WCF; and (6) participates in the review and revision of the Department's WCF policy and operating procedures.

(OVER)

PRIVACY ACT REQUIREMENTS (P.L. 93-579)

The referenced forms are used to evaluate your qualifications for promotion and are authorized under Title 5 of the U.S. Code, Sections 2266 and 3381. Each referenced form must be submitted in order for you to be considered for promotion in the position being advertised. The social security number is not required for this purpose and may be deleted from the forms submitted. Your servicing personnel office or the office named in this announcement will be able to provide information on specific Privacy Act requirements.

CANDIDATES WHO FAIL TO SUBMIT THE REQUIRED FORMS WILL NOT BE CONSIDERED. NONE OF THESE FORMS WILL BE SUBSEQUENTLY LOANED OR RETURNED TO THE APPLICANTS.

CANDIDATES WILL BE EVALUATED ON BASIS OF EXPERIENCE AND EDUCATION. PERFORMANCE APPRAISAL, TRAINING AND AWARDS.

ALL QUALIFIED CANDIDATES WILL BE CONSIDERED REGARDLESS OF RACE, COLOR, RELIGION, SEX OR NATIONAL ORIGIN

QUALIFICATIONS:

General Experience: Applicants must meet the Positive Education Requirement outlined in the OPM X-118 Qualification Standards Handbook for the GS/GM-510 Accounting Series.

Specialized Experience: Applicants must have at least one year of specialized experience at a level of difficulty equivalent to the next lower grade in the Federal service, which is in or related to the line of work of the position and which has equipped the applicant with the specific knowledge, skills, and abilities to successfully perform the duties of the position.

QUALITY RANKING FACTORS: For maximum consideration, address the specific factors listed below including any experience, training, and awards pertinent to each factor.

- Knowledge of commercial accounting practices, working capital funds, revolving funds, industrial funds, trust funds or any entity utilizing cost accounting concepts and processes.
- Ability to analyze complex financial and accounting issues and make recommendations for resolution.
- Ability to evaluate programs and financial/accounting operations and systems for effectiveness and efficiency.
- Ability to communicate both orally and in writing with program, technical, and management audiences.

HOW TO APPLY:

Applicants must submit a Standard Form 171, "Application for Federal Employment," and a current (within 12 months of the closing date of the announcement) performance appraisal form. If a performance appraisal cannot be provided, a statement explaining why it is not possible to obtain an appraisal must be submitted. Applicants should also submit the latest SF-50 which documents competitive status, if available. All forms should be sent to: Personnel Operations Division, M-18, Room 9113, Department of Transportation, 400 Seventh Street, S.W., Washington, D.C. 20590. If additional information is required, please call (202) 366-6613. All applications must be received or postmarked by the closing date of this announcement.

THE USE OF POSTAGE-PAID GOVERNMENT AGENCY ENVELOPES IN FILING APPLICATIONS IS A VIOLATION OF FEDERAL LAW. ANY APPLICATIONS RECEIVED IN POSTAGE-PAID GOVERNMENT ENVELOPES WILL NOT BE CONSIDERED.

U S D A

Agricultural Marketing Service

AGRICULTURAL COMMODITY GRADER

Announcement No. 453

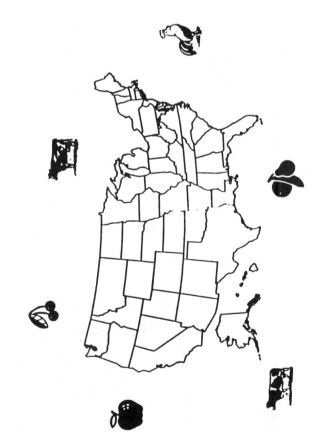

THIS ANNOUNCEMENT COVERS

Agricultural Commodity Grader positions with the specializations of:

DAIRY--GS-5, and 7,* See page 3 for "Special Requirement"

FRESH FRUIT AND VEGETABLE--GS-5, 7, and 9

MEAT--GS-5, 7, and 9

POULTRY--GS-5 and 7

PROCESSED FRUIT AND VEGETABLE--GS-5 and 7

If you apply for more than one specialization, a separate set of application forms must be submitted. See paragraph entitled, "How to Apply."

No previous Federal service experience is required. Applicants must be citizens of the United States.

WHAT THE JOBS ARE

Agricultural Commodity Graders with the U.S. Department of Agriculture compare the quality or condition of agricultural commodities with official standards and related regulations to determine their official U.S. Grade and/or acceptability. The Graders inspect production samples of the product and describe the grade and/or condition of the product by color, taste, shape, or other specific conditions required by official standards, regulations, or purchase contracts. They may also determine if the processing, packaging, storage, or transportation procedures are being followed and if sanitary requirements and contract provisions are being met.

Agricultural Commodity positions may be filled on a full-time, part-time, seasonal, or intermittent basis.

--Full-time: Employees work a regularly prearranged schedule of 40 hours per week. They are entitled to leave and health and life insurance benefits.

--Part-time: Employees work a regularly prearranged schedule of 16-32 hours per week. They are entitled to leave and health and life insurance benefits.

--Intermittent: Employees work on an irregular or occasional basis as needed. They are compensated only for time actually worked, have no pre-arranged schedule, and are not entitled to leave, health, or life insurance benefits.

-- Seasonal: Employees work only during certain times of the year but do that work every year. Only employees who are expected to work 6 months or more in a year are entitled to leave, and health and life insurance benefits.

WHERE THE JOBS ARE

Agricultural Commodity Graders are assigned to duty locations throughout the United States, depending on where they are needed, and may be transferred if necessary.

WORK ENVIRONMENT

Agricultural Commodity Graders perform physically active work, often in freezers and outdoors, and are exposed to hot or cold conditions, dust, dryness, humidity, heights, and wet and slippery floors. Graders must work at a pace largely determined by the marketing or production process typical of the commodity.

QUALIFICATIONS REQUIRED

Requirements for GS-5 (all specializations)

A. Three years of experience that demonstrated possession of the knowledges, skills and abilities required to perform agricultural commodity grading work. For the DAIRY specialization, at least 1 year of that experience must be directly related to the manufacture, processing, or grading of dairy products or other work that demonstrates the ability to perform Agricultural Commodity Grader (Dairy) duties.

OR

B. Successful completion of a full 4-year course in an accredited college or university leading to a bachelor's degree that included the required semester hours (or equivalent) in courses directly related to the commodity specialization of the position being filled. (See education requirement under each specialization).

OR

C. Any time-equivalent combination of experience and education defined in A and B above. In combining education with experience, an academic year of study comprising 30 semester hours or 45 quarter hours is considered equal to 9 months of experience.

The total creditable experience and/or education in A, B, or C above must have demonstrated possession of the following:

-- Knowledge of the general characteristics of common agricultural products of the agricultural commodity group for which the applicant is applying or of another agricultural commodity group;
-- A familiarity with the standard methods or practices related to the products' processing, storage, transportation, or marketing in terms of the effects such factors have on product quality;
-- The ability to learn the methods and procedures of product grading and inspection work.

Brief job descriptions and examples of the experience or education which may provide the required knowledge, skill, and ability related to the various specializations follow. The examples are typical but not all-inclusive of the type of work that may qualify you for the position.

DAIRY GRADERS examine and evaluate the class, quality and condition of cheese, butter, fresh milk, and dry milk to determine official U.S. Grade and/or their acceptability. The determinations are made according to written standards, official specifications, and related regulations. Graders inspect dairy manufacturing plants and enforce applicable Federal and State laws and regulations regarding raw materials, sanitation, and finished products.

SPECIAL REQUIREMENTS
-- Graders selected for this option will be required to pass a sensory evaluation taste test within the first 3 weeks of employment. (Failing this test could result in termination of employment.)

Experience
-- Work that involved grading dairy products by applying government and commercial standards.
-- Work that involved assembling, distributing, or storing dairy products provided the work required familiarity with product grade and quality factors; or

Education
-- Successful completion of a full 4-year course of study in an accredited college or university leading to a bachelor's degree including 9 semester hours (or the equivalent) in Agriculture, Food Technology, Food Science, Chemistry, or Biology that included or was supplemented by one course in Dairy Products Processing or Manufacturing.

FRESH FRUIT AND VEGETABLE GRADERS inspect the condition of fresh fruit and vegetables and determine the official U.S. grade and/or acceptability. The work often includes monitoring the conditions under which the product is processed, stored, or transported when these conditions affect product quality. The grader has frequent contact with producers, distributors, wholesalers, and retailers.

Experience
-- Marketing of fresh fruit or vegetables that involved handling substantial car lot quantities and knowledge of Federal grades and grading;
-- Commercial grading and packing of fresh fruit or vegetables on a substantial scale that involved supervision or instruction of others in commercial grading and packing;
-- Inspection of fresh fruit or vegetables for official certification of quality and condition or for enforcement of standardization laws;
-- Research work in horticulture or marketing of horticultural products provided the studies relate to the standardization or inspection of fresh fruit or vegetables; or

Education
-- A 4-year course of college study including 9 semester hours (or the equivalent) in a related field such as Agriculture, Botany, Food Science, or Horticulture that leads to an understanding of the production, marketing, or quality characteristics of fresh fruit and vegetables.

Some examples of acceptable courses include Berry Production, Vegetable Production, Technology of Fruits, Technology of Vegetables, Basic Botany, Basic Agriculture, Agricultural Marketing, Agricultural Economics, Food Processing, or other related courses.

*   *   *

MEAT GRADERS examine and grade dressed meat, meat carcasses, and wholesale cuts by uniformly applying official quality standards and contract specifications. U.S. standards define classes and grades in terms of such factors as texture and firmness of lean, and degree and character of marbling. Meat Graders also examine and certify meat and meat products for various Government and commercial buyers according to approved purchase specifications.

Experience
-- Technical or supervisory responsibility for a phase of a meat packing production operation requiring technical knowledge of the production process;
-- Directing a meat packing production unit;
-- Ribbing beef carcasses for shipment or breaking beef into primal cuts;
-- Work experience involving livestock production or marketing for the purpose of regularly supplying meat animals of a consistent quality to the market;
-- Buying or selling livestock in quantity as a packer buyer, commission salesperson, commission firm operator, or livestock auction operator;
-- Livestock or meat market reporting under the supervision of a Federal officer; or

Education
-- A 4-year course of college study including 9 semester hours (or the equivalent) in Agriculture, Animal Science, Animal Husbandry, Biology, or other related fields, that included or was supplemented by ONE COURSE IN MEAT.

*   *   *

POULTRY GRADERS determine and certify the class, quality, and condition of poultry, shell eggs, and egg products. They assign the correct U.S. grade to poultry and ensure that various types of poultry are correctly labeled and packaged. They determine the class, quality, quantity, and condition of shell eggs while ensuring compliance with program sanitation requirements. They ensure that graded eggs are properly packaged and identified with the correct USDA grademark. They inspect egg products to ensure that product description, quantity, and condition are in accordance with approved regulations, and oversee the segregation of raw materials, breaking, processing, reexamination of product, pasteurization, freezing or drying, on a continuous basis to ensure wholesomeness. Graders are also responsible for proper handling and identification of inedible products.

Experience
-- Enforcement of Federal, State, or local laws and regulations requiring a knowledge of grading or inspection requirements for poultry, poultry products, shell eggs or egg products;

-- Work experience involving application of Federal, State, or commercial grades in grading agricultural commodities;
-- Work experience raising poultry provided the work required familiarity with product grades and quality factors; or

Education
-- A 4-year course of college study including 9 semester hours (or the equivalent) in Poultry Science, Animal Science, Food Technology, Agriculture, Biology or other closely related courses.

*   *   *

PROCESSED FRUIT AND VEGETABLE GRADERS determine the quality, condition, and wholesomeness of canned, frozen, dried, dehydrated, or otherwise preserved fruits, vegetables, and related products. Determinations are based on official grade standards, written specifications, buyer-seller contracts, or inspection agreements. They review plant sanitation and product formulation compliance and perform laboratory analyses. Graders explain the application of standards, regulations, and Federal contract requirements to financially interested parties.

Experience
-- Experience that involved determining the quality and condition of processed fruits or vegetables in accordance with written standards, specifications, or contracts;
-- Laboratory or analytical work related to quality control, inspection, or classification of processed fruits and vegetables;
-- Other experiences such as teaching, research, extension work, or food processing plant management related to processing, standardizations, grading, or inspection of fruits, vegetables, or similar processed foods; or

Education
-- A 4-year course of college study including 9 semester hours (or the equivalent) in Agriculture, Food Technology, Chemistry, Physical or Biological Science, or Home Economics.

ADDITIONAL REQUIREMENTS FOR POSITIONS ABOVE GS-5 (ALL SPECIALIZATIONS)

For GS-7 level positions:

A. A background of experience or education which demonstrated possession of the following:
-- Specific knowledge of the official U.S. grade standards for products within the relevant commodity group.
-- Knowledge of the specific elements of agricultural product processing, transportation, storage, or condition that affect the products' grade, acceptability, and quality;

-- Skill in applying the procedures, techniques, and methods required to determine product acceptability or grade, and skill in performing various types of inspections;

-- Skill in establishing, maintaining, and developing effective interpersonal relationships with employees, operating supervisors, and managers of agricultural processing firms and facilities.

The following kinds of experience are examples of work which may provide the required knowledge and skill:

-- Work as an Agricultural Commodity Grader which involved grading agricultural products for official U.S. certification;

-- Work which involved developing recognized standards or specifications for classes or grades of products within the relevant commodity group;

-- Work in a food processing plant, warehouse, or similar facility that required extensive technical knowledge of the product's processing, storage, shipment, or marketing provided the work also required specific knowledge of product grades, the factors involved in their determination, and the typical methods of grade determination.

OR

B. Successful completion of 1 year of graduate study in an accredited college or university with major study in a field directly related to the commodity specialization of the position being filled meets all requirements for positions at GS-7 or below. Graduate study alone does not provide sufficient evidence of possession of knowledges and skills required for positions above GS-7. One year of full-time graduate education is determined by the number of credit hours the school attended declares to represent a full year of study in that graduate program. You are responsible for providing evidence that your hours of graduate coursework meet your school's requirement.

C. The following Superior Academic Achievement Standard applies ONLY to the FRESH FRUIT AND VEGETABLE, MEAT and Poultry specializations.

Criteria for GS-7 Eligibility--Persons who have completed all the requirements for or are candidates for the bachelor's degree from an accredited college or university within 9 months (with appropriate majors or course credits, if required) may be rated eligible for GS-7 provided they meet one of the requirements listed below. (Certification from the college or university must be submitted with your Application for Federal Employment).

(A) Standing in the upper third of their class based on completed college work at time of application for the position. This is the upper third of the class in the college or university, or major subdivision (e.g., School of Engineering, School of Business Administration).

(B) College grade average of "B" (3.0 of a possible 4.0) or better or equivalent (2.95 may be rounded up to 3.0). This is either:
(1) the average of all completed college courses at time of application for the position, or
(2) the average of all college courses completed during the last 2 years of the undergraduate curriculum.

(C) College grade average of B+ (3.5) or better (or equivalent, in their major, where such field is fully qualifying and directly applicable to the specialty field of the position to be filled. This is either:
(1) the average of completed courses in the major field at time of application for the position, or
(2) the average of college courses completed in the major field during the last 2 years of the undergraduate curriculum.

(D) Election of membership in Phi Beta Kappa, Sigma Xi, or one of the national honorary scholastic/societies meeting the minimum requirements of the Association of College Honor Societies, other than freshman honor societies.

Senior students may be rated provisionally eligible under b(2) or c(2), provided they had the required average in the junior year. They will be required to submit evidence at the time of appointment that the required average was maintained during the senior year.

All grade-point averages are to be computed on a 4.0 scale (A = 4 points. B = 3 points. C = 2 points. D = 1 points. F = 0 points). If college uses any other system to compute GPA, an official explanation of equivalence to the 4.0 system must be provided.

- -

For GS-9 level positions: (Applies ONLY to the FRESH FRUIT AND VEGETABLE and MEAT specializations).

GS-9 positions require "hands on" grading and/or inspection experience in the commodity specialization applied for. Such experience must have included final responsibility for certifying the condition and grade according to universally accepted standards for the commodity.

QUALITY OF EXPERIENCE

For positions at all grade levels, experience shown must have been at a sufficiently high level of difficulty and responsibility to demonstrate the ability to perform the duties and responsibilities of the position for which the candidate is applying. Therefore, at each grade, 6 months of the required experience must have been at a level of difficulty comparable to that of the next lower grade in the Federal service, or at least 1 year of the experience must have been at a level of difficulty and responsibility comparable to that of the second lower grade in Federal service.

UNPAID EXPERIENCE OR VOLUNTEER WORK

Pertinent unpaid experience or volunteer work will be evaluated on the same basis as paid experience. To receive proper credit you must show the actual time spent on these activities.

STUDENTS

Applications will be accepted from senior students who are otherwise qualified and expect to complete all scholastic coursework needed to qualify within 9 months of the date of filing their application. Courses you expect to complete will be accepted tentatively and should be entered on the list of courses you submit as "Courses to be Completed." You may be offered a job before you graduate, but must show proof that you have finished your coursework before starting work.

HOW YOU WILL BE RATED

No written test will be required. All candidates will be rated on a scale of 100 based on an evaluation of experience, education, and training in relation to the duties of the position to be filled. Work experience and relevant course-work above the minimum required for a particular grade level will be considered in ranking qualified applicants based on the relatedness of the work experience or courses to the position's required knowledges, skills, and abilities. Rating will be based on statements in the application form and the Supplemental Qualifications Statement, and any additional evidence received by the examining office.

ELIGIBILITY

A separate list of eligibles will be established for each specialization. If you are interested in more than one specialization, you must submit a separate set of application forms for each specialization.

TERM OF ELIGIBILITY

Eligibility on these lists will be limited to a period of 12 months. You may, however, have your eligibility extended for an additional 12-month period by submitting a new application or by bringing your original application up to date. This may be done at any time after your name has been on the list 10 months. (The date appearing on your "Notice of Results" represents the date your name was placed on the list.)

PHYSICAL REQUIREMENTS

You must be physically and mentally able to safely and efficiently perform the essential functions of the position. Good near and distant vision and depth perception, (corrective lenses permitted) are required, as is the ability to distinguish basic and fine shades of colors. Usable hearing, speech and a normal sense of smell are essential. Many positions in certain specializations also require a normal sense of taste. However, in most cases, a specific physical condition or impairment other than complete loss of vision, hearing, or speech will not automatically disqualify an applicant for appointment. The loss or impairment of a specific function may be compensated for by the satisfactory use of a prosthesis or mechanical aid. Reasonable accommodation may also be considered in determining an applicant's ability to perform. Reasonable accommodation may include, but is not limited to: job modification, provision of assistive devices, and/or job restructuring.

ADDITIONAL REQUIREMENT

Males born after December 31, 1959, desiring federal employment, must be registered with the Selective Service System.

EQUAL EMPLOYMENT OPPORTUNITY

Qualified applicants, who are U. S. Citizens, will receive consideration for appointment without regard to race, religion, color, national origin, sex, political affiliations, age or any other non-merit factor.

SALARIES

Federal salary rates are adjusted periodically. Current information regarding salaries may be obtained from Federal Job Information Centers.

DRIVING REQUIREMENTS

Some positions require the operation of a motor vehicle. For positions requiring operation of a motor vehicle, you must either hold, or obtain within 30 days of employment, appropriate State and U.S. Government motor vehicle operator's permits.

TRAINING

All applicants selected for Agricultural Commodity Grader (Meat) positions will be required to successfully complete an 8-week training course.

TRAVEL

All positions may require travel of at least 1-5 nights per month.

MOBILITY STATEMENT

Applicants for Agricultural Commodity Grader positions should be aware that all specializations, except Fresh Fruit and Vegetable, require a Mobility Statement at the time of appointment. The applicant will be required to sign a statement indicating willingness to accept a reassignment to other geographical locations throughout the United States whenever the agency encounters a need for Agricultural Commodity Graders in a different geographical location.

HOW TO APPLY

WHAT TO FILE: Please submit one set of the forms listed below for each specialization in which you are interested.

A. SF-171, Application for Federal Employment. Be sure to show the title of the position, the announcement number, the specialization for which you are applying, and the lowest salary you are willing to accept. In order to receive proper credit, list all the jobs you have had and describe fully the experience gained in each. Be sure to include the number of hours worked per week.

B. OPM Form 1170/37, Supplemental Qualifications Statement, Agricultural Commodity Grader. This form must be completed for all specializations except Dairy.

C. OPM Form 1170/65, Supplemental Qualifications Statement, Agricultural Commodity Grader (Dairy). Applicants for the Dairy specialization must complete this form.

D. College Transcript or OPM Form 1170/17. If you are submitting a transcript of college courses, send it with your application. Do not have the school send the transcript directly to the Examining Office.

E. SF-15, Application for 10-Point Veteran Preference. Submit this form with documentary proof required therein, if you are claiming 10-point veteran preference (disability, widow, wife, or mother preference). Documentary proof will be returned to you.

F. Employment Availability Statement--Be sure to provide all information requested.

*Refer to the Geographic Code Listing in this Announcement to identify your geographic availability.

WHERE TO OBTAIN FORMS: The forms listed above may be obtained by writing or calling to the address below.

WHERE TO FILE: Send the completed forms listed above to:

U.S. Department of Agriculture, APHIS
Field Servicing Office, Examining Unit
Butler Square West, 5th Floor
100 North Sixth Street
Minneapolis, MN 55403
PH: (612) 370-2208

WHEN TO FILE: The register will be opened and closed by specialization and/or location. Before you apply, consult the current amendment to this announcement to find out which specializations and locations are open to receipt of applications. If you apply for a specialization or a location that is not open, your application will be returned.

PROFESSIONAL
AGRICULTURAL ENGINEERING POSITIONS

ANNOUNCEMENT NO. AE-NW-1
OPEN ON A CONTINUOUS BASIS

OPPORTUNITIES IN THE FEDERAL GOVERNMENT GS-5/7

The Soil Conservation Service, Special Examining Unit is accepting applications for professional agricultural engineering positions located throughout the country, except Hawaii.

DESCRIPTION OF DUTIES:
The duties of such positions require application of a high level of fundamental scientific knowledge in the development, interpretation, and evaluation of new scientific knowledge, techniques, or products.

BASIC QUALIFICATIONS REQUIREMENTS:
The primary method of qualifying for professional engineering positions is through successful completion of a full 4-year professional engineering curriculum (NOT ENGINEERING TECHNOLOGY) leading to a Bachelor's or higher degree in engineering in an accredited college or university. To be acceptable, the curriculum must:

Be in a school of engineering with at least one curriculum accredited by the Accreditation Board for Engineering and Technology (ABET) as a professional engineering curriculum, OR

Include differential and integral calculus and courses (more advanced than first-year physics and chemistry) in five of the seven areas of engineering science or physics:

(a) statics, dynamics;
(b) strength of materials (stress-strain relationships);
(c) fluid mechanics, hydraulics;
(d) thermodynamics;
(e) electrical fields and circuits;
(f) nature and properties of materials (relating particle and aggregate structure to properties);
(g) any other comparable area of fundamental engineering science or physics, such as optics, heat transfer, soil mechanics, or electronics.

ALTERNATE METHOD OF QUALIFYING:
Applicants who do not meet the basic engineering requirements may qualify for entry-level positions through a combination of college education and professional engineering experience equivalent to a full 4-year professional engineering curriculum and one of the following: (1) professional registration as an engineer; (2) successfully passed Board of Engineering Examiners written test or the Engineer-in-Training Exam; (3) 60 semester hours of specified academic courses for a B.S. in professional engineering; or (4) related degree and at least 1 year of professional engineering experience acquired under professional engineering supervision and guidance.

QUALIFICATION REQUIREMENTS BY GRADE LEVEL:
GS-5 - The basic requirements are fully qualifying for GS-5 positions.

GS-7 - The basic requirements, plus:

* One year of professional experience in an appropriate field comparable in difficulty and responsibility to GS-5 level work in the federal service (if you have a professional engineering degree up to 12 months of appropriate experience gained as a technician equivalent to the GS-5 level or higher may be credited in qualifying for GS-7 - engineer); OR

* Completion of the requirements for a master's or higher degree in engineering; OR

* Successful completion of a 5-year program of study (i.e. one designed to be completed in no less than 5 years) of at least 160 semester hours leading to a Bachelor's Degree in engineering in an accredited college or university; OR

* Appropriate degree and one year of appropriate student trainee experience at the GS-5; OR

* Completion of all requirements for a Bachelor's Degree (NOT A BS IN ENGINEERING TECHNOLOGY) which meets one of the following Superior Academic Achievement Standards:

a. A standing in the upper third of your class or major subdivision (e.g. school of engineering) at the time you apply; OR

b. A grade average of "B" or better (3.0 or higher out of a possible 4.0) for all courses completed:
(a) at the time of application; or (b) during the last 2 years of your undergraduate curriculum; OR

c. A "B" or better (3.5 or higher out of a possible 4.0) average for all courses completed in a qualifying major field of study, either; (a) at the time of application; or (b) during the last 2 years of your undergraduate curriculum; OR

d. Election to membership in one of the national honorary societies (other than freshman societies) that meet the requirements of the Association of College Honor Societies.

If you apply based on Superior Academic Achievement, YOU MUST INDICATE THE BASIS FOR THIS ACHIEVEMENT ON THE LAST PAGE OF OPM-FORM-1170/17, List of College Courses and Certificate of Scholastic Achievement, Part III.

HOW TO APPLY:
Submit a completed Standard Form 171, CSC-Form-1311, and OPM-FORM-1170/17 AND an official transcript.

1. Standard Form-171, Personal Qualification Statement: Include agricultural and engineering background and experience (paid or unpaid) in your application.

2. CSC-Form-1311, Work Location Preference: You may indicate availability for up to six states. If you choose more than one state it is important that you decide which state you most prefer to work in. You will generally receive consideration only for positions located in your state of first preference. However, under certain circumstances, you may also receive consideration in other states, for example, where a shortage of well-qualified candidates exists.

3. TRANSCRIPTS AND OPM-Form-1170/17, List of College Courses and Certificate of Scholastic Achievement: It is necessary for you to show your scholastic achievement on the back page of this form and sign the signature page if you wish to receive credit in this area. Two photocopies of TRANSCRIPTS ARE REQUIRED; however, if your transcript is no longer available from your college, you may list your course work on this form. You must give course numbers and college name for all courses taken. DO NOT HAVE THE SCHOOLS SEND TRANSCRIPTS DIRECTLY TO THE EXAMINING OFFICE. You are responsible for providing evidence that a given course fully meets the specified course requirements. For this purpose, you may be asked to submit a copy of your college department's outline or syllabus which provides the information necessary to evaluate the course content. Letters from faculty members stating the a course is appropriate are not sufficient for purposes of evaluating course content.

WHERE TO OBTAIN FORMS:
You may obtain the forms you will need to apply from any Soil Conservation Service (SCS) state office and Federal Job Information Center (FJIC). SCS and FJIC's offices are listed in the white or blue pages of most major metropolitan phone directories under "U.S. Government."

WHERE TO APPLY:
Application forms should be mailed to the address listed below. You should allow approximately ten weeks to receive notification of a rating.

USDA, SOIL CONSERVATION SERVICE
SPECIAL EXAMINING UNIT
P.O. BOX 37636
WASHINGTON, D.C. 20013

Address for Overnight mail ONLY:
USDA, SOIL CONSERVATION SERVICE
SPECIAL EXAMINING UNIT
14TH STREET & INDEPENDENCE AVENUE, SW
SOUTH BLDG., ROOM 0110-A
WASHINGTON, D.C. 20250

Jobs in HAWAII are filled locally and the Office of Personnel Management in Honolulu issues vacancy announcements for any openings.

EQUAL EMPLOYMENT OPPORTUNITY

All qualified applicants will receive employment consideration regardless of race, religion, sex, political affiliation, or any other non-merit factor.

CDC Position Announcement

CENTERS FOR DISEASE CONTROL

Office of Program Support • Personnel Management • Recruitment and Placement Branch

MERIT PROMOTION

NUMBER: NW-92-459

OPENING DATE:

CLOSING DATE:

POSITION: Architect, GS-808-7/9/11/12/13
(If filled at the GS-7 or GS-9 or GS-11 or GS-12 level, position has promotion potential to the GS-13). Please indicate the grade(s) for which you wish to be considered. You will only be considered for the grade(s) for which you indicate an interest.

NOTE: OPEN CONTINUOUS ANNOUNCEMENT

Your application will remain in our active files for six (6) months. Once selected, your name will be removed from consideration for this position that is being announced.

LOCATION: Office of the Director, Office of Program Support, Engineering Services Office , Facilities Design Branch, Atlanta, Georgia

AREA OF CONSIDERATION: CDC/ATSDR and HHS nationwide employees may apply and be considered in accordance with the Agency's Merit Promotion Program. Concurrent consideration will be extended to Federal employees serving on a permanent appointment in the competitive service and individuals with status, such as reinstatement eligibles. Candidates who have eligibility for non-competitive appointments, such as VRA eligibles, 30% or more disabled veterans and persons with disabilities are encouraged to apply. Proof of eligibility must accompany application. Commissioned Corps Officers are encouraged to apply.

DUTIES: Serves as an architect on the staff of a design and construction organization responsible for the planning, design, and construction of the new and/or extension, conversion, or modernization of existing buildings or facilities. Assignments involve(s) performance of civil and field architectural/engineering review, inhouse design, and/or monitoring and managing construction projects; and (b) building or project sites with diverse climate, geographic and environmental conditions. Applies the latest design, and construction techniques to such structures as office buildings, laboratory buildings, and repair and remodeling of existing facilities. Prepares detailed fee estimates used for negotiating with architect-engineering firms for design services.

QUALIFICATION REQUIREMENTS: Candidates must meet the basic qualification requirements outlined in OPM Qualification Standards Handbook. Candidates must have completed (A) a full 4-year course of study in an accredited college or university leading to a bachelor's or higher degree in architecture; or related field which includes 60 semester hours in architecture or related disciplines and includes, at a minimum, 30 semester hours in architectural design and 6 semester hours in each of the following: structural technology, properties of materials and methods of construction, and environmental control systems OR (B) college-level education, training, and/or technical experience that furnishes (1) a thorough knowledge of the arts and sciences underlying professional architecture and (2) a good understanding, both theoretical and practical, of the architectural principles, methods and techniques and their applications to the design and construction or improvement of buildings. Alternative requirements may be substituted as outlined in the Handbook. In addition, candidates must have completed at least one year of specialized experience equivalent to the next lower grade level in the Federal service.

Specialized experience is in or related to the line of work of the position to be filled and has equipped the applicant with the specific knowledge, skills, and abilities to successfully perform the duties of the position.

Applicants should indicate the extent to which they possess the following knowledges, skills and/or abilities for this position; these will be considered in the rating process:

1. Ability to solve a variety of structural problems.

2. Skill in the design, construction and modification of laboratories and existing facilities.

3. Ability to apply government contracting procedures.

4. Skill in consulting and advising all levels of management on facilities design.

TIME-IN-GRADE: Applicants must meet appropriate time-in-grade requirements for promotion.

EVALUATION METHODS: Employees will be evaluated and ranked as indicated in the CDC Merit Promotion Plan and by HHS Instructions on use of performance appraisals in the promotion process.

HOW TO APPLY: CDC/ATSDR employees should submit completed "Application for Position Vacancy Under CDC Merit Promotion Announcement" (Form CDC 0.996) to the Centers for Disease Control, 1600 Clifton Road, Atlanta, Georgia 30333. Attention: General Personnel Services Branch, Building 1, Room 1073, Mailstop D-43, Personnel Management Office. NCHS Employees should submit completed "Application for Position Vacancy under CDC Merit Promotion Announcement" (Form CDC 0.996) or "Application for Federal Employment" (SF-171). HHS applicants other than CDC/ATSDR employees must submit "Application for Federal Employment" (SF-171), a copy of recent performance appraisal, and a current copy of your SF-50. All applicants must submit Form CDC 0.996 or SF-171 by the closing date for applying or they will not be considered.

U.S. DEPARTMENT OF HEALTH AND HUMAN SERVICES
Public Health Service

– The Centers for Disease Control maintains a smoke-free environment –

DEPARTMENT OF TRANSPORTATION

PROMOTIONAL AND CAREER OPPORTUNITIES

ORGANIZATION OFFICE OF INSPECTOR GENERAL

                        ANNOUNCEMENT NO. I-92-40

POSITION   Auditor, GM-511-13

           OPENING DATE: CLOSING DATE

LOCATION   Assistant Inspector General for Auditing
Office of Surface Transportation & Secretarial Programs, Wash., D.C.

AREA OF CONSIDERATION All Sources

Certain disabled veterans, other disabled individuals, Veterans Readjustment Appointment eligibles, and other candidates eligible for special appointing authorities may apply. Reinstatement eligibles may also apply. Status applicants who wish to be considered under both merit promotion and competitive procedures must submit two (2) complete applications. When only one (1) application is received, it will be considered under the merit promotion announcement only. All nonstatus applicants who meet minimum requirements will be referred to OPM for rating, ranking, and referral

DUTIES

The incumbent plans, develops, and conducts comprehensive audits of programs related to the administrations of the Department of Transportation. Audits involve the evaluation of both the financial and operational aspects of complex programs. The incumbent develops audit objectives and programs, conducts or directs the audit, consolidates audit results, and develops findings and recommendations. Coordinates with OIG investigative staff on suspected cases of fraud and abuse. May serve as a team leader of up to three auditors, providing technical guidance and direction.

QUALIFICATIONS REQUIRED

All applicants must have 1 year of specialized experience equivalent to the GS-12 level in the Federal Service. This specialized experience must be related to the line of work of the position to be filled and have equipped the applicant with the specific knowledge, skills, and abilities to successfully perform the duties of the position as indicated in the OPM Qualification Standards Handbook.

In addition, all applicants must meet time-in-grade requirements as well as the positive education requirements (24 semesters of accounting). The above requirements must be met within 30 days after the closing date of this announcement.

METHOD OF EVALUATION

All qualified candidates will be evaluated based on the relevance and quality of their experience as reflected in the SF-171, supplemental statement, performance appraisal, and other relevant documents submitted by the applicant. For maximum consideration applicants should address the following KSAs:

Major KSAs required to perform
the duties of this position   Weight

1. Ability to plan and perform audits   25%
   in accordance with GAO standards.
   (Specify types and complexity.)

2. Analytical skill to identify, evaluate,   20%
   and recommend solutions to problems.

3. Ability to provide training and technical   15%
   direction on audits or special projects.

4. Ability to write various types of   25%
   communications such as audit reports,
   correspondence, speeches, testimony,
   and briefings.

5. Skill in communicating orally to a wide   15%
   variety of officials.

OTHER ESSENTIAL INFORMATION

1. Candidates may be required to spend up to 50 percent of the time in a travel status in executing assignments.

2. Appointment is contingent upon the selectee being granted a critical-sensitive clearance.

3. This position is covered under the Performance Management and Recognition System.

HOW TO APPLY

Applicants should submit:

(1) SF-171, "Application for Federal Employment;"

(2) A supplemental statement which concisely addresses the KSAs above. The supplemental statement should be brief summary of your experience, education, awards, and outside activities related to each KSA;

(3) A current annual performance appraisal; and

(4) SF-50, "Notification of Personnel Action". This form is required of all reinstatement eligibles as well as current Federal employees.

Mail all forms to:

Attn: Leslie Dexter
Office of Inspector General
Department of Transportation
Office of Human Resources, JP-30
400 7th Street, S.W., Room 7418
Washington, D.C. 20590

Telephone Number (202) 366-2677

NOTE: Applications received in postage-paid Government envelopes will not be considered. Applications must be postmarked by the closing date of this announcement.

FORM CD-260
REV. 11-89LF [WP50]
DAO 202-335

U.S. DEPARTMENT OF COMMERCE

ANNOUNCEMENT NUMBER: OA/W-92-0063DCH

ISSUE DATE:

CLOSING DATE:

Merit Program

VACANCY ANNOUNCEMENT
NATIONAL OCEANIC AND ATMOSPHERIC ADMINISTRATION (NOAA)

Budget Analyst   NATIONAL WEATHER SERVICE
GS-560-13   OFFICE OF THE ASSISTANT ADMINISTRATION
                                          FOR WEATHER SERVICES
PROMOTION POTENTIAL: NONE   MANAGEMENT AND BUDGET OFFICE
COMPETITIVE SERVICE   PLANNING AND RESOURCE MANAGEMENT BRANCH
                                        SILVER SPRING, MARYLAND

WHO MAY APPLY: STATUS APPLICANTS AND APPLICANTS ELIGIBLE FOR NON-
COMPETITIVE APPOINTMENT UNDER SPECIAL APPOINTING AUTHORITIES.

**"PUBLIC LAW REQUIRES ALL NEW APPOINTEES TO PRESENT PROOF OF IDENTITY
AND ELIGIBILITY TO WORK IN THE UNITED STATES (e.g., U.S.
CITIZENSHIP)."**

DUTIES: The incumbent of this position studies various aspects of all
NWS programs, with emphasis on issues/problems having potential
financial implications; analyzes budget proposals to determine the
impact on the relevant program area; provides expert advise and
guidance to NWS program managers on matters pertaining to various
aspects of their budget request; analyzes, combines, and consolidates
budget estimates into formal budget documents; coordinates and reviews
all presentation material for NOAA Monthly Program Reviews; reviews
and recommends approval, disapproval and timing of requests for
reprogramming, and allotment of funds to NWS components and programs;
and participates in the Departmental long-range planning process.
QUALIFICATIONS REQUIRED: Applicants must have one year of specialized
experience that was at a level equivalent or comparable in difficulty
and complexity to the next lower grade in the Federal service.
SPECIALIZED EXPERIENCE is experience which is in or directly related
to the line of work of the position to be filled and which has
equipped the applicant with the particular knowledge, skills, and
ability to successfully perform the duties.
BASIS FOR EVALUATING APPLICANTS: Applicants who meet the minimum
qualification requirements may be further evaluated and ranked on the
basis of the following job-related factors in order to determine the
best qualified: (1) Knowledge and understanding of the Federal budget
process, including knowledge of the Congressional budget process. (2)
Skill in analyzing program-budgetary relationships and evaluating the
adequacy of program/budget information. (3) Skill in analyzing and
projecting program implications of proposed budgetary actions. (4)
Knowledge of the concepts, principles, laws, and regulations for
budgeting of national programs. (5) Ability to provide authoritative
advice to program managers in budget formulation. In addition to the
knowledge, skills, and abilities listed above, full consideration will
be given to education, experience, training, awards and performance
appraisal. To ensure proper consideration, applicants **should** clearly
address each of the above factors by attaching a narrative statement.
WHO AND WHERE TO APPLY: All applicants must submit the forms
specified under **APPLICATION REQUIREMENTS** (see below) to: NATIONAL
OCEANIC AND ATMOSPHERIC ADMINISTRATION, OFFICE OF ADMINISTRATION,
NWS/NESDIS OPERATIONS BRANCH, SILVER SPRING METRO CENTER #1, 1335
EAST-WEST HIGHWAY, SSMC1, OA212, ROOM 2107, SILVER SPRING, MARYLAND
20910.
FOR FURTHER INFORMATION CALL: **DELORIS HAYES (301) 713-0511
                                  TDD # FOR HEARING IMPAIRED:
                                  (301) 713-0973**

BUDGET ANALYST, GS-560-13   OA/W-92-0063DCH
TITLE, SERIES AND GRADE   ANNOUNCEMENT NUMBER   CLOSES

NOTICE TO ALL APPLICANTS

PLEASE READ FORM CD-260S, WHICH CONTAINS IMPORTANT INFORMATION ABOUT THIS ANNOUNCEMENT.

BLM NEW MEXICO Vacancy Announcement

U.S. Department of the Interior, Bureau of Land Management
NEW MEXICO STATE OFFICE, P.O. BOX 27115, SANTA FE, NM 87502-7115

ANNOUNCEMENT: NMSO-92-51*   ISSUING DATE: CLOSING DATE:
POSITION: BLM RANGER
SERIES, GRADE: GS-1801-5/7/9   LOCATION: CUBA NM
AREA OF CONSIDERATION: Governmentwide

POSITION SENSITIVITY: POSITION IS DESIGNATED CRITICAL SENSITIVE. SELECTEE IS
SUBJECT TO COMPLETION OF A FAVORABLE BACKGROUND INVESTIGATION.

THIS IS A PERMANENT FULLTIME POSITION.

POSITION LOCATION:
ALBUQUERQUE DISTRICT. RIO PUERCO RESOURCE AREA, AREA MANAGER'S STAFF.
CUBA, NEW MEXICO

BRIEF DESCRIPTION OF DUTIES:
INCUMBENT ENFORCES A VARIETY OF FEDERAL LAWS AND REGULATIONS RELATED TO PUBLIC
LAND AND RESOURCES BY PERFORMING INVESTIGATIONS, APPREHENDING SUSPECTS AND
VIOLATORS, PERFORMING SURVEILLANCE ACTIVITIES AND MAKING ENFORCEMENT CONTACTS.
INVESTIGATES ACTS OF CRIMINAL ACTIVITIES, THEFT, VANDALISM, OR OFFENSES OF
CRIMINAL LAWS AND REGULATIONS OF THE UNITED STATES THAT RELATE TO PUBLIC LANDS
AND NATURAL RESOURCES. DEVELOPS INFORMATION THROUGH FACTFINDING BY COLLECTING
ON-SITE EVIDENCE, INTERVIEWING WITNESSES OR SUSPECTS, FOLLOWING-UP ON LEADS.
SEARCHING RECORDS, CONDUCTING SURVEILLANCE, OBSERVING SUSPICIOUS ACTIVITY. AND
THROUGH INFORMATION PROVIDED BY INFORMANTS, CONCERNED CITIZENS, AND LOCAL
FEDERAL AND STATE OFFICIALS. HE/SHE WILL REPRESENT THE U.S. GOVERNMENT AS A
PROSECUTOR IN COURT. DEVELOPS AND MAINTAINS LIAISON WITH FEDERAL, STATE AND
LOCAL LAW ENFORCEMENT AGENCIES TO SHARE IN THE RESOURCES IN ORDER TO PROVIDE
ADDITIONAL PROTECTION OF PEOPLE AND PROPERTY ON PUBLIC LANDS. PARTICIPATES AS
A MEMBER OF A MULTI-DISCIPLINARY TEAM IN PERFORMING WORK IN SUPPORT OF
RESOURCE MANAGEMENT ACTIVITIES.

THE FULL PERFORMANCE LEVEL OF THIS POSITION IS GS-09. THE POSITION HAS
PROMOTION POTENTIAL. IF FILLED BELOW THE FULL PERFORMANCE LEVEL, INCUMBENT MAY
SUBSEQUENTLY BE PROMOTED WITHOUT FURTHER COMPETITION AFTER SATISFACTORY
PERFORMANCE AND MEETING TIME-IN-GRADE REQUIREMENTS, UP TO THE FULL PERFORMANCE
LEVEL. However, promotion is not guaranteed and no promise of promotion is
implied.

WHO MAY APPLY: FEDERAL EMPLOYEES WITH COMPETITIVE STATUS, OR FORMER EMPLOYEES
WITH REINSTATEMENT ELIGIBILITY. VRA ELIGIBLE, 30% DISABLED VETERANS, AND
FORMER PEACE CORPS AND VISTA VOLUNTEERS MAY BE CONSIDERED UNDER SPECIAL
HIRING AUTHORITIES.

NON-STATUS CANDIDATES MAY APPLY FOR THIS POSITION. PLEASE CALL
RITA M. MONTOYA AT 505-438-7653 FOR MORE INFORMATION AND APPLICATION
PROCEDURES.

TENTATIVE SELECTEE FOR THIS POSITION WILL BE REQUIRED TO SUBMIT TO URINALYSIS
TO SCREEN FOR ILLEGAL DRUG USE PRIOR TO APPOINTMENT. THIS POSITION CONTAINS
PROCUREMENT DUTIES. THE CANDIDATE SELECTED MUST SIGN A CERTIFICATION OF
COMPLIANCE WITH P.L. 101-189.

BASIC QUALIFICATION REQUIREMENTS:
Applicants must meet the minimum qualification requirements as outlined in OPM
Handbook X-118 (available for review at the Personnel Office). In summary: At
the GS-5 level, applicants must have 3 years of general experience. General
experience is 3 years of progressively responsible experience which
demonstrates (1) the ability to analyze problems to identify significant
factors, gather pertinent data and recognize solutions; (2) plans and
organizes work; and (3) communicates effectively both orally and in writing.
Such experience may have been gained in administrative, professional,
technical, investigative or other responsible work. At the GS-7 and GS-9
levels, applicants must have one year of specialized experience at least
equivalent to the next lower grade in the Federal service. Specialized
experience is experience which has equipped the applicant with the knowledge,
skills and abilities to successfully perform the duties of the position.
Substitution of Education for Experience: At the GS-5 level, a 4-year course
of study above high school leading to a bachelor's degree may be substituted
for experience. One full academic year of graduate level education or law
school or superior academic achievement may be substituted for experience at
the GS-7 grade level. At the GS-9 level, two full academic years of graduate
level education or master's or equivalent graduate degree of LL.B. or J.D.
Equivalent combinations of education and experience are qualifying for all
grade levels for which both education and experience are acceptable.

EVALUATION CRITERIA (KSA's):
Applicants who meet basic qualification requirements will be evaluated
according to the following knowledge, skills, and abilities (KSAs):
1. KNOWLEDGE OF FEDERAL LAWS AND REGULATIONS PERTAINING TO THE PROTECTION OF
   PUBLIC LAND RESOURCES.
2. SKILL IN THE USE OF LAW ENFORCEMENT TECHNIQUES, INCLUDING CONDUCTING BASIC
   INVESTIGATIONS, CARRYING OUT SURVEILLANCE, APPREHENDING VIOLATORS, ISSUING
   CITATIONS AND MAKING ARRESTS.
3. KNOWLEDGE OF FUNCTIONS AND JURISDICTION OF OTHER FEDERAL, STATE AND LOCAL
   LAW ENFORCEMENT ORGANIZATIONS AND HOW THEY RELATE TO LAW ENFORCEMENT AND
   SEARCH AND RESCUE ON PUBLIC LANDS.
4. KNOWLEDGE OF FEDERAL RULES OF CRIMINAL PROCEDURE, RULES OF EVIDENCE AND
   SEARCH AND SEIZURE.

The Narrative Statement, requested as part of the application, provides opportunity for applicants to relate their experience, education, self-development,
training and awards to each KSA. The Narrative Statement should be presented
in the order of the KSA's, as listed above, and may not exceed two
single-spaced pages. Also, the Supervisor's Employee Appraisal, where
requested, should be keyed to the KSA's, in the order listed.

Obligation to give all information to be considered in rating/ranking qualifications is the responsibility of the applicant. Applications and additional information will not be accepted after the closing date of this vacancy announcement. Requests to be considered, either oral or written, are accepted if received on or before the closing date. All documents (e.g., supervisor's appraisal) required to complete the application must be received within 5 working days following the closing date.

HOW TO APPLY: Submit current SF 171 and supplemental forms requested to:

NEW MEXICO STATE OFFICE (953)   EXPRESS MAIL:
BUREAU OF LAND MANAGEMENT   BRANCH OF PERSONNEL
P.O. BOX 27115   BUREAU OF LAND MANAGEMENT
SANTA FE, NM 87502-7115   1474 RODEO ROAD
                                     SANTA FE, NM 87505

* - * - * - * - * - * - * - * - * - * - * - * - * - * - * - * - * - * - *
Privacy Act Requirements (PL93-579): The application forms prescribed are used to determine qualifications for promotion or employment and are authorized under Title 5, United States Code, Sections 3302 and 3361.

Using government postage or envelopes to mail job applications is a violation of OPM and Postal Service regulations. Applications submitted in postage-paid government envelopes will not be considered. Further, violators may be subject to disciplinary action and fine as prescribed by law.
* - * - * - * - * - * - * - * - * - * - * - * - * - * - * - * - * - * - *

FORMS TO SUBMIT:
All Applicants-
  SF 171 (Application for Federal Employment)*
  NARRATIVE STATEMENT (covering KSA's)
  DI 1935 (Applicant Background Survey)
  COPY OF OFFICIAL COLLEGE TRANSCRIPT
Bureau Applicants - additional-
  BLM Form 1400-86(335) (Vacancy Application)
  BLM Form 1400-86a(335) (Supvr's Empl Appraisal)
Non-Bureau Applicants - additional-
  SF-50 (Proof of Status)
  DD-214 (Verify Vet Pref/Mil Svc Time)
Application will be rejected if documents asterisked (*) are not submitted. However, please do not submit extra or extraneous materials, e.g., position descriptions, commendations, training certificates, etc. Your SF 171, Narrative Statement, and other requested forms should adequately cover your total background, including experience, education, awards, self-development, and training, as related to the specific requirements of the position.

All applications and related material submitted in response to this vacancy announcement will be retained as part of the merit promotion file required by BLM Manual 1400-335.51 and will not be returned to the applicant; nor can the application be referred from this file for any other vacancy. Please submit one application for each position for which you desire consideration.

Applicants must meet all eligibility requirements for this position, including time-in-grade requirements, within 60 days of the closing date given above.

A N   E Q U A L   O P P O R T U N I T Y   E M P L O Y E R
All candidates will receive consideration without regard to age, race, color, sex, religion, national origin, or other non-merit factors.

APPOINTMENT INFORMATION:
IF APPOINTED TO THE POSITION, YOU -
>MUST FILE STATEMENT OF EMPLOYMENT/FINANCIAL INTERESTS, 43 CFR 20.735 SUB B.
>CANNOT OWN FINANCIAL INTERESTS THAT CONFLICT/APPEAR TO CONFLICT WITH DUTIES.
>AS A BLM EMPLOYEE, CANNOT HOLD AN ACTIVE REAL ESTATE LICENSE, AND
>CANNOT HAVE AN INTEREST IN FEDERAL LANDS, INCLUDING STOCK IN FIRMS THAT DO.
THE SELECTION OF A BLM APPLICANT WHO HAS NOT BEEN IN HIS OR HER CURRENT DUTY STATION FOR AT LEAST THREE YEARS IS SUBJECT TO APPROVAL BY THE APPROPRIATE OFFICIAL.

NOTE FOR NON-BLM APPLICANTS:
SUPERVISORY APPRAISAL ADDRESSING THE KSA'S SHOWN ABOVE IS REQUESTED OF ALL APPLICANTS (NOT NECESSARY TO BE ON BLM FORM). ALSO MUST SUBMIT SF-50.

VACANCY ANNOUNCEMENT

ANNOUNCEMENT CONTINUED:

- Fills in as a Child Care Giver, supervising children's meals, activities and lessons.
- Decorates bulletin boards, classrooms and center for holidays and seasonal events.
- Constantly observes children for signs of neglect or abuse.
- Observes all aspects of the facility and Family Home Care(FHC) homes for health and safety hazards and cleanliness.
- Maintains accurate records on each Family Home Care (FHC) home to include home certifications, care giver training, documentation of home visits made, children enrolled, contacts with parents.
- Monitors Family Home Care (FHC) homes on a monthly basis, or more often as required, to ensure that all standards and regulations are being followed.
- Perform other duties as assigned.

QUALIFICATION REQUIREMENTS.

IN ADDITION TO MEETING THE TIME IN GRADE RESTRICTIONS, APPLICANTS MUST MEET THE EXPERIENCE RE-QUIREMENT SPECIFIED IN CIVIL SERVICE HANDBOOK X-118, SERIES 1702

JOB-RELATED RANKING ELEMENTS.

A. Knowledge of principals and philosophy of child development and education gained through college/university education and/or work experience

B. Knowledge of skills development in children.

C. Ability to communicate, both orally and in writing to supervisors, employees, patrons and children.

D. Ability to recognize signs of physical, sexual and mental abuse and/or neglect.

NOTE: ATTACH A STATEMENT DESCRIBING HOW YOU MEET THE KNOWLEDGE, SKILL, AND/OR ABILITY REQUIRED BY EACH RANKING ELEMENT AND IDENTIFY WHICH JOB OR WHAT EDUCATION/TRAINING SHOWN ON YOUR SF-171 GAVE YOU THIS KNOWLEDGE, SKILL, AND/OR ABILITY.

NOTE: PLEASE ATTACH A COPY OF YOUR LATEST ANNUAL PERFORMANCE APPRAISAL AND SF-50.

MERIT PROMOTION PROGRAM

DEPARTMENT OF THE NAVY
Consolidated Civilian Personnel Office
Philadelphia, Staten Island Branch
355 Front Street
Staten Island, New York 10304

VACANCY ANNOUNCEMENT

POSITION: CHILD DEVELOPMENT PROGRAM ASSISTANT   ANNOUNCEMENT NO.
GS-1702-07 $23,658.00 P.A.

LOCATION: NAVAL STATION NY, STATEN ISLAND, NY   OPENING DATE:

                                                       CLOSING DATE:

AREA OF CONSIDERATION: ALL FEDERAL ACTIVITIES IN THE NEW YORK/METROPOLITAN AREA, ALL REINSTATEMENT, TRANSFER AND VRA ELIGIBLES

| Competitive Status Required: YES | Written Test: NO | Position Subject to Probationary Period: NO |

THIS POSITION IS LOCATED IN THE CHILD DEVELOPMENT CENTER, RECREATIONAL SERVICES DIVISION, MORALE, WELFARE AND RECREATION DEPARTMENT, U.S. NAVAL STATION NEW YORK STATEN ISLAND, NEW YORK. THE PRIMARY PURPOSE OF THE POSITION IS TO ASSIST THE CHILD DEVELOPMENT DIRECTOR IN THEIR DAY TO DAY OPERATION OR MORE CHILDREN DAILY

DUTIES

- Assists the Child Development Director, Child Care Givers and Family Home Care (FHC) providers to develop, evaluate and/or modify curriculums and activities using knowledge of child development needs, skills, first aid, safety and nutrition

- Collects fees and charges, issuing receipts to patrons and accounting for funds in authorized manner.

- Assists Child Development Director in training staff

- Prepares lists of supplies and equipment for purchase

- Acts as Child Development Director in his/her absence, granting leave, developing work schedules, evaluating performance of other child care givers and handling emergencies and day to day operations

CONTINUED OVER

INSTRUCTIONS AND INFORMATION TO APPLICANTS

Send SF-171 and Supplemental forms, if required, to:
CONSOLIDATED PERSONNEL OFFICE, PHILADELPHIA, STATEN ISLAND BRANCH OFFICE,
355 FRONT STREET, STATEN ISLAND NEW YORK 10304

Applications will not be returned. Only applicants meeting basic qualifications requirements will be ranked. Rating and ranking will be based on appraisals of performance and quality of experience, education, training, knowledge, skill, self-development, and awards as you describe on the SF-171 and additional statements. DO NOT USE COPIES OF POSITION DESCRIPTIONS. Qualifications determinations will be made as of the closing date of this announcement. Do not list positions being filled below the target level, the selectee may be promoted to the target position or as appropriate, through intervening grades without further competition upon meeting Office of Personnel Management qualification requirements, demonstration of ability to perform at the higher level and assignment of increased responsibilities. Promotion however is neither guaranteed nor promised. This announcement does not preclude filling this position by other means such as appointment from OPM register, Reassignment, Transfer or Reinstatement. Any selection will be made without discrimination because of Race, Religion, Color, Sex, Age, Etc. Special consideration for re-promotion has already been given to those known eligible and to be considered further they must make specific application under this announcement and compete with other applicants. THIS ANNOUNCEMENT IS SUBJECT TO RESTRICTIONS IMPOSED BY DOD.

EQUAL OPPORTUNITY EMPLOYER

DEPARTMENT OF THE NAVY
CONSOLIDATED CIVILIAN PERSONNEL OFFICE
PHILADELPHIA STATEN ISLAND BRANCH
355 FRONT STREET
STATEN ISLAND, NEW YORK 10304
OFFICIAL BUSINESS

VACANCY ANNOUNCEMENT

ANNOUNCEMENT CONTINUED:

- Arranges and provides the orientation training for all staff
- Arranges training for food service staff in the United States Department of Agriculture standards for preparing and serving meals and snacks
- Develops the framework for a curriculum to be used by program staff which promotes the physical, emotional, cognitive and social growth of children ages six weeks to twelve years
- Develops a working relationship with local colleges and professional organizations and advises staff about continuing avenues of professional development
- Serves as a point of contact for information on the Child Development Associate (CDA) National Credentialing Program
- Maintains instructor's certification in first aid and CPR
- Perform other related duties as assigned

QUALIFICATION REQUIREMENTS:
IN ADDITION TO MEETING THE TIME IN GRADE RESTRICTIONS, APPLICANTS MUST MEET THE EXPERIENCE REQUIREMENT SPECIFIED IN CIVIL SERVICE HANDBOOK. X-118. SERIES 1701

JOB-RELATED RANKING ELEMENTS:

A. Knowledge of Principals and Philosophy of Child Development, and education gained through college/university education and or work experience

B. Ability to train Child Development Program employees to meet the professional requirements of their positions

C. Knowledge of Child Development Principles, infancy through adolescence and the requirements for curricula, materials and equipment, and children s learning environments

D. Ability to communicate both orally and in writing to supervisor, military, parents and children

NOTE: ATTACH A STATEMENT DESCRIBING HOW YOU MEET THE KNOWLEDGE, SKILL, AND/OR ABILITY REQUIRED BY EACH RANKING ELEMENT AND IDENTIFY WHICH JOB OR WHAT EDUCATION/TRAINING SHOWN ON YOUR APPLICATION FOR FEDERAL EMPLOYMENT (SF 171) GAVE YOU THIS KNOWLEDGE, SKILL AND/OR ABILITY

NOTE: PLEASE ATTACH A COPY OF YOUR LATEST ANNUAL PERFORMANCE APPRAISAL AND SF 50

MERIT PROMOTION PROGRAM
DEPARTMENT OF THE NAVY
Consolidated Civilian Personnel Office
355 Front Street
Staten Island, New York 10304

VACANCY ANNOUNCEMENT

POSITION: CHILD DEVELOPMENT TRAINING AND CURRICULUM SPECIALIST GS-1701-07 $23,658.00 P.A.
(2 POSITIONS AVAILABLE)

ANNOUNCEMENT NO.

OPENING DATE:

CLOSING DATE:

LOCATION: NAVAL STATION NEW YORK, STATEN ISLAND, NY

AREA OF CONSIDERATION: ALL FEDERAL ACTIVITIES IN THE NEW YORK METRO AREA. ALL REINSTATEMENT, TRANSFER AND VRA ELIGIBLES.

Competitive Status Required: YES	Written Test: NO	Position Subject to Probationary Period: NO

NOTE: A BACCALAUREATE DEGREE FROM AN ACCREDITED COLLEGE/UNIVERSITY IN CHILD DEVELOPMENT/EDUCATION IS REQUIRED.

THIS POSITION IS LOCATED IN THE CHILD DEVELOPMENT CENTER RECREATIONAL SERVICES DIVISION, MORAL AND RECREATION DEPARTMENT, U.S. NAVAL STATION NEW YORK, STATEN ISLAND, NEW YORK.
Child Development Services Programs provide safe and developmentally appropriate care for children of military and DOD civilian personnel.
DUTIES: Develops and implements training for child development center staff which help them render safe and developmentally appropriate care for children. Executes the standardized child development training program. Provides orientation training in safety, health and sanitation; fire prevention and evacuation; recognizing, reporting and preventing child abuse; first aid and cardiopulmonary resuscitation (CPR); nutrition and meal service; child growth and development; classroom management; child guidance and discipline techniques.

CONTINUED OVER →

INSTRUCTIONS AND INFORMATION TO APPLICANTS

Send SF-171 and Supplemental forms, if required, to:
CONSOLIDATED PERSONNEL OFFICE, PHILADELPHIA, STATEN ISLAND BRANCH OFFICE, 355 FRONT STREET, STATEN ISLAND NEW YORK 10304

Applications will not be returned. Only applicants meeting basic qualifications requirements will be ranked. Rating and ranking will be based on appraisals of performance and quality of experience, education, training, knowledge, skill, self-development and awards as you describe in the SF 171 and additional statements. DO NOT USE COPIES OF POSITION DESCRIPTIONS. Qualifications determinations will be made as of the closing date of this announcement. for positions being filled below the target level, the selectee may be promoted to the target position, or as appropriate, through intervening grades without further competition upon meeting Office of Personnel Management qualification requirements, demonstration of ability to perform at the higher level and assignment of increased responsibilities. Promotion, however, is neither guaranteed nor promised. This announcement does to preclude filling this position by other means such as appointment from OPM register, Reassignment, Transfer or Reinstatement. Any selection will be made without discrimination because of Race, Religion, Color, Sex, Age, Etc. Special consideration for promotion that are by those known eligible and to be considered further, they must make specific application under this announcement and compete with other applicants. THIS ANNOUNCEMENT IS SUBJECT TO RESTRICTIONS IMPOSED BY DOD.

EQUAL OPPORTUNITY EMPLOYER

United States
Office of
Personnel
Management

Clerical and Administrative Support Positions

Announcement No. WA-8-06
Revised January
Open Continuous

Clerk-Typist, GS-2/3/4   Secretary, GS-3/4

Clerk-Stenographer, GS-3/4/5   *Messenger, GS-2/3/4

Other Clerical and Administrative Support Positions, GS-2/3/4

Do Not Apply Under This Announcement for Summer Jobs

Location of Jobs

Washington, D.C.: Maryland: Counties of Charles, Montgomery, and Prince Georges. **Virginia:** Cities of Alexandria, Fairfax, and Falls Church and Counties of Arlington, Fairfax, King George, Loudoun, Prince William, and Stafford, and **Overseas Atlantic.**

Occupations Covered

GS-029	Environmental Protection Assistant
GS-072	Fingerprint Identification Clerk
GS-086	Security Clerk/Assistant
GS-134	Intelligence Aid/Clerk
GS-203	Personnel Clerk/Assistant
GS-204	Military Personnel Clerk/Technician
GS-302	Messenger*
GS-303	General Clerk/Assistant
GS-304	Information Reception Clerk
GS-305	Mail and File Clerk
GS-309	Correspondence Clerk
GS-312	Clerk-Stenographer
GS-318	Secretary
GS-322	Clerk-Typist
GS-332	Computer Operator
GS-335	Computer Clerk/Assistant
GS-344	Management Clerk/Assistant
GS-350	Office Equipment Operator
GS-351	Printing Clerk
GS-357	Coding Clerk
GS-359	Electronic Accounting Machine Operator
GS-382	Telephone Operator
GS-385	Teletypist
GS-388	Cryptographic Equipment Operator
GS-390	Communications Relay Operator
GS-392	Communications Technician
GS-394	Communications Clerk
GS-503	Financial Clerk/Assistant
GS-525	Accounting Clerk/Technician
GS-530	Cash Processing Clerk
GS-540	Voucher Examining Clerk
GS-544	Payroll Clerk
GS-545	Military Pay Clerk
GS-561	Budget Clerk/Assistant
GS-590	Time and Leave Clerk
GS-592	Tax Accounting Clerk
GS-593	Insurance Accounts Clerk
GS-675	Medical Records Clerk/Technician
GS-679	Medical Clerk
GS-963	Legal Instruments Examining Clerk
GS-986	Legal Clerk/Technician
GS-998	Claims Clerk
GS-1001	Arts and Information Clerk
GS-1046	Language Clerk
GS-1087	Editorial Clerk/Assistant
GS-1101	Business Clerk
GS-1105	Purchasing Agent
GS-1106	Procurement Clerk/Assistant
GS-1107	Property Disposal Clerk/Technician
GS-1152	Production Control Clerk
GS-1411	Library Clerk/Technician
GS-1421	Archives Clerk/Technician
GS-1531	Statistical Clerk/Technician
GS-1802	Compliance Inspection Clerk
GS-1897	Customs Clerk/Aid
GS-2005	Supply Clerk/Technician
GS-2102	Transportation Clerk/Assistant
GS-2131	Freight Rate Clerk
GS-2132	Travel Clerk
GS-2133	Passenger Rate Clerk
GS-2134	Shipping Clerk/Assistant
GS-2151	Dispatching Clerk

Direct-Hire Authority is restricted to the above listed positions

*Under 5 U.S.C. 3310, appointment to Messenger positions is restricted to persons entitled to veteran preference as long as such persons are available.

Qualification Requirements

A WRITTEN TEST IS REQUIRED FOR ALL OCCUPATIONS COVERED BY THIS ANNOUNCEMENT.
The following chart reflects the minimum qualification requirements.

GRADE/POSITIONS	EDUCATION	OR	EXPERIENCE	
			GENERAL	SPECIALIZED
GS-2—ALL POSITIONS	High school graduation or equivalent	OR	3 months	None
GS-3 Clerk-Steno	High school graduation or equivalent	OR	6 months	None
GS-3—ALL OTHER POSITIONS	1 year above high school	OR	6 months	None
GS-4—ALL POSITIONS	2 years above high school	OR	1 year	None
GS-5 Clerk-Steno	4 years above high school	OR	2 years	None

Equivalent combinations of education and experience are qualifying for all grade levels and positions for which both education and experience are acceptable

Salary

Federal salary rates are adjusted periodically. Current information regarding salaries may be obtained from the Federal Job Information/Testing Center in the Office of Personnel Management, 1900 E Street NW, Washington, D.C. 20415.

For all positions requiring a qualified typist the minimum typing speed is 40 wpm with three errors or less. Clerk-Stenographer, GS-3/4, and any other occupation at the GS-3/4 level with a parenthetical title of (Stenography) must have a minimum shorthand speed of 80 wpm with 24 errors or less. Clerk-Stenographer, GS-5, must have a minimum shorthand speed of 120 wpm with 36 errors or less. You may meet these requirements at the time of appointment by indicating these skills on your *Application for Federal Employment* (SF 171), presenting a Certificate of Proficiency (OPM Form 680) or taking a performance test given by the agency

For All Positions

"General experience" is progressively responsible clerical, office OR other work which indicates ability to acquire the particular knowledge and skills needed to perform the duties of the position to be filled

SPECIALIZED EXPERIENCE MAY BE SUBSTITUTED FOR GENERAL EXPERIENCE. Unpaid or volunteer work will be credited on the same basis as salaried experience.

Education

Successfully completed education above the high school level in any field for which high school graduation or the equivalent is a prerequisite may be substituted for the experience required at grades GS-3 through GS-5 for which this education must have been obtained in an accredited business, secretarial or technical school, junior college, college or university. One full year of full-time academic study is 30 semester hours, 45 quarter hours, or the equivalent, of college or at least 20 hours of classroom instruction per week for approximately 36 weeks in a business, secretarial, or technical school.

Intensive Short-Term Training—Completion of an intensive, specialized course of study of less than one year (such as for computer operator) may meet in full the experience requirements for GS-3. Courses of this type normally require completion of up to 40 hours per week of instruction rather than the usual 20 hours per week and are usually of *at least three months* duration. Such courses may have been obtained through a variety of programs such as those offered by business or technical schools, and through military training programs. To be creditable, such a course must have been designed specifically as career preparation for the work of the position being filled and must have provided the applicant with the necessary knowledge, skills, and abilities to do the work.

Certificates of Proficiency

If you wish, you may present a Certificate of Proficiency in typing and/or shorthand which meets the speed and accuracy requirements. To be acceptable, the certification must be made on OPM Form 680 or on an official form or letterhead of the testing organization and include the following information:

- The date the test was administered;
- The length of the test in minutes;
- The total number of words typed per minute on at least a 5-minute test, and the total number of errors made; and
- For stenographer, the rate of dictation in words per minute on a 3-minute test, and the total number of errors made.

We accept Certificates of Proficiency from the following sources:

- Public and parochial schools;
- Accredited private high schools;
- Business, commercial, and secretarial schools accredited by such accrediting organizations as the Association of Independent Colleges and Schools or the appropriate State education department;
- Junior colleges and colleges which are accredited or whose work is accepted for advance credit by the State University of the State in which they are located;
- Schools approved by the Veterans Administration for the education of veterans and their dependents.

- Public and private social and welfare agencies conducting programs sponsored or approved by the U.S. Office of Education or by an appropriate State Office of Education to provide training or retraining of the handicapped or for vocational rehabilitation purposes
- Federal, State or other public or private agencies with programs in support of personnel utilization and economic opportunity, such as the Neighborhood Youth Corps, Job Corps, Opportunities Industrialization Centers, and other agencies that provide training under provisions of the Comprehensive Employment and Training Act;
- State Employment Service Offices
- Military hospitals or agencies and other Federal hospitals or agencies which provide training in connection with occupational therapy or vocational rehabilitation programs in typing and/or shorthand and
- Federal agencies which provide in-service training in typing or shorthand to civilian or military personnel

Time Limitations on Certificates of Proficiency

The test on which the Certificate of Proficiency is based must have been taken within one year of the date on which the certificate was issued. The certificate is good for three years from the date of issue

How to Apply

1. Take the general written test.

Information About the Test

Written Test—The written test consists of two parts, clerical aptitude and verbal abilities. To pass the written test, applicants must make a minimum score of 33 on the verbal abilities part and a minimum combined total score of 80 on both the clerical and verbal parts. The minimum score of 80 will be converted to an eligible numerical rating of 70.0. This test takes about two hours to administer to competitors. The test is given on a walk-in basis every Monday through Friday at 8:30 a.m. at the Office of Personnel Management, 1900 E Street, NW, Washington, D.C., in Room 1416. To accommodate those applicants unable to take the morning test, an afternoon test will be given on a walk-in basis on the third Friday of each month at 1:00 p.m. in Room 1416. Applicants may also take the written test at the locations listed on page 3. OPM PROVIDES SAME-DAY SERVICE FOR ISSUING NOTICES OF WRITTEN TEST RESULTS TO APPLICANTS

Testing of Applicants With Physical Handicaps

The Blind—If you are blind, you will be required to take the test of verbal abilities but not the clerical aptitude test.

The Deaf—If you are deaf, you will be required to take the clerical aptitude test, but not the verbal abilities test.

Other—Appropriate modifications in the testing procedure may be authorized, depending on the nature of the handicap.

For testing in the Washington, D.C. area, applicants with physical handicaps may call the Office of Personnel Management (632-5528 or 653-9260) to arrange for special testing

Minimum Age Requirements

You must meet the age requirements. The usual minimum is 18, but high school graduates may apply at 16. If you are 16 or 17 and are out of school but not a high school graduate you may be hired only if (1) you have successfully completed a formal training program preparing you for work (for example, training provided under the Comprehensive Employment and Training Act or in similar Government or private programs), or (2) you have been out of school for at least three months, not counting the summer vacation, and school authorities write a letter on their official stationery agreeing with your preference for work instead of additional schooling. Appropriate forms will be given to you by the agency that wants to hire you

How to Get a Job

Simplified hiring procedures make it easier for persons seeking Clerical and Administrative Support Positions to be given immediate employment consideration in the Washington, D.C. metropolitan area.

When seeking employment, you should submit an *Application for Federal Employment* (SF 171) and a copy of your *Notice* directly to agencies where you wish to work. Effective April 25, 1988, Notices of Results issued by OPM Area Offices **outside** the Washington, D.C. area are also acceptable if the occupational supplement shown on the notice is "0300-X Clerical Positions". **Be sure to keep the original Notice.**

Job Information

The Office of Personnel Management furnishes information about Federal employment opportunities, qualification requirements, and application procedures without charge. Residents of the Washington, D.C. metropolitan area may call the Federal Job Information/Testing Center on 653-8468 for information. Residents of other areas should check the local telephone directory under "United States Government" for the address and telephone number of the nearest Federal Job Information/Testing Center.

"Civil Service" Schools

The Office of Personnel Management has no connection with any so-called "civil service" school or private employment agency. No "civil service" school or employment agency can guarantee that you will be found qualified for a particular position.

Equal Employment Opportunity

All qualified applicants will receive consideration for appointment without regard to race, religion, color, national origin, sex, political affiliations, handicap, or any other non-merit factor.

Testing Locations

DEPARTMENT OF COMMERCE
Patent and Trademark Office
2011 Crystal Drive, Suite 601,
Room B
Arlington, Virginia 22202
Appointment Only (703) 557-3631

AGRICULTURAL RESEARCH SERVICE
Personnel Division
6305 Ivy Lane
Greenbelt, Maryland 20770-1435
Appointment Only (301) 344-3961

DEPARTMENT OF HEALTH AND HUMAN SERVICES
National Institutes of Health
9000 Rockville Pike
Building 31C, Room B3C02B
Bethesda, Maryland 20892
Walk-in Test Mon., Wed., and Fri. at
8:30 a.m., limited to 16 per test date
(301) 496-2403

ARMY (FORT MYER)
Civilian Personnel Office
Building 469, Room 401
Fort Myer, Virginia 22211-5050
Appointment Only (202) 696-3180/3036

DEPARTMENT OF HEALTH AND HUMAN SERVICES
Public Health Service
5600 Fishers Lane
Parklawn Bldg., Room 3B-55
(Twinbrook Room)
Rockville, Maryland 20857
Walk-in Test Tues., Thurs., and Fri. at
9:00 a.m., limited to 25 per test date
(301) 443-6900

DEPARTMENT OF THE ARMY
Hoffman Civilian Personnel Office
Military District of Washington
200 Stovall Street
Room 1S39, Hoffman II
Alexandria, Virginia 22332-0800
Walk-in Test Friday, 8:00 a.m.,
limited to 18 per test date
(703) 325-8840

NAVY (CRYSTAL CITY)
1921 Jefferson Davis Hwy.
Crystal Mall Building, Building 2
S. Arlington, Virginia 20376-5006
Appointment Only (202) 746-0171

DEFENSE LOGISTICS AGENCY
DASC-KSE Cameron Station
Alexandria, Virginia 22304-6130
Appointment Only (202) 274-7087/88

DEPARTMENT OF VETERANS AFFAIRS
(CENTRAL OFFICE)
810 Vermont Ave., NW., Room 115
Washington, D.C. 20420
Appointment Only (202) 233-2459

GEOLOGICAL SURVEY
12201 Sunrise Valley Drive, Room 1A315,
MS-215
Reston, Virginia 22092
Appointment Only (703) 648-6131

DEPARTMENT OF DEFENSE
(PENTAGON)
Directorate for Personnel and Security
Pentagon, Room 3A346
Washington, D.C. 20310-1155
Appointment Only (202) 695-6213

ENVIRONMENTAL PROTECTION AGENCY
401 M Street, SW, Room G050
Washington, D.C. 20460
Appointment Only (202) 382-3144

AGRICULTURE (HEADQUARTERS)
Room 1078, South Building
14th St. and Independence Ave., SW.
Washington, D.C. 20250
Walk-in Test Tuesday at 8:00 a.m. and
11:00 a.m.; limited to 20 per test date
(202) 447-5625

DEPARTMENT OF COMMERCE
Bureau of the Census
Personnel Division
Suitland, Maryland 20746
Walk-in Test Tues., Wed., and Thurs.
Limited to 30 per test date
(301) 763-7460

BOLLING AFB
Main Entrance
Building P20, Room 240
Washington, D.C. 20332-5000
Appointment Only (202) 767-5449

INTERNAL REVENUE SERVICE
1111 Constitution Ave., NW., Room 1501
Washington, D.C. 20224
Appointment Only (202) 343-0072

DEPARTMENT OF TRANSPORTATION
FAA Headquarters Bldg.
800 Independence Ave., SW
Washington, D.C. 20591
Walk-in Test Thursday at 8:30 a.m.
and 1:00 p.m.; limited to 20 per
test date
(202) 366-9397

DEPARTMENT OF LABOR
200 Constitution Ave. NW
DOL Academy—Room C5515
Seminar Room 5
Washington, D.C. 20210
Appointment Only (202) 523-6525

U.S. DEPARTMENT OF COMMERCE

ANNOUNCEMENT NUMBER: F92-22 KB

ISSUE DATE:

CLOSING DATE:

Merit Program

VACANCY ANNOUNCEMENT

NATIONAL OCEANIC AND ATMOSPHERIC ADMINISTRATION (NOAA)

Computer Specialist
GS-334-11
No Known promotion potential
Competitive Service
Salary Range: $32,423 to $42,152

Data Management Support
Northeast Fisheries Service Center
National Marine Fisheries Service
Woods Hole, MA

WHO MAY APPLY: Career and Career conditional employees, reinstatement eligibles and those with VRA or handicap eligibility.

DUTIES: Designs Fisheries relational data bases which integrate various historical data sets. Analyzes user's needs to determine systems' requirements; develops systems for collection, entry, quality control and archival of data. Prepares data base analysis, design and implementation specifications to be followed by programmers. Maintains user accounts, access authorizations, and disk resources in a mainframe environment.

QUALIFICATIONS: Applicants must have either 3 full academic years of progressively higher level graduate education which provided knowledge equivalent to a major in the computer field OR at least 52 weeks of experience which demonstrated accomplishment of computer requirements and techniques at a level of skill equivalent to GS-9 level OR a combination of education and experience as described in Civil Service Handbook X-118. Time-in-grade restrictions apply to status candidates.

BASIS FOR EVALUATING CANDIDATES: Candidates who meet the minimum qualification requirements described above may be further evaluated and ranked on the basis of job-related factors to determine the best qualified. Consideration will be given to education, training and awards. Date of awards must be included. **1)** Knowledge of database management systems technology, standards and practices sufficient to design database systems **2)** Knowledge of systems analysis and design techniques, **3)** Knowledge of computer system hardware, operating systems, and vendor supplied utility software sufficient to select appropriate design alternatives.

HOW AND WHERE TO APPLY: All applicants must submit an SF-171, Application for Federal Employment, and OPM form 1170, List of College Courses or college transcripts. **NOTE:** Federal employees **must** submit a copy of their most recent annual performance appraisal. Failure to submit this form may affect consideration under this announcement. Send forms to: Eastern Administrative Support Center, room 411, 253 Monticello Avenue, Norfolk, VA 23510, ATTN: Kathlyn Baker. Applications **must be received in the office by closing date.** If you have any questions or desire an application package contact Kathlyn Baker, on 804-441-6880. The Telecommunications Device for the Deaf telephone access number is 804-441-3609. For more information on other EASC Merit Assignment Program recruitment, contact the EASC MAP Vacancy Announcement Hotline on Commercial 804-441-3720.

MERIT PROGRAM
VACANCY ANNOUNCEMENT
SUPPLEMENTAL INFORMATION

ALL QUALIFIED APPLICANTS WILL BE CONSIDERED REGARDLESS OF AGE, RACE, COLOR, SEX, CREED, NATIONAL ORIGIN, LAWFUL POLITICAL AFFILIATION, NON-DISQUALIFYING PHYSICAL HANDICAP, MARITAL STATUS, AFFILIATION WITH AN EMPLOYEE ORGANIZATION OR OTHER NON-MERIT FACTOR.

I. APPLICATION REQUIREMENTS:

A. ALL APPLICANTS MUST:

1. SUBMIT A SIGNED AND DATED COPY OF A CURRENT FORM SF-171.
2. IDENTIFY THE JOB APPLIED FOR BY PLACING THE ANNOUNCEMENT NUMBER IN BLOCK 1 OF FORM SF-171.
3. APPLY AT THEIR OWN EXPENSE; APPLICATIONS MAILED IN GOVERNMENT POSTAGE-PAID ENVELOPES WILL NOT BE ACCEPTED.
4. ENSURE THAT THEIR COMPLETE APPLICATION REACHES THE ISSUING PERSONNEL OFFICE NO LATER THAN THE CLOSING DATE OF THE VACANCY ANNOUNCEMENT. (APPLICATIONS RECEIVED AFTER THE CLOSING DATE WILL NOT BE CONSIDERED.)
5. MEET ALL ELIGIBILITY REQUIREMENTS BY THE CLOSING DATE OF THE VACANCY ANNOUNCEMENT.
6. BE CITIZENS OF THE UNITED STATES (OR OWE ALLEGIANCE TO THE UNITED STATES).

B. SPECIFIC REQUIREMENTS:

1. ALL FEDERAL EMPLOYEE APPLICANTS SHOULD SUBMIT A COPY OF THEIR MOST RECENT PERFORMANCE APPRAISAL.
2. FORMER FEDERAL EMPLOYEES ELIGIBLE FOR REINSTATEMENT SHOULD SUBMIT PROOF OF REINSTATEMENT ELIGIBILITY.
3. HANDICAPPED APPLICANTS, DISABLED VETERANS, OR ANY OTHER APPLICANTS ELIGIBLE FOR NON-COMPETITIVE APPOINTMENT UNDER SPECIAL APPOINTING AUTHORITIES NOT REQUIRING COMPETITIVE STATUS SHOULD CLEARLY SPECIFY THEIR SPECIAL ELIGIBILITY ON THEIR APPLICATION.
4. APPLICANTS WHO ARE NOT FEDERAL EMPLOYEES MUST SUBMIT A COPY OF THEIR OPM NOTICE OF RESULTS FOR VACANCIES OPEN TO NON-STATUS APPLICANTS, IF THEY HAVE RECEIVED SUCH A NOTICE AND IT IS CURRENT.
5. IF SELECTED, MALE APPLICANTS BORN AFTER DECEMBER 31, 1959 MUST CONFIRM THEIR SELECTIVE SERVICE REGISTRATION STATUS. CERTIFICATION FORMS ARE AVAILABLE AT MOST FEDERAL AGENCY PERSONNEL OFFICES OR FROM THE U.S. OFFICE OF PERSONNEL MANAGEMENT.

II. CONSIDERATION OF APPLICATIONS:

A. ALL CAREER AND CAREER-CONDITIONAL COMMERCE EMPLOYEES WHO APPLY WILL BE CONSIDERED.
B. FOR ANY VACANCY EMPLOYEES OF THE DEPARTMENT OF COMMERCE MAY BE CONSIDERED BEFORE OTHER APPLICANTS.
C. DEPARTMENT OF COMMERCE EMPLOYEES IN THE COMMUTING AREA WHO SUBMIT A COPY OF THEIR ACTIVE SPECIFIC RIF NOTICE OR THEIR ACTIVE GENERAL RIF NOTICE WILL RECEIVE PRIORITY CONSIDERATION.
D. COMMERCE EMPLOYEES ENTITLED TO PROMOTION RECONSIDERATION UNDER THE MERIT ASSIGNMENT PLAN RECEIVE IT BEFORE A VACANCY IS ADVERTISED. FOR FURTHER CONSIDERATION FOR THIS VACANCY THESE EMPLOYEES MUST APPLY AND COMPETE.
E. SOME ANNOUNCED VACANCIES ARE NOT FILLED THROUGH THE MERIT PLAN, BUT BY OTHER MEANS, SUCH AS REASSIGNMENT, REINSTATEMENT, NEW APPOINTMENT, OR ON A PRIORITY BASIS FROM THE DEPARTMENT'S PRIORITY PLACEMENT PROGRAM OR REEMPLOYMENT PRIORITY LIST.

III. GENERAL INFORMATION:

A. APPLICATIONS WILL NOT BE RETURNED TO APPLICANTS.
B. APPLICANTS WILL RECEIVE NOTICE OF THE OUTCOME OF A VACANCY ANNOUNCEMENT AS SOON AS POSSIBLE AFTER A SELECTION IS MADE.
C. IF A VACANCY IS FOR A SUPERVISORY OR MANAGERIAL POSITION, THE SELECTEE MAY HAVE TO SERVE A SUPERVISORY/MANAGERIAL PROBATIONARY PERIOD.
D. A TEMPORARY OR TERM PROMOTION MADE THROUGH A VACANCY ANNOUNCEMENT MAY BE CONVERTED TO A PERMANENT PROMOTION WITHOUT FURTHER COMPETITION (THIS IMPLIES NO PROMISE OR GUARANTEE OF A PERMANENT PROMOTION).
E. IF A VACANT POSITION IS FILLED AT A GRADE BELOW THE FULL PERFORMANCE LEVEL, THE SELECTEE MAY BE PROMOTED WITHOUT FURTHER COMPETITION (HOWEVER, THIS IMPLIES NO PROMISE OR GUARANTEE OF PROMOTION).
F. QUALIFICATION REQUIREMENTS IN THE VACANCY ANNOUNCEMENT ARE BASED ON OPM **HANDBOOK X-118,** WHICH CONTAINS FEDERAL QUALIFICATION STANDARDS. IT IS AVAILABLE FOR REVIEW IN MOST FEDERAL PERSONNEL OFFICES.
G. PRIVACY ACT REQUIREMENTS (PL 93-579): THE APPLICATION FORMS PRESCRIBED ARE USED TO DETERMINE QUALIFICATION FOR PROMOTION REASSIGNMENT, OR EMPLOYMENT AND ARE AUTHORIZED UNDER TITLE 5, U.S.C. SECTIONS 3302 AND 3361.
H. THE MERIT ASSIGNMENT PLAN IS AVAILABLE FOR REVIEW AT THE PERSONNEL OFFICE ADDRESS LISTED IN THE ANNOUNCEMENT UNDER "HOW AND WHERE TO APPLY".

NOTICE TO ALL APPLICANTS

PLEASE READ FORM CD-260S, WHICH CONTAINS IMPORTANT INFORMATION ABOUT THIS ANNOUNCEMENT.

Correctional Officer Announcement 431 and General Information

U.S. Department of Justice
Federal Bureau of Prisons
(Open Until Further Notice)

1. SALARY:

Correctional Officers are appointed at the GS-6 level. Salaries of Federal Employees are adjusted periodically. Current salary rates are available at Federal Job Information Centers.

After six months satisfactory service, a Correctional Officer may be advanced to the next higher grade level. Advancement beyond that depends upon available vacancies, personal performance and demonstrated ability.

A strong internal merit promotion system allows advancement opportunities.

2. DUTIES:

- enforcing the rules and regulations governing the operation of a correctional institution and the confinement, safety, health and protection of inmates. This may, at times, require arduous physical exertion in the subduing of recalcitrant inmates who may be armed or assaultive.
- supervising the various work assignments of inmates.
- on occasion, Correctional Officers are required to carry firearms, and
- participating as a member of the corrections team of Case Workers, Psychiatrists, Psychologists, Teachers and others working to help the individual inmate.

3. BENEFITS:

Insurance...... You may elect to be covered by group life insurance and health insurance for which the government shares in the cost.

Retirement...... Your retirement coverage entitles you to retire at 50 after 20 years of service or at any age with 25 years of federal law enforcement service. Retirement at age 55 after 20 years of service is mandatory. Retirement contributions and Federal and state taxes are deducted.

MANDATORY GENERAL REQUIREMENTS

APPLICANTS:

1. Citizenship
Must be a U.S. Citizen.

2. Age:
At time of appointment applicants must not have reached their 35th birthday unless they have previously served in a Federal civilian law enforcement position covered by special civil service retirement provisions, including early or mandatory retirement. The maximum entry age limit has been established under the authority of Public Law 93-350 and the age limit constitutes an exception to normal age discrimina-

tion prohibitions contained in section 15 of the Age Discrimination in Employment Act.

3. EMPLOYMENT INTERVIEW

All qualified candidates will be subject to an employment interview prior to final selection. Interviews will be held within the general area (approximately 250 miles, roundtrip) where the applicant resides. All candidates must pay expenses to interview site and first employment location.

4. PHYSICAL EXAMINATIONS:

All applicants are subject to satisfactory completion of Physical Examination.

5. SECURITY INVESTIGATION:

All applicants are subject to satisfactory completion of Full Field Security Investigation.

SELECTEES:

1. TRAINING:

Must successfully complete training provided by the Bureau as follows:

- 160 hours of formal training within the first year of employment.
- 120 hours of specialized training at our residential training center (located at Glynco, Georgia).

2. MISCELLANEOUS INFORMATION:

Correctional Officers are required to work weekends and rotating shifts. Additional pay is given for evening, Sunday, & Holiday work. Work is performed inside and outside depending on the nature of the assignment. A Uniform Clothing Allowance is provided by the prison service.

BASIC QUALIFICATION REQUIREMENTS

1. QUALIFYING EXPERIENCE:

——— NO WRITTEN TEST IS REQUIRED ———

To become a Correctional Officer you must show that you have had a minimum of 3½ years experience. This experience must have been in one or more of the following or similar types of work:

Supervisory or leadership experience.

Teaching or instructing, especially with adults or disadvantaged groups.

Enforcement of rules and regulations relating to safety, health or protection.

Corrections or rehabilitation.

Counseling in a welfare or other social service agency.

Interviewing and counseling.

Sales work which involved extensive person-to-person relationships.

2. EXAMPLES OF NON-QUALIFYING EXPERIENCE:

Routine clerical - machine operation

Non-supervisory construction or production work

Property maintenance

Checker

Clerk

3. NOTE: Pertinent UNPAID OR VOLUNTEER work will be credited on the same basis as paid employment.

4. SUBSTITUTION OF EDUCATION FOR EXPERIENCE

Education successfully completed in an accredited college, university or resident school above the high school level may be substituted as indicated below:

(1) Two years of study successfully completed in a resident school above the high school level may be substituted for two years of general experience.

(2) Successful completion of a full four-year course of college study may be substituted for three years of general experience.

(3) One full semester of graduate study successfully completed in an accredited college or university may be substituted for 6 months of general experience, and is fully qualifying for grade GS-6.

BASIS OF RATING:

All applicants will be evaluated on the description of experience and training described in the Standard Form 171 and on the response to Elements A, B, and C on the Supplemental Qualifications Statement for Correctional Officers.

HOW TO APPLY

1. Complete the following forms:

   a. SF-171, Application for Federal Employment
   b. OPM Form 1170-35, Supplemental Qualifications Statement for Correctional Officer
   c. OPM Form 1203C, Form A, Employment Availability Statement

2. In addition, if applicable, submit the following:

   a. Copy of college transcript.
   b. Standard Form 15 and letter from Veteran's Administration, (dated within last six months), if you are claiming 10 points veteran preference.

RETURN ALL COMPLETED APPLICATION FORMS TO:

Federal Prison System
Examining Section
Room 400
320 First Street, N.W.
Washington, D.C. 20534

OTHER INFORMATION

Eligible competitors who have not been appointed must submit up-to-date information on their qualifications at intervals of not less than 10 and not more than 12 months, if they wish to remain active on the list of eligibles.

U.S. Department of Justice
Federal Bureau of Prisons

U.S. Department of Justice
Federal Bureau of Prisons
Examining Unit
Room 400
320 First Street, N.W.
Washington, D.C. 20534

INSTRUCTIONS FOR COMPLETING EMPLOYMENT AVAILABILITY STATEMENT (KEES) - FORM A

This form is not as complicated as it may appear at first glance. Read and follow all instructions on this sheet and on the Form A very carefully to avoid any delay in the processing of your forms. Make sure you understand how to properly fill out this form before starting.

Do not fold, staple, tear or paper clip this form! Do not submit photocopies of this form! Do not fill this form out in ink. Use a Number 2 (or softer) lead pencil only! Completely blacken each circle you choose. Completely erase any mistakes or stray marks!

Block 1: Print your name and title of the position for which you are applying.

Block 2: Enter your social security number, one number per block, and then blacken the corresponding circle below each number you have entered. Verify that the social security numbers on Form A and your SF-171 are identical. **An incorrect social security number will delay the processing of your forms.**

Block 3: In the blocks beneath Area office name, print "FEDERAL PRISONS", one letter per block.

The listing of geographic location codes on the back of this sheet are separated into two columns. You may select only 1 (one) location from column 1. This will be considered your first choice location preference. Enter the three digit location code number, which appears in column 1, in the three spaces designated as number 1 in block 3 on Form A.

You may select 2 (two) locations from column 2. (You do not have to select any from this column if you do not want to be considered for other than your first choice location.) Select only those locations where you are able and willing to accept employment. Do not select a location to which you can not realistically move.

If you refuse employment consideration at any location that you indicate you are available for, your name will be removed from the register.

Block 4: Blacken either the Yes or No circle for each question. Do not blacken both circles and do not leave any questions unanswered!

Block 5: Leave blank. Do not leave any marks in this block.

Block 6: Leave blank. Do not make any marks in this book.

Block 7: Name. Self-explanatory

Block 8: Self-explanatory. If space permits, leave a space between the street number, street name, etc. Do not use any punctuation. For example: 1000 Main ST APT 1 or PO BOX 9.

Block 9: Self-explanatory. If space permits, leave a blank space between the words of cities with more than one word. For example: NEW ORLEANS or SAN ANTONIO.

Block 10 through 14: Self-explanatory.

After completing Block 13 and 14 on Page 3, check all of the blocks you have completed and make sure they are accurate. Do not make any other marks on the rest of Page 3 or on Page 4.

GEOGRAPHIC AVAILABILITY

Select only 1 (one) location from column 1 (First Choice), and up to two locations from column 2 (Second Choice) and blacken the corresponding circle under block 3 on the Employment Availability Statement (KEES) Form A.

	COLUMN 1	COLUMN 2
Ashland, KY - FCI	001	051
Englewood, CO - FCI	002	052
Morgantown, WV - FCI	003	053
El Reno, OK - FCI	004	054
• Lompoc, CA-USP	005	055
Milan, MI - FCI	006	056
Petersburg, VA - FCI	007	057
Seagoville, TX - FCI	008	058
Tallahassee, FL - FCI	009	059
Pleasanton, CA - FCI	010	060
Lexington, KY - FCI	011	061
Oxford, WI - FCI	012	062
Miami, FL - MCC	013	063
Bastrop, TX - FCI	014	064
Memphis, TN - FCI	015	065
Talladega, AL - FCI	016	066
Atlanta, GA - USP	017	067
• Leavenworth, KS - USP	018	068
• Lewisburg, PA - USP	019	069
Allenwood, PA - FPC	020	070
• Marion, IL - USP	021	071
Terre Haute, IN - USP	022	072
Ray Brook, NY - FCI	023	073
Otisville, NY - FCI	024	074
Danbury, CT - FCI	025	075
La Tuna, TX - FCI	026	076
Sandstone, MN - FCI	027	077
Terminal Island, CA - FCI	028	078
Texarkana, TX - FCI	029	079
Boron, CA - FPC	030	080
Big Spring, TX - FPC	031	081
Eglin, FL - FPC	032	082
Phoenix, AZ - FCI	033	083
Montgomery, AL - FPC	034	084
Safford, AZ - FPC	035	085
Chicago, IL - MCC	036	086
San Diego, CA - MCC	037	087
New York, NY - MCC	038	088
Alderson, WV - FCI	039	089
Springfield, MO - MCFP	040	090
Butner, NC - FCI	041	091
Fort Worth, TX - FCI	042	092
Tucson, AZ - MCC	043	093
Rochester, MN - FMC	044	094
Duluth, MN - FPC	045	095
Loretto, PA - FCI	046	096
Oakdale, LA - ADC	047	097
** Los Angeles, CA - MDC (10-88)	048	098
Tyndall, FL - FPC	049	099
Marianna, FL - FCI	050	100
** Fairton, NJ - FCI (11-88)	101	201
** Sheridan, OR - FCI (4-89)	102	202
** Lewis Run, PA - FCI (6-89)	103	203
** Jesup, GA - FCI (9-89)	104	204
Pensacola, FL - FPC	105	205
Yankton, SD - FPC	106	206
Victorville, CA - FPC	107	207
Denver, CO. - FPC	108	208
Bryan, TX - FPC	109	209
Lompoc, CA - FPC	110	210
El Paso, TX - FPC	111	211

*NOTE: MALES ONLY MAY APPLY FOR CORRECTIONAL OFFICER POSITIONS AT THE INSTITUTIONS INDICATED BY ASTERISK(*). THIS RESTRICTION APPLIES ONLY TO CORRECTIONAL OFFICERS.

IF YOU *REFUSE* EMPLOYMENT CONSIDERATION AT ANY LOCATION THAT YOU INDICATE YOU ARE AVAILABLE FOR, YOUR NAME WILL BE *REMOVED FROM THE REGISTER.*

**ANTICIPATED TO OPEN ON DATES INDICATED.

United States Department of the Interior
Bureau of Indian Affairs

VACANCY ANNOUNCEMENT

ANNOUNCEMENT NUMBER: _____ ISSUING DATE: _____

CONSIDERATION AREA: ALL SOURCES CLOSING DATE: _____
(STATUS AND/OR INDIAN APPLICANTS ONLY)

POSITION TITLE & GRADE: CRIMINAL INVESTIGATOR (CHILD ABUSE)
GS-1811-9/11/12

SALARY RANGE:
GS-09: $26,798 - $34,835
GS-11: $32,423 - $42,152
GS-12: $38,861 - $50,516

NUMBER OF POSITIONS: SIX (6)

LOCATION: Bureau of Indian Affairs, Office of Tribal Services, Division of Law Enforcement, Washington, D.C.

DUTY LOCATION: One position at each of the following locations:

ABERDEEN, SOUTH DAKOTA
ALBUQUERQUE, NEW MEXICO
BILLINGS, MONTANA
MINNEAPOLIS, MINNESOTA
PHOENIX, ARIZONA
PORTLAND, OREGON

NOTE: Please indicate on the attached form which duty location you would like to be considered for and submit with application forms.

AGE REQUIREMENTS: MAXIMUM AGE FOR AN ORIGINAL APPOINTMENT TO A LAW ENFORCEMENT POSITION IN THE BIA IS PRIOR TO THE APPOINTEE HAVING REACHED THEIR THIRTY-SEVENTH (37) BIRTHDAY.

INDIAN PREFERENCE POLICY: Preference in filling vacancies is given to qualified Indian candidates in accordance with the Indian Preference Act of 1934. (Title 25, USC, Section 472). Verification Form BIA-432 must be submitted with the application if claiming Indian Preference.

BRIEF STATEMENT OF DUTIES: The incumbents of these positions will be commissioned law enforcement officers under 25 USC 2803, specializing in the investigating of crimes involving child abuse, sexual abuse, and other exploitation or victimization of children. Investigations conducted by the incumbent can have nationwide affect often requiring the incumbent to have a lead role and provide guidance to a multi-disciplinary team of personnel which includes criminal investigators and other professionals, such as medical personnel, social workers, counselors, legal personnel, engaged in the investigation of child abuse or other criminal activity.

Duties: continued

Insures that incidents of child abuse are reported and thoroughly investigates incidents of suspected non-reporting. Establishes and maintains effective liaison with all types of law enforcement and intelligence agencies. Develops and maintains intelligence data on suspected illegal activities. Serves as a certified instructor, insuring all area investigative personnel are properly trained and maintain proficiency in the specialized area of child abuse investigation.

POSITION SENSITIVITY: This position has been designated critical-sensitive. The selectee will be subject to the necessary background investigation.

POSITION SUBJECT RANDOM TO DRUG TESTING.

SUMMARY OF QUALIFICATIONS REQUIRED: (Refer to OPM Handbook X-118 and BIA Excepted Standards for additional qualifications requirements and substitutions for education.) Applicants must meet the qualification requirements contained in Office of Personnel Management Handbook X-118 or BIA Excepted standards. The requirements for this position is least one year of specialized experience at a level of difficulty and responsibility comparable to the next lower grade level in Federal service. Specialized experience is experience which is in or directly related to the line of work of the position to be filled and which has equipped the applicant with the particular knowledge, skills and abilities to successfully perform the duties of this position.

ADDITIONAL INFORMATION: Concurrent consideration may be given to VRA eligible, handicapped eligible, disabled veterans, reinstatement and transfer eligible.; 2) Applications become part of the official record and will not be duplicated or returned; 3) Candidates must meet all qualification requirements (including Time-in-Grade) within 30 days after the closing date; 4) All male applicants born after December 31, 1959, will be required to complete the certification document to confirm their selective service status; 5) Position subject to drug testing; 6) Applicant must possess a valid State Driver's License and must qualify to operate a Government owned vehicle; 6) Promotion to the next higher grade maybe made without further competition.

*SUPPLEMENTAL QUESTIONNAIRE

This supplemental will be the principal basis for determining whether or not you are highly qualified for this position. You may add information not identified in your SF-171 or expand on that which is identified. You should consider appropriate work experience, outside activities, awards, training, and education for each of the items listed below.

1. Knowledge of, and sensitivity to, issues related to child abuse, child sexual abuse, and the exploitation of children.

2. Skill in communicating effectively, both orally and in writing; including the ability to prepare complex written reports, containing legal, medical and forensic terminology.

3. Skill in maintaining surveillance, performing undercover work, making arrest, taking part in raids, following leads that indicate a crime will be committed, and interviewing or interrogating suspects, victims and witnesses.

4. Knowledge of Federal, state and tribal laws, court decisions, as applicable to Indian country, especially those Federal statutes regarding child sexual abuse.

5. Skill in the use of firearms and chemical agents.

*On a separate sheet of paper, address the above items in narrative form. Identify the vacancy announcement number across the top. Sign and date your supplemental questionnaire.

APPLICANTS MUST SUBMIT: Current SF-171; BIA Form 4432 (if claiming Indian Preference); Attached Supplemental Questionnaire for Knowledge, Skills and Abilities; DD Form 214 (If claiming Veteran's Preference); College Transcripts (credit for education will not be granted without verification); Supervisory Appraisal (Must be current within the preceding year); Current SF-50 (if status candidates); Form DI-1935 attached (voluntary). MUST SUBMIT THE ATTACHED DUTY LOCATION PREFERENCE FORM.

HOW TO APPLY: Applications must be received by close of business on the closing date of the announcement. However, if the Personnel Office is notified on or before the closing date, applications will be accepted if postmarked within 3 working days after the closing date of the announcement. Applications mailed using Government postage and/or envelopes is in violation of OPM and Postal Regulations and will not be accepted. APPLICANT'S QUALIFICATIONS WILL BE EVALUATED SOLELY ON THE INFORMATION SUBMITTED BY THEM IN THEIR APPLICATIONS.

MAIL APPLICATIONS TO:

Bureau of Indian Affairs   For Additional Info.
Branch of Personnel Services/MS-331-SIB   contact Kay Hayes
1951 Constitution Avenue, NW   (202) 208-2706.
Washington, D.C. 20245

For a copy of the Vacancy Announcement call (202) 208-7581.

Vacancy Hot-Line (202) 208-2682

THE DEPARTMENT OF THE INTERIOR IS AN EQUAL OPPORTUNITY EMPLOYER

U.S. DEPARTMENT OF HEALTH AND HUMAN SERVICES

PHOENIX AREA INDIAN HEALTH SERVICE

PERSONNEL MANAGEMENT BRANCH
3738 N. 16TH STREET, SUITE A
PHOENIX, ARIZONA 85016-5981

Announcement	Opening Date	Closing Date
No. PXIHS-92-99-1		Open Until Filled

POSITION: LOCATION/DUTY STATION:

DENTAL ASSISTANT   PHS Indian Hospital
                                               Keams Canyon Service Unit
SERIES/GRADE/SALARY: Duty Station: Jeddito, AZ
GS-681-2, $12,905 - $16,237 per annum
GS-681-3, $14,082 - $18,303 per annum
GS-681-4, $15,808 - $20,551 per annum

TYPE/NUMBER OF POSITIONS: CONDITIONS OF EMPLOYMENT: AREA OF CONSIDERATION:
2 Number of Positions   X Full-time
X Permanent   ___ Intermittent   **IHS WIDE**
___ Temporary-NTE: ___ Part-time

SUPERVISORY/MANAGEMENT: PHRS: PROMOTION POTENTIAL:
    Yes, may require one year probationary period.   ___ Yes   X Yes, to Grade: GS-4
X No   X No   ___ No known potential

HOUSING: TRAVEL EXPENSES:
___ Yes, government housing available   ___ Travel may be paid in accordance
X Private housing only   with Federal Travel Regulations
                                         X No expenses paid

BRIEF DESCRIPTION OF DUTIES: At the GS-2 and GS-3 employee receives close guidance.
Serves as a trainee at the GS-2, assignments involve steps which are clearly defined. GS-3
performs clinic maintenance and recordkeeping duties and provides chairside assistance to
dentist. GS-4 - Performs chairside assistance duties in all phases of restorative,
prosthodontic, surgical endodontic and peridontal treatment as provided in general dentistry.
Records information related to medical history of patients; charts examination and treatment
information as relayed by dentist. Maintains dental equipment, properly stores and maintains
adequate levels of supplies. Performs other clinical duties including oral health education
consistent with the smooth and efficient operation. Performs other duties as assigned.

QUALIFICATION REQUIREMENTS:

NOTE: Public Law 97-35 requires that persons who administer radiologic procedures meet the
credentialing standards which are set forth in 42 CFR Part 75. Essentially, they must (1) have
successfully completed an educational program which meets or exceeds the standards described in
that regulation and which is accredited by an organization recognized by the Department of
Education and (2) be certified as radiographers in their field.

*TO IDENTIFY ADDITIONAL CANDIDATES. THOSE WHO PREVIOUSLY APPLIED WILL AUTOMATICALLY
BE RECONSIDERED AND NEED NOT REAPPLY.

The following are deemed to have met the requirements of 42 CFR Part 75:

(1) Persons employed by the Federal Government as radiologic personnel prior to the effective
date of the regulation (December 11, 1985) who show evidence of current or fully satisfactory
performance or certification of such from a licensed practitioner such as a doctor of medicine,
osteopathy, dentistry, podiatry, or chiropractic, who prescribes radiologic procedures to
others.

(2) Persons first employed by the Federal Government as radiologic personnel prior to the effective date of the
regulations who (a) received training from institutions in a state or foreign jurisdiction which did not accredit training
in that particular field at the time of graduation, or (b) practice in a state or foreign jurisdiction which did not license
that particular field or which did not allow special eligibility to take a licensure examination for those who did not
graduate from an accredited education program; provided that such persons show evidence of training, experience,
and competence as determined by OPM or the employing agency.

Such persons, however, must meet the requirements below.

EXPERIENC/EDUCATION REQUIREMENTS:

GS-2   Three (3) months of general experience OR high school graduation or equivalent. OR high
        school graduation or equivalent.

GS-3   Six (6) months of general experience OR successful completion of (a) a one 1-year dental
        assistant program or completion of one year of a dental hygiene program accredited by
        the American Dental Association's Commission on Accreditation which included a course in
        radiation physics; radiation biology; radiation health, safety and protection; X-ray
        films and radiographic film quality; radiographic techniques; darkroom and processing
        techniques; and film mounting; or (b) practical nurse training approved by the
        appropriate State or District of Columbia accrediting body.

GS-4   Six (6) months of general experience and six (6) months of specialized experience OR
        successful completion of a 2-year dental assistant program or completion of 1 year of a
        dental hygiene program accredited by the American Dental Association's Commission on
        Accreditation which included at least 12 semester hours of courses such as those listed
        for GS-3 above.

GENERAL EXPERIENCE:

Any type of work which demonstrates the applicants ability to perform the work of the position
or experience which proved a familiarity with the subject matter or processes of the broad
subject area of the occupation.

SPECIALIZED EXPERIENCE:

Experience in dental assistance to general or specialized dentistry, dental assistant (expanded
function) work or any combination of these appropriate to the position being filled.

SELECTIVE PLACEMENT FACTOR: None

SUPPLEMENTAL QUESTIONNAIRE
On Knowledge, Skills, and Abilities

Position applied for: Dental Assistant, GS-681-2/3/4

Announcement No: PXIHS-92-99-1   Closing Date: Open Until Filled

Evaluation Method: Evaluation will be made of experience, Performance Appraisals, Training, Letters of Commendation, Self-Development, Awards and Outside Activities, which are related to this position. To receive full credit for your qualification, provide a narrative statement of experience, training, education, awards, hobbies, self-developed achievements, and any other aspects of your background as they relate to the knowledge, skills and abilities (KSA's) outlined below and show the level of accomplishments and degree of responsibility. This supplement will be the principal basis for determining whether or not you are best qualified for the position. Describe your qualification in each of the following:

1. Knowledge of instruments, materials and standardized dental procedure for making preparations and providing chairside assistance.

2. Knowledge of standard clinical routines and procedures including the use, care, and storage of dental, medical or laboratory instruments.

3. Knowledge of proper cleaning and sterilization techniques.

The information you provide is considered to be a part of your application and as such is certified by your signature on the SF-171 or equivalent.

_____   _____
Signature   Date

TIME-IN-GRADE RESTRICTION: (If selected under the Excepted Service Examining Plan, such individuals may be appointed under Schedule A authority without regard to Time-in-Grade Requirements.) A candidate may be advanced to a position in grade GS-5 or below if: (1) The position is no more than two grades above the lowest grade level he/she held within the proceeding year under nontemporary appointment; or (2) He/she met the above restriction for advancement to the grade of the position to be filled, at any time in the past; or (3) He/she previously held a position at or above the grade level of the position to be filled, at any time under any type of appointment.

MOTOR VEHICLE OPERATION REQUIREMENTS: Incumbent may be required at some locations to operate a government motor vehicle and maintain a current State Driver's license and Government Employee Identification Card.

SELECTIVE SERVICE CERTIFICATION: If you are male, born after December 31, 1959, and you want to be employed by the Federal Government, you must (subject to certain exemptions) be registered with Selective Service System.

LEGAL AND REGULATORY REQUIREMENTS: Candidates must meet time after competitive appointment, time-in-grade restrictions, and qualification requirements 30 days after the opening date of vacancy announcement.

APPLICANTS OR CURRENT FEDERAL SERVICE EMPLOYEES CLAIMING INDIAN PREFERENCE MUST INDICATE in Item 1 ON THEIR APPLICATION IF THEY WISH TO BE CONSIDERED UNDER THE INDIAN HEALTH SERVICE MERIT PROMOTION PLAN, EXCEPTED SERVICE EXAMINING PLAN, OR BOTH. IF NOT, THEY WILL BE CONSIDERED UNDER THE IHS MERIT PROMOTION PLAN ONLY.

PREFERENCE IN FILLING VACANCIES IS GIVEN TO QUALIFIED INDIAN CANDIDATES IN ACCORDANCE WITH THE INDIAN PREFERENCE ACT (TITLE 25, U.S. CODE, SECTION 472 AND 473). IN OTHER THAN THE ABOVE, THE INDIAN HEALTH SERVICE IS AN EQUAL OPPORTUNITY EMPLOYER.

REASONABLE ACCOMMODATION WILL BE GIVEN TO QUALIFIED DISABLE APPLICANTS PURSUANT TO SECTION 501 OF THE REHABILITATION ACT OF 1973, 29 U.S. CODE 791, TITLE 29.

ADDITIONAL SELECTION MAY BE MADE FROM THIS ANNOUNCEMENT WITHIN 90 DAYS FROM THE DATE OF THE CERTIFICATE PROVIDED THE VACANT POSITION IS AN IDENTICAL POSITION, SAME GEOGRAPHICAL LOCATION AND SAME CONDITIONS OF EMPLOYMENT.

Announcement No. VA-0630

Department of Veterans Affairs

DIETITIAN, GS-630-7/11

Applications will be accepted until further notice.

DESCRIPTION OF WORK

Dietitians in medical centers perform or supervise others in performing a full range of professional dietetic duties in areas of program development and organization, food preparation and service, patient therapy, education and research. In selected outpatient clinics, dietitians perform duties in the areas of patient therapy and education, and are responsible for program development, organization, and the nutritional phase of any medical research.

Dietitians work closely with physicians, nurses, social workers, and other allied health personnel to integrate the patient's nutritional care into the total treatment program. The dietitian's contribution as a team member includes the nutritional assessment of patients, the development of a nutritional care plan, and providing individualized nutrition education.

LOCATION OF POSITIONS

Most of the dietitians in the Federal service are employed by the Department of Veterans Affairs (VA) at medical centers in all fifty states and Puerto Rico. Vacancies in other Federal agencies may occasionally be filled through this announcement.

SALARY

Starting salary depends upon the duties and responsibilities of the position being filled. There are opportunities for promotion to higher grade levels, periodic increases within each grade level, additional increases for superior performance, and increases in Federal salaries based on comparability with the private sector.

QUALIFICATION REQUIREMENTS

BASIC REQUIREMENTS

You must be a citizen of the United States.

English Language Proficiency: If you are appointed to a direct patient-care position, you must be proficient in spoken and written English as required by 38 USC 4105 (c).

FOR POSITIONS WITH THE DEPARTMENT OF VETERANS AFFAIRS ONLY: Applicants for VA positions must be registered with the Commission on Dietetic Registration, the credentialing branch of the American Dietetic Association. Nonregistered applicants who otherwise meet the minimum requirements in the basic qualification standard may be appointed subject to obtaining the registration during the first year of employment. Those who fail to obtain ADA registration during that year must be removed from the GS-630 Dietitian series, which may result in termination of employment.

EDUCATION AND EXPERIENCE

Basic educational requirement is a bachelor's degree in dietetics, food, nutrition, food service management, institution management, or related science. The curriculum must have been in accordance with the qualifying

requirements established by The American Dietetic Association (ADA) in effect at the time of graduation. Professional registration as a registered dietitian (R.D.) is evidence of meeting ADA requirements.

GS-7 Education: You qualify for GS-7 positions based on education alone if you have completed a Coordinated Undergraduate Program (CUP), internship, or other clinical component approved by The American Dietetic Association, which was conducted as part of the undergraduate program, or after completion of the basic requirements for a baccalaureate degree. You may also qualify if you have satisfied the superior academic achievement requirements in your bachelor's degree program. Superior academic achievement is described later in this announcement. Completion of one full year of directly related graduate level education is also fully qualifying at this grade level.

GS-7 Experience or ADA Registration: You qualify for GS-7 positions based on experience if you have one year of specialized experience equivalent to the GS-5 level in the Federal service. If you are a Registered Dietitian you meet the requirements for eligibility at the GS-7 level.

GS-9 Education: You qualify for GS-9 positions based on education if you have two full years of directly related graduate level education or a master's or equivalent degree.

GS-9 Experience: You qualify for GS-9 positions based on experience if you have one year of specialized experience equivalent to grade GS-7 in the Federal service.

GS-11 Education: You qualify for GS-11 positions based on education if you have three full years of directly related graduate level or a Ph.D. or equivalent graduate degree.

GS-11 Experience: You qualify for GS-11 positions based on experience if you have one year of specialized experience equivalent to grade GS-9 in the Federal service.

SPECIALIZED EXPERIENCE

Specialized experience is experience which is in or related to the line of work of the position to be filled and which has equipped you with the specific knowledge, skills, and abilities needed to successfully perform the duties of the position.

COMBINING EDUCATION AND EXPERIENCE

Combinations of successfully completed graduate level education and specialized experience may be used to meet total experience requirements.

QUALITY OF EXPERIENCE: For positions at any grade, the required amount of experience will not in itself be accepted as proof of qualification for a position. Your record of education and experience must clearly demonstrate that you have the ability to perform the duties of the position. The primary consideration is the quality and level of experience.

SUPERIOR ACADEMIC ACHIEVEMENT

If you have successfully completed a bachelor's-level program in an American Dietetic Association approved curricula, you may qualify for GS-7 positions on the basis of either:

  a. Standing in the upper third of your class based on completed college work at the time of application for the position. This is the upper third of the class in the college or university, or major subdivision (e.g., school of engineering, school of business administration).

  b. College grade average of "B" (2.95 or better on a 4 point scale). This is either: (1) The average of all completed college courses at the time of application for the position, or (2) The average of all college courses completed during the last 2 years of the undergraduate curriculum.

  c. Maintenance of a "B+" (3.5 or better on a 4 point scale) average in your major field of dietetics, nutrition, institution managment etc., coursework.

  d. Election to membership in Phi Beta Kappa, or other national honorary scholastic society meeting the minimum requirements of the Association of College Honor Societies (other than freshman honor societies).

VHS&RA Supplement, MP-5, Part I
Chapter 338, Appendix 338A
Change 57

QUALIFICATION STANDARD

GS-630

AUTHORITY: 38 U.S.C. 4105

DIETITIAN AND NUTRITIONIST SERIES

a. The Office of Personnel Management (OPM) qualification requirements for DIETITIAN AND NUTRITIONIST, GS-630, found in the Minimum Qualification Requirements for Two-Grade Interval Professional Positions, Handbook X-118, part III, have been approved for use in VA with the following additional requirement:

(1) All applicants must be registered with the Commission on Dietetic Registration, the credentialing branch of the ADA (American Dietetic Association).

(2) All persons permanently employed as GS-630 VA Dietitians at the time this standard is received are considered to have met the registration requirements in full. They may be promoted, demoted or reassigned within the GS-630 occupational series. Any employee initially retained in this manner who leaves this job series loses protected status and must meet the full requirements in effect at the time of reentry.

b. Exceptions:

(1) Nonregistered applicants who otherwise meet the minimum requirements in the basic qualification standard may be given a temporary appointment not to exceed 1 year; OR they may be appointed subject to obtaining the required registration during the probationary period. Those who fail to obtain ADA registration during that year must be removed from the GS-630 Dietitian series, which may result in termination of employment. A statement citing this condition of employment must be signed by each Dietitian appointed under these provisions and filed in the appointee's Official Personnel Folder.

(2) If, after positive recruitment activities, there are no acceptable applicants who meet these requirements, the Assistant Chief Medical Director for Clinical Affairs may authorize a medical center to hire otherwise qualified applicants, provided such persons show evidence of equal competence. Requests which meet the requirements of MP-5, part I, chapter 338, should be submitted, through channels, to the Deputy Assistant Secretary for Personnel and Labor Relations (054C).

BASIS OF RATING

There is no written test. You will be rated on a scale of 100 based on the extent and quality of your education, experience, and training relevant to the duties of the position. Such ratings will be based on your statements in the application and on any additional information obtained by our office.

You will be rated for all grade levels for which you are qualified and for which you will accept employment as indicated in your application.

LENGTH OF ELIGIBILITY

If you are found qualified, your name will be maintained on the list of eligibles established under this announcement for a period of 12 months. You may submit up-to-date information about your qualifications before that time period ends. A letter or an Amendment to Application for Federal Employment (Standard Form 172) may be used for this purpose. Do not submit information until two months before your eligibility expires unless you believe it will help you qualify for a higher grade. **If you do not update your records within the last 60 days of your eligibility period, you will receive no further consideration for Federal employment until you update your application. We will not notify you that your eligibility period is about to end.**

EQUAL EMPLOYMENT OPPORTUNITY

All qualified applicants will receive consideration for appointment without regard to race, religion, color, national origin, sex, political affiliation, age or any other non-merit factor.

HOW TO APPLY

Please submit the following forms:

1. Application for Federal Employment, Standard Form 171. Please show the title of the position for which you are applying, the announcement number, and the lowest salary you are willing to accept. Standard Form 171 also contains instructions for claiming Veteran's Preference.

2. Supplemental Qualifications Statement for Dietitian, OPM Form 1170/56. Please read the instructions carefully and complete the form as directed. **Your rating will be based primarily on the information you give on this form.**

3. List of College Courses and Certificate of Scholastic Achievement, OPM Form 1170/17. This form may be used to furnish a listing of all your completed college courses including semester-hour credits received. Students should also list the courses now being taken, the anticipated dates of completion and credits to be received. **Transcripts of college records may be used, if you prefer.**

4. Claim for 10-point Veteran's Preference, Standard Form 15, (if appropriate). Include copies of documentary evidence required by that form. Original evidence will be returned to applicants. Other veteran's preference information is contained in the instructions of Standard Form 171.

5. VA Employment Availability Form, 5-3447. Retain accompanying Job Locations list for your records.

WHERE TO OBTAIN FORMS

Information about forms or application instructions may be obtained from a VA medical center or an Office of Personnel Management Job Information Center (located in most large cities). Consult the telephone directory for the one nearest you. Information may also be obtained from the VA Delegated Examining Unit by calling toll-free, 800-368-6008. Virginia residents may call toll-free 800-552-3045.

Mail your application to:

Department of Veterans Affairs
Delegated Examining Unit
P.O. Box 24269
Richmond, VA 23224-0269

Delegated Examining Unit for the Office of Personnel Management
United States Environmental Protection Agency
Washington, DC 20460

Announcement Number
EPA-2-DEU-122

Opening Date

Closing Date

❂EPA

Vacancy Announcement
This is a competitive vacancy, open to all candidates, being filled
under a delegated examining authority

The Environmental Protection Agency is an Equal Opportunity Employer

How To Apply: Send completed Standard Form 171, Personal Qualifications Statement, and proof of 10-point Veterans Preference (if applicable) to the address below. Applications must be received or postmarked on or before the closing date. Required forms are obtainable from any EPA Personnel Office or Federal Job Information Center (listed under US Government in local telephone directories). Applications mailed in U.S. Government Postage Paid Envelopes will not receive consideration and will be returned.

Title, Series, Grade, and Salary of Position

Environmental Protection Specialist, GS-028-09
Salary: $26,798 - $34,835 per annum

Address of Personnel Office
Voice: 202-260-3144/Hearing Impaired 202-260-3141
US Environmental Protection Agency
Delegated Examining Unit (PM-212)
Attention: Rona Hunt
401 M Street, SW
Washington, DC 20460

Known Promotional Potential to:
GS-13

Organizational Location and Duty Station of Position EPA, Assistant Administrator for Prevention Pesticide and Toxic Substances, Office of Pesticide Programs, Special Review and Reregistration Division, Accelerated Reregistration Branch, Section I, II, III, Arlington, VA

Duties

Incumbent collects, evaluates and selects all pertinent data required for the issuance of Data Call-In notices or related notices. Evaluates certain responses from registrants and prepares decision packages on notices encompassing relevant findings and conclusions. Identifies the chemical or action in terms of actions required and certain types of data requirements. Assists in preparations from hearings by collecting additional data and reviewing new evidence or studies on the chemical being reviewed. Prepares background and policy memoranda, summaries, or other types of correspondence relevant to the process. Communicates with Branch members and personnel inside and outside of the Office of Pesticide Programs, the regulated Pesticide Industry, State, and local governments and various environmental groups.

Qualification Requirements (Applicants must meet the minimum qualification requirements defined in Qualification Standards Handbook X118 or X118c, which are available in the Personnel Office, and any selective placement factors listed below)
Information regarding X-118, Qualification Standards, can be obtained in G-050 NE Mall
Condition of Employment: All selectees are subject to verification and requirements under the immigration reform and control act of 1986. Proof of citizenship is required.

Ranking Factors
1) Skill in collecting and maintaining environmental and or human health information.
2) Skill in evaluating and analyzing regulatory documents. 3) Knowledge of pesticides laws and regulations. 4) Skill in written communication. 5) Skill in oral communication.

Applicants who meet the basic requirements and any mandatory factors listed above will be further evaluated by a determination of the extent to which their work experience, education, training, awards, and professional recognition are relevant to the position. The above listed factors will be used in making ranking determination. Please indicate in your SF-171 or a separate sheet of paper how the ranking factors listed above are demonstrated. Credit will be given for unpaid or volunteer service such as community, cultural, social service, and professional association activities on the same basis as paid experience. To receive proper credit, the applicant must show the actual time, that is the number of hours per week, spent on such activities. All applicants who claim 10-point veteran's preference must submit proof. If proof is not received by the closing date of the announcement, credit will be given for 5 points only. Qualified applicants will receive consideration without regard to such nonmerit factors as race, color, sex, religion, age, natural origin, political affiliation, marital status, nondisqualifying handicaps, membership in an employee organization, or personal favoritism.

VETERANS AND HANDICAPPED PEOPLE ARE ENCOURAGED TO APPLY.

Military Draft Registration
Male applicants between the ages of 18 and 25 are eligible for appointment only after registering with the Selective Service System.

DEPARTMENT OF TRANSPORTATION

PROMOTIONAL AND CAREER OPPORTUNITIES

		ANNOUNCEMENT NO
ORGANIZATION	FEDERAL AVIATION ADMINISTRATION	
		OPENING DATE
POSITION	**Temporary** (NTE 1 year) Equal Employment Manager GS-260-13 (Multiple Positions)	
		CLOSING DATE
LOCATION	Internal Program, Office of Civil Rights, FAA, DOT, Washington, D.C.	
AREA OF CONSIDERATION	WASHINGTON METRO AREA (Status/Non-Status)	

NOTE: Individuals with disabilities who are eligible for special appointing authorities may also apply. Ingrade/downgrade applicants will be considered.

THIS ANNOUNCEMENT MAY BE USED TO FILL OTHER SIMILAR POSITIONS SUBJECT TO THE PRIOR APPROVAL OF THE HUMAN RESOURCE MANAGEMENT DIVISION.

EQUAL OPPORTUNITY THROUGH AFFIRMATIVE ACTION: The Federal Aviation Administration is committed to a multicultural environment. Minorities and women are strongly encouraged to apply.

DUTIES: The incumbent conducts review and analysis of systematic problems and recommends alternatives and solutions. Performs a cross-section of duties related to equal employment. Provides guidance and direction to field civil rights officers in the development, coordination, review, and evaluation of the national counseling program. Investigates EEO complaints and complaint related issues. Conducts special studies derived from the complaint process. Identifies trends in issues, costs, settlements, etc. Reviews and analyzes discrimination complaints for completeness, appropriateness, sufficiency and involvement of other organizational elements. Identifies the requirements for new, revised, or amended regulations, processes or procedures; prepares recommendations for supervisory approval. Insures the dissemination, promulgation, and implementation of approved changes.

QUALIFICATIONS: All applicants must demonstrate one year of specialized experience equivalent to that of the next lower grade in the Federal government. Specialized experience is experience which is directly related to the line of work of this position which has equipped the applicant with the particular knowledge, skills and abilities (KSA's) to successfully perform the duties of this position. To be creditable, specialized experience must have been at least equivalent to the next lower grade in the normal line of progression for the occupation in the organization.

SELECTIVE FACTOR: In order to be considered for this position all candidates must demonstrate "Skill in the writing clear, concise and logically developed reports, recommendations and correspondence" as demonstrated by two separate samples of such writing.

RATING AND RANKING PROCESS: Qualified candidates will be rated and ranked on the following KSA's:

1. Skill in identifying and evaluating institutionalized, systematic barriers to equal employment opportunity.

2. Skill in the interpretation and application of equal employment and federal personnel system law, regulations, precedents, policies, principles and methods.

3. Skill in program management.

4. Skill in advising, consulting, and/or negotiating issues with a diversity of personnel.

HOW TO APPLY: An SF-171, Application for Federal Employment, must be submitted by all applicants. In addition, the submission of the following supplemental forms/information are encouraged. – The SF-171 **and supplemental materials** must **be submitted as a complete package by the closing date of the announcement.**

1. WA Form 3330.42, Request for Promotional Consideration and Acknowledgement, for acknowledgement of application and final selection notification.

2. WA Form 3330.9, Evaluation of Knowledge, Skills, Abilities, completed by supervisor (current or former).

3. Response to Evaluation Criteria. A supplemental statement for each KSA is highly recommended although KSA's may be addressed in work experience blocks on SF-171.

4. Current SF-50, Notification of Personnel Action, to verify competitive status or reinstatement eligibility.

5. SF-181, Race and National Origin Identification.

6. Two samples of writing prepared by the applicant.

*Applications must be postmarked by the closing date of the announcement and received by the close of business on the 5th working day after close of announcement.

**Applicants must meet the time-in-grade requirements by the closing date of the announcement.

***We are prohibited from considering applications received in penalty and/or interoffice mail or in any other government envelope.

WHERE TO SEND APPLICATION:

Federal Aviation Administration
Human Resource Management Division 151 Team 2
Operations Branch, AHR-151
800 Independence Avenue, S.W.
Washington, D. C. 20591

Applications may be hand-delivered to Room 516.

Please call Marvin Poindexter at (202) 267-8007 for further information or forms.

"SBA - AN EQUAL OPPORTUNITY EMPLOYER"

SBA   U.S. Small Business Administration

Career Opportunity
for
Financial Analyst

ANNOUNCEMENT NO.: 92-31   **OPENING DATE:**   **MUST BE POSTMARKED BY**
                                              CLOSING DATE:

POSITION: Financial Analyst, GS-1160-12/13

            TERM EMPLOYMENT NTE: 2 YEARS

SALARY RANGE: $38,861 - $60,070 per annum

LOCATION: Office of Financial Assistance, Office of Rural Affairs and
                 Economic Development, Washington, D.C.

AREA OF CONSIDERATION: All Recruiting Sources

                                Competitive Status Required: __ Yes X No

---

DUTIES AND RESPONSIBILITIES: The incumbent serves as a Financial Analyst and technical advisor to the Office of Rural Affairs & Economic Development through the Development Company Branch. As such, develops and recommends Agency-wide policies and procedures which govern Small Business Administration's (SBA) economic development programs; reviews and recommends changes or revisions to existing policies and procedures; develops and recommends issuance of SOPs, policy statements, and interim regulations which are utilized by the SBA's field activities in implementing the Agency's economic development programs; plans, develops and implements strategies for outreach activities for continued promotion of the economic development programs; oversees the review analysis and evaluation of applications for certification submitted by development companies; and responds to Congressional or other inquiries directly, or through preparation of replies for the signature of the Administrator, Associate Administrator, etc.

QUALIFICATION REQUIREMENTS: The following is an excerpt from the Office of Personnel Management's Qualification Standard, Handbook X-118, which is available for review in most Federal personnel offices. Applicants must have one year of specialized experience which is in or directly related to the line of work of the position to be filled and which has equipped the applicant with the particular knowledge, skills, and abilities to successfully perform the duties of the position. Specialized experience must have been at least equivalent to the next lower grade level in the Federal service. Time-in-grade requirement applies. Applicants who meet the time-in-grade requirement within 45 days of the closing date will be considered.

Any individual eligible for consideration under special hiring authorities, e.g. handicapped, VRA, etc., may apply for this position, if applicable. Please indicate on your SF-171 if you are applying under a special hiring authority. The VRA hiring authority is limited to positions at the GS-11 level and below.

                   SBA - AN EQUAL OPPORTUNITY EMPLOYER

SBA Form 534

KNOWLEDGE, SKILLS AND ABILITIES (KSAs) USED IN THE RATING PROCESS:

1. Knowledge of concepts, principles, theories, and practices of financial analysis, and commercial lending.
2. Ability to apply technical theories, procedures and practices that govern an economic development program.
3. Ability to research and develop policies and procedures.
4. Ability to communicate orally and in writing.

TO RECEIVE FULL CREDIT FOR YOUR QUALIFICATIONS, YOU SHOULD PROVIDE A SUPPLEMENTAL NARRATIVE THAT PROVIDES DETAILED EVIDENCE OF YOUR EXPERIENCE, TRAINING, EDUCATION, AWARDS, HOBBIES, SELF-DEVELOPMENT, ACHIEVEMENTS AND ANY OTHER ASPECTS OF YOUR BACKGROUND AS THEY RELATE TO THE KNOWLEDGE, SKILLS AND ABILITIES OUTLINED ABOVE.

APPLICATION REQUIREMENTS:

* An SF-171, Application for Federal Employment.
* A copy of your most recent performance appraisal.

PLEASE DO NOT SUBMIT OFFICIAL POSITION DESCRIPTIONS IN LIEU OF NARRATIVE STATEMENTS OF EXPERIENCE. SF-171s MAY BE OBTAINED FROM ANY SBA OFFICE.

NOTE: YOUR APPLICATION WILL BE RETAINED IN THE MERIT PROMOTION FILE AND WILL NOT BE RETURNED TO YOU.

OTHER PERTINENT INFORMATION: Payment of Relocation Expenses is not Authorized.

         COMPLETED FORMS SHOULD BE SUBMITTED TO:

            U.S. Small Business Administration
            409 3rd Street, S.W., 4th Floor
            Washington, D.C. 20416-5223
            Attention: Barbara Belleston
                 (202) 205-6780
               TDD: (202) 205-6189

FEDERAL DEPOSIT INSURANCE CORPORATION
An Equal Opportunity Employer
*****POSITION ANNOUNCEMENT*****

ANNOUNCEMENT NO: FDIC-100-NYR   Opening Date:
                                        Closing Date:

POSITION: Financial Institution Examiner (Trainee) - GG-570-5
          NOTE: All positions have promotion potential to GG-12.

LOCATION: New York Regional Office (New Jersey & New York City)

AREA OF CONSIDERATION: Nationwide

SUMMARY OF DUTIES:

Financial Institution Examiners conduct assessments of financial
institutions to determine the existence of unsafe and unsound practices,
violations of laws and regulations, the adequacy of internal controls and
procedures, and the general character of management. Trainee examiners
work under the immediate supervision of examiners of higher grades and
perform varying tasks required for completion of financial institution
examinations. The job requires a great deal of travel; the amount and
degree of travel varies with duty locations. Trainee examiners are
provided with extensive on-the-job training to prepare them to perform
their functions independently.

QUALIFICATION REQUIREMENTS:

For GG-5 positions: Applicants may qualify with (1) a bachelor's degree
which must have included at least 24 semester hours or the equivalent in
accounting, business administration, finance, economics, or marketing,
with at least 6 semester hours or the equivalent in accounting subjects,
OR (2) at least 3 years of general (nonclerical) financial institution
banking or examining experience.

Applicants with cumulative grade point averages of 3.50 (or equivalent)
or who graduate in the upper 10 percent of their classes or major
university subdivisions may qualify as outstanding scholars and should
submit their applications directly to the FDIC Regional Office(s) of
preference.

Applicants within 9 months of meeting the educational requirements may
apply.

HOW TO APPLY:

All applicants must complete the SUPPLEMENT TO ANNOUNCEMENT NO. FDIC-100
which contains application forms and filing instructions. A separate
supplement must be completed and filed for each region to which
application is being made. Supplements can be obtained by contacting
either of the following:

OPM, Recruitment   Federal Deposit Insurance Corporation
550 17th Street, NW   New York Regional Office
Washington, DC 20429-9990   452 5th Avenue, 21st Floor
1-800-424-4334, Ext. 8890 or (202) 898-8890   New York, NY 10018
                                         (212)-704-1200

When making an inquiry, please reference the vacancy announcement number
which you wish to discuss.

Individuals with certain disabilities, 30% disabled veterans, and Vietnam
Era veterans may be considered under special hiring authorities. If you
believe that you qualify in one of these categories and would like
consideration under a special hiring authority, so indicate in Block 1 of
the SF-171 (Veterans must also complete Blocks 17-22 to indicate
eligibility).

Applications must be <u>postmarked</u> by the closing date of the vacancy
announcement.

ADMINISTRATIVE OFFICE OF THE U.S. COURTS
VACANCY   ANNOUNCEMENT

Announcement #:   Opening Date: Closing Date:

POSITION: (Title, Series, Grade)   **ORGANIZATION LOCATION:**

FINANCIAL REPORTS EXAMINER   OFFICE OF FINANCE BUDGET AND PROGRAM ANALYSIS
GS-503-7/8/9/10

SALARY RANGE: $21,906 TO $38,367   **AREA OF CONSIDERATION:** WASHINGTON METROPOLITAN AREA - ALL SOURCES
APPLICANTS FROM OUTSIDE THE AREA OF CONSIDERATION MAY BE CONSIDERED.
HOWEVER, ANY RELOCATION EXPENSES WILL NOT BE PROVIDED EXCEPT WITH THE
AUTHORIZATION OF THE DIRECTOR UPON REQUEST OF THE SELECTING OFFICIAL.

PROMOTION POTENTIAL: GS-10

DUTIES AND RESPONSIBILITIES:
1. Prepares correspondence for the Committee Chairman's and/or Counsel's to the Judicial Ethics Committee signature regarding discrepancies and issues on Financial Disclosure Reports.
2. Assists the Judicial Conference Committee on Judicial Ethics, Counsel to the Ethics Committee and the Chief of the Judicial Ethics Office in administering the Judicial Ethics program. Interprets the provisions of the Ethics Reform Act of 1989, with responsibility for providing technical counseling to the judicial officers and judicial employees on the Act, on Judicial Financial Disclosure Reports, and on statutory time limits for filing.
3. Performs initial and secondary reviews of Financial Disclosure Reports and of inquiry response to determine if Financial Disclosure Reports and responses are filed in accordance with statutory requirements or requirements of the Judicial Ethics Committee.
4. Performs special analyses on Financial Disclosure Reports at the request of Judicial Ethics Committee members and others.

QUALIFICATIONS REQUIREMENTS: Applicants must have specialized experience as listed below. This requirement is in accordance with the OPM X-118 Handbook, available in your personnel office, which specifies when and how education may be substituted for the experience.

GS-7/8/9/10: ONE YEAR OF SPECIALIZED EXPERIENCE AT LEAST EQUIVALENT TO THE NEXT LOWER GRADE

Specialized Experience: Experience which is in or directly related to the line of work of the position to be filled and which has equipped the applicant with the particular knowledge, skills, and abilities to successfully perform the duties of that position.

QUALITY RANKING FACTORS: APPLICANTS MUST SUBMIT A NARRATIVE STATEMENT ADDRESSING THE FACTORS LISTED BELOW.
(MANDATORY) EACH FACTOR SHOULD BE ADDRESSED INDIVIDUALLY.

1. Skill in analyzing and evaluating auditing procedures.
2. Ability to communicate in writing.

ALL APPLICANTS MUST MEET TIME-IN-GRADE REQUIREMENTS

HOW TO APPLY: Submit to the address indicated below the following: 1) signed and dated Standard Form 171 with the appropriate vacancy announcement number (RESUMES WILL NOT BE ACCEPTED); 2) most recent annual performance appraisal (letter of recommendation for non-status applicants); and 3) any supplemental information required by this announcement. Applications must be received in the Personnel Office no later than the closing date indicated above.
NOTE: APPLICATIONS AND ENCLOSURES WILL NOT BE RETURNED.

FOR FURTHER INFORMATION CONTACT: ADMINISTRATIVE OFFICE SERVICES BRANCH ON (202) 786-6307
ADDITIONAL REQUIRED INFORMATION: NARRATIVE STATEMENT ADDRESSING THE QUALITY RANKING FACTORS (MANDATORY)
ADDRESS: (for hand delivery)   (for mailing):
                      Room 1008   Administrative Office of U.S. Courts
                      1120 Vermont Ave., NW   Administrative Office Services Branch, Room V/1008
                      Washington, D.C.   Washington, D.C. 20544

THE ADMINISTRATIVE OFFICE IS AN EQUAL OPPORTUNITY EMPLOYER

United States
Office of
Personnel
Management

Food Inspector

Opportunities
In the Federal
Government GS-5

Announcement No. 451

Each year the United States Department of Agriculture hires several hundred Food Inspectors at the GS-5 grade level. While promotion possibilities vary by position, most of these Food Inspectors are promoted to the GS-7 grade level after one year of satisfactory performance. Opportunities above the GS-7 level are available through competitive promotion procedures.

DESCRIPTION OF WORK

Food Inspectors ensure that privately owned meat or poultry slaughtering and processing plants comply with Federal laws governing the wholesomeness and purity of meat and poultry products. At the discretion of the Department of Agriculture, inspectors are assigned to either red meat or poultry inspection duties. Most inspectors are trained in the slaughter inspection specialization, while the remainder specialize in processed products inspection. GS-5 level trainees perform the simpler inspection work and receive on-the-job training in the rules, regulations, techniques and responsibilities of the position. Those assigned to slaughter inspection are trained to detect physical and behavioral abnormalities in live animals and head, viscera and carcass irregularities that would make products unfit for human consumption. Those specializing in processed products are trained in food sanitation and processing operations, and the theories of public health sanitation applicable to food processing.

Food Inspectors work in highly mechanized plant environments with moving objects; near operating machinery with moving parts; with poultry or livestock in confined areas; in extreme temperatures and humidity; and on slippery floors. The duties often require working with sharp knives, hands in water, moderate lifting, and walking or standing for long periods.

WHERE THE JOBS ARE

Nearly all Food Inspector jobs are in the Food Safety and Inspection Service, at locations throughout the United States and Puerto Rico. Food Inspectors work at slaughtering or processing plants ranging from small facilities to large mechanized assembly line operations. The plants may be in large metropolitan areas or rural locations close to animal supply sources.

Occasionally, the National Marine Fisheries Service fills entry-level GS-5 positions for Fish inspection in U.S. ports.

QUALIFICATION REQUIREMENTS

To qualify for these jobs, you must pass the written Food Inspector test with a minimum score of 70 out of 100. In addition, you must have 3 full years of work experience or equivalent education as described below.

ACCEPTABLE EXPERIENCE

Except for the educational substitution explained below, you must have had 3 years of full-time experience since your 16th birthday in any combination of the following:

1. Experience with animals gained as a veterinary assistant or field disease control.

2. Experience with livestock or poultry gained in a public stockyard; in manufacturing or preparing veterinary biological products; on a ranch, farm or hatchery; in poultry or livestock management; or other comparable activity.

3. Experience with livestock or poultry slaughtering/ processing; or in marketing or handling these products at sale points.

4. Experience in dairy, poultry, meat or other food processing setting where sanitation measures and quality controls are applied.

NOTE: Some jobs do not provide the type of experience that can be counted toward this requirement. Such jobs include laborer, guard, driver, or sales clerk positions in the activities described above. Only work directly involved with caring for animals or working with meat products will be credited.

SUBSTITUTION OF EDUCATION

Satisfactory completion of a full 4-year course of high school study which included at least two 1-year courses in biology, general science, chemistry, appropriate agricultural subjects, or an equivalent combination of these, may be substituted for 1 year of the required experience. The application form (SF-171) must contain specific information about the courses, if they are substituted for experience.

Successfully completed study beyond high school may be substituted at the rate of one year for nine months of the required experience. This study must have included an average of six semester hours (or equivalent) per year in any combination of the following: zoology, biology, chemistry, veterinary medicine, food technology, or appropriate agricultural subjects.

PHYSICAL REQUIREMENTS

Applicants must be physically and mentally able to efficiently perform the job functions, without hazard to themselves or others. These positions require good vision (including color), hearing, touch, and eye-hand coordination. If the use of a prosthesis or mechanical aid satisfactorily compensates for an impaired function, then applicants may not be automatically disqualified. Some positions may require a valid driver's license.

CONFLICT OF INTEREST POLICY

The Food Safety and Inspection Service prohibits the assignment of employees to any establishment where existing circumstances might prevent impartial performance of assigned duties. Such a situation is considered a conflict of interest. The following are specifically prohibited situations:

1. An appointment to perform official inspection or related duties at an establishment where you have been employed for more than 90 days during the past 3 years.

2. An appointment to perform these duties at an establishment, tenant, or subsidiary thereof, from which you receive an annuity or pension.

3. An appointment to any establishment which employs a member of your immediate family (i.e., parent, spouse, child, or sibling) or which employs other family members living in your household. These include immediate family in-laws, stepparents, stepchildren, grandparents, or grandchildren.

4. An appointment to any establishment which employs your family member (above) in a supervisory, managerial, or policy-making capacity, even if that person does not live in your household.

HOW TO APPLY

To be scheduled for the written test, complete and mail the attached tear-out form, or use an OPM 5000B, to:

OPM-Twin Cities Area Office
Federal Building, Room 501
Fort Snelling, MN 55111

Indicate only one preferred test site on the application. Select this test site using the current test site/calendar information on the amendment to Announcement 451. Note that testing will occur at different sites throughout the year and the location you choose will affect your scheduled test date. If necessary to provide for increasing hiring activity, additional tests/dates may be added. OPM Job Information Centers and State Employment Service Offices will post these opportunities as they become available.

After the test, the results will be mailed to you and, if you achieve a passing score, you will also be sent the necessary application forms. Then, if you meet the education/experience requirement, as vacancies occur and additional candidates are needed, your name will be placed on the List of Eligibles in test score order. Those on the list will receive employment consideration for a one-year period, during which time the test may NOT be retaken. DO NOT submit any applications unless asked to do so - they will be returned.

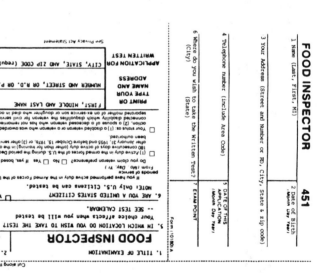

If you fail the written test, you may apply and retake the exam after at least six months have elapsed. If you take the test within the six-month period, your test scores will not be accepted and you will have to wait another six months before retaking the test for acceptable results.

This announcement supersedes all previous versions of announcement 451.

Privacy Act Notice

This information is requested under the authority of sections 1302, 3301, and 3304 of title 5 of the U.S. Code. These sections require the Office of Personnel Management to conduct examinations for competitive positions in the Federal service. The information sought will be used to schedule you for a written examination, serve as an admission card to the exam, and to ascertain whether you may be affected by laws determining who may be tested or employed. Other possible uses of the data include disclosure to a source (e.g., former employer or school) who is requested to furnish information about you that will assist in determining whether to hire you; to a Federal, State, or local agency for checking on law violations; or to the courts where the agency is party to a suit. Your Social Security Number (SSN) is requested under authority of Executive Order 9397, which requires individuals in Government information systems. The furnishing of your SSN and other information is voluntary. Failure to provide your SSN and other information will result in your not being scheduled for an exam.

Dep...tment of Transportation

PROMOTIONAL AND CAREER OPPORTUNITIES

ORGANIZATION   FEDERAL AVIATION ADMINISTRATION

ANNOUNCEMENT NO

OPENING DATE

POSITION   General Engineer GS-801-13/14
Promotion Potential: 14

CLOSING DATE

LOCATION   Tower/TRACON System Engr Div, Fac Sys Eng Svc, Sys Engr and Dev,
FAA, DOT, Washington, D.C

AREA OF CONSIDERATION   WASHINGTON METRO AREA (Status/Non-Status)

NOTE: Individuals with disabilities who are eligible for special appointing authorities may also apply. Ingrade/downgrade applicants will be considered.

THIS ANNOUNCEMENT MAY BE USED TO FILL OTHER SIMILAR POSITIONS SUBJECT TO THE PRIOR APPROVAL OF THE HUMAN RESOURCE MANAGEMENT DIVISION.

EQUAL OPPORTUNITY THROUGH AFFIRMATIVE ACTION: The Federal Aviation Administration is committed to a multicultural environment. Minorities and women are strongly encouraged to apply.

DUTIES: (At the GS-14 level) The incumbent is responsible for the development of plans, procedures and standards pertaining to facility system engineering projects. Conducts a variety of studies (feasibility, acceptability, life-cycle costing, cost-benefit, risk analysis, etc.) to determine the effectiveness, efficiency and economy of established and proposed facility system engineering programs; analyzes and evaluates information, identifies current or potential problems, methods to reduce cost or improve productivity/response or similar positive changes or required revisions and provides, orally or in writing, detailed recommendations for consideration. Formulates, defines, and develops facility system standards, criteria, requirements and related issues. Analyzes state-of-the-art technology and engineering concepts; determines compatibility with established systems, desirability and effectiveness; analyzes trends, developments and performance data; identifies requirements for new, revised, or modified national standards, objectives, policies, plans, procedures, quality control techniques, and/or system or facilities modifications, and modernization; submits recommendations for acquisition, approval, change, modification, etc. Participates in all phases of procurement activities: prepares or reviews specifications, reviews bids, monitors contractor performance, functions as the Contracting Officer's Technical Representative. Proposes specific engineering design criteria for inclusion in the reliability, maintainability, and safety test criteria and/or maintenance procedures.

(At the GS-13 level) The incumbent performs essentially the same duties as described for the GS-14 position but is subject to a more stringent work review, closer supervision and less independence of action.

QUALIFICATIONS: Basic Qualifications: (Primary Method): Successful completion of a 4 year course of study in a college or university leading to a degree in professional engineering. To be acceptable, the curriculum must (1) be in a school of engineering with at least one curriculum accredited be the Accreditation board for Engineering and Technology (ABET) as a professional engineering curriculum; or (2) include differential and integral calculus and courses (more advanced than first year physics and chemistry) in 5 of the following 7 areas of engineering science or physics: (a) statics, dynamics; (b) strength of materials (stress-strain relationships); (c) fluid mechanics, hydraulics; (d) thermodynamics; (e) electrical fields and circuits; (f) nature and properties of materials (relating particle and aggregate structure to properties); and (g) any other comparable area of fundamental engineering science or physics, such as optics, heat transfer, soil mechanics, or electronics.

PRIVACY ACT REQUIREMENTS (P.L. 93-579)

The referenced forms are used to determine qualifications for promotional and are authorized under Title 5 of the U.S. Code, Sections 1302 and 3361 Each specified form must be submitted in order for you to be considered for promotion to the position being advertised. The social security number is not required for this purpose and may be deleted from the forms submitted. Your servicing personnel office or the office named in this announcement will be able to provide information on specific Privacy Act requirements.

CANDIDATES WHO FAIL TO SUBMIT THE REQUIRED FORMS WILL NOT BE CONSIDERED. NONE OF THESE FORMS WILL BE SUBSEQUENTLY LOANED OR RETURNED TO THE APPLICANTS

CANDIDATES WILL BE EVALUATED ON BASIS OF EXPERIENCE AND EDUCATION, PERFORMANCE APPRAISAL, TRAINING AND AWARDS

DOT IS AN EQUAL OPPORTUNITY EMPLOYER

ALL QUALIFIED CANDIDATES WILL BE CONSIDERED REGARDLESS OF RACE, COLOR, RELIGION, SEX OR NATIONAL ORIGIN

FORM DOT F 3300 6

ALTERNATE REQUIREMENTS: Combination of education and experience-college-level education, training, and/or technical experience that furnished (1) a thorough knowledge of the physical and mathematical sciences underlying professional engineering, and (2) a good understanding, both theoretic and practical, of the engineering sciences and techniques and their applications to one of the branches of engineering. The adequacy of such background MUST be demonstrated by one of the following:

OR

(a) Current registration as a professional engineer by any State, the District of Columbia, Guam, or Puerto Rico.

(b) Evidence of having successfully passed the Engineering-in-Training (EIT) examination, or the written test required for professional registration which is administered by the Boards of Engineering Examiners in the various States, the District of Columbia, Puerto Rico, and Guam. OR

(c) Successful completion of at least 60 semester hours of courses in the physical, mathematical, and engineering sciences and in engineering, which included the course specified in the basic requirement. The course must be fully acceptable toward meeting the requirements of a professional engineering curriculum as described in the basic requirements. (Must be documented by a completed OPM Form 1170-17, List of College Courses or copies of official transcripts) OR

(d) Successful completion of a curriculum leading to a bachelor's degree in engineering technology or in an appropriate professional field may be accepted in lieu of a degree in engineering, provided the applicant has at least 1 year of professional engineering experience acquired under professional engineering supervision and guidance. (Must be documented by a completed OPM Form 1170-17 List of College Courses or copies of official transcripts).

SELECTIVE FACTOR: Candidates who do not demonstrate possession of the selective factor will not be eligible for further consideration.

Skill in the application of diverse engineering skills to aviation relevant facility engineering systems.

RATING AND RANKING PROCESS: Qualified candidates will be rated and ranked on the following KSA's:

1. (For GS-14) Skill in the application of advanced theories, techniques, processes, and procedures of a wide range of engineering disciplines (electronic, civil, computer, and/or human factors) to aviation related facility engineering systems.
    (For GS-13) Skill in the application of advanced theories, techniques, processes, and procedures of a wide range of engineering disciplines to aviation relevant facility engineering systems.
    NOTE: In the evaluation process this factor will be weighted at a ratio of 3:1.

2. (For GS-14) Skill in program management.
    (For GS-13) Skill in the application of the principles of program management.
    NOTE: In the evaluation process this factor will be weighted at a ratio of 2:1.

3. (For GS-14) Skill in the conduct of advanced engineering studies (feasibility, acceptability, cost-benefit, etc.).
    (For GS-13) Skill in the conduct of engineering studies.
    NOTE: In the evaluation process this factor will be weighted at a ratio of 1:1.

HOW TO APPLY: An SF-171, Application for Federal Employment, must be submitted by all applicants. In addition, the submission of the following supplemental forms/information are encouraged. – The SF-171 and supplemental materials must be submitted as a complete package by the closing date of the announcement.

1. WA Form 3330.42, Request for Promotional Consideration and Acknowledgement, for acknowledgement of application and final selection notification.

2. WA Form 3330.9, Evaluation of Knowledge, Skills, and Abilities, completed by supervisor (current or former).

ANNOUNCEMENT NO.

3. Response to Evaluation Criteria. A supplemental statement for each KSA is highly recommended although KSA's may be addressed in work experience blocks on SF-171.

4. Current SF-50, Notification of Personnel Action, to verify competitive status or reinstatement eligibility.

5. SF-181, Race and National Origin Identification.

6. A brief narrative addressing the selective factor is required.

*Applications must be postmarked by the closing date of the announcement and received by the close of business on the 5th working day after close of announcement.

**Applicants must meet the time-in-grade requirements by the closing date of the announcement.

***We are prohibited from considering applications received in penalty and/or interoffice mail or in any other government envelope.

WHERE TO SEND APPLICATION:

Federal Aviation Administration
Human Resource Management Division 151 Team 2
Operations Branch, AHR-151
800 Independence Avenue, S.W.
Washington, D. C. 20591

Applications may be hand-delivered to Room 516.

Please call Marvin Poindexter at (202) 267-8007 for further information or forms.

U.S. Office of Personnel Management
Office of Washington Examining Services
Washington, D.C. 20415

Announcement No. WA-8-18

Guard
GS-085-3/4/5

This announcement cancels and supersedes previous Announcements WA-8-18 and all amendments under Announcement No. WA-5-03 (Local) for Police Officer positions.

Competition for these positions is restricted by law to persons entitled to Veterans' Preference. In the event of an insufficient number of preference eligibles, this restriction may be waived by the Office of Personnel Management, and non-preference eligibles may be referred for employment consideration.

Location of Positions

Positions are located in Washington, D.C.; Maryland: Charles, Montgomery, and Prince Georges counties; Virginia: Cities of Alexandria, Fairfax, and Falls Church, and counties of Arlington, Fairfax, King George, Loudoun, Prince William, and Stafford; and Overseas Atlantic.

Duties and Responsibilities

Guards patrol buildings and other Federal properties to prevent fire, theft, damage, accident, or trespass. They protect lives, control traffic, and perform other similar duties. Holiday and weekend work may be required by some positions.

Qualification Requirements

No written test is required. Applicants will be evaluated based upon the extent and quality of experience as described in their applications. Length of experience requirements are:

Grade	General Experience	Specialized Experience	Total
GS-3	½ year		½ year
GS-4	½ year	½ year	1 year
GS-5		1 year*	1 year

*Experience must be at a level of difficulty and responsibility comparable to that of the GS-4 level in the Federal service.

General Experience

Work experience that involved following written directions, rules, or regulations and dealing with co-workers, supervisors, or members of the public in providing a service or responding to inquiries. Such work may include, for example, administrative, technical, clerical, military duty or other responsible work which required substantive contacts with individuals and knowledge of regulations or prescribed procedures.

Specialized Experience

Acceptable specialized experience includes work with a Federal, state, municipal, local, or private protective organization which involved (a) the protection of property against such hazards as fire, theft, damage, accident, or trespass or (b) maintaining order and protecting life. Such experience must have provided a knowledge of protective systems and techniques. Acceptable experience includes service in the Armed Services or Coast Guard which involved the performance of guard duties on a regular or intermittent basis. For security guard positions in a hospital setting, experience as a psychiatric nursing assistant or similar position safeguarding patients is qualifying.

Substitution of Education

GS-3: One year of successfully completed study at an accredited school above the high school level. At least 6 semester hours of the study must be pertinent to guard work.

GS-4: Two years of successfully completed study at an accredited school above the high school level.

Training

Successful completion of a Federal, state, county, or municipal police academy or comparable training course which included at least 40 classroom hours of instruction in police department procedures and methods, and local law and regulations, may be substituted for a maximum of 3 months of specialized experience or 6 months of general experience.

No substitution of education or training may be made for the required specialized experience at the GS-5 level.

Physical Requirements

The duties of this position require moderate to arduous physical exertions and/or duties of a hazardous nature. The following physical requirements apply to all applicants: good vision; ability to distinguish basic colors; and ability to hear the conversational voice. Agencies may establish additional, job-related physical or medical requirements provided the specific position(s) involves the arduous or hazardous duties to which the physical requirements relate.

Motor Vehicle Operator Requirements

For some positions, applicants must possess a driver's license which is currently valid in the state in which they live or work, or must obtain one within 30 days after appointment.

How to Apply

Applicants must submit an SF-171, *Application for Federal Employment*; OPM Form 1170/17, *List of College Courses* or transcript; SSW 580, *Employment Availability Statement*; and, if applicable, SF-15, *Application for 10-Point Veteran Preference* and documentary proof.

Completed forms should be mailed to:
Office of Personnel Management
Washington Examining Services—WEC
P.O. Box 14179
Washington, DC 20044

Equal Employment Opportunity

All qualified applicants will receive consideration for appointment without regard to race, religion, color, national origin, sex, political affiliation, handicap, or any other non-merit factor.

DEFENSE LOGISTICS AGENCY
JOB OPPORTUNITY

JOA# 108-92LS

PERMANENT CHANGE OF STATION (PCS) FUNDS WILL NOT BE AUTHORIZED.

POSITION: Information Specialist, GS-301-12   ANNOUNCEMENT NO.

LOCATION: DLA Administrative Support Center   OPENING DATE: 20 MARCH
Office of Planning and Resource Mgmt.
Administrative Management Division   CLOSING DATE: 06 APRIL
Cameron Station, Alex., VA

**AREA OF
CONSIDERATION:** Competitive Service Career and Career-Conditional Employees of
All Federal Agencies in the Washington, D.C. Metropolitan Area

DUTIES: The incumbent administers the Freedom of Information Act and Privacy
Act for the Defense Logistics Agency (DLA). Duties require the incumbent to
continuously assess public and contractor demands for information and the case
law associated with the statutes in order to develop and promulgate agency
rules, regulations, and notices appropriately responsive to such demands. The
incumbent also oversees field operations and provides staff guidance on
problematic and/or complex cases, administers the programs within HQ DLA and
DASC, and handles selected cases with special sensitivities and administrative
problems. These functions require a broad knowledge of the agency and its
functions, its business methods and impacts on the private sector, and
adversarial administrative processes. The incumbent serves as the principle
technical authority within the agency on the statutes and has broad latitude in
establishing required program actions and reviews. The incumbent also
negotiates with requesters and/or their attorneys in selected cases and may
commit the agency to a course of action in such negotiations.

QUALIFICATION REQUIREMENTS: Applicants must have at least one year of
specialized experience equivalent to the GS-11 level. Specialized experience
is experience typically in or related to the work of the position to be filled
which has equipped the applicant with the particular knowledge, skills, and
abilities to successfully perform the duties of the position. Applicants must
have served at least one year at the GS-11 level to meet OPM time-in-grade
requirements.

EVALUATION METHODS: MAXIMUM POINT VALUE
1. Quality of Experience   65
2. Performance Appraisal   20
3. Education, Training and Self-Development   5
4. Awards   10
     100

AN EQUAL OPPORTUNITY EMPLOYER

SELECTION FOR THIS POSITION IS SUBJECT TO RESTRICTIONS RESULTING FROM
DEPARTMENT OF DEFENSE REFERRAL SYSTEM FOR DISPLACED EMPLOYEES.

METHOD OF RANKING: Applicants competing for promotion will be given a score
on each evaluation method. The combined score on all evaluation methods will
be used in ranking candidates to determine their relative standing.
Applicants meeting the minimum qualification requirements will be evaluated
against the following criteria:

1. **Knowledge of the Freedom of Information Act (FOIA), Privacy Act (PA)
requirements and government policies, principles, and regulations**...in order to
establish agency policy, procedures, and systems.

2. **Ability to communicate orally and in writing**...in order to write directives
and staff communications and provide advice to subordinate activities.

3. **Knowledge of management principles and information systems**...in order to
establish governing policies and procedures.

4. **Ability to plan, organize, and coordinate**...in order to formulate and
implement programs.

OTHER:

1. This position may be filled through means other than the competitive
promotion process. This may include reassignments or repromotion of qualified
eligibles or appointment from an Office of Personnel Management Certificate of
Eligibles. In such case, this announcement will be cancelled and all
applicants so advised.

2. Male applicants who were born after December 31, 1959, are required to
complete a Pre-Employment Certification Statement for Selective Service
Registration prior to appointment. Failure to comply may be grounds for
withdrawal of an offer of employment, or dismissal after appointment.

3. This position is noncritical-sensitive, as defined in DoD 5200.2-R and
therefore requires that a personnel security investigation be adjudicated for
security eligibility on a preappointment basis. This requirement may take 90
days or longer to process.

4. Applications will be accepted from 30 percent or more disabled veterans.

5. Time in grade and qualification requirements must be met by the closing
date of this announcement.

6. All qualified reassignment applicants within the stated area of
consideration will be referred for selection consideration. Employees
competing for promotion are subject to the evaluation methods outlined above.

7. SF-171(s) and related forms transmitted by facsimile equipment will not be
accepted.

HOW TO APPLY: Forward a current, completed and signed SF-171, Application for
Federal Employment, along with the following documents and forms to Defense
Logistics Agency, ATTN: DASC-KSE, Room 6-214, Cameron Station, Alexandria, VA.
22304-6130. **APPLICATION MUST BE POSTMARKED BY THE CLOSING DATE INDICATED ON
THE JOB OPPORTUNITY ANNOUNCEMENT.**

   a. Supplemental Experience Questionnaire.

   b. A copy of current annual performance rating and appropriate
performance standards. (For DLA employees, DLA Forms 46 and 46A (Jun 86
version) or Merit Pay appraisal and standards, if applicable, are to be
submitted. DLA employees serviced by non-DLA personnel offices may submit
their current appraisals and performance standards on the appropriate forms
utilized by their respective systems). **FAILURE TO SUBMIT A CURRENT**

JOA# 108-92LS

SUPPLEMENTAL EXPERIENCE QUESTIONNAIRE

POSITION: Information Specialist, GS-301-12   JOA# 108-92LS

NAME _____   DATE _____

INSTRUCTIONS: Prepare brief but concise responses to the following highly qualifying criteria on how your experience, education and/or training satisfies the knowledge, skills, and abilities cited below. DO NOT REPEAT VERBATIM INFORMATION IN THE SF-171 (Application for Federal Employment).

KSA# 1. Knowledge of the Freedom of Information Act (FOIA), Privacy Act (PA) requirements and government policies, principles, and regulations.

Please provide the following information relating to the above experiences:
Names and telephone numbers of supervisors or other persons who can verify your statements
title, series, and grade of your position (if applicable) _____ ; time period this work was performed (month and year)
From _____ To _____ .

KSA# 2. Ability to communicate orally and in writing.

Please provide the following information relating to the above experiences:
Names and telephone numbers of supervisors or other persons who can verify your statements
title, series, and grade of your position (if applicable) _____ ; time period this work was performed (month and year)
From _____ To _____ .

JOA# 108-92LS

PERFORMANCE APPRAISAL (NO MORE THAN 18 MONTHS OLD) MAY AFFECT APPLICANT'S OVERALL RATING.

c. A list of all awards received within the past 10 years, including the dates of the awards.

d. OPM Form 1386, Background Survey Questionnaire 79-2. (Submission of this form is optional).

e. Copy of recent SF-50, Notification of Personnel Action, for verification of competitive status/reinstatement eligibility.

Annotate Item 1 of the SF-171 to show the announcement number of the specific position applied for. Applicants should not submit official position descriptions but should describe duties and responsibilities in their own words. SF-171'S WILL NOT BE RETURNED SINCE THEY ARE REQUIRED TO BE MAINTAINED FOR AUDIT PURPOSES, THEREFORE, DO NOT SUBMIT OFFICIAL DOCUMENTS.

Failure to submit appropriate application forms may affect applicant's consideration in the evaluation process.

For further information regarding this vacancy, call (703) 274-7087 between the hours of 9:30 a.m. and 3:00 p.m. or Autovon 284-7087. For general vacancy information, call our recorded vacancy listing on (703) 274-7372 or Autovon 284-7372.

After submission of applications, documents, forms, etc., please DO NOT contact the Civilian Personnel Office for "Status" requests. All applicants will be notified of final results after selection for the position has been completed.

ALL QUALIFIED CANDIDATES WILL RECEIVE CONSIDERATION WITHOUT REGARD TO RACE, RELIGION, COLOR, SEX, AGE, NATIONAL ORIGIN, LAWFUL POLITICAL AFFILIATION, MARITAL STATUS, UNION MEMBERSHIP, OR OTHER NONDISQUALIFYING PHYSICAL OR MENTAL HANDICAPS.

SUPPLEMENTAL EXPERIENCE QUESTIONNAIRE

POSITION: Information Specialist, GS-301-12   JOA# 108-92LS

NAME _____   DATE _____

INSTRUCTIONS: Prepare brief but concise responses to the following highly
qualifying criteria on how your experience, education and/or training
satisfies the knowledge, skills, and abilities cited below. DO NOT REPEAT
VERBATIM INFORMATION IN THE SF-171 (Application for Federal Employment).

KSA# 3. **Knowledge of management principles and information systems.**

Please provide the following information relating to the above experiences:
Names and telephone numbers of supervisors or other persons who can verify your
statements
title, series, and grade of your position (if applicable)
From _____ To _____ ; time period this work was performed (month and year)

KSA# 4. **Ability to plan, organize and coordinate.**

Please provide the following information relating to the above experiences:
Names and telephone numbers of supervisors or other persons who can verify your
statements
title, series, and grade of your position (if applicable)
From _____ To _____ ; time period this work was performed (month and year)

RESTRICTED TO STATUS CANDIDATES

Notice of Position Vacancy

U.S. Department of Housing and Urban Development

Smoking is restricted, within the HUD Headquarters Building, to designated smoking areas.

Vacancy No.	OO-MSY-92-0010	Issue Date:	Closing Date*

Position Management Analyst, GS-343-9/11

Location Headquarters, Office of Inspector General, Office of Audit, Planning and Oversight Division, Audit Quality Assurance and Follow-up Staff, Washington, DC

Duties

The incumbent works under the general supervision of a higher graded employee, assisting in the analysis and evaluation of audit recommendations, audit quality control reviews and GAO assignments. Analyzes and studies compiled data to identify and evaluate new methods and procedures necessary to assure timely resolution of audit findings, and quality of the Office of Inspector General's audit products. Assists in oversight responsibilities concerning audit recommendation resolution and GAO assignments. Develops and maintains data bases and spreadsheet applications for support of the Office of Audit. This includes support for the preparation of the Office of Inspector General Semiannual Report to Congress. Prepares and coordinates administrative and automated reports, and correspondence relating to the audit follow-up and GAO liaison functions.

MINIMUM QUALIFICATION REQUIREMENTS: (X-118 Qualification Standards)

Specialized Experience: One year of specialized experience which is in or directly related to the line of work of the position to be filled and which has equipped the applicant with the particular knowledge, skills, and abilities to successfully perform the duties of that position. To be creditable, specialized experience must have been at least equivalent to the next lower grade level in the normal line of progression for the occupation in the organization. Applicants must also meet time-in-grade requirements, where applicable.

IN ADDITION TO THE SF-171, APPLICANTS ARE REQUIRED TO LIST EACH QUALITY RANKING FACTOR SEPARATELY AND PROVIDED A NARRATIVE DESCRIPTION OF HOW THEY SATISFY THE FACTORS SHOWN BELOW. APPLICANTS WILL NOT RECEIVE CONSIDERATION FOR THIS POSITION IF THIS ADDITIONAL DESCRIPTION IS NOT SUBMITTED.

QUALITY RANKING FACTORS:

1. Ability to plan, and conduct analytical reviews to identify problems or weaknesses in order to identify fraud waste mismanagement and/or management control weaknesses.
2. Ability to develop solutions to problems including recommending changes in organizational structure, delegations of authority, information and control systems and operating procedures.
3. Ability to communicate in writing analytical reports, procedure guidelines, or informational documents aimed at diversified audiences.
4. Ability to communicate orally to diversified audiences.
5. Skill in using microcomputer software, e.g. wordprocessing, Lotus 1-2-3, data base or spreadsheet applications.

The Personnel Representative for this vacancy is FOR A COPY OF VACANCY ANNOUNCEMENT CALL (202) 708-3203
Elizabeth Sims (202) 708-0866

The use of postage paid agency envelopes in filing job applications is a violation of Federal law.

How To Apply:

1. *Applications must be received in the Personnel Office by the closing date (office closes at 5:15 p.m.).
2. All applicants must submit: SF-171, Application for Federal Employment, a current Performance Appraisal and any other materials required in the announcement. Do not send position descriptions.
3. If selected, male applicants born after December 31, 1959, must confirm their selective service registration status. Certification forms are available at most Federal agency personnel offices or from the U.S. Office of Personnel Management (OPM).
4. Submit application materials to: Dept. of HUD,
   Office of Personnel and Training, Room 2258
   451 7th Street, S.W.,
   Washington, DC 20410-3100

HUD IS AN EQUAL OPPORTUNITY EMPLOYER

OO-MSY-92-0010
Management Analyst
GS-343-9/11

POINTS FOR AWARDS AND PERFORMANCE APPRAISAL:

A maximum of 4 additional points overall will be credited for awards and performance appraisal related to one or more of the Quality Ranking Factors listed in the vacancy announcement. Failure to provide a narrative description of how candidate's awards and performance appraisal relate to the Quality Ranking Factors will result in no credit for these items.

OTHER ESSENTIAL INFORMATION:

-Maximum grade potential is GS-12.
-EXEMPT UNDER FAIR LABOR STANDARDS ACT, AS AMENDED.
-All applicants must submit a current performance appraisal of record. All pages of appraisal must be submitted.
-Transfer and reinstatement eligibles should submit a copy of their latest SF-50, Notification of Personnel Action, showing proof of eligibility.
-Failure to provide all of the documents required in this announcement will remove applicant form consideration for this vacancy.
-Occasional travel may be required.
-Candidates must meet security clearance prior to appointment.
-Applications will also be accepted from applicants who have eligibility for noncompetitive appointments, such as 30 percent for disabled veterans, certain Vietnam-Era veterans (for positions GS-9 and below), Post Vietnam-Era veterans (for positions GS-9 and below), and handicapped persons. Proof of eligibility must be submitted with the application.

HUD-878.4 (   )

United States
Office of
Personnel
Management

Medical Officer
Dental Officer

**Opportunities
in the Federal
Government**

Announcement No. 442

What the Jobs Are

**Medical Officer GS-11/15
Dental Officer GS-12/15**

Medical and Dental Officers in the Federal Government work in a wide range of health programs that affect the lives of hundreds of thousands of people. Many have access to Federal hospital, laboratory, and research facilities that have earned worldwide professional acclaim.

Where the Jobs Are

The major employers of Medical and Dental Officers are the Department of Defense, the Department of Health and Human Services, and the Veterans Administration. Jobs may also be filled at the Department of Labor, the Department of Justice, and various other Federal agencies. Positions are located throughout the United States and in foreign countries.

See below for special application procedures for some agencies.

Direct Hire Authorities

The Office of Personnel Management has issued two direct-hire authorities for medical officer positions. One was given to the Department of Defense (which includes Army, Navy, and Air Force), covering positions in grades GS-11 through 14; the other was given to the Public Health Service, Department of Health and Human Services, covering positions in grades GS-11 through GS-15.

This means that these agencies may recruit, determine qualifications, and hire qualified applicants without their prior referral from an Office of Personnel Management register of qualified candidates. Therefore, for employment consideration in any of the agencies covered by direct hire authority, you should apply directly to the installation(s) where you wish to work.

Employment in the Veterans Administration

The VA offers employment opportunities in two Departments:

- Medical Officers (Disability Evaluation) in the Department of Veterans Benefits. Those interested in these positions should follow the general application procedures outlined on page 8 of this announcement, or contact directly any VA Regional Office.

- Physicians (most specialties) and Dentists in the Department of Medicine and Surgery receive the same basic benefits as other Federal employees but are employed under a unique personnel system with special "grades" and different salaries. These positions are not filled from a civil service list of eligibles. Persons interested should contact any of the VA hospitals.

(For VA consideration nationwide in either or both the above VA Departments, contact the VA Central Office, Washington, DC 20420.)

MEDICAL OFFICER

Description of Work

Medical Officers may perform functions such as the following:

Practice of medicine or direct service to patients involving the performance of domestic, preventive, and therapeutic services to patients in hospitals, clinics, diagnostic centers, etc.; or

Conduct of medical activities of a preventive nature such as those in an occupational health program, aviation medicine program, etc.; or

Evaluation of medical aspects of claims which may arise under various Federal laws for disability or death compensation or benefits; or

Research and experimental work in various health programs, including causes, methods of prevention and control, and methods of treatment of disease, and research and experimental work in physical limitations and conditions; or

Performance of a variety of medical work pertaining to food, drugs, cosmetics, and devices; or

Administration of Federal medical aid programs; or

Direction or training for interns, residents, and in-service training of medical officers

The difficulty of the work performed and the responsibility assumed will vary with the grade of the position, increasing progressively with the grade.

Basic Minimum Qualification Requirements for all Medical Officer Positions

For all grades, candidates must meet the following educational, training, and licensure requirements

A. Education

Candidates must have a Doctor of Medicine or Doctor of Osteopathy degree from a school in the United States or Canada approved by a recognized accrediting body in the year of the candidate's graduation.

OR

Candidates must have a Doctor of Medicine or equivalent degree from a foreign medical school that provided education and medical knowledge substantially equivalent to accredited schools in the United States. Comparability may be demonstrated by permanent certification by the Educational Commission for Foreign Medical Graduates (ECFMG) or a fifth pathway certificate for American students who completed premedical education in the United States and graduate education in a foreign country. Comparability may also be established through certification by an American specialty board.

B. Graduate Training

Subsequent to obtaining a Doctor of Medicine or Doctor of Osteopathy degree, a candidate must have had at least one year of supervised experience providing direct service in a clinical setting, i.e., a one-year approved internship or the first (transitional) year of a residency program in an institution approved by an accrediting body recognized within the United States or Canada.

Currently, first year intern programs are in hospitals or other institutions accredited for internship training by a recognized body of the American Osteopathic Association (AOA). American Medical Association (AMA) approved internships were integrated into AMA residency programs during the 1970's. Residency programs involve training in a specialized field of medicine in an institution accredited for training in the specialty by a recognized body of AMA or AOA.

C. License

For positions involving patient care responsibility, candidates must have a permanent, current, full, and unrestricted license to practice medicine in a state, District of Columbia, the Commonwealth of Puerto Rico, or a territory of the United States. Applications will be accepted from physicians who are not currently licensed; however, if selected for appointment, an applicant must either obtain a license before entering on duty or, in the case of an applicant that has a temporary license to practice until the next regular session of the licensing board, obtain an unconditional license within one year of appointment.

Applicants who meet basic qualification requirements qualify for GS-11 positions.

Additional Requirements

A. General Practice GS-12 through GS-15

In addition to the basic educational, training, and licensure requirements described above, applicants for general practice positions must also meet requirements for the grade levels shown below. The additional experience and training must have been well rounded to prepare the physician to treat common diseases, ailments, and injuries; conduct physical examinations; and provide immunizations against common diseases

GS-12

2 years of graduate training or equivalent experience and training.

GS-13

3 years of graduate training or equivalent experience and training.

GS-14

In addition to the requirements for GS-13, 1 year of appropriate experience.

GS-15

In addition to the requirements for GS-13, 2 years of appropriate experience.

B. Specialized Positions, GS-13 through GS-15

Special Fields - Anesthesiology, Immunology and Allergy, Dermatology, Emergency Medicine, Internal Medicine, Neurology, Nuclear Medicine, Obstetrics-Gynecology, Ophthalmology, Otolaryngology, Pathology, Pediatrics, Physical Medicine and Rehabilitation, Preventive Medicine, Psychiatry, Radiology, Surgery, and Urology.

Subspecialties - Aerospace Medicine, Radioisotope Pathology, Child Psychiatry, Nuclear Radiology, etc.

In addition to the basic educational, training, and licensure requirements described above, applicants for these specialized fields must also meet the requirements for the grade levels shown below. Graduate training and experience must be related to the specialty and subspecialty of the position. Experience may not be substituted for training essential for performing specialized duties. The length and content of the residency programs depend upon the specialization and requirements of recognized accrediting American medical specialty boards. An exception may be made when a peer panel of physicians, such as an American specialty board, determines and documents that the knowledges, skills, and abilities acquired in professional medical practice are equivalent to those acquired during the same period of time in a graduate training program.

GS-13
3 years of residency training in the specialty of the position to be filled or equivalent experience and training.

GS-14
4 years of residency training in the specialty of the position to be filled or equivalent experience and training.

GS-15
5 years of residency training in the specialty of the position to be filled or equivalent experience and training.

C. Disability Evaluation, GS-12 through GS-15
In addition to the basic educational, training, and licensure requirements described above, applicants for disability evaluation positions must meet the requirements for the grade levels shown below. Most disability evaluation positions are of a generalist nature and may be filled by medical officers who have a background of training or experience in one of the significant areas of work within the broad assignment (e.g., internal medicine, general surgery, psychiatry) as well as by medical officers whose training or experience has been in general practice. When positions involve evaluating specialized medical cases or developing specialized guides and require training and experience in a specific area of medicine (e.g., general surgery, psychiatry, neurology), requirements under "Specialized Positions" must be met.

GS-12
2 years of graduate training or equivalent training and experience that provided knowledges, skills, and abilities for work in the position.

GS-13
3 years of graduate training or equivalent training and experience that included at least 1 year of experience in a disability evaluation program in government or industry.

GS-14
4 years of graduate training or equivalent training and experience that included at least 2 years of experience in a disability evaluation program in government or industry.

GS-15
5 years of graduate training or equivalent training and experience that included at least 3 years of experience in a disability evaluation program in government or industry.

Note: For positions at grades GS-13 and above involved in policy or program development, the requirement for disability evaluation experience may be waved.

D. Aviation Medicine, GS-12 through GS-15
In addition to the basic educational, training, and licensure requirements, applicants for aviation medicine positions must meet the requirements for the grade levels shown below. Knowledges, skills, and abilities for work in this program area may be acquired through a residency program in aerospace medicine or in an area such as internal medicine, pulmonary disease, cardiovascular disease, family practice, preventive medicine, occupational health, public health, etc.

GS-12
2 years of graduate training or equivalent training, education, and experience that provided skills and knowledges for work in the position to be filled.

GS-13
3 years of residency training in aerospace medicine or equivalent training, education, and/or experience that included at least 1 year of experience in aviation medical programs.

GS-14
In addition to meeting the requirements for GS-13, 1 year of appropriate graduate training or experience in aviation or aerospace medical programs.

GS-15
In addition to meeting the requirements for GS-14, 1 year of subsequent work experience at an appropriate level in aviation or aerospace medical programs.

E. Occupational Medicine, GS-12 through GS-15
In addition to meeting the basic educational, training, and licensure requirements, applicants for occupational medicine positions must meet the requirements for the grade levels shown below. Knowledges, skills, and abilities for work in this program area may be acquired through a residency program in occupational medicine or a residency program in family practice, internal medicine, surgery, pathology, dermatology, radiology, physical medicine and rehabilitation, public health, aerospace medicine, or general preventive medicine.

GS-12
2 years of graduate training or equivalent training, education, and experience that provided skills and knowledges for work in the position to be filled.

GS-13
3 years of residency training in occupational medicine or equivalent training, education, and experience in an occupational health program in an industrial or office-type establishment.

GS-14
In addition to meeting the requirements for GS-13, 1 year of appropriate training or experience in occupational health programs.

GS-15
In addition to meeting the requirements for GS-13, 2 years of appropriate graduate training or experience in occupational health programs.

F. Maternal and Child Health, GS-12 through GS-15
In addition to the training, educational, and licensure requirements, applicants for maternal and child health positions must meet the requirements for the grade levels shown below. Examples of medical fields that provide the basic knowledges, skills, and abilities for maternal and child health work include pediatrics, obstetrics-gynecology, family practice, and subspecialties of preventive medicine.

GS-12
2 years of graduate training, education, or appropriate graduate training and experience that provided skills and knowledges for work in the position to be filled.

GS-13
3 years of graduate training or equivalent training, education, and experience in an appropriate field of medicine.

GS-14
In addition to requirements at GS-13, 1 year of appropriate experience in maternal and child health programs.

GS-15
In addition to requirements at GS-13, 2 years of appropriate experience in maternal and child health programs.

G. Research Medical Officer Positions, GS-11 through GS-15
Because medical officers in this program area conduct, supervise, or direct basic and applied medical research that does not involve patient care responsibility, they are not required to have a license to practice medicine. If they do research and have any patient care responsibility, they must meet the licensure requirement described in paragraph C under "Basic Minimum Qualification Requirements for all Medical Officer Positions" and the requirements described in either section A (General Practice) or section B (Special Fields) under "Additional Requirements."

GS-11
In addition to meeting the minimum educational requirement, demonstrated interest in and aptitude for medical research work through participation in research projects such as might have been offered through medical school, residency training, and fellowship programs.

GS-12
1 year of medical research experience; or
1 year of graduate training in which the candidate demonstrated interest and aptitude for medical research, or
1 year of graduate study in an accredited college or university in a field of science (for example, pathology, pharmacology, physiology, microbiology, biochemistry, or zoology) closely related to the work of the position being filled.

GS-13
In addition to the Doctor of Medicine or Doctor of Osteopathy degree, an earned doctorate from an accredited college or university in a field of science directly related to medicine and closely allied to the position to be filled; or
In addition to meeting the requirements for GS-12, 2 years of graduate training or medical research experience that demonstrates ability to do independent major medical research.

GS-14
In addition to the requirements for GS-13, 1 year of medical experience that demonstrates ability to do significant medical research requiring a comprehensive knowledge and outstanding professional competence in a field of medical science.

GS-15
In addition to the requirements for GS-14, 1 year of medical research experience that demonstrates outstanding leadership in the particular medical field.

Quality of Training and Experience

In addition to meeting the requirements set forth above for education, training, licensure, and length and kinds of experience, applicants must present training and experience of the quality described below. Applicants whose training and experience do not meet the quality requirements, even though they meet all of the other requirements, will not be eligible for appointment.

The training and/or experience must have been progressive and responsible, and must have demonstrated that the applicant has a good knowledge of current principles, practices, methods, and techniques in his/her field of medicine.

The experience for clinical positions and for positions in the various fields of preventive medicine must have provided the applicant with knowledges, skills, and abilities equivalent to those which would have been acquired in the same amount of time in approved residency training in the appropriate specialty.

For positions at grades GS-13 and above, 1 year of the required experience in the appropriate specialty must have been at a level of difficulty and responsibility equivalent to that of the next lowest grade in the Federal service.

DENTAL OFFICER

Description of Work

Dental Officers perform professional or scientific work in the prevention, diagnosis, and treatment of diseases, injuries, and deformities of the teeth, the jaws, organs of the mouth, and other structures and connective tissues associated with the oral cavity and the masticatory system. Positions may be in the general practice of dentistry, or in the following specialties officially recognized by the American Dental Association: Oral Surgery, Prosthodontics, Pedodontics, Periodontics, Endodontics, or Orthodontics.

Requirements

I Minimum Educational Requirement
All applicants must be graduates of an accredited United States or Canadian school approved by the Council on Dental Education, American Dental Association, and hold a degree in dental surgery (D.D.S.) or dental medicine (D.M.D.).

II. Licensure Requirement
For all positions, applicants must be currently licensed to practice dentistry in a State, the District of Columbia, the Commonwealth of Puerto Rico, or a territory of the United States.

III. Additional Experience and/or Training Requirements
Applicants must have experience and/or training beyond the dental degree as follows:

Grade	Years
GS-12	
GS-13	3*
GS-14/15	5*

The required experience and/or training may have been one of the following types:

1 Professional experience in the general practice of dentistry.

2. Approved internship or residency training. (This is training in a hospital dental internship or residency, as the case may be, approved by the Council on Dental Education of the American Dental Association.)

3 Graduate-level study in an accredited dental school. (This is either dental school graduate study leading to an advanced degree such as Master of Science or postgraduate (non-degree) dental school study involving a level of instruction comparable to that provided in a graduate degree program.)

4. Professional experience in a specialized area of practice.

5 Other advanced study or training outside a dental school or hospital creditable towards satisfaction of training program requirements for Board eligibility. (Board eligibility is qualification for examination by a national certifying board as a result of having met the advanced training program requirements for a dental specialty.)

For GS-12 positions at least 1 year of the required experience and/or training must have been in professional practice or internship or residency training. Those applicants who have completed an approved internship in which they demonstrated superior achievement and ability will fully meet the requirements for GS-12 ("Superior achievement and ability" is defined as that demonstrated by an intern who, on the basis of an evaluation of all interns who have completed training in the same hospital in the same kind of internship program over the past 5 years, would fall into the upper half of the group.)

Specialist Positions

The required experience and training for specialist positions must clearly establish the applicant's status as a specialist. Three or more years of experience which includes some work in a specialized area of practice does not, of itself, provide the required evidence of specialist qualifications. Specialist qualifications are determined by the types and difficulty* of the cases dealt with, the level of knowledge and understanding of the specialization regularly required, and the degree of diagnostic skills and treatment planning ability involved. Invariably, specialization requires that professional practice be supplemented by pertinent graduate level study

Specialty training and experience for GS-13 positions must have provided the applicant with the advanced knowledges, skills, and abilities needed to diagnose and treat very difficult cases in the specialty with very little or no consultation.

Specialty training and experience for GS-14 specialist positions must have provided the applicant with knowledges, skills and abilities equivalent to those acquired by a Board eligible.

Certification as a diplomat by a national certifying board for a specialized area of practice is qualifying for GS-14 positions. (A national certifying board is an examining board in a special area of dental practice recognized by the Council on Dental Education of the American Dental Association.)

*For specialized fields, the experience and/or training must have been in the appropriate specialty

Quality of Experience and Training

In addition to meeting the requirements set forth above for education, licensure, and length and kinds of experience and/or training, applicants must present training and experience of the quality described below.

The training and/or experience must have been progressive and responsible, and, as a minimum, must give evidence that the applicant has a good knowledge of current principles, practices, methods, and techniques in dentistry. For specialist positions, it must give strong evidence that the applicant has a thorough knowledge of current principles, practices, methods and techniques in his/her specialized areas of dentistry.

For positions at grade GS-13 and above, 1 year of the required experience must have been at a level of difficulty and responsibility equivalent to that of the Federal grade next below the grade for which the applicant is being considered. For specialist positions, such required experience must also have been in the appropriate specialty.

INFORMATION COMMON TO MEDICAL AND DENTAL OFFICERS

Unpaid Experience or Volunteer Work

Credit will be given for unpaid experience or volunteer work such as in community, cultural, social service, and professional association activities on the same basis as for paid experience, provided it is of the type acceptable for these positions. Therefore, you may, if you wish, report such experience if you feel that it represents qualifying experience for the position for which you are applying. However, to receive proper credit, you must show the actual time, such as number of hours per week, spent in such activity.

Basis of Rating

You will be rated on a scale of 70-100 on the extent and quality of your experience, education, and training in relation to the requirements of these positions. Such ratings will be based upon statements in your application and upon any evidence which may be secured by the Office of Personnel Management.

Length of Eligibility

If you are found qualified, your name will be placed on an Office of Personnel Management register, from which names are referred to Federal agencies for job consideration. Your name stays on the register 12 months, after which it will be removed unless you extend your eligibility by submitting up-to-date information after 10 months. (Letters, Standard Form 171, or Standard Form 171A may be used for this purpose.) Information submitted before 10 months will not be accepted unless the updated information will qualify you for a higher grade.

Salary

Federal salary rates are adjusted periodically. Current information regarding salaries may be obtained from Federal Job Information/Testing Centers.

Equal Employment Opportunity

Qualified applicants will be considered for appointment without regard to race, creed, color, age, national origin, handicapping condition, sex, political affiliation, or other nonmerit factor.

Federal Job Information Centers

All forms mentioned in this announcement are available from Federal Job Information Centers, (FJIC) which are located in many large cities across the country. The FJIC's also have information on such subjects as kinds of appointments; veteran preference; and citizenship, age, and physical requirements.

How to Apply

What to File
1. **Standard Form 171, Application for Federal Employment.** Be sure to show the type of position you want, the number of this announcement, and the lowest salary you will accept. Give detailed information about your experience, showing the amount and kind of supervision you receive or exercise, and the proportion of time you spend in the various phases of your work.

2. **OPM Form 1170/29, Supplemental Qualification Statement for Medical and Dental Officer.**

3. **Form 1567, Employment Availability Statement for Medical/Dental Officer Announcement 442.**

4. **Standard Form 15, Claim for 10 Point Veteran Preference.** Submit this form only if you are claiming 10-point veteran preference (disability, widow, widower, spouse, or mother preference). Attach the required documentary proof.

Please be sure to submit all forms fully completed. Failure to do so will delay processing of your application.

Where to File
Send your complete application package to:

U. S. Office of Personnel Management
Office of Washington Examining Services
P. O. Box 14080
Washington, DC 20044.

FORM CD-260
REV. 11-89LF [WP50]
DAO 202-335

U.S. DEPARTMENT OF COMMERCE

ANNOUNCEMENT NUMBER:
ISSUE DATE:
CLOSING DATE:

Merit Program

VACANCY ANNOUNCEMENT
NATIONAL OCEANIC AND ATMOSPHERIC ADMINISTRATION (NOAA)

Meteorological Technician	National Weather Service
(Weather Observations & Radar Spec)	Weather Forecast Service Office
GS-1341-09	Portland, Maine
Salary: $26,798 to $34,385 yearly	
NO PROMOTION POTENTIAL	

COMPETITIVE SERVICE

WHO MAY APPLY: Consideration restricted to status applicants and applicants eligible for appointment under special appointing authorities.

DUTIES: Observes, records and transmits regularly scheduled and special surface, synoptic, and upper air weather observations; operates network radar; provides specialized aviation weather briefing service to pilots; provides climatological data; updates weather releases; prepares scripts for release on NOAA Weather Radio; and assist the forecaster as required; promptly disseminates watches and warnings. **SHIFT WORK IS REQUIRED.**

QUALIFICATIONS REQUIRED: 52 weeks specialized experience equivalent to the next lower grade. **Qualifying Specialized Experience** includes: Measuring meteorological phenomena with scientific equipment and instrumentation; observing and recording atmospheric characteristics, i.e., temperature, air movement, visibility, pressure, air density, cloud types; decoding, plotting, and systematically recording data related to the physical characteristics of the atmosphere, i.e., charts, diagrams, cross sections; and collecting, analyzing, interpreting, adjusting and verifying atmospheric and other meteorological data to confirm and improve accuracy and efficacy.

Education may be substituted as provided by OPM Qualifications Handbook, X-118, Series 1341.

TIME-IN-GRADE REQUIREMENTS: In addition to the above qualifications, applicants must have completed 52 weeks below the grade level for which applying.

BASIS FOR EVALUATING CANDIDATES: Applicants who meet the minimum qualification requirements will be evaluated on type and quality of job-related experience, education, training, awards and performance appraisals. In order to receive appropriate credit consideration applicants should include in their SF-171 a list of courses taken including hours of credit received (or submit a transcript of education); list all training and list all awards including the types of awards (including outstanding performance rating) and their effective dates; list performance ratings for the last three years and list all job-related outside activities or professional associations.

HOW AND WHERE TO APPLY: Submit the required forms as specified on Merit Program Supplemental Information. (Note: Federal employee applicants **must** submit a copy of their most recent annual performance appraisal. **FAILURE TO SUBMIT THIS FORM MAY AFFECT CONSIDERATION UNDER THIS ANNOUNCEMENT. TO:** U.S. Department of Commerce, Eastern Administrative Support Center (EASC), Atmospheric/NON-NOAA Operations Branch, Room 407, 253 Monticello Avenue, Norfolk, Virginia 23510. For further information call Christine Hudson on commercial (804)441-6548 or FTS 827-6548.

For other information on EASC Merit Assignment Program recruitments, contact the EASC MAP Vacancy Announcement Hotline on commercial (804)441-3720 or FTS 827-3720. Telecommunications Device for the Deaf (TDD) is accessible by dialing commercial (804)441-3609 or FTS 827-3609.

(2) Successful completion of a course of study of at least 12 months, including clinical training or preceptorship, specifically designed for professional caliber physician's assistants in that it provided the candidate with the knowledge and ability to take a detailed medical history, to conduct a physical examination, to follow observation procedures, to order and perform diagnostic and therapeutic tasks, and to exercise a degree of judgment in integrating and interpreting findings on the basis of general medical knowledge; or equivalent education and training.

The course of study or training must be approved by a nationally-recognized professional medical body such as the American Medical Association or the Association of American Medical Colleges, or by a panel of physicians established by a Federal Agency for this purpose.

In addition to the basic requirements the following amounts of pertinent professional caliber experience comparable to the work of a physician's assistant are required:

GS-11 - two (2) years of pertinent professional caliber experience.
GS-12 - three (3) years of pertinent professional caliber experience.

The required education, training, and experience must have demonstrated the ability to perform professional-caliber medical work as a physician's assistant with minimal supervision, including the exercise of a degree of judgment in integrating and interpreting diagnostic findings and in determining the need for referral to a physician.

For all grades, at least 6 months of the required experience must have been at the level of difficulty comparable to that of the next lower grade, or 1 year comparable to the second lower grade, in the Federal service.

EXCEPTION TO CUMULATIVE YEARS OF EXPERIENCE REQUIREMENT: Persons who have 1 year of specialized experience equivalent to the next lower level (in the normal line of progression for the occupation), even though they do not meet the cumulative years of experience required above, may be rated eligible if their total backgrounds demonstrate the knowledge, skills, and abilities necessary for successful job performance.

SELECTIVE PLACEMENT FACTOR: Applicant must possess current certification from the National Commission on Certification of Physician Assistants.

New physician assistant graduates (defined as individuals who have obtained a qualifying degree within 12 months of their appointment) have 1 year from the date they enter on duty to provide evidence of certification. During this 1 year period, new physician assistant graduates will be assigned responsibilities under closer supervision than that normally expected of a certified physician assistant.

Certification is required for all Indian Health Service (IHS) physician assistants when moving to a position other than the one presently incumbered. Certification for individuals will be waived only for the position they presently incumber.

U.S. DEPARTMENT OF HEALTH AND HUMAN SERVICES

PHOENIX AREA INDIAN HEALTH SERVICE

PERSONNEL MANAGEMENT BRANCH
3738 N. 16TH STREET, SUITE A
PHOENIX, ARIZONA 85016-5981

Announcement No. PXIHS-92-118

Opening Date _____ Closing Date _____

Personnel: Date:
EEO: Date:

POSITION:
GS-603, Physician's Assistant OR
GS-610, Nurse Practitioner

LOCATION/DUTY STATION:
PHS Indian Health Center
Owyhee Service Unit
Ely, Nevada

SERIES/GRADE/SALARY:
GS-603-11, $32,423 - $42,152 per annum
GS-603-12, $38,861 - $50,516 per annum
GS-610-11, $39,990 - $49,719 per annum
GS-610-12, $46,651 - $58,286 per annum

TYPE/NUMBER OF POSITIONS:
1 Number of Positions
X Permanent
___ Temporary-NTE:

CONDITIONS OF EMPLOYMENT:
X Full-time
___ Intermittent
___ Part-time

AREA OF CONSIDERATION:
IHS-WIDE

SUPERVISORY/MANAGEMENT:
___ Yes, may require one year probationary period.
X No

PMRS:
___ Yes
X No

PROMOTION POTENTIAL:
X Yes, to Grade: GS-12
___ No known potential

HOUSING:
___ Yes, government housing available
X Private housing only

TRAVEL EXPENSES:
X Travel may be paid in accordance with Federal Travel Regulations
___ No expenses paid

BRIEF DESCRIPTION OF DUTIES: Physician Assistant Duties: Serves as Physician's Assistant providing medical and health care for ambulatory patients, emergency cases, individuals and families. Provides diagnostic, preventive, and therapeutic health services to patients and family members in a community based primary care facility as the primary health resource at a Field Clinic.. Performs or requests special screening and developmental tests and laboratory tests and interprets the results. Provides full range of emergency services or crisis intervention including life saving emergency procedures. Evaluates the medical aspects of treatment plans periodically recognizing the need for reassessment by a physician or other health professionals.

QUALIFICATION REQUIREMENTS:

Candidates must meet basic requirements (1) and (2) below:

(1) A broad background of knowledge of the medical environment, practices, and procedures such as would be acquired by a bachelor's degree in a health care occupation such as nursing, medical technology, or physical therapy or by 3 years of responsible and progressive health care experience such as medical corpsman, nursing assistant, or medical technician .

AND

BRIEF DESCRIPTION OF DUTIES: Nurse Practitioner: Plans and provides comprehensive health care to patients of all ages and their families. Orders and/or performs appropriate screening and diagnostic tests and procedures. Identifies and manages acute chronic illnesses. Provides full range of emergency services or crisis intervention. Assesses the health needs of patients, considering socio-economic, epidemiologic, and cultural influences. Serves as a consultant and provides technical assistance to other health care providers and staff.

PROFESSIONAL REGISTRATION REQUIREMENT: All applicants must have active, current registration as a professional nurse in a state, District of Columbia, the Commonwealth of Puerto Rico, or a Territory of the United States. Exception: If you have graduated within the past 12 months from a State approved school of professional nursing, you may be appointed pending professional registration. However, you must attain registration within 6 months after appointment in order to keep your job.

A copy of your current license must be submitted with your application.

BASIC EDUCATION REQUIREMENTS FOR ALL NURSE POSITIONS: Candidates for positions at all grades must meet one of the following requirements.

A. Graduation with a bachelor's or higher degree in nursing from a school of professional nursing, approved by the legally designated State accrediting agency at the time the program was completed by the candidate.

B. Graduation from a 3-year (at least 30 months) diploma program of professional nursing approved by the legally designated State accrediting agency at the time the program was completed by the candidate.

C. Graduation from a diploma program of professional nursing of less than 30 months approved by the legally designated State accrediting agency at the program was completed by the candidate.

D. Graduation from an associate degree program or other program of at least 2 years in a school of professional nursing approved the legally designated State accrediting agency at the time the program was completed by the candidate.

E. Graduation from a school of professional nursing (including foreign schools), of at least 2 years in length other than one covered above, provided that the professional nurse training and the nursing knowledge acquired are substantially comparable and equivalent to that of graduates of an approved school as described above.

In addition the basic qualifications, candidates for positions at GS-11 must have the following amounts of required experience: 1) 4 years of professional experience for Associate degree program or diploma programs of less than 30 months ; 2) 3 years of professional experience for Diploma program of 30 months or more ; 3) 3 years of professional experience for Bacculaureate degree program. One year of professional nursing experience must be sufficiently related to the specialty in both subject-matter and grade-level, to demonstrate the candidate's ability to perform the major duties of the position being filled.

In addition to the basic qualifications, candidates for positions at GS-12 must have at least 1 year of experience at the next lower grade, and must demonstrate a record of accomplishment, professional competence, leadership, and recognition in the profession as in the planning, organizing, directing, and coordinating of nursing projects, or in well-established service as an expert and consultant.

EXCEPTION TO CUMULATIVE YEARS OF EXPERIENCE REQUIREMENT: Persons who have 1 year of specialized experience equivalent to the next lower level (in the normal line of progression for the occupation), even though they do not meet the cumulative years of experience required above, may be rated eligible if their total backgrounds demonstrate the knowledge, skills, and abilities necessary for successful job performance.

TIME-IN-GRADE RESTRICTION: (If selected under the Excepted Service Examining Plan, such individuals may be appointed under Schedule A authority without regard to Time-In-Grade Requirements.) Candidates for GS-11 must have had at least one year of service in a position no more than two grades lower than the position to be filled. Candidates for GS-12 must have had at least one year of service in a position no more than one grade lower than the position to be filled..

MOTOR VEHICLE OPERATION REQUIREMENTS: Incumbent may be required at some locations to operate a government motor vehicle and maintain a current State Driver's license and Government Employee Identification Card.

SELECTIVE SERVICE CERTIFICATION: If you are male, born after December 31, 1959, and you want to be employed by the Federal Government, you must (subject to certain exemptions) be registered with Selective Service System.

LEGAL AND REGULATORY REQUIREMENTS: Candidates must meet time after competitive appointment, time-in-grade restrictions, and qualification requirements within 30 calendar days after the closing date of the vacancy announcement.

APPLICANTS OR CURRENT FEDERAL SERVICE EMPLOYEES CLAIMING INDIAN PREFERENCE MUST INDICATE in Item 1 ON THEIR APPLICATION IF THEY WISH TO BE CONSIDERED UNDER THE INDIAN HEALTH SERVICE MERIT PROMOTION PLAN, EXCEPTED SERVICE EXAMINING PLAN, OR BOTH. IF NOT, THEY WILL BE CONSIDERED UNDER THE IHS MERIT PROMOTION PLAN ONLY.

PREFERENCE IN FILLING VACANCIES IS GIVEN TO QUALIFIED INDIAN CANDIDATES IN ACCORDANCE WITH THE INDIAN PREFERENCE ACT (TITLE 25, U.S. CODE, SECTION 472 AND 473). IN OTHER THAN THE ABOVE, THE INDIAN HEALTH SERVICE IS AN EQUAL OPPORTUNITY EMPLOYER.

REASONABLE ACCOMMODATION WILL BE GIVEN TO QUALIFIED DISABLED APPLICANTS PURSUANT TO SECTION OF THE REHABILITATION ACT OF 1973, 29 U.S. CODE 791, TITLE 29.

INSTRUCTIONS FOR PHS COMMISSIONED CORPS CANDIDATES: Active duty applicants may submit a copy of current billet description, resume or curriculum. If not on active duty but have applied for the Commissioned Corps, submit the same information as above (except billet description).

NOTE: Commissioned Corps applicants claiming Indian Preference will be evaluated by the Area Personnel Office against the applicable Preston standard or the civil service standard, if no Preston standard exists. These applicants must describe the experience gained in their two most recent positions and provide the dates they occupied those positions. In addition, Commissioned Corps Indian Preference applicants must also provide information regarding education, including degrees obtained and schools attended and they must include home/work telephone numbers if this information is not contained in the resumes. When required by the vacancy announcement, these applicants must submit specific information related to any knowledges, skills, and abilities which are being used as selective factors. Commissioned Corps Indian Preference applicants must submit Form BIA - 4432, as proof of Indian Preference and also proof of possession of the appropriate license.

ADDITIONAL SELECTION MAY BE MADE FROM THIS ANNOUNCEMENT WITHIN 90 DAYS FROM THE DATE OF THE CERTIFICATE PROVIDED THE VACANT POSITION IS AN IDENTICAL POSITION, SAME GEOGRAPHICAL LOCATION AND SAME CONDITIONS OF EMPLOYMENT.

SUPPLEMENTAL QUESTIONNAIRE
On Knowledge, Skills, and Abilities

Position applied for: Nurse Practitioner, GS-610-11/12

Announcement No: _____   Closing Date: _____

Evaluation Method: Evaluation will be made of experience, Performance Appraisals, Training, Letters of Commendation, Self-Development, Awards and Outside Activities, which are related to this position. To receive full credit for your qualification, provide a narrative statement of experience, training, education, awards, hobbies, self-developed achievements, and any other aspects of your background as they relate to the knowledge, skills and abilities (KSA's) outlined below and show the level of accomplishments and degree of responsibility. This supplement will be the principal basis for determining whether or not you are best qualified for the position. Describe your qualification in each of the following:

1. Knowledge of primary care principles, practices and processes used in the primary care of patients through extended clinical study and/or experience

2. Ability to collect, organize, record, and communicate data relevant to primary health assessments and express ideas and recommendations verbally and in writing.

3. Ability to interpret special screening and developmental tests and selected laboratory findings.

4. Skill in making diagnoses and choosing, initiating and modifying selected therapies.

5. Knowledge of pharmaceuticals in order to recognize their desired effects, side effects, and complications of their use.

The information you provide is considered to be a part of your application and as such is certified by your signature on the SF-171 or equivalent.

_____
Signature

_____
Date

HOW TO APPLY: Applicants must submit the following required forms to the PHOENIX AREA INDIAN HEALTH SERVICE, PERSONNEL MANAGEMENT BRANCH, 3738 N. 16th STREET, SUITE A, PHOENIX ARIZONA 85016-5981, by the closing date. APPLICANTS WILL NOT BE CONSIDERED IF THE APPLICATION IS RECEIVED AFTER THE CLOSING DATE. ONCE AN APPLICATION HAS BEEN RECEIVED, WE WILL NOT HONOR REQUEST FOR COPIES. APPLICATIONS WILL BE ACCEPTED FROM INDIAN APPLICANTS, CAREER CONDITIONAL OR CAREER FEDERAL EMPLOYEES AND REINSTATEMENT ELIGIBLES BASED ON PRIOR FEDERAL SERVICE. For information regarding this announcement, contact Patsy Mousseau, Personnel Staffing and Classification Specialist, at (602) 640-2070.

1. SF-171, APPLICATION FOR FEDERAL EMPLOYMENT. Must be current, up-to-date and have an original signature.
2. PERFORMANCE APPRAISAL, if available, must be the most recent appraisal.
3. BIA Form 5-4432, VERIFICATION OF INDIAN PREFERENCE SIGNED BY THE APPROPRIATE BIA OFFICIAL, or equivalent form issued by a Tribe authorized by P.L. 93-638 contract to perform the certification function on behalf of the BIA. Applicants currently employed in the Phoenix Area wishing to claim Indian preference, without attaching BIA Form 5-4432 to their SF-171, must state on their application that Indian preference is a matter of record in their Official Personnel Folder. Failure to do so will result in loss of due consideration as an Indian preference applicant.
4. SUPPLEMENTAL QUESTIONNAIRE ON KNOWLEDGE, SKILLS, AND ABILITIES. It is important that you describe your qualifications in detail in order for you to receive proper evaluation in the ranking process.
5. IF CURRENTLY A FEDERAL EMPLOYEE, a copy of latest personnel action (SF-50B) to verify competitive or excepted service status.
6. Copy of DD-214, MILITARY DISCHARGE DOCUMENT, if claiming veterans preference.
7. To obtain educational credit applicants must submit a college transcript.
8. Copy of certification from the National Commission on Certification of Physician Assistants.
9. Copy of Nursing License.

United States Department of the Interior

OFFICE OF THE SECRETARY
Washington, D.C. 20240

EQUAL OPPORTUNITY EMPLOYER

Announcement No.:
Opening Date:
Closing Date:

VACANCY ANNOUNCEMENT

Position Title, Series and Grade: Paralegal Specialist, GS-950-9/11
Number of Vacancies and Nature of Position: One, full-time, permanent position
Promotion Potential: GS-11
Minimum Area of Consideration: All Sources
Position Sensitivity: Non-sensitive
Conflict of Interest Statement Required: No
Limitations on Consideration: Consideration is limited to applicants with Civil Service Status and to individuals eligible for noncompetitive appointment, such as VRA, handicapped, etc. Individuals requiring OPM certification will not be considered.

Location: Office of the Solicitor, Southwest Region, Tulsa OK. Relocation expenses will not be paid.

DUTIES: Serves as a paralegal specialist in a field office of the Solicitor with responsibility for the analysis and evaluation of claims and other matters arising from various legislative acts. Selects, assembles, summarizes, and compiles substantive information by use of statutes, regulations, Department directives and policies, digests, commentaries and other reference material. Receives, analyzes, investigates and recommends decisions or actions of submissions under various Indian claims and tort claim acts. Examines and evaluates requests for information under the Freedom of Information and Privacy Acts. Reviews title evidence submitted by client agencies for land acquisitions and Indian wills submitted for approval and drafts opinions.

Qualifications Required: (Applicants will not be considered further if these requirements are not substantially met): Applicants must meet qualification standards as specified in Office of Personnel Management X-118 Handbook. One (1) year of specialized experience at least equivalent to next lower grade level; OR For GS-9: two (2) full academic years of graduate level education or master's or equivalent graduate degree of LL.B or J.D.; For GS-11: three (3) full academic years of graduate level education or Ph.D or equivalent doctoral degree. Specialized experience is experience directly related to the line of work of the position to be filled and which has equipped the applicant with the particular knowledge, skill and abilities to successfully perform the duties of that position.

Quality Ranking Factors: (Desirable)

1. Knowledge of the Federal laws and statutes.
2. Knowledge of legal terminology.
3. Knowledge of the techniques of records management.
4. Ability to communicate orally and in writing.
5. Knowledge of quasi-judicial functions.

Basis of Evaluation: All qualified status candidates applying for promotion will be evaluated on the basis of experience, education, training, self-development, awards, performance appraisals and supervisory evaluations as they relate to the aforementioned quality ranking factors. IT IS SUGGESTED THAT APPLICANTS ADDRESS THESE FACTORS IN THEIR SF-171 OR SUPPLEMENT. The names of all qualified candidates applying for lateral reassignment or lateral transfer will be certified to the selecting official for consideration. All candidates will receive consideration without regard to age, race, religion, color, national origin, politics, sex, or any other non merit factors.

The application you submit for this position contains information subject to the Privacy Act of 1974. Information regarding this Act is available upon request in the Division of Personnel Services.

HOW TO APPLY: IN ACCORDANCE WITH 18 U.S.C. 1729 & 39 U.S.C.3201, APPLICATIONS WILL NOT BE ACCEPTED FROM APPLICANTS USING A POSTAGE PAID ENVELOPE (PENALTY MAIL). APPLICANTS MUST SUBMIT AN APPLICATION FOR FEDERAL EMPLOYMENT (SF-171). THE ATTACHED SUPERVISORY EVALUATION (OR APPROPRIATE SUBSTITUTE) SHOULD BE COMPLETED AND RETURNED. TO ENSURE CONSIDERATION, SF-171's MUST BE RECEIVED IN THE PERSONNEL OFFICE ON OR BEFORE THE ABOVE CLOSING DATE, AND SHOULD BE SENT TO:

DEPARTMENT OF THE INTERIOR
OFFICE OF THE SECRETARY
DIVISION OF PERSONNEL SERVICES
BRANCH OF PERSONNEL OPERATIONS (B)
1849 C Street, N.W., MS-5459, MIB
Washington, D.C. 20240

TELEPHONE INQUIRIES MAY BE DIRECTED TO (202) 208-4821

OFFICE OF THE SECRETARY

VA 0 -92-18(B)

Supervisory Appraisal for Position of Paralegal Specialist, GS-950-9/11

Applicant _____

Taking into consideration the duties of the position and the qualification requirements indicated in the vacancy announcement, please make an evaluation on each of the elements below based on (1) the applicant's demonstrated performance, or (2) on your estimate of the individual's potential ability. The applicant will be shown a copy of this evaluation upon his/her request.

ELEMENTS	Rating				Opportunity to Judge		
	Superior	Above Average	Average	Needs Improvement	Frequently	Infrequently	None
1. Knowledge of the Federal laws and statues.							
2. Knowledge of legal terminology.							
3. Knowledge of the techniques of records management.							
4. Ability to communicate orally and in writing.							
5. Knowledge of quasi-judicial functions.							
6. Skill in operating a personal computer.							
7. Ability to work under pressure.							
8. Ability to learn tasks (quick to catch on to techniques and procedures, ability to apply new methods, can grasp causes and effects).							
9. Ability to work with minimum supervision.							

COMMENTS:

_____

_____

_____

_____

Immediate Supervisors Signature   Date

MERIT STAFFING
VACANCY ANNOUNCEMENT
U.S. DEPARTMENT OF ENERGY

Announcement No: NV 92-96 (PFT)

Issue Date:

Closing Date:

NEVADA FIELD OFFICE

POSITION: Physical Scientist, GS-1301-13

SALARY RANGE: $46,210 - $60,070

Demonstrated exceptional difficulty in recruiting highly qualified candidates may be the basis for paying a recruitment or relocation bonus (up to 25 percent of base pay), or requesting approval of a dual compensation waiver for civil and uniformed service retirees.

NONCOMPETITIVE
PROMOTION POTENTIAL: NONE

SUBJECT TO MERIT PAY: NO

SUPERVISOR/MANAGER: NO

FLSA: EXEMPT

SUPERVISOR/MANAGER
PROBATIONARY PERIOD: NO

LOCATION: Performance Assessment Branch, Performance Assessment & Quality Division, Las Vegas, Nevada

AREA OF DISTRIBUTION:
Nationwide

Selected candidates will be subject to a comprehensive background investigation for security clearance.

NOTE: All DOE employees may be subject to drug testing in accordance with the DOE Drug-Free Federal Workplace testing implementation program.

Applications will be accepted from current career or career-conditional employees of the federal government, or former federal employees with reinstatement eligibility. Other persons may be eligible for consideration under special employment program appointment authorities such as: those authorized for the severely handicapped; some veterans; some former Peace Corp/VISTA volunteers; and certain former overseas employees.

DUTIES AND RESPONSIBILITIES:

This position provides expertise to the Performance Assessment Branch in the physical sciences as they relate to mining and drilling operations. Plans, leads, conducts, and reports on assessments of complex technical, environmental, and scientific operations and activities under the purview of the DOE/NV. Assessments may include such areas as geological, hydrological, and geophysical aspects of mining and drilling projects. Assists in identifying physical science, mining, and drilling related performance objectives and indicators, analysis of data, and developing recommendations and improvement action plans for senior management consideration and actions. Conducts Total Quality Management (TQM) type technical assessments of the DOE/NV.

QUALIFICATION REQUIREMENTS: Applicants must have general and specialized experience as described below; these requirements are in accordance with OPM X-118 Handbook. The Handbook, available at your personnel office, specifies when and how education may be substituted for the experience. Applicants must also meet any placement factors listed below.

EDUCATION REQUIREMENTS: Successful completion of a full 4-year professional scientific curriculum leading to a bachelor's or higher degree in physical science, engineering, or mathematics that includes 24 semester hours in physical science and/or related engineering science, or meet alternate requirements stated in the OPM X-118 Handbook for GS-1301 Series.

EXPERIENCE REQUIREMENTS: Candidates must have one year of specialized experience at least equivalent to the next lower grade level. Specialized experience is defined as experience which is in or directly related to the line of work of the position to be filled and which has equipped the applicant with the particular knowledges, skills and abilities to successfully perform the duties of that position.

RANKING FACTORS: Applicants who meet the qualification requirements described above may be further evaluated to determine the extent to which their education, work-related experience, training, awards, and supervisory appraisals indicate they possess or have the potential to acquire knowledges, skills, and personal characteristics described in the following factors:

1. Professional knowledge of the theories and practices of the physical sciences to include geology, hydrology, geochemistry and geophysics sufficient to lead Total Quality Management (TQM) teams in assessing the complex technical, environmental, and scientific activities related to mining and drilling conducted at the Nevada Test Site and to provide senior technical expertise in those areas to the Branch Chief.

2. Knowledge of drilling technologies, hydrological investigations, geophysical measurement, mining geology and mining engineering to assess performance in the mining and drilling arena including environmental monitoring, environmental restoration, and underground nuclear weapons testing.

3. Knowledge of management principles and procedures in order to effectively plan, coordinate, and lead performance assessments within a complex technical organization.

4. Knowledge of contract management and administration sufficient to assess technical and scientific performance of activities conducted by contractor organizations.

5. Skill in written and oral communication sufficient to lead teams conducting performance assessments, interface with outside agencies, contractors, laboratories, and the public regarding sensitive and controversial issues.

6. Knowledge of the principles pertaining to the self-assessment process, i.e., performance measurements, for tracking/ trending root cause analysis, lessons learned, etc.

TO APPLY:

(1) Applicants _must_ submit a current, completed and signed APPLICATION FOR FEDERAL EMPLOYMENT (SF-171) AND LISTING OF COLLEGE COURSE WORK (SF-1170), or COLLEGE TRANSCRIPTS. Application _should_ include all pertinent experience, awards, commendations, training, and other information which clearly relates to the evaluation factors listed above; the SUPERVISORY APPRAISAL (see reverse); on a separate sheet of paper, examples of experience/education which best describes the extent and level of your knowledge, skills, and ability for each of the ranking factors listed above; your most recent performance appraisal; the latest copy of your SF-50, NOTIFICATION OF PERSONNEL ACTION; and SF-181, RACE AND NATIONAL ORIGIN IDENTIFICATION (optional).

(2) Qualifications and rankings will be based on information contained in the SF-171; appraisals; the applicant's response to the ranking factors, and any other relevant documents submitted by the applicant. All materials become the property of the personnel office and will not be returned.

(3) APPLICATIONS MUST BE RECEIVED ON OR BEFORE THE CLOSING DATE SHOWN ABOVE. The address is:

U.S. Department of Energy
DOE Nevada Field Office
Federal Personnel Branch
P.O. Box 98518
Las Vegas, NV 89193-8518.

Applications mailed in government postage-free envelopes or over a government fax will not be accepted. Forms or information may be obtained by calling (702) 295-1487.

THE U.S. DEPARTMENT OF ENERGY IS AN EQUAL OPPORTUNITY EMPLOYER

UNITED STATES DEPARTMENT OF ENERGY
NEVADA FIELD OFFICE
SUPERVISORY APPRAISAL

POSITION: Physical Scientist, GS-1301-13   ANNOUNCEMENT NO: NV 92-95 (PFT)

APPLICANT'S NAME: _____

Taking into consideration the duties of the position and qualification requirements indicated in the vacancy announcement, please make an evaluation on each of the elements below based on the applicant's demonstrated performance or your estimate of potential ability. If your evaluation is based on demonstrated performance, put a 1 in the relevant column. If it based on your estimate of potential ability, put a 2 in the column. If you lack the knowledge to make a judgement, check the Don't Know column.

EVALUATION CRITERIA	BELOW AVERAGE	SATISFACTORY	HIGHLY SUCCESSFUL/SUPERIOR	OUTSTANDING	DON'T KNOW
1. Professional knowledge of the theories and practices of the physical sciences to include geology, hydrology, geochemistry and geophysics sufficient to lead Total Quality Management (TQM) teams in assessing the complex technical, environmental, and scientific activities related to mining and drilling conducted at the Nevada Test Site and to provide senior technical expertise in those areas to the Branch Chief.					
2. Knowledge of drilling technologies, hydrological investigations, geophysical measurement, mining geology and mining engineering to assess performance in the mining and drilling arena including environmental monitoring, environmental restoration, and underground nuclear weapons testing.					
3. Knowledge of management principles and procedures in order to effectively plan, coordinate, and lead performance assessments within a complex technical organization.					
4. Knowledge of contract management and administration sufficient to assess technical and scientific performance of activities conducted by contractor organizations.					
5. Skill in written and oral communication sufficient to lead teams conducting performance assessments, interface with outside agencies, contractors, laboratories, and the public regarding sensitive and controversial issues.					
6. Knowledge of the principles pertaining to the self-assessment process, i.e., performance measurements, for tracking/ trending root cause analysis, lessons learned, etc.					

ADDITIONAL REMARKS: _____

_____
SUPERVISOR'S SIGNATURE

_____
SUPERVISOR'S NAME (Print or Type)

_____
DATE

_____
SUPERVISOR'S TITLE

USDA
ANIMAL AND PLANT HEALTH
INSPECTION SERVICE

OPPORTUNITIES IN THE FEDERAL GOVERNMENT FOR

PLANT PROTECTION AND QUARANTINE OFFICER

GS-5 AND GS-7   ANNOUNCEMENT NUMBER 436

THE FEDERAL GOVERNMENT IS AN EQUAL OPPORTUNITY EMPLOYER

The Plant Protection and Quarantine program has positions located throughout the United States, Puerto Rico, and the Virgin Islands. The majority of positions are located at seaports, international airports and border stations. The following is a listing of states with the largest number of Plant Protection and Quarantine Officer positions.

California   New Jersey
Florida   New York
Illinois   Texas
Michigan

We anticipate very few vacancies occurring in any of the remaining states.

BEFORE YOU APPLY, CONSULT THE CURRENT AMENDMENT TO THIS ANNOUNCEMENT FOR THE OPENING AND CLOSING DATES TO SUBMIT APPLICATIONS. (Applications postmarked after the closing date will be returned unrated).

No previous Federal service experience is required. Applicants must be citizens of the United States.

Federal salary rates are adjusted periodically. Current information regarding salaries may be obtained from Federal Job Information Centers.

A register (list of qualified applicants) will be established and certification made by state. As vacancies occur, applicants will only be certified for vacancies in states where they have indicated willingness to accept employment. APPLICANTS CERTIFIED FOR ONE STATE WILL NOT BE CERTIFIED FOR VACANCIES IN ANOTHER STATE AT THE SAME TIME.

A written test is not required. Rating will be based on education, training, and experience (paid or unpaid) as shown on the application form.

DUTIES:

Plant Protection and Quarantine Officers are located in various ports-of-entry at the borders, air terminals and seaports. PPQ Officers enforce Federal laws and regulations designed to prevent the introduction of foreign plant and animal pests and plant diseases potentially harmful to crops, ornamentals, forests, and livestock. PPQ Officers also conduct or coordinate specialized surveys in support of domestic pest programs, such as gypsy moth, golden nematode, exotic fruit flies, plant diseases and weeds of national importance.

WORK WEEK: The Plant Protection and Quarantine Officers work a scheduled 40-hour week which is arranged to cover the duties at an assigned duty station for the period Monday through Saturday. Sunday is excluded from the basic work week and is treated as an overtime day. The work schedule may include night assignments, occasional overtime and holiday work. Overtime rates of pay apply to work performed outside the regularly scheduled tour of duty or in excess of 8 hours per day or 40 hours per week. Work on Sundays, holidays and scheduled night assignments is subject to premium pay.

QUALIFICATION REQUIREMENTS FOR GS-5 LEVEL:

A. A full 4-year course of study in an ACCREDITED college or university leading to a bachelor's or higher degree with major study in one of the biological sciences is required. This course of study must have included at least 20 semester hours of course work in any one, or in any combination of the following subjects: Entomology, botany, plant pathology, nematology, horticulture, mycology, invertebrate zoology, or closely related scientific subjects;

OR

B. A total of at least 30 semester hours of course work in any combination of biological and related natural and physical sciences in an accredited college or university, including at least 20 semester hours of course work in any one, or in any combination, of the following subjects: entomology, botany, plant pathology, nematology, horticulture, mycology, invertebrate zoology, or closely related scientific subjects, plus additional experience, or education, of an appropriate nature to total 4 years of experience and education or 4 years of education.

The quality of this additional experience or education must have been such that, when combined with the required 30 semester hours in biology and related natural and physical sciences, it gives the applicant a technical knowledge comparable to that normally acquired through the successful completion of the full 4-year course of study described in paragraph A above.

QUALIFICATION REQUIREMENTS FOR GS-7 LEVEL:

Basic Qualifications for GS-5 plus:

1. Superior Academic Achievement

    a. A standing in the upper third of your class or major subdivision (i.e., school of agriculture) at the time of application,

    OR

    b. A grade point average of 3.0 or better (on a 4.0 scale) for all courses completed at (a) the time of application, or (b) during the last 2 years of your undergraduate curriculum. Note: Grade-point averages should be rounded to one decimal place. For example: 2.95 should be rounded to 3.0 and 2.94 should be rounded to 2.9.

    OR

    c. A grade point average of 3.5 or better (on a 4.0 scale) for all courses completed in your major field of study by (a) the time of application, or (b) during the last 2 years of your undergraduate curriculum.

    OR

    d. Membership in a national honorary society (other than freshmen societies) that meets the requirements of the Association of College Honor Societies,

    OR

2. One full academic year, or the equivalent amount of graduate education in an appropriate field. One year of full-time graduate education is determined by the number of credit hours the school attended declares to represent a full year of study in that graduate program. You are responsible for providing evidence that your hours of graduate course work meet your school's requirement, OR

3. One year of professional experience. This experience must have been in or directly related to plant protection and quarantine work.

STUDENTS:

Applications will be accepted from senior students who are otherwise qualified and expect to complete all scholastic course work needed to qualify within 9 months of the date of filing their application. Courses you expect to complete will be accepted tentatively and should be entered on the list of courses you submit as "Courses to be Completed." You may be offered a job before you graduate, but must show proof that you have finished your course work before starting work.

All grade-point averages are to be computed on a 4.0 scale (A = 4 points. B = 3 points. C = 2 points. D = 1 point. F = 0 points). If college uses any other system to compute GPA, an official explanation of equivalence to the 4.0 system must be provided.

ADDITIONAL REQUIREMENTS:

1. Automobile Driving Requirements: All Plant Protection and Quarantine Officers are required to operate a motor vehicle and must possess a valid State Driver's License at time of appointment.

2. EMPLOYMENT IS SUBJECT TO SATISFACTORY COMPLETION OF A 1-YEAR PROBATIONARY PERIOD. SATISFACTORY COMPLETION OF THE PROBATIONARY PERIOD INCLUDES:
- Achieving an average final grade of 80 percent for New Officer Training (NOT).
- Demonstrating satisfactory job performance and conduct during the probationary period.

A. NEW OFFICER TRAINING
The purpose of NOT is to provide relevant training to help PPQ officers acquire new skills and knowledge to enable them to accomplish PPQ's mission.

NOT consists of approximately 9 weeks of technical instruction. Most of the instruction will take place at the Professional Develop Center in Frederick, Maryland. Other portions of NOT will be completed at your duty station, either in a self-instructional or computer based format. Your training will begin as soon after your appointment as possible, but no later than 9 months after you enter on duty.

B. PESTICIDE APPLICATOR CERTIFICATION
All PPQ officers must complete a prescribed training program and pass an examination to be certified as Regulatory Pest Control Applicators. Officers must take the certification examination within the probationary period.

3. **Physical requirements:** Physical fitness is an important consideration in this position. Most of the work is conducted out-of-doors and requires considerable standing, stooping and climbing.

4. PPQ Officers must be able to converse in English with the traveling public, read and understand technical manuals written in English, and write reports in English.

5. Males born after December 31, 1959, desiring federal employment must be registered with the Selective Service System.

HOW TO APPLY:

Please submit one set of the following forms:

-- SF-171, Application for Federal Employment: BE SURE TO INDICATE THE ANNOUNCEMENT NUMBER. Include education and experience (paid or unpaid) pertaining to this position in your application. Pertinent unpaid experience or volunteer work will be evaluated on the same basis as paid experience. To receive proper credit, you must show the actual time such as number of hours a week spent on each activity.

-- College Transcripts or OPM Form 1170/17, List of College Courses and Certificate of Scholastic Achievement. This information is needed to determine your rating and must be included with your application. If you are submitting a transcript of college courses, send it with your application. Be certain that it indicates semester hours or quarter hours and contains your GPA(grade point average). Do not have the school send the transcript directly to the Examining Office. (Transcript or OPM Form 1170/17 must be submitted in English).

-- SF-15, Claim for 10-Point Veteran Preference: with documentary proof if you are claiming 10-point veteran preference.

-- Employment Availability Statement is required to automate your records. You may select up to nine states. You will, however, only receive consideration for vacancies in one state/zone at a time. If you select more than nine states, only your first nine selections will be accepted. Do not select a state unless you are willing to accept a permanent job assignment in that state. IF YOU TURN DOWN JOB OFFERS IN A STATE WHERE YOU HAVE INDICATED YOU WILL ACCEPT EMPLOYMENT, YOUR NAME WILL BE REMOVED FROM THE LIST OF QUALIFIED APPLICANTS FOR THAT STATE.

Application forms should be mailed to the following address:

U.S. Department of Agriculture, APHIS
Field Servicing Office, Examining Unit
Butler Square, 5th Floor
100 North Sixth Street
Minneapolis, MN 55403
Phone: (612) 370-2200

ADMINISTRATIVE OFFICE OF THE U.S. COURTS
VACANCY ANNOUNCEMENT

Announcement Number: 37	Opening Date:	Closing Date:

POSITION: (Title, Series, Grade) PROGRAM ASSISTANT GS-303-7/8/9	ORGANIZATION LOCATION: OFFICE OF AUTOMATION AND TECHNOLOGY COURT SYSTEMS DIVISION SYSTEMS ADMINISTRATOR TRAINING AND SUPPORT BRANCH
SALARY RANGE: $22,636 PA to $34,835 PA	AREA OF CONSIDERATION: WASHINGTON METROPOLITAN AREA – ALL SOURCES
	APPLICANTS FROM OUTSIDE THE AREA OF CONSIDERATION MAY BE CONSIDERED. HOWEVER, ANY RELOCATION EXPENSES WILL NOT BE PROVIDED EXCEPT WITH THE AUTHORIZATION OF THE DIRECTOR UPON REQUEST FROM THE SELECTING OFFICIAL.

PROMOTION POTENTIAL: GS-9

DUTIES AND RESPONSIBILITIES:

This position is located in the Systems Administrator Training and Support Branch whose primary purpose is to provide a technical education program and technical assistance to the Federal judiciary in support of automated systems developed and implemented by the Court Systems Division. The incumbent of this position is responsible for providing a wide range of program, management, and administrative support services for the branch with particular attention to support the student registration process, student certification process, and hospitality program. The incumbent will also be responsible for enhancing the processing of one-time, recurring, and continuing projects and for the typing, editing and logistical support for all reports and correspondence generated through the branch.

QUALIFICATIONS REQUIREMENTS: Applicants must have general and specialized experienced as listed below. This requirement is in accordance with the OPM X-118 Handbook, available in your personnel office, which specifies when and how education may be substituted for the experience.

ONE YEAR OF SPECIALIZED EXPERIENCE AT LEAST EQUIVALENT TO THE NEXT LOWER GRADE LEVEL IS REQUIRED TO QUALIFY FOR EACH GRADE LEVEL.

SPECIALIZED EXPERIENCE: is experience which is directly related to the position to be filled and which has equipped the candidate with the particular knowledge, skills, and abilities to successfully perform the duties of that position. To be creditable, specialized experience must have been at least equivalent to the next lower grade level.

QUALITY RANKING FACTORS: Applicants are encouraged to submit a narrative statement addressing the factors listed below. **EACH FACTOR SHOULD BE ADDRESSED INDIVIDUALLY.**

1. Ability to deal with people at various levels with tact and sensitivity.
2. Ability to effectively communicate and express ideas both orally and in writing.
3. End-user proficiency with office automation (WordPerfect, MicroSoft word, spreadsheet software, etc.)
4. Knowledge of education program operations.

ALL APPLICANTS MUST MEET TIME-IN-GRADE REQUIREMENTS

HOW TO APPLY: Submit to the address indicated below the following: 1) signed and dated Standard Form 171 with the appropriate vacancy announcement number (RESUMES WILL **NOT BE ACCEPTED**); 2) most recent annual performance appraisal (letter of recommendation for non-status applicants); and 3) any supplemental information required by this announcement. Applications must be received in the Personnel Office no later than the closing date indicated above. **NOTE:** APPLICATIONS AND ENCLOSURES WILL **NOT BE** RETURNED.

FOR FURTHER INFORMATION CONTACT: HUMAN RESOURCES DIVISION on (202) 786-6307

ADDITIONAL REQUIRED INFORMATION: NONE

ADDRESS:	(for hand delivery): Room V/1008 1120 Vermont Avenue, N.W. Washington, D.C.	(for mailing): Administrative Office of U.S. Courts Human Resources Division, Room V/1008 1120 Vermont Avenue, N.W. Washington, D.C. 20544

THE ADMINISTRATIVE OFFICE IS AN EQUAL OPPORTUNITY EMPLOYER

VACANCY ANNOUNCEMENT

U.S. General Services Administration
Office of Personnel

Vacancy Number
Issue Date
Closing Date

Position: (PC-2-T281A) (1 VACANCY)
Realty Specialist, GS-1170-5/7

Promotion Potential: GS-11

Area of Consideration: REGIONWIDE*

Location: PBS, Real Estate Division, Interstate Branch, New York, NY.

THIS ANNOUNCEMENT SUPERSEDES AND CANCELS ANNOUNCEMENTS #57-92 AND #57A-92 WHICH ARE BEING REANNOUNCED TO EXPAND THE APPLICANT POOL. PERSONS WHO APPLIED UNDER ANNOUNCEMENTS #57-92 AND #57A-92 DO NOT NEED TO REAPPLY.

*The area of consideration is for advertising and distribution purposes only. Applications from outside the area of consideration will be accepted.

APPLICATIONS WILL BE ACCEPTED ONLY FROM GENERAL SERVICES ADMINISTRATION EMPLOYEES. ALL APPLICANTS MUST HAVE CAREER OR CAREER-CONDITIONAL STATUS.

THIS POSITION IS IN THE AFGE BARGAINING UNIT.

RELOCATION EXPENSES WILL NOT BE PAID.

THIS POSITION MAY BE FILLED THROUGH REASSIGNMENT OR CHANGE TO LOWER GRADE. YOU CANNOT BE PROMOTED INTO THIS POSITION UNLESS YOU HAVE PREVIOUSLY SERVED AT THE GRADE OF ENTRY OR AT A HIGHER GRADE.

NOTE: AN EMPLOYEE WHO ACCEPTS A CHANGE TO LOWER GRADE TO ENTER THIS DEVELOPMENTAL AGREEMENT MAY BE ENTITLED TO THE BENEFITS OF SALARY RETENTION.

THIS POSITION IS COVERED BY THE CAREER ADVANCEMENT AND DEVELOPMENTAL AGREEMENT (CADA). THIS TRAINING AGREEMENT PROVIDES A TRAINING PLAN THROUGH WHICH GENERAL SERVICES ADMINISTRATION EMPLOYEES WITH DEMONSTRATED POTENTIAL MAY BE COMPETITIVELY SELECTED AND TRAINED FOR NEW CAREER FIELDS UNRELATED TO THEIR PAST OCCUPATIONS.

THIS POSITION IS PROPERLY CLASSIFIED AT THE GS-11 LEVEL. HOWEVER, IT IS BEING ANNOUNCED ONLY AT GS-5 AND GS-7 AND WILL BE FILLED ONLY AT THOSE LEVELS, DEPENDING UPON THE QUALIFICATIONS OF THE INDIVIDUAL CANDIDATE. THE SELECTED CANDIDATE MAY BE PROMOTED TO THE NEXT HIGHER GRADE LEVEL AS AN EXCEPTION TO THE MERIT PROMOTION PLAN WHEN THE TIME-IN-GRADE AND EXPERIENCE REQUIREMENTS ARE MET AND THE ABILITY TO PERFORM AT EACH

GSA FORM 2507 (REV. 6-89)

SUCCESSIVELY HIGHER LEVEL HAS BEEN DEMONSTRATED. PROMOTIONS WILL BE CONTINGENT UPON CERTIFICATION OF SATISFACTORY PERFORMANCE UNDER THE TRAINING AGREEMENT.

SUMMARY OF DUTIES:
Incumbent assists in the acquisition of real property for the Government by purchase, condemnation, permit, exchange, donation, lease, or other rights of use. Participates in the study, survey, analysis, assignment, and economic utilization of office space occupied by Federal agencies. Researches legal and technical materials and assists in the development of reports. Performs other duties as assigned.

ALL APPLICANTS MUST POSSESS OR BE ABLE TO OBTAIN A VALID STATE DRIVER'S LICENSE.

APPLICATION ON THE BASIS OF EXPERIENCE AND TRAINING:
YEARS OF EXPERIENCE:

GRADE	GENERAL	SPECIALIZED	TOTAL
GS-5	3	0	3
GS-7	0	1	1

SUMMARY OF QUALIFICATIONS:
GENERAL EXPERIENCE:
Three years of progressively responsible experience which demonstrates the ability to:
1. Analyze problems to identify significant factors, gather pertinent data, and recognize solutions;
2. Plan and organize work; and
3. Communicate effectively orally and in writing.

To be creditable, at least one year of general experience must have been equivalent to the next lower grade level.

SPECIALIZED EXPERIENCE:
Experience which is in or directly related to the line of work of the position to be filled and which has equipped the applicant with the particular knowledges, skills, and abilities to successfully perform the duties of that position. For GS-7, one year of the specialized experience must have been at least equivalent to the GS-5 level.

SUBSTITUTION OF EDUCATION FOR EXPERIENCE:
FOR GS-5:
Successful completion of a full 4-year course of study in any field leading to a bachelor's degree, in an accredited college or university.

FOR GS-7:
One full academic year of graduate-level education (including law school education) in an accredited college or university. Education must demonstrate the knowledges, skills, and abilities to do the work.

-OR-

An applicant may qualify at the GS-7 level if the education requirements for GS-5 are met and the applicant meets one of the "superior academic achievement" requirements listed below:

qualifications may then be credited at the rate of two (2) months of experience for one (1) month on the job under the terms of this training agreement. Promotions will be exempt from the Merit Promotion Plan and in all cases will be contingent upon certification of satisfactory performance under the training agreement.

EVALUATION CRITERIA:
The ranking of candidates shall be based on the basis of potential. Job elements such as ability to handle several tasks concurrently, ability to communicate orally, ability to communicate in writing, ability to work under pressure, and ability to work under minimum supervision will be considered in the evaluation and ranking of candidates. All job elements will be given equal weight.

HOW TO APPLY:
GSA employees interested in applying for this position must submit GSA Form 2422, Vacancy Application; SF-171, Application for Federal Employment; and a copy of a current annual performance appraisal. All applicants are also requested to submit GSA Form R2-1464, Background Survey Questionnaire. Application forms are available at any GSA office. All completed applications must be sent to the General Services Administration, Personnel Division, 2CPE, Room 18-110, 26 Federal Plaza, New York, NY 10278. All applications must be received or postmarked on or before June 11,

FAILURE TO SUBMIT THE SF-171 WILL AUTOMATICALLY RESULT IN AN INELIGIBLE RATING. YOUR SF-171 ALONE WILL BE USED TO DETERMINE YOUR BASIC ELIGIBILITY FOR THE POSITION. THEREFORE, IT IS YOUR RESPONSIBILITY TO PROVIDE COMPLETE AND ACCURATE INFORMATION ON THE SF-171. ALL APPLICATION MATERIALS WILL BE RETAINED IN THE MERIT PROMOTION FILE AS A RECORD OF THIS ACTION.

OFFICIAL PERSONNEL FOLDERS WILL NOT BE USED FOR CANDIDATE EVALUATION.

PERSONNEL CONTACT: Please contact Esther Jackman on FTS or (212) 264-8298 for further information.

NOTE: IF YOU ARE HEARING IMPAIRED, FTS OR (212) 264-8298 IS EQUIPPED WITH A SPECIAL TELECOMMUNICATIONS DEVICE (TDD).

USE OF POSTAGE-PAID GOVERNMENT AGENCY ENVELOPES OR ANY OTHER METHOD OF DELIVERY AT GOVERNMENT EXPENSE (SUCH AS THE USE OF OVERNIGHT MAIL) TO FILE JOB APPLICATIONS IS A VIOLATION OF FEDERAL LAW AND REGULATIONS. CANDIDATES SUBMITTING SUCH APPLICATIONS WILL NOT RECEIVE CONSIDERATION.

Consideration will be given to all qualified applicants without regard to race, color, creed, national origin, sex, non-disqualifying handicap, marital status, age, religious affiliation, or membership or non-membership in employer organization.

GSA FORM 2307 BACK (REV. 6-89)

1. Standing in the upper third of the graduating class in the college, university, or major subdivision, such as the College of Liberal Arts or the School of Business Administration, based on completed courses.

2. Grade point average (GPA) of 3.0 or higher out of a possible 4.0 ("B" or better) based on the average of all completed college courses at the time of application or courses completed during the final 2 years of the undergraduate curriculum.

3. GPA of 3.5 or higher out of a possible 4.0 ("B+" or better) based on the average of all completed courses in the major field at time of application or of all such courses completed during the final 2 years of the undergraduate curriculum.

4. Election to membership in Phi Beta Kappa, Sigma Xi, or one of the national honorary scholastic societies meeting the minimum requirements of the Association of College Honor Societies, other than freshman honor societies.

NOTE: Grade point averages are rounded to one decimal place. For example, 2.95 is rounded to 3.0 and 2.94 is rounded to 2.9.

NOTE: If you are applying under the Superior Academic Achievement provision, please include OPM Form 1170/17 or a copy of your college transcript(s) specifying all courses taken.

COMBINATIONS OF SUCCESSFULLY COMPLETED EDUCATION AND EXPERIENCE MAY BE USED TO MEET TOTAL QUALIFICATION REQUIREMENTS.

IF APPLICATION IS MADE ON THE BASIS OF EXPERIENCE AND EDUCATION, THE APPLICANT MUST MEET THE QUALIFICATIONS REQUIREMENTS OF THE POSITION WITHIN 30 CALENDAR DAYS OF THE CLOSING DATE.

APPLICATION ON THE BASIS OF POTENTIAL:
You may apply if you feel you have the potential to perform in the target position, Realty Specialist, GS-1170-11. General Schedule employees may apply if they are serving at GS-5 or if they have served at a higher grade. Wage grade employees may apply if they are serving or have served at a grade level which has demonstrated the possession of a level of experience equivalent, in the opinion of the evaluation panel, to the entry training level.

If you are already in the line of work, the series, and the grade of the target position, Realty Specialist, GS-1170-11, your application will not be accepted, as there would be no advantage in your being trained for a position similar to the one you are already occupying. If you are already serving in the grade of the target position, you may apply if the target position is in a different line of work. You would enter the program as a trainee and be qualified for the new career at the target level at the end of successful training. At the end of successful training, the selected candidate may be promoted to the target position. Before final assignment to the position, the selected candidate must make up the difference in qualifications between what he/she brings into the program and the qualifications required (whether general experience or specialized experience or both) for the target position as published in such Handbook X-118; training time to make up the difference in such

MERIT PROMOTION PROGRAM
DEPARTMENT OF THE NAVY
Consolidated Civilian Personnel Office
Philadelphia, Staten Branch Branch
355 Front Street
Staten Island, New York 10304

VACANCY ANNOUNCEMENT

POSITION: RECREATION AID GS-189-02 $13,937.00 P.A.

ANNOUNCEMENT NO.

LOCATION: NAVAL STATION NEW YORK, STATEN ISLAND, NEW YORK

OPENING DATE:

CLOSING DATE:

AREA OF CONSIDERATION: ALL FEDERAL ACTIVITIES IN THE NEW YORK
METROPOLITAN AREA, REINSTATEMENT, HANDICAPPED AND VRA
ELIGIBLES.

| Competitive Status Required: YES | Written Test: NO | Position Subject to Probationary Period: NO |

AMENDMENT: TO AREA OF CONSIDERATION AND UPDATE SALARY.

THIS POSITION IS LOCATED IN THE MORALE, WELFARE, AND RECREATION DEPARTMENT OF NAVAL STATION NEW YORK.

DUTIES:
The purpose of this position is to provide information and to assist patrons in utilizing the Gym/Fitness Center/Recreation Center.

- Provides information to patrons which assist them in selecting and furthering their interests in the respective area.
- Maintains custody of equipment assigned to the activity.
- Conducts daily inventory of equipment for issue and retail merchandise.
- Operates cash register and ensures accountability of cash receipts in his/her control.
- Perform other duties as assigned.

NOTE: MUST BE ABLE TO LIFT UP TO 50 LBS. OF EQUIPMENT.

CONTINUED OVER →

INSTRUCTIONS AND INFORMATION TO APPLICANTS

Send SF-171 and Supplemental forms, if required, to:
CONSOLIDATED PERSONNEL OFFICE, PHILADELPHIA, STATEN ISLAND BRANCH OFFICE,
355 FRONT STREET, STATEN ISLAND NEW YORK 10304

Applications will not be returned. Only applicants meeting basic qualifications requirements will be ranked. Rating and ranking will be based on appraisals of performance and quality of experience, education, training, knowledge, skill, self-development, and awards as you describe in the SF-171 and additional statements. DO NOT USE COPIES OF POSITION DESCRIPTIONS. Qualifications determinations will be made as of the closing date of this announcement. for positions being filled below the target level, the selectee may be promoted to the target position, or as appropriate, through intervening grades without further competition upon meeting Office of Personnel Management qualification requirements, demonstration of ability to perform at the higher level and assignment of increased responsibilities. Promotion, however, is neither guaranteed nor promised. This announcement does to preclude filling this position by other means such as appointment from OPM register, Reassignment, Transfer or Reinstatement. Any selection will be made without discrimination because of Race, Religion, Color, Sex, Age, Etc. Special consideration for re-promotion has already been given to those known eligible and to be considered further, they must make specific application under this announcement and compete with other applicants. **THIS ANNOUNCEMENT IS SUBJECT TO RESTRICTIONS IMPOSED BY DOD.**

EQUAL OPPORTUNITY EMPLOYER

DEPARTMENT OF THE NAVY
CONSOLIDATED CIVILIAN PERSONNEL OFFICE
PHILADELPHIA, STATEN ISLAND BRANCH
355 FRONT STREET
STATEN ISLAND, NEW YORK 10304
OFFICIAL BUSINESS

FIRST-CLASS MAIL
POSTAGE & FEES
USN
PERMIT NO G-9

VACANCY
ANNOUNCEMENT

ANNOUNCEMENT CONTINUED:

QUALIFICATION REQUIREMENTS:
IN ADDITION TO MEETING THE TIME IN GRADE RESTRICTIONS, APPLICANTS MUST MEET THE EXPERIENCE RE-QUIREMENT SPECIFIED IN CIVIL SERVICE HANDBOOK X-118, SERIES 189.

JOB-RELATED RANKING ELEMENTS:
A. Knowledge of materials to be used for various athletic programs.
B. Ability to advise patrons on proper and safe use of athletic equipment.
C. Ability to meet and deal courteously with all patrons.

NOTE: ATTACH A STATEMENT DESCRIBING HOW YOU MEET THE KNOWLEDGE, SKILL, AND/OR ABILITY REQUIRED BY EACH RANKING ELEMENT AND IDENTIFY WHICH JOB OR WHAT EDUCATION/TRAINING SHOWN ON YOUR SF-171 GAVE YOU THIS KNOWLEDGE, SKILL, AND/OR ABILITY.

NOTE: PLEASE ATTACH A COPY OF YOUR LATEST ANNUAL PERFORMANCE APPRAISAL AND SF-50.

Announcement No. VA-0638

Department of Veterans Affairs

RECREATION/CREATIVE ARTS THERAPIST, GS-638-5/6/7/9/11

Applications will be accepted until further notice.

DESCRIPTION OF WORK

Recreation/creative arts therapist (art, dance, music, or psychodrama) evaluate the history, interest, aptitudes, and skills of patients by interviews, inventories, tests, and measurements. They use such findings, along with medical records and the therapy orders of physicians or nurses, to develop and implement therapy activities for individual patients. These therapy approaches are directed toward achieving such therapeutic objectives as diminishing emotional stress of patients, providing a sense of achievement, channeling energies and interests into acceptable forms of behavior, aiding physical and mental rehabilitation, and promoting successful community re-entry.

OPTIONS

080 Creative Arts Therapist (Art)
081 Creative Arts Therapist (Dance)
082 Creative Arts Therapist (Music)
083 Creative Arts Therapist (Psychodrama)
084 Recreation Therapist

LOCATION OF POSITIONS

The positions to be filled from this announcement are located in VA medical centers and outpatient clinics throughout the United States and Puerto Rico. Some positions may exist in other Federal agencies.

SALARY

Your starting salary depends upon the duties and responsibilities of the position being filled. There are opportunities for promotion to higher grade levels, periodic increases within each grade level, additional increases for superior performance, and increases in Federal salaries based on comparability with the private sector.

QUALIFICATION REQUIREMENTS

BASIC REQUIREMENTS

You must be a citizen of the United States.

English Language Proficiency: If you are appointed to a direct patient-care position, you must be proficient in spoken and written English as required by 38 USC 4105 (c).

EDUCATION

Successful completion of a full four year course of study from an accredited college or university leading to a bachelor's degree with a major in recreational therapy, a creative arts therapy field (art therapy, dance therapy, music therapy, or psychodrama) or a major in an appropriate subject-matter field with therapeutic emphasis or concentration. The degree must have included a minimum of nine (9) semester hours in non-practicum coursework in subjects which are directly related to the therapy field for which you are applying.

EDUCATION AND EXPERIENCE

GS-5: The education described above is fully qualifying.

GS-6: Successful completion of a degree-related program of 6 months (1040 clock hours) clinical practice/practicum planned to assure professional competence in the particular therapy specialty.

GS-7: One full year of appropriate graduate level education or one year of specialized recreation/creative arts therapy experience comparable to the GS-5 level in the Federal service.

GS-9: Two full years of graduate level education, a master's or equivalent graduate degree in an appropriate field or one year of specialized experience comparable to the GS-7 level in the Federal service.

GS-11: Three full years of graduate level education, a Ph.D or equivalent graduate degree in an appropriate field or one year of specialized experience comparable to the GS-9 level in the Federal service.

COMBINING EDUCATION AND EXPERIENCE

Combinations of successfully completed graduate education and specialized experience may be used to meet total qualification requirements.

QUALIFYING EXPERIENCE

Experience must have been in activities or programs which require application of a knowledge of the concepts, principles, and practices of recreational therapy or one of the creative arts therapy specializations. This experience must involve the use of therapeutic approaches to maintain the physical and/or mental health or to achieve the physical and/or mental rehabilitation of persons.

For positions at any grade, the required amount of experience will not in itself be accepted as proof of qualification for a position. Your record of education and experience must clearly demonstrate that you have the ability to perform the duties of the position. The primary consideration is the quality and responsibility level of experience.

SUPERIOR ACADEMIC ACHIEVEMENT

Individuals who have completed all the requirements for or who are candidates for an appropriate bachelor's degree from an accredited college or university within 9 months of the date of application may be rated eligible for GS-7 provided they meet one of the requirements listed below:

a. Standing in the upper third of their class based on completed college work at the time of application for the position. This is the upper third of the class in the college or university, or major subdivision (e.g., school of engineering, school of business administration).

b. College grade average of "B" (3.0 or higher on a 4 point scale). This is either:
  (1) the average of all completed college courses at the time of application for the position, OR
  (2) the average of all college courses completed during the last 2 years of the undergraduate curriculum.

c. College grade average of "B+" (3.5 or higher on a 4 point scale) in the major field, where such field is fully qualifying and directly applicable to the specialty field of the position to be filled. This is either:
  (1) the average of completed courses in the major field at the time of application for the position, OR
  (2) the average of college courses completed in the major field during the last 2 years of the undergraduate curriculum.

Grade-point averages should be rounded to one decimal place. For example, 2.95 should be rounded to 3.0 and 2.94 should be rounded to 2.9. Senior students may be rated provisionally eligible under b(2) or c(2), provided they had the required average in the junior year. They will be required to submit evidence at the time of appointment that the required average was maintained during the senior year.

d. Election to membership in Phi Beta Kappa, Sigma Xi, or one of the other national honorary scholastic societies meeting the minimum requirements of the Association of College Honor Societies, other than freshman honor societies.

BASIS OF RATING

There is no written test. You will be rated on the extent and quality of your education, experience, and training relevant to the duties of the position. Such ratings will be based on your statements in the application and on any additional information obtained by our office. You will be rated for all grade levels for which you are qualified and for which you will accept employment as indicated on your application.

LENGTH OF ELIGIBILITY

If you are qualified, your name will be maintained on the list of eligibles established under this announcement for a period of 12 months. You may submit up-to-date information about your qualifications before that time period ends. A letter or an Amendment to Application for Federal Employment (Standard Form 172) may be used for this purpose. Do not submit information until two months before your eligibility expires unless you believe it will help you qualify for a higher grade.

If you do not update your records within the last 60 days of your eligibility period, you will receive no further consideration for Federal employment until you update your application. We will not notify you that your eligibility period is about to end.

EQUAL EMPLOYMENT OPPORTUNITY

All qualified applicants will receive consideration for appointment without regard to race, religion, color, national origin, sex, political affiliation, age or any other non-merit factor.

HOW TO APPLY

Please submit the following forms:

1. Application for Federal Employment, Standard Form 171. Please show the title of the position for which you are applying, the announcement number, and the lowest salary you are willing to accept. Standard Form 171 also contains instructions for claiming Veteran's Preference.

2. Supplemental Qualifications Statement for Recreation/Creative Arts Therapist, OPM Form 1170/83. Please read the instructions carefully and complete the form as directed.

3. List of College Courses and Certificate of Scholastic Achievement, OPM Form 1170/17. This form may be used to furnish a listing of all your completed college courses including semester-hour credits received. Students should also list the courses now being taken, the anticipated dates of completion and credits to be received. If you wish to qualify for the grade GS-7 on the basis of superior academic achievement, be certain to fill out Part III of this form. Transcripts of college records may be used, if you prefer.

4. Application for 10-point Veteran's Preference, Standard Form 15, (if appropriate). Include copies of documentary evidence required by that form. Original evidence will be returned to applicants. Other veteran's preference information is contained in the instructions of Standard Form 171.

5. VA Employment Availability Form, 5-3447. Retain accompanying Job Locations list for your records.

WHERE TO OBTAIN FORMS

Information about forms or application instructions may be obtained from a VA medical center or an Office of Personnel Management Job Information Center (located in most large cities). Consult the telephone directory for the one nearest you. Information may also be obtained from the VA Delegated Examining Unit by calling toll-free, 800-368-6008. Virginia residents may call toll-free 800-552-3045.

Mail your application to:

Department of Veterans Affairs
Delegated Examining Unit
P.O. Box 24269
Richmond, VA 23224-0269

---

the position to be filled. To be creditable, specialized experience must have been at least equivalent to the next lower grade level in the normal line of progression for the occupation in the organization.

Superior Academic Achievement: The superior academic achievement provision is applicable to all occupations covered by this standard.

Graduate Education: Education in a field of study which provided the knowledge, skills, and abilities necessary to do the work.

Completion of graduate level education in the amounts shown in the table, in addition to meeting the basic requirements, is qualifying for positions at GS-7 through GS-11, and GS-12 research positions. A year of full-time graduate education is considered to be the number of credit hours which the school attended has determined represents 1 year of full-time study. If this number cannot be obtained from the school, 18 semester hours should be considered an academic year of graduate study.

Research Positions: Positions which primarily involve scientific inquiry or investigation, or research-type exploratory development of a creative or advanced scientific nature, where the knowledge required to successfully perform the work is typically and primarily acquired through graduate study (master's or equivalent degree for GS-11, Ph.D. or equivalent for GS-12). The work is such that the academic preparation will equip the applicant to fully perform the professional work of the position after a short orientation period.

1. Qualification on the basis of education—Applicants for such research positions can be considered qualified for GS-11 if they possess an appropriate master's or equivalent graduate degree, and qualified for GS-12 if they possess a Ph.D. or equivalent doctoral degree.

2. Qualification on the basis of experience—Applicants who furnish positive evidence that they have performed highly creative or outstanding research that has led or can lead to major advances in a specific area of research, to a major advance in the discipline or field of science involved, or to major advances in science in general, can be rated under this provision for highly demanding research positions requiring similar abilities. Under these circumstances, applicants can be rated eligible for the next higher grade above that for which they would normally be rated, provided they have not been rated eligible at this higher grade on the basis of meeting the graduate study requirements described in paragraph 1. above. That is, applicants cannot receive an "extra" grade for education, and an additional "extra" grade for appropriate experience.

(p. 4)

ADDITIONAL EXPERIENCE AND EDUCATION REQUIREMENTS FOR GS-7 AND ABOVE

In addition to meeting the basic entry qualification requirements, applicants must have either specialized experience or directly related education in the amounts shown in the table below. Applicants who meet education requirements for a higher grade are also qualified for appropriate positions at lower grades.

Grade	Education	OR	Specialized Experience
GS-7	1 full year of graduate-level education or superior academic achievement	OR	1 year at least equivalent to GS-5
GS-9	2 full years of progressively higher level graduate education or master's or equivalent graduate degree	OR	1 year at least equivalent to GS-7
GS-11	3 full years of progressively higher level graduate education or Ph.D. or equivalent doctoral degree	OR	1 year at least equivalent to GS-9
GS-12 & above			1 year at least equivalent to next lower grade level
Research Positions			
GS-11 research positions	Master's or equivalent graduate degree		1 year at least equivalent to GS-9
GS-12 research positions	Ph.D. or equivalent doctoral degree		1 year at least equivalent to GS-11
GS-13 and above research positions			1 year at least equivalent to next lower grade

NOTE: Education and experience may be combined to meet the above requirements.

Specialized Experience: Experience which has equipped the applicant with the particular knowledge, skills, and abilities to perform successfully the duties of the position and which is typically in or related to the work of

OFFICE OF PERSONNEL MANAGEMENT

QUALIFICATION STANDARDS

(p. 5)

PROFESSIONAL POSITIONS

To receive this rating, the work must have been creative in the sense that it developed a basic principle, product, concept, method, approach, or technique, or provided a body of basic information that opened the way for a major advance in the discipline or field of science involved, or to advances in science in general, by providing a method of solving other problems, opening areas of research, or providing the means of exploiting the application of science in a major area.

Combination of Graduate Education and Professional Experience: Combinations of successfully completed graduate level education and specialized experience may be used to meet total experience requirements. Only graduate level education in excess of the amount required for the next lower grade level may be combined with experience. For example, an applicant with six months of appropriate experience equivalent to GS-7 (50 percent of the experience requirement for GS-9), and 27 semester hours of appropriate graduate education (50 percent of the education requirement for GS-9, in excess of that required for GS-7) would be qualified for a GS-9 position (assuming that there is no evidence that the attended college or university requires more than 18 hours as equivalent to a year of graduate study).

USE OF SELECTIVE FACTORS

Agencies may identify some positions covered by this standard that require knowledge, skills, and abilities (KSA's) or other qualifications that are in addition to the minimum requirements prescribed in the standard. The need for these special requirements can be met through the use of selective factors in both the competitive and inservice recruitment processes for positions at any grade level covered by this standard.

There are a variety of situations where agencies would be warranted in limiting consideration to applicants who possess the particular qualifications required to perform the work of such positions. For example, an agency may require specific kinds of training appropriate for filling positions concerned with scientific research and development activities, or may require specific educational courses or combinations of courses (where the individual occupational requirement permits applicants to qualify based on several combinations of educational course-work) to meet other specialized agency requirements. Also, an agency filling an international economist position may require that applicants for such a position possess certain kinds of knowledge in international economics. In this case, since applicants can qualify on the basis of education, the agency may also require certain types of educational courses. That agency may not, however, require applicants for statistical clerk, or other positions which do not require completion of a degree, to have a degree. Similarly, in some cases, consideration may be limited only to those applicants who possess an appropriate license, registration, or certification, if possession of such is determined to be necessary for carrying out the responsibilities of a position.

Selective factors must be job related, essential for the successful performance of the position and represent KSA's or other qualifications which could not be reasonably acquired on the job during the period of training customary for the position being filled.

ADDITIONAL QUALIFICATION REQUIREMENTS

In addition to meeting basic and additional requirements, all applicants for some positions must also meet special requirements such as certification or licensure in a particular occupation. These situations are noted in individual occupational requirements in the attachment.

GS-638
(p. 52)

RECREATION/CREATIVE ARTS THERAPIST
GS-5/above

Basic Requirements:

Degree: recreational therapy or in a creative arts therapy field (art therapy, dance therapy, music therapy, or psychodrama); or a major in an appropriate subject-matter field with therapeutic emphasis or concentration.

Applicants who have graduated from an approved curriculum in recreational therapy or in a field directly applicable to the specialized creative arts therapy, and who have completed (as part of the degree and/or subsequently) a program of 6 months' (1040 clock hours) clinical practice/practicum planned to assure professional competence in the particular therapy specialty, may be rated eligible at grade GS-6. (A degree-related program of clinical practice/practicum involves, as a general rule, a period of 240 clock hours (6 weeks) pre-clinical training in the sophomore year, followed by up to 400 clock hours (10 weeks) of clinical practice/practicum in the junior and/or senior years. This 400 clock hours of degree-related practicum may be applied against the 6 months' clinical practice required for GS-6 eligibility. To illustrate: When an applicant holds a degree which has included 400 clock hours of practicum, a postgraduate program of clinical practice of 640 clock hours provides the combined total of 1040 clock hours required in qualifying for positions at grade GS-6.)

Evaluation of Experience:

Experience in activities or programs which do not require application of a knowledge of the concepts, principles, and practices of recreational therapy or one of the creative arts therapy specializations covered by this standard and which do not involve the use of therapeutic approaches to maintain the physical and/or mental health or to achieve the physical and/or mental rehabilitation of persons, e.g., Outdoor Recreation Specialist; Commercial Recreation Leader; Vocational Counselor, or other *diversional*-type recreation specialist positions is not qualifying for this series.

These individual occupational requirements have been approved by the Secretary of Veterans Affairs for use within the Veterans Health Services and Research Administration under the provisions of Section 4105, Title 38, U.S.C.

UNITED STATES DEPARTMENT OF STATE
JOB OPPORTUNITY ANNOUNCEMENT
An Equal Opportunity Employer

Position Title: Secretary (Typing)	Announcement Number:
Series and Grade: GS-318-07	Opening Date:
Promotion Potential: GS-08	Closing Date:
Office and Location: INM/C, Room 3418, N.S.	Supervisory: No
Security Clearance Required: Top Secret	Merit Pay: No

AREA OF CONSIDERATION: Applicants must current be career or career-conditional Federal Employees or have reinstatement or non-competitive eligibility

DUTIES:

   This position is located in the Bureau of International Narcotics Matters. The incumbent serves as secretary to the Controller/Executive Director. Duties include, but are not limited to: Typing and proofreading; receiving visitors and directing to appropriate officers as well as personally handling inquiries which need not be referred to others. Reviews incoming correspondence and attaches pertinent background material. Schedules appointments as necessary. Arranges for travel, including authorization, advance, flight schedule, hotels, rental cars and visas when necessary. Upon return of traveler, obtains complete travel information and prepares travel voucher for reimbursement. Uses the WANG word-processor for special projects, using independent judgment to devise new information storage procedures. Types correspondence, forms, reports, cables etc. into final form.

QUALIFICATION REQUIREMENTS (Handbook X-118): Applicants must have the required experience or education as described below and, when specified, any selective factors.

Candidates must have one year of specialized experience equivalent to next lower grade which is directly related to the position to be filled and which has equipped the candidate with the particular knowledge, skills, and abilities to successfully perform the duties of the position. A qualified typist is required.

One year time-in-grade requirements apply.

All applicants not currently employed by the Department of State who are selected for employment will be required to submit to a urinalysis to screen for illegal drug use prior to appointment. Appointment will be contingent upon a negative drug test result.

RANKING FACTORS: Applicants who meet the qualification requirements described above will be further evaluated by determining the extent to which their education, experience, training, awards and supervisory appraisal indicated they possess the knowledges, skills, abilities and other characteristics described below.

1. Ability to plan and coordinate office activities.
2. Ability to comprehend and interpret written material.
3. Ability to establish priorities.
4. Ability to analyze incoming correspondence.
5. Ability to research information.

APPLICATIONS WILL NOT BE ACCEPTED AFTER THE CLOSING DATE OF THE ANNOUNCEMENT
(SEE REVERSE FOR HOW TO APPLY)

SELECTIONS WILL BE MADE WITHOUT DISCRIMINATION AS TO POLITICAL, RELIGIOUS, UNION OR NON-UNION AFFILIATION MARITAL STATUS, COLOR, NATIONAL ORIGIN, RACE, SEX, AGE, OR DISABILITIES WHICH ARE NOT DISQUALIFYING

FORM
2-90 DS-1737

DEPARTMENT OF THE TREASURY
UNITED STATES CUSTOMS SERVICE

MERIT PROMOTION PLAN

VACANCY ANNOUNCEMENT

51325, PAPM

VACANCY ANNOUNCEMENT NUMBER	
92/SECTOR*	
OPENING DATE	CLOSING DATE

POSITION TITLE

Sector Enforcement Specialist

PAY PLAN, SERIES AND GRADE	
GS-1801-5/7/9	

ORGANIZATION AND DUTY STATION

U.S. Customs Service
Office of Enforcement
Duty Station: See Geographic Locations

NUMBER OF VACANCES	At the discretion of the Selecting Official, additional vacancies may be filled within 60 days after the closing date.
Several	

AREA OF CONSIDERATION

GOVERNMENTWIDE: Applications will be accepted from present and former Federal employees with competitive status.

Regardless of the stated Area of Consideration any employee of the Department of the Treasury may apply and be considered for this position.

Note: SEE "GEOGRAPHIC LOCATIONS" FOR SPECIFIC ANNOUNCEMENT NUMBERS.

This announcement is open continuously for 6 months from the opening date. The first cut-off date for the purpose of paneling and issuing the first selection register of this announcement will be 30 days from the opening date, with subsequent cut-off dates as selection registers are requested. Candidates may apply throughout the life of this announcement, but must be within sixty (60) days of meeting all qualification and time-in-grade requirements at the time of submission of their application. To ensure accurate qualifications and consideration, please indicate the date of your last promotion (not with-in-grade increase) under "WORK EXPERIENCE" on your SF-171 (i.e., your current position of record). All applicants should provide a copy of their last SF-50 to offer documentation regarding eligibility.

SUMMARY OF DUTIES: Operating out of one of seven regional SECTOR Communication Centers, the incumbent supports real-time enforcement agencies. Monitors the operation of communication links; develops pertinent background data; researches local, National and International Automated Enforcement Information Systems for the purpose of identifying and developing applicable tactical and operational data; and communicates the results of data searches back to the inquiring parties. The incumbent provides Watch and Duty Officers, the office of Investigations, Regional Intelligence Branches and other concerned individuals/offices with written documentation (e.g., Memorandums of Information Received) noting significant interpretations/analysis/findings provided to the SECTOR user community. Additionally, the incumbent provides emergency assistance to law enforcement personnel; monitors the operation of radio and network equipment; conducts the initial analysis when equipment/transmission problems are encountered; conducts the initiates actions required to restore radio communications as appropriate.

POSITION TITLE

SECTOR ENFORCEMENT SPECIALIST (GS-1801-5/7/9)

VACANCY ANNOUNCEMENT NO.	
92/SECTOR*	
CLOSING DATE	

SUMMARY OF QUALIFICATION REQUIREMENTS: GS-05: Applicants must have 3 years of General Experience, 1 year of which was at least equivalent to the GS-04 in the Federal Service or have a 4-year course of study above high school leading to a bachelor's degree. No specialized experience is required.

GS-07: Applicants are not required to possess any general experience, but must have 1 year of Specialized Experience equivalent to the GS-05 level in the Federal Service or have one full academic year of graduate level education or law school or superior academic achievement.

GS-09: Applicants are not required to possess any general experience, but must have 1 year of Specialized Experience equivalent to the GS-07 level in the Federal Service or two full academic years of graduate level education or a master's or equivalent graduate degree or LL.B or J.D.

GENERAL EXPERIENCE: Is described as progressively responsible experience which demonstrates the ability to: 1) analyze problems to identify significant factors, gather pertinent data, and recognize solutions; 2) plan and organize work; and 3) communicate effectively orally and in writing.

Such experience may have been gained in administrative, professional, technical, investigative or other responsible work.

SPECIALIZED EXPERIENCE: Is experience which is directly related to the line of work for the position to be filled and which has equipped the applicant with the particular knowledge, skills, and abilities to successfully perform the duties of the position.

Equivalent combinations of education and experience are qualifying for all grade levels.

TIME-IN-GRADE: Applicants must have served 52 weeks equivalent to the next lower grade.

ELIGIBLE CANDIDATES WILL BE EVALUATED AS PROVIDED IN THE CUSTOMS SERVICE MERIT PROMOTION PLAN AGAINST THE FOLLOWING PRIMARY CRITERIA:

1. Experience in providing tactical and/or analytical support.

2. Experience in utilizing automated data bases.

3. Knowledge of communications/tactical support systems.

POSITION TITLE | VACANCY ANNOUNCEMENT NO. 92/SECTOR* | CLOSING DATE

SECTOR ENFORCEMENT SPECIALIST (GS-1801-5/7/9)

IMMIGRATION CONTROL ACT: The Immigration Reform Control Act of 1986 weeks to preserve jobs for those who are legally entitled to them: American citizens and aliens who are authorized to work in our country. This law requires employers to verify that persons are eligible to work in the United States and requires employees to provide a document or documents that establish identity and employment eligibility.

GEOGRAPHIC LOCATIONS
SECTOR ENFORCEMENT SPECIALIST

Listed below are 4 vacancy announcement numbers and the applicable Regional Offices relating to each of the 4 vacancy announcements. You may apply for as many locations as you wish, keeping in mind that a separate application package must be submitted for each location for which you wish consideration. On each SF-171, CF-306, CF-307, annual performance appraisal, and a copy of your most recent SF-50 should reference the announcement number. Application packages which lack the identification described above may delay the processing of your application or eliminate you from consideration.

***** EACH LOCATION REQUIRES A SEPARATE APPLICATION PACKAGE ******

SOUTHEAST ENFORCEMENT AREA
ENF2/92-083TB
(202) 634-2976
MIAMI, FL and NEW ORLEANS, LA

SOUTHWEST ENFORCEMENT AREA
ENF2/92-085RDH
(202) 634-5154
HOUSTON, TX

NORTHWEST ENFORCEMENT AREA
ENF2/92-084LJS
(202) 634-2569
CHICAGO, IL and LONG BEACH, CA

NORTHEAST ENFORCEMENT AREA
ENF1/92-086DMN
(202) 634-5036
BOSTON, MA and NEW YORK SEAPORT

POSITION TITLE | VACANCY ANNOUNCEMENT NO. 92/SECTOR* | CLOSING DATE

SECTOR ENFORCEMENT SPECIALIST (GS-1801-5/7/9)

ONLY HIGHLY QUALIFIED CANDIDATES WILL THEN BE EVALUATED AGAINST THE FOLLOWING SECONDARY CRITERIA:

4. Ability to communicate in writing.

5. Ability to communicate orally with various levels of personnel within and outside the agency.

REMARKS:

VACANCIES MAY EXIST IN SOME OR ALL GEOGRAPHIC AREAS LISTED. THIS ANNOUNCEMENT WILL BE USED FOR THOSE LOCATIONS LISTED AS VACANCIES OCCUR. THESE POSITIONS REQUIRE SHIFT WORK WHICH COVERS A 24 HOUR-A-DAY, 7 DAYS-A-WEEK ROTATIONG SCHEDULE. EXTENSIVE AMOUNTS OF OVERTIME MAY ALSO BE REQUIRED.

Applicants must be within 60 days of meeting time-in-grade and qualification requirements at the time of submission of their application. Applications are not to be mailed in U.S. Government "For Official Use Only" postage and fees paid envelopes. Names of individuals submitting applications in Government envelopes may be referred to the office of Internal Affairs for action.

CONSIDERATION WILL BE GIVEN TO THOSE ELIGIBLE UNDER SPECIAL APPOINTMENT AUTHORITIES (E.G., HANDICAP, VRA's, 30% DISABILITIES).

HOW TO APPLY: Customs employees wishing to be considered for this vacancy should (1) forward a completed and originally-signed SF-171 to the Personnel Office listed below; and (2) give a completed Supplemental Qualifications Statement (CF-307), Appraisal for Promotional Opportunities (CF-306), and a copy of their current performance appraisal of record (either CF-188 or CF-281) to their immediate supervisor on or before the closing date. All other applicants (see area of consideration): Forward a completed and originally-signed SF-171 and a copy of your current performance appraisal of record to the Personnel Office listed below. Forms CF-306, Appraisal for Promotional Opportunities, and CF-307, Supplemental Qualifications Statement (or their equivalents), are optional for all other applicants, but should be submitted in order to receive more complete consideration. Forms are available from the Personnel Office listed below or from any Customs personnel office.

(Does not apply unless checked.) This position is covered by Manual Supplement 51335-11 (formerly 51928-80), Selection Procedures for Key Managerial Positions. Applicants are to (1) (1) a completed and originally-signed SF-171 to the Personnel Office listed below; and (2) a copy of their most recent supervisory appraisal of performance and submit CF-308, Employee Supplemental Qualifications Statement and Supervisory Appraisal for SES/Key Managerial Positions, to their current supervisor on or before the closing date. Applicants for these positions should not submit CF-306 or CF-307.

IMPORTANT NOTES:

1. Applicants wishing to be notified of the receipt and disposition of their application should complete a CF-69, Notification to Applicant, and submit it with their SF-171 to the Personnel Office.

2. All applicants are requested to complete and submit an OPM Form 1386, EEO Background Survey Data Questionnaire, with their SF-171 at the time of application; however, completion of this form is strictly voluntary and will in no way impact upon your consideration.

3. Applications or requested supplemental information forms are not to be mailed in U.S. Government "For Official Use Only" postage and fees paid envelopes.

4. The SF-171 must either be postmarked or received in the Personnel Office listed below no later than the closing date of this vacancy announcement. Customs employees must also give their CF-306, CF-307, and most recent performance appraisal to their supervisor on or before the closing date.

5. No additional information or enclosures, other than as specified above, are to be submitted. Do not submit copies of position descriptions, awards, or training certificates.

6. Qualification determinations will be based solely upon information submitted in accordance with the instructions on this vacancy announcement.

MAILING ADDRESS
U.S. Customs Service
Office of Enforcement
P.O. Box 7747
ATTN: 92/SECTOR*
Washington, DC 20044

ADDITIONAL INFORMATION ABOUT THIS VACANCY OR ABOUT THE APPLICATION PROCEDURES MAY BE OBTAINED BY CONTACTING:
For copies only, please call
(202) 634-5240
For information only, please
(202) 634-2569

THIS VACANCY ANNOUNCEMENT INCLUDES AN ADDITIONAL SHEET (CF 48, page 2) WHICH LISTS THE CONDITIONS OF EMPLOYMENT AND OTHER REQUIREMENTS OF THE POSITION(S) TO BE FILLED AS WELL AS ADDITIONAL REMARKS.

Customs Form 48 (071788)

U.S. DEPARTMENT OF HEALTH AND HUMAN SERVICES

PHOENIX INDIAN MEDICAL CENTER

PERSONNEL MANAGEMENT BRANCH
4212 N. 16TH STREET
PHOENIX, ARIZONA 85016

Announcement No. PM-92-24	Opening Date	Closing Date	Personnel: Date:	EEO: Date:

AMENDMENT
AMENDS DUTIES DESCRIPTION

POSITION:
Social Worker

LOCATION/DUTY STATION:
Social Services
Phoenix Indian Medical Center
Phoenix, Arizona

SERIES/GRADE/SALARY:
GS-185-09, $24,705.00 Per Annum
GS-185-11, $29,891.00 Per Annum

TYPE/NUMBER POSITIONS:
1 Number Positions
X Permanent Positions
___ Temporary-NTE:

AREA OF CONSIDERATION:
IHS Wide

SUPERVISORY/MANAGEMENT:
___ Yes, may require one year probationary period.
X No

PWS:
X Yes, to grade: 11
___ No known potential

PROMOTION POTENTIAL:
X Yes, to grade: 11
___ No known potential

HOUSING:
___ Yes, Government housing available
X Private housing only

TRAVEL EXPENSES:
X Yes, relocation expenses paid.
___ No expenses paid.

CONDITIONS OF EMPLOYMENT: If the selectee was born after December 31, 1956, he/she must provide proof of immunity to or evidence of adequate immunization against rubella and measles prior to entry on duty. The duty location may provide immunization or determine immunity or antibody through testing.

BRIEF DESCRIPTION OF DUTIES: Incumbent provides a full range of social work services for hospital and pediatric, obstetrics and gynecology patients, clinic outpatients, and their family members such as initial screening and assessment services for selected patients referred to the Department of Psychiatry; consultation and information services to medical and nursing staff on program and patient matters. Serves as consultant and in a service capacity for the Phoenix Area Indian Health Maternal and Child Health Program. Participates as co-worker and consultant in case and teaching conferences with physicians, residents, nursing staff, and other members of the health team. Serves as counselor for the hospital's employee assistance program. As assigned, plans and supervises assignments for social work graduate students, undergraduate students and summer co-steps. Prepares reports, surveys and studies as assigned. Performs other duties as assigned.

BASIC REQUIREMENTS: Degree - Social work. Must fulfill all of the requirements for the master's degree in social work in a school accredited by the Council on Social Work Education.

ADDITIONAL EXPERIENCE AND EDUCATION REQUIREMENTS: In addition to meeting the basic entry qualification requirements, applicants must have either specialized experience or directly related education as follows:

GRADE	EDUCATION	OR	SPECIALIZED EXPERIENCE
GS-9	2 full years of graduate level education or master's or equivalent graduate degree		1 year at least equivalent to GS-7
GS-11	3 full years of graduate level education of Ph.D. or equivalent graduate degree		1 year at least equivalent to GS-9

GRADUATE EDUCATION: Education above the baccalaureate level in a field of study which provided the knowledge, skills, and abilities necessary to do the work. A year of full-time graduate education is considered to be the number of credit hours which the school attended has determined represents one year of full-time study.

SPECIALIZED EXPERIENCE: Experience which is in or related to the line of work of the position to be filled and which has equipped the applicant with the specific knowledge, skills, and abilities to successfully perform the duties of the position, i.e., providing placement services, casework services to patients/families, serving as liaison with multiple public and private social welfare and health agencies, providing consultation services, etc.

Exception to Cumulative Years of Experience Requirement: Individuals who have 1 year of experience equivalent to the next lower grade may be rated eligible even though they do not meet the cumulative years of experience shown above, provided their background demonstrate the knowledges, skills and abilities necessary for successful job performance.

QUALITY OF EXPERIENCE: For positions at grade GS-9, experience must have been at a level comparable in scope and difficulty to that of grade GS-7 in the Federal service; for grade GS-11, experience must have been comparable in scope and difficulty to that of GS-9 in the Federal service.

TIME-IN-GRADE REQUIREMENTS: Candidates must have at least one year of service in positions no more than two grades lower than the position to be filled. (If selected under the Excepted Service Examining Plan, individuals may be appointed under Schedule A authority without regard to Time-in-Grade Requirements).

MOTOR VEHICLE OPERATION REQUIREMENT: Incumbent must qualify and maintain a current U.S. Government Operator's Identification Card.

SELECTIVE SERVICE CERTIFICATION: If you are male, born after December 31, 1959, and you want to be employed by the Federal Government, you must (subject to certain exemptions) be registered with Selective Service System. The attached PRE-APPOINTMENT CERTIFICATION STATEMENT FOR SELECTIVE SERVICE REGISTRATION, must be signed and dated and returned with your application.

LEGAL AND REGULATORY REQUIREMENTS: Candidates must meet time after competitive appointment, time-in-grade restrictions, and qualification requirements within 30 calendar days after the closing date of the vacancy announcement.

APPLICANTS OR CURRENT FEDERAL SERVICE EMPLOYEES CLAIMING INDIAN PREFERENCE MUST INDICATE IN ITEM 1 ON THEIR APPLICATION IF THEY WISH TO BE CONSIDERED UNDER THE INDIAN HEALTH SERVICE MERIT PROMOTION PLAN, EXCEPTED SERVICE EXAMINING PLAN, OR BOTH. IF NOT, THEY WILL BE CONSIDERED UNDER THE IHS MERIT PROMOTION PLAN ONLY.

ADDITIONAL SELECTIONS MAY BE MADE FROM THIS ANNOUNCEMENT WITHIN 90 DAYS FROM THE DATE OF THE CERTIFICATE PROVIDED THE VACANT POSITION IS AN IDENTICAL POSITION, SAME GEOGRAPHICAL LOCATION AND SAME CONDITIONS OF EMPLOYMENT.

PREFERENCE IN FILLING VACANCIES IS GIVEN TO QUALIFIED INDIAN CANDIDATES IN ACCORDANCE WITH THE INDIAN PREFERENCE ACT (TITLE 25, U.S. CODE, SECTION 472 AND 473). IN OTHER THAN THE ABOVE, THE INDIAN HEALTH SERVICE IS AN EQUAL OPPORTUNITY EMPLOYER.

INSTRUCTIONS FOR PHS COMMISSIONED CORPS CANDIDATES: Active duty candidates must submit a copy of curdes or billet description along with resumes or curriculum vitae showing work experience, dates of employment, names and addresses of supervisors, education, and other information reflecting qualifications for the position. In reference to IHS Circular No. 87-2, dated 07-09-87, Commissioned Corps candidates must meet full qualification requirements. If you are not on active duty and have applied for the Commissioned Corps, submit the same information as above (except billet description). Also, provide information on the current status of your application with the Public Health Service, Commissioned Corps Personnel Division. NOTE: Commissioned Corps applicants claiming Indian Preference will be evaluated by the Personnel Office against the applicable Preston standard of the civil service standard, if no Preston standard exists. These applicants must describe the experience gained in their two most recent positions and provide the dates they occupied those positions. In addition, Commissioned Corps Indian Preference applicants must also provide information regarding education, including degrees obtained and schools attended and they must include home/work telephone numbers if this information is not contained in the resumes. When required by the vacancy announcement, these applicants must submit specific information related to any knowledges, skills, and abilities which are used in the selective process. Commissioned Corps applicants claiming Indian Preference must submit Form BIA 4432, as proof of Indian Preference and also proof of possession of the appropriate license.

HOW TO APPLY: Applicants must submit the following required forms to the PHOENIX INDIAN MEDICAL CENTER, 4212 NORTH 16TH STREET, PERSONNEL MANAGEMENT BRANCH, PHOENIX, ARIZONA 85016 by the closing date. APPLICANTS WILL NOT BE CONSIDERED IF THE APPLICATION IS RECEIVED AFTER THE CLOSING DATE. ONCE AN APPLICATION HAS BEEN RECEIVED, WE WILL NOT HONOR REQUEST FOR COPIES. APPLICATIONS WILL BE ACCEPTED FROM INDIAN APPLICANTS, CAREER CONDITIONAL OR CAREER FEDERAL EMPLOYEES AND REINSTATEMENT ELIGIBLES BASED ON PRIOR FEDERAL SERVICE. For information concerning this announcement contact the Personnel Office at (602) 263-1575.

1. SF-171, APPLICATION FOR FEDERAL EMPLOYMENT, must be current, up-to-date and have an original signature.
2. PERFORMANCE APPRAISAL, if available, must be the most recent appraisal.
3. BIA Form 4432, VERIFICATION OF INDIAN PREFERENCE SIGNED BY THE APPROPRIATE BIA OFFICIAL, certification function on behalf of the BIA authorized by P.L. 93-638 contract to perform the certification function on behalf of the BIA. Applicants currently employed in the Phoenix Area wishing to claim Indian Preference, without attaching BIA Form 4432 to their SF-171, must state on their application that Indian Preference is a matter of record in their Official Personnel Folder. Failure to do so will result in loss of due consideration as an Indian Preference applicant.
4. SUPPLEMENTAL QUESTIONNAIRE ON KNOWLEDGES, SKILLS, AND ABILITIES.
5. Copy of latest Personnel action (SF-50B) to verify competitive status, if applicable.
6. Copy of DD-214, MILITARY DISCHARGE DOCUMENT, if applicable.
7. SELECTIVE SERVICE REGISTRATION, if applicable.
8. If claiming qualification based on education, candidates must submit copies of all transcripts (or proof of degree) or OPM Form 1170/17, List of College Courses.

A SMOKE-FREE WORK ENVIRONMENT IS PIMC POLICY.

SUPPLEMENTAL QUESTIONNAIRE
On Knowledges, Skills, and Abilities

Position applied for: __Social Worker, GS-185-9/11__

Announcement No: __PM-92-24__   Closing Date: ____

Evaluation Method: Evaluation will be made of experience, Performance Appraisals, Training, Letters of Commendation, Self-Development, Awards and Outside Activities, which are related to this position. To receive full credit for your qualification, provide a narrative statement of experience, training, education, awards, hobbies, self-developed achievements, and any other aspects of your background as they relate to the knowledges, skills and abilities (KSA's) outlined below and show the level of accomplishments and degree of responsibility. This supplement will be the principal basis for determining whether or not you are best qualified for the position. Describe your qualification in each of the following:

1. Ability and skill in providing intensive social casework services to clients.

2. Skill in oral and written communication.

3. Knowledge of social systems, community, environment, resources and services.

The information you provide is considered to be a part of your application and as such is certified by your signature on the SF-171 or equivalent.

_____   _____
Signature   Date

PRE-APPOINTMENT CERTIFICATION STATEMENT FOR
SELECTIVE SERVICE REGISTRATION

Important Notice

If you are a male born after December 31, 1959, and you want to be employed by the Federal Government, you must (subject to certain exemptions) be registered with the Selective Service System.

Privacy Act Statement

We need information on your registration with the Selective Service System to see whether you are affected by the laws we must follow in deciding who may be employed by the Federal Government.

Criminal Penalty Statement

A false statement by you may be grounds for not hiring you, or for firing you after you begin work. Also, you may be punished by fine or imprisonment (U.S. Code, Title 18, Section 1001).

Review

If your employing agency has informed you that you cannot be appointed to a position in an executive agency because of your failure to register, and you wish to establish that your non-compliance with the law was neither knowing nor willful, you may write to:

U.S. Office of Personnel Management
NACI Center
IOD-SAB
Boyers, Pennsylvania 16018

CERTIFICATION OF REGISTRATION STATUS

( ) I certify that I am registered with the Selective Service System.

( ) I certify that I am not required to be registered with the Selective Service System.

_____   _____
Legal Signature (please use ink)   Date Signed (please use ink)

OPPORTUNITIES IN THE FEDERAL GOVERNMENT

FOR

SOIL CONSERVATIONIST, SOIL SCIENTIST, RANGE CONSERVATIONIST

ANNOUNCEMENT: LS-NW-1

OPEN UNTIL FURTHER NOTICE

The Special Examining Unit of the Soil Conservation Service is accepting applications for the soil conservation, soil science and range conservation options at grades GS-5 and GS-7 for positions located throughout the country, except Hawaii.

BASIC REQUIREMENTS FOR GS-5

A. Successful completion of a full 4 year course of study leading to a bachelor's or higher, degree from an accredited college or university with a major in the pertinent field. This study must have included the specific coursework requirements as listed in each of the stated options below.

OR

B. A combination of four years of experience and education. The EXPERIENCE must be equivalent at least to the GS-5 level and demonstrate an understanding of the fundamental techniques and principles of the occupation equivalent to that acquired through completion of a 4 year course of study. THE COURSE WORK MUST INCLUDE THE STATED REQUIREMENTS FOR EACH OPTION.

SPECIFIC COURSE WORK REQUIREMENTS

Each disciplinary option has specific course requirements described below in semester hours. Multiply quarter hours by 2/3 to convert to semester hours.

SOIL CONSERVATIONIST

DESCRIPTION OF WORK:

Soil Conservationists advise on, administer, coordinate, perform, or supervise scientific work in a coordinated program of soil, water, and resource conservation which requires the application of a combination of agricultural sciences in order to bring about the proper land use and to improve the quality of the environment.

COURSE REQUIREMENTS:

A degree with a major in soil conservation or closely related agricultural or natural resource disciplines, such as soil science, agronomy, forestry, agricultural education, or agricultural engineering. The study must have included 30 semester hours in natural resources or an agricultural discipline including at least 12 semester hours in a combination of soil and crops or plant science. Of the 12 semester hours, a minimum of 3 semester hours must be in soils and 3 semester hours in crops or plant science.

OR

EDUCATION AND EXPERIENCE REQUIREMENTS:

Combination of education and experience - at least 30 semester hours in one or more of the disciplines as shown above, including at least 12 semester hours in a combination of soils/and crops or plant science, plus appropriate experience or additional education equivalent to a four-year degree.

SOIL SCIENTIST

DESCRIPTION OF WORK:

Soil Scientists study and investigate soils from the standpoint of their morphology, genesis, and distribution; their interrelated physical, chemical, and biological properties and processes; their relationships to climate, physiographic and vegetative influences; and their adaption to use and management in agriculture.

COURSE REQUIREMENTS:

A degree in soil science or a related discipline. The study must have included 30 semester hours or equivalent of biological, physical, or earth science, which includes at least 15 semester hours in such soils courses as soil genesis, pedology, soil chemistry, soil physics, and soil fertility.

OR

EDUCATION AND EXPERIENCE REQUIREMENTS:

Combination of education and experience - courses equivalent to a major in soil science, which includes at least 30 semester hours in the biological, physical, or earth sciences. At least 15 of these semester hours must be in the areas specified above, plus appropriate experience or additional education equivalent to a four-year degree.

RANGE CONSERVATIONIST

DESCRIPTION OF WORK:

Range Conservationists inventory, analyze, improve, protect, utilize and manage the natural resources of rangelands and related grazing lands; regulate grazing on public rangelands; develop cooperative relationships with range users; assist landowners to plan and apply range conservation programs; develop technical standards and specifications; conduct research on the principles underlying rangeland management; and develop new and improved instruments and techniques.

COURSE REQUIREMENTS:

A degree in range management, or a closely related discipline, which included at least 42 semester hours in a combination of plant, animal, and soil sciences and natural resources management, diversified as follows:

(1) 18 semester hours of course work in range management. Course work includes courses such as basic principles of range management; range plants; range ecology; range inventories and studies; range improvements, and ranch or rangeland planning.

(2) 15 semester hours of directly related course work in plant, animal and soil sciences. Course work must have included at least one course in each of these three scientific areas (i.e., plant, animal, and soil sciences). Acceptable course work includes courses such as plant taxonomy; plant physiology; plant ecology; animal nutrition; livestock production; and soil morphology or soil classification.

(3) 9 semester hours of course work in related resource management subjects. Course work includes such areas as wildlife management; watershed management; natural resource or agricultural economics; forestry; agronomy; forages; and outdoor recreation management.

OR

EDUCATION AND EXPERIENCE REQUIREMENTS:

Combination of education and experience - at least 42 semester hours of course work in a combination of the plant, animal and soil sciences and natural resources management, as shown above, plus appropriate experience or additional education equivalent to a four-year degree.

BASIC REQUIREMENTS FOR GS-7:

A. One year of professional experience in an appropriately related field, comparable in difficulty and responsibility to the GS-5 level of work in federal government service; OR

B. One full academic year of graduate education in a directly related field; OR

C. Appropriate degree and 12 months of student trainee experience which included one work period (at least 60 days) at the GS-5 grade level; OR

D. Completion of all academic requirements for a bachelor's degree which meets one of the following Superior Academic Achievements:

1. A standing in the upper third of your class or major subdivision (e.g. school of agriculture) at the time of application.

2. A grade point average of 2.95 or better (on a 4.0 scale) for all undergraduate courses completed by (a) the time of application, or (b) during the last 2 years of your undergraduate curriculum.

3. A grade point average of 3.5 or better (on a 4.0 scale) for all courses completed in your major field of study by (a) the time of application, or (b) during the last 2 years of your undergraduate curriculum.

4. Membership in a national honorary society (other than a freshman society) that meets the requirements of the Association of College Honor Societies.

If you apply for grade GS-7 based on Superior Academic Achievement, YOU MUST INDICATE THE BASIS FOR THIS ACHIEVEMENT IN PART III OF OPM FORM 1170/17, List of College Courses and Certificate of Scholastic Achievement.

HOW TO APPLY

Submit a completed Standard Form 171, CSC-Form 1311, and the Scholastic Achievement page of OPM Form 1170/17 and two photocopies of your university/college transcript from each university/college attended. TRANSCRIPTS ARE REQUIRED FOR MORE COMPLETE DOCUMENTATION. OPM Form 1386 is also requested. Only one set of these forms should be submitted; additional copies will be destroyed. One copy will be evaluated for all options for which you qualify.

1. Standard Form 171, Personal Qualification Statement: Include agricultural background and experience (paid or unpaid) in your application. Your description of experience need not be lengthy, but should include all pertinent information.

2. OPM Form 1311, Work Location Preference: You may indicate up to six states of preference. One state is the state in which you primarily wish to be considered for employment. You will receive consideration in any one of the 5 secondary states in which you indicate an interest only when there is an insufficient number of applicants who indicate that state as their primary state of interest.

3. TRANSCRIPTS AND OPM Form 1170/17, List of College Courses and Certificate of Scholastic Achievement: It is necessary for you to show your scholastic achievement on the back page of this form and sign the signature page if you wish to receive credit in this area. Transcripts are required; however, if your transcript is no longer available from your college, you may list your course work on this form. You must give course numbers and college name for all courses taken. DO NOT HAVE THE SCHOOLS SEND TRANSCRIPTS DIRECTLY TO THE EXAMINING OFFICE. You are responsible for providing evidence that a given course fully meets the specified course requirements. For this purpose, you may be asked to submit a copy of your college department's outline or syllabus which provides the information necessary to evaluate the course content. Letters from faculty members stating that a course is appropriate are not sufficient for purposes of evaluating course content.

4. OPM Form 1386, Background Questionnaire 79-2: An optional form whose submission is requested. This form is used to help insure agency personnel practices meet requirements of federal law.

5. Standard Form 15, Claim for 10-Point Veteran Preference: with documentary proof required therein, if you are claiming 10-point preference (disability, widow, wife, or mother preference). Documentary proof will be returned.

STUDENTS

If you are a senior or graduate student, you may file an application 9 months prior to completing your scholastic requirements. You should indicate all course work to be completed by the time of graduation. You may not enter on duty until proof of successful completion of all required course work is received.

ELIGIBILITY

You will receive consideration for appointment for 12 months from the date on your notice of rating unless you are removed for failure to respond to official correspondence, accept a position from the register of candidates, or you request to be removed. For continued consideration (of an additional 12 months), you must submit a written request, plus any additional education or work experience completed since your initial rating. Do not submit a request earlier than 2 months prior to the expiration date of your notice of rating. (If you qualify for both a GS-5 and GS-7 position, but accept a position at the GS-5 level, you must submit a request to the Special Examining Unit with a completed application and all required forms to remain on the register for the GS-7 option.)

WHERE TO OBTAIN FORMS:

You may obtain the forms you will need to apply from any Soil Conservation Service (SCS) state office and Federal Job Information Center (FJIC). SCS and FJIC offices are listed in the white pages of most major metropolitan phone directories under "U. S. Government."

WHERE TO APPLY:

Application forms should be mailed to the address listed below. You should allow approximately ten weeks to receive notification of a rating.

USDA, SOIL CONSERVATION SERVICE
SPECIAL EXAMINING UNIT
P. O. BOX 37636
WASHINGTON, D.C. 20013

Address for Overnight mail ONLY:

USDA, SOIL CONSERVATION SERVICE
SPECIAL EXAMINING UNIT
14TH STREET & INDEPENDENCE AVENUE, SW
SOUTH BLDG., ROOM 0110-A
WASHINGTON, D.C. 20250

Jobs in HAWAII are filled locally and the Office of Personnel Management in Honolulu issues vacancy announcements for any openings.

EQUAL EMPLOYMENT OPPORTUNITY

All qualified applicants will receive consideration for employment regardless of race, religion, sex, political affiliation, or any other non-merit factor.

U. S. DEPARTMENT OF HEALTH AND HUMAN SERVICES

PHOENIX AREA INDIAN HEALTH SERVICE

PERSONNEL MANAGEMENT BRANCH
3738 N. 16TH STREET, SUITE A
PHOENIX, ARIZONA 85016-5981

Announcement No. PXIHS-	Opening Date	Closing Date	Personnel: LO Date: 4/3/

POSITION:

LOCATION/DUTY STATION:

TECHNICAL PUBLICATIONS WRITER-EDITOR (ENGINEERING)

Office of Environmental Health
Phoenix, Arizona

SERIES/GRADE/SALARY:
GS-1083-11, $32,423 - $42,152 per annum

TYPE/NUMBER OF POSITIONS:
1 Number of Positions
X Permanent
___ Temporary-NTE:

CONDITIONS OF EMPLOYMENT:
X Full-time
___ Intermittent
___ Part-time

AREA OF CONSIDERATION:
Indian Health Service Wide

SUPERVISORY/MANAGEMENT:
___ Yes, may require one year probationary period.
X No

PMRS:
___ Yes
X No

PROMOTION POTENTIAL:
___ Yes, to Grade:
X No known potential

HOUSING:
___ Yes, government housing available
X Private housing only

TRAVEL EXPENSES:
X Travel may be paid in accordance with Federal Travel Regulations
___ No expenses paid

CONDITION OF EMPLOYMENT: Immunization Requirement - If the selectee was born after 12-31-56, he/she must provide proof of immunity to or evidence of adequate immunization against Rubella and Measles prior to entry on duty. The duty location may provide immunization to determine immunity or antibody through testing.

BRIEF DESCRIPTION OF DUTIES: Incumbent prepares and/or edits specific documents, reports, and publications associated with the Office of Environmental Health and Engineering, which includes Environmental Health Services, Sanitation Facilities Construction and the O & M Section to further the goals and objectives of the program. Preliminary engineering reports, agreement documents, technical status reports, final engineering and as-built reports, data processing reports, technical operation manuals and bulletins, newsletters and annual reports on program activities. Interprets information from numerous sources and a variety of subject matters. Evaluates the needs of diverse audiences, and prepares clear, concise, and cogent documents to meet those needs. Insures proper organization of information including a logical sequence of thoughts and ideas, correct grammar and spelling, and proper style and manner of presentation. Performs other duties as assigned.

QUALIFICATION REQUIREMENTS: Applicants must have one year of Specialized experience at least equivalent to the GS-9, OR 3 full academic years of graduate level education or Ph.D. or equivalent doctoral degree.

GENERAL EXPERIENCE: NA

SPECIALIZED EXPERIENCE: Experience which required substantial subject-matter or technical knowledge of the field. This experience must have demonstrated the ability to acquire and present technical information through independent reading, interviews with subject-matter specialists, observation of tests and experiments, interpretation of blueprints or diagrams, or other appropriate methods. Such experience may have been acquired as a writer or editor of technical reports, articles, manuals, or specifications.

Undergraduate and Graduate Education: Must have included a total of 15 semester hours in appropriate scientific, technical or social science field(s), and which included at least one course above the introductory level in the field(s) covered by the position. For technical manuals and specifications writers or editors, the equivalent of 15 semester hours may be gained through vocational or educational training above the high school level at a public, private, or armed forces school.

SUPERVISORY OR MANAGERIAL ABILITIES: None

SELECTIVE PLACEMENT FACTOR: None

TIME-IN-GRADE RESTRICTION: (If selected under the Excepted Service Examining Plan, such individuals may be appointed under Schedule A authority without regard to Time-In-Grade Requirements.)

MOTOR VEHICLE OPERATION REQUIREMENTS: Incumbent is required to operate a government motor vehicle and maintain a current State Driver's license and Government Employee Identification Card.

SELECTIVE SERVICE CERTIFICATION: If you are male, born after December 31, 1959, and you want to be employed by the Federal Government, you must (subject to certain exemptions) be registered with Selective Service System.

LEGAL AND REGULATORY REQUIREMENTS: Candidates must meet time after competitive appointment, time-in-grade restrictions, and qualification requirements by the closing date of the vacancy announcement.

APPLICANTS OR CURRENT FEDERAL SERVICE EMPLOYEES CLAIMING INDIAN PREFERENCE MUST INDICATE in Item 1 ON THEIR APPLICATION IF THEY WISH TO BE CONSIDERED UNDER THE INDIAN HEALTH SERVICE MERIT PROMOTION PLAN, EXCEPTED SERVICE EXAMINING PLAN, OR BOTH. IF NOT, THEY WILL BE CONSIDERED UNDER THE IHS MERIT PROMOTION PLAN ONLY.

PREFERENCE IN FILLING VACANCIES IS GIVEN TO QUALIFIED INDIAN CANDIDATES IN ACCORDANCE WITH THE INDIAN PREFERENCE ACT (TITLE 25, U.S. CODE, SECTION 472 AND 473). IN OTHER THAN THE ABOVE, THE INDIAN HEALTH SERVICE IS AN EQUAL OPPORTUNITY EMPLOYER.

REASONABLE ACCOMMODATION WILL BE GIVEN TO QUALIFIED DISABLED APPLICANTS PURSUANT TO SECTION 501 OF THE REHABILITATION ACT OF 1973, 29 U.S. CODE 791, TITLE 29.

SUPPLEMENTAL QUESTIONNAIRE
On Knowledge, Skills, and Abilities

Position applied for: Technical Publications Writer-Editor (Engineering), GS-1083-11

Announcement No: PXIHS-92-117   Closing Date: May 18, 19

Evaluation Method: Evaluation will be made of experience, Performance Appraisals, Training, Letters of Commendation, Self-Development, Awards and Outside Activities, which are related to this position. To receive full credit for your qualification, provide a narrative statement of experience, training, education, awards, hobbies, self-developed achievements, and any other aspects of your background as they relate to the knowledge, skills and abilities (KSA's) outlined below and show the level of accomplishments and degree of responsibility. This supplement will be the principal basis for determining whether or not you are best qualified for the position. Describe your qualification in each of the following:

1. Knowledge of technical writing-editing techniques and practices.

2. Knowledge of data researching techniques and practices.

3. Knowledge of program policies and computer software and hardware relating to data processing needs.

The information you provide is considered to be a part of your application and as such is certified by your signature on the SF-171 or equivalent.

_____
Signature

_____
Date

INSTRUCTIONS FOR PHS COMMISSIONED CORPS CANDIDATES: Active duty applicants must submit a copy of current billet description, resume or curriculum vitae. If not on active duty but have applied for the Commissioned Corps, submit the same information as above (except billet description).

NOTE: Commissioned Corps applicants claiminig Indian Preference will be evaluated by the Area Personnel Office against the applicable Preston standard or the Civil Service standard, if no Preston standard exists. These applicants must describe the experience gained in their two most recent positions and provide the dates they occupied those positions. In addition, Commissioned Corps Indian Preference applicants must also provide information regarding education, including degrees obtained and schools attended and they must include home/work telephone numbers if this information is not contained in the Resumes. When required by the vacancy announcement, these applicants must submit specific information related to any knowledges, skills, and abilities which are being used as selective factors. Commissioned Corps Indian Preference applicants must submit Form BIA - 4432, as proof of Indian Preference and also proof of possession of the appropriate license.

ADDITIONAL SELECTION MAY BE MADE FROM THIS ANNOUNCEMENT WITHIN 90 DAYS FROM THE DATE OF THE CERTIFICATE PROVIDED THE VACANT POSITION IS AN IDENTICAL POSITION, SAME GEOGRAPHICAL LOCATION AND SAME CONDITIONS OF EMPLOYMENT.

HOW TO APPLY: Applicants must submit the following required forms to the PHOENIX AREA INDIAN HEALTH SERVICE, PERSONNEL MANAGEMENT BRANCH, 3738 N. 16th STREET, SUITE A, PHOENIX ARIZONA 85016-5981, by the closing date. APPLICANTS WILL NOT BE CONSIDERED IF THE APPLICATION IS RECEIVED AFTER THE CLOSING DATE. ONCE AN APPLICATION HAS BEEN RECEIVED, WE WILL NOT HONOR REQUEST FOR COPIES. APPLICATIONS WILL BE ACCEPTED FROM INDIAN APPLICANTS, CAREER CONDITIONAL OR CAREER FEDERAL EMPLOYEES AND REINSTATEMENT ELIGIBLES BASED ON PRIOR FEDERAL SERVICE. For information regarding this announcement, contact Louise Pino, Personnel Staffing and Classification Specialist, at (602) 640-2068.

1. SF-171, APPLICATION FOR FEDERAL EMPLOYMENT, Must be current, up-to-date and have an original signature.
2. PERFORMANCE APPRAISAL, if available, must be the most recent appraisal.
3. BIA Form 5-4432, VERIFICATION OF INDIAN PREFERENCE SIGNED BY THE APPROPRIATE BIA OFFICIAL, or equivalent form issued by a Tribe authorized by P.L. 93-638 contract to perform the certification function on behalf of the BIA. Applicants currently employed in the Phoenix Area wishing to claim Indian preference, without attaching BIA Form 5-4432 to their SF-171, must state on their application that Indian preference is a matter of record in their Official Personnel Folder. Failure to do so will result in loss of due consideration as an Indian preference applicant.
4. SUPPLEMENTAL QUESTIONNAIRE ON KNOWLEDGE, SKILLS, AND ABILITIES. It is important that you describe your qualifications in detail in order for you to receive proper evaluation in the ranking process.
5. IF CURRENTLY A FEDERAL EMPLOYEE, a copy of latest personnel action (SF-50B) to verify competitive or excepted service status.
6. Copy of DD-214, MILITARY DISCHARGE DOCUMENT, if claiming veterans preference.
7. Copy of college transcripts.

DEFENSE LOGISTICS AGENCY
JOB OPPORTUNITY

POSITION: Telecommunications Specialist, GS-391-12

ANNOUNCEMENT NO.

OPENING DATE:

LOCATION: DLA Administrative Support Center
Office of Telecommunications and
Information Systems
ADP/T Operations Division

CLOSING DATE:

AREA OF CONSIDERATION: Competitive Service Career and Career-Conditional Employees of the Department of Defense in the Washington, D.C. Metropolitan Area

DUTIES: Incumbent serves as a Data Communications Node Management Specialist ensuring continuity and operational readiness of DASC-Z telecommunications resources. Responsibilities include evaluating, designing, developing, installing, and maintaining DLA data communications systems used to support worldwide, high-visibility systems. Duties include: (1) Serving as the focal point for DLA HQ on telecommunications with responsibility for attainment of nodal mission, goals, and policy; (2) Insuring correction of all operational problems affecting remote DLA Network terminals supported by the DASC data processing installation (DPI); (3) Identifying and monitoring correction of network failures; (4) Operating manual and on-line/automatic test equipment and network-related ADPE; (5) Developing local procedures, analyzing and resolving data communication problems, and monitoring implementation and activation of DLA Network hardware and software; (6) Analyzing current and planned network usage and developing recommendations to network management for improvements to data communications equipment and its operation; (7) Providing technical guidance to potential DLA Network terminal station users, covering such areas as recommended equipment, equipment configuration, optional facility layout, circuitry requirements, and the most economical methods for providing network access; (8) Providing operational guidance on debugging, system facility information concerning failing job executions, system failure, and equipment failure; and, (9) Developing specifications for large data communications segments serving a varied mix of computers and terminals linked via automated switches, control devices, and transmission media.

QUALIFICATION REQUIREMENTS: Candidates must have one year of specialized experience equivalent to the GS-11 grade level. Specialized experience is experience in evaluating, analyzing, developing, managing, or improving communications systems, procedures, and requirements which demonstrated knowledge of current developments and trends in communications concepts and technology. Candidates must have served at least one year at the GS-11 grade level to meet OPM time-in-grade requirements.

a. Supplemental Experience Questionnaire.

b. A copy of current annual performance rating and appropriate performance standards. (For DLA employees, DLA Forms 46 and 46A (June 86 version) or Merit Pay appraisal and standards, if applicable, are to be submitted. DLA employees serviced by non-DLA personnel offices may submit their current appraisals and performance standards on the appropriate forms utilized by their respective systems). Applicants who have a minimally acceptable or unacceptable annual performance rating will not be certified for selection consideration.

c. A list of all awards received within the past 10 years, including the dates of the awards.

d. OPM Form 1386, Background Survey Questionnaire 79-2. (Submission of this form is optional).

e. Copy of recent SF-50, Notification of Personnel Action, for verification of competitive status/reinstatement eligibility.

Annotate Item 1 of the SF-171 to show the announcement number of the specific position applied for. Applicants should not submit official position descriptions but should describe duties and responsibilities in their own work. **SF-171'S WILL NOT BE RETURNED SINCE THEY ARE REQUIRED TO BE MAINTAINED FOR AUDIT PURPOSES, THEREFORE, DO NOT SUBMIT OFFICIAL DOCUMENTS.**

Failure to submit appropriate application forms may affect applicant's consideration in the evaluation process.

For further information regarding this vacancy, call (703) 274-7087 between the hours of 9:30 a.m. and 3:00 p.m. or Autovon 284-7087. For general vacancy information, call our recorded vacancy listing on (703) 274-7372 or Autovon 284-7372.

After submission of applications, documents, forms, etc., please DO NOT contact the Civilian Personnel Office for "Status" requests. All applicants will be notified of final results after selection for the position has been completed.

ALL QUALIFIED CANDIDATES WILL RECEIVE CONSIDERATION WITHOUT REGARD TO RACE, RELIGION, COLOR, SEX, AGE, NATIONAL ORIGIN, LAWFUL POLITICAL AFFILIATION, MARITAL STATUS, UNION MEMBERSHIP, OR OTHER NONDISQUALIFYING PHYSICAL OR MENTAL HANDICAPS.

SUPPLEMENTAL EXPERIENCE QUESTIONNAIRE

POSITION: Telecommunications Specialist, GS-391-12   JOAs

NAME _____   DATE _____

INSTRUCTIONS: Prepare brief but concise responses to the following highly qualifying criteria on how your experience, education and/or training satisfies the knowledge, skills, and abilities cited below. DO NOT REPEAT VERBATIM INFORMATION IN THE SF-171 (Application for Federal Employment).

KSAe 1. Knowledge of Patch and Test, Technical Control or Network Management functions and operations.

Please provide the following information relating to the above experiences: Names and telephone numbers of supervisors or other persons who can verify your statements
title, series, and grade of your position (if applicable)
_____ ; time period this work was performed (month and year)
From _____ To _____ .

KSAe 2. Ability to perform actions to resolve data communications hardware and software problems.

Please provide the following information relating to the above experiences: Names and telephone numbers of supervisors or other persons who can verify your statements
title, series, and grade of your position (if applicable)
_____ ; time period this work was performed (month and year)
From _____ To _____ .

SUPPLEMENTAL EXPERIENCE QUESTIONNAIRE

POSITION: Telecommunications Specialist, GS-391-12   JOAs

NAME _____   DATE _____

INSTRUCTIONS: Prepare brief but concise responses to the following highly qualifying criteria on how your experience, education and/or training satisfies the knowledge, skills, and abilities cited below. DO NOT REPEAT VERBATIM INFORMATION IN THE SF-171 (Application for Federal Employment).

KSAe 3. Ability to communicate orally.

Please provide the following information relating to the above experiences: Names and telephone numbers of supervisors or other persons who can verify your statements
title, series, and grade of your position (if applicable)
_____ ; time period this work was performed (month and year)
From _____ To _____ .

KSAe 4. Knowledge of formal standards and regulations which establish and control the interfacing and electrical operation between ADP/Communications and Telecommunications.

Please provide the following information relating to the above experiences: Names and telephone numbers of supervisors or other persons who can verify your statements
title, series, and grade of your position (if applicable)
_____ ; time period this work was performed (month and year)
From _____ To _____ .

VACANCY ANNOUNCEMENT

Headquarters, First U.S. Army and Fort George G. Meade
Civilian Personnel Office
Fort George G. Meade, Maryland 20755-5035

AN EQUAL OPPORTUNITY EMPLOYER

THE FILLING OF THIS POSITION IS SUBJECT TO THE DOD PRIORITY PLACEMENT PROGRAM

ANNOUNCEMENT NUMBER
97-111-92

POSITION USAR SCHOOL ADMINISTRATOR GS-301-09

PROMOTION POTENTIAL NONE

LOCATION 97th US ARMY RESERVE COMMAND
FT. BELVOIR USAR CENTER 3
2070 USARF SCHOOL FT. BELVOIR, VA 22060

SALARY $26,798 – $34,835

OPENING DATE

FIRST CUT OFF DATE

CLOSING DATE

CONDITION OF EMPLOYMENT

PCS EXPENSES PAID	
YES	NO X

RELOCATION (DAR SE) PAID	
YES	NO X

ARMY RESERVE TECHNICIAN POSITION – ACTIVE ARMY RESERVE MEMBERSHIP IS REQUIRED

X TPU

☐ SELECTED RESERVE

☐ NOT APPLICABLE

SUPERVISORY MANAGERIAL PROBATIONARY PERIOD REQUIRED

☐ YES

X NO

SECURITY CLEARANCE REQUIRED

X YES ☐ NO

☐ SECRET

☐ TOP SECRET

AREA OF CONSIDERATION X DA CIVILIAN EMPLOYEES WITH COMPETITIVE STATUS X DOD EMPLOYEES WITH STATUS X FEDERAL

EMPLOYEES WITH STATUS ☐ EMPLOYEES WITH REINSTATEMENT ELIGIBILITY, INDIVIDUALS ELIGIBLE FOR APPOINTMENT BY SPECIAL AUTHORITY SUCH AS HANDICAPPED, VETERANS READJUSTMENT, ETC. MILITARY SPOUSES REQUESTING MILITARY SPOUSE PREFERENCE MUST REGISTER IAW PROCEDURES ESTABLISHED UNDER THE DOD PRIORITY PLACEMENT PROGRAM. (SPOUSES BY SUBMITTING DOCUMENTATION REQUIRED TO ESTABLISH ELIGIBILITY (SF 171, LATEST PERFORMANCE APPRAISAL, SF 50, DD 214, SPONSOR'S TRAVEL ORDERS, ETC.)

☐ THIS IS AN EXCEPTED POSITION ALL INTERESTED CANDIDATES MAY APPLY

MAJOR DUTIES:

Serves as the principal administrator to the USAR School Commandant in accomplishing the overall functions of the school which includes training, administration, unit operations, logistics and supply. Receives, interprets, analyzes and develops directives, policies and procedures governing school operations. Prepares or assures the preparation and maintenance of the USAR School master training schedules. This includes the receipt of all course-ware, inventory, material and equipment. Assures that the USAR School has properly staffed faculty who are qualified to teach specific courses assigned. Coordinates action to contract qualified instructors to teach complex courses. Assures the availability of proper education of all facilities and equipment. The incumbent may be called upon to develop program of instructions for nonconfigured courses. Provides support to all instructors and assures that they have the necessary material and equipment to conduct training.

METHODS OF EVALUATION: ALL APPLICANTS WILL BE EVALUATED AGAINST APPROPRIATE QUALIFICATION STANDARDS, MERIT PROMOTION AND OTHER COMPETITIVE CANDIDATES' RESPONSES TO IDENTIFIED RANKING ELEMENTS WILL BE FURTHER EVALUATED TO DETERMINE BEST QUALIFIED

NOTE ANY FORMS NOT FULLY COMPLETED AND SIGNED OR FAILURE TO SUBMIT REQUIRED FORMS MAY RESULT IN AN INELIGIBLE RATING OR LESS THAN FULL CONSIDERATION FOR THE POSITION

HOW TO APPLY SUBMIT THE FOLLOWING DOCUMENTS.

1. APPLICATION FOR FEDERAL EMPLOYMENT (SF-171)
2. SUPPLEMENTAL NARRATIVE & EVALUATION (FGGM FM 45) FOR GS GM POSITIONS
3. COPY OF ANNUAL LATEST PERFORMANCE APPRAISAL
4. COPY OF COLLEGE TRANSCRIPTS (LIST OF COLLEGE COURSES, AS APPROPRIATE
5. GEOGRAPHIC AVAILABILITY FORM (RESERVE TECHNICIAN POSITIONS ONLY)
6. DOCUMENTS VERIFYING ELIGIBILITY, SF 50, DD FORM 214, SF-15, ETC.
7. BACKGROUND SURVEY QUESTIONNAIRE 79 2, OMB No 50-616

BY MAIL CIVILIAN PERSONNEL OFFICE, AFKA ZI-CPR, FORT GEORGE G. MEADE, MD 20755-5035

IN PERSON AT THE ONE STOP INFORMATION CENTER DURING NORMAL DUTY HOURS

AFTER HOURS AND WEEKENDS, USE THE DROP BOX OUTSIDE THE CPO, BLDG 4432 OR THE ONE STOP INFORMATION CENTER, BLDG 4283

APPLICATIONS MUST BE RECEIVED IN THE CIVILIAN PERSONNEL OFFICE BY THE CLOSING DATE OF THE ANNOUNCEMENT

"PEOPLE ALWAYS"

QUALIFICATIONS REQUIRED BY OPM X-118:

GS-09: Candidates must posses at least one year of specialized experience equivalent to the GS-07 level.

"**Specialized experience**" refers to progressively responsible experience in educational administration, development of course materials or training aids or other comparable administrative activity in a secondary school, college, industrial, commercial or military establishment. This experience must have demonstrated ability to determine and analyze operating needs, funding requirements, and the execution of approved budget.

TIME-IN-GRADE REQUIREMENT:

GS-09: Candidates must have completed at least one year at the GS-07 grade level in the Federal Service.

RANKING ELEMENTS: (KNOWLEDGE, SKILLS AND ABILITIES) APPLICANTS MUST ADDRESS THESE ELEMENTS ON THE APPLICANT'S SUPPLEMENTAL NARRATIVE AND SUPERVISORS EVALUATION FORM (FGGM FORM 45):

1. Ability to evaluate and analyze.

2. Ability to communicate in writing.

3. Ability to communicate orally.

4. Ability to establish and review training programs, plans and schedules.

5. Knowledge of organization and administration of military units and the application of military regulations and procedures.

DISTRIBUTION:
X(d) (Less 40)
ARCOMS, AMSAS, CENTERS (MAILING LABELS FORWARDED)

CDC Position Announcement

CENTERS FOR DISEASE CONTROL

Office of Program Support • Personnel Management • Recruitment and Placement Branch   NUMBER: NCHS

MERIT PROMOTION

OPENING DATE:

CLOSING DATE:

POSITION: Visual Information Specialist, GS-1084-5/7/9
(If filled at the GS-5 or GS-7 level, position has promotion potential to GS-9.) Please indicate the grade(s) for which you wish to be considered. You will only be considered for the grade(s) for which you indicate an interest.

LOCATION: Centers for Disease Control, National Center for Health Statistics, Office of Data Processing and Services, Division of Data Services, Publications Branch, Communications Section, Hyattsville, Maryland

DUTY STATION: HYATTSVILLE, MARYLAND

AREA OF CONSIDERATION: CDC/ATSDR and HHS nationwide employees may apply and be considered in accordance with the Agency's Merit Promotion Program. Concurrent consideration will be extended to Federal employees serving on a permanent appointment in the competitive service and individuals with status, such as reinstatement eligibles. Candidates who have eligibility for non-competitive appointments, such as VRA eligibles, 30% or more disabled veterans and persons with disabilities are encouraged to apply. Proof of eligibility must accompany application. Commissioned Corps Officers are encouraged to apply.

DUTIES: At the full performance level, incumbent will design, prepare and instruct vendors in preparing art for presentation aids. Incumbent will be working from rough handwritten copy, hand-plotted or computer-plotted graphs, hand-drawn charts, and material previously prepared for other media.

QUALIFICATION REQUIREMENTS: Candidates must meet the basic qualification requirements outlined in OPM Qualification Standards Handbook. Applicants at the GS-5 level must have three years of general experience one of which must have been at the GS-4 level in the Federal service. Applicants at the GS-7 and GS-9 levels must have 52 weeks of specialized experience equivalent to the next lower grade in the Federal service (GS-5 and GS-7). General experience is experience in administrative, professional, technical, or other responsible work that has demonstrated the skills and creativity needed to use the tools or equipment associated with the work. Specialized experience is actual work in the line of work of the position to be filled and which has equipped the applicant with the particular knowledge, skills, and abilities to successfully perform the duties of the position.

PLEASE ADDRESS THESE SPECIFIC KSA'S IN YOUR APPLICATION. FAILURE TO DO SO COULD RESULT IN YOUR NOT BEING DETERMINED QUALIFIED.

1. Ability to design, prepare and instruct vendors to prepare art for presentation aids.

2. Ability to use and advise clients on the use of presentation graphics software for PC's.

3. Ability to maintain and archive of presentation aids.

4. Ability to produce audiovisual communication programs.

5. Ability to design and produce visual aids and to prepare camera ready art for printing.

6. Ability to setup or coordinate the setup of a wide variety of audiovisual communication equipment according to requests and schedules.

EVALUATION METHODS: Employees will be evaluated and ranked as indicated in the CDC Merit Promotion Plan as modified by HHS Instructions on filing Performance Management and Recognition Systems Positions.

HOW TO APPLY: CDC/ATSDR employees should submit completed "Application for Position Vacancy Under CDC Merit Promotion Announcement" (Form CDC 0.996) to the Centers for Disease Control, P.O. Box 12214, Room A-131. Personnel Office, Research Triangle Park, North Carolina 27709-2214; ATTN: Lu Thomas. NCHS Employees should submit completed "Application for Position Vacancy under CDC Merit Promotion Announcement" (Form CDC 0.996) or "Application for Federal Employment" (SF-171). HHS applicants other than CDC/ATSDR employees must submit "Application for Federal Employment" (SF-171), a copy of recent performance appraisal, and a current copy of your SF-50. All applicants must submit Form CDC 0.996 or SF-171 by the closing date for applying or they will not be considered.

U.S. DEPARTMENT OF HEALTH AND HUMAN SERVICES
Public Health Service

~ The Centers for Disease Control maintains a smoke-free environment ~

All applicants will receive equal consideration without regard to race, religion, color, national origin, sex, political affiliation, **age** (with authorized

Department of Veterans Affairs

VOCATIONAL REHABILITATION SPECIALIST, GS-1715-9/11

Applications will be accepted until further notice.

DESCRIPTION OF WORK

Vocational Rehabilitation Specialists assist individuals entitled to vocational rehabilitation services. They must be able to recognize and understand the limitations and capabilities associated with different disabilities; evaluate individuals' progress towards rehabilitation; assist individuals to successfully pursue training; aid in the adjustment to employment; and provide supportive counseling to disabled individuals and their families.

LOCATION OF POSITIONS

Most of these positions are located in VA medical centers, regional offices, outpatient clinics, and domiciliaries throughout the United States and Puerto Rico. Some positions exist in other Federal agencies.

SALARY

Your starting salary depends upon the duties and responsibilities of the position being filled. There are opportunities for promotion to higher grade levels, periodic increases within each grade level, additional increases for superior performance, and increases in Federal salaries based on comparability with the private sector.

QUALIFICATION REQUIREMENTS

BASIC REQUIREMENTS:

You must be a citizen of the United States.

English language proficiency - If you are appointed to a direct patient-care position, you must be proficient in spoken and written English as required by 38 USC 4105 (c).

EXPERIENCE

AT ALL GRADE LEVELS: At least one year of specialized experience which is in or directly related to vocational rehabilitation. This experience must have equipped you with the particular knowledge, skills, and abilities necessary to successfully perform the duties of Vocational Rehabilitation Specialist positions. For GS-9 level positions, this one year of specialized experience must have been comparable to GS-7 level positions in the Federal service. For GS-11 level positions, you must be able to document one year of specialized experience equivalent to GS-9 level in the Federal service.

SUBSTITUTION OF EDUCATION FOR EXPERIENCE:

GS-9: Two full academic years of graduate level education or a master's (or equivalent) degree in which the major field of study has been vocational rehabilitation, vocational or educational counseling, or other fields directly related to the position, is fully qualifying.

GS-11: Three full academic years of graduate level education or a Ph.D. or equivalent doctorate degree in a major field of study as cited above is fully qualifying.

COMBINING EDUCATION AND EXPERIENCE:

Combinations of successfully completed education and experience may be used to meet total qualification requirements.

QUALITY OF EXPERIENCE: For positions at any grade, the required amount of experience will not in itself be accepted as proof of qualification for a position. Your record of education and experience must clearly demonstrate that you have the ability to perform the duties of the position. The primary consideration is the quality and responsibility level of experience.

BASIS OF RATING

There is no written test. You will be rated on a scale of 70-100 based on the extent and quality of your education, experience, and training relevant to the duties of the position. Such ratings will be based on your statements in the application and on any additional information obtained by our office.

You will be rated for all grade levels for which you are qualified and for which you will accept employment as indicated in your application.

LENGTH OF ELIGIBILITY

If you are qualified, your name will be maintained on the list of eligibles established under this announcement for a period of 12 months. You may submit up-to-date information about your qualifications before the end of that time period. A letter or an Amendment to Application for Federal Employment (Standard Form 172) may be used for this purpose. Do not submit information until two months before your eligibility expires unless you believe it will help you qualify for a higher grade. **If you do not update your records within the last 60 days of your eligibility period, you will receive no further consideration for Federal employment until you update your application.**

EQUAL EMPLOYMENT OPPORTUNITY

All qualified applicants will receive consideration for appointment without regard to race, religion, color, national origin, sex, political affiliation, or any other nonmerit factor.

HOW TO APPLY

Please submit the following forms:

1. Application for Federal Employment, Standard Form 171. Please show the title of the position for which you are applying, the announcement number, and the lowest salary you are willing to accept.

2. Supplemental Qualifications Statement for Vocational Rehabilitation Specialist, OPM Form 1170/89. Please read the instructions carefully and complete the form as directed. Your rating will be based primarily on the information you give on this form.

3. List of College Courses and Certificate of Scholastic Achievement, OPM Form 1170/17. **A transcript of your master's or doctorate college records may be used, if you prefer.** If you are a graduate student, you may use the form 1170/17, Part I, to show the courses and semester hour credits you expect to complete within the next nine months.

4. Application for 10-point Veteran's Preference, Standard Form 15, (if appropriate). Include copies of documentary evidence required by that form. Original evidence will be returned to applicants. Other veteran's preference information is contained in the instructions of Standard Form 171.

5. VA Employment Availability Form, 5-3447. Retain accompanying Job Location list for your records.

Since Vocational Rehabilitation Specialist positions exist in VA medical centers, regional offices, and other Federal agencies, please choose your location codes carefully. If you choose entire State codes (101-152), you may be referred to any location in the State(s) you choose.

WHERE TO OBTAIN FORMS

Information about forms or application instructions may be obtained from a VA medical center, regional office, or an Office of Personnel Management Job Information Center (located in most large cities). Consult the telephone directory for the one nearest you. Information may also be obtained from the VA's Delegated Examining Unit by calling toll-free 800-368-6008. Virginia residents may call toll-free on 800-552-3045.

Mail your application to:

Department of Veterans Affairs
Delegated Examining Unit
P.O. Box 24269
Richmond, VA 23224-0269

GS-1715   VOCATIONAL REHABILITATION
(p. 36)   GS-5/above

Undergraduate and Graduate Education: Major study—vocational rehabilitation, vocational or educational counseling, or other fields related to the position.

General Experience: Experience which provided a knowledge of training practices, techniques, and requirements as they relate to vocational development or rehabilitation.

Specialized Experience: Experience which demonstrated the ability to perform the work. Examples of qualifying specialized experience include:

- Work that required obtaining and applying occupational information for the handicapped, knowledge of the interrelationships of the involved professional and specialist services, and skill in employing the methodology and techniques of counseling to motivate and encourage individuals served by the program.

- Experience which demonstrated knowledge of the vocational rehabilitation problems characteristic of the *disabled*, including familiarity with available resources and skill in identifying, evaluating, and making effective use of such resources to serve disabled individuals; or of the *disadvantaged*, including knowledge of adjustment problems of the educationally or culturally disadvantaged, familiarity with available adult education and training resources, and ability to recognize problem areas needing special attention.

- Experience in vocational guidance or teaching in a recognized vocational rehabilitation program or school; developmental or supervisory work in programs of vocational rehabilitation or training programs for the disadvantaged; or personnel or employment placement work that provided extensive knowledge of the training and adjustment requirements necessary to place persons having disabilities or social adjustment problems.

PRE-EMPLOYMENT DRUG TEST IS REQUIRED FOR NON-DEPARTMENT OF STATE APPLICANTS WHO ARE SELECTED FOR EMPLOYMENT. APPOINTMENT WILL BE CONTINGENT UPON A NEGATIVE DRUG TEST.

United States Department of State

CAREER OPPORTUNITY

This competitive career vacancy is open to all qualified candidates, and it is being filled through the Department of State's Merit Promotion process or through the Office of Personnel Management competitive procedures.

ANNOUNCEMENT NO.:   92-0345 II   OPENING DATE:
                                           CLOSING DATE:
Position Title: Computer Specialist
Series and Grade: GM-334-13
Area of Consideration: All Qualified Sources
Number of Vacancy: One
Location: ·   S/S-IRM/SMD, Washington, D.C.
Security Clearance Required: Critical-Sensitive
Salary: $46,210 - $60,070
Supervisory: NO   Merit Pay: YES

DUTIES: This position is located in the Systems Management Division, Office of Information Resource Management, Executive Secretariat. Incumbent serves as a Computer Specialist under the general supervision of the Chief, Systems Management Division and as such is expected to carry out assignments in the following areas: Performs analysis and design tasks within major project areas of the Secretariat Systems office which is responsible for developing and maintaining minicomputer and microcomputer applications, telecommunications, micro-to-mini-to-mainframe communications, presentation graphics and other subsystems as assigned. Participates generally as a member of a project team in the definition of aspects of operational problems and in determining the applicability, feasibility, and practicability of office automation in areas under study. Develops or participates in the development of cost data on equipment, personnel, training and assists in the development of equipment specifications. Participates in pilot operations to test suitability to basic systems design and in the implementation of new and/or modified data processing systems. Develops operational procedures, instructions, guides, etc. for automated systems and conducts orientation training for personnel affected by the systems. Recommends needed redesign studies.

QUALIFICATION REQUIREMENTS (Handbook X-118): Candidates must have one year of specialized experience equivalent to next lower grade which is directly related to the position to be filled and which has equipped the candidate with the particular knowledge, skills, and abilities to successfully perform the duties of the position.

SELECTIVE PLACEMENT FACTORS: 1) Knowledge of Computer Networks and advanced system programs and design techniques.
                                2) Ability to use Programming Languages.

APPLICANTS MUST SUBMIT SSW FORM 555, SUPPLEMENTAL QUALIFICATIONS STATEMENT FOR COMPUTER SPECIALIST WITH THEIR APPLICATION.

IF A LIST OF ELIGIBLES IS REQUESTED FROM OPM, ALL NONSTATUS CANDIDATES WHO MEET MINIMUM REQUIREMENTS WILL BE REFERRED TO OPM FOR RANKING AND REFERRAL.

RANKING FACTORS: Applicants who meet the qualification requirements described above will be further evaluated by determining the extent to which their education, experience, training, awards and supervisory appraisal indicated they possess the knowledges, skills, abilities and other characteristics described below.

1. Ability to analyze and evaluate.
2. Ability to meet and deal.
3. Skill in written communication.
4. Knowledge of Computer Networks and advanced system programs and design techniques.
5. Ability to use Programming Languages.

APPLICATIONS WILL NOT BE ACCEPTED AFTER THE CLOSING DATE OF THE ANNOUNCEMENT
(SEE REVERSE FOR HOW TO APPLY)

SELECTIONS WILL BE MADE WITHOUT DISCRIMINATION AS TO POLITICAL, RELIGIOUS, UNION OR NON-UNION AFFILIATION, MARITAL STATUS, COLOR, NATIONAL ORIGIN, RACE, SEX, AGE, OR PHYSICAL HANDICAPS WHICH ARE DISQUALIFYING.

HOW TO APPLY

ALL APPLICANTS NOT CURRENTLY EMPLOYED BY THE DEPARTMENT OF STATE WHO ARE SELECTED FOR EMPLOYMENT WILL BE REQUIRED TO SUBMIT TO A URINALYSIS TO SCREEN FOR ILLEGAL DRUG USE PRIOR TO APPOINTMENT. APPOINTMENT WILL BE CONTINGENT UPON A NEGATIVE DRUG TEST RESULT.

DEPARTMENT OF STATE EMPLOYEES must submit the following to PER/CSP/SSD, Room 2819, Main State Building: (1) Application for Vacancy, Form DS-1738; (2) a completed and originally signed Application for Federal Employment, form SF-171; (3) a copy of your current performance appraisal of record (see Note 1); and (4) Background Survey Data Questionnaire, OPM Form 1386 (see Note 5). Application forms are available in PER/CSP/SSD or Bureau Administrative/Executive Offices.

NON-DEPARTMENT OF STATE APPLICANTS *(see Area of Consideration)* must submit the following: (1) a completed and originally signed form SF-171; (2) a copy of your current performance appraisal of record (see Note 1); (3) a copy of your last Notification of Personnel Action (SF-50) verifying your current or previous competitive status; and (4) Background Survey Data Questionnaire, OPM Form 1386 (see Note 5).

NON-STATUS APPLICANTS must submit the following: (1) a completed and originally signed form SF-171; (2) a Background Survey Data Questionnaire, (OPM Form 1386) (see Note 5); and any supplemental forms required by the announcement.

PERSONS WITH DISABILITIES OR DISABLED VETERANS who qualify for this position must be able to show eligibility for appointment under special procedures for employment of persons with disabilities or disabled veterans. If assistance is needed with the application process, you may call (202) 647-6132 or TDD (202) 647-7256.

IMPORTANT NOTES:

1. The SF-171, performance appraisal and other associated application materials should describe specific duties performed and or education which demonstrate the ranking factors listed in the vacancy announcement. If the performance appraisal of record does not fully address the ranking factors, you may submit an Applicant Appraisal, Form DS-1812, or a previous performance appraisal which addresses the ranking factors, in addition to the performance appraisal of record.

2. If you are filing for GS-7 positions on the basis of superior academic achievement (SAA) or combining SAA with subsequent professional work experience to qualify for certain GS-9 positions, complete and submit Form 1170/17, List of College Courses, or submit a letter from an official of your school which verifies that you meet one or more of the criteria for SAA.

3. A copy of the official record for each award received during the last five years must be submitted in order for awards to be considered. These awards shall be considered only in terms of the demonstrated or implied experience or performance that related to the requirements of the vacancy.

4. Applicants with foreign education must submit an evaluation of their coursework by an organization recognized for accreditation or by an accredited U.S. college or university.

5. Your name and Social Security Number must be provided on OPM Form 1386, Background Survey Data Questionnaire. Completion of the rest of the form is strictly voluntary, but it is needed for statistical purposes.

6. DO NOT ATTACH any additional materials such as resumes, position descriptions, certificates of training, publications, etc. unless additional information is asked for in the vacancy announcement.

7. Qualifications and eligibility determination will be made solely on the basis of the SF-171. Follow the instructions in the application and the vacancy announcement for completion of the SF-171.

8. APPLICATIONS WHICH ARE INADEQUATE OR INCOMPLETE OR MAILED IN POSTAGE-PAID GOVERNMENT ENVELOPES WILL NOT BE CONSIDERED. ALL APPLICATIONS AND DOCUMENTS SUBMITTED IN RESPONSE TO THIS ANNOUNCEMENT WILL BECOME THE PROPERTY OF THE DEPARTMENT OF STATE.

9. All applicants will be notified in writing of the results of the considerations given to their application. TELEPHONE CALLS or inquiries concerning the status of applications should not be made until at least three weeks after the closing date of the announcement.

> U.S. Department of State
> Office of Civil Service Personnel Mgt.
> P.O. Box 18657
> Washington, D.C. 20036-8657

PRIVACY ACT INFORMATION: The SF-171, SF-171A, and SF-172 contains information subject to the Privacy Act of 1974 (P.L. 93-579, 5 U.S.C. 552a). Information regarding this Act is available upon request in the Merit Promotion Division, Office of Career Development and Assignments, Department of State.

*AMENDED TO CORRECT THE SELECTIVE PLACEMENT FACTOR (SPF)

United States Department of State

CAREER OPPORTUNITY

POSITION TITLE: Foreign Affairs Officer

ANNOUNCEMENT #

AREA OF CONSIDERATION: All Sources
SERIES & GRADE: GW-130-14
PROMOTION POTENTIAL: None
SECURITY CLEARANCE: Critical-Sensitive
OFFICE & LOCATION: OES/SCT/EAL, Rm. 4330 NS

OPENING DATE:
CLOSING DATE:
SUPERVISORY: No
MERIT PAY: Yes

DUTIES:
This position is located in the European, African and Latin American Affairs Division, Office of Cooperative Science and Technology Programs, Bureau of OES. In the area of assignment, incumbent identifies and analyzes foreign policy issues; evaluates those issues and advises bureau and department officials. Develops recommendations and alternative actions related to policy options; as necessary, coordinates sensitive bilateral agreements/conventions with policy-level officers in other departments, academic community, congressional offices, private sector officials, and foreign government representatives. Acts as liaison with policy-level officials within the Bureau, to ensure that Department views and interests are promoted with respect to current/emerging policy issues, and are taken into consideration in S&T policy development and implementation. Evaluates, reviews and develops new methods and mechanisms to monitor the organizational, operational and funding aspects of S&T programs. Organizes and conducts interagency and bilateral meetings. Prepares request for authority to negotiate, conclude agreements or conventions, including memoranda for cooperation. Drafts documents and reports, position and briefing papers.

QUALIFICATION REQUIREMENTS (Handbook X-118): Applicants must have the required experience or education as described below and, when specified, any selective placement factors.

Applicants must have at least one year of specialized experience at the GS/GM-13 grade level. Specialized experience is that which demonstrates the ability to analyze and evaluate scientific and technological information and/or data in relation to foreign policy.

* SELECTIVE PLACEMENT FACTOR: Knowledge of science and technology organizations, policies, and programs related to the former Soviet Union."

"One year time-in-grade at the next lower grade level requirement applies."

All applicants not currently employed by the Department of State who are selected for employment will be required to submit a urinalysis to screen for illegal drug use prior to appointment. Appointment will be contingent upon a negative drug test result.

RANKING FACTORS: Applicants who meet the qualification requirements described above will be further evaluated by determining the extent to which their education, experience, training, awards and supervisory appraisal indicated they possess the knowledges, skills, abilities and other characteristics described below.

1. Knowledge of science and technological (S&T) developments, programs, and public policy issues as they relate to foreign policy issues.
2. Ability to communicate orally.
3. Ability to communicate in writing.
4. Ability to research, analyze and evaluate information or data.
5. Ability to plan and direct program activities.

APPLICATIONS WILL NOT BE ACCEPTED AFTER THE CLOSING DATE OF THE ANNOUNCEMENT
(SEE REVERSE FOR HOW TO APPLY)

Selections will be made without discrimination as to political, religious, union or non-union affiliation, marital status, color, national origin, race, sex, age, or disabilities which are not disqualifying.

HOW TO APPLY

ALL APPLICANTS NOT CURRENTLY EMPLOYED BY THE DEPARTMENT OF STATE WHO ARE SELECTED FOR EMPLOYMENT WILL BE REQUIRED TO SUBMIT TO A URINALYSIS TO SCREEN FOR ILLEGAL DRUG USE PRIOR TO APPOINTMENT. APPOINTMENT WILL BE CONTINGENT UPON A NEGATIVE DRUG TEST RESULT.

DEPARTMENT OF STATE EMPLOYEES must submit the following to PER/CSP/SSD, Room 2819, Main State Building: (1) Application for Vacancy, Form DS-1738; (2) a completed and originally signed Application for Federal Employment, form SF-171; (3) a copy of your current performance appraisal of record (see Note 1); and (4) Background Survey Data Questionnaire, OPM Form 1386 (see Note 5). Application forms are available in PER/CSP/SSD or Bureau Administrative/Executive Officers.

NON-DEPARTMENT OF STATE APPLICANTS (see Area of Consideration) must submit the following: (1) a completed and originally signed form SF-171; (2) a copy of your current performance appraisal of record (see Note 1); (3) a copy of your last Notification of Personnel Action (SF-50) verifying your current or previous competitive status; and (4) Background Survey Data Questionnaire, OPM Form 1386 (see Note 5).

NON-STATUS APPLICANTS must submit the following: (1) a completed and originally signed form SF-171; (2) a Background Survey Data Questionnaire. (OPM Form 1386) (see Note 5); and any supplemental forms required by the announcement.

PERSONS WITH DISABILITIES OR DISABLED VETERANS who qualify for this position must be able to show eligibility for appointment under special procedures for employment of persons with disabilities or disabled veterans. If assistance is needed with the application process, you may call (202) 647-6132 or TDD (202) 647-7256.

IMPORTANT NOTES:

1. The SF-171, performance appraisal and other associated application materials should describe specific duties performed and or education which demonstrate the ranking factors listed in the vacancy announcement. If the performance appraisal of record does not fully address the ranking factors, you may submit an Applicant Appraisal, Form DS-1812, or a previous performance appraisal which addresses the ranking factors, in addition to the performance appraisal of record.

2. If you are filing for GS-7 positions on the basis of superior academic achievement (SAA) or combining SAA with subsequent professional work experience to qualify for certain GS-9 positions, complete and submit Form 1170/17, List of College Courses, or submit a letter from an official of your school which verifies that you meet one or more of the criteria for SAA.

3. A copy of the official record for each award received during the last five years must be submitted in order for awards to be considered. These awards shall be considered only in terms of the demonstrated or implied experience or performance that related to the requirements of the vacancy.

4. Applicants with foreign education must submit an evaluation of their coursework by an organization recognized for accreditation or by an accredited U.S. college or university.

5. Your name and Social Security Number must be provided on OPM Form 1386, Background Survey Data Questionnaire. Completion of the rest of the form is strictly voluntary, but it is needed for statistical purposes.

6. DO NOT ATTACH any additional materials such as resumes, position descriptions, certificates of training, publications, etc. unless additional information is asked for in the vacancy announcement.

7. Qualifications and eligibility determination will be made solely on the basis of the SF-171. Follow the instructions in the application and the vacancy announcement for completion of the SF-171.

8. APPLICATIONS WHICH ARE INADEQUATE OR INCOMPLETE OR MAILED IN POSTAGE-PAID GOVERNMENT ENVELOPES WILL NOT BE CONSIDERED. ALL APPLICATIONS AND DOCUMENTS SUBMITTED IN RESPONSE TO THIS ANNOUNCEMENT WILL BECOME THE PROPERTY OF THE DEPARTMENT OF STATE.

9. All applicants will be notified in writing of the results of the considerations given to their application. TELEPHONE CALLS or inquiries concerning the status of applications should not be made until at least three weeks after the closing date of the announcement.

U.S. Department of State
Office of Civil Service Personnel Mgt.
P.O. Box 18657
Washington, D.C. 20036-8657

PRIVACY ACT INFORMATION: The SF-171, SF-171A, and SF-172 contains information subject to the Privacy Act of 1974 (P.L. 93-579, 5 U.S.C. 552a). Information regarding this Act is available upon request in the Merit Promotion Division. Office of Career Development and Assignments. Department of State.

DEPARTMENT OF THE ARMY
TRANSATLANTIC DIVISION, CORPS OF ENGINEERS
P.O. BOX 1250
WINCHESTER, VIRGINIA 22601-1432

JOB OPPORTUNITY
Army-Wide

ANN NO:

OPENING DATE:
CLOSING DATE:

SUPERVISORY CONTRACT SPECIALIST, GM-1102-13

US ARMY ENGINEER DIVISION, TRANSATLANTIC
KUWAIT PROGRAM OFFICE
CONTRACTING OFFICE
KUWAIT CITY, KUWAIT

AREA OF CONSIDERATION: All career and career-conditional employees serviced by the Transatlantic Division (TAD) and Department of the Army promotion eligibles. Concurrent consideration may be extended to transfer and reinstatement eligibles; eligibles under special appointing authorities, such as handicapped, VRA, 30% Disabled Veterans, E.O. 12721, and OPM eligibles.

PAY RETENTION WILL BE OFFERED TO SELECTED APPLICANTS OUTSIDE THE GEOGRAPHICAL LOCATION OF THE POSITION WHOSE PAY WOULD OTHERWISE BE REDUCED.

SUMMARY OF DUTIES: Serves as Chief of the Contracting Office, Kuwait Program Office (KPO). As Contracting Officer, is fully responsible for the planning, execution, and awarding of all contracts. Participates, as necessary, and assists in negotiation on unusual and/or complex contracts. Responsible for the timely resolution of Contract Audit Report recommendations for contracts assigned. Responsible for the initiation and completion of appropriate formal contracts for the acquisition of supplies, services, and construction needs to support all customers. Implements and executes established acquisition programs. Resolves all adverse actions associated with the acquisition requirements. Closes out completed contracts. Advises and assists the Government of Kuwait (GOK) and KPO staff in developing justification and documentation for contracts. Participates in joint meetings with representatives of GOK and KPO staff and advises relative resolution of contracting technicalities. Plans, directs, coordinates, and reviews the procurement and contract activities of KPO. Devises internal procedures and controls, interprets and applies regulatory provisions and makes decisions on difficult or controversial matters. Plans, directs, reviews and evaluates the work of other specialists engaged in administering a wide variety of service, supplies, and construction contracts ranging from logistical support to complex multi-million dollar contracts. Conducts internal review of organization efficiency and optimal skill utilization and recommends reorganization of assignments and functions as necessary. Performs full range of supervisory functions.

MINIMUM QUALIFICATION REQUIREMENTS: One (1) year of specialized experience which is at least equivalent to the next lower grade. Specialized experience must have equipped the applicant with the particular knowledge, skills, and abilities to perform successfully the duties of the position to be filled.

HIGHLY QUALIFYING CRITERIA: Applicants will be evaluated in the following areas:
1. Ability to plan, develop, establish, and direct a procurement program.
2. Knowledge of procurement regulations and contracting principles relating to supply, service, and construction contracts.
3. Knowledge of related disciplines and functions, i.e., engineering, construction, etc., and their interrelationships and requirements with the contracting process.
4. Knowledge of personnel management policies and procedures.
5. Ability to deal effectively with all levels of personnel within the Federal service and private sector.

REPROMOTION CONSIDERATION: DOD candidates who have been demoted from this or a higher grade without personal cause will be given consideration for repromotion to position. Candidates who believe they are entitled to such consideration should forward a description of the circumstances with their application. Consideration of candidates for repromotion will precede efforts to fill the position by competitive procedures.

THIS ANNOUNCEMENT MAY BE USED TO FILL MORE THAN ONE VACANCY.

EQUAL EMPLOYMENT OPPORTUNITY: Evaluation of qualifications and consideration for placement will be made on a fair and equitable basis without regard to race, religion, color, lawful political or other affiliation, marital status, sex, age, national origin, or physical or mental handicap provided such handicap does not preclude performance of required duties.

SPOUSE PREFERENCE: The Military Family Act of 1985 provides employment preference for spouses of relocating military members who apply for and are referred in the best qualified groups as competitive promotion candidates for certain positions in the competitive service in the DoD components at grade levels GS-5 and above or equivalent wage system positions. Candidates who believe they are entitled to this preference must indicate such on their applications and submit a copy of the military member's permanent change of station travel orders.

PRIVACY ACT REQUIREMENTS (P.L. 93-579): The forms referenced in this announcement are used to determine candidates' qualifications for the position and are authorized under 5 U.S.C. 3302 and 3361. The social security number is not required for this purpose and may be deleted from the forms submitted.

USE OF US GOVERNMENT INDICIA ENVELOPES TO SUBMIT APPLICATIONS IS A VIOLATION OF FEDERAL LAW.

HOW TO APPLY: Submit the following to the address below:
(1) SF 171, Application for Federal Employment, describing your experience, training, education and awards. Failure to submit an accurate and up-to-date SF 171 may result in not being considered for the position.
(2) Supplemental Application Form (attached) designed to elicit from you specific information related to the highly qualifying criteria. Completion of this form is mandatory. Failure to complete will result in no further consideration.
(3) Supervisory Appraisal (attached), designed to elicit specific rating from your supervisor on the highly qualifying criteria. You MUST submit this appraisal in order to be considered. Exceptions will be made for Reinstatement Eligibles, Overseas Returnees, or applicants who do not have a supervisor available to complete a rating. In such cases, applicants must submit an explanation for the lack of an appraisal. A rating of "2" (Satisfactory) will be assigned for each rating factor provided evidence of experience in the rating factor is reflected in the SF 171 and Supplemental Application Form. The same will apply on those factors the supervisor indicates, "Unable to Appraise."

(4) OPM Form 1386, Background Survey Questionnaire (attached). You are requested to complete and submit this form with your application. Completion is voluntary and personnel selections are not made based on this information.
(5) SF 50, Notification of Personnel Action, if you are NOT serviced by this office. This is used as proof of status of current or last appointment and MUST be submitted.
(6) TAD Form 369, Job Vacancy Application, ONLY by employees serviced by this office.
(7) All MALE applicants born after December 31, 1959 who are between the ages of 18 and 26 are required to complete a certification document to confirm their Selective Service registration status. If this is applicable to you, please contact this office at (703)665-3732 for the appropriate form.
(8) Most recent annual Employee Performance Appraisal.

US Army Corps of Engineers
Transatlantic Division, CETAD-HR-R
P.O. Box 2250
Winchester, VA 22601-1450

ALL APPLICATIONS MUST BE RECEIVED BY CLOSE OF BUSINESS ON THE CLOSING DATE OF THE ANNOUNCEMENT.

ADDITIONAL INFORMATION: Tour of duty is 12 months. Dependents are NOT authorized. SMA authorized. Living quarters and vehicle are provided. There is current a 20% post differential authorized. Post allowance (cost of living allowance) is currently authorized. Sunday premium pay authorized. For further information, contact Alois Egan, Human Resouces, (703) 665-3734; FTS 982-3734; or AV 937-1440, Ext. 3734.

DEPARTMENT OF TRANSPORTATION

PROMOTIONAL AND CAREER OPPORTUNITIES

ORGANIZATION FEDERAL AVIATION ADMINISTRATION

ANNOUNCEMENT NO 4-ACS-
OPENING DATE

POSITION Supervisory Criminal Investigator, GM-1811-15
PROMOTION POTENTIAL: NONE

CLOSING DATE

LOCATION Assistant Administrator for Civil Aviation Security,
Office of Civil Aviation Security Operations, Investigations and
Security Division, Drug Investigations Support Program Branch

AREA OF CONSIDERATION NATIONWIDE (STATUS/NONSTATUS)

NOTE: Certain handicapped individuals and disabled veterans eligible for special appointing authorities may also apply. Ingrade/downgrade applicants will be considered.

THIS ANNOUNCEMENT MAY BE USED TO FILL OTHER SIMILAR POSITIONS SUBJECT TO THE PRIOR APPROVAL OF THE HUMAN RESOURCE MANAGEMENT DIVISION.

EQUAL OPPORTUNITY THROUGH AFFIRMATIVE ACTION: The Federal Aviation Administration is committed to a multicultural environment. Minorities and women are strongly encouraged to apply.

DUTIES: The incumbent, as Manager of the Drug Investigations Support Program Branch, is responsible for developing implementing instructions for policies, procedures, and standards with respect to the Drug Investigations Support Program (DISP), as well as providing oversight and guidance to field operations and serving as the local point within the FAA for the handling of all matters directly or indirectly pertaining to anti-drug operational assistance and as staff advisor to the Assistant Administrator for Civil Aviation Security and key officials of the agency on all matters relating to the DISP. Serves as principal representative of the Office of Civil Aviation Security on all matters regarding aviation-related drug activities. Interfaces with the Department of Transportation (DOT), Office of the Secretary (OST) on aviation-related drug issues involving coordination, support, and/or response to those Congressional or Office of the President Committees or representatives addressing matters related to the national drug effort. Responsible for providing technical information and support to FAA top management regarding its participation in high-level committee activity, e.g., Office of National Drug Control Policy (ONDCP), Border Interdiction Committee (BIC), etc. Has oversight of a field investigative program covering (a) certificate actions against airmen arrested and/or convicted of the drug smuggling provisions of Title 49, (b) deregistration actions against aircraft used in violation of the smuggling provisions of Title 49, (c) integration of ongoing FAA investigations with other Federal, State, and local law enforcement smuggling investigations, both substantive and conspiracy, (d) providing onsite FAA assistance to law enforcement officers, (e) conducting fraudulent document investigations of violations of the felony criminal provisions within Title 49, (f) coordinating unusual law enforcement requests for assistance, (g) the seizure and forfeiture of aircraft used in Title 49 violations. Implement investigative policies, standards, and techniques relating to the FAA-wide DISP, providing assistance and advice to the division manager in matters involving field investigations and interaction with Federal, State, and local law enforcement.

QUALIFICATIONS: Applicants must have at least one year of specialized experience equivalent to the next lower grade level. Specialized experience is experience which is in or directly related to the line of work of the position to be filled and which has equipped the applicant with the particular Knowledge, Skills, Abilities to successfully perform the duties of the position. To be creditable, specialized experience must have been at least equivalent to the next lower grade level in the normal line of progression for the occupation in the organization.

PRIVACY ACT REQUIREMENTS (P.L. 93-579)

The referenced forms are used to determine qualifications for promotional and are authorized under Title 5 of the U.S. Code, Sections 1302 and 3361. Each specified form must be submitted in order for you to be considered for promotion to the position being advertised. The social security number is not required for this purpose and may be deleted from the forms submitted. Your servicing personnel office or the office named in this announcement will be able to provide information on specific Privacy Act requirements.

CANDIDATES WHO FAIL TO SUBMIT THE REQUIRED FORMS WILL NOT BE CONSIDERED. NONE OF THESE FORMS WILL BE SUBSEQUENTLY LOANED OR RETURNED TO THE APPLICANTS.

CANDIDATES WILL BE EVALUATED ON BASIS OF EXPERIENCE AND EDUCATION, PERFORMANCE APPRAISAL, TRAINING AND AWARDS.

DOT IS AN EQUAL OPPORTUNITY EMPLOYER

ALL QUALIFIED CANDIDATES WILL BE CONSIDERED REGARDLESS OF RACE, COLOR, RELIGION, SEX OR NATIONAL ORIGIN

FORM DOT F 3300 6 (Rev. 1-88) SUPERSEDES PREVIOUS EDITION

RATING AND RANKING PROCESS: Applicants who meet the qualification requirements described above will be rated and ranked based on the following Knowledge, Skills, and Abilities (KSA's).

1. Ability to identify the need for, develop, and coordinate the implementation of written regulations, policies, and procedures.

2. Ability to communicate orally and to brief senior management and members of Congress on key program areas.

3. Indepth knowledge of policies, programs, and activities in one or more of the following areas: regulatory/criminal investigations or drug interdiction.

4. Ability to manage the overall programs and to ensure implementation through the conduct of extensive research, analysis, writing/editing, coordination, followup, and or review of action documents and correspondence pertaining to the policies, procedures, and standards for one or more of the following security program areas: regulatory/criminal investigations or drug interdiction.

5. Ability to work with senior management persons and groups within his/her own and other Federal and civil agencies to identify and/or resolve policy issues and to conduct liaison at the national level with outside agencies.

NOTE: SUPERVISORY AND MANAGERIAL PROBATIONARY PERIOD: The candidate selected for this position may be required to complete a probationary period. Employees who as of August 11, 1979, have served in supervisory or managerial positions in the Federal Government are exempt from the comparable probationary period requirement. Satisfactory completion of the probationary period is a prerequisite to continuation in the position. If an evaluation of the selectee's performance reveals supervisory or managerial deficiencies which make him or her unsuited for continued employment in the position, the employee will be returned to a non-supervisory or non-managerial position.

For FAA candidates, permanent promotion or reassignment to this position requires prior successful completion of the Supervisor's Course, Phase I at the Center for Management Development. The person selected for this position will be scheduled for the required course as soon as possible after selection but will not be permanently promoted or reassigned until the course has been successfully completed. For non-FAA candidates, a permanent promotion or reassignment may be made, but the training will be required within 120 days of accession.

THIS POSITION IS COVERED UNDER THE PERFORMANCE MANAGEMENT AND RECOGNITION SYSTEM. THE INCUMBENT'S PERFORMANCE WILL BE EVALUATED ACCORDING TO THE PROVISION OF OPM LETTER 540-1, "DEPARTMENT PERFORMANCE MANAGEMENT AND RECOGNITION SYSTEM."

HOW TO APPLY: An SF-171, Application for Federal Employment, must be submitted by all applicants. In addition, the submission of the following supplemental forms/information are encouraged. – The SF-171 and supplemental materials must be submitted as a complete package by the closing date of the announcement.

1. WA Form 3330.8, transmittal for Position Vacancy Application, for acknowledgement of application and final selection notification.

2. WA Form 3330.9, Evaluation of Knowledge, Skills, and Abilities, completed by supervisor (current or former).

3. Response to Evaluation Criteria. A supplemental statement for each KSA is highly recommended although KSA's may be addressed in work experience blocks on SF-171.

4. Current SF-50, Notification of Personnel Action, to verify competitive status or reinstatement eligibility.

5.   SF-181, Race and National Origin Identification.

6.   Latest performance appraisal.

Applications must be postmarked by the closing date of the announcement and received by the close of business on the 5th working day after close of announcement.

**Applicants must meet the time-in-grade requirements by the closing date of the announcement.

****We are prohibited from considering applications received in penalty and/or interoffice mail or in any other government envelope.

WHERE TO SEND APPLICATION:

Federal Aviation Administration
Human Resource Management Division
Operations Branch, AHR-150
800 Independence Avenue, S.W.
Washington, D. C. 20591

Applications may be hand-delivered to Room 516.

Please call 267-8008 for further information or forms.

All qualified applicants will receive consideration for appointment without regard to race, religion, color, national origin, sex, political affiliation, age, physical or mental handicap, marital status, or any other nonmerit factor.

TITLE, SERIES, AND GRADE: Supervisory Electronics Engineer (Director, Communication and System Control Division), GM-855-13. The full performance level for this position is GM-13.

THIS IS A MERIT PAY POSITION.

LOCATION: Department of Energy, Western Area Power Administration, Billings Area Office, Bismarck District Office, Communication and System Control Division. Duty station: Bismarck, North Dakota.

NOTE: The applicant selected for this position will be required to file upon entrance on duty, a Report of Financial Interest (DOE F 3735.1).

AREA OF CONSIDERATION: Nationwide.

Applications will be accepted from all status candidates. (Status candidates are current career or career-conditional employees of the Federal Government, or former employees with reinstatement eligibility.)

Other persons may be eligible for a special employment program appointment such as those authorized for the severely handicapped, including disabled veterans having a compensable service-connected disability of 30 percent or more, or former Peace Corps/VISTA volunteers. Applicants eligible for one of these programs do not need to be present or former employees of the Federal Government in order to apply under this announcement, but should state the specific program eligibility on line 1 of the SF-171, Application for Federal Employment, if known.

NOTE: Probationary Period. In accordance with the Civil Service Reform Act, the employee selected for this position will serve a 1-year probationary period before the appointment becomes final--unless he/she is now serving or has served in a supervisory/managerial position in the Federal service. Failure to complete probation successfully because of deficiencies in supervisory/managerial performance will mandate the employee's return to a nonsupervisory/nonmanagerial position at no lower grade and pay than the one he/she left to accept the probational appointment.

DUTIES AND RESPONSIBILITIES: The incumbent is responsible for formulating and executing a program for the operation, maintenance, design, installation, and replacement of communications and system control equipment and facilities which support the power system in the Bismarck District.   Plans, manages, and is responsible for the development and execution of an adequate preventive maintenance program involving highly specialized VHF and UHF radio, microwave

communication systems, computer network and data communications equipment, carrier relaying, telemetering, supervisory control and data acquisition, power line carrier, load control equipment, and fault recorders. In addition, is responsible for system implementation and all coordination associated with any future electronic equipment installations.   Directs continuing analysis of day-to-day operations, malfunctions, equipment failures, test and maintenance techniques. Coordinates Division activities with owners of leased power communications facilities to effect optimum performance. Represents the District on problems relating to communications, telemetering, and load control facilities with the Corps of Engineers, interconnected utility systems, and other District offices.   Resolves complicated and controversial problems concerning such items as leased phone circuits,   equipment purchases and specifications, frequency assignment coordination, and load control arrangements. Designs and implements modifications to communication and system control facilities. Conducts field tests and surveys and compiles data required for the location and equipment required for new communication facilities or additions to the existing systems.

QUALIFICATION REQUIREMENTS: Applicants must meet the qualifications outlined in the Office of Personnel Management Qualifications Handbook X-118, for the GS-855 series. The length and type of qualifying experience is described below:

BASIC REQUIREMENTS: A. Degree in professional engineering. To be acceptable, the curriculum must: (1) Be in a school of engineering with at least one curriculum accredited by the Accreditation Board for Engineering and Technology (ABET) as a professional engineering curriculum; or (2) Include differential and integral calculus and courses (more advanced than first-year physics and chemistry) in five of the following seven areas of engineering science or physics: (a) statics, dynamics; (b) strength of materials   (stress-strain relationships); (c) fluid mechanics, hydraulics;   (d) thermodynamics;   (e) electrical fields and circuits; (f) nature and properties of materials (relating particle and aggregate structure to properties); and (g) any other comparable area of fundamental engineering science or physics, such as optics, heat transfer, soil mechanics, or electronics.

OR

B. Combination of education and experience - college-level education, training, and/or technical experience that furnished (1) a thorough knowledge of the physical and mathematical sciences underlying professional engineering, and (2) a good understanding, both theoretical and practical, of the engineering sciences and techniques and their applications to one of the branches of engineering. The adequacy of such background must be demonstrated by one of the following: (a) Current registration as a professional engineer; (b) Evidence of having successfully passed the Engineer-in-Training (EIT) examination; (c) Successful completion of at least 60 semester hours of courses in professional engineering curriculum; or, (d) Related curriculum.

The U.S. Department of Energy is an Equal Opportunity Employer

DEFINITION OF PROFESSIONAL ENGINEERING EXPERIENCE: The professional engineering experience required for grades GS-7 and above is defined as nonroutine engineering work that required and was characterized by (1) professional knowledge of engineering; (2) professional ability to apply such knowledge to engineering problems; and (3) positive and continuing development of professional knowledge and ability.

LENGTH OF QUALIFYING EXPERIENCE:

Specialized

GM-13   One year at least equivalent to next lower grade.

SPECIALIZED EXPERIENCE: Experience which is in or directly related to the line of work of the position to be filled and which has equipped the applicant with the particular knowledges, skills, and abilities to successfully perform the duties of that position.

SUBSTITUTION OF EDUCATION FOR EXPERIENCE: None.

TIME-IN-GRADE RESTRICTIONS: Applicants must meet time-in-grade restrictions within 30 days of the closing date of this announcement.

SELECTIVE PLACEMENT FACTOR(S): None.

BASIS OF EVALUATION: Applicants will be evaluated on the basis of information contained in their Application for Federal Employment (SF-171) and the Supervisory Appraisal included with this announce-ment. Applicants should include all pertinent experience, awards, commendations, training, and other information on the SF-171. Applicants who possess the required experience noted above will be further evaluated according to the degree to which they possess the knowledges, skills, and abilities, described in the following factors:

1. Knowledge of the theories, principles, and practices of communications systems that include microwave, VHF and UHF radio, powerline carrier, leased communications facilities, telephone systems, complex telemetering schemes, supervisory control and data acquisition systems, computer networks, and data communication systems as they are applied to an integrated power system.

2. Knowledge of electrical and electronic engineering principles, practices, and procedures involving power system operation.

3. Ability to supervise and direct the activities of professional engineers, technicians, and wage employees involved in formulating and executing a program for the maintenance of communications and systems control facilities.

4. Ability to meet and deal effectively with people including federal agencies, public and private utilities, and equipment vendors.

5. Ability to communicate technical and administrative requirements effectively, both orally and in writing.

6. Knowledge of and willingness to support equal employment opportunity programs, including programs for the handicapped and disabled veterans.

The above knowledges, skills, and abilities will be the basis for determining which applicants are best qualified for promotion or for grade levels with promotion potential. Applicants are encouraged to address those factors in their SF-171, or as a Narrative Statement on a separate piece of paper.

LIVING CONDITIONS: Bismarck, North Dakota, is a progressive city of approximately 50,000. The housing situation is good. No government housing is available. Some rental housing is available, and there are houses in all price ranges for sale. There are apartments, furnished and unfurnished, available. Rent is moderate. The city has an excellent school system, churches of most faiths, excellent clinics and hospitals, and shopping areas. Bismarck has daily air and bus service, but does not have a public transportation system. A junior college and a 4-year liberal arts college are located in Bismarck.

Western supports the policy of restricting smoking in Federal facilities. Smoking permitted only in designated areas.

CONTACT: For further information, call Personnel (303) 231-1502. For information on other current vacancies, contact Western's jobline on (303) 231-1148. Hearing and speech impaired may call (303) 231-7919 (TDD).

HOW TO APPLY: Applicants should submit all of the following forms to receive consideration for this vacancy announcement:

● Application for Federal Employment (SF-171)   with original signature and date;

● SF-50 (Notification of Personnel Action), showing current Federal status or reinstatement eligibility;

● Veterans should submit a copy of all DD-214's and if applicable a current letter from the Veterans Administration verifying disability, dated within one year;

● Supervisory Appraisal, attached to the vacancy announcement;

● Narrative Statement addressing the knowledges, skills, and abilities as listed in the vacancy announcement under the area entitled BASIS OF EVALUATION.

Submission of the attached Applicant Background Survey is voluntary and will be detached from your application package upon receipt.

Submit complete application package to the Western Area Power Administration, 1627 Cole Blvd., Golden, CO 80401, Attention: Personnel A1220. Applications received in the mail must be postmarked on or before the closing date, and received in the personnel office within 3 working days after the closing date of the vacancy announcement. Applications received in government franked or blue envelopes will not be accepted. Do not send original documents. Applications will not be returned.

FAILURE TO PROVIDE THE SPECIFIC FORMS OUTLINED ABOVE MAY RESULT IN AN APPLICANT RECEIVING A LOWER RATING IN THE EVALUATION PROCESS.

DEPARTMENT OF TRANSPORTATION

PROMOTIONAL AND CAREER OPPORTUNITIES

ORGANIZATION	FEDERAL AVIATION ADMINISTRATION

ANNOUNCEMENT NO

POSITION	Supervisory Personnel Management Specialist, GM-201-14

PROMOTION POTENTIAL: NONE

OPENING DATE

LOCATION   Assistant Administrator for Human Resource Management, Senior Executive Resource Staff, Washington, D.C.

CLOSING DATE

AREA OF CONSIDERATION   NATIONWIDE (Status)

NOTE: Certain handicapped individuals and disabled veterans eligible for special appointing authorities may also apply. Ingrade/downgrade applicants will be considered.

THIS ANNOUNCEMENT MAY BE USED TO FILL OTHER SIMILAR POSITIONS SUBJECT TO THE PRIOR APPROVAL OF THE HUMAN RESOURCE MANAGEMENT DIVISION.

EQUAL OPPORTUNITY THROUGH AFFIRMATIVE ACTION: The Federal Aviation Administration is committed to a multicultural environment. Minorities and women are strongly encouraged to apply.

DUTIES: The incumbent supervises a team of professionals who provide expert advice and support on a wide range of SES personnel matters. Plans the work of the team, establishes goals and objectives, sets priorities, etc. Provides expert advice and support to the FAA Administrator, Deputy Administrator, Assistant Administrator for Human Resource Management and other agency executives on all SES operational personnel matters. Reviews and evaluates request for additional SES resources, changes in classification and compensation for SES positions. Works with staffing, compensation, performance management and employee relations.

QUALIFICATIONS: All applicants must demonstrate one year of specialized experience equivalent to that of the next lower grade in the Federal government. Specialized experience is experience which is directly related to the line of work of this position which has equipped the applicant with the particular knowledge, skills, and abilities (KSA's) to successfully perform the duties to be filled. To be creditable, specialized experience must have been at least equivalent to the next lower grade in the normal line of progression for the occupation for the position.

TIME IN GRADE REQUIREMENT: Applicants must have completed one year of service at the next lower grade as of the closing date of the announcement.

RATING AND RANKING PROCESS: Applicants who meet the qualification requirements described above will be rated and ranked based on the following Knowledge, Skills, and Abilities (KSA's).

1. Knowledge of Federal human resource operations, particularly as they relate to Senior Executive Service level positions, e.g., staffing, classification, compensation, performance management, and employee relations.

2. Skill in formulating and implementing human resource management policy.

3. Skill in representing an organization to outside groups both informally and formally, e.g. briefings/presentations.

4. Ability to supervise others, i.e., planning and assigning work; improving and controlling performance; promoting EEO, human relations, and employee participation.

SELECTIVE REQUIREMENTS (FPL 93-579):

PRIVACY ACT REQUIREMENTS (including leave)

The referenced forms are used to determine qualifications (for promotions) and are authorized under Title 5 of the U.S. Code, Sections 1302 and 3361. Each specified form must be submitted in order for you to be considered for promotion to the position being advertised. The social security number is not required for this purpose and may be deleted from the forms submitted. Your servicing personnel office or the office named in this announcement will be able to provide information on specific Privacy Act requirements.

CANDIDATES WHO FAIL TO SUBMIT THE REQUIRED FORMS WILL NOT BE CONSIDERED. NONE OF THESE FORMS WILL BE SUBSEQUENTLY LOANED OR RETURNED TO THE APPLICANTS.

CANDIDATES WILL BE EVALUATED ON BASIS OF EXPERIENCE AND EDUCATION, PERFORMANCE APPRAISAL, TRAINING AND AWARDS.

DOT IS AN EQUAL OPPORTUNITY EMPLOYER

ALL QUALIFIED CANDIDATES WILL BE CONSIDERED REGARDLESS OF RACE, COLOR, RELIGION, SEX OR NATIONAL ORIGIN

FORM DOT F 3300 6 (Rev. 1-88) SUPERSEDES PREVIOUS EDITION

ANNOUNCEMENT NO.   Continued

HOW TO APPLY: An SF-171, Application for Federal Employment, must be submitted by all applicants. In addition, the following forms/information are encouraged. *ALL APPLICATION MATERIALS MUST BE RECEIVED OR POSTMARKED BY THE CLOSING DATE OF THE ANNOUNCEMENT.*

1. WA Form 3330-8, Transmittal for Position Vacancy Application, for acknowledgment of application and final selection notification.

2. WA Form 3330-9, Evaluation of Knowledges, Skills and Abilities, completed by supervisor (current or former).

3. Response to Evaluation Criteria. A supplemental statement for each KSA is highly recommended although KSA's may be addressed in work experience blocks on SF-171.

4. Latest performance appraisal.

5. Current SF-50, Notification of Personnel Action, to verify competitive status or reinstatement eligibility.

6. SF-181, Race and National Origin Identification.

* Applications must be postmarked by the closing date of the announcement and received by the close of business on the 5th working day after close of announcement.
** Applicants must meet the time-in-grade requirements by the closing date of the announcement.
*** We are prohibited from considering applications received in penalty and/or interoffice mail or in any other government envelope.

WHERE TO SEND APPLICATION:

Federal Aviation Administration
Human Resource Management Division
Operations Branch, AHR-150, Team 1
800 Independence Avenue, S.W.
Washington, D.C. 20591

Applications may be hand-delivered to Room 516.

Please call Natalie Love 267-8007 for further information or forms.

United States Department of the Interior
FISH AND WILDLIFE SERVICE
Washington, D.C. 20240

VACANCY ANNOUNCEMENT

Position Title, Series and Grade:
Supervisory Wildlife Biologist
GM-486-15
(Center Director, NPWRC)

Announcement No.: FWS9-

Opening Date:

Closing Date:

Location:
Region 8
Northern Prairie Wildlife Research
Center
Jamestown, North Dakota

Performance Management and
Recognition System Position:
Yes _X_ No _____

Subject to Supervisory or
Managerial Probation Period:
Yes _X_ No _____

(Status Candidates Only)
Area of Consideration: Governmentwide **Full Performance Level:** GM-15

****

Primary Duties: The incumbent serves as the Director of the Northern Prairie Wildlife Research Center (NPWRC). The Center Director functions as part of the Region 8 directorate and as such is responsible for all aspects of the administration and management of the NPWRC. The incumbent serves as primary liaison to other service components, Federal and state agencies, and private conservation groups. He/She identifies and prioritizes future research issues important to the Service mission, approves research study plans, and supervises the Center's operational and administrative functions to include personnel, field, contracting property management and maintenance. The incumbent has overall responsibility to insure that all support functions are effectively and efficiently conducted within federal guidelines and legal framework. He/She also insures transfer of technical information to resource managers and administrators to aid in the decision making process.

Quality Ranking Factors:

(1) Knowledge of wildlife resources programs and policies.
(2) Ability to manage a natural resources research or related program.
(3) Skill in meeting, dealing and negotiating with diverse individuals and groups.
(4) Ability to supervise.
(5) Ability to implement EEO principles and practices including special emphasis programs.

Qualifications:
In accordance with OPM Handbook X-118, which is available for review in most Federal personnel offices, candidates must meet one of the following basic requirements: [A] A full 4-year course of study in an accredited college or university leading to a bachelor's or higher degree with at least 30 semester hours of course work in biological science. This course work must have included at least 9 semester hours in wildlife subjects, 12 semester hours in zoology and at least 9 semester hours in botany or related plant sciences, OR [B] Course work described in [A] above plus additional appropriate experience or education which when combined with the 30 semester hours will total 4 years of education or 4 years of education and experience. **Additional Experience and Training Requirements:** Candidates must have had one year of professional experience and three years of graduate education or a doctoral degree, or equivalent combinations of education and experience. This year of professional experience must have been in or directly related to wildlife biology and must have equipped the candidate with the knowledge, skill and abilities necessary to perform the duties of this position.

THE SUCCESSFUL CANDIDATE MUST FILE, PRIOR TO APPOINTMENT, A CONFIDENTIAL STATEMENT FO EMPLOYMENT AND FINANCIAL INTERESTS (DI 212).

APPLICANTS MUST MEET TIME-IN-GRADE REQUIREMENTS.

DI Form 1935: The completion of DI Form 1935 is strictly voluntary and is used for statistical purposes by the Office for Human Resources. All DI 1935 forms become the property of the Office for Human Resources and are not shared in the evaluation process or with the Selecting Official.

How To Apply: Submit a complete up-to-date Standard Form 171, Application for Federal Employment, accompanied by a Supervisory Appraisal, a separate statement addressing each quality ranking factor, a copy of most recent Standard Form 50 (Notification of Personnel Action) and a copy of college transcripts, if applicable, to:

U.S. Fish and Wildlife Service
Division of Personnel Management
1849 C Street, N.W.
Mail Stop: ARLSQ - 100
Washington, D.C. 20240
Attention: FWS9-

*Applicants who wish to handcarry their applications should deliver them to 4401 N. Fairfax Drive, Room 100, Arlington, Virginia or who need information can call (703) 358-1743 or TDD: 358-1796.

Method of Evaluating and Ranking Applicants: In addition to your experience and education, other elements such as relevant awards, training, self-development, outside activities, and supervisory appraisals will be evaluated as indicators of your ability to perform the specific ranking factors of the position. To receive full consideration for this position, your application must include concise information regarding the quality of your experience. Identify the knowledge, skills, and abilities involved in carrying out the duties and responsibilities of your current and past positions as they relate to this position.

General Information: The importance of a complete and accurate Standard Form 171 cannot be over-emphasized. In accordance with 39 U.S.C., Section 415, applications will not be accepted in a Federal agency postage paid envelope (Penalty Mail). Position descriptions are not acceptable. Position descriptions submitted with an application will not be considered in the evaluation. All career/career conditional status candidates who wish to be considered under both merit promotion and competitive procedures must submit two (2) complete applications. When only one (1) application is received, it will be considered under the merit promotion procedures only. Applications become the property of the Service and will not be returned or referred for other vacancies.

Privacy Act Information: The application you submit for this position contains information subject to the Privacy Act of 1974 (P.L. 93-579, 5 U.S.C. 552a). Information regarding this Act is available upon request.

Other: Vietnam era veterans, disabled veterans, the handicapped and other individuals eligible for special appointing authorities are encouraged to apply.

THE U.S. FISH AND WILDLIFE SERVICE IS AN EQUAL OPPORTUNITY EMPLOYER.

ALL CANDIDATES WILL RECEIVE CONSIDERATION WITHOUT REGARD TO RACE, COLOR, RELIGION, SEX, NATIONAL ORIGIN, AGE, POLITICAL AFFILIATION OR ANY OTHER NONMERIT FACTOR.

U.S. Fish and Wildlife Service

DEPARTMENT OF THE INTERIOR

SUPERVISORY APPRAISAL FOR MERIT PROMOTION

(This appraisal is used for merit promotion plan purposes only. It is not related to the separate requirement for annual performance evaluation of the employee.)

Position Applying For: Supervisory Wildlife Biologist, GM-486-13   Vacancy Announcement Number: FWS9-92-042

      Title, Series and Grade

Supervisors must complete this appraisal within three days of the employee's request and return to the employee.

NAME OF CANDIDATE	PRESENT POSITION TITLE	SERIES	GRADE

NAME OF IMMEDIATE SUPERVISOR	SUPERVISOR'S TITLE	PERIOD OF SUPERVISION
		FROM: TO:

The employee named has requested consideration for the above position. Your appraisal will be used as one measure in ranking the employee with other candidates. Please complete this form based upon your appraisal of the employee's ability to perform satisfactorily in the position. An appraisal is given to an employee upon his/her request.

IN THE COLUMNS AT THE RIGHT INDICATE YOUR APPRAISAL OF THE EMPLOYEE'S ABILITY IN EACH OF THE FOLLOWING AREAS:

	WOULD EXCEED REQUIRE- MENTS	WOULD FULLY MEET REQUIRE- MENTS	WOULD NEED FURTHER DEVELOP- MENT	UNABLE TO ADDRESS
1) Knowledge of wildlife resources programs and policies.				
2) Ability to manage a natural resources research or related program.				
3) Skill in meeting, dealing and negotiating with diverse individuals and groups.				
4) Ability to supervise.				
5) Ability to implement EEO principles and practices including special emphasis programs.				

Supervisor's Signature _____ Date _____

NATIONAL SCIENCE FOUNDATION

EXCEPTED POSITION VACANCY

ANNOUNCEMENT NO: **OPEN:**   **CLOSE:**

THIS IS A PERMANENT POSITION

POSITION VACANT: Physical Science Education Administrator (PROGRAM DIRECTOR), AD-1301-4. (Salary ranges from $54,607 to $85,500 per annum)

LOCATION: Directorate for Education and Human Resources, Division of Teacher Preparation Enhancement, Institutes and Recognition Section, Teacher Enhancement Program, National Science Foundation, Washington, D.C.

AREA OF CONSIDERATION: ALL SOURCES.

BARGAINING UNIT STATUS: This position is included in the Bargaining Unit and will be filled in accordance with the provisions of the Collective Bargaining Agreement, Article VIII.

THIS POSITION IS OUTSIDE THE COMPETITIVE CIVIL SERVICE

Appointment to this position will be made under the Excepted Authority of the NSF Act. Candidates who do not have civil service status or reinstatement eligibility will not obtain civil service status if selected. Candidates currently in the competitive civil service may be required to waive competitive civil service rights if selected. Usual civil service benefits (retirement, health benefits, insurance, leave) are applicable. Disabled veterans with 30% service-connected disabilities as well as other applicants with severe disabilities will be considered without regard to the closing date if applications are received prior to final selection.

DUTIES AND RESPONSIBILITIES:

- In cooperation with other program directors, manages a program which supports the development of effective approaches and creative materials for the continuing education of elementary, middle and secondary school mathematics and science teachers.
- Develops policies and recommendations in the area of physics education in the precollege classroom and other learning environments.
- Conducts final review of proposals and recommends award or declination, based on scientific merit and continuing evaluation of the availability of resources, priorities and knowledge of NSF policies and goals.
- Designs and implements the proposal review and evaluation process for the program to assure the support of high quality proposals and adequacy of review.

- Manages and monitors grants, contracts, and cooperative agreements to ensure fulfillment of commitments to and by NSF.
- Negotiates revision of proposal budgets when appropriate, and serves as on-going advisor to applicants and grantees concerning NSF policies, requirements, regulations, and program objectives.

QUALIFICATIONS REQUIRED: Candidates must have a Ph.D. or equivalent experience in a field of physical science or physical science education. (Individuals with backgrounds in chemistry, physics, and other relevant physical sciences will be considered.) In addition, six or more years of successful research development, research administration, teaching and/or managerial experience related to teacher training and curricula, methodologies and education research in science, mathematics and technology education for the precollege levels is required.

QUALITY RANKING FACTORS: Qualified candidates will be rated and ranked based on the extent and quality of their total backgrounds. Appropriate credit will be given for job-related experience, training, education, awards and supervisory appraisal of job performance. Final ranking will be based on the required qualifications and on the following knowledge, skills, and abilities:

- Broad knowledge and understanding of the role of teacher training and enhancements in science, mathematics, and technology education at the precollege level.

- Ability to organize, implement and manage a proposal-driven grant program allocating resources to meet a broad spectrum of programs goals.

- Knowledge of and ability to interact with members of the scientific community.

- Research, analytical and technical writing skills which evidences the ability to perform extensive inquiry into a wide variety of significant issues, and make recommendations and decisions based on findings.

HOW TO APPLY: Applicants must submit an SF-171, Application for Federal Employment; Current General Workforce Performance Appraisal or letters of recommendation from professionals who can comment on your capabilities; and (NSF employees only) NSF Form 614, Merit Promotion Interest Statement. In order to ensure full consideration it is recommended that all applicants submit a supplemental statement on plain bond paper which specifically addresses how his/her background/experience relates to each Selective and Quality Ranking Factor listed in this announcement.

Submit required forms to National Science Foundation, Division of Human Resource Management, 1800 G Street, N.W. Room 208, Washington, D.C. 20550. Attn: Announcement Number EX 92-17. ALL FORMS MUST BE RECEIVED BY THE CLOSING DATE OF THIS ANNOUNCEMENT. For additional information call Rhonda Horton on (202) 357-9529. Hearing impaired individuals should call TDD (202) 357-7492.

AN EQUAL OPPORTUNITY EMPLOYER

U.S. Department of Energy

Senior Executive Service

EMPLOYMENT OPPORTUNITY

Mail Distribution Code: 5 ☒   6 ☒
Announcement No.: **ERM-**____ ____
Issue Date: March 09,
Closing Date: April 07,
Area of Consideration:
Government-Wide   ☒
Nation-Wide All Sources   ☒

POSITION: Assistant Administrator for Power Management, Operations and Maintenance, ES-340*

ORGANIZATIONAL LOCATION: Western Area Power Administration, Office of Power Management, Operations and Maintenance

SALARY RANGE: $90,000 - $112,100 per annum
*ANTICIPATED VACANCY -

GEOGRAPHIC LOCATION: Golden, CO

ALL POSITIONS ARE SUBJECT TO THE DEPARTMENT OF ENERGY DRUG TESTING PROGRAM

DUTIES AND RESPONSIBILITIES: The Assistant Administrator is responsible for managing the Western Area Power administration's power marketing, operations, maintenance, and resources programs. Specific duties include establishing and administering policies, standards, and guidelines for conducting power repayment studies; formulating and implementing electric power and transmission service rates and adjustments; developing power planning studies of water and land resource requirements relating to electric power development; and working with other power marketing administrations, utility systems, and Area Reliability Councils in the development of general power utility standards.

QUALIFICATION REQUIREMENTS: To be eligible for consideration, applicants must meet a majority of the following six managerial qualification factors:

1. Integration of internal and external program and policy issues
2. Organizational representation and liaison
3. Direction and guidance of programs, projects, or policy development
4. Resource acquisition and administration
5. Utilization of human resources
6. Review of implementation and results

In addition, applicants must possess the following technical qualifications:

1. Demonstrated experience in managing and directing a complex power marketing activity and the operation and maintenance of a major transmission system.
2. Knowledge of electric power rate development.
3. Knowledge of the legal, regulatory, and operational issues governing the development and administration of contracts for Federally marketed electric power.

EVALUATION METHODS: Applicants will be rated and ranked by a Merit Staffing Committee using only the information submitted for consideration. Failure to document demonstrated experience, training, or education in support of the required qualification requirements may adversely affect an applicant's chance for further consideration. The Committee will rate and rank each applicant based on the criteria identified in the qualification requirements and refer the top applicants to the selecting official. The selecting official will consider the applicants referred based on the information provided and/or personal interview.

TO APPLY: To be considered, all applicants must submit the following information: (1) a current SF-171, Application for Federal Employment; (2) a supplemental statement addressing each of the qualification requirements listed above; and (3) a current performance appraisal. Applications should be sent to the Department of Energy, Executive Resources Management Division, Room 4E-060, 1000 Independence Avenue, SW, Washington, DC 20585, Attention: ERM-92-13. For further information contact Tanja Doy at (202) 586-8450 or FTS 896-8450. Application materials must be postmarked by the closing date of this announcement.

Candidates must provide information covering the six activity areas that provide the focus for the Office of Personnel Management review of executive qualifications. The listing of elements for each activity area is not meant to be exhaustive, but illustrative; nor is it expected that an individual will be a subject matter expert in these activities. What is required in each of these areas is that the individual candidate's record--experience, education, accomplishments, and/or potential--be indicative of competence to provide leadership for the accomplishment of these activities.

1. **INTEGRATION OF INTERNAL AND EXTERNAL PROGRAM/POLICY ISSUES.** This area involves seeing that key national and organization-wide goals, priorities, values, and other issues are taken into account in carrying out the responsibilities of the immediate work unit, including:

   * Responsiveness to the general public and clientele groups
   * Keeping up-to-date with relevant social, political, economic and technological developments
   * Coordinating with other parts of the organization and other organizations, as relevant
   * Understanding the role of political leadership in the Administration and Congress

2. **ORGANIZATIONAL REPRESENTATION AND LIAISON.** This area covers functions related to establishing and maintaining relationships with key individuals and groups outside the immediate work unit and serving as a spokesperson for one's unit and organization. Types of actions generally required to carry out these functions include:

   * Briefings, speeches, congressional testimony, inter-unit staff meetings, professional society presentations, question-and-answer sessions, etc. involving information giving and receiving, recommendations, persuasion, selling, negotiation, program defense

3. **DIRECTION AND GUIDANCE OF PROGRAMS, PROJECTS, OR POLICY DEVELOPMENT.** This area involves activities related to establishing goals and the structure and processes necessary to carry them out. These include:

   * Long-term and short-term planning; needs, forecasts, objectives, priorities, feasibility, options
   * Productivity and other effectiveness-efficiency standards
   * Information gathering and analysis
   * Research and development
   * Work organization structure and operational procedures
   * Scheduling and work assignment

4. **RESOURCE ACQUISITION AND ADMINISTRATION.** This area concerns procedures and activities related to obtaining and allocating the resources necessary to support program or policy implementation. These include:

   * Staffing: work force planning, recruitment and selection, including affirmative action and EEO
   * Budgeting: organizational and congressional procedures and processes
   * Procurement
   * Contracting

5. **UTILIZATION OF HUMAN RESOURCES.** This area involves processes and activities for seeing that people are appropriately employed and dealth with fairly and equitably. These include:

   * Assessment of individual capabilities and needs
   * Delegation of work
   * Provision for career development opportunities
   * Performance standards and appraisal
   * EEO and other special emphasis personnel utilization programs

6. **REVIEW OF IMPLEMENTATION AND RESULTS.** This area involves activities and procedures for seeing that plans are being implemented and/or adjusted as necessary and that the appropriate results are being achieved. These include:

   * Periodic monitoring and review
   * Program evaluation

The content and structure of your application materials should carefully reflect your experience in each of these six activity areas as well as the other qualification requirements found on the front of this announcement.

U.S. Department of Energy

Senior Executive Service

EMPLOYMENT OPPORTUNITY

Mail Distribution Code: 5 ☒   6 ☒
Announcement No.: ERM-_____
Issue Date: ___March 16,___
Closing Date: ___April 7,___
Area of Consideration:
Government-Wide ☐
Nation-Wide All Sources ☒

POSITION: Deputy Director, Office of Special
Projects, ES-819

ORGANIZATION LOCATION: Office of the Assistant Secretary
for Environment, Safety and Health;
Office of Special Projects

SALARY RANGE: $90,000 - $112,100 per annum

GEOGRAPHIC LOCATION: Washington, D.C.

ALL POSITIONS ARE SUBJECT TO THE DEPARTMENT OF ENERGY DRUG TESTING PROGRAM

DUTIES AND RESPONSIBILITIES: The Deputy Director, Office of Special Projects, provides expert advice and analysis to the Director on strategies for monitoring and assessing all aspects of the Department's operating facilities compliance with applicable orders, statutes, and regulations pertaining to environment, safety, and health considerations. Recommends modifications, if appropriate, and addresses items of noncompliance. Advises the Director and other senior level experts on the development and implementation of policy and programs associated with Special Projects. Determines policies, identifies problems, and devises solutions, developing recommendations on the feasibility, nature and scope of the program.

QUALIFICATIONS REQUIREMENTS: To be eligible for consideration, applicants must meet a majority of the following six managerial qualification factors:

(1) Integration of internal and external program or policy issues
(2) Organizational representation and liaison
(3) Direction and guidance of programs, projects, or policy development
(4) Resource acquisition and administration
(5) Utilization of human resources
(6) Evaluating program/policy implementation efforts against achieved results

In addition, applicants must possess the following technical qualifications:

(1) Experience in directing a professional technical staff including scientists and engineers.
(2) Experience that demonstrates detailed knowledge of Federal and State environmental programs (legislation, regulations, implementation plans) including the Resource Conservation and Recovery Act, the Comprehensive Environmental Response, Compensation, and Liability Act, and the Superfund Amendment and Reauthorization Act.
(3) Experience in negotiations with Federal and State agencies and private parties over matters of environmental compliance and remedial actions.
(4) Experience with and understanding of the nuclear fuel cycle, nuclear energy, defense programs, and energy research activities.
(5) Knowledge of and experience with national and international environmental issues.

EVALUATION METHODS: Applicants will be rated and ranked by a Merit Staffing Committee using only the information submitted for consideration. Failure to document demonstrated experience, training, or education in support of the required qualification requirements will adversely affect an applicant's chance for further consideration. The committee will rate and rank each applicant based on the criteria identified in the qualification requirements and refer the top applicants to the selecting official. The selecting official will consider the applicants referred based on the information provided and/or personal interview.

TO APPLY: To be considered, all applicants must submit the following information: (1) a current SF-171, Application for Federal Employment; (2) a supplemental statement addressing each of the qualification requirements listed above; and (3) a current performance appraisal. Applications should be sent to the Department of Energy, Executive Resources Management Division, Room 4E-060, 1000 Independence Avenue, SW, Washington, DC 20585. Attention: ERM-92-16 For further information contact Tanja Doy at (202) 586-8450 or FTS 896-8450. Application materials must be postmarked by the closing date of this announcement.

Candidates must provide information covering the six activity areas that provide the focus for the Office of Personnel Management review of executive qualifications. The listing of elements for each activity area is not meant to be exhaustive, but illustrative; nor is it expected that an individual will be a subject matter expert in these activities. What is required in each of these areas is that the individual candidate's record--experience, education, accomplishments, and/or potential--be indicative of competence to provide leadership for the accomplishment of these activities.

1. **INTEGRATION OF INTERNAL AND EXTERNAL PROGRAM/POLICY ISSUES.** This area involves seeing that key national and organization-wide goals, priorities, values, and other issues are taken into account in carrying out the responsibilities of the immediate work unit, including:

   - Responsiveness to the general public and clientele groups
   - Keeping up-to-date with relevant social, political, economic and technological developments
   - Coordinating with other parts of the organization and other organizations, as relevant
   - Understanding the role of political leadership in the Administration and Congress

2. **ORGANIZATIONAL REPRESENTATION AND LIAISON.** This area covers functions related to establishing and maintaining relationships with key individuals and groups outside the immediate work unit and serving as a spokesperson for one's unit and organization. Types of actions generally required to carry out these functions include:

   - Briefings, speeches, congressional testimony, inter-unit staff meetings, professional society presentations, question-and-answer sessions, etc. involving information giving and receiving, recommendations, persuasion, selling, negotiation, program defense

3. **DIRECTION AND GUIDANCE OF PROGRAMS, PROJECTS, OR POLICY DEVELOPMENT.** This area involves activities related to establishing goals and the structure and processes necessary to carry them out. These include:

   - Long-term and short-term planning; needs, forecasts, objectives, priorities, feasibility, options
   - Productivity and other effectiveness-efficiency standards
   - Information gathering and analysis
   - Research and development
   - Work organization structure and operational procedures
   - Scheduling and work assignment

4. **RESOURCE ACQUISITION AND ADMINISTRATION.** This area concerns procedures and activities related to obtaining and allocating the resources necessary to support program or policy implementation. These include:

   - Staffing: work force planning, recruitment and selection, including affirmative action and EEO
   - Budgeting: organizational and congressional procedures and processes
   - Procurement
   - Contracting

5. **UTILIZATION OF HUMAN RESOURCES.** This area involves processes and activities for seeing that people are appropriately employed and dealth with fairly and equitably. These include:

   - Assessment of individual capabilities and needs
   - Delegation of work
   - Provision for career development opportunities
   - Performance standards and appraisal
   - EEO and other special emphasis personnel utilization programs

6. **REVIEW OF IMPLEMENTATION AND RESULTS.** This area involves activities and procedures for seeing that plans are being implemented and/or adjusted as necessary and that the appropriate results are being achieved. These include:

   - Periodic monitoring and review
   - Program evaluation

The content and structure of your application materials should carefully reflect your experience in each of these six activity areas as well as the other qualification requirements found on the front of this announcement.

AMENDMENT #2 CHANGE IN NUMBER OF VACANCIES

Merit Promotion
Vacancy Announcement

U.S. GOVERNMENT PRINTING OFFICE

Announcement No.:

Position: Clerk-Typist		Issue Date:	Closing Date: OUF
Series/Grade: PG-0322-3/4	Salary: $15,116 - $21,506	Number of Vacancies: 2	Promotion Potential: PG-04

Geographic Location: Columbus, OH	Tour of Duty: Shift 1	Duration of Appointment: (X) Permanent ( ) Temporary

Organization: Printing Procurement Department, Regional Operations Office, Columbus Regional Printing Procurement Office	Civil Service Status Required: SEE NOTE (X) Yes OR (X) No

Area of Consideration: Applicants with Status or OPM Notice of Results in the Columbus Area and Veterans	OPM Notice of Results Required: (X) Yes ( ) No

SUMMARY OF DUTIES/RESPONSIBILITIES:

The incumbent types a variety of material such as form letters, reports, specifications, contracts, contract modifications, abstracts, etc., in final form or rough draft as required. Operates computer terminal using standard typewriter keyboard to enter, retrieve or transmit information. Verifies input data on display screen to insure accuracy, and reviews retrieved information for completeness. Composes and types routine correspondence from brief notes, oral instructions, or on the basis of precedents. Receives, date stamps, logs, and distributes incoming mail, in accordance with established procedures and knowledge of staff responsibilities in the office. Prepares outgoing mail by stuffing and sealing envelopes, or wrapping and labeling packages. Receives and refers visitors and telephone calls, personally handling those for which information is available in files or from own knowledge of office activities.

QUALIFICATIONS: Applicants for PG-3 must show 6 months of general clerical experience. Applicants for PG-4 must show 1 year of general clerical experience. Education may be substituted for experience. Selectee must be a qualified typist. Applicants without status must submit a current OPM Notice of Results to be considered.

NOTE: Those eligibles for VRA appointments are: veterans who served minimum of 180 days of active military service who are honorably discharged between the dates of August 5, 1964, to the present time and Vietnam Veterans who have received a campaign badge/medal or have received a services connected disability. Veterans must submit a copy of their DD-214 at time of application. Civil Service Status not required.

RANKING FACTORS: Applicants who meet the above qualification requirements will be rated on the basis of relevant experience, education, training, supervisory appraisal, job-related awards, and the factors listed below. Applicants should be specific in documenting these areas in their application materials. Applicants must meet time-in-grade and qualification requirements by the closing date of the announcement.

1. Skill in operating electric or automatic typewriter.
2. Knowledge of the format and clerical procedures involved in the work.
3. Knowledge of activities and program carried out in the office.
4. Knowledge of grammar, spelling, punctuation, and specialized terminology.

TO APPLY: Each applicant must submit:
NOTE: Submit GPO Form 2566 "Report of Merit Promotion Action" if you want a report on the status of your application.

(X) Copy of your latest annual performance rating.

( ) Standard Form 171, "Application for Federal Employment"

( ) Special Application Form (Available from GPO Employment Branch)

(X) Copy of SF-50, showing proof of status or reinstatement eligibility.

APPLICATIONS AND REQUESTED FORMS MUST BE RECEIVED NO LATER THAN THE CLOSING DATE OF THIS ANNOUNCEMENT. Please describe duties and responsibilities in your own words; do not submit copies of position descriptions.
Non-GPO applicants who are selected for appointment must successfully pass a drug test.

SUBMIT APPLICATION TO:
VIVIAN WHITE
MANAGER, COLUMBUS, RPPO

U.S. Government Printing Office
Employment Branch, Rm. C106, Stop PSE
North Capitol and H Streets NW.
Washington, DC 20401

For additional information, call:
ANN NOBLE (202) 512-1187
DAVID SEVER (614) 488-4616
GPO Form 2884 (R 2-90) P. 57543-7

THE GOVERNMENT PRINTING OFFICE IS AN EQUAL OPPORTUNITY EMPLOYER

Merit Promotion Vacancy Announcement

U.S. GOVERNMENT PRINTING OFFICE

Announcement No.:

Position: Occupational Health Nurse		Issue Date:	Closing Date: 6/5/92

Series/Grade: PG-0610-9	Salary: $34,008 - $42,282	Number of Vacancies: 1	Promotion Potential: None

Geographic Location: Washington, DC	Tour of Duty: Shift 1	Duration of Appointment: (X) Permanent ( ) Temporary

Organization: Occupational Health and Environmental Services, Occupational Health Division	Civil Service Status Required: ( ) Yes (X) No

Area of Consideration: All Sources	OPM Notice of Results Required: ( ) Yes (X) No

SUMMARY OF DUTIES/RESPONSIBILITIES:

The incumbent performs the health care, counseling, educational and training aspects of employee health programs. Administers emergency care for illnesses of occupational/ non-occupational origin/injuries that occur at the place of work. Makes assessments and determines appropriate plan of care and arranges appropriate transportation to medical facility when necessary. Administers medications/treatments authorized by physicians. Counsels employees on varied health subjects. Notifies supervisor of serious injuries or serious health problems and plan of procedure being used. Prepares written report of each patient seen with his or her condition, medication given and any recommendations made. Follows up by telephone or interview on serious or acute conditions. Performs/interprets laboratory tests. Performs screenings such as: blood pressure, visual acuity, audiometric test, height, weight. Counsels employees in varied health subjects. Notifies employees and management with posters when health screening programs. Maintains an adequate inventory of necessary medicines and supplies and follows up on orders for the replenishment of stock.

QUALIFICATIONS: Applicants must have the certification and experience, education or combination as noted in 1-3 below. Applicants may review Handbook X-118 for complete details on acceptable experience and education.

1. Certification: Applicants must have an active current registration as a professional nurse in a State, DC, Commonwealth of Puerto Rico, or Territory of U.S.
2. Basic Education Requirements:
   A. Graduation with a bachelor's degree or higher in nursing from an approved school of professional nursing; OR
   B. Graduation from a 3-year diploma program of professional nursing; OR
   C. Graduation from an associate degree or other program of at least 2 years in length comparable and equivalent to A, B, or C above; OR
   D. Graduation from an approved school of professional nursing of at least 2 years in length comparable and equivalent to A, B, C, above.
3. Education and Experience Above the Basic: Applicants must show a minimum of 1 year of professional experience in occupational health nursing or graduate education, or an equivalent combination of both, in addition to the basic requirements noted above.

RANKING FACTORS: Applicants who meet the above qualification requirements will be rated on the basis of relevant experience, education, training, supervisory appraisal, job-related awards, and the factors listed below. Applicants should be specific in documenting these areas in their application materials. Applicants must meet time-in-grade and qualification requirements by the closing date of the announcement.

1. Knowledge of the full range of professional occupational health nursing principles, practices, and procedures applied in providing services in a work environment.
2. Knowledge of nursing service administration.
3. Knowledge of Office of Personnel Management, Federal Personnel Manual, U.S. Public Health Service/other administrative orders, procedures and regulatory restrictions.
4. Ability to work with employees with physical, emotional or mental problems.
5. Ability to use specialized medical equipment.
6. Ability to read, understand and use technical information concerning hazardous chemicals.
7. Knowledge of current occupational health practices.

TO APPLY: Each applicant must submit:
NOTE: Submit GPO Form 2566 "Report of Merit Promotion Action" if you want a report on the status of your application.

(X) Copy of your latest annual performance rating.

(X) Standard Form 171, "Application for Federal Employment"

( ) Special Application Form (Available from GPO Employment Branch)

(X) Copy of SF-50, showing proof of status or reinstatement eligibility.

APPLICATIONS AND REQUESTED FORMS MUST BE RECEIVED NO LATER THAN THE CLOSING DATE OF THIS ANNOUNCEMENT. Please describe duties and responsibilities in your own words; do not submit copies of position descriptions. Non-GPO applicants who are selected for appointment must successfully pass a drug test.

SUBMIT APPLICATION TO:
VIVIAN WHITE

U.S. Government Printing Office
Employment Branch, Rm. C106, Stop PSE
North Capitol and H Streets NW.
Washington, DC 20401

For additional information, call:
ANN NOBLE (202) 512-1187
TDD (202) 512-1519
GPO Form 2884 (R 2-90) P. 57543-7

THE GOVERNMENT PRINTING OFFICE IS AN EQUAL OPPORTUNITY EMPLOYER

PEOPLE WHO PREVIOUSLY APPLIED UNDER ANNOUNCEMENT   MUST REAPPLY

Merit Promotion
Vacancy Announcement

Announcement No.:

U.S. GOVERNMENT PRINTING OFFICE
AMENDMENT #1:   CHANGE IN SALARY

Position: Parking Manager		Issue Date:	Closing Date:
Series/Grade: PG-301-7/9	Salary: $22,850-$35,847	Number of Vacancies: 1	Promotion Potential: 9

Geographic Location: Washington, DC	Tour of Duty: Shift 1	Duration of Appointment: (X) Permanent ( ) Temporary

Organization: Security and Support Services, Office of Deputy Director for Support Services Administrative Services Group	Civil Service Status Required: (X) Yes ( ) No

Area of Consideration: Current and Former Federal Employees in the Washington, DC Area	OPM Notice of Results Required: ( ) Yes (X) No

SUMMARY OF DUTIES/RESPONSIBILITIES:

The incumbent is responsible for the continuing and efficient operation of the GPO Pay Parking Program. Participates in the preparation of policies and procedures covering the use of parking facilities on GPO premises, taking into account both the security requirements and the nature of parking as an employee benefit. Determines what reports will be useful in managing the program and oversees development of appropriate computer applications. Conducts continuing evaluations of effectiveness of administration of the parking policy of the agency, preparing and submitting to the Supervisor periodic reports of findings and recommendation for improvement of the program. Conducts the day-to-day operations within the parking office. Conducts recertification of parking assignments. Prepares announcements, assigns parking places, etc. Coordinates all special parking arrangements with security officials in Protective Services Group (PSG) to ensure PSG is aware of arrangements and that necessary security measures can be put in place. Implements decisions concerning the parking program to all levels of GPO personnel as well as individuals who are not employed by the agency but who seek parking privileges. Refers requests for administrative exceptions to the parking policy to supervisor. Informs security officials of violations of parking regulations which would lead to enforcement measures (i.e., ticketing, towing, etc.). Periodically evaluates condition of parking facilities, deciding upon and directing such activities as cleaning, replacement of signage, repainting, etc. Develops special reporting formats and databases using personal computing equipment in order to meet reporting requirements established at higher levels. Answers inquiries and complaints from parking patrons, union officials, and security personnel by telephone or personal visit. Maintains contacts with other GPO organizations as necessary to satisfy problems or situations that require immediate attention.

QUALIFICATIONS: Applicants must show 52 weeks of specialized experience at the next lower grade level, which equipped the applicant with knowledge, skill and abilities to successfully perform duties as described above.

RANKING FACTORS: Applicants who meet the above qualification requirements will be rated on the basis of relevant experience, education, training, supervisory appraisal, job-related awards, and the factors listed below. Applicants should be specific in documenting these areas in their application materials. Applicants must meet time-in-grade and qualification requirements by the closing date of the announcement.

1. Knowledge of analytical and evaluative methods to design studies for analyzing Pay Parking Program elements and operations and to interpret accurately the information gathered.
2. Knowledge of personal computing equipment and of various application programs, procedures, and operations.
3. Knowledge of the activities and programs of the office as well as the regulations and policies concerning the Pay Parking Program.
4. Ability to effectively communicate orally.

TO APPLY: Each applicant must submit:
NOTE: Submit GPO Form 2566 "Report of Merit Promotion Action" if you want a report on the status of your application.

(X) Copy of your latest annual performance rating.

(X) Standard Form 171, "Application for Federal Employment"

( ) Special Application Form (Available from GPO Employment Branch)

(X) Copy of SF-50, showing proof of status or reinstatement eligibility.

APPLICATIONS AND REQUESTED FORMS MUST BE RECEIVED NO LATER THAN THE CLOSING DATE OF THIS ANNOUNCEMENT.
Please describe duties and responsibilities in your own words; do not submit copies of position descriptions.
Non-GPO applicants who are selected for appointment must successfully pass a drug test.

SUBMIT APPLICATION TO:

VIVIAN WHITE

U.S. Government Printing Office
Employment Branch, Rm. C106, Stop PSE
North Capitol and H Streets NW.
Washington, DC 20401

For additional information, call:

ANN NOBLE (202) 512-1187

GPO Form 2884 (R 2-90) P. 57543-7

THE GOVERNMENT PRINTING OFFICE IS AN EQUAL OPPORTUNITY EMPLOYER

Merit Promotion Vacancy Announcement

U.S. GOVERNMENT PRINTING OFFICE

Announcement No.:

Position: Secretary (Typing)		Issue Date:	Closing Date:
Series/Grade: PG-318-6	Salary: $21,981 - $27,831	Number of Vacancies: 1	Promotion Potential: None

Geographic Location: Washington, DC	Tour of Duty: Shift 1	Duration of Appointment: (X) Permanent ( ) Temporary

Organization: Off. of the APP (Ops. & Proc.), Customer Svc. Dept. Typo. & Des. Div., Office of the Superintendent	Civil Service Status Required: (X) Yes ( ) No

Area of Consideration: All Sources	OPM Notice of Results Required: ( ) Yes (X) No

SUMMARY OF DUTIES/RESPONSIBILITIES:

The incumbent serves as a personal assistant to the Superintendent of the Division, and is responsible for the clerical administrative duties performed in connection with the management of the office. Specifically, the work includes the following duties: Receives telephone calls and visitors to the office; determines if calls should be referred to the Superintendent, another staff member, or handled personally; determines if visitors should be directed to a supervisor or other staff person. Answers questions of a routine and non-technical nature. Keeps Superintendent's calendar of scheduled appointments, and arranges timely contacts. Receives incoming mail and maintains control records on incoming correspondence and follow-up actions. Takes dictation notes of meetings; composes and types correspondence based on notes, oral instructions, or precedents. Types a variety of material directly in draft and final form including status reports, correspondence, and tables; ensures correct punctuation, capitalization, spelling, grammar, and conformance to style. Assembles information from computer files, telephone calls, visitors, and other appropriate sources for use by the Superintendent. Compiles one-of-a-kind or recurring reports. Maintains ready reference, organization, and personnel files. Keeps a record of personnel actions, and furnishes personnel data required in preparation of the budget/annual reports. Orders and directs the preparation of requisitions for supplies and materials. In the absence of the Clerical Assistant (timekeeper), maintains leave records and Daily Time and Attendance Report; and reviews and amends the PROBE sheets.

<u>QUALIFICATIONS REQUIRED</u>: Applicants must possess 52 weeks of specialized experience in administrative or clerical work equivalent to the next lower grade level. Specialized experience is experience directly related to the work described above under "Summary of Duties Responsibilities", which demonstrates possession of the knowledge, skills, and abilities required to serve as a principal office assistant.

<u>NOTE</u>: A qualified typist is required. <u>Applicants who have not held a Federal position with "Typing" in the title must pass a GPO test prior to submitting their application.</u> For further information regarding scheduling an appointment to take the typing test, contact one of the persons whose names appear below.

RANKING FACTORS: Applicants who meet the above qualification requirements will be rated on the basis of relevant experience, education, training, supervisory appraisal, job-related awards, and the factors listed below. Applicants should be specific in documenting these areas in their application materials. Applicants must meet time-in-grade and qualification requirements by the closing date of the announcement.

1. Knowledge of office routines and clerical procedures.
2. Knowledge of the rules grammar, spelling, punctuation, and required forms.
3. Skill in operating word processor, computer, and typewriter.
4. Ability to work independently, and willingness to accept responsibility.
5. Ability to exercise tact and discretion in dealing with others.
6. Ability to communicate orally.
7. Ability to communicate routine, non-technical correspondence.
8. Ability to maintain file and control records.

TO APPLY: Each applicant must submit:
NOTE: Submit GPO Form 2566 "Report of Merit Promotion Action" if you want a report on the status of your application.

(X) Copy of your latest annual performance rating.

( ) Standard Form 171, "Application for Federal Employment"
(X)
( ) Special Application Form (Available from GPO Employment Branch)
( ) Copy of SF–50, showing proof of status or reinstatement eligibility.

APPLICATIONS AND REQUESTED FORMS MUST BE RECEIVED NO LATER THAN THE CLOSING DATE OF THIS ANNOUNCEMENT. Please describe duties and responsibilities in your own words; <u>do not submit copies of position descriptions.</u>
Non-GPO applicants who are selected for appointment must successfully pass a drug test.

SUBMIT APPLICATION TO:
VIVIAN WHITE

U.S. Government Printing Office
Employment Branch, Rm. C106, Stop PSE
North Capitol and H Streets NW.
Washington, DC 20401

For additional information, call:
ANN NOBLE (202) 512-1187
TDD (202) 512-1519
GPO Form 2884 (R 2-90) P. 57543-7

THE GOVERNMENT PRINTING OFFICE IS AN EQUAL OPPORTUNITY EMPLOYER

AN EQUAL OPPORTUNITY EMPLOYER

OPENING DATE:

CLOSING DATE:

POSITION TITLE/ SERIES AND GRADE	ORGANIZATION	ANNOUNCEMENT NUMBER

Gardener
WG-5003-6
Salary: $10.98 per hour

Cooper Hewitt Museum
Office of Facilities Management

Duty Location: New York, New York

Area of Consideration: Candidates with civil service competitive status; veterans with VRA or 30% disability eligibility; and handicapped individuals with eligibility under a special appointing authority.

Duties: Performs a wide range of turf maintenance work including mowing, fertilizing, weeding edging, trimming, watering, thatching, aerating, etc. Renovates existing turf areas, prepares and plants new turf areas, observes and controls turf pests, including weeds, insects, fungus, and other diseases. Cultivates and propagates landscape plants, such as trees, shrubs, and floral crops; selects plants for specific location for best growth and development by considering soil conditions, plant hardiness, flowering periods, plant toxicity, and the overall landscape plan. Recommends plants for particular purposes such as shade, ground cover, traffic, and erosion control. Operates power equipment, such as sprayers, blowers, movers, trimmers, chain saws, leaf vacuums, trucks, and scooters.

SPECIAL CONDITIONS OF EMPLOYMENT: The work requires frequent walking, standing, stooping, bending, kneeling, and pushing of carts, mowers, and wheelbarrows. The incumbent occasionally climbs ladders to prune vegetation and frequently lifts heavy objects, weighing up to 50 lbs, including bags of fertilizer, logs, rocks, etc. Incumbent may be exposed to various weather conditions such as sun, rain, snow, dust and mud associated with gardening duties. May be required to wear protective clothing.

Minimum Qualifications: In order to be rated basically qualified or eligible, an applicant's overall experience and training must indicate possession of the minimum skills, knowledge and abilities needed to perform the duties of this position.

Basis of Rating: Selection will be made from among those candidates who demonstrate the highest potential to perform the job as determined by ratings on the following elements.

1. ABILITY TO DO THE WORK OF A GARDENER WITHOUT MORE THAN NORMAL SUPERVISION.
(This is the screen-out element. Applicants who are not rated satisfactory or potentially satisfactory on the screen-out element will not be rated on the remaining elements.)

2. Technical practices related to gardening.
3. Ability to interpret specifications, plans, and so forth (other than blueprints).
4. Ability to use and maintain hand and powered gardening tools and equipment.
5. Knowledge of materials used in gardening work.
6. Dexterity and safety in work practices.

NOTE: RELOCATION EXPENSES WILL NOT BE PAID

In addition to an Application for Federal Employment (SF-171), applicants should submit a supplemental sheet giving specific examples of experience and training which apply to each of the selective and/or quality ranking factors. This experience and training must also be included in the SF-171.

The attached SI-662 form should also be completed by all candidates except Smithsonian Institution employees and returned with the application. This form is to be used for gathering statistical data and will not be a part of the application.

Please note: All Smithsonian positions require fingerprinting of employees hired and may include some additional background checks before employment. In addition to submitting a current SF-171, each applicant should submit a copy of the latest of any performance appraisals received. Smithsonian Institution employees are asked to submit a copy of their latest completed performance plan SI-778 (SI-777 is optional) and a Merit Promotion Interest Statement SI-1426 (Rev. 03-31-81).

The Immigration Reform and Control Act of 1986 requires employers to hire only individuals who are eligible to work in the United States. Upon reporting for work, an individual will be expected to present proper evidence establishing employability.

Applications must be submitted to one of the addresses below and must be received by the closing date. Postmark dates will not be considered.

Send your application to:	OR	Bring your application to:
Smithsonian Institution		955 L'Enfant Plaza, S.W.
Office of Human Resources		Employment Office
Branch 1		Suite 2100
P.O. Box 23762		Washington, DC
Washington, DC 20026-3762		

For further information please call (202) 287-3100 ext. 287

VACANCY ANNOUNCEMENT

Headquarters, First U.S. Army and Fort George G. Meade
Civilian Personnel Office
Fort George G. Meade, Maryland 20755-5035

AN EQUAL OPPORTUNITY EMPLOYER

ANNOUNCEMENT NUMBER

THE FILLING OF THIS POSITION IS SUBJECT TO THE DOD PRIORITY PLACEMENT PROGRAM

POSITION: Heavy Mobile Equipment Repairer WG-5803-08
PROMOTION POTENTIAL:

OPENING DATE:
FIRST CUT OFF DATE:

LOCATION: All Vacancies within the 79th U.S. Army Reserve Command
SALARY: Determined by Location Of Vacancy

CLOSING DATE:

CONDITION OF EMPLOYMENT:

ARMY RESERVE TECHNICIAN POSITION: ACTIVE ARMY RESERVE MEMBERSHIP IS REQUIRED IN:
[ ] TPU
[X] SELECTED RESERVE
[ ] NOT APPLICABLE

SUPERVISORY MANAGERIAL PROBATIONARY PERIOD REQUIRED?
[ ] YES
[X] NO

SECURITY CLEARANCE REQUIRED:
[ ] YES [X] NO
[ ] SECRET
[ ] TOP SECRET

PCS EXPENSES PAID
[ ] YES [X] NO

RELOCATION (DARSE) PAID
[ ] YES [X] NO

AREA OF CONSIDERATION: [X] DA CIVILIAN EMPLOYEES WITH COMPETITIVE STATUS [X] EMPLOYEES WITH STATUS [X] DOD EMPLOYEES WITH STATUS [X] FEDERAL

EMPLOYEES WITH REINSTATEMENT ELIGIBILITY, INDIVIDUALS ELIGIBLE FOR APPOINTMENT BY SPECIAL AUTHORITY SUCH AS HANDICAPPED, VETERANS READJUSTMENT, ETC. MILITARY SPOUSES REQUESTING MILITARY SPOUSE PREFERENCE MUST REGISTER IAW PROCEDURES ESTABLISHED UNDER THE DOD PRIORITY PLACEMENT PROGRAM. BY SUBMITTING DOCUMENTATION REQUIRED TO ESTABLISH ELIGIBILITY (SF 171), LATEST PERFORMANCE APPRAISAL, SF 50, DD 214, SPONSOR'S TRAVEL ORDERS, ETC).

[ ] THIS IS AN EXCEPTED POSITION ALL INTERESTED CANDIDATES MAY APPLY.

MAJOR DUTIES:

Performs repairs on a variety of automotive, heavy mobile and power support equipment. Completes repairs as indicated on work order and troubleshoots to assure no further complications. Performs minor body work. Replaces tail gates and floor boards. Occasionally required to paint entire vehicle. Makes minor adjustments to canvas items such tents and equipment covers. Provides technical assistance to unit personnel on performance of operator and organizational maintenance procedures. Instruction is usually provided as OJT and incumbent serves as part of a team traveling on-site to the unit requesting assistance. Required to operate vehicles for the purpose of moving in and out of shop area and to evacuate items to support installation.

SELECTIVE PLACEMENT FACTORS: Applicants may be required to pass and appropriate physical examination.

QUALIFICATIONS REQUIRED -OPM X-118C: Applicants must have had experience and/or training of sufficient scope and quality to

METHODS OF EVALUATION. ALL APPLICANTS WILL BE EVALUATED AGAINST APPROPRIATE QUALIFICATION STANDARDS, MERIT PROMOTION AND OTHER APPROPRIATE REGULATIONS. QUALIFIED CANDIDATES RESPONSES TO THE IDENTIFIED RANKING ELEMENTS WILL BE FURTHER EVALUATED TO DETERMINE BEST QUALIFIED

HOW TO APPLY. SUBMIT THE FOLLOWING DOCUMENTS:
1 APPLICATION FOR FEDERAL EMPLOYMENT (SF-171)
2 SUPPLEMENTAL NARRATIVE & EVALUATION (FCGM FM 45) FOR GS/GM POSITIONS
3 COPY OF YOUR LATEST PERFORMANCE APPRAISAL
4 COPY OF COLLEGE TRANSCRIPTS, LIST OF COLLEGE COURSES, AS APPROPRIATE
5 COMMISSION VERIFYING ELIGIBILITY FORM (RESERVE TECHNICIAN POSITIONS ONLY)
6 DOCUMENTS VERIFYING ELIGIBILITY SF 50, DD FORM 214, SF 15, ETC.
7 BACKGROUND SURVEY QUESTIONNAIRE 79-2, OMB No. 50-RO-616.

BY MAIL: CIVILIAN PERSONNEL OFFICE, AFKA-ZI-CPR, FORT GEORGE G. MEADE, MD 20755-5035
IN PERSON: AT THE ONE STOP INFORMATION CENTER DURING NORMAL DUTY HOURS
AFTER HOURS AND WEEKENDS, USE THE DROP BOX OUTSIDE THE CPO, BLDG 4432 OR THE ONE STOP INFORMATION CENTER, BLDG 4283

NOTE: ANY FORMS NOT FULLY COMPLETED AND SIGNED OR FAILURE TO SUBMIT REQUIRED FORMS MAY RESULT IN AN INELIGIBLE RATING OR LESS THAN FULL CONSIDERATION FOR THE POSITION

APPLICATIONS MUST BE RECEIVED IN THE CIVILIAN PERSONNEL OFFICE BY THE CLOSING DATE OF THE ANNOUNCEMENT

"PEOPLE ALWAYS"

---

perform the duties of the position. The job element procedure will be used to determine eligibility of the applicants. Applicants will be rated in accordance with their knowledge and skill in the elements listed below.

ELEMENTS: The following questions have been designed to cover a wide range of skills and knowledges in order to be sure that you receive all credit to which entitled. However, you are not expected have full knowledge of every question listed. Failure to give complete answers may be reflected in the rating you receive. Candidates must possess sufficient competence in the screen-out element (Element A) to score at least two points in order to be rated eligible. ACCURATELY ANSWER ALL PARTS OF THIS FORM. YOUR ANSWERS ARE SUBJECT TO VERIFICATION BEFORE YOU ARE SELECTED FOR A JOB VACANCY.

ELEMENT A: ABILITY TO DO THE WORK OF A HEAVY MOBILE EQUIPMENT REPAIRER (SCREEN OUT ELEMENT)

1. What work can you do by yourself, without the help of a boss or supervisor?

2. Give examples of the kinds of instructions your supervisor gives your.

3. What responsibilities have you been give or jobs in the community, in the military, etc.?

ELEMENT B: KNOWLEDGE OF HEAVY MOBILE EQUIPMENT COMPONENTS AND ASSEMBLIES

1. List the kinds of equipment you had to assemble, make, install, test, repair, etc. and show type and size of equipment and where you work with each.

2. Tell about experience you have had in conserving materials, using correct parts, keeping exact tolerances and using "tricks of the trade."

Beside each item listed below circle one of the letters A through D that best describes your knowledge skill or ability.

A. Had study or training.
B. I have used my knowledge, but I have been closely supervised.
C. I have used my knowledge under general supervised.
D. I have used my knowledge on my own.

	Applicant's Self-Rating	Supervisor's Rating
1. Removing and replacing new or rebuilt subassemblies		
a. Voltage regulator	A B C D	A B C D
b. Generators	A B C D	A B C D
c. Carburetors	A B C D	A B C D
d. Alternators	A B C D	A B C D
e. Fuel Pumps	A B C D	A B C D
2. Replacing brake cylinders	A B C D	A B C D
3. Remove and clean or repair fuel tanks	A B C D	A B C D
4. Adjusts tappets, distributors points	A B C D	A B C D
5. Disassemble parts on engines, power transmissions, suspensions, steering and braking assemblies	A B C D	A B C D
6. Recondition parts and assemblies on engines, power transmission, suspensions, steering and braking assemblies	A B C D	A B C D
7. Replacing and repairing tailgates	A B C D	A B C D
8. Using spray enamels and primers	A B C D	A B C D
9. Making minor repairs to canvas and weather equipment	A B C D	A B C D

ELEMENT C: USE OF TEST AND MEASURING INSTRUMENTS

Beside each item listed below, circle one of the letters A through D that best describes your knowledge, skill or ability.

A. Had study or training.
B. I have used my knowledge, but I have been closely supervised.
C. I have used by knowledge under general supervision.
D. I have used my knowledge on my own.

	Applicant's Self-Rating	Supervisor's Rating
1. Calipers	A B C D	A B C D
2. Scales	A B C D	A B C D
3. Rules	A B C D	A B C D
4. Micrometer	A B C D	A B C D
5. Timing lights	A B C D	A B C D

ELEMENT D: ABILITY TO USE REFERENCE MANUAL

Beside each item listed below, circle one of the letters A through D that best describes your knowledge, skill or ability.

A. Have had study or training.
B. Getting limited information about a limited subject as materials to be used, sizes, etc to perform operations.
C. Interpreting occasional changes in instructions.
D. Interpreting frequent changes in instructions, etc. concerning your operations

	Applicant's Self-Rating	Supervisor's Review
1. Manufacturer's specifications	A B C D	A B C D
2. Inventory items list, component diagrams.	A B C D	A B C D
3. Trade Journals	A B C D	A B C D
4. Charts, tables	A B C D	A B C D
5. Technical manuals (mechanical and electrical)	A B C D	A B C D

ELEMENT E: ABILITY TO USE AND MAINTAIN TOOLS AND EQUIPMENT

Beside each of the items listed below, circle one of the letters A through C that best describes your knowledge, skill or ability.

A. Use it on rough or routine work.
B. Use it on fine works, or in unusual or in difficult site or location.
C. Maintained, sharpened, adjusted.

	Applicant's Self-Rating	Supervisor's Review
1. Tachometer	A B C D	A B C D
2. Voltmeter	A B C D	A B C D
3. Compression Gauge	A B C D	A B C D
4. Drill Meter	A B C D	A B C D
5. Drill Press	A B C D	A B C D
6. Wrenches	A B C D	A B C D
7. Pliers	A B C D	A B C D
8. Brake Tools	A B C D	A B C D
9. Ignition Tools	A B C D	A B C D
10. Feeler Gauges	A B C D	A B C D
11. Circuit Testers	A B C D	A B C D
12. Timing Lights	A B C D	A B C D
13. Wheel alignment and frame tools	A B C D	A B C D
14. Honing machines	A B C D	A B C D

ELEMENT F: TROUBLESHOOTING

Beside each item listed below, circle one of the letters A
through D that best describes your knowledge, skill or ability.

A. Able to troubleshoot for common malfunctions.
B. Able to troubleshoot with assistance of supervisor.
C. Can troubleshoot on my own well enough to locate malfunction
    and avoid serious injury or damage.
D. I am consulted by others and am able to discover malfunction
    when others cannot find trouble.

	Applicant's Self-Rating	Supervisor's Review
1. Locate simple trouble such as		
inoperative lights and fuel or oil		
leaks or improperly installed		
parts	A B C D	A B C D
2. Locate trouble by detailed		
inspection and trial runs of		
mechanical equipment	A B C D	A B C D
3. Locate trouble through knowledge		
of relationship of mechanical or		
electrical or hydraulic systems	A B C D	A B C D

REVIEW AND CERTIFICATION

After completing the application and this form, look them over
carefully to make sure that both have been signed and that you
have answered all items. STATEMENTS CONCERNING QUALIFICATION ARE
SUBJECT TO VERIFICATION. EXAGGERATION OR MISSTATEMENTS MAY BE
CAUSE FOR YOU DISQUALIFICATION OR LATER REMOVAL FROM THE FEDERAL
SERVICE.

CERTIFICATION

I CERTIFY THAT ALL OF THE STATEMENTS MADE IN THIS FORM ARE TRUE,
COMPLETE AND CORRECT TO THE BEST OF MY KNOWLEDGE AND BELIEF, AND
ARE MADE IN GOOD FAITH.

Your Signature _____ Date _____

Supervisor's Signature _____ Date _____

United States Department of the Interior

NATIONAL PARK SERVICE

NATIONAL CAPITAL REGION
1100 OHIO DRIVE S.W
WASHINGTON D.C 20242

R E C R U I T M E N T   B U L L E T I N

Bulletin Number: RB92-175
Opening Date: 05-11
Closing Date: 05-20
Area Of Consideration: All Sources

NOTE: THOSE APPLICANTS THAT PREVIOUSLY APPLIED UNDER 92-111, WILL NEED TO REAPPLY TO BE CONSIDERED FOR THIS VACANCY.

An Equal Opportunity Employer - The National Park Service is accepting application for the purpose of filling the vacancy listed below. All applicants will receive consideration without regard to race, sex, color, creed, age, national origin, religion, physical/mental handicap, or any other nonmerit factors.

POSITION TITLE, SERIES, AND GRADE: LOCATION:

Laborer   NPS, National Capital Region
WG-3502-3   John F. Kennedy Center
$8.34 - $9.73 per hour   Branch of Building Maintenance
                                          Washington, D.C.

Note: More than one position may be filled from this announcement.

BRIEF DESCRIPTION OF DUTIES: Loads and unloads material, moves, sorts, and stack supplies. Scrubs, mops, waxes, and vacuums floors. Cleans walls and particians and polishes fixtures. Removes stains from rugs, drapes, floors, and fixtures. Moves furniture, cabinets and equipment in order to clean areas. Assist other workers by carrying supplies and tools, keeping work areas and workbenches clean and orderly, and by lubricating tools and machines. Operates heavy power equipment such as lawn mowers, edgers, trimmers, and woodworking equipment. Rakes, weeds sweeps, and hauls trash. Performs other duties as assigned.

NATURE OF APPOINTMENT: This position is part-time not-to-exceed 24 hours per week.

QUALIFICATIONS REQUIRED: As required in Office of Personnel Management Qualifications Handbook X-118C, applicants must possess the following knowledge, skills, and abilities which are considered essential to successful job performance:

1. Ability to perform work involving heavy physical effort.
2. Ability to keep things neat, clean and in order.
3. Ability to use hand tools and small electrical equipment such as lawn mowers, edgers, trimmers and wood working equipment.

METHODS TO BE USED IN RATING AND RANKING CANDIDATES: Applications will be rated using the criteria listed above. Qualified candidates will be ranked to determine the best qualified for referral to the selecting official.

PRIVACY ACT INFORMATION: The application you submit for this position contains information subject to the Privacy Act of 1974 (P.L. 93-579,5 U.S.C. 522a). We are required to provide you with information regarding our authority and purposes for collecting this data, the routine uses which will be made of it, and the effect, if any, of nondisclosures. You are entitled to the same information as it pertains specifically to disclosure of your Social Security number. Any information you may need regarding Privacy Act regulations and the rights they extend can be obtained by calling 619-7256. Hearing impaired candidates may call on TTY 619-7364 if additional information is needed.

How To Apply - Submit the following:

- An up-to-date Application for Federal Employment (SF-171)
- The attached Supplemental Questionnaire, if applicable
- Your most recent Annual Performance Appraisal
- Applicant Background Survey (DI-1935) optional
- Notification of Personnel Action (SF-50)

Submit all forms to: National Park Service
                       National Capital Region
                       Division of Personnel
                       1100 Ohio Drive, SW
                       Washington, DC 20242

VACANCY ANNOUNCEMENT

U.S. General Services Administration
Office of Personnel

	Vacancy Number
	61-92
	Issue Date
	Closing Date

POSITION: (PC-2-6337)   (1 VACANCY)
Maintenance Worker, WG-4749-5

PROMOTION POTENTIAL: None

AREA OF CONSIDERATION: Regionwide*

LOCATION: PBS, Real Property Management & Safety Division,
Plattsburgh Subfield Office, Rouses Point, N.Y.

THIS ANNOUNCEMENT SUPERCEDES AND CANCELS ANNOUNCEMENT #43-92, WHICH IS
BEING REANNOUNCED IN ORDER TO EXPAND THE APPLICANT POOL. PERSONS WHO
APPLIED UNDER ANNOUNCEMENT #43-92 NEED NOT REAPPLY.

*The area of consideration is for advertising and distribution
purposes only. Applications from outside the area of consideration
will be accepted.

APPLICATIONS WILL BE ACCEPTED ONLY FROM GENERAL SERVICES
ADMINISTRATION EMPLOYEES. ALL APPLICANTS MUST HAVE CAREER OR CAREER-
CONDITIONAL STATUS.

THIS POSITION IS IN THE AFGE BARGAINING UNIT.

THIS POSITION MAY BE FILLED THROUGH PROMOTION, REASSIGNMENT, OR CHANGE
TO LOWER GRADE, DEPENDING UPON THE CURRENT GRADE OF THE SELECTED
CANDIDATE.

RELOCATION EXPENSES WILL NOT BE PAID.

SUMMARY OF DUTIES:
Incumbent serves under the immediate supervision of a higher-graded
Maintenance Worker. Specific duties include: operating a low-pressure
heating plant, including checking controls, maintaining oil burner,
and auxiliary equipment such as pumps; operating and performing minor
maintenance repairs on air-conditioning and water supply systems;
assisting in the maintenance and repair of other equipment; cleaning
offices, corridors, lobbies, toilet rooms, store rooms, shop area,
parking areas, driveways, and walks; assisting in building repairs
including carpentry, plumbing, and minor electrical work; operating
power mowing and snow removal equipment as required; performing other
duties as assigned.

APPLICANTS MUST MEET THE QUALIFICATIONS REQUIREMENTS OF THE POSITION
WITHIN 30 CALENDAR DAYS OF THE CLOSING DATE.

RANKING CRITERIA:
The ranking of candidates shall be based on the examination and
evaluation of the candidate's experience, education, training, awards,
appraisals, hobbies, self-development activities, etc., which are
present in the candidate's application package. A composite of the
numeric value from the crediting plan will constitute the overall
value for ranking of candidates to determine best qualified. All
knowledges, skills, and abilities will be given equal weight.

EACH APPLICANT MUST COPY THE FOLLOWING QUALITY RANKING FACTORS ONTO
GSA FORM 3413, SUPERVISORY APPRAISAL OF DEMONSTRATED PERFORMANCE OR
POTENTIAL, BEFORE GIVING THE FORM TO HIS/HER SUPERVISOR FOR RATING.
FAILURE TO SUBMIT THIS FORM COULD RESULT IN YOUR NOT RECEIVING FULL
CONSIDERATION.

QUALITY RANKING FACTORS (KNOWLEDGES, SKILLS, AND ABILITIES):
87.   Reliability and dependability (screenout).
21.   Shop aptitude and interest.
75.   Ability to follow instructions.
86.   Dexterity and safety.
100. Ability to work with others.

ALL APPLICANTS MUST RESPOND IN WRITING TO THE ATTACHED QUESTIONS ON
GSA FORM R2-1303, SUPPLEMENTAL EXPERIENCE STATEMENT FOR SKILLED
TRADES. EACH QUESTION MUST BE ANSWERED IN SUFFICIENT DETAIL TO ALLOW
AN EVALUATION OF YOUR SKILLS AS THEY RELATE TO THE POSITION FOR WHICH
YOU ARE APPLYING. FAILURE TO COMPLETELY ANSWER ALL THE QUESTIONS
COULD RESULT IN YOUR NOT RECEIVING FULL CONSIDERATION.

HOW TO APPLY:
GSA employees interested in applying for this position must submit GSA
Form 2422, Merit Promotion Application; SF-171, Application for
Federal Employment; GSA Form 3413, Supervisory Appraisal of
Demonstrated Performance or Potential; GSA Form R2-1303, Supplemental
Experience Statement for Skilled Trades; and a copy of a current
annual performance appraisal. Failure to submit all of the above
mentioned forms could result in your not receiving full consideration.
All applicants are also requested to submit GSA Form R2-1464,
Background Survey Questionnaire. Application forms are available at
any GSA office. All completed applications must be sent to the
General Services Administration, Personnel Division, 2CPE, Room 18-
110, 26 Federal Plaza, New York, NY 10278. All applications must be
received or postmarked on or before June 11.

FAILURE TO SUBMIT THE SF-171 WILL AUTOMATICALLY RESULT IN AN
INELIGIBLE RATING. YOUR SF-171 ALONE WILL BE USED TO DETERMINE YOUR
BASIC ELIGIBILITY FOR THE POSITION. THEREFORE, IT IS YOUR
RESPONSIBILITY TO PROVIDE COMPLETE AND ACCURATE INFORMATION ON THE SF-
171. THE ADDITIONAL INFORMATION CONTAINED IN YOUR SUPPLEMENTAL FORMS,
ALONG WITH YOUR SF-171, WILL BE USED FOR RANKING PURPOSES. ALL
APPLICATION MATERIALS WILL BE RETAINED IN THE MERIT PROMOTION FILE AS
A RECORD OF THIS ACTION.

OFFICIAL PERSONNEL FOLDERS WILL NOT BE USED FOR CANDIDATE EVALUATION.

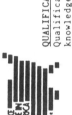

United States Department of the Interior

NATIONAL PARK SERVICE
1100 OHIO DRIVE, S.W.
WASHINGTON, DC 20242

R E C R U I T M E N T   B U L L E T I N

Bulletin Number: RB92-177
Opening Date: 05-15-
Closing Date: 05-28-
Area Of Consideration: All Sources

An Equal Opportunity Employer - The National Park Service is accepting application for the purpose of filling the vacancy listed below. All applicants will receive consideration without regard to race, sex, color, creed, age, national origin, religion, physical/mental handicap, or any other non-merit factors.

POSITION TITLE, SERIES, AND GRADE:

Mobile Equipment Servicer
WG-5806-5
$9.51 - $11.47 per hour

LOCATION:

NPS, National Capital Region
ARD, Administration
Division of Property Management
Branch of Transportation
Washington, DC

BRIEF DESCRIPTION OF DUTIES: The incumbent changes oil and oil filters, greases and otherwise thoroughly lubricates all types of gasoline and diesel powered automotive equipment. Cleans, washes, waxes and polishes automotive equipment. Incumbent keeps radiators properly filled; maintain proper air pressure in tires; installs and remove tire chains; replaces and charges batteries; changes tires and services with antifreeze. Enters required information on repair orders, such as the number of quarts of oil used, etc. Keeps working areas and tools and equipment in a neat and orderly manner. Performs other duties as assigned.

WORKING CONDITIONS: Incumbent works indoors in areas that are damp and drafty. Occasionally works outside in bad weather. Required to wear the prescribed maintenance uniform.

QUALIFICATIONS REQUIRED: As required in Office of Personnel Management Qualifications Handbook X-118C, applicants must possess the following knowledge, skills, and abilities which are considered essential to successful job performance:

    <u>SCREEN OUT ELEMENT:</u> Knowledge of a variety of gasoline and diesel powered automation equipment.

1. Knowledge of various lubricants; the location of points requiring lubrication, and amounts of lubricants to be applied.
2. Ability to use small hand tools associated with the work such as tire irons, wrenches, grease guns, etc.
3. Ability to follow both written and oral instructions.

NOTE: Must possess a valid State or District of Columbia driver's license.

METHODS TO BE USED IN RATING AND RANKING CANDIDATES: Applications will be rated using the criteria listed above. Qualified candidates will be ranked to determine the best qualified for referral to the selecting official.

PRIVACY ACT INFORMATION: The application you submit for this position contains information subject to the Privacy Act of 1974 (P.L. 93-579,5 U.S.C. 522a). We are required to provide you with information regarding our authority and purposes for collecting this data, the routine uses which will be made of it, and the effect, if any, of nondisclosures. You are entitled to the same information as it pertains specifically to disclosure of your Social Security number. Any information you may need regarding Privacy Act regulations and the rights they extend can be obtained by calling 619-7256. Hearing impaired candidates may call on TTY 619-7364 if additional information is needed.

How To Apply - Submit the following:

- An up-to-date Application for Federal Employment (SF-171)
- The attached Supplemental Questionnaire, if applicable
- Your most recent Annual Performance Appraisal
- Applicant Background Survey (DI-1935) optional
- Notification of Personnel Action (SF-50)

Submit all forms to: National Park Service
National Capital Region
Division of Personnel
1100 Ohio Drive, SW
Washington, DC 20242

United States Department of the Interior

NATIONAL PARK SERVICE
1100 OHIO DRIVE S.W.
WASHINGTON, D.C. 20242

V A C A N C Y   A N N O U N C E M E N T

Announcement Number: 92-134
Opening Date: 03-20-
Closing Date: 04-09-
Area Of Consideration: Servicewide

An Equal Opportunity Employer - The National Park Service is accepting applications for the purpose of filling the vacancy listed below. Application will be accepted from qualified status employees of the National Park Service only.

Selection will be made solely on the basis of merit, fitness, and qualifications without regard to race, age, sex, marital status, political affiliation, national origin, religion, non-disqualifying handicap conditions, or any other non-merit factors.

POSITION TITLE, SERIES, AND GRADE:

Tractor Operator
WG-5705-6
$10.55 - $12.34 per hour

LOCATION:

NPS, National Capital Region
George Washington Memorial
Parkway
Division of Maintenance,
Horticultural Group
McLean, Virginia

NOTE: MORE THAN ONE POSITION MAY BE FILLED FROM THIS ANNOUNCEMENT.

BRIEF DESCRIPTION OF DUTIES: The incumbent operates various type tractors. Mows lawns, roadways, etc., by operating tractors equipped with gang mowers, rotary cut and "hammer knife" grass cutting attachments. Prepares acreage for planting and levels earth by operating tractors with blades, springtooth harrows, discs, rakes, drags, etc. Loads and unloads various materials such as gravel, soil, and mulch by using a tractor with a front-end loader. Incumbent also uses tractors with graders and front-end loaders in snow removal operations. The incumbent may be required to operate motor vehicles not exceeding 22,000 gross vehicle weight when necessary, performs other duties as assigned.

CONDITION OF EMPLOYMENT: The incumbent must have a valid operator's license, D.C. or State, and Government.

QUALIFICATIONS REQUIRED: As required in Office of Personnel Management Qualifications Handbook X-118C, applicants must possess the following knowledge, skills, and abilities which are considered essential to successful job performance:

1. Ability to use and maintain tools and equipment.
2. Skilled in the operation of a wide variety of motor vehicles attachments, tools and equipment.
3. Ability to follow oral and/or written instructions.
4. Knowledge of the techniques and operation of a variety of tractors and lawn mowing equipment.

METHODS TO BE USED IN RATING AND RANKING CANDIDATES: Applications will be rated using the criteria listed above. Qualified candidates will be ranked to determine the best qualified for referral to the selecting official.

PRIVACY ACT INFORMATION: The application you submit for this position contains information subject to the Privacy Act of 1974 (P.L. 93-579,5 U.S.C. 522a). We are required to provide you with information regarding our authority and purposes for collecting this data, the routine uses which will be made of it, and the effect, if any, of nondisclosures. You are entitled to the same information as it pertains specifically to disclosure of your Social Security number. Any information you may need regarding Privacy Act regulations and the rights they extend can be obtained by calling 619-7256. Hearing impaired candidates may call on TTY 619-7364 if additional information is needed.

How To Apply - Submit the following:

–   An up-to-date Application for Federal Employment (SF-171)
–   The attached Supplemental Questionnaire, if applicable
–   Your most recent Annual Performance Appraisal
–   Applicant Background Survey, (DI-1935) optional
–   Notification of Personnel Action (SF-50)

United States Department of the Interior

NATIONAL PARK SERVICE

NATIONAL CAPITAL REGION
1100 OHIO DRIVE, S.W.
WASHINGTON, D.C. 20242

VACANCY ANNOUNCEMENT

Announcement Number: 92-124
Opening Date: 03-23-
Closing Date: 04-06-
Area Of Consideration: Regionwide

An Equal Opportunity Employer - The National Park Service is accepting application for the purpose of filling the vacancy listed below. Applications will be accepted from qualified status employees of the National Park Service, National Capital Region only.

Selection will be made solely on the basis of merit, fitness, and qualifications without regard to race, color, age, sex, marital status, political affiliation, national origin, religion, non-disqualifying handicap conditions, or any other non-merit factors.

POSITION TITLE, SERIES, AND GRADE:

Woodcrafter
WG-4605-10
$13.29 - $15.52 per hour

LOCATION:

NPS, National Capital Region
Prince William Forest Park
Division of Maintenance
Triangle, Virginia

BRIEF DESCRIPTION OF DUTIES:
The main purpose of this position is to construct, alter and repair wood cabinets, fittings, panels, partitions and wood or wood substitute articles, along with general carpentry duties when needed. The incumbent makes and repairs high grade wooden items with intricate, precise and fancy features. The incumbent plans and lays out his/her work including final assembly from specifications, blueprints, sketches and oral instructions. He/she uses the full range of hand and power tools and takes into consideration the characteristics of a variety of wood products.

NATURE OF APPOINTMENT:
The incumbent is required to wear the prescribed maintenance uniform.

QUALIFICATIONS REQUIRED:
As required in Office of Personnel Management Qualifications Handbook X-118C, applicants must possess the following knowledge, skills, and abilities which are considered essential to successful job performance:

1. Knowledge of the work practices, procedures and techniques of woodcrafting.
2. Ability to interpret blueprints, specifications, sketches, oral and written information and instructions.
3. Knowledge of the hand and power tools and equipment used in wood crafting.
4. Ability to analyze the characterics of wood and wood substitutes used in planning projects.

METHODS TO BE USED IN RATING AND RANKING CANDIDATES:
Applications will be rated using the criteria listed above. Qualified candidates will be ranked to determine the best qualified for referral to the selecting official.

PRIVACY ACT INFORMATION: The application you submit for this position contains information subject to the Privacy Act of 1974 (P.L. 93-579.5 U.S.C. 522a). We are required to provide you with information regarding our authority and purposes for collecting this data, the routine uses which will be made of it, and the effect, if any, of nondisclosures. You are entitled to the same information as it pertains specifically to disclosure of your Social Security number. Any information you may need regarding Privacy Act regulations and the rights they extend can be obtained by calling 619-7256. Hearing impared candidates may call on TTY 619-7364 if additional information is needed.

How To Apply - Submit the following:

- An up-to-date Application for Federal Employment (SF-171)
- The attached Supplemental Questionnaire, if applicable
- Your most recent Annual Performance Appraisal
- Applicant Background Survey (DI-1935) optional
- Notification of Personnel Action (SF-50)

Submit all forms to: National Park Service
                         National Capital Region
                         Division of Personnel
                         1100 Ohio Drive, SW
                         Washington, DC 20242

RECORDED JOB INFORMATION NUMBER: (202) 619-7111

GOVERNMENT OF THE DISTRICT OF COLUMBIA ★★★

POSITION VACANCY ANNOUNCEMENT

APPLICANTS WHO APPLIED UNDER VACANCY PAH-92-23 MUST REAPPLY
EXECUTIVE OFFICE OF THE MAYOR
DISTRICT OF COLUMBIA OFFICE OF PERSONNEL
SERVICING PERSONNEL OFFICE #2

ANNOUNCEMENT NO.	_____	POSITION	Maintenance Mechanic	PROMOTION POTENTIAL **NONE**

Foreman, SW-4749-09

OPENING DATE _____ AGENCY Dept. of Public & Assisted Housing, MOA DURATION OF APPOINTMENT.

CLOSING DATE _____ WORKSITE Various Sites **XX** Permanent

IF OPEN UNTIL FILLED, FIRST SCREENING DATE _____ SALARY RANGE $15.88 - $18.52 Per hour
TOUR OF DUTY 8:15 a.m. - 4:45 p.m. Monday - Friday

☐ Term (1 to 4 years). Not to Exceed

☐ Temporary. Not to Exceed _____ (Months)

NO OF VACANCIES 14 AREA OF CONSIDERATION Unlimited

☐ This position IS in the collective bargaining unit represented by _____
and you may be required to pay an agency service fee through an automatic payroll deduction.

x This position IS NOT in a collective bargaining unit.

RESIDENCY PREFERENCE AMENDMENT ACT OF 1988

Effective March 16, 1989, an applicant for employment in the Career Service who is a bona fide resident of the District of Columbia AT THE TIME OF APPLICATION may claim a hiring preference over a non-resident applicant by completing a DCSF-171-RP, "D.C. Government Residency Preference for Career Service Employment" form and submitting it with the employment application. SF-171. To be granted preference, an applicant must: (a) be qualified for the position; and (b) submit a claim form at the time of application. Preference will not be granted unless the claim is made at the time of application.

BRIEF DESCRIPTION OF DUTIES: Plans work schedules and sequence of operations for staff. Establishes deadlines and priorities on the basis of work to be performed. Based on workload and priorities, determines the number of assignments to be performed concurrently, the number and type of staff needed to do the work and the availability of materials and equipment.

QUALIFICATIONS REQUIREMENTS:
Applicants will be rated on the job elements listed below. Therefore, your application should show you have such skills:

1. Ability to supervise through subordinate supervisors. (Screen-out)
2. Knowledge of equipment assembly, installation, repair, etc.
3. Technical practices.
4. Use of measuring instruments.
5. Ability to interpret instructions, specifications, etc. (includes blueprint reading).

– Over –

RANKING FACTORS: The following ranking factors will be used in the evaluation process. All applicants MUST respond to the ranking factors ON A SEPARATE SHEET OF PAPER. Please describe specific incidents of sustained achievements from your experience which show evidence of the level at which you meet the ranking factors which have been determined to be of importance for the position for which you are applying. You may refer to any experience, education, training, awards, outside activities, etc., which indicate the degree to which you possess the job-related knowledges, skills, and abilities described in the ranking factors. The information given in response to the ranking factors should be complete and accurate to the best of your knowledge. FAILURE TO RESPOND TO ALL RANKING FACTORS MAY ELIMINATE YOU FROM CONSIDERATION.

RANKING FACTORS

PHYSICAL EFFORT

Work requires standing, stooping, bending, climbing, kneeling, working in hard to reach places and lifting and carrying up to 40 pounds and occasionally 100 pounds.

WORKING CONDITIONS

Work is performed inside and outside during good and bad weather. Incumbent is subject to dirt, dust, grease, unpleasant odors, possibility of bruises, cuts, broken bones, scrapes and infections. In some instances, incumbent is required to wear protective equipment which is heavy and uncomfortable.

DRUG-FREE WORKPLACE ACT OF 1988:

"Pursuant to the requirements of the Drug-Free Workplace Act of 1988, the individual selected to fill this position will, as a condition of employment, be required to notify his or her immediate supervisor, in writing no later than five days after conviction of or a plea of guilty to a violation of any criminal drug statute occuring in the workplace."

OTHER SIGNIFICANT FACTS

Knowledge of at least two (2) trades is required.
Due to field responsibility, incumbent must obtain a valid D.C. Government driver's license within six (6) months of the date of appointment to this position.

APPLICATIONS SUBMITTED FOR CONSIDERATION WILL NOT BE RETURNED TO THE APPLICANT. EXCEPT THAT APPLICATIONS RECEIVED OUTSIDE THE AREA OF CONSIDERATION OR AFTER THE CLOSING DATE WILL BE RETURNED WITHOUT ACTION.

HOW TO APPLY: Each applicant, including departmental employees, MUST submit a SF-171. (Application for Federal Employment).

SUBMIT TO:
D.C. Office of Personnel
Servicing Personnel Office #2
1133 North Capitol Street, N.E., Suite 326
Washington, D.C. 20002

OFFICIAL JOB OFFERS ARE MADE ONLY BY THE D.C. OFFICE OF PERSONNEL

United States Department of the Interior

NATIONAL PARK SERVICE

NATIONAL CAPITAL REGION
1100 OHIO DRIVE S.W.
WASHINGTON, DC 20242

T E M P O R A R Y E M P L O Y M E N T O P P O R T U N I T Y
R E C R U I T M E N T B U L L E T I N

Bulletin Number:
Opening Date:
Closing Date:
Area Of Consideration: All Sources

An Equal Opportunity Employer - The National Park Service is accepting applications for the purpose of filling the vacancy listed below. All applicants will receive consideration without regard to race, sex, color, creed, age, national origin, religion, physical/mental handicap, or any other nonmerit factors.

POSITION TITLE, SERIES, AND GRADE: **LOCATION:**

Laborer Leader   NPS, National Capital Region
WL-03502-3   National Capital Parks-East
$9.16 - $10.72 per hour   Office of Superintendent
                                              Division of Resource Management
                                              Washington, DC

BRIEF DESCRIPTION OF DUTIES: Supervises 10-15 enrollees in environmental and work projects. Provides technical guidance and direction. Required to work in an outdoor environment and is responsible for carrying out field work in a wide variety of trades and crafts such as carpentry, painting, basic grounds and gardening skills, and a wide variety of land resource improvement projects. Assigns duties. Reports adverse social behavior and discipline problems. Counsels enrollees. Must possess a valid state license.

NATURE OF APPOINTMENT: THIS IS A TEMPORARY APPOINTMENT NOT TO EXCEED 9-30-92.

QUALIFICATIONS REQUIRED: As required in Office of Personnel Management Qualifications Handbook X-118C, applicants must possess the following knowledge, skills, and abilities which are considered essential to successful job performance:

1. **SCREEN OUT ELEMENT:** Ability to motivate and lead others in the completion of assignments.
2. Ability to use a variety of hand tools for such jobs as carpentry, painting and grounds maintenance.
3. Knowledge of basic carpentry and painting practices.

METHODS TO BE USED IN RATING AND RANKING CANDIDATES: Applications will be rated using the criteria listed above. Qualified candidates will be ranked to determine the best qualified for referral to the selecting official.

PRIVACY ACT INFORMATION: The application you submit for this position contains information subject to the Privacy Act of 1974 (P.L. 93-579.5 U.S.C. 522a). We are required to provide you with information regarding our authority and purposes for collecting this data, the routine uses which will be made of it, and the effect, if any, of nondisclosures. You are entitled to the same information as it pertains specifically to disclosure of your Social Security number. Any information you may need regarding Privacy Act regulations and the rights they extend can be obtained by calling 619-7256. Hearing impaired candidates may call on TTY 619-7364 if additional information is needed.

How To Apply - Submit the following:

-   An up-to-date Application for Federal Employment (SF-171)
-   The attached Supplemental Questionnaire, if applicable
-   Report of Separation from Active Duty (DD-214), for those applicants claiming 5 or 10 pt. Veterans Preference
-   Application for 10 pt. Veterans Preference (SF-15) and the required proof listed on the form
-   Applicant Background Survey (DI-1935) optional

Submit all forms to: National Park Service
                        National Capital Region
                        Division of Personnel
                        1100 Ohio Drive, SW
                        Washington, DC 20242

RECORDED JOB INFORMATION NUMBER: (202) 619-7111

THE USE OF GOVERNMENT ENVELOPES OR GOVERNMENT MAIL CHANNELS FOR SENDING APPLICATIONS IS UNLAWFUL. APPLICATIONS RECEIVED IN THIS MANNER WILL BE REJECTED BY THIS OFFICE.

Appendix H: Application Forms

The Federal government has many different kinds of applications forms, each suited to a specific purpose. Some are used for a wide range of occupations, others for only a few or one. A number of these forms are reprinted here on pages 486-491. The all-important SF-171 (Application for Federal Employment) provided may actually be used, either by cutting it out or by photocopying it. However, neither the reprints nor photocopies may be submitted for forms intended for computer scanning, such as the Forms B; in those instances, originals must be obtained from either the hiring agency or your local OPM Service Center.

Which forms to submit when applying for a given job are always indicated on the job announcement. The SF-171 is often requested but no longer required by most agencies in their Vacancy Announcements, and is generally also needed when applying to OPM for a rating. However, alternative or supplementary forms are occasionally requested. The supplementary forms included here are not for use, but samples only.

Note: Because many of the Forms B (pp. 507-35) contain duplicated material, we have included only those pages that differ from form to form.

Filling out the SF-171 is discussed in detail in Step 5; worksheets forr this process are provided in Appendix I.

CONTENTS

Standard Form 171
Application for Federal Employment

Read The Following Instructions Carefully Before You Complete This Application

▶ **DO NOT SUBMIT A RESUME INSTEAD OF THIS APPLICATION.**

● **TYPE OR PRINT CLEARLY IN DARK INK.**

▶ IF YOU NEED MORE SPACE for an answer, use a sheet of paper the same size as this page. On **each** sheet write your name, Social Security Number, the announcement number or job title, and the item number. Attach all additional forms and sheets to this application at the top of page 3.

● If you do not answer **all** questions fully and correctly, you may delay the review of your application and lose job opportunities.

● Unless you are asked for additional material in the announcement or qualification information, **do not attach** any materials, such as: official position descriptions, performance evaluations, letters of recommendation, certificates of training, publications, etc. Any materials you attach which were not asked for may be removed from your application and will **not** be returned to you.

● We suggest that you **keep a copy** of this application for your use. if you plan to make copies of your application, we suggest you leave items **1, 48** and **49** blank. Complete these blank items each time you apply. **YOU MUST SIGN AND DATE, IN INK, EACH COPY YOU SUBMIT.**

● **To apply for a specific Federal civil service examination** (whether or not a written test is required) **or a specific vacancy in a Federal agency:**

-- Read the announcement and other materials provided.

-- Make sure that your work experience and/or education meet the qualification requirements described.

-- Make sure the announcement is open for the job and location you are interested in. Announcements may be closed to receipt of applications for some types of jobs, grades, or geographic locations.

-- Make sure that you are allowed to apply. Some jobs are limited to veterans, or to people who work for the Federal Government or have worked for the Federal Government in the past.

-- Follow any directions on "How to Apply". If a written test is required, bring any material you are instructed to bring to the test session. For example, you may be instructed to "Bring a completed SF 171 to the test." If a written test is not required, mail this application and all other forms required by the announcement to the address specified in the announcement.

Work Experience *(Item 24)*

● Carefully complete each experience block you need to describe your work experience. Unless you qualify based on education alone, **your rating will depend on your description of previous jobs. Do not leave out any jobs you held during the last ten years.**

● Under **Description of Work**, write a **clear** and **brief**, but **complete** description of your **major** duties and responsibilities for each job. Include any supervisory duties, special assignments, and your accomplishments in the job. We may verify your description with your former employers.

● If you had a major change of duties or responsibilities while you worked for the same employer, describe each major change as a separate job.

Veteran Preference in Hiring *(Item 22)*

● **DO NOT LEAVE Item 22 BLANK.** If you do **not** claim veteran preference place an **"X"** in the box next to **"NO PREFERENCE"**.

● You **cannot** receive veteran preference if you are retired or plan to retire at or above the rank of major or lieutenant commander, **unless** you are disabled or retired from the active military Reserve.

● To receive veteran preference your separation from active duty must have been under honorable conditions. This includes honorable and general discharges. A clemency discharge does not meet the requirements of the Veteran Preference Act.

● Active duty for training in the military Reserve and National Guard programs is not considered active duty for purposes of veteran preference.

● To qualify for preference you must meet **ONE** of the following conditions:

1. Served on active duty anytime between December 7, 1941, and July 1, 1955; (If you were a Reservist called to active duty between February 1, 1955 and July 1, 1955, you must meet condition 2, below.)

or

2. Served on active duty any part of which was between July 2, 1955 and October 14, 1976 or a Reservist called to active duty between February 1, 1955 and October 14, 1976 **and** who served for more than 180 days;

or

3. Entered on active duty between October 15, 1976 and September 7, 1980 or a Reservist who entered on active duty between October 15, 1976 and October 13, 1982 **and** received a Campaign Badge or Expeditionary Medal **or** are a disabled veteran;

or

4. Enlisted in the Armed Forces after September 7, 1980 or entered active duty other than by enlistment on or after October 14, 1982 **and:**

   a. completed 24 months of continuous active duty or the full period called or ordered to active duty, or were discharged under 10 U.S.C. 1171 or for hardship under 10 U.S.C. 1173 **and** received or were entitled to receive a Campaign Badge or Expeditionary Medal; **or**

   b. are a disabled veteran.

● If you meet one of the four conditions above, you qualify for 5-point preference. If you want to claim 5-point preference **and** do not meet the requirements for 10-point preference, discussed below, place an **"X"** in the box next to **"5-POINT PREFERENCE"**.

● If you think you qualify for 10-Point Preference, review the requirements described in the Standard Form (SF) 15, Application for 10-Point Veteran Preference. The SF 15 is available from any Federal Job Information Center. The 10-point preference groups are:

-- Non-Compensably Disabled or Purple Heart Recipient.

-- Compensably Disabled (less than 30%).

-- Compensably Disabled (30% or more).

-- Spouse, Widow(er) or Mother of a deceased or disabled veteran.

If you claim 10-point preference, place an **"X"** in the box next to the group that applies to you. **To receive 10-point preference you must attach a completed SF 15 to this application together with the proof requested in the SF 15.**

Privacy Act Statement

The Office of Personnel Management is authorized to rate applicants for Federal jobs under sections 1302, 3301, and 3304 of title 5 of the U.S. Code. Section 1104 of title 5 allows the Office of Personnel Management to authorize other Federal agencies to rate applicants for Federal jobs. We need the information you put on this form and associated application forms to see how well your education and work skills qualify you for a Federal job. We also need information on matters such as citizenship and military service to see whether you are affected by laws we must follow in deciding who may be employed by the Federal Government.

We must have your Social Security Number (SSN) to keep your records straight because other people may have the same name and birth date. The SSN has been used to keep records since 1943, when Executive Order 9397 asked agencies to do so. The Office of Personnel Management may also use your SSN to make requests for information about you from employers, schools, banks, and others who know you, but only as allowed

by law or Presidential directive. The information we collect by using your SSN will be used for employment purposes and also may be used for studies, statistics, and computer matching to benefit and payment files.

Information we have about you may also be given to Federal, State and local agencies for checking on law violations or for other lawful purposes. We may send your name and address to State and local Government agencies, Congressional and other public offices, and public international organizations, if they request names of people to consider for employment. We may also notify your school placement office if you are selected for a Federal job.

Giving us your SSN or any of the other information is voluntary. However, we cannot process your application, which is the first step toward getting a job, if you do not give us the information we request. Incomplete addresses and ZIP Codes will also slow processing.

DETACH THIS PAGE – NOTE SF 171-A ON BACK

Application for Federal Employment—SF 171

Read the instructions before you complete this application. *Type or print clearly in dark ink.*

Form Approved:
OMB No. 3206-0012

GENERAL INFORMATION

1 What kind of job are you applying for? *Give title and announcement no. (if any)*

2 Social Security Number

3 Sex ☐ Male ☐ Female

4 Birth date *(Month, Day, Year)*

5 Birthplace *(City and State or Country)*

6 Name *(Last, First, Middle)*

Mailing address *(include apartment number, if any)*

City   State   ZIP Code

7 Other names ever used *(e.g., maiden name, nickname, etc.)*

8 Home Phone
Area Code | Number

9 Work Phone
Area Code | Number | Extension

10 Were you ever employed as a civilian by the Federal Government? If **"NO"**, go to **Item 11.** If **"YES"**, mark each type of job you held with an **"X".**

☐ Temporary ☐ Career-Conditional ☐ Career ☐ Excepted

What is your **highest** grade, classification series and job title?

Dates at **highest** grade: FROM   TO

FOR USE OF EXAMINING OFFICE ONLY

Date entered register

Form reviewed:
Form approved:

Option	Grade	Earned Rating	Veteran Preference	Augmented Rating
			☐ No Preference Claimed	
			☐ 5 Points (Tentative)	
			☐ 10 Pts. (30% Or More Comp. Dis.)	
			☐ 10 Pts. (Less Than 30% Comp. Dis.)	
			☐ Other 10 Points	

Initials and Date

☐ Disallowed ☐ Being Investigated

FOR USE OF APPOINTING OFFICE ONLY

Preference has been verified through proof that the separation was under honorable conditions, and other proof as required.

☐ 5-Point ☐ 10-Point--30% or More Compensable Disability ☐ 10-Point--Less Than 30% Compensable Disability ☐ 10-Point--Other

Signature and Title

Agency   Date

AVAILABILITY

11 When can you start work? *(Month and Year)*

12 What is the **lowest** pay you will accept? *(You will not be considered for jobs which pay less than you indicate.)*

Pay $ _____ per _____ OR Grade _____

13 In what geographic area(s) are you willing to work?

14 Are you willing to work:

	YES	NO
A. 40 hours per week *(full-time)*?..............		
B. 25-32 hours per week *(part-time)*?..........		
C. 17-24 hours per week *(part-time)*?..........		
D. 16 or fewer hours per week *(part-time)*?......		
E. An intermittent job *(on-call/seasonal)*?........		
F. Weekends, shifts, or rotating shifts?.........		

15 Are you willing to take a temporary job lasting:

A. 5 to 12 months *(sometimes longer)*?........		
B. 1 to 4 months?..........................		
C. Less than 1 month?......................		

16 Are you willing to travel away from home for:

A. 1 to 5 nights each month?................		
B. 6 to 10 nights each month?..............		
C. 11 or more nights each month?............		

MILITARY SERVICE AND VETERAN PREFERENCE

17 Have you served in the United States Military Service? *If your only active duty was training in the Reserves or National Guard, answer "NO". If "NO", go to item 22.* ....

YES	NO

18 Did you or will you retire at or above the rank of major or lieutenant commander?................................

MILITARY SERVICE AND VETERAN PREFERENCE *(Cont.)*

19 Were you discharged from the military service under honorable conditions? *(If your discharge was changed to "honorable" or "general" by a Discharge Review Board, answer "YES". If you received a clemency discharge, answer "NO".)* If **"NO"**, provide below the date and type of discharge you received.

YES	NO

Discharge Date *(Month, Day, Year)*	Type of Discharge

20 List the dates *(Month, Day, Year)*, and branch for all **active duty** military service.

From	To	Branch of Service

21 If all your active military duty was after October 14, 1976, list the full names and dates of all campaign badges or expeditionary medals you received or were entitled to receive.

22 **Read the instructions that came with this form before completing this item.** When you have determined your eligibility for veteran preference from the instructions, place an **"X"** in the box next to your veteran preference claim.

☐ NO PREFERENCE

☐ 5-POINT PREFERENCE -- You must show proof when you are hired.

10-POINT PREFERENCE -- If you claim 10-point preference, place an **"X"** in the box below next to the basis for your claim. **To receive 10-point preference you must also complete a Standard Form 15, Application for 10-Point Veteran Preference, which is available from any Federal Job Information Center. ATTACH THE COMPLETED SF 15 AND REQUESTED PROOF TO THIS APPLICATION.**

☐ Non-compensably disabled or Purple Heart recipient.
☐ Compensably disabled, less than 30 percent.
☐ Spouse, widow(er), or mother of a deceased or disabled veteran.
☐ Compensably disabled, 30 percent or more.

THE FEDERAL GOVERNMENT IS AN EQUAL OPPORTUNITY EMPLOYER

PREVIOUS EDITION USABLE UNTIL 12-31-90

NSN 7540-00-935-7150   171-109

Standard Form 171 (Rev. 6-88)
U.S. Office of Personnel Management
FPM Chapter 295

WORK EXPERIENCE *If you have no work experience, write "NONE" in A below and go to 25 on page 3.*

23 May we ask your present employer about your character, qualifications, and work record? *A "NO" will not affect our review of your* | YES | NO
qualifications. *If you answer "NO" and we need to contact your present employer before we can offer you a job, we will contact you first.* . . . .

24 READ **WORK EXPERIENCE** IN THE INSTRUCTIONS BEFORE YOU BEGIN.

- Describe your current or most recent job in Block **A** and work backwards, describing each job you held **during the past 10 years.** If you were **unemployed** for longer than **3 months** within the past 10 years, list the dates and your address(es) in an experience block.

- You may sum up in one block work that you did **more than 10 years ago.** But if that work **is related** to the type of job you are applying for, describe each related job in a separate block.

- INCLUDE VOLUNTEER WORK *(non-paid work)*-**If the work** *(or a part of the work)* **is like the job you are applying for,** complete **all** parts of the experience block just as you would for a paying job. You may receive credit for work experience with religious, community, welfare, service, and other organizations.

- INCLUDE MILITARY SERVICE--You should complete **all** parts of the experience block just as you would for a non-military job, including all supervisory experience. Describe each major change of duties or responsibilities in a separate experience block.

- IF YOU NEED MORE SPACE TO DESCRIBE A JOB--Use sheets of paper the same size as this page (be sure to include **all** information we ask for in **A** and **B** below). On **each** sheet show your name, Social Security Number, and the announcement number or job title.

- IF YOU NEED MORE EXPERIENCE BLOCKS, use the SF 171-A or a sheet of paper.

- IF YOU NEED TO UPDATE (ADD MORE RECENT JOBS), use the SF 172 or a sheet of paper as described above.

A | Name and address of employer's organization *(include ZIP Code, if known)* | Dates employed *(give month, day and year)* | Average number if hours per week | Number of employees you supervise

From: To:

Salary or earnings | Your reason for wanting to leave

Starting $ per

Ending $ per

| Your immediate supervisor | | | Exact title of your job | If Federal employment *(civilian or military)* list series, grade or rank and, if promoted in this job, the date of your last promotion |
| Name | Area Code | Telephone No. | | |

Description of work: Describe your specific duties, responsibilities and accomplishments in this job, **including** the job title(s) of any employees you supervise. *If you describe more than one type of work (for example, carpentry and painting, or personnel and budget), write the approximate percentage of time you spent doing each.*

For Agency Use (skill codes, etc.)

B | Name and address of employer's organization *(include ZIP Code, if known)* | Dates employed *(give month, day and year)* | Average number of hours per week | Number of employees you supervised

From: To:

Salary or earnings | Your reason for leaving

Starting $ per

Ending $ per

| Your immediate supervisor | | | Exact title of your job | If Federal employment *(civilian or military)* list series, grade or rank, and, if promoted in this job, the date of your last promotion |
| Name | Area Code | Telephone No. | | |

Description of work: Describe your specific duties, responsibilities and accomplishments in this job, **including** the job title(s) of any employees you supervised. *If you describe more than one type of work (for example, carpentry and painting, or personnel and budget), write the approximate percentage of time you spent doing each.*

For Agency Use (skill codes, etc.)

Page 2   IF YOU NEED MORE EXPERIENCE BLOCKS, USE SF 171-A *(SEE BACK OF INSTRUCTION PAGE).*

— ⟵ —————— **ATTACH ANY ADDITIONAL FORMS AND SHEETS HERE**

EDUCATION

25 Did you graduate from high school? *If you have a GED high school equivalency or will graduate within the next nine months, answer "YES".*

YES ▶	If **"YES"**, give month and year graduated or received GED equivalency: . . . .
NO ▶	If **NO"**, give the highest grade you completed: .

26 Write the name and location *(city and state)* of the last high school you attended or where you obtained your GED high school equivalency.

27 Have you ever attended college or graduate school? **YES** / **NO** ▶ If **"YES"**, continue with **28**. ▶ If **NO"**, go to **31**.

28 NAME AND LOCATION *(city, state and ZIP Code)* OF COLLEGE OR UNIVERSITY. *If you expect to grad-uate within nine months, give the **month** and **year** you expect to receive your degree:*

Name	City	State	ZIP Code	MONTH AND YEAR ATTENDED From	To	NUMBER OF CREDIT HOURS COMPLETED Semester	Quarter	TYPE OF DEGREE *(e.g. B.A., M.A.)*	MONTH AND YEAR OF DEGREE
1)									
2)									
3)									

29

CHIEF UNDERGRADUATE SUBJECTS *Show major on the first line*	NUMBER OF CREDIT HOURS COMPLETED Semester	Quarter
1)		
2)		
3)		

30

CHIEF GRADUATE SUBJECTS *Show major on the first line*	NUMBER OF CREDIT HOURS COMPLETED Semester	Quarter
1)		
2)		
3)		

31 If you have completed any **other courses or training related to the kind of jobs you are applying for** *(trade, vocational, Armed Forces, business)* give information below.

NAME AND LOCATION *(city, state and ZIP Code)* OF SCHOOL	MONTH AND YEAR ATTENDED From	To	CLASS-ROOM HOURS	SUBJECT(S)	TRAINING COMPLETED YES	NO
School Name 1)						
City State ZIP Code						
School Name 2)						
City State ZIP Code						

SPECIAL SKILLS, ACCOMPLISHMENTS AND AWARDS

32 Give the title and year of any honors, awards or fellowships you have received. List your special qualifications, skills or accomplishments that may help you get a job. *Some examples are: skills with computers or other machines; most important publications (do not submit copies); public speaking and writing experience; membership in professional or scientific societies; patents or inventions; etc.*

33 How many words per minute can you: TYPE? TAKE DICTATION?

Agencies may test your skills before hiring you.

34 List **job-related** licenses or certificates that you have, such as: *registered nurse; lawyer; radio operator; driver's; pilot's; etc.*

	LICENSE OR CERTIFICATE	DATE OF LATEST LICENSE OR CERTIFICATE	STATE OR OTHER LICENSING AGENCY
1)			
2)			

35 Do you speak or read a language other than English *(include sign language)*? *Applicants for jobs that require a language other than English may be given an interview conducted solely in that language.* **YES** / **NO** ▶ If **"YES"**, list each language and place an **"X"** in each column that applies to you. ▶ If **"NO"**, go to **36**.

LANGUAGE(S)	CAN PREPARE AND GIVE LECTURES Fluently	With Difficulty	CAN SPEAK AND UNDERSTAND Fluently	Passably	CAN TRANSLATE ARTICLES Into English	From English	CAN READ ARTICLES FOR OWN USE Easily	With Difficulty
1)								
2)								

REFERENCES

36 List three people who are not related to you and are not supervisors you listed under **24** who know your qualifications and fitness for the kind of job for which you are applying. At least **one** should know you well on a personal basis.

FULL NAME OF REFERENCE	TELEPHONE NUMBER(S) *(Include Area Code)*	PRESENT BUSINESS OR HOME ADDRESS *(Number, street and city)*	STATE	ZIP CODE
1)				
2)				
3)				

Page 3

BACKGROUND INFORMATION--*You must answer each question in this section before we can process your application.*

37 Are you a citizen of the United States? *(In most cases you must be a U.S. citizen to be hired. You will be required to submit proof of identity and citizenship at the time you are hired.)* If **"NO"**, give the country or countries you are a citizen of: _____ | YES | NO |

> NOTE: **It is important that you give complete and truthful answers to questions 38 through 44.** If you answer **"YES"** to any of them, provide your explanation(s) in **Item 45. Include** convictions resulting from a plea of nolo contendere *(no contest)*. **Omit:** 1) traffic fines of $100.00 or less; 2) any violation of law committed before your 16th birthday; 3) any violation of law committed before your 18th birthday, if finally decided in juvenile court or under a Youth Offender law; 4) any conviction set aside under the Federal Youth Corrections Act or similar State law; 5) any conviction whose record was expunged under Federal or State law. We will consider the date, facts, and circumstances of each event you list. In most cases you can still be considered for Federal jobs. However, **if you fail to tell the truth or fail to list all relevant** events or circumstances, this may be grounds for not hiring you, for firing you after you begin work, or for criminal prosecution (18 USC 1001).

	YES	NO
38 During the last **10 years**, were you **fired from any job** for any reason, did you **quit after being told that you would be fired**, or did you leave by mutual agreement because of specific problems?.		
39 Have you **ever** been convicted of, or forfeited collateral for **any felony violation?** *(Generally, a felony is defined as any violation of law punishable by imprisonment of longer than one year, except for violations called misdemeanors under State law which are punishable by imprisonment of two years or less.)*		
40 Have you **ever** been convicted of, or forfeited collateral for **any firearms or explosives violation**?.		
41 Are you **now** under charges for **any** violation of law?.		
42 During the **last 10 years** have you forfeited collateral, been convicted, been imprisoned, been on probation, or been on parole? Do **not** include violations reported in 39, 40, or 41, above.		
43 Have you **ever** been convicted by a military **court-martial?** If no military service, answer **"NO"**.		
44 Are you **delinquent** on any Federal debt? *(Include delinquencies arising from Federal taxes, loans, overpayment of benefits, and other debts to the U.S. Government **plus** defaults on Federally guaranteed or insured loans such as student and home mortgage loans.)*.		

45 If **"YES"** in: 38 - Explain for each job the problem(s) and your reason(s) for leaving. Give the employer's name and address.

   39 through 43 - Explain each violation. Give place of occurrence and name/address of police or court involved.

   44 - Explain the type, length and amount of the delinquency or default, and steps you are taking to correct errors or repay the debt. Give any identification number associated with the debt and the address of the Federal agency involved.

   NOTE: If you need more space, use a sheet of paper, and include the item number.

Item No.	Date (Mo./Yr.)	Explanation	Mailing Address
			Name of Employer, Police, Court, or Federal Agency
			City State ZIP Code
			Name of Employer, Police, Court, or Federal Agency
			City State ZIP Code

	YES	NO
46 Do you receive, or have you ever applied for retirement pay, pension, or other pay based on military, Federal civilian, or District of Columbia Government service?.		

47 Do any of your relatives work for the United States Government or the United States Armed Forces? Include: *father; mother; husband; wife; son; daughter; brother; sister; uncle; aunt; first cousin; nephew; niece; father-in-law; mother-in-law; son-in-law; daughter-in-law; brother-in-law; sister-in-law; stepfather; stepmother; stepson; stepdaughter; stepbrother; stepsister; half brother; and half sister.* . . . .

If **"YES"**, provide details below. If you need more space, use a sheet of paper.

Name	Relationship	Department, Agency or Branch of Armed Forces

SIGNATURE, CERTIFICATION, AND RELEASE OF INFORMATION

YOU MUST SIGN THIS APPLICATION.   Read the following carefully before you sign.

- A false statement on any part of your application may be grounds for not hiring you, or for firing you after you begin work. Also, you may be punished by fine or imprisonment (U.S. Code, title 18, section 1001).
- If you are a male born after December 31, 1959 you must be registered with the Selective Service System or have a valid exemption in order to be eligible for Federal employment. You will be required to certify as to your status at the time of appointment.
- **I understand** that any information I give may be investigated as allowed by law or Presidential order.
- **I consent** to the release of information about my ability and fitness for Federal employment **by** *employers, schools, law enforcement agencies and other individuals and organizations,* **to** *investigators, personnel staffing specialists, and other authorized employees of the Federal Government.*
- **I certify** that, to the best of my knowledge and belief, **all** of my statements are true, correct, complete, and made in good faith.

48 SIGNATURE *(Sign each application in dark ink)* | **49** DATE SIGNED *(Month, day, year)*

Standard Form 171-A— *Continuation Sheet for SF 171*

Form Approved:
OMB No. 3206-0012

● Attach all SF 171-A's to your application at the top of page 3.

1. Name *(Last, First, Middle Initial)*	2. Social Security Number

3. Job Title or Announcement Number You Are Applying For	4. Date Completed

ADDITIONAL WORK EXPERIENCE BLOCKS

☐ Name and address of employer's organization *(include ZIP Code, if known)*

Dates employed *(give month, day and year)*	Average number of hours per week	Number of employees you supervised
From: To:		

Salary or earnings	Your reason for leaving
Starting $ per	
Ending $ per	

Your immediate supervisor

Name	Area Code	Telephone No.	Exact title of your job	If Federal employment *(civilian or military)* list series, grade or rank, and, if promoted in this job, the date of your last promotion

Description of work: Describe your specific duties, responsibilities and accomplishments in this job, **including** the job title(s) of any employees you supervised.   *If you describe more than one type of work (for example, carpentry and painting, or personnel and budget), write the approximate percentage of time you spent doing each.*

For Agency Use (skill codes, etc.)

☐ Name and address of employer's organization *(include ZIP Code, if known)*

Dates employed *(give month, day and year)*	Average number of hours per week	Number of employees you supervised
From: To:		

Salary or earnings	Your reason for leaving
Starting $ per	
Ending $ per	

Your immediate supervisor

Name	Area Code	Telephone No.	Exact title of your job	If Federal employment *(civilian or military)* list series, grade or rank, and, if promoted in this job, the date of your last promotion

Description of work: Describe your specific duties, responsibilities and accomplishments in this job, **including** the job title(s) of any employees you supervised.   *If you describe more than one type of work (for example, carpentry and painting, or personnel and budget), write the approximate percentage of time you spent doing each.*

For Agency Use (skill codes, etc.)

Standard Form **171-A** (Rev. 6-88)
U.S. Office of Personnel Management
FPM Chapter 295

FORM APPROVED
OMB NO. 3206-0040

FORM

A

U.S. OFFICE OF PERSONNEL MANAGEMENT

Employment Availability Statement

USE NO. 2 PENCIL ONLY

WARNING: KEEP RESPONSES WITHIN BOX.

NAME: _____
                                    (PLEASE PRINT)

JOB APPLYING FOR: _____
                                    (PRINT JOB TITLE)

DIRECTIONS FOR COMPLETING APPLICANT INFORMATION

SAMPLE NAME GRID

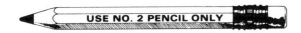

When completing information requested, enter the appropriate letter or number in the box and completely blacken in the corresponding oval below the box. See Sample Name Grid to the right.

DO NOT FOLD, STAPLE, TEAR OR PAPER CLIP THIS FORM.
DO NOT SUBMIT PHOTOCOPIES OF THIS FORM.

BATCH NUMBER
(BNO)

FOR OFFICE
USE ONLY

We can process this information only if you:
- Use only a number 2 lead pencil.
- Completely blacken each oval you choose.
- Completely erase any mistakes or stray marks.

Read the instructions for each item carefully before you begin that item.

OPM FORM 1203-AH (6/88)

018384   ○○○○○○○○○○■○○○■■■■■○■○○○▣   **DO NOT MARK IN THIS AREA**

1 — FIRST NAME (FNM) | **MI (MIN)** | **LAST NAME (LNM)**

A B C D E F G H I J K L M N O P Q R S T U V W X Y Z (bubble fields for each letter position)

2 — SOCIAL SECURITY NO. (SSN)

0 1 2 3 4 5 6 7 8 9 (bubble columns)

3 — TELEPHONE NUMBER (TEL) | **CONTACT TIME (TCT)**

AREA CODE

0 1 2 3 4 5 6 7 8 9 (bubble columns)

DAY ○

NIGHT ○

EITHER ○

4 — STREET ADDRESS (HOUSE AND STREET AND APT. NO. WHERE YOU WANT TO RECEIVE MAIL) (ADR)

0 1 2 3 4 5 6 7 8 9 (bubble columns)

A B C D E F G H I J K L M N O P Q R S T U V W X Y Z (bubble fields)

5 — CITY (CTY)

A B C D E F G H I J K L M N O P Q R S T U V W X Y Z (bubble fields)

6 — STATE CODE (STE)

USE STANDARD STATE CODES

A B C D E F G H I J K L M N O P Q R S T U V W X Y Z (bubble fields)

IF OUTSIDE U.S.A., BLACKEN "OV" AND PRINT COUNTRY HERE →

7 — ZIP CODE +4 (ZIP) — OPTIONAL

0 1 2 3 4 5 6 7 8 9 (bubble columns)

8 EMPLOYMENT AVAILABILITY

(Blacken YES or NO for each question)

ARE YOU AVAILABLE FOR: YES   NO

A) full-time employment   (FTE)
   –40 hours per week?   Ⓨ   Ⓝ

B) part-time employment of   (PTE)
   –16 or fewer hours per week?   Ⓨ   Ⓝ
   –17 to 24 hours per week?   Ⓨ   Ⓝ
   –25 to 32 hours per week?   Ⓨ   Ⓝ

C) temporary employment
   lasting   (TMP)
   –less than 1 month?   Ⓨ   Ⓝ
   –1 to 4 months?   Ⓨ   Ⓝ
   –5 to 12 months?   Ⓨ   Ⓝ

D) jobs requiring travel
   away from home for   (TRV)
   –1 to 5 nights per month?   Ⓨ   Ⓝ
   –6 to 10 nights per month?   Ⓨ   Ⓝ
   –11 or more nights per month?   Ⓨ   Ⓝ

E) other employment
   questions (See directions)   (OEM)
   QUESTION 1?   Ⓨ   Ⓝ
   QUESTION 2?   Ⓨ   Ⓝ
   QUESTION 3?   Ⓨ   Ⓝ
   QUESTION 4?   Ⓨ   Ⓝ

11 DATE AVAILABLE FOR WORK
                                         (EBD)

MONTH			YEAR
Jan ◯	May ◯	Sep ◯	This year ◯
Feb ◯	Jun ◯	Oct ◯	
Mar ◯	Jul ◯	Nov ◯	Next year ◯
Apr ◯	Aug ◯	Dec ◯	

9 GEOGRAPHIC AVAILABILITY   (GFP)

Using the GEOGRAPHIC CODE LISTING and instructions you were given with this form, write the servicing office name in the boxes below. Then, choose up to nine locations where you are willing to accept employment. Write your choices in the boxes and blacken the corresponding oval below each box.

SERVICING OFFICE

(Gridded numeric columns 0–9 for locations 1, 2, 3, 4, 5)

(Gridded numeric columns 0–9 for locations 6, 7, 8, 9)

10 JOB PREFERENCE (JBF)

Follow the directions you were given with this form to complete this item. If no directions were given do not complete this item.

1 ◯	36 ◯
2 ◯	37 ◯
3 ◯	38 ◯
4 ◯	39 ◯
5 ◯	40 ◯
6 ◯	41 ◯
7 ◯	42 ◯
8 ◯	43 ◯
9 ◯	44 ◯
10 ◯	45 ◯
11 ◯	46 ◯
12 ◯	47 ◯
13 ◯	48 ◯
14 ◯	49 ◯
15 ◯	50 ◯
16 ◯	51 ◯
17 ◯	52 ◯
18 ◯	53 ◯
19 ◯	54 ◯
20 ◯	55 ◯
21 ◯	56 ◯
22 ◯	57 ◯
23 ◯	58 ◯
24 ◯	59 ◯
25 ◯	60 ◯
26 ◯	61 ◯
27 ◯	62 ◯
28 ◯	63 ◯
29 ◯	64 ◯
30 ◯	65 ◯
31 ◯	66 ◯
32 ◯	67 ◯
33 ◯	68 ◯
34 ◯	69 ◯
35 ◯	70 ◯

OTHER EMPLOYMENT INFORMATION

For items 12 – 15, follow the directions you were given with this form to complete these items.

If no directions were given do not complete these items.

Be sure to sign the form in item 16.

12 LANGUAGES (LNG)

(Gridded numeric columns 0–9)

13 DATE BLOCK (SDF)

MM   DD   YY

(Gridded numeric columns 0–9)

14 OTHER INFORMATION (MSC)

(Gridded numeric columns 0–9)

15 SPECIAL KNOWLEDGES (SPK)

(Gridded numeric columns 0–9 for 1, 2, 3, 4)

16 SIGNATURE

I certify that all the information on this form is true, complete, and correct to the best of my knowledge and belief.

_____
Signature

_____
Date Signed

018384

DO NOT MARK IN THIS AREA

LEAVE PAGES 4, 5, 6, 7, AND 8 BLANK

FOR OFFICE USE ONLY

US Office of Personnel Management

OCCUPATIONAL SUPPLEMENT FOR MATHEMATICIANS AND RELATED POSITIONS — 1500-X

FORM APPROVED
OMB NO. 3206-0040
(See Page 6 for Public Burden Information)

FORM B

BATCH NUMBER (BNO)

FOR OFFICE USE ONLY

DO NOT FOLD, STAPLE, TEAR OR PAPER CLIP THIS FORM. DO NOT SUBMIT PHOTOCOPIES OF THIS FORM.

We can process this information only if you:
1) Use a number 2 lead pencil only.
2) Completely blacken each circle you choose.
3) Completely erase any mistakes or stray marks.

PRINT YOUR RESPONSE IN THE BOXES AND BLACKEN THE APPROPRIATE CIRCLES.

USE ONLY A NUMBER 2 LEAD PENCIL.

1 NAME

NAME: _____
(Please Print)

2 SOCIAL SECURITY NUMBER (SSN)

3 DATE OF BIRTH (DOB)
MONTH | DAY | YEAR

EXAMPLES

5

	YES	NO
A	●	Ⓝ
B	Ⓨ	●●● Ⓝ
C	● Ⓨ Ⓨ	Ⓝ ●●

5 EMPLOYMENT AVAILABILITY (EMP)

ARE YOU AVAILABLE FOR:

(Blacken YES or NO for each question)

	YES	NO	
A full-time employment			
– 40 hours per week?	Ⓨ	Ⓝ	(FTE)
B part-time employment of			(PTE)
– 16 or fewer hours per week?	Ⓨ	Ⓝ	
– 17 to 24 hours per week?	Ⓨ	Ⓝ	
– 25 to 32 hours per week?	Ⓨ	Ⓝ	
C temporary employment lasting			(TMP)
– 5 to 12 months?	Ⓨ	Ⓝ	
– 1 to 4 months?	Ⓨ	Ⓝ	
– less than 1 month?	Ⓨ	Ⓝ	
D jobs requiring travel away from home for			(TRV)
– 1 to 5 nights per month?	Ⓨ	Ⓝ	
– 6 to 10 nights per month?	Ⓨ	Ⓝ	
– 11 or more nights per month?	Ⓨ	Ⓝ	

4 GEOGRAPHIC AVAILABILITY (GFP)

From the GEOGRAPHIC CODE LISTING furnished with this application, print the name of the Zone you are applying for below.

GEOGRAPHIC ZONE

In the above Zone, choose up to nine (9) locations where you are willing to work. Write the codes corresponding to your choices in the boxes below and blacken the corresponding circles below each box.

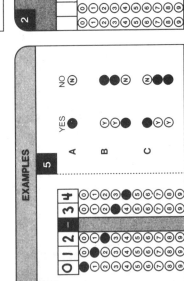

1   2   3   4   5   6   7   8   9

6 LANGUAGES (LNG)

Select up to three languages in which you are proficient. Blacken the circle beside each choice.

○ Any African Language (01)
○ Any Native American Language (Aleut. Navajo, etc.) (02)
○ Any Classical Language (03)
○ Asian/Near East Languages (04)
○ Asian/Far East Languages (other than Chinese) (05)
○ Chinese (06)
○ French (07)
○ German (08)
○ Russian (09)
○ Sign Language (10)
○ Spanish (11)
○ Other European Languages (12)
○ Other Languages (13)

OPM Form 1203-L (Rev. August 1989)
Prior Edition (1/89) Only Is Usable

0392844

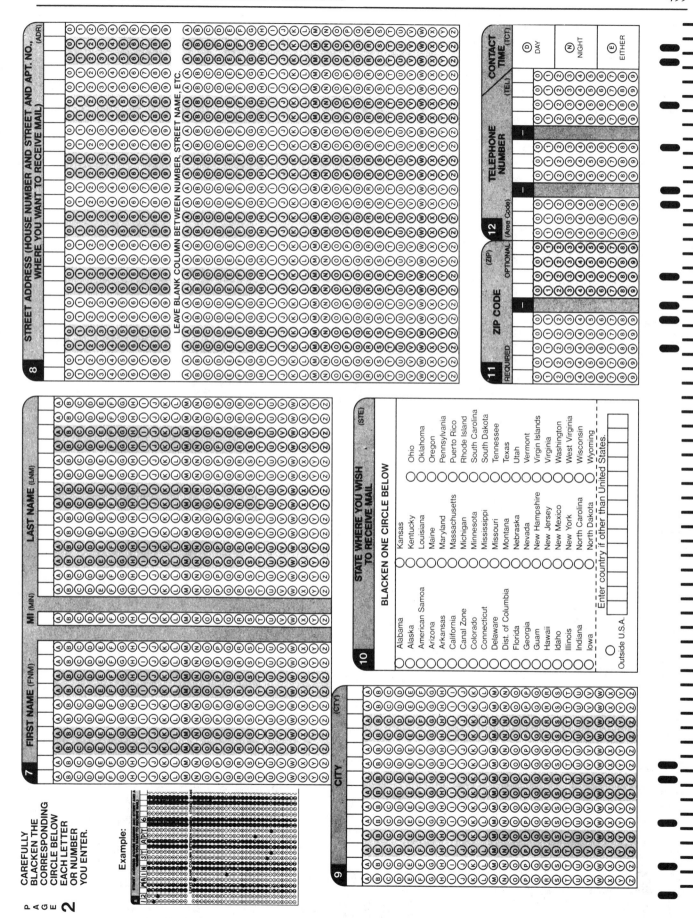

13 ACADEMIC DISCIPLINES

Indicate the academic degree(s) you have completed or will complete within the next 9 months by blackening the appropriate circle(s).

DISCIPLINES	BS DEGREE	1 YEAR GRAD STUDY	MASTERS DEGREE	PhD
ACTUARIAL SCIENCE	O	O	O	O
COMPUTER SCIENCE	O	O	O	O
MATHEMATICS	O	O	O	O
STATISTICS	O	O	O	O
OPERATIONS RESEARCH	O	O	O	O
MATHEMATICAL STATISTICS	O	O	O	O
OTHER	O	O	O	O

Completion of Undergraduate Study

If you have claimed an undergraduate degree, indicate whether or not you have completed the degree.　　O Yes　O No

Completion of Graduate Study

If you have claimed a graduate degree or study, indicate whether or not you have completed the degree or study.　　O Yes　O No

14 SUPERIOR ACADEMIC ACHIEVEMENT (SAC)

If you have a Bachelor's degree (or expect to complete a degree within the next 9 months) and meet any of these Superior Academic Achievement requirements, blacken one or more appropriate circles below.

O GPA of 3.5, all courses completed in your major field of study.

O GPA of 3.5, all courses completed in your major field of study in the last 2 years of your undergraduate curriculum.

O GPA of 3.0, all completed undergraduate courses.

O GPA of 3.0 all courses completed in the last 2 years of your undergraduate curriculum.

O Rank in the upper one-third of the graduating class.

O Membership in a scholastic honorary society (other than a freshman society).

15 ACTUARIAL EXAMINATIONS/COURSEWORK

Have you successfully completed two or more actuarial examinations given by the Casualty Actuarial Society, or obtained 60 credits for Society of Actuary courses?

O Yes　　　　O No

0392844

(OSP)

OCCUPATIONAL SPECIALTIES

YOU WILL NEED TO REFER TO THE QUALIFICATIONS FOR EACH OCCUPATIONAL SPECIALTY TO COMPLETE THIS SECTION. THE QUALIFICATIONS ARE LISTED IN THE QUALIFICATION INFORMATION STATEMENT (QIS). YOUR RESPONSES WILL BE VERIFIED FROM THE INFORMATION ON YOUR SF 171, APPLICATION FOR FEDERAL EMPLOYMENT.

INSTRUCTIONS: You may select up to six (6) specialties from the list provided to you. For each specialty chosen, you must: 1) write the specialty codes in the boxes and blacken the corresponding circles under the boxes; and 2) indicate your answers to the following seven questions by blackening the corresponding circles for each specialty you have chosen.

NOTE: The phrase in the specialty means in the field or discipline for which you are applying and in a related field means a specialty that shares a number of the same or similar basic scientific principles and concepts.

1. Do you meet the basic qualifications requirements (including specific coursework) for the specialty as defined in the Qualification Information Statement?

2. Do you have at least 24 semester hours (36 quarter hours) of undergraduate coursework in the specialty for which you are applying?

3. What is your grade point average of all undergraduate courses taken in the specialty?

  1) 3.00 - 3.09   2) 3.10 - 3.19   3) 3.20 - 3.29
  4) 3.30 - 3.39   5) 3.40 - 3.49   6) 3.50 - 4.00

4. If you have 12 months or more of experience in the specialty, indicate the highest level of experience using the definitions in the LEVELS OF EXPERIENCE section.

5. Did you complete your experience or education in the specialty within the last two years?

6. If you have 12 months or more of experience in a related field, indicate the highest level of experience using definitions in the LEVELS OF EXPERIENCE section.

7. Did you complete your experience or education study in a related field within the last two years?

LEVELS OF EXPERIENCE

a) Performed work as a student trainee which involved duties using common established procedures performed under close supervision.

b) Performed routine duties using basic principles and practices. Work involved following established procedures and instructions. All work was closely supervised and any deviations were coordinated with others.

c) Performed elementary duties using basic principles and practices and adapting them when necessary. Guidelines provided were generally specific, but sometimes were only general and had to be interpreted to cover the work assignment. Work involved some independent action and judgment. Close supervision or guidance was only provided as necessary.

d) Performed a wide range of practices in the field. Work involved applying general guidelines and policies that required judgement or initiative to apply to work assignment. Work involved planning, designing and independently carrying out assignments.

(LAG)

LOWEST GRADE

Blacken the circle of the lowest grade for which you are available and qualified.

○ GS-5   ○ GS-7

(JBF)

18 SPECIALIZED EXPERIENCE / EDUCATION

Blacken only the circle(s) of the specialized fields in which you possess experience or education and are interested in working.

GENERAL

- ○ Actuarial Science (1)
- ○ Computer Science (2)
- ○ Mathematics (3)
- ○ Statistics (4)
- ○ Operations Research (5)
- ○ Mathematical Statistics (6)
- ○ Computer Programming (7)
- ○ Research (8)
- ○ Testing and Evaluation (9)
- ○ Aerospace Technology (10)
- ○ Cost Effectiveness (11)
- ○ Public Information (12)

MATHEMATICS FIELD

- ○ Cryptography (13)
- ○ Linear/Dynamic Programming (14)
- ○ Logic (15)
- ○ Mathematical Analysis (16)
- ○ Mathematical Modeling (17)
- ○ Theoretical Mathematics (18)
- ○ Applied Mathematics (19)
- ○ Computational Mathematics (20)
- ○ Artificial Intelligence (21)
- ○ Probability (22)
- ○ Topology/Geometry (23)
- ○ Numerical Analysis (24)

OPERATIONS RESEARCH FIELD

- ○ Military Tactics/Strategy (25)
- ○ Weapons Systems Related (26)
- ○ Transportation Related (27)
- ○ Communications Related (28)
- ○ Energy/Natural Resource Related (29)
- ○ Logistics/Supply Related (30)
- ○ Organizational Methods/Procedures (31)
- ○ Network Flow Theory (32)
- ○ Queuing Theory (33)

STATISTICAL FIELD

- ○ Survey Statistics (34)
- ○ Agriculture (35)
- ○ Biological Sciences (36)
- ○ Demographics (37)
- ○ Economics (38)
- ○ Education (39)
- ○ Engineering (40)
- ○ Health (41)
- ○ Medicine (42)
- ○ Physical Sciences (43)
- ○ Social Sciences (44)

19 JOB PREFERENCE (JBF)

Follow the instructions you were given with this form to complete this item. If no instructions were given, do not make any entries.

○ (45)	○ (54)	○ (63)
○ (46)	○ (55)	○ (64)
○ (47)	○ (56)	○ (65)
○ (48)	○ (57)	○ (66)
○ (49)	○ (58)	○ (67)
○ (50)	○ (59)	○ (68)
○ (51)	○ (60)	○ (69)
○ (52)	○ (61)	○ (70)
○ (53)	○ (62)	

20 BACKGROUND INFORMATION (SB1)

	YES	NO
1. Are you a citizen of the United States?	○ Y	○ N
2. During the last 10 years, were you fired from any job for any reason or did you quit after being told that you would be fired?	○ Y	○ N
3. Are you now or have you ever been: (Answer the following questions.)		
a) convicted of or forfeited collateral for any felony?	○ Y	○ N
b) convicted of or forfeited collateral for any firearms or explosives violation?	○ Y	○ N
c) convicted, forfeited collateral, imprisoned, on probation, or on parole, during the last 10 years?	○ Y	○ N
d) convicted by a court-martial?	○ Y	○ N
4. Are you currently under charges for any violation of law?	○ Y	○ N

21 VETERAN PREFERENCE CLAIM (VET)

Blacken the circle next to the type of veteran preference you claim.

- ① No preference claimed
- ② 5 points preference claimed

10 POINT PREFERENCE - You must enclose a completed Standard Form 15.

- ③ 10 points preference claimed (award of a Purple Heart or noncompensable service-connected disability)
- ④ 10 points compensable disability preference claimed (disability rating of less than 30%)
- ⑤ 10 points other (wife, widow, husband, widower, mother preference claimed)
- ⑥ 10 points compensable disability preference claimed (disability rating of 30% or more)

22 SIGNATURE / DATE

A false statement on any part of your application may be grounds for not hiring you, or for firing you after you begin work. Also, you may be punished by fine or imprisonment (U.S. Code, title 18, section 1001). I certify that the information on this form is true and correct to the best of my knowledge.

_____
Signature

_____
Date Signed

0392844

US Office of Personnel Management

OCCUPATIONAL SUPPLEMENT FOR PROFESSIONAL ENGINEERING POSITIONS — 0800-X

FORM APPROVED
OMB NO. 3206-0040
(See Page 6 for Public Burden Information)

(BNO)
BATCH NUMBER

FOR OFFICE USE ONLY

FORM B

DO NOT FOLD, STAPLE, TEAR OR PAPER CLIP THIS FORM. DO NOT SUBMIT PHOTOCOPIES OF THIS FORM.

We can process this information only if you:
1) Use a number 2 lead pencil only.
2) Completely blacken each circle you choose.
3) Completely erase any mistakes or stray marks.

PRINT YOUR RESPONSE IN THE BOXES AND BLACKEN THE APPROPRIATE CIRCLES.

USE ONLY A NUMBER 2 LEAD PENCIL.

EXAMPLES

	YES	NO
A	●	Ⓝ
B	Ⓨ Ⓨ	● ● Ⓝ
C	● Ⓨ Ⓨ	Ⓝ ● ●

1 NAME

NAME: _____
(Please Print)

2 SOCIAL SECURITY NUMBER (SSN)

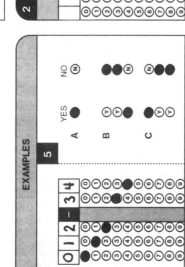

3 DATE OF BIRTH (SDF)

MONTH | DAY | YEAR

4 GEOGRAPHIC AVAILABILITY (GFP)

From the GEOGRAPHIC CODE LISTING furnished with this application, print the name of the Zone you are applying for below.

GEOGRAPHIC ZONE

In the above Zone, choose up to nine (9) locations where you are willing to work. Write the codes corresponding to your choices in the boxes below and blacken the corresponding circles below each box.

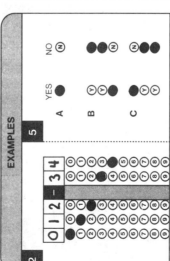

1 2 3 4 5 6 7 8 9

5 EMPLOYMENT AVAILABILITY (Blacken YES or NO for each question)

ARE YOU AVAILABLE FOR:

	YES	NO	
A full-time employment			(FTE)
– 40 hours per week?	Ⓨ	Ⓝ	
B part-time employment of			(PTE)
– 16 or fewer hours per week?	Ⓨ	Ⓝ	
– 17 to 24 hours per week?	Ⓨ	Ⓝ	
– 25 to 32 hours per week?	Ⓨ	Ⓝ	
C temporary employment lasting			(TMP)
– 5 to 12 months?	Ⓨ	Ⓝ	
– 1 to 4 months?	Ⓨ	Ⓝ	
– less than 1 month?	Ⓨ	Ⓝ	
D jobs requiring travel away from home for			(TRV)
– 1 to 5 nights per month?	Ⓨ	Ⓝ	
– 6 to 10 nights per month?	Ⓨ	Ⓝ	
– 11 or more nights per month?	Ⓨ	Ⓝ	

6 LANGUAGES (LNG)

Select up to three languages in which you are proficient. Blacken the circle beside each choice.

○ Any African Language (01)
○ Any Native American Language (Aleut, Navajo, etc.) (02)
○ Any Classical Language (03)
○ Asian/Near East Languages (04)
○ Asian/Far East Languages (other than Chinese) (05)
○ Chinese (06)
○ French (07)
○ German (08)
○ Russian (09)
○ Sign Language (10)
○ Spanish (11)
○ Other European Languages (12)
○ Other Languages (13)

OPM Form 1203-C (Rev. August 1989)
Prior Edition (1/89) Only Is Usable

PAGE 1

0850464

13 — ACADEMIC DISCIPLINES

Indicate the engineering major(s) and the degree(s) or the highest level of study you have completed or will complete within the next 9 months, by blackening the corresponding circle across from the academic discipline(s) which best describes your major and degree level. If you have more than one degree in the same discipline, indicate all degrees.

ENGINEERING DISCIPLINES

Columns: BET | BET (ABET) | 4-YR BS | 4-YR BS (ABET) | 5-YR BS | 5-YR BS (ABET) | 1-YR GRAD STUDY | 2-YR GRAD STUDY/MS | 3-YR GRAD STUDY/PhD

- Aerospace
- Agricultural
- Biomedical
- Ceramics
- Chemical
- Civil
- Computer
- Electrical
- Electronics
- Environmental
- Fire Prevention
- Industrial
- Materials
- Mechanical
- Mining
- Naval Architecture
- Nuclear
- Ocean
- Petroleum
- Safety
- Welding

RELATED ACADEMIC DISCIPLINES

If you have a related degree other than or in addition to an engineering degree, please indicate by blackening the corresponding circles the type of degree and academic discipline.

RELATED DISCIPLINES

Columns: BS | 1 YR GRAD STUDY | MS | PhD

- Architecture
- Astronomy/Space Science
- Bio/Medical Sciences
- Chemistry
- Computer Science
- Geology/Hydrology
- Mathematics (including Operations Research, Statistics, etc.)
- Metallurgy
- Physics
- Other Mathematics and Physical Sciences

Completion of Undergraduate Study
If you have claimed an undergraduate degree, indicate whether or not you have completed the degree.   ○ YES   ○ NO

Completion of Graduate Study
If you have claimed a graduate degree or study, indicate whether or not you have completed the degree or study.   ○ YES   ○ NO

14 — SUPERIOR ACADEMIC ACHIEVEMENT (SAC)

If you have a Bachelor's degree (or expect to complete a degree within the next 9 months) and meet any of these Superior Academic Achievement requirements, blacken one or more appropriate circles below.

1. GPA of 3.5, all undergraduate courses completed in your major field of study.
2. GPA of 3.5, all undergraduate courses completed in your major field of study in the last two years.
3. GPA of 3.0, all undergraduate courses completed.
4. GPA of 3.0, all courses completed in the last 2 years of your undergraduate curriculum.
5. Rank in the upper one-third of the graduating class.
6. Membership in a scholastic honorary society (other than a freshman society).

15 — ALTERNATE QUALIFICATIONS

If you do not have a Bachelor's Degree in engineering from an ABET accredited school, indicate by blackening the appropriate circle, which of the following alternate requirements (described more fully in the Qualifications Information Statement) you meet?

1. A passing score on the Engineering-in-Training test.
2. A passing score on the Engineer-in-Training test with one year of additional training or experience in engineering.
3. Registration as a professional engineer.
4. 60 semester hours of appropriate engineering coursework.
5. Course of study included courses in five of the seven areas of engineering science or physics specified in the basic requirements.
6. A degree in a related field and one year of professional engineering experience.
7. Two or more years of highly technical experience in or directly related to the field of engineering.

20 BACKGROUND INFORMATION (SB1)

YES   NO
Ⓨ   Ⓝ

1. Are you a citizen of the United States?

2. During the last 10 years, were you fired from any job for any reason or did you quit after being told that you would be fired?   Ⓨ   Ⓝ

3. Are you now or have you ever been: (Answer the following questions.)

   a) convicted of or forfeited collateral for any felony?   Ⓨ   Ⓝ

   b) convicted of or forfeited collateral for any firearms or explosives violation?   Ⓨ   Ⓝ

   c) convicted, forfeited collateral, imprisoned, on probation, or on parole, during the last 10 years?   Ⓨ   Ⓝ

   d) convicted by a court-martial?   Ⓨ   Ⓝ

4. Are you currently under charges for any violation of law?   Ⓨ   Ⓝ

21 VETERAN PREFERENCE CLAIM (VET)

Blacken the circle next to the type of veteran preference you claim.

① No preference claimed

② 5 points preference claimed

10 POINT PREFERENCE - You must enclose a completed Standard Form 15.

③ 10 points preference claimed (award of a Purple Heart or noncompensable service-connected disability)

④ 10 points compensable disability preference claimed (disability rating of less than 30%)

⑤ 10 points other (wife, widow, husband, widower, mother preference claimed

⑥ 10 points compensable disability preference claimed (disability rating of 30% or more)

22 SIGNATURE/DATE

A false statement on any part of your application may be grounds for not hiring you, or for firing you after you begin work. Also, you may be punished by fine or imprisonment (U.S. Code, title 18, section 1001). I certify that the information on this form is true and correct to the best of my knowledge.

_____   _____
Signature   Date Signed

18 SPECIALIZED EXPERIENCE/EDUCATION (JBF)

Choose the fields and job functions in which you have specialized experience or education and are interested in working. You will be required to furnish sufficient information to verify your claimed background and degree of expertise. Blacken the circle(s) next to the item(s) you choose.

ENGINEERING DISCIPLINES

○ Aerospace (1)
○ Agricultural (2)
○ Biomedical (3)
○ Ceramics (4)
○ Chemical (5)
○ Civil (6)
○ Computer (7)
○ Electrical (8)
○ Electronics (9)
○ Environmental (10)
○ Fire Prevention (11)
○ Industrial (12)
○ Materials (13)
○ Mechanical (14)
○ Mining (15)
○ Naval Architecture (16)
○ Nuclear (17)
○ Ocean (18)
○ Petroleum (19)
○ Safety (20)
○ Welding (21)

RELATED DISCIPLINES

○ Architecture (22)
○ Astronomy/Space Science (23)
○ Bio/Medical Sciences (24)
○ Chemistry (25)
○ Computer Science (26)
○ Geology/Hydrology (27)
○ Mathematics (including Operations Research, Statistics, etc.) (28)
○ Metallurgy (29)
○ Physics (30)
○ Other Mathematics and Physical Sciences (31)

SPECIALIZED JOB FUNCTIONS:

○ Aerospace Technology (32)
○ Bioengineering (33)
○ Computer Programming (34)
○ Computer Systems Analysis (35)
○ Construction (36)
○ Cost Effectiveness (37)
○ Cost Estimating (38)
○ Design (39)
○ Development (40)
○ Energy Conservation (41)
○ Environmental Protection (42)
○ Experimental Manufacturing (43)
○ Installation, Operation and Maintenance (44)
○ Patent Examiner (45)
○ Production/Quality Control (46)
○ Rates and/or Valuation (47)
○ Regulatory Enforcement and Licensing (48)
○ Reliability/Maintainability (49)
○ Remote Sensing (50)
○ Standards and Specifications (51)
○ Testing and Evaluation (52)

19 JOB PREFERENCE (JBF)

Follow the instructions you were given with this form to complete this item. If no instructions were given, do not make any entries.

○ (53)   ○ (59)   ○ (65)
○ (54)   ○ (60)   ○ (66)
○ (55)   ○ (61)   ○ (67)
○ (56)   ○ (62)   ○ (68)
○ (57)   ○ (63)   ○ (69)
○ (58)   ○ (64)   ○ (70)

OCCUPATIONAL SUPPLEMENT FOR PHYSICAL SCIENCES POSITIONS — 1300-X

US Office of Personnel Management

FORM **B**

FORM APPROVED
OMB NO. 3206-0040
(See Page 5 for Public
Burden Information)

BATCH NUMBER (BNO)

FOR OFFICE USE ONLY

DO NOT FOLD, STAPLE, TEAR OR PAPER CLIP THIS FORM. DO NOT SUBMIT PHOTOCOPIES OF THIS FORM.

We can process this information only if you:
1) Use a number 2 lead pencil only.
2) Completely blacken each circle you choose.
3) Completely erase any mistakes or stray marks.

PRINT YOUR RESPONSE IN THE BOXES AND BLACKEN THE APPROPRIATE CIRCLES.

USE ONLY A NUMBER 2 LEAD PENCIL

1 NAME

NAME: _____

(Please Print)

2 SOCIAL SECURITY NUMBER (SSN)

3 DATE OF BIRTH (SOF)

MONTH | DAY | YEAR

4 GEOGRAPHIC AVAILABILITY

From the GEOGRAPHIC CODE LISTING furnished with this application, print the name of the Zone you are applying for below.

GEOGRAPHIC ZONE

In the above Zone, choose up to nine (9) locations where you are willing to work. Write the codes corresponding to your choices in the boxes below and blacken the corresponding circles below each box.

1 2 3 4 5 6 7 8 9

5 EXAMPLES

	YES	NO
A	●	Ⓝ
B	Ⓨ Ⓨ ●	● ● Ⓝ
C	● Ⓨ Ⓨ	Ⓝ Ⓝ Ⓝ

5 EMPLOYMENT AVAILABILITY

ARE YOU AVAILABLE FOR:

(Blacken YES or NO for each question)

	YES	NO
A full-time employment		
– 40 hours per week?..........	Ⓨ	(FTE) Ⓝ
B part-time employment of		(PTE)
– 16 or fewer hours per week?..	Ⓨ	Ⓝ
– 17 to 24 hours per week?.....	Ⓨ	Ⓝ
– 25 to 32 hours per week?.....	Ⓨ	Ⓝ
C temporary employment lasting		(TMP)
– 5 to 12 months?.............	Ⓨ	Ⓝ
– 1 to 4 months?..............	Ⓨ	Ⓝ
– less than 1 month?..........	Ⓨ	Ⓝ
D jobs requiring travel away from home for		(TRV)
– 1 to 5 nights per month?....	Ⓨ	Ⓝ
– 6 to 10 nights per month?...	Ⓨ	Ⓝ
– 11 or more nights per month?.	Ⓨ	Ⓝ

6 LANGUAGES (LNG)

Select up to three languages in which you are proficient. Blacken the circle beside each choice.

○ Any African Language (01)
○ Any Native American Language (Aleut, Navajo, etc.) (02)
○ Any Classical Language (03)
○ Asian/Near East Languages (04)
○ Asian/Far East Languages (other than Chinese) (05)
○ Chinese (06)
○ French (07)
○ German (08)
○ Russian (09)
○ Sign Language (10)
○ Spanish (11)
○ Other European Languages (12)
○ Other Languages (13)

0656306

OPM Form 1203-K (Rev. August 1989)
Prior Edition (1/89) Only Is Usable

14 SUPERIOR ACADEMIC ACHIEVEMENT (SAC)

If you have a Bachelor's degree (or expect to complete a degree within the next 9 months) and meet any of these Superior Academic Achievement requirements, blacken one or more appropriate circles below.

○ GPA of 3.5, all courses completed in your major field of study.

○ GPA of 3.5, all courses completed in your major field of study in the last 2 years of your undergraduate curriculum.

○ GPA of 3.0, all completed undergraduate courses.

○ GPA of 3.0, all courses completed in the last 2 years of your undergraduate curriculum.

○ Rank in the upper one-third of the graduating class.

○ Membership in a scholastic honorary society (other than a freshman society).

15 ALTERNATIVE QUALIFICATIONS

Health Physics Certification

Do you possess a certificate as a Health Physicist by the American Board of Health Physics?   ○ Yes   ○ No

Land Surveying Registration

Do you possess a current registration as a land surveyor in a State, Territory or the District of Columbia which was obtained by written examination? (Refer to the Qualifications Information Statement.)   ○ Yes   ○ No

13 ACADEMIC DISCIPLINE

Indicate the academic degree(s) you have completed or will complete within the next 9 months by blackening the appropriate circle(s).

DISCIPLINE	BS DEGREE	1 YEAR GRAD STUDY	MASTERS DEGREE	PhD
Astronomy	○	○	○	○
Biological Science	○	○	○	○
Cartography	○	○	○	○
Chemistry	○	○	○	○
Electronics	○	○	○	○
Engineering	○	○	○	○
Environmental Science	○	○	○	○
Geodesy	○	○	○	○
Geology	○	○	○	○
Geophysics	○	○	○	○
Health Physics	○	○	○	○
Hydrology	○	○	○	○
Land Surveying	○	○	○	○
Mathematics	○	○	○	○
Metallurgical Engineering	○	○	○	○
Metallurgy	○	○	○	○
Meteorology	○	○	○	○
Natural Science	○	○	○	○
Oceanography	○	○	○	○
Photogrammetry	○	○	○	○
Physical Science	○	○	○	○
Physics	○	○	○	○
Space Science	○	○	○	○
Other Mathematics and Engineering	○	○	○	○

Completion of Undergraduate Study

If you have claimed an undergraduate degree, indicate whether or not you have completed the degree.   ○ Yes   ○ No

Completion of Graduate Study

If you have claimed a graduate degree or study, indicate whether or not you have completed the degree or study.   ○ Yes   ○ No

PAGE 3

0656306

18 SPECIALIZED EXPERIENCE/EDUCATION (JBF)

Blacken only the circle(s) of the specialized fields in which you possess experience or education and are interested in working.

PHYSICAL SCIENCE FIELDS

- Astronomy and Space Science (01)
- Biology (02)
- Cartography (03)
- Chemistry (04)
- Engineering Science (05)
- Environmental Science (06)
- Geodesy (07)
- Geology (08)
- Geophysics (09)
- Health Physics (10)
- Hydrology (11)
- Land Surveying (12)
- Mathematics (13)
- Metallurgy (14)
- Meteorology (15)
- Oceanography (16)
- Physics (17)

SPECIALIZED JOB FUNCTIONS

- Aerospace Technology (18)
- Computer Programming (19)
- Computer Systems Analysis (20)
- Cost Effectiveness (21)
- Design (22)
- Development (23)
- Energy Conservation (24)
- Environmental Protection (25)
- Experimental Manufacturing (26)
- Patent Advisor/Patent Examiner (27)
- Production/Quality Control (28)
- Public Information Writing (29)
- Regulatory Enforcement and Licensing (30)
- Remote Sensing (31)
- Research (32)
- Research Facilities/Equipment Design (33)
- Research Piloting (34)
- Standards and Specifications (35)
- Testing and Evaluation (36)

19 JOB PREFERENCE (JBF)

Follow the instructions you were given with this form to complete this item. If no instructions were given, do not make any entries.

○ (37)	○ (60)
○ (38)	○ (61)
○ (39)	○ (62)
○ (40)	○ (63)
○ (41)	○ (64)
○ (42)	○ (65)
○ (43)	○ (66)
○ (44)	○ (67)
○ (45)	○ (68)
○ (46)	○ (69)
○ (47)	○ (70)
○ (48)	
○ (49)	
○ (50)	
○ (51)	
○ (52)	
○ (53)	
○ (54)	
○ (55)	
○ (56)	
○ (57)	
○ (58)	
○ (59)	

20 BACKGROUND INFORMATION (SB1)

	YES	NO
1. Are you a citizen of the United States?	Ⓨ	Ⓝ
2. During the last 10 years, were you fired from any job for any reason or did you quit after being told that you would be fired?	Ⓨ	Ⓝ

3. Are you now or have you ever been: (Answer the following questions.)

	YES	NO
a) convicted of or forfeited collateral for any felony?	Ⓨ	Ⓝ
b) convicted of or forfeited collateral for any firearms or explosives violation?	Ⓨ	Ⓝ
c) convicted, forfeited collateral, imprisoned, on probation, or on parole, during the last 10 years?	Ⓨ	Ⓝ
d) convicted by a court-martial?	Ⓨ	Ⓝ
4. Are you currently under charges for any violation of law?	Ⓨ	Ⓝ

21 VETERAN PREFERENCE CLAIM (VET)

Blacken the circle next to the type of veteran preference you claim.

- ① No preference claimed
- ② 5 points preference claimed

10 POINT PREFERENCE - You must enclose a completed Standard Form 15.

- ③ 10 points preference claimed (award of a Purple Heart or noncompensable service-connected disability)
- ④ 10 points compensable disability preference claimed (disability rating of less than 30%)
- ⑤ 10 points other (wife, widow, husband, widower, mother preference claimed)
- ⑥ 10 points compensable disability preference claimed (disability rating of 30% or more)

22 SIGNATURE/DATE

I certify that the information on this form is true and correct to the best of my knowledge.

_____   _____
Signature   Date Signed

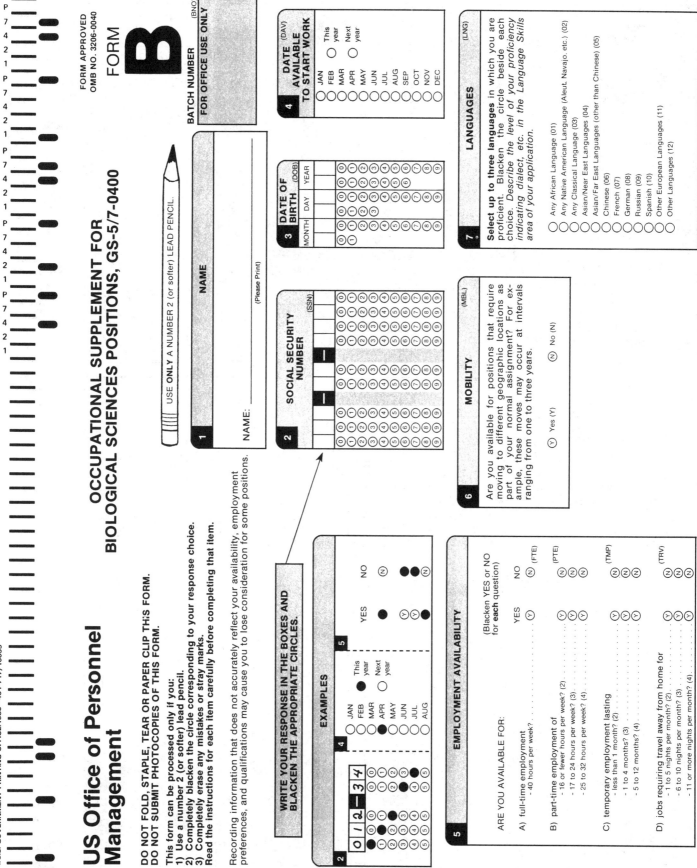

*U.S. GOVERNMENT PRINTING OFFICE:1986—491-717/10059

FORM APPROVED
OMB NO. 3206-0040

FORM **B**

US Office of Personnel Management

OCCUPATIONAL SUPPLEMENT FOR BIOLOGICAL SCIENCES POSITIONS, GS-5/7-0400

DO NOT FOLD, STAPLE, TEAR OR PAPER CLIP THIS FORM.
DO NOT SUBMIT PHOTOCOPIES OF THIS FORM.

This form can be processed only if you:
1) Use a number 2 (or softer) lead pencil.
2) Completely blacken the circle corresponding to your response choice.
3) Completely erase any mistakes or stray marks.
Read the instructions for each item carefully before completing that item.

Recording information that does not accurately reflect your availability, employment preferences, and qualifications may cause you to lose consideration for some positions.

USE **ONLY** A NUMBER 2 (or softer) LEAD PENCIL.

1 NAME

NAME: _____
(Please Print)

2 SOCIAL SECURITY NUMBER (SSN)

3 DATE OF BIRTH (DOB)
MONTH | DAY | YEAR

4 DATE AVAILABLE TO START WORK (DAV)
JAN FEB MAR APR MAY JUN JUL AUG SEP OCT NOV DEC
○ This year
○ Next year

6 MOBILITY (MBL)
Are you available for positions that require moving to different geographic locations as part of your normal assignment? For example, these moves may occur at intervals ranging from one to three years.
Ⓨ Yes (Y)   Ⓝ No (N)

7 LANGUAGES (LNG)
Select up to three languages in which you are proficient. Blacken the circle beside each choice. *Describe the level of your proficiency indicating dialect, etc. in the Language Skills area of your application.*
○ Any African Language (01)
○ Any Native American Language (Aleut, Navajo, etc.) (02)
○ Any Classical Language (03)
○ Asian/Near East Languages (04)
○ Asian/Far East Languages (other than Chinese) (05)
○ Chinese (06)
○ French (07)
○ German (08)
○ Russian (09)
○ Spanish (10)
○ Other European Languages (11)
○ Other Languages (12)

BATCH NUMBER (BNO)
FOR OFFICE USE ONLY

WRITE YOUR RESPONSE IN THE BOXES AND BLACKEN THE APPROPRIATE CIRCLES.

EXAMPLES

4
JAN FEB MAR APR MAY JUN JUL AUG
● This year
○ Next year

5
YES NO
Ⓨ ●
● Ⓝ
● Ⓝ
Ⓨ ●

2
| 0 | 1 | 2 | – | 3 | 4 |

5 EMPLOYMENT AVAILABILITY

(Blacken YES or NO for **each** question)

ARE YOU AVAILABLE FOR:

                                          YES   NO
A) full-time employment
   - 40 hours per week? . . . . Ⓨ   ● (N) (FTE)
B) part-time employment of
   - 16 or fewer hours per week? (2) . . . Ⓨ Ⓝ (PTE)
   - 17 to 24 hours per week? (3) . . . . Ⓨ Ⓝ
   - 25 to 32 hours per week? (4) . . . . ● Ⓝ
C) temporary employment lasting
   - less than 1 month? (1) . . . . Ⓨ Ⓝ (TMP)
   - 1 to 4 months? (2) . . . . Ⓨ Ⓝ
   - 5 to 12 months? (4) . . . . ● Ⓝ
D) jobs requiring travel away from home for
   - 1 to 5 nights per month? (2) . . . . Ⓨ Ⓝ (TRV)
   - 6 to 10 nights per month? (3) . . . . Ⓨ Ⓝ
   - 11 or more nights per month? (4) . . Ⓨ Ⓝ

P
A
G
E
1

180211

0 4 0 0

PRINT YOUR RESPONSES IN THE BOXES AND BLACKEN THE CORRESPONDING CIRCLE BELOW EACH BOX.

PAGE 2

8 FIRST NAME (FNM) · MI (MIN) · LAST NAME (LNM)

9 STREET ADDRESS (HOUSE NUMBER AND STREET AND APT NO., WHERE YOU WANT TO RECEIVE MAIL) (ADR)

10 CITY (CTY)

11 STATE WHERE YOU WISH TO RECEIVE MAIL (STE)

BLACKEN ONE CIRCLE BELOW

- Alabama
- Alaska
- American Samoa
- Arizona
- Arkansas
- California
- Canal Zone
- Colorado
- Connecticut
- Delaware
- Dist. of Columbia
- Florida
- Georgia
- Guam
- Hawaii
- Idaho
- Illinois
- Indiana
- Iowa
- Kansas
- Kentucky
- Louisiana
- Maine
- Maryland
- Massachusetts
- Michigan
- Minnesota
- Mississippi
- Missouri
- Montana
- Nebraska
- Nevada
- New Hampshire
- New Jersey
- New Mexico
- New York
- North Carolina
- North Dakota
- Ohio
- Oklahoma
- Oregon
- Pennsylvania
- Puerto Rico
- Rhode Island
- South Carolina
- South Dakota
- Tennessee
- Texas
- Utah
- Vermont
- Virgin Islands
- Virginia
- Washington
- West Virginia
- Wisconsin
- Wyoming
- Outside U.S.A.

Enter country if other than United States.

12 ZIP CODE (ZIP)

13 TELEPHONE NUMBER (Area Code) (TEL)

CONTACT TIME (TCT)

- D DAY
- N NIGHT
- E EITHER

A. EDUCATION LEVEL AND MAJOR

Questions A through E are designed to assess your qualifications for biologist positions at grades GS-5 and GS-7. Read the Qualifications Information Statement, the Competition Notice and this form to gain a better understanding of the kinds of information we are looking for. You will find it helpful to complete your SF-171 and either complete the List of College Courses or have your college transcript(s) at hand so you can refer to them in completing this form. Be sure to answer the questions carefully and accurately.

Use a soft pencil to mark your answers to questions. Erase cleanly if you change an answer. Make written responses only where instructed to do so.

1. Blacken the appropriate circles below to indicate the highest level of undergraduate AND graduate education you have successfully completed, the undergraduate AND graduate degrees you have received, and the academic discipline(s) in which you majored. Include study or degrees you will complete within the next 9 months if you are currently enrolled.

	UNDERGRADUATE MAJOR (no degree) (1)	BACHELOR'S DEGREE (2)	GRADUATE MAJOR (no degree) (3)	MASTER'S DEGREE (4)	PhD DEGREE (5)
1. Botany					
2. Zoology					
3. Microbiology					
4. Wildlife Biology					
5. Wildlife Management					
6. Fishery Biology					
7. Fishery Management					
8. Ecology					
9. Other Natural Resource Mgmt.					
10. Oceanography					
11. Marine Biology/Science					
12. Bacteriology					
13. Medical Technology					
14. General Biology					
15. Other Biology					
16. Chemistry/Biochemistry					
17. Agricultural Science					
18. Other (Non-biology)					

TOTAL ACADEMIC CREDITS COMPLETED

2. Indicate by writing in the boxes to the right and blackening the corresponding circles beneath them the total number of undergraduate semester hours you have successfully completed or expect to successfully complete within the next 9 months if you are a currently enrolled student. Convert quarter hours to semester hours by multiplying by 2/3.

3. Similarly, indicate the amount of graduate study completed by entering the number of semester hours in the boxes at the right and blackening the corresponding circles beneath them.

4. Indicate here, by blackening the appropriate circles if the undergraduate and graduate study shown above has been completed or if it includes degrees or hours which you have not yet completed but expect to complete within the next 9 months.

Undergraduate - Completed ◯ Graduate - Completed ◯
Will Complete in 9 months ◯ Will Complete in 9 months ◯

14. GEOGRAPHIC AVAILABILITY (GFP)

From the GEOGRAPHIC CODE LISTING provided with this application, CHOOSE AT LEAST ONE BUT NO MORE THAN NINE LOCATIONS and blacken the code for each location you choose.

LOCATIONS (GFP) (Blacken At Least 1 Circle But Not More Than 9)

◯ 01	◯ 15	◯ 29	◯ 43	◯ 57	◯ 71	◯ 85
◯ 02	◯ 16	◯ 30	◯ 44	◯ 58	◯ 72	◯ 86
◯ 03	◯ 17	◯ 31	◯ 45	◯ 59	◯ 73	◯ 87
◯ 04	◯ 18	◯ 32	◯ 46	◯ 60	◯ 74	◯ 88
◯ 05	◯ 19	◯ 33	◯ 47	◯ 61	◯ 75	◯ 89
◯ 06	◯ 20	◯ 34	◯ 48	◯ 62	◯ 76	◯ 90
◯ 07	◯ 21	◯ 35	◯ 49	◯ 63	◯ 77	◯ 91
◯ 08	◯ 22	◯ 36	◯ 50	◯ 64	◯ 78	◯ 92
◯ 09	◯ 23	◯ 37	◯ 51	◯ 65	◯ 79	◯ 93
◯ 10	◯ 24	◯ 38	◯ 52	◯ 66	◯ 80	◯ 94
◯ 11	◯ 25	◯ 39	◯ 53	◯ 67	◯ 81	◯ 95
◯ 12	◯ 26	◯ 40	◯ 54	◯ 68	◯ 82	◯ 96
◯ 13	◯ 27	◯ 41	◯ 55	◯ 69	◯ 83	◯ 97
◯ 14	◯ 28	◯ 42	◯ 56	◯ 70	◯ 84	◯ 98

How many locations did you select?
① ② ③ ④ ⑤ ⑥ ⑦ ⑧ ⑨

15. OCCUPATIONAL SPECIALTIES AND GRADES (OSP/GRD)

By blackening the appropriate circles, indicate the specialties and grade levels for which you wish to be considered and believe you qualify.

SPECIALTY	GRADE LEVEL	
	GS-5	GS-7
General Biology (001)	◯	◯
Microbiology (002)	◯	◯
Wildlife Biology (003)	◯	◯
Fishery Biology (004)	◯	◯

B

COLLEGE COURSEWORK

In this section report the amount of college coursework you have completed (or will complete in the next 9 months if you are currently enrolled) in the types of courses listed below. Under each coursework category, write in the number of semester hours you have, or will have, completed and blacken the corresponding circles beneath the numbers. **Convert quarter hours to semester hours by mul-**

tiplying by 2/3. Count each course only once, and enter it under the category which best describes the course content. Courses listed under each category are illustrative only. Other courses with different titles may be counted under a category if that category best describes the content and emphasis of the course.

CROSS-REFERENCE your responses to this item by writing next to each course on your transcript or college course list the number of the category under which you counted that course. Thus, you would write the number "1" next to all of your wildlife biology courses, the number "2" next to fishery biology courses, etc.

1. Wildlife Biology

Includes courses such as: Wildlife Biology. Animal Ecology. Mammology. Ornithology. Game Management. Wildlife Management. Herpetology. Wildlife Conservation.

2. Fishery Biology

Includes courses such as: Icthyology. Marine Ecology/Biology. Fish Husbandry. Fisheries Management. Aquatic Botany. Phycology. Limnology.

3. Microbiology

Includes courses such as: General Microbiology. Bacteriology. Immunology/Serology. Virology. Cytology. Applied or Environmental Microbiology. Microbial Taxonomy.

4. Zoology

Includes courses such as: General Zoology. Physiology. Anatomy. Embryology. Pathology. Comparative Anatomy. Vertebrate and Invertebrate Zoology.

5. Botany

Includes courses such as: General Botany. Plant Genetics. Plant Anatomy. Plant Taxonomy. Plant Pathology. Dendrology. Silvics. Algology.

6. Natural Resource Management

Includes courses such as: Range Science. Soil Science. Forestry. Silviculture. Natural Resource Management. Conservation.

7. Genetics

8. Ecology

9. Agriculture

Includes courses such as: Agronomy. Husbandry. Agricultural Management.

10. Methods Courses

Includes courses such as: Laboratory Techniques. Experimental Biology. Biological Field Studies. Instrumentation.

11. Electron Microscopy

Courses dealing primarily with the techniques and applications of electron microscopy to the biological or physical sciences.

12. Mathematics and Statistics

13. Computer Science

Includes courses such as: Computer Programming. Data Processing. Computer Systems Analysis.

14. Technical Writing

Courses beyond basic English composition courses which dealt specifically with scientific or technical writing.

15. Physical Sciences - Total of courses listed below:

For each subject, indicate approximate number of semester hours:

	none	1-4	5-8	9+
Organic Chemistry (16)	○	○	○	○
Biochemistry (17)	○	○	○	○
Other Chemistry (18)	○	○	○	○
Physics (19)	○	○	○	○
Geology (20)	○	○	○	○
Other Physical Science (21)	○	○	○	○

P 7 4 2 1 P 7 4 2 1 P 7 4 2 1 P 7 4 2 1 P 7 4 2 1 P 7 4 2 1

C | ACADEMIC ACHIEVEMENT

Refer to the Qualifications Information Statement for a complete explanation of the Superior Academic Achievement requirements. If you qualify, blacken one or more circles to indicate the provision(s) under which you qualify.

① GPA of 2.90, all undergraduate courses.
② GPA of 2.90, last 2 years undergrad.
③ GPA of 3.50, all courses in related major.
④ GPA of 3.50, last 2 years of courses in related major.
⑤ Rank in upper 1/3 graduating class.
⑥ Membership in scholastic honorary society.

Next, indicate your gradepoint average, first for all UNDERGRADUATE courses you have already completed, and then for all UNDERGRADUATE BIOLOGY courses which you entered in item B-1 through 11, above. Calculate gradepoint average on the basis of A = 4.0, B = 3.0, C = 2.0, D = 1.0 and F = 0. If you have a combination of semester hour and quarter hour credits, convert quarter hours to semester hours by multiplying by 2/3. There is space for calculating gradepoint average on the college course list furnished with the application forms. Enter your average by blackening the circle next to the appropriate gradepoint range below.

ALL UNDERGRADUATE COURSEWORK

○ less than 2.00   ○ 3.00 to 3.49
○ 2.00 to 2.49   ○ 3.50 to 4.00
○ 2.50 to 2.99

UNDERGRADUATE BIOLOGY COURSEWORK

○ less than 2.00   ○ 3.00 to 3.49
○ 2.00 to 2.49   ○ 3.50 to 4.00
○ 2.50 to 2.99

PAGE 5

D | BIOLOGY-RELATED WORK EXPERIENCE

In item D, on the next page, describe any work experience related to the biological sciences you have had. If your eligibility for any of the specialties or grades you have applied for is based on work experience, be sure that experience is described fully and accurately. The Qualifications Information Statement (QI-0400) describes the education and/or experience requirements for each specialty and grade. We suggest you first complete your Application for Federal Employment (SF-171) and then refer to it to complete this item.

Read over the responses in item D to get an idea of the kinds of experience which should be reported. Each of the six columns of circles in this item represents a period of work experience by describing it in terms of the AREA OF WORK, TYPE OF WORK, SETTING OF WORK, and LEVEL OF WORK. Also indicate the DURATION of that period of experience, and in the CROSS REFERENCE block at the bottom of each column, write in the letter of the experience block on your SF-171 that gives the narrative description of that period of experience.

Use a separate column of circles to describe each different period of experience. Begin a new period when one or more of the factors (area, type, setting, or level) change, even if your employer did not change. On the other hand if you had several jobs of the same area, type, setting and level, you may report them in one period and combine their durations, entering more than one cross-reference if necessary.

To receive proper credit for a period of experience, the column representing that period must contain a single response next to each of the four factors (AREA, TYPE, SETTING and LEVEL), and a response for DURATION and CROSS REFERENCE.

Do not leave any factor blank, and do not darken more than one response for any factor. Instead, pick one single response for each factor which best describes the job. If a job was truly interdisciplinary, and if space permits, you may split a job into two periods and pro-rate the duration. If you worked on a part-time or intermittent basis, pro-rate duration to reflect the actual time worked in terms of a 40-hour week.

If you have more biology-related work experience than you can fit into the six periods provided, pick the experience most relevant to the specialty and grade level you are applying for.

Assume, for example, that you have the following work experience:

(1) Two summers, 3 months each, as a laboratory aid in a medical laboratory.

(2) One year, 10 hours per week, as a laboratory technician in the quality control lab of a food processing plant.

(3) One year as a beginning level research microbiologist working under the guidance of a senior biologist.

You would complete item D as shown below. The cross-reference numbers refer to the job numbers in our example. Note that the duration of job 2 (12 months at 10 hours per week) was pro-rated as the equivalent of 3 months of full-time experience.

BIOLOGY-RELATED WORK EXPERIENCE (Instructions on preceding page.)

PAGE 6

AREA OF WORK For each period of work, blacken the one circle with the number corresponding to the area of work from the list below which best describes your work.

1 Wildlife Biology
2 Fishery Biology
3 Microbiology
4 Ornithology
5 Zoology
6 Botany

7 Environmental Sciences
8 Agricultural Sciences
9 Health/Medicine
10 Chemistry/Biochemistry
11 Forestry/Range Science
12 General Biology

TYPE OF WORK For each period of work, blacken the one circle with the number corresponding to the type of work from the list below which best describes your work.

1 Research
2 Laboratory Support
3 Teaching
4 Administration
5 Consulting
6 Survey/Inventory
7 Regulation/Inspecting

8 Production/Manufacturing
9 Health Services
10 Animal Care
11 Equipment/Operation
12 Construction/Maintenance/Laborer
13 Tourist Information/Guide
14 Clerical

SETTING OF WORK For each period of work, blacken the one circle with the number corresponding to the work setting from the list below which best describes your work.

1 Laboratory
2 Office
3 Classroom
4 Park
5 Forest/Range/Range

7 Farm/Ranch
8 Plant (Processing Plant)
9 Hatchery/Breeding Facility
10 Museum/Zoo
11 Lake/Stream/Ocean

LEVEL OF WORK For each period of work, blacken the one circle with the number corresponding to the level of work from the list below which best describes your work.

1 Professional/Manager
2 Administrator
3 Professional or Management
4 Intern or Trainee

4 Administrative Assistant or Trainee
5 Student Trainee
6 Technician
7 Aid

DURATION For each period of work, enter the number of months you worked and blacken the corresponding circles under each digit. Pro-rate if less than full time.

CROSS REFERENCE Finally, write in the letter or number of the experience block on your SF-171 where this work is described.

PERIOD TWO, PERIOD FOUR, PERIOD SIX (bubble grid columns)

CONTINUE ON PAGE 6

BIOLOGY-RELATED WORK EXPERIENCE (Instructions on preceding page.)

AREA OF WORK

For each period of work, blacken the one circle with the number corresponding to the area of work from the list below which best describes your work.

1. Wildlife Biology
2. Fishery Biology
3. Microbiology
4. Oceanography/Limnology
5. Zoology
6. Botany
7. Environmental Sciences
8. Agricultural Sciences
9. Health/Medicine
10. Chemistry/Biochemistry
11. Forestry/Range Science
12. General Biology

TYPE OF WORK

For each period of work, blacken the one circle with the number corresponding to the type of work from the list below which best describes your work.

1. Research
2. Laboratory Support
3. Teaching
4. Administration
5. Consulting
6. Survey/Inventory
7. Regulation/Inspecting
8. Production/Manufacturing
9. Health Services
10. Animal Care
11. Equipment Operation
12. Construction/Maintenance/Laborer
13. Tourist Information/Guide
14. Clerical

SETTING OF WORK

For each period of work, blacken the one circle with the number corresponding to the work setting from the list below which best describes your work.

1. Laboratory
2. Clinic
3. Office
4. Classroom
5. Park
6. Forest/Range/Refuge
7. Farm/Ranch
8. Manufacturing/Processing Plant
9. Hatchery/Breeding Facility
10. Museum/Zoo
11. Lake/Stream/Ocean

LEVEL OF WORK

For each period of work, blacken the one circle with the number corresponding to the level of work from the list below which best describes your work.

1. Professional/Manager
2. Administrator
3. Professional or Management Intern or Trainee
4. Administrative Assistant or Trainee
5. Student Trainee
6. Technician
7. Aid

DURATION

For each period of work, enter the number of months you worked and blacken the corresponding circles under each digit. Pro-rate if less than full time.

CROSS REFERENCE

Finally, write in the letter or number of the experience block on your SF-171 where this work is described.

WORK ACTIVITIES

The activities listed in this section cover a wide range of entry-level biologist jobs. Individual biologist positions would typically consist of only a few of these activities. The ability to perform these activities is **not** required of biologist applicants. However, applicants who have demonstrated their ability to perform one or more of these activities should indicate their level of ability here.

ABILITY RATING

If you have **not** had the opportunity to demonstrate your ability in an activity, blacken the circle in the ABILITY RATING column labeled "N/A" (Not Applicable).

If you have demonstrated your ability in any of these activities, use the following scale to rate your level of ability:

1 = Some ability (i.e., would require some on-the-job training to perform the activity)

2 = Satisfactory (i.e., could perform the activity with guidance)

3 = Very good ability (i.e., could perform the activity independently)

4 = Excellent ability (i.e., could provide guidance to others under difficult conditions)

Blacken the circle in the numbered ABILITY RATING column which corresponds to your ability rating for **each** activity.

BASIS FOR ABILITY RATING

For each activity on which you give yourself a numerical ability rating, indicate the basis for that rating by:

– Entering the reference numbers from your coursework listing or transcript in the COURSEWORK NUMBER column if your ability rating is based on specific college coursework.

– Entering the experience block number from your SF-171 in the EXPERIENCE BLOCK column if your ability rating is based on specific work experience.

– Blacken the box under the GENERAL EXPERIENCE/EDUCATION column if you cannot attribute your ability to any specific experience or education.

WORK ACTIVITY

Accurately mark **each** activity to avoid loss of credit.

ABILITY RATING columns: N/A, 1, 2, 3, 4

BASIS FOR ABILITY RATING — Coursework Number(s), Experience Block(s), General Experience Education. Write inside boxes only.

1. Collect and analyze data in a biological experiment and write a report of the results.
2. Collect, record, tabulate, and report biological data.
3. Set up and carry out a biological experiment according to a protocol designed by a senior investigator.
4. Perform quantitative and qualitative analyses in biology.
5. Utilize automated data processing equipment (computers) in the storage, retrieval and analysis of biological data.
6. Collect material, prepare slides and interpret microscopic examinations.
7. Inoculate, isolate, and identify pathogenic and non-pathogenic microorganisms.
8. Prepare experimental compounds and inocula.
9. Maintain, cultivate, and harvest cell cultures.
10. Prepare media and reagents.
11. Utilize sterile techniques when appropriate.
12. Perform laboratory quality control procedures.
13. Direct and/or teach others in the performance of laboratory techniques.
14. Perform immunological and serological assays.
15. Perform analyses using chromatographic, spectrophotometric, and other standard laboratory instruments.
16. Utilize standard safety procedures for handling and disposal of biohazardous material.
17. Trap and band or mark birds and other animals.
18. Conduct surveys and censuses of wildlife populations.
19. Identify and classify wildlife.
20. Conduct a field survey of wildlife habitat employing standard habitat assessment techniques.
21. Collect and maintain records of livestock and wildlife use of land.
22. Perform habitat assessment using aerial photos and/or topographic maps.
23. Formulate plans for the improvement of wildlife habitat.

ACTIVITIES CONTINUED ON NEXT PAGE

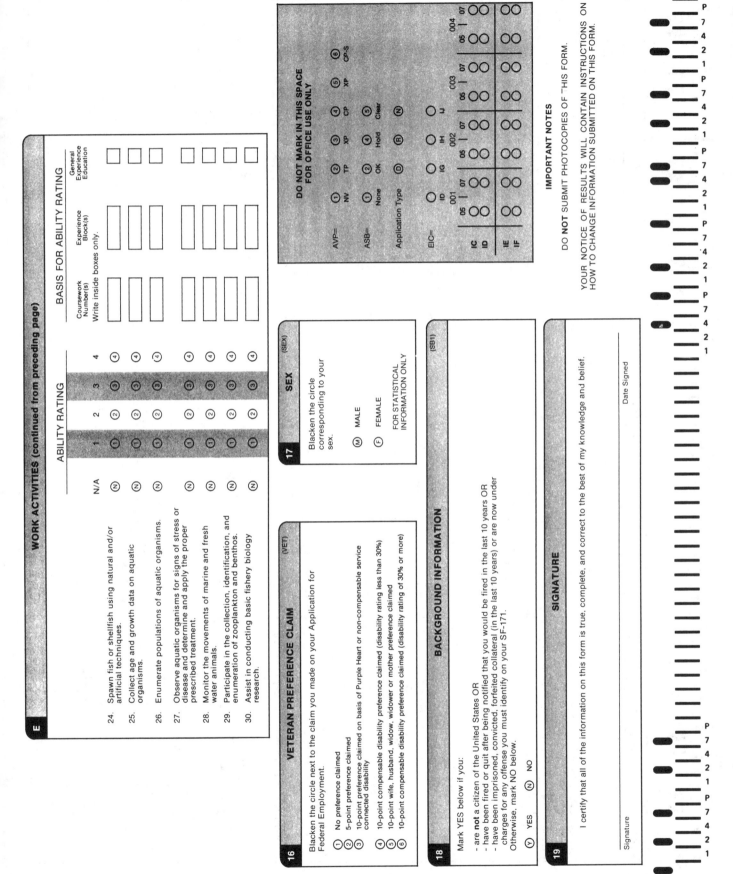

WORK ACTIVITIES (continued from preceding page)

E

ABILITY RATING

	N/A	1	2	3	4
24. Spawn fish or shellfish using natural and/or artificial techniques.	Ⓝ	①	②	③	④
25. Collect age and growth data on aquatic organisms.	Ⓝ	①	②	③	④
26. Enumerate populations of aquatic organisms.	Ⓝ	①	②	③	④
27. Observe aquatic organisms for signs of stress or disease and determine and apply the proper prescribed treatment.	Ⓝ	①	②	③	④
28. Monitor the movements of marine and fresh water animals.	Ⓝ	①	②	③	④
29. Participate in the collection, identification, and enumeration of zooplankton and benthos.	Ⓝ	①	②	③	④
30. Assist in conducting basic fishery biology research.	Ⓝ	①	②	③	④

BASIS FOR ABILITY RATING

Write inside boxes only.

Coursework Number(s)   Experience Block(s)   General Experience Education

DO NOT MARK IN THIS SPACE
FOR OFFICE USE ONLY

AVP= ① ② ③ ④ ⑤ ⑥
     NV TP XP CP XP CP-S

ASB= ① ② ③ ④ ⑤
     None OK Hold Clear

Application Type Ⓓ Ⓑ Ⓝ

EIC= ○ ○ ○ ○
     ID IH IG IJ

	001	05	07	002	06	07	003	06	07	004	06	07
IC		○○	○○		○○	○○		○○	○○		○○	○○
ID												
IE		○○	○○		○○	○○		○○	○○		○○	○○
IF												

IMPORTANT NOTES

DO **NOT** SUBMIT PHOTOCOPIES OF THIS FORM.

YOUR NOTICE OF RESULTS WILL CONTAIN INSTRUCTIONS ON HOW TO CHANGE INFORMATION SUBMITTED ON THIS FORM.

---

16   **VETERAN PREFERENCE CLAIM**   (VET)

Blacken the circle next to the claim you made on your Application for Federal Employment.

① No preference claimed
② 5-point preference claimed
③ 10-point preference claimed on basis of Purple Heart or non-compensable service connected disability
④ 10-point compensable disability preference claimed (disability rating less than 30%)
⑤ 10-point wife, husband, widow, widower or mother preference claimed
⑥ 10-point compensable disability preference claimed (disability rating of 30% or more)

---

17   **SEX**   (SEX)

Blacken the circle corresponding to your sex.

Ⓜ MALE

Ⓕ FEMALE

FOR STATISTICAL INFORMATION ONLY

---

18   **BACKGROUND INFORMATION**   (SB1)

Mark YES below if you:
- are **not** a citizen of the United States OR
- have been fired or quit after being notified that you would be fired in the last 10 years OR
- have been imprisoned, convicted, forfeited collateral (in the last 10 years) or are now under charges for any offense you must identify on your SF-171.
Otherwise, mark NO below.

Ⓨ YES   Ⓝ NO

---

19   **SIGNATURE**

I certify that all of the information on this form is true, complete, and correct to the best of my knowledge and belief.

_____   _____
Signature   Date Signed

180211

* U.S. GOVERNMENT PRINTING OFFICE:1990—262-449/00031

FORM APPROVED
OMB NO. 3206-0040

FORM **B**

US Office of Personnel Management

OCCUPATIONAL SUPPLEMENT FOR
ACCOUNTANT AND AUDITOR POSITIONS, GS-5/7/9-0510

DO NOT FOLD, STAPLE, TEAR OR PAPER CLIP THIS FORM.
DO NOT SUBMIT PHOTOCOPIES OF THIS FORM.

This form can be processed only if you:
1) Use a number 2 (or softer) lead pencil.
2) Completely blacken the circle corresponding to your response choice.
3) Completely erase any mistakes or stray marks.
Read the instructions for each item carefully before completing that item.

Recording information that does not accurately reflect your availability, employment preferences, and qualifications may cause you to lose consideration for some positions.

USE ONLY A NUMBER 2 (or softer) LEAD PENCIL.

BATCH NUMBER (BNO)

FOR OFFICE USE ONLY

1 NAME

NAME: _____
(Please Print)

2 SOCIAL SECURITY NUMBER (SSN)

3 DATE OF BIRTH (DOB)
MONTH | DAY | YEAR

4 DATE AVAILABLE TO START WORK (DAV)

JAN
FEB   ○ This year
MAR
APR   ○ Next year
MAY
JUN
JUL
AUG
SEP
OCT
NOV
DEC

7 LANGUAGES (LNG)

Select up to three languages in which you are proficient. Blacken the circle beside each choice. *Describe the level of your proficiency indicating dialect, etc. in the Language Skills area of your application.*

○ Any African Language (01)
○ Any Native American Language (Aleut, Navajo, etc.) (02)
○ Any Classical Language (03)
○ Asian/Near East Languages (04)
○ Asian/Far East Languages (other than Chinese) (05)
○ Chinese (06)
○ French (07)
○ German (08)
○ Russian (09)
○ Spanish (10)
○ Other European Languages (11)
○ Other Languages (12)

WRITE YOUR RESPONSE IN THE BOXES AND BLACKEN THE APPROPRIATE CIRCLES.

EXAMPLES

4
JAN
FEB
MAR   This year ●   Next year ○
APR ●
MAY
JUN
JUL
AUG

5
                YES   NO
                ●   Ⓝ
        Ⓨ   Ⓨ   ●
                ●   Ⓝ

2 | 0 | 1 | 2 | — | 3 | 4 |

0735373

6 MOBILITY (MBL)

Are you available for positions that require moving to different geographic locations as part of your normal assignment? For example, these moves may occur at intervals ranging from one to three years.

Ⓨ Yes (Y)   Ⓝ No (N)

5 EMPLOYMENT AVAILABILITY

ARE YOU AVAILABLE FOR:
(Blacken YES or NO for **each** question)

	YES	NO
A) full-time employment, - 40 hours per week?	Ⓨ	Ⓝ (FTE)
B) part-time employment of		(PTE)
- 16 or fewer hours per week? (2)	Ⓨ	Ⓝ
- 17 to 24 hours per week? (3)	Ⓨ	Ⓝ
- 25 to 32 hours per week? (4)	Ⓨ	Ⓝ
C) temporary employment lasting		(TMP)
- less than 1 month? (2)	Ⓨ	Ⓝ
- 1 to 4 months? (3)	Ⓨ	Ⓝ
- 5 to 12 months? (4)	Ⓨ	Ⓝ
D) jobs requiring travel away from home for		(TRV)
- 1 to 5 nights per month? (2)	Ⓨ	Ⓝ
- 6 to 10 nights per month? (3)	Ⓨ	Ⓝ
- 11 or more nights per month? (4)	Ⓨ	Ⓝ

9 STREET ADDRESS (HOUSE NUMBER AND STREET AND APT NO., WHERE YOU WANT TO RECEIVE MAIL) (ADR)

8 FIRST NAME (FNM)   MI (MIN)   LAST NAME (LNM)

10 CITY (CTY)

11 STATE WHERE YOU WISH TO RECEIVE MAIL (STE)

BLACKEN ONE CIRCLE BELOW

Enter country if other than United States.

Outside U.S.A.

Alabama	Kansas	Ohio
Alaska	Kentucky	Oklahoma
American Samoa	Louisiana	Oregon
Arizona	Maine	Pennsylvania
Arkansas	Maryland	Puerto Rico
California	Massachusetts	Rhode Island
Canal Zone	Michigan	South Carolina
Colorado	Minnesota	South Dakota
Connecticut	Mississippi	Tennessee
Delaware	Missouri	Texas
Dist. of Columbia	Montana	Utah
Florida	Nebraska	Vermont
Georgia	Nevada	Virgin Islands
Guam	New Hampshire	Virginia
Hawaii	New Jersey	Washington
Idaho	New Mexico	West Virginia
Illinois	New York	Wisconsin
Indiana	North Carolina	Wyoming
Iowa	North Dakota	

12 ZIP CODE (ZIP)

13 TELEPHONE NUMBER (TEL)

(Area Code)

CONTACT TIME

D	DAY
N	NIGHT
E	EITHER (TCT)

A G E

2 RESPONSES IN THE BOXES AND BLACKEN THE CORRESPONDING CIRCLE BELOW EACH BOX.

16 OCCUPATIONAL SPECIALTIES AND GRADES (OSP/GRD)

By blackening the appropriate circles, indicate the specialties and grade levels for which you wish to be considered and believe you qualify.

SPECIALTY	GRADE LEVEL		
	GS-5	GS-7	GS-9
ACCOUNTANT (001)	○	○	○
AUDITOR (002)	○	○	○

Questions A through G are designed to assess your qualifications for Accountant and Auditor positions at grades GS-5, GS-7, and GS-9. Read the Qualifications Information Statement, the Competition Notice and this form to gain a better understanding of the kinds of information we are looking for. You will find it helpful to complete your SF-171 and either complete the List of College Courses or have your college transcript(s) at hand so you can refer to them in completing this form. Be sure to answer the questions carefully and accurately. Entries on this form must be supported by your SF-171 and List of College Courses or transcript.

Use a soft pencil to mark your answers to questions. Erase cleanly if you change an answer. Make written responses only where instructed to do so.

A COLLEGE EDUCATION

Blacken the appropriate circles below to show the **highest** levels **both** of undergraduate and graduate education you have completed, or if you are now enrolled in school, the highest level you will complete within the next 9 months. If you have a combination of quarter hours and semester hours, convert quarter hours to semester hours by multiplying by 2/3. Refer to the Qualifications Information Statement for additional instructions on reporting graduate study.

UNDERGRADUATE STUDY

○ - Less than 30 semester hours (45 quarter hours)
○ - 30 to 59 semester hours (45 to 89 quarter hours)
○ - 60 to 89 semester hours (90 to 134 quarter hours)
○ - 90 semester hours or more (135 quarter hours or more- no degree)
○ - Bachelor's Degree

GRADUATE STUDY

○ - less than 1/2 academic year (e.g., 3 to 11 semester hours)
○ - 1/2 to less than 1 academic year
○ - at least 1 academic year, no degree
○ - at least 1 academic year, graduate degree awarded
○ - at least 2 academic years, no degree
○ - at least 2 academic years, graduate degree awarded

Indicate whether you have already completed the education level(s) claimed above or are currently enrolled in school and will complete that level within the next 9 months.

UNDERGRADUATE
○ Completed
○ Will complete within 9 months

GRADUATE
○ Completed
○ Will complete within 9 months

Indicate your undergraduate and graduate college majors by blackening the appropriate circles below.

MAJOR	UNDERGRADUATE	GRADUATE
Accounting Major	○	○
Other Business or Finance-Related Major	○	○
All Other Majors	○	○

14 WORK SETTING AVAILABILITY (WSA)

Indicate your availability for positions in the following work settings by blackening the appropriate circles.

ENVIRONMENTAL SETTINGS

○ Metropolitan Areas (1)
○ Rural Areas (2)
○ Isolated areas - sparsely inhabited locations (3)

ORGANIZATIONAL SETTINGS

○ DOD contractor audit agencies (4)
○ DOD internal audit agencies* (5)
○ Other contractor auditing jobs* (6)
○ Other internal auditing jobs* (7)
○ Financial institution examining* (8)

* These types of positions frequently require extensive overnight travel.

15 GEOGRAPHIC AVAILABILITY (GFP)

From the GEOGRAPHIC CODE LISTING provided with this application CHOOSE AT LEAST ONE BUT NO MORE THAN NINE LOCATIONS and blacken the code for each location you choose.

○ 01 ○ 15 ○ 29 ○ 43 ○ 57 ○ 71 ○ 85
○ 02 ○ 16 ○ 30 ○ 44 ○ 58 ○ 72 ○ 86
○ 03 ○ 17 ○ 31 ○ 45 ○ 59 ○ 73 ○ 87
○ 04 ○ 18 ○ 32 ○ 46 ○ 60 ○ 74 ○ 88
○ 05 ○ 19 ○ 33 ○ 47 ○ 61 ○ 75 ○ 89
○ 06 ○ 20 ○ 34 ○ 48 ○ 62 ○ 76 ○ 90
○ 07 ○ 21 ○ 35 ○ 49 ○ 63 ○ 77 ○ 91
○ 08 ○ 22 ○ 36 ○ 50 ○ 64 ○ 78 ○ 92
○ 09 ○ 23 ○ 37 ○ 51 ○ 65 ○ 79 ○ 93
○ 10 ○ 24 ○ 38 ○ 52 ○ 66 ○ 80 ○ 94
○ 11 ○ 25 ○ 39 ○ 53 ○ 67 ○ 81 ○ 95
○ 12 ○ 26 ○ 40 ○ 54 ○ 68 ○ 82 ○ 96
○ 13 ○ 27 ○ 41 ○ 55 ○ 69 ○ 83 ○ 97
○ 14 ○ 28 ○ 42 ○ 56 ○ 70 ○ 84 ○ 98

How many locations did you select?
① ② ③ ④ ⑤ ⑥ ⑦ ⑧ ⑨

PAGE 3

0735373

B — COLLEGE COURSEWORK

In this section indicate the number of hours of college coursework you have completed in each of the types of courses listed below. You may include courses you will complete in the next 9 months if you are currently attending school. Coursework is divided into two major categories: Accounting Courses and Other Related Courses. For each course type listed, blacken a circle to indicate the number of semester or quarter hours of coursework you have (or will have) completed. Then indicate your total number of hours in all the course types in each of the two categories. Finally, cross reference your responses to the transcript or List of College Courses submitted with your application. Cross reference by using the course numbers on your form or by numbering the courses on your transcript or Course List (1, 2, 3, 4...etc.) and entering the number(s) in the column labeled "Course Reference Number(s)." Each course should be counted only once; therefore, you should read through the entire list of courses before attempting to complete this section.

1. ACCOUNTING COURSES

Number of undergraduate and graduate hours in listed courses

semester hours— (quarter hours)—	1-4 (1-6)	5-7 (7-11)	8-10 (12-15)	11-13 (16-20)	14+ (21+)	Course Reference Number(s) WRITE INSIDE BOXES ONLY
1. Principles of Accounting	○	○	○	○	○	☐
2. Intermediate Accounting	○	○	○	○	○	☐
3. Advanced Accounting	○	○	○	○	○	☐
4. Cost Accounting	○	○	○	○	○	☐
5. Accounting Systems	○	○	○	○	○	☐
6. Governmental Accounting	○	○	○	○	○	☐
7. Accounting Theory	○	○	○	○	○	☐
8. Principles of Auditing	○	○	○	○	○	☐
9. Advanced Auditing	○	○	○	○	○	☐
10. Internal Auditing (Operations)	○	○	○	○	○	☐
11. Tax Accounting	○	○	○	○	○	☐
12. Managerial Accounting	○	○	○	○	○	☐
13. Financial Statement Analysis	○	○	○	○	○	☐
14. CPA Problems and Review	○	○	○	○	○	☐
15. Accounting Practicum/ Special Problems	○	○	○	○	○	☐
16. Other Accounting Courses	○	○	○	○	○	☐

TOTAL HOURS ABOVE	semester hours (quarter hours)	1-11 (1-17)	12-14 (18-21)	15-17 (22-26)	18-20 (27-30)	21-23 (31-35)	24-29 (36-44)	30+ (45+)
		○	○	○	○	○	○	○

Indicate the total number of hours you claim in the Accounting courses listed above.

continued in next column

2. OTHER RELATED COURSES

Number of undergraduate and graduate hours in listed courses

semester hours— (quarter hours)—	1-4 (1-6)	5-7 (7-11)	8-10 (12-15)	11-13 (16-20)	14+ (21+)	Course Reference Number(s) WRITE INSIDE BOXES ONLY
1. Business Law	○	○	○	○	○	☐
2. Quantitative Methods in Business and Finance	○	○	○	○	○	☐
3. Statistics	○	○	○	○	○	☐
4. Data Processing	○	○	○	○	○	☐
5. Computer Programming	○	○	○	○	○	☐
6. Writing and English Composition	○	○	○	○	○	☐
7. Budget and Finance	○	○	○	○	○	☐
8. Economics	○	○	○	○	○	☐
9. Business and Management	○	○	○	○	○	☐

TOTAL HOURS ABOVE	semester hours (quarter hours)	1-11 (1-17)	12-14 (18-21)	15-17 (22-26)	18-20 (27-30)	21-23 (31-35)	24-29 (36-44)	30+ (45+)
		○	○	○	○	○	○	○

Indicate the total number of hours you claim in the related courses listed above.

C — UNDERGRADUATE GRADE POINT AVERAGE

Indicate your gradepoint average, first for all UNDERGRADUATE courses you have already completed, and then for all UNDERGRADUATE ACCOUNTING courses which you entered in item B-1, above. Calculate gradepoint average on the basis of A = 4.0, B = 3.0, C = 2.0, D = 1.0 and F = 0. If you have a combination of semester hour and quarter hour credits, convert quarter hours to semester hours by multiplying by 2/3. There is space for calculating gradepoint average on the college course list furnished with the application forms. Enter your average by blackening the circle next to the appropriate gradepoint range below.

All undergraduate coursework

○	less than 2.00		○	3.00 to 3.49
○	2.00 to 2.49		○	3.50 to 4.00
○	2.50 to 2.99			

Undergraduate Accounting Coursework

○	less than 2.00		○	3.00 to 3.49
○	2.00 to 2.49		○	3.50 to 4.00
○	2.50 to 2.99			

D · SUPERIOR ACADEMIC ACHIEVEMENT (SAC)

Refer to the Qualifications Information Statement for a complete explanation of the Superior Academic Achievement requirements. If you qualify, blacken one or more circles to indicate the provision(s) under which you qualify.

1. GPA of 2.90, all undergraduate courses.
2. GPA of 2.90, last 2 years undergrad.
3. GPA of 3.50, all courses in related major.
4. GPA of 3.50, last 2 years of courses in related major.
5. Rank in upper 1/3 graduating class.
6. Membership in scholastic honorary society.

E · PROFESSIONAL CERTIFICATION (LIC)

Indicate if you are certified in any of the areas listed below. If YES, write your certificate number and the date and place of issue in item 22-B on your SF-171.

1. Certified Public Accountant ○ YES (01) ○ NO (00)

2. Certified Internal Auditor ○ YES (01) ○ NO (00)

3. Certified Management Accountant ○ YES (01) ○ NO (00)

F · ACCOUNTING WORK EXPERIENCE, AUDITING WORK EXPERIENCE AND RELATED WORK EXPERIENCE

Use section F-1, F-2 and/or F-3 on the next page to describe any work experience you have had which qualifies you for the specialties and grades for which you wish to be considered. The Qualifications Information Statement describes the types and amounts of experience needed to qualify. We suggest that you first complete your Personal Qualifications Statement (SF-171) describing all of your work experience and then refer to that form when responding to the questions in this section.

Select the section (F-1, -2 or -3) which best describes each period of your work experience. Use a column of circles in the appropriate section to describe each period of work experience in terms of its Type, Level and Length. Begin in Column A of the appropriate section with your most recent period of related experience. First darken the SINGLE circle which best describes the level at which you worked. Continue down to the "Length of Work Experience" section and blacken a circle to indicate the length of the experience. Finally, cross-reference this experience to your SF-171 by entering in the box at the bottom of the column the number or letter of the experience block you are describing. Describe other periods of related experience, up to a total of 4 periods of each type, in the same way.

Begin a new column whenever the Type or Level of Work changes. You should use a new column even if the experience is with the same employer and requires the same cross-reference to the SF-171.

For example, if you worked as an accounting technician and were promoted to an accountant position within the same organization, you would use 2 columns (i.e., periods of work experience) in section F-1 to describe these jobs. If you have extensive experience in accounting- or auditing–related jobs, more than can fit into the 4 columns provided in each section, pick your most relevant experience, that is, the experience most related to the type and level of job you are applying for.

For each column you complete to describe a period of experience, be sure to darken only one circle to describe the Type of Work and one circle to describe the Level of Work and be sure to indicate the length of that experience. If a particular period of experience involves more than one Type or Level of Work, pick the single response for Type and Level of Work which best describes that experience. If you worked less than full time, use the equivalent amount of full time experience in describing the Length of Work Experience, e.g., 12 months of 20 hour/week experience should be shown as 6 months.

Assume, for example that you have the following work history:

(1) Two summers, 3-1/2 months each, as an accounting technician in a corporate accounting office. (See F-1, period A)
(2) Two summers as a summer intern in a public accounting firm. (See F-1, period B)
(3) 16 months as a part-time, 10 hours per week, bank teller. (See F-3, period A)
(4) 6 months part time, 20 hours per week, preparing income tax returns. (See F-3, period B)

You would complete item F as shown below. The cross-reference numbers refer to the job numbers in our example.

F-1 · ACCOUNTING WORK EXPERIENCE

F-2 · AUDITING WORK EXPERIENCE

F-3 · RELATED WORK EXPERIENCE

FOLLOW DIRECTIONS CAREFULLY

The instructions for completing this item are on page 5. Failure to follow them exactly may result in your not receiving proper credit for your work experience. For each period of work you describe, be sure to blacken ONE AND ONLY ONE circle under "Type of Work", one circle under "Level of Work", and one circle under "Length of Experience".

CONTINUE ON PAGE 6

F-1 — ACCOUNTING WORK EXPERIENCE

PERIODS OF WORK EXPERIENCE

TYPE OF WORK

1. Financial Accounting (Business)
2. Financial Accounting (Government)
3. Systems Accounting
4. Tax Accounting
5. Cost Accounting
6. Public Accounting (with CPA Firm)
7. Accounting Teaching

LEVEL OF WORK

1. Accounting Clerk
2. Bookkeeper
3. Accounting Technician (Business)
4. Accounting Technician (Government)
5. Student Trainee (Accounting)
6. Trainee/Intern (Accounting)
7. Accountant
8. Senior Accountant
9. Supervisory Accountant

Accounting Teaching:

10. Teacher (High School or Vocational/Technical School)
11. Teaching Assistant (College/University)
12. Instructor (College/University)
13. Professor (College/University)

LENGTH OF WORK EXPERIENCE

1. Less than 2 months
2. 2 to 5 months
3. 6 to 11 months
4. 12 to 23 months
5. 24 to 35 months
6. 36 to 47 months
7. 4 years or more

CROSS REFERENCE EXPERIENCE BLOCK ON SF-171

F-2 — AUDITING WORK EXPERIENCE

PERIODS OF WORK EXPERIENCE

TYPE OF WORK (Audits Performed)

1. Financial
2. Grant
3. Compliance
4. Operational
5. Internal

LEVEL OF WORK

1. Student/Trainee (Auditing)
2. Trainee/Intern (Auditing)
3. Auditor
4. Auditor-in-Charge
5. Supervisory Auditor

LENGTH OF WORK EXPERIENCE

1. Less than 2 months
2. 2 to 5 months
3. 6 to 11 months
4. 12 to 23 months
5. 24 to 35 months
6. 36 to 47 months
7. 4 years or more

CROSS REFERENCE EXPERIENCE BLOCK ON SF-171

F-3 — RELATED WORK EXPERIENCE

PERIODS OF WORK EXPERIENCE

TYPE OF WORK

1. Banking and Finance
2. Management/Program Analysis
3. Contract Administration
4. Taxes
5. Business Administration
6. Budgeting
7. Public Administration
8. Data Processing
9. Statistics
10. Operations Research
11. Economics

LEVEL OF WORK

1. Aid
2. Clerical
3. Student Trainee
4. Technician
5. Administrative Assistant/Trainee
6. Professional or Management Intern/Trainee
7. Administrative/Professional/Managerial

LENGTH OF WORK EXPERIENCE

1. Less than 2 months
2. 2 to 5 months
3. 6 to 11 months
4. 12 to 23 months
5. 24 to 35 months
6. 36 to 47 months
7. 4 years or more

CROSS REFERENCE EXPERIENCE BLOCK ON SF-171

FOLLOW DIRECTIONS CAREFULLY

The instructions for completing this item are on page 5. Failure to follow them exactly may result in your not receiving proper credit for your work experience. For each period of work you describe, be sure to blacken ONE AND ONLY ONE circle under "Type of Work", ONE circle under "Level of Work", and ONE circle under "Length of Experience".

0735373

PAGE 7 G

WORK ACTIVITIES

The activities listed in this section cover a wide range of entry-level accounting and auditing jobs. Individual accounting or auditing positions would typically consist of only a few of these activities. The ability to perform these activities is not required of Accountant or Auditor applicants. However, applicants who have demonstrated their ability to perform one or more of these activities should indicate their level of ability here.

ABILITY RATING

If you have not had the opportunity to demonstrate your ability in an activity, blacken the circle in the ABILITY RATING column labeled "N/A" (Not Applicable).

If you have demonstrated your ability in any of these activities, use the following scale to rate your level of ability:

1 = Some ability (i.e., would require some on-the-job training to perform the activity)

2 = Satisfactory (i.e., could perform the activity with guidance)

3 = Very good ability (i.e., could perform the activity independently)

4 = Excellent ability (i.e., could provide guidance to others under difficult conditions)

Blacken the circle in the numbered ABILITY RATING column which corresponds to your ability rating for each activity.

BASIS FOR ABILITY RATING

For each activity on which you give yourself a numerical ability rating, indicate the basis for that rating by:

– Entering the reference numbers from your coursework listing or transcript in the COURSEWORK NUMBER column if your ability rating is based on specific college coursework.

– Entering the experience block number from your SF-171 in the EXPERIENCE BLOCK column if your ability rating is based on specific work experience.

– Blacken the box under the GENERAL EXPERIENCE/EDUCATION column if you cannot attribute your ability to any specific experience or education.

WORK ACTIVITY

Accurately mark each activity to avoid loss of credit.

Ability Rating columns: N/A, 1, 2, 3, 4

1. Review accounting transactions for accuracy and propriety.
2. Reconcile account or fund balances.
3. Reconcile subsidiary records with general ledger control accounts.
4. Review financial reports for accuracy and completeness.
5. Prepare trial balances.
6. Review or maintain controls over commitments, obligations and/or disbursements to assure they are within authorized limits.
7. Post and balance ledgers, journals and subsidiary accounts.
8. Prepare adjusting or closing entries.
9. Prepare bills or notices regarding accounts.
10. Prepare working papers and/or financial statements.
11. Observe and/or take physical inventory to verify records and/or check on the condition or quantity of items.
12. Advise operating officials and others on financial and accounting policies and procedures.
13. Interpret or apply laws, regulations, decisions and/or rulings affecting the accounting system.
14. Identify and resolve financial reporting problems by working with operating officials or other administrative organizations.
15. Analyze an accounting organization's internal work processes or financial controls to develop and recommend improvements.
16. Prepare an audit plan and identify objectives of audit.
17. Conduct interviews with supervisors, employees, program officials and others to obtain information.
18. Develop statistical sampling plan for examining and testing records and management controls.
19. Check accuracy and reliability of operational reports.
20. Verify that direct costs are actually expended on the product or service contracted for.
21. Verify that accounting system is set up and maintained according to generally accepted accounting procedures.
22. Evaluate the effectiveness of management control systems.
23. Test an organization's operations to determine deviations from prescribed procedures.

ACTIVITIES CONTINUED ON NEXT PAGE

BASIS FOR ABILITY RATING

Write inside boxes only.

Coursework Number(s) | Experience Block(s) | General Experience/Education

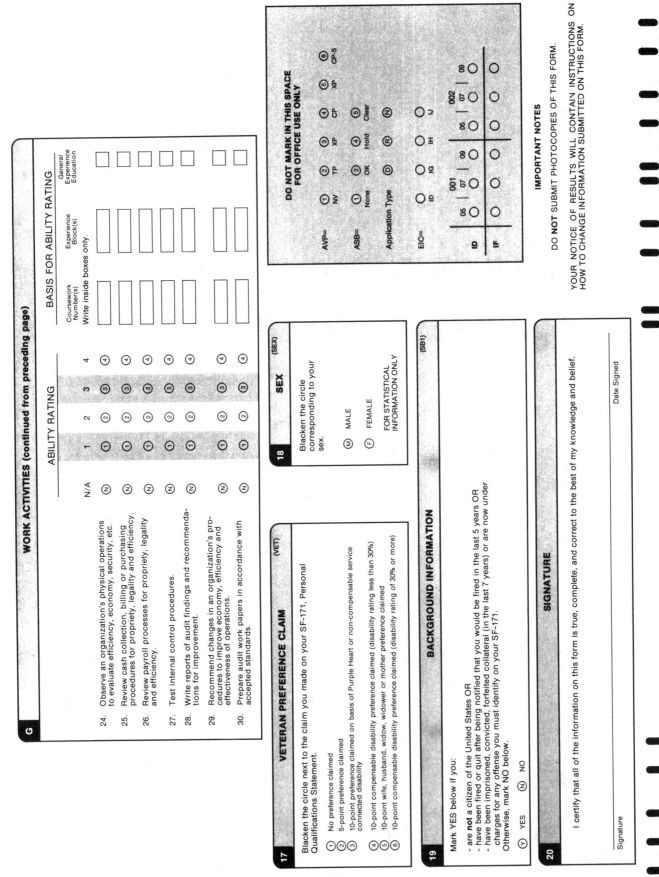

G

WORK ACTIVITIES (continued from preceding page)

ABILITY RATING

BASIS FOR ABILITY RATING

Coursework Number(s)
Experience Block(s)
General Experience Education

Write inside boxes only.

	N/A	1	2	3	4
24. Observe an organization's physical operations to evaluate efficiency, economy, security, etc.	N	1	2	3	4
25. Review cash collection, billing or purchasing procedures for propriety, legality and efficiency.	N	1	2	3	4
26. Review payroll processes for propriety, legality and efficiency.	N	1	2	3	4
27. Test internal control procedures.	N	1	2	3	4
28. Write reports of audit findings and recommendations for improvement.	N	1	2	3	4
29. Recommend changes in an organization's procedures to improve economy, efficiency and effectiveness of operations.	N	1	2	3	4
30. Prepare audit work papers in accordance with accepted standards.	N	1	2	3	4

DO NOT MARK IN THIS SPACE FOR OFFICE USE ONLY

AVP= ① NV ② TP ③ XP ④ CP ⑤ XP ⑥ CP-S

ASB= ① None ② OK ③ ④ Hold ⑤ Clear

Application Type D R N

EIO= ID IG IH IJ

ID | 06 001 | 05 002 09
   07 | 07 08 07 09

IF

17 VETERAN PREFERENCE CLAIM (VET)

Blacken the circle next to the claim you made on your SF-171, Personal Qualifications Statement.

① No preference claimed
② 5-point preference claimed
③ 10-point preference claimed on basis of Purple Heart or non-compensable service connected disability
④ 10-point compensable disability preference claimed (disability rating less than 30%)
⑤ 10-point wife, husband, widow, widower or mother preference claimed
⑥ 10-point compensable disability preference claimed (disability rating of 30% or more)

18 SEX (SEX)

Blacken the circle corresponding to your sex.

Ⓜ MALE
Ⓕ FEMALE

FOR STATISTICAL INFORMATION ONLY

19 BACKGROUND INFORMATION (SB1)

Mark YES below if you:

- are **not** a citizen of the United States OR
- have been fired or quit after being notified that you would be fired in the last 5 years OR
- have been imprisoned, convicted, forfeited collateral (in the last 7 years) or are now under charges for any offense you must identify on your SF-171.

Otherwise, mark NO below.

Ⓨ YES   Ⓝ NO

20 SIGNATURE

I certify that all of the information on this form is true, complete, and correct to the best of my knowledge and belief.

_____ Signature   _____ Date Signed

IMPORTANT NOTES

DO **NOT** SUBMIT PHOTOCOPIES OF THIS FORM.

YOUR NOTICE OF RESULTS WILL CONTAIN INSTRUCTIONS ON HOW TO CHANGE INFORMATION SUBMITTED ON THIS FORM.

0735373

BATCH NUMBER
(BNO)

FOR OFFICE
USE ONLY

U.S. Office of Personnel Management

OCCUPATIONAL SUPPLEMENT FOR
HEALTH, SAFETY and ENVIRONMENTAL OCCUPATIONS (0001H)

FORM APPROVED
OMB NO. 3206-0040

FORM

USE **ONLY** A NUMBER 2 LEAD PENCIL.

DO NOT FOLD, STAPLE, TEAR OR PAPER CLIP THIS FORM.

This form can be processed only if you:
1) Submit an original form (no photocopies).
2) Completely blacken the oval corresponding to your response choice.
3) Completely erase any mistakes or stray marks.

1   **NAME**

NAME: _____
(Please Print)

INSTRUCTIONS AND EXAMPLES

Read the instructions for each item carefully before completing that item. Recording information that does not accurately reflect your availability, employment preferences, and qualifications may cause you to lose consideration for some jobs.

PRINT YOUR RESPONSE IN THE BOXES AND BLACKEN THE APPROPRIATE OVALS.

2   0 1 2 − 2 0

5
- ○ JAN
- ○ FEB
- ○ MAR
- ● APR
- ○ MAY
- ● This year
- ○ Next year

8
YES   NO
●   Ⓝ

2   **SOCIAL SECURITY NUMBER**   (SSN)

3   **DATE OF BIRTH**   (SDF)

MONTH	DAY	YEAR

4   **SEX**

Blacken the oval corresponding to your sex.

○ Male

○ Female

FOR STATISTICAL INFORMATION ONLY

5   **DATE AVAILABLE TO START WORK**   (EBD)

- ○ JAN
- ○ FEB
- ○ MAR
- ○ APR
- ○ MAY
- ○ JUN   This year
- ○ JUL
- ○ AUG   Next year
- ○ SEP
- ○ OCT
- ○ NOV
- ○ DEC

6   **GRADE**

Blacken the oval of the lowest grade for which you wish to be considered. If you select GS-5 you will also be rated for GS-7.

○ GS-5

○ GS-7

7   **OPTIONS**   (OSP)

Mark one or more options for which you wish to be considered by blackening the oval next to the option(s). You must select at least one option. **Note:** Those options with an asterisk (*) have specific qualification requirements which are defined in the Qualification Information Statement.

○ Environmental Protection Specialist (002)

○ Hospital Housekeeping Management* (003)

○ Outdoor Recreation Planning* (004)

○ Public Health Program Specialist (005)

○ Safety and Occupational Health Management* (006)

8   **EMPLOYMENT AVAILABILITY**

ARE YOU AVAILABLE FOR: (Blacken YES or NO for **each** question)

	YES	NO	
A) full-time employment			
- 40 hours per week?.......................Ⓨ		Ⓝ	(FTE)
B) part-time employment of			(PTE)
- 16 or fewer hours per week?...........Ⓨ		Ⓝ	
- 17 to 24 hours per week?...............Ⓨ		Ⓝ	
- 25 to 32 hours per week?...............Ⓨ		Ⓝ	
C) temporary employment lasting			(TMP)
- 5 to 12 months?...........................Ⓨ		Ⓝ	
- 1 to 4 months?............................Ⓨ		Ⓝ	
- less than 1 month?........................Ⓨ		Ⓝ	
D) jobs requiring travel away from home for			(TRV)
- 1 to 5 nights per month?................Ⓨ		Ⓝ	
- 6 to 10 nights per month?...............Ⓨ		Ⓝ	
- 11 or more nights per month?...........Ⓨ		Ⓝ	

* U.S. GOVERNMENT PRINTING OFFICE:1990—262-449/00043

057

0163840

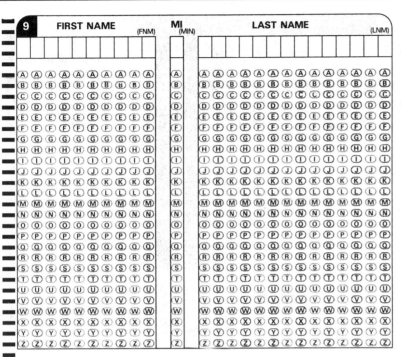

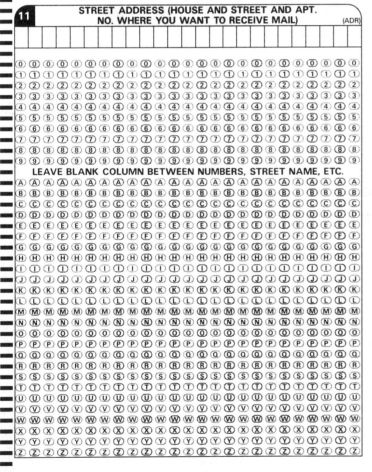

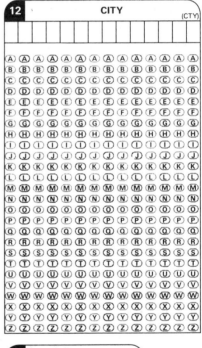

15

EDUCATION: Includes parts A, B, C, D, and E. Skip parts B, C, D, and E if you do **not** have college course work.

A. GENERAL

1) What is the highest level of education you have completed?
- ◯ High School Graduate or Equivalency (GED)
- ◯ Attended Business or Technical School
- ◯ Graduated from Business or Technical School
- ◯ Less than 2 years of college
- ◯ 2 or more years of college, with no degree
- ◯ Associates Degree
- ◯ Bachelors Degree
- ◯ Bachelors Degree and Graduate course work
- ◯ Masters Degree
- ◯ Doctorate or Other Graduate Degree (i.e., J.D.)

2) How long has it been since you attended college for academic credit?
- ◯ Did not attend college
- ◯ Still attending college
- ◯ Less than 2 years
- ◯ 2 or more years, but less than 5 years
- ◯ 5 or more years, but less than 10 years
- ◯ 10 or more years

3) What is your present student status?
- ◯ Not a student
- ◯ Part-time college student
- ◯ Full-time college student

4) Enter the latest year you received any underground degree and blacken the ovals below each number. 19 ☐☐

5) Enter the latest year you received any graduate degree and blacken the ovals below each number. 19 ☐☐

B. COLLEGE STUDY

1) Amount of Course Work

Mark the amount or level of college course work you have completed, or will complete within the next 9 months. Mark all items that apply. Follow the directions listed below each level you indicate.

- ◯ Course work but no undergraduate degree

  Enter the number of semester hours or quarter hours. Only complete both fields if you have course work under each system.

  Semester Hours   Quarter Hours

- ◯ Bachelors Degree

- ◯ Bachelors Degree plus graduate course work but no graduate degree

  a) Enter the number of semester or quarter hours of **graduate course work.** If you have more than 99 hours, enter "99".)

  Semester Hours   Quarter Hours

  b) Enter the number of semester or quarter hours considered by your college as one year of **full-time graduate study.**

  Semester Hours   Quarter Hours

- ◯ Graduate Degree — Masters, Ph.D., J.D., or LL.B.

2) Completion of Course Work

	YES	NO
a) Have you completed the undergraduate study indicated above?	Ⓨ	Ⓝ
b) Have you completed the graduate study listed above?	Ⓨ	Ⓝ

0163840   ○○○○○○■○■■○○○○○○○○○○○○○○○○○○○□

057

15   **EDUCATION (continued)**

C. FIELD OF STUDY (JBF)

Undergraduate Major: Mark your major field(s) of study, or any field in which you completed (or will complete) 24, or more, semester hours (36 quarter hours). Next to your major field(s) of study blacken the oval(s) under the column labeled "Undergraduate Major."

Undergraduate Minor: Mark your minor field(s) of study, or any field in which you completed (or will complete) 12 to 23 semester hours (18 to 35 quarter hours). Next to your minor field(s) of study blacken the oval(s) under the column labeled "Undergraduate Minor."

Graduate Major: Mark your major field of study, or any field in which you meet the requirements for a major as defined by your college or university. Next to your major field(s) of study blacken the oval(s) under the column labeled "Graduate Major."

Columns: UNDERGRADUATE MAJOR / UNDERGRADUATE MINOR / GRADUATE MAJOR

AGRICULTURE
○ ○ ○ Agricultural Economics (1)
○ ○ ○ Other Field (1)

ARCHITECTURE
○ ○ ○ All Fields (2)

BIOLOGICAL, HEALTH AND LIFE SCIENCES
○ ○ ○ Biology (3)
○ ○ ○ Hospital or Health Care Administration (4)
○ ○ ○ Public Health (5)
○ ○ ○ Professional Health Sciences (Pharmacy, Nursing, etc.) (6)

BUSINESS AND MANAGEMENT
○ ○ ○ Accounting (7)
○ ○ ○ Advertising (8)
○ ○ ○ Business Administration (9)
○ ○ ○ Finance or Banking (10)
○ ○ ○ Commerce (11)
○ ○ ○ Contracts (12)
○ ○ ○ Hotel and Restaurant Management (13)
○ ○ ○ Industrial Management (14)
○ ○ ○ Insurance (15)
○ ○ ○ International Trade (16)
○ ○ ○ Marketing (17)
○ ○ ○ Personnel (18)
○ ○ ○ Public Administration (19)
○ ○ ○ Procurement (20)
○ ○ ○ Real Estate (21)
○ ○ ○ Safety Administration (22)
○ ○ ○ Transportation and Public Utilities (23)

COMMUNICATION
○ ○ ○ Creative Writing (24)
○ ○ ○ Public Information or Relations (24)
○ ○ ○ Journalism (24)

COMPUTER SCIENCE
○ ○ ○ Computer Science (25)
○ ○ ○ Information Systems (26)
○ ○ ○ Telecommunications (27)

EDUCATION
○ ○ ○ Vocational Rehabilitation (28)
○ ○ ○ Educational Counseling (28)

ENGINEERING
○ ○ ○ Agricultural (29)
○ ○ ○ Civil (29)
○ ○ ○ Electrical or Electronic (29)
○ ○ ○ Industrial or Safety (29)
○ ○ ○ Sanitation (29)
○ ○ ○ Other Field (29)

LAW
○ ○ ○ Business or Commercial (30)
○ ○ ○ Other Field (30)

MATHEMATICS
○ ○ ○ Mathematics (31)
○ ○ ○ Statistics (31)
○ ○ ○ Quantitative Methods (31)

NATURAL RESOURCES
○ ○ ○ Ecology or Conservation (32)
○ ○ ○ Forestry (33)
○ ○ ○ Natural Resource or Park Management (34)
○ ○ ○ Range Conservation (35)
○ ○ ○ Recreation (36)
○ ○ ○ Wildlife Management (37)
○ ○ ○ Other Field (38)

PHYSICAL SCIENCES
○ ○ ○ Astronomy (39)
○ ○ ○ Chemistry (39)
○ ○ ○ Earth Sciences or Geology (39)
○ ○ ○ Oceanography (39)
○ ○ ○ Physics (39)
○ ○ ○ Other Field (39)

PSYCHOLOGY
○ ○ ○ Industrial Psychology (40)

SOCIAL SCIENCES
○ ○ ○ Anthropology (41)
○ ○ ○ Archeology (42)
○ ○ ○ Cultural Studies (43)
○ ○ ○ Economics (44)
○ ○ ○ History (45)
○ ○ ○ Geography (46)
○ ○ ○ Political Science or International Relations (47)
○ ○ ○ Sociology or Social Work (48)
○ ○ ○ Urban Planning (49)

TRANSPORTATION
○ ○ ○ Motor Mechanics (23)
○ ○ ○ Traffic Management (23)
○ ○ ○ Other Field (23)

○ ○ ○ **OTHER FIELD**

D. ACADEMIC ACHIEVEMENT

Blacken the appropriate oval(s) if you have a Bachelors degree (or expect to complete a degree within the next 9 months) and meet or exceed any of the following provisions. (All Grade-Point Average (GPA) references are based on a 4.00 scale for undergraduate courses only. GPA's should be rounded in the following manner: a 2.94 is rounded down to 2.9; a 2.95 is rounded up to 3.0.)

○ GPA of 3.0, for all completed undergraduate courses.
○ GPA of 3.0, for all courses completed in the last 2 years of your undergraduate curriculum.
○ GPA of 3.5, for all courses completed in your major field of study.
○ GPA of 3.5, for all courses completed in your major field of study in the last 2 years of your undergraduate curriculum.
○ Rank in the upper one-tenth of graduating class.
○ Rank in the upper one-third of graduating class.
○ Membership in a scholastic honorary society. (Do not include Freshmen level societies.)

E. GRADE-POINT AVERAGE

Items 1), 2), and 3) below each describe a portion of your undergraduate course work. Enter your undergraduate Grade-Point Average (GPA) for each item in the blocks provided. Show your GPA based on a 4.00 scale. Blacken the oval below each number.

1) All Undergraduate Course Work Completed

⓪	⓪	⓪
①	①	①
②	②	②
③	③	③
④	④	④
⑤	⑤	⑤
⑥	⑥	⑥
⑦	⑦	⑦
⑧	⑧	⑧
⑨	⑨	⑨

2) Junior and Senior Years
Enter your GPA for courses completed during these years.

⓪	⓪	⓪
①	①	①
②	②	②
③	③	③
④	④	④
⑤	⑤	⑤
⑥	⑥	⑥
⑦	⑦	⑦
⑧	⑧	⑧
⑨	⑨	⑨

3) Major Field of Study
Enter your GPA for courses completed in your major field of study.

⓪	⓪	⓪
①	①	①
②	②	②
③	③	③
④	④	④
⑤	⑤	⑤
⑥	⑥	⑥
⑦	⑦	⑦
⑧	⑧	⑧
⑨	⑨	⑨

057 **0163840**

16.   **EXPERIENCE:** Includes parts A and B. Skip part B if you do <u>not</u> have experience.

A. <u>GENERAL</u>

1) What is your <u>present</u> employment status? (Consider 32 or more hours a week as full-time.)

- ◯ Not employed
- ◯ Part-time non-Federal employee
- ◯ Part-time Federal employee
- ◯ Full-time non-Federal employee
- ◯ Full-time Federal employee
- ◯ On active duty in the military

2) Have you ever been employed as a civilian in the Federal government?

◯ Yes   ◯ No

3) My most recent work evaluation could be classified as:

- ◯ I have no work experience, or have not received an evaluation.
- ◯ Below Average
- ◯ Average
- ◯ Above Average
- ◯ Outstanding

B. <u>QUALIFYING EXPERIENCE</u>

Qualifying experience is progressively responsible work as defined below. It does not include general clerical duties such as typing, filing, or related routine duties. Secretarial or related work, or Trades and Crafts work, is qualifying if it meets the definition. Leave these questions blank if your experience does not fit the following definition.

    Qualifying experience is defined as experience which includes <u>all</u> of the following:
- — Analyzing problems and presenting solutions;
- — Planning and organizing work; and,
- — Communicating verbally and in writing.

Record your qualifying experience as months of specialized <u>or</u> months of general experience below. <u>Do not count the same experience as both specialized and general.</u> For example, if you have a total of 25 months experience, of which 13 fits one of the categories under specialized, enter 13 months under "Months of Specialized Experience" and 12 months (25 minus 13) under "Months of General Experience."

1) Specialized Experience
In part a) below blacken the oval next to each type of experience in which you have at least 12 months of experience. Your experience must be directly in, or related to, the field listed. Once you have indicated your type(s) of experience in part a), you must enter the total number of months of specialized experience in b). Then indicate in part c) how long it has been since you performed this type(s) of work.

If your qualifying experience does not fall into one of the specialized types listed, you should count it in Section 2), "General Experience".

a) Type of Specialized Experience (JBF)
- ◯ Biology (50)
- ◯ Ecology or Conservation (51)
- ◯ Environmental Programs, Plans or Standards (52)
- ◯ Hospital or Health Care Administration (53)
- ◯ Industrial or Safety Engineering (54)
- ◯ Natural Resource or Wildlife (55)
- ◯ Public Health (56)
- ◯ Safety Administration or Occupational Health (57)

b) Months of Specialized Experience

⓪	⓪
①	①
②	②
③	③
④	④
⑤	⑤
⑥	⑥
⑦	⑦
⑧	⑧
⑨	⑨

c) How long has it been since you performed this type of work?
- ◯ No specialized experience
- ◯ Still performing this type of work
- ◯ Less than 2 years ago
- ◯ 2 or more years, but less than 5 years
- ◯ 5 or more years, but less than 10 years
- ◯ 10 or more years

2) General Experience
In part a) below enter the total number of months of qualifying experience which you did not enter as specialized experience above. Blacken the ovals below each number. In part b) blacken the oval next to the item which best indicates how long it has been since you performed this type of work.

a) Months of General Experience

⓪	⓪
①	①
②	②
③	③
④	④
⑤	⑤
⑥	⑥
⑦	⑦
⑧	⑧
⑨	⑨

b) How long has it been since you performed this type of work?
- ◯ No general experience
- ◯ Still performing this type of work
- ◯ Less than 2 years ago
- ◯ 2 or more years, but less than 5 years
- ◯ 5 or more years, but less than 10 years
- ◯ 10 or more years

3) Level of Experience
Mark the definition that best describes the highest level of experience you have completed.
- ◯ Performed duties generally involving established procedures under close supervision.
- ◯ Performed duties sometimes requiring interpretation or independent action and judgment.

17 GEOGRAPHIC AVAILABILITY (GFP)

From the geographic code listing provided, choose up to nine locations where you are willing to work. Print the location code(s) in the boxes and blacken the corresponding oval below each box.

1 ☐☐☐ 2 ☐☐☐ 3 ☐☐☐ 4 ☐☐☐ 5 ☐☐☐

(0)(0)(0) (1)(1)(1) (2)(2)(2) (3)(3)(3) (4)(4)(4) (5)(5)(5) (6)(6)(6) (7)(7)(7) (8)(8) (9)(9)

6 ☐☐☐ 7 ☐☐☐ 8 ☐☐☐ 9 ☐☐☐

(0)(0)(0) (1)(1)(1) (2)(2)(2) (3)(3)(3) (4)(4)(4) (5)(5)(5) (6)(6)(6) (7)(7)(7) (8)(8) (9)(9)

18 LANGUAGES (LNG)

Select up to three languages in which you are proficient. Blacken the oval beside each choice.

- ○ Any African Language (01)
- ○ Any Native American Language (Aleut, Navajo, etc.) (02)
- ○ Any Classical Language (03)
- ○ Asian/Near East Languages (04)
- ○ Asian/Far East Languages (other than Chinese) (05)
- ○ Chinese (06)
- ○ French (07)
- ○ German (08)
- ○ Russian (09)
- ○ Sign Language (10)
- ○ Spanish (11)
- ○ Other European Languages (12)
- ○ Other Languages (13)

19 RECRUITING INFORMATION

Indicate how you learned about these jobs with the Federal Government by blackening the appropriate oval. Select only one response.

- ○ Newspaper, Magazine, TV, or Radio
- ○ State Employment or Unemployment Office
- ○ By contacting a Federal agency
- ○ Through Federal recruiter
- ○ Federal Job Information Center
- ○ College Placement Office
- ○ Friend or relative working for Federal Government
- ○ Other method

20 MOBILITY (OEM-1)

Are you available for positions that require moving to different geographic locations as part of your normal assignment? (For example, these moves may occur at intervals ranging from one to three years.)   ○ Yes   ○ No

21 BICULTURAL (OEM-3)

Are you knowledgeable in the area of Hispanic culture?   ○ Yes   ○ No

22 CERTIFICATION

Internship/Residency: Blacken the oval next to each program you have completed.

- ○ One year Hospital Administration Residency Program
- ○ One year as an Intern in Hospital Administration or Hospital Housekeeping Management

Certification: Blacken the oval for each certification you have obtained.

- ○ Certified Safety Professional
- ○ Certified Industrial Hygienist
- ○ Certified Health Physicist

23 INTERN POSITIONS (OEM-2)

Some positions are filled through intern programs that typically involve formal training in a variety of assignments. Intern positions may also involve temporary duty away from your regular post of duty or permanent relocation. Are you available for intern positions?   ○ Yes   ○ No

24 MILITARY SERVICE

A. Have you ever served on active duty in the United States Military Service?   ○ Yes   ○ No

B. Blacken the oval next to your claimed veteran preference.
  ① NO PREFERENCE
  ② 5-POINT PREFERENCE—Active duty in the armed forces during a war or in a campaign or expedition for which a campaign badge has been authorized or between 12/07/41 and 07/01/55 or more than 180 consecutive days of active duty any part of which occurred between 02/01/55 and 10/14/76. Discharge must have been under honorable conditions. You must show proof when you are hired.

  10-POINT PREFERENCE—You must enclose a completed **Standard Form 15** if you mark 3-6 below.

  ③ Non-compensably disabled or Purple Heart recipient.
  ④ Compensably disabled (less than 30%).
  ⑤ Qualified spouse, widow(er), or mother of a deceased or disabled veteran.
  ⑥ Compensably disabled (30% or more).

25 BACKGROUND INFORMATION (SB1)

	Yes	No
A. Are you a citizen of the United States?	Ⓨ	Ⓝ
B. During the last 10 years, were you fired from any job for any reason or did you quit after being told that you would be fired?	Ⓨ	Ⓝ
C. Are you now or have you ever been: (Answer the following questions.)		
1) convicted of or forfeited collateral for any felony?	Ⓨ	Ⓝ
2) convicted of or forfeited collateral for any firearms or explosives violation?	Ⓨ	Ⓝ
3) convicted, forfeited collateral, imprisoned, on probation, or on parole, during the last 10 years?	Ⓨ	Ⓝ
4) convicted by a military court-martial?	Ⓨ	Ⓝ
D. Are you currently under charges for any violation of law?	Ⓨ	Ⓝ

26 SIGNATURE

I certify that all information on this form is true, complete, and correct to the best of my knowledge. **NOTE:** A false statement on any part of your application may be grounds for not hiring you, or for firing you after you begin work. Also, you may be punished by fine or imprisonment (U.S. Code, title 18, section 1001).

_____   _____
Signature   Date Signed

APPLICANT RACE AND NATIONAL ORIGIN QUESTIONNAIRE

The United States District Court for the District of Columbia, in a decree approved in a lawsuit entitled Luevano v. Newman, Civil Action No. 79-0271, has ordered that Federal Government agencies provide data on the race and national origin of applicants for certain Federal occupations. The position for which you are applying is in one of those occupations.

The collection of this information is authorized for use by the Office of Personnel Management only for the purposes of complying with the requirements of the Luevano v. Newman Decree. The data you supply will be used for statistical analysis pursuant to the requirements of the lawsuit, and will not be shared with employing agencies.

You are requested to complete the following, however, submission of this information is voluntary. Your failure to do so will have no effect on the processing of your application for Federal employment.

PRIMARY GEOGRAPHIC ZONE

Blacken the oval next to the one Zone which includes your first choice for location of employment. This designation is for statistical use only and will not affect your actual consideration for employment. Your geographic area of consideration will be determined by your entries in item 17, GEOGRAPHIC AVAILABILITY. Please mark only one oval.

○ **ATLANTA**	○ **CHICAGO**	○ **DALLAS**	○ **PHILADELPHIA**	○ **SAN FRANCISCO**
Alabama	Illinois	Arizona	Connecticut	California
Florida	Indiana	Arkansas	Delaware	Idaho
Georgia	Iowa	Colorado	Maine	Nevada
Mississippi	Kansas	Louisiana	Maryland	Oregon
North Carolina	Kentucky	Montana	Massachusetts	Washington
South Carolina	Michigan	New Mexico	New Hampshire	
Tennessee	Minnesota	Oklahoma	New Jersey	
Virginia	Missouri	Texas	New York	
	Nebraska	Utah	Pennsylvania	
	North Dakota	Wyoming	Rhode Island	
	Ohio		Vermont	
	South Dakota			
	West Virginia			
	Wisconsin			

○ **ALASKA**
State of Alaska

○ **CARIBBEAN**
Puerto Rico and
the Virgin Islands

○ **HAWAII**
State of Hawaii and
Pacific overseas area

○ **WASHINGTON DC: Washington DC Metropolitan Area** (Charles, Montgomery, and Prince George's Counties in Maryland; Arlington, Fairfax, Prince William, King George, Stafford and Loudoun Counties and Falls Church, Alexandria, and Fairfax cities in Virginia) and **Atlantic overseas area** (African, European, Middle Eastern, Central and South American countries).

RACE AND/OR NATIONAL ORIGIN

The categories below provide descriptions of race and national origins. Read the Definition of Category descriptions and then blacken the oval next to the category with which you identify yourself. If you are of mixed race and/or national origin, select the category with which you most closely identify yourself. Please mark only one oval.

Name of Category	**Definition of Category**
○ American Indian or Alaskan Native	A person having origins in any of the original peoples of North America, and who maintains cultural identification through community recognition or tribal affiliation.
○ Asian or Pacific Islander	A person having origins in any of the original peoples of the Far East, Southeast Asia, the Indian subcontinent, or the Pacific Islands. For example, this area includes China, India, Japan, Korea, the Philippine Islands, and Samoa.
○ Black, not of Hispanic origin	A person having origins in any of the black racial groups of Africa. This does not include persons of Mexican, Puerto Rican, Cuban, Central or South American, or other Spanish cultures or origins.
○ Hispanic	A person of Mexican, Puerto Rican, Cuban, Central or South American, or other Spanish cultures or origins. This does not include persons of Portuguese culture or origin.
○ White, not of Hispanic origin	A person having origins in any of the original peoples of Europe, North America, or the Middle East. This does not include persons of Mexican, Puerto Rican, Cuban, Central or South American, or other Spanish cultures or origins.
○ Other	A person not included in another category.

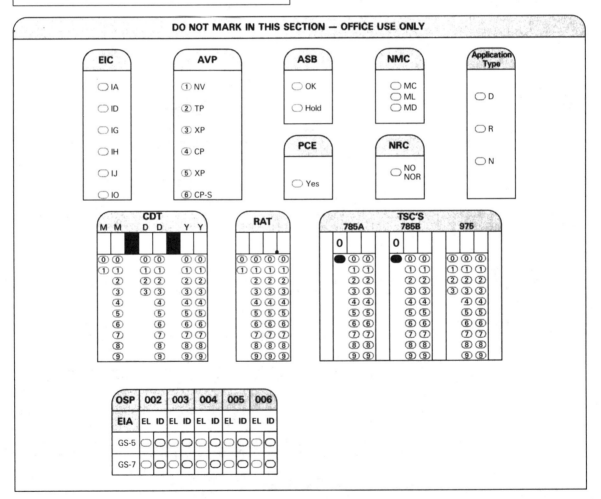

OPTIONAL QUESTIONS (COMPLETE ONLY AS DIRECTED)

PUBLIC BURDEN INFORMATION

The public reporting burden for completing this form is estimated to vary from 20 to 90 minutes with an average of 35 minutes. This estimate includes time for reviewing instructions, gathering data needed, and completing and reviewing entries. Send comments about the burden estimate or any other aspect of this form, including suggestions for reducing this burden to: Reports and Forms Management Officer, U.S. Office of Personnel Management, 1900 E Street, N.W. Room 6410, Washington, D.C. 20415; and to the Office of Management and Budget, Paperwork Reduction Project (3206-0040), Washington, D.C. 20503.

DO NOT MARK IN THIS SECTION — OFFICE USE ONLY

0163840

BATCH NUMBER
(BNO)
FOR OFFICE
USE ONLY

U.S. Office of Personnel Management

OCCUPATIONAL SUPPLEMENT FOR
WRITING and PUBLIC INFORMATION OCCUPATIONS (0001W)

FORM APPROVED
OMB NO. 3206-0040

FORM

B

USE **ONLY** A NUMBER 2 LEAD PENCIL.

DO NOT FOLD, STAPLE, TEAR OR PAPER CLIP THIS FORM.

This form can be processed only if you:
1) Submit an original form (no photocopies).
2) Completely blacken the oval corresponding to your response choice.
3) Completely erase any mistakes or stray marks.

1 **NAME**

NAME: _____
(Please Print)

INSTRUCTIONS AND EXAMPLES

Read the instructions for each item carefully before completing that item. Recording information that does not accurately reflect your availability, employment preferences, and qualifications may cause you to lose consideration for some jobs.

PRINT YOUR RESPONSE IN THE BOXES AND BLACKEN THE APPROPRIATE OVALS.

2

0	1	2	–	2	0

5
- ○ JAN
- ○ FEB
- ○ MAR
- ● APR
- ○ MAY
- ● This year
- ○ Next year

8
YES   NO
●   Ⓝ

2 **SOCIAL SECURITY NUMBER** (SSN)

3 **DATE OF BIRTH** (SDF)

MONTH	DAY	YEAR

4 **SEX**

Blacken the oval corresponding to your sex.

○ Male

○ Female

FOR STATISTICAL INFORMATION ONLY

5 **DATE AVAILABLE TO START WORK** (EBD)

- ○ JAN
- ○ FEB
- ○ MAR
- ○ APR
- ○ MAY
- ○ JUN — This year
- ○ JUL
- ○ AUG — Next year
- ○ SEP
- ○ OCT
- ○ NOV
- ○ DEC

6 **GRADE**

Blacken the oval of the lowest grade for which you wish to be considered. If you select GS-5 you will also be rated for GS-7.

○ GS-5

○ GS-7

7 **OPTIONS** (OSP)

Mark one or more options for which you wish to be considered by blackening the oval next to the option(s). You must select at least one option. **Note:** Those options with an asterisk (*) have specific qualification requirements which are defined in the Qualification Information Statement.

○ Agricultural Market Reporting* (002)

○ Archives Specialist (003)

○ General Arts and Information (004)
(Excluding Fine/Applied Arts.)

○ Public Affairs (005)

○ Technical Information Services* (006)

○ Technical Writing and Editing* (007)

○ Writing and Editing (008)

8 **EMPLOYMENT AVAILABILITY**

ARE YOU AVAILABLE FOR:

(Blacken YES or NO for **each** question)

	YES	NO	
A) full-time employment			
- 40 hours per week?	Ⓨ	Ⓝ	(FTE)
B) part-time employment of			
- 16 or fewer hours per week?	Ⓨ	Ⓝ	(PTE)
- 17 to 24 hours per week?	Ⓨ	Ⓝ	
- 25 to 32 hours per week?	Ⓨ	Ⓝ	
C) temporary employment lasting			
- 5 to 12 months?	Ⓨ	Ⓝ	(TMP)
- 1 to 4 months?	Ⓨ	Ⓝ	
- less than 1 month?	Ⓨ	Ⓝ	
D) jobs requiring travel away from home for			
- 1 to 5 nights per month?	Ⓨ	Ⓝ	(TRV)
- 6 to 10 nights per month?	Ⓨ	Ⓝ	
- 11 or more nights per month?	Ⓨ	Ⓝ	

★ U.S. GOVERNMENT PRINTING OFFICE:1989—262-449/00023

0055238

058

BATCH NUMBER
(BNO)
FOR OFFICE
USE ONLY

U.S. Office of Personnel Management

OCCUPATIONAL SUPPLEMENT FOR
BUSINESS, FINANCE and MANAGEMENT OCCUPATIONS (0001B)

FORM APPROVED
OMB NO. 3206-0040

FORM

B

USE **ONLY** A NUMBER 2 LEAD PENCIL.

DO NOT FOLD, STAPLE, TEAR OR PAPER CLIP THIS FORM.

This form can be processed only if you:
1) Submit an original form (no photocopies).
2) Completely blacken the oval corresponding to your response choice.
3) Completely erase any mistakes or stray marks.

1 **NAME**

NAME: _____
(Please Print)

INSTRUCTIONS AND EXAMPLES

Read the instructions for each item carefully before completing that item. Recording information that does not accurately reflect your availability, employment preferences, and qualifications may cause you to lose consideration for some jobs.

PRINT YOUR RESPONSE IN THE BOXES AND BLACKEN THE APPROPRIATE OVALS.

2 | 0 | 1 | 2 | - | 2 | 0 |

5
○ JAN
○ FEB
○ MAR
● APR
○ MAY
● This year
○ Next year

8
YES   NO
●   (N)

---

2 **SOCIAL SECURITY NUMBER** (SSN)

3 **DATE OF BIRTH** (SDF)
MONTH | DAY | YEAR

4 **SEX**
Blacken the oval corresponding to your sex.

○ Male

○ Female

FOR STATISTICAL INFORMATION ONLY

5 **DATE AVAILABLE TO START WORK** (EBD)
○ JAN
○ FEB
○ MAR
○ APR
○ MAY
○ JUN
○ JUL
○ AUG
○ SEP
○ OCT
○ NOV
○ DEC
○ This year
○ Next year

6 **GRADE**
Blacken the oval of the lowest grade for which you wish to be considered. If you select GS-5 you will also be rated for GS-7.

○ GS-5

○ GS-7

---

7 **OPTIONS** (OSP)

Mark one or more options (but not more than ten) for which you wish to be considered by blackening the oval next to the option(s). You must select at least one option. **Note:** Several of the options cover more than one position. Refer to the Qualification Information Statement (QIS) to identify positions covered by each option. Those options with an asterisk (*) have specific qualification requirements which are defined in the QIS.

○ Agricultural Programs* (002)
○ Business (003)
○ Communications Specialist* (004)
○ Contract Specialist* (005)
○ Financial Institution Examining* (006)
○ Finance* (007)
○ Industrial Programs* (008)
○ Supply (009)
○ Trade Specialist* (010)
○ Transportation* (011)
○ Unemployment Insurance* (012)

* U.S. GOVERNMENT PRINTING OFFICE:1989—262-449/00024

8 **EMPLOYMENT AVAILABILITY**

ARE YOU AVAILABLE FOR:
(Blacken YES or NO for **each** question)

A) full-time employment   YES   NO
- 40 hours per week?........................(Y)   (N) (FTE)

B) part-time employment of
- 16 or fewer hours per week?...........(Y)   (N) (PTE)
- 17 to 24 hours per week?...............(Y)   (N)
- 25 to 32 hours per week?...............(Y)   (N)

C) temporary employment lasting
- 5 to 12 months?...........................(Y)   (N) (TMP)
- 1 to 4 months?.............................(Y)   (N)
- less than 1 month?........................(Y)   (N)

D) jobs requiring travel away from home for
- 1 to 5 nights per month?................(Y)   (N) (TRV)
- 6 to 10 nights per month?..............(Y)   (N)
- 11 or more nights per month?..........(Y)   (N)

059

0107859

BATCH NUMBER
(BNO)

FOR OFFICE
USE ONLY

U.S. Office of Personnel Management

FORM APPROVED
OMB NO. 3206-0040

OCCUPATIONAL SUPPLEMENT FOR
PERSONNEL, ADMINISTRATION and
COMPUTER OCCUPATIONS (0001A)

FORM **B**

USE **ONLY** A NUMBER 2 LEAD PENCIL.

DO NOT FOLD, STAPLE, TEAR OR PAPER CLIP THIS FORM.

This form can be processed only if you:
1) Submit an original form (no photocopies).
2) Completely blacken the oval corresponding to your response choice.
3) Completely erase any mistakes or stray marks.

1   NAME

NAME: _____
(Please Print)

INSTRUCTIONS AND EXAMPLES

Read the instructions for each item carefully before completing that item. Recording information that does not accurately reflect your availability, employment preferences, and qualifications may cause you to lose consideration for some jobs.

PRINT YOUR RESPONSE IN THE BOXES AND BLACKEN THE APPROPRIATE OVALS.

2 `0 1 2 - 2 0`

5
- ○ JAN
- ○ FEB
- ○ MAR
- ● APR
- ○ MAY
- ● This year
- ○ Next year

8
YES   NO
●   (N)

---

2   SOCIAL SECURITY NUMBER   (SSN)

3   DATE OF BIRTH (SDF)

MONTH	DAY	YEAR

4   SEX

Blacken the oval corresponding to your sex.

○ Male

○ Female

FOR STATISTICAL INFORMATION ONLY

5   DATE (EBD) **AVAILABLE TO START WORK**

- ○ JAN
- ○ FEB
- ○ MAR
- ○ APR
- ○ MAY
- ○ JUN   This year
- ○ JUL
- ○ AUG   Next year
- ○ SEP
- ○ OCT
- ○ NOV
- ○ DEC

6   GRADE

Blacken the oval of the lowest grade for which you wish to be considered. If you select GS-5 you will also be rated for GS-7.

○ GS-5

○ GS-7

---

7   OPTIONS   (OSP)

Mark one or more options for which you wish to be considered by blackening the oval next to the option(s). <u>You must select at least one option.</u> **Note:** Several of the options cover more than one position. Refer to the Qualification Information Statement (QIS) to identify positions covered by each option. Those options with an asterisk (∗) have specific qualification requirements which are defined in the QIS.

○ Computer Specialist Trainee (002)
　(Does not require knowledge of computers.)

○ Personnel (003)

○ Administration (004)

○ Program Analysis (005)

○ Vocational Rehabilitation∗ (006)

8   EMPLOYMENT AVAILABILITY

ARE YOU AVAILABLE FOR: (Blacken YES or NO for **each** question)

A) full-time employment   YES   NO
　- 40 hours per week?.........................(Y)   (N)   (FTE)

B) part-time employment of
　- 16 or fewer hours per week?............(Y)   (N)   (PTE)
　- 17 to 24 hours per week?...............(Y)   (N)
　- 25 to 32 hours per week?...............(Y)   (N)

C) temporary employment lasting
　- 5 to 12 months?............................(Y)   (N)   (TMP)
　- 1 to 4 months?..............................(Y)   (N)
　- less than 1 month?........................(Y)   (N)

D) jobs requiring travel away from home for
　- 1 to 5 nights per month?................(Y)   (N)   (TRV)
　- 6 to 10 nights per month?..............(Y)   (N)
　- 11 or more nights per month?..........(Y)   (N)

★ U.S. GOVERNMENT PRINTING OFFICE:1990—262-449/00046

`0271894`

BATCH NUMBER
(BNO)

FOR OFFICE
USE ONLY

U.S. Office of Personnel Management

OCCUPATIONAL SUPPLEMENT FOR
BENEFITS REVIEW, TAX and LEGAL OCCUPATIONS (0001C)

FORM APPROVED
OMB NO. 3206-0040

FORM B

USE **ONLY** A NUMBER 2 LEAD PENCIL.

DO NOT FOLD, STAPLE, TEAR OR PAPER CLIP THIS FORM.

This form can be processed only if you:
1) Submit an original form (no photocopies).
2) Completely blacken the oval corresponding to your response choice.
3) Completely erase any mistakes or stray marks.

1 NAME

NAME: _____
(Please Print)

INSTRUCTIONS AND EXAMPLES

Read the instructions for each item carefully before completing that item. Recording information that does not accurately reflect your availability, employment preferences, and qualifications may cause you to lose consideration for some jobs.

PRINT YOUR RESPONSE IN THE BOXES AND BLACKEN THE APPROPRIATE OVALS.

2 0 1 2 - 2 0

5
○ JAN
○ FEB
○ MAR
● APR
○ MAY
● This year
○ Next year

8
YES   NO
●   Ⓝ

---

2 SOCIAL SECURITY NUMBER (SSN)

3 DATE OF BIRTH (SDF)
MONTH DAY YEAR

4 SEX

Blacken the oval corresponding to your sex.

○ Male

○ Female

FOR STATISTICAL INFORMATION ONLY

5 DATE AVAILABLE TO START WORK (EBD)
○ JAN
○ FEB
○ MAR
○ APR
○ MAY
○ JUN
○ JUL
○ AUG
○ SEP
○ OCT
○ NOV
○ DEC
This year
Next year

6 GRADE

Blacken the oval of the lowest grade for which you wish to be considered. If you select GS-5 you will also be rated for GS-7.

○ GS-5

○ GS-7

---

7 OPTIONS (OSP)

Mark one or more options for which you wish to be considered by blackening the oval next to the option(s). You must select at least one option. **Note:** Several of the options cover more than one position. Refer to the Qualification Information Statement (QIS) to identify positions covered by each option. Those options with an asterisk (*) have specific qualification requirements which are defined in the QIS.

○ Claims Examining (002)

○ Land Law Examining* (003)

○ Paralagal Specialist (004)

○ Social Insurance Administration and Social Insurance Claims Examining (005)

○ Social Services (006)

○ Tax Law Specialist* (007)

○ Tax Technician (008)

8 EMPLOYMENT AVAILABILITY

ARE YOU AVAILABLE FOR: (Blacken YES or NO for **each** question)

A) full-time employment
   - 40 hours per week?......................... Ⓨ   Ⓝ (FTE)

B) part-time employment of
   - 16 or fewer hours per week?............ Ⓨ   Ⓝ (PTE)
   - 17 to 24 hours per week?................ Ⓨ   Ⓝ
   - 25 to 32 hours per week?................ Ⓨ   Ⓝ

C) temporary employment lasting
   - 5 to 12 months?........................... Ⓨ   Ⓝ (TMP)
   - 1 to 4 months?............................. Ⓨ   Ⓝ
   - less than 1 month?........................ Ⓨ   Ⓝ

D) jobs requiring travel away from home for
   - 1 to 5 nights per month?................. Ⓨ   Ⓝ (TRV)
   - 6 to 10 nights per month?............... Ⓨ   Ⓝ
   - 11 or more nights per month?........... Ⓨ   Ⓝ

★ U.S. GOVERNMENT PRINTING OFFICE:1990—262-449/00045

0260874

061

BATCH NUMBER
(BNO)

FOR OFFICE
USE ONLY

U.S. Office of Personnel Management

OCCUPATIONAL SUPPLEMENT FOR
LAW ENFORCEMENT and INVESTIGATION OCCUPATIONS (0001L)

FORM APPROVED
OMB NO. 3206-0040

FORM
B

USE **ONLY** A NUMBER 2 LEAD PENCIL.

DO NOT FOLD, STAPLE, TEAR OR PAPER CLIP THIS FORM.

This form can be processed only if you:
1) Submit an original form (no photocopies).
2) Completely blacken the oval corresponding to your response choice.
3) Completely erase any mistakes or stray marks.

1   **NAME**

NAME: _____
(Please Print)

INSTRUCTIONS AND EXAMPLES

Read the instructions for each item carefully before completing that item. Recording information that does not accurately reflect your availability, employment preferences, and qualifications may cause you to lose consideration for some jobs.

PRINT YOUR RESPONSE IN THE BOXES AND BLACKEN THE APPROPRIATE OVALS.

2 `012-20`

5
○ JAN
○ FEB
○ MAR
● APR
○ MAY
● This year
○ Next year

8
YES   NO
●   Ⓝ

2 **SOCIAL SECURITY NUMBER** (SSN)

3 **DATE OF BIRTH** (SDF)
MONTH DAY YEAR

4 **SEX**
Blacken the oval corresponding to your sex.

○ Male

○ Female

FOR STATISTICAL INFORMATION ONLY

5 **DATE AVAILABLE TO START WORK** (EBD)
○ JAN
○ FEB
○ MAR
○ APR
○ MAY
○ JUN   ○ This year
○ JUL
○ AUG   ○ Next year
○ SEP
○ OCT
○ NOV
○ DEC

6 **GRADE**
Blacken the oval of the lowest grade for which you wish to be considered. If you select GS-5 you will also be rated for GS-7.

○ GS-5

○ GS-7

7 **OPTIONS** (OSP)

Mark one or more options (but not more than ten) for which you wish to be considered by blackening the oval next to the option(s). You must select at least one option. **Note:** One of the options covers more than one position. Refer to the Qualification Information Statement (QIS) to identify positions covered by each option. Those options with an asterisk (∗) have specific qualification requirements which are defined in the QIS.

○ Alcohol, Tobacco and Firearms Inspection (002)
○ Civil Aviation Security Specialist (003)
○ Criminal Investigator (004)
○ Customs Inspector (005)
○ Game Law Enforcement (006)
○ General Investigator (007)
○ Immigration Inspection (008)
○ Internal Revenue Officer (009)
○ Import Specialist and Security (010)
○ Park Ranger∗ (011)
○ Public Health Quarantine Inspection∗ (012)
○ Securities Compliance Examining∗ (013)
○ Wage and Hour Compliance (014)

8 **EMPLOYMENT AVAILABILITY**

ARE YOU AVAILABLE FOR: (Blacken YES or NO for **each** question)

A) full-time employment   YES   NO
   - 40 hours per week?.................Ⓨ   Ⓝ   (FTE)

B) part-time employment of
   - 16 or fewer hours per week?............Ⓨ   Ⓝ   (PTE)
   - 17 to 24 hours per week?...............Ⓨ   Ⓝ
   - 25 to 32 hours per week?...............Ⓨ   Ⓝ

C) temporary employment lasting
   - 5 to 12 months?.....................Ⓨ   Ⓝ   (TMP)
   - 1 to 4 months?......................Ⓨ   Ⓝ
   - less than 1 month?..................Ⓨ   Ⓝ

D) jobs requiring travel away from home for
   - 1 to 5 nights per month?................Ⓨ   Ⓝ   (TRV)
   - 6 to 10 nights per month?...............Ⓨ   Ⓝ
   - 11 or more nights per month?...........Ⓨ   Ⓝ

∗ U.S. GOVERNMENT PRINTING OFFICE:1989—262-449/00027

062

`0004618`

APPLICANT RACE AND NATIONAL ORIGIN QUESTIONNAIRE

The United States District Court for the District of Columbia, in a decree approved in a lawsuit entitled Luevano v. Newman, Civil Action No. 79-0271, has ordered that Federal Government agencies provide data on the race and national origin of applicants for certain Federal occupations. The position for which you are applying is in one of those occupations.

The collection of this information is authorized for use by the Office of Personnel Management only for the purposes of complying with the requirements of the Luevano v. Newman Decree. The data you supply will be used for statistical analysis pursuant to the requirements of the lawsuit, and will not be shared with employing agencies.

You are requested to complete the following, however, submission of this information is voluntary. Your failure to do so will have no effect on the processing of your application for Federal employment.

PRIMARY GEOGRAPHIC ZONE

Blacken the oval next to the one Zone which includes your first choice for location of employment. This designation is for statistical use only and will not affect your actual consideration for employment. Your geographic area of consideration will be determined by your entries in item 17, GEOGRAPHIC AVAILABILITY. Please mark only one oval.

○ **ATLANTA**	○ **CHICAGO**	○ **DALLAS**	○ **PHILADELPHIA**	○ **SAN FRANCISCO**
Alabama	Illinois	Arizona	Connecticut	California
Florida	Indiana	Arkansas	Delaware	Idaho
Georgia	Iowa	Colorado	Maine	Nevada
Mississippi	Kansas	Louisiana	Maryland	Oregon
North Carolina	Kentucky	Montana	Massachusetts	Washington
South Carolina	Michigan	New Mexico	New Hampshire	
Tennessee	Minnesota	Oklahoma	New Jersey	
Virginia	Missouri	Texas	New York	
	Nebraska	Utah	Pennsylvania	
	North Dakota	Wyoming	Rhode Island	
	Ohio		Vermont	
	South Dakota			
	West Virginia			
	Wisconsin			

○ **ALASKA**	○ **CARIBBEAN**	○ **HAWAII**
State of Alaska	Puerto Rico and	State of Hawaii and
	the Virgin Islands	Pacific overseas area

○ **WASHINGTON DC:** **Washington DC Metropolitan Area** (Charles, Montgomery, and Prince George's Counties in Maryland; Arlington, Fairfax, Prince William, King George, Stafford and Loudoun Counties and Falls Church, Alexandria, and Fairfax cities in Virginia) and **Atlantic overseas area** (African, European, Middle Eastern, Central and South American countries).

RACE AND/OR NATIONAL ORIGIN

The categories below provide descriptions of race and national origins. Read the Definition of Category descriptions and then blacken the oval next to the category with which you identify yourself. If you are of mixed race and/or national origin, select the category with which you most closely identify yourself. Please mark only one oval.

Name of Category	Definition of Category
○ American Indian or Alaskan Native	A person having origins in any of the original peoples of North America, and who maintains cultural identification through community recognition or tribal affiliation.
○ Asian or Pacific Islander	A person having origins in any of the original peoples of the Far East, Southeast Asia, the Indian subcontinent, or the Pacific Islands. For example, this area includes China, India, Japan, Korea, the Philippine Islands, and Samoa.
○ Black, not of Hispanic origin	A person having origins in any of the black racial groups of Africa. This does not include persons of Mexican, Puerto Rican, Cuban, Central or South American, or other Spanish cultures or origins.
○ Hispanic	A person of Mexican, Puerto Rican, Cuban, Central or South American, or other Spanish cultures or origins. This does not include persons of Portuguese culture or origin.
○ White, not of Hispanic origin	A person having origins in any of the original peoples of Europe, North America, or the Middle East. This does not include persons of Mexican, Puerto Rican, Cuban, Central or South American, or other Spanish cultures or origins.
○ Other	A person not included in another category.

Type or Print in Ink

1. Title of Examination

2. Social Security Number

3. Announcement No. (If appropriate)

4. Where do you wish to take written test?
City   State

5. Birth Date
(month) (day) (year)

6. Telephone No. (Include Area Code)

7. Where are you willing to work?
City: State:

8. If you have performed active duty in the armed forces of the United States and were separated under honorable conditions, indicate periods of service:
From: (month, day, year)   To: (month, day, year)

9. ☐ Check here if you observe the Sabbath or religious holiday on a day other than Sunday (specify day) or have a disability that will require special or individual testing arrangement. Specify the nature and degree of your disability and the special arrangements you will need.

10. Do you claim veteran preference? ☐ No ☐ Yes   If yes, based on:
☐ (1) Active duty in the armed forces of the U.S. during the period December 7, 1941, through July 1, 1955, (2) more than 180 consecutive days of active duty (other than for training) in the armed forces of the U.S. any part of which occurred after January 31, 1955 and before October 15, 1976, or (3) after service in a campaign for which a campaign badge has been authorized.
☐ Your status as: (1) a disabled veteran or a veteran who was awarded the Purple Heart for wounds or injuries received in action, (2) a spouse of a deceased veteran who has not remarried, (3) the spouse of a veteran who has a service-connected disability which disqualifies the veteran for civil service appointment, or (4) the widowed, divorced or separated mother of an ex-service son or daughter who died in action or who is totally and permanently disabled.

11. Are you a United States citizen? ☐ YES ☐ NO

DO NOT WRITE IN THIS SPACE

Examining Point No.

Give Address Where You Wish To Be Notified of Time and Place For Examination

Name (First, middle and last)

Address (Number and street, or R.D., or post office box no.)

City, state and Zip Code (ZIP Code must be included)

CHECK COPY TO BE SURE IT IS LEGIBLE

IMPORTANT — READ INSTRUCTIONS ON THE OTHER SIDE
IDENTIFICATION MAY BE REQUIRED FOR WRITTEN EXAMINATIONS
The Federal Government Is An Equal Opportunity Employer

ADMISSION NOTICE

This card will be returned to you. Bring it with you when you report for the written test.

OPM Form 5000-B (Rev. 10-80)

Type or Print in Ink

1. Title of Examination

2. Social Security Number

3. Announcement No. (If appropriate)

4. Where do you wish to take written test?
City   State

5. Birth Date
(month) (day) (year)

6. Telephone No. (Include Area Code)

7. Where are you willing to work?
City: State:

8. If you have performed active duty in the armed forces of the United States and were separated under honorable conditions, indicate periods of service:
From: (month, day, year)   To: (month, day, year)

9. ☐ Check here if you observe the Sabbath or religious holiday on a day other than Sunday (specify day) or have a disability that will require special or individual testing arrangement. Specify the nature and degree of your disability and the special arrangements you will need.

10. Do you claim veteran preference? ☐ No ☐ Yes   If yes, based on:
☐ (1) Active duty in the armed forces of the U.S. during the period December 7, 1941, through July 1, 1955, (2) more than 180 consecutive days of active duty (other than for training) in the armed forces of the U.S. any part of which occurred after January 31, 1955 and before October 15, 1976, or (3) after service in a campaign for which a campaign badge has been authorized.
☐ Your status as: (1) a disabled veteran or a veteran who was awarded the Purple Heart for wounds or injuries received in action, (2) a spouse of a deceased veteran who has not remarried, (3) the spouse of a veteran who has a service-connected disability which disqualifies the veteran for civil service appointment, or (4) the widowed, divorced or separated mother of an ex-service son or daughter who died in action or who is totally and permanently disabled.

11. Are you a United States citizen? ☐ YES ☐ NO

DO NOT WRITE IN THIS SPACE

Examining Point No.

Give Address Where You Wish To Be Notified of Time and Place For Examination

Name (First, middle and last)

Address (Number and street, or R.D., or post office box no.)

City, state and Zip Code (ZIP Code must be included)

CHECK COPY TO BE SURE IT IS LEGIBLE

IMPORTANT — READ INSTRUCTIONS ON THE OTHER SIDE
IDENTIFICATION MAY BE REQUIRED FOR WRITTEN EXAMINATIONS
The Federal Government Is An Equal Opportunity Employer

RECORD COPY

This card will be returned to you. Bring it with you when you report for the written test.

OPM Form 5000-A (Rev. 10-80)

SUPPLEMENTAL QUALIFICATIONS STATEMENT
LIST OF COLLEGE COURSES AND CERTIFICATE OF SCHOLASTIC ACHIEVEMENT

Complete and submit this Form with your Application for Federal Employment or as instructed.

Form Approved
OMB No. 3206-0038

1. Name (Last, First, M.I.)	2. Birth date (Month, day, year)	3. Social Security Number

4. Position for which you are applying (Include options, if any)

5. List the undergraduate and/or graduate college degrees you have received or expect to receive (Give name of degree, name of college or university granting degree, and date received or to be received)

6. State your major undergraduate course(s) of study	6a. State your major graduate course(s) of study

PART I — COLLEGE COURSES

List below by appropriate academic field (e.g., biology, mechanical engineering, economics, sociology, etc.) all courses you have taken (including those failed) which appear to satisfy the qualification requirements of positions for which you are applying. List graduate and undergraduate courses separately. Credits for each category should be totaled to determine if you meet the minimum course requirements.

Indicate academic field:

Indicate academic field:

DESCRIPTIVE TITLE	COMPLE-TION DATE	GRADE	CREDIT HOURS			DESCRIPTIVE TITLE	COMPLE-TION DATE	GRADE	CREDIT HOURS		
			SEM.	QTR.	CLASS ROOM				SEM.	QTR.	CLASS ROOM
TOTAL						TOTAL					

U.S. Office of Personnel Management

OPM 1170/17 (Rev. 4/90)

(2)

Indicate academic field:

DESCRIPTIVE TITLE	COMPLE-TION DATE	GRADE	CREDIT HOURS		
			SEM	QTR	CLASS ROOM
TOTAL					

Indicate academic field:

DESCRIPTIVE TITLE	COMPLE-TION DATE	GRADE	CREDIT HOURS		
			SEM	QTR	CLASS ROOM
TOTAL					

Indicate academic field:

DESCRIPTIVE TITLE	COMPLE-TION DATE	GRADE	CREDIT HOURS		
			SEM.	QTR	CLASS ROOM
TOTAL					

Indicate academic field:

DESCRIPTIVE TITLE	COMPLE-TION DATE	GRADE	CREDIT HOURS		
			SEM	QTR	CLASS ROOM
TOTAL					

MISCELLANEOUS COURSES

DESCRIPTIVE TITLE	COMPLE-TION DATE	GRADE	CREDIT HOURS			DESCRIPTIVE TITLE	COMPLE-TION DATE	GRADE	CREDIT HOURS		
			SEM.	QTR.	CLASS ROOM				SEM.	QTR.	CLASS ROOM
TOTAL						TOTAL					

PART II – PRIVACY ACT STATEMENT AND CERTIFICATION

The Office of Personnel Management is authorized by section 1302 of Chapter 13 (Special Authority) and sections 3301 and 3304 of Chapter 33 (Examination, Certification, and Appointment) of Title 5 of the U.S. Code to collect the information on this form.

Executive Order 9397 (Numbering System for Federal Accounts Relating to Individual Persons) authorizes the collection of your Social Security Number (SSN). Your SSN is used to identify this form with your basic application. It may be used for the same purposes as stated on the application.

The information you provide will be used primarily to determine your qualifications for Federal employment. Other possible uses or disclosures of the information are:

1. To make requests for information about you from any source; (e.g., former employers or schools), that would assist an agency in determining whether to hire you;

2. To refer your application to prospective Federal employers and, with your consent, to others (e.g., State and local governments) for possible employment;

3. To a Federal, State, or local agency for checking on violations of law or other lawful purposes in connection with hiring or retaining you on the job, or issuing you a security clearance;

4. To the courts when the Government is party to a suit; and

5. When lawfully required by Congress, the Office of Management and Budget, or the General Services Administration.

Providing the information requested on this form, including your SSN, is voluntary. However, failure to do so may result in your not receiving an accurate rating, which may hinder your chances for obtaining Federal employment.

ATTENTION — THIS STATEMENT MUST BE SIGNED
Read the following paragraph carefully before signing this Statement

A false answer to any question in this Statement may be grounds for not employing you, or for dismissing you after you begin work, and may be punishable by fine or imprisonment (U.S. Code, Title 18, Sec. 1001). All statements are subject to investigation, including a check of your fingerprints, police records, and former employers. All the information you give will be considered in reviewing your Statement and is subject to investigation.

CERTIFICATION	Signature *(Sign in ink)*	Date Signed
I CERTIFY that all of the statements made in this Statement are true, complete, and correct to the best of my knowledge and belief, and are made in good faith.		

COMPLETE PART III ON THE NEXT PAGE IF YOU
CLAIM SUPERIOR ACADEMIC ACHIEVEMENT

(4)

PART III - SCHOLASTIC ACHIEVEMENT

NOTE: This part is for the use of college students and graduates who may qualify for some GS-7 positions on the basis of undergraduate scholastic achievement, as provided in an open job announcement. *See the appropriate job announcement for complete requirements.* Proof of scholastic achievement under one of these provisions should not be submitted with your application, but will be required by the hiring agency at the time of appointment. If you do not wish to qualify on this basis or if you do not meet the scholastic requirements for the position, do not complete this part. In any case, YOU MUST SIGN YOUR NAME AFTER THE CERTIFICATION STATEMENT AT THE BOTTOM OF PAGE 3.

A. **COLLEGE OR CLASS STANDING.** Must be in upper third of your graduating class in the college or university, or major subdivision such as School of Engineering, School of Business Administration, etc.

NUMBER IN CLASS _____   YOUR STANDING _____

Proof of class standing should be in the form of a statement in writing from the institution's registrar, the dean of your course of study, or other appropriate official. This statement of class standing must be based on a suitable measure of your academic performance, such as the results of a comprehensive examination or an overall faculty assessment, and must indicate the basis of the judgment. Class standing must be based on your standing in your college or university or the first major subdivision (e.g., the School of Business Administration, the College of Arts and Sciences, etc.). Subdivisions below this level, i.e., a single academic department within a large university, such as the English Department or the Accounting Department, are not recognized as major subdivisions for this purpose.

B. **COLLEGE-GRADE POINT AVERAGE.** Your grade-point average (GPA) should be recorded in the manner that is most beneficial to you, using one of methods below. Your grade-point average must be expressed in terms of a value on a 4.0 scale based on 4 years, the last 2 years, or courses completed in the major field of study.* If computing your GPA, indicate the method used and period covered by checking the appropriate boxes in item 2 *and* in item 3 below, and compute your average in the space provided below on this page.

1. GPA as recorded on final transcript _____ (Transcript must cover *at least* the last 2 years)

2. (Check One) ☐ Average of undergraduate courses ☐ Average in major field of study

3. (Check One) ☐ At time of filing * ☐ All 4 years ☐ Last 2 years

* You may be rated provisionally eligible if you are a senior student, provided you have the required average in the junior year. You will be required to submit evidence at the time of appointment that you maintained the required average during your senior year.

In computing your grade-point average, round to the first decimal place, (e.g., 2.95 = 3.0 , 2.94 = 2.9, 3.45 = 3.5, etc.). If your college uses a different system, explain below, or on an attachment, how it compares with the grade-point average on a 4.0 scale:

If more than 10 percent of your courses were graded on a pass/fail or similar system rather than on a traditional grading system, you can usually claim credit under the scholastic achievement provision based only on class standing or membership in a national honor society. The exception is if you can document that only your freshman-year courses (25 percent or less of your total credit) were credited on a pass/fail or similar system.

NO. OF SEMESTER OR QUARTER HOURS AT 4.0 ("A") _____	X	4	=	_____
NO. OF SEMESTER OR QUARTER HOURS AT 3.0 ("B") _____	X	3	=	_____
NO. OF SEMESTER OR QUARTER HOURS AT 2.0 ("C") _____	X	2	=	_____
NO. OF SEMESTER OR QUARTER HOURS AT 1.0 ("D") _____	X	1	=	_____
NO. OF SEMESTER OR QUARTER HOURS AT 0.0 ("F") _____	X	0	=	_____

TOTAL (1) _____   TOTAL (2) _____

COMPUTED GRADE-POINT AVERAGE _____
Total (2) divided by Total (1)

C. **HONOR SOCIETY MEMBERSHIP.** Must be one of the national scholastic honor societies meeting the minimum requirements of the Association of College Honor Societies (other than freshman scholarship honor societies).

Name of honor society and date you were elected to membership. _____

*U.S. GPO:1990-277-627/20039

SUPPLEMENTAL QUALIFICATIONS STATEMENT

FOR

SECRETARY, GS-5, 6, 7, 8

NAME (last, first, middle)	Date of Birth	Social Security No.

Instructions: For each section below, follow the specific directions given. The information you provide will be used in conjunction with the experience shown in your Personal Qualifications Statement (SF-171) to determine your eligibility and to rank you. No credit will be given for any experience claimed on this form unless it is demonstrated by the employment history shown in your application (SF-171). You will be evaluated on elements A through F below.

ELEMENT A: ABILITY TO ORGANIZE EFFECTIVELY THE FLOW OF CLERICAL PROCESSES IN AN OFFICE.

Directions: First review all of the items listed below. After reviewing them, select the one that best describes your skill and experience, and place a check mark next to it. DO NOT CHECK MORE THAN ONE. DO NOT place a check mark next to any item if you have not performed such duties. Read carefully before making a decision.

1. ( )   Receive work and complete assignments as directed by supervisor or other staff members.

2. ( )   Teach or advise lower level clerical staff in procedural matters such as the correct steps to follow in preparing correspondence, ordering office supplies, etc.

3. ( )   Screen incoming work, determine which must be handled personally and refer the remainder to appropriate employees for action.

4. ( )   Notify lower level secretaries, or other staff members of administrative and procedural requirements and instructions, and shift subordinate clerical staff around to meet temporary fluctuations in workload.

5. ( )   Organize work assignments on own and set priorities based on knowledge of organization.

6. ( )   Distribute work to other employees to more effectively deal with fluctuating workload and set priorities for day-to-day workflow.

7. ( )   Perform all typing work for supervisor and others.

List the jobs from your SF-171 where you performed the duty checked above.

ELEMENT B: ABILITY TO ORGANIZE AND DESIGN A FILING SYSTEM

Directions: First review all of the items listed below. After reviewing them, select the one that best describes your skill and experience, and place a check mark next it. DO NOT CHECK MORE THAN ONE. DO NOT place a check mark next to any item if you have not performed such duties. Read each item carefully before making a decision.

1. ( )   File correspondence, records, and reports. Receive and file changes to publications or other office manuals or working documents.

2. ( )   Place correspondence or other work in files.

3. ( )   Revise old and design new filing systems as needed, based on changes or new requirements within the organization.

4. ( )   Revise old or design new filing systems as needed, based on changes or new requirements within the organization.

5. ( )   Maintain records and files related to the operations, programs, and activities of the organization. Follow established procedures for the maintenance of records and files. Insure that files contain all required documents.

6. ( )   Maintain files related to the operations, programs, and activities of the organization following established procedures for the maintenance of files and records.

7. ( )   Place phone calls to obtain information from other offices.

List the jobs from your SF-171 where you performed the duty checked above.

ELEMENT C: ABILITY TO MAKE ARRANGEMENTS FOR SUCH THINGS AS TRAVEL, CONFERENCES, AND MEETINGS.

Directions: First review all of the items listed below. After reviewing them, select the one that best describes your skill and experience, and place a check mark next to it. DO NOT CHECK MORE THAN ONE. DO NOT place a check mark next to any item if you have not performed such duties. Read each item carefully before making a decision.

1. ( )   Make hotel or airline reservations.

2. ( )   Make travel arrangements including hotel and airline reservations.

3. ( )   Make extensive travel arrangements and set up conferences, and meetings. Obtain travel and hotel reservations, prepare travel vouchers and/or reports from travelers' records.

4. ( )   Set up appointments for supervisor.

5. ( )   Type reports and other data for distribution at conferences and meetings.

6. ( )   Make arrangements for conferences and meetings.

7. ( )   Make arrangements for conferences and staff meetings.

List the jobs from your SF-171 where you performed the duty checked above.

ELEMENT D: **ABILITY TO LOCATE AND ASSEMBLE INFORMATION FOR VARIOUS REPORTS, BRIEFINGS, AND CONFERENCES.**

Directions: First review all of the items listed below. After reviewing them, select the one that best describes your skill and experience and place a check mark next to it. DO NOT CHECK MORE THAN ONE. DO NOT place a check mark next to any item if you have not performed such duties. Read each item carefully before making a decision.

1. ( )   Upon request, obtain readily available routine and non-technical information, such as status of reports, suspense dates, etc., from file.

2. ( )   Obtain needed information from files or other records and summarize for those requesting the information.

3. ( )   Type reports from rough drafts.

4. ( )   Return files to file cabinets.

5. ( )   Gather material from a variety of sources, such as files, records, other employees, in order to prepare reports, briefings, or conference data.

6. ( )   Arrange for submission of data by other employees and assemble the material.

7. ( )   Type simple forms, labels, addresses, bills, or other simple data.

List the jobs from your SF-171 where you performed the duty checked above.

ELEMENT E: **ABILITY TO COMPOSE NON-TECHNICAL CORRESPONDENCE**

Directions: First review all of the items listed below. After reviewing them, select the one that best describes your skill and experience and place a check mark next to it. DO NOT CHECK MORE THAN ONE. DO NOT place a check mark next to any item if you have not performed such duties. Read each item carefully before making a decision.

1. ( )   On own initiative compose correspondence - e.g., letters of acknowledgement, letters on administrative matters, letters regarding general office policies, etc., -- or write narrative reports or have comparable writing experience.

2. ( )   Prepare drafts of routine correspondence as outlined in regulations and procedures or specifically requested by supervisor. Work must be reviewed and approved by supervisor prior to sending out.

3. ( )   Review correspondence written by others for spelling, typographical errors, errors in grammar, and conformance to format or procedural requirements.

4. ( )   Compose correspondence on administrative support or clerical functions of the office. Compose routine correspondence on other subjects as outlined in regulations or office procedures, or specifically requested by supervisor.

5. ( )   Compose routine correspondence after receiving specific instructions from supervisor on what to say.

6. ( )   Screen incoming correspondence and distribute to proper personnel.

7. ( )   Type letters for supervisor or other staff members. Review own typing when complete for errors in spelling, typing, and conformance to format before turning in to originator for signature.

List the jobs from your SF-171 where you performed the duty checked above.

ELEMENT F: **ABILITY TO PERFORM A VARIETY OF MISCELLANEOUS OFFICE DUTIES**

Directions: PLACE A CHECK MARK NEXT TO ANY ITEMS BELOW WHICH DESCRIBE YOUR EXPERIENCE. (IF YOUR BACKGROUND INCLUDES ALL, CHECK ALL; IF IT DOES NOT INCLUDE ANY, DO NOT CHECK ANY; IF IT INCLUDES ONE OR TWO OF THE ITEMS, PLACE THE CHECK MARK NEXT TO THE ONES THAT APPLY TO YOUR EXPERIENCE, ETC.)

1. ( )   Order office equipment, supplies, publications, manuals, maintenance services, etc.

2. ( )   Answer and refer phone calls.

3. ( )   Receive and refer visitors.

4. ( )   Distribute and/or control mail or distribute and/or control any other variety of incoming work.

5. ( )   Maintain employee leave (time and attendance) records, or other records that require mathematical computations or the collection of statistical data, or any other comparable type of records.

6. ( )   Practice accurate spelling and good grammar and punctuation in everyday work.

<u>List the jobs from your SF-171 where you performed any duty checked above.</u>

- Continued -

GS-318

-6-

AUTHORITY

This information is provided pursuant to Public Law 93-579 (Privacy Act of 1974), December 31, 1974, for individuals completing Federal employment application forms. Sections 1302, 3301, and 3304 of Title 5 of the United States Code give the U. S. Civil Service Commission the authority to recruit, examine, and evaluate applicants' qualifications for employment in the Federal service. Use of the employment application forms is necessary for performing these functions.

PURPOSES AND USES

The principal purpose of employment application forms is to collect information needed to determine qualifications, suitability, and availability of applicants for Federal employment and of current Federal employees for reassignment, reinstatement, transfer, or promotion. Your completed application may be used to examine, rate, and/or assess your qualifications; to determine if you are entitled under certain laws and regulations such as Veterans Preference, and restrictions based on citizenship, members of family already employed, and residence requirements; and to contact you concerning availability and/or for an interview. All or part of your completed Federal employment application form may be disclosed outside the U. S. Civil Service Commission to:

1. Federal agencies upon request for a list of eligibles to consider for appointment, reassignment, reinstatement, transfer, or promotion.

2. State and local government agencies, congressional offices, public international organizations, and other public offices, if you have indicated availability for such employment consideration.

3. Federal agency investigators to determine your suitability for Federal employment.

4. Federal, State, or local agencies to create other personnel records after you have been appointed.

5. Appropriate Federal, State, or local law enforcement agencies charged with the responsibility of investigating a violation or potential violation of the law.

6. Appropriate Federal, State, or local agencies maintaining records on you to obtain information relevant to an agency decision about you.

7. A requesting Federal, State, or local agency to the extent the information is relevant to the requesting agency's decision.

8. Federal agency selecting officials involved with internal personnel management functions.

9. Your college or university placement offices if you are appointed to a career position in some occupations at certain grade levels.

10. Anyone requesting statistical information (without your personal identification) under the Freedom of Information Act.

11. A congressional office in response to an inquiry from the congressional office made at your request.

EFFECTS OF NONDISCLOSURE

Because the employment application forms request both optional (other skills, training, etc.) and mandatory (qualifications and biographical, etc.) data, it is in your best interest to answer all questions. Omission of an item means you might not receive full consideration for a position in which this information is needed.

INFORMATION REGARDING DISCLOSURE OF YOUR SOCIAL SECURITY NUMBER
UNDER PUBLIC LAW 93-579, SECTION 7(b)

Disclosure by you of your Social Security Number (SSN) is mandatory to obtain the services, benefits, or processes that you are seeking. Solicitation of the SSN by the United States Civil Service Commission is authorized under provisions of Executive Order 9397, dated November 22, 1943. The SSN is used as an identifier throughout your Federal career from the time of application through retirement. It will be used primarily to identify your records that you file with the Civil Service Commission or agencies. The SSN also will be used by the Civil Service Commission and other Federal agencies in connection with lawful requests for information about you from your former employers, educational institutions, and financial or other organizations. The information gathered through the use of the number will be used only as necessary in personnel administration processes carried out in accordance with established regulations and published notices of systems and records. The SSN also will be used for the selection of persons to be included in statistical studies of personnel management matters. The use of the SSN is made necessary because of the large number of present and former Federal employees and applicants who have identical names and birth dates, and whose identities can only be distinguished by the SSN.

ATTENTION — THIS STATEMENT MUST BE SIGNED
Read the following paragraph carefully before signing this Statement

A false answer to any question in this Statement may be grounds for not employing you, or for dismissing you after you begin work, and may be punishable by fine or imprisonment (U.S. Code, Title 18, Sec. 1001). All statements are subject to investigation, including a check of your fingerprints, police records, and former employers. All the information you give will be considered in reviewing your Statement and is subject to investigation.

CERTIFICATION I CERTIFY that all of the statements made in this Statement are true, complete, and correct to the best of my knowledge and belief, and are made in good faith.	SIGNATURE (Sign in ink)	DATE SIGNED

(February 1990)

GS-610

U.S. OFFICE OF PERSONNEL MANAGEMENT

SUPPLEMENTAL QUALIFICATIONS STATEMENT FOR PROFESSIONAL NURSING POSITIONS, GS-4/12

Form Approved
OMB No. 3206-XXX

Name (Last, First, MI)	Social Security Number	Date of Birth (Month, Day, Year)

The following questions are designed to assess your qualifications for the specialties and grades you apply for and to determine your rating. Read Announcement No. 419 and all of the questions on this form to gain a better understanding of the kind of information we are looking for. You may find it helpful to complete your narrative application forms first, and then refer to them in completing this form. Answer the questions carefully and accurately. Indicate your response by checking the appropriate columns or boxes.

1. Occupational Specialty and Grade

Indicate the nursing specialties and the grade levels for which you wish to be considered by marking the appropriate columns to the right. For each specialty you choose, mark the column corresponding to the lowest grade you will accept for which you are qualified. Note that the specialties occur only at the higher grades and that all nursing jobs at the GS-4 and GS-5 grade levels are classified as General Nurse.

Refer to Announcement No. 419 for descriptions of the occupational specialties and of the qualification requirements.

OCCUPATIONAL SPECIALTY	GS-4	GS-5	GS-7	GS-9	GS-11	GS-12
A. General Nurse						
B. Clinical Nurse						
C. Community Health Nurse						
D. Operating Room Nurse						
E. Occupational Health Nurse						
F. Psychiatric Nurse						
G. Nurse Anesthetist						
H. Nurse Midwife						
I. Nurse Practitioner						
J. Nurse Educator, Consultant, Specialist, or Researcher						

2. Basic Nursing Preparation

Refer to Announcement No. 419 for an explanation of the basic requirements. Indicate the basic requirement provision(s) you meet or will meet in the next nine months, if you are currently enrolled in a school of nursing.

A. Bachelor's or higher degree from an accredited school of nursing.   A. ☐
B. Graduation from a State-approved diploma program of 30 months or more.   B. ☐
C. Associate degree from an accredited school of nursing.   C. ☐
D. Graduation from a State-approved diploma program of less than 30 months.   D. ☐
E. Military corpsman experience which has been accepted by a State board of nursing registration.   E. ☐

3. Superior Academic Achievement

The announcement explains how you may qualify for GS-7 under the Superior Academic Achievement provision. If you have a Bachelor's Degree in nursing and qualify under this provision, check the box which indicates the provisions you meet. YOU MUST SUPPORT YOUR CLAIM ON YOUR TRANSCRIPT OR COLLEGE COURSE LIST.

A. GPA of 2.90—all undergraduate courses.   A. ☐
B. GPA of 2.90—last 2 years of undergraduate study.   B. ☐
C. GPA of 3.50—all nursing courses.   C. ☐
D. GPA of 3.50—all nursing courses in last 2 years.   D. ☐
E. Rank in upper third of graduating class.   E. ☐
F. Membership in scholastic honorary society   F. ☐

4. Undergraduate Grade Point Average

If you are applying for the GS-4 or -5 grade level, indicate your grade point average for all courses in your basic nursing degree shown in Item 2. Your College Course List must substantiate your claimed grade point average.

A. 2.49 or lower GPA   A. ☐
B. 2.50 to 2.99 GPA   B. ☐
C. 3.00 to 3.49 GPA   C. ☐
D. 3.50 to 4.00 GPA   D. ☐

5. Professional Registration

Mark the box beside the statement which describes your current nursing registration status.

If registered, show the State, your registration number, and the date you received it in the space below.

A. I have active registration as a professional registered nurse (RN) in a State, the District of Columbia, Puerto Rico or a U.S. Territory.   A. ☐
B. I am not registered, but I graduated from an accredited school of nursing within the past 12 months.   B. ☐
C. I am not registered, but I will graduate from an accredited nursing school within the next 9 months.   C. ☐

State	Registration Number	Date Received (Month, Day, Year)

6. Summary of Nursing Experience

Check the appropriate columns in the graph below to summarize a unique period of nursing experience in terms of the Nursing Specialty, the Institutional Setting, the Level of Experience, and the Length of that period of experience.

We suggest that you first complete your SF-171, Personal Qualifications Statement, describing all of your work experience, and then refer to that form when responding to Item E of this section.

Begin with your most recent period of nursing experience in column 1. Check the box which describes the (A) Nursing Specialty in which you worked during that period. Move down in the same column to Item B to show the Institutional Setting in which you worked. Continue down to Item C and show the Level of Experience for that period. In Item D write in the **number of months** you worked in that particular specialty, in that setting and at that level. Finally, write in the box at the bottom of the column the letter or number of the experience block on SF-171 which covers this period of experience (Item E). Describe other periods of nursing experience in the same way, up to a total of six periods.

Begin a new column whenever the Nursing Specialty, Institutional Setting, or Level of Experience changes, even though you may have been working for the same employer and may cross-reference the same experience block on SF-171. For example, if after receiving your diploma, you began working in the pediatric ward of a hospital as a graduate nurse, after registration became a staff nurse on the same ward, and six months later became a charge nurse, you would need three columns to describe your experience.

If you have extensive nursing experience, more than you can fit into the six columns provided, pick your best experience, that is, the experience most related to the type and level of job you are applying for. If you have very little or no work experience as a registered nurse, use this section to describe your practicum experience or any preprofessional experience as a graduate nurse, practical nurse, or nursing assistant.

			PERIOD OF NURSING EXPERIENCE					
			1	2	3	4	5	6

A. Nursing Specialty
Check only one box per column to show the specialty in which you worked during that period of experience.

1. Clinical Nurse	1.
2. Community Health	2.
3. Operating Room	3.
4. Occupational Health	4.
5. Psychiatric Nurse	5.
6. Nurse Anesthetist	6.
7. Nurse Midwife	7.
8. Nurse Practitioner	8.

B. Institutional Setting
Check only one box per column to show the type of medical facility you were working in during each period of work experience you describe.

1. Hospital Inpatient Department	1.
2. Hospital Special Care Unit	2.
3. Hospital Emergency Room	3.
4. Outpatient Unit	4.
5. Extended Care Facility	5.
6. Physician's Office	6.
7. Community Health Facility	7.
8. School Health Facility	8.
9. Employee Health Unit	9.
10. Private Duty Nurse	10.
11. Health Program Agency, Teaching, Research, or other setting in which you were not involved in providing direct care to patients.	11.

C. Level of Experience
Check in each column only the box which best describes the level of your experience during that period.

1. Nursing Assistant	1.
2. Licensed Practical Nurse	2.
3. Student Nurse (undergraduate practicum)	3.
4. Student Nurse (graduate practicum)	4.
5. Graduate Nurse (not yet registered)	5.
6. Beginning level RN under direct supervision of experienced RN	6.
7. RN providing health care or services usually to individual patients or other clientele in a hospital, clinic, doctor's office or other health facility under general supervision, e.g., Staff Nurse	7.
8. RN independently planning and providing health care or services for a group of patients and leading or directing other nurses or non-professional staff, e.g., charge nurse	8.
9. RN exceptionally skilled in providing specialized health care under difficult, unusual, or experimental conditions	9.
10. RN responsible for directing a staff of nurses and other employees in providing health care or services, e.g., head nurse	10.
11. RN functioning primarily in administrative, research, teaching, or supervisory capacity	11.

D. Length of Experience—Write in the length of the period of experience you are describing in months. If you worked less than full-time, be sure to pro-rate. For example, if you worked half-time (20 hours per week) for a year, you would write in "6 months.

MONTHS

E. Cross-Reference With SF-171—Write in the number or letter of the experience block on your SF-171 which covers the period described in each column. If there is no letter or

BLOCK NUMBERS

GS-610

7. Summary Of Postgraduate Nursing Education

Enter the amount of nursing education and training you have completed beyond your basic nursing preparation either in a graduate nursing curriculum (Section A), or in training courses, seminars, etc., (Section B).

Show only **nursing** courses or training in this item. If a particular course is applicable to more than one specialty, count it only once and enter it opposite the specialty that best describes the overall course content and objectives. In evaluating your responses, we will automatically credit education or training in one specialty toward qualification requirements in related specialties.

A. Graduate Nursing Education
Write in the number of semester hours or quarter hours of graduate nursing courses you have completed and any graduate degrees you have received in any of the nursing specialties listed below. Be sure to specify whether you are showing semester hours (s.h.) or quarter hours (q.h.).

B. Other Nursing Education
Write in the number of Contact Hours* of other nursing education and training, such as seminars, training courses, extra undergraduate courses beyond your basic nursing preparation, etc., for each of the specialties listed. Also show the total amount of such training in all specialties.

NURSING SPECIALTY	NO OF HOURS	S H Q H	GRAD DEGREE	NURSING SPECIALTY	CONTACT HOURS
1. Clinical Nursing				1. Clinical Nursing	
2. Community Health				2. Community Health	
3. Operating Room				3. Operating Room	
4. Occupational Health				4. Occupational Health	
5. Psychiatric Nursing				5. Psychiatric Nursing	
6. Nurse Anesthetist				6. Nurse Anesthetist	
7. Nurse Midwife				7. Nurse Midwife	
8. Nurse Practitioner				8. Nurse Practitioner	
9. Other, e.g. nursing education/administration				TOTAL	
TOTAL					

*Contact Hours means the amount of time you spent in classroom, laboratory or demonstration sessions as part of a formal training program. Generally, 1 continuing education unit equals 10 contact hours. 1 semester hour equals 15 contact hours.

8. Advanced Nursing Certification

If you hold any advanced nursing certificates (e.g., Certified Nurse Anesthetist, Nurse Midwife) provide the following information.

Type of Certification	Name of Certifying Agency	Date Issued (Month, Day, Year)

9. Professional Nursing Status

A. Are you now working as a professional nurse or attending an accredited school of nursing?
☐ YES
☐ NO

B. If you answered "NO" to "A," provide the date you last worked as a professional nurse or last attended an accredited nursing school.

C. If it has been more than one (1) year since your last professional experience or education, have you taken nursing refresher courses within the last year?
☐ YES
☐ NO

D. If your answer to "C" was "Yes," provide the following information: Course Was Given By:

Dates of Course (From-To)   Number of Hours

10. Nursing Practice Areas

Check the specialized areas below in which you have had directly related experience/training appropriate to the level of job for which you are applying.

☐ 1. Alcoholism
☐ 2. Allergies
☐ 3. Burn Care
☐ 4. Cardiovascular
☐ 5. Dermatology
☐ 6. Drug Abuse
☐ 7. Emergency Room
☐ 8. Endocrinology
☐ 9. Epidemiology
☐ 10. General Surgery
☐ 11. General Medical
☐ 12. Geriatrics
☐ 13. Gastroenterology

☐ 14. Hearing Conservation
☐ 15. Hematology
☐ 16. Infectious Diseases
☐ 17. Maternal/Child Care
☐ 18. Mental Health
☐ 19. Neonatology
☐ 20. Nephrology/Dialysis
☐ 21. Neurology
☐ 22. Obstetrics/Gynecology
☐ 23. Occupational Health Hazards
☐ 24. Oncology
☐ 25. Ophthalmology
☐ 26. Orthopedics

☐ 27. Otolaryngology
☐ 28. Pediatrics
☐ 29. Plastic Surgery
☐ 30. Preventive Medicine
☐ 31. Proctology
☐ 32. Rheumatology
☐ 33. Suicide Prevention
☐ 34. Thoracic
☐ 35. Toxicology
☐ 36. Transplants
☐ 37. Pulmonary Disorder
☐ 38. Urology
☐ 39. Venereal Disease

☐ 40. Other
   (List Below)
_____
_____
_____
_____

GS-610 4

11. Availability—Check the boxes which indicate your availability.

☐ Day Shift (Approximately 7:00 AM to 3:00 PM) ☐ Night Shift
☐ Evening Shift (Approximately 3:00 PM to 11:00 PM) (Approximately 11:00 PM to 7:00 AM)
☐ Rotating Shifts, including weekends

The list below does not include all employment locations for nurse. It does, however, indicate the locations with the greatest need for nurses. Please check the boxes for the areas and agencies where you will accept employment. You should also complete the availability items on your SF-171, Personal Qualifications Statement. You should submit a separate application package to each area office in whose jurisdiction you wish consideration, except that applications for all Nurse Anesthetist positions at GS 9/12 and all GS 11 and 12 positions should be submitted to the Washington Area Office. (See Announcement No. 419.)

ANCHORAGE AREA OFFICE
Alaska Area Native Health Service
☐ Anchorage
☐ Barrow
☐ Bethel
☐ Kanakanak
☐ Kotzeoue
☐ Mt. Edgecumbe
☐ Tanana

DAYTON AREA OFFICE
Air Force Bases:
☐ Chanute AFB, Illinois
☐ K.I. Sawyer AFB, Michigan
☐ Kincheloe AFB, Michigan
☐ Selfridge AFB, Michigan
☐ Wurtsmith AFB, Michigan
☐ Wright-Patterson, AFB, Ohio
Navy Installations:
☐ Naval Hospital, Great Lakes, Illinois
☐ Naval Avionics Facility, Crane, Indiana
☐ Navy Finance Center, Cleveland, Ohio
Other:
☐ Public Health Service, Chicago, Illinois
☐ Ft. Benjamin Harrison, Indianapolis, Indiana
☐ Public Health Service, Redlake, Minnesota
☐ NASA, Louis Research Center, Cleveland, Ohio
☐ IRS, Covington, Kentucky

DENVER AREA OFFICE
Indian Health Service in:
☐ Browning, Montana
☐ Box Elder, Montana
☐ Crow Agency, Montana
☐ Harlem, Montana
☐ Lame Deer, Montana
☐ Poplar, Montana
☐ St. Ignatius, Montana
☐ Belcourt, North Dakota
☐ Ft. Yates, North Dakota
☐ Eagle Butte, South Dakota
☐ Pine Ridge, South Dakota
☐ Rosebud, South Dakota

☐ Sisseton, South Dakota
☐ Brigham City, Utah
☐ Arapahoe, Wyoming
☐ Fort Washakie, Wyoming
Air Force Bases in:
☐ Grand Forks, North Dakota
☐ Minot, North Dakota
☐ Ellsworth AFB, Rapid City, S.D.
☐ Hill AFB, Salt Lake City, Utah
Other:
☐ Fitzsimons Army Medical Center, Aurora, Colorado

HARTFORD AREA OFFICE
Air Force Bases:
☐ Loring AFB, Limestone, Maine
☐ Hanscom AFB, Bedford, Mass.
☐ Pease AFB, Portsmouth, N.H.
Army Installations:
☐ Ft. Devens, Massachusetts
☐ R&D Command, Natick, Mass.
Naval Bases:
☐ Naval Submarine Base, New London/Groton, Connecticut
☐ Naval Education & Training Center, Newport, R.I.

NEW ORLEANS AREA OFFICE
Air Force Bases:
☐ Barksdale, AFB, Shreveport, Louisiana
☐ Tinker, AFB, Oklahoma City, Oklahoma
Army Installations:
☐ Ft. Bliss, El Paso, Texas
☐ Ft. Hood, Killeen, Texas
Public Health/Indian Health:
☐ PHS, New Orleans, Louisiana
☐ IHS, Albuquerque, New Mexico
☐ PHS, Galveston, Texas

PHILADELPHIA AREA OFFICE
☐ Public Health Service, Baltimore, MD.

RALEIGH AREA OFFICE
Army Installations:
☐ Ft. Benning, Georgia
☐ Ft. Gordon, Georgia
☐ Ft. Campbell, Kentucky

☐ Ft. Knox, Kentucky
☐ Ft. Bragg, North Carolina
☐ Ft. Jackson, South Carolina
Navy & Marine Corps Installations:
☐ Marine Corps Air Station, Cherry Point, N.C.
☐ Naval Hospital, Charleston, South Carolina
Other:
☐ Federal Correctional Institute, Lexington, Kentucky

SAN DIEGO AREA OFFICE
Army Installation:
☐ Letterman Hospital, Presidio, San Francisco, California
Naval Installations:
☐ Medical Center, Long Beach, California
☐ Medical Center, Oakland, CA.
Public Health/Indian Health:
☐ IHS, Keans Canyon, Arizona
☐ IHS, Sells, Arizona
☐ IHS, Window Rock, Arizona
☐ PHS, San Francisco, CA.

SEATTLE AREA OFFICE
☐ Bonneville Power Administration, Portland, Oregon
☐ Fairchild AFB, Spokane, Washington
☐ Madigan Army Hospital, Tacoma, Washington
Naval Installations:
☐ Medical Center, Bremerton, Washington
☐ Whidby Island, Washington
Public Health/Indian Health:
☐ PHS Hospital, Seattle, WA.
☐ IHS, Idaho
☐ IHS, Oregon
☐ IHS, Washington

ST. LOUIS AREA OFFICE
Air Force Bases:
☐ Scott, AFB, Illinois
☐ Richards-Gebaur, AFB, MO.
☐ Offutt, AFB, Nebraska
Army Installations:
☐ Ft. Leavenworth, Kansas

☐ Ft. Riley, Kansas
☐ Ft. Leonard Wood, Missouri
Other:
☐ Bureau of Prisons, Springfield, Missouri
☐ St. Louis, Missouri
☐ Chadron, Nebraska
☐ Winnebago, Nebraska

SYRACUSE AREA OFFICE
Army Installations:
☐ Ft. Dix, N.J.
☐ Ft. Monmouth, N.J.
☐ Ft. Drum, N.Y.
☐ Watervliet Arsenal, N.Y.
☐ West Point Military Academy, N.Y.
Naval Installations:
☐ Lakehurst, N.J.
☐ St. Albans, N.Y.
Air Force Bases:
☐ Hancock AFB, N.Y.
☐ Plattsburgh AFB, N.Y.
Other:
☐ Agriculture Dept., Plum Island, N.Y.
☐ Coast Guard, Governor's Island, N.Y.
☐ Public Health Service, Buffalo, N.Y.
☐ Public Health Service, Staten Island, N.Y.
Puerto Rico:
☐ Navy, Roosevelt Roads
☐ Public Health Service, Castaner
☐ Public Health Service, Rincon

WASHINGTON AREA OFFICE
☐ National Institutes of Health, Bethesda, MD.
☐ Naval Medical Hospital, Bethesda, MD.
☐ St. Elizabeths Hospital, Washington, D.C.
☐ Walter Reed Army Medical Center, Washington, D.C.

PRIVACY ACT INFORMATION

The Office of Personnel Management is authorized by section 1302 of Chapter 13 (Special Authority) and sections 3301 and 3304 of Chapter 33 (Examination, Certification, and Appointment) of Title 5 of the U.S. Code to collect the information on this form.

Executive Order 9397 (Numbering System for Federal Accounts Relating to Individual Persons) authorizes the collection of your Social Security Number (SSN). Your SSN is used to identify this form with your basic application. It may be used for the same purposes as stated on the application.

The information you provide will be used primarily to determine your qualifications and geographic availability for Federal employment. Other possible uses or disclosures of the information are:
1. To make requests for information about you from any source (E.G., former employers or schools), that would assist an agency in determining whether to hire you;

2. To refer your application to prospective Federal employers and, with your consent, to others (e.g., State and local governments) for possible employment;
3. To a Federal, State, or local agency for checking on violations of law or other lawful purposes in connection with hiring, retaining you on the job, or issuing you a security clearance;
4. To the courts when the Government is party to a suit; and
5. When lawfully required by Congress, the Office of Management and Budget, or the General Services Administration.

Providing the information requested on this form, including your SSN, is voluntary. However, failure to do so may result in your not receiving an accurate rating, which may hinder your chances for obtaining Federal employment.

ATTENTION—THIS STATEMENT MUST BE SIGNED
Read the following paragraph carefully before signing this Statement

A false answer to any question in this Statement may be grounds for not employing you, or for dismissing you after you begin work, and may be punishable by fine or imprisonment (U.S. Code, Title 18, Sec. 1001). All statements are subject to investigation, including a check of your fingerprints, police records, and former employers. All the information you give will be considered in reviewing your Statement and is subject to investigation.

CERTIFICATION	SIGNATURE (Sign in ink)	DATE SIGNED
I CERTIFY that all of the statements made in this Statement are true, complete, and correct to the best of		

	APPLICANT APPRAISAL	
NAME OF CANDIDATE	JOA NUMBER 92-196 (LSM)	

INFORMATION AND GUIDANCE

Listed below are seven elements which are to be used to appraise the candidate's performance.

Use the Numeric Code Level (shown below) to most nearly describe the candidate's <u>observed performance</u>. Particular consideration should be given to those characteristics following each element in parentheses.

NUMERIC CODE LEVEL (CL)

4 · OUTSTANDING	2 · AVERAGE
3 · ABOVE AVERAGE	1 · MARGINAL
0 · UNSATISFACTORY	

<u>NOTE</u>: When 1 or 4 appears in the Code Level column, REMARKS block must be completed.

APPRAISAL ELEMENTS	CL	REMARKS
1. Knowledge of communications-electronics principles, methods, and techniques.		
2. Knowledge of the worldwide Defense Communications System, facilities, and equipment used by DISA, MILDEPs, and non-Defense and non-Defense and commercial organizations.		
3. Knowledge of program development and implementation management in government owned and leased tele-communications systems.		
4. Ability to interact with higher echelons both within and outside the organization.		
5. Ability to develop policy and doctrinal guidance and directives on tele-communications projects.		

DCA FORM 651 APR 77

92-196(LSM)

APPRAISAL ELEMENTS	CL	REMARKS
6. Ability to supervise a team of technical personnel.		
7.		

COMMENTS BY IMMEDIATE SUPERVISOR

NAME, TITLE, & CODE	SIGNATURE	DATE

COMMENTS BY SECOND LEVEL SUPERVISOR

NAME, TITLE, & CODE	SIGNATURE	DATE

Request for Promotion Consideration and Acknowledgement

INFORMATION • Part IV will be dated, detached, and returned to you to acknowledge receipt of your application.
• Part V will be returned to you when action on your application has been completed.

INSTRUCTIONS • Please type or print.
• Complete Parts I, III, and IV of this form and attach it to your application.
• A separate form and application must be submitted for each vacancy and location for which you request consideration.

PART I. Request for Promotion Consideration to: _____

(See vacancy announcement to find where application is to be sent.)

I wish to be considered for Position Vacancy No. _____ at _____
(Location)

Title, Series, Grade of Vacancy _____

NAME _____

TITLE/GRADE _____
DUTY
LOCATION _____

_____ _____
Date   Signature

PART II: For use by personnel office ONLY	
ELIGIBLE	INELIGIBLE BECAUSE
Referred ☐	☐ TIME IN GRADE ☐ OTHER
Not Referred ☐	☐ DOES NOT MEET QUALIFICATION REQUIREMENTS

PART III. TO BE COMPLETED BY EMPLOYEE: *(To be used to notify you of the results of your application. Use correct home/office facility mailing address or headquarters routing symbol.)*

☐ Voluntary Application _____
Title, Series and Grade

☐ Vacancy Number _____

Location/Region _____

Enter Name and Routing Symbol or Address below

_____

_____

_____

PART IV. TO BE COMPLETED BY EMPLOYEE: *This part will be returned to acknowledge receipt of your application. Use correct home/office/facility or headquarters routing symbol.)*

☐ Voluntary Application _____
(Title, Series and Grade)

☐ Vacancy Number _____

Location/Region _____

Enter Name and Routing Symbol or Address below

_____

_____

_____ (Date received) _____

FAA Form 3330-42 1-86

PART V. This portion will be completed by the office processing the vacancy announcement.

To The Employee: You were found to be.

Eligible	Ineligible
☐ Placed on Selection List	☐ You did not meet the announcement requirements.
	☐ You did not meet time-in-grade requirements (FPM Ch. 300)
☐ Not placed on Selection List (Did not fall in Best Qualified Group)	☐ You are outside the area of consideration
	☐ Your application was not submitted within required time limits.

Vacancy Announcement	Other
☐ Cancelled ☐ Expired	☐

Privacy Act Information. This form is used to advise the candidate about the status of his/her application. It is authorized under Title 5 of the U.S. Code. Section 3302 and 3361. The information will be used for FAA personnel management related purposed and will not be transmitted outside the agency except as provided by law. This form must be accurately completed in order for the candidate to get a receipt of his/her application and to be advised when action on the application has been completed.

US Department
of Transportation

**Federal Aviation
Administration**

Knowledges, Skills, Abilities, and Other Characteristics (KSAO's) Evaluation

Announcement Number

Name of Applicant

Position Being Filled

Instructions to Applicants: *Complete the above; complete Section I by transposing the KSAO's from the vacancy announcement; have your supervisor complete Section II; sign and date; submit with bid package.*

Instructions to Supervisor: *Complete Section II by indicating by check mark (✓) in the appropriate column your evaluation of the applicant against the criteria in Section I; sign and date; return to the applicant. This evaluation should be based on observed work behaviors. Attach additional sheets, if necessary.*

Section II - Description

Section I	Superior	Satisfactory	Barely Acceptable	Not Observed	Comment

Applicant's Signature

Date

Supervisor's Signature

Title

Date

FAA Form 3330-52 (10-85)

☆U.S. GOVERNMENT PRINTING OFFICE: 1986-659-121/40185

WAPA F 3000.25
(6-82)

DEPARTMENT OF ENERGY
WESTERN AREA POWER ADMINISTRATION
MERIT PROMOTION PROGRAM - SUPERVISORY APPRAISAL

SUPERVISORY POSITIONS

Sup. Electronics Engr., GM-855-13   **W87-92**

Position Title/Series/Grade   Vacancy Announcement Number

Name of Applicant   Present Position Title/Series/Grade

The employee named is being considered for a position which is being filled under the Merit Promotion Program. Your appraisal will be used as one measure in ranking the employee with other candidates for the position. Please complete this form based on your knowledge of the employee's job performance in his/her current position.

This form will be made available to the employee upon his/her request.

IN THE COLUMNS AT THE RIGHT INDICATE YOUR OPINION OF THE EMPLOYEE'S CAPABILITY IN EACH OF THE FOLLOWING AREAS, PLUS THE FREQUENCY OF THE OBSERVATIONS ON WHICH THE OPINION IS BASED.

	PERIOD OF SUPERVISION							
	FROM:			TO:				
	RATING				OPPORTUNITY TO JUDGE			
	OUTSTANDING	HIGHLY SUCCESSFUL	FULLY SATISFACTORY	MINIMALLY SATISFACTORY	FREQUENTLY	INFREQUENTLY	NONE	POTENTIAL
1. Establishing realistic objectives and defining goals.								
2. Planning and directing work priorities.								
3. Delegating authority and defining responsibilities appropriately.								
4. Utilizing subordinates to maximize productivity.								
5. Providing employees with appropriate guidelines and resources for accomplishing duties.								
6. Anticipating long-range and short-range needs.								
7. Presenting new ideas and concepts to the staff.								
8. Providing sound application of position management principles and personnel practices.								
9. Assessing employee performance.								
10. Training subordinates.								
11. Communicating ideas in writing.								
12. Communicating ideas orally.								
13. Supporting organizational policy and reflecting a positive image.								
14. Guiding and counseling employees.								
15. Providing a positive EEO environment.								
16. Keeping superiors and subordinates informed.								
17. Working effectively with people outside of immediate office.								
18. Assuming responsibility for subordinate's duties in unusual circumstances.								
19. Innovative and creative approaches to problems.								
20. Seeking and accepting responsibility.								
21. Complying with schedules and deadlines.								
22. Complying with regulations, directives, and instructions from supervisors.								
23. Making timely decisions under stress or adverse circumstances.								

PLEASE TURN PAGE
APPRAISAL CONTINUED ON REVERSE SIDE

SUPERVISORY APPRAISAL (Continued)

	RATING					OPPORTUNITY TO JUDGE			
	OUTSTANDING	HIGHLY SUCCESSFUL	FULLY SATISFACTORY	MINIMALLY SATISFACTORY		FREQUENTLY	INFREQUENTLY	NONE	POTENTIAL
24. Willingness to try new ideas and adjust to changing requirements and conditions.									
EVALUATION FACTORS									
1. Knowledge of the theories, principles, and practices of communications systems that include microwave, VHF and UHF radio, powerline carrier, leased communications facilities, telephone systems, complex telemetering schemes, supervisory control and data acquisition systems, computer networks, and data communication systems as they are applied to an integrated power system.									
2. Knowledge of electrical and electronic engineering principles, practices, and procedures involving power system operation.									
3. Ability to supervise and direct the activities of professional engineers, technicians, and wage employees involved in formulating and executing a program for the maintenance of communications and systems control facilities.									
4. Ability to meet and deal effectively with people including Federal agencies, public and private utilities, and equipment vendors.									
5. Ability to communicate technical and administrative requirements effectively, both orally and in writing.									
6. Knowledge of and willingness to support equal employment opportunity programs, including programs for the handicapped and disabled veterans.									

IF ANY OF THE ABOVE RATINGS ARE UNSATISFACTORY, PLEASE PROVIDE A BRIEF NARRATIVE.

Signature of supervisor _____   Title _____   Date _____

Signature of second or higher level supervisor*   Title _____   Date _____

*If you do not agree with the above evaluation, please submit a separate one.

GPO 835 - 724

WAPA F 3000 65
(4-90)

U.S. DEPARTMENT OF ENERGY
WESTERN AREA POWER ADMINISTRATION
APPLICANT BACKGROUND SURVEY

GENERAL INSTRUCTIONS

The information from this survey is used to help ensure that agency personnel practices meet the requirements of Federal law. Your responses are voluntary. Please answer each of the questions to the best of your ability. Please print entries in pencil or pen. Use only capital letters. Read each item thoroughly before completing the appropriate code number in each box.

Vacancy Announcement No.: W87-92

Date (Month, Day, Year):

Position:

PRIVACY ACT INFORMATION

GENERAL

This information is provided pursuant to Public Law 935-579 (Privacy Act of 1974.) December 31, 1974. For individuals completing Federal records and forms that solicit personal information.

AUTHORITY

Sections 1302, 3301, 3304, and 7201 of Title 5 of the U.S. Code.

PURPOSE AND ROUTINE USES

The information from this survey is used for research and for a Federal equal opportunity recruitment program to help ensure that agency personnel practices meet the requirements of Federal law.

EFFECTS OF NONDISCLOSURE

Providing this information is voluntary. No individual personnel selections are based on this information.

INFORMATION REGARDING DISCLOSURE OF YOUR SOCIAL SECURITY NUMBER UNDER PUBLIC LAW 93-579. SECTION 7 (b)

Solicitation of the Social Security Number (SSN) by the Office of Personnel Management is authorized under provisions of Executive Order 9397. dated November 22, 1943. It is used to relate this form with other records that you file with Federal agencies.

1. Name (Last, First, MI):

2. Year of Birth: 1 9 ☐ ☐

3. Social Security Number: ☐☐☐ - ☐☐ - ☐☐☐☐

4. How did you learn about the particular position or exam for which you are applying? *(You may circle up to three choices)*

01 — Private Information Service
02 — Newspaper
03 — Magazine
04 — Poster
05 — Private Employment Office
06 — State Employment Office (Unemployment Office)
07 — Agency Personnel Department (Bulletin Board or Other Announcement)

08 — Agency or Other Federal Government Recruitment at School or College
09 — Federal, State, or Local Job Information Center
10 — Religious Organization
11 — School or College Counselor or Other Official
12 — Friend or Relative Working for Agency
13 — Friend or Relative Not Working for Agency
14 — Other (Specify) _____

_____

5. Please categorize yourself in terms of race, sex and handicap using the definitions below.

Race/Ethnic Code: ☐   Sex: Female ☐ Male ☐   Handicap Code: ☐

DEFINITIONS

RACE/ETHNIC CODES:

A — American Indian or Alaskan Native
B — Asian or Pacific Islander
C — Black, Not of Hispanic Origin
D — Hispanic
E — White, Not of Hispanic Origin

HANDICAP CODES:

A — I do not have a handicap.
B — I have a handicap but not listed below. Please state handicap _____
_____ .
C — Speech Impairment

D — Hearing Impairment
E — Vision Impairment
F — Missing Extremities
G — Nonparalytic Orthopedic
H — Partial Paralysis
I — Complete Paralysis

Merit Promotion Announcement

U. S. DEPARTMENT OF ENERGY
SAVANNAH RIVER FIELD OFFICE (SR)
AIKEN, SOUTH CAROLINA

Announcement No.: SR-92-063
Issue Date: 04/30/92
Initial Cutoff: N/A
Closing Date: 05/20/92
Area of Consideration:
1 ☒ DOE, SR (Status Applicants)
2 ☒ DOE-Wide (Status Applicants)
3 ☒ Reinstatement, Transfer Eligibles
4 ☒ Nationwide (Status Applicants)
5 ☐ VRA, Handicapped Applicants

POSITION: GENERAL ENGINEER, GS-0801-12

ORGANIZATION: Office of the Chief Financial Officer, Planning and Budget Division, Planning Branch

PROMOTION POTENTIAL:	☒ To GS- 13	☐ No Known
SUBJECT TO PMRS:	☐ Yes ☒ No	
SUPERVISOR/MANAGER:	☐ Yes* ☒ No	
RELOCATION (Expenses allowed):	☒ Yes** ☐ No	

* Newly appointed supervisors/managers must serve a one year probationary period.
** Except within commuting area.

POSITION SENSITIVITY
☐ Non Sensitive
☐ Non Critical Sensitive
☒ Critical Sensitive
☐ Special Sensitive

FINANCIAL STATEMENT REQUIRED: ☒ Yes ☐ No
TESTING DESIGNATED POSITION: ☐ Yes*** ☒ No
***Subject to random drug testing.

DUTIES AND RESPONSIBILITIES

Responsible for contractor planning, scheduling and work authorization programs, improvement plans, performance tracking, trending, and analysis, and Award Fee support for the Chief Financial Officer (CFO). Responsible for the coordination and oversight of the contractors planning and scheduling programs. Oversees the development of work authorization programs by the contractor; reviews plans for consistency with SR management directives and priorities; and appraise SR management periodically of progress. Reviews contractors and SR staff reporting of progress and problems. Tracks event reporting and resolution, trends and analyses contractor problems and occurrences, and prepares periodic briefings to the Manager, SR on outstanding and anticipated problems.

NOTE: *The position(s) covered by this announcement may be filled on a temporary, provisional or permanent basis. Actions processed on a temporary/provisional basis may be made permanent without further competition.*

QUALIFICATION REQUIREMENTS: Applicants must have general, specific, and specialized experience as described below. This requirement is in accordance with the OPM Handbook X-118, available for review in your personnel office, which specifies when, how and if education may be substituted for experience. When specified, applicants must also meet the Selective Placement Factors listed below.

BASIC REQUIREMENTS: Successful completion of a full four-year professional engineering curriculum leading to a bachelor's, or higher degree in engineering from an accredited college or university, or the equivalent as prescribed in OPM Qualifications Standards for the GS-0800, Professional Engineer series.

SPECIALIZED EXPERIENCE: Experience which is in or directly related to the line of work of the position to be filled which has equipped the applicant with the specific knowledge, skills and abilities to successfully perform the duties of the position. The one year of specialized experience must have at least been equivalent to the GS-11 level.

RANKING FACTORS: Applicants who meet the qualification requirements described above will be further evaluated to determine the extent to which their education, work related experience, training, awards and supervisory appraisals indicate they possess or have the potential to acquire knowledges, skills, abilities, and personal characteristics required to perform the duties and responsibilities described above.

1. Knowledge of planning and scheduling concepts, principles and procedures.

2. Ability to analyze, review and evaluate technical and non-technical activities and requirements.

3. Ability to meet and deal effectively with all levels of management within and outside the organization.

4. Ability to communicate effectively in writing.

TO APPLY: For each announcement under which application is made, submit the following: (a) current completed "Application for Federal Employment" SF-171, with original signature, (b) completed "Supervisory Appraisal for Potential Performance"(see reverse), (c) applicant's statement of knowledge, skills and abilities as they relate to the ranking factors, (d) current performance appraisal of record, (e) SF-50, Notification of Personnel Action and/or other documents to indicate eligibility for Career/Career Conditional appointment. The SF-171 should include all pertinent experience, awards, commendations, training and any other pertinent information. Do not include position descriptions. Ranking will be based on information contained in the applicant's SF-171; the Supervisory Appraisal of Potential Performance; applicant's statement of knowledge, skills and abilities; current performance appraisal; and any other relevant documents submitted by the applicant. Applications submitted in response to this announcement become the property of the personnel office.
APPLICATIONS RECEIVED IN POSTAGE-PAID GOVERNMENT ENVELOPES WILL NOT BE ACKNOWLEDGED OR CONSIDERED. APPLICATIONS MUST BE RECEIVED NO LATER THAN THE CLOSING DATE. They should be sent to the Human Resources Division, P. O. Box A, Aiken, SC 29802-0900.
Telephone: FTS 239-2056; Commercial (803) 725-2056.

EQUAL OPPORTUNITY EMPLOYER

U. S. Department of Energy - Savannah River Field Office
SUPERVISORY APPRAISAL OF PAST/POTENTIAL PERFORMANCE

**PLEASE HAVE THIS APPRAISAL COMPLETED BY YOUR SUPERVISOR
AND SUBMIT IT WITH YOUR APPLICATION, SF-171.**

Announcement No.: SR-92-063

Position: GENERAL ENGINEER
GS-0801-12

Name of Applicant: _____

Basis for Appraisal — Check One				RANKING FACTORS (Knowledges, Skills, Abilities, and Personal Characteristics)	Level of Potential Performance — Please check (√) as appropriate: 4 - Exceptional / 3 - Superior / 2 - Satisfactory / 1 - Weak / 0 - None				
Outside Activities	On-the-Job Performance	Formal Training	Unable to Appraise		4	3	2	1	0
				1. Knowledge of planning and scheduling concepts, principles and procedures.					
				2. Ability to analyze, review and evaluate technical and non-technical activities and requirements.					
				3. Ability to meet and deal effectively with all levels of management within and outside the organization.					
				4. Ability to communicate effectively in writing.					

NARRATIVE: Please include any other information pertinent to the applicant's potential knowledge, skills or abilities and personal characteristics that may not be adequately expressed above.   (Attach additional sheets if needed.)

IN WHAT CAPACITY ARE YOU MAKING THIS APPRAISAL? (Please √ as appropriate)

[ ] Present Immediate Supervisor   [ ] Present 2nd Level Supervisor   [ ] Other *(Specify)*

[ ] Former Immediate Supervisor   [ ] Former 2nd Level Supervisor

Period Covered by this Appraisal:

From: To:

Appraiser:

(Signature)   (Date)   (Phone No.)

Appendix I: SF-171 Experience Block Worksheets

The **SF-171** (Application for Federal Employment) is discussed in detail in Step 5 (pp. 92-97).

This appendix includes a series of worksheets designed to help you respond to block 24 on the SF-171. The importance of this block, which relates to work experience, cannot be overstated. It is the heart of your SF-171, the key to getting an interview and, ultimately, a Federal job (or promotion). These worksheets help you accentuate those aspects of your experience that are most impressive for the job vacancy in question. Completing them takes time, but is well worthwhile. The resulting SF-171 will be much more polished and more impressive to a prospective Federal employer.

Although these worksheets are primarily designed for the SF-171, they may also be used as guides for filling out other types of application forms the government may require for employment.

CONTENTS

WORKSHEET 1: PREVIOUS AND PRESENT JOBS

This worksheet is intended to help you present information about your previous and present jobs in ways that will strengthen your Federal job application. Specifically, it helps you analyze each job you have had by breaking it down into duties, responsibilities, and accomplishments.

Photocopy the blank worksheet provided to make as many as you need. Use one worksheet per job. If you have had more than one job with the same company or organization, use a *separate worksheet for each* and designate it by its appropriate job title.

Federal examiners are most impressed with job experience from the past five years, so try to detail as much of your experience during that period as possible, even if it was spent on one job. However, if a job you held over five years ago matches well with a particular duty or qualification called for by the job for which you are applying, you should certainly cite it as relevant experience. Volunteer experience may be cited as though it were a paid job.

PART I: GENERAL

The information requested here corresponds to that required for each previous or present job you list in block 24 of the SF-171. You may find you need to consult old résumés or even tax records to refresh your memory. The telephone number of your former supervisor should be as up-to-date as possible, as he or she may have since left the organization for which you both had worked. If the company itself has since relocated, provide both the new and old addresses. Under "Employment Dates," say "To: Present" if you are describing your current job.

In addition to the information you will need for your SF-171, you may wish to use your own sequential code: "A" for your most recent (or current) job, "B" for your previous job, and so on. This code will be quite useful when you get to Worksheets 3 and 4.

PART II: DUTIES

A *duty* is a function or specific chore that can be described in a few words, such as "reconciled bank statements," "welded seams in steel plate," "operated EKG," "designed airframes," or "conducted personnel screening interviews." In Part II, number and list each duty of the job you described in Part I. Delineate as many distinct duties as you can. This may require some hard thinking: We tend to think of a job as a unified entity even though it is almost always a series of separate duties.

Supervising others is an important duty to include in this section. When describing your supervisory experience, include both the number and level of those whose work you oversaw; for example, "supervised welder's helper" or "supervised airframe design department of 20 engineers."

PART III: RESPONSIBILITIES

A *responsibility* is something for which you were held accountable by your employer. In Part III, record the responsibilities associated with the job you specified in Part I. Note that these are not necessarily synonymous with the duties you listed in Part II. One way to determine what your responsibilities were is to ask yourself the following: "If things went well, for what did I get credit? If things went badly, for what did I get blamed?" Functions for which you got either credit or blame were those for which you were responsible. Examples are "maintaining the general ledger," "keeping faults in welds below 2%," "accurate and timely EKG tests," and "meeting airframe design objectives."Often one responsibility involves several specific duties. For example, the responsibility "maintaining the general ledger" may include the duties of posting the cash disbursements and keeping cash receipts books. Thus the number of duties is expected to exceed the number of responsibilities; in fact, there may be only one responsibility to list.

Supervision of others, mentioned above as a duty, is also important as a responsibility. Be sure to include and describe such supervisory responsibilities fully: "responsible for the performance and training of welder's helpers" or "responsible for the performance of the 20 engineers in my department." Thinking up words to describe responsibilities may be difficult, but take the time to do it well: This is the very area where your SF-171 (or other Federal application) can stand out.

PART IV: ACCOMPLISHMENTS

Finally, describe in an impressive yet accurate manner what you accomplished at the given job. An accomplishment is something positive and specific that you achieved. Ask yourself, "What did I do particularly well on that job? Exactly why can I say I did it well?" You may have saved time or money, getting a job done with reductions in supplies, equipment, or personnel. Or perhaps you cleaned up a mess inherited with the job, or designed easier ways to do things. Be specific: Rather than saying "saved company money," say "saved company $1,528 in stationery costs in one year." Bear in mind that claims made on applications may be checked with former employers, and that misstatements are considered a serious violation of law that can result in disciplinary action or even dismissal.

WORKSHEET 1, SF-171, Block 24, MASTER

DESCRIPTIONS OF YOUR PREVIOUS OR PRESENT JOBS

List in box all duties, responsibilities, and accomplishments. Include volunteer work and internships.

Previous Job: _____

(Assign each previous job an alphabet letter for later identification.)

Part I.
NAME & ADDRESS OF EMPLOYER

DATES EMPLOYED
From: _____ To: _____

AVERAGE # OF
HOURS PER WEEK

NUMBER OF
EMPLOYEES
YOU SUPERVISE

SALARY OR EARNINGS:

Starting $ _____ per _____

Ending $ _____ per _____

YOUR REASON
FOR LEAVING

_____

YOUR IMMEDIATE SUPERVISOR'S NAME

SUPERVISOR'S
TELEPHONE #

(___) _____

EXACT TITLE OF YOUR JOB

IF FEDERAL GOV'T, CIVILIAN OR MILITARY, LIST: SERIES,
GRADE OR RANK, & DATE OF LAST RAISE

Part II. DUTIES:	
	D1
	D2
	D3
	D4
	D5
	D6
	D7
	D8
	D9
	D10

Part III. RESPONSIBILITIES:	
	R1
	R2
	R3
	R4
	R5
	R6
	R7
	R8
	R9
	R10

Part IV. ACCOMPLISHMENTS:	
	A1
	A2
	A3
	A4
	A5
	A6
	A7

WORKSHEET 1, SF-171, Block 24, Sample A1 - SECRETARY

DESCRIPTIONS OF YOUR PREVIOUS OR PRESENT JOBS

List in box all duties, responsibilities, and accomplishments. Include volunteer work and internships.

Previous Job: _____ A - Office Clerk _____

(Assign each previous job an alphabet letter for later identification.)

Part I.

NAME & ADDRESS OF EMPLOYER

Bland, Bland, Boring & Bland

1800 L Street, NW

Washington, DC 20006

DATES EMPLOYED
From: 5/82 To: Present

SALARY OR EARNINGS:

Starting $ 9,000 per year

Ending $ 10,000 per year

AVERAGE # OF HOURS PER WEEK   40

NUMBER OF EMPLOYEES YOU SUPERVISE

YOUR REASON FOR LEAVING

Career Advancement

YOUR IMMEDIATE SUPERVISOR'S NAME

Sandra Wood

SUPERVISOR'S TELEPHONE #

(202) 555-4321

EXACT TITLE OF YOUR JOB

Office Clerk

IF FEDERAL GOV'T, CIVILIAN OR MILITARY, LIST: SERIES, GRADE OR RANK, & DATE OF LAST RAISE

Part II. DUTIES:
- D1 Type legal briefs, motions, and other correspondence
- D2 Answer telephones
- D3 Refer inquiries
- D4 Take dictation
- D5 Get documents and schedules from computer
- D6 Pick up supplies
- D7
- D8
- D9
- D10

Part III. RESPONSIBILITIES:
- R1 Organize and maintain case files
- R2 Organize and maintain general office files
- R3 Make sure all minor supplies, such as stationery, stocked
- R4
- R5
- R6
- R7
- R8
- R9
- R10

Part IV. ACCOMPLISHMENTS:
- A1 Worked with vendors and helped choose hardware for our office
- A2 Suggested and developed new filing system
- A3
- A4
- A5
- A6
- A7

WORKSHEET 1, SF-171, Block 24, Sample A2 - SECRETARY

DESCRIPTIONS OF YOUR PREVIOUS OR PRESENT JOBS

List in box all duties, responsibilities, and accomplishments. Include volunteer work and internships.

Previous Job: _____ B - Special Olympics _____

(Assign each previous job an alphabet letter for later identification.)

Part I.
NAME & ADDRESS OF EMPLOYER

Arlington County Chamber of

Commerce

2500 Wilson Boulevard

Arlington, VA 22207

DATES EMPLOYED
From: 7/81 To: Present

AVERAGE # OF HOURS PER WEEK
40

SALARY OR EARNINGS:

Starting $ Volunteer per _____

Ending $ _____ per _____

NUMBER OF EMPLOYEES YOU SUPERVISE
_____

YOUR REASON FOR LEAVING

Ongoing

YOUR IMMEDIATE SUPERVISOR'S NAME

George Ward

SUPERVISOR'S TELEPHONE #

(202) 691-2138

EXACT TITLE OF YOUR JOB
volunteer

IF FEDERAL GOV'T, CIVILIAN OR MILITARY, LIST: SERIES, GRADE OR RANK, & DATE OF LAST RAISE

Part II. DUTIES:
D1 Schedule judges in track and field events
D2 Pick up judges and competitors to transport to events
D3
D4
D5
D6
D7
D8
D9
D10

Part III. RESPONSIBILITIES:
R1 Recruit and organize volunteer judges for Special Olympics
R2 Make sure all judges and competitors make it to Olympics
R3
R4
R5
R6
R7
R8
R9
R10

Part IV. ACCOMPLISHMENTS:
A1 Prepared Special Olympics Judges Training Manual now used by
A2   seven communities
A3
A4
A5
A6
A7

WORKSHEET 1, SF-171, Block 24, Sample A3 - SECRETARY

DESCRIPTIONS OF YOUR PREVIOUS OR PRESENT JOBS

List in box all duties, responsibilities, and accomplishments. Include volunteer work and internships.

Previous Job: _____ C - Clerk _____

(Assign each previous job an alphabet letter for later identification.)

Part I.
NAME & ADDRESS OF EMPLOYER

Headquarters Company

82nd Engineer Battalion

APO New York 09139

DATES EMPLOYED
From: 11/78 To: 6/81

AVERAGE # OF HOURS PER WEEK
40

NUMBER OF EMPLOYEES YOU SUPERVISE

SALARY OR EARNINGS:

Starting $ 586 _____ per month

Ending $ 775 _____ per month

YOUR REASON FOR LEAVING
Honorable Discharge

YOUR IMMEDIATE SUPERVISOR'S NAME
SFC Warren Ford

SUPERVISOR'S TELEPHONE #
(_) N/A

EXACT TITLE OF YOUR JOB
Company Clerk

IF FEDERAL GOV'T, CIVILIAN OR MILITARY, LIST: SERIES, GRADE OR RANK, & DATE OF LAST RAISE
Sgt - 1st 6/78

Part II. DUTIES:	D1 Prepare and maintain all unit records
	D2 Reports to parent unit
	D3 Prepare outgoing correspondence
	D4
	D5
	D6
	D7
	D8
	D9
	D10
Part III. RESPONSIBILITIES:	
	R1 Manage administrative functions for unit of 180 men
	R2 Advise company commander and other officers on records
	R3
	R4
	R5
	R6
	R7
	R8
	R9
	R10
Part IV. ACCOMPLISHMENTS:	
	A1 Given credit for Company admin. office being named "Outstanding"
	A2
	A3
	A4
	A5
	A6
	A7

WORKSHEET 1, SF-171, Block 24, Sample B - ELECTRICIAN

DESCRIPTIONS OF YOUR PREVIOUS OR PRESENT JOBS
List in box all duties, responsibilities, and accomplishments. Include volunteer work and internships.

Previous Job: _____ A - Lead Electrician, Foreman, Shop Steward Apprentice _____

(Assign each previous job an alphabet letter for later identification.)

Part I.
NAME & ADDRESS OF EMPLOYER

Brophy Electric

29 Broadway

New York, NY 10020

DATES EMPLOYED
From: 9/79 To: Present

AVERAGE # OF HOURS PER WEEK
50

NUMBER OF EMPLOYEES YOU SUPERVISE

SALARY OR EARNINGS:
Starting $ 14.50 per hour

Ending $ 21.00 per hour

YOUR REASON FOR LEAVING

YOUR IMMEDIATE SUPERVISOR'S NAME
Mike Brophy

SUPERVISOR'S TELEPHONE #
(212) 555-7463

EXACT TITLE OF YOUR JOB
Lead Electrician

IF FEDERAL GOV'T, CIVILIAN OR MILITARY, LIST: SERIES, GRADE OR RANK, & DATE OF LAST RAISE

Part II. DUTIES:
D1 Installation of circuits, breakers, fuses, junctions, controls.
D2 Inspect installations for federal, state, local code integrity.
D3 Train apprentice electricians.
D4 Read and interpret schematics.
D5 Work closely with superiors and contractors.
D6 Perform both interior and exterior wiring.
D7 Locate and troubleshoot problems within the systems.
D8
D9
D10

Part III. RESPONSIBILITIES:
R1 Bring existing wiring up to code.
R2 Order and delivery of supplies.
R3 Responsible for code adherence on site.
R4 Complete needed repairs as they occur.
R5 Adhere to OSHA standards on site.
R6 Keep time records for subordinates.
R7 Supervision of 16 electricians.
R8
R9
R10

Part IV. ACCOMPLISHMENTS:
A1 Illinois State Electricians Merit Award.
A2 Completed "Advanced Wiring and Schematics," Chicago Comm. Col.
A3 UBEW Shop Steward.
A4 Completed upgrade and modification of 200-year-old historic struc-
A5   ture for New York Park Service.
A6
A7

WORKSHEET 1, SF-171, Block 24, Sample C - ACCOUNTANT

DESCRIPTIONS OF YOUR PREVIOUS OR PRESENT JOBS

List in box all duties, responsibilities, and accomplishments. Include volunteer work and internships.

Previous Job: _____ A - Accountant _____

(Assign each previous job an alphabet letter for later identification.)

Part I.
NAME & ADDRESS OF EMPLOYER

Arnold Arthurson, Inc.

3200 Rickville Pike

Rockville, MD 31104

DATES EMPLOYED
From: 3/83 To: Present

AVERAGE # OF HOURS PER WEEK
45-55

NUMBER OF EMPLOYEES YOU SUPERVISE
7

SALARY OR EARNINGS:

Starting $ 350.00 per week

Ending $ 540.00 per week

YOUR REASON FOR LEAVING
N/A

YOUR IMMEDIATE SUPERVISOR'S NAME
Clara Peller

SUPERVISOR'S TELEPHONE #
(312) 345-1212

EXACT TITLE OF YOUR JOB
Accountant, supervisor

IF FEDERAL GOV'T, CIVILIAN OR MILITARY, LIST: SERIES, GRADE OR RANK, & DATE OF LAST RAISE
N/A

Part II. DUTIES:
- D1 All Accounting functions: Accounts Payable, Accounts Receivable,
- D2   Ledger Reconciliation, invoicing, inventory, payroll,
- D3   Federal, State, and Local taxation, employee benefits
- D4   contributions.
- D5 Supervision of 4 Bookkeepers, 2 Cashiers, and 1 Receptionist.
- D6 Manage cash flow.
- D7
- D8
- D9
- D10

Part III. RESPONSIBILITIES:
- R1 Maintain record keeping for tax and creditor review.
- R2 Prepare State, Local, and Federal tax returns for 1.5-Million
- R3   -dollar business.
- R4 Create plan within present departmental guidelines.
- R5 Training personnel of business office.
- R6 Negotiate contracts with suppliers.
- R7
- R8
- R9
- R10

Part IV. ACCOMPLISHMENTS:
- A1 Installed computerized billing and payroll systems.
- A2 Elected Secretary of the Maryland Association of Accountants.
- A3 Produced capital expenditures 3 years running.
- A4
- A5
- A6
- A7

WORKSHEET 2: ANALYSIS OF JOB QUALIFICATIONS

Worksheet 2 is intended to help you specify and understand the exact qualifications sought by the government for a particular job title. This worksheet is easier than the first one because it requires no creative thought; however, it is equally important. Unless you know precisely what qualifications are sought, you cannot show that you have those qualifications.

Fortunately, the Federal government is very precise about the qualifications for each of its jobs. They are described in Qualifications Information Statements (QISs), Competition Notices, and Vacancy Announcements, which can be obtained from job qualification information sources.

Some qualifications are educational; others relate to job experience. There is usually an equivalency relationship between educational and experience qualifications. This means that you can cite experience to make up for a lack of formal education and vice versa.

> **Job qualification** info sources, including the *Handbooks*, are covered in Step 3 (pp. 70-2). General **Federal job descriptions** are reproduced in Appendixes K and N.

PART I

Record the job title for which you are applying, as given in the job announcement (QIS, Competition Notice, Vacancy Announcement) or other vacancy source material. Also record the grade level at which you intend to apply, as well as any job announcement number.

You'll recall from the Overview of Step 1 (p. 7) that there is no limit to the job titles for which you can apply; in fact, the more job titles for which you qualify, the greater your chances of getting a Federal job or promotion quickly. However, you should do a separate worksheet *for each job title* for which you are applying. For entry-level jobs one worksheet (and one basic SF-171) suffices per job title; however, if you are applying at middle or higher grade levels, you should complete different worksheets for every vacancy *even if the job titles are the same*. This is because the special qualifications of higher-level jobs differ for each vacancy.

PART II: BASIC QUALIFICATIONS

Record the basic qualifications of the vacancy as listed in the job announcement or other source. *Basic* or *minimum qualifications* are those required to apply for the position and are usually so indicated in the source material; for example, typing is a basic qualification for a secretary, and knowledge of electrical circuits is a basic qualification for an electrician.

> **Basic (minimum) qualifications** are also discussed in Step 4 (p. 83).

PART III: SPECIAL QUALIFICATIONS

Record the special qualifications of the vacancy as listed in the job announcement or other source. *Special qualifications*—sometimes desig-

> **Special qualifications** are also discussed in Step 4 (p. 83).

nated "Knowledge, Skills, and Abilities" (KSAs), "Ranking Factors," "Evaluation Factors," or "Selective Placement Factors"—enhance an applicant's chances of being selected from a large pool of applications. They are usually more advanced versions of the basic qualifications: For example, a candidate for an aerospace engineering position might be required to have two years of professional experience, but a special qualification might add that this experience be of a specific nature or in a particular area. Because special qualifications often apply to a particular local vacancy, they usually are listed in a Vacancy Announcement but may not appear in a Competition Notice or manuals. The higher the vacancy's grade level, the more important its special qualifications become. At upper levels, special qualifications make a job unique and are the deciding factors in selection.

WORKSHEET 2, SF-171, Block 24, MASTER

ANALYSIS OF JOB QUALIFICATIONS
(FROM JOB ANNOUNCEMENT, HANDBOOK X-118, OR OTHER SOURCE)

PART I.

1. JOB TITLE APPLYING FOR: _____

2. GRADE LEVEL: _____

3. ANNOUNCEMENT NUMBER: _____

4. AGENCY: _____

PART II.	PART III.
BASIC QUALIFICATIONS	SPECIAL QUALIFICATIONS
	(KSAPs, EVALUATION, OR RANKING FACTORS)

BQ1.	SQ1.
BQ2.	SQ2.
BQ3.	SQ3.
BQ4.	SQ4.
BQ5.	
BQ6.	SQ5.
BQ7.	SQ6.
BQ8.	SQ7.
BQ9.	
BQ10.	SQ8.
BQ11.	
BQ12.	SQ9.
BQ13.	

WORKSHEET 2, SF-171, Block 24, Sample

ANALYSIS OF JOB QUALIFICATIONS
(FROM JOB ANNOUNCEMENT, HANDBOOK X-118, OR OTHER SOURCE)

PART I.

1. JOB TITLE APPLYING FOR: _Secretary, GS-0318_

2. GRADE LEVEL: _9_

3. ANNOUNCEMENT NUMBER: _May 4, N0300216_

4. AGENCY: _Defense Logistics_

PART II.   PART III.

BASIC QUALIFICATIONS   SPECIAL QUALIFICATIONS

                                     (KSAPs, EVALUATION, OR RANKING FACTORS)

BASIC QUALIFICATIONS	SPECIAL QUALIFICATIONS
BQ1. Knowledge of various office skills	SQ1. Posession of a certificate as a "Certified Professional Secretary"
BQ2. Working knowledge of different office procedures, such as requesting office equipment, supplies, maintenance	SQ2. Successful completion of in-service courses that offered training in areas related to the secretarial function
BQ3. Ability to organize and design a filing system to classify, retrieve, and dispose of material	
BQ4. Ability to organize effectively the flow of clerical processes	SQ3. Successful completion of work-related educational courses in excess of those used to meet minimum requirements
BQ5. Ability to make arrangements for conferences, meetings, etc.	SQ4. Recognition for exceptional work performance
BQ6. Ability to locate and assemble information from various reports, briefings, and conferences	SQ5.
BQ7. Ability to compose nontechnical correspondence	SQ6.
BQ8. Knowledge of spelling, punctuation, and syntax to identify and correct grammatical errors	SQ7.
BQ9. Refer telephone calls and visitors	
BQ10. Distribute and control mail	SQ8.
BQ11. Maintain leave records	
BQ12. Provide general and nontechnical information	SQ9.
BQ13.	

WORKSHEET 3: MATCHING QUALIFICATIONS

Worksheet 3 is used to identify which of your qualifications (from Worksheet I) match those the government is seeking (from Worksheet 2). As was the case for Worksheet 2, you will want to prepare a separate Worksheet 3 for every different job title (and for every mid or upper grade level for a single job title) in which you are interested.

PART I

Copy the particulars of the job, including job title, grade level, announcement number, and agency from Worksheet 2.

PART II: BASIC AND SPECIAL QUALIFICATIONS

List by number and/or key words the various qualifications being sought by the Federal government. Number them as per Worksheet 2, prefixing a "B" for basic qualifications or "S" for special qualifications. Be sure to include any special qualifications you meet, since they are more important than and usually supersede the basic qualifications.

PART III: APPLICANT'S DUTIES, RESPONSIBILITIES, AND ACCOMPLISHMENTS

Here is where the codes you assigned to your previous and present jobs on Worksheet 1 come in handy. Write in the numbers of the duties (D), responsibilities (R), and accomplishments (A) you listed on Worksheet 1 that match or correspond closely with the basic or special qualifications you just listed in Part II. For example, say Qualification (a) calls for "an ability to operate a word processor," and Worksheet 1 for your Job A shows "operated a word processor" listed second under "Duties" (that is, as D2). In this case, you should enter "D2" in the box where Qualification (a) and Job A intersect.

Although duties are likely to match most clearly with qualifications, you should also examine the Worksheet 1 sections on responsibilities and accomplishments. Under "Responsibilities" you may find an entry that says "responsible for maintaining word processor files," and under "Accomplishments" an entry that reads "organized and implemented a new filing scheme for word processor that made retrieval easier." These too would then be entered where the above-mentioned Qualification (a) and Job A intersect. Consequently, you may have more than one number in a given box.

Having found all the appropriate material for Qualification (a) from Job A, go on to appropriate material for that qualification from Jobs B, C, and of your previous or present jobs. When finished, you will have identified on Worksheet 3 the experiences from each of your jobs that specifically match the qualifications for the job for which you are now applying.

Don't feel compelled to have absolutely every one of your past or current jobs' duties, responsibilities, or accomplishments show up on Worksheet 3 or on your SF-171. Only experience that is *relevant* is important to the Federal examiners; irrelevant experience contributes nothing to your getting a high rating for the job title.

WORKSHEET 3, SF-171, Block 24, MASTER

MATCHING APPLICANT QUALIFICATIONS TO VACANCY QUALIFICATIONS

PART I.

1. JOB TITLE: _____

2. GRADE LEVEL: _____

3. ANNOUNCEMENT NUMBER: _____

4. AGENCY: _____

PART II.
JOB ANNOUNCEMENT QUALIFICATIONS

(FROM WORKSHEET 2) INCLUDE BOTH
BQ AND SQ NUMBERS

PART III.
APPLICANT'S QUALIFICATIONS THAT MATCH

	PREVIOUS JOB A	PREVIOUS JOB B	PREVIOUS JOB C	PREVIOUS JOB D	PREVIOUS JOB E
(USE THIS LINE TO IDENTIFY PREVIOUS JOB BY ABBREVIATED TITLE)					
1.					
2.					
3.					
4.					
5.					
6.					
7.					
8.					
9.					
10.					
11.					
12.					
13.					
14.					
15.					
16.					

WORKSHEET 3, SF-171, Block 24, Sample A

MATCHING APPLICANT QUALIFICATIONS TO VACANCY QUALIFICATIONS

PART I.

1. JOB TITLE: _____ SECRETARY GS-0318 _____

2. GRADE LEVEL: _____ GS-9 _____

3. ANNOUNCEMENT NUMBER: _____ N0300216 _____

4. AGENCY: _____ DEFENSE LOGISTICS _____

PART II.
JOB ANNOUNCEMENT QUALIFICATIONS

(FROM WORKSHEET 2) INCLUDE BOTH
BQ AND SQ NUMBERS

PART III.
APPLICANT'S QUALIFICATIONS THAT MATCH

	PREVIOUS JOB A	PREVIOUS JOB B	PREVIOUS JOB C	PREVIOUS JOB D	PREVIOUS JOB E
	Clerk	S.O.	Clerk	_____	_____
	(USE THIS LINE TO IDENTIFY PREVIOUS JOB BY ABBREVIATED TITLE)				
1. B1 Office skills	D1,D4		D2		
2. B2 Office procedures	D6, A1		R1		
3. B3 Filing system	R1 A2,R2		D1		
4. B4 Flow of clerical process	D5		R2		
5. B5 Arrange conf. meetings, etc.		D1,R1			
6. B6 Locate info., reports, etc.	D5	A1	D2		
7. B7 Compose nontech documents		A1	D3		
8. B8 Spelling, punctuation	D1				
9. B9 Telephone calls and visitors	D2,D3				
10. B10 Mail					
11. B11 Leave records			D1		
12. B12 Gen. nontech information		D1			
13. S1 Certificate					
14. S2 In-service courses					
15. S3 Work-related education					
16. S4 Work performance		A1	A1		

WORKSHEET 4: HIGHLIGHTING MATCHING QUALIFICATIONS

Worksheet 4 is where you will write your actual job-description paragraphs for the SF-171 (block 24) or other application form, based on the work you did in Worksheets 1-3. You will want to use a different Worksheet 4 for every Worksheet 3 you prepared—that is, for every different job title (and for every mid or upper grade level for a single vacancy) for which you are applying. Also, be sure to make enough copies of this worksheet to take you from your preliminary drafts through to the final versions of your job descriptions.

PART I

Copy the job title, grade level, agency, and announcement number as they appear on your Worksheet 3.

PART II: DESCRIPTION

The box marked Job A in Part II (Preliminary) is where you will write the preliminary description of your first job. The paragraph marked Job B is for your next most recent job and so on. You will begin with a rough or preliminary version of each job description; then you will rewrite each description until you are satisfied with it. This will be the final version. You should use this same Worksheet for the preliminary and the final versions.

Step 1: To start, take out Worksheet 1 for your most recent job (Job A) and Worksheet 3 for the job (or one of the jobs) for which you intend to apply. Copy into Worksheet 4's Job A box *only* those descriptive phrases from Worksheet 1 that are relevant to the job for which you are applying-that is, only those duties, responsibilities, and accomplishments you have already listed for Job A on Worksheet 3. (Not all of the experience you gained on Job A job may be relevant to the job for which you are applying.) This collection of descriptive phrases constitutes the first rough version of your eventual paragraph on Job A (see sample "rough"). You should not be concerned with writing style at this point.

For instance, the secretarial candidate of our sample forms had listed D1, D4, D6, Al, R1, A2, R2, D5, D2, and D3 as the relevant experience under Job A in Worksheet 3. Therefore, as step 1 in the preparation of this final worksheet, she has copied all the phrases from Worksheet 1 that correspond to these codes into the Job A box on Worksheet 4.

This procedure is repeated for all other previous or present jobs for which a Worksheet 1 has been completed (Jobs B, C, etc.). (Worksheet 4 has boxes only for Jobs A-C, but these can be relabeled D-F should you wish to describe more than three jobs.) Once all pertinent job decriptions have been roughed out, you are ready for the next step.

Step 2. On clean copies of Worksheet 4, rewrite the "roughs" for each job description into paragraph-form first drafts. These can then be refined as many times as necessary until they comprise strong, concise statements. An example of this process is shown as the "Sample Rough Draft." Keep rewriting your paragraphs until you achieve a forceful, persuasive description of how your previous job experience corresponds directly to the qualifications the government is seeking in candidates for the job title in question. However, be sure you *do not simply duplicate the wording* of the job announcement or *Handbook*: Federal examiners want to see that an applicant can communicate effectively on his or her own, not merely parrot someone else's words.

Step 3. In your final versions, eliminate personal pronouns (I, they, we, etc.) and start each sentencewith phrases containing such active verbs as:

Began	Increased	Motivated	Saved
Created	Led	Organized	Solved
Designed	Maintained	Planned	Supervised
Finished	Managed	Produced	Trained

Your descriptive paragraphs can be as long as you want. If there is not enough room for them on the actual SF-171 form, just cut apart the pages of the SF-171 and add paper. This practice is perfectly acceptable to Federal examiners. As a general rule, a longer SF-171 looks better than a shorter one.

When your paragraphs have been polished to your satisfaction, you are ready to type them onto your SF-171, yielding a dynamic, well presented, and powerful application.

WORKSHEET 4, SF-171, Block 24, MASTER

PRELIMINARY AND FINAL MATCHING QUALIFICATIONS

PART I.
JOB TITLE: _____ 3. ANNOUNCEMENT NUMBER: _____

GRADE LEVEL: _____ 4. AGENCY: _____

PART II. DESCRIPTIONS (Rough / 1st Draft / 2nd Draft / Final)

```
JOB A




```

```
JOB B




```

```
JOB C




```

```
JOB D




```

```
JOB E




```

WORKSHEET 4, SF-171, Block 24, Sample Rough Draft

PRELIMINARY AND FINAL MATCHING QUALIFICATIONS

PART I.

JOB TITLE: _____   3. ANNOUNCEMENT NUMBER: _____

GRADE LEVEL: _____   4. AGENCY: _____

PART II. DESCRIPTIONS (Rough / 1st Draft / 2nd Draft / Final)

JOB A   Type legal briefs, motions, and other correspondence. Take dictation and transcribe. Pick up supplies. Work with vendors and help choose hardware for our
office. Organize and maintain case files. Suggest and develop new filing system. Organize and maintain general office files. Get documents and schedules
from computer. Answer phone. Refer inquiries.

JOB B   Schedule judges in track and field events. Recruit and organize volunteer
judges for Special Olympics. Prepare Special Olympics Judges Training Manual
now used by seven communities.

JOB C   Reports to parent unit. Manage administrative functions for unit of 180 men.
Prepare and maintain all unit records. Advise company commander and other
officers on records. Prepare outgoing correspondence. Given credit for company
administration office being named "Outstanding."

JOB D

JOB E

WORKSHEET 4, SF-171, Block 24, Sample First Draft

PRELIMINARY AND FINAL MATCHING QUALIFICATIONS

PART I.

JOB TITLE: _____ SECRETARY _____

3. ANNOUNCEMENT NUMBER: NO300216 _____

GRADE LEVEL: _____ GS-6 _____

4. AGENCY: NAVY, PENTAGON, DEPT. OF DEFENSE

PART II. DESCRIPTIONS (Rough / 1st Draft / 2nd Draft / Final)

JOB A In this job I type all kinds of papers and letters, such as law briefs, memos, motions, complaints, answers and transcripts, correspondence, accounting charts, etc. I keep straight and up to date the legal case files. I also get legal papers and various schedules from the computer when the attorneys ask for them. I organize and keep track of office files and also clean them out when they are out of date. I take dictation from the attorneys and transcribe it into letter format. I answer the telephone and screen all calls to make sure they go to the proper person. My accomplishments include working with word-processing salespeople to make the new equipment fit our office requirements, and I was responsible for suggesting and then putting into use a new legal filing and management system.

JOB B In this volunteer position I am responsible for finding volunteer judges for Special Olympic meets and also for teaching them how to be judges for events that are for mentally and physically handicapped persons. I was a trainer for judges for the various kinds of track and field events, such as running, long jumping, etc., and explained to them the mental and physical problems of people competing in the Special Olympics. I am proud that I was able to find many judges and taught them for several competitions. I had the idea for and got together a judges training book, which is being used by seven communities to train judges for their Special Olympics.

JOB C This was a U.S. Army position. I was the managing clerk for all the records and various associated duties of a 180-person/soldier battalion. I was responsible for making up and keeping on hand all battalion records and each soldier's records for personnel uses. This was a big task, as the Army requires very detailed records of each individual soldier and each battalion. I had to do reports of all kinds to the next higher authority in the company every day and on a weekly basis. I answered any questions on the records that I was asked by the company commander and other officers and various personnel, and also gave them my opinion on those records when it was necessary. I typed and sometimes wrote up all the correspondence my battalion sent out. I kept files of all that correspondence and organized by month. In two different yearly inspections by the Inspector General's Office, our company was called "Outstanding."

JOB D

JOB E

WORKSHEET 4, SF-171, Block 24, Sample Final Version

PRELIMINARY AND FINAL MATCHING QUALIFICATIONS

PART I.
JOB TITLE: _____SECRETARY_____   3. ANNOUNCEMENT NUMBER: ___NO300216___

GRADE LEVEL: ___GS-6_____   4. AGENCY: NAVY, PENTAGON, DEPT. OF DEFENSE

PART II. DESCRIPTIONS (Rough / 1st Draft / 2nd Draft / (Final))

JOB A DUTIES AND RESPONSIBILITIES: Type legal briefs, memoranda, motions, complaints, answers, and transcripts, general correspondence, and accounting charts; organize and maintain updated legal case files; PRODUCED legal documents and schedules from computer upon request; organize, maintain, and dispose of general office files; take and transcribe dictation; answer telephone and refer inquiries to appropriate attorneys.
    ACCOMPLISHMENTS: 1. Directed wordprocessing vendors toward conforming new hardware to office requirements. 2. Proposed, planned, and implemented new litigation filing and management systems.

JOB B DUTIES AND RESPONSIBILITIES: Recruit and train volunteer event judges for semiannual Special Olympics competition for mentally and physically handicapped persons; instructed judges in track and field events and in mental and physical disability problems of competitors.
    ACCOMPLISHMENTS: 1. Recruited, trained, and supervised over 75 judges for four competitions. 2. Created, researched, designed, and prepared Special Olympics Judges Training Manual, which is now being used by seven communities in Virginia for their Special Olympics programs.

JOB C DUTIES AND RESPONSIBILITIES: Managed administrative functions for a unit of 180 persons; prepared and maintained all unit and individual soldier personnel records; made daily and weekly reports to parent unit; advised company commander, platoon leaders, and company personnel on all aspects of military records; prepared all outgoing correspondence.
    ACCOMPLISHMENTS: Solely responsible for company administrative office being cited as "Outstanding" in two consecutive Inspector General annual inspections.

JOB D

JOB E

Appendix J: Geographic Location of Federal Employment

One of the major factors in determining your speed and success in finding a Federal job will be your choice of locations. As discussed in Step 1 (p. 23), your chances for relatively quick success are maximized by indicating on the SF-171 or other application form that you are willing to work anywhere. (Name requests, as explained on p. 43, are the exception to this general rule.) However, many people are not willing to relocate to just any part of the country, or to relocate at all.

This appendix has two parts: The first is a table of recent Federal employment statistics for various geographic areas; the second provides useful governmental geographic codes.

The importance of **geographic location** is discussed in Step 1 (p. 24) and throughout Step 2.

CONTENTS

PART I: GEOGRAPHICAL EMPLOYMENT STATISTICS

Part I is a tale of 1994 data (the latest available as of this printing) showing the geographic distribution of the Federal civilian work force across 338 Standard Metropolitan Statistical Areas (SMSAs). Note that some of these SMSAs comprise a single city, whereas others include two or more cities, and may even cross state lines. If you cannot find a listing for a particular city, check under the name of another sizable city nearby.

For each SMSA, the number of Federal employees is broken down by pay scale (General Schedule, Wage Grade, and other). Generally, the more current Federal workers in an area, the better the chances of getting a government job there. You may wish to write the OPM Service Center responsible for an area in which you are interested to obtain a list of local agencies that hire candicates in your particular job title.

The table also shows average salaries for each SMSA, again subdivided by pay scale. Recall that the special pay scales mentioned in Step 1 (p. 19) for several metropolitan areas do not apply across the board, but only to specific, high-demand job titles. That is why the average Federal salaries in such areas need not be higher than (and may even be lower than) those in areas without special pay scales.

It should be noted that these data account for only some 1,700,000 Federal employees. Omitted are roughly 1,500,000 others—about 40% of whom are postal workers—whose jobs are either in non-SMSA U.S. locations (such as small towns) or overseas.

Geographic Analysis
of Federal Civil Service

Data Source and Population Coverage

Most data for this survey are obtained from the Central Personnel Data File (CPDF) covering most Federal agencies and full-time employees with the exception of:

a. Members and employees of Congress
b. Congressional Budget Office
c. U.S. Postal Service
d. Postal Rate Commission
e. Foreign Nationals (non-U.S. citizens employed overseas)
f. Judicial Branch

Agencies exempt by law from personnel reporting requirements are:

a. Defense Intelligence Agency
b. Central Intelligence Agency
c. National Security Agency

Non-CPDF agencies responding to this survey are:

a. Architect of the Capitol
b. U.S. Botanic Gardens
c. Copyright Royalty Tribunal
d. Board of Governors of the Federal Reserve System
e. Library of Congress
f. Office of Technology Assessment
g. Tennessee Valley Authority

The White House Office (330 employees in 1991) and Office of the Vice President (25 employees in 1991) have not reported data for this survey since 1989.

Agency changes occurring between March 1990 and March 1991 were:

New Agencies or Changes in Agency Titles

a. Arctic Research Commission
b. James Madison Memorial Fellowship Fund
c. National Commission on AIDS
d. National Commission on Migrant Education
e. National Critical Materials Council
f. National Womens Business Council
g. Office of Nuclear Waste Negotiator

Terminated Agencies

a. Alaska Land Use Council
b. Commission for the Study of International Marketing and Cooperative Economic Development
c. Commission on the Ukraine Famine
d. President's Commission on Catastrophic Nuclear Accidents

Federal Civilian Employment by Major Geographic Area, State, and Selected Agency

Executive Branch, Non-Postal, Full-time, Permanent Employees
(September 1996)

	All Agencies	Percent of Total	Department of Defense	Annuitants	Annuitants + Employees	Percent of Total
Total, All Areas*	1,658,966	100.0	715,573	2,342,112	4,001,078	100.0
Outside United States	29,266	1.8	21,495	31,654	60,920	1.5
United States**	1,628,976	98.2	693,747	2,310,458	3,939,434	98.5
District of Columbia	132,046	8.0	12,869	42,061	174,107	4.4
Fifty States	1,467,523	88.5	674,922	2,255,124	3,722,647	93.0
Washington, DC-MD-VA-WV, MSA	259,106	15.6	74,360	NA	NA	NA
District of Columbia	132,046	8.0	12,869	42,061	174,107	4.4
Maryland counties	55,832	3.4	14,760	NA	NA	NA
Virginia counties and independent cities	68,467	4.1	46,527	NA	NA	NA
West Virginia counties	2,761	0.2	204	NA	NA	NA
Alabama	34,296	2.1	20,734	54,018	88,314	2.2
Alaska	11,145	0.7	4,448	6,046	17,191	0.4
Arizona	25,115	1.5	8,057	44,642	69,757	1.7
Arkansas	10,638	0.6	3,510	23,184	33,822	0.8
California	156,417	9.4	79,651	227,015	383,432	9.6
Colorado	33,389	2.0	11,269	41,261	74,650	1.9
Connecticut	7,838	0.5	3,159	14,456	22,294	0.6
Delaware	2,716	0.2	1,487	5,787	8,503	0.2
Florida	59,730	3.6	26,977	160,804	220,534	5.5
Georgia	59,933	3.6	30,478	68,561	128,494	3.2
Hawaii	19,487	1.2	16,584	22,922	42,409	1.1
Idaho	7,400	0.4	1,314	10,621	18,021	0.5
Illinois	44,569	2.7	14,479	64,542	109,111	2.7
Indiana	20,590	1.2	11,411	33,244	53,834	1.3
Iowa	6,885	0.4	1,252	19,430	26,315	0.7
Kansas	14,734	0.9	5,318	23,072	37,806	0.9
Kentucky	19,604	1.2	8,933	30,203	49,807	1.2
Louisiana	19,932	1.2	7,839	24,697	44,629	1.1
Maine	7,845	0.5	5,395	12,823	20,668	0.5
Maryland	98,316	5.9	34,220	130,380	228,696	5.7
Massachusetts	24,909	1.5	7,812	48,812	73,721	1.8
Michigan	22,098	1.3	8,041	37,519	59,617	1.5
Minnesota	13,123	0.8	2,386	25,009	38,132	1.0
Mississippi	16,681	1.0	9,205	22,639	39,320	1.0
Missouri	36,279	2.2	15,196	49,366	85,645	2.1
Montana	7,729	0.5	1,086	10,048	17,777	0.4
Nebraska	7,894	0.5	3,341	13,194	21,088	0.5
Nevada	6,960	0.4	1,934	16,179	23,139	0.6
New Hampshire	3,324	0.2	1,175	11,375	14,699	0.4
New Jersey	30,931	1.9	18,313	57,229	88,160	2.2
New Mexico	19,706	1.2	7,521	23,476	43,182	1.1
New York	57,958	3.5	12,039	104,333	162,291	4.1
North Carolina	30,064	1.8	16,175	52,162	82,226	2.1
North Dakota	4,599	0.3	1,596	5,652	10,251	0.3
Ohio	46,181	2.8	27,195	72,784	118,965	3.0
Oklahoma	29,259	1.8	17,912	48,403	77,662	1.9
Oregon	17,046	1.0	2,613	29,092	46,138	1.2
Pennsylvania	63,609	3.8	29,388	108,269	171,878	4.3
Rhode Island	5,779	0.3	4,160	9,983	15,762	0.4
South Carolina	15,722	0.9	9,484	36,468	52,190	1.3
South Dakota	5,951	0.4	1,140	8,296	14,247	0.4
Tennessee	20,640	1.2	5,104	36,656	57,296	1.4
Texas	105,618	6.4	48,104	142,170	247,788	6.2
Utah	21,652	1.3	12,241	32,534	54,186	1.4
Vermont	2,579	0.2	505	3,814	6,393	0.2
Virginia	121,311	7.3	85,845	130,669	251,980	6.3
Washington	42,644	2.6	23,311	59,539	102,183	2.6
West Virginia	10,995	0.7	1,587	13,732	24,727	0.6
Wisconsin	11,375	0.7	3,078	23,057	34,432	0.9
Wyoming	4,328	0.3	920	4,957	9,285	0.2
Unspecified	724	0.0	331	0	724	0.0

* includes unspecified geographic location

January 15,1997

** includes U.S. territories

SOURCE: *U.S. OFFICE OF PERSONNEL MANAGEMENT*
Office of Workforce Information
Central Personnel Data Files (CPDF) September Files and the October 1, 1996 Annuity Role

TABLE 2 -- FEDERAL CIVILIAN EMPLOYMENT BY
METROPOLITAN STATISTICAL AREA AND PAY SYSTEM, DECEMBER 31, 1994

	TOTAL	GENERAL SCHEDULE	WAGE SYSTEMS	POSTAL	OTHER
ABILENE, TX	1,029	495	112	418	4
AGUADILLA, PR	234	77	43	70	44
AKRON, OH	3,408	444	108	2,818	38
ALBANY, GA	3,402	1,778	1,277	326	21
ALBANY-SCHENECTADY-TROY, NY	9,282	3,574	1,315	3,402	991
ALBUQUERQUE, NM	13,703	9,177	952	2,512	1,062
ALEXANDRIA, LA	2,109	1,110	372	383	244
ALLENTOWN-BETHLEHEM-EASTON, PA	3,063	327	13	2,701	22
ALTOONA, PA	969	387	75	391	116
AMARILLO, TX	2,014	927	124	684	279
ANCHORAGE, AK	8,894	6,169	1,370	1,251	104
ANN ARBOR, MI	4,254	1,812	266	1,125	1,051
ANNISTON, AL	5,289	2,204	2,754	245	86
APPLETON-OSHKOSH-NEENAH, WI	1,216	226	18	938	34
ARECIBO, PR	149	63	...	85	1
ASHEVILLE, NC	2,479	1,279	202	655	343
ATHENS, GA	1,330	897	43	353	37
ATLANTA, GA	45,459	25,517	1,730	14,210	4,002
ATLANTIC-CAPE MAY, NJ	3,003	1,845	262	867	29
AUGUSTA-AIKEN, GA-SC	7,120	4,625	640	921	934
AUSTIN-SAN MARCOS, TX	9,869	6,124	555	3,010	180
BAKERSFIELD, CA	10,532	3,653	1,324	1,443	4,112
BALTIMORE, MD	48,700	33,253	4,231	8,686	2,530
BANGOR, ME	1,167	502	170	484	11
BARNSTABLE-YARMOUTH, MA	484	68	...	395	21
BATON ROUGE, LA	2,323	669	54	1,501	99
BEAUMONT-PORT ARTHUR, TX	1,817	386	105	1,293	33
BELLINGHAM, WA	778	415	36	321	6
BENTON HARBOR, MI	470	112	4	350	4
BERGEN-PASSAIC, NJ	5,763	664	10	5,008	81
BILLINGS, MT	1,836	1,144	26	617	49
BILOXI-GULFPORT-PASCAGOULA, MS	8,463	5,855	1,438	763	407
BINGHAMTON, NY	1,159	300	24	829	6
BIRMINGHAM, AL	9,728	4,742	401	3,634	951
BISMARCK, ND	1,062	691	72	286	13
BLOOMINGTON, IN	408	89	10	307	2
BLOOMINGTON-NORMAL, IL	1,269	762	14	493	...
BOISE CITY, ID	4,401	2,529	527	1,092	253
BOSTON, MA-NH	37,883	17,228	1,721	15,835	3,099
BOULDER-LONGMONT, CO	2,788	1,453	78	853	404
BRAZORIA, TX	416	59	15	341	1
BREMERTON, WA	16,561	7,778	8,436	337	10
BRIDGEPORT, CT	2,104	645	22	1,409	28
BROCKTON, MA	3,021	976	289	1,374	382
BROWNSVILLE-HARLINGEN-SAN BENITO, TX	1,284	937	34	297	16
BRYAN-COLLEGE STATION, TX	852	471	31	328	22
BUFFALO-NIAGARA FALLS, NY	10,428	4,399	593	4,615	821
BURLINGTON, VT	2,153	1,254	278	593	28
CAGUAS, PR	293	110	14	161	8
CANTON-MASSILLON, OH	1,439	177	21	1,223	18
CASPER, WY	692	443	53	186	10
CEDAR RAPIDS, IA	1,041	257	16	721	47
CHAMPAIGN-URBANA, IL	1,500	770	16	675	39
CHARLESTON-NORTH CHARLESTON, SC	12,443	6,095	3,530	1,137	1,681
CHARLESTON, WV	2,519	720	176	1,540	83
CHARLOTTE-GASTONIA-ROCK HILL, NC-SC	7,132	2,081	504	4,095	452
CHARLOTTESVILLE, VA	1,263	187	26	586	464
CHATTANOOGA, TN-GA	7,822	431	949	2,022	4,420
CHEYENNE, WY	2,248	1,336	392	383	137
CHICAGO, IL	73,506	26,319	2,802	39,050	5,335
CHICO-PARADISE, CA	527	160	12	353	2
CINCINNATI, OH-KY-IN	15,623	7,309	364	7,018	932
CLARKSVILLE-HOPKINSVILLE, TN-KY	3,713	2,103	640	292	678
CLEVELAND-LORAIN-ELYRIA, OH	21,238	10,133	891	8,667	1,547
COLORADO SPRINGS, CO	8,187	5,240	1,343	1,468	136
COLUMBIA, MO	2,305	1,113	189	534	469
COLUMBIA, SC	7,809	3,937	1,081	1,990	801
COLUMBUS, GA-AL	5,009	2,839	1,086	578	506
COLUMBUS, OH	17,182	10,050	1,706	5,174	252
CORPUS CHRISTI, TX	6,113	2,504	2,672	891	46
CUMBERLAND, MD-WV	564	227	55	273	9
DALLAS, TX	30,154	11,140	732	13,298	4,984
DANBURY, CT	1,021	342	46	629	4
DANVILLE, VA	256	42	4	209	1
DAVENPORT-MOLINE-ROCK ISLAND, IA-IL	7,893	5,509	1,320	999	65
DAYTON-SPRINGFIELD, OH	22,421	15,573	2,144	2,977	1,727
DAYTONA BEACH, FL	1,384	270	4	1,084	26
DECATUR, AL	2,121	95	507	229	1,290
DECATUR, IL	396	67	21	305	3
DENVER, CO	35,810	21,275	1,395	10,424	2,716

TABLE 2 -- FEDERAL CIVILIAN EMPLOYMENT BY
METROPOLITAN STATISTICAL AREA AND PAY SYSTEM, DECEMBER 31, 1994

	TOTAL	GENERAL SCHEDULE	WAGE SYSTEMS	POSTAL	OTHER
DES MOINES, IA	7,227	2,001	399	4,446	381
DETROIT, MI	32,919	12,437	1,063	18,635	784
DOTHAN, AL	3,147	2,289	413	294	151
DOVER, DE	1,672	869	543	254	6
DUBUQUE, IA	329	83	13	232	1
DULUTH-SUPERIOR, MN-WI	1,709	672	252	757	28
DUTCHESS COUNTY, NY	1,581	559	174	621	227
EAU CLAIRE, WI	577	138	17	381	41
EL PASO, TX	7,347	5,098	854	1,195	200
ELKHART-GOSHEN, IN	302	41	5	256	...
ELMIRA, NY	499	104	6	388	1
ENID, OK	347	162	26	158	1
ERIE, PA	1,652	516	145	863	128
EUGENE-SPRINGFIELD, OR	1,907	879	129	864	35
EVANSVILLE-HENDERSON, IN-KY	1,139	244	50	798	47
FARGO-MOORHEAD, ND-MN	2,213	963	311	650	289
FAYETTEVILLE, NC	8,637	5,061	1,520	1,022	1,034
FAYETTEVILLE-SPRINGDALE-ROGERS, AR	1,480	601	124	628	127
FITCHBURG-LEOMINSTER, MA	550	260	...	285	5
FLINT, MI	1,537	243	5	1,280	9
FLORENCE, AL	1,986	136	752	250	848
FLORENCE, SC	570	160	13	392	5
FORT COLLINS-LOVELAND, CO	2,039	1,435	142	424	38
FORT LAUDERDALE, FL	7,058	1,712	13	5,168	165
FORT MYERS-CAPE CORAL, FL	1,750	316	9	1,378	47
FORT PIERCE-PORT ST. LUCIE, FL	749	146	6	588	9
FORT SMITH, AR-OK	1,433	552	396	469	16
FORT WALTON BEACH, FL	5,164	3,721	1,092	309	42
FORT WAYNE, IN	2,231	630	278	1,188	135
FORT WORTH-ARLINGTON, TX	13,953	7,480	1,058	5,024	391
FRESNO, CA	8,898	6,219	522	1,790	367
GADSDEN, AL	327	120	21	182	4
GAINESVILLE, FL	3,500	1,487	229	803	981
GALVESTON-TEXAS CITY, TX	967	522	13	429	3
GARY, IN	2,388	420	51	1,824	93
GLENS FALLS, NY	454	65	5	384	...
GOLDSBORO, NC	934	592	164	176	2
GRAND FORKS, ND-MN	1,184	609	237	313	25
GRAND RAPIDS-MUSKEGON-HOLLAND, MI	4,110	979	29	3,014	88
GREAT FALLS, MT	1,370	727	379	254	10
GREELEY, CO	461	168	14	279	...
GREEN BAY, WI	1,046	305	14	723	4
GREENSBORO+WINSTON-SALEM+HIGH PT, NC	6,690	1,570	25	5,051	44
GREENVILLE, NC	360	124	15	215	6
GREENVILLE-SPARTANBURG-ANDERSON, SC	2,821	654	71	2,057	39
HAGERSTOWN, MD	1,511	1,090	91	255	75
HAMILTON-MIDDLETOWN, OH	578	68	2	506	2
HARRISBURG-LEBANON-CARLISLE, PA	13,314	7,978	2,073	2,791	472
HARTFORD, CT	8,928	2,242	328	5,294	1,064
HATTIESBURG, MS	701	209	258	217	17
HICKORY-MORGANTON, NC	879	121	16	741	1
HONOLULU, HI	22,782	13,178	6,346	2,638	620
HOUMA, LA	431	146	11	271	3
HOUSTON, TX	26,239	11,064	785	12,395	1,995
HUNTINGTON-ASHLAND, WV-KY-OH	3,086	1,726	287	775	298
HUNTSVILLE, AL	14,836	13,464	223	844	305
INDIANAPOLIS, IN	19,539	11,215	1,358	5,902	1,064
IOWA CITY, IA	1,644	740	166	232	506
JACKSON, MI	436	53	5	375	3
JACKSON, MS	5,304	2,853	433	1,381	637
JACKSON, TN	513	153	22	279	59
JACKSONVILLE, FL	16,236	8,517	2,739	4,857	123
JACKSONVILLE, NC	3,257	1,530	995	220	512
JAMESTOWN, NY	444	54	3	384	3
JANESVILLE-BELOIT, WI	357	65	...	291	1
JERSEY CITY, NJ	10,898	1,698	1,723	7,379	98
JOHNSON CITY-KINGSPORT-BRISTOL,TN-VA	3,514	1,252	557	1,030	675
JOHNSTOWN, PA	1,291	461	75	742	13
JOPLIN, MO	510	142	19	328	21
KALAMAZOO-BATTLE CREEK, MI	5,044	2,656	561	1,499	328
KANKAKEE, IL	430	126	...	304	...
KANSAS CITY, MO-KS	29,458	17,850	1,112	8,375	2,121
KENOSHA, WI	274	25	6	243	...
KILLEEN-TEMPLE, TX	6,841	4,294	1,590	436	521
KNOXVILLE, TN	6,096	1,954	504	1,687	1,951
KOKOMO, IN	400	40	3	356	1
LA CROSSE, WI-MN	596	201	51	340	4
LAFAYETTE, LA	1,316	454	31	806	25
LAFAYETTE, IN	605	144	...	452	9
LAKE CHARLES, LA	574	168	31	374	1

TABLE 2 -- FEDERAL CIVILIAN EMPLOYMENT BY
METROPOLITAN STATISTICAL AREA AND PAY SYSTEM, DECEMBER 31, 1994

	TOTAL	GENERAL SCHEDULE	WAGE SYSTEMS	POSTAL	OTHER
LAKELAND-WINTER HAVEN, FL	1,460	275	30	1,140	15
LANCASTER, PA	1,764	227	4	1,532	1
LANSING-EAST LANSING, MI	2,934	866	186	1,858	24
LAREDO, TX	1,248	802	14	415	17
LAS CRUCES, NM	3,654	2,913	393	290	58
LAS VEGAS, NV-AZ	7,634	3,904	630	2,899	201
LAWRENCE, KS	429	211	27	190	1
LAWRENCE, MA-NH	2,852	1,983	26	835	8
LAWTON, OK	3,086	2,262	578	224	22
LEWISTON-AUBURN, ME	297	80	11	204	2
LEXINGTON, KY	5,349	2,545	693	1,251	860
LIMA, OH	641	168	9	464	...
LINCOLN, NE	2,797	1,507	306	806	178
LITTLE ROCK-NORTH LITTLE ROCK, AR	9,490	4,395	1,025	2,641	1,429
LONGVIEW-MARSHALL, TX	676	135	4	508	29
LOS ANGELES-LONG BEACH, CA	64,597	23,644	3,785	32,317	4,851
LOUISVILLE, KY-IN	10,299	4,324	1,384	3,341	1,250
LOWELL, MA-NH	973	198	45	681	49
LUBBOCK, TX	1,665	789	107	667	102
LYNCHBURG, VA	744	132	15	589	8
MACON, GA	13,880	7,403	5,189	1,083	205
MADISON, WI	4,379	1,729	374	1,631	645
MANCHESTER, NH	3,032	767	130	1,884	251
MANSFIELD, OH	814	169	96	549	...
MAYAGUEZ, PR	508	256	23	174	55
MCALLEN-EDINBURG-MISSION, TX	1,785	961	146	632	46
MEDFORD-ASHLAND, OR	1,534	875	183	405	71
MELBOURNE-TITUSVILLE-PALM BAY, FL	5,841	4,358	400	967	116
MEMPHIS, TN-AR-MS	16,176	7,731	1,899	5,247	1,299
MERCED, CA	791	397	102	286	6
MIAMI, FL	17,999	8,489	918	6,882	1,710
MIDDLESEX-SOMERSET-HUNTERDON, NJ	7,393	2,114	462	3,928	889
MILWAUKEE-WAUKESHA, WI	11,798	3,909	756	5,972	1,161
MINNEAPOLIS-ST PAUL, MN-WI	23,380	8,124	943	12,497	1,816
MOBILE, AL	2,922	1,547	154	1,159	62
MODESTO, CA	879	244	6	623	6
MONMOUTH-OCEAN, NJ	13,056	8,902	776	3,263	115
MONROE, LA	492	149	31	309	3
MONTGOMERY, AL	6,203	4,018	736	1,136	313
MUNCIE, IN	474	71	...	402	1
MYRTLE BEACH, SC	347	96	...	249	2
NAPLES, FL	555	143	15	394	3
NASHUA, NH	1,106	676	2	420	8
NASHVILLE, TN	11,370	4,926	1,028	3,737	1,679
NASSAU-SUFFOLK, NY	19,260	7,201	754	10,476	829
NEW BEDFORD, MA	510	121	2	379	8
NEW HAVEN-MERIDEN, CT	5,300	1,494	289	2,767	750
NEW LONDON-NORWICH, CT-RI	3,852	2,550	452	781	69
NEW ORLEANS, LA	16,942	9,918	1,104	4,806	1,114
NEW YORK, NY	73,454	25,499	2,305	40,698	4,952
NEWARK, NJ	18,721	8,734	774	8,199	1,014
NEWBURGH, NY-PA	5,515	2,255	1,430	1,529	301
NORFOLK-VA BEACH-NEWPORT NEWS, VA-NC	47,100	29,661	12,425	3,840	1,174
OAKLAND, CA	27,387	10,955	4,958	10,733	741
OCALA, FL	604	145	1	455	3
ODESSA-MIDLAND, TX	755	152	3	594	6
OKLAHOMA CITY, OK	24,890	13,495	6,568	3,732	1,095
OLYMPIA, WA	1,063	419	35	555	54
OMAHA, NE-IA	8,456	4,247	529	2,849	831
ORANGE COUNTY, CA	14,982	4,765	855	7,696	1,666
ORLANDO, FL	9,398	3,777	249	5,234	138
OWENSBORO, KY	272	63	6	203	...
PANAMA CITY, FL	2,932	2,054	434	437	7
PARKERSBURG-MARIETTA, WV-OH	2,152	1,674	112	361	5
PENSACOLA, FL	7,963	4,950	1,941	1,014	58
PEORIA-PEKIN, IL	2,283	977	272	975	59
PHILADELPHIA, PA-NJ	67,049	33,273	7,465	23,427	2,884
PHOENIX-MESA, AZ	18,710	8,053	1,395	8,308	954
PINE BLUFF, AR	1,744	962	547	195	40
PITTSBURGH, PA	21,274	7,456	1,560	10,507	1,751
PITTSFIELD, MA	477	186	2	287	2
PONCE, PR	528	188	46	254	40
PORTLAND, ME	2,247	466	45	1,693	43
PORTLAND-VANCOUVER, OR-WA	18,870	9,976	1,634	5,981	1,279
PORTSMOUTH-ROCHESTER, NH-ME	6,001	2,576	2,577	838	10
PROVIDENCE-FALL RIVER-WARWICK, RI-MA	7,705	1,955	350	4,821	579
PROVO-OREM, UT	869	280	29	558	2
PUEBLO, CO	854	382	90	316	66
PUNTA GORDA, FL	240	17	...	217	6
RACINE, WI	417	67	...	348	2

TABLE 2 -- FEDERAL CIVILIAN EMPLOYMENT BY
METROPOLITAN STATISTICAL AREA AND PAY SYSTEM, DECEMBER 31, 1994

	TOTAL	GENERAL SCHEDULE	WAGE SYSTEMS	POSTAL	OTHER
RALEIGH-DURHAM-CHAPEL HILL, NC	9,045	4,457	459	3,180	949
RAPID CITY, SD	1,546	975	306	258	7
READING, PA	1,283	214	18	1,046	5
REDDING, CA	1,136	567	109	436	24
RENO, NV	3,129	1,376	317	1,127	309
RICHLAND-KENNEWICK-PASCO, WA	1,310	746	143	403	18
RICHMOND-PETERSBURG, VA	16,041	9,529	1,827	3,674	1,011
RIVERSIDE-SAN BERNARDINO, CA	16,857	7,360	2,800	5,914	783
ROANOKE, VA	3,462	1,628	308	1,033	493
ROCHESTER, MN	955	532	44	352	27
ROCHESTER, NY	6,065	1,631	492	3,570	372
ROCKFORD, IL	1,418	217	4	1,170	27
ROCKY MOUNT, NC	571	70	...	500	1
SACRAMENTO, CA	20,497	12,233	4,598	3,179	487
SAGINAW-BAY CITY-MIDLAND, MI	2,010	515	109	1,226	160
ST. CLOUD, MN	1,674	690	241	534	209
ST. JOSEPH, MO	569	163	107	292	7
ST. LOUIS, MO-IL	34,096	19,843	1,769	11,156	1,328
SALEM, OR	1,534	595	98	806	35
SALINAS, CA	4,909	3,156	620	755	378
SALT LAKE CITY-OGDEN, UT	24,781	14,701	5,323	3,926	831
SAN ANGELO, TX	1,013	686	126	189	12
SAN ANTONIO, TX	35,342	20,901	8,071	3,965	2,405
SAN DIEGO, CA	38,944	20,048	6,581	7,569	4,746
SAN FRANCISCO, CA	27,755	12,982	1,368	11,078	2,327
SAN JOSE, CA	12,664	5,631	743	4,917	1,373
SAN JUAN-BAYAMON, PR	10,700	5,170	1,045	2,863	1,622
SAN LUIS OBISPO-ATASCDR-PASO RBLS,CA	708	248	41	404	15
SANTA BARBARA-SANTA MARIA-LOMPOC, CA	3,574	2,039	411	1,094	30
SANTA CRUZ-WATSONVILLE, CA	574	60	...	502	12
SANTA FE, NM	1,556	1,028	164	353	11
SANTA ROSA, CA	1,945	274	25	1,625	21
SARASOTA-BRADENTON, FL	2,070	214	8	1,840	8
SAVANNAH, GA	2,790	1,625	353	774	38
SCRANTON--WILKES-BARRE--HAZLETON, PA	4,515	1,762	266	2,062	425
SEATTLE-BELLEVUE-EVERETT, WA	23,744	12,330	1,094	8,796	1,524
SHARON, PA	313	45	3	262	3
SHEBOYGAN, WI	235	29	...	206	...
SHERMAN-DENISON, TX	318	70	31	206	11
SHREVEPORT-BOSSIER CITY, LA	4,279	1,836	714	1,122	607
SIOUX CITY, IA-NE	931	302	166	424	39
SIOUX FALLS, SD	2,211	899	264	743	305
SOUTH BEND, IN	1,129	263	12	837	17
SPOKANE, WA	3,849	1,720	501	1,443	185
SPRINGFIELD, IL	2,307	922	268	1,039	78
SPRINGFIELD, MO	2,422	983	171	1,202	66
SPRINGFIELD, MA	7,167	1,791	811	4,294	271
STAMFORD-NORWALK, CT	2,043	192	2	1,841	8
STATE COLLEGE, PA	525	209	45	269	2
STEUBENVILLE-WEIRTON, OH-WV	421	35	18	368	...
STOCKTON-LODI, CA	4,728	1,545	1,724	1,455	4
SUMTER, SC	868	542	155	167	4
SYRACUSE, NY	5,032	1,630	353	2,502	547
TACOMA, WA	8,809	4,870	1,922	1,735	282
TALLAHASSEE, FL	1,715	852	80	743	40
TAMPA-ST. PETERSBURG-CLEARWATER, FL	17,659	6,373	884	8,403	1,999
TERRE HAUTE, IN	1,372	614	275	482	1
TEXARKANA, TX-TEXARKANA, AR	4,581	1,734	2,504	338	5
TOLEDO, OH	2,672	516	193	1,931	32
TOPEKA, KS	3,204	1,436	432	985	351
TRENTON, NJ	3,220	1,020	290	1,881	29
TUCSON, AZ	8,194	3,793	1,578	1,923	900
TULSA, OK	4,980	1,979	301	2,555	145
TUSCALOOSA, AL	1,609	792	259	333	225
TYLER, TX	729	161	4	545	19
UTICA-ROME, NY	3,327	1,860	492	965	10
VALLEJO-FAIRFIELD-NAPA, CA	7,503	2,987	3,238	982	296
VENTURA, CA	10,226	6,215	1,028	1,477	1,506
VICTORIA, TX	234	65	...	163	6
VINELAND-MILLVILLE-BRIDGETON, NJ	749	409	55	283	2
VISALIA-TULARE-PORTERVILLE, CA	1,138	413	122	495	108
WACO, TX	2,766	1,471	313	718	264
WASHINGTON, DC-MD-VA-WV	367,528	255,047	19,809	26,387	66,285
WATERBURY, CT	755	86	6	658	5
WATERLOO-CEDAR FALLS, IA	609	137	41	426	5
WAUSAU, WI	520	79	11	428	2
WEST PALM BEACH-BOCA RATON, FL	4,973	968	78	3,795	132
WHEELING, WV-OH	710	227	36	430	17
WICHITA, KS	4,815	1,782	648	2,053	332
WICHITA FALLS, TX	1,969	1,396	180	390	3

TABLE 2 -- FEDERAL CIVILIAN EMPLOYMENT BY
METROPOLITAN STATISTICAL AREA AND PAY SYSTEM, DECEMBER 31, 1994

	TOTAL	GENERAL SCHEDULE	WAGE SYSTEMS	POSTAL	OTHER
WILLIAMSPORT, PA	655	258	32	363	2
WILMINGTON-NEWARK, DE-MD	5,238	1,712	626	2,196	704
WILMINGTON, NC	1,234	657	175	395	7
WORCHESTER, MA-CT	3,013	369	41	2,180	423
YAKIMA, WA	1,334	674	232	415	13
YOLO, CA	2,551	285	8	2,247	11
YORK, PA	3,056	1,178	1,058	815	5
YOUNGSTOWN-WARREN, OH	2,264	516	156	1,579	13
YUBA CITY, CA	997	440	128	422	7
YUMA, AZ	2,187	1,607	347	202	31
MSA TOTAL	2,524,559	1,275,489	248,573	787,720	212,777

Federal Civilian Workforce Statistics Publications available from:

National Technical Information Service   Telephone (703) 487–4650
5285 Port Royal Road   FAX (703) 321–8547
Springfield, Virginia 22161.   TELEX 64617

There is a $3.00 handling charge for each order plus cost of publications as listed below.
Make check payable to NTIS; or charge by MasterCard, VISA, or American Express, provide
card #, expiration date, and signature; or charge to NTIS deposit account.

			October 1991 NTIS Prices					
			Paper		Microfiche		Diskette	
TITLE	Issue	NTIS Number	Code	Price	Code	Price	Code	Price
Occupations of Federal White–Collar and Blue–Collar Workers:								
	Oct 81	PB87–131256/AS	A09	$26.00	A01	$9.00		
	Oct 83	PB87–131264/AS	A10	$35.00	A01	$9.00		
	Oct 85	PB87–131272/AS	A10	$35.00	A01	$9.00		
	Sep 87	PB89–163190/AS	A10	$35.00	A01	$9.00		
	Sep 89	PB91–129908/AS	A09	$26.00	A01	$9.00		
Biennial Report of Employment by Geographic Area:								
	Dec 80	PB87–130308/AS	A06	$26.00	A01	$9.00		
	Dec 82	PB87–130316/AS	A07	$26.00	A01	$9.00		
	Dec 84	PB87–204111/AS	A07	$26.00	A01	$9.00		
	Dec 86	PB88–156609/AS	A07	$26.00	A01	$9.00		
	Dec 88	PB90–120080/AS	A07	$26.00	A01	$9.00		
	Dec 90	PB92–140128/AS	A07	$26.00	A02	$12.50		
Affirmative Employment Statistics:								
	Sep 82	PB87–138129/AS	A10	$35.00	A01	$9.00		
	Sep 84	PB87–138137/AS	A11	$35.00	A01	$9.00		
	Sep 86	PB88–156591/AS	A11	$35.00	A01	$9.00		
	Sep 88	PB90–183666/AS	A11	$35.00	A01	$9.00		
	Sep 90	PB92–140052/AS	A11	$35.00	A03	$17.00		
Pay Structure of the Federal Civil Service:								
	Mar 83	PB87–131090/AS	A04	$19.00	A01	$9.00		
	Mar 84	PB87–131108/AS	A04	$19.00	A01	$9.00		
	Mar 85	PB87–131116/AS	A04	$19.00	A01	$9.00		
	Mar 86	PB87–214615/AS	A04	$19.00	A01	$9.00		
	Mar 87	PB89–163166/AS	A04	$19.00	A01	$9.00		
	Mar 88	PB89–163174/AS	A04	$19.00	A01	$9.00		
	Mar 89	PB90–185448/AS	A04	$19.00	A01	$9.00		
	Mar 90	PB91–129882/AS	A04	$19.00	A01	$9.00		
	Mar 91	PB92–140045/AS	A04	$19.00	A01	$9.00		
Work Years & Personnel Costs of Executive Branch:								
	FY82	PB87–133070/AS	A03	$17.00	A01	$9.00		
	FY83	PB87–130282/AS	A03	$17.00	A01	$9.00		
	FY84	PB87–130290/AS	A03	$17.00	A01	$9.00		
	FY85	PB87–210126/AS	A03	$17.00	A01	$9.00		
	FY86	PB88–158480/AS	A03	$17.00	A01	$9.00		
	FY87	PB89–163182/AS	A04	$19.00	A01	$9.00		
	FY88	PB90–188822/AS	A04	$19.00	A01	$9.00		
	FY89	PB91–129890/AS	A05	$19.00	A01	$9.00		
	FY90	PB92–141019/AS	A05	$19.00	A01	$9.00		
Inventory of Personnel Automation Projects in Federal Agencies								
	Jun 91	PB91–228833/AS	A10	$35.00	A03	$17.00		
	Jun 91	PB91–510032					D02	$90.00

PART II: GEOGRAPHIC CODE LISTING

This reprint of OPM form 1205 (Geographic Code Listing) shows all fourteen Federal employment zones and lists numerical codes for the geographic subdivisions of each one. This listing can be quite helpful. For instance, some Federal job announcements use zones and codes instead of naming the job location. By consulting the list, you will be able to decode thjis important information. Also, when asked on a Federal application form for your geographic area of preference—that is, wher eit is you are willing to work—you can use these zones and codes to make your preference clearly understood and as inclusive or restrictive as necessary. Note that a numerical code alone does not define an area: It is meaningful only when the zone is given as well.

GEOGRAPHIC CODE LIST

United States
**Office of
Personnel Management
Regions**

This booklet contains the geographic codes which you are to enter in the "Geographic Availability" section of the Form B. Follow these directions and any in the Qualifications Information Statement (QIS) for the group of positions for which you are applying. **Keep this listing** to interpret the geographic codes on the Notice of Results you will receive and to make any needed changes or additions to your geographic area of consideration.

The listing is divided into 8 zones: Alaska, Atlanta, Chicago, Dallas, Pacific, Philadelphia, San Francisco, and Washington, D.C. The zones are subdivided into smaller geographic areas such as States, sections of States, or specific cities or Federal installations. A summary of the coverage is listed below. In many cases a separate application is required for each zone. The QIS gives specific information for each examining program.

Please follow all instructions carefully to avoid losing consideration. You must decide where you want to work before you select geographic locations (codes). You are encouraged to select all locations where you are willing to work. However, you should be as precise and specific as possible since for some positions applicants are only referred to one Federal agency at a time for employment consideration. If you select codes where you are not certain you would accept employment, you may miss out on opportunities at locations where you are sure you would like to work.

If you are interested in a specific location, select the code for that location. For example, if you are interested in positions in Huntsville, Alabama, select code 005 which covers "Huntsville."

If you are interested in a location that does not appear in the geographic code listing, select the smallest listed area which includes that location. For example, if you are interested in a location in northern Alabama other than the specific locations listed, select code 002 which covers "Northern Alabama."

If you are interested in a broad area of consideration, select the largest listed location which covers the area for which you wish to be considered. For example, if you will accept any location in Alabama, then select code 001 which covers "Anywhere in Alabama."

You may select up to nine locations (codes) for which you are available. You must select at least one location to be considered for positions. For each location selected, enter the code and grid the circles on the Form B following the instructions on the form. Again, be sure to review any instructions in the application materials provided for the positions to which you are applying.

**United States
Office of
Personnel
Management**

OPM Form 1205
June 1989

SUMMARY OF GEOGRAPHIC ZONE COVERAGE

ATLANTA ZONE
Alabama
Florida
Georgia
Mississippi
N. Carolina
S. Carolina
Tennessee
Virginia

CHICAGO ZONE
Illinois
Indiana
Iowa
Kansas
Kentucky
Michigan
Minnesota
Missouri

Nebraska
N. Dakota
Ohio
S. Dakota
W. Virginia
Wisconsin

DALLAS ZONE
Arizona
Arkansas
Colorado
Louisiana
Montana
New Mexico
Oklahoma
Texas
Utah
Wyoming

PHILADELPHIA ZONE
Connecticut
Delaware
Maine
Maryland
Massachusetts
New Hampshire
New Jersey
New York
Pennsylvania
Puerto Rico
Rhode Island
Vermont
Virgin Islands

SAN FRANCISCO ZONE
California
Idaho

Nevada
Oregon
Washington

WASHINGTON D.C. ZONE
Washington D.C. Metropolitan Area
Atlantic Overseas Area

ALASKA ZONE
Alaska

PACIFIC ZONE
Hawaii
Pacific Overseas Area

ATLANTA ZONE

001 ANYWHERE IN ALABAMA

Only In:
002 Northern Alabama
  003 Anniston
  004 Birmingham
  005 Huntsville
  006 Tuscaloosa (city)
007 Southern Alabama
  008 Dothan-Fort Rucker area
  009 Mobile (city)
  010 Montgomery (city)
  011 Auburn/Tuskegee

015 ANYWHERE IN FLORIDA

Only In:
016 Northwestern Florida (Panhandle)
  017 Pensacola
  018 Eglin-Fort Walton Beach area
  019 Panama City
020 Northeastern Florida
  021 Jacksonville
  022 Gainesville
  023 Lake City
  024 Tallahassee
025 Central Florida
  026 Orlando
  027 Tampa-St. Petersburg
  028 Cocoa (Canaveral-Patrick) area
029 Southern Florida
  030 Fort Lauderdale
  031 Homestead-Miami
  032 Key West
  033 West Palm Beach

035 ANYWHERE IN GEORGIA

Only In:
036 Northern Georgia
  037 Athens
  038 Metropolitan Atlanta area
039 Southern Georgia
  040 Albany
  041 Augusta
  042 Brunswick
  043 Columbus
  044 Fort Stewart-Hinesville
  045 Macon-Dublin-Warner Robins area
  046 Savannah
  047 Valdosta

048 ANYWHERE IN MISSISSIPPI

Only In:
049 Northern Mississippi
  050 Jackson
  051 Vicksburg
  052 Clarksdale-Greenville area
  053 Columbus-Tupelo area
  054 Meridian
055 Southern Mississippi
  056 Gulfport-Biloxi area
  057 Pascagoula
  058 Bay St. Louis (Stennis Center)

060 ANYWHERE IN NORTH CAROLINA

Only In:
061 Eastern North Carolina
  062 Wilmington
  063 Jacksonville (Lejeune)
  064 Cherry Point
  065 Elizabeth City

  066 Goldsboro (Seymour-Johnson)
067 Central North Carolina
  068 Fayetteville
  069 Durham-Raleigh area
  070 Greensboro-Winston-Salem

075 ANYWHERE IN SOUTH CAROLINA

Only In:
076 Eastern South Carolina
  077 Beaufort-Parris Island area
  078 Charleston
  079 Myrtle Beach
  080 Sumter (Shaw) area
  081 Aiken (Savannah River)
082 Western South Carolina
  083 Columbia
  084 Spartanburg-Greenville area

090 ANYWHERE IN TENNESSEE
(includes Crittenden County, Arkansas)

Only In:
091 Eastern Tennessee
  092 Chattanooga
  093 Knoxville-Oak Ridge
094 Central Tennessee
  095 Nashville
  096 Tullahoma
097 Western Tennessee (includes Crittenden County, Arkansas)
  098 Memphis

100 ANYWHERE IN VIRGINIA*

Only In:
101 Northern Virginia*
  102 Warrenton
103 Central Virginia
  104 Richmond
  105 Petersburg

DEFINITIONS OF GROUPS AND SERIES

GS-610—Nurse Series*

This series includes positions that require a professional knowledge of nursing. Positions involve providing care to patients in hospitals, clinics, occupational health units, homes, schools and communities; administering anesthetic agents and supportive treatments to patients undergoing surgery or other medical procedures; promoting better health practices; teaching; performing research in one or more phases of the field of nursing; or consulting and advising nurses who provide direct care to patients.

GS-620—Practical Nurse Series*

This series covers positions which involve a variety of nursing care and practices which do not require full professional nurse education, but are represented by the licensing of practical and vocational nurses by a State, Territory, or the District of Columbia.

GS-621—Nursing Assistant Series*

This series covers positions which involve a variety of personal care, nursing care, or related procedures which do not require (a) the knowledges and skills represented by the licensure of practical and vocational nurses by a State, territory, or the District of Columbia, or (b) fully professional nurse education.

GS-622—Medical Supply Aide and Technician Series*

This series contains positions the duties of which are to provide wards, clinics, operating rooms, and other hospital facilities with medical supplies, instruments, sets, and equipment. Duties require a knowledge of aseptic techniques and sterilization practices; the care, functioning, and uses of supplies, equipment, sets, and instruments; and methods for the preparation, storage, and issue of sterile and nonsterile medical supplies and the maintenance of adequate stock levels.

GS-625—Autopsy Assistant Series*

This series includes all classes of positions the paramount duties and responsibilities of which are to provide technical assistance and related services to pathologists or physicians during autopsies and/or inquests. Characteristic of positions in this series is some knowledge of human anatomy and of embalming processes, and skill in dissecting procedures.

GS-630—Dietitian and Nutritionist Series*

This series includes positions that advise on, administer, supervise, or perform work in human nutrition requiring the application of professional knowledge of dietetics or nutrition directed toward the maintenance and improvement of human health.

Dietetics is an essential component of the health sciences, usually with emphasis on providing patient care services in hospitals or other treatment facilities. The work of the dietitian includes food service management, assessing nutritional needs of individuals or community groups, developing therapeutic diet plans, teaching the effects of nutrition on health, conducting research regarding the use of diet in the treatment of disease, or consulting on or administering a dietetic program.

Nutrition is the science of food and nutrients, their uses, processes, and balance in relation to health and disease. The work of nutritionists emphasizes the social, economic, cultural, and psychological implications of food usually associated with public health care services or with food assistance and research activities. The work includes directing, promoting, and evaluating nutritional components of programs and projects; developing standards, guides, educational and informational material for use in Federally funded or operated nutrition programs; participating in research activities involving applied or basic research; or providing training and consultation on nutrition.

GS-631—Occupational Therapist Series*

This series includes positions requiring professional knowledge of the concepts, principles and practices of occupational therapy to provide clinical services, supervise or train students and therapist, or perform research with people who have impaired capacities for performing activities appropriate to their age group. The work requires knowledge of the structure and function of the human body, environmental influences, human development, physical and psychosocial dysfunctions, and skill in developing treatment plans to teach new skills, restore performance, or learn compensating skills.

GS-633—Physical Therapist Series*

This series includes positions which involve professional work requiring the application of a knowledge of the concepts, principles, and practices of physical therapy for the treatment or prevention of physical disability or disease. Physical therapists plan and carry out treatment utilizing therapeutic exercise, massage, and physical agents such as air, water, electricity, sound, and radiant energy. Therapists perform tests and measurements involving manual or electrical means; and interpret results. Therapists also devise adaptations of equipment to meet the specific needs of patients.

GS-635—Corrective Therapist Series*

This series includes positions which involve professional work requiring the application of a knowledge of the concepts, principles, and practices of physical education and rehabilitation therapy, using physical exercise to maintain the health or to achieve physical or mental rehabilitation of patients. Corrective therapists plan and carry out treatment in which they use or adapt various types of physical exercise, physical activities, and equipment. They evaluate patients for muscle strength, endurance, coordination, and balance; provide individual or group instruction for physical reconditioning or for resocialization of patients; and devise adaptations of equipment to meet the specific needs of patients.

GS-636—Rehabilitation Therapy Assistant Series*

This series includes positions which involve treating, instructing or working with patients in carrying out therapeutic

_____
* Standards published

U.S. OFFICE OF PERSONNEL MANAGEMENT

activities prescribed for their physical or mental rehabilitation. Rehabilitation therapy assistants work in such fields of therapy as occupational, physical, corrective, manual arts, and educational. The work requires the ability to apply a practical knowledge of therapeutic methods and techniques but does not require a full professional knowledge of the concepts, principles, and practices of the specialized field of therapy.

GS-637—Manual Arts Therapist Series*

This series includes positions which involve professional work requiring the application of a knowledge of the concepts, principles, and practices of industrial arts education and rehabilitation therapy to plan and carry out treatment for the physical or mental rehabilitation of patients. Manual arts therapists evaluate vocational potential of patients; devise projects and equipment to maintain or improve skills of patients and promote recovery; and evaluate patient's ability to work in an actual or simulated work environment. Some manual arts therapists participate in the rehabilitation of blind patients.

GS-638—Recreation/Creative Arts Therapist Series*

This series includes positions which involve professional work requiring application of either (1) a knowledge of the concepts, principles, and practices of recreation therapy, and the use of recreational modalities; or (2) a knowledge of the concepts, principles, and practices of a specialized creative arts therapy field (i.e., art, dance, music, and psychodrama) and the use of appropriate specialized activity modalities to maintain the physical and/or mental health or to achieve the physical and or mental rehabilitation of patients. These therapists evaluate the history, interests, aptitudes, and skills of patients by interviews, inventories, tests, and measurements, and use such findings, along with medical records and the therapy orders of physicians or nurses, to develop and implement therapy activities for individual patients. These several therapy approaches are directed toward achieving such therapeutic objectives as diminishing emotional stress of patients, providing a sense of achievement, channeling energies and interests into acceptable forms of behavior, aiding physical and mental rehabilitation, and promoting successful community reentry.

GS-639—Educational Therapist Series*

This series includes positions which involve professional work requiring the application of knowledge of the concepts, principles, and practices of education and rehabilitation therapy. Educational therapists plan and carry out treatment which involves the use of educational situations, equipment, and methods to rehabilitate patients. They evaluate the learning ability or educational level of patients by use of educational tests and measurements. Some educational therapists participate in the rehabilitation of blind patients. The activities of educational therapists are directed to achieving therapeutic objectives such as diminishing emotional stress of a patient, providing a sense of achievement, and channeling energies into acceptable forms of behavior.

GS-640—Health Aid and Technician Series*

This series includes positions involving nonprofessional work of technical, specialized, or support nature in the field of health or medicine when the work is of such generalized, specialized or miscellaneous nature that there is no other more appropriate series. Such work is either (1) characteristic of two or more specialized nonprofessional series in the Medical, Dental, and Public Health Group, GS-600, when no one type of work controls the qualification requirements, or (2) sufficiently new, unique, or miscellaneous that it is not specifically included in a specialized nonprofessional series in the Group.

GS-642—Nuclear Medicine Technician Series

This series includes positions that involve using radionuclides (exclusive of sealed radiation sources) for diagnostic, therapeutic, and investigative purposes. Such positions require a technical knowledge of the principles and practices of nuclear medicine and the ability to perform tests and examinations using radionuclides, radiation detectors, scanning apparatus, and related equipment in medical laboratories and clinics.

GS-644—Medical Technologist Series*

This series includes positions which require professional knowledge and competence in the field of medical technology. Medical technology involves performing, advising on, or supervising clinical laboratory testing of human blood, urine, and other body fluids or tissues, using manual or automated techniques; confirming test results and developing data which may be used by physicians in determining the presence and extent of disease or in support of medical research; modifying or designing laboratory procedures; establishing and monitoring quality control systems and measures; and providing instruction in the basic theory, technical skills, and application of laboratory test procedures. Medical technology includes work in such areas as hematology, bacteriology, mycology, virology, parasitology, immunology, serology, immunohematology (blood banking), clinical chemistry (including endocrinology and toxicology), and urinalysis as they relate to clinical laboratory practice.

GS-645—Medical Technician Series*

This series includes positions which involve nonprofessional technical work in clinical (medical) laboratories in performing tests and examinations in one or more areas of work such as chemistry, blood banking, hematology, or microbiology. The reports of findings of tests and examinations may be used by physicians in diagnosis, care and treatment of patients, or in support of medical research. The work requires a practical knowledge of the techniques of medical laboratory practice in one or more areas of clinical laboratory work (e.g., blood banking, chemistry, hematology, microbiology) and of the chemistry, biology, and anatomy involved.

GS-646—Pathology Technician Series*

This series includes positions which involve technical work subordinate to the work of pathologists or other physicians (or other professional personnel) who make the final diag-

* Standards published

DEFINITIONS OF GROUPS AND SERIES

nostic examinations of specimens of human tissues and/or cell preparations. Technician work in histopathology involves preparing thin sections of tissue specimens including fixing, clearing, infiltrating, embedding, sectioning, staining, and mounting. Technician work in cytology involves preparing, staining, and examining microscopically specimens of body fluids, secretions, and exudations from any part of the body to determine whether cellular structure is normal, atypical, or abnormal. Positions in this series require a practical knowledge of the techniques of anatomical laboratory practice in one or both of the areas of laboratory work (i.e., histopathology and cytology) and of the chemistry, biology, and anatomy involved.

GS-647 – Diagnostic Radiologic Technologist Series*

This series includes positions requiring the performance or supervision of technical work in the field of diagnostic radiologic examinations, performed under the direction of a physician. The work involves the operation of radiologic equipment in a hospital or clinic environments as part of the diagnostic plan for patients.

GS-648 – Therapeutic Radiologic Technologist Series**

This series includes positions which involve supervision or performance of technical work which is subordinate to the work of radiotherapists or other professional or scientific personnel and which involves the operation of ionizing radiation equipment and sealed radiation sources as part of a therapeutic treatment plan for patients.

GS-649 – Medical Instrument Technician Series*

This series includes positions that perform diagnostic examinations or medical treatment procedures as part of the diagnostic or treatment plan for patients. The work involves operating or monitoring diagnostic and therapeutic medical instruments and equipment associated with cardiac catheterization, pulmonary examinations and evaluations, heart bypass surgery, electrocardiography, electroencephalography, hemodialysis, and ultrasonography. Positions in this series require a knowledge of the capabilities and operating characteristics of one or more kinds of instruments and a practical knowledge of human anatomy and physiology. Positions also require a practical understanding of medical data generated by patient/equipment connections. Some positions also require a practical knowledge of chemistry, pharmacology, physics, and mathematics.

GS-650 – Medical Technical Assistant Series*

This series includes all classes of positions the duties of which are to supervise and perform technical work which is subordinate to professional work in medicine and dentistry, in penal and correctional institutions.

GS-651 – Respiratory Therapist Series*

This series includes positions which involve the supervision or performance of technical work concerned with administering therapeutic and diagnostic respiratory care and life support to patients with cardiopulmonary deficiencies and abnormalities. The work involves: Operating and monitoring respiratory equipment such as continuous and intermittent ventilators, medical gas delivery apparatus, incentive breathing/hyperinflation devices, environmental control systems, and aerosol devices; administering medical gases, humidification, aerosols, and respiratory medications; maintaining clearance of patient's natural and artificial airways; obtaining blood samples and interpreting blood gas data; and providing primary assistance in cardiopulmonary resuscitation. Positions in this series require a knowledge of the operating characteristics and daily maintenance of respiratory equipment and devices and practical knowledge of human anatomy, physiology, chemistry, physics, and mathematics.

GS-660 – Pharmacist Series*

This series includes all positions which involve professional and scientific work in the field of pharmacy. The work typically involves the compounding of prescriptions of physicians, dentists, and other licensed practitioners; the formulation, preparation, bulk compounding, selection, dispensing and preservation of drugs, medicines, and chemicals; research and investigation in developing special vehicles or variations of standard formulas to meet the needs of individual patients and in developing original techniques of compounding and making available for use new investigational drugs; advising on drug therapy and usage; or performing administrative, consultive, or staff advisory work concerning the administration of a pharmacy program for hospital, clinic, or other medical care facility. Some positions involve the evaluation of drug proposals submitted by private industry and the surveillance of marketed drugs for safety and efficacy.

GS-661 – Pharmacy Technician Series*

This series includes positions which involve technical support work in a pharmacy under the supervision of a registered pharmacist. The work requires application of a practical knowledge of: Pharmaceutical nomenclature; characteristics, strengths, and dosage forms of pharmaceuticals; pharmaceutical systems of weights and measures; operation and care of pharmacy equipment; and pharmaceutical procedures and techniques.

GS-662 – Optometrist Series*

This series covers positions that require the application of professional optometric knowledges and skills in examining and analyzing the eye for diseases and defects and prescribing correctional lenses or exercises. Except for positions not involving patient care responsibility (e.g., research optometrist) positions in this series require a current license to practice optometry in a State or Territory of the United States or in the District of Columbia.

GS-664 – Restoration Technician Series*

This series includes all classes of positions the duties of which are to advise on, supervise, or perform technical work involving the development, design, fabrication, fitting to patients, and repair of custom-made medically prescribed appliances which are used primarily for cosmetic and restorative purposes. The prime objective of the work is to compensate for loss or damage to various areas of the human body by restoring a normal appearance that will facilitate the patient's social

* Standards published
** Flysheets published

and vocational rehabilitation. This objective is attained through the use of painting, sculpting, molding, and casting techniques, working with a wide variety of materials, in the fabrication of appliances which are as natural in appearance (size, form, texture, translucence, color, etc.) as the original tissues of the patient's normal feature or body member.

GS-665 – Speech Pathology and Audiology Series*

This series covers positions involving professional work in the study and/or treatment of human communications disorders, as reflected in impaired hearing, voice, language, or speech. The work requires professional knowledge of the nature of these disorders, their causes, and methods of therapeutic treatment. The work involves any one or a combination of the following functions: (1) providing direct clinical services in the evaluation and resolution of communications disorders; (2) providing graduate level training in communications disorders; (3) planning and administering a comprehensive program for evaluating and treating communications disorders; and (4) planning, administering, and performing laboratory and clinical research in communications disorders.

GS-667 – Orthotist and Prosthetist Series*

This series includes positions which involve designing, fabricating, or fitting orthotic or prosthetic devices to preserve or restore function to patients with disabling conditions of the limbs and spine or with partial or total absence of limbs. The work requires: (1) knowledge of anatomy, physiology, body mechanics, the application and function of orthoses (braces and orthopedic shoes) and prostheses (artificial limbs), and of the materials available for the fabrication of such devices; (2) skill in the use of tools and specialized equipment; and (3) the ability to deal effectively with patients and their problems and to work with other members of the medical team.

GS-668 – Podiatrist Series

This series includes all classes of positions the duties of which are to perform professional work involved in the care and treatment of the feet, including work in the prevention, diagnosis, and treatment of foot diseases and disorders by physical, medical, and/or surgical methods; the writing of prescriptions for topical medications, corrective exercises, corrective footwear and other purposes; and/or investigative research for analytical evaluations and experimental purposes when such work requires the application of professional podiatry knowledges and skills.

GS-669 – Medical Records Administration Series*

This series includes positions the duties of which are to manage, advise on, preserve, analyze, and supervise the use of diagnostic and therapeutic medical records. Medical records administration personnel develop medical records policies and procedures and provide advice on the use of medical records. The work requires a knowledge of medical records administration and management skills and abilities.

GS-670 – Health System Administration Series*

Positions in this series have full line responsibility for the administrative management of a health care delivery system which may range from a nationwide network including many hospitals to a major subdivision of an individual hospital. The fundamental responsibility of health system administrators is to effectively use all available resources to provide the best possible patient care. This requires an understanding of the critical balance between the administrative and clinical functions in the health care delivery system, and ability to coordinate and control programs and resources to achieve this balance. These positions require the ability to apply the specialized principles and practices of health care management in directing a health care delivery system. They do not require the services of a qualified physician.

GS-671 – Health System Specialist Series*

Positions in this series provide support to health care management officials by analyzing, evaluating, advising on and/or coordinating health care delivery systems and operations. Such positions may be located within an operating health care facility or at a higher organizational echelon. In addition to a high degree of analytical ability, positions in this series require specialized knowledge of the basic principles and practices related to the management of health care delivery systems. These positions do not have line authority.

GS-672 – Prosthetic Representative Series

This series includes positions the duties of which are to administer, supervise, or perform work concerned with rendering prosthetic and sensory aids services to disabled patients. Included in this series is such work as (1) planning, developing, and directing a prosthetic and sensory aids program at either the national, regional, or local level; (2) serving as an advisor to physicians with regard to selection, prescription, and acquisition of prosthetic devices involving furnishing information concerning such matters as new developments in the field of prosthetics, and sources of supply for such devices; (3) counseling and advising patients and their families and representatives regarding eligibility for and the use of prosthetic and sensory aids; (4) interpreting prescriptions of medical officers in order to make certain that proper prosthetic devices are selected for, or by, the patients; (5) authorizing the purchase, fabrication, or repair of prosthetic devices; (6) maintaining continuous liaison with manufacturers and dealers of prosthetic supplies, inspecting their facilities and services, and participating in the award of prosthetic appliance contracts; (7) participating in investigative studies by selecting patients as pilot wearers of newly developed prosthetic items, evaluating the usefulness of such items, and preparing data for the use of research project leaders or manufacturers; and (8) as required, giving technical and administrative advice and assistance on prosthetic problems to outlying stations.

This work requires the application and interpretation of laws concerning benefits available to disabled patients and of the regulations, procedures, and practices based thereon, and,

* Standards published

DEFINITIONS OF GROUPS AND SERIES

in addition, a specialized knowledge of the medical and psychological problems directly related to the use of prosthetic devices; and a specialized knowledge and understanding of the fabrication and satisfactory fitting of prosthetic devices. (These positions are filled by persons who have a major disability and who have demonstrated their ability to wear and use successfully a major prosthetic device.)

This series does not include classes of positions described in, and classifiable to, the Contact Representative Series, GS-962; Orthotist and Prosthetist Series, GS-667; Restoration Technician Series, GS-664; or Speech Pathology and Audiology Series, GS-665, although incidental performance of some elements of the work of these series will not remove a position from the Prosthetic Representative Series.

GS-673 – Hospital Housekeeping Management Series*

This series includes all positions requiring application of administrative ability and technical knowledge in supervising or performing work in the development, coordination, direction, and management of hospital housekeeping programs. The major concern of such programs is the maintenance of environmental sanitation within acceptable levels of bacteriological, as well as visual, cleanliness.

GS-675 – Medical Record Technician Series*

This series includes positions that involve analyzing medical records for completeness, consistency, and compliance with requirements, and performing related functions such as coding medical record information, and selecting and compiling medical record data. The work requires application of a practical knowledge of medical terminology, anatomy, physiology, the internal organization and consistency of the medical record, medical record references and procedures, and the medical and legal significance of medical records.

GS-679 – Medical Clerk Series*

This series includes all positions the primary duties of which are to perform clerical work in support of the care and treatment given to patients in a ward, clinic or other such unit of a medical facility. This work includes functions such as serving as a receptionist, performing recordkeeping duties, performing clerical duties relating to patient care and treatment, and providing miscellaneous support to the medical staff of the unit. This work requires a practical knowledge of the medical facility's organization and services, the basic rules and regulations governing visitors and patient treatment and a practical knowledge of the standard procedures, medical records and a medical terminology of the unit supported.

GS-680 – Dental Officer Series*

This series includes positions which involved advising on, administering, supervising, or performing professional and scientific work in the field of dentistry. Dentistry is concerned with the prevention, diagnosis and treatment of diseases, injuries and deformities of the teeth, the jaws, organs of the mouth, and other structures and connective tissues associated with the oral cavity and the masticatory system. The work

of this series requires the degree of Doctor of Dental Surgery or Doctor of Dental Medicine.

GS-681 – Dental Assistant Series*

This series includes positions the duties of which are to receive and prepare patients for dental treatment; to prepare materials and equipment for use by the dentist; to assist a dentist at chairside or bedside in the treatment of patients; to perform reversible intra-oral procedures under the supervision of the dentist; to perform dental radiography work; and to keep records of appointments, examinations, treatments and supplies. This work requires a practical knowledge of standardized procedures and methods used in dentistry, and skill in the techniques and procedures of dental assistance.

GS-682 – Dental Hygiene Series*

This series includes all positions the duties of which are to perform, under the supervision and direction of a dentist, prophylactic dental treatment which includes application of topical medication and dental health education for patients within a clinical setting.

GS-683 – Dental Laboratory Aid and Technician Series*

This series covers positions that involve technical work in the fabrication and repair of dental prosthetic appliances on prescription of a dentist. This work requires a technical knowledge of dental anatomy and skill in the use of dental laboratory materials and equipment.

GS-685 – Public Health Program Specialist Series*

This series includes all positions that direct, supervise, or perform work which involves providing advice and assistance to State and local governments and to various public, non-profit, and private entities on program and administrative matters relating to the development, implementation, operation, administration, evaluation, and funding by public health activities which may be financed in whole or in part by Federal funds; or, conducting studies and performing other analytical work related to the planning development, organization, administration, evaluation, and delivery of public health programs; or, other similar public health program work. Positions in this series require specialized knowledge of the principles, practices, methods, and techniques of administering public health programs, but do not require full professional education and training in medical, social, or other disciplines.

GS-688 – Sanitarian Series*

This series includes positions that involve planning, developing, administering, evaluating, and promoting programs concerned with the elimination and prevention of environmental health hazards. Also included are positions which involve developing and revising health laws, rules, and regulations. These positions require a broad knowledge of any one or a combination of the health, agricultural, physical or biological sciences sufficient to understand the basic concepts, principles, methods, and techniques of environmen-

---

* Standards published

U.S. OFFICE OF PERSONNEL MANAGEMENT

tal health; and a practical knowledge of health laws, rules, and regulations.

GS-690—Industrial Hygiene Series*

This series includes all classes of positions the duties of which are to advise on, administer, supervise, manage, or perform professional and scientific work in industrial hygiene, including the identification and evaluation of conditions affecting the health and efficiency of employees, or the citizens of the adjacent community, the formulation and recommendation of measures to eliminate or control occupational health hazards, and the promotion of occupational health programs for instructing and motivating managers and employees in the prevention as well as correction of potential health hazards.

GS-696—Consumer Safety Series*

This series includes professional positions concerned with enforcing the laws and regulations protecting consumers from foods, drugs, cosmetics, fabrics, toys, and household products and equipment that are impure, unwholesome, ineffective, improperly or deceptively labeled or packaged, or in some other way dangerous or defective. These positions require knowledge of various scientific fields such as chemistry, biology, pharmacology, and food technology. Consumer safety officers identify substances and sources of adulteration and contamination, and evaluate manufacturing practices, production processes, quality control systems, laboratory analyses, and clinical investigation programs.

GS-698—Environmental Health Technician Series*

This series includes positions that involve investigating, evaluating, and providing information on sanitation practices, techniques, and methods for the purpose of identifying, preventing, and eliminating environmental health hazards. Positions in this occupation require a practical knowledge of basic environmental health concepts, principles, methods, and techniques, including survey and inspection techniques and control and eradication methods.

GS-699—Medical and Health Student Trainee Series

See the series definition for the General Student Trainee Series, GS-099.

GS-700—VETERINARY MEDICAL SCIENCE GROUP

This group includes positions which advise on, administer, manage, supervise, or perform professional or technical support work in the various branches of veterinary medical science.
Series in this group are:

GS-701—Veterinary Medical Science Series*

This series includes positions that involve professional veterinary work to investigate, inspect, and deal with animal diseases, animal pollution, contamination of food of animal origin, health and safety of imported animals and animal products, safety and efficacy of many animal, as well as human, drugs and biological products, and cooperative enforcement activities involving both the public and private sectors. Such positions require the degree of Doctor of Veterinary Medicine or an equivalent degree; a knowledge of current, advanced, or specialized veterinary medical arts and science principles and practices of the profession; and the ability to apply that knowledge in programs established to protect and improve the health, products, and environment of or for the Nation's livestock, poultry, or other species for the benefit of human, as well as animal, well-being.

GS-704—Animal Health Technician Series

This series includes positions that involve technical work concerned with animal health in support of veterinary medical programs. The duties include inspection, quarantine, identification, collection of specimens, vaccination, appraisal and disposal of diseased animals, and disinfection for the control and eradication of infectious and communicable animal diseases. Performance of the work requires a practical knowledge of normal and certain abnormal animal health conditions and the related Federal-State animal health laws and regulations.

GS-799—Veterinary Student Trainee Series

See the series definition for the General Student Trainee Series, GS-099.

GS-800—ENGINEERING AND ARCHITECTURE**

This group includes all classes of positions the duties of which are to advise on, administer, supervise, or perform professional, scientific, or technical work concerned with engineering or architectural projects, facilities, structures, systems, processes, equipment, devices, material or methods. Positions in this group require knowledge of the science or art, or both, by which materials, natural resources, and power are made useful.

Series in this group are:

GS-801—General Engineering Series

This series includes all classes of positions the duties of which are to advise on, administer, supervise, or perform research or other professional and scientific work of a special or miscellaneous character which is not specifically classifiable in any other engineering series, but which involves the application of a knowledge of such engineering fundamentals as the strength and strain analysis of engineering materials and structures, the physical and chemical characteristics of engineering materials such as elastic limits, maximum unit stresses, coefficients of expansion, workability, hardness, tendency to fatigue, resistance to corrosion, engineering adaptability, engineering methods of construction and processing, etc.; or positions involving professional work in several branches of engineering.

---

* Standards published
** Flysheets published

DEFINITIONS OF GROUPS AND SERIES

GS-802 – Engineering Technician Series*

This series includes technical positions that require primarily application of a practical knowledge of (a) the methods and techniques of engineering or architecture; and (b) the construction, application, properties, operations, and limitations of engineering systems, processes, structures, machinery, devices, and materials. The positions do not require professional knowledges and abilities for full performance and therefore do not require training equivalent in type and scope to that represented by the completion of a professional curriculum leading to a bachelor's degree in engineering or architecture. Excluded from this series are positions that are specifically covered by a more specialized technical series.

GS-803 – Safety Engineering Series*

This series includes positions that require the performance of professional engineering work to eliminate or control hazardous conditions resulting from human error, equipment and machine operations which may lead to injury to persons and damage to property. The work requires the application of: (a) advanced mathematical techniques; (b) professional engineering principles, methods, and techniques; (c) safety related elements of the physical sciences, ergonomics, psychology and physiology; and (d) safety principles, standards, practices, and analytical techniques.

GS-804 – Fire Protection Engineering Series

This series includes all classes of positions the duties of which are to advise on, administer, supervise, or perform research or other professional and scientific work in the investigation or development of fire prevention projects, the design, construction, inspection, testing, operation, or maintenance of firefighting or fire prevention apparatus, appliances, devices and systems, or the testing of fire resistant materials.

GS-806 – Materials Engineering Series*

This series includes professional positions in engineering, or in engineering and physical science, which are concerned primarily with the properties, processing, uses, and inservice behavior of engineering materials, where the work performed and the qualifications required are such that the position is not more characteristic of a series appropriate to some other academic discipline. The work is characterized by the following three qualification requirements: (1) a highly developed knowledge of materials and their properties, processing, uses, and behavior under environmental influences; (2) an understanding of and the ability to utilize advances of the fundamental materials sciences, e.g., as they pertain to the interrelationships of composition, structure, and properties; and (3) knowledge of and ability to apply pertinent engineering principles and practices including considerations such as cost, availability, fabrication, performance, and use.

GS-807 – Landscape Architecture Series*

This series includes positions the duties of which are to perform or supervise professional work in the planning and design of land areas and concurrent landscape construction and maintenance for integrated developments to meet specific human needs. It involves the analysis of land characteristics, operational requirements, land use intensities, and commensurate land values and includes the efficient correlation of ground and water forms, plant forms, structures, roads, and walks to serve esthetic, functional, economic, and other interrelated purposes. Positions in this series require professional landscape architectural planning and design ability and require knowledge of the allied physical planning fields of architectural and civil engineering, and the biological sciences of agronomy, plant ecology, horticulture, and botany as they affect land development.

GS-808 – Architecture Series*

This series includes positions the duties of which involve professional architectural work which typically requires: (a) knowledge of architectural principles, theories, concepts, methods, and techniques; (b) a creative and artistic sense; and (c) an understanding and skill to use pertinent aspects of the construction industry, engineering and the physical sciences related to the design and construction of new or the improvement of existing buildings.

GS-809 – Construction Control Series*

This series includes positions which involve on site inspection of construction or the monitoring and control of construction operations. Positions in this occupation require application of (a) practical knowledge of engineering methods and techniques; (b) knowledge of construction practices, methods, techniques, costs, materials, and equipment; and (c) ability to read and interpret engineering and architectural plans and specifications.

GS-810 – Civil Engineering Series*

This series included professional positions in the field of civil engineering, typically requiring application of general knowledge of the physical sciences and mathematics underlying engineering, and specialized knowledge of (a) mechanics of solids, particularly of soils, (b) hydraulics, (c) theory of structure, (d) strength of materials, (e) engineering geology, and (f) surveying. Positions in this series have responsibility for management, supervision or performance of (1) planning, designing, constructing, and/or maintaining structures and facilities that provide shelter, support transportation systems, and control natural resources; (2) investigating, measuring, surveying and mapping the earth's physical features and phenomena; and (3) research and development activities pertaining to (1) or (2).

GS-817 – Surveying Technician Series*

This series includes positions which require primarily the application of a technical knowledge of surveying methods, equipment, and techniques in the measurement or determination of distances, elevations, areas, angles, land boundaries, and other features of the earth's surface. Specifically included are topographic, hydrographic, geodetic, land, control, and construction surveying.

GS-818 – Engineering Drafting Series*

This series includes positions which involve primarily portraying engineering and architectural ideas and information through drawings. The positions require a practical

---

* Standards published

U.S. OFFICE OF PERSONNEL MANAGEMENT

knowledge of drafting methods and procedures, and skill in the application of drafting techniques.

GS-819—Environmental Engineering Series*

This series includes positions that involve professional engineering work to protect or improve air, land, and water resources in order to provide a clean and healthful environment. Such work requires the application of (a) professional knowledge of the principles, methods, and techniques of engineering concerned with facilities and systems for controlling pollution and protecting quality of resources and the environment, and (b) an understanding of and the ability to utilize pertinent aspects of chemistry, biological sciences, and public health that pertain to the control or elimination of pollutants.

GS-828—Construction Analyst Series*

This series includes positions which involve technical work requiring the application of a practical knowledge of both architectural design and construction practices for housing. This work includes the examination of drawings and specifications for compliance with standards and verification that construction complies with these standards; the estimation of costs of construction, extension, alteration, remodeling, or repair of housing; and the collection, analysis, and development of basic cost information on housing construction.

GS-830—Mechanical Engineering Series*

This series includes professional positions in the field of mechanical engineering typically requiring the application of thermodynamics, mechanics, and other physical, mathematical and engineering sciences to problems concerned with the production, transmission, measurement, and use of energy, especially heat and mechanical power.

GS-840—Nuclear Engineering Series*

This series includes positions that involve professional engineering work which is concerned primarily with the engineering principles and considerations relating to the atomic nucleus and the systems, processes, and materials required for the generation, controlled release, and utilization of nuclear energy. Nuclear engineering work requires the application of professional engineering knowledges in the research, development, design, construction, testing, installation, monitoring, operation and maintenance of nuclear reactors (fission or fusion) and other nuclear systems and immediate auxiliary or ancillary systems and equipment.

GS-850—Electrical Engineering Series*

This series includes professional engineering positions which require primarily application of knowledge of (a) the physical and engineering sciences and mathematics, (b) electrical phenomena, and (c) the principles, techniques, and practices of electrical engineering. The work pertains primarily to electrical circuits, circuit elements, equipment, systems, and associated phenomena concerned with electrical energy for purposes such as motive power, heating, illumination, chemical processes, or the production of localized electric or magnetic fields.

GS-854—Computer Engineering Series*

This series includes professional engineering positions which require primarily the application of knowledge of (a) fundamentals and principles of professional engineering, (b) computer hardware, systems software, and computer system architecture and integration, and (c) mathematics, including calculus, probability, statistics, discrete structures, and modern algebra. The work pertains primarily to the research, design, development, testing, evaluation, and maintenance of computer hardware and software systems in an integrated manner.

GS-855—Electronics Engineering Series*

This series includes professional engineering positions which require primarily application of knowledge of (a) the physical and engineering sciences and mathematics, (b) electronic phenomena, and (c) the principles, techniques, and practices of electronics engineering. The work pertains primarily to electronic circuits, circuit elements, equipment, systems, and associated phenomena concerned with electromagnetic or acoustical wave energy or electrical information for purposes such as communication, computation, sensing, control, measurement, and navigation.

GS-856—Electronics Technician Series*

This series includes positions that require (a) the knowledge of the techniques and theories characteristic of electronics such as a knowledge of basic electricity and electronic theory, algebra, and elementary physics, (b) the ability to apply that knowledge to duties involved in engineering functions such as design, development, evaluation, testing, installation and maintenance of electronic equipment, and (c) a knowledge of the capabilities, limitations, operations, design characteristics, and functional use of a variety of types and models of electronic equipment and systems. Such knowledge is related to but less than a full professional knowledge of electronics engineering.

GS-858—Biomedical Engineering Series

This series includes positions which involve professional work in biomedical engineering. The work requires the application of engineering concepts and methodology to investigate problems and phenomena of living systems to advance the understanding of these systems and improve medical practices; to develop materials, instruments, diagnostic and therapeutic devices, and other equipment applicable in the study of life systems and the practice of medicine; and to improve health service delivery systems for communities and within individual institutional components (hospitals, clinics, or other activities). Biomedical engineering work requires in addition to knowledge and skill in engineering disciplines a background in physiology and anatomy, and a practical facility in specialized subject matter areas such as computer applications, electronics, or mathematics.

GS-861—Aerospace Engineering Series*

This series includes professional aerospace engineering positions engaged in planning, research, development, design, testing, evaluation, production, fabrication, operation, and maintenance of aerospace vehicles and integrally associated

DEFINITIONS OF GROUPS AND SERIES

equipment, and investigation of phenomena encountered in aerospace flight. Positions in this series require the application of a wide range of scientific and engineering principles in the field of aeronautics and astronautics such aerodynamics, fluid mechanics, flight mechanics, structural dynamics, thermodynamics, and energy conversion and utilization in adaptation to the aerospace environment.

GS-871—Naval Architecture Series*

This series includes all classes of positions the duties of which are to advise on, administer, supervise, or perform professional engineering work in the field of naval architecture which primarily concerns the form, strength, stability, performance, and operational characteristics of ships. The work of positions in this series includes research, design, development, construction, investigation, testing, arrangement, installation, and maintenance for all types of ships. This work involves the consideration and application of naval architectural principles and concepts; the making of stability and buoyancy calculations and developing data for launching, loading, operation, and drydocking of ships in a safe, efficient, and economical manner; and naval architectural investigations and development of data and criteria leading to improved ship design.

GS-873—Ship Surveying Series

This series includes all classes of positions the duties of which are to administer, supervise, or perform work primarily concerned with surveying Government-owned vessels, Government-operated vessels, or both, or privately owned and operated merchant vessels, including components installed thereon, to determine condition and need for an extent of work required to place the vessels in condition to meet specified requirements. Work of this series includes in combination (1) the preparation of specifications, including estimates of labor and material costs to cover work determined to be necessary as a result of surveys, (2) the inspection and acceptance of the work accomplished to place the vessel in the condition specified, and (3) other work, such as preparation of reports, incidental to ship surveying. This series does not include work primarily concerned with inspection of the construction, assembly, modification, conversion, overhaul, or repair of vessels or inspections involved in the procurement of vessels, chiefly to assure compliance with contracts, plans, and specifications.

GS-880—Mining Engineering Series*

This series includes positions that require primarily the application of professional knowledge of mining engineering. The work requires the ability to apply the principles of mathematics, chemistry, geology, physics, and engineering to mining technology. It also requires general knowledge of construction and excavation methods, materials handling, and the processes involved in preparing mined materials for use. Mining engineer positions are concerned with the search for, efficient removal, and transportation of ore to the point of use; conservation and development of mineral lands, materials, and deposits; and the health and safety of mine workers.

GS-881—Petroleum Engineering Series*

This series includes positions that require primarily the application of a professional knowledge of petroleum engineering. The work is concerned with exploration and development of oil and natural gas fields; production, transportation, and storage of petroleum, natural gas, and helium; investigation, evaluation, and conservation of these resources; regulation of transportation and sale of natural gas; valuation of production and distribution facilities for tax, regulatory, and other purposes; and research on criteria, principles, methods, and equipment.

GS-890—Agricultural Engineering Series*

This series includes professional positions which require primarily the application of the principles of engineering in combination with knowledge of one or more fields of agriculture. The work involves research, development, design, test, evaluation, and application of the fundamentals of engineering to aid in the solution of agricultural problems in such areas as farm structures, soil and water conservation, mechanical power and machinery, and electric power and processing.

GS-892—Ceramic Engineering Series

This series includes professional engineering positions concerned with the development or adaptation of materials, methods, and processes used in the manufacture of ceramic products; and with the design, construction and operation of industrial processes and equipment used in their production. Ceramic products may be considered as those composed of nonmetallic, inorganic minerals which are subjected to high temperature during manufacture or use; and include crystalline materials with desired physical properties, cementitious materials, abrasives, refractories, porcelain enamels, structural clay products, whiteware, and glass products.

GS-893—Chemical Engineering Series*

This series includes positions that involve professional work in chemical engineering, including research, development, design, operation, evaluation, and improvement of processes, plants, equipment, methods, or products. The work involves changes in the chemical composition or physical state of materials and requires primarily application of knowledge of the principles and practices of chemical engineering, chemistry, and other scientific and engineering disciplines.

GS-894—Welding Engineering Series

This series includes all classes of positions the duties of which are to administer, supervise, advise on, coordinate, or perform engineering research or other professional engineering work involving the application of welding and engineering principles to the solution of problems in the development and improvement of welding equipment and processes, the design of welding sequences and welded structures, the establishment and maintenance of standards and quality controls for welding, the giving of advice to design and construction engineers on the production applicability of welding, and similar work regarding metallic joining or cutting processes allied to welding.

---

* Standards published

U.S. OFFICE OF PERSONNEL MANAGEMENT

GS-895 – Industrial Engineering Technician Series*

This series includes nonprofessional technical positions engaged in industrial engineering work. Industrial engineering technician positions are concerned primarily with planning, designing, analyzing, improving, and installing integrated work systems comprised of men, materials, and equipment, for use in producing products, rendering services, repairing equipment, or moving and storing supplies and equipment. The work typically involves studies of engineered time standards, methods engineering, layout design of work centers, control systems, materials handling, or manpower utilization. It requires a knowledge of the principles and techniques of industrial engineering and practical knowledge of pertinent industrial and related work processes, facilities, methods, and equipment.

GS-896 – Industrial Engineering Series*

This series includes positions that involve professional work in industrial engineering. Industrial engineering is that branch of engineering concerned with the planning, design, analysis, improvement, and installation of integrated systems of employees, materials, and equipment to produce a product or render a service. The work requires application of specialized professional knowledge and skill in the mathematical, physical, and social sciences together with the principles and methods of engineering analysis and design to specify, predict, and evaluate the results to be obtained from such systems.

GS-899 – Engineering and Architecture Student Trainee Series

See the series definition for the General Student Trainee Series, GS-099.

GS-900 – LEGAL AND KINDRED GROUP

This group includes positions which advise on, administer, supervise, or perform work of a legal or kindred nature.

Series in this group are:

GS-904 – Law Clerk Series

This series includes positions of law clerk trainees performing professional legal work requiring graduation from a recognized law school or equivalent experience, pending admission to the bar.

GS-905 – General Attorney Series*

This series includes professional legal positions involved in preparing cases for trial and/or the trial of cases before a court or an administrative body or persons having quasi-judicial power; rendering legal advice and services with respect to questions, regulations, practices, or other matters falling within the purview of a Federal Government agency (this may include conducting investigations to obtain evidentiary data); preparing interpretative and administrative orders, rules, or regulations to give effect to the provisions of governing statutes or other requirements of law; draft-

ing, negotiating, or examining contracts or other legal documents required by the agency's activities; drafting, preparing formal comments, or otherwise making substantive recommendations with respect to proposed legislation; editing and preparing for publication statutes enacted by Congress, opinions or discussions of a court, commission, or board; drafting and reviewing decisions for consideration and adoption by agency officials. Included also are positions, not covered by the Administrative Procedure Act, involved in hearing cases arising under contracts or under the regulations of a Federal Government agency when such regulations have the effect of law, and rendering decisions or making recommendations for disposition of such cases. The work of this series requires admission to the bar.

GS-920 – Estate Tax Examining Series

This series includes positions concerned with determining liability for Federal estate or gift taxes. Such work requires knowledge of State, local, and Federal laws and regulations relating to estate and gift taxation; knowledge of accounting principles and theory; knowledge of business methods and practices; and knowledge of property valuation and investigative techniques.

GS-930 – Hearings and Appeals Series

This series includes positions which involve the adjudication of cases that typically include the conduct of formal or informal hearings that accord appropriate due process, arising under statute or under the regulations of a Federal agency when the hearings are not subject to the Administrative Procedure Act; or involve the conduct of appellate reviews of prior decisions. The work requires the ability to review and evaluate investigative reports and case records, conduct hearings in an orderly and impartial manner, determine credibility of witnesses, sift and evaluate evidence, analyze complex issues, apply agency rules and regulations and court decisions, prepare clear and concise statements of fact, and exercise sound judgment in arriving at decisions. Some positions require application of a substantive knowledge of agency policies, programs, and requirements in fields such as personnel management or environmental protection.

GS-945 – Clerk of Court Series

This series includes all classes of positions the duties of which are to administer, supervise, or perform clerical, administrative, and related work in connection with proceedings instituted before courts of justice under the jurisdiction of the District of Columbia Government or of a department or independent establishment in the executive branch of the United States Government, and in connection with the business operations of such courts.

GS-950 – Paralegal Specialist Series*

This series includes positions not requiring professional legal competence which involve various legal assistance duties, of a type not classifiable in some other series in the Legal and Kindred Group, in connection with functions such as hearings, appeals, litigation, or advisory services. The specialists analyze the legal impact of legislative developments and administrative and judicial decisions, opinions, determinations, and rulings on agency programs; conduct

---

* Standards published

DEFINITIONS OF GROUPS AND SERIES

research for the preparation of legal opinions on matters of interest to the agency; perform substantive legal analysis of requests for information under the provisions of various acts; or other similar legal support functions which require discretion and independent judgment in the application of a specialized knowledge of laws, precedent decisions, regulations, agency policies and practices, and judicial or administrative proceedings. Such knowledge is less than that represented by graduation from a recognized law school, and may have been gained from formalized, professionally instructed agency or educational institution training or from professionally supervised on-the-job training. While the paramount knowledge requirements of this series are legal, some positions also require a practical knowledge of subject matter areas related to the agency's substantive programs.

GS-958 – Pension Law Specialist Series

This series includes positions that involve administering, supervising, or performing work requiring specialized knowledge of the provisions governing the administration of employee pension and welfare plans and the management of plan funds. This knowledge is used to: (1) interpret such laws as the Employee Retirement Income Security Act (ERISA), certain provisions of the Federal Employees' Retirement System Act (FERSA) relating to the Thrift Savings Plan, pertinent amendments, and tax law, as well as relevant court decisions, regulations, rulings, opinions, and appeal decisions; (2) prepare associated regulations, rulings, advisory opinions, appeal decisions, exemptions, and other technical guides; (3) examine legislative and public policy issues which affect the management, investment practices, assets, and viability of the nation's employee benefit plans; (4) formulate statutory, regulatory, and policy proposals; and/or (5) provide policy and technical guidance on matters of enforcement.

GS-962 – Contact Representative Series*

This series includes positions that primarily involve personal contacts with the public for the purposes of (1) providing information on rights, benefits, privileges, or obligations under a body of law; (2) explaining pertinent legal provisions, regulations, and related administrative practices and their application to specific cases; and (3) assisting individuals in developing needed evidence and preparing required documents, or in resolving errors, delays, or other problems in obtaining benefits or fulfilling obligations. The work requires (1) a high degree of skill in oral communication; and (2) a good working knowledge of, and ability to apply, governing laws, regulations, precedents, and agency procedures, but less than the degree of legal training equivalent to that represented by graduation from a recognized law school.

GS-963 – Legal Instruments Examining Series*

This series includes all positions concerned with the examination of legal documents, other than claims, which require the application of specialized knowledge of particular laws, or of regulations, precedents, or agency practices based thereon, and which do not require legal training equivalent to that represented by graduation from a recognized law school.

GS-965 – Land Law Examining Series*

This series includes positions the duties of which are to administer, supervise, or perform quasi-legal work involved in processing, adjudicating and advising on applications and claims for rights, privileges, gratuities, or other benefits authorized under the various public land, mineral leasing, and mining laws. The work requires a knowledge of governing public laws and agency policies and procedures regarding the application of these laws, but does not require full professional legal training.

GS-967 – Passport and Visa Examining Series*

This series includes positions the duties of which are to administer, advise on, supervise, or perform quasi-legal work involved in the review, evaluation and examination of applications for United States passports and for other privileges and services that involve citizenship determinations; and/or application for United States visas and for other privileges and services that involve determinations of aliens' fitness for admission to this country.

GS-986 – Legal Clerk and Technician Series*

This series includes all classes of positions the duties of which are to perform or supervise legal clerical or technical work not classifiable in any other series in the Legal and Kindred Group, GS-900. The work requires: (1) a specialized knowledge of legal documents and processes; and (2) the ability to apply established instructions, rules, regulations, precedents, and procedures pertaining to legal activities.

GS-987 – Tax Law Specialist Series

This series includes all classes of positions, not classifiable in any other series, the principal duties of which are to administer, supervise, or perform quasi-legal technical tax work requiring analysis and application of tax principles and specialized knowledges of the Internal Revenue Code and related laws, court decisions, regulations, and precedent rulings of the Internal Revenue Service, not requiring legal training equivalent to that represented by graduation from a recognized law school; in such functions as (1) interpreting the Internal Revenue Code, related laws, regulations, rulings, and precedents, (2) preparing regulations, rulings, and technical guides, and (3) making or reviewing determinations and decisions in such matters.

GS-990 – General Claims Examining Series

This series includes all classes of positions the duties of which are to administer, supervise, or perform quasi-legal work in developing, examining, adjusting, reconsidering, or authorizing the settlement of claims for which separate series have not been provided.

GS-991 – Workers' Compensation Claims Examining Series*

This series includes quasi-legal positions concerned with work involving the examination, development, and adjudication of claims for compensation (monies and medical services) under the Federal Employees' Compensation Act, and/or the Longshoremen's and Harbor Workers' Compensation Act, and/or their statutory extensions. Such work

---

* Standards published

U.S. OFFICE OF PERSONNEL MANAGEMENT

requires a comprehensive knowledge of the workers' compensation program, and an extensive lay medical knowledge of impairments and diseases.

GS-992 – Loss and Damage Claims Examining Series

This series includes all classes of positions the duties of which are to administer, supervise, or perform quasi-legal work involved in developing, examining, adjusting, reconsidering, or authorizing the settlement of claims, by or against the Government, exclusive of claims arising under insurance contracts, because of (1) loss, damage, or rifling of United States mail, or abandonment, capture, loss, damage, or destruction of personal or real property, other than Government materials or supplies in the custody of or under the control of contractors, storekeepers, warehousemen, shippers, transit companies, or others, or under contracts of insurance, and (2) injury or death of individuals where such claims work is not properly classifiable in other series in the Legal and Kindred Group, GS-900.

GS-993 – Social Insurance Claims Examining Series*

This series includes (1) positions the duties of which are to advise on, supervise, or perform quasi-legal work involved in developing, examining, adjusting, adjudicating, authorizing, or reconsidering claims for retirement, survivor, or disability benefits under the Social Security and/or Railroad Retirement Acts, or (2) positions the duties of which consist of studying and preparing operating policies and procedures as they relate to the processing of claims under these programs.

GS-994 – Unemployment Compensation Claims Examining Series*

This series includes all classes of positions the duties of which are to administer, supervise, or perform quasi-legal work involved in developing, examining, adjusting, reconsidering, or authorizing the settlement of claims for unemployment compensation, including sickness benefits.

GS-995 – Dependents and Estates Claims Examining Series

This series includes all classes of positions the duties of which are to administer, supervise, or perform quasi-legal work involved in developing, examining, adjusting, reconsidering, or authorizing the settlement of claims (1) for the payment of monetary allowances or gratuities based upon dependency on an active or deceased former military serviceman, and (2) for assets of a deceased or incompetent person which are in the possession of a Government agency.

GS-996 – Veterans Claims Examining Series*

This series includes positions the duties of which are to administer, supervise, or perform quasi-legal work involved in developing, examining, adjusting, reconsidering, or authorizing the settlement of claims filed by veterans, their dependents and beneficiaries, in regard to disability compensation, disability, pension, death pension, death compensation, National Service Life Insurance and U.S. Government Life Insurance, as well as other Veterans Administration administered benefits.

GS-998 – Claims Clerical Series*

This series includes positions which involve clerical work in the examination, review, or development of claims by or against the Federal Government. Included are (a) clerical positions concerned with examining and developing claims cases for adjudication; (b) clerical positions concerned with determining and verifying entitlement to benefits, where the legal requirements are clear and the examination process is routine; (c) clerical positions concerned with examining, developing, and verifying post-entitlement actions regarding established beneficiaries; and (d) clerical positions concerned with answering general or routine inquiries about benefits or procedures for filing claims. The work in this series requires ability to apply established instructions, rules, regulations, and procedures relative to claims examining activities.

GS-999 – Legal Occupations Student Trainee Series

See the series definition for the General Student Trainee Series, GS-099.

GS-1000 – INFORMATION AND ARTS GROUP

This group includes positions which involve professional, artistic, technical, or clerical work in (1) the communication of information and ideas through verbal, visual, or pictorial means, (2) the collection, custody, presentation, display, and interpretation of art works, cultural objects, and other artifacts, or (3) a branch of fine or applied arts such as industrial design, interior design, or musical composition. Positions in this group require writing, editing, and language ability; artistic skill and ability; knowledge of foreign languages; the ability to evaluate and interpret informational and cultural materials; or the practical application of technical or esthetic principles combined with manual skill and dexterity; or related clerical skills.

Series in this group are:

GS-1001 – General Arts and Information Series

This series includes all positions the duties of which are to administer, supervise, or perform (1) any combination of work characteristic of two or more series in this group where (a) no one type of work is series controlling, (b) the paramount qualification requirements are not characteristic of another series in the group, and (c) the combination of work is not specifically provided for in another series, or (2) other work typical of this group for which no other series has been established.

---

* Standards published

DEFINITIONS OF GROUPS AND SERIES

GS-1008—Interior Design Series**

This series includes positions the duties of which are to perform, supervise, or manage work related to the design of interior environments in order to promote employee productivity, health, and welfare, and/or the health and welfare of the public. Typical duties include investigating, identifying, and documenting client needs; analyzing needs, proposing options and, working with the client, developing specific solutions; developing design documents, including contract working drawings and specifications; and, as appropriate, managing design projects performed in-house or by contract. The work requires applying knowledges from a variety of such fields as (a) interior construction (building systems and components, building codes, equipment, materials, and furnishings, working drawings and specification, codes and standards); (b) contracting (cost estimates, bid proposals, negotiations, contract awards, site visits during construction, pre- and post-occupancy evaluations); (c) facility operation (maintenance requirements, traffic patterns, security and fire protection); (d) aesthetics (sense of scale, proportion, and form; color, texture, and finishes; style and visual imagery); (e) psychology (privacy and enclosure; effects of environmental components (color, texture, space, etc.) on mood, alertness, etc.); and, as appropriate, (f) management (design project and resource coordination).

GS-1010—Exhibits Specialist Series*

This series includes positions which supervise or perform work involved in planning, constructing, installing, and operating exhibits, the preparation of gallery space for exhibits, the preservation of historic buildings, or the restoration or preparation of items to be exhibited. The work requires a combination of artistic abilities, technical knowledge and skills, and ability to understand the subject matter concepts which assigned exhibits projects are intended to convey.

GS-1015—Museum Curator Series*

This series includes all classes of positions the primary duties of which are to administer, supervise, or perform professional work related to research, collections and exhibits in Federal museums, when such work is not classifiable in other professional, scientific, or historical series.

GS-1016—Museum Specialist and Technician Series*

This series includes all classes of positions the duties of which include technical and specialized work in connection with the operation of public museums or the management of museum collections.

GS-1020—Illustrating Series*

This series includes positions which supervise or perform work involved in laying out or executing illustrations in black and white or in color, and with retouching photographs. The work requires artistic ability, the skill to draw freehand or with drawing instruments, and the ability to use art media such as pen-and-ink, pencils, tempera, acrylics, oils, wash, watercolor, pastels, air brush, or computer-generated graphics. It also requires knowledge of the subject matter being depicted sufficient to create accurate visual representations. Knowledge of basic art principles such as color, line, form, and space is required to produce appropriately composed illustrations.

GS-1021—Office Drafting Series*

This series includes positions involving the supervision or performance of drafting work for charts, diagrams, floor plans, office forms, and other types of graphic presentation of statistical, administrative, or related data. Positions in this series require skill in the application of drafting techniques, ability to read statistical tables and make arithmetical computations, and knowledge of the various types of graphic presentation that are appropriate for portrayal of statistical, administrative, and related data.

GS-1035—Public Affairs Series*

This series includes positions responsible for administering, supervising, or performing work involved in establishing and maintaining mutual communication between Federal agencies and the general public and various other pertinent publics including internal or external, foreign or domestic audiences. Positions in this series advise agency management on policy formulation and the potential public reaction to proposed policy, and identify and carry out the public communication requirements inherent in disseminating policy decisions. The work involves identifying communication needs and developing informational materials that inform appropriate publics of the agency's policies, programs, services and activities, and plan, execute, and evaluate the effectiveness of information and communications programs in furthering agency goals. Work in the series requires skills in written and oral communications, analysis, and interpersonal relations.

GS-1040—Language Specialist Series*

This series includes positions the primary duties of which are to administer, supervise, or perform work in rendering from a foreign language into English or from English into a foreign language the spoken or written word where the ultimate objective is accurate translations and/or interpretations.

GS-1046—Language Clerical Series*

This series includes positions the duties of which are to supervise or perform translating and/or interpreting work from and into English where the level of language knowledges and skills required is sufficient only for mutual understanding of basic concepts, phrases, and words, or where the level is limited in breadth because of the routine, repetitive nature of the interpreting and translating assignments, and/or clerical duties are performed in conjunction with such translating or interpreting.

GS-1048—Foreign Language Broadcasting Series

This series includes all classes of positions the duties of which are to administer, supervise, advise on, or perform (1) the adaptation of radio scripts and other written materials in

English into a foreign language for broadcast to foreign countries or geographic area, requiring not only a native ability in the foreign language involved, but also a comprehensive knowledge of the culture, mores, current developments, and thinking of the people in the area of broadcast reception, and a knowledge of the radio style appropriate for specific foreign countries and geographic areas; and/or (2) vocal participation in radio broadcasts in a foreign language for live and recorded programs, requiring a speaking voice suitable for international broadcasting, ability in the language which is comparable to that of a native living in the area of broadcast reception, and vocal qualities and skills necessary in broadcasting news, news analyses, features, documentaries, and dramas.

GS-1051—Music Specialist Series

This series covers positions that require a knowledge of one or more of the music arts such as vocal or instrumental music; composition, theory, and harmony; arranging and orchestration; choral or instrumental conducting; classical or modern dance styles including choreography and notation; or musicology. Music specialists (1) plan, supervise, administer, or carry out educational, recreational, cultural, or other programs in music such as creative music clinics or workshops, or electronic music experiments, (2) produce, stage, direct, or conduct musical productions, concerts, or recitals, (3) instruct or serve as a specialist in conducting; composing; arranging; interpreting classical, modern, ethnic or cultural dance forms; choreography; musicology; or choral or instrumental music, or (4) perform other functions requiring knowledge or skill in music.

GS-1054—Theater Specialist Series

This series covers positions that require a knowledge of the techniques of producing, staging, rehearsing, or performing in theatrical productions; of technical production; or of theatrical history and literature. Theater specialists (1) plan, supervise, administer, or carry out educational, recreational, cultural, or other programs in theater, such as children's theater or creative dramatics; (2) produce, stage, or direct theatrical productions; (3) instruct or serve as a specialist in direction; technical production; dance production; performance techniques; playwriting; play or music theater production; or theater administration, management or promotion; or (4) perform other functions requiring knowledge and skill in the theater arts.

GS-1056—Art Specialist Series

This series covers positions that require a knowledge of the theories and techniques of one or more art forms. Art specialists (1) plan, supervise, administer, or carry out educational, recreational, cultural, or other programs in art, (2) demonstrate the techniques and instruct in one or more of the arts, or (3) perform other functions requiring knowledge and skill in one or more art forms.

GS-1060—Photography Series*

This series includes positions that involve the performance of (a) still, motion picture, television, high-speed, aerial, or other similar camera work, or (b) photographic processing work, or (c) a combination of these two types of work. Positions in this series require, in addition to a knowledge of the equipment, techniques, and processes of photography, either (1) a knowledge about the subject matter of work to be photographed in such fields as scientific, engineering, technical and medical research and operations, or (2) artistic ability in selecting, arranging, and lighting subjects, or in processing negatives, or printing, enlarging, cropping, or retouching prints, or (3) both.

GS-1071—Audio-Visual Production Series*

This series includes positions that involve work connected with the production of motion pictures; filmstrips; live, taped or transmitted television productions, live, taped or recorded radio productions, and such other similar productions as prerecorded slide lectures and sound accompaniments to exhibits or to scenic or historic views. Positions in this series require the ability to plan, organize, and direct the work of writers, actors, narrators, or other speakers, musicians, set designers, recording and sound technicians, and motion picture and television cameramen in order to produce the actions, sounds, or visual effects required for the finished production; or to select and arrange appropriate sequences of action, dialogue, sound effects, visual effects, and music in order to create an effective finished production.

GS-1082—Writing and Editing Series*

This series includes positions that involve as their primary function, writing, rewriting, or editing reports, articles, news stories and releases, which are to appear in publications, reports, periodicals, or the press; or speeches that are to be presented in person, or by means of radio or television; or radio, television, or motion picture scripts. This kind of writing and editing requires the ability to acquire information about different subjects and to analyze, select, and present the information in a form suitable for the intended audience. It does not require substantial subject-matter knowledge.

GS-1083—Technical Writing and Editing Series*

This series includes the performance or supervision of writing and/or editing work which requires the application of (1) substantial subject-matter knowledges, and (2) writing and editing skills, including the ability to determine the type of presentation best suited to the audience being addressed. Positions which require full professional or technical subject-matter knowledges and, in addition, writing or editing abilities, are excluded from this series.

GS-1084—Visual Information Series*

This series includes positions which supervise or perform work involved in communicating information through visual means. Work in this series includes the design and display of such visual materials as photographs, illustrations, diagrams, graphs, objects, models, slides, and charts used in books, magazines, pamphlets, exhibits, live or video recorded speeches or lectures, and other means of communicating. The work requires knowledge of and ability to apply the principles of visual design; knowledge of the

---

* Standards published

DEFINITIONS OF GROUPS AND SERIES

technical characteristics associated with various methods of visual display; and the ability to present subject matter information in a visual form that will convey the intended message to, or have the desired effect on, the intended audience.

GS-1087 – Editorial Assistance Series*

This series covers positions that involve editorial support work in preparing manuscripts for publication and verifying factual information in them. Such support work includes editing manuscripts for basic grammar and clarity of expression as well as marking copy for format. These positions require skill in using reference works to verify information and knowledge of grammar, punctuation, spelling, and good English usage.

GS-1099 – Information and Arts Student Trainee Series

See the series definition for the General Student Trainee Series, GS-099.

GS-1100 – BUSINESS AND INDUSTRY GROUP

This group includes all classes of positions the duties of which are to advise on, administer, supervise, or perform work pertaining to and requiring a knowledge of business and trade practices, characteristics and use of equipment, products, or property, or industrial production methods and processes, including the conduct of investigations and studies; the collection, analysis, and dissemination of information; the establishment and maintenance of contacts with industry and commerce; the provision of advisory services; the examination and appraisal of merchandise or property; and the administration of regulatory provisions and controls.

Series in this group are:

GS-1101 – General Business and Industry Series

This series includes all classes of positions the duties of which are to administer, supervise, or perform (1) any combination of work characteristic of two or more series in this group where no one type of work is series controlling and where the combination is not specifically included in another series; or (2) other work properly classified in this group for which no other series has been provided.

GS-1102 – Contracting Series*

This series includes positions that manage, supervise, perform, or develop policies and procedures for professional work involving the procurement of supplies, services, construction, or research and development using formal advertising or negotiation procedures; the evaluation of contract price proposals; and the administration or termination and close out of contracts. The work requires knowledge of the legislation, regulations, and methods used in contracting; and knowledge of business and industry practices, sources of supply, cost factor, and requirements characteristics.

GS-1103 – Industrial Property Management Series*

This occupation includes positions which primarily require a knowledge of business and industrial practices, procedures, and systems for the management and control of Government-owned property. These positions involve technical work in the administration of contract provisions relating to control of Government property in the possession of contractors, from acquisition through disposition. Also included are positions that involve providing staff leadership and technical guidance over property administration matters.

GS-1104 – Property Disposal Series*

This series includes positions involving administrative, managerial, or technical work concerned with the utilization, redistribution, donation, sale, or other disposition of excess or surplus personal property in Government activities. Work covered by this series primarily requires a knowledge of: (a) characteristics of property items, their proper identification and uses; (b) merchandising and marketing methods and techniques; and (c) the policies, programs, regulations and procedures for the disposition, including redistribution, of excess or surplus property. Some positions also require a knowledge of automatic data processing and ADP systems.

GS-1105 – Purchasing Series*

This series includes positions which involve purchasing, rental, or lease of supplies, services and equipment through (a) informal open market methods and (b) formal competitive bid procedures, when the primary objectives of the work is to assure rapid delivery of goods and services in direct support of operational requirements. The work requires knowledge of commercial supply sources and of common business practices with respect to sales, prices, discounts, deliveries, stocks, and shipments.

GS-1106 – Procurement Clerical and Assistance Series*

This series covers positions that involve clerical and technical support work for purchasing, procurement, contract negotiation, contract administration, and contract termination. Typical work of positions covered by this series includes: (1) preparing, controlling, verifying, or abstracting procurement documents, reports, or industry publications or other clerical and support work related to procurement operations, and (2) technical work in support of such contract and procurement tasks as assembling product and price data for procurement negotiations, reporting on performance of contractors in meeting terms of contracts, and similar support functions. These positions require a practical knowledge of procurement operations, procedures, and programs and the ability to apply procurement policies, regulations, or procedures.

GS-1107 – Property Disposal Clerical and Technician Series*

This series includes positions involving the supervision or performance of clerical or technical support work related to the utilization, redistribution, donation, sale or other

---

* Standards published

U.S. OFFICE OF PERSONNEL MANAGEMENT

disposition of personal property which has been declared excess or surplus to the needs of the owning Federal agency. Included in this occupation, e.g., are duties concerned with processing, verifying, abstracting, or controlling documents, reports, or records when such work requires a knowledge of the operations, regulations, practices, and procedures related to the utilization, redistribution, donation, sale, or other disposition of excess or surplus personal property.

GS-1130—Public Utilities Specialist Series

This series includes positions that require application of knowledges concerning the business practices, rate structures, and operating characteristics of public utilities, in carrying out such functions as: (1) analysis of utility rate schedules to determine their reasonableness and applicability; (2) investigation and analysis of the business management organization and financial structure of public utilities in connection with licensing or regulatory actions, including preparation and presentation of testimony before regulatory bodies; (3) purchase or sale by the Government of utility resources and services; and (4) related functions that require the kind of knowledges indicated above. The utilities with which these positions deal are primarily concerned include telecommunications, electric and gas power, water, steam, and sewage disposal.

GS-1140—Trade Specialist Series*

This series includes positions the duties of which are to administer, supervise, or perform promotional, advisory, or analytical functions pertaining to the commercial distribution of goods and services. The work performed concerns, and requires a practical knowledge of, market structures and trends, competitive relationships, retail and wholesale trade practices, distribution channels and costs, business financing and credit practices, trade restrictions and controls, and principles of advertising and consumer motivation.

GS-1144—Commissary Store Management Series*

This series includes positions the incumbents of which manage, supervise the management of, or advise on the operation of commissary stores or departments thereof, or overall commissary operations. These positions require primarily knowledge of commercial retail food merchandising and food store management.

GS-1145—Agricultural Program Specialist Series*

This series includes positions involving work in developing, reviewing, administering, and coordinating programs for direct farmer-producer participation in production adjustment, price support, land conservation, and similar programs. The work requires a knowledge of agricultural stabilization, conservation, and related programs; farming customs and practices; crop cultivation; production and marketing methods; and related agricultural activities.

GS-1146—Agricultural Marketing Series*

This series includes positions involving management, research, analytical, regulatory, or other specialized work concerned with the marketing of one or more agricultural commodities or products. The work requires a practical knowledge of marketing functions and practices, including, for example, a knowledge of or experience with the commodity exchanges and markets, agricultural trade, or the practices and methods involved in various agricultural marketing or agribusiness operations, or a knowledge of the requirements of one or more statutory provisions relating to an agricultural marketing program.

GS-1147—Agricultural Market Reporting Series*

This series includes all positions primarily concerned with collection, analysis and dissemination of current information on available supplies, movement, demand, prices, marketing trends, and other facts relating to the marketing of agricultural products. This work, in its various aspects, requires: (a) knowledge of the methods and practices characteristic of markets in the assigned commodity area; (b) ability to establish and maintain sound working relationships with the industry; and (c) knowledge of the physical characteristics, production factors, and quality grading or inspection criteria of the assigned group of commodities.

GS-1150—Industrial Specialist Series*

This series includes positions which require primarily a practical knowledge of the nature and operations of an industry or industries, and the materials, facilities and methods employed by the industry or industries in producing commodities. These positions involve the administration, supervision, or performance of one or more of the following functions: (1) developing and carrying out plans for the expansion, conversion, integration or utilization of industrial production facilities, either to meet mobilization or strategic requirements or to strengthen the industrial economy; (2) furnishing technical information, assistance, and advice concerning facilities, machinery, methods, materials and standards for industrial production (which may include exploration, extraction, refining, manufacturing and processing operations); (3) developing and/or administering provisions or regulations covering such matters as materials allocation, tariffs, export-import control, etc.; (4) conducting surveys of industrial plants to evaluate capacity and potential for production of specific commodities; (5) planning, evaluating, and maintaining technical surveillance over Government production operations, either in contractor plants or in Government-operated plants; or (6) performing related functions which require essentially similar knowledges as the functions listed above.

GS-1152—Production Control Series*

This series includes positions involving the supervision or performance of the functions of planning, estimating, scheduling and/or expediting the use of manpower, machines and materials in specific manufacturing operations that employ mechanical production methods in the fabrication or repair of Government equipment and supplies.

* Standards published

DEFINITIONS OF GROUPS AND SERIES

GS-1160 — Financial Analysis Series*

This series includes all positions the duties of which are to direct or perform analytical and evaluative work requiring a comprehensive knowledge of (1) the theory and principles of finance applicable to the full range of financial operations and transactions involved in the general activities of the various types of business corporate organizations; (2) the financial and management organization, operations, and practices of such corporate organizations; (3) pertinent statutory or regulatory provisions; and (4) related basic economic, accounting, and legal principles.

GS-1161 — Crop Insurance Administration Series*

This series includes positions the duties of which are to administer, supervise, or perform program development, sales, loss adjustment, or other technical work in a crop insurance program. Work in this series requires specialized knowledge of (a) applicable Federal crop insurance principles, procedures, and techniques and (b) agriculture, agricultural practices, and related business, social and economic conditions.

GS-1162 — Crop Insurance Underwriting Series*

This series includes positions the duties of which are to administer, supervise, or perform work involved in classifying land, establishing crop insurance premiums, or other technical work related to underwriting insurance policies in a crop insurance program. Work in this series requires the application of training and knowledge in one or more agricultural or biological sciences such as agronomy, soil sciences, agricultural economics, agricultural management, horticulture, etc., as well as requiring knowledge of applicable Federal crop insurance principles, procedures and techniques.

GS-1163 — Insurance Examining Series**

This series includes positions the duties of which are to direct, supervise, or perform work involved in insuring persons or property, determining that adequate insurance to protect Government or private interests has been provided, settling claims arising under insurance contracts, or performing other similar insurance examining work when the duties performed are of a technical, nonclerical nature, requiring (a) knowledge of insurance principles, procedures, and/or practices; the commercial insurance market; commercial insurance operations; or similar specialized insurance knowledges, (b) knowledge of pertinent statutory or regulatory provisions; related administrative regulations, and (c) some knowledge of contract law and of other laws related to the particular kind of insurance involved but not legal training equivalent to that represented by graduation from a recognized law school.

GS-1165 — Loan Specialist Series*

This series includes all positions the duties of which are to direct or perform analytical and evaluative work which requires knowledge of (1) credit risk factors and lending principles involved in loans of specialized types granted, insured, or guaranteed by the Federal Government; (2) financial structures and practices of business organizations concerned with such loans; and (3) pertinent statutory, regulatory, and administrative provisions.

GS-1169 — Internal Revenue Officer Series*

This series includes all classes of positions the duties of which are to collect delinquent taxes, canvass for unreported taxes due and secure delinquent returns where performance of the work requires application of a knowledge of (1) general or specialized business practices; (2) internal revenue laws, regulations, procedures and precedents; (3) judicial processes, laws of evidence, and the interrelationship between Federal and State laws with respect to the collection and assessment processes; and (4) investigative techniques and methods.

GS-1170 — Realty Series*

This series includes positions that involve performing, planning, directing, or advising on one or more of the following functions: acquisition of real estate interests; disposal of real estate at a fair value for the greatest benefit to the Government and to the public; planning and management of real estate to attain its highest and best use from a realty standpoint. This work requires a knowledge of real estate principles, practices, markets, and values.

GS-1171 — Appraising and Assessing Series*

This series covers positions that involve supervising or performing work in appraising real or personal property or interests therein. These positions require technical knowledge and skill in the application of the principles, practices, and techniques of appraisal.

GS-1173 — Housing Management Series*

This series covers positions the duties of which are (1) to manage or assist in managing one or more family housing projects, billeting facilities, or other accommodations such as transient or permanent individual and family living quarters, dormitory facilities and restricted occupancy buildings including adjacent service facilities and surrounding grounds; and/or (2) to administer, supervise, or perform work involved in the evaluation of housing management programs, the development of administrative procedures, and the provision of technical assistance to onsite housing management. Positions in this occupation require a variety of housing management and administrative knowledges and related practical skills and abilities in such housing activities as: operations and maintenance, procurement of services, cost management and financial planning, assignments and utilization, occupancy changes and periodic inspections, scheduled and special requirement surveys, new construction and improvements, control of furnishings and equipment, master planning, and management-tenant relations. While some positions may involve administrative or indirect supervision of trade or craft work, an intensive practical knowledge of skilled trade and craft work techniques and processes is not required.

---

* Standards published
** Flysheets published

U.S. OFFICE OF PERSONNEL MANAGEMENT

GS-1176—Building Management Series*

This series covers positions that involve the management of public buildings or other facilities to provide occupant organizations with appropriate space and essential building services in order to promote occupant welfare, safety, and productivity. Positions in this series typically involve one or more of the following functions: (1) directly managing, or assisting in managing, the operation of one or more public buildings and surrounding grounds; (2) directing comprehensive building management programs; or (3) performing staff level work in the study of building management methods and the development of standard building management practices. This work requires management and administrative skills, the ability to meet and deal effectively with a wide variety of individuals and groups, and knowledge of building operational requirements.

GS-1199—Business and Industry Student Trainee Series

See the series definition for the General Student Trainee Series, GS—099.

GS-1200—COPYRIGHT, PATENT, AND TRADE-MARK GROUP

This group includes all classes of positions the duties of which are to advise on, administer, supervise, or perform professional scientific, technical, and legal work involved in the cataloging and registration of copyrights, in the classification and issuance of patents, in the registration of trade-marks, in the prosecution of applications for patents before the Patent Office, and in the giving of advice to Government officials on patent matters.

Series in this group are:

GS-1202—Patent Technician Series

This series includes positions that have responsibility for supervising or performing technical work in support of professional evaluation and examination of patent applications, including searching for, selecting, evaluating and presenting pertinent background data and documents. The duties of positions in this series require the application of (a) an understanding of the basic principles and practices in a narrow field of physical science or engineering, and (b) quasi-legal knowledges of precedents, practices and procedures under patent laws governing the processing of patent applications. They do not require full professional competence equivalent to that represented by completion of a full 4-year accredited college curriculum leading to a bachelor's degree in engineering or one of the physical sciences.

GS-1210—Copyright Series

This series includes positions that require the exercise of discretion and independent judgment in the application of a broad knowledge of copyright law, precedents, regulations, and practices. The duties include examining, registering, cataloging, disseminating information, and certifying original and renewal copyrights.

GS-1211—Copyright Technician Series

This series includes positions that involve technical work in connection with examination, cataloging, registration, dissemination of information, processing and certification of original and renewal copyrights. The work requires the ability to apply established rules, regulations and procedures.

GS-1220—Patent Administration Series

This series includes all classes of positions the duties of which are to advise on, administer, supervise, or perform professional scientific, technical, and legal work involved in the administration of the patent and trade-mark laws through the issuance of patents for inventions in the various arts and through the registration of trade-marks.

GS-1221—Patent Adviser Series*

This series includes positions involving professional scientific or engineering work and, in addition, legal work pertaining to the analysis of inventions and the evaluation of the patentability thereof. This entails preparing and prosecuting applications for patents; preparing and presenting briefs and arguments and prosecuting appeals and interferences before the Patent Office; making infringement investigations, and rendering opinions on the validity of patents, in order to protect the Government's interest in such inventions.

GS-1222—Patent Attorney Series*

This series includes positions involved with performing professional legal, scientific, and technical work concerning patents, including rendering opinions on validity and infringement of patents, negotiation of patent licenses, settlement of patent claims, negotiation of patent clauses in contracts, providing professional legal advice to contracting officers and other procurement personnel on patent matters, and the preparation and/or presentation of briefs and arguments before the Patent Office or before the Federal Courts. Also included in this series are positions which, in addition to the foregoing, may be involved with performing similar professional legal functions regarding trade-marks. The work of this series requires training equivalent to that represented by graduation (with a degree in one of the scientific or engineering disciplines) from an accredited college or university, in addition to a degree from a recognized law school and admission to the bar.

GS-1223—Patent Classifying Series*

This series includes all professional, scientific, and technical positions which are primarily concerned with developing and/or administering systems for the classification, for patent purposes, of the technological knowledge embodied in United States patents and related material.

GS-1224—Patent Examining Series*

This series includes all classes of positions the duties of which are to advise on, administer, supervise, or perform professional, scientific, technological, and legal work involved in

---
* Standards published

DEFINITIONS OF GROUPS AND SERIES

the examination and disposition of applications for patents, exclusive of design patents, to determine the grant or denial of patents based on such applications, and in the adjudication of petitions and appeals from decisions of such applications. Such work in its various aspects involves the utilization of the basic and advanced concepts of the natural sciences, the techniques of all branches of engineering and of the industrial arts, and the application of those aspects of procedural and substantive law generally, and of the statutory and case law applied to patents specifically, which are applicable to the patent examination process.

GS-1225 – Patent Interference Examining Series*

This series includes all classes of positions the duties of which are to advise on, administer, supervise, or perform professional scientific, technical, and legal work of a specialized nature involved in the conduct of quasi-judicial proceedings instituted for the purpose of determining the question of priority of invention between two or more parties claiming the same patentable invention. The series also includes work involving proceedings to determine the title and other rights of applicants for atomic energy patents. The work of this series requires training equivalent to that represented by graduation from a college of recognized standing with concentration in one of the major fields of physical science or engineering and from a recognized law school. Admission to the bar is not required.

GS-1226 – Design Patent Examining Series*

This series includes all classes of positions the duties of which are to supervise or perform professional, technical and legal work involved in the granting or denial of applications for design patents. Such work involves the employment of basic concepts of the natural sciences, techniques of the industrial arts, fundamentals of aesthetic and functional design, and the application of statutes and precedent decisions in design patent matters.

GS-1299 – Copyright and Patent Student Trainee Series

See the series definition for the General Student Trainee Series, GS-099.

GS-1300 – PHYSICAL SCIENCES GROUP

This group includes all classes of positions the duties of which are to advise on, administer, supervise, or perform research or other professional and scientific work or subordinate technical work in any of the fields of science concerned with matter, energy, physical space, time, nature of physical measurement, and fundamental structural particles; and the nature of the physical environment.

Series in this group are:

GS-1301 – General Physical Science Series*

This series includes positions which involve professional work in the physical sciences when there is no other more appropriate series, that is, the positions are not elsewhere classifiable. Thus, included in this series are positions that involve: (1) a combination of several physical science fields with no one predominant or (2) a specialized field of physical science not identified with other existing series.

GS-1306 – Health Physics Series*

This series includes positions that require application of professional knowledge and competence in health physics, which is concerned with the protection of man and his environment from unwarranted exposure to ionizing radiation.

GS-1310 – Physics Series

This series includes all classes of positions the duties of which are to advise on, administer, supervise, or perform research or other professional and scientific work in the investigation and applications of the relations between space, time, matter, and energy in the areas of mechanics, sound, optics, heat, electricity, magnetism, radiation, or atomic and nuclear phenomena.

GS-1311 – Physical Science Technician Series*

This series includes positions which involve nonprofessional technical work in the physical sciences and which are not specifically included in other series in the Physical Sciences Group. Positions in this series require a knowledge of the principles and techniques of physical science, but do not require competence equivalent to that represented by the completion of a full four-year college curriculum leading to a bachelor's degree in physical science. Positions in this series involve work in the fields of astronomy, chemistry, geology, geophysics, health physics, hydrology, metallurgy, oceanography, physics, and other physical sciences.

GS-1313 – Geophysics Series*

This series includes professional scientific positions requiring application of knowledge of the principles and techniques of geophysics and related sciences in the investigation, measurement, analysis, evaluation, and interpretation of geophysical phenomena and artificially applied forces and fields related to the structure, composition, and physical properties of the earth and its atmosphere.

GS-1315 – Hydrology Series*

This series includes positions which involve professional work in hydrology, the science concerned with the study of water in the hydrologic cycle. The work includes basic and applied research on water and water resources; the collection, measurement, analysis, and interpretation of information on water resources; forecast of water supply and water flows; and development of new, improved or more economical methods, techniques, and instruments.

---

* Standards published

U.S. OFFICE OF PERSONNEL MANAGEMENT

GS-1316—Hydrologic Technician Series*

This occupation includes positions of hydrologic aids and technicians who apply practical knowledge of hydrologic methods and techniques; and of the construction, application, operation, and limitations of instruments, equipment, and materials used in hydrologic investigations. They collect, select, compute, adjust, and process data; prepare charts and reports; and perform related duties supporting professional work in hydrology, the science concerned with the study of water, its quantity, quality, availability, movement, and distribution.

GS-1320—Chemistry Series*

This series includes all positions involving work that requires full professional education and training in the field of chemistry. This work includes the investigation, analysis, and interpretation of the composition, molecular structure, and properties of substances, the transformations which they undergo, and the amounts of matter and energy included in these transformations.

GS-1321—Metallurgy Series*

This series includes positions that require primarily professional education and training in the field of metallurgy, including ability to apply the relevant principles of chemistry, physics, mathematics, and engineering to the study of metals. Metallurgy is the art and science of extracting metals from their ores, refining them, alloying them and preparing them for use, and studying their properties and behavior as affected by the composition, treatment in manufacture, and conditions of use.

GS-1330—Astronomy and Space Science Series*

This series includes professional positions requiring primarily application of the principles and techniques of astronomy and physics in the investigation and interpretation of the physical properties, composition, evolution, position, distance, and motion of extraterrestrial bodies and particles in space.

GS-1340—Meteorology Series*

This series includes positions that involve professional work in meteorology, the science concerned with the earth's atmospheric envelope and its processes. The work includes basic and applied research into the conditions and phenomena of the atmosphere; the collection, analysis, evaluation, and interpretation of meteorological data to predict weather and determine climatological conditions for specific geographical areas; the development of new or the improvement of existing meteorological theory; and the development or improvement of meteorological methods, techniques, and instruments. Positions in this occupation require full professional knowledge and application of meteorological methods, techniques, and theory.

GS-1341—Meteorological Technician Series*

This series includes positions that require application of (a) technical or practical knowledge of meteorological equipment, methods, and techniques and (b) skill in the development and operation of data collection, verification, information dissemination, observation, and forecasting services and systems. These positions do not require full professional knowledge of meteorology.

GS-1350—Geology Series*

This series includes professional scientific positions applying a knowledge of the principles and theories of geology and related sciences in the collection, measurement, analysis, evaluation, and interpretation of geologic information concerning the structure, composition, and history of the earth. This includes the performance of basic research to establish fundamental principles and hypotheses and develop a fuller knowledge and understanding of geology, and the application of these principles and knowledges to a variety of scientific, engineering, and economic problems.

GS-1360—Oceanography Series*

This series includes professional scientific positions engaged in the collection, measurement, analysis, evaluation and interpretation of natural and physical ocean phenomena, such as currents, circulations, waves, beach and near-shore processes, chemical structure and processes, physical and submarine features, depth, floor configuration, organic and inorganic sediments, sound and light transmission, color manifestations, heat exchange, and similar phenomena, and their interrelations with other marine phenomena (e.g., biota, weather, geological structure, etc.) Oceanographers plan, organize, conduct, and administer seagoing and land-based study and research of ocean phenomena for the purpose of interpreting, predicting, utilizing and controlling ocean forces and events. This work requires a fundamental background in chemistry, physics, and mathematics and appropriate knowledges in the field of oceanography.

GS-1361—Navigational Information Series*

This series includes all classes of positions involving the acquisition, collection, evaluation, selection, and preparation of vital aeronautical or marine information for dissemination in official publications concerning safe navigation and related operations, requiring the technical and practical knowledges of air or marine navigation and operations.

GS-1370—Cartography Series*

The Cartography Series, GS-1370, includes positions which require the application of professional knowledge and skills in the mapping and related sciences, and relevant mathematics and statistics to plan, design, research, develop, construct, evaluate and modify mapping and charting systems, products, and technology.

GS-1371—Cartographic Technician Series*

This series includes positions that require primarily a practical knowledge of the processes, practices, methods, and techniques involved in the construction of new or revision of existing maps, charts, and related cartographic products. Cartographic aids and technicians perform precompilation tasks (such as the investigation of source materials, extension of basic geodetic control network, and the plotting map

---

* Standards published

DEFINITIONS OF GROUPS AND SERIES

projection and ground control on base sheets), manual or photogrammetric compilation, assembling aerial photographs into mosaics, drafting, digitizing, and editing or reviewing. The positions do not require full professional knowledges and abilities and, therefore, do not require education equivalent in type and scope to that represented by completion of a professional curriculum leading to a bachelor's degree in cartography or a related science.

GS-1372 – Geodesy Series*

This series includes professional positions requiring primarily application of the principles and techniques of geodesy. The work includes determining the size and shape of the earth and its gravitational field, measuring the intensity and direction of the force of gravity, and determining the horizontal and vertical positions of points on the earth and in space, where consideration of the curvature of the earth is required.

GS-1373 – Land Surveying Series*

This series includes positions that involve professional work in land surveying, which is concerned with establishing, investigating, and reestablishing land and property boundaries, and with preparing plats and legal descriptions for tracts of land. The work requires application of professional knowledge of the concepts, principles and techniques of surveying, including underlying mathematics and physical science, in combination with a practical knowledge of land ownership laws.

GS-1374 – Geodetic Technician Series*

This series includes positions the duties of which are to supervise or perform technical work in the analysis, evaluation, processing, computation, and selection of geodetic survey data. These positions require a practical knowledge of theories and techniques of geodesy particularly as they relate to the identity, reliability, and usefulness of geodetic control data but not a full professional knowledge of geodesy as required in the execution and adjustment of geodetic surveys or the mathematical transformation of geodetic datum systems.

GS-1380 – Forest Products Technology Series

This series includes professional positions concerned with the development, improvement, and utilization of wood or wood products, including the study of preservation and treatment methods, the processing and production of wood products, the properties and structure of wood, and the production of lumber.

GS-1382 – Food Technology Series

This series includes professional positions concerned with the study and analysis of problems related to the development, improvement, and evaluation of food products; their production, utilization, processing and preservation; and the utilization or disposal of by-products.

GS-1384 – Textile Technology Series

This series includes classes of professional positions which involve scientific and technological work concerned with textiles or fibers (plant, animal, and synthetic), including investigation, development, production, processing, evaluation, and application of fibers, yarns, fabrics and finishes.

GS-1386 – Photographic Technology Series*

This series includes professional positions the duties of which are to advise on, administer, supervise, or perform work which requires interdisciplinary knowledge and skills in those scientific and engineering fields that comprise photographic technology. This work includes planning, research, design, development, modification, instrumentation, testing, and evaluation of photographic equipment and techniques involved in the taking, processing, viewing, and printing of photographic images. The work requires the ability to apply a knowledge of the scientific principles of photography and those aspects of chemistry, physics, mathematics, and mechanical, electronic and electrical engineering that relate to photographic technology.

GS-1397 – Document Analysis Series

This series includes all classes of positions the duties of which are to direct, administer, supervise, advise on, or perform technical work in examining and identifying questioned documents. Examinations are conducted in order to determine the genuineness or spuriousness of a document or any of its parts; decipher or restore eradicated or obliterated writings and markings; detect alterations, additions, interlineations, or other tampering with the original document; determine authorship of a signature or other writing; determine the validity of a date or the alleged age of a document or a particular entry; identify the particular machine used to produce a document; or identify the source of a document. The work requires (1) knowledge of the properties, characteristics, and techniques of analysis of handwriting, typewriting, printing, and duplicating, and of inks, papers, and other writing, printing, and recording instruments and materials; (2) knowledge and skill in the use of photographic and laboratory equipment and techniques; and (3) the ability to develop evidence and to present it convincingly in written reports or orally.

GS-1399 – Physical Science Student Trainee Series

See the series definition for the General Student Trainee Series, GS-099.

GS-1400 – LIBRARY AND ARCHIVES GROUP

This group includes all classes of positions the duties of which are to advise on, administer, supervise, or perform professional and scientific work or subordinate technical work in the various phases of library and archival science.

Series in this group are:

GS-1410 – Librarian Series*

This series includes all positions involving work that primarily requires a full professional knowledge of the theories, objectives, principles, and techniques of librarianship.

* Standards published

An inherent requirement of these positions is a knowledge of literature resources. Some positions also require a substantial knowledge of the subject matter involved and/or a substantial knowledge of foreign languages. Such work is concerned with the collection, organization, preservation, and retrieval of recorded knowledge in printed, written, audiovisual, film, wax, near-print methods, magnetic tape, or other media. Typical library functions include the selection, acquisition, cataloging, and classification of materials, bibliographic and readers' advisory services, reference and literature searching services, library management and systems planning, or the development and strengthening of library services.

GS-1411—Library Technician Series*

This series includes positions involving nonprofessional or technical work in libraries which are administered in accordance with the practices and techniques of professional librarianship. Such work primarily requires a practical knowledge of library functions and services; and ability to apply standard library tools, methods, and procedures to the service needs of the particular library.

GS-1412—Technical Information Services Series*

This series includes positions which are primarily concerned with the direction, administration, development, coordination, or performance of work involved in processing and transmitting scientific, technological, or other specialized information. Duties performed require a broad knowledge of one or more professional, scientific, or technical disciplines or fields of interest sufficient to understand the significance and relationship of the concepts and ideas contained in the information; a practical knowledge of documentation or library techniques; and, in some cases, a knowledge of foreign languages.

GS-1420—Archivist Series*

This series includes positions which involve professional archival work in appraising, accessioning, arranging, describing, preserving, publishing, or providing reference service from public records and historic documents. This work requires a professional knowledge of archival principles and techniques, a comprehensive knowledge of the history of the United States and the institutions and organizations of the Federal Government, and a thorough understanding of the needs, methods, and techniques of scholarly research.

GS-1421—Archives Technician Series*

This series includes positions which involve nonprofessional and technical work in accessioning, arranging, describing, preserving, using, and disposing of archives, noncurrent records, and related material kept in record and manuscript depositories. This work requires the application of a practical or technical knowledge of archival methods, procedures, and techniques, and in some assignments a knowledge of the administrative history of specific Federal organizations, past or present. The work does not require full professional preparation in archival science, nor the application of a full professional knowledge of the history of the United States.

GS-1499—Library and Archives Student Trainee Series

See the series definition for the General Student Trainee Series, GS-099.

1500—MATHEMATICS AND STATISTICS GROUP

This group includes all classes of positions the duties of which are to advise on, administer, supervise, or perform research or other professional and scientific work or related clerical work in basic mathematical principles, methods, procedures, or relationships, including the development and application of mathematical methods for the investigation and solution of problems; the development and application of statistical theory in the selection, collection, classification, adjustment, analysis, and interpretation of data; the development and application of mathematical, statistical, and financial principles to programs or problems involving life and property risks; and any other professional and scientific or related clerical work requiring primarily and mainly the understanding and use of mathematical theories, methods, and operations.

Series in this group are:

GS-1510—Actuary Series*

This series includes positions which involve the application of professional knowledge and experience in actuarial science (including mathematics, statistics, and business, financial, and economic principles) to programs or problems related to annuities, and to life, health, or property risks and contingencies.

GS-1515—Operations Research Series*

This series includes positions which involve professional and scientific work requiring the design, development and adaptation of mathematical, statistical, econometric, and other scientific methods and techniques to analyze problems of management and to provide advice and insight about the probable effects of alternative solutions to these problems. The primary requirement of the work is competence in the rigorous methods of scientific inquiry and analysis rather than in the subject matter of the problem.

GS-1520—Mathematics Series*

This series includes all positions the duties of which are to advise on, administer, supervise, or perform work which requires professional education and training in the field of mathematics. This work includes research on basic mathematical principles, methods, procedures, techniques or relationships; the development of mathematical methods in the solution of a variety of scientific, engineering, economic and military problems, where the exactitude of the relationships, the rigor and economy of mathematical operations, and the logical necessity of the results are the controlling considerations.

* Standards published

DEFINITIONS OF GROUPS AND SERIES

GS-1521 — Mathematics Technician Series*

This series includes all classes of positions the duties of which are to supervise or perform work in the reduction and computation of quantitative data where such work requires the use of mathematical techniques in connection with particular engineering and scientific activities, but does not require professional knowledge of the mathematical theories, assumptions, or principles upon which the techniques are based.

GS-1529 — Mathematical Statistician Series*

This series includes all classes of positions the primary duties of which are to advise on, administer, or perform professional work requiring the design, development and adaptation of mathematical methods and techniques to statistical processes, or research in the basic theories and science of statistics.

GS-1530 — Statistician Series*

This series includes all classes of positions the duties of which are to administer or perform professional work, or to provide professional consultation in the application of statistical theories, techniques and methods to the gathering and/or interpretation of quantified information.

GS-1531 — Statistical Assistant Series*

This series includes positions which require primarily the application of knowledge of statistical methods, procedures, and techniques, to the collection, processing, compilation, computation, analysis, editing, and presentation of statistical data. The work does not require the application of professional knowledge of statistics or other disciplines.

GS-1540 — Cryptography Series

This series includes all classes of positions the duties of which are to advise on, administer, supervise, or perform research or other professional and scientific work in the construction and solution of codes and ciphers, or in the design, construction, inspection, testing, operation, and maintenance of new and improved cryptographic code and cipher equipment and methods.

GS-1541 — Cryptanalysis Series

This series includes all classes of positions the duties of which are to supervise or perform subordinate technical work in the solution or analysis of secret communication codes and ciphers.

GS-1550 — Computer Science Series*

This series includes professional positions which primarily involve the application of, or research into, computer science methods and techniques to store, manipulate, transform or present information by means of computer systems. The primary requirements of the work are (a) professional competence in applying the theoretical foundations of computer science, including computer system architecture and system software organization, the representation and transformation of information structure, and the theoretical models for such representations and transformation; (b) specialized knowledge of the design characteristics, limitations, and potential applications of systems having the ability to transform information, and of broad areas of applications of computing which have common structures, processes, and techniques; and (c) knowledge of relevant mathematical and statistical sciences.

GS-1599 — Mathematics and Statistics Student Trainee Series

See the series definition for the General Student Trainee Series, GS-099.

GS-1600 — EQUIPMENT, FACILITIES, AND SERVICES GROUP**

This group includes positions the duties of which are to advise on, manage, or provide instructions and information concerning the operation, maintenance, and use of equipment, shops, buildings, laundries, printing plants, power plants, cemeteries, or other Government facilities, or other work involving services provided predominantly by persons in trades, crafts, or manual labor operations. Positions in this group require technical or managerial knowledge and ability, plus a practical knowledge of trades, crafts, or manual labor operations.

Series in this group are:

GS-1601 — General Facilities and Equipment Series*

This series covers positions involving (1) a combination of work characteristic of two or more series in the Equipment, Facilities, and Services Group when no other series is appropriate for the paramount knowledges and abilities required for the position, or (2) other equipment, facilities, or services work properly classified in this group for which no other series has been established.

GS-1630 — Cemetery Administration Series*

This series includes positions the duties of which are to direct, administer, manage, advise on, or supervise the overall operation of one or more Federal cemeteries.

GS-1640 — Facility Management Series*

This series covers positions that involve managing the operation and maintenance of buildings, grounds, and other facilities such as posts, camps, depots, power plants, parks, forests, and roadways. Such work requires (1) administrative and management skills and abilities and (2) broad technical knowledge of the operating capabilities and maintenance requirements of various kinds of physical plants and equipment. While positions in this series typically involve directing work performed by a variety of trades and labor employees and require specialized knowledge of such work, they do not have as their paramount qualification requirement an intensive knowledge of the specific trades skills utilized.

U.S. OFFICE OF PERSONNEL MANAGEMENT

GS1654 – Printing Management Series*

This series includes all positions which involve planning, administering, supervising, reviewing, evaluating, or performing work in connection with the management of a program which provides printing services. Characteristic of positions in this series is the application of a knowledge of the instructions which a printer must have before he can reproduce manuscript received for publication; knowledge of the capabilities of printing equipment and processes; and ability to manage a printing production organization. Positions in this series may, in addition, involve supervision of related functions such as editing, illustrating, and distributing printed materials.

GS-1658 – Laundry and Dry Cleaning Plant Management Series*

This series includes all positions the duties of which are to advise on or to manage and direct the operation of a laundry, a dry cleaning plant, or a combined laundry and dry cleaning plant, when the duties require (1) skill in performing managerial functions associated with the operation of a laundry and/or dry cleaning plants, and (2) a combination of a practical knowledge of laundry and/or dry cleaning equipment and processing operations.

GS-1667 – Steward Series

This series includes all classes of positions the duties of which are to manage, supervise, or perform work involved in the operation of the food supply service of a Government institution, including storeroom, kitchen, dining room, meat shop, and bakery.

GS-1670 – Equipment Specialist Series*

This series includes positions the duties of which are to supervise or perform work involved in (1) collecting, analyzing, interpreting, and developing specialized information about equipment; (2) providing such information together with advisory service to those who design, test, produce, procure, supply, operate, repair, or dispose of equipment; and/or (3) developing, installing, inspecting, or revising equipment maintenance programs and techniques based on a practical knowledge of the equipment, including its design, production, operational and maintenance requirements. Such duties require the application of an intensive, practical knowledge of the characteristics, properties, and uses of equipment of the type gained from technical training, education and experience in such functions as repairing, overhauling, maintaining, construction, or inspecting equipment.

GS-1699 – Equipment and Facilities Management Student Trainee Series

See the series definition for the General Student Trainee Series, GS-099.

GS-1700 – EDUCATION GROUP**

This group includes positions which involve administering, managing, supervising, performing, or supporting education or training work when the paramount requirement of the position is knowledge of, or skill in, education, training, or instruction processes.

Series in this group are:

GS-1701 – General Education and Training Series*

This series includes positions which primarily involve research or other professional work in the field of education and training when the work is of such generalized or miscellaneous specialized nature that the positions are not more appropriately classifiable in any of the existing professional series in this or any other group. Thus included in this series are positions in the field of education and training when (1) the work has characteristics which may be identified with more than one professional education series with none predominant, or (2) the combination of professional knowledges required by the work is not specifically provided for in another series, or (3) the work is in a specialized professional field not readily identifiable with other existing series in this or any other group.

GS-1702 – Education and Training Technician Series**

This series includes positions involving nonprofessional work of a technical, specialized, or support nature in the field of education and training when the work is properly classifiable in this group and there is no other more appropriate series. Such work characteristically involves knowledge of the program objectives, policies, procedures, or pertinent regulatory requirements affecting the particular education or training activity. The work requires ability to apply a practical understanding or specialized skills and knowledge of the particular education or training activities involved, but does not require full professional knowledge of education concepts, principles, techniques and practices.

GS-1710 – Education and Vocational Training Series*

This series includes positions that require the application of full professional knowledge of the theories, principles, and techniques of education and training in such areas as instruction, guidance counseling, education administration, development or evaluation of curricula, instructional materials and aids, and educational tests and measurements. Some positions also require specialized knowledge of one or more subjects in which the education is given.

GS-1712 – Training Instruction Series*

This series covers positions concerned with administration, supervision, training program development, evaluation, or instruction in a program of training when the paramount requirement of the work is a combination of practical

---

* Standards published
** Flysheets published

DEFINITIONS OF GROUPS AND SERIES

knowledge of the methods and techniques of instruction and practical knowledge of the subject-matter being taught. Positions in this series do not have either a paramount requirement of professional knowledge and training in the field of education, or mastery of a trade, craft, or laboring occupation.

GS-1715 – Vocational Rehabilitation Series*

This series covers positions requiring the application of knowledge of training programs and occupational information in relation to vocational rehabilitation problems of the physically or mentally disabled, or of other individuals whose backgrounds and lack of job skills impairs their employability. The work involves planning training programs for these individuals; placing them in gainful employment; and supervising them while in training and during adjustment to the job. The duties require knowledge of vocational training concepts and practices; of the employment market; of training facilities; and of skill demands and environmental condition in occupations and specific jobs in relation to their suitability for the training and employment of the persons served by the rehabilitation program. The work also involves the application of counseling techniques and methodology in motivating these individuals and helping them to adjust successfully to the training or work situation; however, full professional counseling knowledge is not required.

GS-1720 – Education Program Series*

This series covers professional education positions responsible for promoting, coordinating, and improving education policies, programs, standards, activities, and opportunities in accordance with national policies and objectives. Positions in this series primarily involve the performance, supervision, or management of factfinding, analysis, evaluation, or policy development work concerning education problems and issues. These positions require a professional knowledge of education theories, principles, processes, and practices at elementary, early childhood, or secondary and postsecondary levels, including adult or continuing education, and a knowledge of the Federal Government's interrelationships with state and local educational agencies and with public and private postsecondary institutions.

GS-1725 – Public Health Educator Series

This series includes positions involved in administering, supervising, or performing research or other professional work in public health education. Positions are concerned with providing leadership, advice, staff assistance, and consultation on health education programs. This includes analysis of behavioral and other situational factors affecting good health practices of individuals, groups, and communities; the planning of health education programs designed to meet the needs of particular individuals, groups, or communities; the selection of specialized educational methods, the preparation of educational materials, and the carrying out of such education activities which will best serve to stimulate the interest of individuals and groups in scientific discoveries affecting health in the application of health principles to daily

living. Public health educators consult with State and local health departments, and with national and local voluntary agencies; organize community groups to study health problems and methods of disease prevention; and assist in coordinating mass health programs and in evaluating and improving health education programs.

GS-1730 – Education Research Series*

This series includes positions that primarily involve professional education research work. This includes performance, leadership, management, or supervision of scientific research to solve educational problems or to develop new knowledge bearing on education processes. The paramount qualification requirement for this work is knowledge of and skill in applying research principles and methods and a broad and thorough knowledge of one or more scientific fields or interdisciplinary areas related to the education research work being performed.

GS-1740 – Education Services Series*

This series includes professional positions the duties of which are to administer, supervise, promote, conduct, or evaluate programs and activities designed to provide individualized career-related or self-development education plans. The work requires knowledge of education theories, principles, procedures, and practices of secondary, adult, or continuing education. Some positions require skill in counseling students or enrollees to establish educational and occupational objectives.

GS-1750 – Instructional Systems Series*

This series includes professional positions the duties of which are to administer, supervise, advise on, design, develop, or provide educational or training services in formal education or training programs. The work requires knowledge of learning theory and the principles, methods, practices and techniques of one or more specialties of the instructional systems field. The work may require knowledge of one or more subjects or occupations in which educational or training instruction is provided.

GS-1799 – Education Student Trainee Series

See the series definition for the General Student Trainee Series, GS-099.

GS-1800 – INVESTIGATION GROUP

This group includes all classes of positions the duties of which are to advise on, administer, supervise, or perform investigation, inspection, or enforcement work primarily concerned with alleged or suspected offenses against the laws of the United States, or such work primarily concerned with determining compliance with laws and regulations.

---

* Standards published

U.S. OFFICE OF PERSONNEL MANAGEMENT

Series in this group are:

GS-1801—General Inspection, Investigation, and Compliance Series*

This series includes positions the primary duties of which are to administer, coordinate, supervise or perform inspectional, investigative, analytical, or advisory work to assure understanding of and compliance with Federal laws, regulations, or other mandatory guidelines when such work is not more appropriately classifiable in another series either in the investigation Group, GS-1800 or in another occupational series.

GS-1802—Compliance Inspection and Support Series*

This series includes positions which perform or supervise inspectional or technical support work in assuring compliance with or enforcement of Federal laws, regulations, or other mandatory guidelines and which are not classifiable in another, more specific, occupational series. The work requires a knowledge of prescribed procedures, established techniques, directly applicable guidelines, and pertinent characteristics of regulated items or activities.

GS-1810—General Investigating Series*

This series includes positions that involve planning and conducting investigations covering the character, practices, suitability, or qualifications of persons or organizations seeking, claiming, or receiving Federal benefits, permits, or employment when the results of the investigation are used to make or invoke administrative judgments, sanctions, or penalties. These positions require primarily a knowledge of investigative techniques, a knowledge of the laws, rules, regulations, and objectives of the employing agency; skill in interviewing, following leads, researching records, and preparing reports; and the ability to elicit information helpful to the investigation from persons in all walks of life.

GS-1811—Criminal Investigating Series*

This series includes positions that involve planning and conducting investigations relating to alleged or suspected violations of criminal laws. These positions require primarily a knowledge of investigative techniques and a knowledge of the laws of evidence, the rules of criminal procedure, and precedent court decisions concerning admissibility of evidence, constitutional rights, search and seizure and related issues; the ability to recognize, develop and present evidence that reconstructs events, sequences, and time elements, and establishes relationships, responsibilities, legal liabilities, conflicts of interest, in a manner that meets requirements for presentation in various legal hearings and court proceedings; and skill in applying the techniques required in performing such duties as maintaining surveillance, performing undercover work, and advising and assisting the U.S. Attorney in and out of court.

GS-1812—Game Law Enforcement Series

This series includes all classes of positions the duties of which are to administer, coordinate, supervise, or perform inspectional, investigative, or advisory work to assure public understanding of and compliance with Federal statutes and regulations for the conservation of fish and wildlife resources; in obtaining information on the general condition of such resources; and in the conduct of operations for the abatement of damage to agricultural crops caused by unusual concentrations of wildlife.

GS-1815—Air Safety Investigating Series*

Positions included in this series have duties involving the investigation and prevention of accidents and incidents involving United States aircraft anywhere in the world, and in the establishment of programs and procedures to provide for the notification and reporting of accidents. The investigation includes a report of the facts, conditions, and circumstances relating to each accident and a determination of the probable cause of the accident along with recommendations for remedial action designed to prevent similar accidents in the future. Special studies and investigations on matters pertaining to safety in air navigation and the prevention of accidents are conducted to ascertain what will best tend to reduce or eliminate the possibility of, or recurrence of, accidents. These duties and responsibilities require the application of a broad technical knowledge in the field of aviation, and experience or training which provides a knowledge of investigative techniques and/or legal procedures and practices.

GS-1816—Immigration Inspection Series*

This series includes inspection or examining work involving the enforcement and administration of laws relating to the right of persons to enter, reside in, or depart from the United States, Puerto Rico, Guam, and the Virgin Islands. Inspection work requires knowledge of laws, regulations, procedures and policies concerning entry of persons to the United States and eligibility for various benefits under the immigration laws; ability to acquire information about citizenship and status through interviewing persons and examining documents; ability to make sound decisions to enter or exclude aliens from the United States and to determine eligibility for benefits under the immigration laws; and sound judgment in detaining or apprehending persons at the point of entry who are violating immigration or other laws.

GS-1822—Mine Safety and Health Series*

This series includes positions the paramount duties of which are to perform or supervise work in enforcing, developing, advising on, or interpreting mine safety and health laws, regulations, standards, and practices. Coverage includes positions concerned with underground and surface mining and milling operations associated with coal, and other metal and nonmetal mines. Positions in this series require: (1) practical knowledge of mining and/or milling methods and processes; (2) knowledge of safety and health practices, principles, programs, and hazards applicable to the mining industry; and (3) knowledge of current laws, regulations, and standards for mine safety and health.

---

* Standards published

DEFINITIONS OF GROUPS AND SERIES

GS-1825 – Aviation Safety Series*

This series includes positions that involve primarily developing, administering, or enforcing regulations and standards concerning civil aviation safety, including (1) the airworthiness of aircraft and aircraft systems; (2) the competence of pilots, mechanics, and other airmen; and (3) safety aspects of aviation facilities, equipment, and procedures. These positions require knowledge and skill in the operation, maintenance, or manufacture of aircraft and aircraft systems.

GS-1831 – Securities Compliance Examining Series

This series includes positions the duties of which are to direct, supervise, advise on, or perform examinations of registered broker-dealers, investment advisers, and investment companies to determine compliance with statutory and regulatory requirements of securities acts. The work requires the exercise of discretion and independent judgment in the application of knowledge of the principles and practices of securities compliance examination and a knowledge of the laws and regulations relating to the control and operation of institutions engaged in the trading of securities and the operation of securities markets. The work includes such activities as (1) analyzing financial reports, books, and records, to determine compliance with accounting and auditing requirements, adequacy and accuracy of net capital, overall financial responsibility, and compliance with recordkeeping and other requirements of the securities acts and rules; (2) examining and evaluating customer and broker accounts to determine the existence of improper activity in the accounts; (3) inspecting, reviewing, and evaluating the efficiency and adequacy of procedures for safeguarding funds and securities, and overall supervisory procedures; (4) conducting conferences and interviews with members of brokerage firms, security exchanges, investors, and members of the general public; (5) evaluating findings, making recommendations on further actions and preparing written reports on the compliance of the firm with statutory and regulatory requirements; and (6) conducting oversight examinations of self-regulatory organizations such as national securities exchanges.

GS-1850 – Agricultural Commodity Warehouse Examining Series*

This series includes the administration, supervision, or performance of work involved in (a) examining storage facilities licensed or to be licensed under Federal law for storing agricultural commodities; or (b) in examining facilities approved or to be approved under Government contract or agreement.

GS-1854 – Alcohol, Tobacco and Firearms Inspection Series*

This series includes positions concerned with work involving the qualification and inspection of establishments engaged in the production or use of alcohol or tobacco products; the assurance of full collection of revenue on alcohol and tobacco products; the development and interpretation of regulations applicable to such establishments; and the development, analysis, and improvement of programs, procedures, and techniques for regulating establishments involved in producing and using alcohol and tobacco products. Positions in this series require specialized knowledge of (a) the construction, equipment, and operations of facilities in the alcohol, tobacco, firearms, and related industries together with the laws and regulations that control them, (b) inspectional or examining techniques applicable to these industries, and (c) audit methods.

GS-1862 – Consumer Safety Inspection Series*

This series includes positions that involve primarily developing and conducting inspections, investigations, and related sampling and data collection activities in support of the laws and regulations protecting consumers from foods, drugs, therapeutic devices, cosmetics, fabrics, toys, and household products that are impure, unsanitary, unwholesome, ineffective, improperly labeled, or dangerous. These positions require a practical knowledge of the agency's regulations and programs; a practical knowledge of chemical and biological processes and analytical methods; the characteristics of regulated products; pertinent manufacturing, storage, and distribution methods; and techniques of inspection, sampling, and field testing.

GS-1863 – Food Inspection Series*

This series includes positions that involve the inspection of slaughter, processing, packaging, shipping, and storing of meat and meat products, poultry and poultry products, fish and fish products; meat products derived from equines, and food establishments engaged in these activities in order to determine compliance with law and regulations which establish standards for the protection of the consumer by assuring them that products distributed to them are wholesome, not adulterated, and properly marked, labeled and packaged. Performance of the work in this series requires the knowledge of normal conditions of live and slaughtered meat, poultry, and fish; of standards of wholesomeness and sanitation of meat, poultry and fish products; and of the processing and sanitation of the food production industry or industries inspected.

GS-1864 – Public Health Quarantine Inspection Series*

This series includes all positions the duties of which are to supervise or perform inspectional work in the enforcement of public health quarantine and sanitary regulations governing the entrance of persons and things into the United States or its possessions. The work involves (a) the inspection of persons for the possible presence of quarantinable or communicable diseases and (b) the inspection of carriers engaged in foreign transportation and their cargoes and of vehicles, personal effects, and other things for the presence of disease vectors, infestation, or conditions contrary to approved sanitary procedures and practices.

* Standards published

GS-1884–Customs Patrol Officer Series*

This series includes positions involved in law enforcement concerned with (1) detecting and preventing the smuggling into or out of the United States of contraband and controlled substances and materials; (2) detecting and preventing theft, pilferage, or diversion of merchandise, cargo, or other materials from areas under Customs jurisdiction or custody; and (3) detecting and apprehending suspected violators of the criminal provisions of the Customs Laws of the United States. Enforcement duties are carried out by patrol and surveillance at, around, and between international ports of entry of the United States. Such work requires knowledge and understanding of Customs and related laws, instructions, and precedent decisions; ability to evaluate information; ability to make timely decisions and apply judgment in taking prompt and appropriate actions in all situations and the ability to effectively use basic investigative and law enforcement procedures to enforce the Customs laws and other laws which the Customs Patrol Officer may be called upon to enforce or to assist in enforcing.

GS-1889–Import Specialist Series*

This series includes positions supervising or performing work which involves primarily the acceptance; tariff classification; appraisement; allowance of specified types of drawback claims; and, in some circumstances, liquidation of formal entries of imported merchandise. The major objectives of the work are to assess customs duties and associated taxes to be paid on imported merchandise, and to assure compliance with related laws and regulations. The work requires (a) knowledge of tariff and other import-related laws, regulations, policies, and procedures and of related administrative and judicial rulings; (b) knowledge of the technical or physical characteristics, commercial uses, and trade practices associated with imported merchandise; and (c) judgment in applying these knowledges in order to make decisions on import admissibility, classification, and valuation of merchandise, final settlement of duties and taxes due, and related matters.

GS-1890–Customs Inspection Series*

This series includes positions which involve inspection work in the enforcement and administration of laws governing the importation or exportation of merchandise. The work requires knowledge of laws, regulations, policies, and procedures concerning the entry, examination, classification, and release of merchandise; ability to obtain data about the description, characteristics, value, and country of origin of merchandise by questioning people, examining merchandise, and reviewing documents; ability to search baggage, persons, cargo, and carriers for contraband; ability to make sound decisions to admit and to hold or release merchandise; and sound judgment in detaining and apprehending persons at the point of entry who are violating customs or other laws.

GS-1894–Customs Entry and Liquidating Series*

This series includes all classes of positions the duties of which are to administer, supervise, or perform work involving the examination, acceptance, processing, or issuance of documents required for the entry of imported merchandise into the United States and the initial classification of merchandise covered by the entries; the determination of customs duties and applicable internal revenue taxes accruing on such merchandise; the ascertainment of drawback to be paid on exported articles manufactured with the use of duty-paid or tax-paid imported merchandise or substituted domestic merchandise; and the determination of the validity of protests against liquidation decisions on formal entries.

GS-1895–Customs Warehouse Officer Series*

This series includes positions responsible for maintaining effective control of merchandise stored in customs bonded warehouses until import fees are paid, or other arrangements for the release of the merchandise are approved. These positions oversee all the activities in the warehouse operations to insure compliance with customs regulations for bonded warehouses and to protect the Government from loss of revenue. Positions in this series require application of knowledges of laws and regulations related to customs storage procedures as well as knowledge of appropriate control, inspection and customs examination techniques.

GS-1896–Border Patrol Agent Series*

This series includes positions involved in enforcement work concerned with (1) detecting and preventing the smuggling or illegal entry of aliens into the United States; (2) detecting and apprehending aliens in violation of the conditions under which they were admitted; (3) detecting and apprehending aliens at interior points in the United States who entered illegally; (4) detecting and apprehending aliens falsely claiming United States citizenship or legal status; (5) detecting and apprehending producers, vendors and users of counterfeit, altered and genuine documents used to circumvent the immigration and nationality laws of the United States; and (6) enforcing criminal provisions of the immigration and nationality laws and regulations of the United States. Such work requires knowledge and understanding of the statutes, regulations, instructions and precedent decisions pertaining to the enforcement of the immigration and nationality laws, ability to evaluate information rapidly, make timely decisions and take prompt and appropriate actions, and the ability to use effectively basic investigative and law enforcement procedures to enforce the immigration and nationality laws and other laws which the Border Patrol Agent may be called upon to enforce or assist in enforcing.

---

* Standards published

DEFINITIONS OF GROUPS AND SERIES

GS-1897–Customs Aid Series

This series includes all classes of positions the duties of which are to supervise or perform work that is incidental or subordinate to entry, liquidating, appraising, examining, marine officer, or other technical customs work and which consists of (1) clerical duties requiring the application of specialized knowledge of pertinent provisions of the Tariff Act, the Navigation Laws, or other similar customs laws or (2) quasi-technical duties requiring some, but less than full, technical training in one or more kinds of technical customs work (except such duties when performed as training for the full technical level).

GS-1898–Admeasurement Series

This series includes all classes of positions the duties of which are to administer, supervise, or perform work involved in ascertaining by measurement and computation the gross and net tonnage of vessels, requiring application of provisions of the Navigation Laws of the United States, regulations, and rulings thereunder, Panama Canal rules, and Suez Canal regulations.

GS-1899–Investigation Student Trainee Series

See the series definition for the General Student Trainee Series, GS-099.

GS-1900–QUALITY ASSURANCE, IN-SPECTION, AND GRADING GROUP

This group includes all classes of positions the duties of which are to advise on, supervise, or perform administrative or technical work primarily concerned with the quality assurance or inspection of material, facilities, and processes; or with the grading of commodities under official standards.

Series in this group are:

GS-1910–Quality Assurance Series*

This series includes all positions the duties of which are to perform, administer, or advise on work concerned with assuring the quality of products acquired and used by the Federal Government. The work of this series involves: (1) the development of plans and programs for achieving and maintaining product quality throughout the item's life cycle; (2) monitoring operations to prevent the production of defects and to verify adherence to quality plans and requirements; and (3) analysis

and investigation of adverse quality trends or conditions and initiation of corrective action. The duties of these positions require analytical ability combined with knowledge and application of quality assurance principles and techniques, and knowledge of pertinent product characteristics and the associated manufacturing processes and techniques.

GS-1980–Agricultural Commodity Grading Series*

This series includes positions which administer, supervise, or perform work concerned with examining and evaluating agricultural products to determine their official U.S. grade and/or their acceptability in terms of quality or condition in accordance with official standards and related regulations. The work often includes the inspection or monitoring of the conditions under which the product is processed, stored, or transported insofar as these factors affect product quality.

GS-1981–Agricultural Commodity Aid Series

This series includes all classes of positions the duties of which are to supervise or perform subordinate clerical work such as taking samples, making tests or otherwise assisting in the grading or classing of agricultural commodities in accordance with prescribed standards and regulations. (This series does not include positions the duties of which are to perform subordinate work in one or more branches of agricultural science. Such positions are properly classified in the Biological Technician Series, GS-404. Neither does it include positions the duties of which are to perform nonprofessional work in the physical sciences. Such positions are properly classified in the Physical Science Technician Series, GS-1311.)

GS-1999–Quality Inspection Student Trainee Series

See the series definition for the General Student Trainee Series, GS-099.

GS-2000–SUPPLY GROUP**

This group includes positions which involve work concerned with furnishing all types of supplies, equipment, material, property (except real estate), and certain services to components of the Federal Government, industrial, or other concerns under contract to the Government, or receiving supplies from the Federal Government. Included are positions concerned with one or more aspects of supply activities from initial planning, including requirements analysis and determination, through acquisition, cataloging, storage, distribution, utilization to ultimate issue for consumption or disposal. The work

---

* Standards published
** Flysheets published

U.S. OFFICE OF PERSONNEL MANAGEMENT

requires a knowledge of one or more elements or parts of a supply system, and/or supply methods, policies, or procedures.

Series in this group are:

GS-2001–General Supply Series**

This series includes positions involving: (1) a combination of technical work covered by two or more series in the Supply Group when no other series is appropriate for the paramount knowledges and abilities required for the position; or (2) other technical or administrative supply work not specifically covered by another series.

GS-2003–Supply Program Management Series*

This series includes positions that involve: (1) the management, direction, or administration of a supply program that involves two or more technical supply functions at the departmental, intermediate echelon, or installation level; or (2) in a staff capacity, managerial or administrative work primarily concerned with analyzing, developing, evaluating, or promoting improvements in the policies, plans, methods, procedures, systems, or techniques of such a supply program.

Some positions, in addition, are also concerned with management of activities related to supply (such as procurement, property utilization and disposal, production, maintenance, quality assurance, transportation, funds control, automated data processing) that are classifiable in other occupational groups, provided that supply management knowledge is the paramount qualification requirement.

Positions in this series are concerned with the overall management, or staff work related to overall management, of a supply program encompassing two or more of the technical supply activities included in the GS-2000 Group. (Generally, one of these activities will be work characteristic of the Inventory Management Series, GS-2010, or the Distribution Facilities and Storage Management Series, GS-2030.) The paramount knowledge requirements relate to management of supply programs involving technical work in the GS-2000 Group.

GS-2005–Supply Clerical and Technician Series*

This series includes clerical and technical support work necessary to insure the effective operation of supply management programs, when such work is not covered by another series in the GS-2000 Supply Group. Positions involve supervision or performance of work which requires a knowledge of supply operations and program requirements, and ability to apply established supply policies, management techniques, regulations, or procedures.

GS-2010–Inventory Management Series*

This series includes all positions which involve technical work in managing, regulating, coordinating or otherwise exercising control over supplies, equipment, or other material. Control relates to any one or more phases of material management from initial planning, including provisioning and requirements determination, through acquisition and distribution, up to ultimate issue for consumption, retention, or disposal.

GS-2030–Distribution Facilities and Storage Management Series*

This series covers positions that involve technical or managerial work concerned with receiving, handling, storing, maintaining while in storage, issuing, or physically controlling items within a distribution system. Included is management responsibility for distribution and storage programs. Positions covered by this series require as their primary qualification a knowledge of the principles, practices, and techniques of managing the physical receipt, custody, care, and distribution of material, including the selection of appropriate storage sites and facilities.

GS-2032–Packaging Series*

This occupation includes positions that involve planning, designing, and developing packages to protect supplies, materials, and equipment between the time of purchase and use, including prevention of environmental and mechanical damage during handling, shipping, and storage. The work

---

* Standards published
** Flysheets published

in this occupation involves determining the best method of packaging particular materials; establishing packaging standards; developing or reviewing packaging specifications, evaluating packaging methods; advising on packaging matters, and supervising and managing packaging programs. This occupation requires knowledge of packaging and preservation methods, materials, regulations, specifications, and guidelines.

GS-2050 – Supply Cataloging Series*

This series covers positions which involve technical work in the development, maintenance, or revision of supply catalogs, manuals, stock lists, computer input data, item descriptions, and other documents which identify items of supply. Positions in this series require a knowledge of the characteristics of supply items and of systems for cataloging and classifying such supply items to insure proper identification for management purposes.

GS-2091 – Sales Store Clerical Series*

This series includes all classes of positions the duties of which are to supervise or perform checkout, sales clerk, customer assistance, or other clerical duties which are involved in the retail sale of merchandise or stock items and which require the application of clerical knowledges, procedures, and/or practices that are peculiar to sales store operations.

GS-2099 – Supply Student Trainee Series

See the series definition for the General Student Trainee Series, GS-099.

GS-2100 – TRANSPORTATION GROUP

This group includes all classes of positions the duties of which are to advise on, administer, supervise, or perform clerical, administrative, or technical work involved in the provision of transportation service to the Government, the regulation of transportation utilities by the Government, or the management of Government-funded transportation programs, including transportation research and development projects.

Series in this group are:

GS-2101 – Transportation Specialist Series

This series includes all administrative positions the duties of which are to advise on, supervise, or perform work which involves two or more specialized transportation functions or other transportation work not specifically included in other series of this group.

GS-2102 – Transportation Clerk and Assistant Series

This series includes positions which involve transportation clerical or technical support work of a type not classifiable in other series of this group. The work requires the ability to apply the established instructions, rules, regulations, and procedures of a transportation or traffic management program.

GS-2110 – Transportation Industry Analysis Series*

This occupation includes positions that involve analytical, evaluative, advisory, or similar work pertaining to regulation of the transportation, industry with regard to operations, economics, equity in industry practices, and protection of the public interest. The work requires a knowledge of transportation industry regulatory controls, of the customs and competitive practices of carriers and of carrier operations, services, and facilities. It also requires a general knowledge of economics, statistics, law, business management and related subject-matter areas, but does not require full training and professional competence in any of those fields.

S-2111 – Transportation Rate and Tariff Examining Series

This series includes all classes of positions the duties of which are to administer, supervise, or perform work involved in the examination of transportation rates or tariffs to determine those legally applicable from a regulatory standpoint.

S-2121 – Railroad Safety Series*

This series includes positions that are involved in developing, administering, or enforcing railroad safety standards and regulation or in investigating and preventing railroad accidents. These positions require (1) broad knowledge of railroad operating practices and recordkeeping; (2) practical knowledge of the methods used in installation, maintenance, or manufacture of railroad equipment, signal systems, and track; (3) knowledge of safety practices applicable to the railroad industry and related laws, regulations, and standards; and (4) knowledge of the investigative techniques used in determining the cause of accidents.

GS-2123 – Motor Carrier Safety Series*

This series includes positions the duties of which are to administer, supervise, or perform work involved in promoting or enforcing compliance with Federal laws, standards, and regulations related to the safe operation of commercial motor vehicles on the public highways. Included are positions concerned with promoting safe operating practices and enforcing compliance by shippers of hazardous materials; motor carrier accident investigation and prevention; developing regulations and standards; and providing technical assistance to the industry and other jurisdictions involved in motor carrier safety. The work requires: (1) comprehensive knowledge of the laws, standards, and regulations governing motor carrier safety; (2) knowledge of the safety principles and practices applicable to the motor carrier industry; (3) practical knowledge of the competitive and operating practices, policies, organization, equipment, facilities, and recordkeeping systems of motor carriers; and (4) knowledge of investigative techniques used in compliance enforcement and accident investigation.

---

* Standards published

DEFINITIONS OF GROUPS AND SERIES

GS-2125–Highway Safety Series*

This series includes positions the duties of which primarily involve: (1) development and administration of highway safety regulations, standards and programs to elicit and promote governmental and public support for highway safety; (2) conducting studies or performing other analytical work directed toward identification of current highway safety problems and evaluation of the effectiveness of highway safety programs and methods; or (3) providing State and local governments with technical assistance in planning, developing, monitoring, funding, managing, promoting, or evaluating programs and systems to improve vehicle, passenger, or pedestrian safety and to identify, control, or eliminate the factors that influence highway accidents. All positions in this series require specialized knowledge of highway safety programs and the factors that influence highway safety and the safe performance and operation of motor vehicles. Most positions also require a high degree of analytical ability and a general knowledge of the principles and processes of program management and intergovernmental relations.

GS-2130–Traffic Management Series*

This series includes positions that involve (1) performing, administering, or supervising technical and analytical work concerned with planning, development, and execution of traffic policies and programs; or (2) directing and managing programs to obtain the economical and efficient transportation of freight, personal property, and/or passengers. Positions in this occupation primarily require a knowledge of Federal traffic management principles and policies; transportation industry operations, practices, and capabilities; special handling or movement requirements associated with freight, passengers, or other transportation operations; and the relationship of traffic management to other agency or organizational programs and functions.

GS-2131–Freight Rate Series*

This series includes all classes of positions the duties of which are to administer, supervise, or perform work involved in the procurement of common carrier and other transportation service by rail, motor, air, water, and miscellaneous means, for the domestic and foreign movement of freight. This requires: the study and application of published classification guides, rate tariffs, dockets, agreements, contracts, and related carrier and Federal publications in the classification of freight and the determination of appropriate rates and routes. In addition to positions which determine classification, rates, and/or routes prior to shipment, this series includes positions engaged in the preaudit or the postaudit of freight bills to determine the propriety of the rates paid or to be paid.

GS-2132–Travel Series*

This series includes all classes of positions the duties of which are to administer, supervise, or perform work involved in the procurement of and arrangement for common and other carrier services for the transportation of persons, individually or in groups, within, to, from, and between the United States, its territories and possessions, and foreign countries. Positions in this series require the application of a knowledge of travel regulations and carrier guides, schedules, services, and facilities, but do not require technical knowledge, interpretation, and application of formal tariffs, dockets, agreements, contracts, and related carrier and Federal publications.

GS-2133–Passenger Rate Series*

This series includes all classes of positions the duties of which require technical knowledge, interpretation, and application of published authorized rates and tariffs, dockets, agreements, contracts, and related carrier and Federal publications in the determination of appropriate rates and routes for the transportation of persons, individually or in groups, within, to, from, and between the United States, its territories and possessions, and foreign countries. Particularly included in this series are (a) positions responsible for administering, supervising, or performing work involved in the preaudit or postaudit of passenger transportation bills to determine the propriety of the transportation rates and charges paid or to be paid, and (b) positions responsible for the procurement of or arrangement for transportation when the same technical knowledges are required.

GS-2134–Shipment Clerical and Assistance Series*

This series includes positions which require a practical knowledge of clerical and technical duties involved in shipping or storing freight or personal property by commercial or Government means. Such positions are concerned with preshipment, shipment, or postshipment responsibilities: (1) to arrange for shipment of goods, parcels, or printed materials; (2) to determine extent of personal property shipment and storage entitlements at Government expense; (3) to arrange for storage, pickup, delivery, and other ancillary services required for shipments; (4) to prepare and process shipment and/or storage documents, records, receipts, manifests, etc., for shipping and receiving points; (5) to maintain and update vital shipment and storage records or record control systems; and/or (6) to coordinate shipment scheduling, expediting, delaying, or other disposition. The duties do not require technical knowledge inherent in or associated with the analysis or interpretation of transportation tariffs, classification, or rate structures.

GS-2135–Transportation Loss and Damage Claims Examining Series

This series includes all classes of positions the duties of which are to administer, supervise, or perform work consisting of the examination, development, review, or authorization of claims by or against the Government arising from the loss or damage of goods and merchandise while in the custody of carriers for transporting, when this work does not include the determination of transportation rates nor the development of loss and damage prevention measures as these duties are described in the Freight Rate Series, GS-2131.

* Standards published

* Standards published
** Flysheets published

* Standards published
** Flysheets published

U.S. OFFICE OF PERSONNEL MANAGEMENT

U.S. OFFICE OF PERSONNEL MANAGEMENT

GS-2144—Cargo Scheduling Series**

This series includes all classes of positions the duties of which are to supervise or perform work in controlling or scheduling the movement of cargo into, out of, or through one or more terminals in the proper amounts and time sequence in relationship to the priority of the cargo, the terminals' ability to accommodate the cargo and/or the carriers' ability to move the cargo. This work requires the technical analysis of the transportation considerations which effect the movement of cargo in the proper relationships to the terminal and carrier capacity. Extensive knowledge of transportation systems and of transportation rules and regulations is required but technical knowledge of freight classification and of common carriers' rates is not required.

GS-2150—Transportation Operations Series

This series includes all classes of positions the duties of which are to administer, supervise, or perform work involving the planning, directing, or operating of rail, motor, air, or water transportation systems and service, including positions involving responsibility for operation of both transportation service and terminal facilities.

GS-2151—Dispatching Series**

This series includes all classes of positions the duties of which are to supervise or perform work involved in dispatching or scheduling motor vehicles, trains, aircraft, or vessels used for the transportation of passengers, mail, equipment, or supplies. The duties of these positions are primarily of an office or a clerical nature and involve assigning vehicles, keeping records and reports, and providing route and destination information and instructions to the drivers, engineers, or pilots.

GS-2152—Air Traffic Control Series*

This series includes positions concerned with: (a) the control of air traffic to insure the safe, orderly and expeditious movement along air routes and at airports when a knowledge of aircraft separation standards and control techniques, and the ability to apply them properly, often under conditions of great stress, are required; (b) the providing of preflight and in-flight assistance to aircraft requiring a knowledge of the information pilots need to conduct safe flights and the ability to present that information clearly and concisely; or (c) the development, coordination, and management of air traffic control programs. Positions in this occupation require an extensive knowledge of the laws, rules, regulations and procedures governing the movement of air traffic.

GS-2154—Air Traffic Assistance Series*

This series includes positions that involve the performance of work in support of air traffic control functions. Positions in this series require a knowledge of and skill in applying air traffic control procedures, but do not require knowledge of aircraft separation standards or the ability to provide pre-flight or in-flight safety or weather briefings.

GS-2161—Marine Cargo Series*

This series includes all classes of positions the duties of which are to supervise, administer, monitor, or perform work involved in planning and/or directing the loading and stowage of cargo aboard vessels and the unloading of cargo from vessels.

GS-2181—Aircraft Operation Series*

This series includes all positions primarily involved in: (1) piloting or copiloting of aircraft to carry out various programs and functions of Federal agencies; (2) providing ground and flight instruction and in-flight evaluation in the piloting of aircraft; (3) flight testing of developmental and modified aircraft and components; (4) in-flight inspection and evaluation of air navigation facilities and the environmental conditions affecting instrument flight procedures; and (5) performing staff work concerned with planning, analyzing, or administering agency aviation programs, where the work requires primarily the application of pilot knowledge and skills.

GS-2183—Air Navigation Series*

This series includes positions responsible for assisting the pilot in aircraft operations by determining, planning, and performing the navigational aspects of the flight. Positions in this series require knowledge of the various methods of air navigation, and skill in using navigational instruments, equipment, and systems in conjunction with flight instruments to direct the movement and positioning of the aircraft to accomplish a specific mission or assignment. Some positions may require knowledge of the use and deployment of fighter aircraft ordnance; skill to conduct preflight checks, recognize malfunctions, and coordinate delivery with the pilot; and knowledge of weapon ballistics and skill to operate related avionics systems for fighter aircraft. Also included are positions responsible for providing ground and flight instruction in air navigation.

GS-2185—Aircrew Technician Series*

This series includes all positions the primary duties of which are to perform, instruct, or supervise flight crew work, particularly (1) flight engineering work supporting the operation of heavy multiengine aircraft, (2) controlling and operating aerial refueling systems aboard tanker aircraft, and (3) loading, positioning, and securing cargo in transport aircraft.

GS-2199—Transportation Student Trainee Series

See the series definition for the General Student Trainee Series, GS-099.

---

* Standards published
** Flysheets published

Alphabetical Index to Definitions of Occupational Groups and Series

* Standards published
** Flysheets published

U.S. OFFICE OF PERSONNEL MANAGEMENT

---

* Standards published
** Flysheets published

ALPHABETICAL INDEX

* Standards published
** Flysheets published

U.S. OFFICE OF PERSONNEL MANAGEMENT

Appendix L: White Collar Occupations in Federal Service by Selected Agency

Factors affecting **hiring potential** are discussed in Step 1 (p. 20).

As you'll recall from Step 1, two of the factors affecting hiring potential are the universality of the job title (how many agencies have such positions) and the occupational group (or job family) in which the job title appears. The pie chart and table reproduced in this appendix show the distribution of white-collar Federal jobs by agency, occupational group, and job title. The larger the occupational group, the more vacancies and the greater opportunity to be hired. Likewise, the more agencies in which a job title occurs, the better the chances of finding an opening. By showing how many people in each job title are employed at each of the 25 largest Federal agencies, this appendix can indicate which agencies are likely to offer the best job opportunities in your field.

Because the Federal government periodically updates job classifications and grading, some of the material in this appendix may vary from information presented in other appendixes. The most current list of Federal job series is that appearing in Appendix K. This information is dated 1995 (the latest year available at time of printing). Only small variations in these figures occur from year to year.

FIGURE 2 - WHITE-COLLAR EMPLOYMENT BY DEPARTMENT AND SELECTED AGENCY
SEPTEMBER 30, 1995

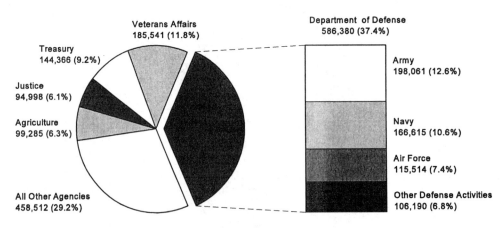

ABLE E   FULL-TIME CIVILIAN WHITE-COLLAR EMPLOYMENT BY OCCUPATION, GENDER, AND SELECTED AGENCY, ALL AREAS, SEPTEMBER 30, 1995

OCCUPATION CODES	TITLES	TOTAL ALL AGENCIES	STATE	TREASURY	ARMY	NAVY	AIR FORCE	DEFENSE LOGIS AGENCY	OTHER DEFENSE	JUSTICE	INTERIOR	AGRI- CULTURE	COM- MERCE
	GRAND TOTAL	1,569,082	14,310	144,366	198,061	166,615	115,514	36,502	69,688	94,998	59,862	99,285	30,046
	PERCENT OF TOTAL	100.0 %	0.9 %	9.2 %	12.6 %	10.6 %	7.4 %	2.3 %	4.4 %	6.1 %	3.8 %	6.3 %	1.9 %
	WOMEN	768,941	6,253	80,192	92,655	68,766	52,783	17,307	40,399	38,233	25,105	40,417	12,513
0006 A	CORRECTIONAL INST ADMIN	1,626	...	...	4	31	...	...	...	1,588	3	...	...
	WOMEN	373	...	...	3	1	...	...	...	369	...	...	...
0007 O	CORRECTIONAL OFFICER	11,808	...	...	...	...	...	...	...	11,801	7	...	...
	WOMEN	1,365	...	...	...	...	...	...	...	1,363	2	...	...
0011 A	BOND SALES PROMOTION	105	...	105	...	...	...	...	...	...	...	...	...
	WOMEN	15	...	15	...	...	...	...	...	...	...	...	...
0018 A	SAFETY & OCCL HEALTH MGT	4,254	4	31	795	998	466	144	42	210	144	60	11
	WOMEN	851	2	5	169	242	56	21	9	24	28	12	5
0019 T	SAFETY TECHNICIAN	238	...	...	64	80	10	8	...	...	15	4	4
	WOMEN	96	...	...	16	45	5	2	...	...	11	2	1
0020 P	COMMUNITY PLANNING	529	...	...	85	39	100	...	...	...	27	18	20
	WOMEN	136	...	...	19	14	17	...	...	...	8	11	5
0021 T	COMMUNITY PLANNING TECH	18	...	...	6	5	...	...	...	...	4	2	...
	WOMEN	13	...	...	5	3	...	...	...	...	4	1	...
0023 A	OUTDOOR RECREATION PLAN	711	...	...	84	...	...	...	...	...	488	133	...
	WOMEN	246	...	...	17	...	...	...	...	...	160	65	...
0025 *	PARK RANGER	6,524	...	...	1,653	...	1	...	...	...	4,868	1	...
	WOMEN	1,836	...	...	286	...	...	...	...	...	1,549	...	...
0028 A	ENVIRONMENTL PROTEC SPEC	5,374	...	2	681	831	408	357	14	2	263	38	11
	WOMEN	2,115	...	...	178	225	193	114	4	...	63	11	3
0029 T	ENVIRONMENTL PROTEC ASST	599	...	...	83	91	75	93	...	...	6	...	1
	WOMEN	425	...	...	35	47	31	80	...	...	4	...	1
0030 A	SPORTS SPECIALIST	620	...	...	325	35	134	1	2	89	...	6	...
	WOMEN	100	...	...	53	4	27	1	...	11	...	3	...
0050 A	FUNERAL DIRECTING	32	...	...	13	1	17	...	1	...	...	...	...
	WOMEN	4	...	...	...	1	3	...	...	...	...	...	...
0060 P	CHAPLAIN	620	...	...	4	1	...	...	...	188	...	...	...
	WOMEN	43	...	...	...	...	...	...	...	25	...	...	...
0062 A	CLOTHING DESIGN	38	...	...	11	7	4	14	...	...	...	...	...
	WOMEN	23	...	...	7	5	4	6	...	...	...	...	...
0072 *	FINGERPRINT IDENTIFICATN	813	...	23	3	3	...	...	...	783	1	...	...
	WOMEN	514	...	4	...	...	...	...	...	510	...	...	...
0080 A	SECURITY ADMINISTRATION	6,292	749	222	1,186	1,056	712	107	783	313	28	13	45
	WOMEN	2,221	82	57	430	434	232	50	350	203	17	3	17
0081 O	FIRE PROTECTION & PREVEN	10,085	...	...	2,529	4,286	2,514	120	...	...	61	...	13
	WOMEN	184	...	...	39	101	37	...	...	...	2	...	...
0082 O	UNITED STATES MARSHAL	91	...	...	...	...	...	...	...	91	...	...	...
	WOMEN	9	...	...	...	...	...	...	...	9	...	...	...
0083 O	POLICE	8,469	...	1,504	657	1,981	131	238	229	110	921	...	...
	WOMEN	611	...	126	40	132	4	17	10	29	65	...	...
0084 O	NUCLEAR MATERIAL COURIER	261	...	...	...	...	...	...	...	...	...	...	...
	WOMEN	...	...	...	...	...	...	...	...	...	...	...	...
0085 O	SECURITY GUARD	4,707	...	...	1,469	709	470	81	112	12	173	18	37
	WOMEN	364	...	...	44	24	7	4	6	5	46	1	1
0086 C	SECURITY CLERICAL & ASST	1,727	20	38	323	583	197	31	231	116	5	5	17
	WOMEN	1,226	17	25	224	394	132	25	185	94	4	3	15
0090 T	GUIDE	171	...	8	9	...	...	...	...	17	117	19	...
	WOMEN	77	...	5	3	...	...	...	...	12	46	11	...
0095 P	FOREIGN LAW SPECIALIST	19	...	...	...	...	...	...	...	...	...	...	...
	WOMEN	9	...	...	...	...	...	...	...	...	...	...	...
0099 O	GENERAL STUDENT TRAINEE	237	...	5	70	43	1	...	3	4	21	16	...
	WOMEN	102	...	2	20	16	...	...	1	3	9	8	...
0000	MISCELLANEOUS OCCUPATIONS	65,968	773	1,938	10,054	10,780	5,230	1,194	1,417	15,324	7,152	333	159
	WOMEN	12,958	101	239	1,588	1,688	658	321	565	2,657	2,018	131	48
0101 P	SOCIAL SCIENCE	5,978	1	2	800	464	731	7	21	1,256	50	105	53
	WOMEN	2,833	1	2	396	287	455	1	12	542	28	42	25
0102 T	SOCIAL SCI AID & TECH	760	...	...	16	32	56	1	1	19	82	239	...
	WOMEN	392	...	...	14	15	44	...	...	15	44	123	...
0105 A	SOCIAL INSURANCE ADMIN	24,353	...	...	...	...	...	...	...	...	...	...	...
	WOMEN	15,892	...	...	...	...	...	...	...	...	...	...	...
0106 A	UNEMPLOYMENT INSURANCE	145	...	...	...	...	...	...	...	...	...	...	...
	WOMEN	60	...	...	...	...	...	...	...	...	...	...	...
0107 A	HEALTH INSURANCE ADMIN	1,537	...	...	...	...	...	...	...	...	...	...	...
	WOMEN	918	...	...	...	...	...	...	...	...	...	...	...
0110 P	ECONOMIST	5,438	977	441	279	9	2	3	11	49	123	714	466
	WOMEN	1,414	227	123	60	1	...	...	4	9	23	163	138
0119 T	ECONOMICS ASSISTANT	129	...	...	6	...	...	1	...	...	...	2	...
	WOMEN	100	...	...	4	...	...	1	...	...	...	1	...
0130 P	FOREIGN AFFAIRS	3,823	2,515	6	3	...	...	...	...	127	...	...	12
	WOMEN	1,160	656	2	...	...	...	...	...	26	...	...	4
0131 P	INTERNATIONAL RELATIONS	129	16	...	18	9	2	...	...	17	...	15	7
	WOMEN	44	6	...	2	2	...	...	...	3	...	11	2
0132 A	INTELLIGENCE	4,732	134	466	1,228	732	818	...	80	1,168	2	5	9
	WOMEN	1,661	49	226	261	187	162	...	10	734	...	3	7

TABLE E, 1995 -- CONTINUED

LABOR	HEALTH & HUMAN SERVICES	HOUSING & URBAN DEVLPMT	TRANSPOR-TATION	ENERGY	EDUCA-TION	VETERANS AFFAIRS	LIBRARY OF CONGRESS	EPA	FDIC	GENERAL SERVICES ADM	OPM	NASA	TVA	ALL OTHER AGENCIES	OCCUPATION CODES
15,575	48,569	11,607	59,969	17,532	4,799	185,541	4,143	16,891	14,398	12,834	3,336	20,695	10,575	113,321	GRAND TOTAL
1.0 %	3.1 %	0.7 %	3.8 %	1.1 %	0.3 %	11.8 %	0.3 %	1.1 %	0.9 %	0.9 %	0.2 %	1.3 %	0.7 %	7.2 %	PERCENT
7,372	30,321	6,902	16,440	7,161	2,911	117,257	2,220	8,150	7,247	6,553	2,077	6,722	3,367	69,618	WOMEN
...	...	...	...	...	...	...	...	...	...	...	...	...	...	...	0006
...	...	...	...	...	...	...	...	...	...	...	...	...	...	...	WOMEN
...	...	...	...	...	...	...	...	...	...	...	...	...	...	...	0007
...	...	...	...	...	...	...	...	...	...	...	...	...	...	...	WOMEN
...	...	...	...	...	...	...	...	...	...	...	...	...	...	...	0011
...	...	...	...	...	...	...	...	...	...	...	...	...	...	...	WOMEN
776	46	...	47	99	3	212	2	14	...	36	...	40	...	74	0018
176	15	...	10	17	2	25	...	2	...	10	...	9	...	12	WOMEN
6	5	...	1	3	...	35	...	...	...	...	...	3	...	...	0019
5	...	...	...	2	...	4	...	...	...	...	...	2	...	...	WOMEN
...	...	14	153	1	...	...	...	1	...	9	...	...	5	57	0020
...	...	3	36	...	...	...	...	...	...	6	...	...	1	16	WOMEN
...	...	...	1	...	...	...	...	...	...	...	...	...	...	...	0021
...	...	...	...	...	...	...	...	...	...	...	...	...	...	...	WOMEN
...	...	...	...	4	...	...	...	...	...	...	...	...	...	2	0023
...	...	...	...	2	...	...	...	...	...	...	...	...	...	2	WOMEN
...	...	...	...	...	...	...	...	...	...	...	...	...	...	1	0025
...	...	...	...	...	...	...	...	...	...	...	...	...	...	1	WOMEN
...	8	29	156	263	...	...	...	2,267	...	1	...	17	...	26	0028
...	4	7	46	103	...	...	...	1,233	...	1	...	11	...	9	WOMEN
...	...	...	2	2	...	...	...	244	...	1	...	...	...	1	0029
...	...	...	1	2	...	...	...	223	...	1	...	...	...	...	WOMEN
...	...	...	...	...	...	1	...	...	...	...	...	...	26	1	0030
...	...	...	...	...	...	1	...	...	...	...	...	...	...	1	WOMEN
...	...	...	...	...	...	...	...	...	...	...	...	...	...	...	0050
...	...	...	...	...	...	...	...	...	...	...	...	...	...	...	WOMEN
...	6	...	...	...	...	416	...	...	...	...	...	...	...	5	0060
...	1	...	...	...	...	17	...	...	...	...	...	...	...	...	WOMEN
...	...	...	2	...	...	...	...	...	...	...	...	...	...	...	0062
...	...	...	1	...	...	...	...	...	...	...	...	...	...	...	WOMEN
...	...	...	...	...	...	...	...	...	...	...	...	...	...	...	0072
...	...	...	...	...	...	...	...	...	...	...	...	...	...	...	WOMEN
4	12	3	67	358	3	101	7	10	15	229	10	72	...	187	0080
1	5	2	29	145	3	12	2	8	10	47	5	24	...	53	WOMEN
...	23	...	59	1	...	440	...	...	...	1	...	18	...	20	0081
...	2	...	2	...	...	1	...	...	...	...	...	...	...	...	WOMEN
...	...	...	...	...	...	...	...	...	...	...	...	...	...	...	0082
...	...	...	...	...	...	...	...	...	...	...	...	...	...	...	WOMEN
...	46	...	1	...	...	2,048	107	...	...	332	...	...	...	114	0083
...	3	...	...	...	...	139	11	...	...	25	...	...	...	10	WOMEN
...	...	...	...	261	...	...	...	...	...	...	...	...	...	...	0084
...	...	...	...	...	...	...	...	...	...	...	...	...	...	...	WOMEN
...	38	...	1	17	...	18	...	...	...	1	...	...	565	986	0085
...	...	...	...	...	...	1	...	...	...	...	...	...	82	143	WOMEN
1	...	...	22	11	...	29	1	...	2	76	...	5	...	24	0086
...	...	...	22	10	...	17	1	...	2	32	...	5	...	19	WOMEN
...	...	...	...	...	...	...	...	...	...	...	...	...	...	1	0090
...	...	...	...	...	...	...	...	...	...	...	...	...	...	...	WOMEN
...	...	...	...	...	...	...	19	...	...	...	...	...	...	...	0095
...	...	...	...	...	...	...	9	...	...	...	...	...	...	...	WOMEN
6	2	...	1	4	3	1	...	17	...	3	...	4	1	32	0099
3	2	...	...	4	3	...	...	11	...	1	...	3	...	15	WOMEN
793	186	46	513	1,024	9	3,301	136	2,553	17	739	10	159	597	1,531	0000
185	32	12	147	285	8	217	23	1,477	12	123	5	54	93	281	WOMEN
32	980	23	52	1	86	967	127	...	...	...	2	1	...	217	0101
21	549	9	36	...	33	262	44	...	...	...	1	...	...	87	WOMEN
5	25	...	2	...	...	260	...	...	...	...	...	...	1	22	0102
5	18	...	2	...	...	94	...	...	...	...	...	...	1	17	WOMEN
...	...	...	...	...	...	...	...	...	...	...	...	...	...	24,353	0105
...	...	...	...	...	...	...	...	...	...	...	...	...	...	15,892	WOMEN
145	...	...	...	...	...	...	...	...	...	...	...	...	...	...	0106
60	...	...	...	...	...	...	...	...	...	...	...	...	...	...	WOMEN
...	1,537	...	...	...	...	...	...	...	...	...	...	...	...	...	0107
...	918	...	...	...	...	...	...	...	...	...	...	...	...	...	WOMEN
1,243	90	90	97	171	2	8	75	92	25	1	...	...	6	465	0110
406	35	18	15	45	...	1	19	27	7	...	...	...	2	91	WOMEN
119	...	...	...	...	...	...	...	...	...	...	...	...	...	1	0119
93	...	...	...	...	...	...	...	...	...	...	...	...	...	1	WOMEN
...	1	...	...	26	...	...	48	...	...	...	...	...	...	1,085	0130
...	...	...	...	8	...	...	15	...	...	...	...	...	...	449	WOMEN
11	...	...	5	19	...	...	...	...	...	...	...	...	...	11	0131
5	...	...	1	9	...	...	...	...	...	...	...	...	...	3	WOMEN
...	...	...	30	53	...	...	...	...	...	...	...	...	...	7	0132
...	...	...	7	14	...	...	...	...	...	...	...	...	...	1	WOMEN

ABLE F   FULL-TIME CIVILIAN WHITE-COLLAR EMPLOYMENT BY OCCUPATION, GENDER, AND SELECTED AGENCY, ALL AREAS, SEPTEMBER 30, 1995

OCCUPATION CODES TITLES	TOTAL ALL AGENCIES	STATE	TREASURY	ARMY	NAVY	AIR FORCE	DEFENSE LOGIS AGENCY	OTHER DEFENSE	JUSTICE	INTERIOR	AGRI-CULTURE	COM-MERCE
0134 C INTELLIGENCE AID & CLERK	527	3	17	127	37	102	...	13	226	...	...	...
WOMEN	424	2	16	112	33	90	...	11	159	...	...	...
0135 P FOREIGN AGRICULT AFFAIRS	195	...	...	...	...	...	...	...	...	...	195	...
WOMEN	35	...	...	...	...	...	...	...	...	...	35	...
0136 A INTERNATIONAL COOPERATN	33	...	...	...	...	...	...	...	...	...	...	...
WOMEN	22	...	...	...	...	...	...	...	...	...	...	...
0140 P MANPOWER RESEARCH&ANALYS	35	...	...	...	...	...	...	...	...	...	...	...
WOMEN	16	...	...	...	...	...	...	...	...	...	...	...
0142 A MANPOWER DEVELOPMENT	488	...	...	1	8	...	...	...	...	1	46	...
WOMEN	218	...	...	...	4	...	...	...	...	...	22	...
0150 P GEOGRAPHY	331	4	...	48	10	1	...	27	1	110	33	89
WOMEN	88	...	...	8	5	1	...	7	...	27	14	26
0160 A CIVIL RIGHTS ANALYSIS	54	1	3	1	...	...	...	...	16	1	...	...
WOMEN	26	1	1	...	...	...	...	...	15	1	...	...
0170 P HISTORY	693	13	3	171	42	161	...	16	11	194	15	5
WOMEN	175	4	2	26	7	27	...	1	2	72	7	...
0180 P PSYCHOLOGY	3,841	...	4	557	294	182	...	35	293	17	8	4
WOMEN	1,270	...	3	206	102	52	...	18	112	8	4	2
0181 T PSYCHOLOGY AID & TECH	850	...	...	23	5	2	...	3	9	...	2	...
WOMEN	402	...	...	14	3	1	...	3	8	...	1	...
0184 P SOCIOLOGY	53	...	...	10	...	...	...	...	...	12	16	1
WOMEN	24	...	...	4	...	...	...	...	...	4	7	...
0185 P SOCIAL WORK	5,225	...	3	354	406	139	2	1	16	71	...	...
WOMEN	2,949	...	2	234	293	95	1	1	8	45	...	...
0186 T SOCIAL SERV AID & ASST	1,020	...	...	277	104	55	2	2	...	159	283	...
WOMEN	560	...	...	227	83	44	2	2	...	77	63	...
0187 A SOCIAL SERVICES	686	1	...	291	76	7	1	...	...	62	3	...
WOMEN	465	...	...	214	59	4	1	...	...	49	2	...
0188 A RECREATION SPECIALIST	1,780	...	2	376	517	391	5	...	394	39	20	...
WOMEN	638	...	1	169	216	174	1	...	50	9	1	...
0189 T RECREATION AID & ASST	1,990	...	1	750	471	494	7	...	...	92	20	...
WOMEN	831	...	1	308	237	193	3	...	...	29	4	...
0190 P GENERAL ANTHROPOLOGY	94	2	...	23	...	5	...	...	...	26	...	2
WOMEN	29	...	...	6	...	1	...	...	...	10	...	2
0193 P ARCHEOLOGY	1,049	...	...	128	10	17	...	...	...	398	477	...
WOMEN	382	...	...	38	3	4	...	...	...	128	204	...
0199 O SOCIAL SCI STUDENT TR	105	...	...	9	1	4	...	1	11	14	20	2
WOMEN	59	...	...	...	1	...	...	1	6	8	18	1
0100 SOC SCI, PSYCH & WELFARE	56,063	3,667	948	5,496	3,227	3,169	28	355	3,468	1,453	2,218	650
WOMEN	33,087	946	379	2,303	1,537	1,349	10	99	1,660	562	725	207
0201 A PERSONNEL MANAGEMENT	11,147	157	773	1,402	1,072	1,132	175	575	715	337	709	242
WOMEN	7,389	119	540	882	711	735	105	365	505	245	511	184
0203 * PERSONNEL CLERICAL &ASST	10,662	22	1,403	1,693	1,300	1,031	290	377	591	334	805	177
WOMEN	9,622	20	1,247	1,521	1,196	928	272	332	533	312	749	163
0204 * MILITARY PERS CLER &TECH	8,157	...	...	4,966	1,640	1,435	23	10	...	...	...	1
WOMEN	5,588	...	...	3,399	1,215	882	19	6	...	...	...	1
0205 A MILITARY PERSONNEL MGT	1,654	...	...	823	163	635	10	10	...	...	...	3
WOMEN	691	...	...	319	89	251	5	...	...	...	...	1
0212 A PERSONNEL STAFFING	2,416	17	317	469	272	116	116	141	107	101	83	14
WOMEN	1,917	14	291	364	219	74	90	124	92	85	63	12
0221 A POSITION CLASSIFICATION	1,404	11	112	334	116	294	65	75	52	64	54	2
WOMEN	850	6	85	180	78	177	43	49	38	41	29	1
0222 A OCCUPATIONAL ANALYSIS	40	...	...	15	3	22	...	...	...	...	...	...
WOMEN	18	...	...	7	2	9	...	...	...	...	...	...
0223 A SALARY AND WAGE ADMIN	146	8	2	1	...	...	...	53	...	...	6	2
WOMEN	96	6	1	1	...	...	...	21	...	...	6	2
0230 A EMPLOYEE RELATIONS	2,008	4	106	289	301	296	89	131	91	65	139	29
WOMEN	1,458	4	83	187	232	196	65	93	77	47	98	22
0233 A LABOR RELATIONS	1,246	2	247	112	201	83	15	40	33	19	25	19
WOMEN	585	1	146	41	97	26	6	15	11	6	5	13
0235 A EMPLOYEE DEVELOPMENT	2,371	2	474	249	304	147	75	76	210	54	110	22
WOMEN	1,547	1	352	155	187	83	43	54	104	40	73	17
0241 A MEDIATION	223	...	...	...	...	...	...	...	...	...	...	...
WOMEN	31	...	...	...	...	...	...	...	...	...	...	...
0243 A APPRENTICESHIP &TRAINING	152	...	...	...	...	...	...	1	...	...	...	...
WOMEN	35	...	...	...	...	...	...	...	...	...	...	...
0244 A LABOR MGT RELATIONS EXAM	406	...	...	...	...	...	...	...	...	...	...	...
WOMEN	143	...	...	...	...	...	...	...	...	...	...	...
0246 A CONTRACTOR INDUSTRL RELS	134	...	...	21	5	4	...	...	...	1	...	...
WOMEN	71	...	...	17	3	...	...	...	...	1	...	...
0249 A WAGE AND HOUR COMPLIANCE	1,013	...	...	...	...	...	...	...	...	...	...	...
WOMEN	368	...	...	...	...	...	...	...	...	...	...	...
0260 A EQUAL EMPLT OPPORTUNITY	2,546	9	270	432	309	116	69	89	81	159	182	61
WOMEN	1,732	7	210	295	227	60	44	56	59	115	123	37
0270 A FED RETIREMENT BENEFITS	483	...	...	...	...	...	...	1	...	...	...	...
WOMEN	327	...	...	...	...	...	...	...	...	...	...	...
0299 O PERSONNEL MGT STUDENT TR	80	...	3	5	16	5	...	2	7	1	8	...
WOMEN	61	...	2	5	15	4	...	2	6	1	8	...
0200 PERSONNEL MGT & IND RELS	46,298	232	3,707	10,811	5,702	5,316	927	1,581	1,887	1,135	2,121	572
WOMEN	32,509	178	2,967	7,373	4,271	3,425	692	1,117	1,425	893	1,665	453

TABLE E, 1995 -- CONTINUED

LABOR	HEALTH & HUMAN SERVICES	HOUSING & URBAN DEVLPMT	TRANSPOR-TATION	ENERGY	EDUCA-TION	VETERANS AFFAIRS	LIBRARY OF CONGRESS	EPA	FDIC	GENERAL SERVICES ADM	OPM	NASA	TVA	ALL OTHER AGENCIES	OCCUPATION CODES
••	•••	•••	•••	2	•••	•••	•••	•••	•••	•••	•••	•••	•••	•••	0134
••	•••	•••	•••	1	•••	•••	•••	•••	•••	•••	•••	•••	•••	•••	WOMEN
••	•••	•••	•••	•••	•••	•••	•••	•••	•••	•••	•••	•••	•••	•••	0135
••	•••	•••	•••	•••	•••	•••	•••	•••	•••	•••	•••	•••	•••	•••	WOMEN
••	•••	•••	•••	•••	•••	•••	•••	•••	•••	•••	•••	•••	•••	33	0136
••	•••	•••	•••	•••	•••	•••	•••	•••	•••	•••	•••	•••	•••	22	WOMEN
32	•••	•••	•••	•••	•••	•••	•••	•••	•••	•••	•••	•••	•••	3	0140
15	•••	•••	•••	•••	•••	•••	•••	•••	•••	•••	•••	•••	•••	1	WOMEN
424	8	•••	•••	•••	•••	•••	•••	•••	•••	•••	•••	•••	•••	•••	0142
190	2	•••	•••	•••	•••	•••	•••	•••	•••	•••	•••	•••	•••	•••	WOMEN
••	•••	•••	•••	2	•••	•••	1	3	•••	•••	•••	•••	•••	2	0150
••	•••	•••	•••	•••	•••	•••	•••	•••	•••	•••	•••	•••	•••	•••	WOMEN
1	•••	•••	1	•••	•••	•••	•••	1	•••	•••	•••	•••	•••	29	0160
1	•••	•••	•••	•••	•••	•••	•••	•••	•••	•••	•••	•••	•••	7	WOMEN
1	9	•••	5	7	1	•••	•••	•••	•••	1	•••	3	1	34	0170
••	5	•••	1	2	•••	•••	•••	•••	•••	•••	•••	•••	1	18	WOMEN
12	261	1	73	2	2	1,990	1	6	1	•••	32	33	1	32	0180
9	127	1	20	•••	2	559	•••	•••	1	•••	19	13	1	11	WOMEN
••	9	•••	9	•••	•••	784	•••	•••	•••	•••	3	•••	•••	1	0181
••	5	•••	5	•••	•••	358	•••	•••	•••	•••	3	•••	•••	1	WOMEN
••	10	•••	1	•••	•••	2	•••	•••	•••	•••	•••	•••	•••	1	0184
••	7	•••	1	•••	•••	1	•••	•••	•••	•••	•••	•••	•••	•••	WOMEN
••	127	•••	2	•••	•••	4,098	•••	•••	•••	•••	3	•••	•••	13	0185
••	90	•••	•••	•••	•••	2,167	•••	•••	•••	•••	2	•••	•••	11	WOMEN
••	26	•••	3	•••	•••	106	•••	•••	•••	•••	•••	•••	•••	3	0186
••	16	•••	3	•••	•••	40	•••	•••	•••	•••	•••	•••	•••	3	WOMEN
••	21	•••	•••	•••	•••	203	•••	•••	•••	•••	•••	•••	•••	21	0187
••	17	•••	•••	•••	•••	112	•••	•••	•••	•••	•••	•••	•••	7	WOMEN
••	6	•••	10	•••	•••	4	•••	•••	•••	•••	•••	•••	9	7	0188
••	5	•••	2	•••	•••	4	•••	•••	•••	•••	•••	•••	2	4	WOMEN
••	1	•••	2	•••	•••	144	•••	•••	•••	•••	•••	•••	2	6	0189
••	1	•••	•••	•••	•••	53	•••	•••	•••	•••	•••	•••	2	•••	WOMEN
••	2	•••	•••	•••	•••	•••	•••	•••	•••	•••	•••	•••	•••	24	0190
••	1	•••	•••	•••	•••	•••	•••	•••	•••	•••	•••	•••	•••	9	WOMEN
••	•••	•••	1	8	•••	•••	•••	•••	•••	•••	•••	•••	3	7	0193
••	•••	•••	•••	4	•••	•••	•••	•••	•••	•••	•••	•••	•••	1	WOMEN
2	12	•••	1	•••	•••	1	•••	•••	•••	•••	2	•••	•••	25	0199
1	7	•••	•••	•••	•••	1	•••	•••	•••	•••	1	•••	•••	13	WOMEN
2,027	3,125	114	204	290	91	8,557	252	102	27	1	42	37	23	26,402	0100
806	1,803	28	93	83	35	3,652	78	27	8	•••	26	13	9	16,649	WOMEN
126	489	87	447	178	46	981	24	138	36	91	230	146	89	750	0201
83	366	60	315	123	26	556	13	99	27	59	105	89	33	513	WOMEN
84	298	53	156	97	7	1,092	15	46	58	72	150	86	34	391	0203
70	271	49	146	91	6	947	12	41	45	69	128	81	32	361	WOMEN
••	20	•••	61	•••	•••	•••	•••	•••	•••	•••	•••	•••	•••	1	0204
••	17	•••	49	•••	•••	•••	•••	•••	•••	•••	•••	•••	•••	•••	WOMEN
••	10	•••	10	•••	•••	•••	•••	•••	•••	•••	•••	•••	•••	•••	0205
••	7	•••	9	•••	•••	•••	•••	•••	•••	•••	•••	•••	•••	•••	WOMEN
31	87	5	55	12	•••	172	•••	7	4	28	145	13	3	101	0212
26	72	3	40	10	•••	131	•••	6	4	19	89	10	2	87	WOMEN
22	25	2	13	12	•••	61	1	2	3	22	22	•••	•••	40	0221
10	13	1	11	6	•••	35	1	1	2	12	7	•••	•••	24	WOMEN
••	•••	•••	•••	•••	•••	•••	•••	•••	•••	•••	•••	•••	•••	•••	0222
••	•••	•••	•••	•••	•••	•••	•••	•••	•••	•••	•••	•••	•••	•••	WOMEN
58	•••	•••	•••	1	•••	15	•••	•••	•••	•••	•••	•••	•••	•••	0223
41	•••	•••	•••	1	•••	7	•••	•••	•••	•••	•••	•••	•••	•••	WOMEN
12	46	18	47	25	6	134	2	10	5	22	11	17	5	108	0230
7	43	15	42	15	6	95	1	6	4	18	8	15	3	76	WOMEN
25	31	9	37	10	4	40	•••	1	8	18	11	5	123	128	0233
12	7	4	13	3	2	12	•••	•••	3	10	5	2	85	60	WOMEN
25	83	11	60	52	9	46	5	23	26	34	44	54	•••	176	0235
19	66	9	40	40	7	28	3	20	19	22	20	31	•••	114	WOMEN
••	•••	•••	•••	•••	•••	•••	•••	•••	•••	•••	•••	•••	•••	223	0241
••	•••	•••	•••	•••	•••	•••	•••	•••	•••	•••	•••	•••	•••	31	WOMEN
139	•••	•••	•••	•••	•••	•••	•••	•••	•••	•••	•••	•••	12	•••	0243
28	•••	•••	•••	•••	•••	•••	•••	•••	•••	•••	•••	•••	7	•••	WOMEN
••	•••	•••	•••	•••	•••	•••	•••	•••	•••	•••	•••	•••	•••	406	0244
••	•••	•••	•••	•••	•••	•••	•••	•••	•••	•••	•••	•••	•••	143	WOMEN
••	•••	47	•••	53	•••	•••	•••	•••	•••	•••	•••	3	•••	•••	0246
••	•••	25	•••	24	•••	•••	•••	•••	•••	•••	•••	1	•••	•••	WOMEN
1,013	•••	•••	•••	•••	•••	•••	•••	•••	•••	•••	•••	•••	•••	•••	0249
368	•••	•••	•••	•••	•••	•••	•••	•••	•••	•••	•••	•••	•••	•••	WOMEN
31	133	14	78	38	11	140	3	27	21	25	1	44	•••	203	0260
19	91	11	45	23	8	84	1	19	11	17	1	29	•••	140	WOMEN
••	•••	•••	•••	•••	•••	•••	•••	•••	•••	•••	481	•••	•••	1	0270
••	•••	•••	•••	•••	•••	•••	•••	•••	•••	•••	326	•••	•••	1	WOMEN
10	4	•••	4	3	•••	1	•••	3	•••	1	1	4	•••	2	0299
7	1	•••	2	1	•••	1	•••	1	•••	•••	•••	3	•••	2	WOMEN
1,576	1,226	246	968	481	83	2,682	50	257	161	313	1,096	372	266	2,530	0200
690	954	177	712	337	55	1,896	31	193	115	226	689	261	162	1,552	WOMEN

TABLE E   FULL-TIME CIVILIAN WHITE-COLLAR EMPLOYMENT BY OCCUPATION, GENDER, AND SELECTED AGENCY, ALL AREAS, SEPTEMBER 30, 1995

OCCUPATION CODES TITLES	TOTAL ALL AGENCIES	STATE	TREASURY	ARMY	NAVY	AIR FORCE	DEFENSE LOGIS AGENCY	OTHER DEFENSE	JUSTICE	INTERIOR	AGRI- CULTURE	COM- MERCE
0301 A MISC ADMIN AND PROGRAM	50,665	545	3,229	7,276	2,756	4,083	424	1,286	2,497	1,751	2,073	993
WOMEN	24,275	306	2,047	2,392	1,435	1,593	174	628	1,542	827	1,060	541
0302 C MESSENGER	112	...	2	18	15	1	7	1	...	...	4	1
WOMEN	22	...	...	4	...	1	1	...	...	...	3	...
0303 * MISC CLERK AND ASSISTANT	61,763	454	7,596	9,129	4,679	3,471	638	1,538	3,465	2,491	2,160	1,218
WOMEN	49,105	340	6,215	6,197	3,675	2,727	520	1,317	2,809	2,240	1,942	1,015
0304 C INFORMATION RECEPTIONIST	1,026	...	54	96	66	43	6	7	121	59	356	4
WOMEN	843	...	41	71	45	34	6	6	106	45	314	4
0305 C MAIL AND FILE	16,058	64	2,654	1,631	1,070	338	191	465	1,829	250	276	96
WOMEN	9,041	43	1,990	668	543	182	73	213	1,403	152	142	41
0309 C CORRESPONDENCE CLERK	289	...	4	30	21	4	...	9	38	2	9	4
WOMEN	233	...	3	28	11	4	...	8	32	2	8	4
0312 C CLERK-STENOGRAPHER &RPTR	222	2	12	63	9	22	3	...	18	4	6	...
WOMEN	213	1	11	60	8	22	3	...	17	4	6	...
0313 C WORK UNIT SUPERVISING	199	...	67	10	3	1	2	1	85	...	1	1
WOMEN	189	...	59	9	3	1	2	1	85	...	1	1
0318 C SECRETARY	78,151	1,498	6,763	12,802	7,425	10,011	1,826	2,844	4,394	2,671	2,672	1,656
WOMEN	76,252	1,466	6,577	12,482	7,237	9,789	1,793	2,748	4,323	2,616	2,615	1,632
0319 C CLOSED MICROPHONE RPTR	161	...	...	28	35	94	...	1	1	...	1	...
WOMEN	133	...	...	21	28	81	...	1	...	...	1	...
0322 C CLERK-TYPIST	5,338	522	572	353	294	79	30	234	151	215	246	15
WOMEN	4,462	393	479	310	240	68	28	194	112	198	232	14
0326 * OFFICE AUTOMATION CLER	17,440	3	1,039	3,346	2,371	1,657	406	444	525	972	1,638	396
WOMEN	15,459	2	916	3,009	2,080	1,490	338	389	451	875	1,514	346
0332 T COMPUTER OPERATION	5,600	25	1,009	980	713	368	139	1,074	129	71	127	111
WOMEN	2,954	14	542	514	370	198	76	570	63	47	94	53
0334 A COMPUTER SPECIALIST	56,212	1,183	5,768	7,048	8,084	3,626	1,784	5,155	1,626	1,926	2,970	2,119
WOMEN	21,927	258	2,425	2,908	3,311	1,227	657	2,036	658	750	1,301	719
0335 * COMPUTER CLERK & ASST	7,788	5	959	1,024	1,109	671	213	758	84	320	872	254
WOMEN	5,358	4	662	712	788	389	143	494	52	229	675	193
0340 A PROGRAM MANAGEMENT	6,961	102	1,489	583	438	222	35	67	126	555	463	48
WOMEN	1,796	30	553	68	80	6	4	14	44	100	129	10
0341 A ADMINISTRATIVE OFFICER	8,527	858	131	952	786	240	80	146	499	651	649	175
WOMEN	5,789	285	85	498	659	84	56	108	396	480	389	152
0342 A SUPPORT SERVICES ADMIN	4,001	206	186	1,126	309	228	53	95	112	96	635	30
WOMEN	2,065	61	94	323	220	116	32	49	56	69	586	13
0343 A MGT AND PROGRAM ANALYSIS	39,784	227	5,653	6,017	5,489	3,133	1,314	1,602	1,212	676	1,385	611
WOMEN	23,927	143	3,595	3,468	3,340	1,642	725	910	810	369	892	375
0344 * MGT & PROGRAM CLER ASST	7,282	28	1,039	1,301	1,411	1,255	542	257	101	98	139	49
WOMEN	6,233	27	891	1,102	1,267	973	468	226	93	80	130	46
0346 A LOGISTICS MANAGEMENT	10,961	6	29	4,079	2,959	3,365	67	96	12	5	2	13
WOMEN	3,219	1	16	1,136	857	992	18	26	7	3	1	4
0350 C EQUIPMENT OPERATOR	1,866	15	324	136	345	29	40	102	30	43	84	120
WOMEN	798	11	175	49	123	13	21	50	16	19	46	76
0351 C PRINTING CLERICAL	184	...	11	16	80	2	...	3	4	9	8	3
WOMEN	137	...	9	15	60	1	...	1	2	6	5	2
0356 C DATA TRANSCRIBER	3,643	6	2,129	136	79	23	31	84	33	23	22	171
WOMEN	3,280	5	1,901	111	69	18	24	74	27	22	18	159
0357 C CODING	226	...	...	28	26	13	...	...	1	13	1	...
WOMEN	185	...	...	23	19	9	...	...	1	12	1	...
0359 C ELECTRIC ACCTG MACH OPER	8	...	...	2	5	1	...	...	...	...	...	...
WOMEN	3	...	...	...	3	...	...	...	...	...	...	...
0360 A EQUAL OPPORTUNITY COMPLI	1,833	...	1	4	...	2	...	2	31	8	62	6
WOMEN	990	...	...	1	...	1	...	...	21	4	37	4
0361 T EQUAL OPPORTUNITY ASST	491	2	40	86	60	20	16	11	12	24	28	7
WOMEN	448	2	37	76	55	19	12	11	11	23	25	7
0362 T ELEC ACCT MACH PROJ PLAN	1	...	...	1	...	...	...	...	...	...	...	...
WOMEN	...	...	...	...	...	...	...	...	...	...	...	...
0382 C TELEPHONE OPERATING	1,622	...	8	212	133	439	10	8	24	10	6	3
WOMEN	1,233	...	8	159	110	334	8	6	22	10	5	1
0390 T TELECOMMUNICATIONS PROCS	922	58	22	245	184	138	25	6	24	114	5	8
WOMEN	329	7	5	61	54	53	6	4	20	62	4	4
0391 A TELECOMMUNICATIONS	7,066	229	703	1,291	737	947	86	651	340	178	202	129
WOMEN	1,681	18	240	215	187	151	21	138	107	46	42	34
0392 T GENERAL TELECOMMUNICATNS	1,338	42	71	244	275	149	20	40	178	62	2	18
WOMEN	516	13	32	73	73	51	7	24	114	31	1	5
0394 C COMMUNICATIONS CLERICAL	310	...	4	65	85	43	7	10	2	3	1	5
WOMEN	245	...	4	54	63	36	5	7	2	2	1	4
0399 O ADM & OFC SPRT STUDNT TR	671	9	23	54	169	33	9	24	18	39	25	24
WOMEN	418	6	11	30	130	23	7	8	14	21	15	10
0300 GEN ADM, CLER & OFC SERVS	398,721	6,089	41,591	60,412	42,220	34,751	8,004	17,021	17,722	13,339	17,130	8,288
WOMEN	263,758	3,436	29,613	36,847	27,143	22,329	5,228	10,261	13,416	9,344	12,235	5,469
0401 P GENRL BIOLOGICAL SCIENCE	8,788	3	1	1,213	113	93	...	49	10	2,470	1,825	110
WOMEN	2,747	1	...	320	36	21	...	24	4	612	437	50
0403 P MICROBIOLOGY	1,984	...	...	156	33	21	...	31	...	38	367	23
WOMEN	815	...	...	52	15	9	...	17	...	17	107	10
0404 T BIOLOGICAL SCIENCE TECH	6,209	...	...	194	48	33	...	45	17	999	3,477	152
WOMEN	2,536	...	...	81	8	10	...	29	13	351	1,355	58
0405 P PHARMACOLOGY	402	...	...	22	...	...	...	13	4	1	5	...
WOMEN	111	...	...	5	...	...	...	4	2	...	1	...
0406 P AGRICULTURAL EXTENSION	54	...	...	...	...	...	...	...	...	...	54	...
WOMEN	18	...	...	...	...	...	...	...	...	...	18	...

TABLE E, 1995 -- CONTINUED

LABOR	HEALTH & HUMAN SERVICES	HOUSING & URBAN DEVLPMT	TRANSPOR-TATION	ENERGY	EDUCA-TION	VETERANS AFFAIRS	LIBRARY OF CONGRESS	EPA	FDIC	GENERAL SERVICES ADM	OPM	NASA	TVA	ALL OTHER AGENCIES	OCCUPATION CODES
591	1,726	1,029	1,944	1,173	438	2,547	109	815	3,450	492	111	716	3,031	5,491	0301
284	1,247	516	859	644	289	1,434	128	477	1,397	256	57	420	796	2,926	WOMEN
1	2	1	...	...	...	10	...	1	4	...	...	...	38	6	0302
...	1	...	...	...	...	4	...	...	...	...	...	...	...	6	2	WOMEN
440	2,108	1,700	1,200	385	247	10,741	188	324	2,137	580	151	219	57	4,447	0303
379	1,816	1,508	1,066	265	201	8,043	136	289	1,727	516	125	198	53	3,786	WOMEN
4	12	7	...	...	...	*58	1	1	56	3	1	...	...	71	0304
2	9	6	...	...	...	40	1	1	51	3	1	...	...	57	WOMEN
99	207	27	42	40	14	3,593	72	8	104	33	134	7	29	2,785	0305
41	104	8	30	12	3	1,199	26	3	55	14	105	6	25	1,960	WOMEN
1	11	...	3	...	...	118	11	2	...	...	...	...	14	8	0309
1	10	...	2	...	...	89	9	1	...	...	...	...	14	7	WOMEN
...	1	...	3	...	...	52	...	...	...	...	...	2	5	20	0312
...	1	...	3	...	...	51	...	...	...	...	...	1	5	20	WOMEN
...	...	...	...	...	...	22	...	...	...	...	...	...	...	6	0313
...	...	...	...	...	...	21	...	...	...	...	...	...	...	6	WOMEN
1,000	3,627	671	2,199	1,410	319	5,967	116	1,066	725	459	120	1,416	335	4,159	0318
974	3,521	650	2,159	1,386	302	5,756	110	1,049	709	451	118	1,403	334	4,052	WOMEN
...	...	...	1	...	...	...	...	...	...	...	...	...	...	...	0319
...	...	...	1	...	...	...	...	...	...	...	...	...	...	...	WOMEN
20	284	48	83	10	12	1,348	25	26	95	24	...	3	279	370	0322
18	240	38	68	9	11	1,146	20	20	86	18	...	3	277	240	WOMEN
189	520	41	186	102	106	1,530	17	120	10	116	74	56	...	1,576	0326
160	435	37	166	84	79	1,352	13	104	10	92	67	51	...	1,399	WOMEN
1	106	2	198	17	...	165	25	1	15	23	39	2	...	260	0332
...	47	2	93	5	...	48	8	...	5	9	19	2	...	175	WOMEN
583	2,092	313	1,405	530	165	3,219	212	500	413	781	172	233	486	3,819	0334
242	890	124	541	195	60	1,089	75	181	137	297	71	113	166	1,496	WOMEN
38	158	22	67	27	3	513	7	13	27	44	43	25	22	510	0335
27	102	16	51	16	3	281	4	9	20	31	30	21	11	395	WOMEN
50	251	58	336	467	45	248	1	291	1	111	43	28	61	842	0340
17	86	12	74	101	21	60	...	100	...	21	12	3	12	239	WOMEN
109	684	74	473	116	30	786	46	74	32	27	6	110	169	624	0341
80	544	56	454	73	23	508	32	72	31	22	4	108	156	434	WOMEN
22	67	27	73	35	4	182	2	33	10	32	7	33	226	172	0342
6	37	16	45	20	2	80	1	20	2	16	3	20	94	84	WOMEN
423	1,674	488	1,473	884	719	1,319	16	1,156	133	557	147	692	186	2,598	0343
270	1,150	308	962	533	446	775	7	737	86	402	76	412	43	1,461	WOMEN
29	111	26	48	70	22	259	42	50	13	58	24	43	6	261	0344
27	92	23	45	66	17	218	35	47	11	50	21	42	...	236	WOMEN
...	6	...	247	15	...	...	...	2	...	...	...	34	...	24	0346
...	2	...	139	3	...	...	...	...	...	...	...	10	...	4	WOMEN
5	29	...	25	...	1	299	2	13	1	13	12	1	41	156	0350
1	9	...	19	...	...	56	1	5	...	7	8	...	11	82	WOMEN
4	2	...	...	2	...	2	...	1	...	3	...	2	...	32	0351
3	1	...	...	1	...	2	...	...	...	2	...	2	...	25	WOMEN
...	23	...	1	...	4	33	...	...	...	9	117	...	30	689	0356
...	23	...	1	...	3	30	...	...	...	6	111	...	24	654	WOMEN
11	34	...	...	...	...	36	...	...	...	1	1	...	40	21	0357
9	33	...	...	...	...	26	...	...	...	...	1	...	36	15	WOMEN
...	...	...	...	...	...	...	...	...	...	...	...	...	...	...	0359
...	...	...	...	...	...	...	...	...	...	...	...	...	...	...	WOMEN
637	168	433	77	1	363	...	...	6	...	...	...	...	6	26	0360
346	96	226	35	...	195	...	...	1	...	...	...	...	3	20	WOMEN
70	15	19	7	5	13	23	1	2	4	1	...	4	...	21	0361
66	15	18	7	5	12	22	1	2	2	1	...	3	...	16	WOMEN
...	...	...	...	...	...	...	...	...	...	...	...	...	...	...	0362
...	...	...	...	...	...	...	...	...	...	...	...	...	...	...	WOMEN
1	71	...	4	...	...	671	2	...	4	...	...	...	11	5	0382
1	68	...	3	...	...	478	2	...	4	...	...	...	11	3	WOMEN
...	...	...	...	...	...	75	...	...	2	...	...	...	...	16	0390
...	...	...	...	...	...	38	...	...	2	...	...	...	...	9	WOMEN
7	96	8	157	47	6	172	21	16	14	573	14	38	35	369	0391
3	37	6	53	12	3	35	6	8	8	171	5	12	21	102	WOMEN
2	1	...	26	15	...	30	3	...	...	33	...	...	...	127	0392
...	1	...	7	7	...	16	3	...	...	23	...	...	...	35	WOMEN
1	11	...	6	...	2	15	...	...	2	22	...	...	2	24	0394
1	10	...	6	...	2	10	...	...	2	15	...	...	2	19	WOMEN
1	31	...	33	33	1	36	...	15	18	12	1	31	...	32	0399
1	17	...	22	21	1	16	...	6	10	9	1	23	...	16	WOMEN
4,339	14,128	4,994	10,317	5,384	2,514	34,069	999	4,536	7,279	4,007	1,217	3,695	5,109	29,567	0300
2,959	10,644	3,570	6,911	3,458	1,673	22,923	618	3,132	4,355	2,432	835	2,853	2,100	19,975	WOMEN
...	1,664	...	2	84	...	166	11	701	...	...	...	32	38	203	0401
...	846	...	...	23	...	74	7	238	...	...	...	10	7	37	WOMEN
...	1,057	...	...	2	...	166	...	89	...	...	...	...	...	1	0403
...	480	...	...	...	...	85	...	23	...	...	...	...	...	...	WOMEN
...	463	...	4	...	...	678	...	76	...	...	...	1	1	21	0404
...	217	...	...	...	...	355	...	50	...	...	...	1	1	7	WOMEN
...	298	...	...	...	...	30	...	24	...	...	...	...	...	5	0405
...	81	...	...	...	...	9	...	5	...	...	...	...	...	4	WOMEN
...	...	...	...	...	...	...	...	...	...	...	...	...	...	...	0406
...	...	...	...	...	...	...	...	...	...	...	...	...	...	...	WOMEN

TABLE E   FULL-TIME CIVILIAN WHITE-COLLAR EMPLOYMENT BY OCCUPATION, GENDER, AND SELECTED AGENCY, ALL AREAS, SEPTEMBER 30, 1995

OCCUPATION CODES	TITLES	TOTAL ALL AGENCIES	STATE	TREASURY	ARMY	NAVY	AIR FORCE	DEFENSE LOGIS AGENCY	OTHER DEFENSE	JUSTICE	INTERIOR	AGRI-CULTURE	COM-MERCE
0408 P	ECOLOGY	760	...	...	154	11	1	...	...	...	220	253	33
	WOMEN	229	...	...	34	4	...	...	...	...	52	113	8
0410 P	ZOOLOGY	103	...	...	7	...	...	...	...	...	18	13	12
	WOMEN	16	...	...	2	...	...	...	...	...	2	3	4
0413 P	PHYSIOLOGY	474	...	...	60	23	24	...	28	...	19	78	8
	WOMEN	106	...	...	12	6	3	...	4	...	6	10	4
0414 P	ENTOMOLOGY	641	...	...	29	15	4	2	1	...	6	514	...
	WOMEN	84	...	...	2	2	...	...	...	...	3	66	...
0415 P	TOXICOLOGY	267	...	...	20	1	13	...	1	...	1	7	...
	WOMEN	82	...	...	5	...	2	...	...	...	...	3	...
0421 T	PLANT PROTECTION TECH	223	...	...	...	...	...	...	...	...	...	223	...
	WOMEN	85	...	...	...	...	...	...	...	...	...	85	...
0430 P	BOTANY	355	...	...	15	2	2	...	...	...	98	214	...
	WOMEN	172	...	...	5	2	...	...	...	...	48	110	...
0434 P	PLANT PATHOLOGY	281	...	...	1	...	...	...	...	...	2	272	...
	WOMEN	52	...	...	1	...	...	...	...	...	...	49	...
0435 P	PLANT PHYSIOLOGY	293	...	...	1	...	...	...	...	...	1	283	...
	WOMEN	59	...	...	1	...	...	...	...	...	...	58	...
0436 P	PLANT PROTECT & QUARANTN	1,453	...	...	...	...	...	...	...	...	...	1,453	...
	WOMEN	318	...	...	...	...	...	...	...	...	...	318	...
0437 P	HORTICULTURE	125	...	...	4	...	...	...	1	1	14	75	...
	WOMEN	37	...	...	...	...	...	...	...	...	3	18	...
0440 P	GENETICS	333	...	...	1	2	...	...	...	...	5	256	11
	WOMEN	68	...	...	...	1	...	...	...	...	...	41	5
0454 P	RANGELAND MANAGEMENT	1,106	...	...	9	...	3	...	...	...	439	652	...
	WOMEN	204	...	...	1	...	...	...	...	...	62	141	...
0455 T	RANGE TECHNICIAN	1,195	...	...	3	...	...	...	...	...	913	276	...
	WOMEN	194	...	...	1	...	...	...	...	...	130	63	...
0457 P	SOIL CONSERVATION	4,391	...	...	8	9	...	...	...	...	50	4,321	...
	WOMEN	678	...	...	1	1	...	...	...	...	2	674	...
0458 T	SOIL CONSERVATION TECH	1,545	...	...	1	1	...	...	...	...	26	1,517	...
	WOMEN	257	...	...	...	...	...	...	...	...	2	255	...
0459 T	IRRIGATION SYSTEM OPER	127	...	...	...	...	...	...	...	...	127	...	...
	WOMEN	1	...	...	...	...	...	...	...	...	1	...	...
0460 P	FORESTRY	4,690	...	12	81	17	15	...	...	...	525	4,026	...
	WOMEN	886	...	1	3	...	...	...	...	...	18	861	...
0462 T	FORESTRY TECHNICIAN	13,968	...	...	74	14	17	...	...	...	1,160	12,700	...
	WOMEN	3,003	...	...	10	...	1	...	...	...	132	2,860	...
0470 P	SOIL SCIENCE	1,449	...	...	8	1	...	...	...	...	79	1,347	...
	WOMEN	147	...	...	...	...	...	...	...	...	5	141	...
0471 P	AGRONOMY	287	...	...	24	1	5	...	...	...	6	236	...
	WOMEN	22	...	...	...	...	...	...	...	...	...	19	...
0475 P	AGRICULTURAL MANAGEMENT	3,218	...	...	...	...	...	...	...	...	...	3,213	...
	WOMEN	640	...	...	...	...	...	...	...	...	...	640	...
0480 P	GEN FISH & WILDLIFE ADM	194	...	...	11	5	...	...	...	...	110	3	61
	WOMEN	30	...	...	...	...	...	...	...	...	22	1	7
0482 P	FISHERY BIOLOGY	2,031	...	...	58	1	...	...	...	...	817	431	680
	WOMEN	411	...	...	3	...	...	...	...	...	129	130	141
0485 P	WILDLIFE REFUGE MGT	636	...	...	...	...	...	...	...	...	636	...	...
	WOMEN	96	...	...	...	...	...	...	...	...	96	...	...
0486 P	WILDLIFE BIOLOGY	2,387	...	...	94	13	9	...	...	...	1,047	1,178	20
	WOMEN	611	...	...	10	3	2	...	...	...	217	371	5
0487 P	ANIMAL SCIENCE	100	...	...	...	...	...	...	2	...	1	73	1
	WOMEN	11	...	...	...	...	...	...	...	...	...	7	...
0493 P	HOME ECONOMICS	23	...	...	3	4	...	...	...	...	...	16	...
	WOMEN	21	...	...	2	4	...	...	...	...	...	15	...
0499 O	BIOLOG SCI STUDENT TR	286	...	...	19	...	...	...	...	...	107	142	4
	WOMEN	142	...	...	8	...	...	...	...	...	62	64	1
0400	BIOLOGICAL SCIENCES	60,378	3	13	2,270	314	240	2	171	32	9,935	39,500	1,115
	WOMEN	14,889	1	1	559	82	48	...	78	19	1,972	9,034	293
0501 A	FINANCIAL ADM & PROGRAM	8,615	83	622	338	669	1,257	90	2,114	374	170	341	80
	WOMEN	5,090	49	387	153	412	709	53	1,236	227	120	253	57
0503 *	FINANCIAL CLER & ASST	7,943	12	2,991	352	453	358	24	1,221	119	231	450	30
	WOMEN	6,178	8	2,393	262	314	303	19	859	101	190	408	28
0505 A	FINANCIAL MANAGEMENT	1,749	129	115	199	246	122	24	66	137	20	56	6
	WOMEN	504	35	54	30	87	25	6	23	44	7	21	1
0510 P	ACCOUNTING	13,585	84	696	1,209	755	357	71	3,380	443	482	953	232
	WOMEN	6,169	52	374	549	321	141	32	1,556	215	228	375	107
0511 P	AUDITING	14,074	83	1,060	1,380	505	769	84	4,893	148	437	395	89
	WOMEN	4,440	37	351	342	153	273	23	1,719	53	144	130	22
0512 P	INTERNAL REVENUE AGENT	16,100	...	16,100	...	...	...	...	...	...	...	...	...
	WOMEN	6,354	...	6,354	...	...	...	...	...	...	...	...	...
0525 *	ACCOUNTING TECHNICIAN	19,801	4	1,178	1,448	2,095	975	139	8,121	794	559	980	216
	WOMEN	16,118	4	995	1,147	1,752	766	115	6,513	679	474	866	177
0526 T	TAX TECHNICIAN	4,388	...	4,388	...	...	...	...	...	...	...	...	...
	WOMEN	3,014	...	3,014	...	...	...	...	...	...	...	...	...
0530 C	CASH PROCESSING	2,034	26	306	148	77	53	...	730	14	160	4	4
	WOMEN	1,636	22	254	121	59	45	...	595	7	117	4	4
0540 C	VOUCHER EXAMINING	3,706	15	13	532	526	78	9	1,585	75	69	76	...
	WOMEN	2,754	10	13	396	397	56	8	1,167	57	57	72	...
0544 *	CIVILIAN PAY	3,407	23	253	195	310	230	7	932	73	132	156	4
	WOMEN	2,816	17	220	155	255	195	5	755	58	108	147	4

TABLE E,   1995 -- CONTINUED

LABOR	HEALTH & HUMAN SERVICES	HOUSING & URBAN DEVLPMT	TRANSPOR-TATION	ENERGY	EDUCA-TION	VETERANS AFFAIRS	LIBRARY OF CONGRESS	EPA	FDIC	GENERAL SERVICES ADM	OPM	NASA	TVA	ALL OTHER AGENCIES	OCCUPATION CODES
...	...	...	1	15	...	...	...	63	...	...	...	...	...	9	0408
...	...	...	...	6	...	...	...	12	...	...	...	...	...	...	WOMEN
...	...	1	...	...	...	...	...	...	...	...	...	...	...	52	0410
...	...	...	...	...	...	...	...	...	...	...	...	...	...	5	WOMEN
...	95	...	3	...	...	97	...	8	...	...	...	26	...	5	0413
...	23	...	...	...	...	25	...	1	...	...	...	8	...	4	WOMEN
...	45	...	...	...	...	...	...	11	...	...	...	...	...	14	0414
...	10	...	...	...	...	...	...	...	...	...	...	...	...	1	WOMEN
...	78	...	...	2	...	4	...	135	...	...	...	...	...	5	0415
...	24	...	...	1	...	...	...	44	...	...	...	...	...	3	WOMEN
...	...	...	...	...	...	...	...	...	...	...	...	...	...	...	0421
...	...	...	...	...	...	...	...	...	...	...	...	...	...	...	WOMEN
...	...	...	...	1	...	...	...	2	...	...	...	...	4	17	0430
...	...	...	...	1	...	...	...	1	...	...	...	...	1	4	WOMEN
...	...	...	...	...	...	...	...	6	...	...	...	...	...	...	0434
...	...	...	...	...	...	...	...	2	...	...	...	...	...	...	WOMEN
...	...	...	...	...	...	...	...	5	...	...	...	2	...	1	0435
...	...	...	...	...	...	...	...	...	...	...	...	...	...	...	WOMEN
...	...	...	...	...	...	...	...	...	...	...	...	...	...	...	0436
...	...	...	...	...	...	...	...	...	...	...	...	...	...	...	WOMEN
...	...	...	...	...	...	8	...	1	...	1	...	...	...	20	0437
...	...	...	...	...	...	4	...	...	...	1	...	...	...	11	WOMEN
...	44	...	...	1	...	4	...	6	...	...	...	...	...	3	0440
...	15	...	...	...	...	1	...	4	...	...	...	...	...	1	WOMEN
...	...	...	...	...	...	...	...	...	...	...	...	...	...	3	0454
...	...	...	...	...	...	...	...	...	...	...	...	...	...	...	WOMEN
...	...	...	...	...	...	...	...	...	...	...	...	...	...	3	0455
...	...	...	...	...	...	...	...	...	...	...	...	...	...	...	WOMEN
...	...	...	3	...	...	...	...	...	...	...	...	...	...	...	0457
...	...	...	...	...	...	...	...	...	...	...	...	...	...	...	WOMEN
...	...	...	...	...	...	...	...	...	...	...	...	...	...	...	0458
...	...	...	...	...	...	...	...	...	...	...	...	...	...	...	WOMEN
...	...	...	...	...	...	...	...	...	...	...	...	...	...	...	0459
...	...	...	...	...	...	...	...	...	...	...	...	...	...	...	WOMEN
...	...	...	...	1	...	...	...	...	...	...	...	...	12	1	0460
...	...	...	...	1	...	...	...	...	...	...	...	...	2	...	WOMEN
...	...	...	...	3	...	...	...	...	...	...	...	...	...	...	0462
...	...	...	...	...	...	...	...	...	...	...	...	...	...	...	WOMEN
...	...	...	...	...	...	...	...	14	...	...	...	...	...	...	0470
...	...	...	...	...	...	...	...	1	...	...	...	...	...	...	WOMEN
...	...	...	...	...	...	...	...	9	...	...	...	3	1	2	0471
...	...	...	...	...	...	...	...	2	...	...	...	1	...	...	WOMEN
...	...	...	...	...	...	...	...	...	...	...	...	...	4	1	0475
...	...	...	...	...	...	...	...	...	...	...	...	...	...	...	WOMEN
...	...	...	...	4	...	...	...	...	...	...	...	...	...	...	0480
...	...	...	...	...	...	...	...	...	...	...	...	...	...	...	WOMEN
...	...	...	...	33	...	...	...	11	...	...	...	...	...	...	0482
...	...	...	...	7	...	...	...	1	...	...	...	...	...	...	WOMEN
...	...	...	...	...	...	...	...	...	...	...	...	...	...	...	0485
...	...	...	...	...	...	...	...	...	...	...	...	...	...	...	WOMEN
...	...	...	7	...	...	...	...	8	...	...	...	...	...	11	0486
...	...	...	...	1	...	...	...	1	...	...	...	...	...	1	WOMEN
...	22	...	...	...	...	...	...	...	...	...	...	...	...	1	0487
...	3	...	...	...	...	...	...	...	...	...	...	...	...	1	WOMEN
...	...	...	...	...	...	...	...	...	...	...	...	...	...	...	0493
...	...	...	...	...	...	...	...	...	...	...	...	...	...	...	WOMEN
...	9	...	...	...	...	...	...	3	...	...	...	2	...	...	0499
...	5	...	...	...	...	...	...	...	...	...	...	2	...	...	WOMEN
...	3,776	...	10	156	...	1,153	11	1,172	...	1	...	66	60	378	0400
...	1,704	...	...	40	...	553	7	385	...	1	...	22	11	79	WOMEN
57	395	249	181	91	119	126	9	133	335	122	6	188	20	446	0501
33	198	186	102	41	83	73	4	92	171	74	2	141	4	230	WOMEN
87	121	6	72	11	2	1,037	39	47	18	26	23	13	1	199	0503
68	108	5	62	11	1	726	35	38	15	25	20	10	1	168	WOMEN
9	29	8	44	29	...	305	4	8	...	6	2	12	45	128	0505
2	8	2	8	8	...	63	1	4	...	2	1	4	36	32	WOMEN
151	532	296	364	477	114	541	17	184	527	219	55	231	164	1,051	0510
65	189	133	187	214	47	289	8	93	206	89	30	141	115	413	WOMEN
252	596	271	267	239	172	235	7	276	256	183	50	102	76	1,249	0511
73	156	67	83	55	52	56	3	119	89	45	17	41	19	318	WOMEN
...	...	...	...	...	...	...	...	...	...	...	...	...	...	...	0512
...	...	...	...	...	...	...	...	...	...	...	...	...	...	...	WOMEN
43	343	106	410	142	9	1,206	36	55	144	319	19	83	16	361	0525
35	272	86	352	132	6	912	26	43	110	241	16	76	15	308	WOMEN
...	...	...	...	...	...	...	...	...	...	...	...	...	...	...	0526
...	...	...	...	...	...	...	...	...	...	...	...	...	...	...	WOMEN
2	6	...	3	1	...	407	2	1	...	...	4	2	...	84	0530
2	4	...	3	1	...	321	2	1	...	...	3	2	...	69	WOMEN
28	20	5	27	21	...	434	1	...	15	15	...	28	...	134	0540
23	19	2	19	16	...	274	1	...	13	12	...	27	...	115	WOMEN
22	33	1	118	25	...	720	...	3	...	32	5	27	13	93	0544
19	27	1	108	24	...	568	...	2	...	25	5	27	10	81	WOMEN

TABLE E   FULL-TIME CIVILIAN WHITE-COLLAR EMPLOYMENT BY OCCUPATION, GENDER, AND SELECTED AGENCY, ALL AREAS, SEPTEMBER 30, 1995

CODES	TITLES	TOTAL ALL AGENCIES	STATE	TREASURY	ARMY	NAVY	AIR FORCE	DEFENSE LO IS AGENCY	OTHER DEFENSE	JUSTICE	INTERIOR	AGRI- CULTURE	COM- MERCE
0545 *	MILITARY PAY	3,215	...	...	613	441	324	...	1,798	...	...	...	2
	WOMEN	2,113	...	...	420	278	228	...	1,165	...	...	...	2
0560 A	BUDGET ANALYSIS	13,196	115	306	3,626	2,822	1,912	178	426	414	384	511	229
	WOMEN	9,286	76	218	2,688	2,127	1,268	125	259	291	284	366	144
0561 *	BUDGET CLERICAL & ASST	3,989	9	79	1,505	1,081	433	25	80	51	209	128	26
	WOMEN	3,516	8	71	1,308	953	389	19	73	43	188	116	24
0570 A	FINANCIAL INST EXAM	5,775	...	3,130	...	...	...	...	...	1	...	...	...
	WOMEN	1,732	...	919	...	...	...	...	...	...	...	...	...
0580 A	CREDIT UNION EXAMINER	77	...	...	...	...	...	...	...	...	...	...	...
	WOMEN	30	...	...	...	...	...	...	...	...	...	...	...
0592 *	TAX EXAMINING	20,723	...	20,723	...	...	...	...	...	...	...	...	...
	WOMEN	15,519	...	15,519	...	...	...	...	...	...	...	...	...
0593 T	INSURANCE ACCOUNTS	83	...	...	...	...	...	...	...	...	...	...	...
	WOMEN	55	...	...	...	...	...	...	...	...	...	...	...
0599 O	FINANCIAL MGT STUDENT TR	138	3	32	17	17	9	1	3	...	5	1	2
	WOMEN	97	1	20	13	14	7	1	3	...	3	...	2
0500	ACCOUNTING AND BUDGET	142,598	586	51,992	11,562	9,997	6,877	652	25,349	2,643	2,858	4,051	920
	WOMEN	87,421	319	31,156	7,584	7,122	4,405	406	15,923	1,775	1,920	2,758	572
0601 P	GENERAL HEALTH SCIENCE	3,883	...	1	106	40	44	...	16	8	1	...	...
	WOMEN	1,963	...	1	64	25	33	...	4	4	...	...	...
0602 P	MEDICAL OFFICER	10,864	55	1	448	97	56	...	47	176	1	2	...
	WOMEN	2,726	8	...	137	30	7	...	8	29	...	...	...
0603 A	PHYSICIAN'S ASSISTANT	2,025	...	1	134	39	18	...	...	643	...	...	...
	WOMEN	597	...	1	29	5	3	...	...	142	...	...	...
0610 P	NURSE	43,752	56	38	2,250	1,034	627	3	58	270	14	26	6
	WOMEN	38,415	52	35	2,089	985	582	3	57	222	12	24	6
0620 T	PRACTICAL NURSE	12,807	1	...	1,075	407	282	...	3	76	3	2	...
	WOMEN	11,024	1	...	882	384	261	...	3	69	3	2	...
0621 T	NURSING ASSISTANT	13,811	1	...	700	27	131	...	5	13	...	...	...
	WOMEN	8,983	1	...	511	25	97	...	5	12	...	...	...
0622 T	MEDICAL SUPPLY AID &TECH	2,346	...	...	99	43	54	...	...	7	...	...	...
	WOMEN	1,000	...	...	38	26	9	...	...	5	...	...	...
0625 T	AUTOPSY ASSISTANT	68	...	...	4	2	1	...	...	...	...	...	...
	WOMEN	10	...	...	1	...	...	...	...	...	...	...	...
0630 P	DIETITIAN & NUTRITIONIST	1,644	...	...	31	23	3	...	2	8	...	95	...
	WOMEN	1,542	...	...	29	23	3	...	2	7	...	82	...
0631 P	OCCUPATIONAL THERAPIST	704	...	...	30	14	2	...	1	...	...	...	...
	WOMEN	600	...	...	29	14	2	...	1	...	...	...	...
0633 P	PHYSICAL THERAPIST	649	...	...	19	10	12	...	1	...	...	...	...
	WOMEN	435	...	...	16	10	4	...	1	...	...	...	...
0635 P	CORRECTIVE THERAPIST	536	...	...	1	...	...	...	...	...	...	...	...
	WOMEN	192	...	...	1	...	...	...	...	...	...	...	...
0636 T	REHABILITATN THERAP ASST	850	...	...	45	3	3	...	...	...	...	...	...
	WOMEN	438	...	...	32	3	1	...	...	...	...	...	...
0637 P	MANUAL ARTS THERAPIST	128	...	...	...	...	...	...	...	...	...	...	...
	WOMEN	11	...	...	...	...	...	...	...	...	...	...	...
0638 P	REC/CREATIVE ARTS THERAP	841	...	...	15	2	...	...	...	8	...	...	...
	WOMEN	468	...	...	15	2	...	...	...	6	...	...	...
0639 P	EDUCATIONAL THERAPIST	30	...	...	...	...	...	...	5	...	...	...	...
	WOMEN	25	...	...	...	...	...	...	5	...	...	...	...
0640 T	HEALTH AID & TECHNICIAN	5,472	...	4	1,330	369	476	3	4	20	4	1	...
	WOMEN	3,103	...	2	700	228	302	2	4	7	3	1	...
0642 T	NUCLEAR MEDICINE TECH	142	...	...	38	3	3	...	...	...	...	...	...
	WOMEN	66	...	...	14	1	...	...	...	...	...	...	...
0644 P	MEDICAL TECHNOLOGIST	5,725	15	...	624	161	163	...	1	34	...	1	...
	WOMEN	3,867	14	...	434	116	111	...	1	21	...	1	...
0645 T	MEDICAL TECHNICIAN	2,099	...	...	434	118	107	...	1	19	...	...	...
	WOMEN	1,353	...	...	309	71	58	...	1	13	...	...	...
0646 T	PATHOLOGY TECHNICIAN	499	...	...	100	28	11	...	1	...	...	...	...
	WOMEN	347	...	...	71	19	9	...	1	...	...	...	...
0647 T	DIAGNOSTIC RADIOL TECH	3,166	2	...	423	83	64	...	...	26	...	...	...
	WOMEN	1,558	2	...	224	45	45	...	...	15	...	...	...
0648 T	THERAPEUTIC RADIOL TECH	124	...	...	21	6	...	...	...	...	...	...	...
	WOMEN	77	...	...	11	5	...	...	...	...	...	...	...
0649 T	MEDICAL INSTRUMENT TECH	2,156	...	1	242	40	83	...	...	2	...	...	...
	WOMEN	1,313	...	1	159	31	49	...	...	2	...	...	...
0650 T	MEDICAL TECHNICAL ASST	3	...	...	...	...	...	...	...	2	...	...	...
	WOMEN	2	...	...	...	...	...	...	...	2	...	...	...
0651 T	RESPIRATORY THERAPIST	457	...	...	127	32	19	...	...	4	...	...	...
	WOMEN	205	...	...	63	11	8	...	...	3	...	...	...
0660 P	PHARMACIST	4,578	...	...	372	102	30	4	...	22	...	...	...
	WOMEN	1,970	...	...	149	60	11	...	...	9	...	...	...
0661 T	PHARMACY TECHNICIAN	3,618	...	...	290	78	90	...	...	11	...	...	...
	WOMEN	2,476	...	...	200	48	45	...	...	11	...	...	...
0662 P	OPTOMETRIST	224	...	...	13	9	3	...	...	...	...	...	...
	WOMEN	75	...	...	3	2	...	...	...	...	...	...	...
0664 T	RESTORATION TECHNICIAN	16	...	...	...	...	1	...	...	...	...	...	...
	WOMEN	2	...	...	...	...	...	...	...	...	...	...	...
0665 P	SPEECH PATHLGY AUDIOLGY	754	...	...	72	56	6	652	15	...	8	...	...
	WOMEN	478	...	...	55	34	3	...	13	...	7	...	...
0667 T	ORTHOTIST & PROSTHETIST	222	...	...	42	3	6	...	...	1	...	...	...
	WOMEN	14	...	...	4	...	...	...	...	...	...	...	...

TABLE E, 1995 -- CONTINUED

LABOR	HEALTH & HUMAN SERVICES	HOUSING & URBAN DEVLPMT	TRANSPORTATION	ENERGY	EDUCATION	VETERANS AFFAIRS	LIBRARY OF CONGRESS	EPA	FDIC	GENERAL SERVICES ADM	OPM	NASA	TVA	ALL OTHER AGENCIES	OCCUPATION CODES
...	13	...	24	...	...	...	...	...	...	...	...	...	...	...	0545
...	8	...	12	...	...	...	...	...	...	...	...	...	...	...	WOMEN
90	425	64	234	286	48	301	9	70	29	228	16	24	1	448	0560
53	294	41	144	172	33	185	5	43	10	159	7	16	1	267	WOMEN
10	52	6	19	26	5	142	...	13	...	40	1	3	...	46	0561
9	49	6	14	24	5	121	...	12	...	37	1	3	...	43	WOMEN
...	...	1	...	...	...	...	...	...	2,632	...	...	...	...	11	0570
...	...	1	...	...	...	...	...	...	305	...	...	...	...	7	WOMEN
...	...	...	...	...	...	...	...	...	...	...	...	...	...	77	0580
...	...	...	...	...	...	...	...	...	...	...	...	...	...	30	WOMEN
...	...	...	...	...	...	...	...	...	...	...	...	...	...	...	0592
...	...	...	...	...	...	...	...	...	...	...	...	...	...	...	WOMEN
...	...	...	...	...	...	83	...	...	...	...	...	...	...	...	0593
...	...	...	...	...	...	55	...	...	...	...	...	...	...	...	WOMEN
...	2	...	2	14	1	8	...	4	4	4	...	4	...	5	0599
...	1	...	2	12	1	4	...	3	2	2	...	1	...	5	WOMEN
751	2,567	1,013	1,765	1,362	470	5,545	124	794	3,960	1,194	181	717	336	4,332	0500
382	1,333	530	1,096	710	229	3,647	85	450	1,421	721	102	489	201	2,086	WOMEN
21	1,345	...	14,	13	...	2,173	...	80	...	...	...	3	...	18	0601
15	674	...	9	7	...	1,077	...	34	...	...	...	2	...	14	WOMEN
11	1,736	...	35	4	...	9,111	1	7	...	...	...	31	7	37	0602
5	527	...	...	1	...	1,959	1	...	...	...	...	6	1	7	WOMEN
...	89	...	...	...	...	1,068	...	1	...	...	...	...	28	4	0603
...	55	...	...	...	...	334	...	1	...	...	...	...	24	3	WOMEN
15	2,894	...	33	9	...	36,243	3	2	2	...	1	1	...	127	0610
15	2,649	...	32	9	...	31,515	3	2	2	...	1	1	...	119	WOMEN
...	400	...	1	...	...	10,538	...	...	...	...	...	...	...	19	0620
...	386	...	1	...	...	9,015	...	...	...	...	...	...	...	17	WOMEN
...	437	...	...	...	...	12,340	...	...	...	...	...	...	...	157	0621
...	392	...	...	...	...	7,813	...	...	...	...	...	...	...	127	WOMEN
...	121	...	...	...	...	2,021	...	...	...	...	...	...	1	...	0622
...	98	...	...	...	...	823	...	...	...	...	...	...	1	...	WOMEN
...	2	...	...	...	...	59	...	...	...	...	...	...	...	...	0625
...	...	...	...	...	...	9	...	...	...	...	...	...	...	...	WOMEN
...	98	...	...	...	...	1,377	...	...	...	...	...	...	1	6	0630
...	89	...	...	...	...	1,301	...	...	...	...	...	...	...	6	WOMEN
...	5	...	...	...	...	651	...	...	...	...	...	...	...	1	0631
...	5	...	...	...	...	548	...	...	...	...	...	...	...	1	WOMEN
...	11	...	...	...	...	593	...	...	...	...	...	...	...	3	0633
...	10	...	...	...	...	394	...	...	...	...	...	...	...	...	WOMEN
...	...	...	...	...	...	535	...	...	...	...	...	...	...	...	0635
...	...	...	...	...	...	191	...	...	...	...	...	...	...	...	WOMEN
...	17	...	...	...	...	777	...	...	...	...	...	...	...	5	0636
...	15	...	...	...	...	385	...	...	...	...	...	...	...	2	WOMEN
...	...	...	...	...	...	128	...	...	...	...	...	...	...	...	0637
...	...	...	...	...	...	11	...	...	...	...	...	...	...	...	WOMEN
...	21	...	...	...	...	790	...	...	...	...	...	...	...	5	0638
...	13	...	...	...	...	430	...	...	...	...	...	...	...	2	WOMEN
...	...	...	...	...	...	25	...	...	...	...	...	...	...	...	0639
...	...	...	...	...	...	20	...	...	...	...	...	...	...	...	WOMEN
...	243	...	2	...	...	2,994	...	...	...	...	...	...	...	22	0640
...	166	...	2	...	...	1,576	...	...	...	...	...	...	...	10	WOMEN
...	8	...	...	...	...	90	...	...	...	...	...	...	...	...	0642
...	7	...	...	...	...	44	...	...	...	...	...	...	...	...	WOMEN
...	595	...	3	...	...	4,126	...	...	...	...	...	...	...	2	0644
...	417	...	3	...	...	2,747	...	...	...	...	...	...	...	2	WOMEN
...	131	...	1	...	...	1,273	...	...	...	...	...	...	12	3	0645
...	101	...	1	...	...	790	...	...	...	...	...	...	7	2	WOMEN
...	20	...	...	...	...	338	...	...	...	...	...	...	...	1	0646
...	17	...	...	...	...	229	...	...	...	...	...	...	...	1	WOMEN
...	218	...	...	...	...	2,349	...	...	...	...	...	...	...	1	0647
...	113	...	...	...	...	1,114	...	...	...	...	...	...	...	...	WOMEN
...	...	...	...	...	...	97	...	...	...	...	...	...	...	...	0648
...	...	...	...	...	...	61	...	...	...	...	...	...	...	...	WOMEN
...	61	...	...	...	...	1,726	1	...	...	...	...	...	...	...	0649
...	39	...	...	...	...	1,031	1	...	...	...	...	...	...	...	WOMEN
...	1	...	...	...	...	...	...	...	...	...	...	...	...	...	0650
...	...	...	...	...	...	...	...	...	...	...	...	...	...	...	WOMEN
...	40	...	...	...	...	235	...	...	...	...	...	...	...	...	0651
...	21	...	...	...	...	99	...	...	...	...	...	...	...	...	WOMEN
...	101	...	...	...	...	3,943	...	...	...	...	...	...	...	4	0660
...	53	...	...	...	...	1,687	...	...	...	...	...	...	...	1	WOMEN
...	131	...	...	...	...	3,014	...	...	...	...	...	...	...	4	0661
...	101	...	...	...	...	2,068	...	...	...	...	...	...	...	3	WOMEN
...	2	...	1	...	...	196	...	...	...	...	...	...	...	...	0662
...	...	...	...	...	...	70	...	...	...	...	...	...	...	...	WOMEN
...	...	...	...	...	...	15	...	...	...	...	...	...	...	...	0664
...	...	...	...	...	...	2	...	...	...	...	...	...	...	...	WOMEN
...	21	...	...	...	...	576	...	...	...	...	...	...	...	...	0665
...	11	...	...	...	...	355	...	...	...	...	...	...	...	...	WOMEN
...	3	...	...	...	...	167	...	...	...	...	...	...	...	...	0667
...	1	...	...	...	...	9	...	...	...	...	...	...	...	...	WOMEN

TABLE E. FULL-TIME CIVILIAN WHITE-COLLAR EMPLOYMENT BY OCCUPATION, GENDER, AND SELECTED AGENCY, ALL AREAS, SEPTEMBER 30, 1995

OCCUPATION CODES TITLES	TOTAL ALL AGENCIES	STATE	TREASURY	ARMY	NAVY	AIR FORCE	DEFENSE LOGIS AGENCY	OTHER DEFENSE	JUSTICE	INTERIOR	AGRI-CULTURE	COM-MERCE
0668 P PODIATRIST	253	...	...	14	...	...	...	...	...	...	...	...
WOMEN	75	...	...	2	...	...	...	...	...	...	...	...
0669 A MEDICAL RECORDS ADMIN	540	1	...	56	38	40	...	...	27	...	...	...
WOMEN	475	1	...	50	33	37	...	...	24	...	...	...
0670 A HEALTH SYSTEM ADMIN	595	1	...	5	2	4	...	...	86	...	...	...
WOMEN	160	...	...	2	...	...	...	...	23	...	...	...
0671 A HEALTH SYSTEM SPECIALIST	1,583	2	...	282	126	176	...	5	20	...	...	...
WOMEN	837	1	...	174	84	89	...	1	11	...	...	...
0672 T PROSTHETIC REPRESENTATIV	205	...	...	...	...	...	...	...	...	...	...	...
WOMEN	64	...	...	...	...	...	...	...	...	...	...	...
0673 A HOSPITAL HOUSEKEEPNG MGT	306	...	...	27	8	2	...	...	3	...	...	...
WOMEN	45	...	...	6	...	...	...	...	2	...	...	...
0675 T MEDICAL RECORDS TECH	3,269	...	3	591	392	290	...	...	147	...	...	...
WOMEN	2,760	...	3	486	321	247	...	...	136	...	...	...
0679 C MEDICAL CLERK	11,701	...	3	2,445	824	765	...	2	32	...	...	...
WOMEN	9,396	...	3	2,120	697	647	...	2	32	...	...	...
0680 P DENTAL OFFICER	847	...	...	38	...	7	...	...	7	...	...	...
WOMEN	99	...	...	11	...	...	...	...	2	...	...	...
0681 T DENTAL ASSISTANT	2,704	...	...	963	220	74	...	...	30	...	...	...
WOMEN	2,533	...	...	890	197	65	...	...	29	...	...	...
0682 T DENTAL HYGIENE	339	...	...	98	38	34	...	...	14	...	...	...
WOMEN	326	...	...	95	37	34	...	...	13	...	...	...
0683 T DENTAL LAB AID & TECH	703	...	...	148	17	60	...	...	2	...	...	...
WOMEN	117	...	...	36	2	2	...	...	1	...	...	...
0685 A PUB HEALTH PROGRAM SPEC	1,601	...	...	1	...	...	...	...	...	...	...	...
WOMEN	769	...	...	...	...	...	...	...	...	...	...	...
0688 A SANITARIAN	40	...	...	4	2	...	...	...	1	6	...	...
WOMEN	13	...	...	...	...	...	...	...	...	3	...	...
0690 P INDUSTRIAL HYGIENE	1,513	2	5	233	299	78	18	6	1	16	6	3
WOMEN	475	...	1	70	80	24	4	...	...	5	1	2
0696 P CONSUMER SAFETY	1,916	...	...	...	...	...	...	...	...	...	...	126
WOMEN	741	...	...	...	...	...	...	...	...	...	...	23
0698 T ENVIRONMENTL HEALTH TECH	161	...	...	32	32	63	...	...	...	4	3	...
WOMEN	38	...	...	8	6	14	...	...	...	3	1	...
0699 O MEDICAL HEALTH STUDNT TR	150	...	...	11	10	3	...	...	3	...	1	...
WOMEN	111	...	...	6	9	1	...	...	3	...	1	...
0600 MED HOSP DENT PUB HEALTH	152,619	136	57	14,033	4,837	3,891	28	173	1,723	57	137	135
WOMEN	104,369	80	47	10,225	3,669	2,803	9	109	855	36	113	31
0701 P VETERINARY MEDICAL SCI	1,952	...	...	6	3	3	...	...	14	1,809	2
WOMEN	353	...	...	...	...	...	...	...	9	307	2
0704 T ANIMAL HEALTH TECHNICIAN	393	...	...	8	...	...	...	...	1	372	...
WOMEN	63	...	...	5	...	...	...	...	...	...	...
0799 O VETERINARY STUDENT TR	3	...	...	...	...	...	...	...	...	...	49	...
WOMEN	2	...	...	...	...	...	...	...	...	...	3	...
0700 VETERINARY MEDICAL SCI	2,349	...	...	14	3	3	...	...	15	2,184	2
WOMEN	418	...	...	5	...	...	...	...	9	358	2
0801 P GENERAL ENGINEERING	20,469	30	269	4,623	3,602	1,921	445	166	7	272	153	180
WOMEN	1,928	3	32	359	219	91	20	8	...	24	14	12
0802 T ENGINEERING TECHNICIAN	20,528	2	23	4,760	6,959	1,418	83	45	104	1,061	1,722	183
WOMEN	2,148	...	2	666	565	122	5	3	13	117	231	2
0803 P SAFETY ENGINEERING	555	...	1	166	58	93	5	3	...	11	...	1
WOMEN	42	...	...	11	5	9	...	...	...	...	...	...
0804 P FIRE PROTECTION ENGINEER	165	...	...	13	49	6	1	2	...	1	...	6
WOMEN	22	...	...	...	6	1	...	1	...	...	...	1
0806 P MATERIALS ENGINEERING	1,171	...	2	160	330	277	8	3	...	15	4	34
WOMEN	167	...	...	12	46	41	1	...	...	3	2	6
0807 P LANDSCAPE ARCHITECTURE	706	1	...	116	24	8	...	...	...	246	279	...
WOMEN	203	...	...	20	3	2	...	...	...	76	100	...
0808 P ARCHITECTURE	2,026	35	31	427	395	200	3	13	52	219	72	3
WOMEN	301	7	7	49	43	19	...	2	13	42	7	...
0809 T CONSTRUCTION CONTROL	2,805	...	6	1,248	383	373	9	2	104	167	139	23
WOMEN	85	...	...	42	12	15	...	...	1	3	2	...
0810 P CIVIL ENGINEERING	13,361	68	4	6,605	997	466	22	27	4	1,138	1,488	64
WOMEN	1,313	2	1	605	82	30	2	2	...	104	214	8
0817 T SURVEYING TECHNICIAN	896	...	...	322	11	9	...	19	...	292	175	46
WOMEN	50	...	...	8	1	1	...	2	...	17	18	2
0818 T ENGINEERING DRAFTING	499	...	2	164	64	90	6	3	4	51	25	23
WOMEN	109	...	...	34	21	15	...	...	2	14	7	5
0819 P ENVIRONMENTAL ENGINEERNG	5,525	...	2	880	1,195	868	12	10	...	65	44	10
WOMEN	1,199	...	...	164	239	151	1	2	...	10	13	1
0828 A CONSTRUCTION ANALYST	515	10	...	1	...	1	...	...	...	...	40	...
WOMEN	44	...	...	...	...	...	...	...	...	...	2	...
0830 P MECHANICAL ENGINEERING	11,413	15	48	2,803	5,815	938	164	27	23	153	40	129
WOMEN	760	...	...	159	399	42	11	...	3	9	5	8
0840 P NUCLEAR ENGINEERING	2,709	1	...	5	1,687	12	6	2	...	9	...	5
WOMEN	149	...	...	...	84	...	1	...	...	...	...	...
0850 P ELECTRICAL ENGINEERING	4,948	17	27	940	1,334	298	25	14	10	173	35	21
WOMEN	446	...	4	85	104	26	2	...	...	15	3	1
0854 P COMPUTER ENGINEERING	2,495	...	9	589	453	184	39	27	6	16	8	12
WOMEN	474	...	1	71	78	30	10	5	...	2	1	3

TABLE E, 1995 -- CONTINUED

LABOR	HEALTH & HUMAN SERVICES	HOUSING & URBAN DEVLPMT	TRANSPOR-TATION	ENERGY	EDUCA-TION	VETERANS AFFAIRS	LIBRARY OF CONGRESS	EPA	FDIC	GENERAL SERVICES ADM	OPM	NASA	TVA	ALL OTHER AGENCIES	OCCUPATION CODES
...	4	...	...	...	...	235	...	...	...	...	...	...	...	...	0668
...	1	...	...	...	...	72	...	...	...	...	...	...	...	...	WOMEN
...	86	...	...	...	...	289	...	...	...	...	...	...	...	3	0669
...	77	...	...	...	...	252	...	...	...	...	...	...	...	1	WOMEN
...	110	...	2	...	...	383	...	...	...	...	...	...	...	2	0670
...	47	...	...	...	...	87	...	...	...	...	...	...	...	1	WOMEN
...	169	...	2	9	...	790	...	...	...	...	...	...	...	2	0671
...	123	...	...	4	...	350	...	...	...	...	...	...	...	...	WOMEN
...	...	...	...	...	...	205	...	...	...	...	...	...	...	...	0672
...	...	...	...	...	...	64	...	...	...	...	...	...	...	...	WOMEN
...	16	...	...	...	...	250	...	...	...	...	...	...	...	...	0673
...	7	...	...	...	...	30	...	...	...	...	...	...	...	...	WOMEN
...	502	...	19	...	...	1,315	...	...	...	...	...	...	...	10	0675
...	470	...	14	...	...	1,074	...	...	...	...	...	...	...	9	WOMEN
...	845	...	3	...	...	6,772	...	...	...	...	...	...	...	10	0679
...	799	...	3	...	...	5,083	...	...	...	...	...	...	...	10	WOMEN
...	26	...	...	...	...	766	...	...	...	...	...	...	...	3	0680
...	10	...	...	...	...	76	...	...	...	...	...	...	...	...	WOMEN
...	501	...	1	...	...	912	...	...	...	...	...	...	...	3	0681
...	492	...	1	...	...	856	...	...	...	...	...	...	...	3	WOMEN
...	7	...	1	...	...	146	...	...	...	...	...	...	...	1	0682
...	7	...	1	...	...	138	...	...	...	...	...	...	...	1	WOMEN
...	21	...	...	...	...	455	...	...	...	...	...	...	...	...	0683
...	8	...	...	...	...	68	...	...	...	...	...	...	...	...	WOMEN
...	1,510	...	...	...	...	...	...	...	...	...	...	...	...	90	0685
...	722	...	...	...	...	...	...	...	...	...	...	...	...	47	WOMEN
...	26	...	...	...	...	...	...	...	...	...	...	...	...	1	0688
...	10	...	...	...	...	...	...	...	...	...	...	...	...	...	WOMEN
516	59	...	9	57	...	144	...	14	...	20	...	9	4	14	0690
185	21	...	5	13	...	42	...	6	...	6	...	3	...	7	WOMEN
...	1,782	...	...	...	...	...	...	6	...	...	...	...	...	2	0696
...	717	...	...	...	...	...	...	...	...	...	...	...	...	1	WOMEN
...	18	...	...	...	...	3	...	...	...	...	...	2	...	4	0698
...	3	...	...	...	...	1	...	...	...	...	...	1	...	1	WOMEN
...	9	...	...	...	...	102	...	...	...	...	...	1	8	2	0699
...	8	...	...	...	...	80	...	...	...	...	...	...	3	...	WOMEN
563	14,442	...	128	92	...	111,375	5	110	2	20	1	48	60	566	0600
220	9,482	...	72	34	...	76,080	5	43	2	6	1	13	36	398	WOMEN
...	88	...	1	...	...	10	...	7	...	...	...	...	...	9	0701
...	25	...	...	...	...	4	...	4	...	...	...	...	...	2	WOMEN
...	2	...	...	...	...	10	...	...	...	...	...	...	...	...	0704
...	2	...	...	...	...	7	...	...	...	...	...	...	...	...	WOMEN
...	...	...	...	...	...	...	...	...	...	...	...	...	...	...	0799
...	...	...	...	...	...	...	...	...	...	...	...	...	...	...	WOMEN
...	90	...	1	...	...	20	...	7	...	...	...	...	...	9	0700
...	27	...	...	...	...	11	...	4	...	...	...	...	...	2	WOMEN
12	94	102	1,010	2,043	...	742	3	40	...	138	...	3,362	454	801	0801
...	9	6	94	270	...	38	1	4	...	5	...	599	47	73	WOMEN
35	260	3	646	141	...	980	...	62	...	50	...	1,138	784	69	0802
5	14	...	50	42	...	39	...	6	...	1	...	92	170	3	WOMEN
74	11	...	4	44	...	34	...	1	...	2	...	10	34	3	0803
10	1	...	...	1	...	3	...	...	...	...	...	...	2	...	WOMEN
1	2	...	8	26	...	3	1	...	...	27	...	4	...	15	0804
...	1	...	...	2	...	...	...	...	...	8	...	...	...	2	WOMEN
...	8	1	3	11	...	...	...	...	...	6	...	271	...	38	0806
...	2	...	1	4	...	...	...	...	...	...	...	47	...	2	WOMEN
...	1	2	3	4	...	13	...	...	...	1	...	...	5	3	0807
...	...	...	2	...	...	...	...	...	...	...	...	...	...	...	WOMEN
1	67	50	59	18	...	77	...	8	1	205	1	13	17	59	0808
...	18	6	14	5	...	8	...	1	...	37	...	3	4	16	WOMEN
...	56	1	79	37	...	32	...	1	...	18	...	8	94	25	0809
...	...	...	1	...	...	1	...	...	...	2	...	...	6	...	WOMEN
32	15	10	1,704	293	...	17	...	5	...	119	...	5	179	99	0810
3	2	...	180	29	...	2	...	...	...	16	...	1	22	8	WOMEN
...	...	...	12	3	...	...	...	...	...	...	...	...	...	7	0817
...	...	...	1	...	...	...	...	...	...	...	...	...	...	...	WOMEN
...	16	...	12	...	...	28	...	...	...	2	...	...	5	4	0818
...	5	...	2	...	...	3	...	...	...	...	...	...	1	...	WOMEN
...	39	...	47	168	...	2	...	2,076	...	8	...	17	71	11	0819
...	9	...	12	43	...	...	...	525	...	2	...	6	18	3	WOMEN
...	...	219	1	...	...	26	...	...	...	...	...	...	...	217	0828
...	...	20	...	...	...	2	...	...	...	...	...	...	...	20	WOMEN
13	86	4	178	162	...	39	...	100	...	139	...	115	331	96	0830
1	15	...	12	17	...	4	...	10	...	12	...	21	21	11	WOMEN
...	...	...	...	373	...	...	...	6	...	...	...	...	77	535	0840
...	...	...	...	23	...	...	...	1	...	...	...	...	7	33	WOMEN
38	34	...	116	518	...	32	...	10	...	90	...	531	611	74	0850
1	6	...	14	52	...	1	...	...	...	2	...	82	47	1	WOMEN
...	19	...	36	6	...	4	2	2	...	...	...	1,080	...	3	0854
...	4	...	6	...	...	1	...	...	...	...	...	262	...	...	WOMEN

TABLE E   FULL-TIME CIVILIAN WHITE-COLLAR EMPLOYMENT BY OCCUPATION, GENDER, AND SELECTED AGENCY, ALL AREAS, SEPTEMBER 30, 1995

OCCUPATION CODES / TITLES	TOTAL ALL AGENCIES	STATE	TREASURY	ARMY	NAVY	AIR FORCE	DEFENSE LOGIS AGENCY	OTHER DEFENSE	JUSTICE	INTERIOR	AGRI-CULTURE	COM-MERCE
0855 P ELECTRONICS ENGINEERING	26,399	145	31	4,192	12,066	5,237	521	442	73	54	52	433
WOMEN	2,137	4	1	329	972	369	36	31	2	6	8	23
0856 T ELECTRONICS TECHNICIAN	12,133	...	46	1,243	5,133	1,490	89	125	650	163	159	789
WOMEN	727	...	1	54	252	87	4	6	20	9	19	19
0858 P BIOMEDICAL ENGINEERING	343	...	...	18	13	11	7	...	...	1	2	1
WOMEN	78	...	...	4	4	4	2	...	...	...	...	1
0861 P AEROSPACE ENGINEERING	8,425	...	1	636	1,691	1,481	132	10	...	...	1	4
WOMEN	823	...	...	35	130	85	3	2	...	...	...	...
0871 P NAVAL ARCHITECTURE	905	...	...	9	849	...	...	2	...	...	...	...
WOMEN	68	...	...	1	64	...	...	...	...	...	...	1
0873 A SHIP SURVEYING	148	...	...	20	62	1	1	...	...	...	...	...
WOMEN	1	...	...	...	...	...	...	...	...	...	...	...
0880 P MINING ENGINEERING	339	...	24	...	...	...	1	...	...	192	11	...
WOMEN	17	...	...	...	...	...	...	...	...	8	2	...
0881 P PETROLEUM ENGINEERING	349	...	44	...	1	1	...	...	...	233	1	...
WOMEN	29	...	8	...	...	...	...	...	...	17	1	...
0890 P AGRICULTURAL ENGINEERING	381	...	...	2	...	...	...	...	...	12	358	...
WOMEN	39	...	...	1	...	...	...	...	...	...	37	...
0892 P CERAMIC ENGINEERING	54	...	...	9	8	1	...	...	...	5	...	8
WOMEN	8	...	...	1	1	...	...	...	...	...	...	2
0893 P CHEMICAL ENGINEERING	1,286	...	7	370	278	79	11	...	...	78	38	38
WOMEN	235	...	1	57	42	19	3	...	...	14	2	11
0894 P WELDING ENGINEERING	62	...	...	3	53	2	...	...	...	...	...	...
WOMEN	3	...	...	...	3	...	...	...	...	...	...	...
0895 T INDUSTRIAL ENGINEER TECH	1,600	...	1	140	510	929	10	...	2	1	1	...
WOMEN	252	...	...	26	77	147	1	...	...	...	...	...
0896 P INDUSTRIAL ENGINEERING	1,964	...	33	477	739	356	266	7	3	11	8	5
WOMEN	322	...	7	75	147	43	28	2	...	4	1	2
0899 O ENGINR & ARCH STUDNT TR	650	...	...	141	100	17	...	1	...	31	28	13
WOMEN	186	...	...	39	22	3	...	...	...	11	12	2
0800 ENGINEERNG & ARCHITECTURE	145,824	324	611	31,082	44,859	16,767	1,866	945	1,042	4,661	4,883	2,032
WOMEN	14,365	16	65	2,907	3,621	1,352	130	66	54	505	701	122
0904 P LAW CLERK	282	3	26	1	7	1	3	1	84	1	...	4
WOMEN	149	1	11	1	2	1	3	...	48	1	...	2
0905 P GENERAL ATTORNEY	25,540	130	2,698	984	543	309	211	248	8,096	319	249	478
WOMEN	9,390	52	900	272	180	52	80	71	2,752	123	83	228
0920 A ESTATE TAX EXAMINING	1	...	1	...	...	...	...	...	...	...	...	...
WOMEN	1	...	1	...	...	...	...	...	...	...	...	...
0930 A HEARING AND APPEALS	1,713	...	1,154	...	...	...	...	...	320	14	117	1
WOMEN	501	...	305	...	...	...	...	...	137	3	31	...
0935 P ADMINISTRATIVE LAW JUDGE	1,323	...	2	...	...	...	...	...	5	12	5	1
WOMEN	146	...	...	...	...	...	...	...	1	3	1	...
0945 A CLERK OF COURT	33	...	...	2	2	...	...	...	...	3	...	...
WOMEN	23	...	...	1	2	...	...	...	...	2	...	...
0950 A PARALEGAL SPECIALIST	5,341	54	495	208	125	57	8	75	1,910	37	33	120
WOMEN	4,147	39	373	175	107	41	8	64	1,531	25	30	104
0958 A PENSION LAW SPECIALIST	118	...	...	...	...	...	...	...	...	...	...	...
WOMEN	69	...	...	...	...	...	...	...	...	...	...	...
0962 T CONTACT REPRESENTATIVE	15,393	57	2,756	331	223	172	1	146	73	75	137	16
WOMEN	11,282	46	1,633	245	187	132	1	86	64	67	97	11
0963 T LEGAL INSTRUMENTS EXAM	2,337	6	244	65	...	16	...	38	360	197	155	565
WOMEN	1,875	5	209	58	...	13	...	30	216	161	152	463
0965 A LAND LAW EXAMINING	296	...	...	...	...	...	...	...	...	270	24	...
WOMEN	245	...	...	...	...	...	...	...	...	222	22	...
0967 A PASSPORT & VISA EXAMININ	1,142	1,137	...	4	...	...	...	...	...	...	...	...
WOMEN	491	489	...	1	...	...	...	...	...	...	...	...
0986 * LEGAL CLERICAL & ASST	9,537	1	503	309	274	124	59	41	3,234	249	82	481
WOMEN	8,771	...	479	283	252	118	57	34	3,034	211	77	362
0987 A TAX LAW SPECIALIST	385	...	384	...	...	...	...	...	...	...	...	...
WOMEN	142	...	141	...	...	...	...	...	...	...	...	...
0990 * GENERAL CLAIMS EXAMINING	1,621	13	49	66	44	44	...	124	4	3	63	...
WOMEN	1,216	10	45	54	37	34	...	86	4	2	47	...
0991 A WORKERS' COMP CLAIM EXAM	868	...	...	...	...	1	...	...	...	...	...	...
WOMEN	495	...	...	...	...	...	...	...	...	...	...	...
0992 T LOSS & DAMAGE CLAIM EXAM	126	3	...	78	4	39	...	...	...	...	1	...
WOMEN	92	3	...	59	3	26	...	...	...	...	1	...
0993 A RAILROAD RETIRE CLM EXAM	3,349	...	...	...	...	...	...	...	...	...	...	...
WOMEN	2,346	...	...	...	...	...	...	...	...	...	...	...
0994 T UNEMPLOY COMP CLAIM EXAM	71	...	...	...	...	...	...	...	...	...	...	...
WOMEN	46	...	...	...	...	...	...	...	...	...	...	...
0995 T DEPEND&ESTATE CLAIM EXAM	31	...	...	...	3	1	...	27	...	...	...	...
WOMEN	25	...	...	...	2	1	...	22	...	...	...	...
0996 A VETERANS CLAIMS EXAM	3,296	...	...	...	...	...	...	...	...	...	...	...
WOMEN	1,524	...	...	...	...	...	...	...	...	...	...	...
0998 C CLAIMS CLERICAL	5,511	...	58	153	87	25	...	...	...	3	28	...
WOMEN	4,608	...	49	123	75	21	...	...	...	3	24	...
0999 O LEGAL OCCUPATN STUDNT TR	27	1	2	2	1	1	...	...	5	...	4	...
WOMEN	18	1	1	1	1	1	...	...	2	...	4	...
0900 LEGAL AND KINDRED	78,341	1,405	8,372	2,203	1,313	790	282	700	14,091	1,183	898	1,666
WOMEN	47,602	647	4,147	1,273	848	440	149	393	7,789	823	568	1,170

TABLE E, 1995 -- CONTINUED

LABOR	HEALTH & HUMAN SERVICES	HOUSING & URBAN DEVLPMT	TRANSPOR-TATION	ENERGY	EDUCA-TION	VETERANS AFFAIRS	LIBRARY OF CONGRESS	EPA	FDIC	GENERAL SERVICES ADM	OPM	NASA	TVA	ALL OTHER AGENCIES	OCCUPATION CODES
9	87	...	1,222	163	...	6	9	7	...	21	...	1,234	...	395	0855
...	10	...	121	8	...	...	...	...	...	1	...	181	...	35	WOMEN
4	45	...	1,356	33	...	149	2	12	...	47	...	354	...	244	0856
1	1	...	204	1	...	2	...	...	...	...	...	29	...	5	WOMEN
...	113	...	1	...	...	175	...	1	...	...	...	...	...	...	0858
...	31	...	...	...	...	31	...	1	...	...	...	...	...	...	WOMEN
...	1	...	499	...	...	...	...	1	...	...	...	3,953	...	15	0861
...	...	...	58	...	...	...	...	...	...	...	...	509	...	1	WOMEN
...	...	...	43	...	...	...	...	...	...	...	...	...	...	1	0871
...	...	...	3	...	...	...	...	...	...	...	...	...	...	...	WOMEN
...	...	...	64	...	...	...	...	...	...	...	...	...	...	...	0873
...	...	...	1	...	...	...	...	...	...	...	...	...	...	...	WOMEN
106	...	...	...	2	...	...	...	1	...	...	...	...	...	2	0880
7	...	...	...	...	...	...	...	...	...	...	...	...	...	...	WOMEN
...	...	...	7	57	...	...	...	2	...	...	...	...	...	3	0881
...	...	...	1	2	...	...	...	...	...	...	...	...	...	...	WOMEN
...	3	...	...	...	...	...	...	3	...	...	...	1	2	...	0890
...	1	...	...	...	...	...	...	...	...	...	...	...	...	...	WOMEN
...	...	...	...	1	...	...	...	...	...	...	...	22	...	...	0892
...	...	...	...	1	...	...	...	...	...	...	...	3	...	...	WOMEN
5	18	...	8	89	...	...	...	150	...	3	...	47	51	16	0893
2	8	...	1	14	...	...	...	39	...	1	...	10	9	2	WOMEN
...	...	...	1	...	...	...	...	...	...	...	...	...	3	...	0894
...	...	...	...	...	...	...	...	...	...	...	...	...	...	...	WOMEN
...	...	...	...	...	...	4	...	...	...	...	...	...	...	2	0895
...	...	...	...	...	...	1	...	...	...	...	...	...	...	...	WOMEN
4	7	1	16	5	...	7	...	...	...	3	...	...	7	9	0896
1	1	...	5	2	...	2	...	...	...	1	...	...	1	...	WOMEN
...	5	...	64	39	...	11	...	21	...	11	...	130	32	6	0899
...	2	...	16	12	...	4	...	6	...	1	...	41	13	2	WOMEN
334	987	393	7,199	4,236	...	2,381	17	2,509	1	890	1	12,295	2,757	2,752	0800
31	140	32	799	528	...	142	1	593	...	89	...	1,886	368	217	WOMEN
16	4	9	3	3	...	...	...	7	1	1	...	...	...	107	0904
12	3	6	2	3	...	...	...	7	1	1	...	...	...	44	WOMEN
617	318	355	475	514	211	671	73	877	1,115	130	23	73	60	5,763	0905
289	156	142	183	200	111	221	29	368	403	55	14	24	11	2,391	WOMEN
...	...	...	...	...	...	...	...	...	...	...	...	...	...	...	0920
...	...	...	...	...	...	...	...	...	...	...	...	...	...	...	WOMEN
4	...	...	...	6	...	77	...	...	...	...	...	...	...	20	0930
1	...	...	...	2	...	13	...	...	...	...	...	...	...	9	WOMEN
66	5	5	14	20	1	...	...	8	...	...	...	...	...	1,179	0935
6	2	1	2	...	...	...	...	1	...	...	...	...	...	129	WOMEN
...	...	...	1	...	...	...	...	...	...	...	...	...	...	25	0945
...	...	...	1	...	...	...	...	...	...	...	...	...	...	17	WOMEN
87	93	35	88	39	44	58	12	57	381	6	14	6	14	1,295	0950
75	60	30	74	37	30	40	7	44	313	6	8	6	13	907	WOMEN
52	...	...	...	...	...	...	...	...	...	...	...	...	...	66	0958
23	...	...	...	...	...	...	...	...	...	...	...	...	...	46	WOMEN
28	81	3	9	...	...	1,335	...	...	...	1	70	...	...	9,879	0962
22	67	2	8	...	...	489	...	...	...	1	61	...	...	8,063	WOMEN
6	39	4	210	8	...	111	...	1	...	...	...	1	...	311	0963
5	33	4	174	8	...	96	...	1	...	...	...	1	...	246	WOMEN
...	...	...	...	2	...	...	...	...	...	...	...	...	...	...	0965
...	...	...	...	1	...	...	...	...	...	...	...	...	...	...	WOMEN
...	1	...	...	...	...	...	...	...	...	...	...	...	...	...	0967
...	1	...	...	...	...	...	...	...	...	...	...	...	...	...	WOMEN
178	60	52	56	61	4	171	1	53	198	6	1	16	...	3,323	0986
168	55	50	50	56	2	141	1	51	176	4	1	16	...	3,090	WOMEN
...	...	...	...	...	...	...	...	...	...	...	...	...	...	1	0987
...	...	...	...	...	...	...	...	...	...	...	...	...	...	...	WOMEN
...	...	2	6	...	83	17	...	...	...	1	89	...	...	1,013	0990
...	...	1	4	...	57	12	...	...	...	1	62	...	...	760	WOMEN
864	...	...	...	...	...	...	...	...	...	...	...	...	3	...	0991
492	...	...	...	...	...	...	...	...	...	...	...	...	3	...	WOMEN
...	...	...	...	...	...	...	...	...	...	...	...	...	...	1	0992
...	...	...	...	...	...	...	...	...	...	...	...	...	...	...	WOMEN
...	...	...	...	...	...	...	...	...	...	...	...	...	...	3,349	0993
...	...	...	...	...	...	...	...	...	...	...	...	...	...	2,346	WOMEN
...	...	...	...	...	...	...	...	...	...	...	...	...	...	71	0994
...	...	...	...	...	...	...	...	...	...	...	...	...	...	46	WOMEN
...	...	...	...	...	...	...	...	...	...	...	...	...	...	...	0995
...	...	...	...	...	...	...	...	...	...	...	...	...	...	...	WOMEN
...	...	...	...	...	...	3,295	...	...	...	...	...	...	...	1	0996
...	...	...	...	...	...	1,523	...	...	...	...	...	...	...	1	WOMEN
58	44	...	...	...	...	1,329	...	...	...	...	37	...	...	3,689	0998
43	42	...	...	...	...	882	...	...	...	...	31	...	...	3,315	WOMEN
...	1	...	1	1	...	1	...	...	...	...	...	...	...	7	0999
...	1	...	1	...	...	1	86	...	...	...	...	...	...	5	WOMEN
1,976	646	465	863	654	343	7,065	86	1,003	1,696	144	234	96	77	30,090	0900
1,136	420	236	499	307	200	3,418	37	472	894	69	177	47	27	21,416	WOMEN

TABLE E   FULL-TIME CIVILIAN WHITE-COLLAR EMPLOYMENT BY OCCUPATION, GENDER, AND SELECTED AGENCY, ALL AREAS, SEPTEMBER 30, 1995

OCCUPATION CODES / TITLES	TOTAL ALL AGENCIES	STATE	TREASURY	ARMY	NAVY	AIR FORCE	DEFENSE LOGIS AGENCY	OTHER DEFENSE	JUSTICE	INTERIOR	AGRI-CULTURE	COM-MERCE
1001 * GENRL ARTS & INFORMATION	3,283	12	47	330	134	134	13	66	28	164	488	19
WOMEN	1,678	7	22	135	57	55	9	30	11	98	380	15
1008 A INTERIOR DESIGN	242	8	7	25	10	32	3	4	...	1	2	1
WOMEN	201	7	5	22	9	26	2	3	...	1	1	1
1010 T EXHIBITS SPECIALIST	368	7	1	38	30	35	2	...	11	86	5	...
WOMEN	61	...	...	6	3	1	...	...	6	9	1	...
1015 P MUSEUM CURATOR	377	3	2	68	23	14	...	...	...	118	3	...
WOMEN	155	3	1	14	5	2	...	...	...	63	2	...
1016 T MUSEUM SPECIALIST & TECH	884	3	1	81	33	32	...	...	...	183	1	2
WOMEN	456	1	1	32	8	9	...	...	...	104	1	1
1020 T ILLUSTRATING	752	...	7	193	141	196	8	13	9	79	9	8
WOMEN	298	...	6	70	56	72	2	6	6	31	7	3
1021 C OFFICE DRAFTING	6	...	1	1	1	2	...	...	...	...	...	...
WOMEN	...	...	...	...	...	...	...	...	...	...	...	...
1035 A PUBLIC AFFAIRS	4,361	67	233	828	343	337	41	69	111	178	537	78
WOMEN	2,499	54	137	398	209	166	19	32	52	101	342	38
1040 A LANGUAGE SPECIALIST	614	37	3	77	13	24	...	16	386	3	1	6
WOMEN	342	18	3	33	4	11	...	7	234	1	1	4
1046 C LANGUAGE CLERICAL	59	...	5	9	4	14	...	...	16	...	3	...
WOMEN	54	...	5	5	3	14	...	...	16	...	3	...
1051 A MUSIC SPECIALIST	21	...	...	7	2	2	...	...	...	...	...	...
WOMEN	5	...	...	3	...	...	...	...	...	...	...	...
1054 A THEATER SPECIALIST	13	...	...	4	...	3	...	...	1	5	...	...
WOMEN	2	...	...	...	...	...	...	...	1	1	...	...
1056 A ART SPECIALIST	136	...	...	67	...	50	...	...	1	2	...	...
WOMEN	67	...	...	29	...	26	...	...	...	1	...	...
1060 T PHOTOGRAPHY	1,439	2	16	359	207	164	14	84	123	47	41	9
WOMEN	303	1	4	62	31	18	3	14	39	7	9	3
1071 A AUDIOVISUAL PRODUCTION	1,219	7	44	247	136	154	7	52	14	41	27	5
WOMEN	246	1	7	36	18	21	2	9	1	13	8	...
1082 A WRITING AND EDITING	1,705	17	50	306	147	129	8	68	57	114	157	66
WOMEN	1,193	15	35	219	99	90	6	52	46	87	111	49
1083 A TECH WRITING & EDITING	1,378	1	...	433	332	153	27	11	12	120	27	16
WOMEN	785	1	...	205	208	58	21	6	8	83	18	12
1084 A VISUAL INFORMATION	1,971	8	60	467	291	188	26	77	50	142	105	43
WOMEN	859	6	28	170	148	57	10	30	16	73	60	17
1087 * EDITORIAL ASSISTANCE	1,030	2	20	204	175	214	13	11	5	125	50	36
WOMEN	944	1	12	190	155	203	13	10	5	121	44	33
1099 0 INFO & ARTS STUDENT TR	45	...	...	5	5	3	1	3	1	2	2	...
WOMEN	28	...	...	4	3	3	1	1	...	1	2	...
1000 INFORMATION AND ARTS	19,903	169	497	3,749	2,027	1,879	163	474	825	1,410	1,458	289
WOMEN	10,176	115	266	1,633	1,016	932	88	200	441	795	990	176
1101 * GEN BUSINESS & INDUSTRY	12,849	8	437	959	1,328	2,161	1,114	324	168	602	4,609	972
WOMEN	11,389	4	262	434	387	815	230	107	74	377	4,391	445
1102 P CONTRACTING	29,317	111	519	5,539	4,582	4,914	4,733	595	659	620	592	208
WOMEN	16,868	60	316	3,347	2,644	2,730	2,524	356	333	372	355	124
1103 A INDUSTRIAL PROPERTY MGT	776	...	...	104	86	52	422	2	5	1	...	...
WOMEN	333	...	...	36	31	22	192	...	1	...	...	...
1104 A PROPERTY DISPOSAL	1,012	4	3	29	25	3	694	...	2	13	22	4
WOMEN	496	1	1	7	9	...	338	...	...	5	15	2
1105 T PURCHASING	6,086	...	154	879	1,489	473	51	76	60	423	553	47
WOMEN	4,847	...	118	725	1,214	376	36	60	45	351	478	43
1106 * PROCUREMENT CLER & TECH	6,729	3	60	1,144	1,339	987	1,724	106	28	156	248	30
WOMEN	5,953	3	48	1,026	1,183	890	1,512	92	24	133	223	26
1107 * PROP DISPOSAL CLER &TECH	538	...	12	4	11	2	432	...	...	6	6	1
WOMEN	439	...	9	3	9	2	355	...	...	3	5	...
1130 A PUBLIC UTILITIES SPEC	627	...	...	10	9	6	6	6	1	6	68	...
WOMEN	256	...	...	4	1	5	5	1	...	2	5	...
1140 A TRADE SPECIALIST	690	...	...	...	...	...	...	...	1	3	3	585
WOMEN	277	...	...	...	...	...	...	...	1	3	2	241
1144 A COMMISSARY MANAGEMENT	1,203	...	...	...	...	...	...	1,203	...	...	...	...
WOMEN	253	...	...	...	...	...	...	253	...	...	...	...
1145 A AGRICULTURAL PROGRM SPEC	617	...	...	...	...	...	...	...	...	...	617	...
WOMEN	153	...	...	...	...	...	...	...	...	...	153	...
1146 A AGRICULTURAL MARKETING	551	...	...	...	...	...	...	...	...	...	550	...
WOMEN	193	...	...	...	...	...	...	...	...	...	193	...
1147 A AGRICULTURAL MARKET RPTR	155	...	...	...	...	...	...	...	...	...	155	...
WOMEN	33	...	...	...	...	...	...	...	...	...	33	...
1150 A INDUSTRIAL SPECIALIST	2,041	...	5	305	422	105	974	16	48	6	34	7
WOMEN	373	...	2	50	49	19	213	2	11	...	5	...
1152 T PRODUCTION CONTROL	5,426	...	3	742	2,116	2,323	64	11	12	6	1	1
WOMEN	1,394	...	...	223	456	640	32	9	3	2	...	...
1160 A FINANCIAL ANALYSIS	1,775	...	105	2	5	1	...	...	222	12	26	7
WOMEN	677	...	38	1	3	1	...	...	145	2	8	1
1161 A CROP INSURANCE ADMIN	2	...	...	...	...	...	...	...	...	...	2	...
WOMEN	1	...	...	...	...	...	...	...	...	...	1	...
1162 A CROP INS UNDERWRITING	64	...	...	...	...	...	...	...	...	...	64	...
WOMEN	7	...	...	...	...	...	...	...	...	...	7	...
1163 A INSURANCE EXAMINING	64	...	...	...	1	...	28	...	...	...	...	...
WOMEN	15	...	...	...	...	...	5	...	...	...	...	...
1165 A LOAN SPECIALIST	3,348	...	...	...	...	...	...	...	...	37	1,169	14
WOMEN	1,532	...	...	...	...	...	...	...	...	19	556	6

TABLE E, 1995 -- CONTINUED

LABOR	HEALTH & HUMAN SERVICES	HOUSING & URBAN DEVLPMT	TRANSPOR-TATION	ENERGY	EDUCA-TION	VETERANS AFFAIRS	LIBRARY OF CONGRESS	EPA	FDIC	GENERAL SERVICES ADM	OPM	NASA	TVA	ALL OTHER AGENCIES	OCCUPATION CODES
9	61	1	18	25	16	24	82	9	2	27	1	22	...	1,551	1001
7	35	...	8	18	15	14	49	5	1	22	...	16	...	670	WOMEN
...	...	...	...	...	...	115	...	...	...	33	...	...	...	1	1008
...	...	...	...	...	...	99	...	...	...	24	...	...	...	1	WOMEN
...	...	...	...	...	...	4	6	...	...	...	...	...	...	148	1010
...	...	...	...	...	...	...	3	...	...	...	...	...	...	32	WOMEN
...	...	...	2	...	...	...	...	...	...	...	...	...	...	144	1015
...	...	...	2	...	...	...	...	...	...	...	...	...	...	63	WOMEN
...	...	...	2	2	...	...	...	...	...	...	...	...	...	544	1016
...	...	...	...	1	...	...	...	...	...	...	...	...	...	298	WOMEN
...	3	...	10	5	1	55	1	1	...	1	...	2	...	10	1020
...	3	...	4	3	1	21	...	...	...	...	...	1	...	6	WOMEN
...	...	...	...	...	...	...	...	...	...	1	...	...	...	...	1021
...	...	...	...	...	...	...	...	...	...	...	...	...	...	...	WOMEN
57	308	12	74	119	30	109	36	125	9	16	8	100	139	397	1035
30	213	6	41	60	13	64	25	74	3	9	6	50	123	234	WOMEN
...	4	...	1	...	...	...	2	...	...	...	...	...	...	41	1040
...	1	...	1	...	...	...	1	...	...	...	...	...	...	23	WOMEN
...	...	...	...	...	...	1	...	...	...	...	...	...	...	7	1046
...	...	...	...	...	...	1	...	...	...	...	...	...	...	7	WOMEN
...	...	...	1	...	...	2	...	...	...	...	...	...	...	7	1051
...	...	...	...	...	...	...	...	...	...	...	...	...	...	2	WOMEN
...	...	...	...	...	...	...	...	...	...	...	...	...	...	...	1054
...	...	...	...	...	...	...	...	...	...	...	...	...	...	...	WOMEN
...	1	...	...	...	...	...	...	...	...	...	...	...	...	15	1056
...	1	...	...	...	...	...	...	...	...	...	...	...	...	10	WOMEN
1	38	...	12	...	1	147	45	1	...	...	1	30	40	57	1060
...	6	...	1	...	...	30	25	...	...	...	...	10	24	16	WOMEN
9	41	1	16	3	2	119	10	4	...	2	1	16	...	261	1071
3	11	...	3	1	...	11	1	1	...	...	1	1	...	97	WOMEN
12	134	4	40	11	20	11	29	14	15	6	1	8	...	282	1082
8	105	3	33	11	12	6	18	9	10	3	...	7	...	159	WOMEN
2	75	...	34	7	...	17	...	6	...	6	...	15	8	76	1083
1	56	...	27	6	...	11	...	3	...	1	...	8	4	48	WOMEN
8	121	6	26	24	5	100	6	12	7	22	2	27	...	148	1084
2	74	2	9	6	3	44	5	5	3	13	...	11	...	67	WOMEN
5	77	3	5	3	...	23	11	3	2	...	...	5	...	38	1087
...	68	2	5	3	...	22	9	3	2	...	...	4	...	34	WOMEN
...	...	...	4	3	...	2	...	2	...	3	...	3	...	6	1099
...	...	...	4	...	...	...	...	2	...	1	...	2	...	4	WOMEN
103	863	27	245	202	75	729	228	177	35	117	14	228	187	3,733	1000
56	573	13	138	109	44	323	135	102	19	73	7	110	151	1,771	WOMEN
57	469	3,020	52	372	366	430	4	117	90	278	...	29	2	1,881	1101
40	339	1,691	29	161	204	143	3	77	35	152	...	14	...	975	WOMEN
56	667	107	764	596	54	752	24	323	140	1,270	15	761	...	716	1102
29	412	55	464	295	32	482	13	191	72	850	9	412	...	391	WOMEN
9	11	...	6	45	...	...	...	3	...	...	...	29	...	1	1103
3	4	...	4	19	...	...	...	...	...	...	...	21	...	...	WOMEN
...	7	...	20	2	...	1	...	...	1	169	1	12	...	...	1104
...	2	...	12	1	...	1	...	...	...	93	...	9	...	...	WOMEN
20	306	7	81	29	...	1,027	...	29	59	128	2	44	58	91	1105
18	234	6	69	25	...	740	...	24	44	111	1	39	23	67	WOMEN
18	129	15	80	40	5	112	5	18	1	204	1	58	...	218	1106
15	116	13	72	37	5	83	4	16	1	176	1	57	...	197	WOMEN
...	1	...	2	...	...	...	...	...	...	52	...	3	...	6	1107
...	1	...	1	...	...	...	...	...	...	44	...	3	...	4	WOMEN
...	...	...	...	445	...	...	...	1	...	14	...	...	36	19	1130
...	...	...	...	214	...	...	...	...	...	5	...	...	9	5	WOMEN
...	...	...	42	2	...	...	...	...	...	...	...	...	...	44	1140
...	...	...	15	...	...	...	...	...	...	...	...	...	...	15	WOMEN
...	...	...	...	...	...	...	...	...	...	...	...	...	...	...	1144
...	...	...	...	...	...	...	...	...	...	...	...	...	...	...	1145
...	...	...	...	...	...	...	...	...	...	...	...	...	...	1	1146
...	...	...	...	...	...	...	...	...	...	...	...	...	...	...	WOMEN
...	...	...	...	...	...	...	...	...	...	...	...	...	...	...	1147
...	...	...	...	...	...	...	...	...	...	...	...	...	...	...	WOMEN
...	...	...	17	53	...	...	...	...	...	...	...	7	6	36	1150
...	...	...	3	11	...	...	...	...	...	...	...	2	1	5	WOMEN
...	3	...	20	1	...	...	2	...	...	...	...	48	70	3	1152
...	...	...	13	1	...	...	1	...	...	...	...	10	1	3	WOMEN
1	16	261	25	44	24	2	...	16	784	6	...	...	30	186	1160
1	3	136	8	14	9	...	...	6	221	3	...	...	18	59	WOMEN
...	...	...	...	...	...	...	...	...	...	...	...	...	...	...	1161
...	...	...	...	...	...	...	...	...	...	...	...	...	...	...	WOMEN
...	...	...	...	...	...	...	...	...	...	...	...	...	...	...	1162
...	...	...	...	...	...	...	...	...	...	...	...	...	...	...	WOMEN
...	...	2	15	1	...	...	...	...	1	...	...	...	...	16	1163
...	...	1	3	...	...	...	...	...	...	...	...	...	...	6	WOMEN
...	1	267	1	...	5	791	...	...	...	...	...	...	...	1,063	1165
...	...	134	1	...	2	472	...	...	...	...	...	...	...	342	WOMEN

TABLE 5. FULL-TIME CIVILIAN WHITE-COLLAR EMPLOYMENT BY OCCUPATION, GENDER, AND SELECTED AGENCY, ALL AREAS, SEPTEMBER 30, 1995

OCCUPATION CODES / TITLES	TOTAL ALL AGENCIES	STATE	TREASURY	ARMY	NAVY	AIR FORCE	DEFENSE LOGIS AGENCY	OTHER DEFENSE	JUSTICE	INTERIOR	AGRI-CULTURE	COM-MERCE
1169 A INTERNAL REVENUE OFFICER	8,166	...	8,166	...	...	...	...	...	...	...	...	...
WOMEN	3,892	...	3,892	...	...	...	...	...	...	...	...	...
1170 A REALTY	3,400	8	5	924	120	227	...	...	14	756	189	23
WOMEN	1,619	3	3	362	54	132	...	...	5	356	112	14
1171 A APPRAISING	1,018	1	63	142	10	...	...	...	3	149	168	...
WOMEN	211	...	21	17	...	...	...	...	1	29	24	...
1173 A HOUSING MANAGEMENT	2,521	...	...	501	1,014	794	1	...	1	20	...	...
WOMEN	1,527	...	...	288	634	451	1	...	1	17	...	...
1176 A BUILDING MANAGEMENT	1,127	109	11	19	6	6	...	68	8	9	7	9
WOMEN	319	4	...	6	2	2	...	29	...	3	5	3
1199 O BUSINESS & IND STUDNT TR	113	...	...	6	35	2	3	1	1	9	10	12
WOMEN	62	...	...	4	17	1	1	1	...	5	2	8
1100 BUSINESS AND INDUSTRY	97,295	244	9,543	11,209	12,598	12,056	10,246	2,408	1,233	2,834	9,093	1,920
WOMEN	53,119	75	4,710	6,533	5,693	6,086	5,444	910	644	1,679	6,573	913
1202 T PATENT TECHNICIAN	15	...	...	1	...	...	...	...	...	...	...	15
WOMEN	13	...	...	1	...	...	...	...	...	...	...	12
1210 A COPYRIGHT	179	...	...	...	...	...	...	...	...	...	...	...
WOMEN	103	...	...	...	...	...	...	...	...	...	...	...
1211 T COPYRIGHT TECHNICIAN	41	...	...	...	...	...	...	...	...	...	...	...
WOMEN	21	...	...	...	...	...	...	...	...	...	...	...
1220 O PATENT ADMINISTRATION	76	...	...	...	...	...	...	...	...	...	...	76
WOMEN	9	...	...	...	...	...	...	...	...	...	...	9
1221 P PATENT ADVISER	28	...	...	7	2	5	...	...	...	...	8	...
WOMEN	8	...	...	...	...	...	...	...	...	...	5	...
1222 P PATENT ATTORNEY	212	...	...	29	52	12	...	...	14	1	2	55
WOMEN	18	...	...	2	1	...	...	...	2	...	...	7
1223 P PATENT CLASSIFYING	77	...	...	...	...	...	...	...	...	...	...	77
WOMEN	14	...	...	...	...	...	...	...	...	...	...	14
1224 P PATENT EXAMINING	2,170	...	...	...	...	...	...	...	...	...	...	2,170
WOMEN	475	...	...	...	...	...	...	...	...	...	...	475
1226 P DESIGN PATENT EXAMINING	55	...	...	...	...	...	...	...	...	...	...	55
WOMEN	31	...	...	...	...	...	...	...	...	...	...	31
1200 COPYRIGHT PATENT TRADEMRK	2,861	...	...	37	54	17	...	...	14	1	10	2,448
WOMEN	692	...	...	3	1	...	...	...	2	...	5	548
1301 P GENERAL PHYSICAL SCIENCE	7,045	58	12	1,003	408	252	2	524	16	586	114	588
WOMEN	1,529	12	3	169	77	44	1	95	2	86	29	102
1306 P HEALTH PHYSICS	841	...	...	75	269	6	4	4	...	...	6	9
WOMEN	169	...	...	12	59	...	...	2	...	...	3	1
1310 P PHYSICS	3,194	...	2	465	1,415	334	...	30	1	24	12	465
WOMEN	220	...	...	24	97	16	...	5	...	1	1	31
1311 T PHYSICAL SCIENCE TECH	2,911	...	13	284	1,117	102	11	...	31	357	336	155
WOMEN	826	...	5	109	219	27	4	...	7	106	168	38
1313 P GEOPHYSICS	509	...	...	17	84	28	...	3	...	325	...	22
WOMEN	56	...	...	2	6	4	...	...	...	42	...	2
1315 P HYDROLOGY	2,632	...	...	48	9	19	...	...	...	1,867	351	265
WOMEN	439	...	...	8	...	1	...	...	...	293	87	36
1316 T HYDROLOGIC TECHNICIAN	1,552	...	...	123	...	...	...	...	...	1,179	231	12
WOMEN	228	...	...	23	...	...	...	...	...	136	60	8
1320 P CHEMISTRY	6,799	...	216	795	631	204	43	19	216	326	739	318
WOMEN	1,842	...	54	182	163	53	8	5	64	85	183	71
1321 P METALLURGY	192	...	2	35	63	10	...	...	1	24	...	24
WOMEN	15	...	1	3	1	1	...	...	...	1	...	3
1330 P ASTRONOMY & SPACE SCIENC	479	...	...	...	130	10	...	...	...	...	...	9
WOMEN	37	...	...	...	11	1	...	...	...	...	...	1
1340 P METEOROLOGY	3,059	...	...	63	86	130	...	...	...	13	28	2,704
WOMEN	267	...	...	5	6	10	...	...	...	1	1	240
1341 T METEOROLOGICAL TECH	1,402	...	...	70	68	136	...	...	...	...	3	1,120
WOMEN	131	...	...	10	2	7	...	...	...	...	1	109
1350 P GEOLOGY	2,128	...	4	281	25	20	...	3	4	1,372	205	4
WOMEN	428	...	2	54	8	3	...	2	3	259	55	3
1360 P OCEANOGRAPHY	680	...	...	30	319	...	...	...	...	48	...	244
WOMEN	112	...	...	5	53	...	...	...	...	6	...	40
1361 A NAVIGATIONAL INFORMATION	333	...	...	3	3	6	...	215	...	...	...	17
WOMEN	69	...	...	...	1	1	...	34	...	...	...	5
1370 P CARTOGRAPHY	4,176	3	...	39	8	9	...	3,073	...	569	117	349
WOMEN	842	...	...	9	3	1	...	586	...	132	36	73
1371 T CARTOGRAPHIC TECHNICIAN	1,296	...	...	126	20	...	...	8	...	670	304	143
WOMEN	431	...	...	32	4	...	...	2	...	190	133	61
1372 P GEODESY	319	...	...	7	1	3	...	209	...	12	...	86
WOMEN	43	...	...	...	...	...	...	26	...	1	...	16
1373 P LAND SURVEYING	504	...	...	15	4	2	...	...	...	319	158	...
WOMEN	21	...	...	...	1	...	...	...	...	6	13	...
1374 T GEODETIC TECHNICIAN	75	...	...	19	3	...	...	5	...	1	...	47
WOMEN	21	...	...	...	...	...	...	3	...	...	...	18
1380 P FOREST PRODUCTS TECHNOL	49	...	...	...	...	...	1	...	...	...	46	...
WOMEN	8	...	...	...	...	...	...	...	...	...	8	...
1382 P FOOD TECHNOLOGY	240	...	...	30	1	...	10	...	...	...	166	12
WOMEN	69	...	...	15	1	...	3	...	...	...	40	4
1384 P TEXTILE TECHNOLOGY	81	...	19	23	19	1	9	...	...	...	6	...
WOMEN	41	...	15	11	7	1	3	...	...	...	1	...

TABLE F,   1995 -- CONTINUED

LABOR	HEALTH & HUMAN SERVICES	HOUSING & URBAN DEVLPMT	TRANSPOR-TATION	ENERGY	EDUCA-TION	VETERANS AFFAIRS	LIBRARY OF CONGRESS	EPA	FDIC	GENERAL SERVICES ADM	OPM	NASA	TVA	ALL OTHER AGENCIES	OCCUPATION CODES
...	...	...	...	...	...	...	...	...	...	...	...	...	...	...	1169
...	...	...	...	...	...	...	...	...	...	...	...	...	...	...	WOMEN
...	26	117	174	54	2	198	...	3	6	651	...	6	...	7	1170
...	18	56	61	32	...	62	...	1	2	339	...	5	...	2	WOMEN
...	...	213	1	4	...	206	...	...	...	42	...	...	15	1	1171
...	...	56	...	...	...	48	...	...	...	14	...	...	1	...	WOMEN
2	4	143	36	...	...	1	...	...	...	...	...	...	...	4	1173
2	1	105	25	...	...	1	...	...	...	...	...	...	...	1	WOMEN
3	4	...	7	9	...	3	...	2	1	787	5	2	...	52	1176
2	2	...	3	1	...	...	...	...	1	246	...	1	...	9	WOMEN
...	5	...	...	4	...	...	...	1	...	16	...	7	...	1	1199
...	4	...	...	4	...	...	...	1	...	9	...	4	...	1	WOMEN
166	1,649	4,152	1,343	1,701	456	3,513	35	513	1,083	3,617	24	1,006	217	4,346	1100
110	1,136	2,253	783	815	252	2,032	21	316	376	2,042	11	577	53	2,082	WOMEN
...	...	...	...	...	...	...	...	...	...	...	...	...	...	...	1202
...	...	...	...	...	...	...	...	...	...	...	...	...	...	...	WOMEN
...	...	...	...	...	...	...	179	...	...	...	...	...	...	...	1210
...	...	...	...	...	...	...	103	...	...	...	...	...	...	...	WOMEN
...	...	...	...	...	...	...	41	...	...	...	...	...	...	...	1211
...	...	...	...	...	...	...	21	...	...	...	...	...	...	...	WOMEN
...	...	...	...	...	...	...	...	...	...	...	...	...	...	...	1220
...	...	...	...	...	...	...	...	...	...	...	...	...	...	...	WOMEN
...	4	...	...	2	...	...	...	...	...	...	...	...	...	...	1221
...	2	...	...	1	...	...	...	...	...	...	...	...	...	...	WOMEN
...	1	...	1	32	...	...	...	1	...	...	...	19	...	...	1222
...	...	...	...	3	...	...	...	...	...	...	...	3	...	...	WOMEN
...	...	...	...	...	...	...	...	...	...	...	...	...	...	...	1223
...	...	...	...	...	...	...	...	...	...	...	...	...	...	...	WOMEN
...	...	...	...	...	...	...	...	...	...	...	...	...	...	...	1224
...	...	...	...	...	...	...	...	...	...	...	...	...	...	...	WOMEN
...	...	...	...	...	...	...	...	...	...	...	...	...	...	...	1226
...	...	...	...	...	...	...	...	...	...	...	...	...	...	...	WOMEN
...	5	...	1	34	...	...	220	.1	...	...	...	19	...	...	1200
...	2	...	...	4	...	...	124	...	...	...	...	3	...	...	WOMEN
13	34	...	36	874	...	2	13	1,778	...	1	...	423	50	258	1301
1	10	...	6	172	...	...	1	577	...	...	...	71	20	51	WOMEN
...	32	...	2	87	...	76	...	27	...	...	...	2	27	215	1306
...	10	...	...	15	...	14	...	3	...	...	...	1	2	47	WOMEN
6	92	...	2	72	...	31	...	9	...	...	...	192	...	32	1310
...	9	...	...	5	...	6	...	...	...	...	...	21	...	4	WOMEN
32	61	...	4	28	...	23	...	61	...	...	...	32	255	9	1311
21	30	...	...	2	...	8	...	17	...	...	...	6	59	...	WOMEN
...	...	...	...	2	...	...	...	1	...	...	...	19	...	8	1313
...	...	...	...	...	...	...	...	...	...	...	...	...	...	...	WOMEN
...	1	...	...	...	...	...	...	55	...	...	...	...	...	12	1315
...	...	...	...	...	...	...	...	13	...	...	...	...	...	...	WOMEN
...	...	...	...	...	...	...	...	...	...	...	...	...	...	17	1316
...	...	...	...	...	...	...	...	...	...	...	...	...	...	1	WOMEN
53	1,932	...	29	102	...	287	4	618	...	22	...	10	95	51	1320
9	645	...	6	30	...	67	...	171	...	6	...	3	24	13	WOMEN
...	...	...	...	2	...	...	...	1	...	...	...	...	14	6	1321
...	...	...	...	...	...	...	...	...	...	...	...	...	4	1	WOMEN
...	...	...	...	...	...	...	...	...	...	...	...	282	...	48	1330
...	...	...	...	...	...	...	...	...	...	...	...	19	...	6	WOMEN
...	...	...	3	7	...	...	...	3	...	...	...	20	4	8	1340
...	...	...	...	1	...	...	...	...	...	...	...	2	...	1	WOMEN
...	...	...	3	1	...	...	...	...	...	...	...	...	...	1	1341
...	...	...	1	1	...	...	...	...	...	...	...	...	...	...	WOMEN
4	2	...	5	25	...	...	...	126	...	...	...	...	2	46	1350
1	...	...	...	6	...	...	...	24	...	...	...	...	...	8	WOMEN
...	...	...	5	...	...	...	...	10	...	...	...	13	...	11	1360
...	...	...	1	...	...	...	...	2	...	...	...	2	...	3	WOMEN
...	...	...	89	...	...	...	...	...	...	...	...	...	...	...	1361
...	...	...	28	...	...	...	...	...	...	...	...	...	...	...	WOMEN
...	...	...	5	2	...	...	...	2	...	...	...	...	...	...	1370
...	...	...	...	...	...	...	...	2	...	...	...	...	...	...	WOMEN
...	...	...	23	2	...	...	...	...	...	...	...	...	...	...	1371
...	...	...	9	...	...	...	...	...	...	...	...	...	...	...	WOMEN
...	...	...	...	...	...	...	...	...	...	...	...	...	...	...	1372
...	...	...	...	...	...	...	...	...	...	...	...	...	...	...	WOMEN
...	...	...	...	6	...	...	...	...	...	...	...	...	...	...	1373
...	...	...	...	1	...	...	...	...	...	...	...	...	...	...	WOMEN
...	...	...	...	...	...	...	...	...	...	...	...	...	...	...	1374
...	...	...	...	...	...	...	...	...	...	...	...	...	...	...	WOMEN
...	...	...	...	...	...	...	...	...	...	2	...	...	...	...	1380
...	...	...	...	...	...	...	...	...	...	...	...	...	...	...	WOMEN
...	21	...	...	...	...	...	...	...	...	...	...	...	...	...	1382
...	6	...	...	...	...	...	...	...	...	...	...	...	...	...	WOMEN
...	...	...	1	...	...	...	...	...	...	1	...	...	...	2	1384
...	...	...	...	...	...	...	...	...	...	1	...	...	...	2	WOMEN

TABLE E   FULL-TIME CIVILIAN WHITE-COLLAR EMPLOYMENT BY OCCUPATION, GENDER, AND SELECTED AGENCY, ALL AREAS, SEPTEMBER 30, 1995

OCCUPATION CODES / TITLES	TOTAL ALL AGENCIES	STATE	TREASURY	ARMY	NAVY	AIR FORCE	DEFENSE LOGIS AGENCY	OTHER DEFENSE	JUSTICE	INTERIOR	AGRI-CULTURE	COM-MERCE
1386 P PHOTOGRAPHIC TECHNOLOGY	31	...	...	6	7	5	...	1	6	2	1	1
WOMEN	1									1		
1397 A DOCUMENT ANALYSIS	106	...	54	2	4	...	...	...	45	...	...	...
WOMEN	44	...	18	1	...	...	...	...	25	...	...	...
1399 O PHYSICAL SCI STUDENT TR	149	...	1	19	6	4	...	2	...	66	17	9
WOMEN	61	...	1	12	1	1	...	...	...	18	10	2
1300 PHYSICAL SCIENCES	40,781	61	323	3,578	4,700	1,371	80	4,096	320	7,760	2,840	6,603
WOMEN	7,949	12	99	686	720	170	19	760	101	1,364	829	864
1410 P LIBRARIAN	2,887	9	24	402	195	232	4	44	45	63	73	48
WOMEN	1,946	7	17	291	145	165	4	37	35	49	54	40
1411 T LIBRARY TECHNICIAN	3,017	6	20	514	352	465	16	112	23	80	88	93
WOMEN	2,277	4	16	414	294	404	14	92	17	66	74	75
1412 A TECH INFORMATION SERVICE	1,314	71	6	79	80	81	6	214	136	38	55	75
WOMEN	909	45	4	59	59	47	5	136	110	24	40	55
1420 P ARCHIVIST	487	...	...	14	12	9	...	3	2	10	...	1
WOMEN	175	...	...	4	6	2	...	2	1	7	...	1
1421 * ARCHIVES TECHNICIAN	899	3	2	21	11	13	...	...	46	11	...	6
WOMEN	492	1	1	16	9	9	...	...	38	7	...	1
1499 O LIBRARY & ARCHIVES STDNT	5	...	...	1	...	1	...	...	...	1	...	...
WOMEN	3	...	...	1	...	1	...	...	...	1	...	...
1400 LIBRARY AND ARCHIVES	8,609	89	52	1,031	650	801	26	373	252	203	216	223
WOMEN	5,792	57	38	785	513	628	23	267	201	154	168	172
1510 P ACTUARY	178	...	28	...	...	1	1	8	...	...	4	...
WOMEN	42	...	6	...	...	...	...	2	...	...	1	...
1515 P OPERATIONS RESEARCH	3,635	...	104	1,692	661	355	68	206	17	18	47	31
WOMEN	837	...	30	402	158	87	15	30	3	4	12	11
1520 P MATHEMATICS	1,787	...	1	300	861	199	...	14	...	21	23	73
WOMEN	518	...	...	68	276	43	...	7	...	5	8	17
1521 T MATHEMATICS TECHNICIAN	29	...	...	5	14	5	...	...	...	...	...	1
WOMEN	24	...	...	3	13	4	...	...	...	...	...	1
1529 P MATHEMATICL STATISTICIAN	1,123	...	34	35	38	14	2	6	5	7	141	315
WOMEN	352	...	14	10	11	5	1	...	2	...	32	111
1530 P STATISTICIAN	2,598	...	57	67	40	12	3	8	47	38	538	1,026
WOMEN	1,005	...	16	27	6	3	1	1	17	9	111	474
1531 * STATISTICAL ASSISTANT	1,226	1	32	90	24	12	4	12	60	34	210	539
WOMEN	1,065	1	24	73	19	9	3	9	54	25	199	482
1541 T CRYPTANALYSIS	17	...	...	...	...	...	...	...	17	...	...	...
WOMEN	10	...	...	...	...	...	...	...	10	...	...	...
1550 P COMPUTER SCIENCE	3,192	...	45	341	1,562	390	...	263	30	56	25	226
WOMEN	995	...	9	119	519	123	...	77	11	11	6	56
1599 O MATH & STAT STUDENT TR	52	...	...	2	27	...	...	...	...	1	3	7
WOMEN	16	...	...	1	8	...	...	...	...	...	...	4
1500 MATHEMATICS & STATISTICS	13,837	1	301	2,532	3,227	988	78	517	176	175	991	2,218
WOMEN	4,864	1	99	703	1,010	274	20	126	97	54	369	1,156
1601 A GENERAL FACILITIES SUPPT	2,622	...	6	761	712	709	20	34	100	52	3	14
WOMEN	415	...	3	156	43	154	1	6	4	13	...	1
1630 A CEMETERY ADMINISTRATION	118	...	...	5	...	...	...	...	...	...	...	...
WOMEN	21	...	...	1	...	...	...	...	...	...	...	...
1640 A FACILITY MANAGEMENT	1,521	...	11	264	208	181	10	12	130	267	30	22
WOMEN	98	...	...	14	25	8	...	...	6	13	1	8
1654 A PRINTING MANAGEMENT	1,486	11	77	72	402	30	9	26	29	38	35	57
WOMEN	537	5	18	29	161	8	4	8	6	15	17	27
1658 A LAUNDRY/DRYCLEAN PLT MGT	155	...	...	13	3	4	...	...	73	...	...	...
WOMEN	20	...	...	3	1	...	...	...	7	...	...	...
1667 A STEWARD	319	...	1	22	1	36	...	25	226	...	...	...
WOMEN	52	...	...	2	...	4	...	25	21	...	...	...
1670 * EQUIPMENT SPECIALIST	8,474	6	23	2,576	2,284	2,372	774	22	7	33	43	13
WOMEN	857	...	...	225	266	213	123	2	...	2	6	1
1699 O EQPT & FACILITY MGT STDT	2	...	...	...	...	...	...	...	...	2	...	...
WOMEN	...	...	...	...	...	...	...	...	...	2	...	...
1600 EQPT FACILITIES & SERVICE	14,697	17	118	3,713	3,610	3,332	813	119	565	392	111	106
WOMEN	2,000	5	21	430	496	397	128	41	44	43	24	37
1701 P GEN EDUCATION & TRAINING	9,801	11	25	1,152	754	949	36	6,198	25	129	23	10
WOMEN	6,584	4	5	891	373	570	22	4,313	13	66	9	9
1702 * EDUCATION &TRAINING TECH	8,056	4	29	2,226	1,712	1,665	22	663	148	1,380	44	4
WOMEN	6,576	4	29	1,601	1,627	1,329	22	632	140	1,045	22	3
1710 P EDUCATION & VOCAT TRAIN	5,702	39	17	118	405	20	3	2,351	474	1,950	117	1
WOMEN	3,858	18	10	86	97	7	2	1,972	234	1,315	50	1
1712 A TRAINING INSTRUCTION	5,818	224	126	2,630	616	1,345	19	64	233	145	54	29
WOMEN	1,396	147	15	556	101	254	11	17	85	59	24	16
1715 A VOCATIONL REHABILITATION	658	...	...	...	...	...	...	...	1	30	...	...
WOMEN	170	...	...	...	...	...	...	...	...	13	...	...
1720 P EDUCATION PROGRAM	456	...	...	1	15	13	...	...	12	9	2	...
WOMEN	261	...	...	1	5	6	...	...	5	3	2	...
1725 P PUBLIC HEALTH EDUCATOR	80	...	...	...	18	1	...	...	2	...	...	...
WOMEN	58	...	...	...	14	1	...	...	2	...	...	...
1730 P EDUCATION RESEARCH	50	...	...	...	1	...	...	...	...	...	...	...
WOMEN	24	...	...	...	1	...	...	...	...	...	...	...

TABLE E, 1995 -- CONTINUED

LABOR	HEALTH & HUMAN SERVICES	HOUSING & URBAN DEVLPMT	TRANSPOR-TATION	ENERGY	EDUCA-TION	VETERANS AFFAIRS	LIBRARY OF CONGRESS	EPA	FDIC	GENERAL SERVICES ADM	OPM	NASA	TVA	ALL OTHER AGENCIES	OCCUPATION CODES
...	...	...	...	...	...	...	1	...	...	...	...	1	...	...	1386
...	...	...	...	...	...	...	...	...	...	...	...	...	...	...	WOMEN
...	...	...	...	...	...	1	...	...	...	...	...	...	...	...	1397
...	...	...	...	...	...	...	...	...	...	...	...	...	...	...	WOMEN
...	11	...	...	3	...	...	...	7	...	...	...	2	...	2	1399
...	9	...	...	1	...	...	...	3	...	...	...	2	...	1	WOMEN
108	2,186	...	205	1,213	...	420	18	2,698	...	26	...	996	447	731	1300
32	719	...	51	234	...	95	1	812	...	7	...	127	109	138	WOMEN
3	146	...	23	5	12	279	999	3	10	4	1	12	19	232	1410
2	127	...	20	4	7	207	538	3	8	3	...	9	15	159	WOMEN
2	111	...	19	5	...	199	771	1	9	4	...	4	...	123	1411
2	79	...	18	5	...	168	440	1	8	2	...	4	...	80	WOMEN
13	210	...	11	25	9	3	91	27	2	1	...	27	...	54	1412
8	163	...	8	21	6	3	36	19	1	...	...	21	...	39	WOMEN
...	...	...	...	1	...	...	20	1	...	...	...	...	...	414	1420
...	...	...	...	1	...	...	10	...	...	...	...	...	...	141	WOMEN
...	...	...	...	...	...	2	10	...	...	...	...	...	...	774	1421
...	...	...	...	...	...	...	5	...	...	...	...	...	...	395	WOMEN
...	...	...	...	...	...	...	...	...	...	...	...	...	...	2	1499
...	...	...	...	...	...	...	...	...	...	...	...	...	...	...	WOMEN
18	467	...	53	36	21	483	1,891	32	21	9	1	43	19	1,599	1400
12	369	...	46	31	13	378	1,029	23	17	5	...	34	15	814	WOMEN
5	30	3	...	1	...	5	...	...	...	...	9	...	...	83	1510
...	7	...	...	...	...	2	...	...	...	...	3	...	...	21	WOMEN
9	48	...	168	122	2	4	...	20	...	15	...	10	...	38	1515
2	18	...	25	26	...	1	...	2	...	2	...	3	...	6	WOMEN
1	16	...	40	21	...	1	...	5	...	...	...	191	2	18	1520
...	5	...	13	10	...	1	...	4	...	...	...	57	...	4	WOMEN
...	1	...	...	1	...	...	...	...	...	...	...	2	...	...	1521
...	1	...	...	...	...	...	...	...	...	...	...	2	...	...	WOMEN
94	294	...	18	39	14	20	...	30	...	...	1	1	...	15	1529
31	81	...	11	18	6	6	...	8	...	...	...	...	...	5	WOMEN
78	362	1	13	44	81	52	...	47	1	1	9	...	3	70	1530
36	172	1	4	16	38	19	...	18	...	...	2	...	3	32	WOMEN
60	47	1	3	1	5	55	...	1	...	1	5	...	...	29	1531
49	43	1	3	1	5	40	...	1	...	1	4	...	...	19	WOMEN
...	...	...	...	...	...	...	...	...	...	...	...	...	...	...	1541
...	...	...	...	...	...	...	...	...	...	...	...	...	...	...	WOMEN
1	37	...	94	6	...	6	...	3	...	...	...	79	...	29	1550
...	5	...	31	2	...	...	...	2	...	...	...	20	...	4	WOMEN
...	...	...	5	1	...	...	...	1	...	...	...	5	...	...	1599
...	...	...	1	...	...	...	...	...	...	...	...	2	...	...	WOMEN
248	835	5	341	236	102	143	...	107	1	17	24	287	5	282	1500
118	332	2	88	73	49	68	...	35	...	3	9	84	3	91	WOMEN
...	...	...	2	51	...	25	...	1	1	14	...	65	31	21	1601
...	...	...	...	3	...	3	...	...	1	6	...	1	10	10	WOMEN
...	...	...	...	...	...	77	...	...	...	...	...	...	...	36	1630
...	...	...	...	...	...	20	...	...	...	...	...	...	...	...	WOMEN
3	17	1	12	9	...	9	7	7	...	1	...	19	229	72	1640
...	2	...	...	1	...	...	...	...	...	...	...	4	5	11	WOMEN
13	51	7	27	16	1	14	5	8	3	36	4	20	...	495	1654
7	20	3	13	4	...	1	2	5	2	16	2	7	...	157	WOMEN
...	...	...	...	...	...	62	...	...	...	...	...	...	...	...	1658
...	...	...	...	...	...	2	...	...	...	...	...	...	...	...	WOMEN
...	...	...	1	...	...	...	...	...	...	...	...	1	...	6	1667
...	...	...	...	...	...	...	...	...	...	...	...	...	...	...	WOMEN
...	19	...	95	19	...	13	3	...	...	145	...	16	...	11	1670
...	3	...	1	6	...	1	...	...	...	6	...	2	...	...	WOMEN
...	...	...	...	...	...	...	...	...	...	...	...	...	...	...	1699
...	...	...	...	...	...	...	...	...	...	...	...	...	...	...	WOMEN
16	87	8	137	95	1	200	15	16	4	194	4	121	260	641	1600
7	25	3	14	14	...	34	2	5	3	28	2	14	15	178	WOMEN
3	117	6	25	19	22	98	...	1	...	4	3	13	15	263	1701
...	72	2	19	9	8	52	...	1	...	2	1	4	8	132	WOMEN
9	10	1	36	2	19	60	1	2	...	1	2	1	...	15	1702
8	9	1	23	2	16	46	1	2	...	1	1	1	...	11	WOMEN
5	7	...	117	...	...	13	...	1	...	...	...	2	...	62	1710
2	6	...	19	...	...	8	...	...	...	...	...	2	...	29	WOMEN
77	24	...	53	23	24	46	6	1	...	20	1	...	...	53	1712
22	10	...	11	3	16	22	3	...	...	5	...	...	...	19	WOMEN
31	...	...	...	...	...	592	...	...	...	...	...	...	4	...	1715
8	...	...	...	...	...	147	...	...	...	...	...	...	2	...	WOMEN
...	...	...	1	...	390	...	...	...	...	...	...	9	...	4	1720
...	...	...	1	...	232	...	...	...	...	...	...	3	...	3	WOMEN
...	57	...	...	...	...	2	...	...	...	...	...	...	...	...	1725
...	39	...	...	...	...	2	...	...	...	...	...	...	...	...	WOMEN
...	...	...	...	...	48	...	...	...	...	...	...	...	...	1	1730
...	...	...	...	...	23	...	...	...	...	...	...	...	...	...	WOMEN

TABLE E   FULL-TIME CIVILIAN WHITE-COLLAR EMPLOYMENT BY OCCUPATION, GENDER, AND SELECTED AGENCY, ALL AREAS, SEPTEMBER 30, 1995

OCCUPATION CODES	TITLES	TOTAL ALL AGENCIES	STATE	TREASURY	ARMY	NAVY	AIR FORCE	DEFENSE LOGIS AGENCY	OTHER DEFENSE	JUSTICE	INTERIOR	AGRI-CULTURE	COM-MERCE
1740 P	EDUCATION SERVICES	1,224	1	7	651	170	283	1	31	19	29	24	...
	WOMEN	565	1	6	303	67	128	...	27	7	14	9	...
1750 P	INSTRUCTIONAL SYSTEMS	1,406	11	1	551	308	259	6	126	8	8	1	7
	WOMEN	648	8	1	265	112	100	4	81	3	5	1	4
1799 O	EDUCATION STUDENT TR	10	...	...	2	6	1	...	...	...	...	...	...
	WOMEN	7	...	...	1	5	...	...	...	...	...	...	...
1700	EDUCATION	33,261	290	205	7,331	4,005	4,436	87	9,433	922	3,680	265	51
	WOMEN	20,147	182	66	3,704	2,402	2,395	61	7,042	489	2,520	117	33
1801 A	GEN INSP, INVEST & COMPL	7,070	12	1,403	138	60	7	...	59	2,520	497	247	174
	WOMEN	2,480	6	383	53	28	2	...	32	1,200	84	43	81
1802 *	COMPLIANCE INSP & SUPPORT	5,838	15	1,120	114	52	70	...	75	3,160	89	502	29
	WOMEN	3,627	15	835	78	43	58	...	68	1,912	36	95	26
1810 A	GENERAL INVESTIGATING	3,867	3	56	33	35	3	13	1,431	378	2	109	...
	WOMEN	1,543	1	30	7	10	2	...	429	157	...	17	...
1811 A	CRIMINAL INVESTIGATING	32,575	46	10,644	141	973	250	22	384	17,633	242	421	89
	WOMEN	4,345	8	1,547	9	145	21	3	61	2,044	19	102	13
1812 A	GAME LAW ENFORCEMENT	390	...	...	16	4	...	...	...	...	236	...	134
	WOMEN	40	...	...	...	...	...	...	...	...	25	...	15
1815 A	AIR SAFETY INVESTIGATING	93	...	...	7	7	...	...	...	...	2	...	...
	WOMEN	10	...	...	...	...	...	...	...	...	...	...	...
1816 A	IMMIGRATION INSPECTION	3,574	...	...	...	...	...	...	...	3,574	...	...	...
	WOMEN	920	...	...	...	...	...	...	...	920	...	...	...
1822 A	MINE SAFETY AND HEALTH	1,339	...	...	...	...	...	...	...	...	...	...	...
	WOMEN	45	...	...	...	...	...	...	...	...	...	...	...
1825 A	AVIATION SAFETY	3,016	...	...	2	...	...	...	...	...	...	...	...
	WOMEN	182	...	...	...	...	...	...	...	...	...	...	...
1831 A	SECURITIES COMPLI EXAM	194	...	...	...	...	...	...	...	...	...	...	...
	WOMEN	100	...	...	...	...	...	...	...	...	...	...	...
1850 A	AGRIC COMMOD WAREHS EXAM	90	...	...	...	...	...	...	...	...	...	90	...
	WOMEN	9	...	...	...	...	...	...	...	...	...	9	...
1854 A	ALCOHOL TOB FIREARM INSP	762	...	762	...	...	...	...	...	...	...	...	...
	WOMEN	354	...	354	...	...	...	...	...	...	...	...	...
1862 T	CONSUMER SAFETY INSPECTN	199	...	...	...	...	...	...	...	...	...	...	29
	WOMEN	92	...	...	...	...	...	...	...	...	...	...	6
1863 T	FOOD INSPECTION	6,559	...	...	1	...	...	...	...	...	...	6,558	...
	WOMEN	1,848	...	...	...	...	...	...	...	...	...	1,848	...
1864 A	PUB HLTH QUARANTINE INSP	32	...	...	...	...	...	...	...	...	...	...	...
	WOMEN	17	...	...	...	...	...	...	...	...	...	...	...
1884 O	CUSTOMS PATROL OFFICER	31	...	31	...	...	...	...	...	...	...	...	...
	WOMEN	2	...	2	...	...	...	...	...	...	...	...	...
1889 A	IMPORT SPECIALIST	1,271	...	1,266	5	...	...	...	...	...	...	...	...
	WOMEN	622	...	621	1	...	...	...	...	...	...	...	...
1890 A	CUSTOMS INSPECTION	6,645	...	6,639	...	6	...	...	...	...	...	...	...
	WOMEN	1,389	...	1,388	...	1	...	...	...	...	...	...	...
1894 A	CUSTOMS ENTRY & LIQUIDAT	454	...	454	...	...	...	...	...	...	...	...	...
	WOMEN	335	...	335	...	...	...	...	...	...	...	...	...
1896 O	BORDER PATROL AGENT	4,876	...	...	...	...	...	...	...	4,876	...	...	...
	WOMEN	198	...	...	...	...	...	...	...	198	...	...	...
1897 *	CUSTOMS AID	982	...	974	1	...	...	7	...	...	...	...	...
	WOMEN	657	...	649	1	...	...	7	...	...	...	...	...
1898 A	ADMEASUREMENT	16	...	...	...	...	...	...	...	...	...	...	...
	WOMEN	1	...	...	...	...	...	...	...	...	...	...	...
1899 O	INVESTIGATION STUDENT TR	57	...	31	...	...	...	...	...	20	...	3	...
	WOMEN	34	...	18	...	...	...	...	...	12	...	2	...
1800	INVESTIGATION	79,930	76	23,330	458	1,137	330	42	1,949	32,161	1,068	7,930	455
	WOMEN	18,850	30	6,162	149	227	83	10	590	6,343	164	2,116	141
1910 A	QUALITY ASSURANCE	10,685	1	24	1,530	1,487	1,170	5,617	5	84	14	23	6
	WOMEN	1,498	1	9	232	202	85	836	...	14	4	3	1
1980 T	AGRIC COMMODITY GRADING	2,231	...	...	...	...	...	...	...	...	...	2,231	...
	WOMEN	694	...	...	...	...	...	...	...	...	...	694	...
1981 T	AGRIC COMMODITY AID	144	...	...	...	...	...	...	...	...	...	144	...
	WOMEN	47	...	...	...	...	...	...	...	...	...	47	...
1999 O	QUALITY INSPECT STUDENT	2	...	...	...	...	...	...	...	...	...	2	...
	WOMEN	1	...	...	...	...	...	...	...	...	...	1	...
1900	QLTY ASSURANCE INSP & GRD	13,062	1	24	1,530	1,487	1,170	5,617	5	84	14	2,400	6
	WOMEN	2,240	1	9	232	202	85	836	...	14	4	745	1
2001 *	GENERAL SUPPLY	3,936	1	7	1,010	1,045	783	405	49	25	65	25	11
	WOMEN	1,658	...	2	465	330	379	180	21	14	25	8	3
2003 A	SUPPLY PROGRAM MANAGEMNT	5,136	19	7	1,542	1,345	713	697	105	34	28	21	3
	WOMEN	2,134	9	4	639	628	240	314	27	19	12	5	3
2005 *	SUPPLY CLERICAL & TECH	19,820	20	160	6,264	3,853	3,688	2,251	520	188	322	205	80
	WOMEN	11,448	5	47	3,369	2,531	2,168	1,481	224	74	172	95	48
2010 A	INVENTORY MANAGEMENT	6,394	22	55	1,363	1,090	1,877	941	118	100	9	2	35
	WOMEN	3,702	7	28	733	604	1,208	579	56	49	3	2	17
2030 A	DISTRIB FACIL & STOR MGT	799	4	10	151	105	11	399	11	5	3	5	4
	WOMEN	188	2	5	29	21	3	98	3	2	2	...	1
2032 A	PACKAGING	337	1	2	70	46	80	131	...	...	...	...	1
	WOMEN	98	...	...	15	11	27	44	...	...	...	...	...
2050 A	SUPPLY CATALOGING	601	...	2	140	49	14	309	25	...	...	...	1
	WOMEN	314	...	1	70	29	5	165	6	...	...	...	1

TABLE E.　1995 -- CONTINUED

LABOR	HEALTH & HUMAN SERVICES	HOUSING & URBAN DEVLPMT	TRANSPOR-TATION	ENERGY	EDUCA-TION	VETERANS AFFAIRS	LIBRARY OF CONGRESS	EPA	FDIC	GENERAL SERVICES ADM	OPM	NASA	TVA	ALL OTHER AGENCIES	OCCUPATION CODES
...	...	...	1	...	...	7	...	...	...	...	...	...	...	...	1740
...	...	...	1	...	...	2	...	...	...	...	...	...	...	...	WOMEN
...	...	1	50	...	...	50	...	...	...	...	...	2	...	17	1750
...	...	...	32	...	...	21	...	...	...	...	...	1	...	10	WOMEN
...	...	...	...	...	...	1	...	...	...	...	...	...	...	...	1799
...	...	...	...	...	...	1	...	...	...	...	...	...	...	...	WOMEN
125	216	7	289	44	503	869	7	5	...	25	6	27	19	415	1700
40	136	3	105	14	295	301	4	3	...	8	2	11	10	204	WOMEN
545	105	2	550	43	...	356	...	5	20	...	...	...	...	327	1801
182	66	2	136	9	...	51	...	3	6	...	...	...	...	113	WOMEN
345	33	...	20	...	3	7	...	...	...	1	52	...	...	151	1802
321	33	...	17	...	3	7	...	...	...	1	45	...	...	134	WOMEN
...	5	...	15	4	34	...	...	44	1	...	462	...	...	1,239	1810
...	3	...	12	1	22	...	...	10	...	...	160	...	...	682	WOMEN
159	286	109	142	56	86	106	1	211	88	129	10	52	...	295	1811
27	57	35	28	15	30	18	...	51	17	16	2	11	...	66	WOMEN
...	...	...	...	...	...	...	...	...	...	...	...	...	...	...	1812
...	...	...	...	...	...	...	...	...	...	...	...	...	...	...	WOMEN
...	...	...	11	...	...	...	...	...	...	...	...	...	...	66	1815
...	...	...	2	...	...	...	...	...	...	...	...	...	...	8	WOMEN
...	...	...	...	...	...	...	...	...	...	...	...	...	...	...	1816
...	...	...	...	...	...	...	...	...	...	...	...	...	...	...	WOMEN
1,339	...	...	...	...	...	...	...	...	...	...	...	...	...	...	1822
45	...	...	...	...	...	...	...	...	...	...	...	...	...	...	WOMEN
...	...	...	3,013	1	...	...	...	...	...	...	...	...	...	...	1825
...	...	...	192	...	...	...	...	...	...	...	...	...	...	...	WOMEN
...	...	...	...	...	...	...	...	...	...	...	...	...	...	194	1831
...	...	...	...	...	...	...	...	...	...	...	...	...	...	100	WOMEN
...	...	...	...	...	...	...	...	...	...	...	...	...	...	...	1850
...	...	...	...	...	...	...	...	...	...	...	...	...	...	...	WOMEN
...	...	...	...	...	...	...	...	...	...	...	...	...	...	...	1854
...	...	...	...	...	...	...	...	...	...	...	...	...	...	...	WOMEN
...	170	...	...	...	...	...	...	...	...	...	...	...	...	...	1862
...	86	...	...	...	...	...	...	...	...	...	...	...	...	...	WOMEN
...	...	...	...	...	...	...	...	...	...	...	...	...	...	...	1863
...	...	...	...	...	...	...	...	...	...	...	...	...	...	...	WOMEN
...	32	...	...	...	...	...	...	...	...	...	...	...	...	...	1864
...	17	...	...	...	...	...	...	...	...	...	...	...	...	...	WOMEN
...	...	...	...	...	...	...	...	...	...	...	...	...	...	...	1884
...	...	...	...	...	...	...	...	...	...	...	...	...	...	...	WOMEN
...	...	...	...	...	...	...	...	...	...	...	...	...	...	...	1889
...	...	...	...	...	...	...	...	...	...	...	...	...	...	...	WOMEN
...	...	...	...	...	...	...	...	...	...	...	...	...	...	...	1890
...	...	...	...	...	...	...	...	...	...	...	...	...	...	...	WOMEN
...	...	...	...	...	...	...	...	...	...	...	...	...	...	...	1894
...	...	...	...	...	...	...	...	...	...	...	...	...	...	...	WOMEN
...	...	...	...	...	...	...	...	...	...	...	...	...	...	...	1896
...	...	...	...	...	...	...	...	...	...	...	...	...	...	...	WOMEN
...	...	...	...	...	...	...	...	...	...	...	...	...	...	...	1897
...	...	...	...	...	...	...	...	...	...	...	...	...	...	...	WOMEN
...	...	...	2	...	...	...	...	...	...	...	...	...	...	14	1898
...	...	...	...	...	...	...	...	...	...	...	...	...	...	1	WOMEN
1	...	...	...	...	...	...	...	...	...	...	...	...	...	2	1899
...	...	...	...	...	...	...	...	...	...	...	...	...	...	2	WOMEN
2,389	631	111	3,753	104	123	469	1	260	109	130	524	52	...	2,298	1800
575	262	37	377	25	55	76	...	64	23	17	207	11	...	1,106	WOMEN
...	18	...	122	50	...	25	15	1	...	119	...	275	90	9	1910
...	11	...	13	14	...	6	4	...	...	22	...	33	7	1	WOMEN
...	...	...	...	...	...	...	...	...	...	...	...	...	...	...	1980
...	...	...	...	...	...	...	...	...	...	...	...	...	...	...	WOMEN
...	...	...	...	...	...	...	...	...	...	...	...	...	...	...	1981
...	...	...	...	...	...	...	...	...	...	...	...	...	...	...	WOMEN
...	...	...	...	...	...	...	...	...	...	...	...	...	...	...	1999
...	...	...	...	...	...	...	...	...	...	...	...	...	...	...	WOMEN
...	18	...	122	50	...	25	15	1	...	119	...	275	90	9	1900
...	11	...	13	14	...	6	4	...	...	22	...	33	7	1	WOMEN
1	60	1	95	25	...	140	1	6	...	91	...	19	...	71	2001
...	19	...	54	10	...	58	...	3	...	45	...	8	...	34	WOMEN
8	29	1	58	20	2	256	3	1	...	167	...	29	...	43	2003
1	7	1	26	7	1	80	...	...	...	75	...	21	...	15	WOMEN
30	215	14	116	22	1	1,226	6	18	2	209	5	13	...	392	2005
11	103	4	74	13	1	621	3	6	2	136	3	10	...	247	WOMEN
1	62	9	149	11	4	342	9	5	...	105	2	9	...	75	2010
1	33	...	99	5	1	166	2	3	...	59	1	8	...	38	WOMEN
2	5	...	9	4	...	10	...	1	...	21	...	4	...	35	2030
...	1	...	2	2	...	2	...	...	...	5	...	1	...	9	WOMEN
...	...	...	...	...	...	...	...	...	...	7	...	...	...	...	2032
...	...	...	...	...	...	...	...	...	...	1	...	...	...	...	WOMEN
...	2	...	25	2	...	4	...	...	...	27	...	1	...	...	2050
...	2	...	13	2	...	1	...	...	...	18	...	1	...	...	WOMEN

TABLE F   FULL-TIME CIVILIAN WHITE-COLLAR EMPLOYMENT BY OCCUPATION, GENDER, AND SELECTED AGENCY, ALL AREAS, SEPTEMBER 30, 1995

OCCUPATION CODES / TITLES	TOTAL ALL AGENCIES	STATE	TREASURY	ARMY	NAVY	AIR FORCE	DEFENSE LOGIS AGENCY	OTHER DEFENSE	JUSTICE	INTERIOR	AGRI-CULTURE	COM-MERCE
2091 C SALES STORE CLERICAL	2,007	...	...	17	10	3	...	1,578	...	...	...	...
WOMEN	1,788	...	...	13	7	3	...	1,394	...	...	...	...
2099 D SUPPLY STUDENT TRAINEE	27	...	...	...	17	...	2	...	...	...	...	...
WOMEN	17	...	...	...	10	...	1	...	...	...	...	...
2000 SUPPLY	39,057	66	243	10,557	7,560	7,169	5,135	2,406	352	427	258	140
WOMEN	21,347	23	87	5,333	4,171	4,033	2,862	1,731	158	214	110	73
2101 A TRANSPORTATION SPECIALST	7,248	...	99	379	115	350	21	12	18	25	43	9
WOMEN	941	...	7	145	37	78	17	7	12	2	16	7
2102 * TRANSP CLERK & ASST	5,100	14	10	1,486	1,179	1,047	635	55	23	17	40	18
WOMEN	3,609	9	6	1,061	908	600	476	42	18	13	24	15
2110 A TRANSP INDUSTRY ANALYSIS	139	...	...	...	...	...	...	...	...	...	...	...
WOMEN	56	...	...	...	...	...	...	...	...	...	...	...
2121 A RAILROAD SAFETY	415	...	...	...	...	...	...	...	...	...	...	...
WOMEN	18	...	...	...	...	...	...	...	...	...	...	...
2123 A MOTOR CARRIER SAFETY	257	...	...	...	...	...	...	...	...	...	...	...
WOMEN	73	...	...	...	...	...	...	...	...	...	...	...
2125 A HIGHWAY SAFETY	277	...	...	...	...	...	...	...	...	1	...	...
WOMEN	61	...	...	...	...	...	...	...	...	...	...	...
2130 A TRAFFIC MANAGEMENT	1,838	39	11	733	181	317	281	45	20	5	22	9
WOMEN	901	11	6	306	93	89	154	16	15	2	10	5
2131 * FREIGHT RATE	851	7	1	242	157	121	220	13	5	1	11	4
WOMEN	590	2	...	156	124	68	174	7	3	1	5	3
2135 T TRANS LOSS-DAMAGE CLM EX	168	...	...	30	55	11	49	19	...	...	...	...
WOMEN	132	...	...	28	37	9	40	16	...	...	...	...
2144 T CARGO SCHEDULING	70	...	...	12	20	31	7	...	...	...	...	...
WOMEN	23	...	...	5	12	4	2	...	...	...	...	...
2150 A TRANSPORTATION OPERATION	942	3	...	60	264	128	3	28	3	3	47	...
WOMEN	255	...	...	7	63	34	1	13	1	...	13	...
2151 C DISPATCHING	434	...	...	149	118	102	15	...	2	18	9	2
WOMEN	159	...	...	51	38	29	6	...	...	14	7	2
2152 A AIR TRAFFIC CONTROL	24,129	...	...	302	166	497	...	...	...	...	...	...
WOMEN	3,339	...	...	28	10	39	...	...	...	...	...	...
2154 T AIR TRAFFIC ASSISTANCE	461	...	...	23	3	74	...	...	...	...	...	...
WOMEN	116	...	...	4	...	9	...	...	...	...	...	...
2161 A MARINE CARGO	59	...	...	27	30	...	...	...	...	...	...	...
WOMEN	10	...	...	3	5	...	...	...	...	...	...	...
2181 T AIRCRAFT OPERATION	2,740	...	318	926	8	1,039	...	...	91	39	86	2
WOMEN	30	...	2	4	...	8	...	...	...	...	8	...
2183 T AIR NAVIGATION	276	...	...	...	...	275	...	...	...	...	...	...
WOMEN	4	...	...	...	...	4	...	...	...	...	...	...
2185 T AIRCREW TECHNICIAN	949	...	12	25	...	905	...	...	...	...	...	...
WOMEN	21	...	...	...	...	21	...	...	...	...	...	4
2199 D TRANSPORTATION STUDNT TR	25	...	...	3	4	...	...	...	...	...	...	...
WOMEN	11	...	...	...	2	...	...	...	...	...	...	...
2100 TRANSPORTATION	46,378	63	451	4,397	2,300	4,897	1,231	172	162	109	258	48
WOMEN	10,248	22	21	1,798	1,329	992	870	101	49	32	83	32
2299 9 UNSPECIFIED SERIES	343	18	...	2	8	34	1	24	...	1	...	...
WOMEN	141	6	...	2	5	10	1	20	...	...	...	...
2200 UNSPECIFIED	343	18	...	2	8	34	1	24	...	1	...	...
WOMEN	141	6	...	2	5	10	1	20	...	...	...	...

TABLE E, 1995 -- CONTINUED

LABOR	HEALTH & HUMAN SERVICES	HOUSING & URBAN DEVLPMT	TRANSPOR -TATION	ENERGY	EDUCA- TION	VETERANS AFFAIRS	LIBRARY OF CONGRESS	EPA	FDIC	GENERAL SERVICES ADM	OPM	NASA	TVA	ALL OTHER AGENCIES	OCCUPATION CODES
...	...	...	...	...	...	356	...	...	...	...	...	...	...	43	2091
...	...	...	...	...	...	332	...	...	...	...	...	...	...	39	WOMEN
...	...	...	...	...	...	...	...	...	...	8	...	...	...	...	2099
...	...	...	...	...	...	...	...	...	...	6	...	...	...	...	WOMEN
42	373	25	452	84	7	2,334	18	31	2	635	7	75	...	659	2000
13	165	5	268	39	3	1,260	5	12	2	345	4	49	...	382	WOMEN
...	3	...	6,014	23	...	...	...	...	...	37	...	15	8	77	2101
...	2	...	556	2	...	...	...	...	...	24	...	5	4	20	WOMEN
...	43	...	94	1	...	181	1	1	...	172	...	5	2	76	2102
...	39	...	76	...	...	135	1	1	...	138	...	5	2	40	WOMEN
...	...	...	86	...	...	...	...	...	...	...	...	...	...	53	2110
...	...	...	30	...	...	...	...	...	...	...	...	...	...	26	WOMEN
...	...	...	402	...	...	...	...	...	...	...	...	...	...	13	2121
...	...	...	18	...	...	...	...	...	...	...	...	...	...	...	WOMEN
...	...	...	257	...	...	...	...	...	...	...	...	...	...	...	2123
...	...	...	73	...	...	...	...	...	...	...	...	...	...	...	WOMEN
...	...	...	273	...	...	...	...	...	...	...	...	...	...	3	2125
...	...	...	60	...	...	...	...	...	...	...	...	...	...	1	WOMEN
...	10	...	28	12	...	1	3	3	...	69	...	25	...	25	2130
...	4	...	17	5	...	...	2	...	...	35	...	14	...	17	WOMEN
1	4	...	8	...	...	2	2	...	...	32	...	6	...	14	2131
...	3	...	6	...	...	1	1	...	...	22	...	5	...	9	WOMEN
...	...	...	1	...	...	...	...	...	...	2	...	...	...	1	2135
...	...	...	1	...	...	...	...	...	...	...	...	...	...	1	WOMEN
...	...	...	...	...	...	...	...	...	...	...	...	...	...	...	2144
...	...	...	...	...	...	...	...	...	...	...	...	...	...	...	WOMEN
...	...	...	71	1	...	...	...	...	...	320	...	8	...	3	2150
...	...	...	7	...	...	...	...	...	...	114	...	2	...	...	WOMEN
...	6	...	6	...	...	6	...	...	...	...	...	...	...	1	2151
...	4	...	6	...	...	2	...	...	...	...	...	...	...	...	WOMEN
...	...	...	23,164	...	...	...	...	...	...	...	...	...	...	...	2152
...	...	...	3,261	...	...	...	...	...	...	...	...	...	...	...	WOMEN
...	...	...	361	...	...	...	...	...	...	...	...	...	...	...	2154
...	...	...	103	...	...	...	...	...	...	...	...	...	...	...	WOMEN
...	...	...	...	...	...	...	...	...	...	...	...	...	...	2	2161
...	...	...	...	...	...	...	...	...	...	...	...	...	...	2	WOMEN
...	...	...	192	17	...	...	...	...	...	...	...	18	4	...	2181
...	...	...	8	...	...	...	...	...	...	...	...	...	...	...	WOMEN
...	...	...	...	...	...	...	...	...	...	...	...	1	...	...	2183
...	...	...	...	...	...	...	...	...	...	...	...	...	...	...	WOMEN
...	...	...	...	...	...	...	...	...	...	...	...	3	...	...	2185
...	...	...	...	...	...	...	...	...	...	...	...	...	...	...	WOMEN
...	...	...	11	...	...	...	...	...	...	3	...	...	...	4	2199
...	...	...	5	...	...	...	...	...	...	3	...	...	...	1	WOMEN
1	66	...	30,968	54	...	190	6	4	...	634	...	81	14	272	2100
...	52	...	4,227	7	...	138	4	1	...	336	...	31	6	117	WOMEN
...	...	1	2	...	1	18	9	3	...	...	...	...	32	189	2299
...	...	1	1	...	1	7	6	1	...	...	...	...	1	79	WOMEN
...	...	1	2	...	1	18	9	3	...	...	...	...	32	189	2200
...	...	1	1	...	1	7	6	1	...	...	...	...	1	79	WOMEN

Appendix M: White-Collar Occupations in Federal Service by Grade

One of the factors discussed in Step 1 as affecting hiring potential is *grade level*. The *educational qualifications* for various General Schedule grade levels are briefly outlined below. Note that these are not absolute requirements: Work experience can generally be substituted for education, at least in part (although not for licensed professionals, such as attorneys and physicians). For instance, three years of general or specific work experience can replace the bachelor's-degree qualification for GS-5.

> Educational and other **qualifications for some specific job categories** are outlined in Appendix B.

Grade Level	Qualifying Education
GS-1	None
GS-2	High school graduation or equivalent
GS-3	1 academic year above high school
GS-4	2 academic years above high school
GS-5	4 academic years above high school leading to a bachelor's degree *or* Bachelor's degree
GS-7	Bachelor's degree with Superior Academic Achievement* for two-grade interval positions *or* 1 academic year of graduate education or law school
GS-9	Master's or equivalent graduate degree *or* 2 academic years of progressively higher-level graduate education *or* LL.B. or J.D. (if specified)
GS-11	Ph.D. or equivalent doctoral degree *or* 3 academic years of progressively higher-level graduate education *or* (for research positions) completion of all requirements for a master's *or* equivalent degree
GS-12	(for research positions) completion of all requirements for a doctoral *or* equivalent degree

*Superior Academic Achievement means having either (1) ranked in the upper third of one's undergraduate class or major subdivision; (2) earned a B average (2.9 on a 4.0 scale) for all courses in one's total undergraduate curriculum for the last two years of attendance; (3) earned a B+ average for all courses in one's major field of study during the last two years of attendance; or (4) belonged to a national honorary scholastic society that meets the requirements of the Association of College Honor Societies (other than freshman societies).

This appendix is a detailed breakdown of Federal white-collar employment by grade level. Data indicate the *total* number of employees in the given job title by grade level (*incumbents*), *not* simply new hires. Because the Federal government tends to hire at entry level and promote from within, the higher the grade level, the less external hiring in general. Job titles that rely on such promotions are those with many employees in one or two entry-level grades but few if any at higher grades. For example, external hiring is relatively infrequent in clerical and administrative fields. It is much more prevalent for professional and technical specialists, as is shown by smoother distributions of employees among grade levels.

The *median grades* shown are useful in evaluating *promotion potential*, with higher medians indicating greater potential for promotion to an upperlevel job. The number of female employees in each job title and at each grade level is also shown.

For a very rough estimate of how many positions are likely to open up annually in each job title or occupational group *overall* (but not at any particular grade level), multiply the total number of employees by 11%—the average Federal attrition rate.

Because the Federal government periodically updates job classifications and grading, some of the material in this appendix may vary from information presented in other appendixes. The most current list of Federal job series is that appearing in Appendix K.

> **Average** and **median** grades are explained in Step 1 (p. 22).

TABLE D-1 FULL-TIME CIVILIAN WHITE-COLLAR EMPLOYMENT BY OCCUPATION, GENDER, GENERAL SCHEDULE AND RELATED GRADE, MEDIAN GRADE, AND AVERAGE GRADE, ALL AREAS, SEPTEMBER 30, 1995

| OCCUPATION | GRAND TOTAL | GENERAL SCHEDULE AND RELATED GRADES | | | | | | | | | |
CODES TITLES		TOTAL	1	2	3	4	5	6	7	8	9
GRAND TOTAL	1,569,082	1,483,419	1,060	2,274	20,138	86,186	156,648	105,723	140,646	44,086	140,385
WOMEN	768,941	717,301	714	1,328	12,615	61,908	113,619	79,359	93,427	28,249	70,497
0006 A CORRECTIONAL INST ADMIN	1,626	1,588	...	...	...	...	...	...	8	...	35
WOMEN	373	371	...	...	...	...	...	...	4	...	11
0007 O CORRECTIONAL OFFICER	11,808	11,808	...	...	...	...	1,296	1,570	3,374	3,543	1,309
WOMEN	1,365	1,365	...	...	...	...	216	225	326	331	214
0011 A BOND SALES PROMOTION	105	105	...	...	...	...	...	...	11	...	1
WOMEN	15	15	...	...	...	...	...	...	5	...	1
0018 A SAFETY & OCCL HEALTH MGT	4,254	4,235	...	...	...	...	36	...	121	1	545
WOMEN	851	847	...	...	...	...	19	...	34	...	137
0019 T SAFETY TECHNICIAN	238	238	...	...	...	8	55	43	82	13	23
WOMEN	96	96	...	...	...	7	21	29	29	3	5
0020 P COMMUNITY PLANNING	529	518	...	...	...	...	1	...	8	...	22
WOMEN	136	134	...	...	...	...	1	...	5	...	10
0021 T COMMUNITY PLANNING TECH	19	18	...	...	...	...	1	3	5	...	4
WOMEN	13	13	...	...	...	...	1	3	4	...	3
0023 A OUTDOOR RECREATION PLAN	711	711	...	...	...	...	8	...	22	...	170
WOMEN	246	246	...	...	...	...	3	...	15	...	88
0025 * PARK RANGER	6,524	5,510	10	13	96	669	989	67	579	...	2,126
WOMEN	1,836	1,832	4	5	55	248	320	21	200	...	583
0028 A ENVIRONMENTL PROTEC SPEC	5,374	5,368	...	...	...	...	37	1	172	...	736
WOMEN	2,115	2,113	...	...	...	...	18	...	99	...	285
0029 T ENVIRONMENTL PROTEC ASST	599	599	...	...	...	15	115	140	284	28	17
WOMEN	425	425	...	...	...	14	80	113	192	22	4
0030 A SPORTS SPECIALIST	620	614	...	...	...	...	33	3	237	16	226
WOMEN	100	97	...	...	...	...	6	1	51	3	28
0050 A FUNERAL DIRECTING	32	32	...	...	...	...	1	...	...	...	1
WOMEN	4	4	...	...	...	...	...	...	...	...	...
0060 P CHAPLAIN	620	619	...	...	...	...	...	...	...	...	...
WOMEN	43	43	...	...	...	...	...	...	...	...	...
0062 A CLOTHING DESIGN	39	39	...	...	...	...	...	...	2	...	10
WOMEN	23	23	...	...	...	...	...	...	1	...	7
0072 * FINGERPRINT IDENTIFICATN	813	813	...	...	...	...	80	58	401	74	33
WOMEN	514	514	...	...	...	...	48	44	302	52	19
0080 A SECURITY ADMINISTRATION	6,292	6,250	...	...	...	...	21	3	132	29	906
WOMEN	2,221	2,218	...	...	...	...	14	...	67	2	442
0081 O FIRE PROTECTION & PREVEN	10,085	10,076	1	3	85	241	2,197	3,786	1,975	597	367
WOMEN	194	184	...	...	6	10	62	44	23	24	6
0082 O UNITED STATES MARSHAL	91	72	...	...	...	...	...	...	...	...	...
WOMEN	9	8	...	...	...	...	...	...	...	...	...
0083 O POLICE	8,469	6,242	...	...	19	294	2,075	2,237	896	374	164
WOMEN	611	419	...	...	...	17	159	148	58	18	9
0084 O NUCLEAR MATERIAL COURIER	261	261	...	...	...	...	...	...	...	145	62
WOMEN	...	...	...	...	...	...	...	...	...	...	...
0085 O SECURITY GUARD	4,707	4,669	...	18	153	1,068	1,961	545	260	510	38
WOMEN	364	364	...	2	13	75	139	50	15	64	3
0086 C SECURITY CLERICAL & ASST	1,727	1,727	...	1	50	247	430	360	524	87	28
WOMEN	1,226	1,226	...	1	23	167	291	279	380	66	19
0090 T GUIDE	171	171	...	1	3	47	60	43	12	3	1
WOMEN	77	77	...	...	3	24	27	15	7	...	1
0095 P FOREIGN LAW SPECIALIST	19	18	...	...	...	...	...	...	...	...	...
WOMEN	9	9	...	...	...	...	...	...	...	...	...
0099 O GENERAL STUDENT TRAINEE	237	231	7	10	18	90	67	1	18	...	17
WOMEN	102	98	5	7	7	36	28	1	7	...	5
0000 MISCELLANEOUS OCCUPATIONS	65,968	63,531	18	46	424	2,679	9,463	8,860	9,123	5,420	6,841
WOMEN	12,958	12,741	9	15	107	598	1,452	973	1,824	585	1,880
0101 P SOCIAL SCIENCE	5,978	5,841	...	...	...	...	52	...	220	1	1,376
WOMEN	2,833	2,800	...	...	...	...	27	...	121	1	695
0102 T SOCIAL SCI AID & TECH	760	759	...	2	15	52	182	133	206	26	118
WOMEN	392	392	...	2	9	21	105	83	128	15	23
0105 A SOCIAL INSURANCE ADMIN	24,353	24,328	...	...	...	...	35	2	315	13	796
WOMEN	15,892	15,882	...	...	...	...	15	1	199	12	592
0106 A UNEMPLOYMENT INSURANCE	145	143	...	...	...	...	...	...	...	...	2
WOMEN	60	59	...	...	...	...	...	...	...	...	1
0107 A HEALTH INSURANCE ADMIN	1,537	1,536	...	...	...	...	8	...	46	...	133
WOMEN	918	917	...	...	...	...	8	...	39	...	107
0110 P ECONOMIST	5,438	4,999	...	...	...	...	9	...	97	...	152
WOMEN	1,414	1,334	...	...	...	...	3	...	38	...	53
0119 T ECONOMICS ASSISTANT	129	129	...	...	...	3	10	59	37	11	7
WOMEN	100	100	...	...	...	2	6	46	27	10	7
0130 P FOREIGN AFFAIRS	3,823	3,208	...	...	...	...	1	...	7	37	279
WOMEN	1,160	1,053	...	...	...	...	1	...	3	13	97
0131 P INTERNATIONAL RELATIONS	129	118	...	...	...	...	...	...	1	...	...
WOMEN	44	43	...	...	...	...	...	...	1	...	...
0132 A INTELLIGENCE	4,732	4,698	...	...	...	...	7	1	97	...	351
WOMEN	1,661	1,655	...	...	...	...	6	1	60	...	253
0134 C INTELLIGENCE AID & CLERK	527	527	...	...	...	4	76	70	159	50	155
WOMEN	424	424	...	...	...	4	60	62	140	41	110

TABLE D-1, 1995 -- CONTINUED

| GENERAL SCHEDULE AND RELATED GRADES | | | | | | MED GRD | AVG GRD | SENIOR PAY LEVELS | OTHER | OCCUPATION |
10	11	12	13	14	15					CODES TITLES
16,659	203,325	248,128	173,700	91,753	52,708	11.0	9.53	15,566	70,037	GRAND TOTAL
7,260	88,689	83,101	46,530	20,094	9,911	7.0	8.26	2,897	48,743	WOMEN
...	134	624	335	328	124	12.0	12.68	38	...	0006 A CORRECTIONAL INST ADMIN
...	59	142	92	48	15	12.0	12.33	2	...	WOMEN
1	642	48	25	...	...	7.0	7.42	...	...	0007 O CORRECTIONAL OFFICER
...	48	4	1	...	...	7.0	7.23	...	...	WOMEN
...	1	65	9	12	5	12.0	11.92	...	...	0011 A BOND SALES PROMOTION
...	...	7	1	1	...	12.0	10.33	...	...	WOMEN
54	1,413	1,220	539	239	67	11.0	11.34	17	2	0018 A SAFETY & OCCL HEALTH MGT
8	306	204	95	37	7	11.0	11.00	3	1	WOMEN
2	7	5	...	...	...	7.0	6.75	...	...	0019 T SAFETY TECHNICIAN
2	...	...	...	...	...	6.0	6.24	...	...	WOMEN
...	67	136	171	78	35	13.0	12.49	10	1	0020 P COMMUNITY PLANNING
...	22	41	41	10	4	12.0	11.92	1	1	WOMEN
...	4	1	...	...	...	8.0	8.33	...	...	0021 T COMMUNITY PLANNING TECH
...	1	1	...	...	...	7.0	7.77	...	...	WOMEN
...	260	162	63	21	5	11.0	10.85	...	...	0023 A OUTDOOR RECREATION PLAN
...	78	46	11	5	...	11.0	10.30	...	...	WOMEN
7	901	578	273	128	74	9.0	8.43	14	...	0025 * PARK RANGER
...	211	110	50	18	7	9.0	7.75	4	...	WOMEN
4	1,219	1,349	1,016	557	277	12.0	11.70	5	1	0028 A ENVIRONMENTL PROTEC SPEC
1	416	553	441	208	92	12.0	11.64	1	1	WOMEN
...	...	...	...	...	...	7.0	6.41	...	...	0029 T ENVIRONMENTL PROTEC ASST
...	...	...	...	...	...	7.0	6.33	...	...	WOMEN
10	45	17	1	26	...	9.0	8.44	...	6	0030 A SPORTS SPECIALIST
3	3	2	...	...	...	7.0	7.79	...	3	WOMEN
2	8	14	4	2	...	12.0	11.56	...	...	0050 A FUNERAL DIRECTING
...	1	3	...	...	...	12.0	11.75	...	...	WOMEN
...	33	464	112	8	2	12.0	12.16	1	...	0060 P CHAPLAIN
...	2	34	6	1	...	12.0	12.14	...	...	WOMEN
...	7	12	5	2	...	11.5	11.00	...	...	0062 A CLOTHING DESIGN
...	4	9	2	...	...	11.0	10.78	...	...	WOMEN
36	17	67	36	10	1	7.0	7.89	...	...	0072 * FINGERPRINT IDENTIFICATN
22	10	16	1	...	...	7.0	7.28	...	...	WOMEN
34	1,607	1,844	940	530	204	12.0	11.56	41	1	0080 A SECURITY ADMINISTRATION
16	669	639	266	87	16	11.0	11.11	2	1	WOMEN
283	274	175	83	7	2	6.0	6.55	...	9	0081 O FIRE PROTECTION & PREVEN
6	3	...	...	...	...	6.0	6.15	...	...	WOMEN
...	...	...	...	...	72	15.0	15.00	19	...	0082 O UNITED STATES MARSHAL
...	...	...	...	...	8	15.0	15.00	1	...	WOMEN
78	77	22	3	3	...	6.0	6.05	...	2,227	0083 O POLICE
6	4	1	...	...	...	6.0	5.95	...	192	WOMEN
45	9	...	...	...	...	8.0	8.69	...	...	0084 O NUCLEAR MATERIAL COURIER
...	...	...	...	...	...	0.0	0.00	...	...	WOMEN
17	18	69	7	1	4	5.0	5.45	3	35	0085 O SECURITY GUARD
...	...	3	...	...	...	5.0	5.54	...	...	WOMEN
...	...	...	...	...	...	6.0	5.83	...	...	0086 C SECURITY CLERICAL & ASST
...	...	...	...	...	...	6.0	5.89	...	...	WOMEN
1	...	...	...	...	...	5.0	5.17	...	...	0090 T GUIDE
...	...	...	...	...	...	5.0	5.04	...	...	WOMEN
...	...	...	1	11	6	14.0	14.29	1	...	0095 P FOREIGN LAW SPECIALIST
...	...	...	1	5	3	14.0	14.22	...	...	WOMEN
...	2	1	...	...	...	4.0	4.74	...	6	0099 O GENERAL STUDENT TRAINEE
...	2	...	...	...	...	4.0	4.55	...	4	WOMEN
574	6,745	6,873	3,623	1,963	879	8.0	9.37	149	2,288	0000 MISCELLANEOUS OCCUPATIONS
64	1,839	1,815	1,008	420	152	9.0	8.96	14	203	WOMEN
14	1,897	892	903	318	268	11.0	11.10	63	74	0101 P SOCIAL SCIENCE
3	911	441	397	126	78	11.0	10.96	18	15	WOMEN
3	16	6	...	...	...	6.0	6.53	...	1	0102 T SOCIAL SCI AID & TECH
2	4	...	...	...	...	6.0	6.19	...	...	WOMEN
20	16,518	4,985	1,117	539	88	11.0	11.24	25	...	0105 A SOCIAL INSURANCE ADMIN
11	11,769	2,619	440	199	25	11.0	11.13	10	...	WOMEN
...	11	49	56	11	14	13.0	12.72	2	...	0106 A UNEMPLOYMENT INSURANCE
...	7	25	19	1	6	12.0	12.49	1	...	WOMEN
...	71	454	629	152	43	13.0	12.20	...	1	0107 A HEALTH INSURANCE ADMIN
...	57	306	326	56	19	12.0	11.85	...	1	WOMEN
...	668	1,152	1,087	1,000	934	13.0	12.78	327	112	0110 P ECONOMIST
...	252	339	277	234	138	12.0	12.40	54	26	WOMEN
1	1	...	...	...	...	6.0	6.57	...	...	0119 T ECONOMICS ASSISTANT
1	1	...	...	...	...	6.0	6.67	...	...	WOMEN
...	786	549	88	649	812	12.0	12.63	609	6	0130 P FOREIGN AFFAIRS
...	283	220	47	198	196	12.0	12.36	100	2	WOMEN
...	9	12	33	28	35	14.0	13.53	11	...	0131 P INTERNATIONAL RELATIONS
...	7	6	12	9	8	13.0	12.98	1	...	WOMEN
4	665	1,548	1,353	480	192	12.0	12.13	29	5	0132 A INTELLIGENCE
1	415	472	321	105	21	12.0	11.44	3	3	WOMEN
10	3	...	...	...	...	7.0	7.32	...	...	0134 C INTELLIGENCE AID & CLERK
5	2	...	...	...	...	7.0	7.21	...	...	WOMEN

TABLE D-1 FULL-TIME CIVILIAN WHITE-COLLAR EMPLOYMENT BY OCCUPATION, GENDER, GENERAL SCHEDULE AND RELATED GRADE, MEDIAN GRADE, AND AVERAGE GRADE, ALL AREAS, SEPTEMBER 30, 1995

OCCUPATION Codes / Titles	GRAND TOTAL	GENERAL SCHEDULE AND RELATED GRADES									
		TOTAL	1	2	3	4	5	6	7	8	9
0135 P FOREIGN AGRICULT AFFAIRS	195	171	...	...	...	...	...	...	...	...	1
WOMEN	35	31	...	...	...	...	...	...	...	...	1
0136 A INTERNATIONAL COOPERATN	33	30	...	...	...	...	...	...	...	...	1
WOMEN	22	19	...	...	...	...	...	...	...	...	1
0140 P MANPOWER RESEARCH&ANALYS	35	35	...	...	...	...	...	...	...	...	1
WOMEN	16	16	...	...	...	...	...	...	...	...	1
0142 A MANPOWER DEVELOPMENT	488	479	...	...	...	...	1	...	10	...	25
WOMEN	218	218	...	...	...	...	...	...	8	...	16
0150 P GEOGRAPHY	331	327	...	...	...	...	...	10	15	...	41
WOMEN	88	89	...	...	...	...	...	5	6	...	12
0160 A CIVIL RIGHTS ANALYSIS	54	46	...	...	...	...	...	...	6	...	12
WOMEN	26	23	...	...	...	...	...	...	...	...	5
0170 P HISTORY	693	681	...	...	...	...	...	3	16	...	56
WOMEN	175	175	...	...	...	...	...	...	...	...	...
0180 P PSYCHOLOGY	3,841	3,736	...	...	...	...	...	3	17	...	173
WOMEN	1,270	1,220	...	...	...	...	...	3	8	...	18
0181 T PSYCHOLOGY AID & TECH	850	849	...	...	2	12	63	166	257	53	270
WOMEN	402	402	...	...	1	5	30	77	117	17	146
0184 P SOCIOLOGY	53	51	...	...	...	...	...	1	...	...	...
WOMEN	24	23	...	...	...	...	...	...	1	...	...
0185 P SOCIAL WORK	5,225	5,194	...	...	...	...	...	1	...	...	286
WOMEN	2,949	2,931	...	...	...	...	...	...	...	...	196
0186 T SOCIAL SERV AID & ASST	1,020	1,018	...	...	9	65	347	142	302	65	75
WOMEN	560	558	...	...	7	53	187	91	146	47	26
0187 A SOCIAL SERVICES	696	682	...	...	...	...	22	25	205	271	127
WOMEN	465	463	...	...	...	...	16	14	148	188	84
0188 A RECREATION SPECIALIST	1,780	1,774	...	...	...	...	61	14	569	54	764
WOMEN	538	537	...	...	...	...	17	8	263	18	253
0189 T RECREATION AID & ASST	1,990	1,942	26	178	552	457	545	113	68	2	...
WOMEN	831	819	8	73	261	188	216	51	21	...	...
0190 P GENERAL ANTHROPOLOGY	84	81	...	...	...	...	1	...	2	...	4
WOMEN	29	28	...	...	...	...	...	...	2	...	2
0193 P ARCHEOLOGY	1,049	1,048	...	...	...	...	39	...	116	...	233
WOMEN	382	382	...	...	...	...	21	...	54	...	102
0199 O SOCIAL SCI STUDENT TR	105	104	...	...	2	20	24	...	32	...	17
WOMEN	59	59	...	...	...	14	10	...	22	...	10
0100 SOC SCI, PSYCH & WELFARE	66,063	64,534	26	180	580	613	1,500	725	2,795	583	5,448
WOMEN	33,087	32,756	8	75	278	287	737	434	1,560	362	2,920
0201 A PERSONNEL MANAGEMENT	11,147	10,992	...	...	5	30	78	...	216	6	928
WOMEN	7,389	7,302	...	...	1	11	44	...	160	...	771
0203 * PERSONNEL CLERICAL&ASST	10,662	10,609	...	3	57	843	2,779	2,489	3,796	526	99
WOMEN	9,522	9,574	...	3	41	732	2,457	2,269	3,470	491	95
0204 * MILITARY PERS CLER&TECH	8,157	9,157	...	1	75	1,967	3,044	1,230	1,493	227	107
WOMEN	5,589	5,589	...	1	55	1,462	2,935	899	924	142	62
0205 A MILITARY PERSONNEL MGT	1,664	1,653	...	...	...	...	4	...	22	2	506
WOMEN	691	680	...	...	...	...	2	...	14	...	278
0212 A PERSONNEL STAFFING	2,416	2,412	...	...	...	...	2	...	14	...	278
WOMEN	1,917	1,914	...	...	...	...	4	...	50	...	251
0221 A POSITION CLASSIFICATION	1,404	1,402	...	...	...	...	2	...	37	...	223
WOMEN	850	848	...	...	...	...	2	...	22	...	66
0222 A OCCUPATIONAL ANALYSIS	40	40	...	...	...	...	2	...	19	...	54
WOMEN	18	18	...	...	...	...	...	...	...	...	...
0223 A SALARY AND WAGE ADMIN	146	146	...	...	...	...	...	...	...	...	22
WOMEN	86	96	...	...	...	...	2	...	4	...	...
0230 A EMPLOYEE RELATIONS	2,008	1,998	...	...	...	...	2	...	2	...	19
WOMEN	1,459	1,451	...	...	...	...	5	1	53	...	243
0233 A LABOR RELATIONS	1,246	1,243	...	...	...	...	3	1	47	...	228
WOMEN	585	585	...	...	...	...	3	...	6	52	31
0235 A EMPLOYEE DEVELOPMENT	2,371	2,348	...	...	...	...	3	...	4	52	26
WOMEN	1,547	1,532	...	...	...	...	6	...	35	...	241
0241 A MEDIATION	223	220	...	...	...	...	6	...	25	...	187
WOMEN	31	31	...	...	...	...	...	...	...	...	...
0243 A APPRENTICESHIP&TRAINING	152	152	...	...	...	...	...	...	...	...	...
WOMEN	35	35	...	...	...	...	...	...	...	...	...
0244 A LABOR MGT RELATIONS EXAM	406	405	...	...	...	...	...	...	10	...	7
WOMEN	143	142	...	...	...	...	...	...	8	...	6
0246 A CONTRACTOR INDUSTRL RELS	134	134	...	...	...	...	...	...	2	...	12
WOMEN	71	71	...	...	...	...	...	...	2	...	10
0249 A WAGE AND HOUR COMPLIANCE	1,013	1,012	...	...	...	...	7	...	51	...	29
WOMEN	369	368	...	...	...	...	3	...	26	...	13
0260 A EQUAL EMPLT OPPORTUNITY	2,546	2,520	...	...	...	...	12	...	46	...	182
WOMEN	1,732	1,716	...	...	...	...	9	...	38	...	142
0270 A FED RETIREMENT BENEFITS	483	483	...	...	...	...	2	...	17	...	142
WOMEN	327	327	...	...	...	...	1	...	14	...	106
0299 Q PERSONNEL MGT STUDENT TR	80	80	...	1	13	19	25	1	11	...	9
WOMEN	61	61	...	1	12	15	15	1	9	...	7
0200 PERSONNEL MGT & IND RELS	46,298	46,016	...	5	150	2,859	5,973	3,721	5,834	813	2,875
WOMEN	32,509	32,329	...	5	109	2,220	4,584	3,170	4,799	685	2,227
0301 A MISC ADMIN AND PROGRAM	50,665	45,983	3	9	18	103	396	52	1,372	243	7,438
WOMEN	24,275	23,050	3	7	8	75	319	38	970	171	5,095
0302 C MESSENGER	112	111	5	50	11	4	38	1	...	...	...
WOMEN	22	22	...	14	...	...	6	...	...	...	...

TABLE D-1, 1995 -- CONTINUED

GENERAL SCHEDULE AND RELATED GRADES						MED GRD	AVG GRD	SENIOR PAY LEVELS	OTHER	OCCUPATION	
10	11	12	13	14	15					CODES	TITLES
...	24	47	...	58	41	14.0	13.24	24	...	0135 P	FOREIGN AGRICULT AFFAIRS
...	6	14	...	8	2	12.0	12.42	4	...		WOMEN
...	...	12	9	7	1	13.0	12.77	...	3	0136 A	INTERNATIONAL COOPERATN
...	...	7	5	6	...	13.0	12.74	...	3		WOMEN
...	...	2	19	6	7	13.0	13.40	...	...	0140 P	MANPOWER RESEARCH&ANALYS
...	...	1	11	2	1	13.0	12.94	...	...		WOMEN
...	62	128	166	51	36	13.0	12.38	8	1	0142 A	MANPOWER DEVELOPMENT
...	38	73	63	13	7	12.0	11.93	...	...		WOMEN
...	68	126	45	14	8	12.0	11.27	4	...	0150 P	GEOGRAPHY
...	24	28	11	1	1	11.0	10.76	...	...		WOMEN
...	9	11	10	3	8	12.0	12.35	5	3	0160 A	CIVIL RIGHTS ANALYSIS
...	7	8	5	...	1	12.0	11.78	2	1		WOMEN
...	111	250	148	73	24	12.0	11.98	5	7	0170 P	HISTORY
...	40	66	26	11	3	12.0	11.44	...	...		WOMEN
1	250	678	1,948	473	193	13.0	12.69	19	86	0180 P	PSYCHOLOGY
...	138	222	601	107	29	13.0	12.30	2	48		WOMEN
10	14	2	...	...	...	7.0	7.42	...	1	0181 T	PSYCHOLOGY AID & TECH
5	4	...	...	...	...	7.0	7.46	...	...		WOMEN
...	6	10	21	8	5	13.0	12.80	1	1	0184 P	SOCIOLOGY
...	5	4	9	4	1	13.0	12.65	...	1		WOMEN
3	3,593	1,070	154	85	2	11.0	11.20	7	24	0185 P	SOCIAL WORK
2	2,113	527	66	27	...	11.0	11.12	2	16		WOMEN
2	11	...	...	...	...	6.0	6.21	...	2	0186 T	SOCIAL SERV AID & ASST
1	...	...	...	...	...	6.0	6.01	...	2		WOMEN
3	11	7	2	6	3	8.0	7.91	2	2	0187 A	SOCIAL SERVICES
2	6	2	1	2	...	8.0	7.80	...	2		WOMEN
64	205	36	6	1	...	9.0	8.51	...	6	0188 A	RECREATION SPECIALIST
18	48	11	1	...	...	9.0	8.24	...	1		WOMEN
...	...	1	...	...	...	4.0	4.00	...	48	0189 T	RECREATION AID & ASST
...	...	1	...	...	...	4.0	3.95	...	12		WOMEN
...	17	22	15	9	11	12.0	12.25	3	...	0190 P	GENERAL ANTHROPOLOGY
...	9	6	4	3	3	12.0	11.96	1	...		WOMEN
...	354	225	65	12	4	11.0	10.28	1	...	0193 P	ARCHEOLOGY
...	127	56	20	2	...	11.0	9.84	...	...		WOMEN
...	8	1	...	...	...	7.0	6.57	...	1	0199 O	SOCIAL SCI STUDENT TR
...	3	...	...	...	...	7.0	6.49	...	...		WOMEN
135	25,388	12,175	7,774	3,983	2,629	11.0	11.04	1,145	384	0100	SOC SCI, PSYCH & WELFARE
51	16,276	5,454	2,662	1,114	538	11.0	10.74	198	133		WOMEN
1	2,265	3,086	2,602	1,227	548	12.0	11.97	86	69	0201 A	PERSONNEL MANAGEMENT
1	1,775	2,200	1,539	571	229	12.0	11.74	35	52		WOMEN
8	7	...	1	1	...	6.0	6.05	...	53	0203 *	PERSONNEL CLERICAL &ASST
8	7	...	1	...	...	6.0	6.08	...	48		WOMEN
9	3	1	...	...	...	5.0	5.40	...	...	0204 *	MILITARY PERS CLER &TECH
7	1	...	...	...	...	5.0	5.34	...	...		WOMEN
12	500	441	138	29	9	11.0	10.82	1	...	0205 A	MILITARY PERSONNEL MGT
3	209	145	25	3	1	11.0	10.38	1	...		WOMEN
...	974	777	285	64	7	11.0	11.35	...	4	0212 A	PERSONNEL STAFFING
...	803	620	187	40	2	11.0	11.27	...	3		WOMEN
...	495	523	240	50	4	12.0	11.67	...	2	0221 A	POSITION CLASSIFICATION
...	326	315	111	21	...	12.0	11.48	...	2		WOMEN
...	9	23	4	3	1	12.0	12.10	...	...	0222 A	OCCUPATIONAL ANALYSIS
...	3	14	1	...	...	12.0	11.89	...	...		WOMEN
...	50	23	31	10	4	11.0	11.40	...	...	0223 A	SALARY AND WAGE ADMIN
...	32	12	14	4	1	11.0	10.98	...	...		WOMEN
...	645	620	347	81	3	12.0	11.42	...	10	0230 A	EMPLOYEE RELATIONS
...	484	422	224	40	2	11.0	11.23	...	7		WOMEN
...	223	423	346	130	29	12.0	12.09	2	1	0233 A	LABOR RELATIONS
...	136	197	124	33	10	12.0	11.58	...	...		WOMEN
...	635	802	448	150	31	12.0	11.69	1	22	0235 A	EMPLOYEE DEVELOPMENT
...	449	522	262	70	11	12.0	11.52	...	15		WOMEN
...	...	14	14	172	20	14.0	13.90	3	...	0241 A	MEDIATION
...	...	3	3	23	2	14.0	13.77	...	...		WOMEN
...	10	88	35	9	10	12.0	12.48	...	...	0243 A	APPRENTICESHIP &TRAINING
...	4	21	6	3	1	12.0	12.31	...	...		WOMEN
...	5	70	209	65	39	13.0	12.94	1	...	0244 A	LABOR MGT RELATIONS EXAM
...	2	39	73	11	3	13.0	12.31	1	...		WOMEN
...	19	45	34	18	4	12.0	12.13	...	...	0246 A	CONTRACTOR INDUSTRL RELS
...	16	23	12	6	2	12.0	11.63	...	...		WOMEN
...	69	679	102	67	8	12.0	11.80	1	...	0249 A	WAGE AND HOUR COMPLIANCE
...	35	253	22	15	1	12.0	11.54	...	...		WOMEN
...	576	750	648	210	96	12.0	11.97	14	12	0260 A	EQUAL EMPLT OPPORTUNITY
...	422	526	410	114	55	12.0	11.83	6	10		WOMEN
...	202	70	40	7	3	11.0	10.63	...	...	0270 A	FED RETIREMENT BENEFITS
...	140	40	21	3	2	11.0	10.46	...	...		WOMEN
...	1	...	...	...	...	5.0	5.21	...	...	0299 O	PERSONNEL MGT STUDENT TR
...	1	...	...	...	...	5.0	5.18	...	...		WOMEN
30	6,688	8,435	5,524	2,293	816	11.0	9.31	109	173	0200	PERSONNEL MGT & IND RELS
19	4,845	5,352	3,035	957	322	9.0	8.84	43	137		WOMEN
655	8,309	10,065	8,184	5,957	4,179	12.0	11.76	2,557	1,125	0301 A	MISC ADMIN AND PROGRAM
319	5,004	4,771	3,219	1,916	1,135	11.0	11.17	617	608		WOMEN
...	1	...	...	1	...	3.0	3.38	...	1	0302 C	MESSENGER
...	1	...	...	1	...	2.0	3.77	...	...		WOMEN

TABLE O-1   FULL-TIME CIVILIAN WHITE-COLLAR EMPLOYMENT BY OCCUPATION, GENDER, GENERAL SCHEDULE AND RELATED GRADE, MEDI N GRADE, AND AVERAGE GRADE, ALL AREAS, SEPTEMBER 30, 1995

OCCUPATION CODES TITLES	GRAND TOTAL	GENERAL SCHEDULE AND RELATED GRADES									
		TOTAL	1	2	3	4	5	6	7	8	9
0303 * MISC CLERK AND ASSISTANT	61,763	60,989	710	547	2,405	10,573	16,364	11,296	14,455	2,792	1,332
WOMEN	49,105	48,537	516	345	1,643	7,912	13,067	9,572	11,493	2,426	1,125
0304 C INFORMATION RECEPTIONIST	1,026	1,009	2	13	210	621	146	8	9	...	...
WOMEN	843	833	2	9	158	522	128	7	7	...	...
0305 C MAIL AND FILE	16,058	16,033	47	229	4,649	6,633	2,518	1,106	484	227	91
WOMEN	9,041	9,034	32	126	2,401	3,588	1,512	766	333	175	65
0309 C CORRESPONDENCE CLERK	289	288	...	...	...	68	153	32	21	7	1
WOMEN	233	233	...	...	...	50	125	27	18	6	1
0312 C CLERK-STENOGRAPHER &RPTR	222	219	...	...	1	94	83	12	2	12	9
WOMEN	213	210	...	...	1	94	80	10	2	11	9
0313 C WORK UNIT SUPERVISING	199	199	...	...	...	...	3	21	41	55	48
WOMEN	189	189	...	...	...	...	3	20	35	54	47
0318 C SECRETARY	78,151	77,667	2	...	33	4,770	29,216	22,100	12,623	5,628	2,389
WOMEN	76,252	75,772	2	...	33	4,546	28,250	21,632	12,452	5,588	2,367
0319 C CLOSED MICROPHONE RPTR	161	161	...	...	...	...	3	7	15	92	39
WOMEN	133	133	...	...	...	...	3	7	11	78	30
0322 C CLERK-TYPIST	5,338	5,056	22	118	769	3,474	303	146	120	71	21
WOMEN	4,462	4,310	18	97	662	2,992	258	117	84	56	15
0326 * OFFICE AUTOMATION CLER	17,440	17,284	31	296	2,342	9,949	3,505	814	336	9	2
WOMEN	15,459	15,313	28	244	2,029	8,784	3,169	741	309	8	1
0332 T COMPUTER OPERATION	5,600	5,577	...	1	4	180	550	730	1,992	803	786
WOMEN	2,954	2,943	...	...	2	126	320	392	1,135	411	357
0334 A COMPUTER SPECIALIST	56,212	55,859	...	...	...	1	254	2	1,222	77	4,732
WOMEN	21,927	21,796	...	...	...	1	126	2	674	22	2,381
0335 * COMPUTER CLERK & ASST	7,788	7,772	3	13	86	621	1,519	1,507	2,512	682	699
WOMEN	5,358	5,344	2	2	40	395	1,009	1,101	1,750	510	460
0340 A PROGRAM MANAGEMENT	6,961	5,278	...	...	...	...	...	...	4	1	23
WOMEN	1,796	1,401	...	...	...	...	...	...	3	1	11
0341 A ADMINISTRATIVE OFFICER	8,527	8,285	...	...	...	...	20	7	267	110	1,977
WOMEN	5,789	5,712	...	...	...	...	18	6	243	106	1,727
0342 A SUPPORT SERVICES ADMIN	4,001	3,978	...	...	...	2	67	282	1,259	523	600
WOMEN	2,065	2,053	...	...	...	1	41	194	645	313	348
0343 A MGT AND PROGRAM ANALYSIS	39,784	39,649	...	...	...	1	94	...	755	11	4,745
WOMEN	23,927	23,879	...	...	...	1	74	...	590	8	3,650
0344 * MGT & PROGRAM CLER ASST	7,282	7,278	...	1	6	84	1,242	1,573	3,848	378	101
WOMEN	6,233	6,230	...	...	4	69	1,036	1,380	3,309	326	79
0346 A LOGISTICS MANAGEMENT	10,961	10,930	...	...	...	...	14	1	191	6	806
WOMEN	3,219	3,214	...	...	...	...	11	1	132	...	336
0350 C EQUIPMENT OPERATOR	1,866	1,861	...	23	248	1,043	408	100	23	12	4
WOMEN	798	798	...	14	120	404	190	55	9	3	3
0351 C PRINTING CLERICAL	184	183	...	1	9	30	82	38	19	3	...
WOMEN	137	136	...	1	7	20	62	29	14	2	...
0356 C DATA TRANSCRIBER	3,643	3,634	10	28	776	2,348	242	47	130	22	4
WOMEN	3,280	3,272	6	18	700	2,110	223	42	125	21	3
0357 C CODING	226	226	...	1	5	80	86	37	13	4	...
WOMEN	185	185	...	...	3	61	74	36	8	3	...
0359 C ELECTRIC ACCTG MACH OPER	8	8	...	...	1	3	2	1	1	...	...
WOMEN	3	3	...	...	...	...	2	...	1	...	...
0360 A EQUAL OPPORTUNITY COMPLI	1,833	1,819	...	...	...	...	16	...	67	...	77
WOMEN	990	987	...	...	...	...	7	...	46	...	42
0361 T EQUAL OPPORTUNITY ASST	491	489	...	...	...	14	104	159	181	22	8
WOMEN	448	446	...	...	...	14	97	147	160	21	6
0362 T ELEC ACCT MACH PROJ PLAN	1	1	...	...	...	...	...	...	...	...	1
0382 C TELEPHONE OPERATING	...	...	...	...	...	...	...	...	...	...	...
WOMEN	1,622	1,619	...	7	345	1,058	111	72	22	3	1
0390 T TELECOMMUNICATIONS PROCS	1,233	1,232	...	5	262	781	93	66	21	3	1
WOMEN	922	922	1	...	12	85	199	203	183	110	65
0391 A TELECOMMUNICATIONS	329	329	...	...	9	48	69	81	70	26	19
WOMEN	7,066	7,044	...	...	...	...	25	3	173	12	1,050
0392 T GENERAL TELECOMMUNICATNS	1,681	1,675	...	...	...	...	14	3	87	7	385
WOMEN	1,338	1,338	...	...	2	77	286	250	316	124	117
0394 C COMMUNICATIONS CLERICAL	516	516	...	...	...	22	124	115	138	45	32
WOMEN	310	310	...	...	6	59	161	41	33	6	4
0399 O ADM & OFC SPRT STUDNT TR	245	245	...	...	4	43	130	36	28	3	1
WOMEN	671	651	40	41	107	219	147	6	46	1	30
0300 GEN ADM, CLER & OFC SERVS	418	405	24	28	88	138	80	3	25	...	11
WOMEN	398,721	390,710	876	1,378	12,045	42,194	58,357	40,654	42,735	12,046	27,200
	263,758	260,437	633	910	8,174	32,797	50,720	36,626	34,927	10,404	18,607
0401 P GENRL BIOLOGICAL SCIENCE	8,788	8,157	...	...	...	...	55	1	239	6	900
WOMEN	2,747	2,539	...	...	...	...	26	...	118	4	458
0403 P MICROBIOLOGY	1,984	1,783	...	...	...	...	4	...	29	1	120
WOMEN	815	745	...	...	...	...	3	...	20	1	79
0404 T BIOLOGICAL SCIENCE TECH	6,209	5,875	36	67	143	495	1,590	635	1,348	419	936
WOMEN	2,536	2,521	13	29	71	230	681	274	622	169	359
0405 P PHARMACOLOGY	402	297	...	...	...	...	...	...	...	...	2
WOMEN	111	78	...	...	...	...	...	...	...	...	2
0406 P AGRICULTURAL EXTENSION	54	50	...	...	...	...	...	...	...	...	...
WOMEN	18	17	...	...	...	...	...	...	...	...	...
0408 P ECOLOGY	760	758	...	...	...	...	5	...	22	1	86
WOMEN	229	229	...	...	...	...	2	...	8	...	50
0410 P ZOOLOGY	103	95	...	...	...	...	1	...	3	...	7
WOMEN	16	15	...	...	...	...	1	...	2	...	3
0413 P PHYSIOLOGY	474	417	...	...	...	...	1	...	1	...	15
WOMEN	106	98	...	...	...	...	1	...	1	...	3

TABLE D-1, 1995 -- CONTINUED

GENERAL SCHEDULE AND RELATED GRADES						MED GRD	AVG GRD	SENIOR PAY LEVELS	OTHER	OCCUPATION	
10	11	12	13	14	15					CODES	TITLES
330	150	20	13	1	1	5.0	5.60	...	774	0303 * MISC. CLERK AND ASSISTANT	
290	126	16	4	1	1	6.0	5.67	...	568		WOMEN
...	...	...	...	...	...	4.0	3.95	...	17	0304 C INFORMATION RECEPTIONIST	
...	...	...	...	...	...	4.0	3.98	...	10		WOMEN
29	16	4	...	...	...	4.0	4.16	...	25	0305 C MAIL AND FILE	
19	14	3	...	...	...	4.0	4.28	...	7		WOMEN
2	1	1	1	1	...	5.0	5.25	...	1	0309 C CORRESPONDENCE CLERK	
2	1	1	1	1	...	5.0	5.32	...	...		WOMEN
2	4	...	...	...	...	5.0	5.12	...	3	0312 C CLERK-STENOGRAPHER &RPTR	
1	2	...	...	...	...	5.0	5.02	...	3		WOMEN
22	8	1	...	...	...	8.0	8.14	...	...	0313 C WORK UNIT SUPERVISING	
21	8	1	...	...	...	8.0	8.17	...	...		WOMEN
612	242	46	5	1	...	6.0	5.95	...	484	0318 C SECRETARY	
611	242	43	5	1	...	6.0	5.96	...	480		WOMEN
4	...	1	...	...	...	8.0	8.08	...	...	0319 C CLOSED MICROPHONE RPTR	
3	...	1	...	...	...	8.0	8.05	...	...		WOMEN
...	10	2	...	...	...	4.0	4.07	...	282	0322 C CLERK-TYPIST	
...	10	1	...	...	...	4.0	4.05	...	152		WOMEN
...	...	...	...	...	...	4.0	4.18	...	156	0326 * OFFICE AUTOMATION CLER	
...	...	...	...	...	...	4.0	4.20	...	146		WOMEN
268	193	59	9	2	...	7.0	7.34	...	23	0332 T COMPUTER OPERATION	
110	74	14	2	...	...	7.0	7.14	...	11		WOMEN
40	11,452	20,770	11,857	4,272	1,180	12.0	11.82	71	282	0334 A COMPUTER SPECIALIST	
14	5,313	8,119	3,821	1,103	220	12.0	11.53	12	119		WOMEN
61	56	12	1	...	...	7.0	6.45	...	16	0335 * COMPUTER CLERK & ASST	
38	31	6	...	...	...	7.0	6.48	...	14		WOMEN
...	83	415	985	1,530	2,237	14.0	14.00	1,664	19	0340 A PROGRAM MANAGEMENT	
...	44	124	340	423	455	14.0	13.75	388	7		WOMEN
64	2,084	1,825	905	542	484	11.0	11.20	184	58	0341 A ADMINISTRATIVE OFFICER	
28	1,516	1,229	460	250	129	11.0	10.74	35	42		WOMEN
93	387	297	196	195	77	8.0	8.95	6	17	0342 A SUPPORT SERVICES ADMIN	
43	189	129	86	49	15	8.0	8.58	2	10		WOMEN
41	7,632	10,783	9,071	4,574	1,942	12.0	11.94	66	69	0343 A MGT AND PROGRAM ANALYSIS	
28	5,320	6,611	5,008	1,953	636	12.0	11.62	15	33		WOMEN
17	10	7	10	1	...	7.0	6.51	...	4	0344 * MGT & PROGRAM CLER ASST	
13	8	5	1	...	...	7.0	6.50	...	3		WOMEN
6	2,086	4,498	2,299	765	258	12.0	11.91	29	2	0346 A LOGISTICS MANAGEMENT	
...	758	1,294	499	143	40	12.0	11.50	4	1		WOMEN
...	...	...	...	...	...	4.0	4.24	...	5	0350 C EQUIPMENT OPERATOR	
...	...	...	...	...	...	4.0	4.26	...	...		WOMEN
1	...	...	...	...	...	5.0	5.21	...	1	0351 C PRINTING CLERICAL	
1	...	...	...	...	...	5.0	5.23	...	1		WOMEN
20	5	...	2	...	...	4.0	4.04	...	9	0356 C DATA TRANSCRIBER	
19	5	...	...	...	...	4.0	4.05	...	8		WOMEN
...	...	...	...	...	...	5.0	4.92	...	...	0357 C CODING	
...	...	...	...	...	...	5.0	4.97	...	...		WOMEN
...	...	...	...	...	...	4.5	4.75	...	...	0359 C ELECTRIC ACCTG MACH OPER	
...	...	...	...	...	...	5.0	5.67	...	...		WOMEN
...	235	838	332	187	67	12.0	12.00	14	...	0360 A EQUAL OPPORTUNITY COMPLI	
...	143	472	161	90	26	12.0	11.87	3	...		WOMEN
1	...	...	...	...	...	6.0	6.25	...	2	0361 T EQUAL OPPORTUNITY ASST	
1	...	...	...	...	...	6.0	6.22	...	2		WOMEN
...	...	...	...	...	...	9.0	9.00	...	...	0362 T ELEC ACCT MACH PROJ PLAN	
...	...	...	...	...	...	0.0	0.00	...	...		WOMEN
...	...	...	...	...	...	4.0	3.99	...	3	0382 C TELEPHONE OPERATING	
...	...	...	...	...	...	4.0	4.03	...	1		WOMEN
25	25	13	...	...	1	6.0	6.54	...	...	0390 T TELECOMMUNICATIONS PROCS	
2	5	...	...	...	...	6.0	6.06	...	...		WOMEN
17	1,531	2,085	1,464	516	168	12.0	11.60	8	14	0391 A TELECOMMUNICATIONS	
4	393	441	263	68	10	11.0	10.98	1	5		WOMEN
49	68	35	11	3	...	7.0	6.98	...	...	0392 T GENERAL TELECOMMUNICATNS	
12	24	4	...	...	...	6.0	6.67	...	...		WOMEN
...	...	...	...	...	...	5.0	5.23	...	...	0394 C COMMUNICATIONS CLERICAL	
...	...	...	...	...	...	5.0	5.22	...	...		WOMEN
1	12	1	...	...	...	4.0	4.37	...	20	0399 O ADM & OFC SPRT STUDNT TR	
1	7	...	...	...	...	4.0	4.14	...	13		WOMEN
2,360	34,600	51,778	35,345	18,549	10,593	7.0	8.42	4,599	3,412	0300 GEN ADM, CLER & OFC SERVS	
1,580	19,238	23,285	13,870	5,999	2,667	7.0	7.44	1,077	2,244		WOMEN
7	2,261	2,166	1,396	712	414	12.0	11.69	152	479	0401 P GENRL BIOLOGICAL SCIENCE	
2	842	541	351	139	58	11.0	11.13	34	174		WOMEN
6	419	366	448	236	154	12.0	12.23	19	182	0403 P MICROBIOLOGY	
3	233	171	143	63	29	12.0	11.67	3	67		WOMEN
61	124	19	2	...	...	6.0	6.43	...	334	0404 T BIOLOGICAL SCIENCE TECH	
23	43	7	...	...	...	6.0	6.34	...	15		WOMEN
...	3	16	137	94	45	13.0	13.52	13	92	0405 P PHARMACOLOGY	
...	1	6	40	21	8	13.0	13.27	...	33		WOMEN
...	...	...	7	24	19	14.0	14.24	4	...	0406 P AGRICULTURAL EXTENSION	
...	...	...	3	11	3	14.0	14.00	1	...		WOMEN
...	177	214	166	71	16	12.0	11.70	1	1	0408 P ECOLOGY	
...	80	52	25	11	1	11.0	10.98	...	...		WOMEN
...	3	13	18	25	25	14.0	13.02	7	1	0410 P ZOOLOGY	
...	1	3	...	3	2	12.0	11.00	1	...		WOMEN
2	49	55	145	89	60	13.0	12.94	15	42	0413 P PHYSIOLOGY	
2	20	18	35	12	7	13.0	12.41	...	8		WOMEN

TABLE D-1 FULL-TIME CIVILIAN WHITE-COLLAR EMPLOYMENT BY OCCUPATION, GENDER, GENERAL SCHEDULE AND RELATED GRADE, MEDIAN GRADE, AND AVERAGE GRADE, ALL AREAS, SEPTEMBER 30, 1995

OCCUPATION CODES TITLES	GRAND TOTAL	GENERAL SCHEDULE AND RELATED GRADES									
		TOTAL	1	2	3	4	5	6	7	8	9
0414 P ENTOMOLOGY	641	637	...	...	...	...	1	...	5	...	22
WOMEN	84	83	...	...	...	...	1	...	3	...	6
0415 P TOXICOLOGY	267	259	...	...	...	...	...	...	...	...	2
WOMEN	82	78	...	...	...	...	...	...	...	...	2
0421 T PLANT PROTECTION TECH	223	223	...	...	25	85	84	8	19	1	1
WOMEN	85	85	...	...	8	40	23	6	8	...	...
0430 P BOTANY	355	354	...	...	...	...	10	...	39	...	89
WOMEN	172	172	...	...	...	...	7	...	19	...	53
0434 P PLANT PATHOLOGY	281	278	...	...	...	...	...	...	2	...	11
WOMEN	52	52	...	...	...	...	...	...	...	...	4
0435 P PLANT PHYSIOLOGY	293	291	...	...	...	...	...	...	1	...	10
WOMEN	59	59	...	...	...	...	...	...	...	...	4
0436 P PLANT PROTECT & QUARANTN	1,453	1,453	...	...	...	...	43	...	61	...	609
WOMEN	319	319	...	...	...	...	16	...	21	...	138
0437 P HORTICULTURE	125	125	...	...	...	...	3	...	2	...	25
WOMEN	37	37	...	...	...	...	1	...	1	...	11
0440 P GENETICS	333	308	...	...	...	...	...	...	2	...	8
WOMEN	68	62	...	...	...	...	...	...	2	...	2
0454 P RANGELAND MANAGEMENT	1,106	1,105	...	...	...	...	10	...	41	...	380
WOMEN	204	204	...	...	...	...	5	...	14	...	118
0455 T RANGE TECHNICIAN	1,195	1,195	...	33	134	200	271	157	228	51	96
WOMEN	194	194	...	4	20	36	61	20	39	5	7
0457 P SOIL CONSERVATION	4,391	4,382	...	...	...	...	27	...	181	...	830
WOMEN	678	675	...	...	...	...	13	...	87	...	249
0458 T SOIL CONSERVATION TECH	1,545	1,545	1	1	12	50	146	416	721	165	33
WOMEN	257	257	...	...	7	21	53	102	66	6	2
0459 T IRRIGATION SYSTEM OPER	127	127	...	...	4	7	74	10	15	2	9
WOMEN	1	1	...	...	...	...	1	...	...	...	...
0460 P FORESTRY	4,690	4,651	...	...	...	...	44	...	64	...	1,285
WOMEN	886	878	...	...	...	...	7	...	19	...	427
0462 T FORESTRY TECHNICIAN	13,968	13,868	11	185	1,460	2,815	3,417	1,242	2,304	299	1,498
WOMEN	3,003	2,962	2	46	330	666	917	209	506	29	203
0470 P SOIL SCIENCE	1,449	1,444	...	...	...	...	6	...	26	...	221
WOMEN	147	147	...	...	...	...	3	...	10	...	36
0471 P AGRONOMY	287	285	...	...	...	...	...	...	4	...	26
WOMEN	22	22	...	...	...	...	...	...	...	...	7
0475 P AGRICULTURAL MANAGEMENT	3,218	3,218	...	...	...	...	20	...	109	...	1,024
WOMEN	640	640	...	...	...	...	8	...	62	...	310
0480 P GEN FISH & WILDLIFE ADM	194	175	...	...	...	...	...	...	...	...	1
WOMEN	30	27	...	...	...	...	...	...	...	...	1
0482 P FISHERY BIOLOGY	2,031	2,025	...	...	...	...	58	...	144	...	371
WOMEN	411	410	...	...	...	...	17	...	44	...	113
0485 P WILDLIFE REFUGE MGT	636	636	...	...	...	...	6	...	21	...	121
WOMEN	96	96	...	...	...	...	...	...	10	...	39
0486 P WILDLIFE BIOLOGY	2,387	2,383	...	...	...	...	49	...	156	...	534
WOMEN	611	611	...	...	...	...	19	...	69	...	221
0487 P ANIMAL SCIENCE	100	97	...	...	...	...	...	...	1	...	3
WOMEN	11	11	...	...	...	...	...	...	...	...	...
0493 P HOME ECONOMICS	23	23	...	...	...	...	...	...	2	...	4
WOMEN	21	21	...	...	...	...	...	...	2	...	3
0499 O BIOLOG SCI STUDENT TR	286	265	1	9	20	94	61	1	40	...	30
WOMEN	142	136	...	7	11	42	28	1	25	...	18
0400 BIOLOGICAL SCIENCES	60,378	58,784	49	295	1,798	3,746	5,986	2,470	5,829	945	9,309
WOMEN	14,889	14,480	15	86	447	1,035	1,894	612	1,778	214	2,928
0501 A FINANCIAL ADM & PROGRAM	8,615	8,484	...	...	...	...	56	2	320	6	1,475
WOMEN	5,090	5,061	...	...	...	...	45	2	235	5	1,131
0503 * FINANCIAL CLER & ASST	7,943	7,933	...	3	174	749	2,038	1,588	2,361	511	268
WOMEN	6,178	6,169	...	1	120	553	1,597	1,260	1,868	399	190
0505 A FINANCIAL MANAGEMENT	1,749	1,613	...	...	...	...	1	...	1	7	8
WOMEN	504	478	...	...	...	...	1	...	1	7	7
0510 P ACCOUNTING	13,585	13,269	...	...	...	...	89	...	368	64	1,272
WOMEN	6,169	6,095	...	...	...	...	62	...	245	51	772
0511 P AUDITING	14,074	13,347	...	...	...	...	38	...	246	3	320
WOMEN	4,440	4,279	...	...	...	...	22	...	129	...	180
0512 P INTERNAL REVENUE AGENT	16,100	16,100	...	...	...	...	216	...	554	...	751
WOMEN	6,354	6,354	...	...	...	...	118	...	282	...	442
0525 * ACCOUNTING TECHNICIAN	19,801	19,768	...	4	46	959	5,014	6,120	6,154	1,043	316
WOMEN	16,118	16,087	...	3	30	761	3,944	4,922	5,167	902	266
0526 T TAX TECHNICIAN	4,388	4,388	...	...	...	...	281	...	652	...	2,890
WOMEN	3,014	3,014	...	...	...	...	219	...	436	...	1,918
0530 C CASH PROCESSING	2,034	2,024	...	10	112	741	719	342	51	33	9
WOMEN	1,636	1,626	...	7	88	596	568	288	42	25	7
0540 C VOUCHER EXAMINING	3,706	3,693	...	1	58	743	1,771	700	264	128	22
WOMEN	2,754	2,744	...	...	46	535	1,296	543	198	101	19
0544 * CIVILIAN PAY	3,407	3,396	...	...	15	251	909	1,289	674	174	58
WOMEN	2,816	2,805	...	...	5	194	732	1,070	579	151	55
0545 * MILITARY PAY	3,215	3,215	...	1	49	285	1,540	709	344	192	53
WOMEN	2,113	2,113	...	1	29	185	1,024	471	229	121	29
0560 A BUDGET ANALYSIS	13,196	13,080	...	...	...	...	61	2	458	6	3,090
WOMEN	9,286	9,250	...	...	...	...	50	1	362	5	2,463
0561 * BUDGET CLERICAL & ASST	3,989	3,977	...	...	3	139	786	1,051	1,872	106	14
WOMEN	3,516	3,505	...	...	1	119	691	936	1,648	92	13
0570 A FINANCIAL INST EXAM	5,775	2,613	...	...	...	...	1	...	26	...	291
WOMEN	1,732	805	...	...	...	...	1	...	12	...	129

TABLE D-1, 1995 -- CONTINUED

10	11	12	13	14	15	MED GRD	AVG GRD	SENIOR PAY LEVELS	OTHER	CODES	TITLES
...	84	155	159	132	79	13.0	12.75	3	1	0414 P	ENTOMOLOGY
...	20	31	10	9	3	12.0	11.72	1	...		WOMEN
...	6	35	111	76	29	13.0	13.31	1	7	0415 P	TOXICOLOGY
...	2	15	32	20	7	13.0	13.09	...	4		WOMEN
...	...	...	...	...	...	5.0	4.63	...	...	0421 T	PLANT PROTECTION TECH
...	...	...	...	...	...	4.0	4.60	...	...		WOMEN
1	100	56	33	17	9	11.0	10.47	1	...	0430 P	BOTANY
1	58	24	5	3	2	11.0	9.99	...	...		WOMEN
...	31	63	82	48	41	13.0	12.82	3	...	0434 P	PLANT PATHOLOGY
...	11	17	17	2	...	12.0	11.87	...	...		WOMEN
...	41	34	93	58	55	13.0	13.04	1	1	0435 P	PLANT PHYSIOLOGY
...	12	9	26	6	2	13.0	12.34	...	...		WOMEN
...	568	84	60	28	...	11.0	10.01	...	...	0436 P	PLANT PROTECT & QUARANTN
...	118	15	7	3	...	9.0	9.69	...	...		WOMEN
...	35	22	17	16	5	11.0	11.38	...	...	0437 P	HORTICULTURE
...	11	6	5	2	...	11.0	10.73	...	...		WOMEN
...	48	47	77	74	52	13.0	12.97	16	9	0440 P	GENETICS
...	18	13	16	9	2	12.0	12.10	3	3		WOMEN
...	505	101	40	18	10	11.0	10.36	1	...	0454 P	RANGELAND MANAGEMENT
...	59	5	2	1	...	9.0	9.48	...	...		WOMEN
12	12	1	...	...	...	5.0	5.60	...	...	0455 T	RANGE TECHNICIAN
...	2	...	...	...	...	5.0	5.34	...	...		WOMEN
...	2,097	930	246	55	16	11.0	10.80	4	5	0457 P	SOIL CONSERVATION
...	244	64	12	4	2	9.0	9.79	1	2		WOMEN
...	...	...	...	...	...	7.0	6.56	...	...	0458 T	SOIL CONSERVATION TECH
...	...	...	...	...	...	6.0	5.88	...	...		WOMEN
...	3	2	1	...	...	5.0	5.84	...	...	0459 T	IRRIGATION SYSTEM OPER
...	...	...	...	...	...	5.0	5.00	...	...		WOMEN
5	1,600	711	686	173	83	11.0	10.97	39	...	0460 P	FORESTRY
...	222	83	97	16	7	9.0	10.29	8	...		WOMEN
189	384	62	2	...	...	5.0	5.73	...	100	0462 T	FORESTRY TECHNICIAN
6	42	6	...	...	...	5.0	5.33	...	41		WOMEN
...	650	270	138	76	57	11.0	11.29	5	...	0470 P	SOIL SCIENCE
...	58	21	14	3	2	11.0	10.56	...	...		WOMEN
1	88	85	46	27	8	12.0	11.78	2	...	0471 P	AGRONOMY
...	6	5	4	...	...	11.0	10.95	...	...		WOMEN
2	697	1,073	276	11	6	11.0	10.71	...	...	0475 P	AGRICULTURAL MANAGEMENT
...	145	103	12	...	...	9.0	9.77	...	...		WOMEN
...	9	14	19	68	64	14.0	13.91	19	...	0480 P	GEN FISH & WILDLIFE ADM
...	...	1	2	12	11	14.0	14.07	3	...		WOMEN
...	525	470	292	131	34	11.0	10.96	6	...	0482 P	FISHERY BIOLOGY
...	114	72	42	6	2	11.0	10.21	1	...		WOMEN
...	184	172	108	24	...	11.0	11.15	...	...	0485 P	WILDLIFE REFUGE MGT
...	26	14	7	...	...	9.0	10.06	...	...		WOMEN
1	827	428	272	92	24	11.0	10.73	3	1	0486 P	WILDLIFE BIOLOGY
...	197	62	34	8	1	9.0	9.90	...	...		WOMEN
...	15	15	21	24	18	13.0	12.97	3	...	0487 P	ANIMAL SCIENCE
...	4	2	3	2	...	12.0	12.27	...	...		WOMEN
...	5	5	6	...	1	12.0	11.22	...	...	0493 P	HOME ECONOMICS
...	5	4	6	...	1	12.0	11.29	...	...		WOMEN
...	9	...	...	...	...	5.0	5.34	...	21	0499 O	BIOLOG SCI STUDENT TR
...	4	...	...	...	...	5.0	5.46	...	6		WOMEN
287	11,559	7,684	5,104	2,399	1,324	11.0	9.19	318	1,276	0400	BIOLOGICAL SCIENCES
37	2,598	1,370	950	366	150	9.0	8.59	56	353		WOMEN
20	2,032	2,210	1,380	625	358	12.0	11.43	75	56	0501 A	FINANCIAL ADM & PROGRAM
15	1,411	1,253	650	217	97	11.0	11.02	16	13		WOMEN
152	50	39	...	...	...	6.0	6.15	...	10	0503 *	FINANCIAL CLER & ASST
118	32	31	...	...	...	6.0	6.16	...	9		WOMEN
1	52	408	412	405	318	13.0	13.28	119	17	0505 A	FINANCIAL MANAGEMENT
1	37	130	136	98	60	13.0	12.86	22	4		WOMEN
21	2,557	4,295	2,761	1,432	410	12.0	11.83	34	282	0510 P	ACCOUNTING
12	1,427	2,084	981	396	65	12.0	11.40	4	70		WOMEN
...	821	6,907	3,155	1,379	479	12.0	12.30	124	603	0511 P	AUDITING
...	308	2,654	738	200	48	12.0	11.91	11	150		WOMEN
...	3,296	4,623	5,738	902	20	12.0	11.86	...	...	0512 P	INTERNAL REVENUE AGENT
...	1,712	2,167	1,468	158	7	12.0	11.45	...	...		WOMEN
81	22	9	...	...	...	6.0	6.13	...	33	0525 *	ACCOUNTING TECHNICIAN
65	20	7	...	...	...	6.0	6.16	...	31		WOMEN
2	381	181	1	...	...	9.0	8.75	...	...	0526 T	TAX TECHNICIAN
2	285	153	1	...	...	9.0	8.76	...	...		WOMEN
7	...	...	...	...	...	5.0	4.91	...	10	0530 C	CASH PROCESSING
5	...	...	...	...	...	5.0	4.92	...	10		WOMEN
3	1	2	...	...	...	5.0	5.24	...	13	0540 C	VOUCHER EXAMINING
3	1	2	...	...	...	5.0	5.25	...	10		WOMEN
17	7	1	1	...	...	6.0	5.96	...	11	0544 *	CIVILIAN PAY
13	5	1	...	...	...	6.0	6.00	...	11		WOMEN
30	9	3	...	...	...	5.0	5.63	...	...	0545 *	MILITARY PAY
17	5	2	...	...	...	5.0	5.61	...	...		WOMEN
22	3,449	3,019	1,782	788	403	11.0	11.16	94	22	0560 A	BUDGET ANALYSIS
15	2,652	2,137	1,084	364	117	11.0	10.91	17	19		WOMEN
2	4	...	...	...	...	7.0	6.27	...	12	0561 *	BUDGET CLERICAL & ASST
2	3	...	...	...	...	7.0	6.27	...	11		WOMEN
...	226	1,078	446	484	61	12.0	12.14	42	3,120	0570 A	FINANCIAL INST EXAM
...	99	405	75	78	6	12.0	11.62	5	922		WOMEN

TABLE D-1 FULL-TIME CIVILIAN WHITE-COLLAR EMPLOYMENT BY OCCUPATION, GENDER, GENERAL SCHEDULE AND RELATED GRADE, MEDIAN GRADE, AND AVERAGE GRADE, ALL AREAS, SEPTEMBER 30, 1995

OCCUPATION CODES TITLES	GRAND TOTAL	GENERAL SCHEDULE AND RELATED GRADES									
		TOTAL	1	2	3	4	5	6	7	8	9
0580 A CREDIT UNION EXAMINER	77	...	...	...	...	...	...	...	...	...	...
WOMEN	30	...	...	...	...	...	...	...	...	...	...
0592 * TAX EXAMINING	20,723	20,723	...	...	12	848	3,582	4,474	8,715	1,617	492
WOMEN	15,519	15,519	...	...	4	588	2,572	3,443	6,440	1,277	405
0593 T INSURANCE ACCOUNTS	83	83	...	...	...	16	18	30	13	5	...
WOMEN	55	55	...	...	...	11	13	18	8	4	...
0599 O FINANCIAL MGT STUDENT TR	138	135	1	3	11	50	50	2	10	...	7
WOMEN	97	95	1	3	8	33	38	2	6	...	3
0500 ACCOUNTING AND BUDGET	142,598	137,841	1	22	480	4,781	17,170	16,309	23,083	3,895	11,336
WOMEN	87,421	96,054	1	15	331	3,575	12,993	12,956	17,887	3,140	8,029
0601 P GENERAL HEALTH SCIENCE	3,883	3,670	...	...	...	...	22	5	98	537	614
WOMEN	1,963	1,848	...	...	...	...	13	1	52	258	338
0602 P MEDICAL OFFICER	10,864	8,913	...	...	...	...	...	...	...	...	...
WOMEN	2,726	2,213	...	...	...	...	...	...	...	...	...
0603 A PHYSICIAN'S ASSISTANT	2,025	958	...	...	...	...	3	1	8	...	11
WOMEN	597	263	...	...	...	...	1	...	6	...	4
0610 P NURSE	43,752	7,427	...	...	...	12	85	...	176	3	2,646
WOMEN	38,415	6,858	...	...	...	9	71	...	158	2	2,451
0620 T PRACTICAL NURSE	12,907	12,725	...	...	322	831	5,783	5,712	75	...	2
WOMEN	11,024	10,957	...	...	243	663	4,945	5,035	69	...	2
0621 T NURSING ASSISTANT	13,811	13,774	32	75	498	5,577	7,096	488	2	6	...
WOMEN	8,983	8,956	18	49	247	3,785	4,586	269	...	2	...
0622 T MEDICAL SUPPLY AID &TECH	2,346	2,346	...	2	72	350	1,304	459	114	34	10
WOMEN	1,000	1,000	...	...	17	146	539	221	51	21	5
0625 T AUTOPSY ASSISTANT	68	68	...	...	...	11	42	15	...	...	...
WOMEN	10	10	...	...	...	3	7	...	...	...	...
0630 P DIETITIAN & NUTRITIONIST	1,644	1,591	...	...	...	...	1	1	47	...	230
WOMEN	1,542	1,494	...	...	...	...	1	1	43	...	213
0631 P OCCUPATIONAL THERAPIST	704	671	...	...	...	...	...	...	22	...	102
WOMEN	600	573	...	...	...	...	...	...	14	...	90
0633 P PHYSICAL THERAPIST	649	619	...	...	...	...	...	...	24	2	131
WOMEN	435	411	...	...	...	...	...	...	11	2	84
0635 P CORRECTIVE THERAPIST	536	536	...	...	...	...	2	5	26	...	50
WOMEN	192	192	...	...	...	...	1	2	11	...	23
0636 T REHABILITATN THERAP ASST	850	850	...	2	15	47	188	554	44	...	...
WOMEN	439	438	...	1	9	21	109	276	22	...	...
0637 P MANUAL ARTS THERAPIST	128	128	...	...	...	...	...	1	4	1	92
WOMEN	11	11	...	...	...	...	...	...	...	...	10
0638 P REC/CREATIVE ARTS THERAP	841	840	...	...	...	...	10	...	29	...	637
WOMEN	468	468	...	...	...	...	7	...	17	...	367
0639 P EDUCATIONAL THERAPIST	30	25	...	...	...	...	...	...	...	...	20
WOMEN	25	20	...	...	...	...	...	...	...	...	17
0640 T HEALTH AID & TECHNICIAN	5,472	5,462	21	25	198	785	1,172	1,407	1,327	234	196
WOMEN	3,103	3,097	4	8	96	474	848	798	658	115	66
0642 T NUCLEAR MEDICINE TECH	142	142	...	...	...	3	5	...	15	40	59
WOMEN	66	66	...	...	...	2	2	...	8	20	25
0644 P MEDICAL TECHNOLOGIST	5,725	5,724	...	...	...	...	29	...	189	4	3,546
WOMEN	3,867	3,866	...	...	...	...	20	...	129	3	2,406
0645 T MEDICAL TECHNICIAN	2,099	2,099	3	2	92	438	433	486	566	44	24
WOMEN	1,353	1,353	2	1	64	301	291	322	336	20	11
0646 T PATHOLOGY TECHNICIAN	499	497	...	...	1	2	28	69	266	53	55
WOMEN	347	345	...	...	1	2	14	46	189	41	39
0647 T DIAGNOSTIC RADIOL TECH	3,166	3,164	...	...	...	1	189	951	749	864	217
WOMEN	1,558	1,557	...	...	...	1	90	517	374	417	102
0648 T THERAPEUTIC RADIOL TECH	124	124	...	...	...	...	3	4	14	63	22
WOMEN	77	77	...	...	...	...	2	...	9	39	14
0649 T MEDICAL INSTRUMENT TECH	2,156	2,156	...	...	8	56	238	583	523	526	149
WOMEN	1,313	1,313	...	...	6	36	159	359	313	329	83
0650 T MEDICAL TECHNICAL ASST	3	3	...	...	...	...	1	...	1	1	...
WOMEN	2	2	...	...	...	...	1	...	1	1	...
0651 T RESPIRATORY THERAPIST	457	456	...	...	...	8	11	143	220	45	16
WOMEN	205	204	...	...	...	2	5	74	96	18	5
0660 P PHARMACIST	4,578	4,397	...	...	...	...	...	...	...	...	52
WOMEN	1,970	1,843	...	...	...	...	...	...	...	...	31
0661 T PHARMACY TECHNICIAN	3,618	3,615	3	3	89	311	2,764	367	67	9	2
WOMEN	2,476	2,474	2	1	53	202	1,930	242	38	4	2
0662 P OPTOMETRIST	224	139	...	...	...	...	...	...	...	...	...
WOMEN	75	32	...	...	...	...	...	...	...	...	...
0664 T RESTORATION TECHNICIAN	16	16	...	...	...	...	...	...	...	...	4
WOMEN	2	2	...	...	...	...	...	...	...	...	1
0665 P SPEECH PATHOLGY AUDIOLGY	754	722	...	...	...	...	...	...	...	...	19
WOMEN	478	449	...	...	...	...	...	...	...	...	17
0667 T ORTHOTIST & PROSTHETIST	222	222	...	...	...	2	4	...	26	2	102
WOMEN	14	14	...	...	...	...	...	...	6	1	3
0668 P PODIATRIST	253	93	...	...	...	...	...	...	...	...	...
WOMEN	75	12	...	...	...	...	...	...	...	...	...
0669 A MEDICAL RECORDS ADMIN	540	540	...	...	...	...	5	1	57	6	180
WOMEN	475	475	...	...	...	...	4	1	47	5	151
0670 A HEALTH SYSTEM ADMIN	595	432	...	...	...	...	...	...	16	...	6
WOMEN	160	144	...	...	...	...	...	...	12	...	2
0671 A HEALTH SYSTEM SPECIALIST	1,583	1,580	...	...	...	...	5	3	46	1	317
WOMEN	837	837	...	...	...	...	5	3	35	...	211
0672 T PROSTHETIC REPRESENTATIV	205	205	...	...	...	...	5	...	16	...	32
WOMEN	64	64	...	...	...	...	4	...	8	...	17

TABLE D-1, 1995 -- CONTINUED

GENERAL SCHEDULE AND RELATED GRADES						MED GRD	AVG GRD	SENIOR PAY LEVELS	OTHER	OCCUPATION	
10	11	12	13	14	15					CODES	TITLES
...	...	...	...	...	...	0.0	0.00	6	71	0580 A	CREDIT UNION EXAMINER
...	...	...	...	...	...	0.0	0.00	1	29		WOMEN
701	141	139	2	...	...	7.0	6.60	...	...	0592 *	TAX EXAMINING
554	119	115	2	...	...	7.0	6.64	...	...		WOMEN
...	1	...	...	...	...	6.0	5.73	...	...	0593 T	INSURANCE ACCOUNTS
...	1	...	...	...	...	6.0	5.75	...	...		WOMEN
...	1	...	...	...	...	5.0	4.79	...	3	0599 O	FINANCIAL MGT STUDENT TR
...	1	...	...	...	...	5.0	4.68	...	2		WOMEN
1,059	13,050	22,914	15,678	6,015	2,048	9.0	9.05	494	4,263	0500	ACCOUNTING AND BUDGET
822	8,118	11,141	5,135	1,511	400	7.0	8.20	76	1,291		WOMEN
97	550	380	481	555	331	11.0	11.23	74	139	0601 P	GENERAL HEALTH SCIENCE
46	298	216	271	232	123	11.0	11.09	23	92		WOMEN
...	1	99	281	1,091	7,441	15.0	14.78	270	1,681	0602 P	MEDICAL OFFICER
...	1	19	106	400	1,687	15.0	14.70	44	469		WOMEN
18	876	40	1	...	...	11.0	10.94	...	1,067	0603 A	PHYSICIAN'S ASSISTANT
17	219	15	1	...	...	11.0	10.86	...	334		WOMEN
1,725	2,039	578	129	30	4	10.0	10.01	5	36,320	0610 P	NURSE
1,598	1,879	533	126	27	4	10.0	10.02	3	31,554		WOMEN
...	...	...	...	...	...	5.0	5.35	...	82	0620 T	PRACTICAL NURSE
...	...	...	...	...	...	5.0	5.37	...	67		WOMEN
...	...	...	...	...	...	5.0	4.53	...	37	0621 T	NURSING ASSISTANT
...	...	...	...	...	...	5.0	4.53	...	27		WOMEN
...	1	...	...	...	...	5.0	5.14	...	...	0622 T	MEDICAL SUPPLY AID &TECH
...	...	...	...	...	...	5.0	5.23	...	...		WOMEN
...	...	...	...	...	...	5.0	5.06	...	...	0625 T	AUTOPSY ASSISTANT
...	...	...	...	...	...	5.0	4.70	...	...		WOMEN
55	789	227	158	74	9	11.0	11.05	1	52	0630 P	DIETITIAN & NUTRITIONIST
53	756	210	141	70	6	11.0	11.04	...	48		WOMEN
182	289	73	1	2	...	11.0	10.41	...	33	0631 P	OCCUPATIONAL THERAPIST
148	254	65	1	1	...	11.0	10.45	...	27		WOMEN
171	212	79	...	...	...	10.0	10.26	...	30	0633 P	PHYSICAL THERAPIST
118	150	46	...	...	...	10.0	10.29	...	24		WOMEN
341	95	17	...	...	...	10.0	9.95	...	...	0635 P	CORRECTIVE THERAPIST
130	22	3	...	...	...	10.0	9.79	...	...		WOMEN
...	...	...	...	...	...	6.0	5.66	...	...	0636 T	REHABILITATN THERAP ASST
...	...	...	...	...	...	6.0	5.63	...	...		WOMEN
10	20	...	...	...	...	9.0	9.30	...	...	0637 P	MANUAL ARTS THERAPIST
1	...	...	...	...	...	9.0	9.09	...	...		WOMEN
38	79	42	3	1	1	9.0	9.29	...	1	0638 P	REC/CREATIVE ARTS THERAP
18	42	15	1	1	...	9.0	9.20	...	...		WOMEN
4	1	...	...	...	...	9.0	9.24	...	5	0639 P	EDUCATIONAL THERAPIST
2	1	...	...	...	...	9.0	9.20	...	5		WOMEN
49	45	3	...	...	...	6.0	5.87	...	10	0640 T	HEALTH AID & TECHNICIAN
10	20	...	...	...	...	6.0	5.71	...	6		WOMEN
12	6	2	...	...	...	9.0	8.47	...	...	0642 T	NUCLEAR MEDICINE TECH
6	3	...	...	...	...	9.0	8.36	...	...		WOMEN
363	1,261	270	60	1	1	9.0	9.60	...	1	0644 P	MEDICAL TECHNOLOGIST
244	851	174	37	1	1	9.0	9.59	...	1		WOMEN
2	9	...	...	...	...	6.0	5.61	...	...	0645 T	MEDICAL TECHNICIAN
2	3	...	...	...	...	6.0	5.51	...	...		WOMEN
9	13	1	...	...	...	7.0	7.23	...	2	0646 T	PATHOLOGY TECHNICIAN
5	7	1	...	...	...	7.0	7.24	...	2		WOMEN
104	71	17	1	...	...	7.0	7.21	...	2	0647 T	DIAGNOSTIC RADIOL TECH
33	17	6	...	...	...	7.0	7.08	...	1		WOMEN
8	6	4	...	...	...	8.0	8.33	...	...	0648 T	THERAPEUTIC RADIOL TECH
6	4	3	...	...	...	8.0	8.45	...	...		WOMEN
49	22	2	...	...	...	7.0	6.91	...	...	0649 T	MEDICAL INSTRUMENT TECH
18	9	1	...	...	...	7.0	6.83	...	...		WOMEN
...	...	...	...	...	...	7.0	6.67	...	...	0650 T	MEDICAL TECHNICAL ASST
...	...	...	...	...	...	7.5	7.50	...	...		WOMEN
9	4	...	...	...	...	7.0	6.85	...	1	0651 T	RESPIRATORY THERAPIST
3	1	...	...	...	...	7.0	6.76	...	1		WOMEN
...	2,782	1,118	331	94	20	11.0	11.46	1	180	0660 P	PHARMACIST
...	1,189	500	107	15	1	11.0	11.38	...	127		WOMEN
...	...	...	...	...	...	5.0	5.01	...	3	0661 T	PHARMACY TECHNICIAN
...	...	...	...	...	...	5.0	5.01	...	2		WOMEN
...	10	22	30	34	43	14.0	13.56	1	84	0662 P	OPTOMETRIST
...	1	10	13	5	3	13.0	12.97	...	43		WOMEN
4	8	...	...	...	...	10.5	10.25	...	...	0664 T	RESTORATION TECHNICIAN
...	1	...	...	...	...	10.0	10.00	...	...		WOMEN
...	100	428	119	49	7	12.0	12.11	...	32	0665 P	SPEECH PATHOLGY AUDIOLGY
...	82	283	~51	15	1	12.0	11.89	...	29		WOMEN
37	34	13	2	...	...	9.0	9.32	...	...	0667 T	ORTHOTIST & PROSTHETIST
2	1	1	...	...	...	8.5	8.57	...	...		WOMEN
...	1	13	13	26	40	14.0	13.98	2	158	0668 P	PODIATRIST
...	...	2	3	3	4	14.0	13.75	1	62		WOMEN
52	147	76	12	4	...	10.0	9.92	...	...	0669 A	MEDICAL RECORDS ADMIN
49	134	69	11	4	...	10.0	9.99	...	...		WOMEN
...	12	76	111	114	97	13.0	13.20	159	4	0670 A	HEALTH SYSTEM ADMIN
...	6	25	41	34	24	13.0	12.76	13	3		WOMEN
5	320	285	479	94	25	12.0	11.48	3	...	0671 A	HEALTH SYSTEM SPECIALIST
3	198	133	207	31	11	11.0	11.09	...	...		WOMEN
3	48	58	39	4	...	11.0	10.94	...	...	0672 T	PROSTHETIC REPRESENTATIV
1	21	10	3	...	...	11.0	9.83	...	...		WOMEN

TABLE D-1 FULL-TIME CIVILIAN WHITE-COLLAR EMPLOYMENT BY OCCUPATION, GENDER, GENERAL SCHEDULE AND RELATED GRADE, MEDIAN GRADE, AND AVERAGE GRADE, ALL AREAS, SEPTEMBER 30, 1995

OCCUPATION — CODES TITLES	GRAND TOTAL	GENERAL SCHEDULE AND RELATED GRADES									
		TOTAL	1	2	3	4	5	6	7	8	9
0673 A HOSPITAL HOUSEKEEPNG MGT	306	305	...	...	...	...	2	...	14	3	27
WOMEN	45	45	...	...	...	...	1	...	6	1	7
0675 T MEDICAL RECORDS TECH	3,269	3,268	...	1	149	621	1,094	968	334	94	16
WOMEN	2,760	2,759	...	1	116	479	932	839	293	84	15
0679 C MEDICAL CLERK	11,701	11,695	8	28	616	7,866	2,671	255	150	71	24
WOMEN	9,396	9,392	5	23	493	6,292	2,164	212	119	58	20
0680 P DENTAL OFFICER	847	818	...	...	...	...	...	...	...	...	...
WOMEN	99	87	...	...	...	...	...	...	...	...	...
0681 T DENTAL ASSISTANT	2,704	2,703	3	16	92	828	1,404	313	44	3	...
WOMEN	2,533	2,532	3	16	90	761	1,324	293	42	3	...
0682 T DENTAL HYGIENE	339	339	...	...	1	3	11	98	141	74	10
WOMEN	326	326	...	...	1	3	11	94	137	70	9
0683 T DENTAL LAB AID & TECH	703	703	...	...	1	3	12	35	95	352	176
WOMEN	117	117	...	...	1	1	3	14	29	54	14
0685 A PUB HEALTH PROGRAM SPEC	1,601	1,560	...	...	...	...	2	...	8	...	217
WOMEN	769	753	...	...	...	...	2	...	6	...	120
0688 A SANITARIAN	40	40	...	...	...	...	1	...	2	...	12
WOMEN	13	13	...	...	...	...	1	...	1	...	4
0690 P INDUSTRIAL HYGIENE	1,513	1,511	...	...	...	...	18	...	27	...	48
WOMEN	475	475	...	...	...	...	10	...	11	...	19
0696 P CONSUMER SAFETY	1,916	1,899	...	...	...	...	5	...	42	...	102
WOMEN	741	737	...	...	...	...	3	...	20	...	40
0698 T ENVIRONMENTL HEALTH TECH	161	161	...	...	1	2	23	15	42	10	53
WOMEN	38	38	...	...	...	1	9	3	10	3	11
0699 O MEDICAL HEALTH STUDNT TR	150	68	...	13	4	18	9	...	6	3	9
WOMEN	111	45	...	12	4	10	6	...	5	3	4
0600 MED HOSP DENT PUB HEALTH	152,619	111,999	70	167	2,150	7,775	24,680	12,939	5,672	3,085	10,237
WOMEN	104,369	71,257	34	112	1,441	13,194	18,120	9,622	3,392	1,574	7,053
0701 P VETERINARY MEDICAL SCI	1,952	1,924	...	...	...	...	...	...	...	...	12
WOMEN	353	349	...	...	...	...	...	...	...	...	8
0704 T ANIMAL HEALTH TECHNICIAN	393	393	...	...	...	7	21	1	24	258	71
WOMEN	63	63	...	...	...	3	7	1	9	28	15
0799 O VETERINARY STUDENT TR	3	3	...	...	...	...	...	...	2	...	...
WOMEN	2	2	...	...	...	...	...	...	1	...	...
0700 VETERINARY MEDICAL SCI	2,348	2,320	...	...	...	7	21	1	26	258	83
WOMEN	418	414	...	...	...	3	7	1	10	28	23
0801 P GENERAL ENGINEERING	20,469	19,684	...	...	...	...	7	...	69	...	161
WOMEN	1,928	1,891	...	...	...	...	2	...	23	...	59
0802 T ENGINEERING TECHNICIAN	20,529	20,522	1	27	76	220	465	420	1,315	985	4,270
WOMEN	2,148	2,148	...	6	18	51	144	108	325	197	502
0803 P SAFETY ENGINEERING	555	555	...	...	...	...	...	...	1	1	14
WOMEN	42	42	...	...	...	...	...	...	...	1	3
0804 P FIRE PROTECTION ENGINEER	165	165	...	...	...	...	2	...	2	...	5
WOMEN	22	22	...	...	...	...	...	...	...	...	...
0806 P MATERIALS ENGINEERING	1,171	1,162	...	...	...	...	...	...	15	...	16
WOMEN	167	167	...	...	...	...	...	...	4	...	3
0807 P LANDSCAPE ARCHITECTURE	706	706	...	...	...	...	4	...	19	...	77
WOMEN	203	203	...	...	...	...	3	...	7	...	46
0808 P ARCHITECTURE	2,026	2,026	...	...	...	...	7	...	20	...	58
WOMEN	301	301	...	...	...	...	2	...	6	...	20
0809 T CONSTRUCTION CONTROL	2,805	2,805	...	...	1	27	39	48	372	306	887
WOMEN	85	85	...	...	...	3	3	6	9	12	27
0810 P CIVIL ENGINEERING	13,361	13,315	...	...	...	...	60	...	235	...	440
WOMEN	1,313	1,313	...	...	...	...	14	...	69	...	123
0817 T SURVEYING TECHNICIAN	896	896	...	7	89	138	178	143	145	95	73
WOMEN	50	50	...	3	8	8	8	5	12	2	3
0818 T ENGINEERING DRAFTING	499	499	...	...	5	41	93	142	177	15	17
WOMEN	109	109	...	...	1	8	26	32	33	4	3
0819 P ENVIRONMENTAL ENGINEERNG	5,525	5,520	...	...	...	...	11	...	102	...	182
WOMEN	1,199	1,197	...	...	...	...	4	...	35	...	75
0828 A CONSTRUCTION ANALYST	515	515	...	...	...	...	2	...	4	...	66
WOMEN	44	44	...	...	...	...	1	...	2	...	6
0830 P MECHANICAL ENGINEERING	11,413	11,397	...	...	...	...	19	...	152	...	236
WOMEN	760	760	...	...	...	...	1	...	26	...	51
0840 P NUCLEAR ENGINEERING	2,709	2,594	...	...	...	...	...	...	...	...	3
WOMEN	149	148	...	...	...	...	...	...	...	...	2
0850 P ELECTRICAL ENGINEERING	4,948	4,940	...	...	...	...	9	...	73	...	106
WOMEN	446	446	...	...	...	...	3	...	13	...	21
0854 P COMPUTER ENGINEERING	2,495	2,488	...	...	...	...	6	...	71	5	54
WOMEN	474	474	...	...	...	...	...	...	9	...	21
0855 P ELECTRONICS ENGINEERING	26,399	26,302	...	...	...	...	26	...	264	...	339
WOMEN	2,137	2,134	...	...	...	...	8	...	44	...	69
0856 T ELECTRONICS TECHNICIAN	12,133	12,133	...	...	...	39	73	49	233	173	1,794
WOMEN	727	727	...	...	...	19	25	8	45	34	174
0858 P BIOMEDICAL ENGINEERING	343	336	...	...	...	...	2	...	9	...	25
WOMEN	78	78	...	...	...	...	...	...	3	...	11
0861 P AEROSPACE ENGINEERING	8,425	8,328	...	...	...	...	2	...	81	...	131
WOMEN	823	822	...	...	...	...	...	...	19	...	29
0871 P NAVAL ARCHITECTURE	905	900	...	...	...	...	...	...	3	...	10
WOMEN	68	68	...	...	...	...	...	...	...	...	3
0873 A SHIP SURVEYING	148	148	...	...	...	...	...	...	...	...	...
WOMEN	1	1	...	...	...	...	...	...	...	...	...

TABLE D-1, 1995 -- CONTINUED

10	11	12	13	14	15	MED GRD	AVG GRD	SENIOR PAY LEVELS	OTHER	OCCUPATION CODES TITLES
9	68	89	78	15	...	12.0	11.49	...	1	0673 A HOSPITAL HOUSEKEEPNG MGT
2	12	12	4	...	...	11.0	10.36	...	...	WOMEN
...	...	...	...	...	...	5.0	5.33	...	1	0675 T MEDICAL RECORDS TECH
...	...	...	...	...	...	5.0	5.37	...	1	WOMEN
6	...	...	...	...	...	4.0	4.29	...	6	0679 C MEDICAL CLERK
6	...	...	...	...	...	4.0	4.29	...	4	WOMEN
...	8	51	27	62	670	15.0	14.63	7	22	0680 P DENTAL OFFICER
...	5	12	13	18	39	14.0	13.85	...	12	WOMEN
...	...	...	...	...	...	5.0	4.76	...	1	0681 T DENTAL ASSISTANT
...	...	...	...	...	...	5.0	4.76	...	1	WOMEN
...	1	...	...	...	...	7.0	6.90	...	...	0682 T DENTAL HYGIENE
...	1	...	...	...	...	7.0	6.89	...	...	WOMEN
19	8	1	1	...	...	8.0	8.04	...	...	0683 T DENTAL LAB AID & TECH
1	...	...	...	...	...	8.0	7.50	...	...	WOMEN
...	148	236	570	254	125	13.0	12.38	12	29	0685 A PUB HEALTH PROGRAM SPEC
...	86	131	260	96	52	13.0	12.16	4	12	WOMEN
...	11	12	1	1	...	11.0	10.48	...	...	0688 A SANITARIAN
...	6	1	...	...	...	11.0	9.69	...	...	WOMEN
4	377	605	321	85	26	12.0	11.85	1	1	0690 P INDUSTRIAL HYGIENE
...	149	177	81	22	6	12.0	11.60	...	...	WOMEN
...	371	449	669	191	70	12.0	12.18	17	...	0696 P CONSUMER SAFETY
...	177	179	256	50	12	12.0	11.96	4	...	WOMEN
7	5	3	...	...	...	7.0	7.63	...	...	0698 T ENVIRONMENTL HEALTH TECH
1	...	...	...	...	...	7.0	7.11	...	...	WOMEN
2	3	1	...	...	...	4.0	5.40	...	82	0699 O MEDICAL HEALTH STUDNT TR
...	1	...	...	...	...	4.0	4.71	...	66	WOMEN
3,394	10,851	5,370	3,918	2,781	8,910	6.0	7.83	553	40,067	0600 MED HOSP DENT PUB HEALTH
2,523	6,607	2,852	1,734	1,025	1,974	6.0	7.07	92	33,020	WOMEN
...	203	1,062	371	213	63	12.0	12.39	17	11	0701 P VETERINARY MEDICAL SCI
...	52	167	77	43	2	12.0	12.27	1	3	WOMEN
7	3	1	...	...	...	8.0	7.95	...	...	0704 T ANIMAL HEALTH TECHNICIAN
...	...	...	...	...	...	8.0	7.54	...	...	WOMEN
...	1	...	...	...	...	7.0	8.33	...	...	0799 O VETERINARY STUDENT TR
...	1	...	...	...	...	9.0	9.00	...	...	WOMEN
7	207	1,063	371	213	63	12.0	11.63	17	11	0700 VETERINARY MEDICAL SCI
...	53	167	77	43	2	12.0	11.53	1	3	WOMEN
...	661	3,469	7,433	5,004	2,880	13.0	13.25	658	127	0801 P GENERAL ENGINEERING
...	100	374	857	344	132	13.0	12.81	31	6	WOMEN
1,744	6,987	3,446	518	42	6	11.0	9.97	6	...	0802 T ENGINEERING TECHNICIAN
167	487	131	10	2	...	9.0	8.74	...	...	WOMEN
...	55	178	197	78	31	13.0	12.61	...	...	0803 P SAFETY ENGINEERING
...	9	14	14	1	...	12.0	11.86	...	...	WOMEN
...	18	34	65	32	7	13.0	12.56	...	...	0804 P FIRE PROTECTION ENGINEER
...	4	8	9	1	...	12.0	12.32	...	...	WOMEN
...	81	370	388	181	111	13.0	12.76	9	...	0806 P MATERIALS ENGINEERING
...	12	78	51	15	4	12.0	12.31	...	...	WOMEN
...	241	209	124	22	10	12.0	11.44	...	...	0807 P LANDSCAPE ARCHITECTURE
...	97	38	8	4	...	11.0	10.65	...	...	WOMEN
...	339	913	464	184	41	12.0	12.14	...	...	0808 P ARCHITECTURE
...	61	120	61	28	3	12.0	11.87	...	...	WOMEN
151	715	177	48	32	2	9.0	9.35	...	...	0809 T CONSTRUCTION CONTROL
1	16	5	1	1	1	9.0	8.86	...	...	WOMEN
...	2,608	5,216	3,143	1,124	489	12.0	12.10	39	7	0810 P CIVIL ENGINEERING
...	412	498	164	30	3	12.0	11.25	...	...	WOMEN
8	14	6	...	...	...	6.0	5.94	...	...	0817 T SURVEYING TECHNICIAN
1	...	...	...	...	...	5.0	5.38	...	...	WOMEN
3	5	1	...	...	...	6.0	6.22	...	...	0818 T ENGINEERING DRAFTING
2	...	...	...	...	...	6.0	6.12	...	...	WOMEN
...	642	2,142	1,737	524	180	12.0	12.28	5	...	0819 P ENVIRONMENTAL ENGINEERNG
...	147	481	381	65	9	12.0	11.97	2	...	WOMEN
...	218	186	34	5	...	11.0	11.21	...	...	0828 A CONSTRUCTION ANALYST
...	23	12	...	...	...	11.0	10.68	...	...	WOMEN
...	1,376	5,646	2,939	760	269	12.0	12.20	13	3	0830 P MECHANICAL ENGINEERING
...	117	421	132	8	4	12.0	11.68	...	...	WOMEN
...	75	1,223	559	415	319	12.0	12.87	107	8	0840 P NUCLEAR ENGINEERING
...	9	74	37	20	6	12.0	12.54	1	...	WOMEN
...	836	2,141	1,325	369	81	12.0	12.15	7	1	0850 P ELECTRICAL ENGINEERING
...	82	218	97	10	2	12.0	11.76	...	...	WOMEN
...	125	786	953	351	137	13.0	12.55	6	1	0854 P COMPUTER ENGINEERING
...	29	160	195	46	14	13.0	12.41	...	...	WOMEN
...	1,711	11,433	8,256	2,892	1,381	12.0	12.53	95	2	0855 P ELECTRONICS ENGINEERING
...	215	1,104	566	102	26	12.0	12.07	3	...	WOMEN
714	4,842	3,345	776	89	6	11.0	10.87	...	...	0856 T ELECTRONICS TECHNICIAN
39	263	78	39	3	...	11.0	9.86	...	...	WOMEN
1	55	93	114	23	14	12.0	12.03	...	7	0858 P BIOMEDICAL ENGINEERING
...	19	23	2	...	...	12.0	11.45	...	...	WOMEN
...	316	1,918	3,201	1,715	964	13.0	13.01	95	2	0861 P AEROSPACE ENGINEERING
...	52	197	388	101	36	13.0	12.56	1	...	WOMEN
...	98	305	268	142	74	13.0	12.70	5	...	0871 P NAVAL ARCHITECTURE
...	8	25	28	3	1	12.0	12.29	...	...	WOMEN
1	18	61	60	8	...	12.0	12.38	...	...	0873 A SHIP SURVEYING
...	...	...	1	...	...	13.0	13.00	...	...	WOMEN

TABLE D-1 FULL-TIME CIVILIAN WHITE-COLLAR EMPLOYMENT BY OCCUPATION, GENDER, GENERAL SCHEDULE AND RELATED GRADE, MEDIAN GRADE, AND AVERAGE GRADE, ALL AREAS, SEPTEMBER 30, 1995

OCCUPATION CODES TITLES	GRAND TOTAL	GENERAL SCHEDULE AND RELATED GRADES									
		TOTAL	1	2	3	4	5	6	7	8	9
0880 P MINING ENGINEERING	339	339	...	...	...	...	1	...	2	...	2
WOMEN	17	17	...	...	...	...	1	...	1	...	...
0881 P PETROLEUM ENGINEERING	349	349	...	...	...	...	1	...	...	...	1
WOMEN	29	29	...	...	...	...	...	...	...	...	...
0890 P AGRICULTURAL ENGINEERING	381	377	...	...	...	...	2	...	19	...	55
WOMEN	39	38	...	...	...	...	2	...	9	...	18
0892 P CERAMIC ENGINEERING	54	54	...	...	...	...	...	...	...	...	...
WOMEN	8	8	...	...	...	...	...	...	...	...	...
0893 P CHEMICAL ENGINEERING	1,286	1,278	...	...	...	...	3	...	26	...	31
WOMEN	235	232	...	...	...	...	2	...	11	...	10
0894 P WELDING ENGINEERING	62	62	...	...	...	...	...	...	...	...	...
WOMEN	3	3	...	...	...	...	...	...	...	...	...
0895 T INDUSTRIAL ENGINEER TECH	1,600	1,600	...	...	...	2	1	13	24	45	513
WOMEN	252	252	...	...	...	1	...	10	5	7	107
0896 P INDUSTRIAL ENGINEERING	1,964	1,963	...	...	...	...	1	...	32	...	38
WOMEN	322	322	...	...	...	...	...	...	10	...	17
0899 O ENGINR & ARCH STUDNT TR	650	649	...	9	54	258	200	14	51	24	31
WOMEN	186	186	...	1	14	84	47	3	16	8	10
0800 ENGINEERNG & ARCHITECTURE	145,824	144,607	1	43	225	725	1,214	829	3,516	1,649	9,635
WOMEN	14,365	14,317	...	10	41	174	296	172	736	265	1,413
0904 P LAW CLERK	282	281	...	...	...	...	1	...	5	...	14
WOMEN	149	149	...	...	...	...	1	...	4	...	5
0905 P GENERAL ATTORNEY	25,540	19,433	...	...	...	...	...	...	...	...	99
WOMEN	9,390	7,534	...	...	...	...	...	...	...	...	64
0920 A ESTATE TAX EXAMINING	1	1	...	...	...	...	...	...	...	...	...
WOMEN	1	1	...	...	...	...	...	...	...	...	...
0930 A HEARING AND APPEALS	1,713	1,711	...	...	...	...	1	...	1	...	35
WOMEN	501	500	...	...	...	...	...	...	1	...	12
0935 P ADMINISTRATIVE LAW JUDGE	1,323	...	...	...	...	...	...	...	...	...	...
WOMEN	146	...	...	...	...	...	...	...	...	...	...
0945 A CLERK OF COURT	33	33	...	...	...	...	3	...	6	3	11
WOMEN	23	23	...	...	...	...	2	...	6	3	5
0950 A PARALEGAL SPECIALIST	5,341	5,312	...	...	...	...	34	5	494	18	1,376
WOMEN	4,147	4,123	...	...	...	...	28	4	357	17	1,178
0958 A PENSION LAW SPECIALIST	118	113	...	...	...	...	1	...	1	...	17
WOMEN	69	68	...	...	...	...	1	...	1	...	10
0962 T CONTACT REPRESENTATIVE	15,393	15,393	...	...	5	342	1,533	1,292	3,020	7,014	1,238
WOMEN	11,282	11,282	...	...	2	264	1,019	987	2,017	5,873	683
0963 T LEGAL INSTRUMENTS EXAM	2,337	2,319	...	...	32	77	159	431	768	483	183
WOMEN	1,875	1,859	...	...	27	63	113	344	655	342	160
0965 A LAND LAW EXAMINING	296	296	...	...	...	...	3	...	31	...	143
WOMEN	245	245	...	...	...	...	3	...	29	...	122
0967 A PASSPORT & VISA EXAMININ	1,142	1,060	...	...	...	...	35	...	48	1	132
WOMEN	491	461	...	...	...	...	13	...	26	1	80
0986 * LEGAL CLERICAL & ASST	9,537	9,520	...	1	13	317	1,767	2,517	2,786	1,736	235
WOMEN	8,771	8,754	...	...	6	249	1,524	2,310	2,640	1,665	223
0987 A TAX LAW SPECIALIST	385	383	...	...	...	...	1	...	...	...	3
WOMEN	142	141	...	...	...	...	1	...	...	...	1
0990 * GENERAL CLAIMS EXAMINING	1,621	1,621	...	...	...	2	59	41	243	82	1,004
WOMEN	1,216	1,216	...	...	...	2	38	31	186	65	764
0991 A WORKERS' COMP CLAIM EXAM	868	867	...	...	...	...	9	...	108	...	49
WOMEN	495	495	...	...	...	...	7	...	69	...	27
0992 T LOSS & DAMAGE CLAIM EXAM	126	126	...	...	...	1	13	22	61	15	10
WOMEN	92	92	...	...	...	...	10	17	45	9	8
0993 A RAILROAD RETIRE CLM EXAM	3,349	3,349	...	...	...	...	53	...	107	48	1,993
WOMEN	2,346	2,346	...	...	...	...	42	...	84	34	1,512
0994 T UNEMPLOY COMP CLAIM EXAM	71	71	...	...	...	...	9	15	14	8	12
WOMEN	46	46	...	...	...	...	8	14	7	3	8
0995 T DEPEND&ESTATE CLAIM EXAM	31	31	...	...	...	...	2	5	7	9	3
WOMEN	25	25	...	...	...	...	1	3	6	8	3
0996 A VETERANS CLAIMS EXAM	3,296	3,296	...	...	...	4	200	...	259	1	965
WOMEN	1,524	1,524	...	...	...	2	115	...	153	1	531
0998 C CLAIMS CLERICAL	5,511	5,511	...	9	47	793	3,472	400	582	74	62
WOMEN	4,608	4,608	...	9	33	621	2,943	326	503	64	50
0999 O LEGAL OCCUPATN STUDNT TR	27	24	2	1	1	6	5	1	5	...	3
WOMEN	18	16	2	1	...	4	4	1	2	...	2
0900 LEGAL AND KINDRED	78,341	70,751	2	11	98	1,542	7,360	4,729	8,546	9,492	7,587
WOMEN	47,602	45,508	2	10	68	1,205	5,873	4,037	6,791	8,085	5,448
1001 * GENRL ARTS & INFORMATION	3,283	3,237	1	4	64	81	266	95	300	35	347
WOMEN	1,678	1,652	1	3	35	51	210	78	211	24	216
1008 A INTERIOR DESIGN	242	242	...	...	...	...	4	...	24	...	61
WOMEN	201	201	...	...	...	...	4	...	21	...	56
1010 T EXHIBITS SPECIALIST	368	368	...	...	...	...	4	...	34	...	133
WOMEN	61	61	...	...	...	...	3	...	8	...	21
1015 P MUSEUM CURATOR	377	358	...	...	...	...	1	...	4	...	43
WOMEN	155	150	...	...	...	...	1	...	4	...	22
1016 T MUSEUM SPECIALIST & TECH	884	884	...	...	16	35	127	2	191	4	208
WOMEN	456	456	...	...	6	17	74	1	103	2	106
1020 T ILLUSTRATING	752	752	...	...	...	...	14	3	124	14	330
WOMEN	298	298	...	...	...	...	9	...	57	4	128
1021 C OFFICE DRAFTING	6	6	...	...	...	1	4	1	...	...	...
WOMEN	...	...	...	...	...	...	...	...	...	...	...

TABLE D-1, 1995 -- CONTINUED

10	11	12	13	14	15	MED GRD	AVG GRD	SENIOR PAY LEVELS	OTHER	OCCUPATION CODES TITLES
...	37	155	103	35	4	12.0	12.37	...	...	0880 P MINING ENGINEERING
...	5	8	1	1	...	12.0	11.18	...	...	WOMEN
...	41	106	135	51	14	13.0	12.65	...	...	0881 P PETROLEUM ENGINEERING
...	3	10	13	3	...	13.0	12.55	...	...	WOMEN
...	129	59	34	41	38	11.0	11.54	1	3	0890 P AGRICULTURAL ENGINEERING
...	7	1	...	...	1	9.0	8.92	...	1	WOMEN
...	4	10	17	17	6	13.0	13.20	...	...	0892 P CERAMIC ENGINEERING
...	...	1	3	4	...	13.5	13.38	...	...	WOMEN
...	112	452	434	154	66	13.0	12.46	4	4	0893 P CHEMICAL ENGINEERING
...	31	83	70	21	4	12.0	11.97	1	2	WOMEN
...	12	29	13	6	2	12.0	12.31	...	...	0894 P WELDING ENGINEERING
...	...	2	1	...	...	12.0	12.33	...	...	WOMEN
25	759	187	30	1	...	11.0	10.30	...	...	0895 T INDUSTRIAL ENGINEER TECH
8	102	10	2	...	...	9.0	9.79	...	...	WOMEN
...	270	1,071	418	108	25	12.0	12.08	1	...	0896 P INDUSTRIAL ENGINEERING
...	63	177	48	6	1	12.0	11.69	...	...	WOMEN
1	5	1	1	...	...	5.0	4.95	...	1	0899 O ENGINR & ARCH STUDNT TR
1	2	...	...	...	...	4.0	5.01	...	...	WOMEN
2,648	23,405	45,368	33,787	14,405	7,157	12.0	11.87	1,051	166	0900 ENGINEERNG & ARCHITECTURE
219	2,375	4,351	3,197	821	247	12.0	11.22	39	9	WOMEN
...	250	10	1	...	...	11.0	10.85	...	1	0904 P LAW CLERK
...	135	3	1	...	...	11.0	10.82	...	...	WOMEN
2	661	1,459	4,707	6,252	6,253	14.0	13.80	3,401	2,706	0905 P GENERAL ATTORNEY
...	345	719	2,031	2,431	1,944	14.0	13.62	855	1,001	WOMEN
...	1	...	...	...	...	11.0	11.00	...	...	0920 A ESTATE TAX EXAMINING
...	1	...	...	...	...	11.0	11.00	...	...	WOMEN
2	82	330	626	510	124	13.0	13.06	2	...	0930 A HEARING AND APPEALS
2	26	168	191	91	9	13.0	12.66	1	...	WOMEN
...	...	...	...	...	...	0.0	0.00	1,323	...	0935 P ADMINISTRATIVE LAW JUDGE
...	...	...	...	...	...	0.0	0.00	146	...	WOMEN
3	4	2	1	...	...	9.0	8.82	...	...	0945 A CLERK OF COURT
2	2	2	1	...	...	9.0	8.70	...	...	WOMEN
7	2,026	893	382	62	15	11.0	10.41	1	28	0950 A PARALEGAL SPECIALIST
7	1,657	662	186	21	6	11.0	10.29	...	24	WOMEN
...	33	19	23	13	6	12.0	11.74	5	...	0958 A PENSION LAW SPECIALIST
...	24	15	10	5	2	11.0	11.41	1	...	WOMEN
413	333	131	56	16	...	8.0	7.50	...	...	0962 T CONTACT REPRESENTATIVE
160	222	48	6	1	...	8.0	7.45	...	...	WOMEN
131	36	18	1	...	...	7.0	7.16	...	18	0963 T LEGAL INSTRUMENTS EXAM
114	31	9	1	...	...	7.0	7.17	...	16	WOMEN
...	95	16	7	1	...	9.0	9.67	...	...	0965 A LAND LAW EXAMINING
...	74	12	4	1	...	9.0	9.55	...	...	WOMEN
23	206	242	1	205	167	12.0	11.79	81	1	0967 A PASSPORT & VISA EXAMININ
16	106	93	1	76	49	11.0	11.34	29	1	WOMEN
124	20	4	...	...	...	7.0	6.54	...	17	0986 * LEGAL CLERICAL & ASST
119	15	3	...	...	...	7.0	6.59	...	17	WOMEN
...	61	28	129	130	31	13.0	13.06	2	...	0987 A TAX LAW SPECIALIST
...	43	20	41	31	4	13.0	12.44	1	...	WOMEN
98	55	28	7	2	...	9.0	8.63	...	...	0990 * GENERAL CLAIMS EXAMINING
70	36	17	6	1	...	9.0	8.51	...	...	WOMEN
...	331	211	126	23	10	11.0	10.99	1	...	0991 A WORKERS' COMP CLAIM EXAM
...	218	116	50	3	5	11.0	10.74	...	...	WOMEN
...	3	1	...	...	...	7.0	7.01	...	...	0992 T LOSS & DAMAGE CLAIM EXAM
...	2	1	...	...	...	7.0	7.01	...	...	WOMEN
408	298	285	128	29	...	9.0	9.61	...	...	0993 A RAILROAD RETIRE CLM EXAM
276	189	140	57	12	...	9.0	9.42	...	...	WOMEN
4	9	...	...	...	...	7.0	7.66	...	...	0994 T UNEMPLOY COMP CLAIM EXAM
3	3	...	...	...	...	7.0	7.22	...	...	WOMEN
2	2	1	...	...	...	8.0	7.81	...	...	0995 T DEPENDS&ESTATE CLAIM EXAM
1	2	1	...	...	...	8.0	8.00	...	...	WOMEN
62	624	924	176	53	29	11.0	10.18	...	...	0996 A VETERANS CLAIMS EXAM
28	306	324	50	11	3	9.0	9.73	...	...	WOMEN
50	18	2	2	...	...	5.0	5.27	...	...	0998 C CLAIMS CLERICAL
43	14	1	1	...	...	5.0	5.29	...	...	WOMEN
...	...	...	...	...	...	5.0	5.17	...	3	0999 O LEGAL OCCUPATN STUDNT TR
...	...	...	...	...	...	5.0	4.88	...	2	WOMEN
1,329	5,148	4,604	6,373	7,296	6,634	9.0	9.69	4,816	2,774	0900 LEGAL AND KINDRED
841	3,451	2,354	2,637	2,684	2,022	9.0	8.72	1,033	1,061	WOMEN
7	569	800	431	150	87	11.0	10.15	16	30	1001 * GENRL ARTS & INFORMATION
3	280	316	151	51	22	9.0	9.30	3	23	WOMEN
12	76	47	16	1	1	11.0	10.31	...	...	1008 A INTERIOR DESIGN
10	57	40	11	1	1	11.0	10.20	...	...	WOMEN
8	130	45	13	1	...	11.0	10.02	...	...	1010 T EXHIBITS SPECIALIST
3	13	7	5	1	...	9.0	9.77	...	...	WOMEN
...	90	92	68	33	27	12.0	11.91	17	2	1015 P MUSEUM CURATOR
...	40	36	27	17	3	12.0	11.58	4	1	WOMEN
2	168	101	24	4	2	9.0	8.55	...	...	1016 T MUSEUM SPECIALIST & TECH
...	85	41	16	4	1	9.0	8.46	...	...	WOMEN
22	206	37	2	...	...	9.0	9.30	...	...	1020 T ILLUSTRATING
11	74	14	1	...	...	9.0	9.17	...	...	WOMEN
...	...	...	...	...	...	5.0	5.00	...	...	1021 C OFFICE DRAFTING
...	...	...	...	...	...	0.0	0.00	...	...	WOMEN

TABLE D-1 FULL-TIME CIVILIAN WHITE-COLLAR EMPLOYMENT BY OCCUPATION, GENDER, GENERAL SCHEDULE AND RELATED GRADE, MEDIAN GRADE, AND AVERAGE GRADE, ALL AREAS, SEPTEMBER 30, 1995

OCCUPATION CODES TITLES	GRAND TOTAL	GENERAL SCHEDULE AND RELATED GRADES									
		TOTAL	1	2	3	4	5	6	7	8	9
1035 A PUBLIC AFFAIRS	4,361	4,297	...	...	...	...	35	4	170	61	706
WOMEN	2,499	2,471	...	...	...	...	25	2	131	52	495
1040 A LANGUAGE SPECIALIST	614	614	...	...	...	...	5	1	25	2	71
WOMEN	342	342	...	...	...	...	4	...	16	2	44
1046 C LANGUAGE CLERICAL	59	59	...	...	1	4	22	16	13	...	3
WOMEN	54	54	...	...	1	3	19	16	12	...	3
1051 A MUSIC SPECIALIST	21	21	...	...	...	...	...	1	2	...	6
WOMEN	5	5	...	...	...	...	...	...	...	...	3
1054 A THEATER SPECIALIST	13	13	...	...	...	...	...	...	5	...	2
WOMEN	2	2	...	...	...	...	...	...	...	...	1
1056 A ART SPECIALIST	136	136	...	...	...	...	1	...	33	6	64
WOMEN	67	67	...	...	...	...	1	...	19	4	26
1060 T PHOTOGRAPHY	1,439	1,439	...	...	...	4	36	37	293	80	432
WOMEN	303	303	...	...	...	2	16	21	82	12	100
1071 A AUDIOVISUAL PRODUCTION	1,219	1,215	...	...	1	4	1	...	38	...	274
WOMEN	246	245	...	...	...	...	1	...	16	...	55
1082 A WRITING AND EDITING	1,705	1,685	...	...	...	1	27	...	99	2	433
WOMEN	1,193	1,183	...	...	...	...	25	...	75	1	340
1083 A TECH WRITING & EDITING	1,378	1,376	...	...	...	...	5	...	33	1	280
WOMEN	785	783	...	...	...	...	3	...	27	1	177
1084 A VISUAL INFORMATION	1,971	1,966	...	...	...	...	13	1	122	4	466
WOMEN	859	856	...	...	...	...	8	1	75	3	238
1087 * EDITORIAL ASSISTANCE	1,030	1,028	...	...	...	35	291	294	372	27	8
WOMEN	944	942	...	...	...	30	268	274	336	26	7
1099 D INFO & ARTS STUDENT TR	45	45	...	...	1	16	12	...	9	...	5
WOMEN	28	28	...	...	1	10	7	...	8	...	2
1000 INFORMATION AND ARTS	19,903	19,741	1	4	82	178	871	456	1,891	236	3,872
WOMEN	10,176	10,099	1	3	43	113	678	393	1,201	131	2,040
1101 * GEN BUSINESS & INDUSTRY	19,849	19,093	...	...	62	381	2,070	1,982	2,096	189	1,625
WOMEN	11,389	11,181	...	...	41	333	1,884	1,718	1,690	133	899
1102 P CONTRACTING	29,317	29,198	...	...	...	...	285	1	1,071	5	3,988
WOMEN	16,868	16,826	...	...	...	...	216	...	782	4	2,826
1103 A INDUSTRIAL PROPERTY MGT	776	776	...	...	...	...	5	...	16	...	87
WOMEN	333	333	...	...	...	...	4	...	14	...	50
1104 A PROPERTY DISPOSAL	1,012	1,011	...	...	...	...	17	...	45	...	412
WOMEN	496	496	...	...	...	...	11	...	28	...	225
1105 T PURCHASING	6,086	6,062	...	...	...	97	1,248	1,871	2,107	361	285
WOMEN	4,847	4,828	...	...	...	78	977	1,481	1,722	302	230
1106 * PROCUREMENT CLER & TECH	6,729	6,719	...	2	58	1,045	2,472	1,770	1,299	52	19
WOMEN	5,953	5,945	...	1	36	883	2,175	1,614	1,171	46	18
1107 * PROP DISPOSAL CLER & TECH	538	538	...	...	3	62	279	82	108	4	...
WOMEN	439	439	...	...	1	48	227	73	88	2	...
1130 A PUBLIC UTILITIES SPEC	627	621	...	...	...	...	1	1	18	...	60
WOMEN	256	256	...	...	...	...	1	1	12	...	49
1140 A TRADE SPECIALIST	680	678	...	...	...	1	3	...	21	...	50
WOMEN	277	277	...	...	...	1	2	...	10	...	33
1144 A COMMISSARY MANAGEMENT	1,203	1,200	...	...	...	...	17	19	103	127	150
WOMEN	253	253	...	...	...	...	6	9	34	29	45
1145 A AGRICULTURAL PROGRM SPEC	617	617	...	...	...	...	...	...	7	...	16
WOMEN	153	153	...	...	...	...	...	...	7	...	10
1146 A AGRICULTURAL MARKETING	551	535	...	...	...	...	...	...	14	...	28
WOMEN	193	191	...	...	...	...	...	...	8	...	22
1147 A AGRICULTURAL MARKET RPTR	155	155	...	...	...	...	1	...	4	...	17
WOMEN	33	33	...	...	...	...	...	...	1	...	11
1150 A INDUSTRIAL SPECIALIST	2,041	2,041	...	...	...	...	1	...	10	...	103
WOMEN	373	373	...	...	...	...	1	...	6	...	48
1152 T PRODUCTION CONTROL	5,426	5,426	...	...	...	4	81	239	980	191	2,158
WOMEN	1,394	1,394	...	...	...	2	48	101	413	63	551
1160 A FINANCIAL ANALYSIS	1,775	1,640	...	...	...	...	3	1	24	...	54
WOMEN	677	630	...	...	...	...	3	1	17	...	33
1161 A CROP INSURANCE ADMIN	2	2	...	...	...	...	...	...	...	...	...
WOMEN	1	1	...	...	...	...	...	...	...	...	...
1162 A CROP INS UNDERWRITING	64	63	...	...	...	...	...	...	1	...	2
WOMEN	7	7	...	...	...	...	...	...	1	...	2
1163 A INSURANCE EXAMINING	64	64	...	...	...	...	...	...	...	...	...
WOMEN	15	15	...	...	...	...	...	...	...	...	...
1165 A LOAN SPECIALIST	3,348	3,340	...	...	...	...	65	...	201	...	850
WOMEN	1,532	1,530	...	...	...	...	43	...	143	...	537
1169 A INTERNAL REVENUE OFFICER	8,166	8,166	...	...	...	...	105	...	613	...	770
WOMEN	3,892	3,892	...	...	...	...	62	...	384	...	475
1170 A REALTY	3,400	3,394	...	...	...	...	32	...	138	1	497
WOMEN	1,619	1,618	...	...	...	...	30	...	100	...	335
1171 A APPRAISING	1,018	1,010	...	...	...	...	...	...	10	2	33
WOMEN	211	210	...	...	...	...	...	...	8	...	15
1173 A HOUSING MANAGEMENT	2,521	2,520	...	...	...	7	261	24	794	41	550
WOMEN	1,527	1,527	...	...	...	7	192	14	507	17	364
1176 A BUILDING MANAGEMENT	1,127	1,126	...	...	...	...	10	...	41	1	113
WOMEN	319	319	...	...	...	...	9	...	24	...	53
1199 D BUSINESS & IND STUDNT TR	113	113	1	5	8	44	28	...	10	...	8
WOMEN	62	62	1	...	4	25	16	...	5	...	5
1100 BUSINESS AND INDUSTRY	97,205	96,108	1	7	131	1,641	6,984	5,990	9,731	974	11,875
WOMEN	53,119	52,789	1	1	82	1,377	5,907	5,012	7,175	596	6,836

TABLE D-1, 1995 -- CONTINUED

10	11	12	13	14	15	MED GRD	AVG GRD	SENIOR PAY LEVELS	OTHER	OCCUPATION CODES TITLES
10	871	1,053	787	388	212	12.0	11.49	30	34	1035 A PUBLIC AFFAIRS
5	545	556	412	172	76	11.0	11.15	13	15	WOMEN
21	274	140	51	16	8	11.0	11.03	...	...	1040 A LANGUAGE SPECIALIST
14	154	76	20	8	4	11.0	10.88	...	...	WOMEN
...	...	...	...	...	...	6.0	5.81	...	...	1046 C LANGUAGE CLERICAL
...	...	...	...	...	...	6.0	5.87	...	...	WOMEN
...	3	1	3	3	2	11.0	10.95	...	...	1051 A MUSIC SPECIALIST
...	...	...	1	1	...	9.0	10.80	...	...	WOMEN
...	5	1	...	...	...	9.0	9.23	...	...	1054 A THEATER SPECIALIST
...	1	...	...	...	...	10.0	10.00	...	...	WOMEN
3	17	1	...	5	6	9.0	9.18	...	...	1056 A ART SPECIALIST
2	7	1	...	2	5	9.0	9.19	...	...	WOMEN
47	372	105	30	2	1	9.0	9.21	...	...	1060 T PHOTOGRAPHY
12	53	5	...	...	...	9.0	8.41	...	...	WOMEN
9	282	374	169	44	19	11.0	11.14	2	2	1071 A AUDIOVISUAL PRODUCTION
1	60	78	23	9	2	11.0	10.91	1	...	WOMEN
2	404	462	186	56	13	11.0	10.77	2	18	1082 A WRITING AND EDITING
1	311	303	106	19	2	11.0	10.53	...	10	WOMEN
3	475	429	128	18	4	11.0	11.02	1	1	1083 A TECH WRITING & EDITING
2	278	216	67	11	1	11.0	10.87	1	1	WOMEN
5	654	508	149	35	9	11.0	10.71	1	4	1084 A VISUAL INFORMATION
...	269	224	30	6	2	11.0	10.38	...	3	WOMEN
1	...	...	...	...	...	6.0	6.09	...	2	1087 * EDITORIAL ASSISTANCE
1	...	...	...	...	...	6.0	6.09	...	2	WOMEN
...	2	...	...	...	...	5.0	5.71	...	...	1099 O INFO & ARTS STUDENT TR
...	...	...	...	...	...	5.0	5.43	...	...	WOMEN
152	4,598	4,196	2,057	756	391	11.0	10.32	69	93	1000 INFORMATION AND ARTS
65	2,227	1,913	870	302	119	11.0	9.86	22	55	WOMEN
42	2,085	4,016	2,547	1,333	665	11.0	9.85	175	581	1101 * GEN BUSINESS & INDUSTRY
11	1,091	2,059	814	373	135	7.0	8.66	29	179	WOMEN
70	6,681	9,577	4,757	2,025	738	12.0	11.48	83	36	1102 P CONTRACTING
42	4,325	5,391	2,255	805	180	12.0	11.17	22	20	WOMEN
2	356	259	44	5	2	11.0	11.13	...	...	1103 A INDUSTRIAL PROPERTY MGT
1	153	100	9	1	1	11.0	10.83	...	...	WOMEN
1	247	193	74	18	4	11.0	10.31	1	...	1104 A PROPERTY DISPOSAL
...	124	79	23	4	2	9.0	10.03	...	...	WOMEN
27	31	30	...	5	...	6.0	6.45	...	24	1105 T PURCHASING
17	15	5	...	1	...	6.0	6.43	...	19	WOMEN
2	...	...	...	...	...	5.0	5.51	...	10	1106 * PROCUREMENT CLER & TECH
1	...	...	...	...	...	5.0	5.54	...	8	WOMEN
...	...	...	...	...	...	5.0	5.45	...	...	1107 * PROP DISPOSAL CLER &TECH
...	...	...	...	...	...	5.0	5.47	...	...	WOMEN
...	83	175	216	51	16	12.0	12.00	6	...	1130 A PUBLIC UTILITIES SPEC
...	54	82	45	9	3	12.0	11.21	...	...	WOMEN
...	54	183	224	94	48	13.0	12.32	1	1	1140 A TRADE SPECIALIST
...	28	90	83	24	6	12.0	11.82	...	...	WOMEN
138	227	246	114	51	8	11.0	10.36	3	...	1144 A COMMISSARY MANAGEMENT
23	47	37	18	5	...	10.0	9.70	...	...	WOMEN
...	36	387	156	12	3	12.0	12.11	...	...	1145 A AGRICULTURAL PROGRM SPEC
...	22	76	36	1	1	12.0	11.70	...	...	WOMEN
...	90	159	136	83	25	12.0	12.25	2	14	1146 A AGRICULTURAL MARKETING
...	41	65	35	15	5	12.0	11.65	...	2	WOMEN
...	67	51	11	4	...	11.0	11.19	...	...	1147 A AGRICULTURAL MARKET RPTR
...	17	4	...	...	...	11.0	10.33	...	...	WOMEN
...	879	674	238	100	36	12.0	11.66	...	...	1150 A INDUSTRIAL SPECIALIST
...	190	89	26	11	2	11.0	11.15	...	...	WOMEN
84	872	697	102	17	1	9.0	9.22	...	...	1152 T PRODUCTION CONTROL
24	148	41	3	...	...	9.0	8.33	...	...	WOMEN
...	298	525	402	261	72	12.0	12.33	13	122	1160 A FINANCIAL ANALYSIS
...	172	213	111	63	17	12.0	11.85	4	43	WOMEN
...	1	1	...	...	...	11.5	11.50	...	...	1161 A CROP INSURANCE ADMIN
...	...	1	...	...	...	12.0	12.00	...	...	WOMEN
...	1	51	8	...	...	12.0	11.94	1	...	1162 A CROP INS UNDERWRITING
...	...	4	...	...	...	12.0	10.43	...	...	WOMEN
...	5	37	6	10	6	12.0	12.61	...	...	1163 A INSURANCE EXAMINING
...	1	10	2	2	...	12.0	12.33	...	...	WOMEN
8	553	1,103	412	112	36	11.0	10.85	7	1	1165 A LOAN SPECIALIST
7	273	393	107	23	4	11.0	10.20	2	...	WOMEN
...	2,670	3,121	755	132	...	11.0	11.05	...	...	1169 A INTERNAL REVENUE OFFICER
...	1,410	1,270	262	29	...	11.0	10.75	...	...	WOMEN
5	1,023	1,023	449	175	51	12.0	11.27	3	3	1170 A REALTY
...	496	468	148	36	5	11.0	10.78	...	1	WOMEN
...	310	468	149	32	6	12.0	11.77	...	8	1171 A APPRAISING
...	92	74	18	3	...	11.0	11.27	...	1	WOMEN
36	312	296	137	48	14	9.0	8.86	...	1	1173 A HOUSING MANAGEMENT
20	178	150	59	17	2	9.0	8.53	...	...	WOMEN
2	319	291	192	126	31	12.0	11.64	...	1	1176 A BUILDING MANAGEMENT
...	104	71	44	12	2	11.0	10.83	...	...	WOMEN
...	7	2	...	...	...	4.0	5.26	...	...	1199 O BUSINESS & IND STUDNT TR
...	5	1	...	...	...	5.0	5.48	...	...	WOMEN
417	17,207	23,565	11,129	4,694	1,762	11.0	10.13	295	802	1100 BUSINESS AND INDUSTRY
146	8,986	10,773	4,098	1,434	365	9.0	9.29	57	273	WOMEN

TABLE D-1 FULL-TIME CIVILIAN WHITE-COLLAR EMPLOYMENT BY OCCUPATION, GENDER, GENERAL SCHEDULE AND RELATED GRADE, MEDIAN GRADE, AND AVERAGE GRADE, ALL AREAS, SEPTEMBER 30, 1995

OCCUPATION CODES / TITLES	GRAND TOTAL	GENERAL SCHEDULE AND RELATED GRADES									
		TOTAL	1	2	3	4	5	6	7	8	9
1202 T PATENT TECHNICIAN	16	16	...	...	...	...	...	...	...	1	...
WOMEN	13	13	...	...	...	...	...	...	...	1	...
1210 A COPYRIGHT	179	177	...	...	...	...	...	...	1	...	13
WOMEN	103	102	...	...	...	...	...	...	1	...	12
1211 T COPYRIGHT TECHNICIAN	41	41	...	...	...	...	...	4	8	28	1
WOMEN	21	21	...	...	...	...	...	...	...	...	...
1220 P PATENT ADMINISTRATION	76	49	...	...	...	...	...	3	4	14	...
WOMEN	9	7	...	...	...	...	...	...	...	...	...
1221 P PATENT ADVISER	28	28	...	...	...	...	...	...	...	...	1
WOMEN	8	8	...	...	...	...	...	...	...	...	1
1222 P PATENT ATTORNEY	219	175	...	...	...	...	...	...	...	...	...
WOMEN	18	14	...	...	...	...	...	...	...	...	...
1223 P PATENT CLASSIFYING	77	77	...	...	...	...	...	...	...	...	...
WOMEN	14	14	...	...	...	...	...	...	...	...	...
1224 P PATENT EXAMINING	2,170	2,168	...	...	...	...	46	...	122	...	196
WOMEN	475	475	...	...	...	...	18	...	30	...	61
1226 P DESIGN PATENT EXAMINING	55	55	...	...	...	...	...	...	2	...	5
WOMEN	31	31	...	...	...	...	...	...	2	...	3
1200 COPYRIGHT PATENT TRADEMRK	2,861	2,786	...	...	...	...	46	4	133	29	216
WOMEN	692	685	...	...	...	...	18	3	37	15	77
1301 P GENERAL PHYSICAL SCIENCE	7,045	6,496	...	...	...	...	14	...	41	2	145
WOMEN	1,529	1,483	...	...	...	...	4	...	20	1	62
1306 P HEALTH PHYSICS	841	832	...	...	...	...	...	...	7	...	18
WOMEN	169	168	...	...	...	...	...	...	4	...	10
1310 P PHYSICS	3,184	3,046	...	...	...	...	1	...	15	...	20
WOMEN	220	209	...	...	...	...	1	...	3	...	2
1311 T PHYSICAL SCIENCE TECH	2,911	2,905	2	8	23	78	209	167	432	298	435
WOMEN	826	822	1	2	11	36	98	72	178	104	131
1313 P GEOPHYSICS	509	497	...	...	...	...	...	...	...	...	10
WOMEN	56	56	...	...	...	...	...	...	...	...	4
1315 P HYDROLOGY	2,632	2,602	...	...	...	...	18	...	69	...	224
WOMEN	438	437	...	...	...	...	6	...	18	...	74
1316 T HYDROLOGIC TECHNICIAN	1,562	1,562	...	9	19	56	168	154	292	194	285
WOMEN	228	228	...	3	8	12	49	32	50	31	27
1320 P CHEMISTRY	6,799	6,441	...	...	...	...	16	1	97	...	293
WOMEN	1,842	1,753	...	...	...	...	9	1	45	...	131
1321 P METALLURGY	182	180	...	...	...	...	...	...	1	...	1
WOMEN	15	15	...	...	...	...	...	...	...	...	1
1330 P ASTRONOMY & SPACE SCIENC	479	428	...	...	...	...	...	...	...	...	2
WOMEN	37	32	...	...	...	...	...	...	...	...	...
1340 P METEOROLOGY	3,069	3,041	...	...	...	...	82	...	194	...	263
WOMEN	267	263	...	...	...	...	23	...	23	...	36
1341 T METEOROLOGICAL TECH	1,402	1,402	...	...	3	20	30	31	77	58	221
WOMEN	131	131	...	...	1	5	11	6	15	8	21
1350 P GEOLOGY	2,128	2,101	...	...	...	...	13	...	37	...	102
WOMEN	428	423	...	...	...	...	2	...	18	...	47
1360 P OCEANOGRAPHY	680	666	...	...	...	...	7	...	4	...	13
WOMEN	112	109	...	...	...	...	5	...	2	...	5
1361 A NAVIGATIONAL INFORMATION	333	333	...	...	...	...	...	1	19	...	11
WOMEN	69	69	...	...	...	...	...	1	9	...	4
1370 P CARTOGRAPHY	4,176	4,167	...	...	...	...	47	...	163	...	136
WOMEN	942	841	...	...	...	...	6	...	38	...	35
1371 T CARTOGRAPHIC TECHNICIAN	1,296	1,296	1	2	15	119	94	79	200	84	426
WOMEN	431	431	1	...	10	65	47	34	70	27	130
1372 P GEODESY	318	318	...	...	...	...	...	...	3	...	13
WOMEN	43	43	...	...	...	...	...	...	2	...	2
1373 P LAND SURVEYING	504	504	...	...	...	...	...	...	8	...	56
WOMEN	21	21	...	...	...	...	...	...	2	...	6
1374 T GEODETIC TECHNICIAN	75	75	...	...	...	...	4	1	2	6	12
WOMEN	21	21	...	...	...	...	3	...	1	3	3
1380 P FOREST PRODUCTS TECHNOL	49	46	...	...	...	...	...	...	...	...	1
WOMEN	8	8	...	...	...	...	...	...	...	...	1
1382 P FOOD TECHNOLOGY	240	236	...	...	...	...	...	...	...	...	11
WOMEN	69	68	...	...	...	...	...	...	...	...	6
1384 P TEXTILE TECHNOLOGY	81	81	...	...	...	...	...	...	2	...	1
WOMEN	41	41	...	...	...	...	...	...	2	...	2
1386 P PHOTOGRAPHIC TECHNOLOGY	31	31	...	...	...	...	...	...	...	...	2
WOMEN	1	1	...	...	...	...	...	...	...	...	1
1397 A DOCUMENT ANALYSIS	106	106	...	...	...	...	...	...	4	2	8
WOMEN	44	44	...	...	...	...	...	...	1	1	5
1399 O PHYSICAL SCI STUDENT TR	149	149	...	...	13	41	40	...	31	...	18
WOMEN	61	61	...	...	7	19	15	...	12	...	6
1300 PHYSICAL SCIENCES	40,781	39,541	3	19	73	314	743	434	1,698	644	2,727
WOMEN	7,949	7,778	2	5	37	137	279	146	513	175	750
1410 P LIBRARIAN	2,887	2,822	...	...	...	...	5	...	25	5	289
WOMEN	1,946	1,902	...	...	...	...	5	...	20	4	206
1411 T LIBRARY TECHNICIAN	3,017	2,989	4	10	118	402	632	555	716	383	144
WOMEN	2,277	2,255	3	8	91	307	478	432	549	276	92
1412 A TECH INFORMATION SERVICE	1,314	1,310	...	...	...	...	14	...	121	4	263
WOMEN	909	908	...	...	...	...	12	...	95	3	200
1420 P ARCHIVIST	487	484	...	...	...	...	...	...	11	...	33
WOMEN	175	175	...	...	...	...	...	...	5	...	12

TABLE D-1, 1995 -- CONTINUED

10	11	12	13	14	15	MED GRD	AVG GRD	SENIOR PAY LEVELS	OTHER	OCCUPATION CODES TITLES
...	15	...	...	...	...	11.0	10.81	...	...	1202 T PATENT TECHNICIAN
...	12	...	...	...	...	11.0	10.77	...	...	WOMEN
...	117	22	16	6	2	11.0	11.28	2	...	1210 A COPYRIGHT
...	66	13	8	2	...	11.0	11.07	1	...	WOMEN
...	...	...	...	...	...	8.0	7.63	...	...	1211 T COPYRIGHT TECHNICIAN
...	...	...	...	...	...	8.0	7.52	...	...	WOMEN
...	...	...	1	5	43	15.0	14.86	27	...	1220 P PATENT ADMINISTRATION
...	...	...	...	2	5	15.0	14.71	2	...	WOMEN
...	...	...	6	18	3	14.0	13.71	...	...	1221 P PATENT ADVISER
...	...	...	...	7	...	14.0	13.38	...	...	WOMEN
...	1	7	20	59	88	15.0	14.29	44	...	1222 P PATENT ATTORNEY
...	1	...	4	3	6	14.0	13.93	4	...	WOMEN
...	2	4	5	52	14	14.0	13.94	...	...	1223 P PATENT CLASSIFYING
...	1	...	...	11	2	14.0	13.93	...	...	WOMEN
...	206	163	517	642	276	13.0	12.42	2	...	1224 P PATENT EXAMINING
...	39	45	142	110	30	13.0	11.90	...	...	WOMEN
...	6	5	10	23	4	13.0	12.67	...	...	1226 P DESIGN PATENT EXAMINING
...	5	1	6	14	...	13.0	12.32	...	...	WOMEN
...	347	201	575	805	430	13.0	12.49	75	...	1200 COPYRIGHT PATENT TRADEMRK
...	124	59	160	149	43	13.0	11.77	7	...	WOMEN
11	417	1,252	1,971	1,418	1,225	13.0	13.12	532	17	1301 P GENERAL PHYSICAL SCIENCE
8	144	383	475	248	138	13.0	12.61	42	4	WOMEN
8	67	255	278	148	51	13.0	12.67	5	4	1306 P HEALTH PHYSICS
3	18	54	49	20	10	12.0	12.27	...	1	WOMEN
...	74	606	927	781	622	13.0	13.36	106	32	1310 P PHYSICS
...	10	73	78	28	14	13.0	12.66	8	3	WOMEN
642	342	231	35	2	1	9.0	8.68	...	6	1311 T PHYSICAL SCIENCE TECH
97	67	25	...	...	...	8.0	7.75	...	4	WOMEN
...	45	128	130	93	91	13.0	13.03	10	7	1313 P GEOPHYSICS
...	8	22	12	6	4	12.0	12.29	...	...	WOMEN
...	526	782	586	252	145	12.0	11.94	24	6	1315 P HYDROLOGY
...	125	131	58	16	9	11.0	11.17	1	...	WOMEN
180	167	38	...	...	...	9.0	7.89	...	...	1316 T HYDROLOGIC TECHNICIAN
8	8	...	...	...	...	7.0	6.68	...	...	WOMEN
2	1,062	1,779	1,723	913	555	12.0	12.41	85	273	1320 P CHEMISTRY
...	427	534	400	145	61	12.0	11.86	14	75	WOMEN
...	7	39	55	37	40	13.0	13.30	2	...	1321 P METALLURGY
...	3	2	5	2	2	13.0	12.60	...	...	WOMEN
...	11	34	120	131	130	14.0	13.76	49	2	1330 P ASTRONOMY & SPACE SCIENC
...	2	2	13	9	6	13.0	13.47	3	2	WOMEN
...	263	752	907	417	163	12.0	11.88	27	1	1340 P METEOROLOGY
...	31	66	58	22	4	12.0	10.86	4	...	WOMEN
211	549	198	4	...	...	11.0	9.98	...	...	1341 T METEOROLOGICAL TECH
17	37	10	...	...	...	9.0	8.92	...	...	WOMEN
...	344	666	471	223	245	12.0	12.35	22	5	1350 P GEOLOGY
...	82	130	101	35	8	12.0	11.69	3	2	WOMEN
...	79	167	212	107	77	13.0	12.71	8	6	1360 P OCEANOGRAPHY
...	22	37	26	9	3	12.0	11.73	...	3	WOMEN
...	143	86	65	8	...	11.0	11.41	...	...	1361 A NAVIGATIONAL INFORMATION
...	29	14	11	1	...	11.0	10.86	...	...	WOMEN
...	1,611	1,399	620	138	53	12.0	11.49	9	...	1370 P CARTOGRAPHY
...	332	273	123	26	8	12.0	11.44	1	...	WOMEN
24	239	11	2	...	...	9.0	8.03	...	...	1371 T CARTOGRAPHIC TECHNICIAN
4	41	2	...	...	...	7.0	7.24	...	...	WOMEN
...	102	119	48	24	9	12.0	11.90	...	...	1372 P GEODESY
...	10	23	2	3	1	12.0	11.65	...	...	WOMEN
...	220	167	46	7	...	11.0	11.27	...	...	1373 P LAND SURVEYING
...	5	8	...	...	...	11.0	10.43	...	...	WOMEN
15	7	27	1	...	...	10.0	10.13	...	...	1374 T GEODETIC TECHNICIAN
7	2	2	...	...	...	9.0	9.00	...	...	WOMEN
...	5	8	19	12	1	13.0	12.83	3	...	1380 P FOREST PRODUCTS TECHNOL
...	2	1	4	...	...	12.5	11.88	...	...	WOMEN
...	46	62	79	27	11	12.0	12.37	1	3	1382 P FOOD TECHNOLOGY
...	14	21	23	4	...	12.0	11.99	...	1	WOMEN
...	15	43	14	4	2	12.0	12.00	...	...	1384 P TEXTILE TECHNOLOGY
...	8	24	7	...	...	12.0	11.73	...	...	WOMEN
1	7	10	10	1	...	12.0	11.90	...	...	1386 P PHOTOGRAPHIC TECHNOLOGY
...	...	...	...	...	...	9.0	9.00	...	...	WOMEN
...	18	22	36	16	...	12.0	11.98	...	...	1397 A DOCUMENT ANALYSIS
...	11	14	8	4	...	12.0	11.57	...	...	WOMEN
...	6	...	...	...	...	5.0	5.69	...	...	1399 O PHYSICAL SCI STUDENT TR
...	2	...	...	...	...	5.0	5.44	...	...	WOMEN
1,094	6,372	8,881	8,359	4,759	3,421	12.0	11.73	883	357	1300 PHYSICAL SCIENCES
144	1,440	1,851	1,453	578	268	12.0	10.95	76	95	WOMEN
86	794	1,017	372	169	60	12.0	11.60	35	30	1410 P LIBRARIAN
61	555	683	237	98	33	12.0	11.52	17	27	WOMEN
9	15	1	...	...	...	6.0	6.06	...	28	1411 T LIBRARY TECHNICIAN
7	11	1	...	...	...	6.0	6.02	...	22	WOMEN
11	333	328	165	58	13	11.0	10.82	2	2	1412 A TECH INFORMATION SERVICE
7	229	211	109	38	4	11.0	10.66	...	1	WOMEN
...	135	167	70	52	16	12.0	11.86	3	...	1420 P ARCHIVIST
...	56	65	19	14	4	12.0	11.67	...	...	WOMEN

TABLE D-1 FULL-TIME CIVILIAN WHITE-COLLAR EMPLOYMENT BY OCCUPATION, GENDER, GENERAL SCHEDULE AND RELATED GRADE, MEDIAN GRADE, AND AVERAGE GRADE, ALL AREAS, SEPTEMBER 30, 1995

OCCUPATION CODES / TITLES	GRAND TOTAL	GENERAL SCHEDULE AND RELATED GRADES									
		TOTAL	1	2	3	4	5	6	7	8	9
1421 * ARCHIVES TECHNICIAN	899	899	...	3	60	89	174	188	130	26	108
WOMEN	482	482	...	1	33	46	103	102	67	18	60
1499 O LIBRARY & ARCHIVES STDNT	5	5	...	...	...	1	3	...	1	...	...
WOMEN	3	3	...	...	...	...	2	...	1	...	...
1400 LIBRARY AND ARCHIVES	8,609	8,509	4	13	178	492	828	743	1,004	418	837
WOMEN	5,792	5,725	3	9	124	353	600	534	737	301	570
1510 P ACTUARY	178	168	...	...	...	...	3	...	4	...	12
WOMEN	42	41	...	...	...	...	1	...	2	...	4
1515 P OPERATIONS RESEARCH	3,635	3,566	...	...	...	...	3	...	18	...	42
WOMEN	837	830	...	...	...	...	...	...	8	...	17
1520 P MATHEMATICS	1,787	1,760	...	...	...	...	...	...	5	...	17
WOMEN	518	512	...	...	...	...	...	...	4	...	9
1521 T MATHEMATICS TECHNICIAN	29	29	...	...	1	4	...	2	7	5	2
WOMEN	24	24	...	...	...	3	...	2	5	5	2
1529 P MATHEMATICL STATISTICIAN	1,123	1,079	...	...	...	...	...	...	6	...	30
WOMEN	352	339	...	...	...	...	...	...	3	...	13
1530 P STATISTICIAN	2,598	2,545	...	...	...	...	5	...	51	...	98
WOMEN	1,005	984	...	...	...	...	4	...	29	...	50
1531 * STATISTICAL ASSISTANT	1,226	1,225	...	...	38	222	212	225	300	89	115
WOMEN	1,065	1,064	...	...	32	193	189	194	260	78	101
1541 T CRYPTANALYSIS	17	17	...	...	...	...	...	...	...	...	1
WOMEN	10	10	...	...	...	...	...	...	...	...	1
1550 P COMPUTER SCIENCE	3,192	3,144	...	...	...	...	5	...	71	...	60
WOMEN	995	988	...	...	...	...	4	...	29	...	22
1599 O MATH & STAT STUDENT TR	52	52	1	...	3	20	20	...	5	...	...
WOMEN	16	16	...	...	1	4	7	...	3	...	...
1500 MATHEMATICS & STATISTICS	13,837	13,585	1	...	42	246	248	227	467	94	377
WOMEN	4,864	4,808	...	...	33	200	205	196	343	83	218
1601 A GENERAL FACILITIES &EQPT	2,622	2,620	...	...	...	7	147	91	182	67	297
WOMEN	415	414	...	...	...	3	63	43	62	13	77
1630 A CEMETERY ADMINISTRATION	118	118	...	...	...	...	...	3	2	6	27
WOMEN	21	21	...	...	...	...	...	3	2	6	27
1640 A FACILITY MANAGEMENT	1,521	1,464	...	...	...	...	3	...	22	5	265
WOMEN	98	98	...	...	...	...	1	...	5	...	27
1654 A PRINTING MANAGEMENT	1,486	1,478	...	...	...	1	11	1	97	1	217
WOMEN	537	536	...	...	...	...	6	...	60	...	122
1658 A LAUNDRY/DRYCLEAN PLT MGT	155	155	...	...	...	...	1	...	14	23	47
WOMEN	20	20	...	...	...	...	...	...	1	1	9
1667 A STEWARD	319	295	...	...	...	...	1	3	23	1	21
WOMEN	52	28	...	...	...	...	1	2	3	...	2
1670 * EQUIPMENT SPECIALIST	8,474	8,474	...	...	...	...	20	4	235	13	2,129
WOMEN	857	857	...	...	...	...	1	2	61	...	375
1699 O EQPT & FACILITY MGT STDT	2	2	...	...	...	...	1	...	1	...	...
WOMEN	...	...	...	...	...	...	...	...	...	...	...
1600 EQPT FACILITIES & SERVICE	14,697	14,606	...	...	...	8	184	102	576	116	3,003
WOMEN	2,000	1,974	...	...	...	3	72	47	192	14	615
1701 P GEN EDUCATION & TRAINING	9,801	2,975	...	...	...	...	23	...	421	53	1,000
WOMEN	6,584	2,192	...	...	...	...	20	...	392	52	884
1702 * EDUCATION &TRAINING TECH	8,056	6,409	6	54	197	1,902	1,943	441	970	119	576
WOMEN	6,576	5,182	5	52	190	1,780	1,773	354	660	76	221
1710 P EDUCATION & VOCAT TRAIN	5,702	1,166	...	...	...	...	23	...	102	4	291
WOMEN	3,858	606	...	...	...	...	16	...	83	4	158
1712 A TRAINING INSTRUCTION	5,818	5,786	...	...	...	...	39	1	443	11	2,252
WOMEN	1,396	1,387	...	...	...	...	26	...	120	4	562
1715 A VOCATIONL REHABILITATION	658	658	...	...	...	...	9	...	11	3	142
WOMEN	170	170	...	...	...	...	5	...	4	2	45
1720 P EDUCATION PROGRAM	456	428	...	...	...	...	...	...	20	...	12
WOMEN	261	245	...	...	...	...	...	...	13	...	6
1725 P PUBLIC HEALTH EDUCATOR	80	78	...	...	...	...	...	...	...	...	4
WOMEN	58	57	...	...	...	...	...	...	...	...	3
1730 P EDUCATION RESEARCH	50	45	...	...	...	...	...	...	...	...	...
WOMEN	24	19	...	...	...	...	...	...	...	...	...
1740 P EDUCATION SERVICES	1,224	1,193	...	...	...	...	2	...	8	...	388
WOMEN	565	538	...	...	...	...	1	...	7	...	204
1750 P INSTRUCTIONAL SYSTEMS	1,406	1,350	...	...	...	...	1	...	8	...	48
WOMEN	648	596	...	...	...	...	...	...	7	...	31
1799 O EDUCATION STUDENT TR	10	10	...	1	...	...	1	...	5	...	3
WOMEN	7	7	...	1	...	...	1	...	4	...	1
1700 EDUCATION	33,261	20,098	6	55	197	1,902	2,041	442	1,988	190	4,716
WOMEN	20,147	10,999	5	53	190	1,780	1,842	354	1,290	138	2,115
1801 A GEN INSP, INVEST & COMPL	7,070	7,051	...	...	...	...	114	...	300	2	1,067
WOMEN	2,480	2,476	...	...	...	...	53	...	154	1	401
1802 * COMPLIANCE INSP & SUPPRT	5,838	5,838	...	...	...	145	743	1,060	2,336	708	602
WOMEN	3,627	3,627	...	...	...	99	521	830	1,446	504	113
1810 A GENERAL INVESTIGATING	3,867	3,850	...	...	...	...	10	...	69	...	141
WOMEN	1,543	1,542	...	...	...	...	7	...	43	...	76
1811 A CRIMINAL INVESTIGATING	32,575	32,247	...	...	...	...	154	...	507	...	687
WOMEN	4,345	4,332	...	...	...	...	37	...	119	...	161
1812 A GAME LAW ENFORCEMENT	390	390	...	...	...	...	4	...	22	4	37
WOMEN	40	40	...	...	...	...	...	...	5	...	6

TABLE D-1, 1995 -- CONTINUED

| \multicolumn{6}{GENERAL SCHEDULE AND RELATED GRADES} | | | | | | MED GRD | AVG GRD | SENIOR PAY LEVELS | OTHER | OCCUPATION | |
10	11	12	13	14	15					CODES TITLES
1	38	26	27	21	8	6.0	6.82	...	...	1421 * ARCHIVES TECHNICIAN
1	18	11	14	6	2	6.0	6.64	...	...	WOMEN
...	...	...	...	...	...	5.0	5.20	...	...	1499 O LIBRARY & ARCHIVES STDNT
...	...	...	...	...	...	5.0	5.67	...	...	WOMEN
107	1,315	1,539	634	300	97	9.0	9.04	40	60	1400 LIBRARY AND ARCHIVES
76	869	971	379	156	43	9.0	8.81	17	50	WOMEN
...	7	20	53	39	30	13.0	12.82	10	...	1510 P ACTUARY
...	2	7	10	8	7	13.0	12.39	1	...	WOMEN
...	165	822	1,306	772	438	13.0	13.05	68	1	1515 P OPERATIONS RESEARCH
...	68	285	291	109	52	13.0	12.61	7	...	WOMEN
...	106	671	630	217	114	13.0	12.70	14	13	1520 P MATHEMATICS
...	42	216	182	47	12	12.0	12.44	3	3	WOMEN
2	5	1	...	...	...	8.0	7.76	...	...	1521 T MATHEMATICS TECHNICIAN
1	5	1	...	...	...	8.0	8.08	...	...	WOMEN
...	87	269	335	242	110	13.0	12.87	19	25	1529 P MATHEMATICL STATISTICIAN
...	45	104	98	57	19	13.0	12.50	5	8	WOMEN
2	219	871	716	432	151	13.0	12.48	29	24	1530 P STATISTICIAN
2	107	387	262	117	26	12.0	12.14	9	12	WOMEN
9	10	4	1	...	...	6.0	6.14	...	1	1531 * STATISTICAL ASSISTANT
6	8	3	...	...	...	6.0	6.12	...	1	WOMEN
...	...	3	11	2	...	13.0	12.71	...	...	1541 T CRYPTANALYSIS
...	...	...	10	...	...	13.0	13.00	...	...	WOMEN
...	160	1,449	755	417	227	12.0	12.49	40	8	1550 P COMPUTER SCIENCE
...	60	524	210	101	38	12.0	12.23	5	2	WOMEN
...	3	...	...	...	...	5.0	4.96	...	...	1599 O MATH & STAT STUDENT TR
...	1	...	...	...	...	5.0	5.38	...	...	WOMEN
13	762	4,110	3,807	2,121	1,070	13.0	12.09	180	72	1500 MATHEMATICS & STATISTICS
9	338	1,527	1,063	439	154	12.0	10.93	30	26	WOMEN
22	370	696	432	229	80	12.0	10.86	...	2	1601 A GENERAL FACILITIES &EQPT
4	69	64	10	5	1	9.0	8.69	...	1	WOMEN
1	34	25	15	4	1	11.0	10.79	...	...	1630 A CEMETERY ADMINISTRATION
...	8	9	1	...	...	11.0	11.24	...	...	WOMEN
44	358	472	195	75	25	12.0	11.34	49	8	1640 A FACILITY MANAGEMENT
1	33	19	8	2	2	11.0	10.67	...	...	WOMEN
3	261	576	185	91	34	12.0	11.30	5	3	1654 A PRINTING MANAGEMENT
1	121	191	24	8	3	11.0	10.54	...	1	WOMEN
37	19	13	1	...	...	9.0	9.41	...	...	1658 A LAUNDRY/DRYCLEAN PLT MGT
5	4	...	...	...	...	9.0	9.50	...	...	WOMEN
8	147	53	37	...	1	11.0	10.88	...	24	1667 A STEWARD
...	15	5	...	...	...	11.0	10.04	...	24	WOMEN
34	3,416	2,298	280	38	7	11.0	10.72	...	...	1670 * EQUIPMENT SPECIALIST
4	310	93	10	1	...	9.0	9.95	...	...	WOMEN
...	...	...	...	...	...	6.0	6.00	...	...	1699 O EQPT & FACILITY MGT STDT
...	...	...	...	...	...	0.0	0.00	...	...	WOMEN
149	4,605	4,133	1,145	437	148	11.0	10.85	54	37	1600 EQPT FACILITIES & SERVICE
15	560	381	53	16	6	11.0	9.89	...	26	WOMEN
39	548	350	305	160	76	9.0	10.23	152	6,674	1701 P GEN EDUCATION & TRAINING
35	375	193	162	55	24	9.0	9.69	15	4,377	WOMEN
34	107	48	7	4	1	5.0	5.59	...	1,647	1702 * EDUCATION &TRAINING TECH
3	47	21	...	...	...	5.0	5.17	...	1,394	WOMEN
...	404	150	110	63	19	11.0	10.57	71	4,465	1710 P EDUCATION & VOCAT TRAIN
...	201	73	44	22	5	11.0	10.16	2	3,250	WOMEN
22	1,825	825	304	52	12	11.0	10.15	...	32	1712 A TRAINING INSTRUCTION
1	435	176	50	11	2	9.0	9.95	...	9	WOMEN
16	402	71	3	1	...	11.0	10.50	...	...	1715 A VOCATIONL REHABILITATION
4	97	12	...	1	...	11.0	10.23	...	...	WOMEN
...	12	88	168	95	33	13.0	12.72	11	17	1720 P EDUCATION PROGRAM
...	6	59	106	42	13	13.0	12.57	6	10	WOMEN
...	28	15	25	5	1	12.0	11.97	...	2	1725 P PUBLIC HEALTH EDUCATOR
...	19	12	18	5	...	12.0	12.00	...	1	WOMEN
...	...	1	6	19	19	14.0	14.24	1	4	1730 P EDUCATION RESEARCH
...	...	1	3	8	7	14.0	14.11	1	4	WOMEN
...	496	169	107	14	9	11.0	10.70	...	31	1740 P EDUCATION SERVICES
...	219	67	35	3	2	11.0	10.46	...	27	WOMEN
...	395	520	277	84	17	12.0	11.93	1	55	1750 P INSTRUCTIONAL SYSTEMS
...	200	207	120	28	3	12.0	11.76	...	52	WOMEN
...	...	...	...	...	...	7.0	6.90	...	...	1799 O EDUCATION STUDENT TR
...	...	...	...	...	...	7.0	6.29	...	...	WOMEN
111	4,217	2,237	1,312	497	187	9.0	8.97	236	12,927	1700 EDUCATION
43	1,599	821	538	175	56	7.0	7.86	24	9,124	WOMEN
353	1,158	2,165	1,145	592	155	12.0	11.35	18	1	1801 A GEN INSP, INVEST & COMPL
76	383	844	397	147	20	12.0	11.14	4	...	WOMEN
126	54	62	2	...	...	7.0	6.97	...	...	1802 * COMPLIANCE INSP & SUPPRT
88	17	9	...	...	...	7.0	6.71	...	...	WOMEN
...	1,631	1,428	433	98	40	12.0	11.55	3	14	1810 A GENERAL INVESTIGATING
...	609	634	139	23	11	12.0	11.43	...	1	WOMEN
769	1,736	8,801	14,664	3,702	1,227	13.0	12.52	326	2	1811 A CRIMINAL INVESTIGATING
166	349	1,524	1,591	318	67	12.0	12.09	12	1	WOMEN
1	46	179	73	16	8	12.0	11.53	...	...	1812 A GAME LAW ENFORCEMENT
...	13	10	4	1	1	11.0	10.83	...	...	WOMEN

TABLE D-1 FULL-TIME CIVILIAN WHITE-COLLAR EMPLOYMENT BY OCCUPATION, GENDER, GENERAL SCHEDULE AND RELATED GRADE, MEDIAN GRADE, AND AVERAGE GRADE, ALL AREAS, SEPTEMBER 30, 1995

OCCUPATION CODES TITLES	GRAND TOTAL	GENERAL SCHEDULE AND RELATED GRADES									
		TOTAL	1	2	3	4	5	6	7	8	9
1815 A AIR SAFETY INVESTIGATING	93	92	...	...	...	...	...	...	1	...	2
WOMEN	10	10	...	...	...	...	...	...	1	...	...
1816 A IMMIGRATION INSPECTION	3,574	3,572	...	...	...	...	367	...	401	...	1,478
WOMEN	920	920	...	...	...	...	107	...	114	...	375
1822 A MINE SAFETY AND HEALTH	1,339	1,337	...	...	...	...	3	...	11	...	58
WOMEN	45	45	...	...	...	...	3	...	4	...	8
1825 A AVIATION SAFETY	3,016	3,013	...	...	...	...	...	...	1	...	4
WOMEN	182	182	...	...	...	...	...	...	1	...	1
1831 A SECURITIES COMPLI EXAM	194	193	...	...	...	...	1	...	71	...	63
WOMEN	100	100	...	...	...	...	1	...	39	...	34
1850 A AGRIC COMMOD WAREHS EXAM	90	90	...	...	...	...	...	...	...	...	...
WOMEN	9	9	...	...	...	...	...	...	...	...	...
1854 A ALCOHOL TOB FIREARM INSP	762	760	...	...	...	...	5	...	16	...	96
WOMEN	354	353	...	...	...	...	3	...	8	...	84
1862 T CONSUMER SAFETY INSPECTN	199	199	...	...	...	2	14	17	20	25	86
WOMEN	92	92	...	...	...	2	6	10	13	15	31
1863 T FOOD INSPECTION	6,559	6,559	...	...	...	...	258	...	2,975	1,159	1,922
WOMEN	1,848	1,848	...	...	...	...	79	...	1,274	287	191
1864 A PUB HLTH QUARANTINE INSP	32	32	...	...	...	...	...	...	4	...	...
WOMEN	17	17	...	...	...	...	...	...	4	...	...
1884 O CUSTOMS PATROL OFFICER	31	31	...	...	...	...	...	...	...	...	27
WOMEN	2	2	...	...	...	...	...	...	...	...	2
1889 A IMPORT SPECIALIST	1,271	1,271	...	...	...	...	9	...	93	4	48
WOMEN	622	622	...	...	...	...	8	...	59	...	31
1890 A CUSTOMS INSPECTION	6,645	6,645	...	...	...	...	155	2	463	14	2,329
WOMEN	1,389	1,389	...	...	...	...	36	...	184	3	475
1894 A CUSTOMS ENTRY & LIQUIDAT	454	454	...	...	...	...	1	...	11	1	46
WOMEN	335	335	...	...	...	...	1	...	7	1	36
1896 O BORDER PATROL AGENT	4,876	4,875	...	...	...	...	588	...	501	...	2,232
WOMEN	198	198	...	...	...	...	48	...	20	...	90
1897 * CUSTOMS AID	982	982	...	...	2	53	408	95	365	12	41
WOMEN	657	657	...	...	1	32	279	64	254	10	16
1898 A ADMEASUREMENT	16	16	...	...	...	...	...	...	...	...	4
WOMEN	1	1	...	...	...	...	...	...	...	...	1
1899 O INVESTIGATION STUDENT TR	57	57	...	...	...	4	30	15	...	7	1
WOMEN	34	34	...	...	2	17	8	...	6	...	1
1800 INVESTIGATION	79,930	79,554	...	...	6	230	2,849	1,174	8,174	1,929	10,971
WOMEN	18,850	18,831	...	...	3	150	1,197	904	3,755	821	2,133
1910 A QUALITY ASSURANCE	10,685	10,682	...	...	...	...	21	5	96	21	1,818
WOMEN	1,498	1,497	...	...	...	...	6	2	31	7	299
1980 T AGRIC COMMODITY GRADING	2,731	2,729	...	...	...	...	123	...	287	215	1,081
WOMEN	694	694	...	...	...	...	71	...	153	105	297
1981 T AGRIC COMMODITY AID	144	144	...	...	1	36	94	2	11	...	...
WOMEN	47	47	...	...	1	23	23	...	...	...	...
1999 O QUALITY INSPECT STUDENT	2	2	...	...	...	1	1	...	...	...	...
WOMEN	1	1	...	...	...	1	...	...	...	...	...
1900 QLTY ASSURANCE INSP & GRD	13,062	13,057	...	...	1	37	239	7	394	236	2,899
WOMEN	2,240	2,239	...	...	1	24	100	2	184	112	596
2001 * GENERAL SUPPLY	3,936	3,934	...	...	...	...	7	5	312	46	1,847
WOMEN	1,658	1,657	...	...	...	...	4	4	162	20	843
2003 A SUPPLY PROGRAM MANAGEMNT	5,136	5,124	...	...	...	...	13	1	58	1	888
WOMEN	2,134	2,132	...	...	...	...	11	1	38	...	495
2005 * SUPPLY CLERICAL & TECH	19,820	19,568	1	8	359	3,090	7,690	3,339	4,443	413	179
WOMEN	11,448	11,296	...	2	175	1,880	4,411	1,961	2,568	198	80
2010 A INVENTORY MANAGEMENT	6,394	6,391	...	...	...	...	33	3	470	12	2,580
WOMEN	3,702	3,702	...	...	...	...	20	3	328	5	1,569
2030 A DISTRIB FACIL & STOR MGT	799	799	...	...	...	...	2	...	7	1	269
WOMEN	188	188	...	...	...	...	1	...	4	...	92
2032 A PACKAGING	337	337	...	...	...	...	1	...	7	...	80
WOMEN	98	98	...	...	...	...	1	...	1	...	32
2050 A SUPPLY CATALOGING	601	600	...	...	...	...	4	...	20	...	286
WOMEN	314	314	...	...	...	...	3	...	14	...	157
2091 C SALES STORE CLERICAL	2,007	1,623	...	18	977	278	165	131	47	6	1
WOMEN	1,788	1,430	...	14	853	241	150	121	46	4	1
2099 O SUPPLY STUDENT TRAINEE	27	27	...	1	6	15	3	...	2	...	...
WOMEN	17	17	...	1	5	7	3	...	1	...	...
2000 SUPPLY	39,057	38,403	1	27	1,342	3,383	7,918	3,479	5,366	479	6,130
WOMEN	21,347	20,834	...	17	1,033	2,128	4,604	2,090	3,162	227	3,269
2101 A TRANSPORTATION SPECIALST	7,248	7,221	...	...	...	1	4	5	79	21	303
WOMEN	941	935	...	...	...	1	1	3	40	5	139
2102 * TRANSP CLERK & ASST	5,100	5,099	...	1	75	678	1,661	1,204	991	280	172
WOMEN	3,609	3,608	...	1	50	498	1,257	920	629	145	83
2110 A TRANSP INDUSTRY ANALYSIS	139	139	...	...	...	...	...	...	1	...	20
WOMEN	56	56	...	...	...	...	...	...	1	...	15
2121 A RAILROAD SAFETY	415	412	...	...	...	...	...	...	...	...	17
WOMEN	18	18	...	...	...	...	...	...	...	...	5
2123 A MOTOR CARRIER SAFETY	257	257	...	...	...	...	2	...	7	...	8
WOMEN	73	73	...	...	...	...	1	...	4	...	5
2125 A HIGHWAY SAFETY	277	276	...	...	...	...	...	...	...	...	3
WOMEN	61	61	...	...	...	...	...	...	...	...	2
2130 A TRAFFIC MANAGEMENT	1,838	1,837	...	...	...	...	7	1	36	5	422
WOMEN	801	800	...	...	...	...	6	...	24	3	226

TABLE D-1, 1995 -- CONTINUED

10	11	12	13	14	15	MED GRD	AVG GRD	SENIOR PAY LEVELS	OTHER	CODES TITLES
...	5	10	32	26	16	13.0	13.26	1	...	1815 A AIR SAFETY INVESTIGATING
...	...	...	4	5	...	13.5	12.90	...	...	WOMEN
...	797	330	134	57	8	9.0	9.33	2	...	1816 A IMMIGRATION INSPECTION
...	190	80	27	23	4	9.0	9.23	...	...	WOMEN
...	90	892	222	40	21	12.0	12.02	2	...	1822 A MINE SAFETY AND HEALTH
...	5	16	8	1	...	12.0	10.67	...	...	WOMEN
...	110	237	1,236	1,113	312	13.0	13.42	3	...	1825 A AVIATION SAFETY
...	20	28	76	37	19	13.0	12.98	...	...	WOMEN
...	18	22	5	11	2	9.0	9.22	1	...	1831 A SECURITIES COMPLI EXAM
...	12	9	2	3	...	9.0	8.92	...	...	WOMEN
...	76	10	3	1	...	11.0	11.21	...	...	1850 A AGRIC COMMOD WAREHS EXAM
...	8	...	1	...	...	11.0	11.22	...	...	WOMEN
...	290	154	138	43	18	11.0	11.45	2	...	1854 A ALCOHOL TOB FIREARM INSP
...	126	65	52	12	3	11.0	11.00	1	...	WOMEN
25	9	1	...	...	...	9.0	8.32	...	...	1862 T CONSUMER SAFETY INSPECTN
10	5	...	...	...	...	8.5	8.08	...	...	WOMEN
170	34	34	4	3	...	8.0	7.82	...	...	1863 T FOOD INSPECTION
14	2	...	1	...	...	7.0	7.31	...	...	WOMEN
...	21	3	4	...	...	11.0	10.84	...	...	1864 A PUB HLTH QUARANTINE INSP
...	10	2	1	...	...	11.0	10.29	...	...	WOMEN
...	4	...	...	...	...	9.0	9.26	...	...	1884 O CUSTOMS PATROL OFFICER
...	...	...	...	...	...	9.0	9.00	...	...	WOMEN
1	553	226	266	63	8	11.0	11.35	...	...	1889 A IMPORT SPECIALIST
1	295	103	112	11	2	11.0	11.03	...	...	WOMEN
...	2,635	733	255	45	14	11.0	10.09	...	...	1890 A CUSTOMS INSPECTION
...	531	100	51	5	4	9.0	9.79	...	...	WOMEN
...	213	144	35	3	...	11.0	11.17	...	...	1894 A CUSTOMS ENTRY & LIQUIDAT
...	172	96	21	1	...	11.0	11.10	...	...	WOMEN
...	760	557	115	100	22	9.0	9.19	1	...	1896 O BORDER PATROL AGENT
...	19	13	2	1	...	9.0	8.36	...	...	WOMEN
...	6	...	...	...	...	6.0	6.02	...	...	1897 * CUSTOMS AID
...	1	...	...	...	...	6.0	5.97	...	...	WOMEN
...	7	1	3	1	...	11.0	11.13	...	...	1898 A ADMEASUREMENT
...	...	...	...	...	...	9.0	9.00	...	...	WOMEN
...	...	...	...	...	...	4.0	4.65	...	...	1899 O INVESTIGATION STUDENT TR
...	...	...	...	...	...	4.0	4.85	...	...	WOMEN
1,445	10,253	15,980	18,769	5,914	1,851	12.0	10.90	359	17	1800 INVESTIGATION
355	2,767	3,539	2,489	588	131	11.0	9.72	17	2	WOMEN
56	6,132	1,895	495	125	18	11.0	10.91	3	...	1910 A QUALITY ASSURANCE
10	869	214	50	9	...	11.0	10.69	1	...	WOMEN
44	269	121	63	24	2	9.0	9.02	...	2	1980 T AGRIC COMMODITY GRADING
3	52	9	4	...	...	9.0	8.21	...	...	WOMEN
...	...	...	...	...	...	5.0	4.90	...	...	1981 T AGRIC COMMODITY AID
...	...	...	...	...	...	4.0	4.47	...	...	WOMEN
...	...	...	...	...	...	4.5	4.50	...	...	1999 O QUALITY INSPECT STUDENT
...	...	...	...	...	...	4.0	4.00	...	...	WOMEN
100	6,401	2,016	558	149	20	11.0	10.52	3	2	1900 QLTY ASSURANCE INSP & GRD
13	921	223	54	9	...	11.0	9.79	1	...	WOMEN
45	973	490	151	32	17	9.0	9.93	1	1	2001 * GENERAL SUPPLY
18	382	171	41	9	3	9.0	9.69	...	1	WOMEN
55	1,428	1,643	681	283	74	12.0	11.39	9	3	2003 A SUPPLY PROGRAM MANAGEMNT
10	689	584	206	78	20	11.0	11.04	1	1	WOMEN
32	12	2	...	...	...	5.0	5.54	...	252	2005 * SUPPLY CLERICAL & TECH
15	5	1	...	...	...	5.0	5.52	...	152	WOMEN
59	2,175	756	216	77	10	11.0	10.09	...	3	2010 A INVENTORY MANAGEMENT
26	1,262	381	77	28	3	9.0	9.92	...	...	WOMEN
19	218	170	89	22	3	11.0	10.78	...	...	2030 A DISTRIB FACIL & STOR MGT
5	43	29	13	2	...	9.0	10.20	...	...	WOMEN
1	166	62	18	2	...	11.0	10.73	...	...	2032 A PACKAGING
...	50	13	1	...	...	11.0	10.40	...	...	WOMEN
3	168	80	26	10	3	9.0	10.16	...	1	2050 A SUPPLY CATALOGING
2	87	39	11	1	...	9.0	9.96	...	...	WOMEN
...	...	...	...	...	...	3.0	3.74	...	384	2091 C SALES STORE CLERICAL
...	...	...	...	...	...	3.0	3.77	...	358	WOMEN
...	...	...	...	...	...	4.0	4.04	...	...	2099 O SUPPLY STUDENT TRAINEE
...	...	...	...	...	...	4.0	3.94	...	...	WOMEN
214	5,140	3,211	1,180	426	107	7.0	7.68	10	644	2000 SUPPLY
76	2,518	1,217	349	118	26	7.0	7.21	1	512	WOMEN
21	1,145	3,486	1,498	526	132	12.0	12.04	24	3	2101 A TRANSPORTATION SPECIALST
7	152	353	155	57	22	12.0	11.46	5	1	WOMEN
14	13	6	4	...	...	6.0	5.81	...	1	2102 * TRANSP CLERK & ASST
8	11	3	3	...	...	5.0	5.69	...	1	WOMEN
...	16	17	29	34	22	13.0	12.59	...	...	2110 A TRANSP INDUSTRY ANALYSIS
...	12	10	7	5	6	11.5	11.52	...	...	WOMEN
...	9	275	75	22	14	12.0	12.25	3	...	2121 A RAILROAD SAFETY
...	4	7	2	...	...	11.5	11.06	...	...	WOMEN
...	8	232	...	...	...	12.0	11.68	...	...	2123 A MOTOR CARRIER SAFETY
...	3	60	...	...	...	12.0	11.38	...	...	WOMEN
...	1	72	121	58	21	13.0	13.05	1	...	2125 A HIGHWAY SAFETY
...	...	14	22	17	6	13.0	13.11	...	...	WOMEN
8	555	507	212	70	14	11.0	11.08	...	1	2130 A TRAFFIC MANAGEMENT
5	256	201	64	13	2	11.0	10.72	...	1	WOMEN

ABLE D-1 FULL-TIME CIVILIAN WHITE-COLLAR EMPLOYMENT BY OCCUPATION, GENDER, GENERAL SCHEDULE AND RELATED GRADE,
          MEDIAN GRADE, AND AVERAGE GRADE, ALL AREAS, SEPTEMBER 30, 1995

OCCUPATION CODES / TITLES	GRAND TOTAL	GENERAL SCHEDULE AND RELATED GRADES									
		TOTAL	1	2	3	4	5	6	7	8	9
2131 * FREIGHT RATE	851	851	...	...	...	6	102	132	265	131	140
WOMEN	590	590	...	...	...	2	80	103	198	98	74
2135 T TRANS LOSS-DAMAGE CLM EX	168	168	...	...	...	4	72	45	16	24	2
WOMEN	132	132	...	...	...	2	58	36	12	21	...
2144 T CARGO SCHEDULING	70	70	...	...	...	1	1	11	34	10	9
WOMEN	23	23	...	...	...	...	...	3	12	5	3
2150 A TRANSPORTATION OPERATION	942	942	...	...	...	...	14	...	56	2	164
WOMEN	255	255	...	...	...	...	9	...	47	...	67
2151 C DISPATCHING	434	434	...	...	57	130	90	21	115	15	5
WOMEN	159	159	...	...	21	46	25	9	47	10	1
2152 A AIR TRAFFIC CONTROL	24,129	24,115	...	...	...	...	1	...	24	2	503
WOMEN	3,338	3,337	...	...	...	...	...	...	...	9	111
2154 T AIR TRAFFIC ASSISTANCE	461	461	...	...	...	...	5	3	405	27	19
WOMEN	116	116	...	...	...	...	...	1	110	3	2
2161 A MARINE CARGO	59	59	...	...	...	...	2	...	4	...	18
WOMEN	10	10	...	...	...	...	...	...	...	...	5
2181 T AIRCRAFT OPERATION	2,740	2,727	...	...	...	...	1	...	...	...	9
WOMEN	30	30	...	...	...	...	...	...	...	...	...
2183 T AIR NAVIGATION	276	276	...	...	...	...	...	...	1	...	1
WOMEN	4	4	...	...	...	...	...	...	...	...	1
2185 T AIRCREW TECHNICIAN	949	949	...	...	...	...	5	5	16	37	395
WOMEN	21	21	...	...	...	...	1	...	...	3	10
2199 0 TRANSPORTATION STUDNT TR	25	25	...	...	3	12	6	...	3	...	1
WOMEN	11	11	...	...	2	5	3	...	...	...	1
2100 TRANSPORTATION	46,378	46,318	...	1	135	832	1,973	1,427	2,063	554	2,211
WOMEN	10,248	10,239	...	1	73	554	1,441	1,075	1,133	293	750
2299 9 UNSPECIFIED SERIES	343	20	...	1	1	2	...	1	2	1	...
WOMEN	141	8	...	1	...	1	...	...	1	1	...
2200 UNSPECIFIED	343	20	...	1	1	2	...	1	2	1	...
WOMEN	141	8	...	1	...	1	...	...	1	1	...

TABLE D-1, 1995 -- CONTINUED

GENERAL SCHEDULE AND RELATED GRADES						MED GRD	AVG GRD	SENIOR PAY LEVELS	OTHER	OCCUPATION	
10	11	12	13	14	15					CODES	TITLES
26	34	11	2	2	...	7.0	7.41	...	...	2131 * FREIGHT RATE	
9	19	5	2	...	...	7.0	7.20	...	...		WOMEN
5	...	...	...	...	...	6.0	6.06	...	...	2135 T TRANS LOSS-DAMAGE CLM EX	
3	...	...	...	...	...	6.0	6.03	...	...		WOMEN
3	1	...	...	...	...	7.0	7.36	...	...	2144 T CARGO SCHEDULING	
...	...	...	...	...	...	7.0	7.35	...	...		WOMEN
22	267	265	101	28	13	11.0	10.89	...	...	2150 A TRANSPORTATION OPERATION	
2	54	52	17	7	...	11.0	9.94	...	...		WOMEN
1	...	...	...	...	...	5.0	5.18	...	...	2151 C DISPATCHING	
...	...	...	...	...	...	5.0	5.31	...	...		WOMEN
648	2,148	5,957	2,096	9,903	1,933	13.0	12.98	14	...	2152 A AIR TRAFFIC CONTROL	
122	422	965	437	1,083	188	13.0	12.64	1	...		WOMEN
2	...	...	...	...	...	7.0	7.13	...	...	2154 T AIR TRAFFIC ASSISTANCE	
...	...	...	...	...	...	7.0	7.05	...	...		WOMEN
...	25	9	1	...	...	11.0	10.10	...	...	2161 A MARINE CARGO	
...	5	...	...	...	...	10.0	10.00	...	...		WOMEN
1	42	690	1,621	344	19	13.0	12.84	...	13	2181 T AIRCRAFT OPERATION	
...	...	13	10	6	1	13.0	12.93	...	...		WOMEN
...	12	241	14	7	...	12.0	12.03	...	...	2183 T AIR NAVIGATION	
...	2	1	...	...	...	11.0	10.75	...	...		WOMEN
283	191	15	2	...	...	10.0	9.65	...	...	2185 T AIRCREW TECHNICIAN	
6	...	1	...	...	...	9.0	9.10	...	...		WOMEN
...	...	...	...	...	...	4.0	4.68	...	...	2199 O TRANSPORTATION STUDNT TR	
...	...	...	...	...	...	4.0	4.55	...	...		WOMEN
1,034	4,467	11,783	6,676	10,994	2,168	12.0	11.55	42	18	2100 TRANSPORTATION	
162	940	1,685	719	1,188	225	9.0	9.24	6	3		WOMEN
...	...	3	2	4	3	12.0	10.20	69	254	2299 9 UNSPECIFIED SERIES	
...	...	1	...	2	1	10.0	9.50	10	123		WOMEN
...	...	3	2	4	3	12.0	10.20	69	254	2200 UNSPECIFIED	
...	...	1	...	2	1	10.0	9.50	10	123		WOMEN

Appendix N: Wage Grade Occupations in Federal Service

This appendix contains official summary definitions of Federal blue-collar job titles and is the Wage Grade counterpart to Appendix K. Again, bear in mind that governmental positions do not always coincide with similar job titles in the private sector; you should therefore never assume that your private-sector experience applies directly to Federal service. On the other hand, there are probably Federal job titles for which you do qualify but with which you are not familiar. The descriptions presented here will help you determine which blue-collar job titles are most suitable for you. Salaries are not indicated because most occupations cover a range of grade levels; moreover, Wage Grade salaries may vary geographically.

For further information regarding a particular job title, consult *Handbook X-118C*, which you can find at OPM Service Centers, agency personnel offices, or some public libraries. It presents the exact duties and qualifications by grade level for every occupation series described here. You might also wish to obtain a QIS for any job title in which you are seriously interested.

Note: The material in this appendix is reproduced from an OPM document that was last updated in 1986, and some of its classifications numbers or descriptions may have changed in the interim. It appears here, however, because it is the only succinct description of Federal blue-collar jobs available and, despite some possible inaccuracies, is still quite useful in identifying job titles.

> **Job title choice** is discussed throughout Step 1; Appendixes A and B provide further useful information.

> Sources of **job information,** including the *Handbook* and **QISs,** are covered in Step 3.

CONTENTS

ALPHABETICAL INDEX TO DEFINITIONS OF TRADES AND LABOR
JOB FAMILIES AND OCCUPATIONS[1]

*Job grading standard published.

---

*Job grading standard published.

---

*Job grading standard published.

DEFINITIONS OF TRADES AND LABOR JOB FAMILIES AND OCCUPATIONS

2500 WIRE COMMUNICATIONS EQUIPMENT INSTALLATION AND MAINTENANCE FAMILY

This job family includes occupations involved in the construction, installation, maintenance, repair, and testing of all types of wire communications systems and associated equipment which are predominantly electrical-mechanical. WORK INVOLVED IN THE INSTALLATION AND REPAIR OF COMMUNICATIONS EQUIPMENT WHICH REQUIRES IN-DEPTH KNOWLEDGE OF OPERATING ELECTRONIC PRINCIPLES SHOULD BE CODED TO THE ELECTRONIC EQUIPMENT INSTALLATION AND MAINTENANCE FAMILY, 2600.

Occupations in this family are:

2502 Telephone Mechanic*

This occupation includes jobs involved in installing, modifying, repairing, and maintaining telephone systems including central office, private branch automatic, and operator-attended exchanges and customer telephone sets. The work requires knowledge of telephone equipment and installation procedures; knowledge of basic electrical principles as they pertain to the telephone system; the ability to understand and follow such technical guidance as circuit descriptions, schematics, and layout sheets; and the ability to locate and repair trouble within the telephone system.

2504 Wire Communications Cable Splicing

This occupation includes jobs involved in splicing, diagnosing trouble, repairing, and testing aerial, ground, underground, and/or submarine multiple-conductor cables.

2508 Communications Line Installing and Repairing

This occupation includes jobs that involve installing, maintaining, and repairing aerial and underground communications lines and auxiliary equipment such as conduits, insulators, and poles. The work does not require completing line connections.

2511 Wire Communications Equipment Installing and Repairing

This occupation includes jobs involved in installing, repairing, reconditioning, modifying, and adjusting wire communications equipment such as telegraph and teletype equipment, intercom and public address systems, alarm and signaling systems, and wire carrier equipment; includes installing and repairing inside wiring and connecting equipment to outside service wires.

2600 ELECTRONIC EQUIPMENT INSTALLATION AND MAINTENANCE FAMILY

This job family includes occupations involved in the installation, repair, overhaul, fabrication, tuning, alignment, modification, calibration, and testing of electronic equipment and related devices, such as radio, radar, loran, sonar, television, and other communications equipment; industrial controls; fire control, flight/landing control, bombing-navigation, and other integrated systems; and electronic computer systems and equipment.

Occupations in this family are:

2602 Electronic Measurement Equipment Mechanic*

This occupation includes jobs involved in maintenance, repair, calibration, and certification of electronic test, measurement, and reference equipment used for precise measurement of a variety of electrical and electronic values, quantities, and relationships such as voltage, resistance, capacitance, frequency, and inductance. This equipment is also used to maintain and assure the functional accuracy and operational precision of industrial, experimental, airborne, marine, and ground electronic systems and equipment. This work requires a working knowledge and practical application of electronic principles and the ability to perform precise measurement of electrical and electronic values, quantities, and relationships. The work also requires skill in performing such processes as troubleshooting, repairing, modifying, overhauling, testing, installing, and calibrating a variety of measurement equipment, instruments, and consoles.

2604 Electronics Mechanic*

This occupation includes jobs involved in the assembly, fabrication, overhaul, installation, maintenance, and repair of various fixed, semifixed, ground, airborne, and marine electronic equipment such as radar, radio, cryptographic, sonar, navigational aids, and related devices. This work requires a knowledge of the practical application of operating electronic principles, the ability to determine malfunctions, and the skill to perform proper maintenance and repairs to a variety of electronic equipment.

2606 Electronic Industrial Controls Mechanic

This occupation includes jobs involved in the installation, troubleshooting, repair, and calibration of electronic controls and indicating and recording systems used on industrial machinery or engines, or in aircraft engine and similar test facilities. Characteristically, this work requires a knowledge of electronics theory and circuits as applicable to power, timing, motion control, indicating devices, program timing controls, and pulse and counting mechanisms, as well as a knowledge of industrial equipment operation and process control.

2608 Digital Computer Mechanic

This occupation includes jobs involved in the repair, troubleshooting, calibration, and testing of electronic digital computer systems and their components and auxiliary equipment. Includes repairing and maintaining computer subsystems/components of integrated aircraft and weapons control systems where the work does not require considering the interaction of the items worked on with the total integrated system. The work requires general comprehension of the operating electronic principles and mechanics of the computer and auxiliary components, understanding of computer logic, and ability to use a variety of electronic test equipment.

2610 Electronic Integrated Systems Mechanic*

This occupation includes jobs involved in rebuilding, overhauling, installing, troubleshooting, repairing, modifying, calibrating, aligning, and maintaining integrated electronic systems, i.e., where the output of a number of sensor subsystems is integrated in a logic subsystem and the resultant used to modify the operation of the total system. Examples are: fire control, flight/landing control, bombing-navigation, and electronic warfare or multiple integrated electronic systems composed of several of these systems which are closely interrelated and interdependent. This work requires knowledge of electronics principles involved in a number of applications such as radar, data processing, and data display as well as mechanical and hydraulic knowledges involved in operation of equipment such as control valves, gyros, turrets and mounts, and mechanical computing devices.

2800 ELECTRICAL INSTALLATION AND MAINTENANCE FAMILY

This job family includes occupations involved in the fabrication, installation, alteration, maintenance, repair, and testing of electrical systems, instruments, apparatus, and equipment.

---

*Job grading standard published.

Occupations in this family are:

2805 Electrician*

This occupation includes jobs involved in the installation, maintenance, and repair of electrical wiring systems, fixtures, controls, and equipment. These jobs require knowledge and application of electrical principles, materials, and safety standards.

2810 Electrician (High Voltage)*

This occupation includes jobs involved in installation, test, repair, and maintenance of electric power plant and/or overhead and underground primary electrical distribution systems. These jobs require knowledge and application of electrical principles, procedures, materials, and safety standards governing work on electrical systems above 550 volts.

2854 Electrical Equipment Repairing*

This occupation includes jobs involving the assembly, fabrication, troubleshooting, testing, repair, overhaul, modification, and general maintenance of electrical equipment such as automatic alternator synchronizing equipment, amplidyne control units, voltage regulating equipment, generators, switching and control panels, junction boxes, AC and DC motors, electrical harnesses, transformers, and power amplifiers. Electrical equipment repair at the full performance level and above requires an in-depth knowledge of electrical circuitry, electrical principles and formulas, and their practical application to the equipment and systems repaired.

2892 Aircraft Electrical Systems Installing, and Repairing

This occupation includes jobs involved in the troubleshooting, installation, testing, modification, and repair of electrical systems and equipment on aircraft, missiles, test vehicles, and aircraft training devices. Includes installation of electrical systems, diagnosis and elimination of trouble in the systems, and modification of systems by replacement of individual components or installation of new systems. The work requires knowledge; and skill in locating and tying in the electrical systems with the aircraft armament, electronics, and instrument systems; adjusting and calibrating the components of the various electrical systems so that operation is within established limits; and reading and interpreting blueprints, wiring diagrams, and schematics so as to follow a system through to diagnose malfunctions and check continuity, resistance, voltages, and amperage.

3100 FABRIC AND LEATHER WORK FAMILY

This job family includes occupations involving the fabrication, modification, and repair of clothing and equipment made of (a) woven textile fabrics of animal, vegetable, or synthetic origin; (b) plastic film and filaments; (c) natural and simulated leather; (d) natural and synthetic fibers; and (e) paper. Work involves use of handtools and mechanical devices and machines to lay out, cut, sew, rivet, mold, fit, assemble, and attach findings to articles such as uniforms, rainwear, hats, belts, shoes, brief cases, holsters, equipage articles, tents, gun covers, bags, parachutes, upholstery, mattresses, brushes, etc.

Occupations in this family are:

3103 Shoe Repairing

This occupation includes jobs involved in the resoling, reheeling, and repairing of boots and shoes by hand or by using such machines as sanders, stitchers, trimmers, and rough rounders.

3105 Fabric Working*

This occupation includes jobs involved in making, modifying, altering, and repairing fabric equipment, clothing, and other articles, such as awnings, tents, containments, gun covers, sleeping bags, parachutes, belts, carrying cases, flags, bed linens, protective clothing, work clothes, dress clothes, suits, coats, and uniforms. Fabrics include wool, cotton, linen, canvas, nylon, polyester, rayon, acetate, acrylic, olefin, saran, metallic fabrics, fabrics made of rubber yarns or plastic filaments, leather, felt, fiberglass, vinyl, asbestos, and other similar materials. Fabric work involves taking measurements, making patterns and layouts, marking, cutting, fitting, and sewing or cementing parts together, using hand or power tools and equipment and knowledge of fabrics and construction methods.

3106 Upholstering*

This occupation includes jobs involved in repairing and replacing upholstery, including fabrics, springs, webbing, filling, and padding on items such as furniture, seats, and structural framework in houses, rooms, offices, aircraft, ships, boats, railroad cars, automobiles, trucks, buses, and other vehicles or equipment. Upholstering work involves taking measurements, making patterns and layouts, cutting fabrics, fitting and joining cover pieces, and installing and fastening upholstery materials in place, using hand or power tools and equipment and knowledge of fabrics and upholstery methods.

3111 Sewing Machine Operating*

This occupation includes jobs which involve operating power sewing machines to sew, alter, or repair wearing apparel, linens, blankets, and other fabric articles. This includes operation of automatic sewing machines when the operator must know how to thread the machine, wind bobbins, adjust tension, and oil parts.

3114 Mattress Making and Repairing

This occupation includes jobs involved in manufacturing, repairing, or renovating mattresses by hand or machine. This may include tearing apart old, worn, or dirty mattresses, conditioning the material from which mattresses are made, and assembling the material into renovated units.

3118 Embroidering

This occupation includes jobs involved in hand embroidering designs and patterns on standards, colors, combat ribbons'-streamers, and special flags. Includes blending colored toss in accordance with paintings or drawings which indicate the desired effect of color scheme and shading.

3119 Broom and Brush Making

This occupation includes jobs involved in the hand and machine manufacture of brooms, brushes, sweepers, and dusters made of hair, tampico or palmyra fiber, corn, hickory splints, and other material.

3300 INSTRUMENT WORK FAMILY

This job family includes occupations that involve fabricating, assembling, calibrating, testing, installing, repairing, modifying, and maintaining instruments and instrumentation systems for measuring, regulating, and computing physical quantities such as mass, moment, force, acceleration, displacement, stress, strain, vibration or oscillation frequency, phase and amplitude, linear or angular velocity, space-time position and attitude, pressure, temperature, density, viscosity, humidity, thermal or electrical conductivity, voltage, current, power, power factor, impedance, and radiation. Examples of such instruments and equipment are: gyro, optical,

---

*Job grading standard published.

photographic, timekeeping, electrical, metered, pressure, and geared instruments, test equipment, and navigation, flight control, and fuel totalizing systems. The work requires knowledge of electrical, electronic, mechanical, optical, pneumatic, and/or hydraulic principles. WORK THAT PRIMARILY INVOLVES FABRICATING AND REPAIRING ELECTRONIC INSTRUMENTS SHOULD BE CODED TO THE ELECTRONIC EQUIPMENT INSTALLATION AND MAINTENANCE FAMILY, 2600.

Occupations in this family are:

3306 Optical Instrument Repairing*

This occupation includes jobs involved in troubleshooting, overhauling, modifying, maintaining, and testing optical instruments such as binoculars, telescopes, cameras, sextants, gunsights, periscopes, and cinetheodolites. These jobs primarily require knowledge and application of optical principles, procedures, and materials and, in addition, knowledge of mechanical and electrical methods of mounting and controlling optical systems.

3309 Timekeeping Instrument Repairing

This occupation includes jobs involved in cleaning, adjusting, repairing, rebuilding, and regulating watches, clocks, chronographs, timers, and other precision timing instruments and mechanisms.

3314 Instrument Making*

This occupation includes jobs involved in planning and fabricating complex research and prototype instruments that are made from a variety of materials and are used to detect, measure, record, and regulate heat, pressure, speed, vibration, sound, illumination, biomedical phenomena, and other areas of interest to scientific, engineering, or medical personnel. The work requires skill and knowledge of more than one specific trade.

3315 Nuclear Reactor Instrument Systems Mechanic

This occupation includes jobs involved in maintaining and modifying the control and instrumentation systems, auxiliary systems, safety systems, and radiation and activity monitoring systems associated with a light- or heavy-water or liquid metal cooled and moderated, heterogeneous or homogeneous core nuclear reactor. Includes repairing and adjusting individual instruments which are part of integrated instrumentation systems; maintaining and modifying instrumentation for experiments with dynamic test articles; and maintaining, modifying, or restoring operational safety and continuity when trouble is experienced during operation. The work requires knowledge of: (a) the dynamics of the entire reactor complex, including the interrelationships of the control and instrumentation systems and the effects they have on continuous and safe operation of the reactor; (b) causes and effects of reactor power level variations and causes and effects of variations in combinations of related system circumstances and/or conditions; (c) causes and symptoms of abnormal or dangerous instrumentation indications; (d) characteristics of fallacious or erratic instrumentation system operation in contrast to characteristics of faulty reactor or related system operations; (e) troubleshooting procedures used to determine the cause of incidental scramming of the reactor during operation; and (f) the operation and use of equipment involved in the reactor control and, safety systems, including nuclear, electronic, electrical, and mechanical instrumentation systems and components.

3341 Scale Building, Installing, and Repairing

This occupation includes jobs involved in constructing, installing, testing, calibrating, and repairing various types and sizes of weighing scales such as railroad scales, platform scales, truck scales, and scales used to weigh explosives; mail, parcel post, and shipping scales; and precision scales,

balances, and automatic weighing machines that use troy weights for weighing bullion, assays, and coins. May include making, testing, and adjusting replacement parts such as weights.

3359 Instrument Mechanic*

This occupation includes jobs involved in troubleshooting, repairing, overhauling, modifying, testing, calibrating, and installing mechanical, electrical, and/or pneumatic instruments, test equipment, and functionally related assemblies, data processing equipment, and controls related to the operation of industrial, power generation, airborne, marine, and precision measurement equipment and systems. The work includes the repair, maintenance, and calibration of precision measurement instruments and standards such as flow stands, test consoles, recorders, analyzers, converters, and other general and special purpose test equipment. The work requires knowledge and application of mechanical and electrical principles, procedures, and materials; knowledge of the pneumatic and hydraulic mechanisms used to convert pressure and flow into measurable units; and knowledge of the basic operating principles of electronics.

3364 Projection Equipment Repairing

This occupation includes jobs that involve the overhaul and testing of sound and silent motion picture projectors, opaque or transparency projectors, and any integrated or associated audio components. The work includes disassembly, repair, replacement of parts, reassembly, and testing of equipment and requires knowledge of mechanical parts fitting and timing adjustments, maintenance of fractional horsepower electrical motors and related circuitry, and repair of multiple-stage electronic amplifiers in audio components.

3400 MACHINE TOOL WORK FAMILY

This job family includes occupations that involve setting up and operating machine tools and using handtools to make or repair (shape, fit, finish, assemble) metal parts, tools, gages, models, patterns, mechanisms, and machines; and machining explosives and synthetic materials.

Occupations in this family are:

3414 Machining*

This occupation includes jobs involved in the manufacture and repair of parts and items of equipment which require the use of various types of standard and special machine tools and their attachments to machine metals, metal alloys, and other materials. The work requires skill in the initial planning of necessary work sequences, laying out reference points and lines to be followed in the machining processes, planning for and setting up the work in the machine, selecting and shaping metal cutting tools, operating all types of machine tools, and performing precision handwork to fit, finish, and assemble machined parts and equipment; a knowledge of the makeup of blueprints and drawings and the skill necessary to interpret them; and skill in working from other types of specifications such as sketches, models of parts to be manufactured, or work order's.

3416 Toolmaking*

This occupation includes jobs involved in the fabrication, manufacture, calibration, reconditioning, and repair of machine tools, jigs, fixtures, dies, punches, and gages used in the manufacture, overhaul, and repair of equipment.

3417 Tool Grinding

This occupation includes jobs involved in reconditioning tools, dies, punches, cutters, jigs, and fixtures by reshaping, sharpening, and refinish-

---

*Job grading standard published.

ing them by hand, using files, abrasives, and other hand equipment, and by machine, using grinding wheels.

3422 Power Saw Operating

This occupation includes jobs involved in sawing metal materials, using do-all saws, band saws, circular saws, friction saws, cut-off saws, or other similar types of saws.

3428 Die Sinking*

This occupation includes jobs involved in machining and grinding matched impressions in steel blocks to repair and make metal dies which are used in forging shops.

3431 Machine Tool Operating*

This occupation includes jobs involved in the set up, adjustment, and operation of conventional machine tools to perform machining operations in the manufacture of castings, forgings, or parts from raw stock made of various metals, metal alloys, and other materials; or machining operations required in the repair of such items. Work assignments normally involve standard or repetitive operations that can be performed on one machine. The work requires a knowledge of basic machining processes and skill in performing machining operations such as boring, drilling, planing, milling, and turning on milling machines, radial or multiple spindle drill presses, planers, lathes, or equivalent types of conventional machine tools.

3500 GENERAL SERVICES AND SUPPORT WORK FAMILY

This job family includes occupations not specifically covered by another family that require little or no specialized training or work experience to enter. These occupations usually involve work such as moving and handling materials (e.g., loading, unloading, digging, hauling; hoisting, carrying, wrapping, mixing, pouring, spreading); washing and cleaning laboratory apparatus, cars and trucks, etc.; cleaning and maintaining ship decks, living quarters, hospital rooms and wards, office buildings, grounds, and other areas; and doing other general maintenance work, by hand or using common handtools and power equipment. They may involve heavy or light physical work and various skill levels. Skills are generally learned through job experience and instruction from supervisors or, in some instances, formal training programs lasting a few days or weeks or longer.

Occupations in this family are:

3502 Laboring*

This occupation includes jobs which require mainly physical abilities and effort in doing laboring duties involving little or no specialized skill or prior work experience. Typical of this occupation are such duties as: loading and unloading trucks and boxcars; moving furniture, supplies, etc., by hand or handtruck; digging ditches; mowing lawns; washing cars; etc. Such jobs are found in a wide variety of work situations, such as road maintenance, railroad maintenance, ground maintenance, warehouses, shops, etc.

3506 Summer Aid/Student Aid

This occupation includes ONLY (1) Summer Aids employed under Schedule A authority 213.3102(v); and (2) Student Aids employed under Schedule A authority 213.3102(w) paid at special rates established under agency authority.

3507 Deckhand-Sailor

This occupation includes jobs that involve doing general maintenance work and handling gear and equipment in the deck department of a vessel,

e.g., maintaining, repairing, cleaning, and painting the deck, hull, superstructure, living quarters, storage areas, and launches; raising and lowering launches and small craft; operating cargo gear and deck machinery; rigging booms; handling lines during docking, mooring, and departure operations and to make up tows; mending lines and canvas; standing lookout and security watches; shipkeeping; operating launches and small boats engaged in survey and other activities; connecting, disconnecting, and caring for pipelines; steering pipelines; cleaning suction hose; removing snags; destroying water hyacinths; assisting in the erection of tide gages and hydrographic signals; and operating fishing gear.

3508 Pipeline Working

This occupation includes jobs involved in the assembly, movement, and disassembly of discharge pipeline, and the construction and repair of pipeline trestles, dikes, ditches, and spillways for the disposal and drainage of material dredged from waterways.

3511 Laboratory Working*

This occupation includes jobs requiring ability to clean, prepare for sterilization, sterilize, and assemble laboratory and hospital glassware, instruments, and related items. This work includes such tasks as sorting and loading items into washing machine baskets; operating washing machines, sterilizers, water stills, and centrifuges; preparing flasks, beakers, vials, test tubes, and dishes by capping, corking, plugging, and wrapping; assembling special purpose apparatus by arranging and connecting various types and sizes of glassware, instruments, tubings, adapters, connectors, etc., into a composite unit.

3512 Studio-Property Handling

This occupation includes jobs involved in handling, striking, storing, and making minor repairs to studio equipment such as reflectors, mirrors, parallels, scaffolds, canvas tops, and awnings; handling, installing, and removing set properties and scenery; constructing and rigging runways, scaffolds, platforms, backings, and framework, and using blocks and falls and other tackle necessary for the erection and placement of sets and set elements required for production of motion pictures; operating, moving, propelling, and caring for cranes, lifts, dollies, and other rolling equipment required for completion of camera shots; and assembling, setting up, and storing track required for making movie camera shots.

3513 Coin/Currency Checking

This occupation includes jobs involved in visually examining (1) finished coins and medals for finish, appearance, discoloration, missing letters, etc., or (2) U.S. currency, stamps, bonds, and other paper securities and documents to detect imperfections.

3514 Choker Setting

This occupation includes jobs involved in fastening wire, cable, or chain nooses to logs which have been felled and bucked into saw log lengths preparatory to skidding by tractor or overhead cable into log decks or loading areas.

3515 Laboratory Support Working

This occupation includes jobs involved in performing manual work in laboratories, clinics, etc., in support of educational, research, or similar activities. Work includes such tasks as preparing samples by measuring, grinding, drying, sieving, chopping, and mixing materials and solutions; transporting, setting up, dismantling, and arranging models, exhibits, equipment, and supplies; checking equipment for proper operation; and operating and making minor repairs to auxiliary equipment such as water stills, electric power distribution panels, pH meters, and spectropho-

---

*Job grading standard published.

tometers. Does not include jobs that primarily require technical knowledge of the biological or agricultural sciences, physical sciences, medicine, or other scientific activities.

3543 Stevedoring

This occupation includes jobs involved in operating winches and in working under ship's tackle or dockside or floating cranes to load and unload ships, barges, and other vessels; transporting materials between dockside or lighter and ship's deck or hold; and performing necessary rigging, lashing, and stowing.

3545 Pier Facilities Working

This occupation includes jobs involved in assembling and transporting cargo-handling gear on piers; installing, replacing, and repairing equipment, including frayed lines, hawsers, rigging rope, and lashing; splicing ropes; and shifting and placing dock floats and gangways.

3546 Railroad Repairing*

This occupation includes jobs involved in installing, removing, aligning, maintaining, and repairing rails, ties, ballast, switches, frogs, joints, and other parts of railroad tracks and roadbeds, using hand operated power tools and other manually operated equipment. The work requires a knowledge of the layout and maintenance requirements of tracks, roadbeds, and their parts, and ability to find and repair defects in them using specialized railroad maintenance equipment.

3566 Custodial Working*

This occupation includes jobs involving janitorial and custodial work, such as sweeping, scrubbing, and waxing floors; washing windows and walls; dusting and polishing furniture and fixtures; and emptying waste cans. Work is done by hand or with powered equipment.

3600 STRUCTURAL AND FINISHING WORK FAMILY

This job family includes occupations not specifically covered by another family that involve doing structural and finishing work in construction, maintenance, and repair of surfaces and structures, e.g., laying brick, block, and stone; setting tile; finishing cement and concrete; plastering; installing, maintaining, and repairing asphalt, tar, and gravel; roofing; insulating and glazing.

Occupations in this family are:

3602 Cement Finishing*

This occupation includes jobs involved in construction and repair of cement and concrete surfaces and structures.

3603 Masonry*

This occupation includes jobs involved in maintenance, repair, alteration, and construction of masonry structures of brick, block, stone, firebrick, and similar materials.

3604 Tile Setting

This occupation includes jobs involved in the application of structural and/or glazed tile to walls, floors, and ceilings according to specified designs.

3605 Plastering*

This occupation includes jobs involved in the application and finishing of plaster surfaces in the construction and repair of interior walls and ceilings and stucco exterior walls.

3606 Roofing*

This occupation includes jobs involved in maintenance, installation, repair, and weatherproofing of roofs.

3609 Floor Covering Installing

This occupation includes jobs involved in laying tile, linoleum, vinyl sheet goods, and/or carpeting on floors. May include installing coverings on walls and cabinet tops.

3610 Insulating*

This occupation includes jobs involved in fabrication and installation of insulating materials on tanks, boilers, turbines, pumps, pipes, valves, ducts, and other structures to reduce heat loss or absorption, prevent moisture condensation, or reduce sound levels. This work requires a knowledge of insulating materials and their insulating properties and the ability to lay out, form, and install a variety of insulating materials on regular and irregular shaped objects.

3611 Glazing

This occupation includes jobs involved in cutting, fitting, polishing, and installing window or skylight glass and structural and plate glass or glass substitutes; and/or setting and replacing broken windshields and window glass in automotive and engineering type equipment.

3653 Asphalt Working*

This occupation includes jobs involved in maintenance, repair, and construction of roads, pavements, parking areas, or similar surfaced areas of asphalt.

3700 METAL PROCESSING FAMILY

This job family includes occupations which involve processing or treating metals to alter their properties or produce desirable qualities such as hardness or workability, using processes such as welding, plating, melting, alloying, casting, annealing, heat treating, and refining.

Occupations in this family are:

3702 Flame/Arc Cutting

This occupation includes jobs involved in cutting metal, using gas burning or electric arc cutting equipment.

3703 Welding*

This occupation includes jobs involved in welding metals and alloys. The work requires a knowledge of electric, gas, and other welding processes such as electron beam welding, and the skill to apply these processes in manufacturing, repairing, modifying, rebuilding, and assembling various types of metal and alloy parts, equipment, systems, and structures such as buildings, aircraft, and ships.

---

*Job grading standard published.

3707 Metalizing

This occupation includes jobs involved in dipping or spraying molten metal coatings, such as tin, zinc, or copper, on metal objects by hand or by use of equipment such as metal spraying machines or galvanizing equipment.

3708 Metal Process Working

This occupation includes jobs involved in performing support-type operations in a foundry, refinery, or other plant concerned with heating, melting, pouring, or casting metal, e.g., dressing molds, charging furnaces, skimming slag from the surface of molten metal, pouring metal, removing castings from molds, and removing excess metal from castings and forgings using chipping hammers and grinding wheels.

3711 Electroplating

This occupation includes jobs involving the use of electrolytic and chemical processes to plate, coat, and treat surfaces of metals and metal alloys for purposes of protection, repair, maintenance, and fabrication of parts and equipment. The work requires a knowledge of the preparation, testing, and maintenance of various electrolytic and chemical solutions; and skill in controlling and using them in performing the processes required to prepare, plate, coat, or otherwise treat various types of surfaces.

3712 Heat Treating

This occupation includes jobs involved in heat treating metals in a furnace or preheated chemical bath to alter the physical and chemical properties of the metal to produce a specific degree of hardness, toughness, or strength by an established process of controlled heating and cooling; and/or operating an annealing furnace and a series of vats to anneal, treat, wash, and rinse metal components.

3716 Leadburning

This occupation includes jobs involved in burning (welding) lead and lead alloy parts in fabricating, repairing, and installing lead fixtures and equipment.

3720 Brazing and Soldering

This occupation includes jobs involved in cleaning and positioning items to be hand brazed, applying flux, preheating, and operating gas or induction brazing equipment to braze metal joints, using copper, silver alloy, or similar high melting point material to form the bond between ferrous items and steel or cemented carbide items such as cutting tools and wear inserts, fixtures, and gage parts; and/or preparing work, applying flux, heating, and joining metal surfaces using low melting point soldering materials.

3722 Cold Working

This occupation includes jobs involved in cold working partially machined tubes, cylinders, rocket parts, shells, bombs, and barrels to improve their physical characteristics and to detect weaknesses.

3723 Casting Machine Operating

This occupation includes jobs involved in setting up, adjusting, and operating die casting, permanent mold, and other types of casting machines to produce metal castings.

3725 Battery Repairing

This occupation includes jobs involved in disassembling, repairing, reassembling, and charging batteries used in aircraft, electric trucks, motor vehicles, and other types of equipment, including breaking down batteries (removing compound, connector, and cell groups), washing down and diagnosing extent of repairs needed, and repairing and/or rebuilding batteries according to diagnosis requirements (assembling new cell groups, replacing compounds and lead burning connections, and replacing or rebuilding terminal posts).

3727 Buffing and Polishing

This occupation includes jobs involved in finishing metal surfaces by buffing, polishing, deburring, burnishing, filing, grinding, and barrel tumbling, using hand tools or powered equipment such as grinders, files, chisels, polishing wheels, and wire brushes.

3735 Metal Phototransferring

This occupation includes jobs involved in making metal templates, name plates, warning and informational signs, dial facings, switch covers, test plates, schematic drawings, and other items, using photographic methods to transfer drawings to light-sensitized surfaces of metal stock. (This process is used in metalworking operations; it is not used in printing or lithographic shops or in preparing conventional photographs for generalized use.)

3736 Circuit Board Making

This occupation includes jobs involved in making printed circuit boards for use in electronic assemblies by photosensitizing prepared laminate sheets, photoetching prepared pattern on laminate sheets, deep-etching circuits, and electroplating circuits as necessary.

3740 Forgings Heating

This occupation includes jobs involved in setting automatic controls to operate oil or gas fired furnaces at the proper temperature to heat metal parts, bars, and billets prior to forging; placing metal in furnaces and determining when properly heated; and removing materials from furnace using long-handled tongs.

3741 Furnace Operating

This occupation includes jobs involved in operating and controlling electric, oil, or gas fired furnaces to melt ferrous, nonferrous, and precious metals or alloys for casting into ingots, bars, slabs, sponges, etc. May include transferring molten metal to ladle and pouring metal into molds.

3744 Refining Equipment Operating

This occupation includes jobs involved in operating chlorinators, furnaces, vacuum pumps, retorts, electrolytic cells, leach tanks, thickeners, filters, agitators, centrifuges, kilns, or other similar equipment required in the refining of gold and silver bullion; the production or processing of ores, metals, or minerals; or the recovery of metals from waste materials.

3769 Shot Peening Machine Operating

This occupation includes jobs involved in setting up and operating an air blast shot peening machine to harden or strengthen metal surfaces, e.g., the bending and twisting surfaces of landing gear struts, propeller caps, master rods, fulcrums, propeller shafts, and crankshafts. Includes examining parts received to determine areas to be shot peened and to reject those with imperfections; setting up machine; making test runs on identical parts using Almen metal testing strips, and making necessary adjustments after

*Job grading standard published.

test runs to obtain adequate peening prior to peening parts on a production basis; and checking and maintaining shot peening machine in operating condition.

3800 METAL WORKING FAMILY

This job family includes occupations involved in shaping and forming metal and making and repairing metal parts or equipment. Includes such work as the fabrication and assembly of sheet metal parts and equipment; forging and press operations; structural iron working, boilermaking, shipfitting, and other plate metal work; rolling, cutting, stamping, riveting, etc. Does not include machine tool work.

Occupations in this family are.

3802 Metal Forging*

This occupation includes jobs involved in the process of forging metal into desired shapes by compressing between a hammer or ram and an anvil in forging machines such as drop hammers, forging presses, coining presses, forging rolls, and upsetters. The work includes setting up, adjusting, operating, and making minor repairs to the forging machines, and the application of heat treating processes such as annealing, tempering, and hardening.

3804 Coppersmithing

This occupation includes jobs involved in the fabrication and repair of pipe sections, pipefittings, and other parts from copper, brass, and other nonferrous metals.

3806 Sheet Metal Mechanic*

This occupation includes jobs involved in the fabrication, modification, repair, assembly, and installation of sheet metal parts, items, and assemblies. Metals include but are not restricted to galvanized and black iron, aluminum and aluminum alloys, stainless steel, copper, and brass sheets, lead alloys, and bronze. Sheet metal has no specific thickness. Although metals one-fourth inch thick or leas are usually considered to be sheet metal, hard and brittle metals are usually thinner while soft metals and alloys may be up to one-half inch.

3807 Structural/Ornamental Iron Working

This occupation includes jobs involved in fabricating, installing, and repairing steel framework and other metal parts of buildings, bridges, and other structures and equipment; fitting together and installing iron grills, gratings, stairways, enclosures, and other ornamental ironwork; and/or assembling prefabricated metal parts such as slotted angle iron and panels into items such as work stands, scaffolds, dollies, and positioning devices. The work includes following blueprints, measuring for correct alignment, cutting pieces to size, drilling holes, and fastening members together by bolting, riveting, welding, etc.

3808 Boilermaking*

This occupation includes jobs involved in the modification, fabrication, repair, assembly, and installation of boilers, tanks, condensers, uptakes, stacks, other pressure vessels, and similar structures of heavy-gauge metal plate.

3809 Mobile Equipment Metal Mechanic*

This occupation includes jobs involved in maintaining and repairing mobile equipment bodies and mainframe groups. The work requires a knowledge of mobile equipment body construction, the ability to determine the extent of damage and most economical methods of repair, and the

skill to remove, fabricate, reshape, and replace or repair such damage as dents, tears, wrinkles, cuts and creases by cutting, knocking out, welding, filling, and sanding. Work is performed on such mobile equipment as passenger cars, trucks, buses, warehouse tractors, fork lifts, ambulances, cranes, fire trucks, and mobile construction equipment.

3812 Heavy-Duty Fabricating Machine Operating

This occupation includes jobs involved in the setup, adjustment, and operation of metal fabricating machines such as bending machines, punch presses, shears, brakes, rolls, nibblers, and hydraulic presses to bend, form, straighten, notch, punch, and cut heavy-gauge metal plates and structural shapes.

3815 Pneumatic Tool Operating

This occupation includes jobs involved in chipping, calking, drilling, riveting, sawing, and grinding heavy metal plates, castings, and structural shapes, using portable pneumatic and electric tools and hand tools such as calking and chipping hammers, drilling machines, riveting hammers, etc., to shape and close seams and fasten metal parts together.

3816 Engraving

This occupation includes jobs involved in engraving lettering and ornamental designs on metal and plastic pieces such as nameplates, silverware, trophies, lighters, and jewelry according to sketches, diagrams, photographs, or sample workpieces, using hand tools or pantograph engraving machine.

3817 Locksmithing*

This occupation includes jobs involved in repairing, overhauling, modifying, testing, and installing a variety of locking devices typically found on doors, desks, compartments, mobile equipment, safes, vaults, and other secured locations. The work includes the manufacture and duplication of keys and the keying and combinating of locking mechanisms. The work requires a knowledge of the construction, operation, and functional characteristics of locking devices, and skill in manufacturing replacement parts, devising or changing combinations, establishing master keying systems, neutralizing lockouts, and a variety of installation and repair process such as filing, drilling, chiseling and grinding.

3818 Springmaking

This occupation includes jobs which involve setting up and operating machines to manufacture tension, compression, and torsion springs; includes operating machine tools to fabricate the forming blocks and turning mandrels used in forming and shaping.

3819 Airframe Jig Fitting

This occupation includes jobs involved in assembling, fitting, and aligning airframe jigs used in the reworking of aircraft control surfaces, wings, and fuselage sections. The work requires the ability to visualize the configuration of the jig from multiple, cross referenced engineering prints and to determine the tolerances with which the jig must conform; skill in using optical alignment equipment to measure and spot distances and angles so that reference points can be physically located, mechanically adjusted, and set on the jig framework within close tolerances; and knowledge of solid geometry, trigonometry, and algebra to compute reference locations.

3820 Shipfitting*

This occupation includes jobs involved in the modification, fabrication, repair, assembly, and installation of various metal structural parts of ships and other vessels. The work requires knowledge of shipfitting equipment,

---

*Job grading standard published.

structures, and metals; skill in laying out, cutting, and shaping of metal parts; and ability to position, align, and secure parts and subassemblies on ships and other vessels.

3830 Blacksmithing

This occupation includes jobs involved in hand forging wrought iron and other metal objects such as horseshoes, hooks, hitches, hubs, wheel rims, axles, and other metal parts on caissons, buggies, and harnesses. In this process, the metal is usually heated repeatedly in a furnace and beaten into the desired shape with a hammer on an anvil, then hardened and tempered. The work includes Farriery, the practice of shoeing horses and other hoofed mammals by nailing rims of iron or other metals to their hooves.

3831 Rolling and Cutting Machine Operating

This occupation includes jobs involved in operating rolling mills (breakdown and finishing mills), annealing furnaces, slitting machines and related equipment to reduce metal ingots and slabs to finished strips or sheets for production to coinage blanks or other metallic items. May involve using bridge cranes, hoists, or materials handling equipment to lift and position workpieces.

3832 Medal Making

This occupation includes jobs involved in the operation of machine and hand tools such as lathes, annealing equipment, knuckle action or hydraulic presses, crank type and drill presses, sandblasting machines, buffing and polishing lathes, and spray guns to produce official gold, silver, and bronze medals, badges, decorations, and insignia.

3833 Transfer Engraving

This occupation includes jobs involved in plaster of paris casting, electroforming (electrometallurgy), and setting up and operating Janvier die cutting machines (transfer engraving machines) to make exact reproductions or reductions, master dies and hubs, brass intermediates, wax enlargements, plaster of paris molds, and electrotypes (galvanos) from sculptors' original models of United States and foreign coinage, medals, military insignia, governmental and special award citations, emblems, and lapel buttons.

3835 Electron Tube Making

This occupation includes jobs involved in fabricating, assembling, and processing parts and complete tube mounts for experimental electron tubes; constructing cathodes, grids, plates, shields, filaments, and heaters; winding wire of various dimensions; cutting., shaping, folding, and welding solid stock, wire, and sheet metal into tube elements; cutting, grinding, polishing, and cleaning glass parts; operating annealing ovens and furnaces; filling electron tubes with plastic; and operating X-ray machines to locate concealed structures in tubes.

3840 Reinforcing Iron Working

This occupation includes jobs involved in selecting and placing steel bars, stirrups, and spirals in concrete; fastening rods together with wire or patented fasteners; cutting rods with hacksaws or oxyacetylene torches; and bending rods, using rod bending machines.

3858 Metal Tank and Radiator Repairing

This occupation includes jobs which involve the troubleshooting, repair, modification, and testing of aircraft and automotive radiators, air coolers, oil temperature regulators, pontoons, and aircraft tanks and reservoirs made of various kinds of metal such as aluminum, copper, brass, stainless steel, and black iron. The work includes locating and repairing leaks, removing defective parts, and installing new parts.

3869 Metal Forming Machine Operating

This occupation includes jobs that involve setting up, adjusting, and operating metal forming machines such as sheet metal rolls, brakes, shears, hydraulic or mechanical presses, band saws, blanking presses, punch presses, cut-off saws, flanging machines, combination beading machines, planishing machines, shrinking machines, nibblers, power riveters, turret punches, metal stitching machines, drop hammers, "Yoder" hammers and rivet making machines which cut, punch, stamp, draw, shape, and roll metal sheets, strips, or wire into desired shapes or contours (e.g., coin production jobs that involve setting up and operating knuckle action or hydraulic presses and drop hammers to produce proof and finished coins; drill and cranktype presses to perform trimming, piercing, and blanking operations; and upsetting equipment to form a raised edge along the periphery of coin and medal blanks to produce a planchet acceptable for stamping). The work includes installing dies, punches, and other accessories; aligning the mating parts allowing for clearances; feeding the sheet metal into the machine; and manipulating the controls to perform the operations.

3872 Metal Tube Making, Installing, and Repairing

This occupation includes jobs involved in laying out, fabricating, bending, repairing, testing, and installing rigid and flexible metal tubing and welded tube assemblies for use in aircraft hydraulic, fuel, oxygen, and oil systems, and conduits for wiring or cable installations; and forming flat, angular, and channel sheet metal parts into metal tubing and pipe of varying radii. Includes working from blueprints; determining dimensions; selecting or manufacturing bending dies, clamps, and mandrels and mounting them on the machine; making tube bending templates which are used to indicate the number of bends, bend radii, and angle and rotation of bends; and setting up, adjusting, and operating manual, pneumatic, and/or small and large hydraulic tube bending machines, spinning swagers, hydraulic forming machines, hydraulic presses, milling machines, and engine lathes to bend pipe, tubing, and sheet metal stock to accurately determined angles and specified radii, to cold draw, expand, bead, and double flare pipe and tubing, and to cut and finish tubing.

3900 MOTION PICTURE, RADIO, TELEVISION, AND SOUND EQUIPMENT OPERATION FAMILY

This job family includes occupations involved in setting up, testing, operating, and making minor repairs to equipment such as microphones, sound and radio controls, sound recording equipment, lighting and sound effects devices, television cameras, magnetic video tape recorders, motion picture projectors, and broadcast transmitters used in the production of motion pictures and radio and television programs. Also includes occupations that involve related work such as operating public address system equipment.

Occupations in this family are:

3910 Motion Picture Projection*

This occupation includes jobs involved-in the operation and operational maintenance of motion picture equipment such as 8mm, 16mm, fixed and portable 35mm or film strip silent and sound projectors, slide projectors, accessory and associated equipment.

3911 Sound Recording Equipment Operating

This occupation includes jobs involved in operating, testing, adjusting, and making minor repairs to sound recording, re-recording, and sound

---

*Job grading standard published.

mixing equipment such as mixing consoles, amplifiers, recorders, equalizers, filters, reproducers, reverberation chambers, speakers, headsets, and other associated equipment used in the production of motion pictures and radio and television programs. Equipment is used to record voice, music, and sound impulses on discs, magnetic recording tape or film, or motion picture optical film; re-record sound impulses from one or a variety of sources on additional discs, films, or tapes; mix, blend, and control the various sources of sound into a completed composite recording; and perform such operations as lip synchronization, playback of pre- and post-orchestral scoring, narration, and multi-track recording.

3919 Television Equipment Operating

This occupation includes jobs involved in operating television controls, tape recorders, monochrome and color cameras, film projectors, and other equipment to afford simultaneous integration of sound and picture in television programs. The work requires a knowledge of impedance matching and attenuating networks and frequency standards and skill in operating and making minor repairs to television control monitors, processing amplifiers, camera control panels, colorplexers or encoders, synchronizing generators, distribution amplifiers, switching equipment, special effects equipment, test equipment, visual demodulators, oscilloscopes, television transmitters, and microwave equipment.

3940 Broadcasting Equipment Operating

This occupation includes jobs involved in operating and adjusting transmitters and associated antennas and switchgear, broadcast studio consoles, tape and disk playback and reproduction equipment, recording lathes, and other related equipment and facilities used for originating, recording, receiving, and transmitting radio or television broadcasts, including starting up and shutting down transmitters; adjusting tone, volume, and picture quality of programs; monitoring through loudspeaker, headphone, or video equipment; observing volume indicators; making minor repairs and changing parts; keeping operating log; and receiving news messages.

3941 Public Address Equipment Operating

This occupation includes jobs involved in setting up, adjusting, and operating sound-amplifying equipment (public address systems or circuits) used to transmit lectures, announcement, instructions, or programs, either inside of buildings or outside in the field. Includes operating gasoline driven motor generators as necessary for power source.

4000 LENS AND CRYSTAL WORK FAMILY

This job family includes occupations involved in making precision optical elements, crystal blanks or wafers, or other items of glass, crystalline substances, synthetics, polished metals, or similar materials, using such methods as cutting, etching, grinding, polishing, etc.

Occupations in this family are:

4005 Optical Element Working

This occupation includes jobs involved in blocking, grinding, etching, polishing, coating, cementing, silvering, and assembling optical elements such as reticles, prisms, lenses, and optical test plates of glass or other materials for use in precision instruments.

4010 Prescription Eyeglass Making

This occupation includes jobs that involve grinding and polishing eyeglass lenses to prescription specifications and/or cutting, edging, and mounting lenses in frames.

4015 Quartz Crystal Working

This occupation includes jobs involved in cutting, etching, dicing, lapping, orienting, plating, testing, and finishing quartz crystals to specified frequencies for use in aircraft, radio, radar, and signal equipment; and/or calibrating, assembling, and testing crystal units.

4100 PAINTING AND PAPERHANGING FAMILY

This job family includes occupations which involve hand or spray painting and decorating interiors and exteriors of buildings, structures, aircraft, vessels, mobile equipment, fixtures, furnishings, machinery, and other surfaces; finishing hardwoods, furniture, and cabinetry; painting signs; covering interiors of rooms with strips of wallpaper or fabric; etc.

Occupations in this family are:

4102 Painting*

This occupation includes jobs involved in applying coating materials (for example, paint, varnish, lacquer, shellac, epoxy resin, and teflon) on wood, metal, glass, synthetic, concrete, and other surfaces. This coating work is done with brushes, rollers, spray guns, and other related methods and techniques, and is performed on the insides and outsides of buildings, aircraft, vessels, mobile equipment, fittings, furnishings, machinery, and other surfaces.

4103 Paperhanging

This occupation includes jobs involved in the papering or covering of room interiors with strips of wallpaper or fabric.

4104 Sign Painting*

This occupation includes jobs that involve producing, signs and posters, decorating models and displays, painting markings on vehicles, ships, or aircraft, or performing other functions requiring skill in lettering. The work involves the ability to design, lay out, and decorate signs and execute freehand and mechanical lettering, and skill in various production techniques such as silk screen printing, application of reflective sheeting, and lettering with machines.

4110 Scenery Painting

This occupation includes jobs involved in painting scenery, backdrops, or scenery parts from work drawings; blending and mixing paint; and painting woodwork for exteriors and interiors which are photographed as part of a motion picture set. Does not include jobs that primarily require artistic skill and ability.

4157 Instrument Dial Painting

This occupation includes jobs concerned with hand painting instrument dial faces, using radium active or other luminescent material.

4200 PLUMBING AND PIPEFITTING FAMILY

This job family includes occupations that involve the installation, maintenance, and repair of water, air, steam, gas, sewer, and other pipelines and systems, and related fixtures, apparatus, and accessories.

4204 Pipefitting*

This occupation includes jobs involved in the installation, maintenance, and repair of high-temperature water and high-pressure piping systems such as hydraulic, nitrogen, oxygen, steam heating, and steam-generating systems.

---

*Job grading standard published.

4206 Plumbing*

This occupation includes jobs involved in the installation, modification, and repair of utility, supply, and disposal systems, fixtures, fittings, and equipment such as sewage, water, gas, and oil lines, compressed air, vacuum, and acid systems, water closets, water heaters, hydrants, valves, and pumps.

4255 Fuel Distribution System Mechanic

This occupation includes jobs involved in the maintenance and overhaul of pumps, control valves and meters, gages, filters, separators, tanks, pipelines, and other equipment of one or more mechanical, aqua, or hi-speed hydrant fueling and defueling systems.

4300 PLIABLE MATERIALS WORK FAMILY

This job family includes occupations involved in shaping, forming, and repairing items and parts from non-metallic moldable materials such as plastic, rubber, clay, wax, plaster, glass, sand, or other similar materials.

Occupations in this family are:

4351 Plastic Molding Equipment Operating

This occupation includes jobs involved in manufacturing plastic items and parts using a variety of molding equipment. The work involves the set up and operation of molding equipment, using such manufacturing techniques as injection, extrusion, compression, transfer, and slush molding, and a knowledge of the physical properties of plastics and compound materials such as fillers, dyes, and catalysts. May involve the operation of preheaters, shredding machines, and hand tools.

4352 Plastic Fabricating*

This occupation includes jobs which involve fabricating, modifying, repairing, and installing plastic items, paints, assemblies, and structures. The work requires a knowledge of the physical properties and working characteristics of plastics and compound ingredients; ability to use a variety of low pressure shaping, forming, and casting processes; skill in using casting and low pressure processing techniques such as potting, encapsulation, foaming, hand lay-up, thermoforming, and vacuum and pressure bag molding: skill in making master molds, patterns, and form blocks and in performing cutting and finishing operations.

4360 Rubber Products Molding

This occupation includes jobs involved in manufacturing natural and synthetic rubber articles such as hose, tubes, gaskets, packings, and washers, using molding and extruding machines and curing ovens.

4361 Rubber Equipment Repairing

This occupation includes jobs involved in repairing, modifying, testing, and installing synthetic and natural rubber equipment such as oil, water, and alcohol cells and tanks, life rafts, weather and pressure seals, and tiles and tubes, using cold patching and vulcanizing repair procedures. Includes checking items for damage, selecting materials and preparing surface for repair, and operating low pressure forming and curing equipment.

4370 Glassblowing

This occupation includes jobs involved in the development, fabrication, construction, and repair of all types of blown glass such as bottles and pressed or blown scientific, technical, and industrial glassware.

4371 Plaster Pattern Casting

This occupation includes jobs involved in making plaster patterns, molds, coreboxes, forms, and splash casts used in the production of aircraft mechanical parts, shaping or forming dies, etc.

4373 Molding

This occupation includes jobs involved in making bench, floor, or sweep molds for producing foundry castings.

4374 Core Making

This occupation includes jobs involved in making sand cores in molds to produce holes or hollows in castings. This includes the operation of screw core making machines and core blowing machines.

4400 PRINTING FAMILY

This job family includes occupations involved in letterpress (relief), offset-lithographic, gravure (intaglio), or screen printing; includes layout, hand composition, typesetting from hot metal type, platemaking, printing, and finishing operations.

Occupations in this family are:

4402 Bindery Working*

This occupation includes jobs that involve setting up, operating, and making minor repairs to powered and manually operated gathering, stitching, folding, gluing, embossing, papercutting, stapling, drilling, punching, collating, sorting, and binding machines and equipment used in making books, pamphlets, brochures, etc., in quantity.

4403 Hand Composing

This occupation includes jobs involved in the setting and breakdown of type by hand, combined with the proofreading of work for composition and typographical detail.

4405 Film Assembly-Stripping*

This occupation includes jobs involved in the assembly, stripping, and opaquing of photographic negatives and positives used in the offset reproduction of black and white and multicolor subjects. Requires an understanding of the relationship between assembly-stripping and subsequent processes essential to offset reproduction.

4406 Letterpress Operating

This occupation includes jobs involved in the operation and maintenance of presses used for printing material by the letterpress (relief) method from cast metal type or plates on which the printing areas are raised above the non-printing areas.

4407 Linotype Machine Operating

This occupation includes jobs involved in the operation of an automatic machine that selects and assembles matrices of letters into lines and casts strips of type from hot type metal for use in printing. Includes starting and/or adjusting machine, operating automatic casting mechanisms, transferring lines of type, with copy, to composing or bank table for taking proof, and adding new pigs of type metal to melting pot to replenish supply.

---

*Job grading standard published.

4410 Monotype Casting Machine Operating

This occupation includes jobs involved in operating and making minor repairs to an automatic machine that casts and assembles type in composed form for printing.

4413 Negative Engraving*

This occupation includes jobs involved in negative-cutting activities ranging from simply opaquing the background of the negative by painting in pinholes with a solution of asphaltum, lampblack, or turpentine, to making intricate corrections and revisions of film and plastic negatives.

4414 Offset Photography *

This occupation includes jobs involved in operating and making minor repairs to copying cameras used to produce line, halftone, and color separation negatives which are in turn used to produce offset plates.

4416 Platemaking*

This occupation includes jobs involved in processing photographic images onto metal, paper, or plastic plate materials to produce lithographic plates which are used in the offset reproduction of printed matter. Also included are jobs involved in producing paper or plastic masters using photo-direct or electrostatic equipment, as well as jobs that involve other related platemaking processes such as color proofing and making peel coats, scribecoats, and hand transfers. This work requires knowledge of the various types of plates, plastic media, processing and developing solutions, and platemaking equipment (e.g., vacuum frames, whirling machines, automatic plate processors, photo-direct and electrostatic platemaking equipment) and skill in using them to perform platemaking and other related processes necessary in the offset reproduction process.

4417 Offset Press Operating *

This occupation includes jobs involved in the operation and maintenance of offset presses used for printing material by the offset lithographic method from plates on which the printing and non-printing areas are essentially on the same plane. ,

4419 Silk Screen Making and Printing

This occupation includes jobs involved in preparing silk-screen stencils by hand or photographic process, and screen printing letters, diagrams, and designs on various objects such as decals, posters, and instrument dials.

4422 Dot Etching

This occupation includes jobs that involve analyzing continuous-tone color separation negatives and positives in comparison with original films or water colors to determine the amount of color correction and the percentage of color required for high-fidelity color reproduction, and altering tone values to achieve correct color percentages. Requires ability to determine the color value of half-tone dots and use such techniques as extensive masking or staining and tray or local etching.

4425 Photoengraving

This occupation includes jobs involved in making zinc, brass, and copper plates for use in letterpress printing.

4440 Stereotype Platemaking

This occupation includes jobs involved in making stereotype plates for letterpress printing, including preparing the form, molding it into the matrix, and preparing the plates for the press.

4441 Bookbinding

This occupation includes jobs involved in hand binding, rebinding, recasing, and restoring hardback books, manuscripts, musical scores, unbound material, etc. Includes all operations entailed in affixing covers to form books and in finishing same.

4445 Bank Note Designing

This occupation includes jobs involved in drawing, designing, and preparing various kinds of models used in determining the design of engraved plates from which bonds, currency, postage and revenue stamps, and other securities are produced, employing a style and manner calculated to prevent counterfeiting.

4446 Bank Note Engraving

This occupation includes jobs involved in drawing and engraving script, lettering, lathe work, and designs of various kinds on steel dies or plates, and in producing portraits, landscapes, figures, and ornamental engravings on steel dies from which intaglio printing plates are reproduced, employing a style and manner designed to prevent counterfeiting.

4447 Sculptural Engraving

This occupation includes jobs involved in tracing from banknote designer models, transferring tracings to metal, and engraving designs on steel embossing dies which are subsequently used in the manufacture of securities and seals.

4448 Siderographic Transferring

This occupation includes jobs involved in reproducing engravings on steel plates and rolls from original dies, making it possible to produce a single design from individual engravings (lettering, ornamental scrolls, portraits, vignettes, and geometric lathe work) according to models and layouts, and reproducing multiple-subject plates from single-subject dies for printing bank notes, bonds, and other securities.

4449 Electrolytic Intaglio Platemaking

This occupation includes jobs involved in manufacturing intaglio printing plates by electroforming or galvanoplastic reproduction and in examining and coating or recoating electrolytic and steel intaglio printing plates and miscellaneous machine parts with chromium by electroplating.

4450 Intaglio Die and Plate Finishing

This occupation includes jobs involved in finishing, altering, and restoring engraved areas of intaglio dies and plates and making spot repairs of injuries in the printing plates on the presses. This includes scraping, punching, rolling, grinding, and burnishing the unengraved areas of intaglio dies, rolls, and plates and requires the skillful use of hand and/or machine tools to prepare plates to meet the operational requirements of the various printing presses without disturbing the engraving.

4454 Intaglio Press Operating

This occupation includes jobs involved in the operation and maintenance of intaglio presses (die-stamping or gravure presses) used for printing material by the intaglio method from plates which use a sunken or depressed surface for the printing area.

---

*Job grading standard published.

4600 WOOD WORK FAMILY

This job family includes occupations involved in the construction, alteration, repair, and maintenance of wooden buildings and other structures, and the fabrication and repair of wood products such as furniture, foundry patterns, and form blocks, using power and hand tools.

Occupations in this family are:

4602 Blocking and Bracing*

This occupation includes jobs involved in blocking, bracing, staying, and securing cargo for shipment by land, sea, or air. It requires skill in constructing, placing, and installing wooden blocks, wedges, bracing structures, and other staying devices, as well as skill in securing items using wires, ropes, chains, cables, plates, and other hardware.

4604 Wood Working*

This occupation includes jobs involved in making, installing, and repairing supply, shipping, materials handling, and storage items such as boxes, crates, pallets, gates, dividers, and storage bins from wood and wood substitutes. This work requires skill in using hand and powered tools and machines to measure, cut, install, and fasten wooden parts, and the knowledge and ability to follow, select, or adapt patterns, templates, and procedures to make, disassemble, install, and repair wooden items.

4605 Wood Crafting*

This occupation includes jobs involved in making and repairing high-grade wooden items such as fine cabinetry and furniture. The work involves shaping and contouring surfaces; precise, intricate joining and decorating; skilled use of the full range of woodworking tools, machines, and techniques; and application of extensive knowledge of the appearance, durability, strength, and machining characteristics of a wide range of wood and wood substitutes.

4607 Carpentry*

This occupation includes jobs involved in constructing, altering, and repairing buildings and structures, fittings, panels, partitions, and other wood or wood substitute articles.

4608 Saw Mill Operating

This occupation includes jobs involved in preparing logs for cutting, cutting logs into lumber, and storing cut lumber in a sawmill.

4616 Patternmaking*

This occupation includes jobs which involve planning, laying out, and constructing patterns and core boxes used in forming molds for castings of ferrous and nonferrous metals and other substances. The patterns and core boxes are made from a variety of materials such as wood, wood products, and wood substitutes.

4618 Woodworking Machine Operating

This occupation includes jobs involved in setting up and operating woodworking machines such as power saws, moulders, planers, shapers, tenoners, moticers, joiners, carver machines, wood lathes, routers, surfacers, and universal woodworking machines to fabricate wood products such as sashes, window and door frames, doors, furniture parts, and dressed lumber.

4620 Shoe Last Repairing

This occupation includes jobs involved in the repair, modification, and reconditioning of shoe lasts, including cleaning, altering, reconditioning, replacing parts, polishing, buffing, waxing, and other work processes, utilizing a variety of tools and mechanical equipment such as drill presses, buffers, polishers, and grinding wheels.

4639 Timber Working

This occupation includes jobs involved in constructing, installing, maintaining, and repairing piers, wharves, moorings, gangways, and similar docking facilities; fender piling around wharves and dolphin structures for offshore mooring of ships; pontoons, camels, rafts; wooden bridges and trestles; tunnel and sewer supports; and other framing or supporting structures from timbers and planking.

4654 Form Block Making

This occupation includes jobs involved in laying out and constructing solid wood and wood substitute form blocks used by sheet metal, plate metal, plastic, and fiber glass workers to produce commercial and aircraft parts. Includes laying out parts with multiple contours and irregular shapes from assembly blueprints, and studying and interpreting technical information such as loft tables, blueprints, technical orders, and microfilm.

4700 GENERAL MAINTENANCE AND OPERATIONS WORK FAMILY

This job family includes occupations which (1) consist of various combinations of work such as are involved in constructing, maintaining, and repairing buildings, roads, grounds, and related facilities; manufacturing, modifying, and repairing items or apparatus made from a variety of materials or types of components; or repairing and operating equipment or utilities; and (2) require the application of a variety of trade practices associated with occupations in more than one job family (unless otherwise indicated), and the performance of the highest level of work in at least two of the trades involved.

Occupations in this family are:

4714 Model Making*

This occupation includes jobs involved in planning and fabricating complex research and prototype models which are made from a variety of materials and are used in scientific, engineering, developmental, experimental, and test work. The work requires skill and knowledge of more than one specific trade.

4715 Exhibits Making/Modeling

This occupation includes jobs involved in constructing, installing, and maintaining full size or scale model visual displays, training devices, or exhibits for educational and informational purposes from a variety of materials such as wood, metal, plastic, rubber, and plaster, using work processes of more than one trade. Some examples are: making scale model steambeds, inlets, overhang areas, dams, spillways, outlet works, etc., by placing and molding materials such as sand, gravel, ground or crushed coal, haydite, and concrete to form features, and shaping and smoothing concrete mixes to finish surfaces; constructing relief map models in plastic, plaster, cardboard, clay, or other materials, using hand carving tools, pantographic routing machine, and orthographic projector; reproducing mock-ups of ships, aircraft, vehicles, and other objects; etc. May include installing and maintaining animation and control devices and mechanisms. This occupation does not include jobs that primarily require technical knowledge of cartography, artistic ability, specialized subject matter knowledge, or technical knowledge and skill in museum or exhibits techniques.

---

*Job grading standard published.

4716 Railroad Car Repairing

This occupation includes jobs involved in building, repairing, dismantling, painting, and upholstering passenger and freight cars, using skills in more than one specific trade. Also includes the repair of narrow-gage, cable drawn dollies.

4717 Boat Building and Repairing

This occupation includes jobs involved in constructing and repairing aluminum, fiberglass, and plywood hulls of small craft and vessels. Includes fitting replacement blanks, ribs, keelson, deadwood and keel; calking seams; repairing decks and topsides; replacing canvas and moldings; installing deadlite, metal, or wood coamings and marine hardware; and boring shaft logs and constructing cradles to fit hulls. The work requires skill and knowledge of more than one specific trade.

4737 General Equipment Mechanic

This occupation includes jobs involved in installing, maintaining, and repairing two or more different kinds of machinery or equipment (optical instruments, electronic controls, industrial machinery, electrical equipment, hydraulic systems, electromechanical devices, heavy mobile or automotive equipment, artillery systems and components, communications equipment, etc.). The work requires the use of a variety of trade practices associated with occupations in more than one job family, and the performance of the highest level of work in at least two of the trades involved.

4741 General Equipment Operating

This occupation includes jobs involved in operating a combination of transportation, construction, or other mobile equipment and stationary or portable industrial equipment, machinery, tools, or utility systems. The work requires application of skills and knowledges falling within two (or more) job families, neither of which predominates for recruitment, promotion, reduction-in-force, pay setting, or other personnel processes.

4742 Utility Systems Repairing-Operating*

This occupation includes jobs that primarily involve repairing and operating one or more utility systems (air conditioning, heating, water, sewage, electricity generation and distribution, etc.). The work requires the ability to start, stop, and regulate the utility or utilities for optimum efficiency and troubleshoot, maintain, and repair them, and knowledge of the locations and functions of all equipment in the system(s) and the kind and quality of materials to be used in repairs. The levels of work performed in repair and operation must be the same and must represent the highest level of work performed.

4745 Research Laboratory Mechanic

This occupation includes jobs involved in the fabrication, installation, maintenance, operation, modification, and repair of research laboratory facilities or unique types of experimental equipment used in research and development programs. The work requires skill and knowledge of more than one specific trade. Illustrative examples of work include: (1) fabrication and modification of test stands and rigs for supporting engines or structures during ultra-high-velocity wind tunnel studies; (2) finishing of surfaces to micro specifications for air flow effect studies; and (3) maintaining, modifying, and operating test facilities and related equipment such as altitude simulators to achieve and hold prescribed environments for particular research studies.

4749 Maintenance Mechanic*

This occupation includes jobs involved in the maintenance and repair of grounds, exterior structures, buildings, and related fixtures and utilities, requiring the use of a variety of trade practices associated with occupations such as carpentry, masonry, plumbing, electrical, air conditioning, cement work, painting, and other related trades, and the performance of the highest level of work in at least two of the trades involved.

4754 Cemetery Caretaking

This occupation includes jobs involved in the maintenance and upkeep of cemeteries, requiring the use of a variety of trade practices associated with occupations such as motor vehicle operating, gardening, tractor operating, laboring, and fork lift operating. Such work includes digging graves, setting and aligning headstones, erecting mourners' shelters, setting up casket-lowering devices, and maintaining the appearance of the surrounding grounds.

4800 GENERAL EQUIPMENT MAINTENANCE FAMILY

This job family includes occupations involved in the maintenance or repair of equipment, machines, or instruments which are not coded to other job families because the equipment is not characteristically related to one of the established subject-matter areas such as electronics, electrical, industrial, transportation, instruments, engines, aircraft, ordnance, etc., or because the nature of the work calls for limited knowledge/skill in a variety of crafts or trades as they relate to the repair of such equipment, but not a predominate knowledge of any one trade or craft.

Occupations in this family are:

4802 Musical Instrument Repairing

This occupation includes jobs involved in repairing musical instruments, including placing pads on keys, soldering seams, polishing and buffing parts, reshaping parts over mandrels, cutting valve parts, gluing together parts of stringed instruments, sawing, carving, and finishing new wooden parts of instruments, and removing dents from brass instruments.

4805 Medical Equipment Repairing*

This occupation includes jobs involved in the installation, maintenance, overhaul, repair, and testing of various medical and dental equipment used in patient diagnosis and treatment and in research laboratories. This work requires a knowledge and application of mechanical, electrical, and electronic principles and circuitry, the ability to determine malfunctions, and the skill to repair and maintain a variety of medical, laboratory, and dental equipment.

4806 Office Appliance Repairing*

This occupation includes jobs involved in the maintenance, overhaul, and repair of office machines and appliances such as typewriters, calculating and adding machines, addressing and embossing machines, cash registers, time-stamping, numbering, and checkwriting machines, and duplicating machines such as mimeograph. Work is performed on machines and appliances which incorporate mechanical and electrical features.

4807 Chemical Equipment Repairing

This occupation includes jobs involved in fabricating component parts, modifying, overhauling, and repairing chemical equipment such as flame throwers, smoke generators, air compressors, and hand and power driven decontaminating devices, impregnating plants, and collective protectors.

---

*Job grading standard published.

4808 Custodial Equipment Servicing

This occupation includes jobs involved in servicing custodial equipment such as waxing machines, vacuum cleaners, power scrubbing machines, and wall washing machines. Work includes disassembling, making minor repairs, cleaning, oiling, and greasing equipment and replacing worn gears, gaskets, belts, brushes, and roller bearings. May include building ladders and steps and making push brooms and wash applicators.

4812 Saw Reconditioning

This occupation includes jobs involved in filing, gumming, setting, joining, tensioning, and brazing saw blades for both power and hand saws.

4814 Survey Equipment Servicing

This occupation includes jobs involved in the servicing of survey equipment, including range poles, tripods, tide gages, stadia boards, levels, transits, and their boxes. Work includes making minor repairs, cleaning, oiling, and painting equipment; replacing worn or broken parts; and making survey and sounding lines.

4816 Protective and Safety Equipment Fabricating and Repairing

This occupation includes jobs involved in the assembly, fabrication, modification, and/or repair of a variety of protective and safety equipment, including but not limited to gas masks, hoods, respirators, filters, canisters, collective protectors, boots, detection kits, manually-operated decontaminating equipment, safety glasses, and goggles.

4819 Bowling Equipment Repairing*

This occupation includes jobs involved in maintaining and repairing bowling equipment. The work includes making operational and test equipment checks, diagnosing malfunctions, disassembling, repairing and replacing parts, reassembling, adjusting, and making final operational tests. In addition, the work involves conditioning and minor repair of bowling lanes, approaches, and pins. The work requires a knowledge and application of mechanical and electrical operating principles of the equipment, the ability to determine malfunctions, and the skill to repair and maintain a variety of bowling equipment.

4820 Vending Machine Repairing

This occupation includes jobs involved in repairing vending machines in wholesale, retail, service, or recreational establishments. Includes installing, troubleshooting, repairing, and adjusting a variety of components, assemblies, and systems such as ice-making, refrigeration, carbonation, dispensing, electrical, coin-handing, and evaporation systems.

4839 Film Processing Equipment Repairing

This occupation includes jobs involved in installing, maintaining, and repairing motion picture film processing equipment such as developing and printing equipment and recirculation equipment used for processing black and white or color film.

4840 Tool and Equipment Repairing

This occupation includes jobs involved in maintaining, adjusting, sharpening, and repairing a variety of tools, safety equipment, and portable power equipment such as pipe wrenches, acetylene cutting torches, pneumatic hammers, hydraulic rivet guns, portable pumps, high-pressure airless spray guns, hand-held electric power tools, grinders, drills, cutters, chisels, picks, axes, shovels, mowing equipment, etc., that are issued from shop tool rooms and equipment areas to production and maintenance workers.

4841 Window Shade Assembling, Installing, and Repairing

This occupation includes jobs involved in the fabrication, assembly, installation, maintenance, servicing, and repair of roll window shades and venetian blinds, including their mechanisms. May include repair of related items such as drapery hardware.

4843 Navigation Aids Repairing

This occupation includes jobs involved in installing, modifying, and repairing the mechanisms for sound and light equipment used in aids to navigation.

4844 Bicycle Repairing

This occupation includes jobs involved in repairing and reconditioning bicycles.

4845 Orthopedic Appliance Repairing

This occupation includes jobs involved in making and repairing orthopedic appliances such as artificial arms and legs, braces, arch supports, and shoes on prescription of an orthopedic surgeon or other medical officer.

4848 Mechanical Parts Repairing

This occupation includes jobs involved in assembling, disassembling, adjusting, modifying, repairing, reworking, reconditioning, and testing mechanical parts or components such as gear boxes, clutch assemblies, engine control pedestal assemblies, control columns, transmitters, differentials, rudder pedal assemblies, landing gear assemblies, pumps, valves, hose assemblies, or similar components or accessories of aircraft, missiles, trainers, helicopters, test stands, or other equipment where significant knowledge of component relationships and their functions in the major end item is not required. Includes riveting, pinning, fitting, connecting, drilling, reaming, and tapping parts (not machining) using hand and power tools.

4850 Bearing Reconditioning*

This occupation includes jobs involved in reconditioning various types of bearings from aircraft, engines, instruments, propellers, ground equipment, or other property. Includes identifying and visually examining bearings to either condemn them or determine the type of further processing required; replacing and matching parts on selected types of bearings; and calibrating, precision gaging, and testing bearings with specialized equipment.

4851 Reclamation Working

This occupation includes jobs involved in dismantling unserviceable and obsolete automotive and engineering equipment, engines, accessories, and associated equipment; radio and electronic equipment; and all types of shop equipment, machine tools, instruments, industrial internal combustion engines, electrical power units, electric motors, electrical accessories, communications equipment, office furniture and equipment, and miscellaneous equipment, usually in reclamation shops or yards. Does not include jobs involved exclusively in disassembling aircraft or other similar items that represent a single occupation.

4855 Domestic Appliance Repairing

This occupation includes jobs that involve installing, maintaining, and repairing major appliances such as electric and gas ranges and stoves, dishwashers, automatic clothes washers, and dryers. Includes examining units to determine malfunctions, disassembling units, replacing parts and components, reassembling, adjusting, and testing appliances. The work

---

*Job grading standard published.

requires knowledge of mechanical, electrical, and plumbing techniques as associated with the functioning of household appliances, and skill in the use of hand and power tools and testing devices.

5000 PLANT AND ANIMAL WORK FAMILY

This job family includes occupations involved in general or specialized farming operations; gardening, including the general care of grounds, roadways, nurseries, greenhouses, etc.; trimming and felling trees; and propagating, caring for, handling, and controlling animals and insects, including pest species.

Occupations in this family are:

5002 Farming

This occupation includes jobs involved in producing food and feed crops or plants on a general farm or in an agricultural research or experimental setting. The work includes plowing, tilling soil, planting, transplanting, cultivating, irrigating, pruning, spraying, fertilizing, harvesting, and storing farm products. May also include, in addition to general farm work, caring for, breeding, feeding, and butchering livestock raised for food purposes; building and maintaining fences; operating farm equipment; and maintaining farm buildings.

5003 Gardening*

This occupation includes jobs requiring knowledge of gardening procedures and skill in growing and tending lawns, flowers, shrubs, and trees. The work includes preparing soil for plants, seeding, thinning, transplanting, trimming, pruning, fertilizing, aerating, mulching, spraying, and dusting of grass, ground cover, flowers, shrubs, and trees.

5026 Pest Controlling*

This occupation includes jobs requiring knowledge of pest species and the ability to locate and recognize them and to use toxic materials and other measures for their control. The pests controlled typically include insects, small animals, birds, and parasites (may also include fungus growths) which are injurious to plants, materials, or buildings or detrimental to human health, activities, or comfort. The work is performed in urban, rural, and industrial areas in and around buildings, open fields, forests, and watered areas.

5031 Insects Production Working*

This occupation includes jobs involved in reproducing, collecting, treating (as with radiation) and caring for insect collections. The work requires practical knowledge of the characteristics of insects and their needs, and skill in observing and handling them.

5034 Dairy Farming

This occupation includes jobs involved in operating a dairy farm, including caring for, feeding, and breeding the dairy herd; cleaning, washing, and maintaining sanitary conditions throughout the physical plant; sterilizing, adjusting, maintaining, and operating milking machines; preparing feed and feeding the dairy herd; pasteurizing, sterilizing, cooling, weighing, bottling, and storing milk; protecting the animals against disease and abuse; maintaining charts and records pertaining to production; and making minor repairs to buildings and equipment.

5035 Livestock Ranching/Wrangling

This occupation includes jobs involved in operating a livestock ranch, including rounding up livestock on ranges for branding, castrating, vaccinating, and marketing; and maintaining fences, traps, and water supply for livestock. Requires riding horses which are not of a gentle nature and using a lariat with accuracy. This occupation also includes jobs involved in gathering stray and trespass livestock from the Federal range and assisting with counting cattle or sheep on the Federal range.

5042 Tree Trimming and Removing

This occupation includes jobs involved in trimming, topping, and cutting down trees on roadways, grounds, parks, or other public lands. Includes thinning, pruning, trimming, and cutting away dead branches or excess branches from large trees, felling and cutting up trees, and removing stumps. Requires knowledge of ropes, knots, rigging, and hitches; climbing trees; and operating equipment such as chain saws, motorized winches, block and tackle, and shredder-grinder machines.

5048 Animal Caretaking*

This occupation includes jobs which involve providing care for mammals, reptiles, birds, and fish. This work requires knowledge of the animals' characteristics, needs, and behavior, and skill in observing, handling, and controlling them.

5200 MISCELLANEOUS OCCUPATIONS FAMILY

This job family includes occupations which are not covered by the definition of any other job family or which are of such a general or miscellaneous character as to preclude placing them within another job family.

Occupations in this family are:

5205 Gas and Radiation Detecting

This occupation includes jobs involved in placing, reading, and calibrating various types of instruments and using chemical reagents to make standard tests of tanks, compartments, and other enclosures or areas for indications of radiation, oxygen deficiency, or presence of toxic or explosive gases. Does not include jobs that primarily require technical knowledge of the health, medical, or allied sciences.

5210 Rigging*

This occupation includes jobs involved in the selection, installation, and use of cables, ropes, chains, and other weight handling gear to lift, move, and position heavy loads; and the assembly, repair, and installation of standing and running rigging used to support, secure, or operate equipment, machinery, and other items. This work requires a knowledge of rigging practices and weight handling techniques; the ability to plan and select the appropriate gear; and the skill to assemble, repair and install rigging on a variety of objects.

5220 Shipwright*

This occupation includes jobs involved in the dry-docking of marine craft and in the maintenance of marine dry-docking equipment.

5221 Lofting

This occupation includes jobs involved in laying out the lines of a ship and its parts to scale on the mold loft floor and developing and making full-size wooden or paper templates or molds to conform to these layouts.

5222 Diving

This occupation includes jobs that involve diving underwater to repair vessels, raise sunken vessels and aircraft, and remove underwater obstructions to navigation. Includes underwater examination, survey, salvage,

---

*Job grading standard published.

and repair of floating plants, sunken vessels, hulls, ship damage, aircraft, and obstructions to navigation; setting of underwater demolition charges; flame cutting, welding, and removal of propellers and rudders; rigging and fastening of slings; and tending of equipment and gear on diving barge.

5230 Airplane Cargo Dropping

This occupation includes jobs involved in dropping material related to forestry and agricultural operations by parachute or free-fall from air-planes to a designated location on the ground. This may involve evaluating how a parachute carrying cargo will act under various conditions of wind and weather and judging the proper point at which to drop packages so they will land in an accessible and desirable spot without damage to the contents.

5235 Test Range Tracking

This occupation includes jobs involved in tracking missiles, ships, and other objects by operating electronic, photographic, mechanical, and optical tracking equipment to obtain permanent records of tests.

5300 INDUSTRIAL EQUIPMENT MAINTENANCE FAMILY

This job family includes occupations involved in the general maintenance, installation, and repair of portable and stationary industrial machinery, tools, and equipment such as sewing machines, machine tools, wood-working and metalworking machines, printing equipment, processing equipment, driving machinery, power generating equipment, air con-ditioning equipment, heating and boiler plant equipment, and other types of machines and equipment used in the production of goods and services.

Occupations in this family are:

5306 Air Conditioning Equipment Mechanic*

This occupation includes jobs involved in repairing and modifying a variety of equipment and systems that achieve regulated climatic con-ditions. This work requires a knowledge of principles of air conditioning the ability to recognize and determine the best method for correcting malfunctions, and the skill to make repairs to a variety of air conditioning and cooling unit systems.

5307 Shoe Machine Repairing

This occupation includes jobs involved in the repair, adjustment, dis-assembly, replacement of parts, reassembly, and major overhaul of power-driven or hand-operated shoe machines such as shoe sole stitching ma-chines, shoe sole rough rounding machines, shoe finishing line machines, shoe patching machines, sanders, sole cutters, and leather splitting or skiving machines.

5309 Heating and Boiler Plant Equipment Mechanic*

This occupation includes jobs involved in installing, maintaining, re-pairing, and modifying equipment such as coal, gas, and oil fired heaters and hot air furnaces, high and low pressure steam and hot water boilers, power generating equipment, and similar systems. The systems provide heat, hot water, or steam for use in the operation of industrial and institutional facilities and equipment. This work requires a knowledge of the principles of combustion and heat or power distribution; the ability to recognize and determine the best methods for correcting malfunctions; and the skill to install and make repairs to a variety of heat and power producing systems.

5310 Kitchen/Bakery Equipment Repairing

This occupation includes jobs involved in the installation, repair, over-haul, alteration, rebuild, parts replacement, and adjustment of commercial kitchen and/or bakery equipment such as electric and gas ranges, fryers, steam tables, disposers, dishwashers, meat and bread slicers, bone and meat cutters, potato peelers, bread and dough mixers, doughnut machines, dividers and dough hoppers, dough rounders, flour handling machines, proofers, and other food equipment used in cafeterias, hospitals, etc.

5312 Sewing Machine Repairing

This occupation includes jobs involved in the examination, lubrication, adjustment, and repair of all types of sewing machines.

5313 Elevator Mechanic*

This occupation includes jobs involved in the repair and maintenance of high speed elevator systems and moderate or low speed elevators, dumb-waiters, leveling ramps, and escalators to meet regulatory codes and work requirements. The work requires a knowledge of the construction, function, and maintenance procedures of dispatching or scheduling sys-tems, systems components, driving and hoisting machinery, control mecha-nisms, guide structures, and car or platform equipment and counter-weights. Skill is required in planning and carrying out tasks such as tracing and locating troubles, aligning and balancing the network of controls, adjusting and resetting safety devices, and repairing and servicing electro-mechanical parts and equipment located in the machinery penthouse, shaftway, pit, or on the car or platform.

5317 Laundry and Dry Cleaning Equipment Repairing

This occupation includes jobs involved in repair work on laundry, dry cleaning, and related equipment.

5318 Lock and Dam Repairing

This occupation includes jobs involved in the repair of flood-control or navigation lock and dam equipment and machinery and the maintenance and repair of buildings, grounds, and structures peculiar to operations of locks and dams.

5320 Coffee Plant Equipment Repairing

This occupation includes jobs involved in the diagnosis, disassembly, adjustment, repair, and operational testing of various types of coffee plant equipment such as blending, cleaning, roasting, cooling, grinding, con-veying, and packaging equipment.

5323 Oiling and Greasing

This occupation includes jobs involved in lubricating the moving parts or wearing surfaces of mechanical equipment such Is shaft and motor bearings, sprockets, drive chains, gears, and- pulleys; forcing grease into bearings with grease gun; filling grease cups; filling or changing oil in machine sumps, using hand, pneumatic, or electric pumps, and changing filters; and cleaning dust, dirt, grease, and other adhering material from machinery and equipment, using rags, brushes, or a compressed air blower. Includes making minor repairs to equipment.

5324 Powerhouse Equipment Repairing

This occupation includes jobs involved in maintaining and repairing mechanical equipment in a hydroelectric plant, including related pumping plant or dam equipment, e.g., turbines, generators, motors, pimps, pres-

---

*Job grading standard published.

sure regulators, eductors, valves, pipes, penstocks, intakes, spillways, diversion dam and wasteway gates, and appurtenant mechanical and electrical controls. Includes dismantling and reconstructing machinery; machining parts as required; erecting scaffolding, platforms, and hoisting devices; operating crane's, hoists, and industrial tractors; and performing rigging incidental to lifting, moving, dismantling, assembling, overhauling, or repairing hydroelectric power plant machinery and related equipment.

5326 Drawbridge Repairing

This occupation includes jobs involved in the repair of drawbridges, including greasing; removing and replacing cables, span guides, sheaves, rollers, and heavy gears; splicing rope and steel cables; shifting counterweights; and scraping, chipping, and painting.

5330 Printing Equipment Repairing

This occupation includes jobs involved in the installation, repair, and overhaul of printing equipment such as printing presses, offset presses, and allied equipment such as lamps, collating equipment, stitching and gathering machines, cutters, folders, bindery presses, and whirlers.

5333 Sponging Equipment Repairing

This occupation includes jobs involved in the lubrication, diagnosis, adjustment, repair, and overhaul of sponging plant equipment such as wetting-out tanks and "J" feed attachments, loop driers, rolling and measuring machines, londonizing machines, fans and blowers, and related machines and equipment.

5334 Marine Machinery Mechanic*

This occupation includes jobs involved in dismantling, repairing, relocating, modifying, maintaining, aligning, overhauling, and installing a wide variety of marine machinery, equipment, and systems such as propulsion machinery, lifeboat davits, anchor handling gear, and missile tube equipment that are located aboard submarines, ships, and other floating craft. The work requires a practical knowledge of the mechanical, hydraulic, and pneumatic systems and components of diverse marine machinery and their attachments. This includes detailed knowledge of the operating characteristics of the involved machinery, equipment, and systems, their functional relationships, and the applicable installation and repair procedures, methods, and trade practices.

5335 Wind Tunnel Mechanic

This occupation includes jobs that involve repairing and maintaining wind tunnel facilities, preparing wind tunnels for tests, installing specialized equipment, installing, and calibrating instrumentation, and recording data during tunnel operation. Includes installing and maintaining instrumentation and equipment such as fans and compressors, balance system, sting suspension system, survey rake equipment, image system, manometer equipment, angle of attack control mechanism, and unique features such as plates, wedges, screens, and safety nets; adjusting wind tunnels for particular test conditions, for example, by adjusting moveable walls, nozzles, and slot conditions; installing full scale test articles such as aircraft engines; installing schlieren or other photographic equipment; and fabricating manometer boards, pressure tubes, and lines. The work requires a knowledge of the characteristics, operational range, assembly techniques, fits and tolerance, calibration settings, and adjustments of wind tunnel equipment; ability to diagnose and eliminate equipment malfunctions; and comprehension of the relationships among various equipment in providing special tunnel test conditions.

5341 Industrial Furnace Building and Repairing

This occupation includes jobs involved in constructing, installing, maintaining, and repairing electric and gas furnaces used for melting and refining metals and for annealing and heat treating blanks and dies.

5342 Mail Processing Equipment Repairing

This occupation includes jobs involved in testing, maintaining, repairing, and modifying automatic, semiautomatic, and related mechanical equipment, including a combination of mechanical, electrical, electronic, pneumatic, or hydraulic control and operating mechanisms, comprising an extensive mechanized mail processing system.

5345 Fish Facilities Repairing

This occupation includes jobs involved in overhauling and repairing equipment at a fish screen installation (e.g., fish screens, motors, by-pass channels and gates, and appurtenant mechanical and electric controls). May include erecting scaffolds, platforms, and hoisting devices; operating cranes; and performing rigging incidental to lifting, moving, dismantling, assembling, overhauling, or repairing the equipment.

5350 Production Machinery Mechanic*

This occupation includes jobs involved in dismantling, repairing, relocating, modifying, maintaining, aligning, overhauling, and installing fixed and semi-fixed production machinery, equipment, and systems such as various standard and numerically controlled machine tools, woodworking and metalworking machines used in the production of goods. The work requires a practical knowledge of the mechanical, hydraulic, and pneumatic systems and components of diverse industrial production machinery and their attachments. This includes detailed knowledge of the operating characteristics of the involved machinery, equipment, and systems, their functional relationships, and the applicable installation and repair procedures, methods, and trade practices.

5352 Industrial Equipment Mechanic*

This occupation includes jobs involved in dismantling, repairing, aligning, overhauling, and installing general nonproduction industrial plant machinery, equipment, and systems such as bridge cranes, towveyor/ conveyor and pneumatic tube systems, sandblasting machines, and other industrial plant support machinery and equipment; service, industrial waste and flood control equipment such as compressors, pumps, and valves; and engraving machines, aircraft test block equipment, and fire extinguishing systems. The work requires a practical knowledge of the mechanical, hydraulic, and pneumatic systems and components of diverse industrial plant support machinery and equipment, and other equipment that control industrial waste and provide service to establishments such as industrial plants, machine tool repair shops, and hospitals. This includes detailed knowledge of the operating characteristics of the involved systems and equipment, and the applicable installation and repair procedures, methods, and trade practices.

5364 Door Systems Mechanic

This occupation includes jobs involved in installation, adjustment, maintenance, and repair of door operating equipment, including fully automatic and semiautomatic hydraulic, pneumatic, electrical, and spring-loaded mechanical operators and controls. Work includes examination, disassembly, parts condition evaluation, parts replacement, reassembly, and adjustment of door opener and closer devices (excluding locks) requiring knowledge of a variety of types of door operator devices supplied by a number of different manufacturers. May also include installation and repair of overhead and sliding/ swinging door assemblies, including structural support, framework, and door.

---

*Job grading standard published.

5365 Physiological Trainer Mechanic

This occupation includes jobs involved in the overhaul, modification, installation, relocation, and testing of physiological training devices including altitude indoctrination flight chambers. Physiological training equipment simulates altitude, weightlessness, acceleration and deceleration, and other conditions or form of gravity and space. The equipment is used for the purpose of training, testing, and conditioning personnel in the safety, emergency, and counter procedures which are a necessary part of high altitude or space flight.

5378 Powered Support Systems Mechanic*

This occupation includes jobs involved in general mechanical work in making a variety of repairs to powered ground and similar support equipment used for air-craft ground servicing; missile, aircraft, air control, and radar installations' powered support; field combat support; engineering and construction project support; and general utilities, including standby and emergency power generating systems. The systems repaired are made up of combinations of components such as: gasoline, diesel, multi-fuel, or turbine engines; electrical systems; gears; combustion powered generators, compressors, and similar power supply units, including those with heating and cooling applications; and the electric, hydraulic, or pneumatic systems which are part of the equipment repaired.

5384 Gasdynamic Facility Installing and Repairing

This occupation includes jobs involving the installation of systems, equipment, and components comprising a gasdynamic facility; diagnosis of facility malfunctions, and teardown, repair, replacement, and servicing of integrated equipment and components; monitoring and adjustment of systems and equipment to achieve prescribed test conditions, and recording of data observed during tests; and fabrication of parts, fittings, components, test articles, and/or measuring instruments, using machine tools. Facilities are characterized by the integrated use of extreme high temperature heating, high pressure, and/or high vacuum techniques to create fluid dynamic flow of high enthalpy gases for experimental simulation of the flight of hypersonic vehicles. Associated equipment and components include such items as gas fired ceramic storage heaters; high voltage electric arc heaters; mechanical, oil diffusion, and cryogenic vacuum and/or pressure pumps; piping network for coolants, propane gas, nitrogen, hydrogen, carbon dioxide, oxygen, argon, and/or compressed air; electric, hydraulic, and pneumatic valves and control devices; and synchronous and wound rotor motors. Facilities are typically constructed on a fail-safe basis utilizing component and system interlocks.

5400 INDUSTRIAL EQUIPMENT OPERATION FAMILY

This job family includes occupations involved in the operation of portable and stationary industrial equipment, tools, and machines to generate and distribute utilities such as electricity, steam, and gas for heat or power; treat and distribute water; collect, treat, and dispose of waste; open and close bridges, locks and dams; lift and move workers, materials, and equipment; manufacture and process materials and products; etc.

Occupations in this family are:

5402 Boiler Plant Operating*

This occupation includes jobs which involve the firing or operation of one or more types or a combination of automatic or hand-fired, high- or low-pressure boilers. These boilers produce steam or high-temperature water to provide heat for buildings, for use in the generation of electricity, and for use in the operation of industrial and institutional facilities and equipment.

5403 Incinerator Operating

This occupation includes jobs involved in the operation of a wood-fire, gas, or oil burning incinerator to burn garbage and trash.

5406 Utility Systems Operating*

This occupation includes jobs concerned primarily with operating two or more utility systems such as boiler plants, air conditioning, sewage disposal, water treatment, and natural gas distribution systems, for large buildings or small complexes, on a continuing basis. Operators should be familiar with and have the ability to adjust and regulate a variety of automatic or manually controlled auxiliary equipment to insure maximum operating efficiency of the systems. This occupation includes jobs that entail operation of two or more utility systems when no single skill or knowledge of a single utility is predominant for recruitment, promotion, reduction-in-force, paysetting, and other personnel processes.

5407 Electric Power Controlling*

This occupation includes jobs involved in controlling the generation or distribution of electric power. The jobs are located at power generating plants, power distribution centers, and substations. This work requires ability to anticipate load changes due to work schedules, weather, etc., in order to engage or cut out power sources; to interpret wiring diagrams for a complete primary power system in order to plan routings and locate failures; and to determine need for and follow emergency procedures in order to insure safety and provide continuous electric service. Employees must know how to operate electric power generating and controlling equipment, such as high voltage generators, rotary converters, transformers, motor-generators, and remotely operated switches and circuit breakers.

5408 Sewage Disposal Plant Operating*

This occupation includes jobs which involve the operation of sewage disposal plant equipment used to collect, treat, and dispose of water-borne domestic and industrial waste.

5409 Water Treatment Plant Operating*

This occupation includes jobs which involve the operation of water treatment plants to pump or treat water for domestic or industrial use.

5412 Coal Unloader Operating

This occupation includes jobs involved in unloading coal from cars into bins or onto conveyors for storage or further processing by positioning cars over dump areas and releasing locking device on bottom of cars to release coal.

5413 Fuel Distribution System Operating*

This occupation includes jobs involved in working at one or several work stations of a fuel distribution system, or operating a complete system, to receive, store, transfer, and issue petroleum and other products such as liquid oxygen, liquid nitrogen, and anhydrous ammonia.

5414 Baling Machine Operating

This occupation includes jobs involved in the operation of a baling machine to bale (compress) paper, cloth, steel scrap, tobacco, or other loose materials to facilitate handling.

5415 Air Conditioning Equipment Operating*

This occupation includes jobs concerned primarily with the operation of air conditioning systems for large buildings or complexes of buildings.

---

*Job grading standard published.

Also included are jobs that involve the operation and regulation of cold storage and specialized climate simulation facilities. The work requires the ability to adjust equipment for maintaining desired temperatures and humidity: start, operate, and stop the air handling equipment and centrifugal compressors or absorbers; and detect and diagnose malfunctions in equipment. Operators must know the purposes and locations of all equipment in the systems and the auxiliary equipment (cooling towers, water pumps, air compressors, liquid circulating pumps, fans, etc.).

5419 Stationary-Engine Operating

This occupation includes jobs involved in operating and maintaining stationary diesel and gas engines and mechanical equipment such as compressors, generators, motors, turbines, steam engines, fans, and pumps used in buildings and industrial processes. Includes observing meters and gages to determine operating condition of equipment, and making adjustments or minor repairs necessary to insure efficient performance.

5421 Rubber Compounding

This occupation includes jobs involved in compounding ingredients and chemicals of established and newly developed formulas into batches of synthetic rubber. Includes combining ingredients and operating rubber mills to produce raw rubber stock. May involve test molding of rubber parts and equipment to determine the quality and consistency of batch.

5423 Sandblasting*

This occupation includes jobs involved in setting up, operating, and performing preventive maintenance on complete stationary and portable sandblasting equipment and machines used for cleaning metal and nonmetal surfaces. The work requires a knowledge of the operating and preventive maintenance features of sandblasting equipment and machines, cleaning characteristics of metals and nonmetals, cutting or abrasive quality of a wide variety of sand-like abrasives, and the optimum air pressures with specific abrasives to obtain the desired finish without damage to workpieces. The work requires the skill to position and hold workpieces and blasting nozzles, and carry out blasting operations and procedures in a safe manner.

5424 Weighing Machine Operating

This occupation includes jobs involved in the operation and maintenance of weighing scales to weigh cars, products, or materials in or out of an installation (e.g., to weight coinage metals, including bullion, ingots, blanks, planchets, coins, medals, clippings, and other residue, using troy weights, in minting operations: weigh mail and parcel post items in postal operations; etc.)

5426 Lock and Dam Operating*

This occupation includes jobs which involve primarily the operation of navigation lock and dam equipment and machinery to allow river traffic to pass from one level to another because of the differences in elevation between the bodies of water, and to maintain required pool levels.

5427 Chemical Plant Operating

This occupation includes jobs involved in operating and maintaining chemical plant equipment utilized in the development, manufacture, and processing of chemicals and chemical products or the development of chemical and related processes. Typically, such equipment includes reactors, filter, compressors, pumps, valves, furnaces, fractionating columns, generators, centrifuges, meters, stripping units, blenders, mixers, filling machines, evaporators, distillation columns, and other similar equipment. Work includes controlling temperatures, pressures, flows,

and reaction time by reading and recording data, adjusting temperature, flow rate, pressure, and similar gages and instruments, and performing routine chemical analyses and calculations.

5430 Drawbridge Operating

This occupation includes jobs involved in the operation of equipment used to raise, turn, and lower a drawbridge to regulate river traffic. Includes making minor repairs to moving parts of bridge jacks and other related equipment.

5432 Fish Facility Operating

This occupation includes jobs involved in operating and making minor repairs to fish facilities, including fish ladders, locks, and collection systems; regulating water flow; and operating fish counting stations at a multipurpose project.

5433 Gas Generating Plant Operating

This occupation includes jobs involved in the operation and operational maintenance of plants manufacturing compressed and liquefied gases (e.g., oxygen, nitrogen, carbon dioxide, acetylene, helium) to supply storage tanks, pipelines, or gas charging manifolds. Includes operating equipment such as engines, compressors, generators, motors, pumps, fractionating columns, purifying towers, and heat exchangers; observing gages and controlling temperatures, pressures, flow, etc.; and testing the end product for purity.

5435 Carton/Bag Making Machine Operating

This occupation includes jobs involved in setting up, adjusting, and operating production machines to cut, score, slit, fold, crease, slot, stitch, glue, or seal corrugated cardboard, paper, plastic sheet, cellophane, metal foil, or other similar materials to make cartons, carton spacers, liners, or bags for packing items.

5438 Elevator Operating*

This occupation includes jobs involved in the running of freight or passenger elevators. The work includes opening and closing elevator gates and doors, working elevator controls, loading and unloading the elevator, giving information and directions to passengers such as on the locations of offices, and reporting problems in running the elevator.

5439 Testing Equipment Operating

This occupation includes jobs involved in testing materials such as metals or plastics and/or products such as vehicle parts for physical characteristics or defects, using powered or manually operated test equipment such as hardness and shock testers, vibration equipment, temperature-humidity chambers, acceleration test machines, pressure test wells, hydraulic test cabinets, soil compaction machines, mechanical sieve shakers, soil constants apparatus, water retentivity apparatus, cement testing apparatus (flow table, needles, autoclave, and other devices), electrical test equipment, frequency test instruments, optical comparators, profilometers, ultrasonic testing devices, magnetic particle and liquid penetrant equipment, and radiographic and roentgenological fluoroscopic devices. Includes setting up and operating test equipment, using test apparatus to apply tests to materials or products, recording readings, observing and recording established reactions, and classifying according to defined categories. This occupation does not include jobs which primarily require (1) knowledge/skill in the work processes involved in producing or repairing the materials or products tested, or (2) technical knowledge of engineering or the physical, biological, or other sciences.

---

*Job grading standard published.

5440 Packaging Machine Operating

This occupation includes jobs involved in the setup, adjustment, operation, and operational maintenance of automatic machines to fill, mark, fasten, seal, pack, or wrap tubes, cylinders, containers, bags, cartons, or packages of items such as coins, hardware, or other articles.

5444 Food/Feed Processing Equipment Operating

This occupation includes jobs involved in the operation and operational maintenance of equipment and machines that process food products or foodstuffs. Processing procedures include comminution, extraction, carbonation, concentration, dehydration, drying, crystallization, distillation, centrifuging, vacuum evaporation, separation, refining, canning, cooking, sieving, grinding, blending, sifting, mixing, baking, and other related processes.

5446 Textile Equipment Operating

This occupation includes jobs involved in the operation and operational maintenance of textile processing and/or fabricating equipment and machinery used in one, or more major operations such as cleaning and ginning operations involved in producing cotton; opening, picking, carding, combing, and drafting operations involved in producing various hank rovings for use in yarns, twines, and cords; wrapping, slashing, and weaving operations involved in developing fabrics; sponging, scouring, carbonizing, fulling, dyeing, and other chemical and physical treatment operations involved in finishing fabrics; and spreading, die-cutting, pinking, and other similar operations involved in preparing fabric for sewing.

5450 Conveyor Operating

This occupation includes jobs involved in operating and making minor repairs to an endless-conveyor, belt or chain, for the purpose of moving and transporting supplies, materials, and equipment within a plant, terminal, central receiving area, mine, or warehouse, or between buildings and areas. Includes operating an electronic or electrical control panel to sort and control the flow of cargo.

5454 Solvent Still Operating

This occupation includes jobs involved in the operation and maintenance of solvent stills used to reclaim industrial-type cleaning solvents by settling, filtration, heat, and pressure methods. May include receiving dirty solvent and issuing reclaimed solvent incidental to still operation.

5455 Paper Pulping Machine Operating

This occupation includes jobs involved in operating and servicing an industrial-type paper pulping machine to reduce classified documents to pulp.

5473 Oil Reclamation Equipment Operating

This occupation includes jobs involved in operating equipment consisting of pumps, chemical injectors, pipe lines, gages, thermometers, settling tanks, oil skimming devices, and treating tanks to remove water, sludge, and other impurities from contaminated fuel oil or other petroleum products.

5475 Preparation Plant Operating

This occupation includes jobs involved in operating machinery and equipment to convey, blend, grind, crush, sieve, sort, size, or separate waste material from quarry rock, stone, ore, coal, sweeps, or other material to prepare it for use or further processing. The work includes adjusting panel controls to regulate crushers, driers, screens, and conveyors, and cleaning, lubricating, and making minor repairs to machinery.

---

*Job grading standard published.

5477 Concrete/Mortar Mixer Operating

This occupation includes jobs involved in operating a concrete mixing machine to mix sand, gravel, cement, and water to make concrete; a large concrete-mixing plant, usually consisting of two or more large mixing drums and materials storage hoppers centrally located on a construction project; or a block-making machine used to make concrete blocks.

5478 Portable Equipment Operating

This occupation includes jobs involved in the operation of portable (including mounted or towed) construction equipment and power tools such as pneumatic tools, drilling machines, winches, hoists, lifts, compressors, engines, pumps, generators, and other similar equipment powered by a vehicle engine with a power takeoff or by an independent engine or generator.

5479 Dredging Equipment Operating

This occupation includes jobs involved in operating drags and dumping gates aboard a seagoing hopper dredge or operating dredging equipment on a hydraulic pipeline dredge (operating levers and/or winches to move the dredge and make required cuts) to dredge mud, silt, and sand from rivers and harbors.

5481 Nuclear Reactor Operating

This occupation includes jobs involved in operating a light- or heavy-water or liquid metal cooled and moderated, heterogeneous or homogeneous core nuclear reactor. This work requires (1) a comprehension of the configuration, performance characteristics, limitations, and interrelationships of a nuclear reactor complex including integrated supporting systems which must be safely operated and controlled under variable conditions; (2) a knowledge of specific operating procedures, reactor control and safety mechanisms, control console instruments, radiation monitoring equipment, and methods of shutting down the reactor, operating primary, secondary and auxiliary cooling systems and environmental auxiliary facilities, handling fuel, and refueling the reactor; and (3) an understanding of safety devices and health physics standard operating procedures.

5484 Counting Machine Operating

This occupation includes jobs involved in setting up, operating, and making minor repairs to automatic machines that count coins in bulk quantities and make up rolls or bags containing specific amounts. Includes visually examining medals, proof coins, coins, and planchets and removing uncurrent, counterfeit, mutilated, and foreign pieces.

5485 Aircraft Weight and Balance Operating

This occupation includes jobs that involve examining single and multiple engine aircraft for weight and balance purposes, weighing the aircraft, computing weight and balance factors, and releasing the aircraft for flight with respect to weight and balance. This work requires knowledge of the general aircraft structure and the location of various aircraft components, operation of aircraft weighing scales, procedures for weighing each-type of aircraft, and methods of computing weight and balance data.

5486 Swimming Pool Operating

This occupation includes jobs involved in operating and maintaining swimming pools and related equipment and facilities.

5700 TRANSPORTATION/MOBILE EQUIPMENT OPERATION FAMILY

This job family includes occupations involved in the operation and operational maintenance of self-propelled transportation and other mobile equipment (except aircraft) used to move materials or passengers, including motor vehicles, engineering and construction equipment, tractors, etc., some of which may be equipped with power takeoff and controls to operate special purpose equipment; ocean-going and inland waterway vessels, harbor craft, and floating plants; and trains, locomotives, and train cars. VESSEL JOBS THAT ARE EXCLUDED FROM THE FEDERAL WAGE SYSTEM BY 5 U.S.C. 5342 ARE LISTED IN APPENDIX A.

Occupations in this family are:

5702 Amphibian Truck Operating

This occupation includes jobs involved in operating, navigating, and making minor repairs to amphibious vehicles used over streets and highways and in open waters, harbors, and connecting waterways to transport personnel and supplies and make hydrographic surveys or inspections of various river, harbor, and flood-control projects.

5703 Motor Vehicle Operating*

This occupation includes jobs involved in the operation of gasoline, diesel, or electric powered vehicles, some of which may be equipped with special purpose powered equipment. The vehicles are used within or between Government installations, commercial and industrial facilities, or over public roads. They may be used to haul cargo or passengers, or to tow equipment.

5704 Fork Lift Operating*

This occupation includes jobs which involve the operation of electric, diesel, or gasoline powered fork lift trucks to move, stack and unstack, and load and unload materials in and about warehouses, storage areas, loading docks, and on and off vehicles, etc.

5705 Tractor Operating*

This occupation includes jobs which require skill in operating tractors and attached or towed equipment and knowledge of their purpose and operating characteristics. The work performed typically includes transporting materials and equipment, digging, loading, planting, harvesting, clearing, mowing, and dispensing liquid and solid materials. The tractors operated are wheel mounted and powered by gasoline, diesel, and electric motors and typically have single axle drive. Examples of the attached and towed equipment include trailers, towbars, plows, harrows, planters, mowers, post hole diggers, combines, bailers, spreaders, backhoes, and front-end loaders.

5706 Road Sweeper Operating

This occupation includes jobs involved in the operation of a road-sweeping machine on which is mounted heavy brushes for sweeping roads.

5707 Tank Driving

This occupation includes jobs involved in the operation of tanks, including test driving.

5716 Engineering Equipment Operating*

This occupation includes jobs which involve the operation of gasoline or diesel-powered engineering and construction equipment with wheeled or crawler-type traction, such as graders, tractors with bulldozer or angle-dozer blades, front-end loaders, backhoes, trench diggers, and large industrial tractors with pan or scraper attachments. This equipment is used to perform such functions as cutting, moving, digging, grading, and rolling earth, sand, stone, and other materials, and to maintain ditches, road shoulders and beds, and firelines.

5723 Boat Operating

This occupation includes jobs involved in operating inboard or outboard motor boats or barges (generally under 65 feet in length) to transport personnel and supplies, move non-self-propelled floating plants, control harbor pollution, remove and destroy water hyacinths and similar marine growth, make hydrographic surveys or inspections of river, harbor, and flood control projects, etc. Work requires the ability to navigate the boat, operate the engine, and make operating repairs to the engine and the boat itself

5724 Ship Operating

This occupation includes jobs involved in the operation of ships, riverboats, towboats, tugs, barges, dredges, fishing vessels, or other similar water craft (generally 65 feet or more in length) engaged in transporting passengers and freight, moving non-self-propelled vessels and floating plants, making hydrographic and oceanographic surveys, drilling or probing subaqueous holes, dredging and maintaining waterways, conducting fishing operations, etc. The work includes navigating and steering the ship; standing watch; setting and maintaining speed and course and computing position, using navigational aids; signaling passing ships; operating navigational devices such as radio, sonar, and radar; maintaining log; and coordinating activities of members of the crew. This occupation also includes piloting jobs involved in bringing vessels in and out of harbors or moving them from one location to another where a specialized knowledge of the local channels, currents, and bearings is required.

5725 Crane Operating*

This occupation includes jobs involved in the operation of cranes to lift, transport, and position materials; to dig and move earth or other materials; to drive pilings; or to destroy obsolete structures. Cranes use attachments such as hooks, clamshell buckets, orangepeel buckets, dragline buckets, magnets, piledrivers, demolition hammers, and other special material handling devices.

5729 Drill Rig Operating*

This occupation includes jobs involved in moving in, setting up, operating, maintaining, and moving out heavy mobile drill rigs and associated tools and equipment which are used for geologic drilling at field locations. The work requires knowledge of the operating characteristics of core, churn, calyx, auger, or probe type drill rigs and tools; and skill in manipulating controls to adjust to any drilling conditions.

5731 Mining/Tunneling Machine Operating

This occupation includes jobs that involve setting up, operating, adjusting, and making minor repairs to mining and tunneling machines such as cutting and drilling machines, loading machines, and roof-bolting machines to gather and load rock, ore, or coal; cut channels and drill blasting holes; install roof-support bolts; etc.

5734 Wheel Operating

This occupation includes jobs that involve working in a ship's quartermaster department steering the ship to maintain proper course as indicated by pilot, mate, or captain; operating bridge communication systems; making entries in ship's log; maintaining custody and care of navigation instruments; correcting navigation charts; and communicating by flags, semaphore, and blinker lights. Also includes standing gangway and security watches.

---

*Job grading standard published.

5736 Braking-Switching and Conducting*

This occupation includes jobs involved in coordinating (onsite) the movement, makeup, or breakup of trains, locomotives, and train cars. The work requires knowledge of the layout of a railroad track system; knowledge of and ability to follow numerous safety, signaling, switching, track use, train car, and train movement procedures, restrictions, and requirements; and knowledge of the movement and braking characteristics of locomotives, train cars, and various sizes of trains under a variety of weather, visibility, speed, cargo, track, and other operating conditions. Some work also requires ability to plan efficient work sequences in making up, breaking up, and overseeing (onsite) the safe movement of trains; ability to coordinate the work of a train crew; and ability to enforce numerous operational and safety procedures and requirements.

5737 Locomotive Engineering*

This occupation includes jobs involved in operating all types of locomotives and trains to transport supplies, equipment, conveyances, and personnel. This work requires skill in operating locomotives under various conditions, and knowledge of the layout of a track system and the safety, signaling, and track use requirements or restrictions in various areas of operation.

5738 Railroad Maintenance Vehicle Operating*

This occupation includes jobs involved in the operation of self-propelled, flanged wheel railroad maintenance vehicles and equipment to lay, remove, repair, elevate, align, and maintain ties, rails, ballast, and other parts of the railway, and to transport maintenance supplies, tools, equipment, and personnel. This work requires the ability to safely operate one or more flanged wheel railroad maintenance vehicles, knowledge of railway maintenance and repair methods and requirements, and knowledge of track system layout, operating rules, and maintenance procedures.

5767 Airfield Clearing Equipment Operating

This occupation includes jobs involved in operating airfield clearing equipment, including snow removal equipment and vacuum type sweepers (not conventional snow removal equipment or sweepers used primarily on streets, parking areas, ramps, etc.). This equipment typically consists of gasoline or diesel powered units equipped with specially designed attachments used separately or simultaneously in clearing runways, taxiways, and aprons of snow or foreign objects where conventional equipment and techniques are ineffective. Representative of such equipment are Sno-Gos, Rollovers, Vacuum Sweepers, and other vehicles which include comparable auxiliary equipment.

5800 TRANSPORTATION/MOBILE EQUIPMENT MAINTENANCE FAMILY

This job family includes occupations involved in repairing, adjusting, and maintaining self-propelled transportation and other mobile equipment (except aircraft), including any special-purpose features with which they may be equipped.

Occupations in this family are:

5803 Heavy Mobile Equipment Mechanic*

This occupation includes jobs involved in the repair and modification of combustion-powered heavy duty vehicles and heavy mobile equipment such as bulldozers, road graders, crawler tractors, power shovels, locomotives, combat tanks, cranes, large missile transporters, and fire trucks. These vehicles have utility systems or special hydraulic, pneumatic, or mechanical systems, features, and controls which are designed for construction, combat, earth moving, ship loading, firefighting, and comparable heavy duty, industrial or special applications. The repair of major systems (such as engine, transmission, drive line, and hydraulic utility systems) is included whether accomplished as part of or apart from repair of the total or complete heavy mobile equipment involved. The work requires knowledge of how heavy duty engines, hydraulic systems, transmissions and other parts and systems work. It requires ability to detect faulty items, determine causes of malfunction, and determine best repair methods. It requires skill to assemble, disassemble, repair, or modify mechanical components and systems.

5806 Mobile Equipment Servicing*

This occupation includes jobs involved in servicing automotive and mobile equipment such as automobiles, trucks, buses, ambulances, forklifts, and bulldozers. Typical service includes dispensing gasoline, checking fluid levels and tire pressures, inflating tires, washing cars, lubricating vehicles, installing simple accessory items, and changing and repairing tires and tubes.

5823 Automotive Mechanic*

This occupation includes jobs involved in the maintenance and repair of combustion-powered automotive vehicles, over-the-road trucks, and comparable vehicles such as passenger cars, pick-up trucks, buses, semi-trailer truck tractors, warehouse tractors, farm tractors, forklifts, motorcycles, light combat vehicles such as jeeps and trucks, and other vehicles with similar characteristics, including their engines, transmissions, and other mechanical systems.

5876 Electromotive Equipment Mechanic

This occupation includes jobs involved in the overhaul and repair of electric-powered material handling and other self-propelled mobile equipment such as electric-powered fork lifts, cranes, platform lifts, and electric tugs, including magnetically controlled types. The work requires the application of general mechanical skills and knowledges together with a specialized knowledge of electric motors and circuitry from which such equipment derives motive power.

6500 AMMUNITION, EXPLOSIVES, AND TOXIC MATERIALS WORK FAMILY

This job family includes occupations involved in the manufacturing, assembling, disassembling, renovating, loading, deactivating, modifying, destroying, testing, handling, placing, and discharging of ammunition, propellants, chemicals and toxic materials, and other conventional and special munitions and explosives.

Occupations in this family are:

6502 Explosives Operating*

This occupation includes jobs involved in the manufacture of powder, propellant grains, solid or liquid explosives, and mixtures for flares or signals, and the manufacture, assembly, disassembly, renovation, modification, and deactivation of ammunition, explosives, or chemical or toxic filled munitions. Included are jobs which involve operation of equipment, jigs, or machines that were designed or modified to perform particular munitions operations. This work requires a knowledge of explosives and explosives safety practices, the ability to operate equipment that is designed or modified for munitions operations, and the skill to safely perform operations with explosives.

---

*Job grading standard published.

6505 Munitions Destroying*

This occupation includes jobs involved in the destruction of ammunition, explosives, propellants, and toxic munitions. This work requires a knowledge of demolition procedures, the ability to recognize various types of bulk explosives, and the skill to place munitions and initiating charges.

6510 Blasting

This occupation includes jobs involved in placing and discharging explosives to dislodge, break up, or otherwise move earth, rock, and other solid masses. Typical operations are blasting tree stumps from ground, breaking up boulders or rock strata, blasting ditches or ponds in ground, etc. These jobs may include responsibility for correctly drilling holes, loading holes with explosives, detonating explosives, and making provisions for safety of equipment and personnel within the area.

6511 Missile/Toxic Materials Handling

This occupation includes jobs involved in the readying and handling, for storage, transfer or shipment, of explosive or toxic munitions such as poison gases, radioactive materials, or solid propellant ballistic missiles which require strictly controlled temperature or humidity, limitation of shock and vibration, or frequent checks to prevent physical or chemical changes which would make them unsafe or prevent proper operations. This work requires knowledge of the explosive or toxic materials and of mechanical details of containers and controls. Readying and handling include mechanical assembly and disassembly of munitions and containers, such as checking and replacing environmental controls, attaching parts, positioning parts precisely and tightening to close tolerance; frequent checking of condition for replacement or repair of containers or components; and, often, careful transporting in order not to exceed critical acceleration, vibration, temperature, or similar characteristic limitations.

6517 Explosives Test Operating*

This occupation includes jobs involved in the functional testing of explosives, pyrotechnics, propellant grains, and ammunition to discover characteristics such as dispersion patterns, velocity and range. This requires knowledge of explosives, explosive devices, and environmental conditioning and functional testing practices.

6600 ARMAMENT WORK FAMILY

This job family includes occupations involved in the installation, repair, rebuilding, adjustment, modification, and testing of small arms and artillery weapons and allied accessories. Artillery includes, but is not limited to, field artillery, antitank artillery, anti-aircraft weapons, aircraft and shipboard weapons, recoilless rifles, rocket launchers, mortars, cannon, and allied accessories. Small arms includes, but is not limited to, rifles, carbines, pistols, revolvers, helmets, body armor, shoulder-type rocket launchers, machine guns, and automatic rifles.

Occupations in this family are:

6605 Artillery Repairing*

This occupation includes jobs involved in repairing, rebuilding, and modifying mounted, towed, motorized, or shipboard artillery. This includes work on major components such as gun tubes, mounts, turrets, and carriages. This work requires detailed knowledge of mechanical, and a practical working knowledge of hydraulic, electrical, and pneumatic systems; the ability to recognize improper operation, locate the cause, and determine the best methods for correcting defects; and the skill to fit and adjust parts and assemblies.

6606 Artillery Testing

This occupation includes jobs involved in the testing of guns such as light field artillery, 20-mm air cannon, tank guns, and small caliber guns used for testing armor plate, by emplacing, loading, and firing guns to determine mechanical characteristics and ballistic properties. Also included is the testing of heavy guns and howitzers such as field guns from 105-mm to 240-mm howitzers, anti-aircraft guns from 90-mm to 120-mm, and tank mounts from 90-mm to 105-mm.

6610 Small Arms Repairing*

This occupation includes jobs involved in repairing, rebuilding, and modifying small arms which includes such weapons as machine guns, mortars, rocket launchers, recoilless rifles, and portable flame throwers. The work requires a knowledge of weapons mechanical systems, the ability to recognize and determine the best method to correct malfunctions, and the skill to fit and adjust mechanical parts and assemblies.

6641 Ordnance Equipment Mechanic*

This occupation includes jobs involved in maintaining and overhauling major items and assemblies of ordnance systems and equipment. The work requires the knowledge and application of mechanical and electrical principles and the skill to perform intricate repair and adjustment of hydraulic and pneumatic components and devices. The work also requires skill in such processes as troubleshooting, repairing, modifying, rebuilding, assembling, testing, and installing a variety of equipment such as missiles, torpedoes, mines, depth charges, and associated testing equipment and transporting, handling, erecting, and launching devices.

6652 Aircraft Ordnance Systems Mechanic*

This occupation includes jobs involved in troubleshooting, repair, installation, modification, and operational and functional testing and adjustment of aircraft ordnance systems, equipment, and components. These systems and components involve electrical, mechanical, pneumatic, and hydraulic principles of operation, for example, ejection seats, decoys, canopies, module ejection equipment, pylons, and pressure regulators. The work requires a knowledge of aircraft ordnance systems, the ability to recognize and determine the best method to correct malfunctions, and the ability to use test equipment and measuring devices common to the occupation.

6656 Special Weapons Systems Mechanic

This occupation includes jobs that involve examining, disassembling, repairing, modifying, assembling, calibrating, and testing various types of advanced weapons systems and components; reconditioning and repairing weapon skin sections such as airframes and fins; and maintaining special handling equipment and containers. Weapon components include such items as motor generators, hydrostats, differential switches, accelerometer gages, control boxes, fusing components, batteries, radar, etc. The work requires knowledge of pneumatic, hydraulic, mechanical, electrical, and electronic systems and circuitry, and of radioactive, explosive, electrical, and other hazards unique to advanced weapons.

6900 WAREHOUSING AND STOCK HANDLING FAMILY

This job family includes occupations involved in physically receiving, storing, handling, and issuing supplies, materials, and equipment; handling, marking, and displaying goods for selection by customers; identifying and condition classifying materials and equipment; and routing and expediting movement of parts, supplies, and materials in production and repair facilities.

---

*Job grading standard published.

Occupations in this family are:

6902 Lumber Handling

This occupation includes jobs involved in the physical receipt, storage, and issue of lumber. Work processes include the grading, measuring, unloading, stacking, sorting, drying, and seasoning of various types of lumber required in construction, maintenance, and other work.

6903 Coal Handling

This occupation includes jobs involved in the physical receipt, storage, and issue of coal. Work includes directing the unloading of coal in the coal yard or in bins, verifying quantities of coal received, turning coal, directing the issuance and movement of coal to prescribed consuming locations, and coal sampling.

6904 Tools and Parts Attending*

This occupation includes jobs which involve receiving, storing, issuing, signing out, and checking in various tools, equipment, shop supplies, and repair parts to and from such using maintenance, construction, and shop personnel as machinists, carpenters, and automotive and aircraft mechanics. Such work requires knowledge of the kinds of tools, parts, and equipment in stock and how to locate them, and an ability to identify and issue specific items requested by using personnel.

6907 Warehouse Working*

This occupation includes jobs involved in receiving, storing, assembling for issue or shipment, and shipping a variety of bin and bulk supplies, materials, and equipment. Performance of the work requires a knowledge of the methods used in processing material into and out of the supply system, including the methods used in tallying types and quantities of items against receiving and shipping documents; skill in palletizing, stacking, and otherwise placing and arranging items in storage locations in consideration of their size, shape, weight, quantity, type, stock number, letter and number codes, and other storage factors; and an understanding of procedures to be followed in removing from storage and assembling for shipment or issue quantities, units of issue, and types of items shown in issue requests. Such jobs are located in freight terminals, mechanized and non-mechanized warehouses, open storage areas, and other similar operations.

6910 Materials Expediting*

This occupation includes jobs involved in routing and expediting the movement of parts, end items, supplies, and materials within production and repair facilities to meet priority needs. This work requires knowledge of material characteristics, uses, condition, industrial production shop procedures, shop layout, and internal supply sources.

6912 Material Sorting and Classifying*

This occupation includes jobs involved in identifying, condition classifying, categorizing, and processing materials and equipment. The work involves examining materials to establish or insure their identity and observable physical condition, and processing them according to established procedures.

6914 Store Working*

This occupation includes jobs involved in handling, marking, and preparing displays of merchandise or other items for selection by customers. This requires skill in observing, counting, and maintaining stock levels, and in matching names, codes, numbers, or sizes of items on shelves or counters to lists on which these items are shown. Workers acquire and use a knowledge of the various kinds, sizes, and locations of stocked items and how they should be displayed. They also use knowledge of the general characteristics of items handled in recognizing obvious poor or unacceptable quality or in identifying items by type, kind, or variety for pricing.

6920 Train-Baggage Handling

This occupation includes jobs involved in maintaining control of passengers' baggage, mail, and express during a scheduled run of a train, including receiving baggage and organizing it in cars for orderly distribution along the train route.

6941 Bulk Money Handling

This occupation includes jobs involved in receiving, storing, maintaining custody of, and issuing bulk currency, securities, coin items (new domestic, foreign, and proof coins, and uncurrent and mutilated coins), and gold and silver bullion; controlling storage vaults; and preparing large orders of items for shipment.

6967 Personal Flight Equipment Handling

This occupation includes jobs involved in the receipt, examination, storage, and issue of personal flight clothing and equipment directly to flight crews. The work includes storing and issuing flight clothing, survival equipment, parachutes, oxygen masks, protective helmets, and bail-out bottles; performing periodic examination of equipment for obvious defects; and maintaining necessary records of issue and examination.

6968 Aircraft Freight Loading

This occupation includes jobs involved in loading, placing, securing, and unloading air cargo in the air terminal and on the aircraft when such work includes responsibility for maintaining the proper weight and balance of the loaded aircraft, positioning cargo based on destination and priority of shipment, and insuring that incompatible cargoes are not loaded in the same aircraft.

7000 PACKING AND PROCESSING FAMILY

This job family includes occupations involved in determining the measures required to protect items against damage during movement or storage; selecting proper method of packing, including type and size of container; cleaning, drying, and applying preservatives to materials, parts, or mechanical equipment; and packing equipment, parts and materials.

Occupations in this family are:

7002 Packing*

This occupation includes jobs involved in packing and repacking various loose and packaged equipment, parts, tools, printed materials, and other items in prefabricated containers (wood, cardboard, fiberboard, metal, etc.), mailing tubes, cushioned envelopes, and other packing materials and devices to protect them from being crushed, soiled, or otherwise damaged during shipment and storage. The work includes wrapping, arranging, and cushioning items, using slot hanging, bracketing, suspending, and other similar techniques, and banding, stapling, sealing, and labeling containers.

7004 Preservation Packaging*

This occupation includes jobs involving the application of preservation coatings and materials to parts, tools, and materials, in the process of packing them, to protect them from corrosion, deterioration, and damage. The work requires: knowledge of various types and uses of preservatives and packaging coatings, materials, and processes; knowledge of general

---

*Job grading standard published.

types of items and surfaces requiring preservation treatment and protective packaging; skill in operating preservation and packaging equipment and using application devices and materials; and ability to follow detailed processing instructions and procedures which have many variations.

7006 Preservation Servicing*

This occupation includes jobs involved in preserving mechanical and metal items, and large, powered mechanical systems, vehicles, craft, and weapons against corrosion, deterioration, and similar damage, and performing related disassembly and assembly. Fighter planes, combat tanks, automobiles, ships, trucks, engineering equipment, engines, transmissions, weapons, and combustion powered generators are examples of the mechanical equipment processed. The work typically requires: knowledge of various types and uses of preservatives which protect metal and material against corrosion and deterioration; skill in applying preservatives using specialized equipment and processes; ability to partly disassemble and assemble a variety of mechanical systems or equipment; ability to learn and precisely follow a variety of detailed processing instructions, and, at some levels, use judgement in planning work sequences and selecting processes.

7009 Equipment Cleaning*

This occupation includes jobs involved in the cleaning of such equipment as aircraft, ships, engines, electronic equipment, storage and fuel tanks, immersion vats, grease pits, pumps, and traps. This work is accomplished using ultrasonic vibration methods, automated and non-automated immersion tanks, industrial washers, steam cleaners, brushes, buffers, scrapers, sanders, grinders, files, and other necessary tools or processes to remove paint, sludge, grease, carbon, oil, corrosion, rust and radioactive contaminants. The final product must meet specified finish requirements such as smoothness, brightness, thickness, and cleanliness.

7010 Parachute Packing*

This occupation includes jobs that involve unpacking, cleaning, examining, assembling, and packing cargo, drag (deceleration), special weapons, personnel, experimental, and other similar types of parachutes and parachute systems. The work requires a knowledge of parachute packing procedures.

7300 LAUNDRY, DRY CLEANING, AND PRESSING FAMILY

This job family includes occupations involved in receiving, sorting, washing, drying, dry cleaning, dyeing, pressing, and preparing for delivery clothes, linens, and other articles requiring laundering, dry cleaning, or pressing.

Occupations in this family are:

7304 Laundry Working*

This occupation includes jobs involved in receiving, sorting, and marking soiled linen and apparel; processing flatwork and roughdry items; and assembling and issuing clean laundry. This includes classifying and marking; shaking out wet laundry; feeding into the flatwork ironer; catching, folding, and stacking ironed flatwork; folding roughdry laundry; sorting by identification number; and wrapping bundles.

7305 Laundry Machine Operating*

This occupation includes jobs involved in the operation of commercial-type laundry washers, extractors, tumblers, or conditioners. This includes loading, unloading, and operating controls of machines to wash, dye, starch, roughdry, or condition items for pressing.

7306 Pressing*

This occupation includes jobs involved in the shaping and pressing of laundered or dry cleaned garments and articles by operation of steam press machines and hand irons; also the shaping and pressing of seams and garments during and after tailoring.

7307 Dry Cleaning

This occupation includes jobs involved in the dry cleaning of wearing apparel and other articles requiring cleaning by other than the laundering process, including spot and stain removal.

7400 FOOD PREPARATION AND SERVING FAMILY

This job family includes occupations involved in the preparation and serving of food.

Occupations in this family are:

7402 Baking*

This occupation includes jobs involved in the preparation of regular and special diet bakery products such as bread, rolls, cakes, cookies, pies, doughnuts, pastries, puddings, fillings, and icings.

7404 Cooking*

This occupation includes jobs involved in cooking regular or special diet foods and meals. This includes cooking meats, fowl, fish, and seafood; cooking frozen, canned, dried, or fresh vegetables; measuring and mixing ingredients for soups, stews, sauces, and special dishes; adding seasoning to food; and regulating cooking temperatures.

7405 Bartending*

This occupation includes jobs involving the mixing and serving of beverages and the support services required for operating a bar. The work requires the ability to mix and serve alcoholic and nonalcoholic beverages, meet and converse with the public, and maintain the bar in a presentable and sanitary condition.

7407 Meatcutting*

This occupation includes jobs involving cutting, trimming, and removing bones from meat, usually whole carcasses, quarters, or sides, and preparing and processing fish and poultry. This includes cutting meat into steaks, roasts, chops, cutlets, ground meat, and other small cuts, using powered equipment such as meat saws, slicers, grinders, and hand tools such as meathooks, knives, saws, and cleavers.

7408 Food Service Working*

This occupation includes jobs involved in food service or simple food preparation, or a combination of both. This includes setting and waiting on tables; attending food counters; serving food; assembling trays for hospital patients; washing dishes, pots, and pans; transporting food, equipment, and supplies by manual or motorized carts; assisting in food preparation by cutting vegetables, making salads, etc.

7411 Livestock Slaughtering

This occupation includes jobs involved in slaughtering animals and fowls, and trimming, splitting, skinning, and cleaning carcasses to prepare meat for further processing, using knives, saws, and cleavers.

---

*Job grading standard published.

7420 Waiter*

This occupation includes jobs concerned with setting up tables in a dining room, serving the requested selections in the prescribed manner, and clearing the tables upon completion of the meal.

7600 PERSONAL SERVICES FAMILY

This job family includes occupations concerned with providing grooming, beauty, or other personal services to individuals, patrons, guests, passengers, entertainers, etc., or attending to their personal effects.

Occupations in this family are:

7603 Barbering*

This occupation includes jobs involved in cutting and arranging the hair of the head and face, and conditioning the hair, scalp, face, and neck to suit the individual patron. The work requires a knowledge of barbering, and skill in shaving, cutting, and styling hair, mustaches, and beards by applying barbering techniques and tools.

7607 Mortuary Attending

This occupation includes jobs involved in processing the remains, caskets, and clothing of deceased persons (exclusive of embalming) for reshipment, and doing other work involving the physical handling of remains at a mortuary.

7608 Wardrobe Handling

This occupation includes jobs that involve checking on costumes and uniforms required by performers; seeing that performers are in correct costume or uniform; checking in wardrobes; and maintaining records of and safekeeping of all costumes, uniforms, and other wardrobe items stored for projects.

7640 Bus Attending

This occupation includes jobs involved in lifting, carrying, and otherwise helping crippled children, wheel chair patients, mentally disturbed patients, or other disabled persons in and out of buses or other vehicles. Includes accompanying the driver on assigned trips to maintain order (not to guard persons) if necessary.

7641 Beautician*

This occupation includes jobs involved in conditioning and beautifying the skin, hair, and nails of the patron. The work requires a knowledge of hair dressing and beauty services; and the skill in applying hairdressing and beauty procedures, implements, appliances, and materials to bring out appropriate and becoming features of the individual.

8200 FLUID SYSTEMS MAINTENANCE FAMILY

This job family includes occupations that involve repair, modification, assembly, and testing of fluid systems and fluid system components of aircraft, aircraft engines, missiles, and mobile and support equipment. These fluid systems store, supply, distribute, and move gases or liquids in regulated amounts primarily to produce power, transmit force, and pressurize, cool, and condition cabins. Typical of such devices and systems are pumps, governors, regulators, flow control valves, regular valves, air turbines, actuating or slave cylinders, and major accessories which are components of fuel and oil systems; landing gear, brake, flap, door, and other hydraulic actuating and shock absorbing systems; and oxygen, fire prevention, and other pneumatic systems. The most characteristic knowledges and skills required by the work are those of controlling leakage of fluid under pressure; controlling vibration and heating in high speed turbine operation; and understanding the principles, schematics, and sensing mechanisms involved in regulating fluid flow. WORK ON INSTRUMENTS THAT CONTAIN PNEUMATIC AND HYDRAULIC COMPONENTS SHOULD BE CODED TO THE INSTRUMENT WORK FAMILY, 3300.

Occupations in this family are:

8255 Pneudraulic Systems Mechanic*

This occupation includes jobs involved in the maintenance, modification, and repair of hydraulic and/or pneumatic systems and components that actuate mechanisms or produce, control, and regulate fluid flow. The work requires: a knowledge of the physical principles governing the behavior of fluids (liquids and gases) as they pertain to hydraulic and pneumatic systems or components; knowledge of basic electrical and mechanical principles; the ability to use technical manuals and schematics to test for and isolate malfunctions in hydraulic and pneumatic systems or components; and the skill to effect modification, repairs, or the complete disassembly an@ overhaul of such devices.

8268 Aircraft Pneudraulic Systems Mechanic*

This occupation includes jobs involved in the maintenance, modification, and repair of hydraulic and pneumatic systems associated with aircraft. The work requires: a knowledge of the physical principles governing the behavior of fluids (liquids and gases) as they pertain to hydraulic and pneumatic systems and their components; knowledge of aircraft structures and the relationship of hydraulic and pneumatic systems to the structure and other aircraft systems; knowledge of basic electrical and mechanical principles; the ability to use technical manuals and schematics and to test for and isolate malfunctions in hydraulic and pneumatic systems; and the skill to effect modifications, repairs, or maintenance required.

8600 ENGINE OVERHAUL FAMILY

This job family includes occupations concerned primarily with the manufacture, repair, modification, and major overhaul of engines (except where covered by another job family), including the disassembly, reassembly, and test phases of engine overhaul programs.

Occupations in this family are:

8602 Aircraft Engine Mechanic*

This occupation includes jobs involved in the maintenance, troubleshooting, repair, overhaul, modification, and test of aircraft turbine and reciprocating engines. Work involving engine accessories such as starters, generators, anti-icers, and fuel control devices is included when such assignments are incidental to work on the complete engine.

8610 Small Engine Mechanic

This occupation includes jobs involved in diagnosing malfunctions, determining needed repairs, repairing, and testing small gasoline and diesel engines such as those found on motor boats, lawn mowers, power saws, and other similar equipment.

8675 Liquid Fuel Rocket Engine Mechanic

This occupation includes jobs involving troubleshooting and correcting malfunctions of liquid fuel rocket engines. This work includes diagnosing the cause of failure, disassembling engine to the point where the failure can be corrected, replacing defective parts, reassembling engine, operating test stand to check out various systems of the engine, and making final adjustments.

---

*Job grading standard published.

8800 AIRCRAFT OVERHAUL FAMILY

This job family includes occupations concerned primarily with the overhaul of aircraft, including the disassembly, reassembly, and test phases of aircraft overhaul programs. SPECIALIZED WORK PRIMARILY INVOLVED IN MAINTAINING AND REPAIRING SINGLE AIRCRAFT SYSTEMS, ENGINES, OR ACCESSORIES SHOULD BE CODED TO THE APPROPRIATE JOB FAMILY FOR THE KIND OF WORK DONE.

Occupations in this family are:

8807 Aircraft Propeller/Rotor Mechanic

This occupation includes jobs that involve troubleshooting, repairing, overhauling, modifying, and testing aircraft propellers or helicopter rotors, and straightening blades. The work requires an overall knowledge of electric and/or hydraulic types of controls and drive mechanisms and their subassemblies and parts fit tolerances; of blade straightening and balance and alignment techniques; and of the interrelationships of the mechanisms, valves, and other components of the complete installation.

8852 Aircraft Mechanic*

This occupation includes jobs involved in the maintenance and repair of fixed and rotary wing aircraft systems, airframes, components, and assemblies. Aircraft worked on include a variety of models, are single and multi-engine types, and have reciprocating and jet engines.

8862 Aircraft Servicing

This occupation includes jobs concerned with arrival, parking, servicing, and departure of military, civilian, or foreign aircraft. Work includes meeting incoming aircraft, guiding aircraft into parking position, securing aircraft in parking position, assembling and operating ground support equipment such as power supply and engine starting units, and servicing the systems of the aircraft with needed supplies of oil, fuel, greases, oxygen, etc.

8863 Aircraft Tire Mounting

This occupation includes jobs that involve the disassembly of aircraft tire, tube, and wheel assemblies removed from the aircraft; the visual and physical examination of the tire, tube, and wheel for serviceable condition; the repair and replacement of parts; the reassembly of the tire, tube, and wheel for installation on the aircraft; and the inflation of the tire to specified pressure.

8865 Flight Mechanic

This occupation includes jobs that involve operating the aircraft flight control panel under preflight and flight conditions and repairing and servicing the aircraft before and during flight to assure the aircraft is in safe operating condition. Does not include jobs that primarily involve assisting the pilot in the operation of the aircraft rather than maintaining and repairing the aircraft and equipment

8882 Airframe Test Operating

This occupation includes jobs involved in setting up and operating equipment to test the structural integrity of airframes or other similar structures such as re-entry vehicles. Includes assembling and disassembling test structures, constructing and erecting testjigs, and installing test devices and supporting electrical, mechanical, and hydraulic equipment. The work requires a knowledge of airframe assembly, structural steel jig building and handling, tension patch forming and attachment, load application methods, and load measuring devices and their adjustment; ability to understand test objectives and relationships among airframe, jig, loading devices, and load measuring instruments; and knowledge of the sequence, methods, and procedures of test operations.

9000 FILM PROCESSING FAMILY

This job family includes occupations that involve processing film, for example, operating motion picture developers and printers; cleaning, repairing, matching, cutting, splicing, and assembling films; and mixing developing solutions. Does not include processing work that requires specialized subject-matter knowledge or artistic ability.

Occupations in this family are:

9003 Film Assembling and Repairing

This occupation includes jobs involved in examining, cleaning, modifying, cutting, splicing, and assembling motion picture film, filmstrips, and film prints, deleting damaged sections, and repairing defects; joining, assembling, synchronizing, and preparing preprint motion picture film for printing; matching, cutting, splicing, and synchronizing negative film in picture and sound sequence to an edited work print of a completed motion picture production; etc. This work involves the operation of equipment such as automatic inspection machines, film cleaning machines, film splicers, rewinders, synchronizers, magnetic sound readers, moviolas, film coding machines, and/or film lacquering machines, and may involve the incidental operation of projectors and other similar viewing and/or sound equipment.

9004 Motion Picture Developing/Printing Machine Operating

This occupation includes jobs involved in the operational maintenance of motion picture developing machines and/or printing machines.

9055 Photographic Solution Mixing

This occupation includes jobs involved in measuring and combining various chemicals and liquids to prepare film developing solutions.

---

*Job grading standard published.

APPENDIX A. VESSEL JOBS EXCLUDED FROM

THE FEDERAL WAGE SYSTEM BY 5 U.S.C. 5342

Section 5342 of title 5, United States Code, provides that subchapter IV, except Section 5348, is not applicable to officers and members of crews of vessels excepted from chapter 51 of title 5 by section 5102 (c) (8) of that title. Agencies should use the following codes for reporting work force information on those vessel employees whose pay is fixed and adjusted in accordance with maritime rates and practices.

9802	Master	9837	Refrigeration Engineer (Day)
9803	Deck Officer	9838	Machinist
9804	Junior Deck Officer	9839	Plumber
9805	Radio Officer	9840	Plumber-Machinist
9806	Radio Officer (Freighter)	9841	Deck Engineer-Machinist
9807	Relief Deck Officer	9842	Student Observer (Unlicensed Junior Engineer)
9808	Alaska Pilot	9843	Yeoman (Engine)
9809	Damage Control Instructor	9844	Storekeeper (Engine)
9810	Deck Cadet	9845	Yeoman-Storekeeper (Engine)
9811	Boatswain	9846	Pumpman
9812	Boatswain (Freighter)	9847	Assistant Electrician
9813	Carpenter	9848	Electrician (Watch)
9814	Carpenter (Freighter)	9849	Electrician
9815	Master-at-Arms	9850	Electrician (Day)
9816	Watchman (Fire)	9851	Electrician-Maintenance
9817	Yeoman (Deck)	9852	Electrician (Watch P-2 Turbo-Electric)
9818	Storekeeper (Deck)	9853	Engine Utilityman
9819	Yeoman-Storekeeper (Deck)	9854	Evaporator-Utilityman
9820	Boatswain's Mate	9855	Oiler
9821	Boatswain's Mate (Heavy Lift Operator)	9856	Oiler (Diesel)
9822	Boatswain's Mate (Day)	9857	Refrigeration Oiler
9823	Boatswain's Mate (Watch)	9858	Fireman (Oil)
9824	Carpenter's Mate	9859	Wiper
9825	Able Seaman	9860	Steward
9826	Able Seaman Maintenance	9861	Steward (Freighter)
9827	Chief Engineer	9862	Steward (Troop Mess)
9828	Assistant Engineer	9863	Steward (Sanitation)
9829	Assistant Engineer (Day)	9864	Stewardess
9830	Relief Engineer	9865	Steward-Cook (Freighter)
9831	Engine Cadet	9866	Chief Cook
9832	Deck Engineer	9867	Chief Cook (Freighter)
9833	Chief Electrician (P-2 Turbo-Electric)	9868	Yeoman (Steward)
9834	Chief Electrician	9869	Storekeeper (Steward)
9835	Refrigeration Engineer (Refrigerated Cargo)	9870	Yeoman-Storekeeper (Steward)
9836	Refrigeration Engineer (Passenger and Dry Cargo)	9871	Baker

---

*Job grading standard published.

Appendix O: Wage Grade Occupations in Federal Service by Selected Agency

This appendix is the blue-collar counterpart to Appendix L. Recall that two of the factors affecting hiring potential are the universality of the job title (how many agencies have such positions) and the occupational group (or job family) in which the job title appears. The pie chart and table reproduced here show the distribution of blue-collar Federal jobs by agency, occupational group, and job title. As was the case for white-collar jobs, the larger the occupational group, the more vacancies and the greater opportunity to be hired. Likewise, the more agencies in which a job title occurs, the better the chances of finding an opening. To indicate which agencies are likely to offer the best job opportunities in your field, this appendix shows how many people in each job title are employed at each of the 25 largest Federal agencies.

> Factors affecting **hiring potential** are discussed in Step 1 (p. 20).

FIGURE 2 - BLUE-COLLAR EMPLOYMENT BY DEPARTMENT AND SELECTED AGENCY
SEPTEMBER 30, 1995

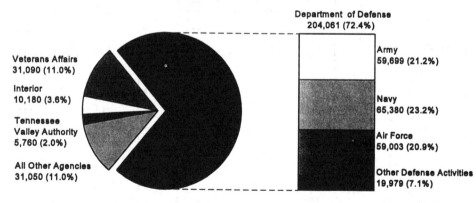

Department of Defense
204,061 (72.4%)

Veterans Affairs
31,090 (11.0%)

Interior
10,180 (3.6%)

Tennessee
Valley Authority
5,760 (2.0%)

All Other Agencies
31,050 (11.0%)

Army
59,699 (21.2%)

Navy
65,380 (23.2%)

Air Force
59,003 (20.9%)

Other Defense Activities
19,979 (7.1%)

TABLE B   FULL-TIME CIVILIAN BLUE-COLLAR EMPLOYMENT BY OCCUPATION AND SELECTED AGENCY, ALL AREAS, SEPTEMBER 30, 1995

OCCUPATION CODES TITLES	TOTAL, ALL AGENCIES	STATE	TREASURY	ARMY	NAVY	AIR FORCE	DEFENSE LOGIS AGENCY	OTHER DEFENSE	JUSTICE	INTERIOR	AGRI-CULTURE	COMMERCE
GRAND TOTAL	282,141	72	4,123	59,699	65,380	59,003	12,991	6,988	4,588	10,180	3,888	1,096
PERCENT OF TOTAL	100.0 %	0.0 %	1.5 %	21.2 %	23.2 %	20.9 %	4.6 %	2.5 %	1.6 %	3.6 %	1.4 %	0.4 %
2501 MISC WIRE COMM EQPT INST &MAIN	18	...	...	9	2	3	...	...	...	1	...	...
2502 TELECOMMUNICATIONS MECHANIC	663	...	4	254	114	201	11	18	...	...	5	...
2504 WIRE COMM CABLE SLICING	130	...	...	36	38	52	...	1	...	...	...	...
2508 COMM LINE INSTALLING REPAIRING	32	...	...	19	8	1	4	...	...	...	...	...
WIRE COMM EQPT INSTALL & MAINT	843	...	4	318	162	257	15	19	...	1	5	...
2601 MISC ELECTRONIC EQPT INST MAIN	407	...	...	168	37	59	1	11	...	12	...	5
2602 ELECTRONIC MEASUREMT EQPT MECH	1,391	...	...	238	494	654	...	...	...	...	...	...
2604 ELECTRONICS MECHANIC	9,545	...	26	4,038	2,185	2,619	34	29	5	67	3	9
2606 ELECTRONIC INDUSTR CONTRL MECH	1,118	...	156	202	238	337	91	29	...	7	...	...
2608 ELECTRONIC DIGITL COMPUTR MECH	625	...	8	90	59	362	27	9	...	6	...	6
2610 ELECTRONIC INTEGR SYSTEMS MECH	4,564	...	3	509	477	3,526	9	...	...	4	...	...
ELECTRONIC EQPT INSTALL & MAINT	17,650	...	193	5,245	3,490	7,557	162	78	5	96	3	20
2801 MISC ELECTRICAL INSTALL &MAINT	216	...	...	46	67	54	1	7	...	14	...	...
2805 ELECTRICIAN	7,224	...	78	749	3,554	654	77	69	162	163	34	27
2810 ELECTRICIAN (HIGH VOLTAGE)	3,510	...	...	493	668	301	20	1	...	216	3	5
2854 ELECTRICAL EQUIPMENT REPAIRER	1,140	...	22	186	326	411	7	...	117	4	...	...
2892 AIRCRAFT ELECTRICIAN	2,720	...	...	264	642	1,790	...	...	1	...	...	...
ELECTRICAL INSTALLATION & MAINT	14,810	...	100	1,738	5,257	3,210	105	77	280	397	37	32
3101 MISC FABRIC AND LEATHER WORK	29	...	...	19	1	1	2	...	...	1	...	5
3103 SHOE REPAIRING	8	...	...	5	3	...	...	...	...	...	...	...
3105 FABRIC WORKING	1,225	...	1	272	308	486	40	...	107	...	...	...
3106 UPHOLSTERING	160	...	...	34	35	11	2	...	40	...	...	...
3111 SEWING MACHINE OPERATING	263	...	1	92	13	...	5	...	...	...	1	...
3119 BROOM AND BRUSH MAKING	8	...	...	...	...	...	...	...	8	...	...	...
FABRIC AND LEATHER WORK	1,693	...	2	422	360	498	49	...	155	1	1	5
3301 MISC INSTRUMENT WORK	13	...	...	9	2	...	1	...	...	...	...	1
3306 OPTICAL INSTRUMENT REPAIRING	286	...	...	167	75	34	6	1	...	...	...	...
3314 INSTRUMENT MAKING	418	...	...	21	12	12	3	...	...	1	5	20
3359 INSTRUMENT MECHANIC	1,649	...	1	112	586	621	...	1	...	28	83	2
3364 PROJECTION EQUIPMENT REPAIRING	12	...	...	12	...	...	...	...	...	...	...	...
INSTRUMENT WORK	2,378	...	1	321	675	667	10	2	...	29	88	23
3401 MISC MACHINE TOOL WORK	384	...	8	245	46	81	...	...	...	...	...	...
3414 MACHINING	5,730	...	86	1,181	2,476	1,125	17	9	11	34	21	11
3416 TOOLMAKING	634	...	27	160	256	174	1	...	10	1	...	...
3417 TOOL GRINDING	52	...	...	17	35	...	...	...	...	...	...	...
3422 POWER SAW OPERATING	9	...	...	3	5	...	...	...	...	...	...	1
3428 DIE SINKING	6	...	...	4	2	...	...	...	...	...	...	...
3431 MACHINE TOOL OPERATING	792	...	43	194	126	434	...	...	1	...	1	3
MACHINE TOOL WORK	7,607	...	164	1,794	2,946	1,814	18	9	22	35	22	15
3501 MISC GEN SERVICES & SUPPORT WK	966	1	5	47	23	11	...	...	1	7	821	...
3502 LABORING	6,652	4	206	1,527	695	676	201	170	7	991	635	27
3508 PIPELINE WORKING	9	...	...	9	...	...	...	...	...	...	...	...
3511 LABORATORY WORKING	153	...	1	16	5	2	...	2	8	1	15	...
3513 COIN/CURRENCY CHECKING	411	...	411	...	...	...	...	...	...	...	...	...
3515 LABORATORY SUPPORT WORKING	44	...	4	1	1	...	1	...	...	...	29	...
3543 STEVEDORING	102	...	...	...	102	...	...	...	...	...	...	...
3546 RAILROAD REPAIRING	45	...	...	22	20	2	1	...	...	...	...	...
3566 CUSTODIAL WORKING	14,045	2	40	428	606	70	40	623	95	332	27	62
GENERAL SERVICES & SUPPORT WORK	22,427	7	667	2,050	1,452	761	243	795	111	1,331	1,527	89
3601 MISC STRUCTURAL & FINISHING WK	53	...	...	33	12	4	...	...	...	...	...	...
3602 CEMENT FINISHING	144	...	...	16	36	85	...	...	...	1	1	...
3603 MASONRY	744	...	4	92	193	109	4	5	17	102	6	...
3604 TILE SETTING	83	...	...	3	77	...	...	...	...	...	...	...
3605 PLASTERING	100	...	2	8	29	5	...	2	1	1	...	...
3606 ROOFING	173	...	...	24	96	28	7	4	...	1	...	...
3609 FLOOR COVERING INSTALLING	74	...	...	4	60	...	...	...	...	...	...	5
3610 INSULATING	968	...	2	29	790	75	...	4	...	...	...	...
3611 GLAZING	33	...	...	11	20	...	...	...	...	...	...	...
3653 ASPHALT WORKING	56	...	...	12	20	21	...	...	...	2	1	...
STRUCTURAL AND FINISHING WORK	2,429	...	8	232	1,333	327	11	15	18	107	8	5
3701 MISC METAL PROCESSING	72	...	5	30	31	4	...	...	...	...	...	...
3702 FLAME/ARC CUTTING	22	...	...	13	7	...	2	...	...	...	...	...
3703 WELDING	3,596	...	5	846	2,084	377	37	1	24	39	21	1
3705 NON-DESTRUCTIVE TESTING	907	...	...	34	137	735	...	...	...	...	...	...

TABLE B, 1995 -- CONTINUED

HEALTH & HUMAN SERVICES	TRANSPOR-TATION	ENERGY	VETERAN AFFAIRS	ARCHI-TECT OF CAPITOL	GPO	FEMA	GENERAL SERVICES ADM	NASA	PANAMA CANAL COMM	ARMED FORCES RET HOME	SMITH-SONIAN INST.	TVA	US INFO AGENCY	ALL OTHER AGENCIES	OCCUPATION CODES
2,675	2,533	1,451	31,090	1,705	1,935	164	3,376	497	297	292	983	5,750	193	1,192	GRAND TOTAL
0.9 %	0.9 %	0.5 %	11.0 %	0.6 %	0.7 %	0.1 %	1.2 %	0.2 %	0.1 %	0.1 %	0.3 %	2.0 %	0.1 %	0.4 %	PERCENT
...	...	...	...	...	2	...	...	...	...	1	...	...	...	...	2501
...	1	1	10	...	...	...	37	...	3	...	...	...	...	4	2502
...	3	...	...	...	...	...	...	...	...	...	...	...	...	...	2504
...	...	...	...	...	...	...	...	...	...	...	...	...	...	...	2508
...	4	1	10	...	2	...	37	...	3	1	...	...	...	4	2500
3	...	...	...	...	13	29	...	66	...	...	3	...	...	...	2601
...	...	5	...	...	...	...	...	...	...	...	...	...	...	...	2602
9	105	124	198	31	...	4	6	31	...	...	14	...	...	8	2604
...	...	...	40	7	...	...	11	...	...	...	...	...	...	...	2606
...	...	...	47	...	...	...	...	...	...	...	11	...	...	...	2608
...	1	11	...	...	...	...	4	4	...	...	7	3	...	...	2610
12	106	140	295	38	13	33	71	101	...	...	35	9	...	8	2600
...	2	8	...	...	...	...	4	...	...	...	1	...	5	7	2801
92	221	9	932	84	32	9	126	24	11	7	50	...	...	60	2805
9	3	685	12	22	...	...	30	12	1	1	6	1,015	5	2	2810
1	3	...	32	...	...	...	...	...	...	...	4	27	...	...	2954
...	23	...	...	...	...	...	...	...	...	...	...	...	...	...	2892
102	252	702	976	106	32	9	160	36	12	8	61	1,042	10	69	2800
...	...	...	...	...	...	...	...	...	...	...	...	...	...	...	3101
...	...	...	...	...	...	...	...	...	...	...	...	...	...	...	3103
7	...	...	4	...	...	...	...	...	...	...	...	...	...	...	3105
...	7	...	12	17	1	...	...	...	...	...	1	...	...	...	3106
4	...	...	147	...	...	...	...	...	...	...	...	...	...	...	3111
...	...	...	...	...	...	...	...	...	...	...	...	...	...	...	3119
11	7	...	163	17	1	...	...	...	...	...	1	...	...	...	3100
...	...	...	...	...	...	...	...	...	...	...	...	...	...	3	3301
14	...	...	2	...	...	...	...	16	...	...	...	308	...	...	3306
...	...	4	...	...	...	...	...	...	...	...	...	...	...	...	3314
7	7	97	9	6	...	...	1	...	4	...	3	80	...	1	3359
...	...	...	...	...	...	...	...	...	...	...	...	...	...	...	3364
21	7	101	11	6	...	...	1	16	4	...	3	388	...	4	3300
...	...	1	...	...	...	...	...	...	3	...	...	...	...	...	3401
1	51	4	31	8	32	1	3	2	9	3	9	603	...	2	3414
...	4	...	...	...	...	...	...	...	1	...	...	...	...	...	3416
...	...	...	...	...	...	...	...	...	...	...	...	...	...	...	3417
...	...	...	...	...	...	...	...	...	...	...	...	...	...	...	3422
...	...	...	...	...	...	...	...	...	...	...	...	...	...	...	3428
...	...	...	...	...	...	...	...	...	...	...	...	...	...	...	3431
1	55	5	31	8	32	1	3	2	13	3	9	603	...	2	3400
3	19	...	...	...	...	3	11	...	...	...	4	...	...	10	3501
54	24	2	746	310	99	...	26	...	...	8	77	47	3	117	3502
...	...	...	...	...	...	...	...	...	...	...	...	...	...	...	3508
65	...	...	35	...	...	...	...	...	...	...	...	...	...	3	3511
...	...	...	...	...	...	...	...	...	...	...	...	...	...	...	3513
3	1	...	...	...	4	...	...	...	...	...	...	...	...	...	3515
...	...	...	...	...	...	...	...	...	...	...	...	...	...	...	3543
...	...	...	...	...	...	...	...	...	...	...	...	...	...	...	3546
635	12	20	9,417	379	70	5	671	...	6	22	221	196	...	66	3566
760	56	22	10,198	689	173	8	708	...	6	30	302	243	3	196	3500
...	...	...	...	...	4	...	...	...	...	...	...	...	...	...	3601
...	...	4	...	...	...	...	...	...	...	...	...	...	...	1	3602
2	6	1	147	21	...	...	15	...	...	2	19	...	...	...	3603
...	...	...	1	1	...	...	...	...	...	1	...	...	...	...	3604
...	...	...	43	7	...	...	1	...	...	...	1	...	...	...	3605
...	2	...	7	...	...	...	1	...	...	...	3	...	...	...	3606
...	...	...	3	7	...	...	...	...	...	...	...	...	...	...	3609
2	7	...	25	8	...	...	18	...	...	...	3	...	...	...	3610
...	...	...	1	...	...	...	...	...	...	...	...	...	...	1	3611
...	...	...	...	...	...	...	...	...	...	...	...	...	...	...	3653
4	15	5	227	44	4	...	35	...	...	3	25	...	...	2	3600
...	...	...	...	...	...	...	...	2	...	...	...	...	...	...	3701
...	...	...	...	...	...	...	...	...	...	...	...	...	...	...	3702
1	94	12	27	2	1	...	...	2	3	...	6	...	...	3	3703
...	...	...	...	...	...	...	...	...	...	...	...	...	...	...	3705

TABLE B   FULL-TIME CIVILIAN BLUE-COLLAR EMPLOYMENT BY OCCUPATION AND SELECTED AGENCY, ALL AREAS, SEPTEMBER 30, 1995

OCCUPATION CODES TITLES	TOTAL, ALL AGENCIES	STATE	TREASURY	ARMY	NAVY	AIR FORCE	DEFENSE LOGIS AGENCY	OTHER DEFENSE	JUSTICE	INTERIOR	AGRI-CULTURE	COMMERCE
3707 METALIZING	127	...	...	15	29	83	...	...	...	...	...	...
3708 METAL PROCESS WORKING	11	...	...	3	6	...	...	...	...	...	...	...
3711 ELECTROPLATING	628	...	5	166	226	230	...	...	...	...	...	...
3712 HEAT TREATING	162	...	35	32	40	55	...	...	...	...	...	...
3720 BRAZING AND SOLDERING	4	...	...	...	...	4	...	...	...	...	...	...
3722 COLD WORKING	2	...	...	2	...	...	...	...	...	...	...	...
3725 BATTERY REPAIRING	101	...	...	36	17	24	14	...	...	...	...	...
3727 BUFFING AND POLISHING	68	...	43	4	15	6	...	...	...	...	...	...
3735 METAL PHOTOTRANSFERRING	29	...	...	18	6	5	...	...	...	...	...	...
3736 CIRCUIT BOARD MAKING	33	...	...	1	15	17	...	...	...	...	...	...
3741 FURNACE OPERATING	17	...	4	3	10	...	...	...	...	...	...	...
3769 SHOT PEENING MACHINE OPERATING	68	...	...	2	21	45	...	...	...	...	...	...
METAL PROCESSING	5,837	...	97	1,205	2,644	1,586	53	1	24	39	21	1
3801 MISC METAL WORK	637	...	32	63	508	21	...	...	3	4	...	...
3802 METAL FORGING	61	...	...	8	50	2	...	...	...	...	...	...
3806 SHEET METAL MECHANIC	8,556	...	17	788	3,080	4,374	8	10	21	6	7	6
3807 STRUCTURAL/ORNAMENTAL IRON WRK	89	...	3	39	38	5	...	...	...	...	1	...
3808 BOILERMAKING	806	...	1	1	490	1	...	...	...	13	...	...
3809 MOBILE EQPT METAL MECHANIC	611	...	...	255	145	197	9	...	...	...	...	...
3815 PNEUMATIC TOOL OPERATING	6	...	...	...	3	...	...	...	...	...	...	...
3816 ENGRAVING	16	...	...	3	5	4	...	...	...	...	...	...
3818 SPRINGMAKING	4	...	...	2	...	2	...	...	...	...	...	...
3819 AIRFRAME JIG FITTING	5	...	...	...	...	5	...	...	...	...	...	...
3820 SHIPFITTING	1,598	...	...	...	1,545	...	...	...	...	...	...	...
3830 BLACKSMITHING	3	...	...	1	...	...	...	...	...	2	...	...
3832 MEDAL MAKING	4	...	4	...	...	...	...	...	...	...	...	...
3833 TRANSFER ENGRAVING	3	...	3	...	...	...	...	...	...	...	...	...
3858 METAL TANK AND RADIATOR REPAIR	71	...	...	28	...	43	...	...	...	...	...	...
3869 METAL FORMING MACHINE OPERATNG	375	...	318	17	3	14	...	...	23	...	...	...
3872 METAL TUBE MAKING INST REPAIR	56	...	...	11	4	41	...	...	...	...	...	...
METAL WORK	12,901	...	378	1,216	5,871	4,709	17	10	47	25	8	6
3901 MISC MOVIE RADIO TV SOUND EQPT	53	...	7	27	4	...	...	...	...	...	...	6
3910 MOTION PICTURE PROJECTION	34	...	...	9	2	4	1	2	3	6	1	...
3911 SOUND RECORDING EQPT OPERATING	5	...	...	1	...	3	...	...	...	1	...	...
3919 TELEVISION EQUIPMENT OPERATING	8	...	...	7	...	1	...	...	...	...	...	...
3940 BROADCAST EQUIPMENT OPERATING	154	...	...	20	...	...	...	...	...	...	...	...
3941 PUBLIC ADDRESS EQPT OPERATING	13	...	...	10	...	...	...	...	...	...	...	...
MOVIE RADIO TV & SOUND EQPT OPER	267	...	7	74	6	8	1	2	3	7	1	6
4001 MISC LENS AND CRYSTAL WORK	3	...	...	...	...	...	...	...	...	...	...	2
4005 OPTICAL ELEMENT WORKING	2	...	...	1	...	1	...	...	...	...	...	...
4010 PRESCRIPTION EYEGLASS MAKING	39	...	...	35	...	...	...	...	4	...	...	...
LENS AND CRYSTAL WORK	44	...	...	36	...	1	...	...	4	...	...	2
4101 MISC PAINTING AND PAPERHANGING	66	...	...	20	31	3	...	2	...	10	...	...
4102 PAINTING	5,072	...	23	735	1,832	1,260	94	19	81	112	8	3
4103 PAPERHANGING	18	...	...	5	...	...	...	...	...	...	...	...
4104 SIGN PAINTING	207	...	...	62	40	50	8	...	...	28	3	...
4157 INSTRUMENT DIAL PAINTING	3	...	...	...	...	3	...	...	...	...	...	...
PAINTING AND PAPERHANGING	5,366	...	23	822	1,903	1,316	102	21	81	150	11	3
4201 MISC PLUMBING AND PIPEFITTING	36	...	1	5	23	1	1	...	3	2	...	...
4204 PIPEFITTING	5,630	...	28	370	3,541	221	28	29	54	25	6	7
4206 PLUMBING	1,539	...	10	395	377	390	18	13	79	62	6	2
4255 FUEL DISTRIBUTION SYSTEM MECH	201	...	...	19	17	165	...	...	...	...	...	...
PLUMBING AND PIPEFITTING	7,406	...	39	789	3,958	777	47	41	136	89	12	9
4301 MISC PLIABLE MATERIALS WORK	95	...	...	64	31	...	...	...	...	...	...	...
4351 PLASTIC MOLDING EQPT OPERATING	21	...	...	...	21	...	...	...	...	...	...	...
4352 PLASTIC FABRICATING	434	...	...	62	205	161	...	...	6	...	...	...
4360 RUBBER PRODUCTS MOLDING	42	...	...	4	24	14	...	...	...	...	...	...
4361 RUBBER EQUIPMENT REPAIRING	58	...	...	29	9	19	...	...	...	...	...	...
4370 GLASSBLOWING	5	...	...	...	...	1	...	...	...	1	...	1
4371 PLASTER PATTERN CASTING	1	...	...	...	1	...	...	...	...	...	...	...
4373 MOLDING	79	...	...	8	52	19	...	...	...	...	...	...
PLIABLE MATERIALS WORK	735	...	...	167	343	214	...	...	6	1	...	1
4401 MISCELLANEOUS PRINTING	477	3	24	12	56	7	1	27	10	18	5	18
4402 BINDERY WORKING	860	7	43	8	273	13	...	32	14	14	5	22
4403 HAND COMPOSING	212	...	...	...	...	1	...	...	...	...	...	...
4405 FILM ASSEMBLY-STRIPPING	55	...	...	1	21	1	...	...	...	...	4	3
4406 LETTERPRESS OPERATING	157	...	132	...	2	1	...	...	...	...	...	13
4413 NEGATIVE ENGRAVING	170	...	...	...	...	...	...	81	...	...	...	13
4414 OFFSET PHOTOGRAPHY	187	3	1	12	51	7	...	36	4	8	15	13
4416 PLATEMAKING	119	...	...	...	7	1	...	32	4	5	...	4
4417 OFFSET PRESS OPERATING	903	11	22	43	254	37	1	51	36	27	54	24
4419 SILK SCREEN MAKING & PRINTING	31	...	...	8	1	5	...	...	16	1	...	...
4425 PHOTOENGRAVING	29	...	29	...	...	...	...	...	...	...	...	...
4441 BOOKBINDING	153	...	152	...	...	...	...	...	...	...	...	1
4445 BANK NOTE DESIGNING	5	...	5	...	...	...	...	...	...	...	...	...
4446 BANK NOTE ENGRAVING	18	...	18	...	...	...	...	...	...	...	...	...

TABLE B, 1995 -- CONTINUED

HEALTH & HUMAN SERVICES	TRANSPOR -TATION	ENERGY	VETERAN AFFAIRS	ARCHI- TECT OF CAPITOL	GPO	FEMA	GENERAL SERVICES ADM	NASA	PANAMA CANAL COMM	ARMED FORCES RET HOME	SMITH- SONIAN INST.	TVA	US INFO AGENCY	ALL OTHER AGENCIES	OCCUPATION CODES
...	...	...	...	...	...	...	...	...	...	...	...	...	...	...	3707
...	...	...	...	...	2	...	...	...	...	...	...	...	...	...	3708
...	1	...	...	...	...	...	...	...	...	...	...	...	...	...	3711
...	...	...	...	...	...	...	...	...	...	...	...	...	...	...	3712
...	...	...	...	...	...	...	...	...	...	...	...	...	...	...	3720
...	...	...	...	...	...	...	...	...	...	...	...	...	...	...	3722
...	...	...	...	...	10	...	...	...	...	...	...	...	...	...	3725
...	...	...	...	...	...	...	...	...	...	...	...	...	...	...	3727
...	...	...	...	...	...	...	...	...	...	...	...	...	...	...	3735
...	...	...	...	...	...	...	...	...	...	...	...	...	...	...	3736
...	...	...	...	...	...	...	...	...	...	...	...	...	...	...	3741
...	...	...	...	...	...	...	...	...	...	...	...	...	...	...	3769
1	95	12	27	2	13	...	...	4	3	...	6	...	...	3	3700
...	5	...	...	...	...	...	...	...	...	...	...	...	...	1	3801
...	1	...	...	...	...	...	...	...	...	...	...	...	...	...	3802
11	115	6	38	30	7	2	12	2	3	3	10	...	...	...	3806
...	2	...	...	...	...	...	...	...	1	...	...	...	...	...	3807
...	...	...	...	...	...	...	...	1	...	...	...	299	...	...	3808
...	3	...	...	...	...	...	4	...	1	...	...	...	...	...	3809
...	...	...	...	...	...	...	...	...	...	...	...	...	...	...	3815
...	...	...	3	...	...	...	1	...	...	...	...	...	...	...	3816
...	...	...	...	...	...	...	...	...	...	...	...	...	...	...	3818
...	...	...	...	...	...	...	...	...	...	...	...	...	...	...	3819
...	51	...	...	...	...	...	...	...	2	...	...	...	...	...	3820
...	...	...	...	...	...	...	...	...	...	...	...	...	...	...	3830
...	...	...	...	...	...	...	...	...	...	...	...	...	...	...	3832
...	...	...	...	...	...	...	...	...	...	...	...	...	...	...	3833
...	...	...	...	...	...	...	...	...	...	...	...	...	...	...	3858
...	...	...	...	...	...	...	...	...	...	...	...	...	...	...	3869
...	...	...	...	...	...	...	...	...	...	...	...	...	...	...	3872
11	177	6	41	30	7	2	17	3	7	3	10	299	...	1	3800
3	...	...	...	...	...	...	...	...	...	...	...	...	4	2	3901
1	...	...	1	...	...	...	...	1	...	...	3	...	...	...	3910
...	...	...	...	...	...	...	...	...	...	...	...	...	...	...	3911
...	...	...	...	...	...	...	...	...	...	...	...	...	...	...	3919
...	...	...	...	...	...	...	...	...	...	...	...	...	134	...	3940
...	...	...	...	3	...	...	...	...	...	...	...	...	...	...	3941
4	...	...	1	3	...	...	...	1	...	...	3	...	138	2	3900
...	1	...	...	...	...	...	...	...	...	...	...	...	...	...	4001
...	...	...	...	...	...	...	...	...	...	...	...	...	...	...	4005
...	...	...	...	...	...	...	...	...	...	...	...	...	...	...	4010
...	1	...	...	...	...	...	...	...	...	...	...	...	...	...	4000
25	75	4	662	55	11	4	26	...	...	5	30	...	...	8	4101
...	...	...	13	...	...	...	...	...	...	...	...	...	...	...	4102
...	...	...	14	2	...	...	...	...	...	...	...	...	...	...	4103
...	...	...	...	...	...	...	...	...	...	...	...	...	...	...	4104
...	...	...	...	...	...	...	...	...	...	...	...	...	...	...	4157
25	75	4	689	57	11	4	26	...	...	5	30	...	...	8	4100
...	...	...	...	...	...	...	...	...	...	...	...	...	...	...	4201
32	78	3	630	68	16	...	55	5	3	7	14	401	...	8	4204
9	9	3	120	11	...	6	17	...	2	2	7	...	...	2	4206
...	...	...	...	...	...	...	...	...	...	...	...	...	...	...	4255
41	86	6	750	79	16	6	72	5	5	9	23	401	...	10	4200
...	...	...	...	...	...	...	...	...	...	...	...	...	...	...	4301
...	...	...	...	...	...	...	...	...	...	...	...	...	...	...	4351
...	...	...	...	...	...	...	...	...	...	...	...	...	...	...	4352
...	...	...	...	...	...	...	...	...	...	...	...	...	...	...	4360
...	1	...	...	...	...	...	...	...	...	...	...	...	...	...	4361
2	...	...	...	...	...	...	...	...	...	...	...	...	...	...	4370
...	...	...	...	...	...	...	...	...	...	...	...	...	...	...	4371
...	...	...	...	...	...	...	...	...	...	...	...	...	...	...	4373
2	1	...	...	...	...	...	...	...	...	...	...	...	...	...	4300
...	...	5	...	...	248	...	...	...	...	...	...	...	...	43	4401
3	5	1	...	...	319	...	41	4	...	...	4	...	...	53	4402
...	...	...	...	...	211	...	...	...	...	...	...	...	...	...	4403
...	...	...	...	...	23	...	...	...	...	...	...	...	...	2	4405
...	...	...	...	...	22	...	...	...	...	...	...	...	...	...	4406
...	...	...	...	...	76	...	...	...	...	...	...	...	...	...	4413
...	2	3	...	...	25	...	2	...	...	...	...	...	...	5	4414
...	...	...	...	...	66	...	...	...	...	...	...	...	...	...	4416
1	13	9	9	...	209	5	36	1	...	2	6	...	...	53	4417
...	...	...	...	...	...	...	...	...	...	...	...	...	...	...	4419
...	...	...	...	...	...	...	...	...	...	...	...	...	...	...	4425
...	...	...	...	...	...	...	...	...	...	...	...	...	...	...	4441
...	...	...	...	...	...	...	...	...	...	...	...	...	...	...	4445
...	...	...	...	...	...	...	...	...	...	...	...	...	...	...	4446

TABLE B   FULL-TIME CIVILIAN BLUE-COLLAR EMPLOYMENT BY OCCUPATION AND SELECTED AGENCY, ALL AREAS, SEPTEMBER 30, 1995

OCCUPATION CODES / TITLES	TOTAL, ALL AGENCIES	STATE	TREASURY	ARMY	NAVY	AIR FORCE	DEFENSE LOGIS AGENCY	OTHER DEFENSE	JUSTICE	INTERIOR	AGRI-CULTURE	COMMERCE
4447 SCULPTURAL ENGRAVING	1	...	1	...	...	...	...	...	...	...	...	...
4448 SIDEROGRAPHIC TRANSFERRING	5	...	5	...	...	...	...	...	...	...	...	...
4449 ELECTROLYTIC INTAGLIO PLATEMAK	21	...	21	...	...	...	...	...	...	...	...	...
4450 INTAGLIO DIE & PLATE FINISHING	2	...	2	...	...	...	...	...	...	...	...	...
4454 INTAGLIO PRESS OPERATING	211	...	211	...	...	...	...	...	...	...	...	...
PRINTING	3,616	24	666	84	665	73	2	259	84	73	83	98
4601 MISC WOOD WORK	112	...	4	28	67	3	3	...	2	1	...	...
4602 BLOCKING AND BRACING	342	...	...	139	80	13	110	...	...	...	...	...
4604 WOOD WORKER	1,016	...	...	117	234	189	446	1	...	3	2	2
4605 WOOD CRAFTING	619	...	9	52	231	127	5	4	9	45	5	3
4607 CARPENTER	3,360	...	28	723	918	385	35	58	50	261	42	9
4616 PATTERNMAKING	68	...	...	10	33	25	...	...	...	...	...	...
4618 WOODWORKING MACHINE OPERATING	125	...	...	3	3	...	10	...	...	108	...	...
4639 TIMBER WORKING	73	...	...	3	70	...	...	...	...	...	...	...
4654 FORM BLOCK MAKING	11	...	...	...	...	11	...	...	...	...	...	...
WOOD WORK	5,726	...	41	1,075	1,636	753	609	63	169	310	49	14
4701 MISC GEN MAINTENANCE OPERATION	3,059	...	4	362	1,757	199	9	35	1	156	9	7
4714 MODEL MAKING	614	...	...	104	260	125	...	...	...	7	3	6
4715 EXHIBITS MAKING/MODELING	117	...	...	97	5	9	...	...	...	1	2	...
4716 RAILROAD CAR REPAIRING	8	...	...	3	5	...	...	...	...	...	...	...
4717 BOAT BUILDING AND REPAIRING	106	...	...	3	54	...	...	...	...	...	...	...
4737 GENERAL EQUIPMENT MECHANIC	256	...	1	96	4	6	80	1	...	7	3	...
4741 GENERAL EQUIPMENT OPERATING	45	...	...	11	5	...	...	...	...	9	...	1
4742 UTILITY SYSTEMS REPAIR-OPERATE	2,435	...	32	388	195	287	9	67	335	157	44	39
4745 RESEARCH LABORATORY MECHANIC	166	...	...	4	19	27	...	...	...	...	1	14
4749 MAINTENANCE MECHANIC	11,939	...	130	2,488	1,259	1,076	128	154	710	3,077	321	77
4754 CEMETERY CARETAKING	568	...	...	33	...	...	...	...	...	...	...	...
GENERAL MAINTENANCE & OPERATION	19,312	...	167	3,589	3,563	1,729	226	257	1,046	3,414	383	144
4801 MISC GENERAL EQPT MAINTENANCE	451	...	14	331	39	33	3	4	...	...	1	...
4804 LOCKSMITHING	360	...	1	83	113	45	3	4	6	2	1	2
4805 MEDICAL EQUIPMENT REPAIRING	405	...	...	129	9	34	2	3	1	...	...	...
4806 OFFICE APPLIANCE REPAIRING	87	...	31	19	5	1	5	1	2	...	...	...
4807 CHEMICAL EQUIPMENT REPAIRING	29	...	...	29	...	...	...	...	...	...	...	...
4808 CUSTODIAL EQUIPMENT SERVICING	14	...	...	1	1	...	...	1	...	...	...	...
4812 SAW RECONDITIONING	16	...	...	2	11	2	1	...	...	...	...	...
4816 PROTEC & SAFETY EQPT FABR REPR	92	...	...	87	...	5	...	...	...	...	...	...
4818 AIRCRAFT SURVIV FLIGHT EQPT RP	529	...	...	95	...	434	...	...	...	...	...	...
4819 BOWLING EQUIPMENT REPAIRING	16	...	...	...	7	9	...	...	...	...	...	...
4839 FILM PROCESSING EQPT REPAIRING	5	...	...	...	...	6	...	...	...	...	...	...
4840 TOOL AND EQUIPMENT REPAIRING	215	...	...	13	161	36	...	...	...	...	...	...
4843 NAVIGATION AIDS REPAIRING	11	...	...	...	...	...	...	...	...	3	...	...
4845 ORTHOPEDIC APPLIANCE REPAIRING	6	...	...	...	...	...	3	...	...	...	...	...
4848 MECHANICAL PARTS REPAIRING	81	...	...	2	10	69	...	...	...	...	...	...
4850 BEARING RECONDITIONING	106	...	...	28	38	39	1	...	...	...	...	...
4851 RECLAMATION WORKING	6	...	...	6	...	...	...	...	...	...	...	...
4855 DOMESTIC APPLIANCE REPAIRING	35	...	...	10	7	18	...	...	...	...	...	...
GENERAL EQUIPMENT MAINTENANCE	2,556	...	46	935	400	731	13	13	9	5	2	2
5001 MISC PLANT AND ANIMAL WORK	274	...	...	11	4	6	...	...	...	49	129	...
5002 FARMING	41	...	...	...	...	...	...	...	3	14	23	...
5003 GARDENING	1,139	...	7	90	79	181	3	2	82	171	64	10
5026 PEST CONTROLLER	605	...	2	166	192	104	19	3	1	8	4	...
5031 INSECTS PRODUCTION WORKING	104	...	...	3	...	...	...	...	...	...	101	...
5034 DAIRY FARMING	8	...	...	...	...	...	...	...	8	...	...	...
5035 LIVESTOCK RANCHING/WRANGLING	25	...	...	7	...	...	...	...	1	17	...	...
5042 TREE TRIMMING AND REMOVING	74	...	...	9	3	1	...	...	...	50	3	...
5048 ANIMAL CARETAKING	565	...	8	56	8	29	...	22	1	125	145	...
PLANT AND ANIMAL WORK	2,896	...	17	342	285	321	22	27	96	434	469	10
5201 MISC OCCUPATIONS	224	...	5	22	18	102	1	...	...	61	2	5
5205 GAS AND RADIATION DETECTING	64	...	...	49	15	...	...	...	...	...	...	...
5210 RIGGING	2,071	...	1	73	1,824	16	39	...	...	10	...	2
5220 SHIPWRIGHT	490	...	...	1	481	...	...	...	...	...	...	...
5221 LOFTING	67	...	...	...	66	...	...	...	...	...	...	...
5235 TEST RANGE TRACKING	15	...	...	...	15	...	...	...	...	...	...	...
MISCELLANEOUS OCCUPATIONS	2,931	...	6	145	2,419	118	40	...	...	71	2	7
5301 MISC INDUSTRL EQPT MAINTENANCE	928	...	18	368	411	71	14	5	...	4	1	2
5306 AIR CONDITIONING EQPT MECHANIC	3,404	...	7	413	1,106	606	43	31	110	19	27	13
5309 HEATING & BOILER PLANT EQ MECH	833	...	4	203	267	291	7	6	1	9	3	...
5310 KITCHEN/BAKERY EQPT REPAIRING	79	...	...	50	18	4	...	...	...	2	...	...
5312 SEWING MACHINE REPAIRING	8	...	...	4	...	...	4	...	...	...	...	...
5313 ELEVATOR MECHANIC	201	3	3	1	24	1	2	1	4	5	...	7
5317 LAUNDRY & DRY CLEANING EQT REP	62	...	...	7	5	1	...	...	...	...	...	...
5318 LOCK AND DAM REPAIRING	503	...	...	489	...	...	...	...	...	11	...	...
5323 OILING AND GREASING	86	...	...	43	41	...	1	...	...	...	...	...
5330 PRINTING EQUIPMENT REPAIRING	29	...	...	8	3	1	2	7	...	3	...	3
5334 MARINE MACHINERY MECHANIC	2,650	...	...	129	2,370	...	...	...	...	14	...	...
5335 WIND TUNNEL MECHANIC	29	...	...	5	...	...	...	...	...	...	...	...
5341 INDUSTRIAL FURNACE BUILD & REP	6	...	6	...	...	...	...	...	...	...	...	...

TABLE B, 1995 -- CONTINUED

HEALTH & HUMAN SERVICES	TRANSPOR-TATION	ENERGY	VETERAN AFFAIRS	ARCHI-TECT OF CAPITOL	GPO	FEMA	GENERAL SERVICES ADM	NASA	PANAMA CANAL COMM	ARMED FORCES RET HOME	SMITH-SONIAN INST.	TVA	US INFO AGENCY	ALL OTHER AGENCIES	OCCUPATION CODES
...	...	...	...	...	...	...	...	...	...	...	...	...	...	...	4447
...	...	...	...	...	...	...	...	...	...	...	...	...	...	...	4448
...	...	...	...	...	...	...	...	...	...	...	...	...	...	...	4449
...	...	...	...	...	...	...	...	...	...	...	...	...	...	...	4450
...	...	...	...	...	...	...	...	...	...	...	...	...	...	...	4454
4	20	18	9	...	1,198	5	79	5	...	2	10	...	...	156	4400
...	...	...	...	...	...	...	...	...	...	4	...	...	...	...	4601
...	...	...	...	...	...	...	...	...	...	...	...	...	...	...	4602
2	15	...	...	...	...	...	1	...	...	...	...	...	4	...	4604
6	11	1	22	34	...	1	14	...	...	1	26	...	...	8	4605
54	54	11	632	16	17	5	32	...	...	5	6	...	...	19	4607
...	...	...	...	...	...	...	...	...	...	...	...	...	...	...	4616
...	...	...	...	...	...	...	...	...	...	...	1	...	...	...	4618
...	...	...	...	...	...	...	...	...	...	...	...	...	...	...	4639
...	...	...	...	...	...	...	...	...	...	...	...	...	...	...	4654
62	80	12	559	50	17	6	47	...	...	10	33	...	4	27	4600
30	21	...	339	...	4	2	76	4	5	5	9	12	...	13	4701
1	9	...	2	...	...	...	...	97	...	...	...	...	...	...	4714
...	...	...	...	...	...	...	...	...	...	...	3	...	...	...	4715
...	...	...	...	...	...	...	...	...	...	...	...	...	...	...	4716
...	49	...	...	...	...	...	...	...	...	...	...	...	...	...	4717
...	7	...	49	...	1	...	...	1	...	...	...	...	...	...	4737
6	...	7	...	...	...	...	...	...	...	...	...	...	...	6	4741
197	21	19	284	...	...	6	202	1	...	7	91	...	...	64	4742
...	...	...	...	...	...	...	...	101	...	...	...	...	...	...	4745
323	303	36	786	10	17	...	824	...	...	3	53	85	1	77	4749
...	...	...	535	...	...	...	...	...	...	...	...	...	...	...	4754
547	410	62	1,995	10	22	8	1,102	204	5	15	156	97	1	160	4700
1	3	...	16	...	7	...	...	...	...	...	...	...	...	...	4801
7	...	...	90	3	...	...	2	...	...	...	8	...	...	...	4804
23	...	...	294	...	...	...	...	...	...	...	...	...	...	...	4805
...	...	...	11	...	...	...	...	...	...	...	...	6	...	6	4806
...	...	...	...	...	...	...	...	...	...	...	...	...	...	...	4807
...	...	...	10	1	...	...	...	...	...	...	...	...	...	...	4808
...	...	...	...	...	...	...	...	...	...	...	...	...	...	...	4812
...	...	...	...	...	...	...	...	...	...	...	...	...	...	...	4816
...	...	...	...	...	...	...	...	...	...	...	...	...	...	...	4818
...	...	...	...	...	...	...	...	...	...	...	...	...	...	...	4819
...	...	...	...	...	...	...	...	...	...	...	...	...	...	...	4839
...	4	...	2	...	...	...	...	...	...	...	...	...	...	...	4840
...	8	...	3	...	...	...	...	...	...	...	...	...	...	...	4843
...	...	...	...	...	...	...	...	...	...	...	...	...	...	...	4845
...	...	...	...	...	...	...	...	...	...	...	...	...	...	...	4848
...	...	...	...	...	...	...	...	...	...	...	...	...	...	...	4850
...	...	...	...	...	...	...	...	...	...	...	...	...	...	...	4851
...	...	...	...	...	...	...	...	...	...	...	...	...	...	...	4855
31	15	...	416	4	7	...	2	...	...	...	8	6	...	6	4800
...	1	...	...	...	...	...	...	...	...	2	72	...	...	...	5001
...	...	...	...	...	...	...	...	...	...	...	1	...	...	...	5002
12	12	1	209	48	...	...	16	...	...	5	45	136	...	27	5003
3	2	...	91	...	2	2	3	...	...	1	2	...	...	...	5026
...	...	...	...	...	...	...	...	...	...	...	...	...	...	...	5031
...	...	...	...	...	...	...	...	...	...	...	...	...	...	...	5034
...	...	...	...	...	...	...	...	...	...	...	...	...	...	...	5035
...	...	...	...	7	...	...	...	...	...	...	1	...	...	...	5042
88	...	...	84	...	...	...	...	...	...	...	...	...	...	...	5048
103	15	1	384	55	2	2	19	...	...	8	121	136	...	27	5000
...	...	...	...	...	...	...	...	...	2	...	...	...	...	6	5201
...	...	...	...	...	...	...	...	...	...	...	...	...	...	...	5205
...	71	7	...	...	...	...	5	...	...	...	19	...	...	4	5210
...	8	...	...	...	...	...	...	...	...	...	...	...	...	...	5220
...	1	...	...	...	...	...	...	...	...	...	...	...	...	...	5221
...	...	...	...	...	...	...	...	...	...	...	...	...	...	...	5235
...	80	7	...	...	...	...	5	...	2	...	19	...	...	10	5200
6	1	...	...	...	...	8	...	10	3	2	...	...	...	4	5301
32	22	...	685	125	...	9	96	8	6	7	30	...	...	4	5306
7	10	...	12	9	...	3	...	...	...	1	...	...	...	...	5309
...	...	...	3	...	...	...	...	...	...	2	...	...	...	...	5310
...	...	...	...	...	...	...	...	...	...	...	...	...	...	...	5312
11	...	1	38	49	18	...	29	...	...	...	2	...	...	2	5313
...	...	...	49	...	...	...	...	...	...	...	...	...	...	...	5317
...	1	...	...	...	...	...	...	...	...	...	...	...	...	2	5318
...	1	...	...	...	...	...	...	...	...	...	...	...	...	...	5323
...	...	...	...	...	1	...	1	...	...	...	...	...	...	...	5330
...	136	...	...	...	...	...	...	...	1	...	...	...	...	...	5334
...	...	...	...	...	...	...	...	24	...	...	...	...	...	...	5335
...	...	...	...	...	...	...	...	...	...	...	...	...	...	...	5341

TABLE B   FULL-TIME CIVILIAN BLUE-COLLAR EMPLOYMENT BY OCCUPATION AND SELECTED AGENCY, ALL AREAS, SEPTEMBER 30, 1995

OCCUPATION CODES / TITLES	TOTAL, ALL AGENCIES	STATE	TREASURY	ARMY	NAVY	AIR FORCE	DEFENSE LOGIS AGENCY	OTHER DEFENSE	JUSTICE	INTERIOR	AGRI-CULTURE	COMMERCE
5350 PRODUCTION MACHINERY MECHANIC	807	...	59	193	313	150	77	...	9	...	1	...
5352 INDUSTRIAL EQUIPMENT MECHANIC	1,625	...	...	439	395	224	199	4	...	161	4	1
5364 DOOR SYSTEMS MECHANIC	36	...	...	7	1	23	2	...	...	...	...	...
5365 PHYSIOLOGICAL TRAINER MECHANIC	18	...	...	...	5	13	...	...	...	...	...	...
5378 POWERED SUPPORT SYSTEMS MECH	2,216	...	...	241	258	1,681	10	...	...	8	...	9
5384 GASDYNAMATIC FACIL INSTALL REP	20	...	...	...	...	12	...	...	...	...	...	...
INDUSTRIAL EQUIPMENT MAINTENANCE	13,540	3	97	2,600	5,217	3,078	361	54	124	236	36	35
5401 MISC INDUSTRIAL EQPT OPERATING	430	...	133	160	34	33	21	10	...	9	...	...
5402 BOILER PLANT OPERATOR	2,616	...	...	412	875	469	36	13	...	9	18	6
5403 INCINERATOR OPERATING	59	...	...	6	2	9	...	...	...	...	2	...
5406 UTILITY SYSTEMS OPERATOR	859	...	11	93	165	257	4	8	1	28	9	...
5407 ELECTRIC POWER CONTROLLER	2,335	...	2	363	166	25	...	6	...	163	...	...
5408 WASTEWATER TREATMENT PLANT OPR	576	...	...	140	243	117	2	...	12	36	9	...
5409 WATER TREATMENT PLANT OPERATOR	575	...	...	221	170	103	...	...	2	47	7	...
5413 FUEL DISTRIBUTION SYSTEM OPER	1,138	...	...	146	346	622	1	...	...	21	...	...
5414 BALING MACHINE OPERATING	38	...	17	...	...	...	...	1	...	...	...	...
5415 AIR CONDITIONING EQPT OPERATOR	365	...	6	37	46	32	...	...	...	2	...	...
5419 STATIONARY-ENGINE OPERATING	67	...	...	3	30	5	...	...	...	...	...	...
5423 SANDBLASTING	582	...	...	139	323	79	14	...	...	3	...	...
5424 WEIGHING MACHINE OPERATING	68	...	65	2	...	1	...	...	...	...	...	...
5426 LOCK AND DAM OPERATING	1,420	...	...	1,379	...	...	...	...	...	3	...	...
5427 CHEMICAL PLANT OPERATING	109	...	...	64	7	...	...	...	...	...	...	...
5430 DRAWBRIDGE OPERATING	6	...	...	...	6	...	...	...	...	...	...	...
5433 GAS GENERATING PLANT OPERATING	41	...	...	...	5	...	...	...	...	36	...	...
5435 CARTON/BAGMAKING MACHINE OPER	55	...	...	2	...	...	52	...	...	...	...	...
5438 ELEVATOR OPERATING	33	...	...	1	...	...	...	1	...	4	...	...
5439 TESTING EQUIPMENT OPERATING	65	...	...	29	2	31	3	...	...	...	...	...
5440 PACKAGING MACHINE OPERATING	95	...	79	13	...	...	3	...	...	...	...	...
5444 FOOD/FEED PROCESSING EQPT OPER	6	...	...	...	...	...	...	...	...	...	6	...
5446 TEXTILE EQUIPMENT OPERATING	37	...	...	...	...	...	1	...	17	...	19	...
5450 CONVEYOR OPERATING	14	...	...	1	...	...	9	...	...	...	...	...
5454 SOLVENT STILL OPERATING	10	...	...	...	...	10	...	...	...	...	...	...
5455 PAPER PULPING MACHINE OPERATNG	17	...	...	1	5	3	...	3	3	...	...	...
5478 PORTABLE EQUIPMENT OPERATING	26	...	...	4	22	...	...	...	...	...	...	...
5479 DREDGING EQUIPMENT OPERATING	44	...	...	25	2	...	...	...	...	17	...	...
5484 COUNTING MACHINE OPERATING	40	...	40	...	...	...	...	...	...	...	...	...
5485 AIRCRAFT WEIGHT & BALANCE OPER	20	...	...	...	10	10	...	...	...	...	...	...
5486 SWIMMING POOL OPERATING	8	...	...	1	6	1	...	...	...	...	...	...
INDUSTRIAL EQUIPMENT OPERATION	11,754	...	353	3,242	2,465	1,807	146	42	35	378	70	6
5701 MISC TRANS/MOBILE EQPT OPERATN	644	...	8	157	137	53	177	6	...	20	1	1
5703 MOTOR VEHICLE OPERATOR	8,213	32	215	1,961	1,454	1,131	501	200	58	594	145	56
5704 FORK LIFT OPERATING	897	...	38	328	139	57	167	53	...	1	2	6
5705 TRACTOR OPERATOR	1,208	...	1	293	126	236	34	9	4	190	83	...
5706 ROAD SWEEPER OPERATING	34	...	...	6	9	5	...	1	3	...	...	...
5707 TANK DRIVING	6	...	...	3	...	1	2	...	...	...	...	...
5716 ENGINEERING EQPT OPERATING	3,498	...	...	820	273	442	25	...	6	1,039	480	...
5725 CRANE OPERATING	1,173	...	...	325	595	101	93	...	...	11	...	...
5729 DRILL RIG OPERATING	186	...	...	106	...	4	...	...	...	65	4	...
5736 BRAKING-SWITCHING & CONDUCTING	102	...	...	46	46	5	3	...	...	2	...	...
5737 LOCOMOTIVE ENGINEERING	78	...	...	36	30	6	3	...	...	3	...	...
5738 RAILROAD MAINTNC VEHICLE OPER	28	...	...	22	6	...	...	...	...	...	...	...
5767 AIRFIELD CLEARING EQPT OPERAT	70	...	...	...	8	62	...	...	...	...	...	...
5782 SHIP OPERATING	263	...	...	98	10	...	...	...	...	10	...	...
5784 RIVERBOAT OPERATING	108	...	...	108	...	...	...	...	...	...	...	...
5786 SMALL CRAFT OPERATING	278	...	...	140	48	1	...	...	...	41	5	5
5788 DECKHAND	306	...	...	257	31	1	...	...	...	15	...	...
TRANSPORTATION/MOBILE EQPT OPER	17,092	32	262	4,706	2,912	2,105	1,005	269	71	1,991	720	68
5801 MISC TRANS/MOBILE EQPT MAINT	740	...	3	493	93	73	8	3	...	10	3	...
5803 HEAVY MOBILE EQPT MECHANIC	10,531	...	...	7,631	1,470	930	132	...	15	197	14	1
5806 MOBILE EQUIPMENT SERVICING	318	...	...	135	87	22	6	...	1	19	5	...
5823 AUTOMOTIVE MECHANIC	6,139	...	8	3,530	631	907	76	8	297	159	120	6
5876 ELECTROMOTIVE EQPT MECHANIC	152	...	2	14	69	10	23	...	...	...	...	...
TRANSPORTATION/MOBILE EQPT MAINT	17,880	...	13	11,803	2,350	1,942	245	11	313	385	142	7
6501 MISC AMMUN EXPL & TOXIC MAT WK	769	...	...	234	499	30	6	...	...	...	...	...
6502 EXPLOSIVES OPERATING	1,074	...	...	837	236	1	...	...	...	...	...	...
6505 MUNITIONS DESTROYING	67	...	...	66	1	...	...	...	...	...	...	...
6511 MISSILE/TOXIC MATERIALS HANDL	308	...	...	272	15	19	2	...	...	...	...	...
6517 EXPLOSIVES TEST OPERATING	115	...	...	82	33	...	...	...	...	...	...	...
AMMUNITION EXPLOSIVES TOXIC MAT	2,333	...	...	1,491	784	50	8	...	...	...	...	...
6601 MISC ARMAMENT WORK	113	...	...	110	2	...	1	...	...	...	...	...
6605 ARTILLERY REPAIRING	449	...	...	396	50	...	3	...	...	...	...	...
6606 ARTILLERY TESTING	55	...	...	55	...	...	...	...	...	...	...	...
6610 SMALL ARMS REPAIRING	387	...	2	334	36	3	8	...	3	1	...	...
6641 ORDNANCE EQUIPMENT MECHANIC	1,464	...	...	163	785	502	...	...	...	...	...	...
6652 AIRCRAFT ORDNANCE SYSTEMS MECH	1,485	...	...	35	89	1,360	...	...	...	...	...	...
6656 SPECIAL WEAPONS SYSTEMS MECH	78	...	...	19	47	12	...	...	...	...	...	...
ARMAMENT WORK	4,031	...	2	1,112	1,009	1,877	12	...	3	1	...	...

TABLE B, 1995 — CONTINUED

HEALTH & HUMAN SERVICES	TRANSPOR-TATION	ENERGY	VETERAN AFFAIRS	ARCHI-TECT OF CAPITOL	GPO	FEMA	GENERAL SERVICES ADM	NASA	PANAMA CANAL COMM	ARMED FORCES RET HOME	SMITH-SONIAN INST.	TVA	US INFO AGENCY	ALL OTHER AGENCIES	OCCUPATION CODES
...	5	...	...	...	...	...	...	...	...	...	...	...	...	...	
9	14	2	166	2	...	...	1	...	...	...	...	...	...	...	5350
...	...	...	3	...	...	...	...	...	...	...	...	...	...	4	5352
...	...	...	...	...	...	...	...	...	...	...	...	...	...	...	5364
...	4	...	...	3	...	...	...	...	...	...	...	...	...	...	5365
...	...	...	...	...	...	...	...	...	...	...	...	...	...	...	5378
...	...	...	...	...	...	...	...	8	...	...	...	...	2	...	5384
65	199	3	956	188	19	20	127	50	10	12	32	...	2	16	5300
10	2	6	...	...	6	...	...	...	...	...	...	...	...	6	5401
53	8	5	586	5	...	...	18	22	...	10	...	51	...	...	5402
7	...	...	33	...	...	...	...	...	...	...	...	...	...	20	5403
11	...	...	216	33	...	...	20	1	...	2	...	...	...	...	5406
...	...	186	...	...	...	8	...	...	8	...	...	1,403	...	5	5407
...	...	...	15	...	...	...	...	...	...	...	...	...	...	2	5408
4	...	...	9	...	...	5	...	...	2	...	...	...	...	3	5409
...	2	...	...	...	...	...	...	...	...	...	3	...	...	...	5413
...	...	...	1	11	...	...	1	...	...	...	...	...	...	7	5414
...	4	...	202	...	...	...	28	1	1	...	...	...	...	1	5415
...	2	...	...	...	27	...	...	...	...	...	5	...	...	...	5419
...	24	...	...	...	...	...	...	...	...	...	...	...	...	...	5423
...	...	...	...	...	...	...	...	...	21	...	...	...	...	...	5424
...	17	...	...	...	...	...	...	...	...	...	...	...	...	...	5426
...	...	...	...	...	...	...	...	...	...	...	...	38	...	...	5427
...	...	...	...	...	...	...	...	...	...	...	...	...	...	...	5430
...	...	...	...	...	...	...	1	...	...	...	...	...	...	...	5433
5	...	...	2	19	...	...	...	...	...	1	...	...	...	...	5435
...	...	...	...	...	...	...	...	...	...	...	...	...	...	...	5438
...	...	...	...	...	...	...	...	...	...	...	...	...	...	...	5439
...	...	...	...	...	...	...	...	...	...	...	...	...	...	...	5440
...	...	...	3	...	...	...	...	...	...	...	...	...	...	...	5444
...	...	...	...	...	1	...	...	...	...	...	...	...	...	...	5446
...	...	...	...	...	...	...	...	...	...	...	...	...	...	...	5450
...	...	...	...	...	...	...	2	...	...	...	...	...	...	...	5454
...	...	...	...	...	...	...	...	...	...	...	...	...	...	...	5455
...	...	...	...	...	...	...	...	...	...	...	...	...	...	...	5478
...	...	...	...	...	...	...	...	...	...	...	...	...	...	...	5479
...	...	...	...	...	...	...	...	...	...	...	...	...	...	...	5484
...	...	...	...	...	...	...	...	...	...	...	...	...	...	...	5485
...	...	...	...	...	...	...	...	...	...	...	...	...	...	...	5486
90	59	197	1,066	68	34	13	70	24	32	13	8	1,492	...	44	5400
...	4	5	...	9	24	...	14	...	6	1	14	...	...	8	5701
233	30	40	1,128	27	56	11	33	...	8	14	28	104	10	144	5703
...	...	...	2	2	75	...	1	...	...	...	2	...	...	24	5704
13	1	...	122	...	...	...	6	...	...	...	3	3	...	11	5705
...	...	...	...	7	...	...	3	...	...	...	...	...	...	...	5706
8	38	23	163	2	...	7	...	1	1	1	3	145	...	21	5707
...	37	1	...	...	1	...	...	...	5	...	1	3	...	...	5716
1	4	...	...	...	...	...	...	...	2	...	...	...	...	...	5725
...	...	...	...	...	...	...	...	...	...	...	...	...	...	...	5729
...	...	...	...	...	...	...	...	...	...	...	...	...	...	...	5736
...	...	...	...	...	...	...	...	...	...	...	...	...	...	...	5737
...	...	...	...	...	...	...	...	...	...	...	...	...	...	...	5738
...	11	...	...	...	...	...	...	...	132	...	...	2	...	...	5767
...	...	...	...	...	...	...	...	...	7	...	...	...	...	...	5782
...	31	...	...	...	...	...	...	...	...	...	...	...	...	...	5784
...	...	...	...	...	...	...	...	...	2	...	...	...	...	...	5786
...	...	...	...	...	...	...	...	...	...	...	...	...	...	...	5788
255	156	69	1,485	46	156	18	57	1	163	19	51	257	10	208	5700
...	9	...	...	1	...	...	4	...	31	1	...	...	...	8	5801
6	27	36	41	...	...	2	9	...	...	...	1	5	...	14	5803
...	...	...	10	...	...	...	27	...	...	...	...	6	...	...	5806
7	6	...	97	6	3	17	179	...	1	3	15	61	...	2	5823
...	...	...	...	2	...	...	31	...	...	...	...	...	...	1	5876
13	42	36	148	9	3	19	250	...	32	4	16	72	...	25	5800
...	...	...	...	...	...	...	...	...	...	...	...	...	...	...	6501
...	...	...	...	...	...	...	...	...	...	...	...	...	...	...	6502
...	...	...	...	...	...	...	...	...	...	...	...	...	...	...	6505
...	...	...	...	...	...	...	...	...	...	...	...	...	...	...	6511
...	...	...	...	...	...	...	...	...	...	...	...	...	...	...	6517
...	...	...	...	...	...	...	...	...	...	...	...	...	...	...	6500
...	...	...	...	...	...	...	...	...	...	...	...	...	...	...	6601
...	...	...	...	...	...	...	...	...	...	...	...	...	...	...	6605
...	...	...	...	...	...	...	...	...	...	...	...	...	...	...	6606
...	14	...	...	...	...	...	...	...	...	...	...	...	...	...	6610
...	...	...	...	...	...	...	...	1	...	...	...	...	...	...	6641
...	...	...	...	...	...	...	...	...	...	...	...	...	...	...	6652
...	...	...	...	...	...	...	...	1	...	...	...	...	...	...	6656
...	14	...	...	...	...	...	...	...	...	...	...	...	...	...	6600

TABLE B   FULL-TIME CIVILIAN BLUE-COLLAR EMPLOYMENT BY OCCUPATION AND SELECTED AGENCY, ALL AREAS, SEPTEMBER 30, 1995

OCCUPATION CODES TITLES	TOTAL, ALL AGENCIES	STATE	TREASURY	ARMY	NAVY	AIR FORCE	DEFENSE LOGIS AGENCY	OTHER DEFENSE	JUSTICE	INTERIOR	AGRI-CULTURE	COMMERCE
6901 MISC WAREHOUSING & STOCK HANDL	788	...	29	135	138	123	304	...	...	...	...	3
6902 LUMBER HANDLING	4	...	...	3	...	...	1	...	...	...	...	...
6903 COAL HANDLING	203	...	...	5	5	7	...	...	...	...	...	...
6904 TOOLS AND PARTS ATTENDING	2,778	...	6	1,528	617	494	37	1	10	14	2	1
6907 MATERIALS HANDLER	18,429	4	332	3,818	2,830	2,145	4,944	802	733	236	99	104
6910 MATERIALS EXPEDITING	1,248	...	32	333	270	488	90	...	...	...	...	2
6912 MATERIALS EXAMINR & IDENTIFIER	2,752	...	3	376	107	309	1,913	6	...	7	...	...
6914 STORE WORKING	2,424	...	...	11	23	4	...	2,373	...	...	...	2
6941 BULK MONEY HANDLING	347	...	347	...	...	...	...	...	...	...	...	...
6968 AIRCRAFT FREIGHT LOADING	172	...	...	...	103	65	1	...	...	3	...	...
WAREHOUSING AND STOCK HANDLING	29,145	4	749	6,209	4,093	3,635	7,290	3,182	743	260	101	112
7001 MISC PACKING AND PROCESSING	110	...	...	24	6	22	58	...	...	...	...	...
7002 PACKING	2,425	...	14	239	234	157	1,671	28	8	...	4	6
7004 PRESERVATION PACKAGING	398	...	...	38	21	13	316	...	...	...	...	...
7006 PRESERVATION SERVICING	245	...	...	16	47	37	122	...	...	...	...	...
7009 EQUIPMENT CLEANING	766	...	...	95	352	308	4	...	...	...	...	...
7010 PARACHUTE PACKING	10	...	...	...	...	10	...	...	...	...	...	...
PACKING AND PROCESSING	3,954	...	14	412	660	542	2,171	28	8	...	4	6
7301 MISC LAUNDRY DRYCLEAN PRESSING	79	...	...	3	2	...	...	...	...	...	...	...
7304 LAUNDRY WORKING	1,386	1	...	101	35	11	...	...	15	...	...	...
7305 LAUNDRY MACHINE OPERATING	407	...	2	19	9	...	...	...	38	3	...	...
7306 PRESSING	35	...	...	10	12	1	...	...	...	...	...	...
7307 DRY CLEANING	7	...	...	2	3	1	...	...	...	...	...	...
LAUNDRY, DRY CLEANING & PRESSING	1,914	1	2	135	61	13	...	...	53	3	...	...
7401 MISC FOOD PREPARATION SERVING	40	...	...	21	5	...	...	...	...	...	...	...
7402 BAKING	94	...	...	36	16	30	...	...	...	2	...	...
7404 COOK	4,184	...	3	505	248	238	...	8	904	201	73	...
7407 MEATCUTTER	1,709	...	...	10	...	2	...	1,691	...	...	2	...
7408 FOOD SERVICE WORKER	8,373	...	1	1,090	360	437	...	11	1	66	1	...
7420 WAITER	35	...	...	3	...	13	...	...	...	...	...	...
FOOD PREPARATION AND SERVING	14,435	...	4	1,665	629	720	...	1,710	905	269	76	...
7601 MISC PERSONAL SERVICES	352	...	...	12	1	...	...	...	...	...	...	...
7603 BARBERING	40	...	...	16	21	...	...	...	2	...	...	...
7641 BEAUTICIAN	2	...	...	...	2	...	...	...	...	...	...	...
PERSONAL SERVICES	394	...	...	28	24	...	...	...	2	...	...	...
8201 MISC FLUID SYSTEMS MAINTENANCE	78	...	...	22	47	9	...	...	...	...	...	...
8255 PNEUDRAULIC SYSTEMS MECHANIC	1,625	...	...	161	448	1,013	...	...	...	...	...	...
8268 AIRCRAFT PNEUDRAULIC SYST MECH	1,492	...	...	105	45	1,339	...	...	...	...	...	...
FLUID SYSTEMS MAINTENANCE	3,195	...	...	288	540	2,361	...	...	...	...	...	...
8601 MISCELLANEOUS ENGINE OVERHAUL	6	...	...	...	4	1	...	...	...	1	...	...
8602 AIRCRAFT ENGINE MECHANIC	4,330	...	...	262	451	3,604	...	...	...	...	...	...
8610 SMALL ENGINE MECHANIC	104	...	...	47	23	17	...	...	...	10	5	...
8675 LIQUID FUEL ROCKET ENGINE MECH	23	...	...	...	...	23	...	...	...	...	...	...
ENGINE OVERHAUL	4,463	...	...	309	478	3,645	...	...	...	11	5	...
8801 MISC AIRCRAFT OVERHAUL	996	...	...	84	161	716	3	...	...	...	...	...
8810 AIRCRAFT PROPELLER MECHANIC	193	...	...	72	37	84	...	...	...	...	...	...
8840 AIRCRAFT MECHANICAL PARTS REPR	691	...	...	358	78	222	...	...	...	...	...	...
8852 AIRCRAFT MECHANIC	12,604	...	1	2,591	1,138	8,654	...	...	35	8	2	6
8862 AIRCRAFT ATTENDING	251	...	...	21	123	98	...	...	...	9	...	...
8863 AIRCRAFT TIRE MOUNTING	13	...	...	...	...	13	...	...	...	...	...	...
8882 AIRFRAME TEST OPERATING	3	...	...	...	...	3	...	...	...	...	...	...
AIRCRAFT OVERHAUL	14,741	...	1	3,126	1,537	9,790	3	...	35	17	2	6
9001 MISC FILM PROCESSING	11	...	...	...	...	...	...	2	...	...	...	...
9003 FILM ASSEMBLING AND REPAIRING	15	...	...	7	8	...	...	...	...	...	...	...
9004 MOTION PICT DEV/PRINT MACH OPR	6	...	...	...	...	6	...	...	...	...	...	...
FILM PROCESSING	32	...	...	7	8	6	...	2	...	...	...	...
9799 UNSPECIFIED BLUE-COLLAR SERIES	143	1	...	67	...	5	...	1	...	4	...	...
UNSPECIFIED	143	1	...	67	...	5	...	1	...	4	...	...
9901 MISC VESSEL JOBS EXCL FROM FWS	66	...	...	...	...	...	...	...	...	...	...	46
9902 MASTER	71	...	...	...	62	...	...	...	...	2	...	...
9903 CHIEF OFFICER CABLE	1	...	...	...	1	...	...	...	...	...	...	...
9904 SHIP PILOT	36	...	...	...	36	...	...	...	...	...	...	...
9905 FIRST OFFICER	67	...	...	...	66	...	...	...	...	1	...	...
9906 SECOND OFFICER	75	...	...	...	75	...	...	...	...	...	...	...
9907 THIRD OFFICER	86	...	...	...	86	...	...	...	...	...	...	...
9909 RADIO OFFICER	2	...	...	...	2	...	...	...	...	...	...	...
9911 RADIO ELECTRONICS OFFICER	5	...	...	...	5	...	...	...	...	...	...	...
9912 FIRST ASST RADIO ELECTR OFFICER	2	...	...	...	2	...	...	...	...	...	...	...
9913 RELIEF DECK OFFICER	1	...	...	...	1	...	...	...	...	...	...	...
9914 DAMAGE CONTROL OFFICER	10	...	...	...	10	...	...	...	...	...	...	...
9915 ASST DAMAGE CONTROL OFFICER	14	...	...	...	14	...	...	...	...	...	...	...
9916 MASTER-MATE (FISHING VESSEL)	4	...	...	...	...	...	...	...	...	...	...	3
9918 DAMAGE CONTROL LEADER	7	...	...	...	7	...	...	...	...	...	...	...

TABLE B, 1995 — CONTINUED

HEALTH & HUMAN SERVICES	TRANSPOR-TATION	ENERGY	VETERAN AFFAIRS	ARCHI-TECT OF CAPITOL	GPO	FEMA	GENERAL SERVICES ADM	NASA	PANAMA CANAL COMM	ARMED FORCES RET HOME	SMITH-SONIAN INST.	TVA	US INFO AGENCY	ALL OTHER AGENCIES	OCCUPATION CODES
17	...	...	11	1	21	...	...	3	...	...	...	...	...	3	6901
...	...	...	...	4	...	...	2	...	...	...	...	...	...	...	6902
8	15	...	30	13	...	...	2	...	...	...	...	180	...	...	6903
108	135	38	1,036	24	144	5	497	1	...	35	16	162	14	167	6904
2	31	...	...	...	...	...	...	...	...	...	...	...	...	...	6907
2	20	...	...	...	...	...	9	...	...	...	...	...	...	...	6910
10	...	...	...	...	...	...	...	...	...	...	...	...	...	...	6912
...	...	...	...	...	...	...	...	...	...	...	...	...	...	1	6914
...	...	...	...	...	...	...	...	...	...	...	...	...	...	...	6941
147	201	38	1,077	42	165	5	510	4	...	35	16	342	14	171	6900
7	21	...	...	...	2	...	26	...	...	...	...	...	...	...	7001
...	10	...	...	...	...	...	...	...	...	...	...	...	1	7	7002
...	28	...	...	...	...	...	...	...	...	...	...	...	...	...	7004
5	2	...	...	...	...	...	...	...	...	...	...	...	...	...	7006
...	...	...	...	...	...	...	...	...	...	...	...	...	...	...	7009
...	...	...	...	...	...	...	...	...	...	...	...	...	...	...	7010
12	61	...	...	...	2	...	26	...	...	...	...	...	1	7	7000
...	...	...	74	1	...	...	...	...	...	...	...	...	...	...	7301
2	...	...	1,219	...	...	...	...	...	...	...	...	...	...	...	7304
4	...	...	332	...	...	...	...	...	...	...	...	...	...	1	7305
1	...	...	3	...	...	...	...	...	...	...	...	...	...	...	7306
...	...	...	1	...	...	...	...	...	...	...	...	8	...	...	7307
7	...	...	1,629	1	...	...	...	...	...	...	...	8	...	1	7300
...	...	...	3	5	...	...	...	...	...	8	5	...	...	1	7401
210	1	...	1,722	34	...	4	...	...	...	1	...	...	...	...	7402
...	...	...	1	1	...	1	...	...	...	26	...	...	...	7	7404
134	...	...	6,110	93	...	...	...	...	...	62	...	...	...	7	7407
...	...	...	...	19	...	...	...	...	...	2	...	...	...	...	7408
344	1	...	7,836	152	...	5	...	...	...	99	5	...	...	15	7420
...	...	...	...	...	...	...	...	...	...	9	...	329	...	1	7601
...	...	...	...	...	...	...	...	...	...	1	...	...	...	...	7603
...	...	...	...	...	...	...	...	...	...	...	...	...	...	...	7641
...	...	...	...	...	...	...	...	...	...	10	...	329	...	1	7600
...	1	...	...	...	...	...	2	...	...	...	...	...	...	...	8201
...	3	...	...	...	...	...	...	...	...	...	...	...	...	...	8255
...	4	...	...	...	...	...	...	...	...	...	...	...	...	...	8268
...	8	...	...	...	...	...	2	...	...	...	...	...	...	...	8200
...	13	...	...	...	...	...	...	...	...	...	...	...	...	...	8601
...	...	...	...	...	...	...	...	...	...	...	...	...	...	...	8602
...	...	...	...	...	...	...	...	...	...	...	...	...	...	...	8610
...	...	...	...	...	...	...	...	...	...	...	2	...	...	...	8675
...	13	...	...	...	...	...	...	...	...	...	2	...	...	...	8600
...	15	...	...	...	...	...	...	7	...	...	...	...	...	...	8801
...	33	...	...	...	...	...	...	...	...	...	...	...	...	...	8810
...	130	4	...	...	...	...	...	...	...	...	...	...	...	...	8840
...	...	...	...	...	...	...	...	33	...	...	...	2	...	...	8852
...	...	...	...	...	...	...	...	...	...	...	...	...	...	...	8862
...	...	...	...	...	...	...	...	...	...	...	...	...	...	...	8863
...	...	...	...	...	...	...	...	...	...	...	...	...	...	...	8882
...	178	4	...	...	...	...	...	40	...	...	...	2	...	...	8800
...	...	...	...	...	...	...	...	...	...	...	...	...	...	9	9001
...	...	...	...	...	...	...	...	...	...	...	...	...	...	...	9003
...	...	...	...	...	...	...	...	...	...	...	...	...	...	...	9004
...	...	...	...	...	...	...	...	...	...	...	...	...	...	9	9000
...	2	...	22	1	6	...	...	...	...	...	...	34	...	...	9799
...	2	...	22	1	6	...	...	...	...	...	...	34	...	...	9700
...	20	...	...	...	...	...	...	...	...	...	...	...	...	...	9901
...	7	...	...	...	...	...	...	...	...	...	...	...	...	...	9902
...	...	...	...	...	...	...	...	...	...	...	...	...	...	...	9903
...	...	...	...	...	...	...	...	...	...	...	...	...	...	...	9904
...	...	...	...	...	...	...	...	...	...	...	...	...	...	...	9905
...	...	...	...	...	...	...	...	...	...	...	...	...	...	...	9906
...	...	...	...	...	...	...	...	...	...	...	...	...	...	...	9907
...	...	...	...	...	...	...	...	...	...	...	...	...	...	...	9909
...	...	...	...	...	...	...	...	...	...	...	...	...	...	...	9911
...	...	...	...	...	...	...	...	...	...	...	...	...	...	...	9912
...	...	...	...	...	...	...	...	...	...	...	...	...	...	...	9913
...	...	...	...	...	...	...	...	...	...	...	...	...	...	...	9914
...	...	...	...	...	...	...	...	...	...	...	...	...	...	...	9915
...	...	...	...	...	...	...	...	...	...	...	1	...	...	...	9916
...	...	...	...	...	...	...	...	...	...	...	...	...	...	...	9918

TABLE B   FULL-TIME CIVILIAN BLUE-COLLAR EMPLOYMENT BY OCCUPATION AND SELECTED AGENCY, ALL AREAS, SEPTEMBER 30, 1995

OCCUPATION CODES — TITLES	TOTAL, ALL AGENCIES	STATE	TREASURY	ARMY	NAVY	AIR FORCE	DEFENSE LOGIS AGENCY	OTHER DEFENSE	JUSTICE	INTERIOR	AGRI-CULTURE	COMMERCE
9919 DAMAGE CONTROL ASST LEADER	3	...	...	...	3	...	...	...	...	...	...	...
9920 BOATSWAIN	71	...	...	...	60	...	...	...	...	...	...	11
9921 CARPENTER	12	...	...	...	12	...	...	...	...	...	...	...
9923 BOATSWAIN'S MATE	141	...	...	...	130	...	...	...	...	...	...	11
9924 ABLE SEAMAN	339	...	...	...	306	...	...	...	...	4	...	29
9925 ABLE SEAMAN-MAINTENANCE	372	...	...	...	366	...	...	...	...	...	...	6
9926 QUARTERMASTER	8	...	...	...	...	...	...	...	...	...	...	8
9927 SEAMAN-FISHERMAN	40	...	...	...	...	...	...	...	...	...	...	40
9928 ORDINARY SEAMAN	138	...	...	...	118	...	...	...	...	...	...	20
9929 DAMAGE CONTROLMAN	4	...	...	...	4	...	...	...	...	...	...	...
9931 CHIEF ENGINEER	94	...	...	...	63	...	...	...	...	2	...	21
9932 FIRST ASSISTANT ENGINEER	69	...	...	...	55	...	...	...	...	...	...	14
9933 SECOND ASSISTANT ENGINEER	89	...	...	...	77	...	...	...	...	...	...	12
9934 THIRD ASSISTANT ENGINEER	137	...	...	...	122	...	...	...	...	...	...	15
9935 RELIEF ENGINEER	3	...	...	...	3	...	...	...	...	...	...	...
9936 ENGINEER MIDSHIPMAN	3	...	...	...	3	...	...	...	...	...	...	...
9939 CHIEF ELECTRICIAN	22	...	...	...	22	...	...	...	...	...	...	...
9940 ELECTRICIAN	25	...	...	...	20	...	...	...	...	...	...	5
9942 SECOND ELECTRICIAN	55	...	...	...	55	...	...	...	...	...	...	...
9944 ELECTRONICS TECHNICIAN	32	...	...	...	32	...	...	...	...	...	...	...
9945 REFRIGERATION ENGINEER	39	...	...	...	39	...	...	...	...	...	...	...
9946 SECOND REFRIGERATION ENGINEER	6	...	...	...	6	...	...	...	...	...	...	...
9947 THIRD REFRIGERATION ENGINEER	8	...	...	...	8	...	...	...	...	...	...	...
9950 PLUMBER-MACHINIST	2	...	...	...	2	...	...	...	...	...	...	...
9952 DECK ENGINEER-MACHINIST	80	...	...	...	80	...	...	...	...	...	...	...
9953 DECK ENGINEER-MECHANIC	4	...	...	...	4	...	...	...	...	...	...	...
9954 UNLICENSED JUNIOR ENGINEER	69	...	...	...	56	...	...	...	...	...	...	13
9955 PUMPMAN	16	...	...	...	16	...	...	...	...	...	...	...
9957 ENGINE UTILITYMAN	146	...	...	...	136	...	...	...	...	...	...	10
9959 MACHINIST	2	...	...	...	...	...	...	...	...	...	...	2
9960 OILER	11	...	...	...	1	...	...	...	...	...	...	10
9961 OILER DIESEL	26	...	...	...	14	...	...	...	...	1	...	...
9963 FIREMAN	3	...	...	...	...	...	...	...	...	...	...	3
9965 WIPER	83	...	...	...	74	...	...	...	...	...	...	9
9968 CHIEF STEWARD	49	...	...	...	33	...	...	...	...	...	...	16
9969 THIRD STEWARD	7	...	...	...	7	...	...	...	...	...	...	...
9971 CHIEF COOK	40	...	...	...	29	...	...	...	...	...	...	11
9972 STEWARD COOK	14	...	...	...	14	...	...	...	...	...	...	...
9973 SECOND COOK	29	...	...	...	10	...	...	...	...	...	...	19
9974 THIRD COOK	11	...	...	...	11	...	...	...	...	...	...	...
9975 ASSISTANT COOK	42	...	...	...	42	...	...	...	...	...	...	...
9976 COOK-BAKER	38	...	...	...	35	...	...	...	...	...	...	3
9977 SECOND COOK-BAKER	31	...	...	...	31	...	...	...	...	...	...	...
9978 NIGHT COOK AND BAKER	18	...	...	...	18	...	...	...	...	...	...	...
9979 STEWARD-BAKER	7	...	...	...	7	...	...	...	...	...	...	...
9982 LAUNDRYMAN	16	...	...	...	14	...	...	...	...	...	...	2
9984 MESSMAN	15	...	...	...	...	...	...	...	...	...	...	15
9985 STEWARD-UTILITYMAN	409	...	...	...	409	...	...	...	...	...	...	...
9988 PURSER	41	...	...	...	33	...	...	...	...	...	...	8
9989 JUNIOR PURSER	3	...	...	...	1	...	...	...	...	...	...	2
9991 SUPPLY OFFICER	27	...	...	...	27	...	...	...	...	...	...	...
9992 ASSISTANT SUPPLY OFFICER	9	...	...	...	9	...	...	...	...	...	...	...
9993 JUNIOR SUPPLY OFFICER	16	...	...	...	16	...	...	...	...	...	...	...
9994 ASSISTANT STOREKEEPER	69	...	...	...	69	...	...	...	...	...	...	...
9996 MEDICAL SERVICES OFFICER	42	...	...	...	42	...	...	...	...	...	...	...
9998 YEOMAN-STOREKEEPER	134	...	...	...	134	...	...	...	...	...	...	...
VESSEL JOBS EXCLUDED FROM FWS	3,666	...	...	...	3,245	...	...	...	...	10	...	364

TABLE B, 1995 -- CONTINUED

HEALTH & HUMAN SERVICES	TRANSPOR -TATION	ENERGY	VETERAN AFFAIRS	ARCHI- TECT OF CAPITOL	GPO	FEMA	GENERAL SERVICES ADM	NASA	PANAMA CANAL COMM	ARMED FORCES RET HOME	SMITH- SONIAN INST.	TVA	US INFO AGENCY	ALL OTHER AGENCIES	OCCUPATION CODES
...	...	...	...	...	...	...	...	...	...	...	...	...	...	...	9919
...	...	...	...	...	...	...	...	...	...	...	...	...	...	...	9920
...	...	...	...	...	...	...	...	...	...	...	...	...	...	...	9921
...	...	...	...	...	...	...	...	...	...	...	...	...	...	...	9923
...	...	...	...	...	...	...	...	...	...	...	...	...	...	...	9924
...	...	...	...	...	...	...	...	...	...	...	...	...	...	...	9925
...	...	...	...	...	...	...	...	...	...	...	...	...	...	...	9926
...	...	...	...	...	...	...	...	...	...	...	...	...	...	...	9927
...	...	...	...	...	...	...	...	...	...	...	...	...	...	...	9928
...	...	...	...	...	...	...	...	...	...	...	...	...	...	...	9929
...	8	...	...	...	...	...	...	...	...	...	...	...	...	...	9931
...	...	...	...	...	...	...	...	...	...	...	...	...	...	...	9932
...	...	...	...	...	...	...	...	...	...	...	...	...	...	...	9933
...	...	...	...	...	...	...	...	...	...	...	...	...	...	...	9934
...	...	...	...	...	...	...	...	...	...	...	...	...	...	...	9935
...	...	...	...	...	...	...	...	...	...	...	...	...	...	...	9936
...	...	...	...	...	...	...	...	...	...	...	...	...	...	...	9939
...	...	...	...	...	...	...	...	...	...	...	...	...	...	...	9940
...	...	...	...	...	...	...	...	...	...	...	...	...	...	...	9942
...	...	...	...	...	...	...	...	...	...	...	...	...	...	...	9944
...	...	...	...	...	...	...	...	...	...	...	...	...	...	...	9945
...	...	...	...	...	...	...	...	...	...	...	...	...	...	...	9946
...	...	...	...	...	...	...	...	...	...	...	...	...	...	...	9947
...	...	...	...	...	...	...	...	...	...	...	...	...	...	...	9950
...	...	...	...	...	...	...	...	...	...	...	...	...	...	...	9952
...	...	...	...	...	...	...	...	...	...	...	...	...	...	...	9953
...	...	...	...	...	...	...	...	...	...	...	...	...	...	...	9954
...	...	...	...	...	...	...	...	...	...	...	...	...	...	...	9955
...	...	...	...	...	...	...	...	...	...	...	...	...	...	...	9957
...	...	...	...	...	...	...	...	...	...	...	...	...	...	...	9959
...	...	...	...	...	...	...	...	...	...	...	...	...	...	...	9960
...	11	...	...	...	...	...	...	...	...	...	...	...	...	...	9961
...	...	...	...	...	...	...	...	...	...	...	...	...	...	...	9963
...	...	...	...	...	...	...	...	...	...	...	...	...	...	...	9965
...	...	...	...	...	...	...	...	...	...	...	...	...	...	...	9968
...	...	...	...	...	...	...	...	...	...	...	...	...	...	...	9969
...	...	...	...	...	...	...	...	...	...	...	...	...	...	...	9971
...	...	...	...	...	...	...	...	...	...	...	...	...	...	...	9972
...	...	...	...	...	...	...	...	...	...	...	...	...	...	...	9973
...	...	...	...	...	...	...	...	...	...	...	...	...	...	...	9974
...	...	...	...	...	...	...	...	...	...	...	...	...	...	...	9975
...	...	...	...	...	...	...	...	...	...	...	...	...	...	...	9976
...	...	...	...	...	...	...	...	...	...	...	...	...	...	...	9977
...	...	...	...	...	...	...	...	...	...	...	...	...	...	...	9978
...	...	...	...	...	...	...	...	...	...	...	...	...	...	...	9979
...	...	...	...	...	...	...	...	...	...	...	...	...	...	...	9982
...	...	...	...	...	...	...	...	...	...	...	...	...	...	...	9984
...	...	...	...	...	...	...	...	...	...	...	...	...	...	...	9985
...	...	...	...	...	...	...	...	...	...	...	...	...	...	...	9988
...	...	...	...	...	...	...	...	...	...	...	...	...	...	...	9989
...	...	...	...	...	...	...	...	...	...	...	...	...	...	...	9991
...	...	...	...	...	...	...	...	...	...	...	...	...	...	...	9992
...	...	...	...	...	...	...	...	...	...	...	...	...	...	...	9993
...	...	...	...	...	...	...	...	...	...	...	...	...	...	...	9994
...	...	...	...	...	...	...	...	...	...	...	...	...	...	...	9996
...	...	...	...	...	...	...	...	...	...	...	...	...	...	...	9998
...	46	...	...	...	...	...	...	...	...	...	1	...	...	...	9900

Appendix P: Job Opportunities Overseas

Federal jobs are not restricted to the continental United States. U.S. government employees also work in Alaska, Hawaii, the U.S. territories, and in many foreign countries. When a vacancy exists in a foreign country, a determination is made whether to recruit from among local candidates or to seek qualified applicants from the United States. If the position is to be filled locally, the appointee may be a U.S. citizen residing or traveling in the area, the spouse or dependent of a citizen employed or stationed in the area, or a foreign national.

Approximately 36,000 jobs overseas are filled by U.S. citizens. Roughly 70% of these are in Defense Department agencies, and another 25% are in the State Department, the International Communications Agency, and the International Development Cooperation Agency. Generally the salary rates for these positions are equal to those of employees on the U.S. mainland; however, cost-of-living allowances of 5–25% apply in Alaska, Guam, Hawaii, Puerto Rico, and the Virgin Islands.

Federal agencies frequently employ foreign nationals for some overseas jobs; many overseas clerical or lower-level blue-collar jobs, for example, are opened to them so that the Federal government can avoid the expense of bringing in U.S. citizens. Such positions are in the Excepted Service and therefore not subject to the competitive requirements of the Civil Service Act and its associated rules. However, in many cases where the United States has installations in foreign countries, formal agreements have been drawn up to govern the hiring of foreign nationals in the host country.

Thousands of technical, administrative, and supervisory positions in foreign countries are usually in the Competitive Service, such as those in the Foreign Service, the Department of Defense Dependent Schools, and the attaché offices of U.S. embassies and consulates, as well as most clerk-translator, translator, and interpreter positions. As vacancies occur, they are generally filled by transferral of Federal career employees from the United

States. When such employees are not available for transfer and qualified U.S. citizens cannot be recruited locally, these vacancies are filled through the regular competitive examining process. The examinations cover a variety of business and economics, engineering and scientific, medical, social, educational, and trades positions. Applications for these positions should be made directly to the agency in which you are seeking employment. Your local OPM Service Center can provide a list of agencies that are hiring overseas.

Federal employers abroad generally cannot hire U.S. citizens who travel overseas on their own because the travel visas granted to them by the host country do not permit them to work. On the other hand, work visas cannot be obtained from foreign nations unless the individuals have a prior commitment from an employer. Since the U.S. government is reluctant to give such prior commitment, the situation is a catch-22; however, sometimes this can be circumvented. After identifying suitable overseas vacancies, phone potential Federal employers about the possibility of coming to work for them.

The agencies discussed in the following sections employ overseas personnel on an ongoing basis.

CONTENTS

DEPARTMENT OF AGRICULTURE

The Foreign Agricultural Service has agricultural attachés and secretaries at its foreign posts. Contact:

Personnel Division
Foreign Agricultural Service
Department of Agriculture
Washington, DC 20250

DEPARTMENT OF COMMERCE

The Department of Commerce carries out the U.S. government's nonagricultural foreign trade activities. It encourages and promotes U.S. exports of manufactured goods, administers U.S. statutes and agreements, and advises on international policy. Candidates with business and economics backgrounds should write to the following address:

Department of Commerce
Room 3226
14th & Constitution Avenue, NW
Washington, DC 20230

NATIONAL OCEANIC AND ATMOSPHERIC ADMINISTRATION

The National Oceanic and Atmospheric Administration has positions at weather stations in Alaska, Puerto Rico, Mexico, Hawaii, Wake Island, Guam, American Samoa, the Trust Territories, and Antarctica for people with meteorological and electronics background. Qualified candidates should write:

Personnel Officer
National Oceanic and Atmospheric Administration
Herbert Hoover Bldg.
14th & Constitution Avenue, NW
Washington, DC 20230

U.S. TRAVEL AND TOURISM ADMINISTRATION

The U.S. Travel and Tourism Administration, which promotes travel to the United States from foreign countries, has positions for those with appropriate international sales and promotional work experience in travel and tourism and fluency in the language of the country where assigned. Jobs are in London, Paris, Frankfurt, Mexico City, Toronto, Buenos Aires, Sydney, and Tokyo. Contact:

Personnel Officer, Operations Division
Office of the Secretary
U.S. Department of Commerce
Herbert C. Hoover Building
14th Street & Constitution Ave., NW
Washington, DC 20230

DEPARTMENT OF DEFENSE

NON-APPROPRIATED FUND POSITIONS OVERSEAS

NAF positions are discussed in Step 2 (p. 36); to apply, use pathway 3.

Many overseas installations—mostly military bases—have several Non-Appropriated Fund (NAF) positions. These might include such job titles as Bartender, Waitress, Usher, and Cashier. Several of these installations maintain contracts with the host country that require the hiring of foreign nationals for NAF and some other positions; obviously, U.S. citizens have the best chance of obtaining NAF jobs at overseas installations that have no such agreement. Most often, NAF jobs are filled by the dependents of civilian or military personnel who have been stationed overseas.

DEPARTMENT OF DEFENSE DEPENDENT SCHOOLS (DODDS)

The Department of Defense maintains schools (grades K–12) for the children of military personnel stationed at defense bases around the world.

Each year the agency recruits some 300 teachers in all grades. Applicants must have certification in either elementary or secondary education. The DOD provides its own application form. For information about such overseas educational job opportunities, write:

Department of Defense
Office of Overseas Dependent Schools
2461 Eisenhower Avenue
Alexandria, VA 22331

DEPARTMENT OF THE ARMY

Overseas jobs are normally filled through the reassignment of career Army employees from the United States. For information about jobs that require highly unusual or scarce skills, write:

Department of the Army
Civilian Management Field Agency
Attn: PECM, Forrestal Building
Washington, DC 20314.

DEPARTMENT OF THE NAVY

Vacancies are usually filled by the assignment of Navy and Marine Corps career employees. Contact the Civilian Personnel Officer at your nearest Navy or Marine Corps installation.

DEPARTMENT OF THE INTERIOR

Most positions are located in Alaska and are in the Competitive Service. Vacancies occur from time to time in engineering, metallurgy, geology, forestry, and teaching. Contact:

Department of the Interior
Office of the Secretary
Interior Building
18th & C Streets, NW
Washington, DC 20240

DEPARTMENT OF STATE

FOREIGN SERVICE

The Foreign Service recruits career Foreign Service Officers, who fill virtually all professional positions in the more than 240 embassies and consu-

Foreign Service positions are discussed in some depth in Appendix B (p. 165).

lates in 140 countries worldwide. Appointments are made from among those who take competitive Foreign Service Officer examinations. Contact:

Department of State
Recruitment Division FSBE
P.O. Box 12226
Arlington, VA 22219

There is also a continuing need for secretaries and communications and records assistants in the Foreign Service to staff the overseas embassies and consulates. Requests for information concerning positions not filled through the competitive Foreign Service Office examinations should be addressed to one of the recriutment offices listed below:

FOR GENERAL NON-OFFICER POSITIONS
Recruitment Branch
Employment Division
Main State Department Building
2201 C Street, NW
Washington, DC 20520

FOR FOREIGN SERVICE SECRETARY
Recruit Division
Foreign Service Secretary Program
U.S. Department of State
Box 12209, Rosslyn Station
Arlington, VA 22209-0317

AGENCY FOR INTERNATIONAL DEVELOPMENT (AID)

The Agency for International Development is the principal administrator of U.S. economic and technical assistance to developing countries in Africa, Asia, and Latin America. Most appointees on the AID staff are at the mid or upper level, but the agency also has internships for accountants, management auditors, economists, and financial managers. Training is provided in Washington, DC and at overseas missions. Contact:

Chief, Recruitment Branch
Agency for International Development
Recruitment Division
Main State Department Building
2201 C Street, NW
Washington, DC 20523

DEPARTMENT OF TRANSPORTATION

The Federal Highway Administration takes part in highway design, construction, maintenance, and technical assistance programs abroad. Experienced applicants should write:

Office of Personnel and Training
Federal Highway Administration
400 7th Street, SW
Washington, DC 20590

INDEPENDENT AGENCIES

PEACE CORPS

The Peace Corps, established in 1961 to assist developing countries to train personnel for their needs, provides opportunities for skilled Americans to serve two-year terms as volunteers overseas. The program is interested in people with technical vocational training or special skills, particularly in agriculture. While most volunteers work in educational and community development programs and require a college degree, there are positions available in more than 300 skill areas for which a degree is not required.

As of 1971, the activities of the Peace Corps have been coordinated by ACTION, an independent U.S. agency that manages several Federal volunteer programs. Contact the ACTION office in your state or write to:

Office of Recruitment and Communications
Peace Corps
1990 K Street, NW
Washington, DC 20526

U.S. INFORMATION AGENCY (USIA)

USIA Officers are involved with the dissemination of information about our country through the foreign news media. All but a few specialized positions are filled from within the ranks of USIA's career Foreign Service. The agency may also appoint Foreign Service Limited Reserve Officers (experienced professionals for information and cultural work overseas) for a maximum of five years. There are also opportunities for USIA secretarial jobs. Contact:

> See the section on the **Foreign Service** in Appendix B (p. 165).

Special Service Branch
U.S. Information Agency
301 4th Street, SW
Washington, DC 20547

The USIA's international broadcast arm, the Voice of America (VoA), hires International Radio Broadcasters as well as a number of technical support positions. Contact:

Office of Personnel
Voice of America
HHS North Building
300 Independence Ave., SW
Washington, DC 20547

Appendix Q: Special Recruitment and Hiring Programs

Certain groups of people qualify for special assistance in securing Federal employment—most notably military veterans and the disabled. Some qualifying groups receive preferential treatment of their job applications in the normal Competitive Service. For other groups, the government runs special programs in the Excepted Service. This appendix will help you ascertain whether you qualify for one or more Federal special recruitment and hiring programs.

CONTENTS

PROGRAMS FOR VETERANS

Veterans receive certain advantages in the Federal hiring process. For instance, when OPM evaluates applicant work experience, it awards full credit for time spent in the Armed Forces: Military service is considered either as an extension of your past employment or as a subsequent job in which you gained new skills, whichever will benefit you the most. Also, as you'll recall from the discussion of the Rule-of-Three (Step 2, p. 40), an agency cannot appoint a nonveteran (without documented justification) if a veteran is among the three candidates selected for consideration and is the higher rated.

> See also "**Disabled Veterans** Affirmative Action Program" and "**Summer Jobs** for Veterans," below.

Veterans who were employed by a Federal agency in a nontemporary job immediately before entering active duty may have a right to return to their old jobs. They also may be entitled to certain benefits (such as pay increases) that would have accrued had they remained in those jobs. These *reemployment rights* generally expire 90 days after separation from active duty. To determine whether such rights apply in their cases, veterans should contact their former federal employers.

There are also special hiring programs for veterans, including both *rating enhancement* (veterans preference) and *noncompetitive programs* (Veterans Readjustment Appointment). These are discussed in the ensuing sections.

> **Rating enhancement** and **noncompetitive programs** are described in Step 2 (p. 53).

VETERANS PREFERENCE

If you receive a rating of at least 70 (out of 100) on either a written test or unassembled exam (say, an SF-171) and you qualify for veterans preference, you will automatically have 5 or 10 points added to your score. This procedure was instituted in order to give veterans a competitive edge when a Register of Eligibles is used.

> More information on **veterans preference** is available from any OPM Service Center.

Some registers, including those for Custodians, Guards, Elevator Operators, and Messengers, are open only to *veterans preference eligibles*— that is, those who have veterans preference and are eligible for a particular vacancy—as long as there are such persons willing and able to do the job. Veterans preference eligibles are accorded a similar advantage regarding job titles for which experience in the military is useful (such as Military Pay Clerk, Electronics Mechanic, and Aircraft Mechanic).

10-Point Veterans Preference

The following persons are eligible for 10-point veterans preference:

Disabled veterans: You are eligible if you served on active duty at any time, were honorably separated, and either have a service-connected disability or receive compensation or disability retirement benefits from the Department of Veterans Affairs or the Armed Forces. If you received the Purple Heart for wounds received in action, you are considered to have a service-connected disability.

Spouses of disabled veterans: You are eligible if your spouse would be eligible but, because of a service-connected disability, has been unable to qualify for Federal employment.

Widows or widowers of veterans: You are eligible if you are the unremarried spouse of an honorably separated veteran who served on active duty during any war, or between April 28, 1952 and July 1, 1955, or in any campaign or expedition for which a campaign badge or service medal was authorized. This includes the widow or widower of a veteran meeting any of these service requirements and who died under honorable conditions while, in the Armed Forces.

Mothers of veterans: You are eligible if you are the mother of a veteran who died under honorable conditions while on active duty in a war or in a campaign or expedition for which a campaign badge or service medal has been authorized, or between April 28, 1952 and July 1, 1955, or who became permanently and totally disabled because of a service-connected disability. In addition, you must be divorced, separated, or widowed from the father of the veteran, unless the father is permanently and totally disabled. If you have remarried, you may be granted preference only if your new husband is permanently and totally disabled, or if you have since been divorced, legally separated, or widowed.

Veterans with a 10-point preference have special latitude with regard to application filing dates, in that they may file anytime for any position for which (a) there is a register, (b) for which a register is about to be established, or (c) for which a nontemporary appointment has been made within the past three years.

5-Point Veterans Preference

To qualify for 5-point veterans preference you must meet one of the following conditions:

1. served on active duty any time between December 7, 1941, and July 1, 1955 (if you were a reservist called to active duty between February 1 and July 1, 1955, you must meet condition 2); *or*
2. served on active duty any part of which was between July 2, 1955, and October 15, 1976, or was a reservist called to active duty between February 1, 1955, and October 14, 1976, *and* who served for more than 180 days; *or*
3. entered on active duty between October 15, 1976, and September 7, 1980, or was a reservist who entered on active duty between October 15, 1976, and October 13, 1982 *and* received a campaign badge or expeditionary medal or are a disabled veteran; *or*

4. enlisted in the Armed Forces after September 7, 1980, or entered active duty other than by enlistment on or after October 14, 1982 *and:*

   a. completed 24 months of continuous active duty or the full period called or ordered to active duty, or were discharged under 10 U.S.C. 1173 or for hardship under 10 U.S.C. 1173 and received or were entitled to receive a campaign badge or expeditionary medal; *or*

   b. are a disabled veteran.

Note that to receive veterans preference your separation from active duty must have been under honorable conditions (that is, either an honorable or general discharge); a clemency discharge does not meet the requirements. Active duty for training in the military reserve and National Guard programs is not considered active duty for purposes of veterans preference. Finally, you cannot receive preference if you are retired or plan to retire at or above the rank of major or lieutenant commander, unless you are disabled or retired from the active military reserve.

EXAMPLE
Jeff, our Vietnam veteran, qualifies for a 10-point veterans preference because he is a recipient of the Purple Heart.

VETERANS READJUSTMENT APPOINTMENT (VRA)

Veterans Readjustment Appointment is a special program whereby a limited number of jobs are specifically set aside for qualifying veterans on a noncompetitive basis. This means that some veterans may be appointed to jobs without being rated by the OPM or competing with the general public on OPM registers. As of January 1, 1990, veterans eligible for the VRA program include the following:

> Additional information about **VRA** can be obtained from any OPM Service Center.

1. veterans of the Vietnam era who have a compensable service-connected disability;
2. those who served on active duty in the Armed Forces during the Vietnam era in any campaign or expedition for which a campaign badge or expeditionary medal has been authorized;
3. veterans who served *after* the Vietnam era (May 7, 1975) for more than 180 days of active duty (unless separated for service-connected disability) and were separated other than dishonorably.

The noncompetitively appointed veteran agrees to participate in a training program tailored to meet his or her career aspirations and the needs of the hiring agency. Such a program may include any of the following: on-the-job training, rotational job assignments, classroom training, community volunteer projects, remedial education, vocational education, scientific and technical education, high school or high school equivalency education, or college education.

VRA appointments can be made at grades GS-1-11. Positions are converted to regular Competitive Service appointments once employees have served satisfactorily in the program for two years. In addition, a VRA appointment automatically becomes eligible for in-grade pay increases and all other fringe benefits that accompany regular Federal civil service employment.

OPM Service Centers can supply information on current or anticipated VRA job openings to which you may be referred, as well as a list of participating agencies in your area. Since VRA opportunities are available directly through most Federal agencies nationwide, you can also contact agency personnel offices directly.

See appendix D for list of **agency addresses.**

EXAMPLE

Jeff, because he served on active duty in Vietnam, also qualifies for a VRA appointment.

EMPLOYMENT PROGRAMS FOR THE DISABLED

If disabled, you have a good shot at landing a Federal job. The Federal government, which hires more than 124,000 disabled employees, is by far the largest employer of handicapped persons in the United States. This achievement-the result of an active, ongoing recruitment effort—is promising news for handicapped Americans, plagued by the highest unemployment rate of any group in the country. The Federal government is one of the best places for the disabled to find work, and presents excellent opportunities for promotion.

As required by law, each Federal agency has an affirmative action plan to encourage the hiring, placement, and promotion of the handicapped. Each and every agency, including the Postal Service, is required to establish:

1. annual written affirmative action plans that list goals for the employment and advancement of handicapped applicants and employees;
2. an affirmative action plan for disabled veterans with documented 30% disabilities; and
3. goals and timetables for making their buildings and facilities accessible to the handicapped.

To ensure that handicapped employees are able to succeed, hiring agencies have the authority to appoint readers, interpreters, and personal assistants and buy any special equipment necessary for the employee to function on the job.

For more on the **EEOC,** see Appendix R.

Moreover, the Equal Employment Opportunity Commission (EEOC) has identified those with severe handicaps—such as deafness, paralysis, blindness, convulsive disorders, mental illness, missing extremities, mental retardation, or distortion of the limbs or spine—as targets for special recruitment and hiring programs. Agencies with more than 500 employees must establish numerical goals for hiring people with these targeted disabilities.

Special OPM regulations specify agency requirements with respect to reasonable accommodation, employment criteria, preemployment inquiries, and physical access to buildings.

OPM has also established procedures for agencies to follow in hiring the handicapped. These provide for special testing for handicapped applicants whenever a test is required, using such aids as readers for the blind, interpreters for the deaf, modified tests if necessary, and extra time to take them (including an optional meal break). Extra time is also provided for the completion and filing of applications, including extension of the closing date.

OPM Service Centers have designated selective placement specialists able to help handicapped applicants with job information, examination procedures, any special testing needed, and referrals. In addition, each Federal agency has a coordinator responsible for its handicapped .recruitment program at each facility, including field offices.

DISABLED VETERANS AFFIRMATIVE ACTION PROGRAM

This is a special employment program for veterans who are entitled to compensation from the Department of Veterans Affairs (VA) or who have been discharged or released from active duty because of a service-connected disability. Each Federal agency has a national plan designed to attract such candidates. The program provides for a special *Excepted Appointment Authority* (that is, authority for appointment to the Excepted Service) fur veterans certified as 30% or more disabled by either the VA or the military service that discharged or released them. Agencies are required to recruit such veterans actively and provide them with internal advancement opportunities.

> See also the section below on unpaid work experience for **disabled veterans.**

SELECTIVE PLACEMENT PROCEDURES FOR THE PHYSICALLY DISABLED

Temporary Appointment Not to Exceed 700 Hours

A Federal agency can hire a severely physically handicapped applicant for any GS-1–15 or Wage Grade position as long as employment does not exceed 700 hours, or about four months, during 12 consecutive months. This trial appointment period gives handicapped applicants a chance to demonstrate their abilities to the hiring agency.

To be eligible for consideration under this temporary appointing authority, present a VA or state vocational rehabilitation agency certificate (*verification statement*) specifying your disability and your ability to do the job. You can also qualify if the agency applies OPM's minimum qualification standards for the position and establishes that you have a severe physical impairment. By hiring you under this authority, the agency is making no commitment for a permanent appointment; however, it is possible, at the end of your four-month tenure, to have the position converted to an Excepted Service appointment.

Excepted Appointment

If you have a severe physical impairment, you may be appointed to an Excepted Service (Schedule A, Section 213.3102(u)) position without the temporary trial appointment described above. To qualify, you must provide a certificate from either the VA or a state vocational rehabilitation agency verifying that you have a severe physical handicap meeting OPM's qualification standards for either a temporary trial appointment or Schedule A (Excepted Service) appointment. Eligibility for this kind of appointment is based primarily on the severity of the physical impairment, "severe" being defined for these purposes as relatively permanent and seldom fully correctable by medical treatment, therapy, or surgery. The certificate should state that, in the counselor's judgment, you have the ability to perform the duties of the position and are physically qualified to do the work without hazard to yourself or to others. It must be accompanied by a medical examination report. The hiring agency will also look at the effect of the disease or physical impairment upon how you function in a particular job.

Agencies are authorized to convert such noncompetitive excepted appointments to full competitive status after two years of successful performance in a permanent position. (If you initially served under a temporary trial appointment, that period does *not* count toward the two years.) This conversion authority is used frequently and requires only the recommendation of one's supervisor. For many disabled employees, it is virtually automatic .

Competitive Appointment

Many physically handicapped individuals find employment through normal competitive hiring procedures in the same manner as nonhandicapped persons. Nevertheless, even under the competitive application process, the following assistance is available:

1. OPM Service Centers provide advisory services on job qualifications and appropriate Federal civil service examinations. They may also have information about how to get additional training (if needed) and special examination arrangements for applicants whose handicaps prevent them from competing on an equal footing.
2. Agency coordinators provide information about and help with placement, advancement, retention, and job and work-site modification, if needed.

3. Agencies often give handicapped applicants considerable extensions on application filing deadlines. Therefore, when a job in which you are interested is listed, be sure to request a copy of the vacancy announcement regardless of the specified closing date: The fine print will say whether the job is earmarked with an application filing extension for handicapped applicants. Note that this procedure does not apply to every Federal vacancy: It is up to the hiring agency to determine which jobs should be kept open beyond their announced closing dates for this purpose.

SELECTIVE PLACEMENT PROCEDURES FOR THE MENTALLY ILL

Employment of Persons with Mental Retardation

In addition to the normal competitive service procedures, a special Excepted Service appointing authority (Schedule A, Section 213.3102(t)) is available for mentally retarded persons who have been certified by a state vocational rehabilitation counselor as being competent and capable of performing the duties of a position. After two years of successful continuous performance, an employee in the Excepted Service under this program may be noncompetitively converted to a competitive appointment upon the supervisor's recommendation.

Employment of Mentally Restored Persons

The special appointing authorities described above for recruiting and hiring severely physically handicapped persons also apply to mentally restored people, with some definitional changes. Appointees must meet the minimum requirements for a position (including passing a test if this is required) before being given either a temporary trial or Excepted Service appointment.

Excepted appointment (Schedule B, Section 213.3202(k)) is available for mentally restored persons who:

1. have a documented history of mental illness that was treated within the previous two years;
2. are unemployed or have had a substantial work interruption due to emotional problems; and
3. have been certified directly to a position by a state vocational rehabilitation or VA counselor.

This program provides employment for up to two years, *including* time served in a special 700-hour temporary trial appointment. Unlike the special appointing authorities for physically handicapped or mentally retarded persons, there is *no* conversion to competitive status at the end of the two-year appointment authorized under this procedure.

The *competitive appointment* process for mentally restored persons includes no provisions for special testing.

UNPAID WORK EXPERIENCE PROGRAM FOR DISABLED PERSONS

Many Federal agencies have unpaid (volunteer) work experience programs for the disabled. These allow fur the acquisition of skills and training and may lead to paying positions. Normally, you have one year after completing your volunteer service to take advantage of any special hiring procedures that may be available.

Before applying for any of these programs, contact your state vocational rehabilitation or VA counselor to ensure that you are indeed eligible. Some agencies, including the U.S. Postal Service, are exempted by law from offering these special employment programs; the nearest OPM Service Center can tell you which other agencies are exempt.

Clients of State Vocational Rehabilitation Agencies

See also the section above on affirmative action for **disabled veterans.**

If you are unemployed, disabled, and a client of a state vocational rehabilitation agency, you may be eligible for participation in unpaid work experience at a Federal agency, possibly leading to a paid position upon completion of the initial assignment. Federal agencies may enter into a written agreement with a state vocational rehabilitation agency in which you perform certain outlined duties and perhaps receive related training. Although a paid job is not always available upon completion, you will have acquired skills and training that will assist you in competing for a job at a later date, whether in the public or private sector. If you are interested in this program, contact your nearest state vocational rehabilitation office.

Clients of the Veterans Administration

If you are a disabled veteran with a service-connected disability, meet certain economic criteria, and are already a Federal employee, you may be eligible for on-the-job training under so-called Plan I, in which a contract is drawn up between the VA and the agency providing the training.

If you meet the first two of the above criteria but do not presently work for the Federal government, you may qualify (under Plan II) for unpaid work experience and/or training, also under an agreement between the VA and the employing agency. This may ultimately lead to a noncompetitive appointment to the position for which you have been trained, once OPM determines that you meet all the requirements.

For more information on these training programs, contact your nearest VA office.

SPECIAL STUDENT EMPLOYMENT PROGRAMS

Thousands of high school, junior college, community college, college, and graduate students participate every year in a variety of Federal work-study programs sponsored by OPM. Each program involves fully paid (as per GS level), Excepted Service positions and entails the possibility of a permanent, full-time job after graduation. Detailed information about specific programs can be obtained from any OPM Service Center or school guidance counselor.

See also **"Summer Jobs"** below.

HIGH SCHOOL COOPERATIVE EDUCATION PROGRAM

Full- and part-time jobs in paraprofessional fields, technical or office skills, and trades and crafts are available for high school students. These jobs are open to both citizens and noncitizens, with pay at the GS-1 level or Federal Wage Grade equivalent.

STAY-IN-SCHOOL PROGRAM

Needy high school or post-secondary school students may be appointed to jobs for periods of one year or less, with reappointment possible. This program is open to U.S. citizens and some noncitizens. An exception to its economic need requirement is made for mentally retarded and severely physically handicapped students.

ASSOCIATE DEGREE COOPERATIVE EDUCATION PROGRAM

This work-study program is designed for students attending community colleges, junior colleges, or technical institutes. It is open to U.S. citizens, including natives of American Samoa and Swain's Island. After graduation, participants may be noncompetitively appointed to a Competitive Service job at the GS-4 or WG-7 level. Some jobs are part-time, others full-time; there are also some positions in the Excepted Service.

COLLEGE STUDENTS COOPERATIVE EDUCATION PROGRAM (STUDENT TRAINEE PROGRAM)

This is a study-related, fully paid program in which over 1,000 two- and four-year colleges participate. Full-time students, preferably beyond their first academic year, qualify regardless of their economic status, but must be U.S. citizens and recommended by their school. A grade-point average (GPA) of at least 2.0 is required, as well as a "C" average or equivalent in all major fields of study. Work periods correspond to semesters, trimesters, or quarters, depending upon the school's schedule. After graduation, positions can be noncompetitively converted to GS-5 Competitive Service appointments.

GRADUATE STUDENTS COOPERATIVE EDUCATION PROGRAM

This program encompasses all entry-level occupations for which a master's or doctoral degree satisfies the experience requirements specified in OPM *Handbook* X-118 for the GS-9 and GS-II levels, respectively. To qualify, the position must permit education to be substituted for experience (as per the *Handbook*'s substitution criteria). The field of study must relate to the job, and agencies may recruit directly or seek referrals from schools. Master's degree candidates are employed at the GS-5/7 level. Ph.D. candidates who have completed the master's degree requirements may be appointed at the GS-9 level. Appointments can be for as long as three to four years and are limited to U.S. citizens or *nationals* (spouses or dependents of citizens). At the end of the work period and after graduation, participants may be noncompetitively appointed to a job at the GS-9/11 level.

FEDERAL INTERN PROGRAMS

Career Intern Programs

Federal agencies have paid career intern programs in administrative, professional, and technological fields. For instance, the Department of Education has a career intern program for recent college graduates interested in educational research and program analysis. Programs vary from one agency to the next. Interns are recruited by OPM and through colleges and universities, and are usually employed at the GS-5 or GS-7 level. Candidates can request information from their college or university placement office.

Presidential Management Intern Program

This program is very competitive, but well worth consideration. Each year, 250 outstanding college graduates are selected as Presidential Management Interns. Appointments are for two-year Excepted Service positions throughout the government, beginning at the GS-9 level. After the internship, most who so desire and who have performed satisfactorily can be converted noncompetitively to Competitive Service positions within the same agency. Promotion to GS-12 is common on conversion.

Candidates must have an educational background in public management or a related field (broadly construed) and be nominated by their school. Although most participating schools send only one intern to this program, as many as ten have been selected from the same school.

SUMMER JOBS

As a rule, agencies will accept applications for summer employment between March 15 and April 15; however, there are many exceptions to this rule listed, along with a great deal of other pertinent information, in the annual OPM Publication 414 (Summer Jobs), available from any OPM Service Center.

SUMMER JOBS FOR STUDENTS

The Federal Government hires several thousand young people each year to fill summer positions. Summer jobs are available in virtually all fields and located in Federal agencies nationwide, with most in large urban areas. Pay is in the range GS-1-4 for clerical and subprofessional occupations and GS-5-9 for certain professional occupations. To apply for most student summer jobs, you must be at least 16 years old; if you are under 18, check with their state or local authorities to determine whether you will need a work permit.

Applications for summer jobs usually include an SF-171 (Application for Federal Employment) and OPM Form 1170/17 (List of College Courses and Certificate of Scholastic Achievement). The Form 1170/17 is required of all applicants applying for employment based on education. List all undergraduate courses you will have completed by the end of the current school year, including credit hours you expect to earn, and compute your grade-point average.

> **SF-171** and **Form 1170/17** are introduced in Step 4.

For most jobs, your application will be considered only for the agency and position for which you are applying, so be sure to apply to more than one agency. Specify on your applications the types of jobs for which you wish to be considered, the lowest grade level you will accept, and where you want to work. Be sure to use your permanent home address on all applications and correspondence with agencies.

SUMMER JOBS FOR NEEDY YOUTHS

This program is specifically designed to provide jobs for young people from low-income families and for those who need incomes from summer jobs to return to school in the fall. The rate of pay is the Federal minimum wage. Those who meet the eligibility criteria, including family income limits, may be referred for these jobs by registering with the local office of their state employment service (sometimes called an unemployment office). If there is no local office of the state employment service, or where these offices are unable to provide job referrals, contact the nearest OPM Service Center.

SUMMER JOBS FOR VETERANS

Veterans are also able to apply for summer jobs. If you qualify for 5- or 10-point veterans preference, submit Form SF-15 along with a photocopy of your appropriate qualifying proof. Contact your local OPM Service Center or agencies directly.

OTHER SPECIAL HIRING PROGRAMS

FEDERAL EQUAL OPPORTUNITY RECRUITMENT PROGRAM (FEORP)

Each Federal agency has an affirmative action program designed to attract minority and women applicants. Each hiring office within an agency must have a plan, updated annually, to encourage such recruits. Equal employment opportunity (EEO) counselors are located in each field office to assist applicants who qualify for special assistance on the basis of race, color, religion, gender, or national origin. In addition, each agency must have a Federal Women's Program and a Hispanic Employment Program. These are part of the overall EEO program and, in the hiring context, are designed primarily to seek out and encourage applicants from the serviced groups. More information about these programs is available from OPM Service Centers.

PEACE CORPS/VISTA/ACTION VOLUNTEERS

Former VISTA, Peace Corps, and ACTION community volunteers, as well as Volunteer Leaders, are given special opportunities in seeking Federal employment. If you have been serving as such a volunteer, you may apply for any Competitive Service job administered by OPM within 120 days of your return even if the examination is closed and applications are no longer being accepted from the general public. This applies as long as the register established as a result of the examination is being used to refer applicants.

Under special hiring procedures, you may also apply directly to and be hired noncompetitively by an agency for a position in which you are interested simply by establishing that you meet the minimum qualifications of the job; however, you will need proof that you are eligible under those special procedures. A service statement certifying your volunteer service can be obtained via written request to:

Certifying Officer, Peace Corps or VISTA Volunteers
ACTION
Maiatico Bldg.
806 Connecticut Ave., NW
Washington, DC 20525

When you fill out an SF-171, be sure to indicate your volunteer civilian service in block 10. In block 11, write "Eligible for noncompetitive appointment as Peace Corps/VISTA/ACTION volunteer.

NATIVE AMERICAN PREFERENCE

In accordance with the Indian Reorganization Act (25 U.S.C. 479), Congress extended preference in employment in the Bureau of Indian Affairs to qualified Native Americans. It further determined that proper fulfillment of its trust required providing Native Americans greater control of their own destinies.

A Supreme Court decision of 1974 (Morton *v.* Mancari) stated that Indian Preference is an employment criterion designed to further the cause of Native American self-government and to make the Bureau of Indian Affairs more responsible to the needs of its constituent groups. The decision also states that "preference is granted to [American] Indians not as a discrete racial group, but rather as members of quasi-sovereign tribal entities whose lives and activities are governed by the BIA in a unique fashion." The bureau is therefore required by law to give preference to persons of Indian descent in filling positions whether through initial appointment, promotion, reassignment, or transfer.

In accordance with 25 C.F.R. Part 5, preference will be extended to persons of Indian descent who are:

a. members of any recognized Indian tribe now under Federal jurisdiction;
b. descendants of such members who were, on June 1, 1934, residing within the present boundaries of an Indian reservation;
c. all others of one-half or more Indian blood of tribes indigenous to the United States; and
d. Eskimos and other aboriginal people of Alaska.

OUTSTANDING SCHOLAR PROGRAM (OSP)

The Outstanding Scholar Program (OSP) is a special hiring authority, separate from any OPM inventories, that fills entry-level positions (GS-5/7) based strictly on one's academic achievement. Applicants who qualify—this is, college graduates who have an overall academic grade-point average (GA) of 3.45 or better, or who graduated in the top 10% of their class—need only submit an SF-171 and proof of their outstanding scholarship (Form 1170/17, List of College Courses . . .). Under OSP candidates apply directly to the hiring agency at any time. Write or visit the Personnel Director of the agency for which you are interested in working.

FEDERAL EMPLOYMENT INFO LINE

22

Outstanding Scholars

WHAT IS THE OUTSTANDING SCHOLAR PROGRAM?

The **Outstanding Scholar Program** is a special hiring authority established for entry-level *administrative* positions at the GS-5 and GS-7 grade levels. The **Outstanding Scholar Program** is authorized under the terms of a consent decree (*Luevano vs. Newman*) and can only be used for the specific series and job titles listed on the reverse side of this information sheet. It is **not applicable** for other entry-level professional jobs such as accountants, engineers, physical science careers, or jobs in the biological sciences or mathematics. The Outstanding Scholar Program is also **not applicable** at grades below GS-5 or above GS-7.

If you meet the requirements below, you may be offered a direct appointment by a Federal agency without having to go through the normal competitive hiring procedures. The direct appointment process cuts through all of the red tape and can save you weeks of time.

REQUIREMENTS FOR THE OUTSTANDING SCHOLAR PROGRAM

To qualify for consideration, you must be a college graduate and have maintained a grade-point average (GPA) of 3.45 or better on a 4.0 scale for all undergraduate course work, or have graduated in the upper 10 percent of your class or major university subdivision.

A college degree in any major is qualifying for most of the career fields covered by the Outstanding Scholar Program. A few, however, require some course work in subjects related to the job. You may apply a few months before

graduation, but you must have the GPA or class standing at such time as you are offered a job.

HOW TO APPLY AS AN OUTSTANDING SCHOLAR

You should contact Personnel Offices of Federal agencies directly to inquire about their hiring needs. Send a resume or the Optional Application for Federal employment (OF 612), attach a transcript and a cover letter identifying yourself as an Outstanding Scholar applicant. Frequently, Federal recruiters will visit college campuses, giving you an additional opportunity to make contact.

On the reverse-side of this sheet is a listing of common *career fields for the Outstanding Scholar Program*.

(OVER)

United States Office of Personnel Management

Employment Service

Employment Information Office

Pg. 1 of 2

EI-22

11-01-95

Outstanding Scholars

CAREER FIELDS FOR THE OUTSTANDING SCHOLAR PROGRAM

HEALTH, SAFETY, AND ENVIRONMENTAL JOBS

Safety and Occupational Health
Outdoor Recreation Planning
Environmental Protection
Hospital Housekeeping
Public Health Programs

Writing and Public Information Jobs

General Arts and Information
Public Affairs
Writing and Editing
Technical Writing and Editing
Agricultural Market Reporting
Technical Information Services

Business, Finance and Management Jobs

Bond Sales Promotion
Unemployment Insurance
Food Assistance Programs
Logistics Management
Communications
Financial Administration
Budget Analysis
Financial Institution Examining
General Business and Industry
Contract Specialist
Industrial Property Management
Property Disposal
Public Utilities Specialist
Trade Specialist
Agricultural Program Specialist
Agricultural Marketing
Wage and Hour Law Administration
Industrial Specialist
Financial Analysis
Insurance Examining
Loan Specialist
Realty
Appraising and Assessing
Housing Management
Building Management
Quality Assurance
General Supply
Supply Program Management

Inventory Management
Distribution Facilities and Storage
  Management

Packaging
Supply Cataloging
Transportation Specialist
Transportation Industry Analysis
Highway Safety Management
Traffic Management
Transportation Operations

PERSONNEL, COMPUTER AND ADMINISTRATIVE JOBS

Manpower Development
Personnel Management
Military Personnel Management
Personnel Staffing
Position Classification
Occupational Analysis
Salary and Wage Administration
Employee Relations
Labor Relations
Employee Development
Labor-Management Relations
Examining
Contractor Industrial Relations
Miscellaneous Administration
Computer Specialist — Trainee
Administrative Officer
Management Analysis
Program Analysis
Vocational Rehabilitation

BENEFITS REVIEW, TAX AND LEGAL JOBS

Social Insurance Administration
Social Services
Tax Technician
Paralegal Specialist
Contact Representative
Land Law Examining
Passport and Visa Examining
Tax Law Specialist
General Claims Examining
Worker's Compensation
Claims Examining
Social Insurance Claims

Unemployment Compensation
  Claims Examining
Veterans Claims Examining Federal
  Retirement Benefits

Law Enforcement and Investigative Jobs

Park Ranger
Security Administration
Intelligence
Wage and Hour Compliance
Internal Revenue Officer
Civil Aviation Security
General Investigations
Criminal Investigations
Game Law Enforcement
Immigration Inspection
Securities Compliance Examining
Alcohol, Tobacco, and Firearms Inspection
Public Health Quarantine Inspection
Import Specialist
Customs Inspector

Professional-Related Administrative Jobs

Archives Specialist
Archivist
Archeology
Community Planning
Economics
Educational Programming
Foreign Affairs
General Anthropology
General Education and Training
Geography
History
International Relations
Manpower Research and Analysis
Museum Management (Curator)
Psychology
Social Science
Sociology

Leading the way as an
  equal opportunity employer.

Appendix R: Federal Benefits and Work Conditions

This appendix is a brief overview of the benefits and conditions of Federal employment with respect to schedules, pay, leave, retirement, grievances, and pension plans. It is intended only as an outline, a succinct guide to the plans and programs that make Federal employment an attractive and secure career option; it is not meant to be complete, as many of the areas described have specific limitations and restrictions.

CONTENTS

WORK SCHEDULES, HOLIDAYS, AND LEAVE

WORK SCHEDULES

For a full-time Federal employee, the basic 40-hour, nonovertime administrative workweek consists of five eight-hour days, Monday through Friday. *Overtime* is officially ordered or approved work performed in excess of eight hours in a day or 40 hours in a week. No full-time, regular employee can be required to work overtime on more than five consecutive days in a week.

Alternative work scheduling, or *flextime*, is of two basic types. The first, *flexible scheduling*, has two components: *core time*, the period when an employee is required to be at work, and *flexible time*, that part of the schedule within which employees may choose times of arrival and departure consistent with their duties. Employees must work their basic workweek, but may also work additional hours *optionally*. These so-called *credit hours* that can be carried over (accredited) to the next pay period, decreasing the number of hours that have yet to be worked in that period and allowing one to vary the length of days or weeks in one's work schedule.

The second type of alternative work schedule is *compressed time*. In this case, the two-week work requirement of 80 hours (at five eight-hour days per workweek) is fulfilled in less than ten workdays by increasing the number of hours worked per day. The two most common compressed schedules are "4/10" and "5 4/9." The 4//0 schedule allows for four ten-hour workdays and one day off per workweek. The 5 4/9 schedule allows for eight workdays at ninehours, one at eight hours, and a day off every two workweeks. Although employees generally work some combination of weekdays, other schedules may be arranged.

HOLIDAYS

The Federal government recognizes ten holidays per year: New Year's Day, Martin Luther King Day, Washington's Birthday, Memorial Day, Independence Day, Labor Day, Columbus Day, Veterans' Day, Thanksgiving, and Christmas. If a holiday falls on a Saturday, it is observed on the preceding Friday. If it falls on a Sunday, it is observed on the following Monday.

When Inauguration Day (January 20) falls during the workweek, it is observed as a holiday by Federal employees in the Washington, DC area only.

LEAVE

The amount of leave time allowed to Federal employees annually for vacation and other absences for personal reasons varies with the nature and length of employment. *Full-time* employees with less than 3 years of service earn 13 days annually; those with more than 3 years but less than 15 years earn 20 days; and those with 15 years or more of service earn 26 days. Part-time employees are given leave based not only on length of service but on *pay status*, or number of hours in their workweek. Those with less than 3 years of service earn no leave time; those with between 3 and 15 years earn 1 hour for each 20 hours in pay status; and those with 15 years or more earn 1 hour of leave for each 10 hours in pay status. Thus a part-timer who has worked 25 hours a week for 10 years would get (25 x 52)/20 = 65 hours, or just over eight workdays off.

In general, Federal employees are permitted to accumulate 30 days of annual leave under a "use it or lose it" system. Thus, an employee entitled to 20 days annual leave who uses only 7 may carry 13 over to the next year and receive 33. For those overseas, the maximum is 45 days, but there is no maximum for employees in the Senior Executive Service.

Employees who require or desire leave in excess of time earned (or their annual maximum) can request temporary nonpay status and absence from duty, known as *leave without pay* (LWOP).

In addition to regular leave, employees are entitled to *sick leave:* time off for physical incapacity, to prevent the spread of contagious diseases, or to obtain medical, dental, or eye examination or treatment. Full-timers earn 13 days of sick leave per year; part-timers earn 1 hour of sick leave for each 20 hours in pay status. Employees are required to provide evidence of illness (doctor's note) for sick leaves over three days long. Sick leave may be donated from one employee to another who has to handle a health emergency.

FAMILY AND MEDICAL LEAVE ACT OF 1993

The Family and Medical Leave Act of 1993 allows covered employees up to 12 weeks unpaid time off for one of the following reasons: (1) the birth or adoption of a child by the employee or the arrival of a new foster child; (2) to care for an ill family member or relative; (3) for theemployee's own illness if that requires time off. The employee's job is protected during this time off, according to the law.

The Federal Employees Family Friendly Leave Act of 1994 allows Federal employees 13 days of additional leave per year for reasons other than their own illnesses, such as to care for an ill family member, a new baby, or for bereavement. The Office of Personnel Management released a report to Congress in June 1997 stating that more than 335,000 Federal employees used the Federal Employees Family Friendly Leave Act of 1994 for the purpose of caring for an ailing family member or to arrange or attend a family funeral.

SALARY ENHANCEMENTS

PAY DIFFERENTIALS

Pay schedules are introduced in Step 1 (p. 16) and shown in Appendix F.

As was explained in Step 1, most Federal employees are paid either fixed General Schedule annual salaries or hourly Wage Grade rates determined by those paid locally for similar work in the private sector. However, there are various pay *differentials* (additional compensations) available. For instance, there are differentials of 25% (time-and-a-quarter) for working on

Sunday, of 50% (time-and-a-half) for overtime, and of 100% (double time) for holiday work. General Schedule employees are also entitled to a 100/o differential for working at night (between 6 P.M. and 6 A.M.). Pay differentials may also be offered for certain jobs as incentives to compensate for difficult or unhealthful work conditions or excessive physical hardships. For example, there may be an environmental differential for duties involving unusually severe hazards or working conditions.

COST-OF-LIVING ALLOWANCES

The pay schedule in a given area, as you'll recall from Step 1, can be affected by extreme shortages of qualified applicants and the local cost-of-living index. Special salary rates may include *cost-of-living allowances,* based on annual surveys of living costs in a given area compared to those in the vicinity of Washington, DC. Allowance rates range from a minimum of 5% to a maximum of 25%. In several metropolitan areas, such higher pay applies only to specific job titles for which the demand is high. Federal employees (including postal workers) living in Alaska, Guam, Hawaii, Puerto Rico, or the Virgin Islands can also receive cost-of-living allowances.

GRIEVANCES

Agencies are required to maintain *agency grievance systems* (exceptions are the CIA, FBI, Defense Intelligence Agency, National Security Agency, Nuclear Regulatory Commission, Tennessee Valley Authority, Postal Rate Commission, and U.S. Postal Service), which are reviewed by OPM from time to time. Acting singly or jointly, employees may seek personal reliefvia their agency's grievance system with regard to some aspect of the terms of employment under the agency's control. The following matters, however, are excluded from the system's purview: nonselection for promotion, adverse actions, reassignment or termination of SES appointment, performance standards of employees position, performance awards, and merit pay determinations. Regulations encourage resolution of grievances at the earliest possible stage, and a written determination must be made by the agency for those submitted in writing.

> Complaints regarding **discrimination** are discussed under "Equal Opportunity Employment," below.

The agency grievance system may be used by any employee regardless of type of appointment: competitive, excepted, temporary, or career. However, employees represented by a bargaining unit (for example, union employees of the Postal Service) must instead use the grievance system of that unit.

EQUAL EMPLOYMENT OPPORTUNITY

The Federal government is prohibited from discrimination on the basis of race, color, religion, gender, national origin, age, and/or handicap. Under the Federal Equal Opportunity Recruitment Program (FEORP), each Federal agency is required to establish and maintain an affirmative action program to pursue equal employment opportunity aggressively. Moreover, the Equal Pay Act prohibits discrimination regarding the earnings received by men and women in the same agency performing the same functions. Enforcement and guidance authority in all these matters lies with the Equal Employment Opportunity Commission (EEOC).

> For more on the **EEOC, FEORP,** and **employment of the disabled,** see Appendix Q.

DISCRIMINATION COMPLAINTS AND APPEALS

Several steps are involved in filing a discrimination complaint with a Federal agency. The first course of action is to discuss the situation with an Equal Employment Opportunity counselor of the employing agency within 30 calendar days of the occurrence of the alleged discrimination. If no resolution is achieved, a formal complaint is filed with an appropriate official of the employing agency within 21 days after the initial contact with the counselor. (If the initial counseling lasts longer than 21 days, the formal complaint may be filed 15 days after the final counseling session.) After an investigation made by an official from another jurisdiction within the agency is completed, an attempt is made to resolve the complaint informally. If this proves unsuccessful, a final agency determination will be made with or without a hearing. If a hearing is requested, an Administrative Law Judge is assigned by the EEOC, who submits a recommendation to the agency head; the agency then makes a final decision. If this final decision is unsatisfactory, the employee may file an appeal within 20 days, or file a civil action with the U.S. District Court within 30 days.

At any time during this process, the complainant has the right to legal representation of his or her own choosing.

If you are handicapped and believe you may have been subjected to discrimination during the Federal hiring process, you may file a complaint with the EEOC.

Complaints under the Equal Pay Act are filed with the EEOC. The identity of a complainant and informants may not be revealed without prior permission. The right to file a civil action is provided for as above.

The administrative procedures outlined above do al)ply to age discrimination complaints, except that no specific time limitations are set forth. Civil actions in such cases are also provided for as described above.

SEXUAL HARASSMENT

Sexual harassment is defined as occurring when:

1. submission to a sexual action is made a condition or term of an individual's employment;
2. submission to or rejection of a sexual action is used as a basis of employment decisions; or
3. an unsolicited sexual action has the effect of creating a hostile, intimidating, or offensive workplace.

Cases 1 and 2 are described as *quid pro quo* harassment; case 3 is called *hostile environment* harassment. In quid pro quo harassment cases, the employer is legally responsible for the action of its employees regardless of whether these actions were known to the employer or even forbidden by the same. Under hostile environment cases, the employer's responsibility depends on the Agency Law principles governing liability. If the employer knew or should have known of the harassment and took no immediate action, the employer is responsible. An employer may even be responsible for nonemployees if the employer knew or should have known of the harassment and took no action to correct the situation.

CLASS COMPLAINTS

This form of complaint is fried by an applicant, former employee, or current employee in cases where the individual and other members of a group or class feel they have been discriminated against as a single entity. Before filing a complaint, a complainant must contact a designated Equal Employment Opportunity counselor at the employing agency, usually within 30 days. If the initial counseling is unsuccessful, a complaint may be filed by an individual on behalf of the class as whole. If it is accepted as a class complaint and a hearing granted, a recommendation is provided by an EEOC Administrative Law Judge and a final agency determination is reached. If that decision is not reached within 180 days, a class action civil suit may be filed.

DEATH AND DISABILITY

The Federal Employees' Compensation Act provides compensation in the event any Federal civilian employee suffers injury or death in the performance of his or her job function. Such death and disability insurance is negotiated and administered by OPM.

The term *injury* covers any disease caused by the employment. Besides injury in the line of duty, the Act covers nonwork injury due to war-risk hazard while employed overseas. Coverage also extends to the damage of prosthetic devices. An injured employee is entitled to the continuation of full pay for up to 45 calendar days; this is still considered salary, notcompensation, and all taxation and deductions apply. However, if the employee is disabled beyond this period, compensation is then provided.

Disability compensation is based on the monthly pay received at the time of the injury (or its recurrence, if less than six months after the initial trauma). A written report of the injury must be presented to the employee' s supervisor within 30 days of the occurrence, and a claim must be filed within three years. *Total disability* compensation is equal to two-thirds of the employee's monthly pay, increased to three-quarters if the disabled party is married or has any dependents. Maximum compensation is three-quarters of the employee' s monthly pay at the GS-15 level; minimum compensation is three-quarters of that monthly pay or three-quarters of that at the GS-2 level, whichever is lower. Disability benefits are paid (after a five-month waiting period) for the duration of the disability up to age 65, at which point they are converted to old-age benefits.

Other benefits include medical attention required because of the injury, rehabilitation, and the services of an attendant. For instance, an employee who is permanently disabled may be provided with vocational rehabilitation services and an additional allowance of up to $200.

Death benefits include coverage of burial expenses of up to $&00. Additionally, $200 is paid to the representative of the deceased for reimbursement of the cost of terminating the deceased's status as a U.S. employee. Survivors eligible for death compensation include spouses and dependents.

GROUP LIFE INSURANCE

Postretirement life insurance is duscussed below under "Retirement."

All civilian Federal employees are automatically covered by group life insurance unless they specifically request otherwise. The basic cost is 18.5 cents per $1,000 of basic coverage, with most employees paying two-thirds of this via salary withholdings. (Postal workers are an exception, with their agency contributing 100% of basic costs.) Two are actually kinds of coverage provided: life insurance and accidental death and dismemberment insurance. The coverage for each equals the employee's annual pay rounded off to the next highest thousand plus $2,000, with a minimum of $10,000 and a maximum of $92,000.

Under a standard option, an employee may elect to buy an extra $10,000 worth of life insurance, the cost of which depends on the employee's age and is withheld in full from his or her salary.

Optional family insurance is also available, with the employee bearing the full cost. Premiums depend on the employee's age and are withheld from salary. A spouse is covered for $5,000, and each eligible child for $2,500,

HEALTH CARE

The Federal Employees Health Benefits Program established July 1, 1960, helps protect eligible employees and their families against the cost of illness or accident. Enrollment can be for the employee alone, or for eligible members of his or her family, including spouse, unmarried dependent children, recognized children born out of wedlock, foster children, and stepchildren. In some cases, former spouses are also eligible.

There are two basic types of health plans available: *Fee-for-service plans* reimburse the employee or the health care provider for covered services. *Prepaid plans* are Comprehensive Medical Plans/Health Maintenance Organizations (CMP/HMOs), which arrange for health care through designated physicians, hospitals, and (in certain locations) other providers. The government pays 60-75% of the health insurance costs, depending on the plan selected.

RETIREMENT

All Federal employees hired after December 31, 1983 are covered by the *Federal Employees Retirement System* (FERS), a three-tiered system that includes Social Security, basic annuity, and a Thrift Savings Plan. These benefits are subject to cost-of-living increases, making them inflation-proof. In addition, employees hired on or before December 31, 1983 are covered by the *Civil Service Retirement System* (CSRS) and receive an annuity based on age and length-of-service requirements. Federal employees who also worked outside Federal service long enough to qualify additionally for Social Security have their CSRS payments reduced relative to the amount of their Social Security payments.

The *Federal Thrift Savings Plan* (TSP), a tax-deferred retirement savings plan for Federal employees, is similar to a 401(k) plan offered in the private sector. Those in the plan have a portion of their salary invested automatically, thereby reducing their taxable income before taxes are withheld. Employees covered under CSRS may contribute up to 5% of their basic pay, whereas the maximum deductible investment for FERS members is 10%. TSP contributions made by FERS employees are also partially matched by the government. Of course, workers may also directly fund Individual Retirement Accounts (IRAs), protecting up to $2,000 a year from taxes until the funds are distributed at retirement.

Upon retirement or at age 65, whichever is later, the amount of a Federal employee's basic life insurance is decreased at 2% per month until it equals 25% of the total amount held before retirement. An employee may elect a lesser or no reduction after retirement by paying additional premiums.

Medicare is available to retirees to cover most hospital and hospital related costs.

DUAL COMPENSATION
(MILITARY RETIREES)

Individuals who are paid for a full-time Federal position while receiving a retirement annuity for prior military service are said to have *dual compensation*. In certain instances, the annual remuneration to which these individuals are entitled is regulated. For example, a restriction applies to officers or enlisted members of the Regular or Reserve Service who retire after January 11, 1979 and are then employed in Federal civilian jobs: If necessary, their military retirement pay will be reduced such that when added to their full civilian pay it does not exceed the salary for Level V of the Executive Schedule (presently $104,800); any civilian salary increase thereafter will cause a compensatory downward adjustment in military retirement pay to maintain the Level V maximum.

VETERANS BENEFITS

Pensions are paid to veterans of active military service who have at least 90 days of active wartime service, were honorably discharged, and are totally disabled, over 65 years old, and unemployed. Dollar amounts are determined based on the medical needs and familial obligations of the recipient. Hospitalization and outpatient care are available to veterans at VA and other Federal hospitals. Veterans' benefits also provide for medical care needed by a veteran's dependents or survivors.

Additionally available under the GI Bill are education loans, a matching contributory plan for future education expenses, and education benefits to dependents and survivors. Guaranteed loans also may be obtained through the VA for purchases of homes. Moreover, veterans are entitled to apply for Federal Housing Administration (FHA) loans with lower down payments than are generally available.

There are also a variety of life insurance programs for veterans, as well as readjustment counseling for Vietnam Era veterans. Burial benefits to veterans and their survivors are available both within and outside of the National Cemetery System, with headstones and gravemarkers provided to eligible veterans.

OTHER FEDERAL BENEFITS PROGRAMS

FEDERAL EMPLOYEE EDUCATION AND
ASSISTANCE FUND

The Federal Employee Education and Assistance Fund provides educational grants and scholarships to Federal employees and their dependents. Funds are allocated to various cities and regions in proportion to the amounts raised from each area through contributions to the Combined Federal Campaign, an employee contribution fund.

INCENTIVE AWARDS PROGRAM

A Federal agency can pay an employee up to $425,000 for a suggestion, invention, or other contribution that reduces costs or improves government operations.

Glossary of Federal Employment Terms

Accretion of Duties Promotion: A promotion that may be made without competition because the current position is reconstituted at a higher grade because of additional duties and responsibilities.

Acknowledgment of Application Receipt: Possible preliminary governmental response to receiving an application. Provides no clues as to applicant's eligibility, but acknowledges receipt and advises if there are any problems with the application.

active position: Position that opens up regularly.

Administrative Careers With America (ACWA): Refers to administrative (white collar non-technical) jobs at grades GS-5 and 7 often targeted for recent college graduates but others may apply. At one time, these jobs were filled from a written test, but now they are usually filled by responding to individual vacancy announcements. Applicants are evaluated on the basis of their qualifications although agencies at their option may still use a written test as part of the rating process, but that is hardly ever done.

affirmative action: Policy followed closely by the Federal civil service that requires agencies to take positive steps to ensure equal opportunity in employment, development, advancement, and treatment of all employees and applicants for employment, regardless of race, color, sex, religion, national origin, or physical or mental handicap. Affirmative action also requires that specific actions be directed at the special problems and unique concerns of minorities, women, and other disadvantaged groups.

agency: Any administrative division of the U.S. government, regardless of whether its official name includes the word "agency," "bureau," "department," or "organization."

agency grievance system: System required of most agencies by the OPM to address employee grievances regarding those aspects of the terms of employment under the agency's control. It may be used by any employee regardless of type of appointment; however, employees represented by a bargaining unit (e.g., union) must instead use the grievance system of that unit.

announcement number: Special identification number appearing on each Federal Vacancy Announcement.

appeal rights: Rights of some employees to appeal to the Merit Systems Protection Board regarding an imposed disciplinary action, such as a reduction in grade (demotion), temporary suspension, or dismissal.

applicant: Anyone who has filed an application for current Federal employment, whether it has been accepted or rejected. *Compare* candidate.

applicant supply file: List of candidates who are likely to qualify (based on a preliminary evaluation of their examinations) but have not yet been rated.

Application for Federal Employment, *see* SF-171.

application package: Government-issued informational kit that tells you the qualifications required for a given job title and provides your application form(s). Also called "qualifications information package."

application window: The time period, defined by the opening and closing dates, during which a candidate may apply for a position or to be placed on a register. Also called the "filing period."

appointing officer: Person empowered by law to make appointments.

appointment: Actual employment by an agency. See also specific type.

apprentice: Second career level of Wage Grade employment (WG-6-8), just above helper. Still learning the full range of duties in a specified occupation, apprentices receive both on-the-job and classroom training.

area of consideration: Explanation on a Vacancy Announcement of who may apply for a job; for example, those with competitive status or with a Notice of Results-Rating. *Compare* geographic area of consideration.

assembled examination: Examination that includes, as one of its parts, a written or performance test for which applicants are required to assemble at appointed times and places. *Compare* unassembled exam.

attrition rate: Rate at which positions open up due to retirements, resignations, illnesses, and so on.

average grade, *see* mean grade.

basic qualifications, see minimum qualifications.

basic workweek: For a full-time employee, the 40-hour nonovertime work schedule within an administrative workweek. The usual workweek consists of five eight-hour days, Monday through Friday although some times employees are permitted to work alternate schedules such as four 10-hour days. *See* compressed time.

blue-collar worker: Generally a salaried employee whose job entails manual labor and/or protective clothing. *Compare* Wage Grade employee.

break in service: Time between separation and reemployment that may cause a loss of rights or privileges. For transfer purposes, it means not being on an agency payroll for one working day or more. For the three-year career-conditional period or for reinstatement purposes, it means not being on an agency payroll for more than 30 days.

"bubble sheet," *see* closed-end form.

bumping: During a reduction in force, the displacement of one employee by another employee in a higher group or subgroup.

candidate: Anyone pursuing Federal employment, whether or not an application has yet been filed. *Compare* applicant.

candidate list: A list of eligible candidates ranked, according to regulations, for appointment or promotion consideration. Also called a "certificate."

career appointment: Permanent appointment to a government position in the Competitive Service, entailing the full range of rights and privileges associated with Federal employment (i.e., competitive status).

Career Bargaining: Type of Postal Service appointment including the most populated postal occupations (Clerk, Mail Handler, and Letter Carrier). Candidates must take the postal exam.

career brochure: Agency publication providing an overview of an agency's mission, its major career paths, and the minimum qualifications for those paths.

career-conditional appointment: Appointment to a permanent Competitive Service position, but one in which a new employee must demonstrate satisfactory work performance for three years, the first of which is probationary, before being granted a career appointment.

career-conditional tenure: Tenure of a permanent employee in the Competitive

Service who has not completed three years of substantially continuous creditable Federal service.

career counseling: Service available to Federal employees to assist them in: (1) assessing their skills, abilities, interests, and aptitudes; (2) determining qualifications required for occupations within the career system and how those requirements relate to their individual capabilities; (3) defining their career goals and developing plans for reaching these goals; (4) identifying and assessing education and training opportunities and enrollment procedures; (5) identifying factors that may impair career development; and (6) learning about resources for additional help inside their agency.

career development: Systematic development designed to increase an employee's potential for advancement and career change. It may include classroom training, reading, work experience, and so on.

career ladder: Series of developmental positions of increasing difficulty in the same line of work, through which an employee may progress to a full-performance level in that series.

career level: One or more grade levels comprising a single rung on the career ladder. Wage grade career levels are helper, apprentice, and journeyman.

Career Nonbargaining: Type of Postal Service appointment including all management and administrative positions (e.g., Postmasters and Supervisors). Often filled from the ranks of Career Bargaining employees.

career promotion: Noncompetitive promotion of an employee the employee has been competitively selected from a register or under competitive promotion procedures for an assignment at a lower grade intended as preparation for the full performance level at a higher grade position.

career-reserved position: Position within the Senior Executive Service with a specific requirement for impartiality. May be filled only by career appointment.

career status, *see* competitive status.

career tenure: Tenure of a permanent employee in the Competitive Service who has completed three years of substantially continuous creditable Federal service.

case examining: Examining method that has become the most common method used by agencies; it involves announcing individual jobs and rating and ranking applicants against requirements specifically developed for the position being filled.

Casual: Temporary, part-time Postal Service appointment involving much the same work as Career Bargaining positions but at hourly rates. No exam is required.

ceiling personnel: Maximum number of employees authorized at a given time.

certificate, *see* candidate list.

civil service, Federal: Administrative service of the U.S. government, exclusive of military (noncivilian) personnel in the armed forces. Includes the Competitive Service, Excepted Service, and Senior Executive Service, but not Non-Appropriated Fund positions.

Civil Service Retirement System (CSRS): Federal retirement system granting annuities based on age and length-of-service requirements to employees hired on or before December 31, 1983.

class of positions: All positions sufficiently similar in (1) subject matter of work, (2) level of difficulty and responsibility, and (3) qualification requirements to warrant similar treatment in personnel and pay administration; for example, all GS-3 Clerk-Typist positions.

Classified Service, *see* Competitive Service.

closed-end form: Examination form, such as the Form B, setup for multiple-choice answers regarding the candidate's education and prior job experience. *Compare* open-end form.

closing date: Filing deadline, usually the date by which a Federal job application must be received by the hiring agency. Occasionally refers to the date by which the application must be postmarked.

commuting area, *see* geographic area of consideration.

compensable disability preference ("CP"): Ten-point preference awarded to a veteran who is compensably disabled. Eligible "CP" veterans are placed at the top of civil service Registers of Eligibles, except for scientific and professional positions at GS-9 or higher. *Compare* disability preference ("XP"); 30% or more disabled preference ("CPS").

compensably disabled: Receiving a Federal compensation of 10% or more as an honorably discharged veteran with a service-connected disability.

compensatory time off: Time off (hour for hour) granted an employee in lieu of overtime pay.

competitive promotion: Selection of a current or former Federal civil service employee for a higher-grade position by means of procedures that compare the candidates on merit.

Competitive Service: Federal positions normally filled through open competitive examination under civil service rules and regulations. About 60% of all Federal positions are in the Competitive Service. *Compare* Excepted Service.

competitive status: Basic eligibility of a person to be selected to fill a position in the Competitive Service without open competitive examination. Competitive status may be acquired by career-conditional or career appointment through open competitive examination, or may be granted by statute, executive order, or civil service rules without competitive examination. A person with competitive status may be promoted, transferred, reassigned, reinstated, or demoted subject to the conditions prescribed by civil service rules and regulations. Retention of status after leaving a Federal job is called "reinstatement eligibility."

compressed time: Alternative work schedule in which the two-week work requirement of 80 hours is fulfilled in less than ten workdays by increasing the number of hours worked per day. The two most common such schedules are "4/10" and "5 4/9." *Compare* flexible scheduling.

consultation: Obligation of an agency to consult the labor organization (union) on particular personnel issues. This process falls between *notification,* which may amount simply to providing information to the labor organization, and *negotiation,* which implies agreement on the part of the labor organization.

continuous, *see* open continuously.

conversion: Procedure by which a position may be reclassified from one type of civil service to another; for example, from Excepted Service to Competitive Service.

cooperative education: Work-study program for certain students.

core time: Under flexible scheduling, period when an employee is required to be at work.

cost-of-living allowance (nonforeign area): Compensatory allowance of 5-25% for Federal employees based on annual surveys of living costs in Alaska and Hawaii, Puerto Rico, the Virgin Islands, and Guam compared to those in the vicinity of Washington, DC.

court leave: Time allowed to employees for jury duty and certain types of witness services.

cover letter: Explanatory letter that, although generally unwelcome, may be submitted *under certain circumstances* to a hiring agency along with a job application.

CP, *see* compensable disability preference.

credit hour: Under flexible scheduling, hour of optional work (in addition to the basic workweek) that can be carried over (accredited) to the next pay period.

death benefits: Compensation in the event any Federal civilian employee dies in the performance of his or her job function.

Delegated Examining Authority: Examining Authority delegated by OPM to an agency. As of 1996, OPM has been required to delegate most examining authority to agencies although for a fee OPM can still do the examining for an agency.

department only: As an area of consideration on a Vacancy Announcement, dba1() means that applicants must be affiliated with a particular department of the executive branch—almost always the department of the agency that is issuing the announcement.

detail: Temporary assignment of an employee to different duties or to a different position for a specified time, with the employee returning to his or her usual duties at the end of the detail.

developmental level: Level of a career ladder position at which an employee has not yet learned the full range of duties in a specified occupation. For Wage Grade employees, this is equivalent to the helper and apprentice levels. Delineation is less precise in the General Schedule, where lower-grade entry-level positions are clearly developmental and higher-grade ones may or may not be, depending on the job. *Compare* full-performance level.

differential: Additional compensation, as for working overtime or nights, or on Sundays or holidays. May also serve as an incentive justified by extraordinarily difficult living conditions, excessive physical hardships, or notably unhealthy conditions. *See also* specific type.

disability compensation: Compensation in the event any Federal civilian employee suffers injury (i.e., any disease caused by the employment) in the performance of his or her job function.

disability preference ("XP"): Ten-point preference in hiring for a veteran separated under honorable conditions from active duty who has a service-connected disability or receives compensation, pension, or disability retirement from the VA or a uniformed service. Similar preference may be available to the mother or widow(er)/spouse of a deceased or disabled military veteran. *Compare* compensable disability preference ("CP"); 30% or more disabled preference ("CPS").

disciplinary action: Action taken to correct the conduct of an employee. May range from admonition to reprimand, suspension, reduction in grade or pay, or removal.

DOD: Department of Defense.

dual compensation: Compensation for more than one Federal position if an employee worked more than 40 hours during the week. Also used regarding compensation from both a full-time Federal position and a retirement annuity for prior military service.

duty station: Geographical area in which an employee is permanently assigned.

eligible: Applicant for appointment or promotion who meets the minimum qualification requirements. Thus, in the Competitive Service, an eligible would be someone who passes a Federal examination.

employee development: Term comprising career development and upward mobility. May refer to development for better performance on an employee's current job, learning a new policy or procedure, or enhancing an employee's potential for advancement.

Employment Availability Statement (Form A): Form used to confirm that an applicant is still interested in and available for a given position (e.g., when referred off a register).

employment narrative: Supplemental statement used to relate special technical and managerial qualifications when applying for the Senior Executive Service.

entry level: The grade levels of a pay schedule at which a newcomer is most likely to be hired. Specifically, the lowest career level in the General Schedule, comprising grade levels GS-1-7.

environmental differential: Additional pay authorized for duty involving unusually severe hazards or working conditions.

equal employment opportunity: Federal policy to provide equal employment opportunity for all: to prohibit discrimination on the grounds of age, race, color, religion, sex, national origin, or physical or mental handicap: and to promote the full realization of employees' potential through a continuing affirmative action program in each executive department and agency.

Equal Employment Opportunity Commission (EEOC): Regulates and enforces the Federal program for ensuring equal employment opportunity, and oversees the development and implementation of Federal agencies' affirmative action programs.

equal pay for substantially equal work: Underlying principle to provide the same pay level for work at the same level of difficulty and responsibility.

equilibrium: Condition in which the demand of candidates equals the supply. *Compare* oversupply; undersupply.

evaluation factors, *see* special qualifications.

examination: Means of measuring, in a practical and suitable manner, the qualifications of applicants for employment in specific positions. *See also* assembled examination; unassembled examination.

Examination Announcement: Official announcement of an upcoming assembled examination.

Examining Authority: The legal authority to develop examinations and to evaluate and rate candidates who take them. Originating in (but not necessarily remaining with) OPM, such authority pertains only to the Competitive Service (including the SES).

excepted agency: Agency all of whose positions are excepted from the Competitive Service by law. Also called an "independent employment system." Examples include the U.S. Postal Service, the Foreign Service, and the FBI.

Excepted Appointment Authority: Authority to appoint to Excepted Service positions. **Excepted Service:** Positions in the Federal civil service not subject to the appointment requirements of the Competitive Service. Exceptions to the normal competitive requirements are authorized by law, executive order, or regulation.

exclusive Examining Authority: Rating of candidates by one agency only, whether it be OPM or the agency to which such authority has been delegated. *Compare* nonexclusive Examining Authority.

Executive and Administrative Salary (EAS) Structure: Postal Service pay structure applicable to executives, professionals, supervisors, postmasters, and technical, administrative, and clerical nonbargaining employees.

executive branch: Branch of Federal government that implements laws enacted by the legislative branch. With few exceptions, the job titles for which one may apply with the help of this book are for positions in executive branch agencies.

Executive Competency Review Factors: Set of six: general managerial qualification requirements for all government Senior Executive Service positions

Executive Inventory: OPM computerized file that contains background information on all members of the Senior Executive Service, Senior Level Pay Schedule employees, and those at the highest General Schedule grades who have been certified as meeting the managerial criteria for SFS. It is used as an aid to agencies in executive recruiting and as a planning and management tool.

Executive Resources Board: Panel of top agency executives responsible under the law for conducting the merit staffing process for Career Appointment to Senior Executive Service positions in the agency. Most Boards are also responsible for setting policy on and overseeing such areas as SES position planning and executive development.

Executive Schedule: The highest positions, almost all of which are presidential appointments requiring Senate confirmation. It has five levels, with the lowest number reflecting the highest salary.

exempt employee: Employee exempt from the overtime provisions of the Fair Labor Standards Act.

external hiring, *see* outside hiring.

extra compensation, *see* differential.

Federal Apprenticeship Exam: Test given locally and infrequently--usually by a

DOD base--to compile a register for entry-level Wage Grade positions.

Federal Career Opportunities: Privately published source of Federal vacancy information.

Federal Directory: Government publication listing contact information for Federal agency headquarters.

Federal Employees Retirement System (FERS): Three-tiered system including Social Security, basic annuity, and a Thrift Savings Plan.

Federal Equal Opportunity Recruitment Program (FEORP): Program requiring each Federal agency to establish and maintain an affirmative action program to pursue equal employment opportunity aggressively.

Federal Jobs Digest: Privately published biweekly (fortnightly) source of Federal vacancy information, covering all occupations and geographic areas. Each issue lists over 4,000 Federal job opportunities.

Federal Labor Relations Authority (FLRA): Organization that administers Federal service labor-management relations programs. Resolves questions of union representation of employees, prosecutes and adjudicates allegations of unfair labor practices; decides questions of what is or is not negotiable; and, on appeal, reviews decisions of arbitrators.

Federal Thrift Savings Plan (TSP): Tax-deferred retirement savings plan for Federal employees, similar to a 401(k) plan offered in the private sector.

Federal Wage System (FWS): Body of laws and regulations governing the administrative processes related to trades and laboring (blue-collar) occupations in the Federal service.

fee-for-service plan: Type of Federal health plan that reimburses the employee or the health care provider for covered services. *Compare* prepaid plan.

filing period, *see* application window.

fitness-for-duty examination: Agency-directed or offered examination, given by a Federal medical officer or employee-designated , agency-approved physician to determine the employee's physical, mental, or emotional ability to perform assigned duties safely and efficiently.

5 4/9 schedule: System under compressed time scheduling that allows for eight workdays at nine hours, one at eight hours, and a day off every two workweeks. *Compare* 4/10 schedule.

flexible scheduling: Alternative work schedule in which employees must work their basic workweek, but may also work additional "credit hours" optionally. *Compare* compressed time.

flexible time: Under flexible scheduling, part of the schedule within which employees may choose times of arrival and departure consistent with their duties.

flextime: Alternative work scheduling in general.

Foreign Service: Strictly speaking the career corps of diplomatic personnel who represent the United States abroad.

Form A, *see* Employment Availability Statement.

Form B: Type of closed-end, unassembled-examination form of the type known as a "bubble sheet" (i.e, one with mostly fill-in-the-circles-type answers) that can be scored quickly and inexpensively by computer. Used for entry-level professionals, such as Accountants, Biologists, Engineers, and Mathematicians.

4/10 schedule: System under compressed time scheduling that allows for four ten-hour workdays and one day off per workweek. *Compare* 5 4/9 schedule.

full-field investigation: Detailed investigation of an applicant's background to determine whether he or she meets fitness standards for a critical, sensitive Federal position. *Compare* National Agency Check and Inquiry.

full-performance level: Lowest level of a career ladder position at which an employee has learned the full range of duties in a specified occupation. For Wage Grade employees, this is known as the journeyman level depending on the job. *Compare* developmental level.

general position: Position within the Senior Executive Service that may be filled by a career, noncareer, or limited appointment.

General Schedule (GS): Graded pay system for classifying most Federal white-collar positions. It comprises 15 grade levels, divided into three career levels.

geographic area of consideration: The area from which applicants may apply for a specific position. It may be the commuting area around where the position is located, a larger region, or the whole country.

grade level: Level (representing work experience and/or education) within a salary rate schedule or system. Represents classes of positions that, although different with respect to kind or subject matter of work, are related closely enough in (i) level of difficulty and responsibility and (2) level of qualification requirements to warrant inclusion within one range of basic compensation rates.

grade-point average (GPA): College student's computed average academic score, with 4.0 being the highest possible.

grade retention: Right of a General Schedule or Prevailing Rate (WG) employee, when demoted for *certain reasons,* to retain the higher grade for most purposes for two years.

grievance: Any complaint or expressed dissatisfaction by an employee against an action by management that affects his or her job, pay, or other aspect of employment. Whether such complaint or expressed dissatisfaction is formally recognized and handled as a grievance under a negotiated procedure depends on the scope of that procedure.

Handbook of Occupational Groups and Series of Classes: Government publication describing the duties and responsibilities of each type of Federal position.

Handbook X-118C: *Official OPM publication, Blue-Collar* Occupations in Federal Service. Describes the qualifications required at each grade level for each blue-collar Competitive Service job.

helper: Lowest career level of Wage Grade employment (WG-1-5), at which an employee is still learning the full range of duties in a specified occupation. Helpers receive on-the-job, but not classroom, training.

hiring agency: Federal agency authorized to recruit applicants and appoint qualified candidates to positions within it.

hiring pathway, *see* pathway.

hiring volume: Relative number of employees hired, whether for a particular job title or by a particular agency.

holiday differential: Additional 100% compensation (double time) for working on a holiday.

inactive position: Position that opens up infrequently or irregularly.

incentive award: Any award granted under Part 4.51 of OPM regulations, including (but not limited to) the following: an award for a suggestion submitted by an employee and adopted by management; a special achievement award for performance exceeding job requirements: an honorary award in the form of a certificate, emblem, pin, or other item.

incumbent: Person established in a Federal position, as opposed to a new hire.

indefinite tenure: Tenure of a nonpermanent employee hired for an unlimited time. Independent employment system, see excepted agency.

Indian preference: As an area of consideration on a Vacancy Announcement, means Native Americans are hired preferentially for that position.

Individual Achievement Record (IAR): Section of the ACWA examination that credits candidates for achievements within the scope of their opportunities and is designed to help evaluate such personal attributes such as achievement, motivation, and self- esteem. Because the written test is now rarely used, this is now the major part of ACWA.

ineligible: Applicant who has not qualified for a rating (i.e., scored below the cutoff).

intergovernmental personnel assignment: Assignment of personnel to or from the executive branch of the Federal government, state and local government agencies, and institutions of higher education for up to two years (with a possible two-year extension) to provide short-term technical assistance or expertise as needed.

intermittent appointment: Less than full-time employment requiring irregular work hours that cannot be prescheduled.

intern program: providing temporary jobs for college.

internal placement: Procedure in which a Federal agency recruits applicants from a restricted pool of individuals, such as those already working for the agency.

job announcement: General term covering Competition Notices, Vacancy Announcements, and Examination Announcements.

job enrichment: Work assignments and/or training carefully planned (1) to use and upgrade employee skills, abilities, and interests; (2) to provide opportunity for growth; and (3) to encourage self-improvement.

job fair: Federal recruitment event held in large cities, usually featuring positions for which there are candidate shortages.

job family: Occupational group of Wage Grade (blue-collar) positions.

job freeze: Restriction by administrative or legislative standards on hiring and/or promotion.

job series: Those job titles related closely enough to be designated by the same number in the Federal job classification system. Also called ''series of classes.''

job service office: State unemployment office.

job title: Formal name of a position as determined by official classification standards.

journeyman: First full-performance level for Wage Grade employees, corresponding to levels WG-9-11. Journeyman status is equivalent to holding a state license.

judicial branch: Branch of Federal government that applies and interprets laws enacted by the legislative branch. It includes the U.S. Courts and the Supreme Court.

knowledge, skills, and abilities (KSAs), *see* special qualifications.

known promotion potential: The highest grade to which an employee may be promoted in a position without further competition. It is usually stated on the vacancy announcement.

lead agency: Under the Federal Wage System, the Federal agency with the largest number of Federal wage workers within a geographical area; hence, the one having the primary role for determining wage rates for all Federal employees in that area.

leader, *see* Wage Leader.

leave: Time allowed to employees annually for vacation and other absences for personal reasons. *See* also specific type.

leave without pay (LWOP): Temporarily granted nonpay status and absence from duty, as requested by an employee.

legislative branch: Branch of Federal government responsible for enacting laws. Includes Congress and various agencies (e.g., General Accounting Office, Library of Congress, Government Printing Office).

level of difficulty: Relative ranking of duties and responsibilities. *Compare* grade level.

limited appointment, *see* temporary limited appointment.

List of College Courses and Certificate of Scholastic Achievement: Supplemental Qualifications Statement form used to document educational background.

locality pay: The percentage by which General Schedule salaries are increased depending on where the position is located. The country is divided into 30 locality areas, each with a different percentage.

lottery: Means of awarding seats for postal examinations in areas of extreme candidate oversupply.

major duty: Any duty or responsibility (or group of closely related tasks) of a position that determines qualification requirements for the position, occupies a significant amount of the employee's time, and is regular or recurrent.

management official: Individual whose duties and responsibilities require or authorize him or her to formulate, determine, or influence agency policy.

Management Sectional Center: Unit responsible for a series of Postal Section Centers.

managerial qualifications, *see* Executive Competency Review Factors.

mean grade: Average grade level determined for a particular job title by multiplying the number of people employed in each grade by that grade (e.g., 200 employees at level 7 = 1,400), adding all the results, and dividing by the total number employed.

median grade: Grade level that divides employees in a particular job title into two groups of roughly equal size. Used as an indicator of promotion potential.

merit principles: Set of legally prescribed personnel rules and regulations followed by the Federal government to ensure (among other things) that it hires and promotes qualified individuals competitively, according to their relative ability, knowledge, and skills.

merit promotion system: System in the Competitive Service under which agencies consider an employee for internal personnel actions (e.g., promotion) on the basis of personal merit and qualifying past experience.

merit system: Overall Federal civil service system, set up to implement the merit principles.

Merit Systems Protection Board (MSPB): Independent agency that monitors the administration of the Federal civil service system, prosecutes and, adjudicates allegations of merit principle abuses, and hears and decides other civil service appeals.

mid level: Intermediate career level in the General Schedule, comprising grade levels GS-8-12.

minimum qualifications: Minimum standards (education, experience, training) that an applicant must meet to qualify for a particular position. Also called "basic qualifications." Full descriptions of these are found in OPM's *Qualifications Standards Operating Manual* and *Handbook X-118C.*

monopolized occupation: Job title or series that occurs only in the Federal government (e.g., Postal Clerk, Foreign Service Officer). (Note: This is not an official government term, but used in this volume for convenience.)

multiple-use occupation: Job title or series used by more than one agency (e.g., Secretary, Accountant). *Compare* predominant-use occupation; unique-use occupation.

name request: Request by an agency for referral of a specific candidate once his or her name is among the top three on the appropriate register.

National Agency Check and Inquiry (NACI): Investigation of applicants for nonsensitive Federal positions by means of a name check through national investigative files and voucher inquiries. *Compare* full-field investigation.

national register: Centrally maintained list of eligibles for entry-level positions that are active nationwide.

new hire: Person newly hired for Federal employment, as opposed to one already so employed (i.e., an incumbent).

night differential: Extra 10% compensation for GS employees working at night (between 6 P.M. and 6 A.M.). Certain Postal Service employees also receive night differentials.

nominating officer: Subordinate officer of an agency to whom authority has been delegated by the head of the agency to nominate for appointment, but not actually appoint, employees.

Non-Appropriated Fund (NAF) position: Federal job compensated out of the earnings of the organization employing such persons, rather than the budget granted the agency by Congress. NAF positions, such as military PX jobs, are not part of the Federal civil service proper.

noncompetitive appointment: Employment without competition—that is, without regard to competitive examination, registers, and related Federal hiring procedures. Includes reinstatements, transfers, reassignments, demotions, and promotions, as well as certain special hiring programs (as for the disabled and Native Americans).

nonexempt employee: Employee not exempt from the overtime provisions of the Fair Labor Standards Act.

nonstatus candidate: Candidate who does not have competitive status, such as one never previously employed by the Federal government (i.e., a first-time hire) or a Federal employee in a non-status-conveying program (i.e., the Excepted Service).

Notice of Results: Government document advising an applicant that he or she has been found qualified for Federal employment at a particular grade (or range of grades). A *Notice of Results-Rating* means assignment to a *national* register with a stated rating (but does not give one's rank on that register). A *Notice of Results-Eligibility* means assignment to a *local* register (or to an applicant supply file). A copy of one's Notice of Results may be required when applying directly to an agency.

objection: Written statement by an agency of the reasons it believes an eligible candidate whose name is on a candidate list is not qualified for the position for which he or she was referred. If the examining office sustains the objection, the agency may eliminate the person from consideration.

occupational code: Numerical code assigned to each Federal occupational specialty: for example, WG-2805 for Electrician or GS-630 for Dietician.

occupational group: Positions of differing kinds but within the same general field; for example, the GS-500 Accounting and Budget Occupational Group (which includes the General Accounting Clerical and Administrative Series, Financial Management, Internal Revenue Agent Accounting Technicians, Payroll, etc.). Occupational groups of blue-collar positions are known as "job families."

Occupational Supplement, *see* Form B.

Office of Personnel Management (OPM): Federal government agency that oversees agency hiring and from which job seekers may obtain employment information and assistance for the Competitive Service. OPM sets and carries out personnel policies for a work force of over 1 million employees. As the government's central personnel agency, OPM's management tasks include recruitment and examination, executive development, training, job classification, personnel investigations, evaluation of agency personnel programs, and pay administration. OPM also negotiates and administers Federal employee retirement and insurance programs, and provides primary leadership in the areas of labor relations and affirmative action.

open continuously: Indication, appearing on a Vacancy Announcement, that the hiring agency will accept publications for the position(s) on a continuous basis until its needs are met. May mean that multiple candidates are needed whereas relatively few are expected to apply.

open-end form: Examination form that allows the candidate unlimited commentary to relate any information that may improve his or her rating. Examples of this type are the SF-171 and résumés. Open-end forms are expensive and time consuming to score, as each must be evaluated individually by a trained examiner. *Compare* closed-end form.

open until filled: Indication, appearing on a Vacancy Announcement, that the hiring agency will continue to consider all applicants received until the job has been offered to and accepted by a qualified candidate.

opening date: Date on which a hiring agency begins accepting applications for a specific Federal job.

OPM, *see* Office of Personnel Management.

OPM Qualifications Standards Operating Manual: Official OPM publication, *White-Collar Occupations in Federal Service.* Describes the qualifications required at each grade level for each white-collar Competitive Service job.

outside hiring: Procedure in which a Federal agency recruits applicants from the broadest possible sources, including current and former Federal employees, as well as persons not currently employed by the government.

Outstanding Scholar Program (OSP): Special hiring program for college graduates with an overall academic grade-point average of at least 3.5. Such candidates may approach any agency about ACWA openings without having to take the ACWA exam, and may be hired directly by the agency at GS-517 for any ACWA job title.

oversupply (of candidates): Case in which the supply of candidates exceed the demand. *Compare* equilibrium; undersupply.

overtime compensation: Compensation for overtime work, generally paid at a rate of one-and-one-half times the base hourly rate.

overtime work: Under Title 5, United States Code, officially ordered or approved work performed in excess of eight hours in a day or 40 hours in a week. Under the Fair Labor Standards Act, work in excess of 40 hours in a week by a nonexempt employee. No full-time, regular employee is required to work overtime on more than five consecutive days in a week.

pass over: To eliminate from consideration of appointment an eligible applicant on a candidate list with a veterans' preference, in order to appoint a lower-ranking nonveteran. The agency must submit reasons that OPM finds sufficient.

pathway: Set of procedures an applicant must follow to be considered for a Federal position. (*Note:* Though ''pathway'' is not an official government term, it is used throughout this volume for convenience.)

pay retention: Right of a General Schedule or Prevailing Rate (WG) employee to continue to receive the higher rate following a period of grade retention (or at other specified times when the rate of basic pay would otherwise be reduced). Pay is retained indefinitely.

pay schedule: Government table showing salaries for each grade level. The two most commonly used pay schedules are the General Schedule and the Wage Grade Schedule.

performance appraisal (PA): Systematic comparison of an employee's actual performance with the performance standards previously established for the position. Also, form used to report the results of such an appraisal.

periodic increase, *see* within-grade increase.

permanent appointment: One of only two kinds of appointment available at independent employment systems (excepted agencies), the other being temporary. Allows for within-agency tenure and reinstatement eligibility, as well as for limited appeal rights.

personnel action: Process necessary to appoint, separate, reinstate, or make other changes affecting an employee, such as change in position assignment, tenure, and so on.

personnel management: Management of human resources to accomplish a mission and provide individual job satisfaction. It is the line responsibility of the operating supervisor and the staff responsibility of the personnel office.

personnel office: Subdivision of a Federal agency that recruits and hires new employees.

plum: High-level political appointment, subject to change with each new Administration or presidential term.

position: Specific job consisting of all the current major duties and responsibilities assigned or delegated by management.

position change: Promotion, demotion, or reassignment.

position classification: Analysis and categorization of jobs by occupational group, series, class, and grade according to like duties, responsibilities, and qualification requirements.

position description: Official written statement of the major duties, responsibilities, and supervisory relationships of a position.

position title: Job title appearing on the Vacancy Announcement.

Postal Section Center: Organizational grouping of post offices, headed by a Management Sectional Center.

Postal Service Salary (PSS) structure: Pay structure applicable to bargaining unit Postal Service personnel, such as Postal Clerks and Letter Carriers, but not to Rural Letter Carriers and Mailhandlers.

predominant-use occupation: Job title or series used largely (but not only) by a single agency (e.g., Soil Conservationist). *Compare* multiple-use occupation; unique-use occupation.

preference: Advantage awarded to some candidates; for example, bonus points on an examination for certain types of military disability or service. *See also* specific type.

premium pay, *see* differential.

prepaid plan: Type of Federal health plan involving Comprehensive Medical Plans Health Maintenance Organizations (CMP/HMO), which arranges for health care through designated physicians, hospitals, and (in certain locations) other providers. *Compare* fee-for-service plan.

prep(aratory) book, *see* study guide.

prep(aratory) course: Nongovernmental course provided to prepare one for taking a particular Federal exam (e.g., the Postal Exam).

Prevailing Rate employee: Federal government blue-collar worker.

Prevailing Rate System: Subsystem of the Federal Wage Grade System used to determine employee pay in a particular wage area. The determination requires comparing the rate of pay with the private sector for similar duties and responsibilities.

private sector: That part of the economy that is privately owned, including joint stock companies, whether their stock be privately or publicly held.

probationary period: Trial period that is a condition of the initial competitive (i.e., career-conditional) appointment. Provides the final test of ability, that of actual performance on the job.

Program Coordinator: Agency personnel in charge of special hiring programs. Usually located at larger Federal facilities.

promotion: Change of an employee to a higher grade when both the old and new positions are under the same job classification system and pay schedule, or to a position with higher pay in a different job classification system and pay schedule. *See also* specific type.

promotion certificate: List of best-qualified candidates to be considered to fill a position under competitive promotion procedures.

promotion potential: Likelihood of eventual promotion into an upper-level job.

promotion rate: Percentage of employees in a given position who were promoted during the previous year.

Public sector: That part of the economy that is publicly owned, including all government departments and agencies and all public corporations.

Purple Heart: Medal awarded to all armed forces members wounded or killed in action. Wounds need not have been permanently disabling.

qualification standard: Official description of the duties of a position and the necessary qualifications (education, experience, etc.) for applicants. Used in rating a candidate.

qualifications information package, *see* application package.

qualifications requirements: Education, experience, and other prerequisites to employment or placement in a position.

Qualifications Review Board: Panel attached to OPM that determines whether a candidate for career appointment in the Senior Executive Service meets the managerial and executive criteria established by law.

quality graduate: College graduate who was a superior student and can be hired at a grade higher than that to which he or she would otherwise be entitled.

quality step increase: Additional within-grade increase granted to General Schedule employees for high-quality performance above that ordinarily found in the type of position concerned.

rank: Relative position on a register, based on one's rating.

ranking factors, *see* special qualifications.

rating: Numerical score indicating eligibility for employment in a given job title (or group of job titles) at a specified grade level or range. Applicants who score below the cutoff (70) are considered ineligible for employment in that particular position.

rating enhancement: Special hiring program involving the actual or effective addition of points to an applicant's rating (e.g., veterans preference).

reassignment: Change of an employee from one position to another, without promotion or demotion, while serving continuously within the same agency.

recruitment: Process of attracting a supply of qualified eligible employees for employment consideration.

recruitment bonus: A one-time payment of up to 25% of a position's salary given to a new employee as an incentive for him or her to accept the position.

reduction in force (RIF): Agency personnel cutback. Action involving separating an employee from his or her present position, but does not necessarily result in discharge or downgrading. May be required due to lack of work or funds, changes resulting from reorganization, downward reclassification of a position, or the need to make room for an employee with reemployment or restoration rights.

reduction in grade: Demotion.

Re-employment Priority List: List of employees with career or career-conditional tenure who have been separated by a reduction in force, prioritized for reemployment to competitive positions in the agency in the commuting area where the separations occurred.

reemployment rights: Rights of an employee to return to an agency after detail, transfer, or appointment to: (1) another executive agency during an emergency, (2) an international organization; or (3) other statutorily covered employment, such as the Peace Corps.

register: List of eligible applicants for Federal jobs in a specific occupational field, compiled in the order of their relative standing for referral after Competitive Service examination. Also called "Register of Eligibles." May be national or local in scope.

Register of Eligibles, *see* register.

reinstatement: Noncompetitive reemployment in the competitive service based on previous service under a career or career-conditional appointment.

reinstatement eligibility (RE): Designation indicating that a former Federal employee has retained full competitive status and is eligible to apply for a Federal job on a noncompetitive basis (i.e., to be reinstated into the Federal civil service system).

removal: Separation of an employee for cause or because of continual unacceptable performance.

resignation: Separation, prior to retirement, at the request of the employee. Resignation is a voluntary expression of the employee's desire to leave the organization and must not be demanded as an alternative to some other action to be taken or withheld.

restoration rights: Entitlement of employees who enter military service or sustain a compensable job-related injury or disability to be restored to the same or higher employment status held before their absence.

retention preference: Relative standing of employees competing in a reduction in force. Determined by veterans' preference, tenure group, length of service, and performance appraisal.

retention register: List of all employees, arranged by competitive level, describing their retention preference during reductions in force.

retirement: Under the Civil Service Retirement System, payment of an annuity after separation from a position based on meeting age and length-of-service requirements.

Rule-of-Three: Rule under which the three most highly rated eligibles must be the first considered for a position. Any of these three can then be appointed regardless of their relative ratings; however, the agency cannot unjustifiably appoint a nonveteran if a veteran is among them and is the higher rated.

Schedules A-C: Three groups of positions that are *always* in the Excepted Service. Of these, only positions in Schedules A and B provide any tenure. Also, the types of appointments involving these positions.

secretary: Word used to describe two very different types of jobs: (1) employee who handles correspondence and manages routine and detail work for a superior: (2) officer of state who superintends a government administrative department.

selection: The decision by a management official to choose an applicant for a position. It precedes the appointment that is made by the personnel office, which ensures that the selection met all legal and regulatory requirements.

selective certification: Certification of only those eligibles who have special qualifications required to fill particular vacant positions.

selective placement factors, *see* special qualifications.

selective placement procedures: Special noncompetitive hiring procedures available to certain applicants, such as the physically and mentally disabled, the mentally restored, and former prisoners.

Senior Executive Service (SES): Separate personnel system comprising most top supervisory and managerial jobs in the executive branch (aside from Presidential appointees). Its pay schedule has six grade levels, essentially unlinked to duties and responsibilities.

Senior Level Pay Schedule (SLPS): Pay schedule just above the General Schedule. It includes two parallel subscales (SL and ST) and has minimum and maximum salaries but no grade levels: An individual's pay may fall anywhere within the prescribed range.

separation: Termination of employment.

series of classes, *see* job series.

SF-171: An application form once required for most Federal positions, now it is optional with the applicant. It provides a structured way for applicants to list experience, education, skills and awards. Agencies may not require its use. Applicants may use résumés, but they must include all the information required in the vacancy announcement.

sick leave: Time allowed to employees for physical incapacity, to prevent the spread of contagious diseases, or to obtain medical, dental, or eye examination or treatment.

SL: Senior Level Pay Schedule subscale for managers and administrators.

special qualifications: Requirements added to the minimum standards for a position to distinguish among minimally qualified candidates. Frequently referred to as "knowledge, skills, and abilities (KSAs)," "ranking factors," "selective placement factors," or "evaluation factors."

special salary rates: Salary rates higher than the regular, statutory schedule: established for occupations for which (1) there are shortages of qualified applicants and

(2) the private sector pays substantially more than the regular Federal schedule.

ST: Senior Level Pay Schedule subscale for scientific, medical, legal, and other technical professionals.

Standard Form 171, *see* SF-171.

Standard Metropolitan Statistical Area (SMSA): Geographical areas into which the United States is divided for the purpose of presenting various government social and economic statistics. Some comprise a single city, whereas others include two or more cities, and may even cross state lines.

status, *see* competitive status.

status candidate: Candidate who has competitive status.

step: Subdivision of a grade level's salary range.

step increase, *see* within-grade increase.

structured interview: Intensive, directed job interview, often conducted by a panel. Used to test applicant's ability to think fast and handle stress, as required in law enforcement and air traffic control.

study guide: Privately published book to prepare one for taking a particular Federal exam (e.g., the Postal Exam), of which it includes samples. Also called a "prep book."

suitability: Applicant's or employee's fitness for Federal employment, as indicated by character and conduct.

Sunday differential: Additional 25% compensation for working on Sunday.

Superior Academic Achievement: Level of undergraduate academic performance deemed equivalent to having had a year of postgraduate study. Qualifies one for employment at GS-7.

superior qualifications appointment: An appointment of a new employee above the first step of the General Schedule because of his or her superior qualifications or special need of the Government for his or her services combined with the need to match his or her current earnings in the private sector or to match a job offer from the private sector. These appointments are not available to current employees of the Federal Government.

supervisor: Individual employed by an agency having authority (1) to hire, direct, assign, promote, reward, transfer, furlough, lay off, recall, suspend, discipline, or remove employees in the interest of the agency; (2) to adjust their grievances; and (3) to effectively recommend such action, if the exercise of such authority is not merely routine or clerical in nature, but requires the consistent exercise of independent judgment. With respect to any unit that includes firefighters or nurses, the term "supervisor" includes only those individuals who devote most of their employment time exercising such authority. Wage Supervisor is the highest career level in the Wage Grade system, comprising grade levels WS-16-19.

Supplemental Qualifications Statement: Form used to Supplement the SF-171 if additional space is needed to document educational background or special qualifications.

survey classification: Intensive study of all positions in an organization or organizational segment to ensure their correct classification.

TAPER: Abbreviation for "temporary appointment pending establishment of a register." Employment made under an OPM authority granted to an agency when there are insufficient eligibles on a register appropriate to fill the position involved. Those appointed under TAPER authority may be converted to career status after three years.

technician: Generally, a worker in a professional field who is at a level somewhat below that of a full professional.

temporary limited appointment: Nonpermanent appointment of an employee hired for a specified time of one year or less, or for a seasonal or intermittent position. Involves no promotion or transfer rights. *Compare* TAPER.

tentative preference ("TP"): Five-point candidate veteran's preference tentatively awarded an eligible who served on active duty during specified periods and was separated from military service under honorable conditions, Must be verified by the appointing officer.

tenure: Time an employee may reasonably expect to serve under a current appointment. Governed by the type of appointment, without regard to whether the employee has competitive status.

tenure groups: Categories of employees ranked in priority order (I = highest priority) for retention during reductions in force. Within each group, veterans are ranked above nonveterans.

term appointment: Nonpermanent Competitive Service appointment to work on a project expected to last more than one year but less than four years. Includes within-agency promotion privileges.

test scheduling card (OPM 5000 A/B): Registration form for a written test if required as part of the application process. The completed form, once submitted, is returned with the date, time, and place where the test is to be taken.

30% or more disabled preference ("CPS"): Preference for disabled veteran whose disability is rated at 30% or morel applicable with regard to appointment and during reduction in force. *Compare* compensable disability preference ("CP"); disability preference ("XP").

time-in-grade restrictions: Requirement intended to prevent excessively rapid promotions. Generally, an employee may not be promoted more than two grades within 52 weeks to positions of up to GS-5; at GS-5 and above, an employee must serve a minimum of 52 weeks in a grade, and cannot be promoted more than one grade (or two, if that is the normal progression).

time-limited appointment: Excepted Service appointment with a specific time limitation. Unlike term appointments in the competitive service, which may not exceed four years, there is no maximum length for these appointments.

top-of-the-register certification: Certification in regular order, beginning with the eligibles at the top of the register.

total disability compensation: Disability compensation equal to two-thirds of the employee's monthly pay, increased to three-quarters if the disabled party is married or has any dependents.

tour of duty: Hours of a day (a daily tour of duty) and days of an administrative workweek (weekly tour of duty) scheduled in advance and during which an employee is required to work regularly.

transfer eligibility: Eligibility to move between agencies, employees in the competitive service can move to other agencies in the competitive service. There are some special authorities that permit employees of some excepted agencies to move to competitive service agencies without competing in an examination.

unassembled examination: Examination (using closed- or open-end forms) in which applicants are rated on their education, experience, and other qualifications through the use of an application and any supportive evidence that may be required, without assembling for a written or performance test. *Compare* assembled exam.

undersupply (of candidates): Case in which the demand for candidates exceeds the supply. *Compare* equilibrium; oversupply.

unemployment compensation: Income maintenance payments to former Federal employees who: (1) are unemployed; (2) file a claim at a local employment office for unemployment compensation; and (3) register for work assignment. The program is administered through state and District of Columbia employment service offices, which determine eligibility and make the payments.

unions, Federal: The Civil Service Reform Act of 1978 gave Federal unions statutory bargaining rights, postal unions acquired such rights under the 1970 Postal Reorganization Act. More than 61% of all government workers are represented by unions, which have played a large and honorable part in the successful fight to improve the working conditions and benefits of government workers, as well as the prestige and efficiency of the merit system.

unique-use occupation: Job title or series used by only one agency (e.g., Bond Sales Promoter). *Compare* multiple-use occupation; predominant-use occupation.

universality: Measure of the degree to which a given job title is used among Federal agencies. (*Note:* This is not an official government term, but used in this volume for convenience.)

unpaid work experience program: Special Federal volunteer work program for the disabled, allowing for the acquisition of skills and training and possibly leading to paying positions.

upward mobility: Systematic career development requiring competitive selection in positions that provide experience and training leading to future assignments in other, more responsible positions.

VA: Department of Veterans Affairs (formerly Veterans Administration).

vacancy: Job opening in a Federal agency.

Vacancy Announcement: Job announcement issued by a specific agency, usually for a job that is currently available. *Compare* Competition Notice.

verification statement: Confirmatory certificate, as from a state vocational rehabilitation counselor confirming a disabled person's disability and his or her ability to perform the work required of a specific Federal job.

veteran: Former member of the armed forces.

veterans preference: Special hiring program giving a five- or ten-point numerical advantage given to certain veterans or members of their families in the scoring involved in competing for a Federal job. The statutory right (under 5 USC 2108) to special advantage in appointments or separations, based on a person's honorable discharge from the armed forces, for service during wartime or certain other designated periods. Not applicable to the Senior Executive Service.

Veterans Readjustment Appointment (VRA): Special noncompetitive hiring procedure available to certain veterans. Those with VRA positions receive special career training and are converted to Competitive Service after two years of satisfactory performance.

voucher: Formal inquiry to employers, references, professors, and others who presumably know a job applicant well enough to describe job qualifications and personal character.

Wage Grade employee: One employed in trades, crafts, or labor occupations covered by the Federal Wage System, whose pay is fixed and adjusted periodically in accordance with prevailing rates. Blue-collar worker.

Wage Grade Schedule: Graded pay system for blue-collar occupations covered by the Federal Wage System. It comprises 19 grade levels, divided into five career levels.

Wage Leader: Lower of two supervisory Wage Grade career levels, comprising WL-12-15 and corresponding to foreman in the private sector.

Wage Supervisor: Higher of two supervisory Wage Grade career levels, comprising WS-16-19.

white-collar worker: Generally, a salaried employee whose job does not entail manual labor and/or protective clothing.

within-grade increase: Salary increase without promotion, provided in certain government pay plans based upon time in grade and acceptable or satisfactory work performance. Also known as "periodic increase" or "step increase."

"within reach": Listed among the top three on a register and thus ready for selection under the Rule-of-Three.

workweek, *see* basic workweek.

XP, *see* disability preference.

Index

*Note: **Bold** page numbers refer to definitions.*